Handbook of Public Policy Analysis

Theory, Politics, and Methods

PUBLIC ADMINISTRATION AND PUBLIC POLICY

A Comprehensive Publication Program

Executive Editor

JACK RABIN
Professor of Public Administration and Public Policy
School of Public Affairs
The Capital College
The Pennsylvania State University—Harrisburg
Middletown, Pennsylvania

Assistant to the Executive Editor
T. Aaron Wachhaus, Jr.

Available Electronically

Handbook of Public Policy Analysis

Theory, Politics, and Methods

Edited by

Frank Fischer
Rutgers University
Newark, New Jersey, U.S.A.

Gerald J. Miller
Rutgers University
Newark, New Jersey, U.S.A.

Mara S. Sidney
Rutgers University
Newark, New Jersey, U.S.A.

CRC Press
Taylor & Francis Group
Boca Raton London New York

CRC Press is an imprint of the
Taylor & Francis Group, an informa business

CRC Press
Taylor & Francis Group
6000 Broken Sound Parkway NW, Suite 300
Boca Raton, FL 33487-2742

© 2007 by Taylor & Francis Group, LLC
CRC Press is an imprint of Taylor & Francis Group, an Informa business

International Standard Book Number-10: 1-57444-561-8 (Hardcover)
International Standard Book Number-13: 978-1-57444-561-9 (Hardcover)

Library of Congress Cataloging-in-Publication Data

Handbook of public policy analysis: theory, politics, and methods / edited by Frank Fischer, Gerald J. Miller, and Mara S. Sidney.
    p. cm. -- (Public administration and public policy ; 125)
  Includes bibliographical references and index.
  ISBN-13: 978-1-57444-561-9 (alk. paper)
  ISBN-10: 1-57444-561-8 (alk. paper)
  1. Policy sciences--Handbooks, manuals, etc. 2. Public administration--Handbooks, manuals, etc.
I. Fischer, Frank, 1942- II. Miller, Gerald. III. Sidney, Mara S., 1964- IV. Title. V. Series.

H97.H3583 2007
352.3'4--dc22
      2006031906

Visit the Taylor & Francis Web site at
http://www.taylorandfrancis.com

and the CRC Press Web site at
http://www.crcpress.com

Contributors

Clinton J. Andrews is an associate professor in the Edward J. Bloustein School of Planning and Public Policy at Rutgers University and director of the Urban Planning Program. He has published widely on energy and environmental management and policy, and his most recent book is *Humble Analysis*.

Thomas A. Birkland directs the Center for Policy Research, State University of New York at Albany, where he is also a professor. He is the author of *After Disaster: Agenda Setting, Public Policy, and Focusing Events*.

Susan E. Clarke is professor of political science at the University of Colorado at Boulder. She teaches a graduate seminar on context-sensitive research methods. She is an editor of *Urban Affairs Review*. Her most recent book is *The Work of Cities* (co-authored with Gary Gaile).

Caroline Danielson is a policy analyst at the Public Policy Institute of California, in San Francisco. She earned her doctorate in political science from the University of Michigan, Ann Arbor.

Peter deLeon earned his Ph.D. from the Rand Graduate School. Dr. deLeon is the author of *Democracy and the Policy Sciences* as well as *Advice and Consent*.

Tansu Demir, PhD, is assistant professor in the Department of Public Administration at the University of Central Florida. He received his Ph.D. in public administration from Florida Atlantic University in 2005.

Frank Fischer is professor of political science and member of the faculty of the Edward J. Bloustein School of Planning and Public Policy at Rutgers University. His recent publications include *Reframing Public Policy: Discursive Politics and Deliberative Practice*, and *Citizens, Experts, and the Environment: The Politics of Local Knowledge*.

John Forester is professor of city and regional planning at Cornell University. His best known work includes *The Deliberative Practitioner, Planning in the Face of Power* (University of California Press, 1989), and *The Argumentative Turn in Policy Analysis and Planning* (co-edited with Frank Fischer).

Jan-Eric Furubo, an evaluator and has been at the National Audit Office in Sweden, is the author of many articles and publications in the field of decision making, and was co-editor of the *International Atlas of Evaluation* (2002). He is president of the Swedish Evaluation Society.

Yaakov Garb is a lecturer at the Jacob Blaustein Institutes for Desert Research at the Ben-Gurion University of the Negev, and a visiting assistant professor in the Global Environmental Program at the Watson Institute for International Studies, Brown University. He has worked on a range of environmental and urban issues internationally, often drawing on perspectives from Science and Technology Studies (STS). He has recently completed essays on the "construction of inevitability" in megaprojects, on changing retail travel patterns in Central Europe, and on the politics of mobility in Israel and Palestine.

Herbert Gottweis is director at the Department of Political Science of the University of Vienna. His publications include *Governing Molecules*: *The Discursive Politics of Genetic Engineering in Europe and in the United States*.

Steven Griggs is lecturer in public policy at the Institute of Local Government Studies at the University of Birmingham in the UK. His current research centres on discourses of community protest campaigns against the expansion of airports in the UK.

John Grin is a professor of policy science at the Department of Political Science at the University of Amsterdam. He is also Director of the Amsterdam School for Social Science Research, and co-director of the Dutch Knowledge Network on System Innovations, a research program on fundamental transitions to a sustainable society.

Hubert Heinelt is professor for public administration, public policy and urban and regional research at Darmstadt University of Technology. He is a member of the executive committee of the European Urban Research Association and the Standing Group on Urban Research of the German Political Science Association.

Robert Hoppe is a professor in the Faculty of Business, Public Administration, and Technology (BBT), University of Twente, Netherlands. He is chair of Policy and Knowledge and editor-in-chief of *Beleidswetenschap*. His key research interests are in methods of policy analysis and science/policy boundary work.

Helen Ingram is Warmington Endowed Chair of Social Ecology at the University of California at Irvine. She has joint appointments in the Departments of Planning, Policy and Design, Political Science, and Criminology, Law and Society.

Werner Jann holds the chair for Political Science, Administration and Organisation at the University of Potsdam, Germany. He was associate professor at the Postgraduate School of Administrative Sciences Speyer, and has been research fellow at the University of California, Berkeley.

Patrick Kenis is professor at Tilburg University, the Netherlands, where he is also head of Department Organisation Studies. He earned his Ph.D. in social and political sciences from the European University Institute in Florence, Italy.

David Laws is principal research scientist and lecturer in the Department of Urban Studies and Planning at the Massachusetts Institute of Technology. His recent publications include *Reframing Regulation: Changing Forms of Law and Practice in U.S. Environmental Policy*, and *The Practice of Innovation: Institutions, Policy, and Technology Development*.

Anne Loeber is a post-doctoral researcher and lecturer in public policy at the Department of Political Science at the University of Amsterdam, the Netherlands. She is also a member of the Technology Assessment steering committee, an independent advisory body to the Dutch Ministry of Agriculture, Nature Managment, and Fisheries.

Martin Lodge is lecturer in political science and public policy at the Department of Government and the ESRC Centre for Analysis of Risk and Regulation, London School of Economics and Political Science. His key research interests are in comparative executive government, in particular in the area of regulation.

Miriam Manon is a graduate of the University of Massachusetts, Amherst's Commonwealth Honors College, where she earned an interdisciplinary B.A. in social justice and the environment. She completed a semester at the Arava Institute for Environmental Studies in Israel and plans to continue her studies on the interface of environmental and social issues.

Kuldeep Mathur recently retired as academic director at the Centre for the Study of Law and Governance, and professor at the Centre for Political Studies, Jawaharal Nehru University (JNU), New Delhi, India. He was formerly rector at JNU and director of India's National Institute of Education Planning and Administration.

Navdeep Mathur is research fellow at the Institute of Local Government Studies, School of Public Policy, University of Birmingham, UK. He is also forums editor of the *Journal of Critical Policy Analysis.*

Igor Mayer is an associate professor in the faculty of Technology, Policy and Management at Delft University of Technology, the Netherlands. He is also the director of the Delft-Rotterdam Centre for Process Management and Simulation.

Gerald J. Miller is professor of public administration at Rutgers University, where he teaches government and nonprofit budgeting and financial management. He has published numerous books and research articles, including *The Handbook of Debt Management* and *Government Financial Management Theory.*

Hugh T. Miller is professor of public administration and director of the School of Public Administration at Florida Atlantic University. His most recent books are *Postmodern Public Administration: Revised Edition,* with the late Charles J. Fox and *Tampering with Tradition: The Unrealized Authority of Democratic Agency,* co-edited with Peter Bogason and Sandra Kensen.

Jerry Mitchell is professor of public affairs at Baruch College, The City University of New York. His is the author of a new book published by SUNY Press, *The Business of BIDS.*

Changhwan Mo is currently a research fellow at the Korea Transport Institute and has been advisor at the Regulatory Reform Group in the Prime Minister's Office in South Korea. He is the author or co-author of several articles in the areas of public policy, budgeting, and globalization.

Wayne Parsons is professor of public policy at Queen Mary, University of London. Amongst his publications are *The Political Economy of British Regional Policy; The Power of the Financial Press: Keynes and the Quest for a Moral Science,* and *Public Policy* and he is editor of the New Horizons in Public Policy series for Edward Elgar.

Deike Peters is currently a German Research Foundation (DFG) fellow with the Center for Metropolitan Studies at the Technical University in Berlin. She has a Ph.D. in planning and policy development from Rutgers University and master's degrees in urban planning and international affairs from Columbia University.

Helga Pülzl is currently a post-doctoral researcher at the Department of Economics and Social Sciences at the University of Natural Resources and Applied Life Sciences, Vienna (BOKU). In addition she is a lecturer in comparative politics at the Department of Political Science at the University of Vienna.

Jörg Raab is assistant professor of policy and organisation studies at Tilburg University, the Netherlands. His research focuses mainly on governance mechanisms in the state, economy and society and on different topics in organization theory with an emphasis on inter-organizational networks.

Bernard Reber is research fellow on moral and political philosophy at CNRS-University Paris V. He has also taught at l'Ecole Nationale Supérieure des Mines de Paris, Sorbonne. He is the coeditor of *Pluralisme moral, juridique et politique* and *Les sciences humaines et sociales à l'heure des TIC*.

Donijo Robbins is associate professor for the School of Public & Nonprofit Administration at Grand Valley State University in Grand Rapids, Michigan, where she teaches graduate and undergraduate courses in public budgeting, financial management, and research methods. She holds a Ph.D. in public administration from Rutgers University.

Paul A. Sabatier is professor in the Department of Environment and Policy at the University of California, Davis. He has published *Theories of the Policy Process*.

Alan R. Sadovnik is professor of education, public affairs and administration, and sociology at Rutgers University. Among his publications are *Equity and Excellence in Higher Education; Exploring Education: An Introduction to the Foundations of Education*; and *Knowledge and Pedagogy: The Sociology of Basil Bernstein*.

Thomas Saretzki is professor of environmental policy and politics at the Center for the Study of Democracy, University of Lueneburg (Germany). Currently he is visiting research scholar at Northwestern University in Evanston, Illinois.

Anne Larason Schneider is professor, School of Justice and Department of Political Science, Arizona State University, Tempe. She is co-editor (with Helen Ingram) of *Deserving and Entitled* and co-author (also with Helen Ingram) of *Policy Design for Democracy* (University Press of Kansas, 1997).

Mary Segers is professor of political science at Rutgers University. Her books include *A Wall of Separation? Debating the Role of Religion in American Public Life* (1998) and *Abortion Politics In American States* (1995, co-edited with Timothy Byrnes).

Mara S. Sidney is Associate Professor of Political Science at Rutgers University, Newark. She is the author of *Unfair Housing: How National Policy Shapes Local Action*.

Diane Stone is Marie Curie Chair in the Center for Policy Studies at the Central European University in Budapest, and reader in Politics and International Studies at the University of Warwick. Among her books is *Global Knowledge Networks and International Development* (with Simon Maxwell). She co-edits the journal *Global Governance*.

Eileen Sullivan is a lecturer of political science at Rutgers University. She has been a research director for the New York City Department of Employment, the U.S. Government Accountability Office (GAO), and the Vera Institute of Justice; and she has served as research consultant to the New York City Economic Development Corporation.

Douglas Torgerson is professor of politics at Trent University in Canada. He is a past editor of the journal *Policy Sciences*, and his publications include several critical studies on the theory and history of the field.

Oliver Treib is assistant professor in the Department of Political Science, Institute for Advanced Studies, Vienna. His research topics include EU social policy, new modes of governance and political cleavage structures in international politics.

Michel J.G. van Eeten is an associate professor in the School of Technology, Policy and Management, Delft University of Technology, the Netherlands. He is also a winner of the Raymond Vernon Prize of the Association for Public Policy Analysis and Management and the author (with Emery Roe) of *Ecology, Engineering, and Management.*

Danielle M. Vogenbeck, Ph.D., public affairs, University of Colorado at Denver, is an associate behavioral scientist at RAND, where she specializes in applying social network analysis to organizational change, network governance, and community development projects.

Hendrik Wagenaar is a professor of public policy with the Department of Public Administration at Leiden University. He is the author of *Government Institutions* (Kluwer) and co-editor (with M. A. Hajer) of *Deliberative Policy Analysis* (Cambridge University Press).

Peter Wagner is professor of social and political theory at the European University Institute in Florence, Italy, and professor of sociology at the University of Warwick, UK. His recent book publications include *Varieties of World-Making: Beyond Globalization* (co-edited with Nathalie Karagiannis, 2006) and *A History and Theory of the Social Sciences.*

Christopher M. Weible is an assistant professor in the School of Public Policy, Georgia Institute of Technology in Atlanta. His research interests focus on policy processes and environmental politics, and his work has been published in the *Policy Studies Journal*, *Political Research Quarterly*, and *Journal of Public Administration Research and Theory.*

Kai Wegrich is senior policy analyst at RAND Europe. He received his Ph.D. from Potsdam University. His areas of special interest include public sector reform and regulation.

Hellmut Wollmann is professor (emeritus) of public policy and public administration at the Institute of Social Science of Humboldt University, Berlin, Germany. He was a co-founder and president (1998/1999) of the European Evaluation Society. He is editor of *Evaluation in Public Sector Reform* (2003, with V. Hoffmann-Martinot), *Comparing Public Sector Reform in France and Germany* (2006), and *The Comparative Study of Local Government and Politics* (2006, with H. Baldersheim).

Kaifeng Yang is assistant professor in public administration at Askew School of Public Administration and Policy, Florida State University. He is research associate at the National Center for Public Productivity at Rutgers University and the DeVoe Moore Center for Economic Development at Florida State University.

Dvora Yanow holds the Strategic Chair in Meaning and Method at the Vrije Universiteit, Amsterdam. She is the author of *How Does a Policy Mean?; Conducting Interpretive Policy Analysis; Constructing American "Race" and "Ethnicitiy"* and co-editor of *Knowing in Organizations and Interpretation and Method: Empirical Research Methods and the Interpretive Turn.*

Contents

Part IV
Policy Decision Making: Rationality, Networks, and Learning

Part V
Deliberative Policy Analysis: Argumentation, Rhetoric, and Narratives

Part VI
Comparative, Cultural, and Ethical Perspectives

Part VII
Quantitatively Oriented Policy Methods

Part VIII
Qualitative Policy Analysis: Interpretation, Meaning, and Content

Part IX
Policy Decisions Techniques

Part X
Country Perspectives

Introduction

The study of public policy, including the methods of policy analysis, has been among the most rapidly developing fields in the social sciences over the past several decades. Policy analysis emerged to both better understand the policymaking process and to suppy policy decision makers with reliable policy-relevant knowledge about pressing economic and social problems. Dunn (1981, 35) defines policy analysis as "an applied social science discipline which uses multiple methods of inquiry and arguments to produce and transform policy-relevant information that may be utilized in political settings to resolve policy problems."

By and large, the development of public policy analysis first appeared as an American phenomenon. Subsequently, though, the specialization has been adopted in Canada and a growing number of European countries, the Netherlands and Britain being particularly important examples. Moreover, in Europe a growing number of scholars, especially young scholars, have begun to identify with policy analysis. Indeed, many of them have made important contributions to the development of the field.

Although policy advice-giving is as old as government itself, the increasing complexity of modern society dramatically intensifies the decision makers' need for information. Policy decisions combine sophisticated technical knowledge with complex social and political realities, but defining public policy itself has confronted various problems. Some scholars have simply understood policy to be whatever governments choose to do or not to do. Others have spelled out definitions that focus on the specific characteristics of public policy. Lowi and Ginsburg (1996, 607), for example, define public policy as "an officially expressed intention backed by a sanction, which can be a reward or a punishment." As a course of action (or inaction), a public policy can take the form of "a law, a rule, a statute, an edict, a regulation or an order."

The origins of the policy focus are usually attributed to the writings of Harold Lasswell, considered to be the founder of the policy sciences. Lasswell envisioned a multidisciplinary enterprise capable of guiding the political decision processes of post-World War II industrial societies (see Torgerson, chapter 2). He called for the study of the role of "knowledge in and of the policy process." The project referred to an overarching social-scientific discipline geared to adjusting democratic practices to the realities of an emerging techno-industrial society. Designed to cut across various specializations, the field was to include contributions from political science, sociology, anthropology, psychology, statistics and mathematics, and even the physical and natural sciences in some cases. It was to employ both quantitative and qualitative methods.

But the policy-analytic enterprise largely failed to take up Lasswell's bold vision, following instead a much narrower path of development. Policy analysis, as it is known today, has taken an empirical orientation geared more to managerial practices than to the facilitation of democratic government per se (see deLeon and Vogenbeck, chapter 1). In contrast to a multidisciplinary methodological perspective, the field has been shaped by a more limiting methodological framework derived from the neopositivist/empiricist theories of knowledge that dominated the social sciences of the day. This has generated an emphasis on rigorous quantitative analysis, the objective separation of facts and values, and the search for generalizable findings whose validity would be independent of the particular social context from which they were drawn. That is, the limited framework becomes a policy science that would be able to develop generalizable rules applicable to a range of problems and contexts. In no small part, this has been driven by the dominant influence of economics and its positivist scientific methodologies on the development of the field.

By and large, this contemporary policy orientation has met with considerable success. Not only is policy analysis prominently featured in the social sciences, the practice is widely found throughout government and other political organizations. In addition to academia, policy analysts are employed as researchers in government agencies at all levels of government, in public policy think tanks, research institutions, consulting firms, interest group associations, and nongovernmental organizations. Increasingly they are employed in the public affairs departments of major companies to monitor and research economic and regulatory policies.

At the same time, the discipline has not been without its troubles. It has often been criticized for failing to produce an abundance of problem-oriented knowledge bearing directly on the policy process, or what has been described as "usable knowledge." In the late 1970s and early 1980s, studies showed that empiricist policy research was used far less than anticipated. Research into the utilization of policy findings illustrated that only about a third of the administrators who received such information could identify a concrete use to which it was put. deLeon summed this up by ironically noting that a cost-benefit economist would be hard pressed to explain why so much effort had been given to an exercise with so little payoff.

This is not to say that policy research has been without an impact, but it has not always been of the nature that it set out to supply, namely, knowledge directly applicable to problem solving. Often the contribution has been more of an enlightenment function that has helped politicians, policy decision makers, and the public think about public issues, but not to solve them per se. In view of these difficulties others have sought out new directions. Looking more closely at the nature of social problems and their epistemological implications for a policy science, they have emphasized the inherently normative and interpretive character of policy problems. Policy analysis and policy outcomes, noted such scholars, are infused with sticky problems of politics and social values requiring the field to open itself to a range of other types of methods and issues.

This has lead to a turn to the processes of policy argumentation and deliberative policy analysis. This position, presented in Part IV, challenges the neopositivist or empiricist orientation that has shaped the field, suggesting that it cannot alone produce the kinds of knowledge needed for policy making. Needed is a more normative emphasis that brings empirical and normative inquiry together.

The book is divided into ten parts. Part I, "Historical Perspectives," deals with the basic origins and evolution of the field. The first of three chapters in this part by Peter deLeon and Danielle Vogenbeck, who offer a survey of the development of the field—its successes and failures—and emphasize the political and methodological issues that shaped its evolution, in particular its problem orientation, multidisciplinary perspective, and the normative nature of its research. Based on these considerations, they offer suggestions for future development in the field. Douglas Torgerson focuses more specifically on the contribution of the field's founder, Harold Lasswell. He sketches out in some detail Lasswell's multidisciplinary perspective, his concept of the "policy sciences of democracy," and the need to pay attention to the role of social and political context in both the analysis of policy problems and application of policy objectives in the world of action. Peter Wagner concludes part I by stepping further back to examine development of the policy perspective in terms of the evolution of the modern state and its needs for policy knowledge. Tracing the development of social knowledge for human betterment back to the Enlightenment, he discusses the various theoretical traditions of political intervention, the need for empirical knowledge, and the close relationship of such knowledge to the managerial functions of the modern state. He closes the essay with an analysis of the increasing "scientification" of policy making, and political life more generally, that has accompanied these developments.

The second part of the book, "Policy Processes," examines the stages of the policy-making process. Werner Jann and Kai Wegrich lead off by considering the utility of the "policy stages" or "cycle model" of the policy process. Paradoxically, they argue, this model is constantly criticized but yet frequently employed to structure research. The authors argue that most scholars have discarded the faulty assumptions associated with the model, using it to structure diverse literatures and to answer important questions about the nature of policy processes. The second chapter, by Thomas Birkland, examines the first stage of the policy process, agenda setting, which is the process by which problems and alternative solutions gain or lose attention. He considers groups' differential ability to control the agenda, the strategies used to draw attention to policy issues, and the range of forces that contribute to movement onto or off of the agenda. He reviews common approaches to measuring and tracking the agenda status of a policy issue. Mara Sidney follows with a discussion of the applied and academic approaches to policy formulation, emphasizing the role of design and the choice of policy instruments or tools. As the stage in the policy process where participants generate alternative solutions to deal with issues that have made it onto the agenda, research on policy formulation sheds light on how policy choices are made. Recent work is shown to bring normative criteria to bear on policy designs, and expands to include nongovernment organizations as policy designers in their own right, including expert policy communities and think tanks. Helga Pülzl and Oliver Treib then explore the implementation stage of the policy process, comparing top-down, bottom-up, and hybrid approaches. They suggest that assessments to date have overlooked the value of these different approaches. Toward this end, they outline a range of insights that can be drawn from them. They also urge policy implementation scholars to focus on implementation problems that confront the European Union, given its unique multicultural problems and, in this respect, argue that interpretive-analytic approaches can offer promising new directions. Finally, Hubert Heinelt takes up Lowi's path-breaking policy typology and examines in particular his proposition that "policies determine politics." Situating the original work within the policy scholarship of that time, he shows how it can be updated and still useful in dealing with contemporary policy issues. He suggests extending and refining the typology by incorporating the role that institutional settings and policy networks play in generating varied political dynamics, and by attending to the mutability of policy boundaries and problem perceptions.

Part III, titled "Policy Politics, Advocacy, and Expertise," turns to the role of political advocacy and expertise in the policy process. It leads off with the influential advocacy coalition framework developed by Paul Sabatier. Christopher Weible and Sabatier outline the framework, illustrating the way coalitions, organized around policy belief systems, struggle to change public policy. The model emphasizes the role of external shocks to political systems and the role of technical knowledge and expert communities in influencing belief systems. They illustrate the model with a brief case study. Hugh Miller and Tansu Demir focus more specifically on the role of policy communities that form around particular policy issues. Policy communities are constituted by professional experts and others who closely follow and participate in debates about a policy problem. The members of these communities share common interests and concerns for the particular issue domain and are engaged in various ways in bringing about policy change. Concentrating on ideas and solutions for policy reform, such communities play an important role in shaping the deliberations about public policy, particularly in the policy agenda-setting and policy formulation phases of the policy-making process. Finally, Diane Stone takes up the topic of policy think tanks, which have also emerged to influence and shape policy ideas. Such institutions, having now emerged in developing as well as developed countries, have become important actors on the political landscape. In some countries they are closely related to political parties or orientations; in others they are relatively free-standing. Supplying or interpreting new knowledge for policy-relevant decisions, policy think tanks are seen to deal with both domestic and foreign policy issues.

The fourth part of the book focuses on rationality in policy decision making and the role of policy networks and learning. Clinton Andrews's chapter on rationality in policy decision making contrasts the idea of "rationality" as science and as metaphor. He extends his analysis across the relevant disciplines, economics, policy analysis, and management science. In particular, he focuses on the the differences between the rational approach to decision making and the more publicly oriented concept of practical reason. Steven Griggs follows by focusing on the influential theory of rational choice. He critically analyzes the approaches of policy researchers using this analytical model to deal with a number of important topics: collective action, coalition building, bureaucracies, and the political-business cycle. His analysis challenges both rational choice theory in policy making and, not less important, the problems it poses for policy researchers using other competing approaches. Putting the theory in political context, he warns against those who argue that rational choice techniques are neutral and pliable tools. In the next chapter of the section, Jörg Raab and Patrick Kenis focus on "policy networks." Observing the attraction that the concept has had for many policy rearchers, particularly the multidisciplinary interest that it has attracted, they report a substantial range of research findings about policy networks. In particular, they emphasize the relevance of networks in promoting innovation. They also discuss questions involving the relation of policy networks in promoting innovation, the diffusion of ideas, resource dependencies, and the implications of unequal resources among policy networks. They conclude by noting that research in this area has often not clearly demonstrated a number of the central claims advanced by policy network theorists. In the section's final chapter, John Grin and Anne Loeber focus on the related concept of policy learning. Policy learning is described as a theoretical orientation often advanced to rival the concept of power as a way of explaining policy change. They contrast policy learning with other theoretical orientations—the stages approach, systems theory, and game theory in particular, examine its role in the transfer of policy ideas, and survey its applications and implications in different research domains.

Part V of the book, "Deliberative Policy Analysis," turns to the role of argumentation, rhetoric, and narratives in the policy-analytic process. Deliberative policy analysis emerges in large part as an epistemological alternative to the neopositivist, technocratic tendencies that have had a strong influence on the discipline. In this approach the focus is on language and argumentation rather than evidence narrowly conceived. In particular, the orientation stresses the enlightenment functions of policy analysis. The article by Frank Fischer opens the section. After surveying the limits of the neopositivist epistemology of mainstream policy analysis and its failures to produce "usable knowledge," the chapter turns to a communications model of policy argumentation. The model, as presented, rests on an informal logic of evaluation, illustrated briefly with a policy illustration related to nuclear power. Herbert Gottweis takes up the age-old perspective of rhetoric and updates it to suit the needs and interests of policy analysis. Particularly important, he shows that a rhetorical perspective permits the inclusion of the emotional elements of policy politics, normally neglected by conventional approaches. It emphasizes, in this respect, the need to attend to particular audiences in the construction and presentation of findings. Finally, Michel van Eeten explores a particular method of argumentative policy analysis focused on story-telling and the narrative form of communication. Drawing on the perspective developed by Emery Roe, he shows the way narratives are employed by both citizens and policy makers. The argument is illustrated with two case studies.

Part VI explores the comparative, cultural, and ethical aspects of public policy. Martin Lodge considers the goals of comparative public policy analysis, identifying its core objective as explaining the determinants of state action by investigating patterns in policy choices and outcomes across contexts. Comparative studies share a common logic, if not common methodologies. They seek to understand issues ranging from how governments raise and spend money, how they acquire and use knowledge, how they organize and deliver services, and what policies they choose to intervene in society. In the second chapter, Robert Hoppe argues that policy analysts should systematically assess the role of culture when analyzing a policy problem or process. He offers group-grid cultural theory as a tool to understand policy discourses that are sensitive to pluralism and that can constructively move stalemated policy processes toward action. Eileen Sullivan and Mary Segers bring prevailing theories of ethical decision making to bear on cases of public officials who confronted difficult questions. Examining cases that include U.S. officials' response to genocide in Rwanda, and decision making about the use of torture in wartime, the authors offer a model for analyzing the ethical considerations in public decisions. They argue for increased application of deontological ethics to decision making. In the final chapter, Anne Larason Schneider and Helen Ingram discuss the many implications for democratic citizenship that are embedded in and shaped by public policies. They consider how policies influence access to the public sphere and how they affect the material conditions that enable or constrain active citizenship. The authors suggest that policies ultimately contribute to a group's degree of identification with the nation, and to their conceptions of their worth in the polity.

The seventh part of the book takes up the primary quantitative-oriented analytical methods employed in policy research. In the first chapter, Kaifeng Yang discusses the development of social science's use of quantitative methods in policy analysis in the United States. He then examines the nature and uses of various methods. These include univariant and bivariate analysis, multiple regression analysis, time series analysis, path analysis, event history analysis, and game theory. In the second chapter on surveys, research, Jerry Mitchell argues that polling attracts and fascinates many policy analysts. Exploring the nature and process of survey research, he describes uses for survey research and its various approaches in policy analysis and ends with a critique, pointing out survey research's pitfalls. In particular, he raises questions about the democratic implications of the use of surveys in the policy decision-making process. Caroline Danielson, writing about social experimentation, examines the claim that experiments have become the "gold standard" in policy evaluation, serving as a rigorous, straightforward arbiter among political choices. She highlights issues involving causation and methodological transparency. By surveying the history of experimentation in policy analysis and examining the content of an experiment, she concludes that any experiment rests on crucial assumptions and has important limitations. The final chapter in the section turns to the methods of evaluation research. Here Hellmut Wollmann inventories the concepts that underlie policy evaluation and raises various political and methodological issues to which they give rise. Exploring the evolution of this form of policy analysis, he emphasizes the institutionalization of evaluation theory and practices in many countries.

Part VIII explores the qualitative sides of policy analysis. It shifts the focus to the subjective dimensions of the analytical assignment, examining the role of interpretation, social meaning, and situational context. Dvora Yanow focuses on the interpretively oriented qualitative methods employed in policy research. She characterizes these methods as word-based and writer-reflexive oriented to the identification and analysis of social meaning. She describes a variety of approaches to data gathering, such as observation, interviewing, reading documents, as well as methods of analyzing the data, such as frame, narrative, and category analyses. Alan Sadovnik contrasts qualitative and quantitative research, tracing qualitative research's history in sociology and education in the United States. He surveys several modern paths qualitative research has followed, from ethnography through case studies and grounded research. He then provides criteria for evaluating such research in policy analysis. Henk Wagenaar turns to deeper epistemological issues underlying interpretive analysis. He argues for the need to systematically investigate the meaningful intentions of the behaviors and actions observed in both policy analysis and policy making. The chapter presents two major approaches to interpretation in policy analysis, the hermeneutical and the tradition-generating social interaction approaches. Susan Clarke closes this section with an analysis of the role of context in choosing to use particular policy methods. Focusing on areas of policy analysis where observations alone may not promote insight or understanding, she shows that context is essential to the full range of data observations. Toward this end, she surveys and critiques a number of context-sensitive methods. She concludes that the context sensitivity of observation will help to balance research rigor with flexibility, reliability, and validity in making persuasive and accessible arguments and providing evidence to back claims.

Part IX, "Policy Decisions Techniques," examines various tools employed to help refine policy choices. In the first chapter on cost-benefit analysis (CBA), Gerald Miller and Donijo Robbins explore the roots of this form of analysis, examine the logic and uses of CBA, and explore its use of contingent valuation in decisions aimed to improve social welfare. They also critique CBA as a form of policy analysis limited by its exclusive use of economic reasoning. The well-established technique of environmental impact assessment (EIA) is the focus of the essay by Yaakov Garb, Miriam Manon, and Deike Peters in the next chapter of this section. Examining the ways it is employed to assess environmental impacts, they trace the history of its use, and suggest ways that it might be helpful in the developing world. They also evaluate the technique in terms of hard science criteria, concluding that EIA is not a hard science, but argue that it can and does contribute to social learning. Bernard Reber then explores the techniques of technology assessment, designed to evaluate the present and future impacts—short- and long-term—of both existing and newly emerging technologies. He first describes the initial development of technology assessment in the United States and then examines its adoption in various European countries. In particular, he outlines the practices of participatory technology assessment (e.g., citizens juries and consensus conferences) that have been innovations in Europe. He then concludes with a discussion of technology assessments' social and normative implications. David Laws and John Forester turn to the uses of dispute mediation and describe the practice and process of mediated negotiation in a world of plural perspectives brought to policy analysis. After discussing its uses with several examples from the U.S. and Canada, they conclude that mediation's practical bent can usefully compel mediators and involved stakeholders to map their relationships to a policy issue, to better understand the issue in terms of their own interest, and to examine those interests in terms of the other parties engaged in this form of negotiation.

The final section of the book, "Country Perspectives," traces the development of policy analysis in selected national contexts. As we noted at the outset, policy analysis emerged as a rather unique American disciplinary field, but, as this section is designed to show, it has subsequently developed in a wide range of other countries around the globe. The authors here review the emergence of the field in different countries, the dominant approaches to policy analysis that have been adopted, and the actors and organizations—both within and outside of government—who practice policy analysis today. The first four of these chapters examine European countries. Wayne Parsons opens with a discussion of policy analysis in Britain. He examines the central role that economic analysis long has played in Britain's policy-making process, and traces the development of policy studies within Britain's universities. New Labour called on the social sciences to "become relevant" by informing government what works and why, but the author is skeptical that the move toward "evidence-based policy making" will solve problems. Igor Mayer subsequently describes the origins and evolution of multiple government agencies responsible for policy analysis in the Netherlands from the post-World War II era to the present, along with the rise of non-state research institutes and think tanks. He traces a pendulum swing from adherence to technocratic, rationalistic models of analysis toward innovative participatory models, with a swing back in the late 1990s toward a public management approach stressing indicators and output measures. Jan-Eric Furubo focuses on Sweden's emphasis on the methods of evaluation research. He discusses the ways the positive orientation in Sweden toward the state as a mechanism for problem solving led to a widespread system of commissions connecting research to politics. This institutional structure easily incorporated tools of program evaluation and budgeting from the United States during the 1960s and 1970s in the context of Sweden's ongoing cultural development. Then Thomas Saretzki dates Germany's increasing interest in policy analysis to the 1970s, under the social-liberal governing coalition, and examines the concomitant shifts as universities and research institutes adapted to demands for usable knowledge. He highlights disciplinary divides among German political scientists, and the growth of a set of research centers that developed distinctive approaches to policy analysis. He describes how political notions of civil society, Europeanization, and ideational approaches have become incorporated into public policy research, and charts a general increase in interest among younger scholars in public policy as a field of study.

The last two chapters focus on developments outside of Europe. India is discussed by Kuldeep

Mathur and Navdeep Mathur. They show that policy analysis in their country has traditionally been framed in terms of development planning, with economistic modes of analysis having long dominated the field. There has been, though, a recent rise of non-state research organizations and community-based groups offering local knowledge that challenges the longstanding economic approach to problem solving within the state. Universities now produce policy research beyond program evaluation, bringing institutional and neo-Marxist approaches to the table. NGOs are shown to increasingly present alternative perspectives on state failures and emphasize the need for democratic, participatory processes of policy making. In the final chapter of the book, Changhwan Mo shows how the shifts in Korean political regimes coincided with and shaped the development of policy analysis. Government agencies dating from the 1960s and 1970s served the interests of an authoritarian regime, producing studies to support its policy preferences, often incorporating American economic analysis techniques. As Korea shifted to a democracy in the late 1980s, policy scholars shifted toward process studies, to analyze the surge of citizen participation and conflict across social and political groups.

SUMMARY

The book's ten sections and forty chapters provide a broad, comprehensive perspective on the field of public policy analysis. The book covers the historical development of policy analysis, its role in the policy process, the empirical methods that have defined the endeavor, the theory that has been generated by these methods, and the normative and ethical issues that surround its practice. The chapters discuss the theoretical debates that have defined the field in more recent years, including the work of postpositivist, interpretivist, and social constructionist scholars. In this respect, the guiding theme throughout the book is the interplay between empirical and normative analysis, a crucial issue running through the contemporary debates of the field.

Part I

Historical Perspectives

1 The Policy Sciences at the Crossroads

Peter deLeon and Danielle M. Vogenbeck

INTRODUCTION

From the time of Harold Lasswell's (1951) first articulation of the policy sciences concept, the benchmark of their field of inquiry was relevance to the political and social worlds. Responding directly to the questions posed by Robert Lynd's (1939) *Knowledge for What?* and John Dewey's relentless pressing of pragmatism (deLeon and Vogenbeck 2006), both its salient theories and real-world applications were at the center of the policy sciences. It was, in many ways, seen by the academic and the administrator as the ultimate culmination of the town and gown orientation.

Seemingly, as the world's problems have become increasingly complex, this orientation should be likewise even more central, as it tries to resolve the problems pressing society and its governments. And, indeed, over the past few decades, virtually every governmental bureaucracy or agency (as well an numerous nonprofit groups) has established some sort of analytic charter and attendant desk (especially those dealing with policy analysis and/or evaluation) to underpin its administrative decisions and agenda (see Radin 2000). At the same time, however, others have described the general abandonment in political circles of rational, analytic thought, with policy scholars often voicing the perception that their work is not being utilized. Donald Beam (1996, 430–431) has characterized policy analysts as fraught with "fear, paranoia, apprehension, and denial" and that they do not "have as much confidence…about their value in the political process as they did 15 or 20 years ago." Heineman and his colleagues (2002, 1 and 9) are equally distressed in terms of access accorded policy research and its results:

> …despite the development of sophisticated methods of inquiry, policy analysis has not had a major substantive impact on policymakers. Policy analysts have remained distant from power centers where policy decisions are made.…In this environment, the values of analytical rigor and logic have given way to political necessities.

More recently, author Ron Suskind described a meeting with an official of the George W. Bush White House; that official's comments directly affect the ways in which policy scholars address their stock and trade:

> The aide said that guys like [Suskind] were "in what we call the reality-based community," which he defined as people who "believe that solutions emerge from your judicious study of discernible reality." I nodded and murmured something about enlightenment principles and empiricism. He cut me off. "That's not the way the world really operates any more," he continued. "We're an empire now, and when we act, we create our own reality. And

while you're studying that reality—judiciously, as you will—we'll act again, creating other new realities, which you can study too, and that's how things will sort out. We're history's actors...and you, all of you, will be left to study what we do." (Suskind 2004, 51)

To this observer, a prescriptive policy analysis was being subverted to a descriptive and mostly irrelevant historical or after-the-fact analysis.

Still, to be fair, the history of post-WW II American public policy represents numerous important achievements. In many ways, the American quality of political life has benefited directly and greatly from public policymaking, ranging from the Truman Doctrine and Marshall Plan (that effectively halted the march of European communism after WW II) to the GI Bill (that brought the benefits of higher education to an entire generation of American men and, with it, the broad dissemination of higher education into the fabric of the American society) to the original Medicare/Medicaid policies (1964) to the American civil rights movements to an flowering of environmental programs to (literally) men on the moon. However, as Derek Bok (1997) has pointed out, American expectations and achievements have hardly produced universal progress compared to other industrialized nations, with crime, the environment, health care, and K-12 education being only four of the United States' shortcomings, thereby recalling Richard Nelson's (1977) trenchant question, "if we can put a man on the moon, why can't we solve the problems of the urban ghetto?" All of which leads one—roughly fifty years after Lasswell's initial articulation of the policy sciences—to ask a series of critical evaluative questions as to their continued vitality: Why are some examples of policy research more successful than others? Or, is there a policy sciences' learning curve? What represents a success and what is its trajectory? Can we calculate the respective costs and benefits? And, ultimately, how do we evaluate the policy sciences in terms of both process and results?

To understand the validity of these concerns, it is necessary to place them in the context of the development of the policy sciences. This chapter examines the political, methodological, and philosophical underpinnings in the development of the policy sciences to trace out their role in the contemporary political setting. It also permits us to propose ways in which the policy sciences might be amended.

THE EVOLUTION OF THE POLICY SCIENCES

For the sake of the discussion, let us quickly set out the central touchstones of the policy sciences approach.[1] The policy sciences approach and its advocates deliberately distinguished themselves from early scholars in (among others) political science, public administration, communications, psychology, jurisprudence, and sociology by posing three defining characteristics that, in combination, transcended the individual contributions from those more traditional areas of study:

1. The policy sciences were consciously framed as being *problem-oriented*, quite explicitly addressing public policy issues and posing recommendations for their relief, while openly rejecting the study of a phenomenon for its own sake (Lasswell 1956); the societal or political question—So what?—has always been pivotal in the policy sciences' approach. Likewise, policy problems are seen to occur in a specific context, a context that must be carefully considered in terms of the analysis, methodology, and subsequent recommendations. Thus, necessarily, the policy approach has not developed an overarching theoretic foundation.

2. The policy sciences are distinctively *multi-disciplinary* in their intellectual and practical approaches. This is because almost every social or political problem has multiple compo-

---

1. Greater detail and explanation can be found in deLeon (1988); "archival" materials might include Lasswell 1951a, 1951b, and 1971; Lasswell and Kaplan 1950; Dewey 1927; Merriam 1926; and Merton 1936.

nents closely linked to the various academic disciplines without falling clearly into any one discipline's exclusive domain. Therefore, to gain a complete appreciation of the phenomenon, many relevant orientations must be utilized and integrated. Imagine, if you can, policy research in urban redevelopment (or, for that matter, international terrorism) that did not entail a constellation of disciplinary approaches and skills.

3. The policy sciences' approach is deliberately *normative* or *value oriented*; in many cases, the recurring theme of the policy sciences deals with the democratic ethos and human dignity.[2] This value orientation was largely in reaction to behavioralism, i.e., "objectivism," in the social sciences, and in recognition that no social problem nor methodological approach is value free. As such, to understand a problem, one must acknowledge its value components. Similarly, no policy scientist is without her/his own personal values, which also must be understood, if not resolved, as Amy (1984) has discussed. This theme later achieved a central role in the policy sciences' movement to a post-positivist orientation (see, among others, Dryzek 1990, and Fischer 2003).

Beryl Radin (2000) and Peter deLeon (1988) have both described the institutional and political evolutions of the policy sciences.[3] Although they are not in obvious opposition to one another, their respective chronologies offer contrasting emphases. Radin (2000) argued that the policy analysis approach knowingly drew upon the heritage of American public administration scholarship; for instance, she suggested that policy analysis represent a continuation of the early twentieth century Progressive Movement (also see Fischer 2003) in particular, in terms of its scientific analysis of social issues and the democratic polity. Her narrative particularly focused on the institutional (and supporting educational) growth of the policy analysis approach. Radin suggested a fundamentally linear (albeit gradual) progression from a limited analytic approach practiced by a relatively few practitioners (e.g., by the Rand Corporation in California; see Smith 1966) to a growing number of government institutions, "think tanks," and universities.

Following the introduction and apparent success of systems analysis (which many see as the direct precursor of policy analysis) in Secretary Robert McNamara's Department of Defense in the early 1960s (see Smith 1966), its applications spread out into other government agencies, such as the Department of Health, Education, and Welfare in the mid-1960s, with the explicit blessing of President Lyndon Johnson. Although systems analysis never again enjoyed the great (and, to be fair, transitory) success that it did in the Defense Department (see Wildavsky 1979), the analytic orientation soon was adopted by a number of federal offices, state agencies, and a large number of analytic consultant groups (see Fischer 1993, and Ricci 1984). Thus, Radin (2000) viewed the development of the policy analysis as a "growth industry," in which a few select government agencies first adopted an explicitly innovative analytic approach, others followed, and an industry developed to service them. Institutional problems, such as the appropriate bureaucratic locations for policy analysis, arose but were largely overcome. However, this narrative pays scant attention to three hallmarks of the policy sciences approach: there is little direct attention to the problem orientation of the activity, the multidisciplinary themes are largely neglected, and the normative groundings of policy issues (and recommendations) are often overlooked. As such, Radin's very thoughtful analysis described the largely successful institutional (but basically apolitical) process of formal policy research finding a bureaucratic home in governments.

---

2. In one of its earliest founding declarations, H. D. Lasswell and Abraham Kaplan (1950, xii and xxiv) dedicated the policy sciences to provide the "intelligence pertinent to the integration of values realized by and embodies in interpersonal relations," which "prizes not the glory of a depersonalize state of the efficiency of a social mechanism, but human dignity and the realization of human capabilities."

3. For the present purposes, let us assume that the policy sciences rubric encompasses the differences described by the terms "policy analysis," "systems analysis," and "policy sciences." Fischer (2003, fns. 1 and 4, pp. 1 and 3, respectively) is in agreement with deLeon (1988) in this usage.

DeLeon (1988) offered a parallel but somewhat more complicated model in which he links analytic activities related to specific political events (what he terms *supply*, that is, events that supplied analysts with a set of particular conditions to which they could apply their skills, a learning activity, if you will) with an evolving requirement for policy analysis within government offices (*demand*, i.e., a growing requirement for analytic skills). In particular, he suggested a series of five political events as having been pivotal in the development of the policy sciences, in terms of lessons learned:[4]

The Second World War. The United States assembled an unprecedented number of social scientists—economists, political scientists, operations researchers, psychologists, etc.—to apply their particular skills to further the Allied war efforts. These activities established an important precedent, illustrating the ability of the social sciences to direct problem-oriented analysis to urgent public issues, in this case, assuring victory over the Axis powers. Indeed, Lasswell and his policy sciences collaborator Abraham Kaplan spent the war studying propaganda techniques employed by the Library of Congress. These collective efforts (and their apparent successes) led directly to the postwar establishment of the National Science Foundation (admittedly more concerned at first with the physical sciences) and the Council of Economic Advisors, as well as research facilities such as the Rand Corporation (Smith 1966) and the Brookings Institution (Lyons 1969). However, in general, while the *supply* side of the policy equation was seemingly battle-tested and ready, there was little on the *demand* side from the government, perhaps because of the post-WW II society's desire to return to normalcy.

The War on Poverty. In the early 1960s, largely fueled by the emerging civil rights demonstrations and the new visibility of major nonprofit organizations (e.g., the Ford Foundation) on the U.S. political scene, Americans finally took notice of the pervasive, demeaning poverty extant in "the other America" (Harrington 1963) and realized that as a body politic they were remarkably uninformed. Social scientists moved aggressively into this knowledge gap with enthusiasm but little agreement, producing what Moynihan (1969) called "maximum feasible misunderstanding." A vast array of social programs was initiated to address this particular war, with important milestones being achieved, especially in the improved statistical measures of what constituted poverty and evaluation measures to assess the various anti-poverty programs (see Rivlin 1970), and, of course, civil rights (i.e., the 1964 Civil Rights Act). Walter Williams (1998), reminiscing about his earlier days in the Office of Economic Opportunity (O.E.O.), has suggested that these were the "glory days" of policy analysis. Other O.E.O. veterans, such as Robert Levine (1970), were more reserved, while some, such as Murray (1984), went so far as to indicate that with the advent of the antipoverty, anticrime, and affirmative action programs, the American poor was actually "losing ground." At best, policy analysts were forced to confront the immense complexity of the social condition and discover that in some instances, there were no easy answers. DeLeon (1988, 61) later summarized the result of the War on Poverty as "a decade of trial, error, and frustration, after which it was arguable if ten years and billions of dollars had produced any discernible, let alone effective, relief."[5]

The Vietnam War. The Vietnam War brought the tools of policy analysis to combat situations, a massive analytic exercise that was exacerbated by the growing domestic unrest as to its conduct and, of course, the loss of lives suffered by its participants. The war was closely monitored by Secretary of Defense McNamara's office, with on-going scrutiny from Presidents Kennedy, Johnson, and Nixon;[6] these participating personnel, in the words of David Halberstam (1972), were "the best and the brightest." But it became increasingly obvious that analytic rigor—specified in terms such as

---

4. These are elaborated upon in deLeon (1988). Fischer (2003) and Dryzek (1993) have adopted much of his interpretation.
5. For details regarding the War on Poverty, see Aaron (1978), Kershaw (1970), and Nathan (1985).
6. As was reflected by the publication by the *New York Times* of the McNamara review of the Vietnam commitment, widely known as The Pentagon Papers (Sheenan 1972).

body counts, *ordnance expended*, and *supplies moved*—and rational decision making were largely rendered irrelevant by the growing public sentiment against the war often critically described in the American media, and finally reflected in the 1972 American presidential elections. Too often there was evidence that the hard and fast numbers were being purposively manipulated to serve military and political ends. Moreover, even on its relatively good days, systems analysts were not intellectually able to encompass the almost daily changes in the war's activities occurring in both the international and domestic arenas. At the time, Colin Gray (1971) argued that systems analysis, one of the apparent U.S. advantages of defense policymaking, turned out to be a major shortcoming of the American war effort and was a partial contributor to the ultimate U.S. failures in Vietnam. Finally, and most tellingly, Defense Department analysts could not reflect the (respective) political wills necessary to triumph, or, in the case of this war, outlast the opponent. Cost-effective approaches against the North Vietnamese did little to diminish their war-fighting capacity (see Gelb and Betts 1979), until U.S. troops were finally literally forced to abandon the nation they had sacrificed over fifty thousand lives to protect.

The Watergate Scandal. The most troubling activities surrounding the re-election of President Richard Nixon in the 1972 campaign, his administration and the Committee to Re-elect the President's (CREEP) heavy-handed attempts to "cover up" the tell-tale incriminating signs, and his willingness to covertly prosecute Vietnam war protester Daniel Ellsberg led to impeachment charges being leveled against an American President, which were only averted because President Nixon chose to resign in ignominy rather than face congressional impeachment proceedings (Lukas 1976; Olson 2003).[7] The undeniable evidence of culpability in the highest councils of the U.S. government led to the clear recognition by the public that moral norms and values had been violated by the associates of the president with the almost sure connivance by the president himself. These unsanctioned activities of government, e.g., the amassing of illegal evidence (probably through unconstitutional means) undermined the public norm and constituted an unpardonable political act. Indeed, many observers have argued that President Gerald Ford (who, as President Nixon's appointed vice president, succeeded him) lost to candidate Jimmy Carter in the 1976 presidential election because he chose to pardon President Nixon, thus protecting him from possible criminal prosecution. Few can look back on the Watergate scandal without reflecting on its effect of the public's trust in its elected government. Jimmy Carter's remarkable campaign pledge that "I will never lie to you" and the Ethics in Government Act (1978) were only the most visible realizations that normative standards were central to the activities of government, validating, as it were, one of the central tenets of the policy sciences.

The Energy Crisis of the 1970s. If the early 1960s' wellspring of analytic efforts was the War on Poverty and the late 1960s' was the Vietnam engagement, the 1970s' energy crisis provided ample grounds for the best analytic efforts the country could offer. Beset with nation-wide high gasoline prices, the public was all-but-awash with descriptions of and recommendations for a national energy policy; its elements might have addressed the level of petroleum reserves (domestic and world-wide) and competing energy sources (e.g., nuclear vs. petroleum vs. solar), all over differing (projected) time horizons (e.g., see Stobaugh and Yergin 1979). With this veritable ocean of technical data, the analytic community was seemingly prepared to knowingly inform the energy policymakers, up to and including the president. But, this was not to be the case. As Weyant was later to note, "perhaps as many as two-thirds of the [energy] models failed to achieve their avowed purposes in the form of direct application to policy problems" (Weyant 1980, 212). The contrast was both striking and apparent: energy policy was replete in technical, analytic considerations (e.g., untapped petroleum reserves and complex technical modeling; see Greenberger et al. 1983), but the basic decisions

---

7. The impeachment episode was made more sordid by the earlier resignation of President Nixon's Vice President, Spiro Agnew, rather than face charges of political corruption incurred while he was the Governor of Maryland (see Cohen and Witcover 1974).

were decidedly political in nature (that is, *not* driven by analysis)—President Nixon established Project Independence, President Carter declared that energy independence represented the "moral equivalency of war," President Ford created a new Department of Energy (see Commoner 1979), with President Carter expanding the alternatives option by creating the Solar Energy Research Institute (Laird 2001). There was seemingly a convergence between analytic supply and government demand, yet no policy coherence, let alone consensus, was achieved, a condition that did little to endear the policy sciences approach with either its immediate clients (government officials) or its ultimate beneficiaries (the citizenry).

Since deLeon's (1988) analysis, a final historical event seemingly has cast its shadow on the development of the policy sciences, namely *the end of the Cold War*.[8] The Cold War basically dictated American politics from the end of the Second World War until the very end of the 1980s and, in retrospect, was almost as much an analytic activity as it was political.[9] Given that the central occupation of the American Central Intelligence Agency (CIA), virtually since it was created, was the careful and thorough monitoring of the (then) Soviet Union, it was particularly remarkable that U.S. policymakers were caught almost totally unawares when Mikhail Gorbachev (and later Boris Yeltsin) presided over the demise of the "evil empire," almost as demanded by President Ronald Reagan a few years earlier. Without questioning the personal courage and (later) flexibility of U.S. and Russian leaders, it was telling that neither system seemed to have the analytic wherewithal that was capable of developing friendly overtures toward one another. One standard explanation was that the U.S. defense budget (and its impending arsenal of weapons systems) forced the Soviets into a ruinously costly arms race, a race in which it found itself unable to compete economically, let alone technically. This disparity led the Soviet to abandon the Cold War, even if this meant the certain loss of the Soviet "empire." While not without its merits, this interpretation sorely neglects the effects of the American antinuclear movement (deLeon 1987) on its leaders. In short, the analytic fumblings of the CIA and the mis-estimation of the effects of American public opinion did much to set the existing Cold War in the public's conscience and did little to suggest how it might have ended. That is, the end of the Cold War, however salutary, did not represent a feather in the policy sciences' cap.

We need to observe that while the fruits of the policy sciences might not have been especially bountiful when observed through a set of political lenses, nevertheless, political activities and results are not synonymous with the policy sciences. But it is equally certain that the two are coincident, that they reside in the same policy space. If the policy sciences are to meet the goals of improving government policy through a rigorous application of its central themes, then the failures of the body politic naturally must be at least partially attributed to failure of, or at least a serious shortfall in the policy sciences' approach. To ask the same question from an oppositional perspective: Why should the nominal recipients of policy research subscribe to it if the research and the resulting policy does not reflect the values and intuitions of the client policymaker, that is, in their eyes, does not represent any discernable value added? To this question, one needs to add the issue of democratic governance, a concept virtually everybody would agree upon until the important issues of detail emerge (see deLeon 1997; Barber, 1984; Dahl 1970/1990), e.g., does direct democracy have a realistic place in a representative, basically pluralist democracy. Still, this is an issue repeatedly raised by contemporary observers (e.g., Dionne 1991; Nye et al. 1997), none more pointedly than Christopher Lasch: "does democracy have a future?... It isn't a question of whether democracy *can* survive...[it] is whether

---

8. Certainly other political events since 1990 have weighed heavily on the American body politics (e.g., the impeachment trial of President William Clinton and the various events surrounding the war on terrorism including the invasions of Afghanistan and Iraq), but the historical record on these events, let alone their effects on the policy research communities, have yet to be written.

9. There is a lengthy literature on this monumental topic; see Gaddis (1992) and Beschloss and Talbott (1993) for two timely analyses.

democracy *deserves* to survive" (1995, 1 and 85; emphases added). In light of legislation such as the USA PATRIOT Act (passed in the immediate aftermath of the September 11, 1991 attacks on Washington D.C. and New York City), this question becomes even more germane.

BACKWARD TO THE FUTURE

It is important to realize that the challenges to the policy sciences are not unexpected; any orientation explicitly predicated on normative values is certain to be contentious, just as a range of value issues is fractious. Moreover, the founders of the policy sciences recognized that their approaches were certain to change, as the dilemmas and challenges faced by the policy sciences changed. We can look more closely at two areas in which changes are more likely for the policy sciences, in its interactions with the world of political reality and an expansion of its theoretic constructs.

The first dilemma, one which seems as intractable as the changing political scene would imagine, is reflected in what Douglas Torgerson (1986, 52–53; emphases in original) has depicted as:

> The dynamic nature of the [policy sciences] phenomenon is rooted in an internal tension, a *dialectic opposition between knowledge and politics*. Through the interplay of knowledge and politics, different aspects of the phenomenon become salient at different moments...the presence of dialectical tension means that the phenomenon has the potential to develop, to change its form. However, no particular pattern of development is inevitable.

The described tension is hardly novel; C. P. Snow (1964) described this inherent conflict in terms of "two cultures," in his case, politics and science. What with the increases polarization of the American body politic, almost any given issue is well-fortified with (at least) two sets of orthogonal policy analytic-based positions, each carefully articulated in both the policy and normative modes (Rich 2004). And the growing complexity within policy issues (and between policy issues and the natural environment; see Wilson 1998) only make the roles staked out by the policy sciences more difficult to operationalize. In many ways, the three-tiered characteristics central to the policy sciences' approach that were spelled out earlier have been largely accommodated: the policy focus is increasingly on social problems, however and whoever is defining them; few would argue nowadays that politico-social problems are anything else than grounds for multidisciplinary research, with the only real debate is over which disciplines have particular standing; and most would agree that norms—not "objective" science—are at the heart of most politico-social disputes. For example, nobody would suggest that President G. W. Bush's education initiatives are mal-intended, but proponents and opponents will argue endlessly over the thrust and details of the No Child Left Behind program and, more generally, the role of the federal government in elementary education.

The problem then, lies more in the reconciliation of differing policy research activities. This resolution is often confounded by differing stances and positions, neither of which is particularly amendable to compromise by those involved. The effect of the policy research orientation is that all sides to any given arguments have their supportive analytic evidence, thus neatly reducing the argument to the underlying values. Which, of course, is the heart of the problem. The policy sciences only promised to bring greater intelligence to government; nobody ever made claims that they would *ipso facto* make government and its accompanying politic more intelligent. The intellectual and organizational format, then, is widely accepted but the exact content and the end results remain under almost constant dispute, so participants can argue over the most basic (and often intractable) points, such as the appropriate roles of the federal government and the private market.

The major epistemological thrust that has emerged over the past decade in the policy sciences has been reflected in the transition from an empirical (often described as a "positivist") methodology to a more context-oriented "post-positivist" methodology, and, with it, a return to the democratic orientation that Lasswell and his colleagues had earlier championed. In many ways, this movement had three components. First, as noted above, the policy sciences' record of historical successes was much less than impressive. Many scholars suggested that the shortcomings of the policy sciences were possibly due to its positivist methodologies, one historically based on the tenets of social welfare economics (e.g., benefit/cost analysis) that were fundamentally flawed; as such, it should not be surprising that the resulting analyses were also flawed. John Dryzek (1990, 4–6) was scathing in his assessments of positivism, especially over what he (and others; see Fischer 2003; Hajer and Wagenaar 2003) referred to "instrumental rationality," which he claims,

> destroys the more congenial, spontaneous, egalitarian, and intrinsically meaningful aspects of human association... represses individuals... is ineffective when confronted with complex social problems... makes effective and appropriate policy analysis impossible... [and, most critically] is antidemocratic.

Second, the post-positivist epistemological orientation argued for an alternative policy approach, one that has featured different variations of greater citizen participation (as opposed to technical, generally removed elites), often under the phrase of "participatory policy analysis" (deLeon 1997; Fischer 2003; Dryzek 1990; Mayer 1997) or "deliberative democracy" (see Dryzek 2000; Elster 1998; Gutmann and Thompson 2004). In a more applied set of exercises, James Fishkin (1991; 1995) has engaged citizen-voters in a series of discursive panels as a way of bringing public education, awareness, and deliberation to the political policymaking arena. While many have described these meetings as "new," in truth, they would have been familiar and welcomed to a host of political philosophers as far back as Aristotle (and the Athenian fora) to Jean-Jacques Rosseau to John Stuart Mills to New England town meetings to John Dewey.

Third, policy theorists began to realize that the socio-politico was too complex to be reduced by reduction approaches, and that differing context often required very different perspectives and epistemologies; that is, objectivism was inadequate to the policy tasks. Moreover, many of the perceived conditions were subjectively ascribed to the situation and the participants. If, in fact, the socio-politico context and the individuals within it were a function of social construction, as these theorists (Schneider and Ingram 1997; Fischer 2003; Schneider and Ingram 2005) have contended, then a deliberative democracy model (or some variant) becomes even more essential as affected parties try to forge an agreement, and a benefit-cost analysis (as an example of the historic policy analysis) becomes even more problematic.

But while deliberative democracy or participatory policy analysis has been promising—even illuminating—to many theorists, it has also been severely criticized by others as being "too cumbersome" or demanding too much time or including too many participants to move toward policy closure, especially in today's mega-polities (deLeon 1997); some have characterized it as little more than a publicity exercise in which the opposing group that has the more strident vocal chords or lasting power is the invariable winner. Furthermore, as Larry Lynn (1999) has convincingly argued, many lucid and powerful (and in some cases, unanticipated) insights have been gleaned from the collective analytic (read: positivist) corpus conducted over the past fifty years and there is little reason to suspect that future analysts would want to exorcise these findings or overlook these approaches. Rivlin (1970) observed years ago that policy research has been slow and it might not have arrived at many definitive answers to social problems, but it has at least discerned appropriate questions to be posed. These insights and capability should not be treated lightly, for asking the right questions is surely a necessary step in deriving the right answers. The question then becomes one of problem recognition and when and where to use the methodologies suggested by the problem itself (deLeon 1998).

Some years back, Hugh Heclo (1978) introduced the concept of "issue networks," in which he noted that "…it is through networks of people who regard each other as knowledgeable…that public policy issues tend to be refined, evidence debated, and alternative options worked out—though rarely in any controlled, well-organized way." These horizontal relationships can include individuals, organizations, lobbyists, legislators, or whoever plays a role in policy development. Heclo's work evolved into the concept of *social network analysis* (Wasserman and Faust 1994; Scott 1991), particularly those under a democratic, participative regimen (see Hajer and Wagenaar 2003). This concept is characterized by its use of "networks" as the temporal unit of analysis. That is, public policy issues are no longer the exclusive domain of specified governmental units (i.e., the Department of Commerce for globalization issues or Homeland Security for terrorism) per se. Rather, they tend to reside in *issue* networks, including governmental units on the federal *and* state *and* municipal levels; these are constantly seen to be interacting with important nonprofit organizations on both the national and local levels, and various representations from the private sector as well. Public policies in health care, education, social welfare, and the environment suggest the centrality of the social network phenomenon; President G.W. Bush's programs in "faith-based" initiatives manifest social networks. All of these actors are engaging in what Hajer (1993) called "policy discourses," hopefully, but not always, in a cooperative nature.

Hanf and Scharpf (1978, 12) viewed the policy network approach as a tool to evaluate the "large number of public and private actors from different levels and functional areas of government and society." More traditional forms of policy research have tended to focus on the *hierarchical* policy process. The network approach looks at the policy process in terms of the *horizontal* relationships that define the development of public policies. Thus, Rhodes (1990, 304; also see Carlsson 2000) has defined policy networks as "cluster[s] or complexes of organizations connected to each other by resource dependencies and distinguished from other clusters or complexes by breaks in the structure of resource dependencies." Although there are certainly shortcomings (i.e., for instance, in bounding the scope of the analysis), in many ways social network analysis provides the policy sciences with a methodological approach that is more consonant with the wide range of institutional actors who constitute the policy process than those aggregated under the positivists' approaches.

A final conceptual trend emerging over the past decade has been the movement in most of the industrialized nations toward a more decentralized (or devoluted) polity. While this is most readily observed in the new public management literature,[10] it is easily observed in a host of recent legislation, such as the Welfare Reform Act and the Telecommunications Act (both 1996), as well as in the federal government's recent willingness to defer policy initiatives to the state without sufficiently funding them. In many ways, devolution resonates with a more democratic participatory policy approach, since both are more directly involved with the local units of government and the affected citizen.

CONCLUSIONS

As we have noted above, proponents of the policy sciences can point to a half century of activity, with some success (e.g., the widespread acceptance of the policy approach and its three central conceptual touchstones), some trepidation, or misgivings (what we referred to as the "policy paradox"). Moreover, the importance accorded to the policy analysis processes has implicitly turned policymakers' attention to the more normative aspects of policy, which is ultimately the least amenable to the traditional (read: accepted) forms of policy analysis.

---

10. "Devolution" became the hallmark of the Clinton-Gore administration and their National Performance Review—largely driven by Osborne and Gaebler's (1992) work—but has continued unabated under the administration of George W. Bush, with the important exception of issues dealing with Homeland Security.

We pose two suggestions to possibly reinvigorate the policy approach. The first has to do with the training of future analysts (also see Fischer 2003), implying that the traditional analytic toolkit is, at best, incomplete or, at worst (in Dryzek's words), "ineffective . . . and antidemocratic . . ." Newer policy approaches—sometimes to compliment, other times to replace the more traditional forms of policy analysis—need to be articulated from the post-positivist epistemologies and the social networks analysis approach. Again, the focus should be on choosing the appropriate approach as a function of the problem at hand, rather than always using the same approach for whatever problem occurs (deLeon 1998). One obvious requirement is that policy researchers will need to acquire a new set of analytic skills dealing with public education and negotiation and mediation, that is, helping to foster new policy design models that are less hierarchical than has been the case, rather than simply advising policymakers.

Likewise, the policy scientist should become more fluent and practiced in addressing the potential effects of decentralized authority, for it is obvious that American government and its offices are moving at the moment toward a more localized, state-centered form of government; indeed, many conservatives (and their policy research efforts) are devising ways to minimize governmental services in general and the federal government in particular. These trends raise troubling issues, such as what measures would be necessary to ensure public accountability? This segues into another recurring dilemma for the policy sciences, namely, how does one insure analyst's impartiality or balance, or, alternatively, are these virtues outmoded in an era characterized by and accustomed to fractious policy debates and interchanges?

One would strongly suspect that Lasswell and Lerner and Merton and Kaplan et al., who first articulated the policy sciences' founding premises, would not have expected them to remain untouched or somehow sacred through the vicissitudes of political events and intellectual challenges. Nor would they have dared to predict a string of unvarnished successes or even widespread acceptance. The challenge, then, for the contemporary policy sciences—if indeed they are at a turning point—is to assimilate how and why the world has changed. With this knowledge in mind, it is imperative that they to re-examine their conceptual and methodological cupboards to make sure they well stocked in order to understand the contemporary exigencies and to offer appropriate wisdom and recommendations. If they falter in those endeavors, then indeed the policy sciences are at a perilous crossroad.

REFERENCES

Aaron, Henry J. (1978). *Politics and the Professor: The Great Society in Perspective.* Washington, DC: The Brookings Institution.

Amy, Douglas J. (1984). "Why Policy Analysis and Ethics are Incompatible." *Journal of Policy Analysis and Management.* Vol. 3, No. 4 (Summer). Pp. 573-591 .

Barber, Benjamin (1984). *Strong Democracy: Participatory Politics for a New Age.* Berkeley: University of California Press.

Bean, David R. (1996). "If Public Ideas Are So Important Now, Why Are Policy Analysts So Depressed?" *Journal of Policy Analysis and Management.* Vol. 15, No. 3 (Fall). Pp. 430-437

Beschloss, Michael R., and Strobe Talbott (1993). *At the Highest Levels: The Inside Story of the End of the Cold War.* Boston: Little, Brown.

Carlsson, Lars (2000). "Policy Networks as Collective Action." *Policy Studies Journal.* Vol. 28, No. 3. Pp. 502-527.

Cohen, Ricahrd M., and Jules Witcover (1974). *A Heartbeat Away.* New York: Viking.

Commoner, Barry (1979). *The Politics of Energy.* New York: Alfred A. Knopf.

Dahl, Robert A. (1970/1999). *After the Revolution.* New Haven, CT: Yale University Press.

deLeon, Peter (1987). *The Altered Strategic Environment.* Cambridge, MA: Ballinger Press.

———— (1988). *Advice and Consent.* New York: Russell Sage Foundation.

———— (1997). *Democracy and the Policy Sciences*. Albany: SUNY Press.

———— (1998). "Models of Policy Discourse: Insights vs. Prediction." *Policy Studies Journal*. Vol. 26, No. 1 (Spring). Pp. 147-161.

———— and Danielle M. Vogenbeck (2006-forthcoming). "Back to Square One: A History and Promise of the Policy Sciences." In Jack Rabin, W. Bartley Hildreth, and Gerald J. Miller (eds.). *Handbook of Public Administration*. New York: Marcel Dekker. Third Edition.

Dewey, John (1927). *The Public and Its Problems*. Denver: Allan Swallow.

Dionne, E. J. (1991). *Why Americans Hate Politics*. New York: Simon & Schuster.

Dryzek, John S. (1990). *Discursive Democracy: Politics, Policy, and Political Science*: Cambridge, UK: Cambridge University Press.

———— (1993). "Policy Analysis and Planning: From Science to Argument." In Frank Fischer and John Forester (eds.). *The Argumentative Turn in Policy Analysis and Planning*. Durham, NC: Duke University Press. Pp. 213-232.

———— (2000). *Deliberative Democracy and Beyond*. New York: Oxford University Press.

Elster, Jon (ed.) (1998). *Deliberative Democracy*. New York: Cambridge University Press.

Fischer, Frank (1993). "Policy Discourse and the Politics of Washington Think Tanks." In Frank Fischer and John Forester (eds.). *The Argumentative Turn in Policy Analysis and Planning*. Durham, NC: Duke University Press. Pp. 21-42.

———— (2003). *Reframing Public Policy*. Oxford, UK: Oxford University Press.

Fishkin, James S. (1991). *Democracy and Deliberation*. New Haven, CT: Yale University Press.

———— (1995). *The Voice of the People: Public Opinion and Democracy*. New Haven, CT: Yale University Press.

Gaddis, John Lewis (1992). *The US and the End of the Cold War*. New York: Oxford University Press.

Gelb, Leslie H., with Richard K. Betts (1979). *The Tragedy of Vietnam: The System Worked*. Washington DC: The Brookings Institution.

Gray, Colin (1971). "What Has Rand Wrought?" *Foreign Policy*. No. 4 (Fall). Pp. 111-129.

Greenberger, Martin, Garry D. Brewer, Thomas Schelling (1984). *Caught Unawares: The Energy Decade in Retrospect*. Cambridge, MA: Ballinger.

Gutmann, Amy, and Dennis Thompson (2004). *Why Deliberative Democracy?* Princeton: Princeton University Press.

Hajer, Maarten A. (1993). "Discourse Coalitions and the Institutionalization of Prace: The Case of Acid Rain in Great Britain." In Frank Fischer and John Forester (eds.). *The Argumentative Turn in Policy Analysis and Planning*. Durham, NC: Duke University Press. Pp. 43-76.

Hajer, Maarten A., and Hendrik Wagenaar (2003). "Introduction." In Maarten A., Hajer and Hendrik Wagenaaar (eds). *Deliberative Policy Analysis: Understanding Governance in the Network Society*. Cambridge, NY: Cambrige University Press. Pp. 1-33.

Halberstam, David (1972). *The Best and the Brightest*. New York: Random House.

Hanf, Kenneth, and Fritz W. Scharpf (1978), "Introduction." In Kenneth Hanf and Fritz W. Scharpf (eds.). *Interorganizational Policy Making: Limits to Coordination and Control*. London: Sage. Pp. 1-15.

Harrington, Michael (1963). *The Other America: Poverty in the United States*. New York: Macmillan

Heclo, Hugh (1978). "Issue Networks and the Executive Establishment." In Anthony King (ed.) (1978). *The New American Political System*. Washington DC: American Enterprise Institute.

Heineman, Robert A., William T. Bluhm, Steven A. Peterson, and Edward N. Kearny (2002). *The World of the Policy Analyst*. Chatham, NJ: Chatham House Publishers. Third Edition.

Kershaw, Joseph A, with Paul N. Courant (1970). *Government Against Poverty*. Chicago: Markham, for the Brookings Institution.

Laird, Frank N. (2001). *Solar Energy, Technolgy Policy, and Institutional Values*. New York. Cambridge University Press.

Lasch, Christopher (1995). *The Revolt of the Elites and the Betrayal of Democracy*. New York: W.W. Norton.

Lasswell, Harold D. (1951a). "The Policy Orientation," in Daniel Lerner and Harold D. Lasswell (eds.), *The Policy Sciences*. Palo Alto, CA: Stanford University Press, Chap. 1.

———— (1951b). *The World Revolution of Our Time: A Framework for Basic Policy Research*. Palo Alto, CA: Stanford University Press. Reprinted in Harold D. Lasswell and Daniel Lerner (eds.), *World Revolutionary Elites*. Cambridge, MA: The MIT Press, 1965, Chap. 2.

——— (1956). "The Political Science of Science." *American Political Science Review.* Vol. 50, No. 4 (December). Pp. 961-979.

——— (1971). *A Pre-View of Policy Sciences.* New York: American Elsevier.

——— and Abraham Kaplan (1950*). Power and Society.* New Haven, CT: Yale University Press.

Levine, Robert A. (1970). *The Poor Ye Need Not Have With You: Lessons from the War on Poverty.* Cambridge, MA: The MIT Press.

Lukas, J. Anthony (1976). *Nightmare: The Underside of the Nixon Years.* New York: Viking.

Lynd, Robert S. (1939). *Knowledge for What? The Place for Social Science in the American Culture.* Princeton, NJ: Princeton University Press.

Lynn, Laurence E., Jr. (1999). "A Place at the Table: Policy Analysis, Its Postpositivist Critics, and the Future of Practice." *Journal of Policy Analysis and Management.* Vol. 18, No. 5 (Summer). Pp. 411-424.

Lyons, Eugene M. (1969). *The Uneasy Partnership.* New York: Russell Sage Foundation.

Mayer, Igor (1997). *Debating Technologies: A Methodological Contribution to the Design and Evaluation of Participatory Policy Analysis.* Tilburg, NL: Tilburg University Press.

Merriam, Charles E. (1926). Progress in Political Research," *American Political Science Review.* Vol. 20, No. 1 (February). Pp. 1-13.

Merton, Robert K. (1936). "The Unanticipated Consequences of Purposive Social Action." *American Sociological Review.* Vol. 1, No. 4 (December). Pp. 894-904.

Moynihan, Daniel P. (1969). *Maximum Feasible Misunderstanding: Community Action in the War on Poverty.* New York: The Free Press.

Murray, Charles (1984). *Losing Ground.* New York: Basic Books.

Nathan, Richard P. (1985). "Research Lessons from the Great Society." *Journal of Policy Analysis and Management.* Vol. 4, No. 3 (Spring). Pp. 422-26.

Nelson, Richard N. (1977). *The Moon and the Ghetto.* New York: W.W. Norton.

Nye, Joseph S., Jr., Philip D. Zelikow, and David C. King (eds.) (1997) *Why People Don't Trust Government.* Cambridge, MA: Harvard University Press.

Olson, Keith W. (2003). *Watergate: The Presidential Scandal that Shook America.* Lawrence, KS: The University Press of Kansas.

Osborne, David, and Thomas Gaebler (1992). *Reinventing Government.* Reading, MA: Addison-Wesley.

Radin, Beryl A. (2000). *Beyond Machiavelli: Policy Analysis Comes of Age.* Washington, DC: Georgetown University Press.

Ricci, David M. (1984). *The Transformation of American Politics: The New Washington and the Rise of Think Tanks.* New Haven, CT: Yale University Press.

Rich, Andrew (2004). *Think Tanks, Pubilc Policy, and the Role of Expertise.* New York: Cambridge University Press.

Rivlin, Alice M. (1970). *Systematic Thinking for Social Action.* Washington DC: The Brookings Institution.

Rhodes, R.A.W. (1990). "Policy Networks: A British Perspective." *Journal of Theoretical Politics.* Vol. 2, No. 3. Pp. 293-317.

Schneider, Anne Larason, and Helen Ingram (1997). Policy Design for Democracy. Lawrence: University of Kansas Press.

——— (eds.) (2005). *Deserving and Entitled: Social Construction and Public Policy.* Albany: SUNY Press.

Sheenan, Neil (1972). *The Pentagon Papers.* New York: Bantam for the *New York Times.*

Smith, Bruce L.R. (1966). *The RAND Corporation.* Cambridge, MA: Harvard University Press.

Snow, C.P. (1064). *The Two Cultures.* New York: Cambridge University Press.

Stobaugh, Roger, and Daniel Yergin (eds.) (1979). *Energy Futures.* New York: Random House.

Suskind, Ron (2004). "Without A Doubt." *New York Times Magazine.* October 17. Pp. 46-61, 64, 102, 105.

Wasserman, Stanley, and Katherine Faust (1994). *Social Network Analysis: Methods and Applications.* Cambridge, UK: Cambridge University Press.

Weyant, John P. (1980). "Quantitative Models in Energy Policy." *Policy Analysis.* Vol. 6, No. 2 (Spring). Pp.

Wildavsky, Aaron (1979). *The Politics of the Budgetary Process.* Boston: Little, Brown. Third Edition.

Williams, Walter (1998). *Honest Numbers and Democracy.* Washington DC: Georgetown University Press.

Wilson, Edmund (1998). *Consilience: The Unity of Knowledge.* New York: Alfred A. Knopf.

2 Promoting the Policy Orientation: Lasswell in Context

Douglas Torgerson

When *The Policy Sciences: Recent Trends in Scope and Method* appeared in the early 1950s (Lerner and Lasswell, 1951), the book represented a challenge to an orientation then prevailing in the social sciences. That orientation saw the social scientific project as a patient and painstaking accumulation of knowledge about society. The application of knowledge was not ruled out, but it was also not something to be rushed into prematurely. The contributors to *The Policy Sciences*, a host of distinguished figures from a broad range of the social sciences, generally took a different approach. This approach was particularly given voice by Harold D. Lasswell, a co-editor of the volume, in the book's central chapter, "The Policy Orientation" (Lasswell, 1951b). Following a direction set by the pragmatist philosopher John Dewey in the early part of the twentieth century, Lasswell conceived the social sciences as methods of social problem-solving and thus proposed that they be understood as policy sciences.[1]

Lasswell's proposal in *The Policy Sciences* that the social sciences be shaped through a policy orientation was a public expression of an idea that he had been working on since the early 1920s. As a student and later faculty member at the University of Chicago, Lasswell came under the influence there of Charles E. Merriam—a leading figure in American political science—and, by the 1930s, Lasswell was to emerge as the outstanding representative of the Chicago school of political science. Despite its disciplinary base, the Chicago school was highly interdisciplinary and, responding to both philosophical pragmatism and political progressivism, focused on the identification and solution of practical social problems. This practical focus did not mean a lack of theoretical concern. Especially in the case of Lasswell, there was indeed serious attention to theoretical questions. As a consequence, his conception of the policy orientation was both original and sophisticated.

Context was a chief theoretical and practical concern for Lasswell, and the aim of this chapter is to understand that focus while placing Lasswell himself in context. The policy orientation was Lasswell's proposed solution to what Dewey had, in the 1920s, formulated as "*the* problem of the public" in regard to the potential of developing an intelligent, democratic civilization (1984, 365). The policy orientation thus takes on a key historical role for Lasswell, as he emphasizes with his argument that "developmental constructs" are of central significance to the contextual focus of inquiry (1971a, 67–69). As we shall see, Lasswell's idea of using developmental constructs to orient inquiry in the context of historical change is profoundly indebted to a view of history advanced in Marxian theory. Lasswell, however, also signals a clear departure from Marx not only by identifying quite a different historical hero, but also by stressing that inquiry and action in the face of an indeterminate future have a necessarily speculative character.

The protagonist in the story Lasswell tells is a critically enlightened policy profession devoted to the cause of democracy. Lasswell portrays the emergence of a policy orientation in the social sciences as an historical development of major importance, and—by drawing attention to it and encouraging it—he seeks to give it shape and direction. However, his promotion of the policy orientation emerged from a context in which liberal democracy, having been severely challenged by the anti-democratic forces of Fascism and Bolshevism, could easily seem the only viable form of democracy.

Discussions of policy professionalism and democracy have since Lasswell's time taken on a different tenor, rendering dubious his confidence in advancing the "policy sciences of democracy" (1951b). Not only have the apparent technocratic implications of that phrase become widely suspect, but democracy itself is being rethought along discursive—or deliberative—lines (e.g., Dryzek, 2000). The image of discursive democracy envisions vital public discourses playing a significant role in shaping the policy domain. At the same time, critical approaches to policy inquiry have emerged to reinforce connections between policy discourse and public discourse (e.g., Forester, ed., 1985; Fischer and Forester, eds., 1993; Hajer and Wagenaar, eds., 2003). Although these approaches often owe clear conceptual debts to Lasswell, they also anticipate democratic developments in the policy orientation that would prove unsettling to his position.

THE EMERGENCE OF THE POLICY ORIENTATION

The story that Lasswell tells is in a broad sense a version of the story of modern progress, and his promotion of a policy sciences profession certainly has something in common with nineteenth century positivism and its anticipation of governance by a "priesthood" of experts (Aaron, 1969, ch. 2). There is, however, a paradox in this connection. By the time Lasswell was to promote his proposal for a policy orientation, there was already a distinctly technocratic tone to the policy field, one troubling enough for him that he registered a clear objection.

Lasswell was displeased by the common image of policy-analytic work as mere tinkering to adjust the operations of an existing mechanism. "Running through much of the modern work that is being done on the decision process," Lasswell complained, "is the desire to abolish discretion on the part of the chooser and to substitute an automatic machine-like routine" (1955, 387). He especially took exception to the formalism of rational decision-making models guided by game theory: "In effect the player becomes a computing machine operating with 'built-in' rules in order to maximize built-in preferences" (1955, 387). Against this "preference for automation," Lasswell endorsed a "preference for creativity" (1955, 389). His proposal for the policy orientation thus includes a distinctly critical note (cf. Tribe, 1972). To grasp the significance of this critical element, the main sources of his approach need attention.

On the central role of pragmatism, he was quite explicit: "The policy sciences are a contemporary adaptation of the general approach to public policy that was recommended by John Dewey and his colleagues in the development of American pragmatism" (1971a, xiii–xiv). During the early twentieth century, pragmatism signalled a break with formalism—with an intellectual propensity to take at face value culturally established categories and frames of reference (see Torgerson, 1992). Although tending to share the embrace of science characteristic of the progressive era, pragmatism also recognized science as a thoroughly human and fallible institution. Scientific knowledge could prove itself useful for human purposes, but it could not provide any certain foundation for a "religion of humanity," as nineteenth century positivism had imagined (Aaron, 1969, ch. 2; Torgerson, 1992).

In a pragmatist vein, Lasswell portrayed the social process as ultimately a seamless fabric, indicating that the identification of seams for the purpose of research pertained to "the context of culture" (1971a, 17–8). The perspective of a participant in a cultural context was the point of departure for conceptualization and observation; inquiry involved a continuous, interwoven process of participant-observation (1971a, 3, 58, 74–75). As Lasswell developed a framework for the conduct of inquiry, he thus proposed mapping the social process and the policy process in terms of categories and symbols drawn from a cultural context, and his framework came with no more guarantee than that it appeared helpful *in this context*.

Disavowing any claim to absolutely valid categories, Lasswell leaves everything open, in principle, to question and revision. What, then, might sustain confidence in his approach? If his categories and procedures are simply elements in a cultural envelope folding back upon itself, does inquiry not remain within its limitations? What Lasswell does is to focus upon inquiry itself as a process that, even though a seam within a cultural fabric, possesses a unique significance. Inquiry has a special status within culture. This is because of the reflexive capacity of inquiry, its peculiar capacity to turn back upon itself and, in doing so, to alter the very culture that envelops it.

Already in his first book, Lasswell had recognized a key principle for inquiry: "We must, as part of our study, expose ourselves to ourselves" (Atkins and Lasswell, 1924, 7). Reflexive insight into self and context holds a central place in Lasswell's proposed policy orientation. In elaborating the reflexive character of inquiry, Lasswell looked beyond pragmatism to two key figures, Freud and Marx. In Freudian psychoanalysis and the Marxian critique of ideology, Lasswell saw a point of methodological convergence necessary in mapping the context of inquiry. Insight provided a means for breaking through both psychopathological and ideological constraints on inquiry.

Lasswell repeats the story of modern progress, but in a version that departs from the conventional storyline. For he introduces a standpoint of critical reflection able to expose psychopathological and ideological features of the modern world. Lasswell's critical posture leads him to question specific elements of modernity, but not to dismiss its promise. Modernity, in his view, is an incomplete project that comes with no guarantee of a happy ending. The path of modern development conceivably leads in a desirable direction, but quite undesirable outcomes are also distinct prospects. No longer is it possible, on this account, to naively rely upon the positivist notion of the inevitable progress of humanity to an orderly industrial civilization. In Lasswell, the smooth, dynamic exterior of the modern world at times appears as a front for irrational forces, the constraints and threats of which pose a problem that can potentially be resolved only if consciously recognized (see Torgerson. 1990). A fixation on machine-like routines would not be part of the solution, but central to the problem. In Lasswell's narrative of the policy orientation, the policy professional clearly emerges as the hero of the story. Yet crucial to the story is how this hero is to become self-aware in the context of a larger pattern of historical development.[2]

WORLD REVOLUTION AND THE POLICY ORIENTATION

Lasswell portrays the emergence of the policy orientation as a major event in world history, elaborating his conception in a manner parallel with, and in contradistinction to, the Marxian vision of a world revolution brought about through the agency of the proletariat. The policy orientation, on Lasswell's account, is part of a development that is "distinctive" of his times: "the rise to power of the intellectual class." The world, he argues, is in the midst of a "permanent revolution of modernizing intellectuals": a crucial role for intellectuals is inescapable, in his view, because of the problems presented by "the complexities of large-scale modern civilization" (1968, 185; cf. 1965b).

The increasing importance of intellectuals comes, in his view, with both promise and threat. Intellectuals could simply form part of oligarchic and bureaucratic structures operating for the benefit of the few at the cost of the oppression and indignity of the many. A policy profession devoted to democracy would depend on a critical stance toward context, and crucial to this posture would be a questioning of the obvious. Although the examination of a familiar world might seem to promise little in the way of interesting results, Lasswell emphasizes the importance of what is not readily apparent—"The world about us is much richer in meanings than we consciously see" (1977, 36) —and he offers a striking exaggeration, "to put the truth paradoxically": "The whole aim of the scientific student of society is to make the obvious unescapable..." (1977, 250). The emergence of a critically oriented policy profession would, in Lasswell's view, count among those developments in intellectual life that have promoted "'breakthroughs'...in the decision processes of history" (1958b, 190).

When first advancing the importance of a critical orientation to context, Lasswell in the mid-1930s explicitly invokes a central text of Marxian theory—first published in the early 1920s—the "exposition of the dialectical method" in Georg Lukács's *History and Class Consciousness* (Lasswell, 1965a, 18n; cf. Lukács, 1971). What Lasswell proposes is a reflexive project that recapitulates much of the form, if not the content, of Lukács's critique of capitalism. Especially significant is Lasswell's accent on grasping the whole both as an objective configuration and as a site of action. It is thus that Lasswell recommends "an act of creative orientation" allowing inquirers to locate themselves in an "all-encompassing totality" (1965a, 12). A comprehension of the whole is not to be gained by objective analysis alone, but also requires an active posture in regard to the field of social relationships. No such comprehension can, in principle, ultimately be completed. Inquiry not only is an open-ended process, but is itself part of the pattern of historical development through which the overall totality is constituted—part of an emerging process that remains always open to change.

Lasswell, of course, does not invoke the standpoint of the proletarian class or of revolutionary theory inspired by it. He is also highly suspicious, on methodological grounds, of any Marxian account of future historical development that suggests inevitability rather than emphasizing indeterminacy. In stressing the world historical rise of intellectuals, Lasswell replaces the proletarian class and revolutionary theory with a critically informed policy profession. His move here bears a similarity to Karl Mannheim's (1936) claim that modern intellectuals have a significant capacity to free themselves from ideological constraints. At the same time, Lasswell's move is subject to the same suspicion that critics influenced by Lukács have cast upon Mannheim's claim: that it is oblivious to the full force of dominant interests and, as such, is part of the ideological constraints helping to constitute and reinforce that power (e.g., Adorno, 1967).

What is nonetheless striking in Lasswell is the manner in which he proposes a deliberate project to overcome irrational constraints. The aim of the project is to gain insight into what Lasswell's terms the "self-in-context" (1971a, 155). By this term, Lasswell understands the self in terms of both world history and depth psychology. Indeed, psychoanalytic insight offers a complement to the Marxian dialectic to help in grasping "the symbolic aspects of historical development" (1965a, 19). In Lasswell's conception, insight discloses to a person features of the self-in-context that are "ordinarily excluded from the focus of full waking attention by smooth working mechanisms of 'resistance' and 'repression'" (1958a, 97). It is through such insight that one lessens the constraint of "anxieties" that inhibit inquiry (1958a, 97; cf. 1977, ch. 3).

By seeking to reduce constraints on inquiry, Lasswell aims to enhance rationality. Well aware that no narrow rationalism is capable of this task, Lasswell invokes the psychoanalytic technique of free-fantasy as necessary to overcome both "self-deception" and the bounds of logical thought (1977, 36–37). What he takes from psychoanalysis is the lesson that "logic" is not only insufficient to rational inquiry, but is by itself a constraint. The constraint of the logical must be relaxed in order to gain insight into what is obvious, even though normally obscure. "The mind," he argues, "is a fit instrument for reality testing when both blades are sharpened—those of logic and free-fantasy" (1977, 37). Insight into the self-in-context brings into focus surreptitious forces, thereby denying them their hidden and "privileged position" (1951a, 524).

Although Lasswell's touchstone here is psychoanalysis, he introduces a qualification that is of key significance in focusing inquiry: "Traditional psychoanalysis laid so much emphasis on the 'deeper' motivations that it failed to provide for proportionate, contextual insight into social reality at different levels." What Lasswell suggests is that psychoanalytic technique be adapted to a broader "reality critique," so as to increase individual and collective awareness of the overall institutional context (1971a, 158; cf. 1976, 168).

Reaching intellectual maturity in the period following the First World War, Lasswell is hopeful that a civilization guided by intelligence can overcome the grim realities and irrationalities of the post-war world. He is impressed by the potential of emerging technology and social planning not only to alleviate wants, anxieties, and hostilities, but also to thereby provide leisure conducive to intellectual and aesthetic creativity. Yet this promise of an intelligent civilization comes with no guarantee. This is so especially in Europe, which had long fascinated Lasswell from afar and which he directly encounters through a series of extended visits during the 1920s (see Torgerson, 1987, 1990). There the post-war scene of the early 1920s presents a frightful panorama of irrationalities—antagonism, vindictiveness, brutalizing scarcity—suggesting the distinct prospect that the potential for an intelligent civilization will be eclipsed by criminality and violence. Even in America, the hopes that progressivism had pinned on the advance of science and democracy are dimmed by the advent of professionalized propaganda capable of targeting and manipulating a mass society.

It is in the wake of the First World War that propaganda emerges as a perplexing problem. Shaped in his outlook by progressivism and concerned that the public might be "bamboozled" by propaganda techniques (Lasswell, quoted in Torgerson, 1990, 349), Lasswell focuses on the problem in his Ph.D. thesis, published in 1927 under the title *Propaganda Technique in the World War*. Propaganda, as Lasswell describes it (1971b, 221–222; cf. 1928), involves "the management of opinions and attitudes by the direct manipulation of social suggestion"; but with an increasingly educated populace, propaganda is also "a concession to the rationality of the modern world." For, with its pretensions to being a "rational epoch," modernity thrives on "argument" and prefers "decorum and the trappery of intelligence." The rise of propaganda makes it possible to envision the dystopian prospect of an apparently democratic society being governed by "an unseen engineer" (as he quotes an earlier writer). Lasswell's point in studying propaganda, however, is to render this prospect impossible by bringing "much into the open that is obscure."

Lasswell's effort to promote a critically informed policy profession can thus be read, in large part, as a response to the increasing significance of professional propagandists, who depend upon the rationality of the modern world, yet also undermine it through systematic efforts to mobilize the irrationalities of psychopathology and ideology. Through their critical orientation, the policy sciences promise intelligence capable of leading modern civilization away from an irrational path. This task requires not routine thinking, but reflexivity and creativity. For a key "feature of the policy orientation," according to Lasswell, is the significance it attaches to an "act of creative imagination" that is able to introduce an innovative policy "into the historical process" (1951b, 12).

THE TASK OF CONTEXTUAL MAPPING

In promoting the policy orientation, Lasswell developed a conceptual framework that was designed for a project of "mapping" the policy process in relation to the larger social process (see Brunner, 1991). His often terse specification of the elements of this framework—an enumeration of professional tasks and values together with sequential phases of decision making—gives a surface appearance that hardly distinguishes his framework from the standard check lists that now abound in conventional policy textbooks. This superficial impression is quickly belied, however, by the substance of his proposal and its most distinguishing feature, the principle of "contextuality" (Lasswell, 1971a, ch. 2).

The mapping of the policy process in connection with the social process involves a deliberate task of mapping self-in-context whereby inquirers orient themselves to the overarching context in which they are located—and of which they and their work are a part. Lasswell's proposal for the policy orientation thus crucially depends upon a project of contextual mapping and orientation. "It is…impossible," Lasswell maintains, "for anyone to escape an *implicit* map of the self-in-context" (1971a, 155). A common practical feature of social life, the mapping of context poses a particular problem for professional inquirers because they must render the map explicit as part of a sustained effort to refine their orientation to context.

The inquirer is not a detached observer, but "a participant observer of events who tries to see things as they are" (Lasswell, 1971a, 3; cf. 58, 74–75), an actor trying to make sense of self and world. As one who is never entirely separate from the process nor ever entirely absorbed by it, the inquirer must crucially possess the flexibility of one able to engage as well as disengage; of one who, taking nothing as finally fixed, grasps how the emerging patterns of the process influence—and are reciprocally influenced by—the actors within it (Lasswell, 1965a, 4–6, 16–17, ch. 2). Yet as an actor, the inquirer does not simply map self-in-context so as to gain an orientation to an immediate domain of action. A bigger picture, a "total configuration" (1965a, 19), is also of pressing relevance. Hence, even though one is concerned with specifics, one is at the same time aware that "subtle ties bind every part to the whole" (1971a, 2).

This emphasis on the whole does not mean that the project of contextual orientation ever comes to rest in a final conclusion. Always unfinished, the project develops through one's continuing effort to come to grips with a vast, complex, and at times bewildering world. Although a complete grasp of the whole is, in a sense, continuously presupposed in the course of any inquiry, the whole can never be directly apprehended once and for all. An understanding of the whole is constructed, rather, through meticulous work, disciplined and refined in a continuing search for relevant evidence. "The meaning of any detail depends," moreover, "upon its relation to the whole context of which it is a part" (Lasswell, 1976, 218). The whole, then, can never be seized as a final conclusion because it remains an inexhaustible context enveloping the process of inquiry.

Not only is the context inexhaustible in its scope and complexity; it is also constantly changing. The inquirer shifts between focusing on an overall configuration as something stabilized in form at a particular moment and as a pattern that changes in an historical process (1965a, 4–5). Contextual orientation, in other words, turns on a "principle of temporality" (Lasswell and Kaplan, 1950, xiv). Within a changing context, the inquirer seeking improved contextual orientation must examine history in order to consciously elaborate developmental constructs (cf. Eulau, 1958).

A developmental construct draws upon evidence of historical trends and conditions, formulating the image of a future that can be anticipated, but not predicted. Although aiming for "nothing less than correct orientation in the continuum which embraces past, present, and future" (Lasswell, 1965a, 4), the image of development that the inquirer constructs is unavoidably tentative, open-ended, and subject to revision. Uncertainty is inescapable because future events remain matters that "are partly probable and partly chance" (1971a, 11). As a model, a developmental construct is "speculative" (Lasswell and Kaplan, 1950, xxiii); based in concrete evidence, but necessarily going beyond it, the model is an imaginative creation.

Nonetheless, imagination is not to run counter to the evidence, and Lasswell thus sharply differentiates between developmental constructs that are deemed probable and ones that are thought preferable. Although it is necessary to set out preferable paths of historical development when determining the possibility and plausibility of different courses of action, Lasswell insists upon distinguishing clearly between wishful thinking and what we expect to actually happen (1971a, 68). Elaborated in the course of unfolding events, a developmental construct is disciplined, in particular, by the "crucial test" of emerging events and is subject to revision as potentialities of the future become "actualized in the past and present of participant observers" (1965a, 13).

There is, however, a significant twist in Lasswell's argument that complicates the otherwise clear distinction between developmental constructs as being either probable or simply preferable. For the elaboration of a developmental construct is itself an historical event and, by changing how people see themselves and direct their actions, has a capacity to shape future potentialities. Alluding to notions of self-fulfilling and self-denying prophecies, Lasswell formulates the point in this way: "The act of considering the shape of things to come is itself an event that is not without effect on the ensuing events" (1980, 518). Simply by focusing attention on a future prospect as a goal, a developmental construct can, in principle, make it more likely. Indeed, Lasswell's very conception of the policy orientation as an emerging historical phenomenon involves the promotion of such a future goal.

POLICY PROFESSIONALISM

Lasswell's promotion of the policy orientation emerged from explicit plans he formulated during the 1940s while a policy advisor in Washington during World War II (Goldsen, 1979; cf. Lasswell, 1943a, 1943b, 1941c). However, these formulations were themselves refinements of ideas that were a part of his thinking in the mid-1920s when, in the midst of European chaos following World War I, he identified a potential for intellectual leadership to guide an intelligent civilization. Noting ambivalent tendencies in modernity, he could perceive the potential for a rationally ordered society that would combine technological advancement with intelligent communication and artistic cultivation. Yet, for Lasswell, this potential remained haunted by the distinct possibility of its opposite, a world of violence and scarcity, of psychopathology and propaganda (see Torgerson, 1990).

As Lasswell comes to promote the policy orientation, he explicitly locates his conception within an elaboration of developmental constructs. What he takes as given is the historical rise of intellectuals. His call for a clear policy orientation in the social sciences is a call to focus on this historical development and to shape it. For, regarding the advent of intellectuals with some ambivalence, he emphasizes as a "fundamental issue" the question of democracy versus oligarchy: "whether the overriding aim of policy should be the realization of the human dignity of the many, or the dignity of the few (and the indignity of the many)" (1971a, 41).

Although Lasswell endorses a policy profession devoted to democracy, he readily envisions—especially with rise of specialists on violence—the possibility of a profession devoted to oligarchy (1968, 186; 1971a, 43; cf. 1941b). In his principal attempt to elaborate concrete developmental constructs, indeed, Lasswell draws attention to two sharply divergent possible futures: (1) a democratic commonwealth, and (2) a "garrison-police state" (1965b, 37; cf. 1941b). A "democratically oriented policy science" (1951b, 11) appears, for Lasswell, to be necessary both to attain a commonwealth of general human dignity and to avert the "threatened…regimentation of a garrison-police state," which—in a provocatively dystopian formulation—he conceives as "a world concentration camp" (1976, 222; cf. 1958b, 197). "If we are in the midst of a permanent revolution of modernizing intellectuals," he argues, "the succeeding phase obviously depends in no small degree on perfecting the policy sciences that aid in forestalling the unspeakable contingencies latent in tendencies already more than faintly discernable" (1965b, 96).

Commitment to a policy science of democracy is, according to Lasswell, not to be derived from any abstract, transcendent principle. Nonetheless, he indicates that there is something about inquiry itself that tends to foster professional commitment to democracy. In a pragmatist gesture, Lasswell stresses the process of inquiry as itself being valuable. The upshot of this, for Lasswell, is that the process of contextual mapping is itself of indispensable value to the policy orientation. Without seeking to ground professional commitment to democracy in a principle external to the process of inquiry, Lasswell finds it hard to see how someone committed to the contextual principle of inquiry could avoid a commitment as well to a democratic commonwealth (1968, 182).

The policy scientist, by Lasswell's conception, has an orientation distinguished by a "principal value goal": "*enlightenment* about the policy process and its interaction with the social context…" (1974, 181). For Lasswell, consistent commitment to this goal is a matter of principle for inquiry. In actual situations, such a commitment is typically subject to pressures undermining it. To be sustained, it requires vigilance counteracting "the threats and temptations of power" (1974, 177). The policy profession is faced with the task of creating a space where distorting pressures can be effectively resisted: no relevant information can be withheld, and unconventional insights are not only to be heard, but deliberately encouraged. Those engaged in a common project of inquiry demand openness from themselves and others (1971a, 3). As portrayed by Lasswell, the policy professional depends upon both collective support and a "life-long cultivation of the...potential for rationality" (1958a, 97).

The obvious pressures arising from a context of power are only part of the problem. Basic to the whole enterprise are matters of personal and collective identity. The identity of a person is bound to collective identity through a symbolic medium—through "myth and ideology" (Lasswell, 1958b, 168, 31, 214; cf. Lasswell and Kaplan, 1950, ch. 6)—and, once they are formed, collective symbols of identity exhibit a remarkable persistence (1958b, 169). However, a collective project of inquiry requires that conventional symbols not be taken for granted, but questioned as part of an effort to develop a "distinctive" professional identify (1971a, 120): "Do we not...discover among social scientists some unwillingness to give prominence to hypotheses that may be widely interpreted as inconsistent with prevailing ideology?" By posing this rhetorical question (1961, 112), Lasswell draws attention to ir-rationalities that pose barriers to inquiry, a problem that leads him to seek "procedures" able to make "the mind...fit for rational clarity" (1958a, 90).

A deliberate project of contextual mapping is needed to expose irrationalities and thereby di-minish the distortions they might work on the process of inquiry: "The enlightened person is aware of his assumptions about the past, present, and future of himself, his cultural environment, and his natural environment. Our recommended goal is to provide undogmatic access to inclusive versions of reality, so that the chances are increased that the individual will use his own capacities of imagination and judgment" (Lasswell, 1971a, 155–56). This need is of decisive importance in "policy training operations" because "the cognitive map is rarely brought deliberately or fully into the open unless the individual is exposed to an instructional experience that rewards him by bringing the implicit image of reality to the full focus of waking awareness" (1971a, 155). Lasswell thus stresses that the individual inquirer depends upon an institutional context, upon "agencies of enlightenment" (1971a, 97), in order to gain educational experiences able to enhance insight into self-in-context (1971a, ch. 8) as part of the collective development of professional identity (1971a, ch. 7).[3]

To diminish the effect of irrational constraints on the conduct of inquiry, a project of contextual mapping brings key formative influences to full, conscious attention. The purpose is to diminish socio-psychological resistances—to employ "the contextual principle," not only to counter individual psychopathologies detrimental to inquiry, but also "to remove the ideological blinders from our eyes" at a collective level (Lasswell, 1976, 220): "The conscious process itself may be under the domination of repetitive compulsions which are outside the awareness of the thinker" (Lasswell, 1958a, 92). Here the point of the policy sciences is not to effect control, but to free inquiry:

> It is insufficiently acknowledged that the role of scientific work in human relations is *free-dom* rather than prediction. By freedom is meant the bringing into the focus of awareness of some feature of the personality which has hitherto operated as a determining factor upon the choices made by the individual, but which has been operating unconsciously. Once elevated to the full focus of waking consciousness, the factor which has been op-erating "automatically and compulsively" is no longer in this privileged position. The individual is now free to take the factor into consideration in the making of future choices. (Lasswell, 1951a, 524)

Freeing inquiry from psychopathological and ideological constraints is possible because any ordering of social relationships depends upon "meanings" that are, as Lasswell puts it, "subject to change *with* notice (with insight)"; it is the force of "insight" and "awareness" that provides for changes in "the current meaning" and, indeed, the "context" of action (1965b, 33–34). Following Freud's affirmation of "the efficacy of insight," Lasswell maintains that scientific conclusions about "hu-man interactions" should be placed in "a special category" precisely because they "may produce insight," thus modifying "future events" and "changing the scientifically established relationships themselves" (1956, 114–15)

Lasswell's conception of the policy orientation ultimately depends upon the efficacy of such insight. The contextual mapping of policy professionals involves "a quest for identity" through which individuals "loosen the bounds of the culture into which they are born by becoming aware of it…" (Lasswell, 1958b, 194). The process is one that both breaks the hold of "current stereotypes" and creates new "key symbols of identity" (1958, 193). Policy professionalism thus develops through the deliberate testing and fashioning of personal and collective identities.

THE POLICY ORIENTATION AND THE PUBLIC

When John Dewey published *The Public and Its Problems* in 1927, he was responding to significant doubts about the democratic capacity of the public that had arisen among fellow progressives in the wake of the First World War. The honeymoon of the progressive marriage of science and democracy came to an abrupt end in light of the effectiveness of wartime propaganda in manipulating mass society. The crucial figure in underscoring the shortcomings of public opinion was Walter Lippmann (1965), who concluded that an enlightened elite of experts was needed to avoid irrationality in modern society. In a direct response to Lippmann, Dewey agreed that experts were important, but explicitly insisted on the greater importance of enlightening the public: "The enlightenment of public opinion still seems to me to have priority over the enlightenment of officials and directors" (1983, 344).

In *The Public and Its Problems*, Dewey warned of an oligarchy of experts and identified the central problem for the public as that of that of creating conditions of communication in which the citizenry could be enlightened through discourse: "The essential need…is the improvement of the methods and conditions of debate, discussion and persuasion. That is *the* problem of the public" (1984, 365). Recognizing the substantial difficulty posed by propaganda, Dewey indicated that solving "*the* problem of the public" would require an expertise in propaganda sufficient to counteract its influence.

By the mid-1920s, Lasswell was establishing himself as the leading scholarly expert on propaganda, and he saw irrationality among the public as linked to the problem of the irrationality of experts. In the 1930s, he called for improvements in "the methods and the education of social administrators and social scientists" (1977, 203) as being of key importance in developing a "politics of prevention" (1977, ch. 10) capable of reducing the social tensions that exacerbate irrationalities in society. In the context of such irrationalities, he feared, politics typically becomes a projection of irrational impulses that intensifies problems rather than resolving them.

Lasswell's case for a preventative politics is based on the concern that "the public may be dissolved into a crowd" (1977, 192). He takes it as characteristic of democracy that policy be determined significantly more by "discussion" than by "coercion" (1977, 192). In the midst of psychopathological projections of private motives onto public concerns, he is doubtful of the potential of "belligerent crusades to change the world" (1977, 94). He also is dubious about the contention of democratic theorists that "social harmony depends upon discussion," particularly discussion that formally involves all who are affected by a policy issue (1977, 196). Of what, then, is the "politics of prevention" to consist? "In some measure it will proceed by encouraging discussion among all those who are affected by social policy, but this will be no iron-clad rule. In some measure it will proceed by improving the machinery of settling disputes, but this will be subordinated to a comprehensive program, and no longer treated as an especially desirable mode of handling the situation" (1977, 197). Lasswell is vague on how such a comprehensive program is to be instituted in the face of powers resistant to it, but it is clear that he sees a power in rationality itself, in the discovery of a truth: "Our problem is to be ruled by the truth about the conditions of harmonious human relations, and the discovery of the truth is the object of specialized research…" (1977, 197). Knowledge develops and spreads throughout society, he suggests, while advancing a formulation that a Marxian critic might brand as a kind of idealism: "The politics of prevention does not depend upon a series of changes in the organization of government. It depends upon a reorientation in the minds of those who think about society…" (1977, 198; cf. 203).

Lasswell's manifest concern here is less to enlighten the population than to immunize it. During a time when he sees the forces of Fascism and Bolshevism mounting clear threats, he wants to protect the future of liberal democracy from the anti-democratic potentials of an irrational mass society. In this context, he even endorses propaganda in the cause of democracy. His politics of prevention would be the project of a psychoanalytically enlightened elite of "political psychiatrists" (1965a, 19–20, 181). Here Lasswell formulates the most technocratic version of his position (cf. Horwitz, 1962; Bachrach, 1967, ch 5).

Inclined more toward Dewey than Lippmann, however, Lasswell does not accept disillusionment with public opinion. Indeed, in the early 1940s, he looks back to his European travels of the 1920s and recalls antidemocratic dismissals, during that period, of liberal democratic institutions, such as open public discourse and parliamentary assemblies. Proclaiming in the title of a book the potential of *Democracy through Public Opinion*, he maintains that what democracy needs is "a new way to talk" (1941a, ch. 7): a mode of informed public discourse that is resistant to the irrationality of propaganda. This potential can be realized if the professional adopts the role of "clarifier" in educating and enlightening public opinion (1941a, 89).

Realizing this potential is the task that Lasswell (1951b) assigns to the policy sciences of democracy following World War II. Policy professionals are to oppose oligarchy through a commitment to widespread participation in the "shaping and sharing" of power (1971a, 44–48): "The aim," as Lasswell puts it, "is to subordinate the particular interests of a profession to the discovery and encouragement of public interest. This implies direct community participation as well as client service" (1971a, 119). The profession is thus devoted to the "encouragement of continuous general participation" (1971a, 117).

The policy profession stands in an educative role with regard to the public, addressing *the* problem of the public—as Dewey conceived it—by fostering conditions that would diminish forces of irrationality while eliciting and developing the potential of the populace for involvement in intelligent communication: "The contemporary policy scientist perceives himself … as a specialist in eliciting and giving effect to all the rationality of which individuals and groups are capable at any given time" (1971a, 120). Lasswell saw such development of the public as a way of encouraging democracy in a complex society reliant upon specialist knowledge. Indeed, he believed that democracy would be reinforced if the provision were made to give "everyone who is involved in a public controversy an expert who can say whatever there is to say on his behalf." The effect, he hoped, would be to "serve rationality" by bringing "to the focus of attention" matters that might otherwise be neglected in the policy process (1971a, 121). Arguing that critical insight should extend beyond the policy profession, he advocated "the dissemination of insight on a vast scale to the adult population" (1976, 196). Practiced in the context of a critically enlightened public, politics could become something other than a projection by individuals of their psychological problems onto public issues, as Lasswell had conceived it in 1930 in his *Psychopathology and Politics* (Lasswell, 1970). Political participation could, indeed, become part of the development of a "democratic character" (Lasswell, 1951a; 1976, ch. 7).

Yet, contrary to Lasswell's hopes for the policy orientation, the actual tendency has been the development of a professional identity marked by institutional allegiances to a sphere of organizations—that primarily of state agencies and large private corporations—that tends to reinforce tendencies toward oligarchy and bureaucratism. This observation would not have shocked Lasswell, who once noted that the effect of "professional training" was typically one of promoting "self deception rather than self analysis" (1977, 37). Alert to "pitfalls," he anticipated the failure of "many initiatives" (1971a, 132). He knew that intellectuals must learn "the conditions of survival in the arenas of power" (1971a, 125) as they "find themselves caught in a net of interlocking interest" (1965b, 91). Despite these problems, Lasswell (1970b) insisted upon the importance of developing a professional identity that would offer institutional protection against irrationalities wrought by political power. A commitment to inquiry was "no private act" (1974, 183) and, as he had learned from pragmatism, depended upon a community of inquirers.

Lasswell's account of the policy orientation thus culminates in a paradox. He announces a world revolution of intellectuals whose task it is to lead society away from irrationality and toward an intelligent democratic civilization. However, the policy profession that Lasswell portrays as the agent of historical change is—as he himself clearly recognizes—liable to be entrapped by the very oligarchical and bureaucratic forces that should be opposed in the name of democracy. Still, on its own grounds, there is a plausible rationale to Lasswell's proposal, for he believes that intellectuals are going to be important whatever course history might take. Thus the orientation of intellectuals is bound to be important.

Lasswell's view of history focused perhaps too much on the prospect of an apocalyptic confrontation between forces of coercive oligarchy and liberal democracy for him to adequately grasp the dangers of more subtle kinds of oligarchy, particularly ones that operate surreptitiously through a technocratic idiom. The notion of the professional, for Lasswell, involves critical enlightenment, unwavering integrity, and courageous devotion to public service. However, in a context dominated by technocratic discourse, how can professionalism develop and sustain an adequately critical focus on the mystique of professionalism?

By Lasswell's account, the policy orientation appears in the singular, manifest as the development of a single profession with a distinctive identity. But is policy professionalism here not pictured too much as a discrete, cohesive entity? What is needed, perhaps, is to focus on the diversity of the range of policy-relevant inquiries, rather than trying to place them all under one heading. Indeed, when we examine concretely the relationships among various intellectual orientations and specific political interests, the beguiling images of calm technocratic discourse give way to the recognition of a politics of expertise, in which experts contend with one another (Fischer, 1990).

Lasswell did not want a policy orientation fractured along political lines. He insisted, rather, on a community of inquirers as a coherent collective enterprise capable of guiding the development of an intelligent civilization. As he witnessed the post-war chaos of European civilization in the early 1920s, Lasswell believed that intellectuals were capable of developing a consensual orientation for this purpose (Torgerson, 1987, 11–17, 20–27). Since that time, he supposed that inquiry could issue in a shared professional orientation through which the public could be enlightened. Central to his own effort was the development of a framework for policy professionals that would identify key symbols able to adequately guide the focus of attention in policy inquiry. He did not claim, however, that his framework was the only one possible, allowing that it was "one of many possible approaches to the policy sciences" (1971, xiv). Indeed, at the end of his career, he made a notable shift away from the notion that a single consensual map might guide policy professionals and the public. As he faced blatant differences among professionals, he allowed for a plurality of maps by suggesting that the public should be systematically exposed to alternative perspectives (1979, 63).

Exhibiting no narrow rationalism, Lasswell focuses on the importance of an enlightened public for an intelligent, democratic civilization. In the end, nonetheless, his account of the policy orientation not only recapitulates the old rationalist pattern of reason ruling the passions, but also repeats the gesture of making a rational elite the hero of the story. Despite Lasswell's pragmatism and careful democratic qualifications, it can be said with little exaggeration that the basic image is one of reason on top, calming and ordering a mass of unruly impulses below. The centrality of this image in Lasswell's account can readily be recognized by contrasting it with the inverse image to be found in Lukács's Marxian conception. There the very possibility of critical insight arises from the social position of the subordinate class. What Lukács saw as a source of critical insight, Lasswell views as a site of irrational impulses that are prone to propagandistic manipulation.

As its direct significance declined in the late twentieth century, the Marxian perspective came to inspire post-Marxian strategies seeking the democratization of advanced industrial societies. In these strategies, a fixation on the agency of one class-based social movement gave way to a recognition of the diversity of new social movements. Bringing strikingly unconventional perspectives to political discourse, moreover, these movements came to fashion themselves as publics (see, e.g., Angus, 2003).

At the same time, the impetus toward a radically democratic transformation of society was attenuated by a concern with immediate reform and the consequent adoption of policy orientations. The emerging publics were not enlightened from above or supplied with experts of the kind envisioned by Lasswell. Instead, these publics found themselves in ambivalent positions, creating critical distances between themselves and the official institutions dominating policy processes while—at the same time—seeking to intervene in policy deliberations (Torgerson, 2003, 1999). The publics of a diverse civil society thus found their own voices and shaped their own experts, ones knowledgeable about specific policy matters and able to engage in the politics of expertise (Fischer, 1992).

Challenging Lasswell's account of the policy orientation, these developments minimally suggest a need for revisions. The story now becomes more complicated, as Lasswell seems to have partly anticipated with his late allowance for a diversity of professional perspectives. No longer do we have a story of *the* policy orientation of professionals, who are housed within established institutions while paradoxically working to critically enlighten themselves and the public. Rather, we have a story of a plurality of policy orientations based not only in established institutions, but also in diverse publics of civil society. There are still professionals in this story, but their privileged position as agents of an intelligent civilization is at least partially displaced. If professionals are to promote democratization, they cannot simply retain secure positions in connection with state agencies and other powerful organizations, but must seek critical distances from them, taking as a point of reference the multiple publics whose voices now enter into the domain of policy discourse.

NOTES

1. This essay draws upon the results of previous treatments of Lasswell (see Torgerson, 1985, 1987, 1990, 1992, 1995).
2. Lasswell's own promotion of a critically reflexive policy profession itself becomes part of the story he tells, though this is not the place to fully discuss the implications that the narrative form of the policy orientation might have for the study of policy discourse.
3. On specific recommendations by Lasswell for an educational program (e.g., insight training, devil's advocacy, continuous decision seminars), see Torgerson (1985, 247).

REFERENCES

Aaron, R. (1969). *Main Currents of Sociological Thought,* Vol. 1. Garden City, NY: Anchor Books.

Adorno, T.W. (1967). *The sociology of knowledge and its consciousness. prisms.* S. Weber, (trans), pp. 35–50. London: Neville Spearman.

Angus, I. (2001). *Emergent Publics: An Essay on Social Movements and Democracy.* Winnipeg: Arbeiter Ring Publishing.

Atkins, W.E. and H.D. Lasswell (1924). *Labor Attitudes and Problems.* New York: Prentice-Hall.

Bachrach, P. (1967). *The Theory of Democratic Elitism: A Critique.* Boston: Little, Brown.

Brunner, R.D. (1991). The policy movement as a policy problem. *Policy Sciences,* 24, 65–98.

Dewey, J. (1983). Review of W. Lippmann, Public Opinion. In J.A. Boydston (ed), *John Dewey: The Middle Works,* Vol. 13, pp. 337–344. Carbondale and Edwardsville: Southern Illinois University Press (originally published, 1922).

Dewey, J. (1984). The Public and Its Problems in J.A. Boydston (ed), *John Dewey: The Later Works,* Vol. 2, pp. 235–372. Carbondale and Edwardsville: Southern Illinois University Press (originally published, 1927).

Dryzek, J. (2000). *Deliberative Democracy and Beyond.* Oxford: Oxford University Press.

Eulau, H. (1958). H.D. Lasswell's developmental analysis. *The Western Political Quarterly,* 11, 229–241.

Fischer, F. (1990). *Technocracy and the Politics of Expertise.* Newbury Park, CA: Sage.

Fischer, F. (1992). Participatory expertise: toward the democratization of policy science. In W.N. Dunn and

R.M. Kelly (eds), *Advances in Policy Studies Since 1950,* pp. 351–376. New Brunswick, NJ: Transaction Press.

Fischer, F. and Forester, J. (eds). (1993). *The Argumentative Turn in Policy Analysis and Planning*. Durham, NC: Duke University Press.

Forester, J. (ed). (1985). *Critical Theory and Public Life*. Albany, NY: SUNY Press.

Goldsen, J.M. (1979). Harold Lasswell as policy adviser and consultant. In M.S. McDougal et al., *Harold Dwight Lasswell, 1902–1978*, pp. 78–81. New Haven: Yale Law School.

Hajer, M. and Wagenaar, H. (eds), (2003). *Deliberative Policy Analysis: Understanding Governance in the Network Society*. Cambridge: Cambridge University Press.

Horwitz, R. (1962). Scientific propaganda: Harold D. Lasswell. In H.J. Storing (ed), *Essays on the Scientific Study of Politics*, pp. 225–304. New York: Holt, Rinehart and Winston.

Lasswell, H.D. (1926). Review of W. Lippmann, The Phantom Public. *American Journal of Sociology*, 31, 533–535.

Lasswell, H.D. (1928). The function of the propagandist. *International Journal of Ethics*, 38, 258–268.

Lasswell, H.D. (1941a). *Democracy through Public Opinion*. Menasha, WI: George Banta Publishing Company.

Lasswell, H.D. (1941b). The garrison state. *American Journal of Sociology*, 46, 455–468.

Lasswell, H.D. (1941c). Letter to Anna P. and Linden Lasswell, May 25. *Harold. D. Lasswell Papers* (Box 56), Manuscripts and Archives, Yale University Library, New Haven, CT.

Lasswell, H.D. (1943a). Personal policy objectives. Memorandum, October 1. *Harold D. Lasswell Papers* (Box 145), Manuscripts and Archives, Yale University Library, New Haven, CT.

Lasswell, H.D. (1943b). Proposal: the institute of policy sciences. Memorandum, October 1. *Harold D. Lasswell Papers* (Box 145), Manuscripts and Archives, Yale University Library, New Haven, CT.

Lasswell, H.D. (1951a). Democratic character. In *The Political Writings of Harold D. Lasswell*, pp. 465–525. Glencoe, IL: The Free Press.

Lasswell, H.D. (1951b). The policy orientation. In D. Lerner and H.D. Lasswell (eds), *The Policy Sciences*, pp. 3–15. Stanford: Stanford University Press.

Lasswell, H.D. (1955). Current studies of the decision process: automation versus creativity. *The Western Political Quarterly*, 8, 381–399.

Lasswell, H.D. (1956). Impact of psychoanalytic thinking on the social sciences. In L.D. White (ed), *The State of the Social Sciences*, pp. 84–115. Chicago: University of Chicago Press.

Lasswell, H.D. (1958a). Clarifying value judgment: principles of content and procedure. *Inquiry*, 1, 87–98.

Lasswell, H.D. (1958b). *Politics: Who Gets What, When, How*. New York: Meridian Books.

Lasswell, H.D. (1961). The qualitative and the quantitative in political and legal analysis. In D. Lerner (ed), *Quantity and Quality*, pp. 103–116. New York: The Free Press of Glencoe.

Lasswell, H.D. (1965a). *World Politics and Personal Insecurity*. New York: The Free Press (originally published, 1935).

Lasswell, H.D. (1965b). The world revolution of our time: a framework for basic policy research. In H.D. Lasswell and D. Lerner (eds), *World Revolutionary Elites*, pp. 29–96. Cambridge, MA: The MIT Press.

Lasswell, H.D. (1968). Policy sciences. *International Encyclopedia of the Social Sciences,* 12, 181–189.

Lasswell, H.D. (1970). Must science serve political power? *American Psychologist*, 25, 117–125.

Lasswell, H.D. (1971a). *A Pre-View of Policy Sciences*. New York: American Elsevier.

Lasswell, H.D. (1971b). *Propaganda Technique in World War I*. Cambridge, MA: The MIT Press (originally published as Propaganda Technique in the World War, 1927).

Lasswell, H.D. (1974). Some perplexities of policy theory. *Social Research*, 14, 176–189.

Lasswell, H.D. (1976). *Power and Personality*. New York: W.W. Norton (originally published, 1948).

Lasswell, H.D. (1977). *Psychopathology and Politics*. Chicago: University of Chicago Press (originally published, 1930).

Lasswell, H.D. (1979). *The Signature of Power*. New Brunswick, NJ: Transaction Books.

Lasswell, H.D. (1980). The future of world communication and propaganda. In H.D. Lasswell, D. Lerner and H. Speier (eds), *Propaganda and Communication in World History,* Vol. 3, pp. 516–534. Honolulu: University Press of Hawaii.

Lasswell, H.D. and Kaplan, A. (1950). *Power and Society: A Framework for Political Inquiry*. New Haven: Yale University Press.

Lerner, D. and H.D. Lasswell (eds), *The Policy Sciences: Recent Trends in Scope and Method*. Stanford: Stanford University Press.

Lippmann, W. (1965). *Public Opinion*. New York: The Free Press (originally published, 1922).

Lukács, G. (1971). *History and Class Consciousness: Studies in Marxist Dialectics*. R. Livingstone (trans.). London: Merlin Press (originally published in German, 1923).

Mannheim, K. (1936). *Ideology and Utopia: An Introduction to the Sociology of Knowledge*. L. Wirth and E. Shils (trans.). New York: Harcourt, Brace and World (originally published in German, 1929).

Torgerson, D. (1985). Contextual orientation in policy analysis: the contribution of Harold D. Lasswell. *Policy Sciences,* 18, 241–261.

Torgerson, D. (1987). Political vision and the policy orientation: Lasswell's early letters. Paper presented at the Annual Meetings of the American Political Science Association, Chicago, September 3–6.

Torgerson, D. (1990). Origins of the policy orientation: the aesthetic dimension in Lasswell's political vision. *History of Political Thought,* 11, 339–351.

Torgerson, D. (1992). Priest and jester in the policy sciences: developing the focus of inquiry. *Policy Sciences,* 25, 225–235.

Torgerson, D. (1995). Policy analysis and public life: the restoration of phronesis? In J. Farr, J.S. Dryzek, and S.T. Leonard (eds), *Political Science in History: Research Programs and Political Traditions*, pp. 225–252. Cambridge: Cambridge University Press.

Torgerson, D. (1999). *The Promise of Green Politics: Environmentalism and the Public Sphere*. Durham, NC: Duke University Press.

Torgerson, D. (2003). Democracy through policy discourse. In M. Hajer and H. Wagenaar (eds), *Deliberative Policy Analysis: Understanding Governance in the Network Society*, pp. 113–138. Cambridge: Cambridge University Press.

Tribe, L.H. (1972). Policy science: analysis or ideology? *Philosophy and Public Affairs*, 2, 66–110.

3 Public Policy, Social Science, and the State: An Historical Perspective

Peter Wagner

The idea of developing social knowledge for the purpose of social betterment took the form in which we still know it today during the Enlightenment. In many respects, the American and French revolutions were a culmination of that development and the first large-scale "application" of modern social and political theory. At the same time, the revolutions were often interpreted as having brought about a social situation in which good social knowledge would permit the gradual but incessant amelioration of social life. The ways of thinking of the social sciences were also created in that context (Heilbron, Magnusson, and Wittrock 1998; see also Therborn 1976; Hawthorn 1976).[1]

The new, post-revolutionary situation altered the epistemic position for the social sciences, even though this was only gradually being acknowledged. Any attempt at understanding the social and political world now had to deal with the basic condition of liberty; but an emphasis on liberty alone—as in the tradition of early-modern political theorizing during the seventeenth and eighteenth century—was insufficient to understand a social order. Thus, in the words of Edmund Burke (1993 [1790], 8–9), if "the effect of liberty to individuals is, that they may do what they please [, we] ought to see what it will please them to do, before we risque congratulations." It is the ambivalence of this situation that created the demand for novel forms of social knowledge. Before those revolutions, a policy-oriented social science had existed in many European states. But it was clearly an approach that was serving the interests of the absolute ruler in knowing about the subjects of his principality and about the state of its resources. It was thus known as "state sciences," but also, and even more tellingly, as "police and cameral sciences." In the latter term, "cameral" refers directly to the chamber of the ruler, and the concept "police" had not yet become differentiated into what we now refer to as the institution for the safeguarding of law and order, known as "police," on the one hand, and the planned intervention into the social world by a state or by an organization, known now as "policy," on the other. After the rise of the idea of liberty in the late-eighteenth century revolutions, a widely held assumptions was that only "police" in its current meaning, but very little "policy" was needed, because society would regulate itself on the basis of the free expression of the wills of the individuals. Critics of this latter idea, such as Burke, but also Hegel and later Marx, knew that this would not be the case, but that a new kind of public intervention based on the assumption of abstract liberty would be required. Any long-term history of the policy orientation of the social sciences will need to start out from this novel social-political constellation and investigate the variety of ways of dealing with this situation. Most fundamentally, two strategies could be pursued; they were initially separate strategies, but were combined during the twentieth century in novel ways. Aiming at finding out what it pleased individuals to do, the emerging social sciences, on the one hand, embarked on developing empirical research strategies to provide useful knowledge. The concern for the practical order of the world in those social sciences translated, on the other hand, into attempts at identifying some theoretical order inherent in the nature of human beings and their ways of socializing, namely the predictability and stability of human inclinations and their results.

THE USES OF THE THEORETICAL TRADITIONS

The roots of the *theoretical* traditions in the social sciences lie not least in this *political* problématique. The concern of social scientists for the predictability of human action and the stability of the collective order entered into the four major forms of reasoning that have characterized the social sciences through all of their two-century history. Some theorists argued that their social location determined the orientations and actions of human beings. There are two major variants of such thinking. What one might call a cultural theory, first, emphasized proximity of values and orientations due to a common background. The nation as a *cultural-linguistic* entity was then seen as a major collectivity of belonging that gave a sense of identity to human beings in Europe; and, *mutatis mutandis*, *cultural anthropology* translated this perspective into other parts of the world. An interest-based theory, second, placed the accent on the similarity of *socio-structural* location and, thus, commonality of interest. In this approach, which strongly shaped the discipline of *sociology*, social stratification and class were the key categories determining interest and, as a derivative, action.

The third approach to discursively stabilize human activity appears as directly opposed to culturalist and sociological thinking, in the sense described above. In *individualist-rationalist* theorizing, full reign is given to the individual human beings and no social order constrains their actions. In the tradition that reaches from political economy to neoclassical *economics* to rational choice theorizing, intelligibility is here achieved by different means: Though they appear to be fully autonomous, the individuals are endowed with rationalities such that the uncoordinated pursuit of their interests will lead to overall societal well-being. These three kinds of reasoning make for a very peculiar set in the sense that this latter one locates the determinant of action almost completely inside the human being, and the former two almost completely in the outside socio-cultural world. In the fourth approach, the *behavioral-statistical* one, no such assumptions are made, but attitudes and behaviors of individuals are counted, summarized and treated with mathematical techniques so as to discover empirical regularities. This approach can be, and has been, combined with all the other three.

These four approaches to social life are all well established, and discussions about their strengths and weaknesses have gone on for a long time. What is important in our observations on the uses of the social sciences is that they have all been developed not as purely intellectual projects, but with a view to identifying and enhancing those elements of social life that bring stability into the social world. The rationalistic-individualistic idea that a society composed of free individuals would maximize wealth lent itself to argue for the dismantling of barriers to action, such as in the introduction of the liberty of commerce, but occasionally also to prohibit collective action, such as in the restrictions to form associations, be it trade unions or business cartels. The socio-economic idea of defining the interests of human beings according to social position revealed fundamental conditions for harmony or contradictions in society, such as in structural functionalism or in Marxism. The connection between Durkheim's theory of solidarity and the political ideology of solidarism in the French Third Republic is an important instance of such use of basic modes of social theorizing. The cultural-linguistic idea informed the understanding of the grouping together of larger collectivities; it was at the root of the idea of the nation as the unit polity, thus of nationalism. The behavioral-statistical approach allowed the aggregation of people into collectivities, not unlike the former two, but it worked with less predetermined assumptions about the social bond behind the aggregation. It flourished not least in state-organized statistical institutes aimed at monitoring the population, but also, in particular in Britain and the United States, in private organizations interested in issues such as poverty and deviance.

These modes of reasoning became the intellectual basis for the formation of some of the key disciplines of the social sciences—cultural anthropology, sociology, economics and statistics—during a period of internal consolidation of the universities as sites of scholarly research, roughly at the end of the nineteenth century. In our context here, though, it is more important to underline that all the above ways of relating social theories to societal issues have also been used throughout the twentieth century and keep being used, even though their plausibility and application varies across space and time. Their current forms of use, however, are hardly ever pure any longer (with the exception of neoclassical economics), but blended with forms of positive knowledge as provided by empirical social research.

THE DEMAND FOR EMPIRICAL SOCIAL KNOWLEDGE

In parallel to the elaboration of the basic modes of social theorizing, and with very much the same objective and ambition, attempts to increase positive knowledge about the novel social world were increasingly made across the nineteenth century. Whereas theories tried to provide *reasons* why such social world could hold together, research explored *experiences* of its harmonies or, more often and more consistently, its strains and tensions. A starting point for many empirical research endeavors was indeed the observation that the Enlightenment, or: liberal, promise of automatic harmonization of social life was not kept (on the following see in more detail Wagner, Wittrock, and Wollmann 1991). The wide-ranging effects of the new urban and industrial civilization that was rapidly changing living and working conditions for ever larger parts of the populations in Europe and America during the nineteenth century gave increasingly rise for concern. Thus, these changes, often summarizingly referred to as "the social question" (or "the labor question"), were forcing themselves on the agenda of parliamentary bodies, governmental commissions, and private reform-minded and scholarly societies. The impetus for the search for new knowledge often came from modernizing political and social groupings that favored industrialization but that also advocated more or less far-reaching social reforms. These groupings gradually came to embrace the notion that political action to address the "social question" should be based on extensive, systematic and empirical analysis of the underlying social problems. The rising awareness of deep social problems shaped the social sciences in their period of institutionalization.

In France, social research had been encouraged and pursued since the early nineteenth century by "enlightened administrators" who had grown up with the intellectual traditions of the Revolution and the institutional innovations of the Napoleonic period. They were, therefore, inclined toward an active modernization-oriented view of society and the state's role in bringing about reforms. By mid-century, a more conservative alternative arose with the thinking of Frédéric LePlay who aimed at maintaining and restoring the traditional structures of society, but who equally relied on the systematic observation of society. In Britain, reform-minded individuals, often belonging to the establishment of Victorian England, came together in a number of reform societies, some of which had close links to the scholarly world (see, for example, Rothblatt 1981). Concern for health mounted, for example, when recruitment to the army during the Boer War revealed the appalling conditions under which much of the British population lived. Among the reform societies, the Fabian Society came to play a leading role in the establishment of the London School of Economics and Political Science, a university and research center that has remained marked by its double commitment to academic inquiry and problem-oriented research (Rueschemeyer and van Rossem 1996). In Germany, immediately after the founding of the Bismarckian state, the Verein für Socialpolitik became the main initiator and organizer of empirical research on the "social question." In the United States, social-science research originally had the same characteristics of associational organization and ameliorative orientation as it had in the European countries. The American Social Science Association (ASSA), created in 1865, embraced the notion that the social scientist was a model citizen helping to improve the life of the community, not a professional, disinterested researcher. By the turn of the nineteenth century, this model was overwhelmed by the emerging disciplinary associations, initially splintering off from ASSA and later subdividing further (Haskell 1977; Manicas 1991).

While the range of comparative observations could easily be enlarged, the apparent parallelism in attention to problems cross-nationally must not conceal the fact that both solutions sought and, indeed, the precise nature of the problems perceived were premised on significantly different discourses and institutional constellations. For our context, the role of the state in problem-solving and the position of knowledge-producers in state and society are the key aspects to be considered comparatively (on the following see in more detail Wittrock and Wagner 1996).

STATES, PROFESSIONS, AND THE TRANSFORMATION OF LIBERALISM

The emerging variety of forms of social knowledge and forms of policy intervention can, in a first step, be traced to different ways of transcending the limitations of a liberal conception of society. For France, this change is closely related to the experience of the failed revolution of 1848. It thus became evident that the mere form of a democratic polity did not yet provide a solution to the question of societal organization. In Italy and Germany, in contrast, liberal-minded revolutionary attempts had failed, and the emergence of the social question tended to coincide with the very foundation of a national polity. The process of nation-building in the decade between 1861 and 1871 profoundly changed the terms of both political debate and of the orientations of political scientists in both countries. The idea of social betterment through social knowledge appeared to have found its addressee: the nation-state. The founders of the Verein für Socialpolitik left no doubt about the intimate linkage between the creation of their association and the inauguration of the Reich: "Now that the national question has been solved, it is our foremost duty to contribute to solving the social question" (Schöneberg, quoted in Schäfer 1971, 286).

On the basis of a great variety of social inquiries, the construction of national social policies was argued for on the European continent toward the end of the nineteenth century. Such policies would in practice extend the idea of a community of responsibility, as it was developed in collectivist social theories during that period, be they of a social-interest-based or of a cultural-linguistic kind (Zimmermann and Wagner 2004). In the given intellectual and political situation, it could relatively easily be argued that the nation was the relevant, responsibility-bearing community and the state its collective actor, the head and hand, as it were, in the design and implementation of social policies. The nation-state was regarded as the "natural" container of rules and resources extending over, and mastering, a defined territory. This, however, was much less the case in the United States, where a strong central state did not as yet exist. In contrast to both France and Germany (disregarding for a moment the intellectual variety in these contexts), social researchers in the United States tended to be reluctant to posit state and society as collective entities over or beside individuals. Even if the case for individualist liberalism as the predominant politico-intellectual tradition throughout U.S. history is overstated (see Hartz 1955, for the classical statement), the counterpart to such thought in the United States, civic republicanism, is still comparatively much more liberal and individualist than the variants of nationalism, socialism and organicism that have inspired European social reformers. One consequence of the individualistic inflection of U.S. political culture is that psychology and social psychology have been much more important in the social sciences than elsewhere. Many social problems are dealt with on the level of individual psychology.

This intellectual specificity of the situation in the United States can be connected, in a second step, to an institutional feature that has shaped the strategies of those academic entrepreneurs who advocated social reform. In the United States, such advocates of reform based on inquiry were opposed to the politics of corruption and patronage in particular, but also often distrustful of increasing the power of the state in general. Instead, they tended to advocate the complementary strategy of reform and competence, a type of profession-based social policy. If, as in continental Europe, the widening of social responsibility was the issue, then professions were designed as a non-statist way to exert authority over spheres of social-political action. The specific form of academic institutionalization of social science in the United States, namely as disciplinary associations, was the result of such considerations. At the time, however, it was far from becoming the dominant model; as such, it asserted itself only after the Second World War.

For professors in high-prestige, state-run academic institutions on the European Continent, in Germany in particular, in contrast, it was quite natural—in intellectual, institutional and social terms—to see the state as the key policy institution and themselves as its brain. While U.S. social reformers were not only doubtful about the rightness of state interventions in terms of liberal political theory, they also had no strong reason to connect a reputation-seeking strategy to the state. Their authority was to be based in the knowledge claims inherent in the existence of strong autonomous professions rather than, as in Europe, on the intellectual and social status of representatives of the university as a key institution in the process of nation-building.

KNOWLEDGE FORMS OF MASS DEMOCRACY AND INDUSTRIAL CAPITALISM: THE TRANSFORMATION OF THE EPISTEMIC CONSTELLATION

As the combined result of the processes described up to this point, a variety of *ways of theorizing* society, *empirical research strategies* and *organizational forms* for the production of social knowledge, as profession and as state-run university, were available early in the twentieth century. During the first half of the twentieth century, these elements were reassembled, both in the form of an epistemic reorientation, to be discussed in this section, and in the form of a major shift in organizational outlook and addressee of the research, to be analyzed subsequently. The result of this process was the emergence of knowledge practices that are oriented toward use by organizational oligarchies, be it in state, business, or associations. Such practices redirected the explanatory ambitions of the social sciences and, without abandoning them, deflected the basic theoretical modes of social sciences.

Thus, *economic theorizing* enters into a variety of historically changing relations with the concept of a central societal organization, the state. Keynesianism or theories of the welfare state alter neoclassical economics by limiting its reach into the social world or by introducing additional assumptions with a view to changing the societal outcome of economic activities. But they keep drawing on its basic theoretical ideas. In a different way, the economic way of thinking was modified when social welfare concerns were introduced, this time toward a historico-institutional economics that saw the application of economic thinking as dependent on the detail of social situations to be made known through social inquiry (a similar consideration is also at the basis of Keynes' thinking). The concern for social welfare, though, also provided for an application of *socio-structural thinking*, which could serve for identifying social causes for poverty, thus shifting responsibility from the individual toward the social situation and allowing for the argument that public policies could justifiably intervene in such circumstances.

As in the United States the welfare situation of African-American families was of particular concern, the study of welfare became connected to the concept of race in rather precisely the same way, namely as a way to give nonindividual reasons—*cultural* or *biological* in this case, rather than socio-structural—for a particular social state. This, however, was an argument that would only gradually evolve over the twentieth century. From the late nineteenth century onward, the main use of racial theorizing was to provide arguments for setting boundaries of polities in the era of nationalism and for introducing means to improve a state's population, on the basis of eugenic theorizing. Large-scale emigration (for many European countries) and immigration (for the United States) provided the background for such concern. Even though the origins of modern thinking about differences between human beings emphasized cultural-linguistic features, such thinking increasingly resorted to biological features during the later nineteenth century, allegedly revealed by properly scientific methods. The refutation of those findings, together with the political discreditation of race-based policies after the defeat of Nazism, led to a return to the cultural approach. (Re-)emerging in anthropological debate during the inter-war years, cultural relativism is the contemporary form of theorizing differences between human beings. During the past two decades, it has increasingly been linked to political claims for the institutional acknowledgement, and also promotion, of diversity. The claim to the right to diversity is not only made on behalf of cultural, linguistic, religious or ethnic minorities, but also in gender relations, after the earlier emphasis of the women's movement and of feminist scholarship had been on the right to equality.

Finally, the *behavioral-statistical* mode of reasoning finds one of its most significant use-oriented expressions in the twentieth century in survey research. It had never been entirely detached from policy purposes, since statistical institutes emerged and inquiries flourished first in the realm of the state, before the claim to become a, even *the*, science of society was voiced by statisticians. Methodologically dependent on a concept of sampling, which in principle though was known as early as the late eighteenth century (Desrosières 1991), it developed strongly when political actors in mass democracy needed information about the orientations of the voters, whom they no longer knew, and when producers for mass-consumption markets faced the same problem.

KNOWLEDGE FORMS OF MASS DEMOCRACY AND INDUSTRIAL CAPITALISM: THE BREAKTHROUGH OF A POLICY ORIENTATION IN THE SOCIAL SCIENCES

The case of survey research makes particularly clear what the characteristic features of the emerging policy orientation in the social sciences were and what impact it had on the theory and epistemology of the social sciences. As we have seen, it did not mark any radical rupture; the modes of reasoning that were developed earlier remained alive. However, it considerably redirected research practices and organizational forms. Significantly, the policy orientation itself was dependent on its relation to a feature of social organization that to some extent was novel, to some extent just had not moved into the interest of the empirical social sciences before. This is the large-scale bureaucratic-hierarchical social organization in all its forms, be it as the central state administration, overarchingly powerful in particular on the European continent, or the giant business corporation and other forms of private organizations, which should become an increasingly dominant feature of U.S. society.

In this light, a brief look needs to be taken at the history of organizational analysis. In particular from a use-oriented point of view, one could have expected an empirical science of state activities to emerge together with rising interest in welfare and other policies. However, in particular in Europe, the state long remained above all social actors in the sense that it also was kept hidden from the empirical gaze. Despite several attempts, there was no successful establishment of *political science* as an academic discipline, at least outside the United States, during the "classical" period of the social sciences, i.e. the late nineteenth and early twentieth centuries. Comprising elements as various as public law, half-aborted administrative sciences, election studies, or social-policy research, the study of things political had become a rather incoherent remainder after the modern disciplines had split off (Wagner 2001, chapter 2). Such development can best be understood against the background of the post-Enlightenment ambition to understand the social world through its own laws of motion, as described above, rather than through orders from a center.

When bureaucracies in state, business, and parties rose to ever increasing importance toward the end of the nineteenth century, however, it became unmistakably clear that there would be no withering away of the state and no self-organization of society. Such observations were at the origins of a political sociology of organizations and bureaucracy, which later turned into an *organizational theory* that became almost something like the main paradigm in management studies and the new discipline of political science after the Second World War. As such, the study of organizations with a view to enhancing their functioning became one of the major forms of use-oriented social science in the twentieth century. It formed the backbone of much of the directly policy-oriented research that should develop over the twentieth century, in particular after the Second World War.

Organizational concerns were the characteristic feature of the emerging policy orientation in the social sciences. They demanded considerable shifts in orientation, in several respects. First, as just indicated, an *actor* orientation emerged toward policy actors in a broad sense, i.e., to the top-level of decision-makers in public administration and business organization. Second, the *substantive* focus of research shifted increasingly toward policy areas as objects of public administration, voters as target objects of political parties and consumers as analogously targets of market-oriented organizations. Third, the *conceptual* perspective increasingly emphasized the functioning of goal-oriented organizations in their social environment.

In all three respects, significant changes in the mode of operation of the social sciences can be observed. First, often modeled after the Bureau of Applied Research at Columbia University, research institutes were created that pursued research on commission. The institutes could be university-based, public or private, for-profit or not-for-profit; and the differences in organizational setting led to quite a variety of different research orientations. Always, however, the institute was dependent on the commissioning of research projects, be it through the market or through institutional links. Second, the sponsors were obviously organizations of such a scale of operation that they could afford to pay for the production of knowledge on their demand. Clearly, the main types of such organization were those mentioned above: public administration, big business, including importantly the media, and political parties. New fields of social science inquiry were formed along the lines of interest and activity of such organizations, such as education and social welfare, market and opinion research. Third, the knowledge that was demanded had to address the problems of those who demanded it. In the inclusive mass societies of the twentieth century, organizations increasingly directed their activities to large numbers of people about whose motivations and orientations they knew very little. Ever larger shares of social-science research went into the production of knowledge about these people and of such a kind as was of interest to, and concern for, these organizations in the pursuit of their objectives.

Even though occasional criticism had also been raised earlier, such as in Adorno's observation of the rise of "administrative society" with its concomitant form of social knowledge, such developments started to meet an increasingly critical reception in the social science communities during the 1970s. The expansion of funding and the increase in the number of research institutes as well as university departments was widely welcomed, but concern was raised about the undermining of the scholarly base of the social sciences because of the increasing imbalance between demand-driven knowledge production and academic research. Many of such statements of concern, however, just took the disciplinary constitution of the social sciences in academic institutions for granted and saw such arrangement as the normative baseline against which new developments could be evaluated. An analysis, in which the knowledge practices and modes of theoretical reasoning are themselves set into the context of a more long-term historical development of the relation between knowledge production and socio-political institutions, considerably alters the picture. It does not assume that there can be any pure form of social knowledge, uncontaminated by the situation in which it is created, which could provide the measuring rod with which any "drift of epistemic criteria" (Elzinga 1985) as a result of science policy and research-funding activities could be assessed. Rather, it leads to a historical political sociology that is fully interrelated with a sociology of knowledge and of the (social) sciences.

TRANSFORMATIVE MOMENTS: WARS, EXTERNAL AND INTERNAL

In continuation of precisely such a view, some key aspects of the twentieth-century developments need to be analyzed in more detail. The first such aspect is provided by the observation that there clearly was no steady rise of the "administrative society," but at the very least leaps and spurts in such transformation. Thus, for instance, one needs to emphasize the significance of wars as accelerating or transformative moments in the development of the social sciences.

In the United States, the Civil War marked a first such moment, indeed providing the ground for the development of organized social science. In Europe, the wars of the 1860s, at the end of which the Italian and German nation-state were created and the Third Republic established in France, provided social-science research with a more significant impetus. In Spain, similarly, early social science grew out of formative events in the history of this nation, namely the experience of losing imperial status in the wake of the Spanish-American War (1898). The 1870s witnessed thriving social research activities, many of which were indeed devoted to providing the knowledge required for organizing the national societies. Theoretical, much less disciplinary, consolidation, in contrast, was of little concern. It moved into the center of attention only later, broadly from the 1890s onward, the period known as the "classical era" for sociology, for instance.

For the development of novel forms of knowledge utilization, however, the First World War was even much more significant than the wars of the late nineteenth century. The war effort itself, much prolonged beyond initial expectations and involving the population and the economy much more than preceding wars, required more profound and more detailed knowledge about both. Psychological knowledge and its applications, including psychiatric treatment and intelligence testing, were used to assess the abilities of human beings so as to make best use of them in the war, on the one hand, and the impact of the war experience on them, on the other, such as in the studies of shell shock and other forms of war trauma. Doubts about the viability and desirability of the workings of the market mechanism in the economy had already arisen during the closing decades of the nineteenth century. The transformation toward a managerial economy or to organized capitalism was well under way, at least in the then most quickly growing economies of the United States and Germany. However, it was the need to mobilize all productive forces within a short time-span and for a particular purpose, military production and organization that led to deliberate state efforts toward increasing economic efficiency by public intervention and planning. Economic, statistical, and organizational knowledge was sought toward that end.

One of the most important consequences of the war, and of the peace at its end, was the disruption of the trends toward internationalization that had characterized the pre-war decades in many areas. Even more than after 1870, the development of the resources within the national societies themselves rose to priority, and the social sciences were involved in that effort. Unlike after 1870, however, the conviction that the increase of knowledge would rather directly translate into enhanced understanding and better means to act was shaken. If scholarly opinion during the 1920s still oscillated between the hope that industrial societies would return to a smooth path of development and the despair that the conditions for them to do that had forever disappeared, during the 1930s the view gained ground that these societies had embarked onto an entirely different trajectory for which novel knowledge and novel forms of public intervention were required. But the responses to such insight varied widely. On the one hand, the techniques for the observation of mass society, such as survey research and statistical inquiry, were refined and increasingly used to improve knowledge of the state of the population and the economy, both in democratic and in totalitarian societies (Tooze 1999). On the other hand, the ongoing societal transformation was taken to spell the failure of the fragmented and overspecialized social science disciplines and to require the elaboration of entirely new theoretical and research programs, such as the one that was later to be called "critical theory," initially proposed by Max Horkheimer in 1931 (Horkheimer 1931). As a kind of intermediate view and strategy, thirdly, the emerging soft steering of the economy, later to be called Keynesianism, and "democratic planning" tried to adapt just as much to the new circumstances as was needed to keep the institutions of society and politics intact (Hall 1989; Wagner 2003).

The Second World War had a double effect in this context. On the one hand, and quite similar to the experience of the first war, the war effort itself led to the increasing development and application of the techniques of the first kind. On the other hand, its outcome seemed to indicate that the third strategy, Keynesian democratic interventionism, was viable in principle, even though its application was initially limited to the "First World." A war of a different kind, namely the Cold War, domestically accompanied by the War on Poverty in the United States, enlisted the social sciences, called either "modern" or "bourgeois" depending on the perspective, in the attempt to prove the superiority of this model. The most systematic effort since the "classical era" to propose a comprehensive social theory and research strategy for the analysis of contemporary societies and their logic of evolution, the modernization theory of the 1950s and 1960s, was elaborated in precisely this context.

In how far this theory offered a useful understanding of Western societies remains contested. It is certain, however, that social research efforts of an unprecedented scale took place under its umbrella. They were driven not least by the hope and expectation that, since the general concepts were available, only some knowledge gaps needed to be closed by well-targeted empirical research. At the same time, the idea that good knowledge stands in an entirely unproblematic relation to its usefulness revived. It was only during the 1970s, after signs of crisis had emerged and accumulated, that the presuppositions of "the rationalistic revolution" were doubted even by its proponents. The first response to this crisis was, not to question its validity, but to inquire into its mode of operation. Research on "knowledge utilization" was one of the thriving areas of the social sciences during the 1970s, initially geared to detecting the obstacles to the good use of knowledge, with the hope of making it possible to remove them once they were detected. In the course of this research campaign, however, it became increasingly clear that the rather technocratic assumption of the very model of knowledge use had to be questioned. The "reflexive turn" of much of the social sciences during the 1980s has one of its sources in this experience (Wittrock 1985; Beck and Bonß 1984).

THE CRISIS OF USEFUL SOCIAL KNOWLEDGE: CRITIQUE, RETREAT, AND REFINEMENT

Reviewing the twentieth century experience of the use of the social sciences up to this point, two key observations can be made. On the one hand, mass-democratic, industrial-capitalist societies have been marked by intense efforts to increase the social knowledge about their modes of functioning and about their very members. It seems even justifiable to relate the demand for knowledge to a failure, in a rather specific way, of the Enlightenment project. At least in its most optimistic versions, the latter had assumed that, once autonomy was granted to human strivings, the use of reason would lead to a harmonic development of social life, in a self-steered, self-organized way. Forms of economic and political freedom were indeed introduced in mass-democratic, industrial-capitalist societies (even though such a statement needs many qualifications), but the novel institutional arrangements, far from solving all problems for good, created new social and political issues that required new knowledge and understanding.

On the other hand, however, this very foundation of the search for useful knowledge rules out, as a matter of principle, that any logic of control, with "scientification" of human life as its means, can assert itself in any unequivocal way. Unlike Adorno and Foucault appeared to assume, there is no totalizing logic of disciplinization or of the rise of administrative society. There is a variety of arguments why this is so. First, the resistance to objectification can be stressed, in terms of a *political* argument, as it was from the late 1960s onward in Western debates as well as in what is now known as postcolonialist discourse. Second, one may argue that there are limits to objectification even on the grounds of the *methodology* of the modernist social sciences. The "complexity," a key term that would be evoked in such context, of modern societies escapes even the most sophisticated research technology. And third, in terms of the *philosophy of the social sciences*, the historicity of social life and the agential capacities of human beings, both of which lead to ever again unique and unpredictable situations, can be emphasized. Agentiality and historicity are amenable to interpretation rather than to explanation, and every interpretation takes place in language, with its infinitely open range of possibilities of expression.

As a result of a combination of such arguments, the precise mix of which is impossible to assess, the implications of the use of the social sciences have been effectively criticized during the last three decades of the twentieth century. Two different adjustments to such criticism can be distinguished. More moderately, there has been a move from the mere application of general models or theories toward an increasing sophistication in the design of theory and of research. Various approaches are mixed, and their use is made dependent on the assessment and empirical specification of the situation to which they are being applied. This kind of reaction can best be observed in the analyses of the management of the economy and of accounting practices. More radically, although this may on occasion just be one more step in the same direction, the abandoning of any overarching rationalities can be observed, with a subsequent conceptualization in terms of varieties of particular and potentially competing rationalities. The most obvious examples for such change may be the move from culturalist-holist theories of society, radicalized in-between by biologically based theories of race, toward cultural relativism, on the one hand, and the move from gender studies that emphasized equality to those that emphasize diversity, on the other. Elements of such a radical rethinking of the dominance of any singular rationality can, however, also be found in the areas of modernization, accounting, or planning.

In some countries, notably the United States and the UK, such critical rethinking was accompanied by a crisis of political demand created by the Thatcher and Reagan governments in the early 1980s. Well perceiving the critique of prevailing models of knowledge utilization and linking them to a more deeply ingrained conviction that the social sciences are married to strong and interventionist states, funding for basic as well as commissioned research was reduced and restructured. Neoliberalism as a broad economic ideology indeed revives doctrines of societal self-regulation, in which there is neither place nor need for detailed empirical evidence about social situations. (Just in passing it may be noted that even biologist theories of the social resurface in this context, since with new genetic knowledge they can claim to refer to the individual and be linked to issues of rational choice.)

PERSISTENT VARIATION, PERSISTENT PROBLÉMATIQUES

By way of conclusion, it would be tempting to paint a picture in which such a neoliberal understanding of the relation between the state and the economy lives forever in harmonious relation with a postmodernist understanding of society and culture. The former would need social science only as an underlying framework for thinking the relation between markets and hierarchies; the latter allows for plurality, diversity and complexity and thus would need social science of the kind of cultural studies. However, in the light of precisely the recent criticism of nonreflexive social science, one should not let oneself be so tempted.

On the one hand, there is *persistent variation* in the use of the social sciences across countries and across areas. It remains to be the case that social sciences that orient themselves to state and government and whose practical orientation is one of relevance for public policy and state intervention are more significant in Europe than in the United States. In contrast, research on individuals and their development with possible applications by the caring professions, including self-help groups and movements, is more developed in the United States. Most methodological development in research on the ways large-scale organization can interact with society, such as opinion and survey research for business and political parties, certainly keeps coming from U.S. sources. However, the importance of such knowledge tools has considerably increased in Europe as well. (And we have not touched here at all on the proliferation of research institutes tied in various ways to social actors, including also trade unions, social movements, and nongovernmental organizations.)

On the other hand, neither the thesis of an increasing penetration of life-worlds by a power/knowledge complex nor the opposite view of a retreat to a self-regulation model of society can be sustained. There are *persistent problématiques* in post-Enlightenment societies which will always sustain the demand for useful social knowledge without, however, such knowledge ever solving those problems for good. (This observation in itself supports the prior argument about the persistence of differences, across namely the variety of possible interpretations of the socio-political situation in which one finds oneself.) The demand for knowledge may be driven by the hope to make organizational strategies more predictable. But it may also be meant to justify existing difference and diversity. In either case, it will not succeed in controlling a socio-political situation, since human beings may ever again act in unknowable ways. Nevertheless, across societies and historical periods there is considerable variation in the degree to which the hope of perfectly knowing the social world is upheld, in the ends toward which this hope is entertained, and in the intellectual, institutional and political means that are used are to realize this ambition.

NOTE

1. An earlier but different version of parts of this discussion appeared in Wagner, Peter (2003), "Social Sciences and Social Planning During the Twentieth Century," in Theodore M. Porter and Dorothy Ross, eds, *The Cambridge History of Science*, vol. 7: *The Modern Social Sciences*, Cambridge: Cambridge University Press.

REFERENCES

Beck, Ulrich, and Wolfgang Bonß (1984), "Soziologie und Modernisierung," *Soziale Welt*, vol. 35, 381–406.

Burke, Edmund (1993 [1790]), *Reflections on the Revolution in France* (ed. L.G. Mitchell), Oxford: Oxford University Press.

Desrosières, Alain (1991), "The part in relation to the whole? How to generalise. A prehistory of representative sampling," in Martin Bulmer, Kevin Bales, and Kathryn Kish Sklar, eds, *The Social Survey in Historical Perspecive 1880-1940*, Cambridge: Cambridge University Press, 217–44.

Elzinga, Aant (1985), "Research, bureaucracy, and the drift of epistemic criteria," in Björn Wittrock and Aant Elzinga, eds, *The university research system: Public policies of the home of scientists*, Stockholm: Almqvist and Wiksell.

Hall, Peter A., ed. (1989), *The political power of economic ideas: Keynesianism across nations*, Princeton, NJ: Princeton University Press.

Hartz, Louis (1955), *The Liberal Tradition in America*, New York: Harcourt, Brace and World.

Haskell, Thomas L. (1977), *The emergence of professional social science: The American Social Science Association and the nineteenth-century crisis of authority*, Urbana: University of Illinois Press.

Hawthorn, Geoffrey (1976), *Enlightenment and despair. A history of sociology*, Cambridge: Cambridge University Press.

Heilbron, Johan, Lars Magnusson, and Björn Wittrock, eds (1998), *The rise of the social sciences and the formation of modernity*, Dordrecht: Kluwer, Sociology of the Sciences Yearbook, vol. 20.

Horkheimer, Max (1931), *Die gegenwärtige Lage der Sozialphilosophie und die Aufgaben eines Instituts für Sozialforschung* (Frankfurter Universitätsreden, vol. XXXVII), Frankfurt/M: Englert und Schlosser.

Manicas, Peter (1991), "The social science disciplines: The American model," in Peter Wagner; Björn Wittrock and Richard Whitley, eds., *Discourses on society. The shaping of the social science disciplines*, Dordrecht: Kluwer, 45–71.

Rothblatt, Sheldon (1981), *The Revolution of the Dons. Cambridge and society in Victorian England*, Cambridge: Cambridge University Press.

Rueschemeyer, Dietrich, and Ronan van Rossem (1996), "The Verein für Sozialpolitik and the Fabian Society: a study in the sociology of policy-relevant knowledge," in Dietrich Rueschemeyer, and Theda Skocpol, eds, *Social knowledge and the origins of modern social policies*, Princeton and New York: Princeton University Press and Russell Sage Foundation, 117–62.

Schäfer, Ursula (1971), *Historische Nationalökonomie und Sozialstatistik als Gesellschaftswissenschaften*, Wien: Böhlau.

Therborn, Göran (1976), *Science, class and society*, London: New Left Books.

Tooze, J. Adam (1999), "La connaissance de l'activité économique. Réflexions sur l'histoire de la statistique économique en France et en Allemagne," in Bénédicte Zimmermann, Claude Didry and Peter Wagner, eds, *Le travail et la nation. Histoire croisée de la France et de l'Allemagne*, Paris: Editions de la Maison des Sciences de l'Homme, 55–79.

Wagner, Peter (2001), *A History and Theory of the Social Sciences*, London: Sage.

Wagner, Peter (2003), "Social sciences and social planning during the twentieth century," in Theodore M. Porter and Dorothy Ross, eds, *The Cambridge History of Science*, vol. 7: *The Modern Social Sciences*, Cambridge: Cambridge University Press, 591–607.

Wagner, Peter, Björn Wittrock and Hellmut Wollmann (1991), "Social sciences and modern states," in Peter Wagner, Carol H. Weiss, Björn Wittrock and Hellmut Wollmann, eds, *Social sciences and modern states. National experiences and theoretical crossroads*, Cambridge: Cambridge University Press, 28–85.

Wittrock, Björn (1985), "Social knowledge and public policy: Eight models of interaction," in Helga Nowotny and Jane Lambiri Dimaki, eds, *The difficult dialogue between producers and users of social science research*, Vienna: European Centre for Social Welfare Training and Research, 89–109

Wittrock, Björn, and Peter Wagner (1996), "Social science and the building of the early welfare state," in Dietrich Rueschemeyer, and Theda Skocpol, eds, *Social knowledge and the origins of modern social policies*, Princeton, NJ and New York: Princeton University Press and Russell Sage Foundation, 90–113.

Zimmermann, Bénédicte, and Peter Wagner (2003), "Nation," in Stephan Lessenich, ed, *Wohlfahrtsstaatliche Grundbegriffe*, Frankfurt/M: Campus.

Part II

Policy Processes

4 Theories of the Policy Cycle

Werner Jann and Kai Wegrich

From its origins in the 1950s, the field of policy analysis has been tightly connected with a perspective that considers the policy process as evolving through a sequence of discrete stages or phases. The policy cycle framework or perspective has served as a basic template that allows to systematize and compare the diverse debates, approaches, and models in the field and to assess the individual contribution of the respective approaches to the discipline. At the same time, the framework has regularly been criticized in terms of its theoretical construction as well as in terms of its empirical validity. We are therefore confronted with an almost paradoxical situation: on the one hand of the policy research continues to rely on the stages or cycle perspective or is linked to one of its stages and research questions. On the other hand, the very concept of the stages perspective has become discredited by a variety of criticisms, including attacks on the theoretical status of the policy cycle as a *framework*, *model* or *heuristic* (we use the terms *framework* and *perspective* interchangeably, but return to a discussion of this issue in this chapter's conclusion).

This chapter seeks to assess the limitations and utility of the policy cycle perspective by surveying the literature that analyses particular stages or phases of the policy cycle. Following an initial account of the development of the policy cycle framework, the chapter offers an overview of the different stages or phases of the policy process, highlighting analytical perspectives and major research results. Then we turn to the burgeoning critique of the policy cycle framework in the wider policy research literature. The chapter concludes with a brief overall assessment of the framework, considering, in particular, its status as an analytical tool for public policy research.

THE POLICY CYCLE—A SIMPLIFIED MODEL OF THE POLICY PROCESS

The idea of modeling the policy process in terms of stages was first put forward by Lasswell. As part of his attempt to establish a multidisciplinary and prescriptive policy science, Lasswell introduced (in 1956) a model of the policy process comprised of seven stages: intelligence, promotion, prescription, invocation, application, termination, and appraisal. While this sequence of stages has been contested (in particular that termination comes before appraisal), the model itself has been highly successful as a basic framework for the field of policy studies and became the starting point of a variety of typologies of the policy process. Based on the growth of the field of policy studies during the 1960s and 1970s, the stages models served the basic need to organize and systemize a growing body of literature and research. Subsequently, a number of different variations of the stages typology have been put forward, usually offering further differentiations of (sub-)stages. The versions developed by Brewer and deLeon (1983), May and Wildavsky (1978), Anderson (1975), and Jenkins (1978) are among the most widely adopted ones. Today, the differentiation between *agenda-setting*, *policy formulation*, *decision making*, *implementation*, and *evaluation* (eventually leading to termination) has become the conventional way to describe the chronology of a policy process.

Arguably, Lasswell's understanding of the model of the policy process was more prescriptive and normative rather than descriptive and analytical. His linear sequence of the different stages had been designed like a problem-solving model and accords with other prescriptive rational models of planning and decision-making developed in organization theory and public administration. While empirical studies of decision-making and planning in organizations, known as the behavioral theory of decision making (Simon 1947), have repeatedly pointed out that real world decision-making usually does not follow this sequence of discrete stages, the stages perspective still counts as an ideal-type of rational planning and decision-making. According to such a rational model, any decision-making should be based on a comprehensive analysis of problems and goals, followed by an inclusive collection and analysis of information and a search for the best alternative to achieve these goals. This includes the analysis of costs and benefits of the different options and the final selection of the course of action. Measures have to be carried out (implemented) and results appraised against the objectives and adjusted if needed. One of the major reasons of the success and durability of the stages typology is therefore its appeal as a normative model for ideal-type, rational, evidence-based policy making. In addition, the notion is congruent with a basic democratic understanding of elected politicians taking decisions which are then carried out by a neutral public service. The rational model therefore also shows some tacit concurrence with the traditional dichotomy of politics and administration, which was so powerful in public administration theory until after World War II.

Lasswell was, of course, highly critical of this politics/administration dichotomy, so his stages perspective moves beyond the formal analysis of single institutions that dominated the field of traditional public administration research by focusing on the contributions and interaction of different actors and institutions in the policy process. Furthermore, the stages perspective helped to overcome the bias of political science on the input-side (political behavior, attitudes, interest organizations) of the political system. Framing the political process as a continuous process of policy-making allowed to assess the cumulative effects of the various actors, forces, and institutions that interact in the policy process and therefore shape its outcome(s). In particular, the contribution of administrative and bureaucratic factors across the various stages of the policy process provided an innovative analytical perspective compared to the traditional analysis of formal structures (Scharpf 1973).

Still, the stages of policy-making were originally conceived as evolving in a (chrono)logical order—first, problems are defined and put on the agenda, next. policies are developed, adopted and implemented; and, finally these policies will be assessed against their effectiveness and efficiency and either terminated or restarted. Combined with Easton's input-output model this stages perspective was then transformed into a cyclical model, the so-called policy cycle. The cyclical perspective emphasizes feed-back (loop) processes between outputs and inputs of policy-making, leading to the continual perpetuation of the policy process. Outputs of policy processes at t_1 have an impact on the wider society and will be transformed into an input (demands and support) to a succeeding policy process at t_2. The integration of Easton's input-output model also contributed to the further differentiation of the policy process. Instead of ending with the decision to adopt a particular course of action, the focus was extended to cover the implementation of policies and, in particular, the reaction of the affected target group (impact) and the wider effects of the policy within the respective social sector (outcome). Also, the tendency of policies to create unintended consequences or side-effects became apparent through this policy process perspective.

While the policy cycle framework takes into account the feedback between different elements of the policy process (and therefore draws a more realistic picture of the policy process than earlier stages models), it still presents a simplified and ideal-type model of the policy process, as most of its proponents will readily admit. Under real-world conditions, policies are, e.g., more frequently *not* the subject of comprehensive evaluations that lead to either termination or reformulation of a policy. Policy processes rarely feature clear-cut beginnings and endings. At the same time, policies have always been constantly reviewed, controlled, modified, and sometimes even terminated; policies are perpetually reformulated, implemented, evaluated, and adapted. But these processes do not evolve in a pattern of clear-cut sequences; instead, the stages are constantly meshed and entangled in an ongoing process. Moreover, policies do not develop in a vacuum, but are adopted in a crowded policy space that leaves little space for policy innovation (Hogwood and Peters 1983). Instead, new policies (only) modify, change, or supplement older policies, or—more likely—compete with them or contradict each other.

Hogwood and Peters (1983) suggested the notion of policy succession to highlight that new policies develop in a dense environment of already existing policies. Therefore, earlier policies form a central part of the systemic environment of policy-making; frequently other policies act as key obstacles for the adoption and implementation of a particular measure. At the same time, policies create side-effects and become the causes of later policy problems—across sectors (e.g., road construction leading to environmental problems) as well as within sectors (e.g., subsidies for agricultural products leading to overproduction)—and, hence, new policies themselves ("policy as its own cause," Wildavsky 1979, 83–85).

Despite its limitations, the policy cycle has developed into the most widely applied framework to organize and systemize the research on public policy. The policy cycle focuses attention on generic features of the policy process rather than on specific actors or institutions or particular substantial problems and respective programs. Thereby, the policy cycle highlighted the significance of the policy domain (Burstein 1991) or subsystem (Sabatier 1993; Howlett, Ramesh 2003) as the key level of analysis. However, policy studies seldom apply the whole policy cycle framework as an analytical model that guides the selection of questions and variables. While a number of textbooks and some edited volumes are based on the cycle framework, academic debates in the field of policy studies have emerged from research related to particular stages of the policy process rather than on the whole cycle. Starting at different times in the development of the discipline, these different lines of research developed into more or less separate research communities following a distinct set of questions, analytical perspectives and methods. In other words, the policy cycle framework has guided policy analysis to generic themes of policy-making and has offered a device to structure empirical material; the framework has, however, not developed into a major theoretical or analytical program itself.

With these limitations of the policy cycle perspective in mind, the following briefly sketches theoretical perspectives developed to analyze particular stages of the cycle framework and highlights main research findings. While this overview does only offer a very limited and selective review of the literature, the account stresses how research related to particular stages has shaped the general understanding of the policy process and the policy cycle framework.

THE STAGES OF THE POLICY CYCLE

AGENDA-SETTING: PROBLEM RECOGNITION AND ISSUE SELECTION

Policy-making presupposes the recognition of a policy problem. Problem recognition itself requires that a social problem has been defined as such and that the necessity of state intervention has been expressed. The second step would be that the recognized problem is actually put on the agenda for serious consideration of public action (agenda-setting). The agenda is nothing more than "the list of subjects or problems to which governmental officials, and people outside the government closely associated with those officials, are paying some serious attention at any given time" (Kingdon 1995, 3). The government's (or institutional) agenda has been distinguished from the wider media and the overall public (or systemic) agenda (Cobb and Elder 1972). While the government's (formal and informal) agenda presents the center of attention of studies on agenda-setting, the means and mechanisms of problem recognition and issue selection are tightly connected with the way a social problem is recognized and perceived on the public/media agenda.

As numerous studies since the 1960s have shown, problem recognition and agenda-setting are inherently political processes in which political attention is attached to a subset of all possibly relevant policy problems. Actors within and outside government constantly seek to influence and collectively shape the agenda (e.g., by taking advantage of rising attention to a particular issue, dramatizing a problem, or advancing a particular problem definition). The involvement of particular actors (e.g., experts), the choice of institutional venues in which problems are debated and the strategic use of media coverage have been identified as tactical means to define issues (cf. Kingdon 1995; Baumgartner and Jones 1993). While a number of actors are involved in these activities of agenda control or shaping, most of the variables and mechanisms affecting agenda-setting lie outside the direct control of any single actor.

Agenda-setting results in a *selection* between diverse problems and issues. It is a process of structuring the policy issue regarding potential strategies and instruments that shape the development of a policy in the subsequent stages of a policy cycle. If the assumption is accepted that not all existing problems could receive the same level of attention (and some are not recognized at all; see Baumgartner and Jones 1993, 10), the questions of the mechanisms of agenda-setting arise. What is perceived as a policy problem? How and when does a policy problem get on the government's agenda? And why are other problems excluded from the agenda? Moreover, issue attention cycles and tides of solutions connected to specific problems are relevant aspects of policy-studies concerned with agenda-setting.

Systematic research on agenda-setting first emerged as part of the critique of pluralism in the United States. One classic approach suggested that political debates and, hence, agenda-setting, emerge from conflict between two actors, with the less politically powerful actor seeking to raise attention to the issue (conflict expansion) (Schattschneider 1960). Others suggested that agenda-setting results from a process of filtering of issues and problems, resulting in non-decisions (issues and problems that are deliberately excluded from the formal agenda). Building on the seminal community-power literature, policy-studies pointed out that non-decisions result from asymmetrical distribution of influence through institutional structures that exclude some issues from serious consideration of action (Bachrach and Baratz, 1962; see also Crenson, 1971; Cobb, Ross, and Ross, 1976).

The crucial step in this process of agenda-setting is the move of an issue from its recognition—frequently expressed by interested groups or affected actors—up to the formal political agenda. This move encompasses several substages, in which succeeding selections of issues under conditions of scarce capacities of problem-recognition and problem-solving are made. Several studies of environmental policy development, for example, showed that it is not the objective problem load (e.g., the degree of air pollution) which explains the intensity of problem recognition and solving activities on the side of governments (Prittwitz 1993; Jaenicke 1996). Instead, a plausible definition of a problem (see Stone 2001) and the creation of a particular policy image (Baumgartner and Jones 1993) allowing to attach a particular solution to the problem, have been identified as key variables affecting agenda-setting.

While problem recognition and problem definition in liberal democracies are said to be largely conducted in public, in the media or at least among domain-specific professional (public) communities, the actual agenda-setting is characterized by different patterns in terms of actor composition and the role of the public (cf. May 1991, Howlett and Ramesh, 2003). The *outside-initiation* pattern, where social actors force governments to place an issue on the systemic agenda by way of gaining public support, presents but one of different types of agenda-setting. Equally significant are processes of policies without public input such as when interest groups have direct access to government agencies and are capable of putting topics on the agenda without major interference or even recognition of the public (cf. May, 1991). The agriculture policy in certain European countries would be a classic example for such *inside-initiation* patterns of agenda-setting. Another pattern has been described as the *mobilization* of support within the public by the government after the initial agenda-setting has been accomplished without a relevant role for non-state actors (e.g., the introduction of the Euro or, rather, the campaign prior the implementation of the new currency).

Finally, Howlett and Ramesh (2003, 141) distinguish *consolidation* as a fourth type whereby state actors initiate an issue where public support is already high (e.g., German unification).

Despite the existence of different patterns of agenda-setting, modern societies are characterized by a distinctive role of the public/media for agenda-setting and policy-making, especially when novel types of problems (like risks) emerge (see Hood, Rothstein, and Baldwin 2001). Frequently, governments are confronted with forced choice situations (Lodge and Hood, 2002) where they simply cannot ignore public sentiment without risking the loss of legitimacy or credibility, and must give the issue some priority on the agenda. Examples range from incidents involving aggressive dogs, and Mad Cow Disease to the regulation of chemical substances (see Lodge and Hood 2002; Hood, Rothstein, and Baldwin 2001). While the mechanisms of agenda-setting do not determine the way the related policy is designed and implemented, policies following so-called knee-jerk responses of governments in forced choice situations tend to be combined with rather intrusive or coercive forms of state interventions. However, these policies frequently have a short life cycle or are recurrently object of major amendments in the later stages of the policy cycle after public attention has shifted towards other issues (Lodge and Hood, 2002).

The confluence of a number of interacting factors and variables determines whether a policy issue becomes a major topic on the policy agenda. These factors include both the material conditions of the policy environment (like the level of economic development), and the flow and cycle of ideas and ideologies, which are important in evaluating problems and connecting them with solutions (policy proposals). Within that context, the constellation of interest between the relevant actors, the capacity of the institutions in charge to act effectively, and the cycle of public problem perception as well as the solutions that are connected to the different problems are of central importance.

While earlier models of agenda-setting have concentrated on the economic and social aspects as explanatory variables, more recent approaches stress the role of ideas, expressed in public and professional discourses (e.g., epistemic communities; Haas 1992), in shaping the perception of a particular problems. Baumgartner and Jones (1993, 6) introduced the notion of policy monopoly as the "monopoly on political understandings" of a particular policy problem and institutional arrangements reinforcing the particular "policy image"; they suggested that agenda-setting and policy change occurs when "policy monopolies" become increasingly contested and previously disinterested (or at least "non-active") actors are mobilized. Changing policy images are frequently linked to changing institutional "venues" within which issues are debated (Baumgartner and Jones, 1993, 15; 2002, 19–23).

How the different variables—actors, institutions, ideas, and material conditions—interact is highly contingent, depending on the specific situation. That also implies that agenda-setting is far from a rational selection of issues in terms of their relevance as a problem for the wider society. Instead, the shifting of attention and agendas (Jones 2001, 145–47) could eventually lead governments to adopt policies that contradict measures introduced earlier. The most influential model that tries to conceptualize the contingency of agenda-setting is Kingdon's multiple streams model that builds on the garbage can model of organizational choice (Cohen, March, and Olsen 1972). Kingdon introduced the notion of windows of opportunity that open up at a specific time for a specific policy (Kingdon, 1995). The policy window opens when three usually separate and independent streams—the policy stream (solutions), the politics stream (public sentiments, change in governments, and the like), and the problem stream (problem perception)—intersect. (The classical garbage can model distinguishes solutions, problems, actors, and decision opportunities.)

In a long-term perspective, attention cycles and the volatility of problem perception and reform moods for particular issues can be revealed (see the classic article by Downs 1972, his "issue-attention cycle" has been criticized for omitting the impact of agenda-setting on future policies by shaping institutional structures; Peters and Hogwood, 1985; Baumgartner and Jones 1993, 87). Within such cyclical processes, single issues appear on the agenda, will be removed later on, and may reappear on that agenda as part of a longer wave. Examples include the cyclical perception of environmental, consumer protection and criminal issues, in which (combined with economic and political conditions) single events (like accidents, disasters, and the like) could trigger agenda-setting. A longitudinal perspective also points at changes in perceptions of a single issue, with some prior solutions later becoming problems (e.g., nuclear power). Baumgartner and Jones (1993; 2002) highlight the existence of both periods of stable policy agendas and periods of rapid change and take these findings as a starting point for the development of a policy process model (punctuated equilibrium) that challenges conventional notions of incrementalism.

POLICY FORMULATION AND DECISION-MAKING

During this stage of the policy cycle, expressed problems, proposals, and demands are transformed into government programs. Policy formulation and adoption includes the definition of objectives—what should be achieved with the policy—and the consideration of different action alternatives. Some authors differentiate between formulation (of alternatives for action) and the final adoption (the formal decision to take on the policy). Because policies will not always be formalized into separate programs and a clear-cut separation between formulation and decision-making is very often impossible, we treat them as substages in a single stage of the policy cycle.

In trying to account for different styles, patterns, and outcomes of policy formulation and decision-making, studies on this stage of the cycle framework have been particularly theory-oriented. Over the last two decades or so, a fruitful connection with organizational decision theories has evolved (see Olsen 1991). A multiplicity of approaches and explanations has been utilized, ranging from pluralistic and corporatist interest intermediation to perspectives of incrementalism and the garbage can approach. Others are public choice approaches and the widely utilized neo-institutionalist perspectives (both in its economical and historical-institutionalist variant; for an overview see Parsons 1995, 134).

At the same time, studies of policy formulation have long been strongly influenced by efforts to improve practices within governments by introducing techniques and tools of more rational decision-making. This became most evident during the heyday of political planning and reform policy in the 1960s and 1970s. Policy analysis was part of a reform coalition engaged in developing tools and methods for identifying effective and cost-efficient policies (see Wittrock, Wagner, and Wollmann 1991, 43–51; Wollmann 1984). Western governments were strongly receptive to these ideas given the widespread confidence in the necessity and feasibility of long-term planning. Pioneered by attempts of the U.S. government to introduce Planning Programming Budgeting Systems (PPBS), European governments engaged in similar efforts of long-term planning.

Among parts of the policy research community and government actors, PPBS was perceived as a basis for rational planning and, hence, decision-making. The establishment of clearly defined goals, output targets within the budget statement, and the application of cost-benefit analysis to political programs were regarded as tools facilitating the definition of long-term political priorities. From this perspective an ex-ante, rather rationalistic branch of policy analysis as analysis for policy developed, inspired by micro-economics and operational research (Stokey and Zeckhauser 1978). Right from the beginning, these concepts of decision-making and political planning were heavily criticized from a political science background for being over-ambitious and technocratic ('rescuing policy analysis from PPBS', Wildavsky 1969). The role of economics and political science-based policy analysis in the wider reform debate of political planning provided a fertile ground for the prosperous development of the discipline. As policy advice (analysis for policy-making) became a major aspect of the planning euphoria during the 1970s, empirical research on decision-making practices (analysis of policy-making) was initiated for the first time (e.g., through the project group of governmental and administrative reform in Germany; Mayntz and Scharpf 1975).

Especially political scientists argued from the beginning (Lindblom 1968; Wildavsky 1979) that decision-making comprises not only information gathering and processing (analysis), but foremost consists of conflict resolution within and between public and private actors and government departments (interaction). In terms of patterns of interdepartmental interaction, Mayntz and Scharpf (1975) argued that these usually follow the type of negative coordination (based on sequential participation of different departments after the initial policy program has been drafted) rather than ambitious and complex attempts of positive coordination (pooling suggested policy solutions as part of the drafting), thus leading to the typical process of reactive policy-making. The aim of political science based policy analysis was, therefore, to suggest institutional arrangements which would support more active policy-making.

While these (earlier) studies pointed to the crucial role of the ministerial bureaucracy and top civil servants in policy formulation (Dogan 1975; Heclo and Wildavsky 1974), governments and higher civil servants are not strictly separated from the wider society when formulating policies; instead, they are constantly interacting with social actors and form rather stable patterns of relationships (policy networks). Whereas the final decision on a specific policy remains in the realm of the responsible institutions (mainly cabinet, ministers, Parliament), this decision is preceded by a more or less informal process of negotiated policy formation, with ministerial departments (and the units within the departments), organized interest groups and, depending on the political system, elected members of parliaments and their associates as major players. Numerous policy studies have convincingly argued that the processes in the preliminary stages of decision-making strongly influence the final outcome and very often shape the policy to a larger extend than the final processes within the parliamentary arena (Kenis and Schneider 1991). Moreover, these studies made a strong case against the rational model of decision-making. Instead of a rational selection among alternative policies, decision-making results from bargaining between diverse actors within a policy subsystem—the result being determined by the constellation and power resources of (substantial and institutional) interest of the involved actors and processes of partisan mutual adjustment. Incrementalism, thus, forms the typical style (Lindblom 1959, 1979) of this kind of policy formation, especially in allocation of budgets (Wildavsky 1964, 1988).

During the 70s and 80s, traditional theories of pluralism in policy-making (many, competing interests without privileged access) were, at least in Western Europe, substituted by theories of corporatist policy-making (few, privileged associations with strong influence, cf. Schmitter and Lehmbruch, 1979). At the same time, more elaborate theories of policy networks became prominent (Heclo 1978; Marin and Mayntz, 1991). Policy networks are, generally, characterized by nonhierarchical, horizontal relationships between actors inside the network. Generalized political exchange (Marin 1990) represents the characteristic mode of interaction and diffuse reciprocity (opposed to market-type direct reciprocity) is the corresponding social orientation of actors in the inner circle of networks. In contrast, a higher degree of conflict is to be expected as far as the access to these policy networks is concerned. However, as Sabatier (1991, cf. Sabatier, Jenkins-Smith 1993, 1999) stressed, a policy subsystem frequently consists of more than one network. The different networks (or advocacy coalitions) then compete for the dominance in the respective policy domain.

Despite the considerable level of self-governance within policy networks, governments still play a crucial role in influencing the actor constellation within these networks, for example by altering the portfolio of ministries, creating new ones or establishing/abolishing agencies. (The renaming of the German federal Ministry of Agriculture to the Ministry of Consumer Protection, Food, and Agriculture during the BSE [Bovine Spongiform Encephalopathy] crisis serves as an example of a deliberate attempt to break up long-established policy networks in the agriculture sector as a prerequisite for policy change. Similar changes occurred also in the UK.) One major reason for the strong inclination of ministerial bureaucracies to defend their turf lies in the linkage between the allocation of responsibilities within government and the venues provided for social actors to the policy-making system (Wilson 1989). While these access points are of crucial importance for social actors seeking to influence policy formulation, established relationships with interest groups at the same time provide the power-basis of departments in interdepartmental relationships and conflicts. Any redistribution of organizational structures and institutional arrangements will favor some and discriminate against others and will, therefore, become a contested issue.

While patterns of interaction between governments and society in policy networks are regarded as an omnipresent phenomenon, the particular constellation of actors within policy networks vary between policy domains, as well as between nation states with different political/administrative cultures, traditions of law (cf. Feick and Jann 1988) and differences regarding the wider constitutional setting. As the historical-institutional approach in policy research has pointed out, countries have developed particular types of policy networks resulting from the interaction of the pre-existing state structure and the organization of society at critical junctures in history (Lehmbruch 1991). These differences are said to foster national styles of policy-making in terms of preferred policy instruments and patterns of interaction between state and society (Richardson, Gustafsson, and Jordan 1982; Feick and Jann 1988). It remains, however, a debated issue in comparative policy research if policy networks are to a larger degree shaped by the (different) basic national institutional patterns or if the policies within specific policy subsystems are, to a larger extent, shaped by sectoral, domain-specific governance structures (with the implication of more variety between sectors within one country than between countries regarding one sector) (see e.g., Bovens, t'Hart, and Peters 2001). Some have argued that the emphasis on the pervasive nature of policy networks obscured national variations of patters of policy-making that are in fact related to (different) underlying institutional arrangements and state architectures (Döhler and Manow 1995).

In order to allow for the analysis of different structural patterns of state-society interaction, policy research has developed taxonomies of policy networks. While considerable variation (and maybe even confusion, cf. Dowding 2001) prevails, one major distinction has been made between *iron triangles*, *sub-governments*, or *policy communities* on the one hand and *issue networks* centered around a particular policy issues (e.g., abortion, fuel taxes, speed limits) on the other hand. These two basic types are differentiated along the dimensions of actor composition and the insulation of the network from the wider environment. Iron triangles typically consist of state bureaucracies, parliamentary (sub-) committees, and organized interests generally sharing policy objectives and ideas. Others suggested the notion of policy communities to emphasize the latter aspect of coherent world-views and shared policy objectives (however, the term has been defined in many ways, including a meaning that resembles the notion of issue networks). Heclo (1978) has contrasted iron triangles with issue networks consisting of a multitude of actors, and with comparatively open boundaries and a looser coupling between the actors involved.

When it comes to the final adoption of a particular policy option, the formal institutions of the governmental system move into the center. But even during this substage, modes of self-regulation, sometimes in the shadow of hierarchy, have increasingly been regarded as a widespread pattern of policy-making (Mayntz and Scharpf 1995). Which of the proposed policy options will be finally adopted depends on a number of factors; two of them should be highlighted. First, the feasible set of policy options is reduced by basic substantial parameters. Some policies are excluded because of scarcity of resources—not only in terms of economic resources, but also because political support presents a critical resource in the policy-making process. Second, the allocation of competencies between different actors (e.g., government) plays a crucial role in decision-making. For example, tax policy in Germany is one of the domains in which the federal government is not only dependent on the support of the Federal Parliament (Bundestag, which is most of the time assured in parliamentary systems), but also on the consent of the Federal Council (Bundesrat, the representation of the Länder governments). The scope for substantial policy changes is, all others things being equal, more restricted in federal systems, where second chambers of parliaments and also (more frequently) constitutional courts are in a position of the potential veto player (Tsebelis 2002). At the same time, subnational levels of government possess more leeway to initiate policies in countries with a federal or a decentralized structure than in centralized countries.

Another crucial aspect of policy formulation represents the role of (scientific) policy advice. While earlier models differentiated between technocratic (policy decisions depending on superior knowledge provided by experts) and decisionist (primacy of politics over science) models of the science/policy nexus (see Wittrock 1991), the dominant normative understanding favored a pragmatic and cooperative interaction at eye level (pragmatic model, see Habermas, 1968). Empirically, policy advice was recognized as a 'diffuse process of enlightenment', in which politicians and bureaucrats (contrary to conventional wisdom, especially in the academic world) are not influenced by single studies or reports. Instead, policy advice has an impact on the middle- and long-term changes of general problem perceptions and world views (Weiss 1977). Moreover, scientific research is only one of diverse sources of information and knowledge that is being brought into the policy-making process (Lindblom and Cohen 1979, 10–29).

Over the last years, the role of think tanks in these processes has formed a focal point in debates on changing ways of policy-making, for example in the formulation of neoliberal policies in the 1980s (Weiss 1992). Think tanks and international organizations are regarded as catalysts fostering the exchange and transfer of policy ideas, solutions, and problem perceptions between governments and beyond (Stone 2004). Some have argued that policy transfer has become a regular, though distinctive, part of contemporary policy formulation (Dolowitz and Marsh 2000). However, while the practice and existence of processes of transfer and learning are hardly deniable, the literature has difficulties in drawing clear boundaries between policy transfer and other aspects of policy-making, especially as the notion of lesson drawing (as one pattern of policy transfer) resembles the rational model of decision-making (cf. James and Lodge 2003). The study of policy transfer and learning has been advanced by insights drawn from organizational theory, in particular the notion of institutional isomorphism that differentiates between coercive, mimetic and professional mechanisms of emulation (DiMaggio and Powell 1991; for applications see, among others, Lodge and Wegrich, 2005b; Jann 2004; Lodge 2003).

Most studies dealing with the role of knowledge in policy formulation agree that, in the contemporary age, knowledge is more widely spread beyond the boundaries of (central) governments than some decades ago. Experts and international institutions (like the Organization for Economic Co-operation and Development [OECD]) are said to play an increasingly visible role in communicating knowledge within the public debate on political issues (Albaek, Christiansen, and Togeby 2003). Therefore, the perception of a monopoly of information on the side of the bureaucracy (Max Weber's *Dienst- and Herrschaftswissen*) is obsolete. Policy formulation, at least in western democracies, proceeds as a complex social process, in which state actors play an important but not necessarily decisive role.

IMPLEMENTATION

The decision on a specific course of action and the adoption of a program does not guarantee that the action on the ground will strictly follow policy makers' aims and objectives. The stage of execution or enforcement of a policy by the responsible institutions and organizations that are often, but not always, part of the public sector, is referred to as implementation. Policy implementation is broadly defined as "what happens between the establishment of an apparent intention on the part of the government to do something, or to stop doing something, and the ultimate impact in the world of action" (O'Toole 2000, 266). This stage is critical as political and administrative action at the frontline are hardly ever perfectly controllable by objectives, programs, laws, and the like (cf. Hogwood and Gunn 1984). Therefore, policies and their intentions will very often be changed or even distorted; its execution delayed or even blocked altogether.

An ideal process of policy implementation would include the following core elements:

- Specification of program details (i.e., how and by which agencies/organizations should the program be executed? How should the law/program be interpreted?);
- Allocation of resources (i.e., how are budgets distributed? Which personnel will execute the program? Which units of an organization will be in charge for the execution?);
- Decisions (i.e., how will decisions of single cases be carried out?).

The detection of the implementation stage as a missing link (Hargrove 1975) in the study of policy-making can be regarded as one of the most important conceptual innovations of policy research in the 1970s. Earlier, implementation of policies was not recognized as a separate stage within or element of the policy-making process. What happens after a bill becomes a law (Bardach 1977) was not perceived as a central problem—not for the decision makers and, therefore, also not for policy analysis. The underlying assumption was that governments pass laws, and this is where the core business of policy-making ends.

This perception has fundamentally changed since the seminal study by Pressman and Wildavsky (1984 [1973]) on the implementation of a program targeting unemployment among members of minority groups in Oakland, California. Subsequently, the study of implementation as a core and often critical stage of the policy-making process became widespread currency. The starting point of Pressman and Wildavsky's analysis of the substeps involved in the implementation of the federal program, that was part of the ambitious social policy reform agenda put forth by President Johnson, was the unexpected failure of the program. Based on the analysis of the multitude of decision and clearing points at which involved actors were able to influence the policy along the lines of their particular interests, any successful policy implementation seemed to be more surprising than implementation failure (note the subtitle, *How Great Expectations in Washington Are Dashed in Oakland, or Why It's Amazing that Federal Programs Work at All*).

Following the path-breaking study, implementation research developed into *the* central field of policy research in the 1970s and early 1980s. Initially, implementation was regarded from a perspective that was later called the top-down approach. Implementation studies followed the hierarchical and chronological path of a particular policy and sought to assess how far the centrally defined goals and objectives are achieved when it comes to implementation. Most studies centered on those factors leading to deviations from these objectives. Intra- and inter-organizational coordination problems and the interaction of field agencies with the target group ranked as the most prominent variables accounting for implementation failures. Another explanation focused the policy itself, acknowledging that unsuccessful policy implementation could not only be the result of bad implementation, but also bad policy design, based on wrong assumptions about cause-effect relationships (cf. Pressman and Wildavsky 1984 [1973]; Hogwood and Gunn 1984).

Implementation studies of the first generation thus shared a hierarchical, top-down understanding of governance, at least as a normative yardstick for the assessment of outcomes of implementation. Implementation research was interested in developing theories about what works. One way to do this has been to assess the effectiveness of different types of policy instruments based on particular theories about cause and effect relations. Policy instruments have been classified into regulatory, financial, informational, and organizational policy tools (cf. Hood 1983; Mayntz 1979; Vedung 1998, see Salomon, 2002, for a more differentiated classification). One of the most prominent outcomes of the policy instruments perspective in implementation research has been the importance of the relationship between tool selection and policy implementation: Different policy instruments are vulnerable to specific types of implementation problems, with regulatory policies being aligned with control problems and subsidies with windfall gains on the side of the target group (see Mayntz 1979). Another result of this line of research has been that the reliance on wrong theories about cause and effect relations frequently leads to negative side-effects or even reverse effects of state interventions (see Sieber 1981).

Since the mid 1970s, implementation studies based on the top-down perspective have been increasingly challenged on analytical grounds, as well as in terms of their normative implications (see Hill and Hupe 2002, 51–57). Empirical evidence, showing that implementation was not appropriately described as a hierarchical chain of action leading directly from a decision at the center to the implementation in some field agency, provided the ground for a competing concept of implementation. The so-called bottom-up perspective suggested a number of analytical reorientations that subsequently became accepted in the wider implementation and policy literature. First, the central role of implementation agencies and their personnel in shaping the actual policy outcome has been acknowledged (street level bureaucracy, Lipsky 1980); in particular the pattern of coping with diverse and often contradictory demands associated with policies is a recurring theme in this line of research (see also Lin 2000; Hill 2003; deLeon and deLeon 2002). Second, the focus on single policies regarded as inputs into the implementation process was supplemented, if not replaced, by a perspective that regarded policy as the outcome of implementation resulting from the interaction of different actors *and* different programs. Elmore (1979/80) suggested the notion of backward mapping for a corresponding research strategy that begins at the last possible stage, when "administrative actions intersects with private choices" (Elmore 1979/80, 604). Third, the increasingly widespread recognition of linkages and networks between a number of (governmental and social) actors within a particular policy domain, cutting across the implementation/policy formulation borderline, provided the ground for the eventual abandonment of the hierarchical understanding of state/society interaction.

In sum, implementation research played a major role in triggering the move of policy research away from a state-centered endeavor, which was primarily interested in enhancing the internal administrative and governmental capacities and in fine-tuning program design and implementation. Since the late 1980s, policy research is primarily interested in patterns of state-society interaction and has shifted its attention toward the institutional set-up of organizational fields in the wider society (e.g., the health, education, or science section). Based on the multiplicity of empirical studies in numerous policy areas, the classic leitmotiv of hierarchical governance has been abandoned. Policy networks and negotiated modes of coordination between public and private actors are not only (analytically) regarded as a pervasive pattern underlying contemporary policy-making, but also (normatively) perceived as an effective mode of governance that reflects conditions of modern societies. Studies of policy-making were decreasingly following the traditional stages model, but encompassed all kinds of actors in the organizational and regulatory field, thereby undermining the policy cycle framework.

EVALUATION AND TERMINATION

Policy-making is supposed to contribute to problem solving or at least to the reduction of the problem load. During the evaluation stage of the policy cycle, these intended outcomes of policies move into the center of attention. The plausible normative rationale that, finally, policy-making should be appraised against intended objectives and impacts forms the starting point of policy evaluation. But, evaluation is not only associated with the final stage in the policy cycle that either ends with the termination of the policy or its redesign based on modified problem perception and agenda-setting. At the same time, evaluation research forms a separate subdiscipline in the policy sciences that focuses on the intended results and unintended consequences of policies. Evaluation studies are not restricted to a particular stage in the policy cycle; instead, the perspective is applied to the whole policy-making process and from different perspectives in terms of timing (ex ante, ex post).

Evaluation research emerged in the United States in the context of political controversies centered on the social reform programs of the Great Society of the 1960s. This early debate was concerned with methodological issues and sought to demonstrate its own relevance (cf. Weiss 1972; Levine et al. 1981; Wholey 1983). Evaluation research subsequently spread across OECD countries and was concerned with the activities of the interventionist welfare state (Albaek 1998) and reform policies in general. Evaluation was, for example, perceived as a way to systematically apply the idea of experimental testing of (new) policy options in a controlled setting (Hellstern and Wollmann 1983). Despite the inclination of evaluation research toward a rigorous application of quantitative research tools and quasi-experimental research designs, the general problem of isolating the influence and impact of a specific policy measure on policy outcomes has not been solved (given the variety of variables shaping policy outcomes). Moreover, attempts to establish evaluation exercises as part of politics-free policy-making have been widely regarded as failures. Their results were contested as being largely dependent on the inherent and often implicit values on which the evaluation was based (see, e.g., Fischer 1990).

Moreover, the role of evaluation in the policy process goes far beyond the scope of scientific evaluation studies. Policy evaluation takes place as a regular and embedded part of the political process and debate. Therefore, scientific evaluation has been distinguished from administrative evaluations conducted or initiated by the public administration and political evaluation carried out by diverse actors in the political arena, including the wider public and the media (cf. Howlett and Ramesh 2003, 210–16). Not only scientific studies, but also government reports, the public debate and activities of respective opposition parties embrace substantial elements of evaluation. Also the classical forms of overseeing government and public services in liberal democracies by law courts and legislators as well as audit offices can be grouped as evaluations.

While evaluation research sought to establish evaluation as a central part of rational evidence-based policy-making, activities of evaluation are particularly exposed to the specific logic and incentives of political processes in at least two major ways, both of them related to blame games (Hood 2002). First, the assessment of policy outputs and outcomes is biased according to the position and substantial interest, as well as the values, of a particular actor. In particular, the shifting of blame for poor performance is a regular part of politics. Second, flawed definition of policy aims and objectives presents a major obstacle for evaluations. Given the strong incentive of blame-avoidance, governments are encouraged to avoid the precise definition of goals because otherwise politicians would risk taking the blame for obvious failure. Even outside constellations that may be seen as shaped by partisan politics, the possibility of a self-evaluating organization has been strongly contested, because it conflicts with some of the fundamental values and interests of organizations (e.g., stability; Wildavsky 1972).

Evaluations can lead to diverse patterns of policy-learning, with different implications in terms of feed-back mechanisms and a potential restart of the policy process. One pattern would be that successful policies will be reinforced; a pattern that forms the core idea of so-called pilot projects (or model experiment), in which a particular measure is first introduced within a (territorial, substantive, or temporal) limited context and only extended if the evaluation is supporting. Prominent examples range from school reforms, the introduction of speed limits (and related measures in the field of transport policy), to the whole field of genetic engineering. However, instead of enhancing evidence-based policy-making, pilot projects may represent tools that are utilized for purposes of conflict avoidance; contested measures are not finally adopted but taken up as a pilot projects and thereby postponed until the political mood is ripe for a more enduring course of action.

Evaluations could also lead to the termination of a policy. Reform concepts and management instruments like Sunset Legislation and Zero-Based-Budgeting (ZBB) have been suggested as key tools that encourage terminating prior policies in order to allow for new political priorities to materialize. ZBB is supposed to replace traditional incremental budgeting (the annual continuation of budget items with minor cuts and increases reflecting political moods and distribution of power).

Instead, a new budget should be developed for single policy areas (and the responsible agencies) that expires at a predetermined date (sunset). All programs have to be periodically reassessed, designed, and budgeted. While ZBB proved to be overtly rationalistic and technocratic and, therefore, remained a short-lived reform idea, the notion of sunset legislation has regained more widespread currency (at least on the level of reform debates) since the mid-1990s in connection with the so-called regulatory policy agenda (OECD 2002).

The primary idea of policy termination—a policy problem has been solved or the adopted policy measures have been recognized to be ineffective in dealing with the set policy goals—seems rather difficult to enforce under real-world conditions of policy-making (see Bardach 1976; Behn 1978; deLeon 1978; Kaufman 1976). Rather large-scale budget cuts (e.g., related to subsidies) or windows of opportunity (e.g., changing governments, public sentiments) could trigger policy termination (Geva-May 2004). These processes are frequently connected with partisan motivations, like the implementation of election promises (see the change in energy policy introduced at the beginning of President George W. Bush's first term, or the first Schröder government's withdrawal of pension reforms introduced by the Kohl-Government in Germany).

However, the literature on policy termination suggests that attempts of policy termination are neither widespread nor successful in overcoming resistance of influential actors, allowing for the growth of a "Jurassic Park of programs" (Pollitt 2003, 113). Studies of policy termination, therefore, are frequently concerned with why policies and programs "live on" although they have "outlived their usefulness" (Geva-May 2004, 309). Counter-strategies against termination efforts range from window-dressing activities (instead of substantial changes) to the formation of cross-cutting anti-termination coalitions formed by beneficiaries of programs (e.g., delivery agencies, affected interest groups, local politicians; Bardach 1976). These coalitions can rely on a comparative advantage, because they are easier able to overcome collective action problems than any pro-termination coalition (given the threat of a potential loss of resources provided by the policy). In addition, politicians face greater incentives towards the declaration of new programs rather than the termination of old ones that include the admission of failures. The short-term political, as well as financial, costs of termination may outweigh the long-term benefits (cf. Bardach 1979; deLeon 1978; Geva-May 2004).

Apart from cases of unsuccessful termination, dynamic developments of policy booms (Dunleavy, 1986) as well as phenomena of extinction and reversal (Hood 1994) are alternative patterns of policy development. Among the most important variables accounting for policy reversals (the most important ones being economic policy changes since the late 1970s) are changing ideas and political coalitions supporting a new packaging of policy problems and solutions.

Overall, the analysis of the final stage of the policy cycle has witnessed a substantial departure from its initial focus on evaluation towards wider issues of policy change and inertia and the variables affecting these patterns.

CRITIQUE

While the numerous empirical studies and theoretical debates concerned with *single* stages of the policy cycle have substantially contributed to a better understanding of the prerequisites, elements, and consequences of policy-making, they also have triggered a rising critique challenging the underlying policy cycle framework. This critique is primarily questioning the analytical differentiation of the policy process into separate and discrete stages and sequences. As mentioned above, implementation research has played a crucial role in preparing the ground for that critique; implementation studies revealed that a clear-cut separation between policy formation and implementation is hardly reflecting real-world policy-making, neither in terms of any hierarchical or chronological sequence (first formation, then implementation), nor in terms of the involved actors.

Starting from empirical observations referring to single aspects of the cycle model an increasingly fundamentalist critique evolved, challenging the whole cycle framework. The approach was named, rather polemically, the textbook approach (Nakamura 1987). While the role of the stages heuristic in transforming political research and allowing the analysis of different stages of the policy process involving various institutional actors has been acknowledged even by its fiercest critics, it is said that the model has outlived its usefulness and should be replaced by more advanced models (Sabatier 1999). According to Sabatier, the uncritical application of the stages model prevents scientific progress rather than promotes it. Calls for the utilization of alternative frameworks and theories have criticized the stage heuristic in particular on these grounds (cf. Sabatier 1999; Sabatier, Jenkins-Smith, 1993):

- With regard to description, the stages model is said to suffer from descriptive inaccuracy because empirical reality does not fit with the classification of the policy process into discrete and sequential stages. Implementation, for example, affects agenda-setting; or a policy will be reformulated while some field agencies try to enforce ambiguous programs; or policy termination has to be implemented. In a number of cases it is more or less impossible, or at least not useful, to differentiate between stages. In other cases, the sequence is reversed; some stages miss completely or fall together.
- In terms of its conceptual value, the policy cycle lacks defining elements of a theoretical framework. In particular, the stages model does not offer causal explanations for the transition between different stages. Hence, studies of particular stages draw on a number of different theoretical concepts that have not been derived from the cycle framework itself. The specific models developed to explain processes within single stages were not connected to other approaches referring to other stages of the policy cycle.

The policy cycle is based on an implicit top-down perspective, and as such, policy-making will be framed as a hierarchical steering by superior institutions. And the focus will always be on single programs and decisions and on the formal adoption and implementation of these programs. The interaction between diverse programs, laws, and norms and their parallel implementation and evaluation does not gain the primary attention of policy analysis.

Moreover, by adopting the policy cycle perspective, the elements of the policy process that are not related to problem-solving activities are systematically ignored. Symbolic or ritual activities and activities purely related to the maintenance of power (Edelman 1971) do not feature in the stages model. However, rather than being the main objective of political action, policy-making frequently results as a by-product of politics. While the political process could be analyzed in terms of its impact on problem-solving, this should not be confused with an interpretation that regards actors as primarily taking a problem-solving orientation. Finally, the policy cycle framework ignores the role of knowledge, ideas and learning in the policy process as influential independent variables affecting all stages of the policy process (and not only in the evaluation stage).

Overall, the cycle framework leads toward an oversimplified and unrealistic world-view. Policy-making appears to be too straightforward; the whole process is reduced to initiating and continuing programs. As mentioned earlier, the role of prior policies in shaping policy-making as well as the interaction between diverse cycles, stages and actors is not systematically taken into account. However, a central feature of the policy process in modern societies is the interaction between policy-related activities at different levels (local, regional, national, inter- and supranational) and arenas (governmental, parliamentary, administrative, scientific communities, and the like) of governance. Policies are constantly debated, implemented, enforced, and evaluated. For example, environmental policy-making in the United States and in the European Union is not appropriately understood without the acknowledgement of interaction between initiatives from the different levels of government and without taking the impact of activities in other policy areas (e.g., transport, energy, or the wider economic policy) into account. Even the assumption of clearly defined and separated policy subsystems seems to be unrealistic.

The fundamental critique of Sabatier and others has triggered the development of alternative approaches beside. The advocacy coalition framework developed by Sabatier, the multiple-stream framework, the institutional rational choice approach, policy diffusion models, and the punctuated equilibrium theory are regarded as particularly promising alternative frameworks (see Sabatier 1999).

LIMITATIONS AND UTILITY OF THE POLICY CYCLE PERSPECTIVE

With that fundamental critique in mind, what would be an overall assessment of the limitations and the utility of the policy cycle framework? First of all, most of the different single points of criticism are reasonable. Like any framework, the cycle framework draws an extremely simplified picture of reality, highlighting some aspects while disregarding others. Above all, the policy cycle does not offer a causal model of the policy process with clearly defined dependent and independent variables. Therefore, the policy cycle or stages perspective could, according to Sabatier, not act as a theoretical framework of the policy process.

However, as Renate Mayntz has already emphasized in 1983, policy research is not only, and frequently not primarily concerned with the application of the analytical scientific theory (*analytische Wissenschafts-therorie*) (testing hypothesis, causal relations between variables) (see the debate on different logics of research in Brady and Collier 2004). Instead, the detailed and differentiated understanding of the internal dynamic and peculiarities of complex processes of policy-making counts as distinctive and relevant objectives of policy research (Mayntz 1983, 14).

Against these objectives, the policy cycle perspective has proven to provide an excellent heuristic device. Studies following the policy cycle perspective have enhanced our understanding of the complex preconditions, central factors influencing, and diverse outcomes of the policy process. The diverse concepts developed in studies seeking to understand specific parts of the policy cycle have offered a number of useful tools to classify various elements of the whole process. Hence, the policy cycle perspective will continue to provide an important conceptual framework in policy research, as long as the heuristic purpose of the framework is considered and the departure from the hierarchical top-down perspective and the receptivity for other and new approaches in the wider political science literature is taken into account.

The cycle framework also fulfils a vital role in structuring the vast amount of literature, the abundance of theoretical concepts, analytical tools and empirical studies, and therefore is not only crucial for teaching purposes (Parsons 1995, 80). The framework is also essential as a basic (background) template for assessing and comparing the particular contributions (and omissions) of more recent theories of the policy process. Therefore, the critique of the policy cycle, which is centered on general criteria for frameworks, theories and models, neglects the crucial role of the perspective in providing a base-line for the 'communication' between the diverse approaches in the field. In that respect, we agree with Schlager (1999, 239, 258), who highlights the openness of the cycle perspective for different theoretical and empirical interests in the field of policy studies (and agree with the critique of any application of the cycle perspective as a theoretical framework or model in a strict sense), but would add and emphasize the vital role of the cycle perspective for the integration of the diverse literature.

Numerous empirical studies and theoretical considerations have been conducted along the lines of single stages; these studies made important contributions not only to the policy literature, but also to the wider political science literature. For example, the whole debate on (new forms of) governance and the development from government to governance builds on results of and debates within policy research (Jann 2003; Lodge and Wegrich 2005a, b). Research on implementation has prepared the ground for the governance debate by detecting non-hierarchical modes of governance and patterns of co-governance between state and social actors, and through the recognition of the crucial role of civil society (organizations) for policy delivery.

Central research questions in the academic policy literature as well as in applied research are (more or less explicitly) still derived from the heuristic offered by the policy cycle framework. Questions concerning the actual impacts of particular interventions (evaluation) or concerned with the consequences following from the results of evaluations (termination, new problem perception and recognition) will remain important ones. The same applies to the other stages of the policy process; of course, it is still of central importance if and why a policy drifts away from the original design during implementation, or which actors are the most important ones in defining a policy problem or during the formal adoption of a particular policy.

In terms of democratic governance and from the perspective of public administration research, it remains of central relevance in which stage which actors are dominant and which are not. Which role do parties, parliaments, the media, interest groups, single agencies, or scientific communities play in defining which problems should be addressed or how laws should be applied and enforced? Could it be that, contrary to our normative models, crucial policies are formulated without major interference of elected politicians, which then are only capable to initiate minor adaptations during implementation? The risk exists that empirical findings concerning the complex policy process—pictured as a densely entangled space in which numerous parallel processes operate with frequent interactive feedback loops—leads to the negligence of these central research questions concerning actors' different roles in the different stages of the policy process. Elected officials and appointed bureaucrats, interest groups and corporations, and scientists and experts have different responsibilities in democratic processes—and these roles are linked to the different stages of the policy process, with the maturity of the respective policy.

Therefore, the policy cycle framework does not only offer a yardstick for the evaluation of the (comparative) success or failure of a policy; it also offers a perspective against which the democratic quality of these processes could be assessed (without following the assumption of a simple, discrete sequence and clear separation of stages). Additionally, the cycle framework allows the use of different analytical perspectives and corresponding research questions that will stay among the most important ones in policy research, although the stages heuristic of the policy cycle does not offer a comprehensive causal explanation for the whole policy process and even if the fundamental theoretical assumptions, on which initial versions of the framework were based, have long been left behind; of course, it is still of central importance if and why a policy drifts away from the original design during implementation. Similarly, it is still a relevant question, which actors are the most important in defining a policy problem or formally adopting a particular policy.

REFERENCES

Albaek, E. (1998). Knowledge, interests and the many meanings of evaluation: a development perspective. *Scandinavian Journal of Social Welfare, 7,* 94–98.

Albaek, E., Christiansen, P.M., and Togeby, L. (2003). Experts in the Mass Media: Researchers as Sources in Danish Daily Newspapers, 1961–2001. *Journalism & Mass Communication,* 80(4), 937–948.

Anderson, J.E. (1975). *Public Policymaking.* New York: Praeger.

Bachrach, P., and Baratz, M.S. (1962). Two faces of power. *American Political Science Review,* 56(4), 947–952.

Bardach, E. (1976). Policy Termination as a Political Process. *Policy Sciences,* 7(2), 123–131.

Bardach, E. (1977). *The Implementation Game: What Happens After a Bill Becomes Law.* Cambridge, MA: MIT Press.

Baumgartner, F.R., and Jones, B.D. (1993). *Agendas and Instability in American Politics.* Chicago: University of Chicago Press.

Baumgartner, F.R., and Jones, B.D. (2003). Positive and negative Feedback in Politics. In F.R. Baumgartner and B.D. Jones (eds.), *Policy Dynamics*, pp. 3–28. Chicago: University of Chicago Press.

Behn, R.D. (1978). How to Terminate a Public Policy: A Dozen Hints for the Would-be Terminator. *Policy Analysis*, 4(3), 393–314.

Bovens, M., t'Hart, P., and Peters, G.B. (eds.) (2001). *Success and Failure in Public Governance: A Comparative Analysis*. Cheltenham: Edward Elgar.

Brady, H.E., and Collier, D. (eds.) (2004). *Rethinking Social Inquiry. Diverse Tools, Shared Standards*. Lanham, MD: Rowman & Littlefield.

Brewer, G., and deLeon, P. (1983). *The Foundations of Policy Analysis*. Monterey, Cal.: Brooks, Cole.

Burstein, P. (1991). Policy Domains: Organization, Culture, and Policy Outcomes. *American Review of Sociology* 17: 327–350.

Cobb, R.W.. Elder, C.D. (1972). *Participation in American Politics: The Dynamics of Agenda Building*. Boston, MA: Allyn and Bacon.

Cobb, R.W., Ross, J.K., and Ross, M.H. (1976). Agenda Building as a Comparative Political Process. *American Political Science Review*, 70(1), 126–38.

Cohen, M.D., March, J., and Olsen, J.P. (1972). A Garbage Can Model of Organizational Choice. *Administrative Science Quarterly*, 17(1), 1–25.

Crenson, M.A. (1971). *The Unpolitics of Air Pollution*. Baltimore: Johns Hopkins University Press.

deLeon, P. (1978). A Theory of Policy Termination. In J.V. May and A. Wildavsky (eds.), *The Policy Cycle*, pp. 279–300. Berverly Hills: Sage.

deLeon, P. (1999). The Stages Approach to the Policy Process. In P.A. Sabatier (ed.), *Theories of the Policy Process*, pp. 19–32. Boulder, CO: Westview Press.

DeLeon, P., and deLeon, L. (2002). What ever happened to Policy Implementation. An alternative Approach. *Journal of Public Administration Research and Theory*, 12(4), 467–492.

DiMaggio, P.J., and Powell, W.W. (1991). The Iron Cage Revisited: Institutional isomorphism and Collective Rationality in Organization Fields. In W.W. Powell and P.J. DiMaggio (eds.), *The New Institutionalism in Organisational Analysis*, pp. 63–82. Chicago: Chicago University Press.

Döhler, M., and Manow, P. (1995). *Strukturbildung von Politikfeldern. Das Beispiel bundesdeutscher Gesundheitspolitik seit den fünfziger Jahren*. Opladen: Leske + Budrich.

Dogan, M. (1975). *The Mandarins of Western Europe. The Political Role of Top Civil Servants*. New York: Sage.

Dolowitz, D.P., and Marsh, D. (2000). Learning from Abroad: The Role of Policy Transfer in Contemporary Policy-Making. *Governance*, 13(1), 5–24.

Dowding, K. (2003). There Must Be End to Confusion: Policy Networks, Intellectual Fatigue, and the Need for Political Science Methods Courses in British Universities. *Political Studies*, 49(1), 89–105.

Downs, A. (1972). Up and Down with Ecology. The Issue-Attention Cycle. *The Public Interest*, 28, 38–50.

Dunleavy, P.J. (1986). Explaining the Privatization Boom. *Public Administration*, 64(1), 13–34.

Edelman, M. (1971). *Politics as Symbolic Action*. Chicago: Markham.

Elmore, R.F. (1979/1980). Backward Mapping: Implementation Research and Policy Decisions. *Political Science Quarterly*, 94, 601–616.

Feick, J., and Jann, W. (1988). 'Nations Matter'—aber wie? Vom Eklektizismus zur Integration in der vergleichenden Policy-Forschung. In M.G. Schmidt (ed.), *Staatstätigkeit. International und historisch vergleichende Analysen*, pp. 196–220. Opladen: Westdeutscher Verlag (Special Issue 19 of *Politische Vierteljahresschrift* 29).

Fischer, F. (1990). *Technocracy and the Politics of Expertise*. Newbury Park, CA: Sage.

Geva-May, I. (2004). Riding the Wave of Opportunity: Termination in Public Policy. *Journal of Public Administration Research and Theory*, 14(3), 309–333.

Haas, P.M. (1992). Introduction: Epistemic Communities and International Policy Coordination. *International Organization*, 42(1), 1–35.

Habermas, J. (1968). *Technik und Wissenschaft als Ideologie*. Frankfurt, M.: Suhrkamp.

Hargrove, E.C. (1975). *The Missing Link: The Study of Implementation of Social Policy*. Washington, DC: Urban Institute.

Heclo, H., (1978). Issue networks and the executive establishment. In A. King (ed.), *The New American Political System*, pp. 87–124. Washington, D.C.: American Enterprise Institute.

Heclo, H., and Wildavsky, A. (1974). *The Private Government of Public Money: Community and Policy Inside British Politics*. London: Macmillan.

Hellstern, G.M., and Wollmann, H. (eds.) (1983). *Experimentelle Politik. Reformstrohfeuer oder Lernstrategie*. Opladen: Leske + Budrich.

Hill, H.C. (2003). Understanding Implementation: Street-Level Bureaucrats' Resources for Reform. *Journal of Public Administration Research and Theory*, 13(3): 283–309.

Hill, M., and Hupe, P. (2002). *Implementing Public Policy. Governance in Theory and Practice*. London: Sage.

Hogwood, B.W., and Gunn, L.A. (1984). *Policy-analysis for the real world*. Oxford: Oxford University Press.

Hogwood, B., and Peters, G.B. (1983). *Policy Dynamics*. Brighton: Wheatsheaf.

Hood, C. (1983). *The Tools of Government*. London: Macmillan.

Hood, C. (1994). *Explaining Economic Policy Reversals*. Buckingham, Philadelphia: Open University Press.

Hood, C. (2002). The Risk Game and the Blame Game. *Government and Opposition*, 37(1), 15–37.

Hood, C., Rothstein, H., and Baldwin, R. (2001). *The Government of Risk. Understanding Risk Regulation Regimes*. Oxford: Oxford University Press.

Howlett, M., and Ramesh, M. (2003). *Studying Public Policy. Policy Cycles and Policy Subsystems*. 2nd Edition. Oxford: Oxford University Press.

James, O., and Lodge, M. (2003). The Limitations of 'Policy Transfer' and 'Lesson Drawing' for Contemporary Public Policy Research. *Political Studies Review*, 1, 179–193.

Jann, W. (2003). State, administration and governance in Germany: competing traditions and dominant narratives. *Public Administration*, 81(1), 95–118.

Jann, W. (2004). Einleitung: Instrumente, Resultate und Wirkungen—die deutsche Verwaltung im Modernisierungsschub. In W. Jann, J. Bogumil, G. Bouckaert, D. Budäus, L. Holtkamp, L. Kißler, S. Kuhlmann, E. Mezger, C. Reichard, and H. Wollmann. *Status-Report Verwaltungsreform. Eine Zwischenbilanz nach zehn Jahren*, pp. 9–21. Berlin: Edition Sigma.

Jenkins, W.I., (1978). *Policy-Analysis. A Political and Organisational Perspective*. London: Martin Robertsen.

Jones, B.D. (2001). *Politics and the Architecture of Choice. Bounded Rationality and Governance*. Chicago, London: University of Chicago Press.

Kaufman, H. (1976). *Are Government Organizations Immortal?* Washington, DC: Brookings.

Kenis, P., and Schneider, V. (1991). Policy Networks and Policy Analysis: Scrutinizing an new analytical toolbox. In B. Marin and R. Mayntz (eds), *Policy Networks. Empirical Evidence and Theoretical Considerations*, pp. 25–59. Frankfurt and Boulder, CO: Campus and Westview Press.

Kingdon, J.W. (1995). *Agenda, Alternatives, and Public Policies*. 2nd Edition. New York: HarperCollins College Publishers.

Kuhn, T.S. (1962). *The Structure of Scientific Revolutions*. Chicago: University of Chicago Press.

Lasswell, H.D. (1956). *The Decision Process: Seven Categories of Functional Analysis*. College Park: University of Maryland Press.

Lehmbruch, G. (1991). The organization of society, administrative strategies, and policy networks: Elements of a developmental theory of interest systems. In R. Czada and A. Windhoff-Héritier (eds.), *Political Choice: Institutions, Rules, and the Limits of Rationality*, pp. 121–158. Frankfurt, M. and Boulder, Col: Campus and Westview Press.

Levine, R.A., Salomon, M.A., Hellstern, G.M., and Wollmann, H. (eds.) (1981). *Evaluation Research and Practice: Comparative and International Perspectives*. Beverly Hills, London: Sage.

Lin, A.C. (2000). *Reform in the Making. The Implementation of Social Policy in Prison*. Princeton, NJ: Princeton University Press.

Lindblom C.E. (1959). The Science of Muddling Through. *Public Administration Review*, 19(2), 79–88.

Lindblom C.E. (1968). *The Policy-Making Process*. Englewood Cliffs, N.J.: Prentice Hall, (1st ed.).

Lindblom C.E. (1979): Still Muddling, Not yet Through. *Public Administration Review*, 39(6), 517–526.

Lindblom, C.E., and Cohen, D.K. (1979). *Usable Knowledge. Social Science and Social Problem Solving*. New Haven, London: Yale University Press.

Lipsky, M. (1980). *Street-Level Bureaucracy: Dilemmas of the Individual in Public Services*. New York: Russell Sage Foundation.

Lodge, M., and Hood, C. (2002). Pavlovian Policy Responses to Media Feeding Frenzies? Dangerous Dogs Regulation in Comparative Perspective. *Journal of Contingencies and Crisis Management*, 10(1), 1–13.

Lodge, M. (2003). Institutional Choice and Policy Transfer: Reforming British and German Railway Regulation. *Governance*, 16(2), 150–178.

Lodge, M., and Wegrich, K. (2005a). Governing Multi-Level Governance: Comparing Domain Dynamics in German Land-local Relationships and Prisons. *Public Administration*, 88(2).

Lodge, M., and Wegrich, K. (2005b). Control over Government: Institutional Isomorphism and Governance Dynamics in German Public Administration. *Policy Studies Journal*, 33(2), 213–234.

Marin, B. (1990). Generalized Political Exchange. Preliminary Considerations. In B. Marin (ed.), *Generalized Policy Exchange*, pp. 27–66. Boulder, CO: Westview Press.

Marin, B., and Mayntz, R. (eds) (1991): *Policy Networks. Empirical Evidence and Theoretical Considerations*. Frankfurt, M./Boulder, CO: Campus and Westview.

May, P.J. (1991). Reconsidering policy design: policies and publics. *Journal of Public Policy*, 11(2), 187–206.

May, J.P., and Wildavsky, A. (ed.) (1978). *The Policy Cycle*. Beverly Hills, CA: Sage.

Mayntz, R. (1979). Public Bureaucracies and Policy Implementation. *International Social Science Journal*, 31(4), 633–645.

Mayntz, R. (ed) (1983). Einleitung: Probleme der Theoriebildung in der Implementationsforschung. In R. Mayntz (ed), *Implementation politischer Programme II. Ansätze zur Theoriebildung*, pp. 7–24. Opladen: Westdeutscher Verlag.

Mayntz, R., and Scharpf, F.W. (1975). *Policy-Making in the German Federal Bureaucracy*. Amsterdam: Elsevier.

Mayntz, R., and Scharpf, F.W. (1995). Der Ansatz des akteurzentrierten Institutionalismus. In R. Mayntz and F.W. Scharpf (eds.), *Gesellschaftliche Selbstregulierung und politische Steuerung*, pp. 39–71. Frankfurt and New York: Campus.

Nakurama, R., (1987). The Textbook Process and Policy Implementation Research. *Policy Studies Review*, 1, 142–154.

O'Toole, L.J. (2000). Research on Policy Implementation. Assessment and Prospects. *Journal of Public Administration Research and Theory*, 19(2), 263–288.

OECD (2002). *Regulatory Policies in OECD Countries. From Interventionism to Regulatory Governance*. Paris: OECD.

Olsen, J.P. (1991). Political Science and Organisation Theory: Parallel Agendas but Mutual Disregard. In R. Czada and A. Windhoff-Héritier (eds.), *Political Choice. Institutions, Rules, and the Limits of Rationality*, pp. 887–119. Frankfurt, M. and Boulder, CO: Campus and Westview Press.

Parsons, W. (1995). *Public Policy. An introduction to the Theory and Practice of Policy Analysis*. Aldershot: Edward Elgar.

Pollitt, C. (2003). *The Essential Public Manager*. Maidenhead and Philadelphia: Open University Press/McGraw Hill.

Pressman, J.L., and Wildavsky, A. (1984). *Implementation. How great expectations in Washington are dashed in Oakland*. (1st ed. 1973), Berkeley: University of California Press.

Prittwitz, V. v. (1993). Katastrophenparadox und Handlungskapazität. Theoretische Orientierungen der Politikanalyse. In A. Héritier (eds.), *Policy-Analyse. Kritik und Neuorientierung*, pp. 328–355. Opladen: Westdeutscher Verlag.

Jänicke, M. (1996). The political system's capacity for environmental policy. In M. Jänicke and H. Weidner (eds.), *National environmental policies. A comparative study of capacity-building*, pp. 1–24. Berlin: Springer.

Richardson, J.J., Gustafsson, G., and Jordan, G. (1982). The concept of policy style. In J.J. Richardson. (ed), *Policy styles in Western Europe*, pp. 1–16. London: Allen & Unwin.

Sabatier, P.A. (1991). Toward Better Theories of the Policy Process. *Political Science and Politics*, 24, 147–156.

Sabatier, P.A. (1993). Advocacy-Koalitionen, Policy-Wandel und Policy-Lernen: Eine Alternative zur Phasen-heuristik. In A. Héritier (ed.), *Policy-Analyse. Kritik und Neuorientierung* (Special Issue 24 of *Politische Vierteljahresschrift* 34), pp. 116–148 Opladen: Westdeutscher Verlag.

Sabatier, P.A., (1999): The Need for Better Theories. In P.A. Sabatier (ed.), *Theories of the Policy Process*, pp. 3–17. Boulder, CO: Westview.

Sabatier, P.A., and Jenkins-Smith, H. (eds.) (1993). *Policy change and learning: an advocacy coalition approach*. Boulder, CO: Westview.

Salamon, L.M. (ed.) (2002). *The Tools of Government. A Guide to the new Governance*, Oxford: Oxford University Press.

Scharpf, F.W. (1973). Verwaltungswissenschaft als Teil der Politikwissenschaft. In F.W. Scharpf, *Planung als politischer Prozeß: Aufsätze zur Theorie der planenden Demokratie*, pp. 3–32. Frankfurt: Suhrkamp.

Schattschneider, E.E. (1960). *The Semi-Sovereign People*. New York: Holt, Rinehart and Winston.

Schlager, E. (1999). A Comparison of Frameworks, Theories, and Models of Policy Processes. In P.A. Sabatier (ed.), *Theories of the Policy Process*, pp. 233–260. Boulder, CO: Westview.

Schmitter, P.C., and Lehmbruch, G. (eds.) (1979): *Trends toward Corporatist Intermediation*. London: Sage.

Sieber, S. (1981). *Fatal Remedies. The Ironies of Social Intervention*. New York, London: Plenum Press.

Simon, H.A. (1947). *Administrative Behavior. A Study of decision-making Processes in administrative Organizations*. New York: Macmillan.

Stone, D. (2001). *Policy Paradox. The Art of Political Decision Making*. Revised Edition. New York: Norton.

Stone, D. (2004). Transfer Agents and Global Networks in the 'Transnationalisation' of Policy. *Journal of European Public Policy*, 11(3), 545–66.

Tsebelis, G. (2002). *Veto Players. How Political Institutions Work*. Princeton, NJ: Princeton University Press.

Vedung, E. (1998). Policy Instruments: Typologies and Theories. In M.-L. Bemelmans-Videc, R.C. Rist, and E. Vedung (eds.), *Carrots, Sticks & Sermons. Policy Instruments & Their Evaluation*, pp. 21–58. New Brunswick and London: Transaction Publishers.

Wittrock, B., Wagner, P., and Wollmann, H. (1991). Social science and the modern state: policy knowledge and political institutions in Western Europe and the United States. In P. Wagner, C.H. Weiss, B. Wittrock and H. Wollmann (eds.), *Social Sciences and Modern States*, pp. 28–85. Cambridge: Cambridge University Press.

Weiss, C.H. (1972). *Evaluating Action Programs*. Boston: Allyn & Bacon.

Weiss, C.H. (ed.) (1977). *Using Social Research in Public Policy Making*. Lexington, MA: Lexington Books.

Weiss, C.H. (1992). *Organizations for Policy Analysis: Helping Government Think*. Newbury Park, CA: Sage.

Wittrock, B. (1991). Social knowledge and public policy: eight models of interaction. In P. Wagner, C.H. Weiss, B. Wittrock, and H. Wollmann (eds.), *Social Sciences and Modern States*, pp. 333–353. Cambridge: Cambridge University Press.

Wholey, J.S. (1983). *Evaluation and effective Public Management*. Boston, MA: Little Brown.

Wildavsky, A. (1964). *The Politics of the Budgetary Process*. Boston, MA: Little Brown.

Wildavsky, A. (1969). Rescuing Policy Analysis for PPBS. *Public Administration Review*, 29(2), 189–202.

Wildavsky, A. (1972). The Self-Evaluating Organization. *Public Administration Review*, 32(5), 509–520.

Wildavsky, A. (1979). *Speaking Truth to Power. The Art and Craft of Policy Analysis*. Boston, MA: Little Brown.

Wildavsky, A. (1988). *The New Politics of the Budgetary Process*. Glenview, Illinois and Boston, MA: Scott Foresman/Little Brown.

Wollmann, H. (1984). Policy Analysis. Some Observations on the West German Scene. *Policy Sciences*, 17, 27–47.

5 Agenda Setting in Public Policy

Thomas A. Birkland

In *The Semisovereign People*, E. E. Schattschneider asserts, "the definition of the alternatives is the supreme instrument of power" (Schattschneider 1960/1975, 66). The definition of alternative issues, problems, and solutions is crucial because it establishes which issues, problems, and solutions will gain the attention of the public and decision makers and which, in turn, are most likely to gain broader attention. This chapter considers the processes by which groups work to elevate issues on the agenda, or the process by which they seek to deny other groups the opportunity to place issues. Of particular importance is the fact that is not merely issues that reach the agenda, but the construction or interpretation of issues competes for attention. The discussion is organized into four major parts. In the first, I review the agenda-setting process and our conceptions of how agendas are set. In the second part, I consider the relationships between groups, power, and agenda setting. In the third part, I discuss the relationship between the construction of problems and agenda setting. I conclude this chapter with a discussion of contemporary ways of measuring and conceiving of the agenda as a whole and the composition of the agenda.

THE AGENDA-SETTING PROCESS

Agenda setting is the process by which problems and alternative solutions gain or lose public and elite attention. Group competition to set the agenda is fierce because no society or political institutions have the capacity to address all possible alternatives to all possible problems that arise at any one time (Hilgartner and Bosk 1988). Groups must therefore fight to earn their issues' places among all the other issues sharing the limited space on the agenda or to prepare for the time when a crisis makes their issue more likely to occupy a more prominent space on the agenda. Even when an issue gains attention, groups must fight to ensure that their depiction of the issue remains in the forefront and that their preferred approaches to the problem are those that are most actively considered. They do so for the reasons cited by Schattschneider: the group that successfully describes a problem will also be the one that defines the solutions to it, thereby prevailing in policy debate. At the same time, groups fight to keep issues off the agenda; indeed, such blocking action is as important as the affirmative act of attempting to gain attention (Cobb and Ross 1997).

Central to understanding agenda setting is the meaning of the term *agenda*. An agenda is a collection of problems, understandings of causes, symbols, solutions, and other elements of public problems that come to the attention of members of the public and their governmental officials. An agenda may be as concrete as a list of bills that are before a legislature, but also includes a series of beliefs about the existence and magnitude of problems and how they should be addressed by government, the private sector, nonprofit organizations, or through joint action by some or all of these institutions.

Agendas exist at all levels of government. Every community and every body of government—Congress, a state legislature, a county commission—has a collection of issues that are available for discussion and disposition, or that are being actively considered. All these issues can be categorized based on the extent to which an institution is prepared to make an ultimate decision to enact and implement or to reject particular policies. Furthest from *enactment* are issues and ideas contained in the *systemic agenda*, in which is contained any idea that could possibly be considered by participants in the policy process. Some ideas fail to reach this agenda because they are politically unacceptable in a particular society; large-scale state ownership of the means of production, for example, is generally off the systemic agenda in the United States because it is contrary to existing ideological commitments.

It is worthwhile to think of several levels of the agenda, as shown in Figure 5.1. The largest level of the agenda is the *agenda universe*, which contains all ideas that could possibly be brought up and discussed in a society or a political system. In a democracy, we can think of all the possible ideas as being quite unconstrained, although, even in democracies, the expression of some ideas is officially or unofficially constrained. For example, in the United States, aggressively racist and sexist language is usually not tolerated socially in public discourse, while Canada has laws prohibiting hate speech and expression. Canada's laws are unlikely to be copied and enacted in the United States because they would likely conflict with the First Amendment of the United States Constitution. But laws may not be the most effective way of denying ideas access to the agenda. Social pressure and cultural norms are probably more important. Thus, ideas associated with communism or fascism are so far out of bounds of politically appropriate discourse in the United States that they rarely are expressed beyond a fringe group of adherents. Indeed, sometimes people paint policy ideas with terms intended to place these ideas outside the realm of acceptable discussion. For example, health care reforms that would involve an increase in government activity are often dismissed as socialized medicine, with the threat of "socialism" invoked to derail the idea. In a democracy that prizes freedom of speech, however, many ideas are available for debate on the systemic agenda, even if those ideas are never acted upon by governments.

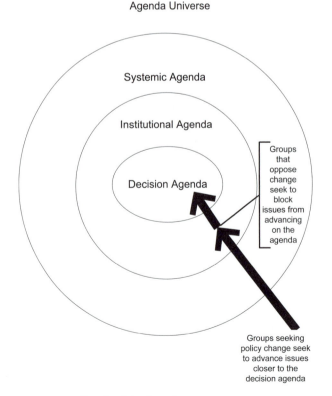

FIGURE 5.1 Levels of the Agenda.

Cobb and Elder say that "the systemic agenda consists of all issues that are commonly perceived by members of the political community as meriting public attention and as involving matters within the legitimate jurisdiction of existing governmental authority." The boundary between the systemic agenda and the agenda universe represents the limit of "legitimate jurisdiction of existing governmental authority" (Cobb and Elder 1983, 85). That boundary can move in or out to accommodate more or fewer ideas over time. For example, ideas to establish programs to alleviate economic suffering have waxed and waned on the agenda when the national mood is more expansive toward the poor, as it was during the 1960s, or less compassionate, as during the 1990s.

If a problem or idea is successfully elevated from the systemic agenda, it moves to the institutional agenda, a subset of the broader systemic agenda. The institutional agenda is "that list of items explicitly up for the active and serious consideration of authoritative decision makers" (Cobb and Elder 1983, 85–86) The limited amount of time or resources available to any institution or society means that only a limited number of issues is likely to reach the institutional agenda (Hilgartner and Bosk 1988; O'Toole 1989). However, institutions can increase their carrying capacity and can address more issues simultaneously (Baumgartner and Jones 2004; Talbert and Potoski 2002), either when there are many pressing issues, or when resources or technology are available to manage this increased load.

Even with this increased carrying capacity, however, relatively few issues will reach the decision agenda, which contains items that are about to be acted upon by a governmental body. Bills, once they are introduced and heard in committee, are relatively low on the decision agenda until they are reported to the whole body for a vote. Notices of proposed rule making in the *Federal Register* are evidence of an issue or problem's elevation to the decision agenda in the executive branch. Conflict may be greatest at this stage, because when a decision is reached at a particular level of government, it may trigger conflict that expands to another or higher level of government. Conflict continues and may expand; this expansion of conflict is often a key goal of many interest groups. The goal of most contending parties in the policy process is to move policies from the systemic agenda to the institutional agenda, or to prevent issues from reaching the institutional agenda. Figure 5.1 implies that, except for the agenda universe, the agenda and each level within it are finite, and no society or political system can address all possible alternatives to all possible problems that arise at any time. While the carrying capacity of the agenda may change, the agenda carrying capacity of any institution ultimately has a maximum bound, which means that interests must compete with each other to get their issues and their preferred interpretations of these issues on the agenda.

Even when a problem is on the agenda, there may be a considerable amount of controversy and competition over how to define the problem, including the causes of the problem and the policies that would most likely solve the problem. For example, after the 1999 Columbine High school shootings, the issue of school violence quickly rose to national prominence, to a much greater extent than had existed after other incidents of school violence. So school violence was on the agenda: the real competition then became between depictions of school violence as a result of, among other things, lax parenting, easy access to guns, lack of parental supervision, or the influence of popular culture (TV, movies, video games) on high school students. This competition over *why* Columbine happened and *what* could be done to prevent it was quite fierce, more so than the competition between school violence and the other issues vying for attention at the time (Lawrence and Birkland 2004).

POLITICAL POWER IN AGENDA SETTING

The ability of groups—acting singly or, more often, in coalition with other groups—to influence policy is not simply a function of who makes the most persuasive argument, either from a rhetorical or empirical perspective. We know intuitively that some groups are more powerful than others, in the sense that they are better able to influence the outcomes of policy debates. When we think of power, we might initially think about how people, governments, and powerful groups in society can compel people to do things, often against their will. In a classic article in the *American Political Science Review*, Peter Bachrach and Morton Baratz argue that this sort of power—the ability of actor A to cause actor B to do things—is one of two faces of power. The other face is the ability to keep a person from doing what he or she wants to do; instead of a coercive power, the second face is a blocking power.

> Of course power is exercised when A participates in the making of decisions that affect B. But power is also exercised when A devotes his energies to creating or reinforcing social and political values and institutional practices that limit the scope of the political process to public consideration of only those issues which are comparatively innocuous to A. To the extent that A succeeds in doing this, B is prevented, for all practical purposes, from bringing to the fore any issues that might in their resolution be seriously detrimental to A's set of preferences. (Bachrach and Baratz 1962, 952)

In the first face of power, A participates in the making of decisions that affect B, even if B does not like the decisions or their consequences. This is the classic sort of power that we see in authoritarian or totalitarian regimes, but we can also see this sort of power in the United States and other democracies, because there are many groups that have very little power to influence decisions made on their behalf or even against their interests. Prisoners, for example, have little power to influence the conditions of their sentencing and incarceration, while minors have little say in policies made on their behalf or in their interests, such as policies influencing education or juvenile justice. This is not to say that other people and groups do not speak for prisoners or minors. But these spokespeople are working on behalf of groups that are either constructed as "helpless" or "deviant" (Schneider and Ingram 1993).

In the second face of power, A *prevents* B's issues and interests from getting on the agenda or becoming policy, even when actor B really *wants* these issues raised. Environmentalism, for example, was, until the late 1960s and early 1970s, not a particularly powerful interest, and groups that promote environmental protection found that their issues rarely made the agenda because these issues in no way were those of the major economic and political forces that dominated decision making. Not until the emergence of high-profile environmental crises, such as the revelation of the problems with the pesticide DDT or the Santa Barbara oil spill of 1969, were these problems coupled with broad-based group mobilization, thereby elevating these issues to where mainstream actors paid attention to it. Even then, one can argue that actor A, representing the business and industrial sector, bent but did not break on environmental issues and is still able to prevent B, the environmental movement, from advancing broader (or radical, depending on one's perspective) ideas that could have a profound effect on the environment.

The blocking moves of the more powerful interests are not simply a function of A having superior resources to B, although this does play a substantial role. In essence, we should not think of the competition between actor A and actor B as a sporting event on a field, with even rules, between two teams, one vastly more powerful than the other. Rather, the power imbalance is as much a function of the nature and rules of the policy process as it is a function of the particular attributes of the groups or interests themselves. As Schattschneider explains:

> All forms of political organization have a bias in favor of the exploitation of some kinds of conflict and the suppression of others because *organization is the mobilization of bias*. Some issues are organized into politics while others are organized out. (Schattschneider 1960/1975, 71)

In other words, some issues are more likely to reach the agenda because the bias of the political system allows them to be raised, while others are, according to the bias of the system, unfit for political consideration. Housing, education, a job, or health care are not provided as a matter of right in America because the bias of the American political system rests on cultural values of self-reliance, which means that the United States lags behind other nations in the state provision of these services. This bias is not static or God-given, but changes rather slowly as some interests oppose the provision of these things as a matter of right.

Other scholars of political power have conceived of a third face of power, which differs substantially from the second face of power in that large groups of people who objectively have a claim that they are disadvantaged remain quiescent—that is, passive—and fail to *attempt* to exert their influence, however small, on policy making and politics. This is the story John Gaventa tells in his book *Power and Powerlessness* (1980, 168). Gaventa explains why a community of Appalachian coal miners remained under the repressive power of a British coal mining company and the local business and social elite. As Harry G. Reid (1981) notes, Gaventa takes on the traditional idea that political participation in Appalachia is low because of the people's own shortcomings, such as low educational attainment and poverty. Rather, in the third face of power, social relationships and political ideology are structured over the long term in such a way that the mining company, remains dominant and the miners cannot conceive of a situation in which they can begin to participate in the decisions that directly affect their lives. When the miners show some signs of rebelling against the unfair system, the dominant interests are able to ignore pressure for change. In the long run, people may stop fighting as they become and remain alienated from politics; quiescence is the result.

This necessarily brief discussion of the idea of power is merely an overview of what is a very complex and important field of study in political science in general. It is important to us here because an understanding of power helps us understand how groups compete to gain access to the agenda *and* to deny access to groups and interests that would damage their interests.

GROUPS AND POWER IN AGENDA SETTING

E. E. Schattschneider's theories of group mobilization and participation in agenda setting rest on his oft-cited contention that issues are more likely to be elevated to agenda status if the scope of conflict is broadened. There are two key ways in which traditionally disadvantaged (losing) groups expand the scope of conflict. First, groups go public with a problem by using symbols and images to induce greater media and public sympathy for their cause. Environmental groups dramatize their causes by pointing to symbols and images of allegedly willful or negligent humanly caused environmental damage.

Second, groups that lose in the first stage of a political conflict can appeal to a higher decision-making level, such as when losing parties appeal to state and then federal institutions for an opportunity to be heard, hoping that in the process they will attract others who agree with them and their cause. Conversely, dominant groups work to contain conflict to ensure that it does not spread out of control. The underlying theory of these tendencies dates to Madison's defense, in *Federalist* 10, of the federal system as a mechanism to contain political conflict.

Schattschneider's theories of issue expansion explain how in-groups retain control over problem definition and the way such problems are suppressed by dominant actors in policy making. These actors form what Baumgartner and Jones (1993, 142) call policy monopolies, which attempt to keep problems and underlying policy issues low on the agenda. Policy communities use agreed-upon symbols to construct their visions of problems, causes, and solutions. As long as these images and symbols are maintained throughout society, or remain largely invisible and unquestioned, agenda access for groups that do not share these images is likely to be difficult; change is less likely until the less powerful group's construction of the problem becomes more prevalent. If alternative selection is central to the projection of political power, an important corollary is that powerful groups retain power by working to keep the public and out-groups unaware of underlying problems, alternative constructions of problems, or alternatives to their resolution. This argument reflects those made by elite theorists such as C. Wright Mills (1956) and E. E. Schattschneider himself, who famously noted that "the flaw in the pluralist heaven is that the heavenly chorus sings with a strong upper-class accent" (1960/1975, 35) This does not deny the possibility of change, but acknowledges that change is sometimes slow in coming and difficult to achieve.

OVERCOMING POWER DEFICITS TO ACCESS THE AGENDA

Baumgartner and Jones argue that when powerful groups lose their control of the agenda, less powerful groups can enter policy debates and gain attention to their issues. This greater attention to the problem area tends to increase negative public attitudes toward the status quo, which can then produce lasting institutional and agenda changes that break up policy monopolies.

There are several ways in which groups can pursue strategies to gain attention to issues, thereby advancing issues on the agenda. The first set of ways for less advantaged interest groups to influence policy making relates to Kingdon's streams metaphor of agenda change (Kingdon 1995). "Windows of opportunity" for change open when two or more streams—the political, problem, or policy streams—are coupled. In the political stream, electoral change can lead to reform movements that give previously less powerful groups an opportunity to air their concerns. An example is policy making during the Lyndon Johnson administration's Great Society program, which contained a package of policies that sought to attack poverty, poor health, racial discrimination, and urban decline, among other problems. This package of programs was made possible by an aggressively activist president and a large Democratic majority in the Congress, the result of the Democratic landslide of 1964.

Second, changes in our perception of problems will also influence the opening of a "window of opportunity" for policy change. In the 1930s, people began to perceive unemployment and economic privation not simply as a failure of individual initiative, but as a collective economic problem that required governmental solutions under the rubric of the New Deal. In the 1960s and 1970s, people began to perceive environmental problems, such as dirty air and water and the destruction of wildlife, not as the function of natural processes but as the result of negative human influences on the ecosystem. And, third, changes in the policy stream can influence the opening of the window of opportunity. In the 1960s, poverty and racism were seen as problems, but were also coupled with what were suggested as new and more effective policies to solve these problems, such as the Civil Rights Acts, the Voting Rights Act, and the War on Poverty.

Lest we think that all this change is in the liberal direction, it is worth noting that other periods of change, notably the Reagan administration, were also characterized by the joining of these streams. These include changes in the political stream (more conservative legislators, growing Republican strength in the South, the advent of the Christian right as a political force), the problem stream (government regulation as cause, not the solution, of economic problems, American weakness in foreign affairs), and the policy stream (ideas for deregulation and smaller government, increased military spending and readiness) that came together during the first two years of the Reagan administration. These factors help explain policies favoring increased military spending, an increase in attention to moral issues, and a decrease in spending on social programs.

In each of these instances, it took group action to press for change. Groups worked to shine the spotlight on issues because, as Baumgartner and Jones argue, increased attention is usually negative attention to a problem, leading to calls for policy change to address the problems being highlighted. But the simple desire to mobilize is not enough. Groups sometimes need a little help to push issues on the agenda; this help can come from changes in indicators of a problem or focusing events that create rapid attention. And groups often need to join forces to create a more powerful movement than they could create if they all acted as individuals.

GROUP COALESCENCE AND STRATEGIES FOR CHANGE

A major shortcoming of elite theory and of power theories is that some interests simply accept their fate and give elite groups relatively little trouble. Related to this is the assumption that the elite is somehow a monolith, single-mindedly marching toward the same class-related goals. Neither of these assumptions is true. Less advantaged interests in the United States can enter policy disputes without inviting the wrath of the state; their major risk is irrelevance or impotence. And powerful social and economic interests often conflict with each other, such as when producers of raw materials, such as oil and steel, want to raise prices and producers of goods that use these inputs, such as automobile makers, seek to keep raw material costs low, or when broadcasters battle powerful values interests over the content of music, movies, or television. Within industries, vicious battles over markets and public policy can result, as in the ongoing legal and economic battles between Microsoft and its rivals, or between major airlines and discount carriers (Birkland and Nath 2000). And many movements that seek policy change are led by people whose socioeconomic condition and background are not vastly different from that of their political opponents. In this section, we will review how less advantaged interests, led by bright and persistent leaders, can and sometimes do overcome some of their power deficits.

The first thing to recognize about pro-change groups is that they, like more powerful interests, will often coalesce into advocacy coalitions. An advocacy coalition is a coalition of groups that come together based on a shared set of beliefs about a particular issue or problem (see Hank Jenkins Smith's chapter in this volume). These are not necessarily these groups' core belief systems; rather, groups will often coalesce on their more peripheral beliefs, provided that the coalition will advance all groups' goals in the debate at hand.

This is one way in which the dynamics of groups and coalitions can work to break down the power of dominant interests. This strength in numbers results in greater attention from policy makers and greater access to the policy-making process, thereby forming what social scientists call *countervailing power* against the most powerful elites. But where should a group begin to seek to influence policy once it has formed a coalition and mobilized its allies and members? This question is addressed by Baumgartner and Jones in their discussion of "venue shopping" (Baumgartner and Jones 1993, 31).

Venue shopping describes the efforts groups undertake to gain a hearing for their ideas and grievances against existing policy (e.g., Pralle 2003). A *venue* is a level of government or institution in which the group is likely to gain the most favorable hearing. We can think of venues in institutional terms—legislative, executive, or judicial—or in vertical terms—federal, state, local government. The news media are also a venue, and even within a branch of government, there are multiple venues.

Groups can seek to be witnesses before congressional committees and subcommittees where the chair is known to be sympathetic to their position or at least open-minded enough to hear their case. This strategy requires the cooperation of the leadership of the committee or subcommittee, and unsympathetic leaders will often block efforts to include some interests on witness lists. But the many and largely autonomous committees and subcommittees in Congress allow groups to venue shop within Congress itself, thereby increasing the likelihood that an issue can be heard.

After a major focusing event (discussed below), it is particularly hard to exclude aggrieved parties from a congressional hearing, and members whose support was formerly lukewarm may be more enthusiastic supporters when the magnitude of a problem becomes clearer.

Groups that cannot gain a hearing in the legislative branch can appeal to executive branch officials. For example, environmentalists who cannot get a hearing in the House Resources Committee may turn to the Environmental Protection Agency, the Fish and Wildlife Service, the various agencies that compose the Department of the Interior, and other agencies that may be more sympathetic and might be able to use existing legal and regulatory means to advance environmental goals. Or the environmentalists may choose to raise their issues at the state level. While an appeal to these agencies may raise some conflict with the legislative branch, this tactic can at least open doors for participation by otherwise excluded groups. Groups often engage in litigation as a way to get their issues on the agenda, particularly when other access points are closed to the group.

Groups may seek to change policies at the local or state level before taking an issue to the federal government, because the issue may be easier to advance at the local level or because a grass-roots group may find it can fight on an equal footing with a more powerful group. This often happens in NIMBY (not in my back yard) cases, such as decisions on where to put group homes, cell phone towers, expanded shopping centers, power plants, and the like. And, of course, groups sometimes must address issues at the state and local level because these governments have the constitutional responsibility for many functions not undertaken by the federal government, such as education or, as became clear in the same-sex marriage issue in 2003 and 2004, the laws governing marriage. In this example, it's clear that gay rights groups have adopted a state by state or even more local strategy because it makes no sense to seek change at the federal level.

On the other hand, groups may expand conflict to a broader level—from the local level to the state level, or from the state to federal level—when they lose at the local level. E. E. Schattschneider calls this "expanding the scope of conflict." This strategy sometimes works because expanding the scope of conflict often engages the attention of other actors who may step in on the side of the less powerful group. An example of the expanding scope of conflict is the civil rights movement, which in many ways was largely confined to the South until images of violent crackdowns on civil rights protesters became more prominent on the evening news, thereby expanding the issue to a broader and somewhat more sympathetic public. Indeed, groups often seek media coverage as a way of expanding the scope of conflict. Media activities can range from holding news conferences to mobilizing thousands of people in protest rallies. Sometimes an issue is elevated to greater attention by the inherent newsworthiness of the event, without preplanning by the protest groups, such as the just-cited example of media coverage of civil rights protests.

Finally, gaining a place on the agenda often relies on coalescing with other groups, as was discussed earlier. Many of the great social movements of our time required that less powerful interests coalesce. Even the civil rights movement involved a coalition, at various times, with antiwar protestors, labor unions, women's groups, antipoverty workers, and other groups who shared an interest in racial equality. By coalescing in this way, the voices of all these interests were multiplied. Indeed, the proliferation of interest groups since the 1950s has resulted in greater opportunities for coalition building and has created far greater resources for countervailing power.

Before concluding this discussion, we must recognize that elevating issues on the agenda in hopes of gaining policy change is not always resisted by political elites. Cobb and Elder (1983) argue that, when political elites seek change, they also try to mobilize publics to generate mass support for an issue, which supports elite efforts to move issues further up the agenda. Such efforts can constitute either attempts to broaden the influence of existing policy monopolies or attempts by some political elites (such as the president and his staff) to circumvent the policy monopoly established by interest groups, the bureaucracy, and subcommittees (the classic iron triangle model). The president or other key political actors may be able to enhance the focusing power of an event by visiting a disaster or accident scene, thereby affording the event even greater symbolic weight.

THE SOCIAL CONSTRUCTION OF PROBLEMS AND ISSUES

Problems can be defined and depicted in many different ways, depending on the goals of the proponent of the particular depiction of a problem and the nature of the problem and the political debate. The process of defining problems and of selling a broad population on this definition, is called social construction. Social construction refers to the ways in which we as a society and the various contending interests within it structure and tell the stories about how problems come to be the way they are. A group that can create and promote the most effective depiction of an issue has an advantage in the battle over what, if anything, will be done about a problem.

At the same time, there remain many social problems that people believe should be solved or, at least, made better. Poverty, illiteracy, racism, immorality, disease, disaster, crime, and any number of other ills will lead people and groups to press for solutions. Often, these social problems require that governmental action be taken because services required to alleviate public problems that are not or cannot be addressed by private actors are *public goods* that can primarily be provided by government actors. While in the popular mind, and often in reality, economic and social conservatives believe in limited government activity, these conservatives also believe there are public goods, such as regulation of securities markets, road building, national defense, and public safety, that are most properly addressed by government. In the end, though, it is probably best to think about problems by thinking first about a clear definition of the problem itself, before concerning ourselves with whether public or private actors must remedy the problem. Beyond this, whether a problem really is a problem at all is an important part of political and policy debate: merely stating a problem is not enough, one must persuade others that the problem exists or that the problem being cited is the *real* problem.

The way a problem is defined is an important part of this persuasive process and is important in the choice of solutions. The social construction of a problem is linked to the existing social, political, and ideological structures at the time. Americans still value individual initiative and responsibility, and therefore make drinking and driving at least as much a matter of personal responsibility as social responsibility. The same values of self-reliance and individual initiative are behind many of our public policies, dealing with free enterprise, welfare, and other economic policies. These values differentiate our culture from other nations' cultures, where the community or the state takes a more important role. In those countries, problems are likely to be constructed differently, and different policies are the result.

CONDITIONS AND PROBLEMS

Conditions—that is, things that exist that are bothersome but about which people and governments cannot do anything—can develop over time into problems as people develop ways to address these conditions. A classic example is polio: until Dr. Jonas Salk developed the polio vaccine, millions of children and their parents lived in fear of this crippling disease. Without the polio vaccine, this disease was simply a dreaded condition that could perhaps be avoided (people kept their kids away from swimming pools, for example, to avoid contracting polio) but certainly not treated or prevented without very high social costs. With the vaccine, polio became a *problem* about which something effective could be done.

When people become dependent on solutions to previously addressed problems, then the interruption of the solution will often constitute a major problem, resulting in efforts to prevent any such interruptions. One hundred and fifty years ago, electricity as public utility did not exist; today, an interruption in the supply of electricity and other utilities is a problem that we believe can be ameliorated—indeed, we believe it should never happen at all! An extreme example is the power outage that struck Auckland, New Zealand, in February 1998. The outage lasted for over ten days, closing businesses, forcing evacuations of apartments due to water and sewer failures, and ending up costing New Zealanders millions of dollars. The cause of the outage was the failure of overtaxed power cables; regardless of its cause, people do not expect, nor lightly tolerate, the loss of something taken for granted for so long. Indeed, while the blackouts that struck eight eastern states and two Canadian provinces in August 2003 lasted hours, not days, for most locations, but led to significant social and economic disruption as elevators failed, subways ceased to work, computer systems shut down, and all the modern features on which urban societies rely were unavailable.

Many problems are not as obvious and dramatic as these. After all, it did not take a lot of argument to persuade those evacuated from their apartments or those who spent the night in their offices because subways and trains didn't work that there was some sort of problem. But other problems are more subtle, and people have to be persuaded that something needs to be done; still more persuasion may be necessary to induce a belief that *government* needs to do something about a problem.

Symbols

Because a hallmark of successful policy advocacy is the ability to tell a good story, groups will use time-tested rhetorical devices, such as the use of symbols, to advance their arguments. A symbol is "anything that stands for something else. Its meaning depends on how people interpret it, use it, or respond to it" (Stone 2002, 137). Politics is full of symbols—some perceived as good, others as bad, and still others as controversial. Some symbols are fairly obvious: the American flag, for example, is generally respected in the United States, while flying a flag bearing the Nazi swastika just about anywhere in the world is considered, at a minimum, to be in poor taste, and, indeed, is illegal in many countries.

Deborah Stone outlines four elements of the use of symbols. First, she discusses *narrative stories*, which are stories told about how things happen, good or bad. They are usually highly simplified and offer the hope that complex problems can be solved with relatively easy solutions. Such stories are staples of the political circuit, where candidates tell stories about wasteful bureaucrats or evil businessmen or lazy welfare cheats to rouse the electorate to elect the candidate, who will impose a straightforward solution to these problems. Stories are told about how things are getting worse or *declining*, in Stone's term, or how things were getting better until something bad happened to stop progress, or how "change-is-only-an-illusion" (142). An example of this last is the stories told on the campaign trail and on the floor of the legislature in which positive economic indicators are acknowledged but are said not to reflect the real problems that real people are having.

Helplessness and control is another common story of how something once could not be done but now something can be done about an issue or problem. This story is closely related to the condition/problem tension.

Often used in these stories is a rhetorical device called *synecdoche* (sin-ECK'-do-key), "a figure of speech in which the whole is represented by one of its parts" (Stone 2002, 145). Phrases such as "a million eyes are on the Capitol today" represent great attention to Congress's actions on a particular issue. In other cases, people telling stories about policy use *anecdotes* or *prototypical cases* to explain an entire phenomenon. Thus, as Stone notes, the idea of the cheating "welfare queen" took hold in the 1980s, even though such people represented a small and atypical portion of the welfare population. Related to such stories are horror stories of government regulation run amok. Such stories are usually distorted: Stone cites the example of how those opposed to industry regulation claimed that the Occupational Safety and Health Administration (OSHA) "abolished the tooth fairy" by requiring that dentists discard any baby teeth they pulled; the actual regulation merely required that appropriate steps be taken to protect health workers from any diseases that may be transmitted in handling the teeth.

TABLE 5.1
Types of Causal Theories with Examples

	Consequences	
Actions	**Intended**	**Unintended**
Unguided	Mechanical cause intervening agents brainwashed people machines that perform as designed, but cause harm	Accidental cause nature weather earthquakes machines that run amok
Purposeful	Intentional cause oppression conspiracies that work programs that work as intended, but cause harm	Inadvertent cause intervening conditions unforeseen side effects avoidable ignorance carelessness omission

Source: Stone 2002

CAUSAL STORIES

An important part of story telling in public policy is the telling of *causal stories*.[31] These stories attempt to explain what caused a problem or an outcome. These stories are particularly important in public policy making, because the depiction of the cause of a problem strongly suggests a solution to the problem. In general, Stone divides causal stories into four categories: mechanical causes, accidental causes, intentional causes, and inadvertent causes. These examples are shown in Table 5.1.

INDICATORS, FOCUSING EVENTS, AND AGENDA CHANGE

John Kingdon discusses changes in indicators and focusing events as two ways in which groups and society as a whole learn of problems in the world. Changes in indicators are usually changes in statistics about a problem; if the data various agencies and interests collect indicate that things are getting worse, the issue will gain considerable attention. Examples include changes in unemployment rates, inflation rates, the gross domestic product, wage levels and their growth, pollution levels, crime, student achievement on standardized tests, birth and death rates, and myriad other things that sophisticated societies count every year.

These numbers by themselves do not have an influence over which issues gain greater attention and which fall by the wayside. Rather, the changes in indicators need to be publicized by interest groups, government agencies, and policy entrepreneurs, who use these numbers to advance their preferred policy ideas. This is not to say that people willfully distort statistics; rather, it means that groups will often selectively use official statistics to suggest that problems exist, while ignoring other indicators that may suggest that no such problem exists. The most familiar indicators, such as those reflecting the health of the economy, almost need no interpretation by interest groups or policy entrepreneurs—when unemployment is up and wages lag behind inflation, the argument is less about whether there is an economic problem but, rather, what to do about it. But even then, the choice of which indicator to use is crucial: in the 2004 presidential campaign, the Bush administration focused on the relatively low national unemployment rate, while the Kerry campaign focused on the numbers of jobs that had allegedly been lost between 2001 and 2004. These are two rather different ways of measuring a similar problem.

An example of indicators used by less advantaged groups to advance claims for greater equity is the growing gap between rich and poor in the United States. According to the *Statistical Abstract of the United States* (United States Department of Commerce, 1999 #3110, table 742), in 1970, those households making $75,000 or more per year, in constant (1997) dollars, comprised 9 percent of all American households; by 1997, this group had doubled its share to 18.4 percent of all households. Where did the other groups shrink to make up this difference? The middle categories, those earning between $25,000 and $49,999, saw their share decrease from 37.2 percent of households in 1970 to 29.6 percent. This kind of evidence is used to argue that the rich are getting richer, while the middle class and, to some extent, the lowest economic classes are worse off in terms of their share of the wealth (see, for example, Phillips, 1990). While these numbers are not in great dispute, the *meaning* of the numbers is in dispute, and the numbers have not had much of an impact on public policy. Indeed, these trends were accelerated with the tax cuts implemented under the Bush administration, which tended to benefit the wealthy more than middle-class and lower-class workers. On the other hand, indicators of educational attainment do have an impact on the agenda, causing periodic reform movements in public education. This is due, in large part, to the activism of the very influential teachers' unions, parent-teacher associations, and other groups that use these indicators to press for greater resources for schools. In the end, the numbers have to be interpreted by groups and advanced on the agenda in order to induce mass and policy maker attention.

Focusing events are somewhat different. Focusing events are sudden, relatively rare events that spark intense media and public attention because of their sheer magnitude or, sometimes, because of the harm they reveal (Birkland 1997). Focusing events thus attract attention to issues that may have been relatively dormant. Examples of focusing events include terrorist attacks (September 11, 2001 was, certainly, a focusing event), airplane accidents, industrial accidents such as factory fires or oil spills, large protest rallies or marches, scandals in government, and everyday events that gain attention because of some special feature of the event. Two examples of the latter are the alleged beating of motorist Rodney King by the Los Angeles Police Department in the early 1990s and O. J. Simpson's murder trial in 1995; the Rodney King incident was noteworthy because, unlike most such incidents, the event was caught on videotape, while the Simpson trial was noteworthy because of the fame of the defendant.

Focusing events can lead groups, government leaders, policy entrepreneurs, the news media, or members of the public to pay attention to new problems or pay greater attention to existing but dormant (in terms of their standing on the agenda) problems, and, potentially, can lead to a search for solutions in the wake of perceived policy failure.

The fact that focusing events occur with little or no warning makes such events important opportunities for mobilization for groups that find their issues hard to advance on the agenda during normal times. Problems characterized by indicators of a problem will more gradually wax and wane on the agenda, and their movement on or off the agenda may be promoted or resisted by constant group competition. Sudden events, on the other hand, are associated with spikes of intense interest and agenda activity. Interest groups—often relatively powerful groups that seek to keep issues off the agenda—often find it difficult to keep major events off the news and institutional agendas. Groups that seek to advance an issue on the agenda can take advantage of such events to attract greater attention to the problem.

In many cases, the public and the most informed members of the policy community learn of a potential focusing event virtually simultaneously. These events can very rapidly alter mass and elite consciousness of a social problem. I say "virtually" because the most active members of a policy community may learn of an event some hours before the general public, because they have a more direct stake in the event, the response to it, and its outcome.

MEASURING AGENDA STATUS OF ISSUES

In a volume on policy analysis it is important to understand how we analyze the status of issues on the agenda. We can do so both qualitatively and quantitatively, and the way we approach this analysis is clearly influenced by the nature of the questions we ask. The two basic categories of questions are What is on the agenda? and What is the agenda status? of any particular issue.

It is probably easiest to measure issues on the national institutional agenda, because the Congress and executive branch have historically kept remarkably good records, and because these records have been put into databases that are reasonably easily searched. Thus, a researcher can use the Congressional Information Service (CIS) index to track the substance of Congressional hearings, the Library of Congress's THOMAS database to track legislation or debate in the *Congressional Record* and various legal research tools to review and track rulemaking in the *Federal Register.* The *Congressional Quarterly* also provides a good source of information about the important issues on the federal agenda. While information on the federal agenda is relatively easy to obtain, there is so much of it that one can easily become lost in a sea of potential data. It is important that the researcher have a well thought out coding scheme for placing data into appropriate subject matter categories while avoiding the temptation to split the difference by putting items—congressional testimony, for example, or entries in the *Congressional Record*—into several categories.

Fortunately, a great deal of the work of involved in gathering and categorizing important agenda information has been achieved under the auspices of the Policy Agendas Project at the Center for American Politics and Public Policy at the University of Washington (http://www.policyagendas. org/) (see also Baumgartner, Jones, and Wilkerson 2002). This project is the outgrowth of Frank Baumgartner and Bryan Jones's efforts to understand the dynamics of agenda setting over many years. The project has collected data on the federal budget, *Congressional Quarterly Almanac* (herein after *CQ Almanac*) stories, congressional hearings from 1946 to 2000, executive orders from 1945 to 2001, front page stories in the *New York Times*, the Gallup Poll's "most important problem" question (which reflects public opinion on the agenda status of key issues), and public laws from 1948–1998. The goal of this project is to provide a base of agenda data, using a comparable coding scheme over time and between the different agendas or "arenas," that researchers can use to study agenda setting. The founders of this effort intended for these databases to be extended, supplemented, and studied in greater depth by researchers. At least two workshops on the use of these data have been held at the annual meeting of the American Political Science association, and the data set was the foundation of the studies published in Baumgartner and Jones's volume *Policy Dynamics* (2002).

The key value of the Agendas Project data is the ability to show the change in the composition of the United States national agenda over time. Because the data set is comprehensive and because it uses a consistent coding scheme, we can see the ebb and flow of issues, and we can understand the expansion and contraction of the agenda as a whole, suggesting that the carrying capacity of the agenda can change with changes in the nature of the institution, including, as Talbert and Potoski note, when "legislative institutions are adapted to improve information processing" (2002, 190) Such improvements can include increases in the numbers of committee, increases in staff support to the members of the legislature, improvements in information processing and retrieval systems, devoting more time to legislative business, among other things.

We can see the results of this increase in carrying capacity, as well as the individual will of the legislative branch to attack more issues, if we plot the number of congressional hearings held each year, a figure easily calculated from the Agenda Project's data, and plotted in Figure 5.2. Clearly, the House and Senate's agendas grew during the 1960s; I will leave it to other analysts to decide whether this increase in the agenda was a response to executive initiative, perceived public demand for legislation, legislators' motivations to hold more hearings, or some combination of these elements.

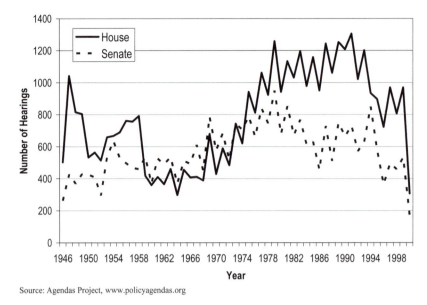

Source: Agendas Project, www.policyagendas.org

FIGURE 5.2   House and Senate Agendas, 1947–2000.

What is interesting about the data is the degree to which both agendas show a saw tooth pattern, reflecting the much greater volume of hearings in odd-numbered, non-election years. Interestingly, the Senate and House held roughly the same number of hearings in 1973, but the growth in the House's hearing agenda continued and then remained much larger than the Senate's agenda well into the early 1990s, while the size of the Senate's agenda remained relatively static. This growth in the House's agenda is likely the result of the proliferation of House subcommittees that followed the post-1974 legislative reforms, coupled with rules changes that allowed subcommittees to act independently of the committee chairs. Many of these newly empowered subcommittees were chaired by activist members who used the rules changes to react to the suppression of the agenda by House leadership and by the executive branch until the early 1990s. The agenda then shrinks in both the House and Senate as the Republican Party becomes ascendant and as party discipline restricts the size of the agenda. While it is clear that the size and composition of the agenda is in many ways out of the control of legislators (Walker 1977), these data suggest that legislators can control the overall size of the agenda through the promotion and management of institutional structures, as Talbert and Potoski note.

Much as the legislative agenda is elastic, so is the news media agenda, and the agenda as measured by the volume of stories in the *CQ Almanac*. The raw number of news stories in the *New York Times* might be somewhat related to the size of the congressional agenda, in large part because the *Times* is considered (and considers itself) the national newspaper of record; presumably, weighty matters of state handled in the Congress would be reflected in the *Times*. The *CQ Almanac,* on the other hand, occupies an intermediate position between the news media and the Congress; the *CQ Almanac* is very closely tied to congressional activity. The relative size of the *Times, CQ Almanac,* and the House and Senate agendas are shown in Figure 5.3. Because we want to compare relative sizes, the agendas are indexed so that all four agendas in 1973 equal 100; 1973 was chosen because it is the middle year in the data and because it is the year in which the Senate and House hearings volumes were nearly equal.

Clearly, the agenda, as represented by the *CQ Almanac* and the *Times*, is reasonably elastic. The major growth period for the *Times* came in the late 1960s, likely a result of the political turmoil

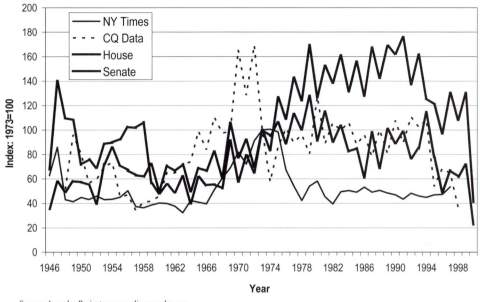

Source: Agendas Project, www.policyagendas.org

FIGURE 5.3 Relative Size of Key Agendas, 1947–2000.

surrounding the Vietnam War and the civil rights movement, and peaked in 1974 with the Watergate scandal. The *CQ Almanac* shows the saw tooth trend evident in the hearings data, but tends to peak during election years; its peaks in the early 1970s appear to be related to the institutional changes in the Congress, coupled with the growing confrontation between the executive and legislative that preceded the Watergate period.

This discussion is merely suggestive, and the reasons for the dynamics of the agenda are deserving of further analysis. But we do know that the agenda is fluid, and that the data available to the analyst are rich, varied, and lead to immensely useful insights. Indeed, a deeper analysis of the relative position of issues on the agenda is beyond the scope of this chapter, but one can, for example, use the agendas data to show the relative decline of defense as an agenda item in the 1970s as other issues gained prominence. The relative position of issues on the agenda is an important feature of the policy history and of the political development of the United States, and is of interest to policy analysts and historians alike.

CONCLUSION

The study of agenda setting is a particularly fruitful way to begin to understand how groups, power, and the agenda interact to set the boundaries of political policy debate. Agenda setting, like all other stages of the policy process, does not occur in a vacuum. The likelihood that an issue will rise on the agenda is a function of the issue itself, the actors that get involved, institutional relationships, and, often, random social and political factors that can be explained but cannot be replicated or predicted. But theories of agenda setting, coupled with better and more readily available data, are enabling researchers to understand why and under what circumstances policy change is likely to occur.

REFERENCES

Bachrach, Peter, and Morton Baratz. 1962. The Two Faces of Power. *American Political Science Review* 56:947–952.

Baumgartner, Frank R., and Bryan D. Jones. 1993. *Agendas and Instability in American Politics*. Chicago: University of Chicago Press.

Baumgartner, Frank R., and Bryan D. Jones. 2002. *Policy Dynamics*. Chicago: University of Chicago Press.

Baumgartner, Frank R., and Bryan D. Jones. 2004. Representation and Agenda Setting. *Policy Studies Review* 32(2):1–24.

Baumgartner, Frank R., Bryan D. Jones, and John D. Wilkerson. 2002. Studying Policy Dynamics. In *Policy Dynamics*, edited by F. R. Baumgartner and B. D. Jones. Chicago: University of Chicago Press.

Birkland, Thomas A., and Radhika Nath. 2000. Business and the Political Dimension in Disaster Management. *Journal of Public Policy* 20 (3):279–303.

Cobb, Roger W., and Charles D. Elder. 1983. *Participation in American Politics: The Dynamics of Agenda-Building* (2nd ed.). Baltimore: Johns Hopkins University Press.

Cobb, Roger W., and Marc Howard Ross. 1997. *Cultural strategies of agenda denial: avoidance, attack, and redefinition*. Lawrence: University Press of Kansas.

Gaventa, John. 1980. *Power and Powerlessness: Quiescence and Rebellion in an Appalachian Valley*. Urbana: University of Illinois Press.

Hilgartner, James, and Charles Bosk. 1988. The Rise and Fall of Social Problems: A Public Arenas Model. *American Journal of Sociology* 94(1):53–78.

Kingdon, John W. 1995. *Agendas, Alternatives and Public Policies* (2nd ed.). New York: Harper Collins.

Lawrence, Regina G., and Thomas A. Birkland. 2004. Guns, Hollywood, and Criminal Justice: Defining the School Shootings Problem across Public Arenas. *Social Science Quarterly* 85(5):1193–1207.

Mills, C.W. 1956. *The Power Elite*. Oxford: Oxford University Press.

O'Toole, Laurence J. 1989. The Public Administrator's Role in Setting the Policy Agenda. In *Handbook of Public Administration*, edited by J. L. Perry. San Francisco: Jossey Bass.

Pralle, Sarah B. 2003. Venue Shopping, Political Strategy, and Policy Change: The Internationalization of Canadian Forest Advocacy. *Journal of Public Policy* 23(3):233–260.

Reid, Herbert G. 1981. Review of John Gaventa, Power and Powerlessness: Quiesence and Rebellion in an Appalachian Valley. *Journal of Politics* 43(4):1270–1273.

Schattschneider, E.E. 1960/1975. *The Semisovereign People*. Hinsdale, IL: The Dryden Press.

Schneider, Anne, and Helen Ingram. 1993. The Social Construction of Target Populations: Implications for Politics and Policy. *American Political Science Review* 87(2):334–348.

Talbert, Jeffrey C., and Matthew Potoski. 2002. The Changing Public Agenda over the Postwar Period. In *Policy dynamics*, edited by F. R. Baumgartner and B. D. Jones. Chicago: University of Chicago Press.

Walker, Jack L. 1977. Setting the Agenda in the U.S. Senate: A Theory of Problem Selection. *British Journal of Political Science* 7:423–445.

6 Policy Formulation: Design and Tools

Mara S. Sidney

In a traditional stages model of the public policy process, policy formulation is part of the pre-decision phase of policy making. It involves identifying and/or crafting a set of policy alternatives to address a problem, and narrowing that set of solutions in preparation for the final policy decision. According to Cochran and Malone, policy formulation takes up the "what" questions: "What is the plan for dealing with the problem? What are the goals and priorities? What options are available to achieve those goals? What are the costs and benefits of each of the options? What externalities, positive or negative, are associated with each alternative?" (1999, 46). This approach to policy formulation, embedded in a stages model of the policy process, assumes that participants in the policy process already have recognized and defined a policy problem, and moved it onto the policy agenda. Formulating the set of alternatives thus involves identifying a range of broad approaches to a problem, and then identifying and designing the specific sets of policy tools that constitute each approach. It involves drafting the legislative or regulatory language for each alternative—that is, describing the tools (e.g., sanctions, grants, prohibitions, rights, and the like) and articulating to whom or to what they will apply, and when they will take effect. Selecting from among these a smaller set of possible solutions from which decision makers actually will choose involves applying some set of criteria to the alternatives, for example judging their feasibility, political acceptability, costs, benefits, and such.

In general, we expect fewer participants to be involved in policy formulation than were involved in the agenda-setting process, and we expect more of the work to take place out of the public eye. Standard policy texts describe formulation as a back-room function. As Dye puts it, policy formulation takes place in government bureaucracies, in interest group offices, in legislative committee rooms, in meetings of special commissions, in think tanks—with details often formulated by staff (2002, 40–41). In other words, policy formulation often is the realm of the experts, the "hidden participants" of Kingdon's policy stream (1995), the technocrats or knowledge elites of Fischer's democracy at risk (2000).

Policy formulation clearly is a critical phase of the policy process. Certainly designing the alternatives that decision makers will consider directly influences the ultimate policy choice. This process also both expresses and allocates power among social, political, and economic interests. As Schattschneider reminds us, "...the definition of the alternatives is the choice of conflicts, and the choice of conflicts allocates power" (1960, 68). Contemporary interest in policy formulation can be traced to Dahl and Lindblom who urged scholars in 1953 to take up the study of public policies rather than to continue to focus on ideologies as the critical aspects of political systems. They argued that broad debates about the merits of capitalism versus socialism were less important to the well being of society than was careful consideration of the myriad "techniques" that might be used to regulate the economy and to advance particular social values. In part they suggest that the details matter—that is, capitalism or socialism may be advanced through any number of specific public policies, and the selection among them will have important consequences that scholars should consider.

Scholarship on policy formulation takes up a variety of issues. It examines the factors that influence how actors craft alternatives, it prescribes means for such crafting, it examines how and why particular policy alternatives remain on or fall off of the decision agenda. Research considers particular policy tools and trends in their use, as well as their underlying assumptions about problems and groups. As scholars answer such questions, they consider the array of interests involved and the balance of power held by participants, the dominant ideas and values of these participants, the institutional structure of the alternative-setting process, more broadly the historical, political, social, and economic context. The best work on policy formulation and policy tools brings together the empirical and normative. That is, it sets out trends and explains relationships while also proposing normative criteria for evaluating the processes and the tools, and considering their implications for a democratic society.

APPROACHES TO POLICY FORMULATION

The literature on policy design or formulation is somewhat disconnected. Policy formulation is an explicit object of inquiry in studies of policy design and policy tools. But attention to policy formulation also is embedded in work on subsystems, advocacy coalitions, networks, and policy communities (see Weible and Sabatier; Miller and Demir; Raab and Kenis, this volume). Even classic works on agenda-setting take up aspects of policy formulation (e.g., Kingdon 1995; Birkland, this volume). These various frameworks and theories of policy change consider the coalitions of actors taking part in (or being excluded from) the policy making process. Identifying these actors, and understanding their beliefs and motivations, their judgments of feasibility, and their perceptions of the political context, goes a long way toward explaining the public policies that take shape (Howlett and Ramesh 1995).

POLICY DESIGN

The most recent wave of literature explicitly focused on policy formulation uses the concept of policy design. Work on policy design emerged in response to implementation studies of the 1970s that held bureaucratic systems responsible for policy failure. Policy design theorists argued that scholars should look further back in the causal chain to understand why policies succeed or fail, because the original policy formulation processes, and the policy designs themselves, significantly contribute to implementation outcomes. Undergirding many of these works is an assumption of bounded rationality (Simon 1985). That is, limits to human cognition and attention, and limits to our knowledge about the social world inevitably lead policy makers to focus on some aspects of a problem at the expense of others, and to compare only a partial selection of possible solutions (see Andrews, this volume). Research on policy formulation thus seeks to understand the context in which the decision makers act and to identify the selectivity in attention that occurs. Often the aim is to bring awareness of the "boundaries" of rationality to the design process in order to expand the search for solutions, in hopes of improving the policies that result.

Under the rubric of policy design, some scholars have written from the perspective of professional policy analysts, exploring how notions of policy design can improve the practice of policy analysis and the recommendations that analysts make. Their purpose is an applied one—they hope to improve the process of designing policy alternatives. They propose that improving the search for, and generation of, policy alternatives will lead to more effective and successful policies. Essentially, these scholars seek to reduce the randomness of policy formulation (e.g., as portrayed in the garbage can model) by bringing awareness to, and then consciously structuring, the process.

For example, Alexander recommends a "deliberate design stage" in which policy makers search for policy alternatives (1982). Typically, designing policy involves some degree of creativity, or extra-rational element, in addition to rational processes of search and discovery, but Alexander argues that "a conscious concern with the systematic design of policy alternatives can undoubtedly effect a significant improvement in decisions and outcomes" (ibid., 289). Linder and Peters elaborate by proposing a framework that policy analysts can use to generate and compare alternative solutions, resulting in a less random process of policy design (1985). They echo a call made by many de-sign theorists for analysts to suspend judgment on alternatives until they have generated the most comprehensive possible set. An effective framework to guide this process would enable analysis, comparison, and matching of the characteristics of problems, goals, and instruments.

Weimer agrees that consulting broad lists of policy instruments can systematize policy formula-tion, but warns that developing truly innovative solutions involves crafting designs that fit specific substantive, organizational, and political contexts (1992). He urges policy designers to think in terms of institution-building. That is, policies as institutions shape behavior and perceptions, so policies can be structured in such a way as to bring about desired changes in problematic conditions, but also the political coalitions to support them. Bobrow and Dryzek (1987) also advocate contextual designs that explicitly incorporate values, and urge policy analysts to draw from a range of perspectives on policy analysis, from welfare economics, public choice, and structural approaches to political philosophy when searching for alternatives. They suggest that analysts take care to include in a list of alternatives policy designs that offer no intervention, the status quo, and solutions vastly different from current practice. Fischer (2000) and Rixecker (1994) suggest that innovation and creativity will emerge from attention to the voices that contribute to the policy dialogue. Rixecker urges conscious inclusion of marginalized populations in the design process. Fischer examines the epistemology that leads citizens to defer to experts on policy matters, arguing that local contextual knowledge has an important role to play both in improving policy solutions and in advancing democracy.

Scholars who approach policy design from an academic research perspective typically seek to develop a framework that can improve our understanding, analysis, and evaluation of policy processes and their consequences. Many of these works aim to identify aspects of policy making contexts that shape policy design. They draw on institutional theories that suggest laws, constitu-tions, and the organization of the political process channel political behavior and choices. That is, institutions shape actors' preferences and strategies by recognizing the legitimacy of certain claims over others, and by offering particular sorts of opportunities for voicing complaints (Immergut 1998). Some focus on discourse and dominant ideas. Politics consists of competing efforts to make meaning as much as to win votes. Indeed, the pursuit and exercise of power includes constructing images and stories, and deploying symbols (Fischer and Forester 1993; Rochefort and Cobb 1994; Schneider and Ingram 1997, 2005; Stone 2001; Yanow 1995). Ideas about feasibility, dominant judicial interpretations, ideas about groups affected by the policy, all play a role in shaping the policy alternatives that emerge.

May proposes that political environments vary in terms of the level of public attention focused upon them, having important consequences for the policy design process. The degree to which or-ganized interests have developed ideas about an issue will entail particular dynamics and challenges in the policy design process. For instance, on some issues, many interest groups will take an active part in defining the problem and proposing alternatives; they will offer an array of opposing ideas. The design challenge in such a scenario is to find solutions that will be acceptable to participants but also will achieve desired outcomes: "A dilemma arises when policy proposals that balance the competing interests do not necessarily lead to optimal outcomes" (1991,197). On the other hand, on some issues, few groups pay attention and discussions about solutions occur far from the public eye. The dilemmas here involve concerns about democratic process, but also policy designers may have trouble capturing the attention of decision makers. Here the challenge is sometimes to mobilize interest, to mobilize publics to care about, and eventually to comply with, policies.

Ingraham considers environment in terms of institutional setting, proposing that the level of design interacts with the locus of design to shape the policy prescription (1987). She contrasts the legislative setting with the bureaucratic setting to illustrate how different institutions carry particular kinds of expertise and decision processes to policy design. For example, legislative settings often require compromise among diverse opinions, which may lead to the broadening or blurring of a policy's purpose and content. On the other hand, bureaucratic settings enable technical and scientific expertise to be brought to bear on the design process, but at the expense of democratic legitimacy.

In addition to the distinction between applied and traditional scholarly work, researchers diverge in their conceptions of the activity of formulating or designing policy. Some see it as a technical endeavor, leading them to characterize policies as "more" or "less" designed, as "well" or "poorly" designed (e.g., Ingraham 1987; Linder and Peters 1985). For example, these authors would describe a policy as well-designed if a careful analysis of means-end relationships had been conducted prior to its adoption (Ingraham 1987). For others, designing policy does not by definition include certain kinds of analytic tasks. These scholars tend to understand policy design as a political process preceding every policy choice (Bobrow and Dryzek 1987; Kingdon 1995; Schneider and Ingram 1997; Stone 2001). Rather than hoping for a rational policy design to emerge, they expect designs to lack coherence or consistency as a result of the contested process that produces them.

APPROACHES TO POLICY TOOLS

Over time, a subset of policy literature has focused explicitly on policy tools. In part, these studies catalog the generic types of tools that might be used in a policy design. Additionally, this body of work charts the trends in usage of particular policy tools across time and space. This research seeks to discern the range of instruments, detached from their association with particular policy programs, both to broaden the alternatives that policy designers consider, and to look for patterns in the dynamics and politics of program operation that arise across policy areas where similar tools are used (Salamon 1989, 2002). It also often looks to theorize about the assumptions and implications of various policy tools.

Bardach offers the appendix "Things Governments Do" in his eight-step framework of policy analysis, describing taxes, regulation, grants, services, budgets, information, rights, and other policy tools (2005). For each tool, he suggests why and how it might be used, and what some of the possible pitfalls could be, aiming to stimulate creativity in crafting policy. Hood analyzes a range of government tools in significantly more detail (1986) with the ultimate aim of making sense of government complexity, generating ideas for policy design and enabling comparisons across governments (115). Recent literature on policy tools documents trends away from direct provision of government services and toward measures that embed government officials in complex collaborative relationships with other levels of government, private-sector actors, and non-government organizations. These arrangements grant government parties much greater discretion than the close supervision and regulation of the past (Salamon 2002). These indirect measures include contracting, grants, vouchers, tax expenditures, loan guarantees, government-sponsored enterprises and regulations, among others; many do not appear on government budgets, which Salamon suggests helps to explain their popularity (ibid., 5).

Like some of the work on policy design, research on policy tools highlights the political consequences of particular tools, as well as their underlying assumptions about problems, people, and behavior. Salamon characterizes the choice of tools as political as well as operational: "What is at stake in these battles is not simply the most efficient way to solve a particular public problem, but also the relative influence that various affected interests will have in shaping the program's postenactment evolution" (11). Additionally, tools require distinctive sets of management skills and knowledge, thus the choice of tools ultimately influences the nature of public management. Literature on tools offers various dimensions according to which tools may be compared, such as directness, visibility, automaticity, and coerciveness, matching these with likely impacts (such as equity, efficiency, political support, manageability) (ibid.). Tools also carry with them particular assumptions about cause and about behavioral motivations. For example, inducements that offer payoffs to encourage behavior assume "that individuals respond to positive incentives and that most will choose higher-valued alternatives" (Schneider and Ingram 1990, 515). Capacity tools that provide information or training assume that barriers to desired behavior consist of lack of resources rather than incentives (ibid., 517).

POLICY DESIGN BEYOND THE STAGES MODEL

The most recent advance in the study of policy formulation and policy tools is Schneider and Ingram's policy design framework (1997). In their book, *Policy Design for Democracy,* the authors present a framework that pushes past a simple stages model by conceptualizing an iterative process. It brings the discrete stages of the policy process into a single model, and emphasizes the connections between problem definition, agenda setting, and policy design on the one hand, policy design, implementation and impact on society on the other. It offers some predictions about the types of policy designs that will emerge from different types of political processes, and it explicitly incorporates normative analysis by considering the impact of policy designs on target groups and on democratic practice.

Schneider and Ingram's framework answers calls for integrative approaches to policy research. Lasswell and other policy scientists consistently emphasized the importance of integrative approaches to policy scholarship, and political scientists also have begun to acknowledge the limitations of analysis that focuses exclusively on interests, ideas, or institutions. The policy design perspective offers a framework to guide empirical research that integrates these three dimensions: Ideas and interests interact within an institutional setting to produce a policy design. This policy design then becomes an institution in its own right, structuring the future interaction of ideas and interests. While complex, this model can be used to guide empirical analysis; and studies can test and refine Schneider and Ingram's predictions about policy designs and their impact.

With their framework, Schneider and Ingram also incorporate critical approaches to policy studies that explore how government and policy create and maintain "systems of privilege, domination, and quiescence among those who are the most oppressed" (1997, 53). They theorize that policy designs reflect efforts to advance certain values and interests, that they reflect dominant social constructions of knowledge and groups of people, and existing power relations. Moreover, policy designs influence not merely policy implementation, but also political mobilization and the nature of democracy. Schneider and Ingram elevate the status and importance of public policies beyond bundles of technical instruments that may or may not solve contemporary problems; they call public policies "the principal tools in securing the democratic promise for all people" (Ingram and Schneider 2005, 2). Viewing policies in this way calls for analysis that considers how effectively policies mitigate social problems, but also the degree to which they advance democratic citizenship—that is, inspire political participation and remedy social division.

Schneider and Ingram are particularly concerned about the impacts of policy designs that result from "degenerative" political processes (see also Schneider and Ingram, this volume). During such processes, political actors sort target populations into "deserving" and "undeserving" groups as justification for channeling benefits or punishments to them. While political gain can be achieved this way, they argue that policies formulated based upon such arguments undermine democracy and hinder problem solving. The language and the resource allocation tend to stigmatize disadvantaged groups, reinforce stereotypes, and send the message—to group members and to the broader pub-lic—that government does not value them.

POLICY DESIGNS

Central to the policy design perspective is the notion that every public policy contains a design—a framework of ideas and instruments—to be identified and analyzed. Rather than a "random and chaotic product of a political process," policies have underlying patterns and logics (Schneider and Ingram 1997, chap. 3). This framework posits policy designs as institutional structures consisting of identifiable elements: goals, target groups, agents, an implementation structure, tools, rules, ra-tionales, and assumptions. Policy designs thus include tools, but this approach also pushes scholars to look for the explicit or implicit goals and assumptions that constitute part of the package.

POLICY FORMULATION: CONTEXT AND AGENCY

To understand and explain why a policy has a particular design, one must examine the process leading to its selection. Schneider and Ingram's framework draws on institutional and ideational theories, the stages model, and theories of decision making, such as bounded rationality. Policy making is seen to occur in a specific context, marked by distinctive institutions and ideas. Institutional arenas, whether Congress, the courts, the executive branch, and the like, have rules, norms, and procedures that af-fect actors' choices and strategies. Additionally, policy making takes place at a particular moment in time, marked by particular dominant ideas related to the policy issue, to affected groups, to the proper role of government, etc. These ideas will influence actors' arguments in favor of particular solutions, and their perceptions and preferences when they take specific policy decisions.

Analysis of a particular context might lead to broad predictions about the policy design that will emerge from it. But because designs have so many "working parts" (goals, problem definitions, target groups, tools, agents, and such), such analysis cannot specify in advance the particular pack-age of dimensions that actors will build at a particular point in time. Prediction also is complicated by the human dimension of policy making. Actors might reimagine a constraining context, reframe the structure of opportunities before them, as they attempt to create policy solutions to pressing problems. In considering agency—leadership, creativity, debate, and coalition-building—Schneider and Ingram essentially turn to the insights of agenda-setting and problem-definition literature, which characterize policy making as interested actors struggling over ideas (Edelman 1988; Fischer and Forester 1993; Rochefort and Cobb 1994; Stone 1989). Adding attention to the problem definitions that these actors hold offers a richer understanding of what political support and "interest" mean in a given policy process. Beyond examining who participates, we can consider whether actors succeed in expanding or restricting such participation, and how this mobilization affects the policy choice (Cobb and Elder 1972; Schattschneider 1960).

CONSEQUENCES OF PUBLIC POLICY

Here, Schneider and Ingram take up the original impetus for policy design research—to better un-derstand implementation. They suggest that policy designs act as institutional engines of change, and analysis can trace how their dimensions influence political action. Policy implementation distributes benefits to some groups, while imposing burdens on others. In doing so, designs estab-lish incentives for some groups to participate in public life, and offer them resources for doing so. Other groups receive negative messages from policies. For example, if benefits are distributed in a stigmatizing way, individuals may be intimidated by government, withdraw from public life, or feel alienated from it (Soss 1999).

Schneider and Ingram's framework builds on arguments about policy feedback. These suggest a number of ways through which policies shape the course of future politics. Groups receiving benefits from government programs are likely to organize to maintain and expand them. Mobilization is facilitated when policies provide resources to interest groups such as funding, access to decision makers, and information (Pierson 1994, 39–46). Consequently, target groups whose understanding of the problem differs or who lack the expertise needed to use a policy's administrative procedures, will not receive the same degree of support or legitimacy from the policy; they will have greater barriers to overcome in order to achieve their goals. The selection of a particular policy design also imposes lock-in effects. Once a choice is taken, the cost of adopting alternative solutions to the problem increase. The significance of the policy formulation process is that much greater because the barriers to change—such as investments in its programs and commitments to its ideas—cumulate over time.

Empirical applications of the policy design framework are beginning to accumulate, and to extend and refine the perspective itself (e.g., Schneider and Ingram 2005). Sidney tracks the development, designs, and impact of two policies intended to fight housing discrimination (2003). She shows how the social construction of target groups, and the causal stories that legislators told as they advocated for and revised policy alternatives, became embedded into the resulting policy choices, constraining the impact on the problem, and importantly shaping the trajectories of implementing agents. Her work situates the policy design perspective within the context of federalism and posits nonprofit organizations as important mediating agents between policy design and target group members.

Soss traces the impact of several means-tested welfare policy designs on recipients' attitudes toward government and disposition toward participation. Comparing Aid to Families with Dependent Children (AFDC) with Social Security disability insurance (SSDI), he shows that programs designs have significant consequences for client perceptions, with AFDC clients likely to develop negative views of government and to avoid speaking up, while SSDI recipients think of government as helpful and interested in their views (2005). In the process, he raises questions about the causal claims that are possible in this framework, since individuals simultaneously belong to many target groups, thus receiving cues from multiple policy designs at once.

CRITIQUE AND NEW DIRECTIONS

Critiques of literature on policy formulation and policy tools may focus on the limitations of the stages model itself. That is, the specification of policy alternatives and the selection of policy tools does not follow neatly from the agenda setting process nor lead neatly into implementation. Rather, selection of alternatives might occur prior to or during the agenda setting process, and implementation often involves reformulation of policy design as well. Thus to the extent that studies offer recommendations for generating alternatives as if problem framing has already occurred, and as if the resulting design will simply be passed on to the implementers, they are flawed at their root. On the other hand, if researchers conceive of policy formulation as a function rather than as a stage that begins and ends in a certain sequence of stages, they are likely to search the empirical record of particular policy arenas more broadly. With their integrative framework that places policy designs at its center, Schneider and Ingram depart from the stages model and, with a growing community of scholars, offer a theory of public policy that directly addresses the question of who gets what, when, and how from government (Schneider and Ingram 2005). Critics charge that it lacks a clear mechanism of policy change that can be tested across cases (deLeon 2005).

The judiciary is the governmental sphere most absent from scholarship on public policy analysis.

Although many researchers study the court's role in public policy making and implementation, this body of work is largely disconnected from theoretical work on the policy process generally, and policy formulation in particular. In part, the traditional understanding of courts as interpreting rather than making law may serve as a barrier, although this conventional wisdom is increasingly challenged (e.g., Miller and Barnes 2004). Many scholars argue that the work of the courts by nature constitutes policy making (e.g., Van Horn, Baumer, and Gormley Jr., chap. 7). Certainly courts represent a distinctive institutional setting, whose actors, procedures, language, and processes of reasoning differ from those that prevail in legislatures and bureaucracies. Yet we can conceptualize court cases as processes of policy formulation, with plaintiffs, defendants, and amici as participants proposing alternatives, and judges as the decision makers. Courts thus offer a potentially fruitful comparative case for studies of the impact of institutions on policy formulation. In the U.S. context at least, many policy issues eventually reach the court system.

Attention to the nonprofit sector's role in policy formulation and tools has steadily increased. Recent work on policy instruments emphasizes that "non-profitization" constitutes a policy tool—and one that is more commonly used across policy arenas, from education (e.g., charter schools) to welfare to housing among others. But non-government organizations (NGOs) also are policy makers in their own right. Research about the kinds of policy designs that NGOs formulate is beginning to emerge, building on a longstanding research tradition about the third sector (e.g., Boris 1999; Smith and Lipsky 1993). Although most extant studies of policy formulation presume a legislative or executive-branch site of activity, recent work examines NGOs as policy designers.

Neighborhood organizations, for example, have quite different motivations and incentives when designing policy than do legislators, so theories of policy design that presume a legislative context may not be helpful in understanding policy making at this small, and extra-governmental, scale (Camou 2005). In Baltimore's poor neighborhoods, organizations targeted their policies to the most needy, framing individuals as redeemable, in contrast to Schneider and Ingram's expectations that policy makers eschew directing benefits to the most marginalized groups. In cities across the country, community-based organizations have designed numerous innovative policies and successfully implemented them (Swarts 2003). More attention to policy formulation outside the bureaucracy, and below the national level can broaden our theories and substantive knowledge of this important function. Such work would build on research about national policy that increasingly finds policy formulation to occur outside of government offices—that is, in think tanks and within the loose networks of advocacy and interest groups that together with government officials make up policy communities (see Miller and Demir, and Stone, this volume).

Research on policy formulation and policy tools draws on, overlaps with, and contributes to research on agenda setting, problem definition, implementation, and policy coalitions, among others. Its singularity emerges in its focus on the micro-level of public policies—that is the specific policy alternatives that are considered, how they differ in terms of policy tools, and how what may seem on the surface, or at a macro-level, to be small differences actually have significant consequences for problem-solving, and for the allocation and exercise of power. Attention to policy design essentially reminds us that democracy is in the details.

REFERENCES

Alexander, Ernest R. 1982. "Design in the Decision-Making Process." *Policy Sciences* 14:279–292.

Bardach, Eugene. 2005. *A Practical Guide for Policy Analysis: The Eightfold Path to More Effective Problem Solving*. Washington, D.C.: CQ Press.

Bobrow, Davis B. and John S. Dryzek. 1987. *Policy Analysis by Design*. Pittsburgh: University of Pittsburgh Press.

Camou, Michelle. 2005. "Deservedness in Poor Neighborhoods: A Morality Struggle." Pp. 197–218 in *De-*

serving and Entitled: Social Constructions and Public Policy, edited by A. L. Schneider and H. M. Ingram. Albany: SUNY Press.

Cobb, R. and C. D. Elder. 1972. *Participation in American Politics: The Dynamics of Agenda Building*. Baltimore: Johns Hopkins University Press.

Cochran, Charles L. and Eloise F. Malone. 1999. *Public Policy: Perspectives and Choices*. Boston: McGraw-Hill.

Dahl, Robert A. and Charles E. Lindblom. 1953. *Politics, Economics, and Welfare*. New York: Harper.

Dye, Thomas R. 2002. *Understanding Public Policy*. Upper Saddle River: Prentice Hall.

Fischer, Frank. 2000. *Citizens, Experts, and the Environment: The Politics of Local Knowledge*. Durham and London: Duke University Press.

Fischer, Frank and John Forester. 1993. "The Argumentative Turn in Policy Analysis and Planning." Durham: Duke University Press.

Hood, Christopher C. 1986. *The Tools of Government*. Chatham, NJ: Chatham House Publishers Inc.

Howlett, Michael and M. Ramesh. 1995. *Studying Public Policy: Policy Cycles and Policy Subsystems*. New York: Oxford University Press.

Immergut, Ellen M. 1998. "The Theoretical Core of the New Institutionalism." *Politics and Society* 26:5–34.

Ingraham, Patricia. 1987. "Toward a More Systematic Consideration of Policy Design." *Policy Studies Journal* 15:611–628.

Ingram, Helen M. and Anne L. Schneider. 2005. "Introduction: Public Policy and the Social Construction of Deservedness." Pp. 1–28 in *Deserving and Entitled: Social Constructions and Public Policy*, edited by A. L. Schneider and H. M. Ingram. Albany: SUNY Press.

Kingdon, John W. 1995. *Agendas, Alternatives, and Public Policies*. New York: HarperCollins College Publishers.

Linder, Stephen H. and B. Guy Peters. 1985. "From Social Theory to Policy Design." *Journal of Public Policy* 4:237–259.

May, Peter. 1991. "Reconsidering Policy Design: Policies and Publics." *Journal of Public Policy* 11:187–206.

Pierson, Paul. 1994. *Dismantling the Welfare State? Reagan, Thatcher, and the Politics of Retrenchment*. Cambridge: Harvard University Press.

Rixecker, Stefanie S. 1994. "Expanding the Discursive Context of Policy Design: A Matter of Feminist Standpoint Epistemology." *Policy Sciences* 27:119–142.

Rochefort, D. and R.W. Cobb. 1994. "Problem Definition: An Emerging Perspective." in *The Politics of Problem Definition*, edited by D. Rochefort and R. W. Cobb. Lawrence: Kansas University Press.

Schattschneider, E.E. 1960. *The Semi-Sovereign People*. New York: Rinehart and Wilson.

Schneider, Anne and Helen Ingram. 1990. "Behavioral Assumptions of Policy Tools." *Journal of Politics* 52:510–522.

Schneider, Anne Larason and Helen Ingram. 1997. *Policy Design for Democracy*. Lawrence: University of Kansas Press.

Sidney, Mara S. 2003. *Unfair Housing: How National Policy Shapes Local Action*. Lawrence: University Press of Kansas.

Simon, Herbert A. 1985. "Human Nature in Politics: The Dialogue of Psychology with Political Science." *American Political Science Review*: 293–304.

Soss, Joe. 1999. "Lessons of Welfare: Policy Design, Political Learning, and Political Action." *American Political Science Review* 93:363–380.

———. 2005. "Making Clients and Citizens: Welfare Policy as a Source of Status, Belief, and Action." Pp. 291–328 in *Deserving and Entitled: Social Constructions and Public Policy*, edited by A. L. Schneider and H. M. Ingram. Albany: SUNY Press.

Stone, Deborah. 2001. *Policy Paradox: The Art of Political Decision Making*. New York: W.W. Norton.

Swarts, Heidi J. 2003. "Setting the State's Agenda: Church-based Community Organizations in American Urban Politics." Pp. 78–106 in *States, Parties, and Social Movements*, edited by J. A. Goldstone: Cambridge University Press.

Weimer, David L. 1992. "The Craft of Policy Design: Can it be More than Art?" *Policy Studies Review*: 370–388.

Yanow, D. 1995. "Editorial: Practices of Policy Interpretation." *Policy Sciences* 28:111–126.

7 Implementing Public Policy

Helga Pülzl and Oliver Treib

1 INTRODUCTION

Implementation studies are to be found at the intersection of public administration, organizational theory, public management research, and political science studies (Schofield and Sausman 2004, 235). In the broadest sense, they can be characterized as studies of policy change (Jenkins 1978, 203).

Goggin and his colleagues (1990) identified three generations of implementation research. Implementation studies emerged in the 1970s within the United States, as a reaction to growing concerns over the effectiveness of wide-ranging reform programs. Until the end of the 1960s, it had been taken for granted that political mandates were clear, and administrators were thought to implement policies according to the intentions of decision makers (Hill and Hupe 2002, 42). The process of "translating policy into action" (Barrett 2004, 251) attracted more attention, as policies seemed to lag behind policy expectations. The first generation of implementation studies, which dominated much of the 1970s, was characterized by a pessimistic undertone. This pessimism was fuelled by a number of case studies that represented shining examples of implementation failure. The studies of Derthick (1972), Pressman and Wildavsky (1973), and Bardach (1977) are the most popular. Pressman and Wildavsky's work (1973) had a decisive impact on the development of implementation research, as it helped to stimulate a growing body of literature. This does not mean, however, that no implementation studies were carried out before, as Hargrove (1975) suggested when writing about the discovery of a "missing link" in studying the policy process. Hill and Hupe (2002, 18–28) point out that implementation research was conducted under different headings before the 1970s. Nevertheless, the most noteworthy achievement of the first generation of implementation researchers was to raise awareness of the issue in the wider scholarly community and in the general public.

While theory building was not at the heart of the first generation of implementation studies, the second generation began to put forward a whole range of theoretical frameworks and hypotheses. This period was marked by debates between what was later dubbed the top-down and bottom-up approaches to implementation research. The top-down school, represented for example by scholars like Van Meter and Van Horn (1975), Nakamura and Smallwood (1980) or Mazmanian and Sabatier (1983), conceived of implementation as the hierarchical execution of centrally-defined policy intentions. Scholars belonging to the bottom-up camp, such as Lipsky (1971, 1980), Ingram (1977), Elmore (1980), or Hjern and Hull (1982) instead emphasized that implementation consisted of the everyday problem-solving strategies of "street-level bureaucrats" (Lipsky 1980).

The third generation of implementation research tried to bridge the gap between top-down and bottom-up approaches by incorporating the insights of both camps into their theoretical models. At the same time, the self-proclaimed goal of third-generation research was "to be more *scientific* than the previous two in its approach to the study of implementation" (Goggin et al. 1990, 18, emphasis in original). Third-generation scholars thus lay much emphasis on specifying clear hypotheses, finding proper operationalizations and producing adequate empirical observations to test these hypotheses. However, as observers like deLeon (1999, 318) and O'Toole (2000, 268) note, only a few studies have so far followed this path.

While the largest part of implementation research stemmed from the United States, the second generation was also especially marked by important theoretical contributions from European authors like Barrett, Hanf, Windhoff-Héritier, Hjern, Mayntz, or Scharpf. Europe was also the origin of a new strand of literature that focused on the issue of implementation in the context of European integration studies.

It is the aim of this chapter to summarize the theoretical lessons to be drawn from the wealth of literature produced by more than thirty years of implementation research. The chapter is structured as follows: Section 2 discusses three different analytical approaches in traditional implementation theory in more detail: top-down models, bottom-up critiques, and hybrid theories that try to combine elements of the two other strands of literature. We explicate the theoretical underpinnings and discuss the pros and cons of the respective approaches. Section 3 then provides an overview of more recent theoretical approaches to implementation, all of which depart from central underpinnings of traditional implementation studies. In particular, we address insights gained from the study of implementation processes in the context of the European Union and we discuss the interpretative approach to implementation, which follows an alternative ontological path. Section 4 focuses on the main insights gained from more than thirty years of implementation research for a proper understanding of implementation processes. Moreover, it discusses the contributions of implementation analysis to the wider field of policy analysis and political science. Finally, Section 5 identifies a number of persistent weaknesses of implementation analysis and concludes by suggesting possible directions of future research to overcome these weaknesses in the years to come.

2 TOP-DOWN, BOTTOM-UP, AND HYBRID THEORIES OF IMPLEMENTATION

The three generations of implementation research presented earlier can be subdivided into three distinct theoretical approaches to the study of implementation:

1. Top-down models put their main emphasis on the ability of decision makers' to produce unequivocal policy objectives and on controlling the implementation stage.
2. Bottom-up critiques view local bureaucrats as the main actors in policy delivery and conceive of implementation as negotiation processes within networks of implementers.
3. Hybrid theories try to overcome the divide between the other two approaches by incorporating elements of top-down, bottom-up and other theoretical models.

The following discussion will briefly outline the theoretical underpinnings of these approaches. It is only possible to present some of the key contributions within the confines of this chapter (see Figure 7.1).

The selection of presented contributions is based on the suggestions of leading scholars (Hill and Hupe 2002; deLeon 1999, 2001; Parsons 1995; Sabatier 1986a) as well as on our own views on the relative importance of the studies discussed.

2.1 TOP-DOWN THEORIES

Top-down theories started from the assumption that policy implementation starts with a decision made by central government. Parsons (1995, 463) points out that these studies were based on a

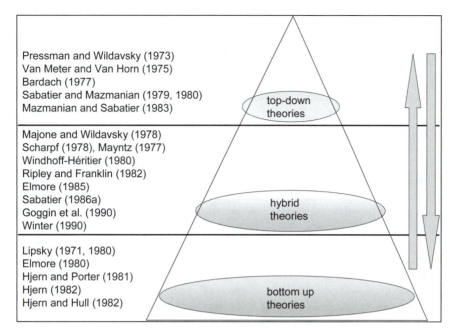

Pressman and Wildavsky (1973)
Van Meter and Van Horn (1975)
Bardach (1977)
Sabatier and Mazmanian (1979, 1980)
Mazmanian and Sabatier (1983)

top-down
theories

Majone and Wildavsky (1978)
Scharpf (1978), Mayntz (1977)
Windhoff-Héritier (1980)
Ripley and Franklin (1982)
Elmore (1985)
Sabatier (1986a)
Goggin et al. (1990)
Winter (1990)

hybrid
theories

Lipsky (1971, 1980)
Elmore (1980)
Hjern and Porter (1981)
Hjern (1982)
Hjern and Hull (1982)

bottom up
theories

FIGURE 7.1   Top-down, bottom-up, and hybrid theories: key contributions.

"blackbox model" of the policy process inspired by systems analysis. They assumed a direct causal link between policies and observed outcomes and tended to disregard the impact of implementers on policy delivery. Top downers essentially followed a prescriptive approach that interpreted policy as input and implementation as output factors. Due to their emphasis on decisions of central policy makers, deLeon (2001, 2) describes top-down approaches as a "governing elite phenomenon". The following authors are classical top-down scholars: Pressman and Wildavsky (1973), Van Meter and Van Horn (1975), Bardach (1977), as well as Sabatier and Mazmanian (1979, 1980, see also Mazmanian and Sabatier 1983).

Pressman and Wildavsky's original work followed a rational model approach. They started from the assumption that policy objectives are set out by central policy makers. In this view, implementation research was left with the task of analyzing the difficulties in achieving these objectives. Hence, they saw implementation as an "interaction between the setting of goals and actions geared to achieve them" (Pressman and Wildavsky 1973, xv). The authors underlined the linear relationship between agreed policy goals and their implementation. Implementation therefore implied the establishment of adequate bureaucratic procedures to ensure that policies are executed as accurately as possible. To this end, implementing agencies should have sufficient resources at their disposal, and there needs to be a system of clear responsibilities and hierarchical control to supervise the actions of implementers. Pressman and Wildavsky's book, a study of the implementation of a federal program of economic development in Oakland, California, highlighted the importance of the number of agencies involved in policy delivery. They argued that effective implementation becomes increasingly difficult, if a program has to pass through a multitude of "clearance points." As most implementation settings, especially in the United States, are of a multi-actor type, the thrust of their analysis was rather skeptical as to whether implementation could work at all.

American scholars Van Meter and Van Horn (1975) offered a more elaborate theoretical model. Their starting point, however, was very similar to the one of Pressman and Wildavsky. They were concerned with the study of whether implementation outcomes corresponded to the objectives set out in initial policy decisions. Their model included six variables that shape the relationship between policy and performance. While many of these factors had to do with organizational capacities and hierarchical control, the authors also highlighted two variables that slightly departed from the top-down "mainstream": They argued that the extent of policy change had a crucial impact on the likelihood of effective implementation and that the degree of consensus on goals was important. Hence, significant policy change was only possible if goal consensus among actors was high. Unlike other representatives of the top-down school, the model of Van Meter and Van Horn was less concerned with advising policy makers on successful implementation but with providing a sound basis for scholarly analysis.

Bardach's book *The Implementation Game*, published in 1977, provided a classical metaphor for the implementation process. He acknowledged the political character of the implementation process and therefore promoted the idea of using game theoretic tools for explaining implementation. Bardach thus provided ideas that also influenced bottom-up scholars (see below). However, his preoccupation with advising policy makers on how to improve implementation makes him a clear member of the top-down camp. His core recommendation was to give attention to the "scenario writing" process, which meant that successful implementation was possible if policy makers succeeded in structuring the implementation games thoughtfully.

Sabatier and Mazmanian (1979, 1980, see also Mazmanian and Sabatier 1983) are among the core authors of the top-down approach. Like Van Meter and Van Horn (1975), Sabatier and Mazmanian started their analysis with a policy decision that was made by governmental representatives. Therefore, they assumed a clear separation of policy formation from policy implementation. Their model lists six criteria for effective implementation: (1) policy objectives are clear and consistent, (2) the program is based on a valid causal theory, (3) the implementation process is structured adequately, (4) implementing officials are committed to the program's goals, (5) interest groups and (executive and legislative) sovereigns are supportive, and (6) there are no detrimental changes in the socioeconomic framework conditions. Although Sabatier and Mazmanian (1979, 489–92, 503–4) acknowledged that perfect hierarchical control over the implementation process was hard to achieve in practice and that unfavorable conditions could cause implementation failure, they argued that policy makers could ensure effective implementation through adequate program design and a clever structuration of the implementation process.

2.2 BOTTOM-UP THEORIES

In the late 1970s and early 1980s, bottom-up theories emerged as a critical response to the top-down school. Several studies showed that political outcomes did not always sufficiently relate to original policy objectives and that the assumed causal link was thus questionable. Theorists suggested studying what was actually happening on the recipient level and analyzing the real causes that influence action on the ground. Studies belonging to this strand of research typically started from the "bottom" by identifying the networks of actors involved in actual policy delivery. They rejected the idea that policies are defined at the central level and that implementers need to stick to these objectives as neatly as possible. Instead, the availability of discretion at the stage of policy delivery appeared as a beneficial factor as local bureaucrats were seen to be much nearer to the real problems than central policy makers. The classical bottom-up researchers are: the American researchers Lipsky (1971, 1980) and Elmore (1980) as well as the Swedish scholar Hjern (1982), also in collaboration with other authors such as Porter and Hull.

Lipsky (1971, 1980) analyzed the behavior of public service workers (e.g., teachers, social workers, police officers, doctors), which he called "street-level bureaucrats." In his seminal article, published in 1971, Lipsky argued that policy analysts needed to consider the direct interactions between social workers and citizens. Hudson (1989) argues that the power held by street-level bureaucrats' stretches beyond the control of citizens' behavior. Street-level bureaucrats are also considered to have considerable autonomy from their employing organizations. The main source of their autonomous power thus stems from the considerable amount of discretion at their disposal.

According to Hill and Hupe (2002, 52–53), Lipsky's work has been widely misinterpreted as he did not only underline the difficulties in controlling street-level bureaucrats' behavior. Still more important, Lipsky showed that street-level policy making created practices that enable public workers to cope with problems encountered in their everyday work. The importance of Lipsky's work lies in the fact that his approach was, on the one hand, used as justification for methodological strategies that focus on street-level actors. On the other hand, it showed that top-down approaches failed to take into account that a hierarchical chain of command and well-defined policy objectives are not enough to guarantee successful implementation.

The main concern of Elmore (1980) was the question of how to study implementation. Instead of assuming that policy makers effectively control implementation, his concept of "backward mapping" suggested that analysis should start with a specific policy problem and then examine the actions of local agencies to solve this problem.

The Swedish scholar Hjern, in close cooperation with colleagues like Porter and Hull, developed an empirical network methodology to the study of the implementation process (Hjern 1982; Hjern and Porter 1981; Hjern and Hull 1982). In their view, it was essential for researchers to acknowledge the multi-actor and inter-organizational character of policy delivery. Therefore, they suggested that implementation analysis should start with the identification of networks of actors from all relevant agencies collaborating in implementation and then examine the way they try to solve their problems. According to Sabatier (1986a), this approach offers a useful tool to describe the "implementation structures" (Hjern and Porter 1981) within which policy execution takes place. However, he also criticizes the lack of causal hypotheses on the relationship between legal and economic factors and individual behavior.

2.3 COMPARATIVE DISCUSSION

There are several characteristics of top-down and bottom-up theories that account for the wide gulf that separates these two schools of thought in implementation theory: They are marked by competing research strategies, contrasting goals of analysis, opposing models of the policy process, inconsistent understandings of the implementation process, and conflicting models of democracy (see Table 7.1).

It was due to their contrasting research strategies that the two camps came to be known as "top-down" and "bottom-up" approaches. Top-downers typically start from a policy decision reached at the "top" of the political system and work their way "down" to the implementers. Bottom-uppers, in contrast, start out with the identification of actors involved in concrete policy delivery at the "bottom" of the politico-administrative system. Analysis then moves "upwards" and "sideways" in order to identify the networks of implementing actors and their problem-solving strategies.

The goal of analysis of top-down scholars is to reach a general theory of implementation. This theory should be parsimonious enough to allow for predictions as to whether an individual piece of legislation is likely to be implemented effectively.[1] Moreover, the theory should enable scholars to derive recommendations for policy makers with a view to improving implementation. The aim

---

1. It has to be noted, however, that the models proposed by top-down scholars do not always meet the standard of theoretical parsimony. For example, the model proposed by Sabatier and Mazmanian (1981, 7) lists no less than seventeen independent variables.

TABLE 7.1
Top-down and Bottom-up Theories Compared

	Top-down theories	Bottom-up theories
Research strategy	Top-down: from political decisions to administrative execution	Bottom-up: from individual bureaucrats to administrative networks
Goal of analysis	Prediction/policy recommendation	Description/explanation
Model of policy process	Stagist	Fusionist
Character of implementation process	Hierarchical guidance	Decentralized problem-solving
Underlying model of democracy	Elitist	Participatory

of bottom-up studies, in contrast, is rather to give an accurate empirical description and explanation of the interactions and problem-solving strategies of actors involved in policy delivery. As Sabatier (1986b, 315) critically notes, many of the bottom-up studies do not go beyond providing descriptive accounts of the large amount of discretion available to implementers. However, some of them actually tried to transcend the sphere of description. This resulted in rather complex heuristic models of the network structures or "implementation structures" (Hjern and Porter 1981) within which implementation takes place.

Both schools of thought rest upon contrasting models of the policy process. Top-downers are heavily influenced by what has been called the "textbook conception of the policy process" (Nakamura 1987, 142). This "stagist" model assumes that the policy cycle may be divided into several clearly distinguishable phases. Top-down analyses thus do not focus on the whole policy process, but merely on "what happens after a bill becomes a law" (Bardach 1977). In contrast, bottom-up approaches argue that policy implementation cannot be separated from policy formulation. According to this "fusionist" model, policy making continues throughout the whole policy process. Hence, bottom-up scholars do not just pay attention to one particular stage of the policy cycle. Instead, they are interested in the whole process of how policies are defined, shaped, implemented and probably redefined.

Both approaches contain widely differing views on the character of the implementation process. Top-downers understand implementation as "the carrying out of a basic policy decision" (Mazmanian and Sabatier 1983, 20). In this view, implementation is an apolitical, administrative process. Power ultimately rests with central decision-makers, who define clear policy objectives and are capable of hierarchically guiding the process of putting these objectives into practice. Bottom-up scholars reject the idea of hierarchical guidance. In their view, it is impossible to formulate statutes with unequivocal policy goals and to control the implementation process from top to bottom. Instead, the model suggests that implementers always have a large amount of discretion. Rather than considering implementation an apolitical process of following orders "from above," bottom-uppers hold that the implementation process is eminently political and that policies are even shaped to a decisive extent at this level. Hence, policies are not so much determined by the statutes emanating from governments and parliaments but by the largely autonomous political decisions of the actors directly involved in policy delivery. The focus thus lies on the decentral-problem-solving of local actors rather than on hierarchical guidance.

Finally, the two approaches are based on fundamentally different models of democracy. Top-down approaches are rooted in traditional, elitist conceptions of representative democracy. In this view, elected representatives are the only actors within a society who are legitimized to take collectively binding decisions on behalf of the whole citizenry. It is thus a matter of proper democratic governance to ensure that these decisions are carried out as accurately as possible. In other words, any deviation from the centrally defined policy objectives is seen as a violation of democratic standards. Bottom-up approaches contest this model of democracy. They stress that local bureaucrats, affected target groups and private actors have legitimate concerns to be taken into account as well. In their view, the elitist model disregards these concerns and thus leads to illegitimate decisions. Deviating from the centrally defined policy objectives thus does not contravene democratic principles. Seen from this angle, legitimate democratic governance is only possible in a participatory model of democracy which includes those who are affected by a particular decision (lower-level administrative actors, interest groups, private actors etc.) in policy formation.

The comparison between both approaches shows that the debate between top-down and bottom-up scholars focused on more than the proper empirical description of the driving forces behind implementation. It is true that this is one important dimension of the dispute. But if this aspect had been the only bone of contention, the debate indeed would have been as sterile as some observers seem to have perceived it (O'Toole 2000, 267). It is certainly true that both sides exaggerated their respective positions and thereby oversimplified the complex implementation process (Parsons 1995, 471). As Sabatier (1986a) rightly notes, top-downers overemphasized the ability of central policy makers to issue unequivocal policy objectives and to meticulously control the process of implementation. In criticizing this "law-makers' perspective," bottom-uppers at the same time overestimated the amount of discretion of local bureaucrats and thus overemphasized the autonomy of the "bottom" vis-à-vis the "top." As scholars gathered more and more empirical evidence that demonstrated the relevance of both approaches, it would have been easy to agree on mutually acceptable theoretical models of implementation that pay attention to both central steering and local autonomy (see e.g., O'Toole 2000, 268). This is the path followed by some of the "hybrid theories" discussed in the next section.

2.4 HYBRID THEORIES

As a reaction to growing uneasiness with the heated debate between top-downers and bottom-uppers, researchers such as Elmore (1985), Sabatier (1986a), and Goggin et al. (1990) tried to synthesize both approaches. The new models presented by these scholars combined elements of both sides in order to avoid the conceptual weaknesses of top-down and bottom-up approaches. Other key contributions were made by scholars like Scharpf (1978), Windhoff-Héritier (1980), Ripley and Franklin (1982), and Winter (1990). Taking the top-downers' concern with effective policy execution as their starting point, they blended several elements of the bottom-up perspective and of other theories into their models. This is why we discuss this group of scholars under the heading of "hybrid theories."

Elmore, previously discussed as a member of the bottom-up camp, combined in his later work (1985) the concept of "backward mapping" with the idea of "forward mapping." He argued that program success is contingent upon both elements, as they are intertwined (Sabatier 1986a). Policy makers should therefore start with the consideration of policy instruments and available resources for policy change (forward mapping). In addition, they should identify the incentive structure of implementers and target groups (backward mapping).

Backing away from his earlier theoretical contributions together with Mazmanian, Sabatier (1986a) gave an account of a different theoretical approach to policy implementation. In his seminal article on implementation research, he argued that not distinguishing between policy formation and implementation would disqualify the study of policy change and evaluation research. He put forward an "advocacy coalition framework" which he developed further in his later work together with Jenkins-Smith (1993). The advocacy coalition framework rejected the "stage heuristic" of the policy process and aimed at empirically explaining policy change as a whole. This conception has some resemblance with the bottom-up approach as the analysis starts from a policy problem and proceeds in reconstructing the strategies of relevant actors to solve this problem. In addition, it emphasizes the role of policy learning and recognizes the importance of extraneous social and economic conditions that may impact on the policy making. However, the advocacy coalition approach seems to neglect the social and historical context in which change occurs. This problem is addressed by discourse analysts, who argue that discourses shape actors' perceptions and may thus influence political elites' interpretation of social events (for further discussion, see Fischer 2003, 99).

Wildavsky, another prominent representative of the top-down school, also turned his back on the linear approach that had marked his earlier contributions. Together with Majone (Majone and Wildavsky 1978), he presented a model that pointed in a similar direction as the advocacy coalition framework. The core argument was that implementation is an evolutionary process in which programs are constantly reshaped and redefined. The conception thus started from policy inputs defined by central policy makers. At the same time, it also embraced the idea that these inputs will almost inevitably be changed in the course of their execution. Thus incremental learning processes were at the heart of this approach.

Winter (1990) contributed to overcoming the separation of policy formation and implementation. Still embracing the "stagist" model of the policy process, he points to the effect of the policy formulation process on implementation. Unlike top-downers, however, he is not interested in the design of the policy itself but looks at how characteristics of the policy formulation process (like the level of conflict or the level of attention of proponents) impacts on implementation.

Goggin, Bowman, Lester, and O'Toole (1990), the self-proclaimed founders of the "third generation" of implementation research, tried to bridge the gap between top-down and bottom-up approaches. Like top-downers, they continued to accept the perspective of a centrally defined policy decision to be implemented by lower-level actors. Their goal of developing a general theory of implementation on the basis of rigorous methods also owes much to the top-down perspective. However, their conception of the implementation process embraced the fact that implementers are political actors in their own right and that the outcome of this endeavor entailed complicated negotiation processes between implementers and central authorities. Drawing on empirical case studies that involved the implementation of federal programs by state authorities in the United States, they developed a communicative model of intergovernmental implementation. As Hill and Hupe (2002, 66–68) point out, the specific focus on the interactions between federal and state layers of government in American federalism raises doubts about the general applicability of the model.

Scharpf (1978) was one of the earliest writers who tried to reconcile the idea of political steering by central governments with the argument of bottom-up scholars that the transformation of policy goals into action depends upon the interaction of a multitude of actors with separate interests and strategies. Introducing the concept of policy networks to implementation research, he suggested giving more weight to processes of coordination and collaboration among separate but mutually dependent actors. The concept of policy networks later became a major approach to the study of policy change as a whole (see e.g., Marin and Mayntz 1991).

A further line of argument places emphasis on a factor that was almost completely neglected by both top-down and bottom-up scholars: the type of policy to be implemented. Building on the seminal article by Lowi (1972), Ripley and Franklin (1982) distinguish between distributive, regulatory, and redistributive policies, arguing that each of these policy types involves different groups of stakeholders as well as different types and levels of conflict in implementation. Windhoff-Héritier (1980) makes a similar argument. She distinguishes between distributive and redistributive policies. This distinction includes regulatory policy, which can fall into either of the two categories depending on whether or not a regulatory program involves clearly identifiable winners and losers.[2] Her book reveals that distributive policies may be implemented in any implementation structure,

---

2. Mayntz (1977), another German scholar, followed a similar line of reasoning with regard to policy types. She distinguishes between different types of policy instruments (imperatives and restraints, positive and negative incentives, procedural regulations, public provision of services) and discusses the different implementation problems typically associated with these policy instruments.

while redistributive policies need a hierarchical implementation structure to be executed effectively (Windhoff-Héritier 1980, 90).

In sum, the approaches we summarized under the heading of "hybrid theories" brought two important innovations to implementation theory. First, they tried to overcome the conceptual weaknesses of the polarized debate between bottom-up and top-down scholars. Leaving aside the normative aspects of the controversy, they focused instead on empirical arguments about the proper conceptualization of the implementation processes and pragmatically blended the extreme arguments of both sides into models that embraced both central steering and local autonomy. Second, some of the hybrid theorists pointed to important factors that had hitherto received little attention.

Scholars like Sabatier or Winter raised the awareness that implementation cannot be analyzed without looking at the policy formulation process. Sabatier stressed the need to view implementation processes (or processes of policy change in general) not in isolation. Instead, his advocacy coalition framework recognizes that extraneous factors such as external economic developments or influences from other policy fields have to be taken into account as well. Finally, Ripley and Franklin, Windhoff-Héritier and others hinted at the impact of different policy types on the way policies are executed.

What is overlooked by advocates of a synthesis of top-down and bottom-up approaches are the fundamentally different views of both sides on the proper conceptualization of the policy process and the legitimate allocation of power over the determination of policy outcomes in the light of democratic theory. Hence, while it seems possible to combine some of the insights of both models, Parsons is also right in pointing out that some of the differences are so fundamental that the effort to seek a comprehensive synthesis of both approaches is like trying to combine "incommensurate paradigms" (Parsons 1995, 487, see also deLeon 1999, 322–23).

The theoretical approaches discussed so far, despite differing in important respects from each other, have two things in common: They all study implementation processes within nation states rather than at the international level, and they share a common positivist worldview in terms of ontology and epistemology. In what follows, we will discuss a number of recent contributions that take the study of implementation beyond these traditional paths.

3 NEW DEVELOPMENTS IN IMPLEMENTATION ANALYSIS

While the origins of implementation research lay in the study of policy change within nation states, the growing importance of policy making at the international level has given rise to a substantial body of literature that addresses the implementation of these "international" policies at the domestic level. There has been some interest in the effectiveness of implementing international agreements (Brown-Weiss and Jacobson 1998; Victor et al. 1998). Even more scholars have addressed issues of implementation within the European Union.

3.1 IMPLEMENTATION IN AN INTERNATIONAL CONTEXT: NEWS FROM EUROPEAN INTEGRATION STUDIES

The first wave of studies addressing implementation issues in the context of European integration started out with largely descriptive accounts of implementation failures. To the extent that theoretical conclusions were drawn at all, these primarily mirrored the insights of the top-down school in implementation theory. The domestic implementation of European legislation was portrayed as a rather apolitical process whose success primarily depended on clearly worded provisions, effective administrative organization and streamlined legislative procedures at the national level (Siedentopf and Ziller 1988; Schwarze et al. 1990; Schwarze et al. 1991, 1993). Problems in policy execution were not put down to political resistance by domestic implementation actors, but to "technical" parameters such as insufficient administrative resources, inter-organizational co-ordination problems or cumbersome legislative or administrative procedures at the domestic level.

As far as the general analytical perspective is concerned, most of the research on the implementation of EU legislation continued to be characterized by a top-down view. Implementation processes are usually approached from a perspective that asks for the fulfillment of centrally defined policy goals. Any deviation from the original goals is seen as an implementation problem obstructing the even execution of European-level policies rather than the legitimate problem-solving strategy of "street-level bureaucrats." What changed over time, however, was the increasing awareness among scholars that implementation is a political process and that the execution of policies is obstructed often enough by the political resistance of domestic actors. EU implementation research thus moved into the direction of what we dubbed "hybrid theories."

The political character of implementation processes was embraced by the second wave of implementation studies, which evolved in the 1990s. Most of the studies of this second wave focused on European environmental policy, one of the policy areas where implementation gaps had become particularly visible. The theoretical innovation of this strand of literature was the incorporation of frameworks and arguments from comparative politics. One particularly prominent line of argument was based on historical institutionalist assumptions about the "stickiness" of deeply entrenched national policy traditions and administrative routines, which poses great obstacles to reforms aiming to alter these arrangements. Starting from the observation that many member state governments struggled to "upload" their own policy models to the European level (Héritier et al. 1996), it was only a short way to the argument that the "downloading" process becomes problematic if this strategy of policy export should fail (Börzel 2002).

The degree of "misfit," that is the extent to which a particular supranational policy required member states to depart from their traditional ways of doing things in terms of policy legacies and organizational arrangements, thus moved to the forefront in explaining implementation outcomes. Seen from this angle, European policies face deeply rooted institutional and regulatory structures. If both fit together, implementation should be a smooth and unproblematic process. If European policies do not match existing traditions, however, implementation should be highly contested, leading to considerable delays, and involving a high risk of total failure (see in particular Duina 1997, 1999; Duina and Blithe 1999; Knill and Lenschow 1998, 2000; Börzel 2000, 2003).

It soon became clear that this theoretical argument was too parsimonious to hold in a broader set of empirical cases. Although acknowledging the political character of implementation, the "misfit" argument laid too much emphasis on structural parameters, assuming that domestic actors merely acted "as guardians of the status quo, as the shield protecting national legal-administrative traditions" (Duina 1997, 157). This one-dimensional view was challenged by scholars who argued that the implementation behavior of domestic government parties, interest groups and administrations was independent of the degree of fit or misfit (Haverland 2000; Treib 2004; Falkner et al. 2005).

Thus, researchers increasingly acknowledged that implementation analysis had to pay attention to a multiplicity of domestic actor networks including the variegated preferences and institutional properties of these networks. As suggested by some of the approaches we dubbed "hybrid theories" above, scholars now began to take into account the complexities of the "implementation games" played at the domestic level, and they fully embraced the political character of bringing EU legislation into practice. Again building on theories from the field of comparative politics, domestic implementation processes were seen to be shaped not only by the fit with existing policy legacies, but also by factors like the number of veto players, the presence or absence of a consensus-oriented decision-making culture, or the support or opposition of interest groups (Cowles et al. 2001; Héritier et al. 2001).

The problem with these broader approaches is well-known from "national" implementation research: the more factors we include in our theoretical models, the less are we able to decide which of these factors are the crucial ones and which circumstances determine whether they become relevant (e.g., O'Toole 2000, 268). One tentative solution to this problem is offered by a recent study that analyzed the implementation of EU social policy in fifteen member states (Falkner et al. 2005). Starting from a broad theoretical perspective that incorporated a wide range of hypotheses suggested by previous research, the authors conclude that most of these hypotheses had some explanatory power, but none of them could explain the whole range of implementation patterns observed in the total of ninety case studies. As a solution to this puzzle, they then offer a typology of three "worlds of compliance," which result from the varying importance of a culture of law-abidingness in the political and administrative systems of the different member states. Hence, the analysis highlights the importance of country-specific cultural conditions. These cultural conditions then determine which sets of other factors are relevant in a particular country setting.

In sum, EU scholars enriched the study of implementation processes by two notable innovations. First, they adopted new methodological strategies. In contrast to "national" implementation research, where "solid cross-national investigations are still rare" (O'Toole 2000, 268), the specific setting of the European Union encouraged an approach that was much more comparative in nature. As a result, cross-country comparison has meanwhile become the standard methodological approach in this field of study. Unlike traditional implementation researchers, EU scholars thus increasingly became aware of systematic institutional and cultural differences in the typical implementation styles of different countries. Moreover, there is a growing number of statistical analyses using the official data on infringement procedures initiated by the European Commission against noncompliant member states (Mendrinou 1996; Lampinen and Uusikylä 1998; Börzel 2001; Mbaye 2001). Although these studies are struggling with all kinds of methodological problems,[3] they could serve to counteract the case study bias that has marked large parts of implementation research so far.

The second innovation is that EU implementation research, instead of seeking to establish a specific "implementation theory," became more and more receptive to general theories, especially from the field of comparative politics. This is an important development because the incorporation of concepts from historical institutionalism, game theory or cultural approaches facilitates communication with other fields of study and might thus increase the visibility of implementation research in the wider scholarly community.

3.2 THE INTERPRETATIVE APPROACH TO POLICY IMPLEMENTATION

The interpretative approach to policy implementation departs from a different ontological stance than the theoretical contributions previously discussed. It considers the strict distinction between facts and values underlying the positivist philosophy of science as untenable, and it challenges the possibility of neutral and unbiased observations. In Yanow's (2000, ix) words, this means that "…interpretative policy [implementation] analysis shifts the discussion from values as a set of costs, benefits, and choice points to a focus on values, beliefs, and feelings as set of meanings, and from a view of human behavior as, ideally, instrumentally and technically rational to human action as expressive (of meaning)."

The interpretative approach does not take the factual essence of problems as its main point of reference, but shows that multiple and sometimes ambiguous and conflicting meanings, as well as a variety of interpretations, coexist in parallel. While traditional analysis concentrates on explaining the implementation gap between policy intention and outcome, interpretative analy-

---

3. Since this data only represents the cases of noncompliance that were actually detected and prosecuted by the Commission, there are serious doubts as to whether they can be taken as an indicator for the true level of noncompliance with EU law. In other words, they might represent no more than the tip of the iceberg, which does not necessarily say much about the size or the shape of those parts that remain below the waterline (Falkner et al. 2005, chap. 11).

sis focuses on the analysis of "how policy means" (Yanow 1996). It also rejects the assumption that policy implementation can be studied without looking at the process of policy formation. In contrast, it assumes that prior debates and policy meanings have an impact on policy execution as they influence implementers' understanding of the policy problem. Implementing actors are also confronted with multiple policy meanings as policy formation frequently involves the accommo- dation of contradicting interests. Moreover, the written content of policies may only reflect goals that are publicly expressible, while implementing agencies are also confronted with the need of implementing so-called "verboten goals" (Yanow 1996, 205) that are only tacitly communicated. In this sense, interpretative analysis studies the very definition of the problem or, in other words, it examines the "struggle for the determination of meanings" (Yanow 1996, 19) and scrutinizes "how those meanings are communicated" (Yanow 1996, 222).

Rather than assuming that policy statements are purely rational and goal-oriented, Yanow suggests that statements also have an expressive character. Through them, a polity may reveal its distinct identity (Yanow 1996, 22). In her case study on the establishment of community centers in Israel, Yanow highlighted that the use of the metaphor "functional supermarket" had shaped the concept of community centers' identity in terms of programs, administrative practices and staff roles. It thus had turned into an organizational metaphor (Yanow 1996, 129–53).

The focus of the interpretative approach therefore lies on the interpretation of meaning passed on by policy actors, implementation agencies and target populations (for a similar argument, see Pülzl 2001). Symbols, metaphors, and policy language, which embody multiple meanings, are em- bedded in what Yanow (1987, 108) calls policy "culture." It is the analysts' main task to examine how different actors interpret this policy culture and then track down the effect of these multiple understandings on the implementation process. Furthermore, the analysis focuses on the context in which policy is transformed into practice. In this sense, the examination of the context-specific meaning of policy reveals essential features of the implementation process, as Yanow's (1996) empirical analysis has also demonstrated.

4 THIRTY YEARS OF IMPLEMENTATION RESEARCH: WHAT HAVE WE LEARNED?

More than thirty years after the publication of Pressman and Wildavsky's pioneering study, the time seems right to take stock of the lessons we learned from implementation research. We will start by summarizing what seem to us the most relevant insights gained with regard to the area of imple- mentation itself. Second, we will discuss a number of contributions of implementation research to the wider field of policy analysis and political science.

What has implementation research taught us about the driving forces behind implementation? The following five points seem to be worth highlighting:

1. After years of debate between top-down and bottom-up scholars, both sides seem to agree that implementation is a continuum located between central guidance and local autonomy. The preferences of street-level bureaucrats and the negotiations within implementation networks have to be taken into account to the same extent as centrally defined policy objectives and efforts at hierarchical control. The actual position of individual implementation processes on this continuum is an empirical rather than a theoretical question.
2. Bottom-uppers have successfully convinced the wider community of implementation scholars that implementation is more than the technical execution of political orders from above. It is itself a political process in the course of which policies are frequently reshaped, redefined or even completely overturned.

3. What bottom-up scholars already suggested a long time ago has become more and more accepted also among the proponents of "hybrid" or "synthesizing" theories: implementation and policy formulation are highly interdependent processes. If not abandoning the "stagist" model of the policy process altogether, it now seems to be widely accepted that it is at least necessary to take into consideration the impact of policy formulation on implementation.

4. Especially the work of Sabatier has alerted us to the fact that implementation processes (and processes of policy change more generally) should not be viewed in isolation. Instead, exogenous influences from other policy fields or external economic developments need to be taken into account.

5. Recent EU implementation analysis has highlighted that different countries seem to have different "implementation styles." To learn more about the contrasting logics of implementation in different country settings, more research with an explicit focus on cross-country comparison (national, regional and local studies) is needed. Moreover, this strand of the literature demonstrated that rather than searching for a unique "implementation theory", theoretical arguments from comparative politics, such as the veto player theorem or insights from historical institutionalisms, can shed new light on implementation processes.

Further to these insights on the forces that drive the process of putting policy into practice, implementation studies have also contributed to three wider debates in policy analysis and political science.

First, implementation research contributed decisively to the debates in public administration and organizational theory about the character of modern bureaucracies. As bottom-up scholars persistently argued that administrative actors are often not tightly enough controlled by politicians and have quite some autonomy in determining how policies are actually executed, they delivered a serious blow to the conviction that modern public administrations resembled the Weberian model of a hierarchically organized and technocratic bureaucracy that is subordinate to the authority of political leaders. What has come to the fore, instead, is the view that public administrations have much more complex organizational structures and are much less hierarchically ordered than assumed by the Weberian model. Above all, implementation analysis has shown that administrative actors have their own political goals and that they use the considerable discretion they often have to pursue these goals rather than the ones prescribed by the political echelons above them. In this sense, Palumbo and Calista (1990, 14) are right in concluding that "implementation research has finally laid to rest the politics–administration dichotomy". Instead, implementation scholars paved the way for a more realistic conception of the institutional features and the role of modern public administration in politics.

Second, the wider debates on political steering and governance, which have been particularly lively in Europe, especially in Germany, owe much to the insights of implementation scholars (for an overview, see Mayntz 1996, 2004). In the 1960s and early 1970s, the dominant view in this debate was characterized by political planning approaches (Mayntz and Scharpf 1973). These approaches started from the assumption of a simple hierarchical relationship between an active state and a passive society. In this view, the ability of political leaders to shape society according to politically defined goals found its limits only in the availability of scientific knowledge about the most pressing problems to be solved and in the effectiveness of the state machinery to devise the proper political strategies to address them. Neither the actual execution of policies by administrations nor the reactions by target groups were seen as a major problem. The findings of implementation scholars about the complexities and problems of policy execution meant a serious setback to this model. The second attack came from interest group research, which discovered, especially in Europe, various forms of neocorporatist patterns where governments cooperated with strong interest associations in policy formation and implementation or even delegated certain public tasks to "private interest governments" (Schmitter and Lehmbruch 1979; Streeck and Schmitter 1985). In theoretical terms, a fundamental critique of the paradigm of hierarchical steering was added by autopoietic systems theory, which argues that society is made up of a set of autonomous subsystems, each of them functioning according to a specific logic. The relative closure of each individual subsystem makes it hard for other subsystems (and therefore also for the political system) to influence them in a deliberate fashion (Luhmann 1985). All of these developments finally gave rise to a new, nonhierarchical model of political steering. The new keyword of this model is "governance" within policy networks or negotiation systems where public actors from different levels cooperate with private actors in the production and execution of policies (Rhodes 1997; Scharpf 1997; Pierre and Peters 2000, chaps. 6 and 9).

Third, implementation scholars, especially those from the bottom-up camp, were among those who voiced serious concerns as to whether classical liberal democratic theory was still appropriate for a world in which not only elected representatives but also administrative actors and interest groups have a decisive say in shaping and delivering policies. Hence, implementation analysis gave an important impulse for the development of alternatives to the model of representative democracy.

Admittedly, the efforts to develop such an alternative model of democracy have only produced some preliminary results. However, there are two strands of theorizing that should be noted here. The first one centers on the Habermasian notion of deliberative democracy, which is based on the idea that democratic decisions are the outcome of consensus-oriented, rational discourses among all affected actors (Habermas 1987; Miller 1993). In implementation research, scholars like deLeon (2001) have taken up the notion of deliberative democracy, and interpretative approaches to implementation (such as Yanow 1996) are also built upon this model of democracy. The other strand does not presuppose consensus-orientation and arguing, but tries to develop democratic standards for the interactions of public and private actors within negotiation systems or policy networks. One example is the model of "associative democracy" (Cohen and Rogers 1992; Hirst 1994), which is based on the assumption that in modern societies, many nonelected actors, especially interest associations, have a crucial say in policy making. Rather than seeing this as a danger for democracy, the authors suggest that these actors, to the extent that they are representatives of certain groups of citizens and their common interests, can also add to the legitimacy of political decisions.

5 CONCLUSIONS AND FURTHER OUTLOOK

We have demonstrated in this chapter that implementation research has produced a number of important insights with regard to both the field of implementation itself and the wider context of the social sciences. Nevertheless, it is not particularly prominent in the wider scientific community. For example, neither the *New Handbook of Political Science* (Goodin and Klingemann 1996) nor the volume on *Theories of the Policy Process* edited by Sabatier (1999) include more than a few scattered paragraphs on the issue of implementation. In our view, the visibility of implementation analysis was severely hampered by three persistent weaknesses.

First, implementation research has been characterized by a lack of cumulation. For a long time, constructive cumulative research was impeded by the fundamental clash between top-down and bottom-up scholars (Lester et al. 1987, 210). However, as the discussion above has shown, this problem also persists after synthesizing or hybrid theories had tried to bridge the gap between these approaches. For example, the findings of European integration scholars have thus far been largely neglected by "national" implementation research.[4]

---

4 Neither the recent summarizing articles by O'Toole (2000) or deLeon (2001) nor the latest handbook on
   implementation research by Hill and Hupe (2002) or the recent symposium on implementation analysis in
   Public Administration (Schofield and Sausman 2004) include any reference to this strand of research.

Second, the theoretical models presented by implementation scholars, no matter whether they emerged in the context of the first, second, or third generations of research, typically comprise a multitude of potential explanatory variables. Yet we know little about which of these factors are more or less important under what kind of background conditions.

Third, the largest part of implementation research has been characterized by a shared positivist ontology and epistemology that largely ignores the role of discourses, symbols, and cultural patterns.

However, these weaknesses do not suggest that implementation research should be abolished altogether, as has been argued by scholars like Ingram or Sabatier, who moved on to other subjects such as policy design or the study of policy change more generally. Unlike this group of scholars, who have recently been dubbed "terminators" (Lester and Goggin 1998, 3), we think that it is still very useful to invest time and money into the study of how policies are transformed into action. Unlike the advocacy coalition framework and many network approaches, we think a separate analysis of implementation is useful since the actors involved in policy formation and implementation, while partly overlapping, are certainly not always exactly the same. Hence, keeping the stages of the policy process separate and focusing on one of them in more detail still seems to be worthwhile, although the interdependencies between the stages have to be taken into account as well.

But in order to advance our understanding of implementation beyond the level that has already been achieved, implementation research needs to take new directions. In particular, implementation analysis should strive to avoid the weaknesses that have hitherto curtailed its impact on the study of policy change. In this sense, we belong to the group of what Lester and Goggin (1998, 2) have called "reformers." First, more mutual awareness of the findings of other scholars in the field could certainly boost more cumulative research. Processes of cross-fertilization could thus improve our understanding of implementation processes.

Second, the problem of overcomplex theoretical models might be mitigated by moving toward what deLeon (1999: 318) has dubbed "contingency concepts," which take institutional properties of implementation structures, policy types, or country-specific cultural variables as framework conditions that make certain types of implementation processes and certain clusters of explanatory variables more likely than others. There have been some initial attempts in this direction (e.g., Matland 1995; Windhoff-Héritier 1980), but the potential of this approach has certainly not been used to the fullest extent possible. Careful comparative investigations of cases that have been selected with a view to systematically varying different policy types, institutional settings, countries and (more or less) successful or failed instances of implementation, could complement these theoretical efforts.

While these two strategies point into a similar direction as the one suggested by third-generation scholars (see e.g., Lester and Goggin 1998), notably to continue implementation studies in a more sophisticated way, there is also another sphere which previous research has only touched upon rudimentarily. There is much to be learned from interpretative and constructivist approaches, which argue that policy contents and objectives as well as implementation problems often cannot be discerned on an objective basis. Instead, the nature of what is at stake in processes of policy execution may be subject to fundamentally different perspectives that are shaped by language, culture, and symbolic politics.

REFERENCES

Bardach, E. (1977). *The Implementation Game. What Happens After a Bill Becomes a Law*. Cambridge: MIT Press.

Barett, S., and Fudge, C. (eds.) (1981). *Policy and Action*. London: Methuen.

Barrett, S. (2004). Implementation Studies. Time fore a Revival? Personal Reflections on 20 Years of Implementation Studies. *Public Administration*, 82, 249–262.

Börzel, T.A. (2000). Why There Is No 'Southern Problem'. On Environmental Leaders and Laggards in the European Union. *Journal of European Public Policy*, 7, 141–162.

Börzel, T.A. (2001). Non-Compliance in the European Union. Pathology or Statistical Artifact? *Journal of European Public Policy*, 8, 803–824.

Börzel, T.A. (2002). Pace-Setting, Foot-Dragging, and Fence-Sitting. Member State Responses to Europeanization. *Journal of Common Market Studies*, 40, 193–214.

Börzel, T.A. (2003). *Environmental Leaders and Laggards in Europe. Why there is (Not) a 'Southern Problem'.* Aldershot: Ashgate.

Brown-Weiss, E., and Jacobson, H.K. (eds) *Engaging Countries. Strengthening Compliance with International Environmental Accords.* Cambridge: MIT Press.

Cohen, J., and Rogers, J. (1992). Secondary Associations and Democratic Governance. *Politics and Society*, 20, 393–472.

Cowles, M.G., Caporaso, J., and Risse, T. (eds) (2001). *Transforming Europe. Europeanization and Domestic Change.* Ithaca: Cornell University Press.

deLeon, P. (1999). The Missing Link Revisited. Contemporary Implementation Research. *Policy Studies Review*, 16, 311–338.

deLeon, P. (2001). A Democratic Approach to Policy Implementation. Paper prepared for presentation at the Annual Meeting of the American Political Science Association, August 31, San Francisco.

Derthick, M. (1972). *New Towns in Town. Why a Federal Program Failed.* Washington, DC: Urban Institute.

Duina, F.G. (1997). Explaining Legal Implementation in the European Union. *International Journal of the Sociology of Law*, 25, 155–179.

Duina, F.G. (1999). *Harmonizing Europe. Nation-States within the Common Market.* Albany: State University of New York Press.

Duina, F.G., and Blithe, F. (1999). Nation-States and Common Markets. The Institutional Conditions for Acceptance. *Review of International Political Economy*, 6, 494–530.

Elmore, R.F. (1980). Backward Mapping. Implementation Research and Policy Decisions. *Political Science Quarterly*, 94, 601–616.

Elmore, R.F. (1985). Forward and Backward Mapping. In K. Hanf and T.A.J. Toonen (eds), *Policy Implementation in Federal and Unitary Systems*, pp. 33–70. Dordrecht: Martinus Nijhoff.

Falkner, G., Treib, O., Hartlapp, M., and Leiber, S. (2005). *Complying with Europe. EU Harmonisation and Soft Law in the Member States.* Cambridge: Cambridge University Press.

Fischer, Frank (2003). *Reframing Public Policy.* Oxford: Oxford University Press.

Goggin, M.L., Bowman, A.O.M., Lester, J.P., O'Toole, L.J. Jr. (1990). *Implementation Theory and Practice. Toward a Third Generation.* New York: Harper Collins.

Goodin, R.E., and Klingemann, H.-D. (eds) (1996). *A New Handbook of Political Science.* New York: Oxford University Press.

Habermas, J. (1987). *The Theory of Communicative Action. Vol. 2: Lifeworld and System. A Critique of Functionalist Reasoning.* Boston: Beacon.

Hargrove, E.C. (1975). *The Missing Link. The Study of the Implementation of Social Policy.* Washington, DC: Urban Institute.

Haverland, M. (2000). National Adaptation to European Integration. The Importance of Institutional Veto Points. *Journal of Public Policy*, 20, 83–103.

Héritier, A., Kerwer, D., Knill, C., Lehmkuhl, D., Teutsch, M., and Douillet, A.-C. (eds) (2001). *Differential Europe. The European Union Impact on National Policymaking.* Lanham: Rowman and Littlefield.

Héritier, A., Knill, C., and Mingers, S. (1996). *Ringing the Changes in Europe. Regulatory Competition and Redefinition of the State.* Berlin: de Gruyter.

Hill, M., and Hupe, P. (2002). *Implementing Public Policy. Governance in Theory and in Practice.* London: Sage.

Hirst, P. (1994). *Associative Democracy. New Forms of Economic and Social Governance.* Amherst: University of Massachusetts Press.

Hjern, B. (1982). Implementation Research. The Link Gone Missing. *Journal of Public Policy*, 2, 301–308.

Hjern, B. and Hull, C. (1982). Implementation Research as Empirical Constitutionalism. *European Journal of Political Research*, 10(2), 105–116.

Hjern, B. and Porter, D.O. (1981). Implementation Structures. A New Unit of Administrative Analysis. *Organization Studies*, 2, 211–227.

Hudson, B. (1989). Michael Lipsky and Street Level Bureaucracy. A Neglected Perspective. In L. Barton (ed), *Disability and Dependency*, pp. 42–45. London: Falmer Press. [Reprinted in M. Hill (ed) (1993), *The Policy Process. A Reader*, pp. 393–403. New York: Harvester Wheatsheaf.]

Ingram, H. (1977). Policy Implementation through Bargaining. Federal Grants in Aid. *Public Policy*, 25, 499–526.

Jenkins, W.I. (1978). *Policy Analysis. A Political and Organisational Perspective*. London: Martin Robertson.

Knill, C., and Lenschow, A. (1998). Coping with Europe. The Impact of British and German Administrations on the Implementation of EU Environmental Policy. *Journal of European Public Policy*, 5, 595–614.

Knill, C., and Lenschow, A. (eds) (2000). *Implementing EU Environmental Policy. New Approaches to an Old Problem.* Manchester: Manchester University Press.

Lampinen, R., and Uusikylä, P. (1998). Implementation Deficit. Why Member States Do Not Comply with EU Directives? *Scandinavian Political Studies*, 21, 231–251.

Lester, J.P. and Googin, M.L. (1998). Back to the Future. The Rediscovery of Implementation Studies. *Policy Currents*, 8, 1–9.

Lester, J.P., Bowman, A. O'M., Goggin, M.L. and O'Toole, J., Jr. (1987). Public Policy Implementation. Evolution of the Field and Agenda for Future Research. *Policy Studies Review*, 7, 200–216.

Lipsky, M. (1971). Street Level Bureaucracy and the Analysis of Urban Reform. *Urban Affairs Quarterly*, 6, 391–409.

Lipsky, M. (1980). *Street-Level Bureaucracy. The Dilemmas of Individuals in the Public Service*. New York: Russell Sage Foundation.

Lowi, T.J. (1972). Four Systems of Policy, Politics and Choice. *Public Administration Review*, 32, 298–310.

Luhmann, N. (1985). *Social Systems*. Stanford: University of California Press.

Majone, G., and Wildavsky, A. (1978). Implementation as Evolution. In H. Freeman (ed). *Policy Studies Review Annual*, pp. 103–117. Beverly Hills: Sage.

Marin, B., and Mayntz, R. (eds) (1991). *Policy Networks. Empirical Evidence and Theoretical Considerations*. Frankfurt/M.: Campus.

Matland, R.E. (1995). Synthesizing the Implementation Literature. The Ambiguity-Conflict Model of Policy Implementation. *Journal of Public Administration Research and Theory*, 5, 145–174.

Mayntz, R. (1977). Die Implementation politischer Programme. Theoretische Überlegungen zu einem neuen Forschungsgebiet. *Die Verwaltung*, 10, 51–66.

Mayntz, R. (1996). Politische Steuerung. Aufstieg, Niedergang und Transformation einer Theorie. In K. von Beyme and C. Offe (eds), *Politische Theorien in der Ära der Transformation*, pp. 148–168. Opladen: Westdeutscher Verlag.

Mayntz, R. (2004). Governance Theory als fortentwickelte Steuerungstheorie? MPIfG Working Paper 04/1. Köln: Max-Planck-Institut für Gesellschaftsforschung <http://www.mpi-fg-koeln.mpg.de/pu/work-pap/wp04-1/wp04-1.html>.

Mayntz, R., and Scharpf, F.W. (eds) (1973). *Planungsorganisation. Die Diskussion um die Reform von Regierung und Verwaltung*. München: Piper.

Mazmanian, D. and Sabatier, P. (1983). *Implementation and Public Policy*. Glenview: Scott

Mbaye, H.A.D. (2001). Why National States Comply with Supranational Law. Explaining Implementation Infringements in the European Union 1972–1993. *European Union Politics*, 2, 259–281.

Mendrinou, M. (1996). Non-Compliance and the European Commission's Role in Integration. *Journal of European Public Policy*, 3, 1–22.

Miller, D. (1993). Deliberative Democracy and Social Choice. In D. Held (ed), *Prospects for Democracy. Noth, South, East, West*, pp. 74–92. Cambridge: Polity.

Nakamura, R., and Smallwood, F (1980). *The Politics of Policy Implementation*. New York: St.Martin's Press.

Nakamura, R.T. (1987). The Textbook Policy Process and Implementation Research. *Policy Studies Review*, 7, 142–154.

O'Toole, L.J. Jr. (2000). Research on Policy Implementation. Assessment and Prospects. *Journal of Public Administration Research and Theory*, 10, 263–288.

Palumbo, D.J., and Calista, D.J. (1990). Opening up the Black Box. Implementation and the Policy Process. In D.J. Palumbo and D.J. Calista (eds), *Implementation and the Policy Process. Opening up the Black Box*, pp. 3–18. New York: Greenwood Press.

Parsons, W. (1995). *Public Policy. An Introduction to the Theory and Practice of Policy Analysis*. London: Edward Elgar.

Pierre, J., and Peters, B.G. (2000). *Governance, Politics and the State*. New York: St. Martin's Press.

Pressman, J. and Wildavsky, A. (1973). Implementation. How great expectations in Washington are dashed in Oakland; or why it's amazing that federal programs work at all. This being a saga of the Economic Development Administration as told by two sympathetic observers who seek to build morals on a foundation of ruined hopes. Berkeley: University of California Press.

Pülzl, H. (2001). Can Discourse Analysis Be Used to Investigate the Implementation of Public Policy? Implementing a European Environmental Directive on the Local Level. Paper prepared for presentation at the European Consortium for Political Research Joint Sessions, Workshop "Policy, Discourse & Institutional Reform," 7–11 April 2001, Grenoble, France.

Rhodes, R.A.W. (1997). *Understanding Governance. Policy Networks, Governance, Reflexivity and Accountability*. Buckingham: Open University Press.

Ripley, R.B. and Franklin, G.A. (1982). *Bureaucracy and Policy Implementation*. Homewood: Dorsey Press.

Sabatier, P.A. (1986a). Top-down and Bottom-up Approaches to Implementation Research. A Critical Analysis and Suggested Synthesis. *Journal of Public Policy*, 6, 21–48.

Sabatier, P.A. (1986b). What Can We Learn from Implementation Research? In F.-X. Kaufmann, G. Majone, and V. Ostrom (eds), Guidance, Control, and Evaluation in the Public Sector. *The Bielefeld Interdisciplinary Project*, pp. 313–326. Berlin: de Gruyter.

Sabatier, P.A. (ed) (1999). *Theories of the Policy Process*. Boulder: Westview.

Sabatier, P.A., and Jenkins-Smith, H.C. (1993). *Policy Change and Learning. An Advocacy Coalition Approach*. Boulder: Westview.

Sabatier, P.A., and Mazmanian, D. (1979). The Conditions of Effective Implementation. *Policy Analysis*, 5, 481–504.

Sabatier, P.A., and Mazmanian, D. (1980). A Framework of Analysis. *Policy Studies Journal*, 8, 538–60.

Sabatier, P.A., and Mazmanian, D.A. (1981). The Implementation of Public Policy. A Framework of Analysis. In D.A. Mazmanian and P.A. Sabatier (eds), *Effective Policy Implementation*, pp. 3–35. Lexington: Lexington Books.

Scharpf, F.W. (1978). Interorganizational Policy Studies. Issues, Concepts and Perspectives. In K. I. Hanf and F.W. Scharpf (eds.), *Interorganizational Policy Making. Limits to Coordination and Central Control*, pp. 345–370. London: Sage.

Scharpf, F.W. (1997). *Games Real Actors Play. Actor Centered Institutionalism in Policy Research*. Boulder: Westview.

Schmitter, P.C., and Lehmbruch, G. (eds) (1979). *Trends Towards Corporatist Intermediation*. London: Sage.

Schofield, J., and Sausman, C. (2004). Symposium on Implementing Public Policy. Learning from Theory and Practice Introduction. *Public Administration*, 82, 235–248.

Schwarze, J., Becker, U., and Pollack, C. (1991). The 1992 Challenge at National Level. A Community-Wide Joint Research Project on the Realization and Implementation by National Governments and Business of the Internal Market Programme. Reports and Conference Proceedings 1990. Baden-Baden: Nomos.

Schwarze, J., Becker, U., and Pollack, C. (1993). The 1992 Challenge at National Level. A Community-Wide Joint Research Project on the Realization and Implementation by National Governments and Business of the Internal Market Programme. Reports and Conference Proceedings 1991/92. Baden-Baden: Nomos.

Schwarze, J., Govaere, I., Helin, F., and Van den Bossche, P. (1990). The 1992 Challenge at National Level. A Community-Wide Joint Research Project on the Realization and Implementation by National Governments and Business of the Internal Market Programme. Reports and Conference Proceedings 1989. Baden-Baden: Nomos.

Siedentopf, H., and Ziller, J. (eds) (1988). *Making European Policies Work. The Implementation of Community Legislation in the Member States*. 2 Volumes. London: Sage.

Streeck, W., and Schmitter, P.C. (eds) (1985). *Private Interest Government. Beyond Market and State*. London: Sage.

Treib, O. (2004). *Die Bedeutung der nationalen Parteipolitik für die Umsetzung europäischer Sozialrichtlinien*. Frankfurt/M.: Campus.

Van Meter, D., and Van Horn, C. (1975). The Policy Implementation Process. A Conceptual Framework. *Administration and Society*, 6, 445–488.

Victor, D.G., Raustiala, K., and Skolnikoff, E.B. (eds) (1998). *The Implementation and Effectiveness of International Environmental Commitments*. Cambridge: MIT Press.

Windhoff-Héritier, A. (1980). *Politikimplementation. Ziel und Wirklichkeit politischer Entscheidungen*. Königstein/Ts.: Anton Hain.

Winter, S. (1990). Integrating Implementation Research. In D.J. Palumbo and D.J. Calista (eds), *Implementation and the Policy Process. Opening up the Black Box*, pp. 19–38. New York: Greenwood Press.

Yanow, D. (1987). Toward a Policy Culture Approach to Implementation. *Policy Studies Review*, 7, 103–115.

Yanow, D. (1996). *How Does a Policy Mean? Interpreting Policy and Organizational Actions*. Washington, DC: Georgetown University Press.

Yanow, D. (2000). *Conducting Interpretive Policy Analysis*. Newbury Park: Sage.

8 Do Policies Determine Politics?

Hubert Heinelt

1 INTRODUCTION

One influential thesis for analyzing the policy process has been formulated by Theodore Lowi.[1] He has argued, "Policies determine politics" (Lowi 1972, 299). In this chapter, the context will first be outlined against which Lowi developed his thesis (section 1). The chapter will then address the influence of this thesis on the academic debate as well as on the doubts raised about its explanatory potential for analyzing individual policy sectors like labor market policy, public old age pension policy, environment policy, or migration policy. The main focus of this chapter will be on how to make use of Lowi's thesis in respect of individual policy fields. However, such an attempt is limited because policies cannot effectively be considered separately from their related historical and locational structures and actor constellations related to them. What this implies and how to cope conceptually with this problem will be addressed in the chapter's final sections.

2 LOWI'S THESIS "POLICIES DETERMINE POLITICS". . .

Lowi's thesis was initially related to basic policy mechanisms or policy types, namely, distributive, redistributive, and regulatory policies.[2] Its relevance has first of all to be seen in the time during which it was formulated. It was Lowi's ambition to develop a framework for categorizing case studies (see Benz 1997, 303). At the same time, he wanted to draw attention to the question: what does policy making (in the sense of politics) depend on? This was a key issue because at that time studies were strongly influenced by Easton's (1965) model of the political system according to which the political-administrative system remains a black box between political input (demands of and support from citizens) and political outputs (laws, programs and such). Processes within the political system remained unanalyzed. Lowi's thesis pointed in the direction in which one should look for an answer—at the content of a policy and the kind of problems associated with it.

Because the content of a policy—in the sense of its distributive, redistributive, or regulatory character (see Table 8.1)—implies particular outcomes, this results in particular responses from those affected, which, in turn, have an impact on political debate in terms of decision making as well as implementation. Or as Lowi (1964, 707) put it, "It is not the actual outcomes but the expectations as to what the outcomes can be that shape the issues and determine their politics." This leads to different kinds of "policy arenas" that exhibit particular features of conflict or consensus. They are crucially shaped by the costs and benefits identified by those involved. In summary, a policy aimed at redistribution and an unequal allocation of costs and benefits will be found in an arena

---

1. This paper has been finished during a stay as a visiting fellow at the School for Policy Studies, University of Bristol. I have benefited a lot from fruitful discussion there, especially with Alex Marsh and Randall Smith.

2. Later on (Lowi 1972) *constituent policy* was added, i.e., procedural policy setting the rules for policy making, which will not be addressed in detail in the following.

TABLE 8.1
Classification of Policy Types

Policy Type	Characteristics of the Policy	Characteristics of the Arena	Examples	Guiding Principles
Distributive	Collective public provision	Consensual No opposition/resistance	Research grants General tax reduction	Incentives
Redistributive	Relation between costs and benefits obvious	Conflictual Polarization between winners and losers Ideological framing	Progressive taxation Labor market policy Social assistance	Imposition by the state
Regulatory	(Legal) norms for behavior/interaction	Changing coalitions according to the distribution of costs and benefits	Consumer protection Safety at work Protection of environment	Imposition by the state Persuasion Guidance by exemplary models Self-regulation

Translated and modified from Windhoff-Héritier 1987, 52–53.

characterized by conflict. By way of contrast, a policy trying to offer universally available services or goods with unclear consequences for the distribution of costs and benefits will be found in an arena characterized by conflict-free processes of policy making. The same applies to a regulatory policy which includes a binding code that does not result in observable benefit. It may imply costs and benefits but they are hard to calculate or predict. Or to put it precisely: "In all components of conventional politics—legislative, administrative, judicial and civil society—the choice of policy mechanisms imposes predictable constraints on the outcomes of public actions and is not simply derivative from either the electoral process or the configuration of interest groups" (Nicholson 2002, 165 with reference to Lowi 1972, 300).

The emphasis given by Lowi to the linkage between the mentioned policy mechanisms and policy arenas characterized by a certain degree of conflict or consensus was inspired by a certain approach: Lowi was interested in "the choices about how to apply the power of the state and not primarily on what goals the sate should pursue" (Nicholson 2002, 163). This led to a microanalysis of how public power has been applied coming to the result that this could be done in different ways and that policy choices are possible—namely between the mentioned policy mechanisms or types. In other words, because perceptions of policy outcomes are relevant, strategic policy makers—in a position to influence those perceptions—can increase the likelihood of a direct influence on the policy process.

This is addressed in the policy analysis literature by the key phrase "issue relabelling" (see Windhoff-Héritier 1987, 56–57 for an overview). This means that by relabelling a policy, the perception of what a policy is about can be influenced—and by this the policy process is also affected. For example, regional policy aiming at equalizing or at least balancing regional and social disparities is apparently redistributive. However, to calm down controversies resulting from the redistributive effects of this policy, emphasis can also be placed on related measures that are of general benefit. The development of the infrastructure, for instance, can improve the accessibility of regions, in relation to the exchange of products (the market) or the mobility of people (for the workforce as well as for tourists) (see Heinelt 1996, 20).

The success of "issue relabelling" depends crucially on the specific context. This applies for the expressions used and the notions to which they are related. A good example is the opening up of a debate about immigration policy in Germany in 2000 by the discussion about a "green card." The expression "green card" was related to its particular American context, and thus to a "demand-driven" and selective immigration policy.

This example also points in another way to the importance of embedding "issue relabelling" in a particular context. Chancellor Schroeder introduced this issue at a specific place and in front of a particular audience. It was the opening speech at Cebit Hanover, the world's largest fair for computers, communication, and information technology, where he could be sure (against the background of a labor shortage in this sector of the German economy) that his rearticulation of the immigration agenda would find not only support from his listeners, but also be picked up by the media.

3 ...AND ITS IMPACT ON DEBATES IN POLITICAL SCIENCE

Although this line of thinking has been very influential not only in policy analysis but in political science in general (see Benz 1997, 303) and reflections on the distributive, redistributive, or regulatory effects of policies have become usual starting points in analyzing policy processes, Lowi's approach has also been criticized.

For instance, it can be argued that the emphasis placed on expectations or perceptions by Lowi (when stating that it "is not the actual outcomes but the expectations as to what the outcomes can be that shape the issues and determine their politics") does not lead to clarification in respect of policies or policy types. Instead, because perceived outcomes are determining politics, the clarity gets lost in linking particular policies to conflictual or consensual arenas. Indeed, when one-sided restrictions or disadvantages are perceived in respect of a law with a regulatory content, it can lead to political conflict just like redistributive policy, even though such a law may be generally binding and affecting everyone.

One example of this is the European Union directive about the employment of workers from other member states in addressing issues like social security contributions and benefits, as well as wages according to national wage agreements. This directive has caused major arguments in some countries (like Germany) where the negative impact on the endogenous workforce has been obvious. In the light of this example, one can question Majone's thesis (1994) that the future of the EU is that of a "regulatory state," i.e., the EU will be capable only of regulative (market-correcting) and not redistributive policies, because the latter implies conflict and goes beyond the decision making capacity of the EU (see Heinelt 1996, p. 17–20). The same argument could apply to a distributive policy. Consider the provision of kindergartens in a time when the proportion of households without children is increasing. In such a context this "classical" distributive policy, can be perceived as redistributive one, as a one-sided support for families or a redistributive burden sharing between households with and without children.

The academic debate on Lowi's thesis has also been taken further in another direction. The thesis (policies determine politics) has been de-coupled from the types of redistributive, distributive, and regulatory policies insofar as attempts have been made to relate it to policy sectors like labor market, public old-age pension, environment, immigration, and the like. This approach to providing an answer to the question of how and why policies determine politics has been linked to the increasing focus of policy analysis on specific policy sectors (Windhoff-Héritier 1983, 351). But in looking at individual policy sectors, the focus on the three policy types appears not to be very fruitful, because within policy sectors distributive, redistributive, and regulatory policies as well as consensual or conflictual policy arenas can be found at the same time as well as sequentially. For instance (like in Germany; see Egner et al. 2004), in housing policies rent allowance and legal protection of tenants can be complementary, i.e., instruments supporting tenants in the housing sector comprising, in the first, case a redistributive and, in the second case, a regulatory policy mechanism. Further, these instruments can (at least in some countries) rely on social housing built in the past by developers who have received subsidies which represent a redistributive policy, Finally, one can consider measures for the improvement of the infrastructure in a neighborhood, which can be labeled as distributive policies.

Attempts to make clear statements on the nature of policy-politics interdependencies by individual policy sectors are not only confronted by the phenomenon that regulatory, redistributive and distributive policies can be of relevance for a certain policy field at the same time. Furthermore—and providing that such an attempt should start from Lowi's model—it has to be clear that Lowi offers a tool of microanalysis (as mentioned above), i.e., to explain or even to predict why a certain program characterized by one of the mentioned policy mechanisms is leading to particular policy processes. "This is not a fatal flaw and it does not, in and of itself, undermine the utility of the model so long as one applies it safely within particular historical eras and specified institutional frameworks" (Nicholson 2002, 170). But attempts to make clear statements on the nature of policy-politics interdependencies by individual policy sectors are clearly not restricted to the application of a certain model (like that of Lowi) to a historically given institutional setting. Instead, a more general approach is in play clarifying general characteristics of policy processes in policy fields. Additionally, it can be argued that "policy choices," i.e., choices between a regulatory, redistributive, and distributive policy (as assumed by Lowi's approach of microanalysis of the policy process) are hard to make (or even hardly possible). Instead reflections on structural constraints and opportunities for policy making or tools of macro analysis seem to be necessary—not least as argued in this chapter regarding policy sectors.

However, in looking for such tools to identify structural constraints and opportunities for policy making by individual policy sectors contingent factors, labeled by Windhoff-Heritier "policy contingencies" (1983, 359), can hardly be denied. These policy contingencies mean that policy sectors should not be seen as unchanging or independent, but as contingent, that is, dependent on institutional structures as well as affected by the specific perceptions and actions of actors. Benz (1997) has tried to address the challenge to consider specific policy-politics relations as well as "policy contingencies" from the perspective of an actor-centered institutionalism. According to him, the interests of actors define what a policy is or should be about. However, this actor, or interested-related definition of policies, has to be connected with (1) a "feasible set" given at a certain point in time and with (2) an already existing institutional structure (Benz 1997, 306). In other words, simply through the definition of a policy a problem becomes subject to political decision and therefore a task of politics. Nevertheless, institutional conditions and power relations impact on the definition of a policy, but they do not totally determine decisions. They leave room for discretion (see Benz 1997, 305, 310) according to the particular (historical) situation in which actors have to solve a problem or define it.

This argument avoids the difficulty that academic policy analysts can get into if they strictly follow the thesis "policies determine politics" regarding policy sectors and if this thesis is not combined with reflections on policy contingencies. Specifically, the would imply—given that a policy sector would be seen as the only relevant variable for explaining politics—that institutions, parties, forms of interest mediation, political culture, etc. do not matter, only the policy sector does.

In fact, the statement that only the policy sector matters is inadequate for academic policy analysts. For example, studies in comparative public policy start from national variations in individual policy sectors and try to explain them by institutions, parties, forms of interest mediation, and political culture (see the seminal work of Heidenheimer et al. 1975 and for different approaches to explain national differences Heidenheimer et al. 1990, p. 6 ff.). Again, in policy studies focused at the local level differences in urban policies are explained by diverging institutional conditions, particular situations ("feasible sets"), as well as actor-related definitions or perceptions of problems and ways to solve them (see for an overview of recent studies Haus et al. 2005).

However, in these studies on policy sectors, generalized arguments on policy-politics interdependencies are missing, or are conceptually underdeveloped (this is also true for the work of Heidenheimer et al. 1975). This is not so surprising: "the comparison of a single policy sector across nation-states prioritizes institutional variation" (John and Cole 2000, 251), and a comparison of case studies of cities in a single country with more or less the same institutional settings leads to a focus on local particularities.

John and Cole (2000) try to provide an empirical answer to the question "When do institutions, policy sectors, and cities matter?" and concluded that the "research findings do not neatly confirm one of the three hypotheses" (John and Cole 2000, 264)—namely "policy sectors matter," "institutions matter," and "cities matter" (where the latter would relate not only to place but also to a certain "feasible set" at a particular point in time). But the study made clear (based on local economic development and secondary education two French and two British cities) that policy sectors play a role insofar as nationally divergent institutional settings are embedded in them, which influence the formation of local particularities and certain "feasible sets" at particular points in time in general. This can be linked to a concept of "policy institution" according to which "a particular policy arena has a set of formal and informal rules that determine the course of public decision making" (John and Cole 2000, 249 with reference to Mazzeo, 1997).

In the following, the formation of different policy institutions (or policy-specific arenas) will be linked to two elements characteristic of a particular policy sector: the distinctiveness of the problems to be addressed, and specificity of the consequent effects of a policy.

The first element points to specific conditions (challenges as well as options) to address a problem according to its very nature. The second element refers to specific impacts on those affected.

In practical terms, this means that in the case of public pension policy, for example, a centralized structure of the delivery system is likely as well as conditionally structured policy instruments, i.e., particular conditions that have to be met for someone to benefit from the provision offered by this policy. Furthermore, the potential beneficiaries of such a policy are likely to remain passive. This means meeting the conditions laid down—those which apply to them not just as individuals but to a social category or a collective entity (e.g., older people). It also means being guaranteed to receive a clearly defined provision from a centralized delivery system. The situation is different in the case of social services. Here decentralization, an orientation toward a certain policy objective (e.g., social inclusion in general or drug prevention in particular), is linked to an individual (e.g., a drug addict) and the active involvement of that person is crucial.

Although changes over time in individual policy sectors as well as international comparisons of public policies demonstrate major variations, they also point to some general policy-specific institutional arrangements—such as those just mentioned regarding public pension policy and social services—and the prevalence of certain forms of policy making in different policy sectors. Such features will be considered in the next section.

4 DIMENSIONS FOR DISTINGUISHING POLICY-POLITICS RELATIONS

Let us start from the point discussed earlier—the perception of a problem as well as the impact of the solution of a problem play a crucial role in conceptualizing policy-politics relations. Additionally, three further aspects are connected to perceptions of how a problem can be solved politically—differences in predictability, shifting or static policy boundaries, and interdependencies between policy sectors (see Table 8.2).

4.1 DIFFERENTIAL OR GENERAL IMPACT OF A PROBLEM

Assuming policy making is analyzed as a process of solving problems—as is usual for policy analysis (Mayntz 1982, 72)—the kind of problem to be solved politically cannot be ignored. Problems transferred from the societal environment into the political system and taken up by the latter to be solved by a societally binding decision can be classified in different ways. In this section, the emphasis is on the distinction between problems affecting everyone and those that just affect some. This distinction is important because it refers to the level of conflict that can occur if something (or nothing) happens to address a particular problem.

TABLE 8.2
Dimensions for Distinguishing Policy-Politics Relations

Dimensions	Examples	
	(Active) Labor Market Policy	**Public Old Age Pension Policy**
Application of a problem: selective vs. universal	(socially) selective	universal
Policy effects: individualizing vs. collective	individualizing	collective
Predictability	relatively clear	clear
Policy boundaries*	shifting	stable
Policy interdependencies*	substantial	limited

*The aspects of policy boundaries and policy interdependencies will be considered tobether in section 4.4.

This becomes clear when looking at standard risks of employees addressed by different social policies. Everyone gets older and every employee is confronted with the prospect of not being able to earn his/her own living. Unemployment differs from these standard risks because it may threaten every employee but actually affects only some, and it affects some in such a way that the chance of earning one's living is placed in question over a long time so that social exclusion is likely to occur. The fact that unemployment is a socially selective risk may explain why unemployment—in contrast to the social risk of not being able to earn one's living beyond a certain age—is addressed politically in a rhetorical sense but not with real priority. When unemployment is high on the public policy agenda (beyond political rhetoric, as in the case of the ongoing "workfare" reforms; see for an overview Finn 2000) it is usually done for other reasons, such as to reduce public spending.

However, the difference between a problem affecting some people but not everyone is not all that clear and, moreover, can be dynamicized due to political debate. In comparing countries, it becomes clear that views on those affected, as well as the perception of reasons why they are affected, differs between countries. For instance, the perception that it is one's personal responsibility if one is unemployed is widespread in the UK, whereas in Germany the prevailing perception is that unemployment is a societal (and not an individual) problem to be solved politically (see Cebulla 2000).[3] However, as the recent reform of labor market policy in Germany shows (Heinelt 2003) this can change.

4.2 INDIVIDUALIZING AND COLLECTIVE POLICY EFFECTS

That political actors can respond, for example, to the problem of unemployment cannot be explained adequately by the structure of the problem according to the distinction outlined above. What also has to be considered is whether or not the effect or the objective of a policy is regarded as something related to individuals or to a group. This becomes clear when considering labor market policy. An active labor market policy consists of measures aimed at bringing the unemployed back into the work force. A "passive" labor market policy consists of providing cash benefits for the unemployed (see Schmid et al. 1992).

---

3. This fits in with Luhmann's (1991, 1993) distinction between "risk" and "danger." According Luhmann, a risk refers to action or nonaction by an actor, whereas a danger refers to something beyond the scope of individual influence. However, as argued above, what is perceived as a risk or as a danger varies. Furthermore, it can be said that a thunderstorm may be a danger, but it is a risk to walk over an open plain during a thunderstorm or when a thunderstorm is expected.

Because active labor market policy focuses directly on improving "employability" (to use the EU jargon) or creating employment, it implies an individualization as it depends on how individuals do or do not make use of job offers, job qualifications, and job creation schemes and so forth.[4]

The situation for public old age pension policy is different from unemployment and labor market policy. It addresses not only the (collective) security of living beyond a certain age for older people in society but also for younger people, because they have an interest in having secure prospects for the later stages of their lives.

The profile of an active labor market policy implies that (key) policy makers can point to the individual use (or nonuse) of policy instruments available for (re)integration into the employment system that may reduce political demands to do more. In the case of public pension policy, arrangements have to be made which include collective entitlements to withdraw from the labor market. However, the importance of a fixed retirement age depends on a politically secured level of income enabling those reaching this age (as a social group) actually to withdraw from the labor market.

Therefore, differences in specific policy sectors do not only result from the fact that some problems just affect some (i.e., that some problems are socially selective) and other problems affect everyone but also from individualizing and collective policy effects. These two dimensions, through the different responses by citizens and policy makers, lead to further specific features of the politics of the policy making process.

4.3 Predictability

The predictability of both the development of the societal environment of the political system, as well as of the effects of political decisions or interventions, are crucial issues for politics which differ by policy sectors.

The predictability of the effects of political decisions is related to the range of choices available. As more options become available, the effects of political decisions are harder to predict and the more contested the debate becomes on how to solve a problem. This becomes clear when looking at the political debates on how to combat unemployment. The more diagnosis about the reasons for unemployment and measures to solve this problem are not only manifold but also contradictory, the more the predictability of the outcomes of certain programs is questioned from the very beginning.

However, looking at labor market and employment policy further, policy sector-related particularities linked to predictability of policy outcomes can be clarified. In the case of active labor market policy, the effects of political decisions on the labor market are relatively easy to predict because they are directly linked to employment or training offers for specific (groups of) persons and can directly decrease the number of unemployed. Such a decrease is quantitatively predictable. In the case of employment policy, i.e., a policy aimed at reducing unemployment indirectly through an increase in public demand/spending, the financial support of private investment or a reduction in the working week/month the circumstances are different because the effects of such measures on the labor market depend on spillovers and the behavioral responses of independent (economic) agents, which can hardly be influenced politically. For instance, a reduction in working hours per week does not necessarily imply that the workforce will increase proportionately.

Even more clear is predictability in public (old age) pension policy. In this case, using known demographic structures and actuarial calculations, it is statistically simple to measure the future financial consequences of a new regulation.

---

4. Furthermore, the majority of unemployed people do not see unemployment as a problem determining their lives but as a transitory phenomenon.

4.4 Interdependencies and Policy Boundaries

In the case of labor market policy, further fundamental challenges appear, reflecting some of the characteristics of policy-politics interdependencies. On the one hand, effects and feedbacks from other policy sectors are harder to assess than in other areas—for example, public pension policy. This is due to the fact that labor market policy does not have clear boundaries. Instead, it is characterized by shifting boundaries in relation to education, early retirement, (urban) regeneration, or family policy. On the other hand, dependency on economic development is more striking than in the case of public pension policy. For the latter, benefit demands are predictable against the background of a more or less stable demographic development, and pension policy is dependent on economic development only on the income side and not additionally in the short term on the spending side, as in the case of labor market policy.

Interdependencies and shifting boundaries of a policy imply more than uncertainty in policy processes in respect to predicting, planning, and taking decisions. Shifting policy boundaries are also associated with an actor constellation being many layered, many faceted, fragile, and muddled. Actors may enter or leave the arena; new linkages may evolve, loosen or even get cut; policy objectives may move, be newly established, or even abolished. Whereas this applies particularly to policy sectors like the labor market, public pension policy is an example of a policy sector in which the involvement of actors is relatively stable and the dominant policy objectives do not shift.

However, in some respects the impact of shifting policy boundaries and interdependencies can also be ambiguous. Linking a policy sector with others can strengthen it in respect to agenda setting, allocation of funding, etc. But the other side of the coin is that the more there are interlinkages with other policy sectors and the more a variety of actors are involved, the bigger the danger of blurred policy objectives that can, in turn, negatively impact agenda setting, allocation of funding, and the like. Which situation applies depends on (as discussed in section 3) the perception of problems and the definition of what a policy is or should be about, and this is the result of the objectives and interests of actors. But this is connected with a certain institutional context and a particular "feasible set" at a given point in time (see, as an example, the development of housing policy in Germany; Egner et al. 2004).

5 "POLICY INSTITUTIONS"

To exploit the explanatory potential of the just described framework for distinguishing and clarifying policy-politics relations within policy sectors against the background of John and Cole's (2000) definition of "policy institutions" as well as the ideas of Benz (1997) inspired by an actor-centered institutionalism, mentioned before the following seems to be appropriate.

One should start from the distinctiveness of problems to be addressed in a policy sector and the particularities of effects linked to it. To do this the dimensions developed for distinguishing policy-politics offer guidance. Building on these dimensions, specific institutional settings (including their formal and informal rules) of policy sectors to be found in individual countries (or even at subnational level) and at certain points in times should be scrutinized. Through such an empirical approach, historically specific features of policy sectors will emerge, as will the relevance of core patterns of actor constellations over time and variation between countries and cities. Such constellations can be seen as *sector-specific* patterns of *policy networks* comprising of particular executive, legislative and societal organizations or actors typically involved in the development, decision making and implementation of a particular policy. Therefore, policy sectors can differ over time and by country or city, but attention should be paid to specific policy networks characteristic of a particular policy sector (for overviews about different typologies of policy networks see Jorden and Schubert, 1992; Waarden, 1992).

For instance, the kind of actors involved, as well as their constellation or the linkages between them, can differ with respect to centralization or decentralization of implementation as a result of the particular problem to be addressed (see public pension policy and social services above). Furthermore, the kind of actors clearly differs when looking at local level policies aiming at economic competitiveness or social inclusion (see Klausen and Sweeting 2005) because in the one case a limited number of highly resourced economic and public actors are involved, whereas in the other a multitude of societal actors are usually integrated beside different public ones. In these two policy sectors the ways the actors are interacting or taking decisions are strikingly different, which has without any doubt effects on how policy is made (by majority, hierarchy, bargaining, or arguing; see Klausen et al. 2005). In the field of economic competitiveness, the participation of highly resourced economic actors is decisive to achieve policy objectives and the relevance of majoritarian decision making by a representative body and hierarchical interventions by public administration officials is limited because the economic actors should not feel frustrated. Instead bargaining plays a crucial role. In the sector of social inclusion societal actors (e.g. from the voluntary sector) have limited opportunities for negotiating with public authorities. Instead, they have to convince them by "good reasons" or public argument, and majoritarian decision by a representative body and hierarchical interventions by public servants are usually crucial for redistributing financial resources, and defining and securing the claims of single individuals as well as of groups, such as disabled people.

The institutional setting embedded in policy sectors, i.e., "policy institutions" goes beyond actor constellations or policy networks, although there is a link between institutions determining a "feasible set" of choices for actors and actors reproducing and reshaping institutional imperatives.

The explanatory value of the notion of "policy institutions" is clarified by the following examples (see Heinelt and Meinke-Brandmeier 2005). Environment protection is usually characterized as a regulatory policy, but it can also rely on financial incentives or support and therefore on redistributive or distributive policies. When it comes to the application of regulatory rules hierarchical decisions by public authorities (by planning acceptances or rejections) are crucial. Additionally, the approval or rejection of hierarchical decisions can play a role. Both can be perceived as "policy institutions" determining the course of policy making in the phase of implementation of environment protection. These *sector-specific* "policy institutions" in the phase of implementation of environment protection differ from those in consumer protection, although the latter is also primarily a regulatory policy relying (as in the case of environment protection) on financial incentives or support. Consumer protection regulates relations between producer, customer, and standards of food safety. It employs therefore prescriptions subject to legal review by courts. However, a main policy instrument for food safety is labeling. This leaves the decision of buying or not buying a certain commodity (e.g., genetically modified products) to the customer, and the institution through which individual consumer choices might lead to a particular outcome (production or availability of a certain commodity) is the market or its so-called "invisible hand."

The consequences of these two "policy institutions"—public administrations intervening (together with courts) hierarchically in society in the one case and guidance and control through the invisible hand of the market in the other—for politics are obvious—for example, looking at room for political maneuvering for civil society. Whereas environment groups see themselves in an unfavorable situation because they are forced to transform their ecological reasoning into a legal argument and mount protests (which do not usually impress public administrations or courts), consumer protection groups are in a better position because they can try to influence consumer choices by public reason and persuasion—the heart of their repertoire of political actions (for more detail, see Heinelt and Meinke-Brandmeier 2005).

If we take particular institutional setting and policy-specific networks in the way outlined above, then Lowi's thesis "policies determine politics" makes sense insofar as characteristics of policy processes can be related to institutional settings and actor constellations typically involved in the development, the decision making, and implementation of a particular policy.

6 CONCLUSION

To realize what Lowi's thesis intended, namely to offer a basis for the development of a "policy theory" by a typology of policy-related structural features, three points are crucial. First, Lowi's orientation to policy choices and its focus on microanalysis has to be broadened by reflections on a macro level. Second, the systematic distinction of perceived problems as well as policy outcomes has to be taken further. The reflections on different dimensions for distinguishing policy-politics relations (see section 4) offer some progress in this respect. Third, specific "policy institutions," i.e., "a particular policy arena [with] a [certain] set of formal and informal rules that determine the course of public decision making" (John and Cole 2000, 249), should be analyzed to answer the question why they allow for policy processes with certain characteristics—and not for others. Although such an analysis would be empirical and historically oriented, options for generalization are not impossible per se. On the contrary, options for generalization are mostly available and should be more strongly used.

REFERENCES

Benz, A. (1997). Policies als erklärende Variable in der politischen Theorie. In A. Benz & W. Seibel (Eds.), *Theorieentwicklung in der Politikwissenschaft – eine Zwischenbilanz* (pp. 303–322). Baden-Baden: Nomos.

Cebulla, A. (2000). The final instance - Unemployment Insurance going private? A study of a future social security scenario in the UK and Germany. *Innovation*, 13, 389–400.

Easton, D. (1965). *A Systems Analysis of Political Life*. New York/London: John Wiley.

Egner, B., Georgakis, N., Heinelt, H., & Bartholoäi, R. (2004). *Wohnngspolitik in Deutschland*. Darmstadt: Schader-Foundation.

Finn, D. (2000). Welfare to Work. *Journal of European Social Policy*, 10, 43–57.

Haus, M., Heinelt, H., & Stewart, M. (Eds.) (2005). *Urban Governance and Democracy. Leadership and Community Involvement*. London: Routledge.

Heidenheimer, A., Heclo, H., & Adams, C. (1975[1]) and (1990[3]) *Comparative Public Policy. The Politics of Social Choice in America, Europe and Japan*. 1st edition New York: St. Martin's Press and 3rd edition Basingstoke: Mcmillan.

Heinelt, H. (1992). Local Labour Market Policy—Limits and Potentials, in: *International Journal of Urban and Regional Research*, 4, 522–528.

Heinelt, H. (1996). Multilevel Governance in the European Union and the Structural Funds. In H. Heinelt & R. Smith (Eds.), *Policy Networks and European Structural Funds* (pp. 9–25). Aldershot: Avebury.

Heinelt, H. (2003). Arbeitsmarktpolitik—von "versorgenden" wohlfahrtsstaatlichen Interventionen zur "aktivierenden" Beschäftigungsförderung. In A. Gohr and M. Seeleib-Kaiser (Eds.), *Sozialpolitik unter Rot-Grün* (pp. 125–146). Wiesbaden: Westdeutscher Verlag.

Heinelt, H., & Meinke-Brandmeier, B. (2005). Comparing Civil Society Participation in European Environmental Policy and Consumer Protection. In St. Smismans (Ed.), *Civil Society and Legitimate European Governance*, Edward Elgar (forthcoming).

Héritier, A. (1993). Policy-Analyse. Elemente der Kritik und Perspektiven der Neuorientierung. In A. Héritier (Ed.), *Policy-Analyse. Kritik und Neuorientierung* (pp. 9–36). Opladen: Westdeutscher Verlag.

John, P., & Cole, A. (2000). When do Institutions, Policy Sectors, and Cities Matter? Comparing Networks of Local Policy Makers in Britain and France. *Comparative Political Studies*, 33, 248–268.

Jordan, G., & Schubert, K. (1992). A Preliminary Ordering of Policy Network Labels. *European Journal of Political Research*, 21, 7–27.

Klausen, J.E., & Sweeting, D. (2005). Legitimacy and community involvement in local governance. In M. Haus, H. Heinelt & M. Stewart (Eds.), *Urban Governance and Democracy* (pp. 214–233). London: Routledge.

Klausen, J.E., Sweeting, D., & Howard, J., (2005). Community involvement, urban leadership and legitimacy. An empirical analysis. In H. Heinelt, P. Getimis & D. Sweeting (Eds.), *Legitimacy and Urban Governance: A Cross-National Comparative Study*. London: Routledge (forthcoming).

Lowi, T. (1972). Four Systems of Policy, Politics and Choice. *Public Administration Review* 33, 298–310.

Lowi, T. (1964). American Business, Public Policy, Case Studies and Political Theory. *World Politics,* 16, 677–715.

Luhmann, N. (1991). *Soziologie des Risikos*. Berlin/New York: de Gruyter.

Luhmann, N. (1993). Risiko und Gefahr. In W. Krohn & G. Krücken (Eds.), *Riskante Technologien—Reflexion und Regulation. Einführung in die sozialwissenschaftliche Risikoforschung* (pp. 138–185). Frankfurt a.M.: Suhrkamp.

Majone, G. (1994). The Rise of the Regulatory State in Europe. *West European Politics*, 17, 131–156.

Mayntz, R. (1982). Problemverarbeitung durch das politisch-administrative System. Zum Stand der Forschung. In J.J. Hesse (Ed.): *Politikwissenschaft und Verwaltungswissenschaft* (pp. 74–89). Opladen: Westdeutscher Verlag.

Mazzeo, C. (1997). From Policy Change to Institutional Change. Persistence Change and Policy Frameworks. Paper presented at the annual meeting of the American Political Science Association, Washingten, D.C.

Nicholson, N. (2002). Policy Choices and the Use of State Power, The work of Theodore J. Lowi. *Policy Sciences*, 35, 163–177.

Schmid, G., Reissert, B., & Bruche, G. (1992). *Unemployment Insurance and Active Labor Market Policy. An International Comparison of Financing Systems*. Detroit: Wayne State University Press.

Waarden, F. van (1992). Dimensions and Types of Policy Networks. *European Journal of Political Research*, 21, 29–52.

Windhoff-Héritier, A. (1983). Policy und Politics. Wege und Irrwege einer politikwissenschaftlichen Policy-Theorie. *Politische Vierteljahresschrift*, 24, 347–360.

Windhoff-Héritier, A. (1987) *Policy-Analyse. Eine Einführung*. Frankfurt/New York: Campus.

Part III

Policy Politics, Advocacy, and Expertise

9 A Guide to the Advocacy Coalition Framework

Christopher M. Weible and Paul A. Sabatier

The Advocacy Coalition Framework (ACF) is a policymaking framework developed to deal with intense public policy problems (Sabatier and Jenkins-Smith 1988, 1993, 1999). It is best served as a lens to understand and explain belief and policy change when there is goal disagreement and technical disputes involving multiple actors from several levels of government, interests groups, research institutions, and the media (Hoppe and Peterse 1993). The ACF has proven to be one of the more useful public policy frameworks (Schlager 1995; Schlager and Blomquist 1996; Johns 2003).

Since the ACF's inception in 1988, there have been dozens of ACF case studies and publications. Recent examples are listed in Table 9.1.[1] Most applications deal with energy and environmental policy in the United States, Canada, and Europe (e.g., air pollution, marine/coastal policy, water policy, oil/minerals, and climate change). But researchers have increasingly applied the ACF to policy areas outside of energy and environmental policy (e.g., domestic violence, drug policy, and public heath). There has also been an increase in the number of researchers applying the ACF to issues in Asia, Africa, Australia, and South America.

Despite the worldwide applications of the ACF in a variety of policy areas, we are observing a need for a more digestible version of the ACF for public and private managers.[1] This chapter provides a field guide to the ACF. It is written for people without a strong public policy or political science background who are interested in formally and informally applying the ACF to think criti-

TABLE 9.1
Recent Examples of ACF Applications

Author	Year	Geographic Scope	Substantive Topic
		Applications by ACF Authors and Students	
Herron and Jenkins-Smith	2002	U.S.	Nuclear security
Zafonte and Sabatier	2004	U.S.	Air pollution
Weible and Sabatier	2005	U.S.	Marine protected areas
Leach and Sabatier	2005	U.S.	Watershed partnerships
		Applications by Other Researchers	
Jordan and Greenaway	1998	U.K.	Coastal water policy
Sato	1999	Japan	Smoking control
Abrar, Lovenduski, and Margetts	2000	U.K.	Domestic violence
Liftin	2000	Canada	Climate change policy
Carvalho	2001	Brazil	Metallurgical development
Kübler	2001	Switzerland	Drug policy
Bryant	2002	Canada	Public health
Chen	2003	Australia	Censorship
Farquharson	2003	Global	Tobacco policy
Kim	2003	Korea	Water policy
Beverwijks	2004	Mozambique	Education policy
Green and Haulihan	2004	Canada and U.K.	Sport policy
Sewell	2005	U.S., the Netherlands, and Japan	Climate change policy

cally about, or to help understand and explain, policy processes. In doing so, we describe a trimmed down version of the ACF, notably overlooking discussion of the hypotheses and revisions. More detailed descriptions of the ACF can be found in Sabatier and Jenkins-Smith (1988; 1993; 1999).

We begin by explaining the components in the ACF flow diagram (Figure 9.1) and then explain how these components interact to affect belief and policy change. One of the best ways to understand, learn, and use the ACF is through an application. To help explain the ACF, we utilize a case study of water quality policy in the Lake Tahoe Basin where we have applied the ACF to help understand more than 30 years of belief and policy change (Sabatier, Hunter, and McLaughlin 1987; Sabatier and Hunter 1989; Sabatier and Pelkey 1990; Sabatier and Brasher, 1993; Sabatier, Weible, Hulsman, and Nechodom 2003; Weible and Sabatier 2004). We conclude this chapter with a summary of the ACF's strengths and limitations.

STRUCTURE OF THE ACF

Figure 9.1 shows a structural diagram of the ACF (Sabatier and Jenkins-Smith 1999). Generally, policymaking occurs in a policy subsystem, which is a policy area that is geographically bounded and encompasses policy participants from all levels of government, multiple interests groups, re-

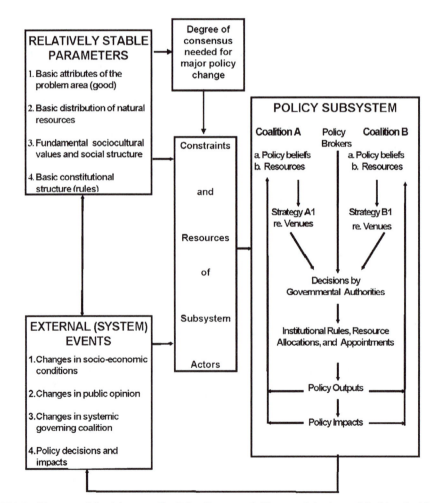

FIGURE 9.1 Diagram of the Advocacy Coalition Framework (Source: Sabatier and Jenkins-Smith, 1999).

TABLE 9.2
Summary of Application of the ACF Applied to the Lake Tahoe Basin

ACF Component	Lake Tahoe Water Quality Application
Relatively Stable Parameters	
Basic Attribute of the Problem Area	Deep and clear lake
Basic distribution of natural resources	Dispute of land use in the Lake Tahoe Basin
Fundamental cultural values and social structure	Property rights and environmental values
Basic constitutional structure	Fragmented governance including the federal agencies, two states, and five local governments.
Policy Subsystem	
Territorial Scope	Lake Tahoe Basin
Substantive Scope	Water quality policy
Policy Participants	U.S. Environmental Protection Agency, CA Department of Parks and Recreation, Tahoe Regional Planning Agency, city and county governments, businesses (e.g., casinos), Sierra Preservation Council (property rights group), League to Save Lake Tahoe (environmental group), university researchers, and *Tahoe Tribune* (local newspaper)
Belief Systems	
Deep Core Beliefs	Neoconservative beliefs
Policy Core Beliefs	Pro-development beliefs
Secondary Beliefs	Specific policy proposals regarding water quality (e.g., prohibiting housing on steep lots)
Advocacy Coalitions	Pro-development vs. Pro-water quality coalitions
Policy Broker	Bill Morgan mitigated consensus in 1987
Resources	Scientific information
Venues	Federal and state courts, state legislatures, regional agency decisions, collaborative institutions
Mechanisms of Policy Change	
Accumulation of Evidence	Science showing declining water quality from 1960s to present and atmospheric deposition as a major cause of nutrient input.
Hurting Stalemate	Political impasse in 1984 led to compromise between coalitions.
External Shock	Growth of the environmental movement 1960s to 1970s

Note: Based on Sabatier and Pelkey (1990), Sabatier, Hunter, and McLaughlin (1993); Sabatier and Brasher (1993), Sabatier et al., (2003), and Weible and Sabatier (2004).

search institutions, and the media. Within a policy subsystem, policy participants coordinate their behavior with allies in advocacy coalitions to influence policy. The policy subsystems are set within, are affected by, and sometime affect, a broader societal context. The ACF groups the broad societal context into two categories: relatively stable parameters and external events. In the space below, we describe the three main components of Figure 9.1. First, we describe the relatively stable parameters, then discuss policy subsystems, and finally describe external events.[2] We summarize the application of the ACF to the Lake Tahoe Basin water quality policy subsystem in Table 9.2.

RELATIVELY STABLE PARAMETERS

The upper left box of Figure 9.1 lists a set of relatively stable parameters: (1) basic attributes of the problem area, (2) basic distribution of natural resources, (3) fundamental socio-cultural values and social structure, and (4) basic constitutional structure (Sabatier and Jenkins-Smith, 1993; 1999). The relatively stable parameters are stable over long periods of time, approximately 100 years or more. They are important because they structure the nature of the problem, constrain the resources available to policy participants, establish the rules and procedures for changing policy and reaching collective decisions, and broadly frame the values that inform policymaking. Because of their resistance to change, the relatively stable parameters are usually not strategically targeted by policy participants.

In the context of our case study, the basic attribute of the Lake Tahoe Basin is a very unique geological setting. The Lake Tahoe Basin has a predominately granite basin (covering 70 percent of the watershed), which limits the amount of nutrients leached into the water. Since the Lake's surface area is rather large compared to the watershed, Lake Tahoe receives 40 percent of its precipitation directly from rainfall. Lake Tahoe's unique geological condition has created one of the largest and clearest lakes in the world. The geological conditions also make the Lake susceptible to nutrient input from changes in the land use, which potentially darkens Lake Tahoe's clear waters.

The basic distribution of Tahoe's water is not disputed, but land use in the Basin is. From the 1850s to the early 1900s, the first Euro-American explorers mined and forested the Basin. The economy shifted to summer tourism in the early twentieth century and then to year-round tourism in the 1960s after a major highway made the area more assessable and after the 1964 Winter Olympics brought notoriety to the Basin. The number of residents and tourists boomed in the Basin (Kauneckis, Koziol, and Imperial 2000; Elliot-Fisk et al. 1996).[3] While many small lots were developed, many more were bought with the expectation of building primary and secondary homes in the future (Sabatier and Pelkey 1990). It was at this time that scientists started to monitor Lake Tahoe water quality, recording gradual declines in clarity (Jassby et al. 2001).

The Lake Tahoe Basin is set within a very diverse U.S. social-cultural landscape. To generalize, the U.S. culture is based on the fundamental beliefs of limited government and of the protection of personal liberties, especially regarding private property rights. Like many societies, the U.S. grapples with the clash between individual rights versus the public interest (Stone 1997). This clash is evident in the Tahoe Basin where pristine, clear waters are open to public use and enjoyment while the thousands of privately owned, subdivided lots are, or are ready to be, developed.

The constitutional structure framing the governance of the Lake Tahoe Basin is complex. Straddling California and Nevada within the United States, the jurisdiction is shared within a federal system under the constitutions of two state governments and the federal government. At the local level, authority is granted to five counties (Washoe, Douglas, Ormsby/Carson City, El Dorado, and Placer) and one incorporated city (South Lake Tahoe). The shared jurisdiction makes it very difficult to reach collective decisions in the Basin and makes a supermajority a necessity for policy making. To address the fragmented decision making in the Basin, policymakers established a regional agency in 1960s to coordinate policymaking (Sabatier and Pelkey 1990).

POLICY SUBSYSTEM

The relatively stable parameters frame the policymaking process within a policy subsystem (Sabatier and Jenkins-Smith 1999). A policy subsystem is defined by its territorial boundary, a substantive topic, and by the hundreds of policy participants from all levels of government, multiple interest groups, the media, and research institutions.[4] To influence policy, policy participants both specialize in a policy subsystem to effectively achieve their objectives and maintain their participation over long periods of time to ensure their objectives are achieved (Sabatier and Jenkins-Smith 1993).

For the Lake Tahoe water quality policy subsystem, the geographic boundary is enclosed by the Lake Tahoe watershed and substantively bounded by water quality policy—indirectly including land use and development in the Basin. The Lake Tahoe Basin involves hundreds of policy participants, who seek to influence water quality policy decisions. The policy participants include federal agencies (e.g., U.S. Environmental Protection Agency), state agencies (e.g., California Department of Parks and Recreation), regional agencies (e.g., Tahoe Regional Planning Agency), local governments (e.g., city and county governments), businesses (e.g., casinos), property rights groups (e.g., Tahoe-Sierra Preservation Council), environmental groups (e.g., League to Save Lake

Tahoe), researchers (e.g., University of California, Davis and University of Reno, Nevada), and journalists (e.g., *Tahoe Tribune*). We have found that some policy participants have been involved in Lake Tahoe water quality policy for more than 30 years.

Sometimes it is difficult to define the geographic and substantive boundaries of a policy subsystem because some policy subsystems are nested within broader policy subsystems and because some policy participants are active in more than one policy subsystem. For example, Lake Tahoe water quality policy subsystem is nested within both state (i.e., California and Nevada) and federal water policy subsystems (Sabatier and Jenkins-Smith 1999). There is no single rule for defining policy subsystems. This flexibility gives the ACF applicability but makes it hard to apply. We suggest that policy subsystem boundaries be ascertained empirically. For most cases, we recommend that ACF applicators identify the appropriate policy subsystem scope by conducting preliminary interviews of policy participants and asking them to identify the territorial and substantive boundary of the issue and the major interest groups and government agencies involved.

Within a policy subsystem, the ACF makes several assumptions and hypotheses regarding (1) the cognitive abilities, motivations, and beliefs of policy participants (called the "model of the individual"), (2) the tendency for most policy participants to join advocacy coalitions, (3) the likelihood that few policy participants remain neutral as policy brokers, (4) the use of resources by coalitions, and (5) the venues within which coalitions influence policy. In the subsections that follow, we describe these assumptions and hypotheses.

Model of the Individual

The ACF presumes that individuals are rationally motivated but are bounded by their imperfect cognitive ability to learn about, and comprehend, a complex world (Simon 1985). Having cognitive constraints, individuals are limited by their capacity to acquire and learn new information. To simplify events and the world around them, ACF individuals filter perceptions through their belief system (Lord, Ross, and Lepper 1979; Scholz and Pinney 1995). They tend to filter or ignore information that challenges their beliefs and readily accept information that bolsters their beliefs. These perceptual filters tend to discount even high-quality technical information if it conflicts with their beliefs and accept technical information with high uncertainty if it supports their beliefs. People viscerally associate themselves with their beliefs, making them very suspicious of people with dissimilar beliefs. They also remember lost policy battles—which they internalize as a painful personal loss—more than previous victories (Quattrone and Tversky 1988). This increases their emotional fear of their opponents, bypassing more rational thinking (McDermott 2004). This makes individuals highly susceptible to exaggerating the influence and maliciousness of their opponents, which in turn strengthens their ties with others who have similar beliefs (Sabatier et al. 1987; Sabatier and Jenkins-Smith 1999). In sum, the ACF's model of the individual motivates policy participants to seek out like-minded allies and form advocacy coalitions (see below).

The ACF assumes that individuals have a three-tiered hierarchical belief system. On the top tier are deep core beliefs, which are normative/fundamental beliefs that span multiple policy subsystems and are very resistant to change. Sabatier and Jenkins-Smith (1999) define four components of deep core beliefs that span from relative value priorities (e.g., individual rights vs. social rights) to socio-cultural identify (e.g., ethnicity and religion).[5]

In the middle tier are policy core beliefs, which are normative/empirical beliefs that span an entire policy subsystem. Policy core beliefs are still resistant to change but are more pliable than deep core beliefs. The ACF identifies eleven categories of policy core beliefs, including perceptions of the severity and causes of subsystem-wide problems, orientation on basic value priorities directly related to the policy subsystem, the effectiveness of policy instruments, and the proper distribution of authority between the market and government (Sabatier and Jenkins-Smith 1999).[6]

We found the best way to operationalize policy core beliefs is through preliminary interviews with policy participants. We typically ask policy participants to comment on the seriousness of a problem, their perceptions of the causes of the problem, or their preferences for resolving a problem. We find that policy participants often have short 10 to 20 second statements that summarize their beliefs regarding a particular policy issue. We take their narrative responses and use them—often word for word—as our policy core belief questions in a survey.

On the lowest tier are secondary beliefs, which are empirical beliefs and policy preferences that relate to a subcomponent (either substantively or territorially) of a policy subsystem. Secondary beliefs include policy participants' preferences for specific government tools for achieving objectives or their perceptions of problems in specific locales.[7] Of the three layers of beliefs, secondary beliefs are most susceptible to change in response to new information and events.

Advocacy Coalitions

The success of policy participants depends upon their ability to translate their policy core beliefs into actual policy. To increase their chances for success, policy participants seek out allies with similar policy core beliefs and coordinate their actions with these allies in advocacy coalitions. Thus, advocacy coalitions include policy participants that both (1) share similar policy core beliefs and (2) engage in nontrivial degree of coordination (Sabatier and Jenkins-Smith 1999).[8]

In the Lake Tahoe Basin, we found evidence of at least two advocacy coalitions (Sabatier et al. 1987; Sabatier and Brasher 1993; Sabatier et al. 2003).[9] One coalition is a pro-development advocacy coalition consisting of developers, business owners, property rights groups, and local governments. The second coalition is a pro-water quality advocacy coalition consisting of environmental groups, research institutions, and regional, state, and federal agencies. Our data suggests that these two advocacy coalitions have been fighting over the land use and environmental protection since the early 1970s when the first regional plan for the management of the Basin was developed (Costantini and Hanf 1972; Sabatier et al. 2003). Conflict between these coalitions escalated for more than a decade, peaking in 1984 when members of both coalitions filed lawsuits after a new regional management plan was adopted. In June 1984, a court order enjoined all construction to stop in the Basin until an acceptable plan was put into affect. This moratorium put the pro-water quality coalition in control, but only temporarily. In response, the 1985 Nevada Legislature threatened to withdraw that state from the bi-state compact with California, which would have thrown water quality regulation in the Basin into utter chaos (Sabatier and Pelkey 1990; Elliot-Fisk et al. 1996; Kauneckis et al. 2000). This ushered in a period that the ACF calls a "hurting stalemate" (see below), where policy participants on both sides of the issue consider the status quo unacceptable and perceive no alternate venues for achieving their objectives (Sabatier and Jenkins-Smith 1999).

Policy Brokers

In a policy subsystem, most policy participants coordinate with allies in advocacy coalitions and work together to translate their beliefs into policy. In competitive policy subsystems, policy disagreements between advocacy coalitions often escalate into intense political conflicts. These conflicts are often mediated by "policy brokers." Whereas most policy participants seek to influence policy processes and outcomes in advocacy coalitions, policy brokers seek to find reasonable compromise among hostile coalitions. Many different actors play the policy broker role. Policy brokers include elected officials (Munro 1993), high civil servants (Doggan 1975), and courts (Mawinney 1993). Policy brokers are usually trusted by both coalitions and have some decision making authority. There is a thin line between policy brokers and policy activists. Sometimes policy activists, concerned about the maintenance and survival of a policy subsystem, will seek to act as a policy broker. Other times, a facilitator is hired from outside the policy subsystem to be the policy broker.

After more than 15 years of political conflict in the Lake Tahoe Basin and during a hurting stalemate between the pro-development coalition and the pro-water quality coalition, a compromise was brokered in 1986/87 by Bill Morgan (Sabatier and Pelkey 1990). Bill Morgan was an executive director of a regional planning agency. Because he was trusted by both coalitions, sufficiently knowledgeable about the nature of the problem, and held a position of authority in a regional agency, Bill Morgan was in a unique position to be a policy broker. He brokered a compromise between the coalitions, which included a new parcel evaluation system, several lot acquisition programs, a right of all property owners to build eventually, a housing allocation system, and several programs for transferable development rights (Sabatier and Pelkey 1990). This compromise is still in effect today.

Resources

The ACF assumes that individuals employ a variety of resources that enable them to develop strategies to influence policy through a variety of venues. These resources include: (1) formal legal authority to make decisions, (2) public opinion, (3) information, (4) mobilizable troops, (5) financial resources, and (6) skillful leadership (Sabatier and Weible 2005). The ACF predicts that stakeholders will strategically use their resources to influence policy in various venues.[10]

In the Lake Tahoe Basin, one of the important resources, especially for the pro-water quality coalition, was scientific information. For more than 30 years, scientists have been monitoring water quality, and results have shown decreases in water quality levels since the 1960s.

Venues

Venues are potential arenas within which stakeholders have the opportunity to influence beliefs or policy.[11] Stakeholders spend considerable amount of time venue shopping, looking for an arena where they might have competitive advantage. They often launch initiatives in several venues simultaneously and defend their interests in several venues simultaneously. Coalitions attempt to influence the view of decision makers to shape policy processes and outcomes. Coalitions focus their attempt on changing institutional rules, resource allocations, and appointments (Sabatier and Jenkins-Smith 1993). These actions have certain policy outputs and impacts which feedback into the policy subsystem but also affect policy outside of the subsystem.

In the Lake Tahoe Basin, the two coalitions have sought to achieve their objectives in several venues. These venues include the state legislatures in California and Nevada, state and federal courts, agency rulemaking, and the media (Sabatier and Pelkey 1990).

External Events

The lower left box of figure one lists a set of external events that can affect a policy subsystem (Sabatier and Jenkins-Smith 1999): (1) major socioeconomic changes (Eisner 1993), (2) changes in public opinion, (3) changes in the systematic governing coalition (Brady 1988), and (4) policy decisions and impacts from other subsystems (Muller 1995).

External events are important because they often shift public attention (and thus resources) toward or away from a policy subsystem. For example, one of the big shifts in public opinion came in the 1960s and early 1970s with increased public priority for environmental values. This led to a large number of national and state environmental regulatory statutes and grants and the creation of many new environmental policy subsystems.

External events can change very gradually in a decade or so. For example, the gradual rise of the national environmental movement in the 1960s and 1970s most likely affected the rise in public concern for Lake Tahoe water quality at about the same time. External events can also shock a policy system. For examples, severe forest fires outside of the Tahoe Basin have affected policy participants' beliefs and water quality policy within the Basin (Weible, Sabatier, and Nechodom 2005).

BELIEF AND POLICY CHANGE

The ACF distinguishes between major and minor policy change.[12] Major policy change is subsystem-wide alterations of policy (changes in policy core aspects of the subsystem). The ACF defines minor policy changes as changes of a specific subcomponent of the policy subsystem (changes in secondary aspects of the policy subsystem). Minor policy changes occur more frequently and have a smaller magnitude in either the substantive or territorial scope of a policy subsystem.

The ACF defines three mechanisms leading to minor or major policy change: (1) external shocks, (2) a hurting stalemate, and (3) the general accumulation of scientific/technical evidence (Sabatier and Jenkins-Smith 1999).

External shocks are events that occur outside of a policy subsystem, e.g., changes in socioeconomic conditions, changes in governing coalitions, and impacts from other subsystems (Sabatier and Jenkins-Smith 1999). External shocks can lead to policy change in at least two ways. First, external shocks might shift resources or open/close venues because of renewed attention of the public or key decision makers. This adjusts the power among coalitions, thereby tipping the advantage to a different coalition with different policy core beliefs and potentially leading to major policy change. In other words, external shocks can replace one dominant advocacy coalition within another (Sabatier and Jenkins-Smith 1999, 148). Second, external shocks can change the policy core beliefs of a dominant advocacy coalition in the policy subsystem, leading to major policy change. For example, a pro-regulatory advocacy coalition may reconsider the adverse economic effects from stringent controls during an economic recession.

A second mechanism of policy change is through belief change via policy-oriented learning from the gradual accumulation of information, such as a scientific study, policy analysis, etc. (Weiss 1977). The ACF defines policy-oriented learning as, "relatively enduring alterations of thought or behavioral intentions that result from experience and/or new information that are concerned with the attainment or revision of policy objectives" (Sabatier and Jenkins-Smith 1999, 123). Policy-oriented learning affects the beliefs of actors within the policy subsystem, which can lead to minor and even major policy change over extended time periods. Learning is inhibited, however, because individuals face cognitive constraints and filter or avoid belief-conflicting information. Whereas external shocks can lead to rapid changes in individual policy core beliefs and, consequently, the policy core aspects of a policy subsystem, policy oriented learning may take ten years or more.

A third mechanism of policy change is a hurting stalemate (Zartman 1991). The basic precondition to successful negotiations is a situation in which all parties involved in the dispute view a continuation of the status quo as unacceptable and run out of alternate venues to achieve their objectives. The assumption is that individuals satisfied with the status quo have little incentive to give up anything in negotiations; thus, negotiating with them is probably a waste of time. Only when both coalitions are out of options and dissatisfied with the current situation are they willing to compromise and negotiate major policy change.

In the Lake Tahoe Basin, we have found three major changes in beliefs or policy that illustrate the ACF's three mechanisms of change.

The first major policy change in the Basin occurred in the late 1960s early 1970s with the creation of a regional agency and a general plan for management in the Basin (Sabatier and Pelkey 1990). This established standards, rules and procedures for water quality management in the Basin and formed the Lake Tahoe water quality policy subsystem. While pinpointing the exact cause is impossible, we hypothesize that the cause of this policy change springs from at least three major sources. First, there were changes in public opinion related to increased public priority of environmental values and especially increased awareness of Lake Tahoe water brought about by the winter Olympics and a major highway, making the area more assessable. Second, there were changes in socioeconomic conditions from major influx of residents and tourists in the Basin in the 1960s, which brought more environmental stress to the Basin and raised the need for coordinated collective action decisions. Third, there was a scientific report that sewage (e.g., leaky septic tanks) was a major threat to the Lake Tahoe's water quality (McGauhey et al. 1963). The multiple governments in the area responded with a new system that collected and exported all sewage out of the Basin by 1975. This also raised the collective need for regional governing agency (Sabatier and Pelkey 1990). The Basin's response to sewage is clearly an example of policy-oriented learning in response to technical information.

The second big change in Lake Tahoe water quality policy came in the 1986/87 compromise between the pro-development advocacy coalition and the pro-water quality advocacy coalition. As discussed above, the two competing advocacy coalitions were experiencing a "hurting stalemate" after a judge halted all building in the Basin and Nevada threatened to pull out of a bi-state compact with California. Since both coalitions perceived the status quo as unacceptable and ran out of venues to achieve their objectives, a compromise was possible. In 1986/87, Morgan brokered a new management plan between the two advocacy coalitions, radically altering future land use management in the Basin.

A third major change in the Basin involved shifts in beliefs regarding the seriousness and causes of the severity of water quality declines. We already discussed the Basin's response to sewage in the 1960s, which suggests that policy participants learned from a scientific report and decided to pump sewage out of the Basin. Basin scientists have also collected more than 30 years of evidence showing declines in water clarity (Jassby et al. 2001). Our research shows that the pro-development coalition radically shifted their perception of the severity of water quality declines between 1984 and 2001 (Sabatier et al. 2003; Weible and Sabatier 2004). Between 1984 and 2001, Basin scientists also found that atmospheric deposition was a major source of nutrient input (Jassby et al. 1995). Paralleling this discover, we found most coalition members are more likely to perceive atmospheric deposition as a major cause of nutrient input in 1984 than in 2001 (Weible and Sabatier 2004).[13]

CONCLUSIONS

We have found that the ACF has provided a good lens for understanding belief and policy change in the Lake Tahoe Basin. In addition, the extensive use of the ACF around the world in a variety of policy subsystems suggests that it has utility beyond Lake Tahoe water quality policy. To summarize the usefulness of the ACF, we conclude this chapter with a discussion of its strengths and limitations.

STRENGTHS

1. The ACF provides an alternate lens to de facto policymaking frameworks. Traditionally, the policy process has been based on *stages heuristic*, which sequentially distinguishes between problem identification, agenda setting, adoption, implementation, monitoring, and enforcement (Lasswell 1951).[14] The ACF is a healthy alternative to the stages heuristic because it has clear causal assumptions, empirically testable hypothesis, an explicit role of information, an explicit model of the individual, and multiple interaction cycles involving hundreds of actors (Sabatier and

Jenkins-Smith 1993). The ACF is also a good comparative lens to the Institutional Analysis and Development Framework (IADF; Ostrom 1990, 1999). Whereas the ACF assumes that public policy is the translation of normative and empirical beliefs of competing advocacy coalitions, the IADF assumes that public policy (i.e., institutions) result from people's efforts to reduce the transaction costs of collective action. We strongly encourage more comparative analysis using the ACF and IADF (Leach and Sabatier 2005).

2. The ACF highlights the magnitude and the nature of political conflicts. For example, Barke's (1993) study of the conflict involving telecommunication policy in the mid-twentieth century highlighted that—even though the issue involved millions of dollars—the disagreement was over secondary beliefs (e.g., choice of television technology) and not over policy core beliefs (e.g., public vs. private ownership). Thus, the telecommunications disagreement was a low magnitude conflict with a relatively easy path to compromise. The ACF can also reveal weak links in a belief system—such as a faulty causal argument—that is susceptible over long periods of time to change from the accumulation of counterevidence. This may help coalition members or policy brokers strategically achieve their goals or negotiate collective decisions.

3. The ACF provides an alternative view to the de facto assumption that policy participants' institutional affiliation is primordial (Sabatier and Jenkins-Smith 1999). Instead, the ACF encourages researchers to view policymaking as conflicts among advocacy coalitions and provides a different means of aggregating the hundreds of actors attempting to influence policy.

4. The ACF includes a significant role of scientific and technical information in policy and political disputes. Many public policy frameworks ignore the scientific and technical information or assume that researchers, policy analysts, and scientists are neutral players. Over the years, ACF research has shown that scientists often are active members in advocacy coalitions and the important role that technical information has in fostering policy-oriented learning and policy change (Zafonte and Sabatier 1998; Herron, Jenkins-Smith, and Silva 2005).

5. The ACF is very applicable to different governing structures, cultural-societies, and policy areas. Our brief literature review in the beginning of this chapter shows that the ACF has been applied to a wide variety of public policy areas and in many different countries. We expect that researchers will continue to apply and test the ACF in different sociopolitical contexts.

LIMITATIONS

1. The ACF can be difficult to apply. To understand political conflict and policy change, the ACF assumes a perspective of a decade or more and typically involves questionnaire and interview data. This is both time-consuming and costly. If resources are not available, we encourage researchers to conduct quick, qualitative ACF-style analysis of policy subsystems. These might include a few informal interviews and an analysis of documents and reports.

2. The ACF loses some of its utility in policy subsystems without clear coalitions (May, 1989) or with just one dominant advocacy coalition (Stewart 1991). These policy subsystems tend to involve issues of low salience, involving new and often highly technical policy issues that are expert-driven and operate outside the public's eye, or in remote locations. On the flip side, the ACF is most useful in salient issues that incite political conflicts involving hundreds of policy participants representing dozens of public and private organizations in fairly well defined policy subsystems.

3. A long-standing critique of the ACF is that shared beliefs are not enough to overcome the temptation to free ride on the efforts of other coalition members (Schlager 1995; Schlager and Blomquist 1995). Recent ACF research has shown that policy core beliefs explain coordination networks and has provided some qualitative illustrations of coordination (Weible 2005; Weible and Sabatier 2005; Sabatier and Weible 2005). More research is needed, however, to verify these results and to depict what types of activities coalitions engage in.

4. The ACF argues that people primarily use shared policy core beliefs to structure their interactions into advocacy coalitions. Certainly, however, cross-coalition interactions occur. For example, state agency officials may be required to coordinate some of their interactions with commercial fishermen to manage a fishery even if fishermen are members of the opposing coalition (Weible 2005). The ACF has yet to define the minimum amount of coordinated behavior needed to define coalitions, nor the affect of these cross-coalition interactions on policy subsystem outcomes. This is particularly important with the rise of policy network analysis, which shows, for example, that ties to people in different social groups (ties to opposing coalition members) are more valuable than redundant ties to one's own social group (Granovetter 1973; Burt 1992).

5. There are some missing links in the causal processes depicted by the ACF that need additional theoretical and empirical investigation. Two of these missing links include understanding how advocacy coalitions use resources and venues and identifying the factors that structure policy subsystems to favor the existence of one dominate advocacy coalition, two or more competing advocacy coalitions, or no advocacy coalitions. Understanding these missing links is critical for piecing together and testing the subsystem processes of belief and policy change predicted by the ACF. Some of these missing links are being investigated (Sabatier and Weible 2005).

In sum, we hope to have provided a useful guide to the structure of the ACF, a good illustration of its utility in the Lake Tahoe Basin, and a summary of its strengths and limitations. We suspect that additional applications and empirical testing of hypotheses will lead to further refinement and hopefully better explanations of policy processes. We encourage others to partake in these activities.

NOTES

1. For example, the United Nations Educational, Scientific, and Cultural Organization is considering the ACF for one of its social science frameworks to help design sustainability policy (Nechodom 2005)
2. We are currently updating the constraints and resources of a policy subsystem.
3. The permanent population in the Basin grew from less than 20,000 prior to 1960 to 55,000 in 1998 (USDA, 2000, 607–608). From 1960 to 1980, the number of homes in the Basin increased from 500 to 19,000 units, and Tahoe's population reached 60,000 people by the end of the century (Kauneckis et al. 2000; Elliot-Fisk et al. 1996).
4. Following Heclo (1978) and Kingdom (1994), the ACF sets itself apart from traditional conceptions of policy participants (e.g., iron triangles) to include journalists and researchers/scientists.
5. An example of a neoclassical conservative deep core belief scale found in Sabatier and Zafonte (2005) includes the following four statements asked on 7-point scales with 1 = strongly disagree and 7 = strongly agree:
    a. "A first consideration of any good political system is the protection of property rights."
    b. "The best government is the one that governs the least."
    c. "Government planning almost inevitably results in the loss of essential liberties and freedoms."
    d. "The "welfare state" tends to destroy individual initiative."
6. An example of a policy core belief scale for the Lake Tahoe environmental policy subsystem includes the following three statements (asked on 7-point scale with 1 = Strongly Disagree and 7 = Strongly Agree):
    a. "We cannot afford to let policies claiming to promote 'environmental quality' prevent the continued economic development of the Basin."
    b. "Protection of water quality requires that regulations be rigorously enforced, even when they create hardships for property owners. (question reversed on scale)."
    c. "There is too much concern for restricting growth in the Basin and not enough concern for encouraging it."
7. Examples of secondary beliefs that were asked on a recent questionnaire to policy participants in the Lake Tahoe Basin include the following policy proposals (asked on 7-point scale with 1 = Strongly Disagree and 7 = Strongly Agree):
    a. "Sharply increasing the miles of shore line available for public beaches and use."
    b. "Prohibiting all housing development on high hazard lots (i.e., those won steep slopes o in stream environment zones)."
    c. "Banning off-road vehicles (ORVs) from use on public lands in the Basin."

8. Weible and Sabatier (2005) and Weible (2005) used network data to show that policy core beliefs structure coordination networks into at least two advocacy coalitions.
9. A systematic network analysis of the policy participants in the Tahoe Basin is forthcoming.
10. This is one of the areas of the ACF that needs theoretical and empirical refinement.
11. In former versions of the ACF, venues were formally called guidance instrument. This is another area within the ACF that needs theoretical and empirical refinement.
12. The ACF assumes that policies are translations of stakeholder beliefs. The policy core beliefs of a coalition are translated into policy core aspects of a policy subsystem. Similarly, a coalition's secondary beliefs are translated into secondary aspects of a policy subsystem. Just as coalition structure and individual beliefs remain stable for periods of a decade or more so do policies in a subsystem.
13. We have yet connected the belief changes from 1984 to 2001 to policy change.
14. Critiques and a defense of stages heuristic can be found in Sabatier and Jenkins-Smith, (1993) and Deleon (1999), respectively.

REFERENCES

Abrar, S., Lovenduski, J,, and Margetts, H. (2000). Feminist ideas and domestic violence policy change. *Political Studies,* 48, 239–262.

Alford, J.R., and Hibbing, J.R. (2004). The Origin of Politics: An Evolutionary Theory of Political Behavior. *Perspectives on Politics*, 2(4), 707–723.

Barke, R. P. (1993). Managing technological change in federal communications policy: The role of industry advisory groups. In P.A. Sabatier and H. Jenkins-Smith (eds.), *Policy Change and Learning: An Advocacy Coalition Approach*, pp. 129–146. Boulder, CO: Westview Press.

Beverwijks, J. (2005). The genesis of a system: Coalition formation in Mozambique higher education, 1993–2003. PhD dissertation, Universiteit Twente, The Netherlands.

Brady, D. (1988). *Critical Elections and Congressional Policy Making.* Stanford, CA: Stanford University Press.

Bryant, T. (2002). Role of knowledge in public health and health promotion policy change. *Health Promotion International,* 17(1), 89–98.

Burt, R.S. (1992). *Structural Holes*. Cambridge, MA: Harvard University Press.

Carvalho, G.O. (2001). Metallurgical development in the Carajas area: A case study of the evolution of environmental policy formation in Brazil. *Society and Natural Resources,* 14, 127–143.

Chen, P. (2003). Advocating online censorship. *Australian Journal of Public Administration,* 62(2), 41–64.

Costantini, E., and Hanf, K. (1972). Environmental concern and Lake Tahoe: A study of elite perceptions, backgrounds, and attitudes. *Environment and Behavior,* 4, 209–242.

Deleon, P. (1999). The stages approach to the policy process: What has it done? Where is it going? In P. Sabatier (ed), *Theories of the Policy Process*, pp. 19–34, Boulder, CO: Westview Press.

Doggan, M. (1975). *The Mandarins of Western Europe.* New York, NY: Wiley.

Elliot-Fisk, D.L., Rowntree R.A., Cahill T.A., Goldman C.R. Gruell G., Harris R., Leisz D., Lindström S., Kattelmann R., Machida D., Lacey R., Rucks P., Sharkey D.A., and Ziegler D.S. (1996). Lake Tahoe case study. In *Status of the Sierra Nevada. Sierra Nevada ecosystem project. Final report to Congress.* Wildland Resources Center Report number 38. University of California, Davis, California.

Eisner, M.A. (1993). *Regulatory Politics in Transition.* Baltimore, MD: Johns Hopkins University Press.

Farquharson, K. (2003). Influencing policy transnationally: Pro- and anti- tobacco global advocacy coalitions. *Australian Journal of Public Administration,* 62(4), 80–92.

Granovetter, M.S. (1973). The strength of weak ties. *American Journal of Sociology*, 78, 1360–1380.

Green, M. and Houlihan, B. (2004). Advocacy coalitions and elite sport policy change in Canada and the United Kingdom. *International Review for the Sociology of Sport,* 39(4), 387–403.

Heclo, H. (1978). Issue networks and the executive establishment. In A. King (ed.), *The New American Political System,* pp. 87–124. Washington, DC: American Enterprise Institute.

Herron, K.G., Jenkins-Smith, H.C., and Silva, C.L. (2005). Scientists, Belief Systems, and Advocacy Coalitions in Environmental Policy. In P.A. Sabatier (ed.), An Advocacy Coalition Lens on Environmental Policy, in preparation.

Herron, K.G. and Jenkins-Smith, H.C. (2002). U.S. perceptions of nuclear security in the wake of the cold ware: Comparing public and elite belief systems. *International Studies Quarterly,* 46, 451–479.

Hoppe, R., and Peterse, A. (1993). *Handling Frozen Fire*. Boulder, CO: Westview Press.

Jassby, A.D., Goldman C.R., Reuter J.E., Richards R.C., and Heyvaert, A.C. (2001). Lake Tahoe: diagnosis and rehabilitation of a mountain lake. In M. Munawar and R.E. Hecky (eds.), *The Great Lakes of the World (GLOW): Food-Web, Health and Integrity*, pp. 431–454. Leiden, The Netherlands: Backhuys Publishers.

Johns, P. (2003). Is there life after policy streams, advocacy coalitions, and punctuations: Using evolutionary theory to explain policy change? *Policy Studies Journal*, 31(4), 481–498.

Jordan, A. and Greenaway, J. (1998). Shifting agendas, changing regulatory structures and the 'new' politics of environmental pollution: British coastal water policy, 1955–1995. *Public Administration*, 76, 669–694.

Kauneckis, D., Koziol, L., and Imperial, M. (2000). *Tahoe Regional Planning Agency: The Evolution of Collaboration*. Washington, DC: NAPA.

Kim, S. (2003). Irresolvable cultural conflicts and conservation/development arguments: Analysis of Korea's Saemangeum project. *Policy Sciences*, 36, 125–149.

Kingdom, J.W. (1995). *Agendas, Alternatives, and Public Policies*, 2d ed. New York: Addison-Wesley Educational Publishers.

Kübler, D. (2001). Understanding policy change with the advocacy coalition framework: an application to Swiss drug policy. *Journal of European Public Policy*, 8(4), 623–641.

Lasswell, H. (1951). The policy orientation, In D. Lerner and H. Lasswell (eds.), *The Policy Sciences*. Stanford, CA: Stanford University Press.

Leach, W.D., and Sabatier, P.A. (2005). To trust an adversary: Integrating rational and psychological models of collaborative policymaking. *American Political Science Review*, forthcoming.

Liftin, K.T. (2000). Advocacy coalitions along the domestic-foreign frontier: Globalization and Canadian climate change policy. *Policy Studies Journal*, 28(1), 236–252.

Lord C., Ross L., and Lepper, M. (1979). Biased assimilation and attitude polarization: The effects of prior theories on subsequently considered evidence. *Journal of Personality and Social Psychology*, 37, 2098–2109.

Mawhinney, H.B. (1991, May). Policy change in education: An assessment of Sabatier's advocacy coalition framework. Paper presented to the conference Theory into Practice: Policy Research and Development in Canada, Calgary, AB: University of Calgary.

May, P.J. (1989). Reconsidering policy design: Polices and publics. *Journal of Public Policy*, 11(2), 187–206.

McDermott, R. (2004). The feeling of rationality: The meaning of neuroscience for political science. *Perspectives on Politics*, 2(4), 691–706.

McGauhey, P.H., Eliassen, H.R., Rohlich, G., Ludwig, H.F., Pearson, E.A., and Engineering Sciences, Inc. (1963). *Comprehensive Study on Protection of Water Resources of Lake Tahoe Basin through Controlled Waste Disposal*. Prepared for the Lake Tahoe Area Council. San Francisco, CA: Engineering Sciences, Inc.

Muller, P. (1995). Les politiques publiques comme construction d'un rapport au monde. In A. Faure, G. Pollet, and P. Warrin, (eds), *La Construction du Sens Dans les Politiques*, pp. 153–179. Paris, France: L'Harmattan.

Munro, J. (1993). California water politics: Explaining policy change in a cognitively polarized subsystem. In P.A. Sabatier and H. Jenkins-Smith (eds.), *Policy Change and Learning*, pp. 105–128. Boulder, CO: Westview Press.

Nechodom, M. (2005, March). Institutional and policy contexts of biosphere reserves: Potential roles for social science in sustainable development strategies. Paper presented at the GLOCHAMORE Workshop on Sustainable Development in UNESCO Mountain Biosphere Reserves. Grenada, Spain.

Ostrom, E. (1990). *Governing the Commons: The Evolution of Institutions of Collective Action*. Cambridge, MA: Cambridge University Press.

Ostrom, E. (1999). Institutional rational choice: An assessment of the institutional analysis and development framework. In P. Sabatier (ed.), *Theories of the Policy Process*, pp. 35–72, Boulder, CO: Westview Press.

Quattrone, G., and Tversky, A. (1988). Contrasting Rational and Psychological Analysis of Political Choice. *American Political Science Review*, 82, 719–736.

Sabatier, P.A., Hunter S., and McLaughlin, S. (1987). The devil shift: Perceptions and misperceptions of opponents. *Western Political Quarterly*, 41, 449–476.

Sabatier, P.A., and Jenkins-Smith, H. (1988). An advocacy coalition model of policy change and the role of policy orientated learning therein. *Policy Sciences*, 21, 129–168.

Sabatier, P.A., and Hunter, S. (1989). The incorporation of causal perceptions into models of elite belief systems. *Western Political Quarterly*, 42 (September), 229–261.

Sabatier, P.A., and Pelkey, N.W. (1990). *Land Development at Lake Tahoe*. Davis, CA: Institute of Ecology.

Sabatier, P.A., and Jenkins-Smith, H. (1993). *Policy Change and Learning: An Advocacy Coalition Approach*, Boulder, CO: Westview Press.

Sabatier, P.A. and Brasher, A. (1993). From vague consensus to clearly-differentiated coalitions: Environmental policy at Lake Tahoe, 1964–1985. In P.A. Sabatier and H Jenkins-Smith (eds.), *Policy Change and Learning*, pp. 149–176. Boulder, CO: Westview Press.

Sabatier, P.A., and Jenkins-Smith, H. (1999). The advocacy coalition framework: An assessment. In P. Sabatier (ed.), *Theories of the Policy Process*, pp. 117–166. Boulder, CO: Westview Press.

Sabatier, P.A., Weible, C.M., Hulsman, M., and Nechodom M. (2003). Stakeholder belief change in the Lake Tahoe Basin: 1970–2001. Department of Environmental Science and Policy, University of California, Davis. A final report to the USDA Forest Service, Pacific Southwest Research Station.

Sabatier, P.A., and Zafonte, M. (2005). Are bureaucrats and scientists members of advocacy coalitions? Evidence from an intergovernmental water policy subsystem." In P.A. Sabatier (ed.), *An Advocacy Coalition Lens on Environmental Policy*, in preparation.

Sabatier, P.A., and Weible, C.M. (2005, April). Innovations in the advocacy coalition framework. Paper presented at the American Society for Public Administration meeting, Milwaukee, WI.

Sato, H. (1999). The advocacy coalition framework and the policy process analysis: The case of smoking control in Japan. *Policy Studies Journal*, 27(1), 28–44.

Schlager, E. (1995). Policy making and collective action: Defining coalitions within the advocacy coalition framework. *Policy Sciences*, 28, 242–270.

Schlager, E., and Blomquist, W. (1996). A comparison of three emerging theories of the policy process. *Political Research Quarterly*, 49(Sept.), 651–672.

Scholz, J., and Pinney, N. (1995). Duty, fear, and tax compliance: The heuristic basis of citizenships behavior. *American Journal of Political Science*, 39(May), 490–512.

Sewell, G.C. (2005). Actors, coalitions, and the framework convention on climate change. PhD dissertation, Massachusetts Institute of Technology, Cambridge, MA.

Simon, H. (1985). Human nature in politics: The dialogue of psychology with political science. *American Political Science Review*, 79, June, 293–304.

Stewart, J.J. (1991). Policy models and equal educational opportunity. *PS: Political Science and Politics*, 24, 167–173.

Stone, D. (1997). Policy Paradox: The Art of Political Decision Making. New York: W.W. Norton.

USDA. (2000). Lake Tahoe Watershed Assessment: Volume 1. Pacific southwest region of the USDA forest service, Tahoe Regional Planning Agency, University of California at Davis, University of Nevada at Reno, the Desert Research Institute, Reno, Nevada.

Weible, C.M., and Sabatier, P.A. (2004, September). Perceptions of Lake Tahoe quality in collaborative and adversarial policymaking contexts. American Political Science Association meeting, Chicago, United States.

Weible, C.M., Sabatier, P.A., and Nechodom, M. (2005). No sparks fly: Policy participants agree on thinning trees in the Lake Tahoe Basin. *Journal of Forestry*, 103(1), 5–9.

Weible, C.M. (2005). Beliefs and perceived influence in a natural resource conflict: An advocacy coalition framework approach to policy networks. *Political Research Quarterly*, 58(3).

Weible, C.M., and Sabatier, P.A. (2005). Comparing policy networks: Marine protected areas in California. *Policy Studies Journal*, 33(2), 181–202.

Weiss, C. (1977). Research for Policy's Sake: The enlightenment function of social research. *Policy Analysis*, 3(Fall), 531–545.

Zafonte, M., and Sabatier P.A. (1998). Shared beliefs and imposed interdependencies as determinants of ally networks in overlapping subsystems. *Journal of Theoretical Politics*, 10(4), 473–505.

Zafonte, M. and Sabatier, P.A. (2004). Short-term versus long-term coalitions in the policy process. *Policy Studies Journal*, 32(1), 75–107.

Zartman, W.I. (1991). Conflict and resolution: Contest, cost and change. *Annals of the American Academy of Political and Social Science*, 518, 11–22.

10 Policy Communities

Hugh T. Miller and Tansu Demir

INTRODUCTION

The term *policy community* is part of an idiom used by policy researchers, political scientists, and public administration scholars to signify the extra-formal interactions (i.e., interactions taking place beyond or outside the formal processes of government) that occur in the interstices between and among government agencies, interest groups, corporations, industry associations, elected officials, and other institutions and individuals. It is a grouping of interrelated policy actors pursuing a matter of public policy important to them for instrumental reasons.

A policy community is a special type of interconnected social formation, wherein communication and influence may flow in nonhierarchical patterns and the resultant policy activism is associated with governmental fragmentation and political particularism. The catena of near-synonyms for policy communities includes iron triangles, issue networks, regulatory sub-governments, policy subsystems, professional networks, whirlpools, cozy triangles and policy networks. The term *policy community* is often juxtaposed against issue network to emphasize the closed, tight-knit aspects of policy communities versus the accessible, loosely bounded aspects of issue networks. Policy communities, too, are suggestive of epistemic communities—discursive groups in possession of problem-solving projects upon which their inquiries and efforts are focused.

Because these terms depict policy processes that are not necessarily contained within the formal structures of government, they have given rise to additional notions such as *governance* (as opposed to government) and the *horizontal government* (Rhodes 1992; Peters 1998). In all variations, the terms direct attention away from formal institutional structures and toward the relations of power, political action, political conflict, and coalition-building as additional loci of meaningful activity. Activities in policy networks and policy communities may precede policy formulation on one hand, and may influence policy enactment and administration on the other.

The term *policy community* is an important innovation in redescribing policy making processes in industrialized societies. Policies are determined by those most affected, most interested, most expert, or most sentimentally attached to the issue, regardless of whether they want to maintain the status quo or are committed to radical change. Policy communities indicate a policy process in which organized interests and governmental actors play a major role in shaping the direction and outcome of public policies. A policy community is neither market nor hierarchy (Williamson 1975), but does respond to the increasing fragmentation and complexity of the policy environment in a plural society. As the policy environment becomes complex, any single center of authority would face difficulty coping with the totality of it (Hanf and Scharpf 1978). The result is the fragmentation of policy making into sectors and the transference of policymaking authority from centralized decision makers to a narrow setting where policymaking frequently takes place. Exchange theorists note the participation in policymaking by those who share an interest in a particular industry or policy subject and focus on the exchange of resources, an exchange presumed to reinforce relationships while maximizing shared objectives.

THEORETICAL IMPORT

After the academic notice, in the 1940s, of the increased role of lobbyists and special interest groups in the processes of government, suspicions turned to the sometimes informal relations among for-hire lobbyists representing special interest groups seeking profit, the elected officials and their staff seeking re-election, and governmental officials from particular agencies seeking larger budgets. The concern was that collaboration among these presumably self-interested policy estates (private interests, elected officials, and bureaucratic elites) in the smoky back offices of legislative houses would generate public policy of benefit only to those in the room—policies nonetheless paid for by the citizenry as a whole. These informal relations were often perceived as preempting legitimate, formal processes of government whereby legislators are beholden only to the electorate.

In the formal representative democracy model that many citizens accept as familiar, voters—who are presumed to have clear policy choices and willingness to exercise their power through participation in elections—make selections among political candidates running for legislative positions. Legislators then translate aggregated citizen preferences into concrete policy proposals that are presumed to serve a larger public interest. In the model, bureaucracy is presupposed to be operating as a neutral and efficient implementer of policies with little or no involvement in policymaking. The model depicts a unidirectional and intermittent influence among the trilogy of citizens, legislators, and bureaucracy. But in policy communities, one finds political administration, not neutral administration, and one finds a multidirectional pattern of interactions (e.g., Cigler 1990).

Hence, in its benign interpretation, policy community is able to slice through the grandiose presumptions associated with sovereignty—the presumption, for example, that the electoral system represents The People while the administrative apparatus implements The People's will. Policy community opens the field for a different kind of politics—a politics that does not force means and ends into separate corners—and generates a different sort of discursive, situation-regarding interaction among those tracking the problems and issues. This is a much less extravagant grounding for political action than those that arise from The People. At the same time *policy community* is observable, situation-based, and open to contingency in ways that do not comport well with a conception of policy as universal good. The term has a tendency toward disaggregating the state and constituting it according to sector. The movement of power to the sector, to the policy communities, and to the various other networks of attentive policy actors, has a centrifugal effect. "The distinction between state and society virtually disappears in this formulation…" (Atkinson and Coleman 1992, 164).

Whether this is a good thing or a bad thing is a matter of dispute (see Hay 1998). One may be pleased with the normative resonance of nonbureaucratic, consensual, harmonious, organic social formations that lead to conciliatory practices and can respond to situational contingencies in a flexible and responsive manner. Such policy communities can be a forum for people conversant in a set of policy problems to innovate in a relatively noncompetitive arena.

In its pejorative connotations, this particularism of policy communities is precisely the problem with them. They are exclusionary, out-of-the-public-eye gatherings of vested interests, bent on spending tax payers' money on their own private projects. The historical suspicion attached to concepts such as "iron triangle" and "pork barrel politics" summarizes this unsympathetic interpretation, which casts the spotlight on the insider politics of narrowly focused policy communities.

What makes policy communities troubling is their appropriation of politics—the theft from the people of their sovereignty. Lowi (1969) developed a theoretical basis for such criticism in *The End of Liberalism*. He critiques interest group liberalism, which he sees as a by-product of pluralist ideology. According to Lowi, the pluralistic, interest-group conception and practice of government is fraught with far-reaching consequences for democratic theory. Had the term policy community been in currency at the time, it would also have been criticized for "favoring the best organized competitors, specializing politics around agencies, [and] ultimately limiting participation to channels provided by pre-existing groups" (63). For example, depression-era programs designed to restore and maintain, say, the economic vitality of farmers whose livelihoods were at risk, has over the years become a series of practices aimed at maintaining the status quo. In the United States, farm price supports remain in place today thanks to the iron triangle of agricultural agencies, agribusiness lobbies, and legislators from rural farming districts. Lowi's solution to the problems caused by informal bargaining is to restore formal institutions of representative democracy. As it is, democratic accountability is highly problematic under informal government as exemplified by policy communities.

The notion of iron triangle is a simplification of Lowi's demur. It reduces policymaking to a bargaining process among congressional members, public bureaucracies, and interest groups operating in a closed and autonomous manner. However, actual policymaking processes are more complex than that. By describing this type of informal interaction as an "issue network," Heclo (1978) recast these informal exchanges as places where political values, intellectual discourse, and human feelings might be expressed.

> Unfortunately, our standard political conceptions of power and control are not very well suited to the loose-jointed play of influence that is emerging in political administration . . . Looking for the few who are powerful, we tend to overlook the many whose webs of influence provoke and guide the exercise of power. (Heclo 1978, 102)

Indeed, the webs of influence that exist in between organizations, above and beyond formal roles, and aside from official job descriptions are multitudinous and multifarious. These extra-formal interactions modify the way the power is exercised and influence the actions that government takes. Participation is not necessarily based on narrow economic interests, and the boundaries of these networks are not so closed or well-defined that entry is inaccessible. The vagueness of these boundaries makes them a difficult unit of analysis for policy researchers, but also opens them up to democratic influences.

> In the old days—when the primary problem of government was assumed to be doing what was right—policy knowledge could be contained in the slim adages of public administration . . . Nowadays, of course, political administrators do not execute but are involved in making highly important decisions on society's behalf . . . Instead of power commensurate with responsibility, issue networks seek influence commensurate with their understanding of the various, complex social choices being made. (Heclo 1978, 103)

DEFINITIONS

Though frequently deployed by policy scholars to describe complex relationships in the policy-making process, there still remain certain definitional problems and ambiguities with the concept policy communities. In the policy literature, scholars struggle with terminology and category usage, seeking to fine-tune their descriptions. Two efforts are prominent. The first effort is to use some related concepts (e.g., issue networks) as foil to better explain the meaning of policy communities, and the second effort is to elucidate a list of characteristics such as membership, level of integration, conflict-cooperation patterns, etc. (see, for example, Rhodes 1997; Klijn 1996). In this way, the supposedly distinctive characteristics of policy communities are spelled out, eventually leading to the development of various typologies. In the first effort, overlaps are unavoidable, and this overlapping begets further ambiguities. In the second effort, it is difficult to see an underlying dimension that helps make much sense with the overall typology and this lack reduces the utility of the typologies.

The problem in comparing policy communities with related concepts is the increasing ambiguity. Campbell (1989) argues that the term *policy communities* overlaps with other ideas that indicate sectorized policy making, with policy community indicating a common perception about the contour of the problems and solutions. In an early effort of clarification, Wilks and Wright (1987) proposed a three-fold typology including "policy universe," "policy community," and "policy network." According to the authors, policy universe is the large population of actors and potential actors who share a common interest in industrial policy, and may contribute to the policy process on a regular basis. Policy community, on the other hand, refers to a more disaggregated system involving those actors and potential actors who share an interest in a particular industry and who interact with one another to mutual benefit. Finally, policy network, in their thinking, becomes a linking mechanism between and among policy communities.

A large part of the literature referentially employs the so-called Rhodes model as point of departure. According to this model, policy networks are categorized along a continuum from policy communities at one end to issue networks at the other (Rhodes 1997). Rhodes (1997) contrasts policy communities with issue networks along four dimensions such as membership, integration, resources, and power. As compared to issue networks, in policy communities the number of participants is very limited and some groups are consciously excluded. For that reason, Atkinson and Coleman (1992) direct attention to the discriminatory nature of policy communities in contrast to issue networks in which anyone can gain membership. Similarly, Bache (2000) states that the nature of linkages between organizations can range from tightly integrated policy communities to loosely coupled issue networks. "If the ideal types of policy communities and issue networks are on extreme ends of the same spectrum, in between lie typologies of networks with some features of both" (Bache, 576).

Dowding (1994) both explicated and ridiculed some of these analytical attempts to categorize notions such as policy community, issue network, and policy network. Though the lack of coherence is not for lack of effort, the attempts to parse differences into categories—as between a policy community and a policy network (Wright 1988)—have given ammunition to critics who would fault the literature for being mostly concerned about developing typologies. Some typologies use dimensions such as micro-, meso-, and macro-level, and others employ sectoral and sub-sectoral level as well as geographic or political region. Sometimes these categories are arranged so as to vary along some underlying dimension such as number of participants; range of interests involved, level of conflict, exclusivity, or solidarity of membership (Rhodes 1997).

As Rhodes (1997, 45) put it, "Obviously, the implication of using a continuum is that any network can be located at some point along it." But with five or more continua, the location of the network (and the type of network it should be called) is not actually a "point." Indeed, the oft-cited Rhodes classification makes use of a continuum that possesses no underlying dimension whatsoever.

Even without an underlying dimension, these conceptualizations emphasize the many ways in which policy activists may be interconnected; in all of them communication and authority may flow in untraditional and nonhierarchical patterns (Hill 1991). Despite the importance of network-style conceptualization, definitional problems persist and inherent ambiguities make it difficult for researchers to utilize *policy community* as a strong denotative instrument through which policymaking processes can be analyzed and the complex relationships can be mapped out more clearly.

| Policy ____ | Professional ____ | Intergovernmental ____ | Producer ____ | Issue |
| Community | Network | Network | Network | Network |

FIGURE 10.1 The Rhodes Classification. Adapted from Dowding (1994, 62).

At the same time, the term seems to point toward something discernable. The "community" metaphor implies people, close interaction, and strong ties (Atkinson and Coleman 1992). Stone et al. (2001) define policy communities as stable networks of policy actors from both inside and outside government, echoing an echo-prone literature that frequently notes the integrated character of policy communities. Policy communities are based on common understandings of problems within a particular policy domain. The community label reflects the emphasis placed on strong and close relationships built among participants. These close relationships along with ground rules accepted by all members presumably prevent conflict from becoming dysfunctional or unmanageable.

Exchange theorists, including transaction-cost analysts (e.g., Hindmoor 1998) assume that all participants have resources and the basic relationship is one of exchange among members. Every member has some resource upon which other members are dependent. Although there may be equilibrium of power among members, one group may be dominant. With or without domination, the persistence of community requires a positive-sum game, according to Rhodes (1997). Possessing technical capacity and detailed information about a policy issue is a crucial feature of effective participation. For those who have such expertise, the exchange of information between state and private actors can create privileged relationships from which the uninitiated can be excluded (Atkinson and Coleman 1992, 157).

A policy community can include journalists and policy analysts, as well as influential politicians and bureaucratic officials. In addition, researchers and professors can gain membership in a policy community if their ideas conform to the normative orientation of the group. Experts from universities, think tanks, or the law are likely to be given insider status if they share the basic values and accept the legitimacy of the outcome. Trust and shared appreciation characterize the relationships in the policy communities and cases of conflict are nested in a general consensus, according to Jordan and Maloney (1997). "The important point is that the policy community provides the institutional mechanism to resolve differences of interests between regular actors" (574). Hence policy communities have become identified with stability and normal politics. Because of the strength of its practices and the durability of its norms, a policy community is perhaps the most institutionalized iteration among the policy network concepts (Klijn 1997).

The emphasis placed on the role of experts and their contribution indirectly implies the existence of an ongoing conversation. Policy learning and discovery can take place, and change to the status quo can occur. Campbell et al. (1989, 88) pay attention to the role of environmental disturbances in leading to major policy changes:

> One possibility is a developmental process, in which an issue network is created around some new concern when activists and experts arouse the interest of some politicians. The resulting pressure leads to a policy change, which becomes institutionalized in a new bureaucratic agency, a stable legislative committee and a growing clientele. The new policy community starts with a commitment to further change, and many new ideas are developed, but eventually its problems and solutions become less interesting. Especially when threatened from the outside, the members will become more concerned with protecting what they have gained, and the policy community turns into a cozy triangle.

The question of what affects the organization and composition of policy communities is answered by exchange theorists as rational utility maximizing. Yet a number of macro-level variables appear in the literature, as well as some case studies that indicate the importance of political culture (especially when it is relevant to political participation and assumptions about hierarchy and conflict), party systems and state structure (see, Campbell et al. 1989). While the quality of the interaction is known or assumed in markets (rational self-interest) as well as hierarchies (superior-subordinate obedience), the nature of the interaction is indeterminate in networks and communities.

CRITIQUE

Research on policy communities may need to reassess its analytical tradition, as it has reached several stumbling blocks. If every policy community represents a specialized segment, what is the role of broader institutions? Atkinson and Coleman (1992) caution that, "proceeding to analyze the policy process as if broad state institutions are irrelevant is a misuse of the concepts network and community" (168). And there are research challenges. If one assumes that there are sectors populated by policy communities, a question arises as to what sort of methodological approach should be used? What is the appropriate unit of analysis? Micro-analysis of actors and relationships (as Dowding (2001) recommends) risks neglecting the substantive content of the political impact of policy communities. The focus on operating modes and norms in policy communities carries a similar risk. The economically rationalistic assumption, that policy actors are in it to exchange resources, crowds out of the picture cultural phenomena such as habit and tradition, identity and sense of belonging, ideological and value-rational motivations, and even political conflict.

Policy communities operate in political arenas characterized by different types and intensities of conflict. Often but not necessarily, these political arenas are manifestations of economic interests. Mostly, they are fields where political conflict expresses itself or is suppressed. The meanings that participants in the network ascribe to their interactions and activities are not necessarily preformed; they may emerge from situations. Decisions, actions, group conflict, and policy change occur as a consequence of interactions. In the process of interaction, participants in a policy community are engaged in a process of meaning construction, and thereby they reinforce one another's sense of importance of the set of issues under question. This meaning construction process might lead to articulation of political demands in ways that can be acted upon. It is also possible that participants abandon the game when events and issues lose their salience or importance. Yet the contingency of political alliances is difficult to appreciate in models that propose static categories for analysis. To rescue *policy community* from its denotative difficulties, it might be useful to adopt a political formulation that takes account of shifting alliances and situational conflict.

TYPES OF POLITICAL CONFLICT

In the following four descriptions, different types and intensities of conflict take place on different fields of play. Varying from low-intensity conflict (as in the policy community) to broad-based, ideological conflict over the role of government, four fields are presented in order of increasing potential for political conflict. The fields are identified as distributive, regulatory, tragedy of the commons, and welfare of the commons.

DISTRIBUTIVE FIELD

In this field, wherein policy community is situated, "All participants share basic values and accept the legitimacy of the outcome" (Rhodes 1997, 44). Though replete with definitional problems, some of the commonly accepted features of British policy communities include:

- Bargaining in sectoral environments,
- Predictable and enduring coalitions,
- Substantial agreement on problem definition,
- Low public profile (visibility) of decisions,
- Well-defined jurisdiction over relevant decision area,
- Low party political level attention,

- Narrow and low scope of conflict within the community,
- A small number of participants, and
- Restricted access for dissenting perspectives. (Jordan and Maloney 1997, 558).

We can gather from this list that policy communities are usually used in association with the major functional categories of government (e.g., agriculture, energy, or transportation) called sectors. The American policy literature would more likely point toward the distributive policy arena described by Lowi (1964; see also Ripley and Franklin 1982). In this policy arena, actors seek favor and subsidy from the government. Private interests and lobbyists petition the government in pursuit of their proffers, be they price support payments, procurement contracts, construction contracts, payment for services rendered, or other means of dispensation (Ripley and Franklin 1982, 90). The exception proves the rule. These cozy arrangements are stable over time, but can sometimes erupt into a more conflictual field of play. A distributive policy is "sprung" from its nourishing policy community when its effects begin to spill over and affect a broader constituency. The classic pork barrel water projects have occasionally been flushed from the routines of the policy community for several possible reasons, including the specter of the growing budget deficit, the emergence of water as a contentious scarce resource, conflicts with environmental groups, or, in the case of agriculture policy in Britain (Smith 1991) a salmonella outbreak. The process of a broad discourse can be most damaging to the pet projects of policy communities. Once broader discourse gains traction, particularistic lines of argument carry less weight. The opportunity for the expression of a wider range of values improves.

Even in the narrow confines of a policy community, a rationale which justifies a distributive policy in terms of some broader interest is usually put forth during policy formulation. For example, the U.S. Food Stamp Program, supported by a policy community situated in the sector identified with the U.S. Department of Agriculture, subsidizes agri-business and grocers. One can imagine being a member of this policy community and convincing the government to issue special money that can only be used to purchase products manufactured by members of that same policy community. In further testimony to the sectorialism of policy communities, the program is administered by the U.S. Department of Agriculture (not by the Department of Health and Human Services). But it is nonetheless justified in the broader political arena in terms of values such as compassion and helping the needy. Hence, distributive policies involve government payments or subsidies to organizations associated with particular policy communities. And it should also be noted that if powerful policy communities did not provide political support for this government program, it probably would not exist. So it also seems reasonable to conclude—as exchange theory would predict—that the underlying theme is instrumental gain.

Regulatory Field

Much of what is nominally referred to as regulatory policy—tariffs, rate-setting, licensing—benefits identifiable policy communities. The dynamics are very similar to the dynamic of regulatory policy in that policy communities want government to rig the rules in their favor. However, Lowi (1964) described how tariff policy could no longer be contained in a closed-off policy community arena because diverse groups (e.g., the victims of retaliatory tariffs on an unrelated product imposed by other nations) would revitalize their own policy communities to oppose the policy. Regulatory practices have effects which are at first blush distributive, but ultimately may activate different policy communities who bear the costs of the regulation. This is what makes the regulatory field different from the distributive field. Pluralistic notions such as the clash of competing interests come into play. Conflict is either present or latent in this policy field.

Tragedy of the Commons

A political field closely related to the regulatory field we name "tragedy of the commons" in honor of Garrett Harding's (1968) seminal article. In this field, there is not necessarily present a competing policy community. Yet if the in-place policy communities, organized around industry interests, get their way (e.g., absence of control on carbon dioxide emissions and other pollutants) the commons—in this case a reference to clean, breathable air—deteriorates to the detriment of all. On most days, the unorganized populace is no match for the tightly-knit, utility-maximizing, and influential policy communities. But when the politics in this field become salient, conflict erupts amidst moral indignation, justified ire, and ideological fervor.

Welfare of the Commons

The fourth political field transcends particularistic policy communities. National defense, social security, and national health care are possible examples. The benefits of policies accrue to the diverse population, as do the benefits. This is not to suggest that some dynamics of national defense policy (e.g., munitions contracts) do not functionally operate according to the politics of the distributive field, in which the policy communities, whose members include major defense contractors, are the major actors. But the politics in this field are likely to be debated at the macro-level, where peak associations (Ripley and Franklin 1982) conduct the debate at a societal level, in view of public media. Conflict about the appropriate role of the state plays out on this field, sometimes heated to boiling point as ideologies clash over highly symbolic macro issues such as capitalism, socialism, war, or the welfare state.

The point of mentioning these four contrasting policy fields is to demonstrate, in a different way, the limits of the *policy community* perspective. While it may be the case that policy communities dominate everyday, outside-the-limelight policy making, it is also possible that the deliberation of these close-knit groups can be exposed to a broader hearing in certain cases or with certain issues.

PUBLIC ADMINISTRATION

Critics point to the long-term negative consequences of the trend toward a network style of politics, most particularly by policy communities. They are "displacing political parties, chief executives, and other political institutions that once served to centralize power in our fragmented governmental system" (Skok 1995, 330). However, once "bureaucracy," or "the executive," or "the party" or "the state" are understood as reified concepts—as contingencies that are mistakenly objectified as immutable forces of nature—then the hard boundaries between and among agencies, institutions, and bureaucracy (and these distinguished from the citizenry) can be made permeable. Instead of looking at policy and administrative processes as a series of power transactions between walled institutions, think instead of an energy field (Fox and Miller 1995). A public energy field is composed of a multiplicity of malleable, discursive social formations. Discourse formations such as policy communities, policy networks, interagency task forces and consortia, negotiated regulatory constraints, adhocracies and the like are in abundant evidence in practice, but political and administrative scholars have only begun to theorize this phenomenon.

The complex web of relationships well represented by the network metaphor bears major implications on the distinction between politics and administration once presumed to exist. The conception of public administrators as neutrally competent and efficiency-guided public employees fails the admissibility test in political-administrative life. Public administrators might participate in network-style policy communities due to knowledge and expertise on substantive policy issues without being identified with one political position or another. Yet, as participants in policy communities, public administrators are political administrators. Public administrators maintain an activist role in policymaking process in that they freely put their knowledge and skills into use to accomplish certain policy outcomes. This proactive engagement in the policymaking process is consistent with long-expressed ideals by many public administration scholars (Harmon 1981). With different agendas, other public administration scholars spoke up on behalf of a more active stance on the part of administrators. The analytical turn of New Public Management expresses itself as managerialism (Kickert, Klign, and Kippenjan 1997), which aims to control and manage policy communities for administrative purposes.

Fox and Miller (1995) proposed an active administrative involvement in public policymaking, but they framed their proposal with standards of authentic discourse, against which actual policy discourse may be judged democratic or not. More recently, Denhardt and Denhardt (2000) proposed a public conversation that is instrumental in bringing administrators and citizens together to work out solutions to pressing policy problems.

Common in all these models is that public administrators are advised to be engaged in "what to do" questions of public policy, not just "how to do" questions. They mobilize key actors and help make policy an actuality. With knowledge as their key resource, they lead others to value their expertise and understanding of the important dimensions of the problem. Knowledgeable people, along with others in need of answers, join efforts and work together. In the process of interaction and reciprocal influence, the issues become clarified, relevant evidence shared and debated, and alternative solutions proposed.

The policy communities model, and its related network models, makes it clear that political interaction is prevalent in the practice of public administration. Political administrators frequently find themselves interacting among members of the public, struggling to sort out meanings and values, trying to establish or modify institutional arrangements, working to channel public resources in desired directions. The conflict that arises through the process provides a means by which to enlarge public discourse and shape public action.

Some political scientists focus attention on integrative functions of such extra-formal interactions, a feature that seems to make these relationships spread despite strong protestations of government formalists. Lowi (1969) calls for return to a formal democracy. Yet this may be a nostalgic wish in the face of ever-increasing presence of extra-formal political dynamics that reflect a desire for say-so in public policy debates. It would be hard to claim, anymore, that these informal dynamics that operate in policy-making processes are a new phenomenon. Throughout the policymaking apparatus of government, there are collections of issue-conscious groups influencing events in a complex system of interrelationships. Participants in this process often represent economic interests, but they typically bring into play technical expertise and specialized knowledge contributions to important questions of public policy.

Policy communities (and policy networks) play critical roles in public policy processes, among which the most important ones are those related to integration tasks performed. Professional associations operate as functional subsystems linking numerous program professionals through all levels of government. These coordinative and communicative competences make policy communities potentially more valuable than autonomous and closed iron triangles. In some cases, the existence of policy communities appears to have reconciled the need of coordinating and integrating public action in a complex and dynamic policy environment that is more fragmented than ever. Without them policy implementation likely would be more complicated and disorderly than it is now.

In a nutshell, the functional utility of policy communities is both political and administrative. Policy communities are political in the sense that they are instrumental in the process of extracting funds from the larger political system. Policy communities are also administrative because critical management functions such as coordination, communication, and integration are facilitated through them. Economic, professional, or intellectual interests represented by the actors in the networks help link various policy actors located at different levels of government. And yet, constant vigilance is required to assure that policy communities do not usurp the vague yet contentious desires of the larger political community.

REFERENCES:

Atkinson, M. and W.D. Coleman (1992). Policy networks, policy communities, and the problems of governance. *Governance*, 5 (2), 154–180.

Bache, I. (2000). Government within governance: Network steering in Yorkshire and the Humber. *Public Administration*, 78 (3), 575–592.

Blom-Hansen, J. (1997). A new institutional perspective on policy networks. *Public Administration*, 75, 669–693.

Campbell, J. C. (1989). Bureaucratic primacy: Japanese policy communities in an American perspective. *Governance*, 2, 5–24.

Campbell, J.C., M.A. Baskin, F.R. Baumgartner, N.P. Halpern (1989). Afterword on policy communities: A framework for comparative research. *Governance*, 2, 86–94.

Cigler, B. A. (1990). Public administration and the paradox of professionalism. *Public Administration Review*, 50 (6), 637–653.

Denhardt, R.B. and J.V. Denhardt (2000). The new public service: Serving rather than steering. *Public Administration Review*, 60 (6), 549–559.

Dowding, K. (1994) Roundtable: The theory of policy communities and policy networks. In P. Dunleavy and J. Stanyer (eds.) *Contemporary Political Studies*. Vol 1. Belfast: Political Studies Association.

Dowding, Keith. 2001. There must be end to confusion: Policy networks, intellectual fatigue, and the need for political science methods courses in British universities. *Political Studies* 49, no. 1 (2001), pp. 89–105

Dudley, G. (2003). Ideas, bargaining, and flexible policy communities: Policy change and the case of the Oxford transport strategy. *Public Administration*, 81 (3), 433–458.

Fox, C. J. and Miller. H. T. (1995). *Postmodern public administration: Toward discourse*. Thousand Oaks, CA: Sage Publications.

Gormley, W. T., Jr., (1986). Regulatory issue networks in a federal system. *Polity*, Summer, 595–620.

Hanf, K. and F.W. Scharpf (1978). *Interorganizational Policy Making: Limits to Coordination and Central Control*. Beverly Hills, CA: Sage Publications.

Hardin, G. (1968). The tragedy of the commons. *Science*, 162 (1968), 1243–1248.

Harmon, M. M. (1981). *Action theory for public administration*. New York: Longman.

Hay, C. (1998). "The tangled webs we weave: the discourse, strategy and practice of networking." In David Marsh, ed., *Comparing Policy Networks*. Buckingham: Open University Press.

Heclo, H. (1978). Issue networks and the executive establishment. In Anthony King (ed.), *The American Political System*. Washington, D.C.: American Institute for Public Policy Research, Ch. 3, pp. 87–124.

Hill, L. B. (1991). Who governs the American administrative state? A bureaucratic-centered image of governance. *Journal of Public Administration Research and Theory*, 1 (3), 261–294.

Hindmoor, A. (1998). The importance of being trusted: Transaction costs and policy network theory. *Public Administration*, 76 (Spring), 25–43.

Jordan, G. and W.A. Maloney (1997). Accounting for subgovernments: Explaining the persistence of policy communities. *Administration & Society*, 29 (5), 557–583.

Kickert, Walter J.M., Erik-Hans Klijn, and Joop F.M. Koppenjan, eds., 1997. *Managing Complex Networks: Strategies for the Public Sector*. London: Sage Publications.

Klijn, E. H. (1997) 'Policy networks: An overview. In Walter J. M. Kickert, Erik-Hans Klijn & Joop F. M. Koppenjan (Eds.) *Managing Complex Networks: Strategies for the Public Sector*. London: Sage.

Klijn, Eric-Hans (1996). Analyzing and managing policy processes in complex networks: A theoretical examination of the concept policy network and its problems. *Administration and Society*, 28 (1), 90–119.

Lowi, T. (1964). American business, public policy, case-studies, and political theory. *World Politics*, 16 (4), 677–715.

Lowi, T. (1969). *The end of liberalism*. New York: Norton.

Peters, B. Guy. 1998. Managing horizontal government: The politics of coordination. Research Paper No. 21, Canadian Centre for Management Development. Ottawa: Minister of Supply and Services. http://www. myschool-monecole.gc.ca/Research/publications/pdfs/p78.pdf

Rhodes, R.A.W. (1997). Understanding Governance: Policy Networks, Governance, Reflexivity and Accountability. Buckingham, U.K.: Open University Press.

Ripley, R.B. and G.A. Franklin (1982). *Bureaucracy and Policy Implementation.* Homewood, Ill: Dorsey Press.

Skok, J. E. (1995). Policy issue networks and the public policy cycle: A structural-functional framework for public administration. *Public Administration Review*, 55 (4), 323–332.

Smith, M.J. (1991) "From Policy Community to Issue Networks: Salmonella in Eggs and the New Politics of Food." *Public Administration,* 69 (Summer), 234–255.

Stone, D., S. Maxwell, and M. Keating (2001). *Bridging research and policy.* An International Workshop Funded By The UK Department For International Development. Radcliffe House, Warwick University.

Wilks, S. & Wright, M. (Eds.) (1987). Comparative government-industry relations: Western Europe, United States, and Japan. Oxford: Clarendon Press.

Williamson, O.E. (1975). *Markets and hierarchies.* New York: Free Press.

Wright, M. (1988). Policy community, policy network, and comparative industrial policies. *Political Studies,* 36, 593–612.

11 Public Policy Analysis and Think Tanks

Diane Stone

The term *think tank* is used here to mean policy research institutes involved in the research and analysis of a particular policy area or a broad range of policy issues, seeking to advise policy makers or inform public debate on policy issues. Generally, these organizations are constituted as non-governmental organizations (NGOs) but some are either semi-governmental agencies or quasi-autonomous units within government. Additionally, some European political parties have created in-house think tanks in the form of party institutes or foundations such as the Konrad Adenauer Stiftung associated with the Christian Democratic Party in Germany. In parts of North Asia, think tanks are often affiliated with business corporations such as the Mitsubishi Research Institute a profit-making institute founded in 1970. Despite this increasing divergence in legal constitution, the roles and functions of think tanks put them at the intersection of academia and politics where they aim to make connection between policy analysis and policy making. However, there is considerable diversity among think tanks in terms of size, ideology, resources, and the quality or quantity of analytic output. Notwithstanding the prosperous, well- known think tanks like RAND, the Brookings Institution, or the Council on Foreign Relations in the United States, the majority of think tanks around the world are relatively small organizations. Most operate with a dozen or so research staff and annual budgets of approximately US$2–$3.5 million (Boucher et al. 2004).

Aside from policy analysis, these organizations also perform a range of ancillary activities that help amplify their policy analysis and sometimes propel their policy products into decision-making circles. Their diversity of activities and functions has presented dilemmas in defining think tanks (reflected in the broad description above), compounded by their dramatic proliferation, hybrid forms, and world-wide spread over the past two decades. In tandem, think tank modes of policy analysis range, at one end of the spectrum, from being highly scholarly, academic, or technocratic in style, to overtly ideological, partisan, and advocacy driven, at the other end, with vastly different standards of quality throughout. The interplay of applying knowledge to policy problems is complemented by strategic practices to develop advisory ties to government, industry or the public as brokers of policy analysis. Accordingly, think tank policy analysis is not simply an intellectual exercise that is manifest through expert commentary or policy documents. Instead, policy analysis is also action-oriented, reliant on policy entrepreneurship, institution building, and the competitiveness of think tanks in the market-place of ideas.

This positivist and pluralist conception of think tanks competing nationally and internationally in their advocacy toward governments and international organization is complicated by understandings of think tank influence that dwell on the longer term capacity to shape the climate of opinion and develop narratives that structure world views and policy beliefs. Consequently, the strategies to directly affect the course of a piece of legislation, or the wording of policy initiatives, must be considered alongside the longer term, indirect, and subtle influence over discourses of governance.

WAVES OF DEVELOPMENT

The waves of think tank development from early in the twentieth century parallel the evolution of policy analysis. Three broad stages can be identified: the first generation of think tank prior to World War II; the second wave of Cold War, peace research and development studies institutes alongside those with a domestic social and economic policy focus; and third, the global think tank boom from the 1980s onward (Stone and Denham 2004). Often with funding support from the National Endowment for Democracy, USAID (United States Agency for International Development), the World Bank or private philanthropic foundations, the Western organisational format of think tank has been spread internationally. In tandem, Western models and norms of policy analysis have also spread.

First generation think tanks were responses to societal and economic problems spawned by urbanization, industrialization, and economic growth. Think tanks became established in English-speaking countries, but most prominently in the United States. Many reasons for uneven development have been posited: the strong philanthropic sector, a conducive tax system, weak political parties, a pluralistic political system, and the division of powers in its federal structure as well as between executive and legislature of the United States (Smith 1991; Abelson 2002). These factors presented favorable political opportunities and policy niches for think tank development. In general, think tanks emerged in North America and the British dominions as a response to the growth of the state—the "progressive era"—expansion of universities with increased literacy and professionalization of public service that facilitated demand for independent policy analysis for the rational improvement of society (Heineman 2003). Organizations such as the Brookings Institution, the 20th Century Fund, and the Russell Sage Foundation in the United States, and the Fabian Society and National Institute for Economic and Social Research in the UK are typical of the first wave.

The post-World War II era brought more extensive role for the state in social and economic affairs, prompting a second wave of think tank developments in North America and in European liberal and social democracies. In the United States, the New Deal and the Great Society period along with the Korean and Vietnam wars prompted the development of government contract research institutions. In the United States, RAND and the Hudson Institute were exemplary of the new breed of think tank increasingly reliant on government contracts rather than private philanthropy. A number of other institutes acquired substantial input into social policy, most notably the Urban Institute. Created in 1968, it had the mission of researching and analyzing American social problems such as the inner city and urban decline, state work-welfare programs, Medicare payments, transport policy, and so forth. Similar institutes emerged in other developed countries: the Institut für Sozialpolitik und Sozialreform in Austria in 1953, the Studiefsbundet Näringsliv och Samhälle in Sweden in 1948, and the Institute of Public Affairs (IPA) in 1943 in Australia. Many of the second generation think tanks pioneered applications of new statistical techniques, economic modeling and cost-benefit analysis. As government demand for this kind of analysis expanded, so, too, did the number and variety of think tanks. Institutes with a social policy focus were increasingly out-numbered by the proliferation of foreign policy institutes, centers for the study of security, and development studies institutes, in an era defined by the Cold War, superpower rivalries, and Third World issues

From the 1980s, a world-wide boom of think tanks was apparent. In Anglo-American political systems, think tank communities matured. Whether as a cause or a consequence of the rise of environmental considerations, environmental policy institutes have burgeoned. Specialization has evolved on other fronts: inter alia, women's policy institutes, business ethics think tanks, and centers for democracy promotion. Many of the new institutes adopted a more strident ideological stance alongside a greater organizational propensity for advocacy (Abeson 2004). The rise of so-called New Right think tanks such as the Adam Smith Institute in London also illustrates how free market and conservative think tanks were one set of actors constitutive of the paradigm shift from Keynesian policy making toward neoliberal principles government organisation (Denham and Garnett 2004). Today, as governments clamor for evidence-based policy, think tanks are ready to provide their evidence in support of policy reform and innovation.

Outside the OECD (Organisation for Economic Co-operation and Development), think tanks exhibit an evolution that occurred later in the twentieth century. In the newly industrialized countries of Asia, rapid economic growth freed resources for policy research while increasing levels of literacy and greater opportunity for university education created new generations of intellectuals. Northeast Asian institutes are relatively numerous but are also more likely to be affiliated with a government ministry or large corporation. A number of Latin American countries such as Argentina, Peru, and Chile also have a healthy population of research institutes; many are affiliated with universities, and have had a new breath of life with democratization in the region. Western-style independent think tanks in former Soviet Union appeared after 1989. Examples include the Center for Social and Economic Research in Poland and the Center for Liberal Strategies in Bulgaria, but the bureaucratic legacy of the old, if impoverished, Soviet-style Academies of Science still looms (Minggui-Pippidi 2004). As relatively young organizations, with limited resources, the new policy institutes are often over-stretched in their policy focus on the problems of transition. This is even more pronounced with think tanks in many African countries (Johnson 2000). In weak and failed states, the presence of think tanks tends to be very limited. Elsewhere the weak policy environment of Bosnia and Herzegovina and the dominance of the Office of the High Representative post-1995 in structuring both the demand and supply of policy analysis has curtailed think tank development (Miller and Struyk 2003).

The global reach of think tank development is reflected in the cottage industries that have evolved around the phenomenon. There are practical guides on how to manage think tanks (Struyk 2002). Workshops are convened regularly by USAID, the Konrad Adenauer Stiftung, Freedom House, the World Bank, UNDP (United Nations Development Programme) and the Open Society Institute (among many others) on how to start and then manage a think tank. Specialist consultants and firms cater to both think tanks that need management advice and to their donors who require evaluation of the think tank analysis they have funded. There are parallels in the development of the academic literature. Into the 1990s, analysis of think tanks was devoted almost exclusively to think tank growth within Anglo-American systems as "third sector" organizational solutions applying knowledge and expertise to public problems (see inter alia, Smith 1991; Weiss 1992). Current research trends are comparative and focused on think tank political roles in developing and post-communist states (McGann and Weaver 2000), in global governance (Stone 2003; Ladi 2004), and addressing issues of think tank influence in policy networks and public discourse (Ullrich 2004; Lucarelli and Radaelli 2004).

In a maturing world-wide industry, think tanks are in a constant state of reinvention. The scaling down of Open Society Institute offices in Central and Eastern Europe has seen the transformation of some of these capacity building NGOs into independent policy institutes, reflective of the so-called policy turn of the Soros funded OSI (Krizsan and Zenta, 2004). In other contexts, some think tanks evolve into, or evolve from, consulting firms (Minggiu-Pippidi 2003). Some institutes might be better defined as "vanity tanks" that help launch the political careers of aspiring leaders (Abeslon 2004).

As think tanks proliferate and diversify, there is less agreement on how they might be defined. The think tank idea has been stretched. Journalists, academics, and other commentators have applied the term haphazardly as a label for any institution undertaking policy-related technical or scientific research and analysis. This could be an international agency, a non-governmental organization, a scientific laboratory, a commercial research enterprise, or policy analysis units inside government. Increasingly, the boundaries between think tanks and other groups are blurring. Pressure groups and NGOs such as Amnesty or Transparency International have their own capacity for policy analytic research. Some think tanks are not devoted exclusively to research and policy analysis but are "think-and-do-tanks" involved in advocacy, technical assistance, and training. Many institutes are informally incorporated or coopted into policy development whereas in other political systems, institutes conform to the strictures of state monitoring and censorship. Consequently, the variety of think tanks in operation defies simple generalization about their standards of research and integrity of policy analysis.

MODES OF POLICY ANALYSIS

One of the most important functions of think tanks is the specialized research activity that leads to policy analysis. The primary targets of think tank analysis are legislatures and executives as well as bureaucrats and politicians at local, national, and international levels of governance, but other actors in society interact with or support think tanks. Further distinctiveness lies in: (1) their capacity to act as a clearinghouse, (2) their involvement in the advocacy of ideas, (3) their incorporation in domestic and transnational policy networks, and (4) their specialized intellectual and scholarly base providing expertise on policy issues.

As a clearinghouse, think tanks represent a concentration of cheap or free information and expertise. The revolution in information technology has made think tank products—working papers, books, training manuals, draft legislation, e-forums—a readily accessible source of policy relevant research and analysis. In addition, think tanks are a repository of "independent" and "scholarly" experts who can provide information that frequently represents a credible alternative to information coming from government or from the corporate sector. This information is used readily by the media, interest groups, business associations, trade unions, churches, NGOs, and social movements; it is often made available as a "public good."

As "advocates" think tank scholars/activists are driven by ideological, scholarly, or professional principles to broadcast and spread specific practices or policies. In general, later generations of American, Canadian, British, and Australian think tanks have been more advocacy-oriented in order to maintain both media and political attention in the increasingly competitive market place of ideas. Stylistically, this has meant that think tanks do not communicate ideas solely through the policy professional domains of seminars, conferences and publications. Think tanks also seek to press their views in public domains such as television and radio or through newspaper commentary where there is increasingly a symbiotic relationship via sound bite policy analysis.

Both individuals in think tanks and the organization need to act as policy entrepreneurs; that is, as educators, advocates, and networkers. Effective communication to policy audiences is as important to the success of a think tank as the production of high-quality policy analysis. Many think tanks are not only more adept at political communication than universities and NGOs, but the organizational format of think tank is itself an institutional response to the difficulties of bridging research and policy and applying (social) science to national problems of economy and society.

Where advocacy is often the strategy of the "outsider" think tank, some think tanks become "insiders" to policy communities. These networks are a sectoral mode of governance incorporating actors from inside and outside government to facilitate decision-making and implementation. As suppliers of expertise and analysis, think tank staff can be coopted into policy deliberation either informally through consultations and personal interactions or more formally through appointment to advisory bodies. In such circumstances, there is a relationship of trust between a think tank and a government ministry or set of officials where the think tank's expertise is recognized in return for some policy access (Ullrich 2004). The Overseas Development Institute in London, for instance, has a strong and long-standing relationship with the UK Department for International Development. Additionally, as conveners of conferences and research projects, think tanks represent interlocutors among business executives, government officials, and other experts, and thereby provide environs conducive for off-the-record discussions. Indeed, a number of think tanks around the world that enjoy the trust of governments have played a quiet but effective behind the scenes role as agents of "track two diplomacy" (Simon, 2001).

As centers for policy analysis, think tanks need to sustain their professional credibility and reputation as repositories of policy knowledge. Chief think tank staff members are usually highly qualified, with a PhD, and continue to participate in the professional meetings of their discipline. Some teach on a part-time basis as adjunct faculty of universities (that also provides opportunity to recruit new talent for the think tank); a small percentage of think tanks are formally linked with universities. However, the primary orientation is the production of policy analysis, not higher education. Nevertheless, think tanks are a vehicle for policy training and a site for political "wannabes" to hone their rhetorical skills and induct themselves into policy communities. Think tanks produce human capital in the form of specialized analysts who often move between think tank, university, and government service. The long-term ramifications indirectly interweave the think tank with government agencies via its former fellows.

Some have spent careers working with governments or international organizations before bringing their professional experience to the think tank while other think tank scholars regularly seek appointment to official committees and advisory boards. Usually, staff can legitimately claim knowledge and detailed awareness of the internal workings of government. Consequently, the mix of staff experiences and formal qualifications is important for the organization to establish credibility with political audiences as reliable "thinking outfits" providing rigorous policy analysis. In short, the human capital of a think tank is its primary asset in producing policy analysis and sustaining reputation.

TRANSNATIONALIZATION OF THINK TANKS

Think tanks are an excellent barometer of the transnationalization of policy analysis. The dual dynamic of globalization and regionalization has transformed the research agendas of these organizations. Institutes have been compelled to look beyond primarily local and national matters to address global issues. Many think tanks have been at the forefront of public debate, policy analysis and research into the global reach and ramifications of policy concerns such as the environment, security, trade, refugees and human rights. In conjunction with academics in universities, a notable number of think tank researchers have been leading commentators on globalization. Their transnational research agendas have been complemented by global dissemination of policy analysis via the Internet.

In the evolving shape of global civil society, think tanks are also prominent players. It is common for think tanks to liaise with like-minded bodies from other countries. The Open Society Institute PASOS association in CEE is a regional network that operates in the same field as the Transition Policy Network of think tanks coordinated by the Urban Institute. Global ThinkNet, convened by the Japan Center for International Exchange, hosts meetings of think tank directors and senior scholars. The Global Development Network is an extensive international federal network primarily of economic research institutes. There are many more. These networks provide an infrastructure for global dialogue and research collaboration, but institutes generally remain committed to the nation-state where they are legally constituted. Nevertheless, there is a nascent global marketplace of ideas. Although North American and European think tanks dominate this marketplace, it provides a rich source of radical thinking as well as orthodox policy analysis.

International organizations like the World Bank, European Union (EU), the World Trade Organization (WTO) or UNDP are important financiers and consumers of research and policy analysis.

They have provided capacity building and training programs throughout the world for local elites to establish new think tanks and policy networks (UNDP 2003). They also require independent policy analysis and research. This is not only to support problem definition and outline policy solutions, but as civil society actors or as highly reputed expert organizations, think tanks are often effective bodies to monitor and evaluate existing policy as well as to provide scholarly legitimating for policy development. Moreover, a few think tanks have become transnational in orientation; for instance, the Evian Group revolves in the orbit of the WTO but is an independent body that convenes meetings of, and studies by, trade experts in support of an open world economy.

Think tanks have become key actors in a thickening web of global/regional institutions, regulatory activities and policy practices. Global governance structures such as the Global Water Partnership or UNAIDS are in response to the increasing prevalence of global policy problems that do not respect national boundaries. These contemporary policy problems provide a structural dynamic for research collaboration, sharing of responsibilities, regularized communication, and expert consultation. Global public policy networks are neocorporatist arrangements that act alongside international organizations, government officials, business representatives, and stakeholders to a policy area to provide policy analysis (Reinicke and Deng 2000). Within these networks, selected think tanks have become useful in building the infrastructure for communication between transnational policy actors; that is, Web sites, newsletters, organizing international meetings, and managing the flow of information coming from numerous sources. Consequently, through their policy analysis and participation in global or regional policy dialogue, the transnationalization of think tanks can be regarded as one transmitter of global policy processes.

Think tank activity within the European Union has been considerable, reflecting the deepening of European integration (Boucher et al. 2004). Despite differences between think tanks in relation to specific policy remits, structural and membership profiles, and ideological perspectives on European integration, they have common features such as close relations with the European Commission and a research focus on distinctively European issues (Ladi 2004; Ullrich 2004). CEPS (the Center for European Policy Studies in Brussels) is the exemplar of this style. Think tanks have also been key players in European harmonization of national structures through cross-national processes of policy transfer, where they go beyond detached policy analysis to spread certain European standards and bench marks (Ladi 2004). Regionalism elsewhere in the world—ASEAN, the African Union, or NAFTA—has also acted as a magnet for think tank activity.

THE INFLUENCE OF THINK TANK POLICY ANALYSIS

One of the most vexed questions concerning think tanks is whether or not they have policy influence. Notwithstanding extensive growth, think tanks do not enjoy automatic political access. Attempting to broker policy analysis to decision makers does not equate with immediate policy impact on forthcoming legislation or executive thinking. Relatively few think tanks make key contributions to decision making in local, national, or regional global fora, or exert paradigmatic influence over policy thinking. Instead, it is more appropriate to view them as cogs in the wider machineries of governance. Furthermore, think tank research and reports do not escape challenges or criticism from other knowledge actors in universities, whilst they may be ignored or patronized at will by governments, corporations, and international organizations. However, this is not to suggest that these organizations are without intellectual authority or policy influence.

First, think tanks appropriate authority on the basis of their scholarly credentials as quasi-academic organizations focused on the rigorous and professional analysis of policy issues. Many use their presumed "independent" status as civil society organizations to strengthen their reputation as beholden neither to the interests of market nor the state. These endowments give think tanks some legitimacy in seeking to intervene with knowledge and advice in policy processes. However, a recent empirical survey of European decision makers, journalists, and academics' views about the impact of think tanks discovered critical and cautious perceptions of influence:

> All (interviewees) insisted on the importance of a healthy think tank sector for E.U. policy making while criticising their relative lack of strength and ability to provide added-value, sometimes their lack of impact and relevance; and finally an approach seen as too technocratic and elitist. (Boucher et al. 2004, 85)

Nevertheless, these organizations acquire political credibility by performing services for states and for non-state actors. In short, the sources of demand help explain think tank relevance and utility if not direct policy influence. Think tanks respond to demand for high-quality and reputable research and analysis, ideas, and argumentation. In addition, they provide services such as ethics or policy training for civil servants, or by organizing conferences or seminars. Similarly, they have become useful translators of the abstract modeling and dense theoretical concepts characteristic of contemporary social science. For governments concerned about evidence-based policy, think tanks potentially help create a more rational policy process by augmenting in-house research capacities, circumventing time and institutional constraints, and alerting elites to changing policy conditions (Dror 1984). Thus, it may be less the case that think tanks have an impact on government and more the case that governments or certain political leaders employ these organizations as tools to pursue their own interests and provide intellectual legitimation for policy.

Think tanks also contribute to governance and institution building by facilitating exchange between official and other private actors as interlocutors and network entrepreneurs. Networks are important to think tanks both in embedding them in a relationship with more powerful actors, and in increasing their constituency, thereby potentially amplifying their impact. However, such relationships also pull think tanks toward advocacy and ideological polemic or partisanship and politicization. Too close an affinity with government, a political party, or NGOs can seriously undermine their authority and legitimacy as objective (or at least balanced) knowledge providers, and potentially dissolve important distinctions between the research institute and advocacy group.

Rather than organizations for rational knowledge utilization in policy, think tank development is also indicative of the wider politicization of policy analysis. In a few countries, think tanks are a means of career advancement or a stepping stone for the politically ambitious. This has lead to the hollowing out of British think tanks after election of a new government (Denham and Garnett 2004). The revolving-door of individuals moving between executive appointment and think tanks, law firms, or universities is a well-known phenomenon in the United States and is increasingly seen in Central and Eastern Europe and sub- Saharan African countries. In short, rather than the policy analysis papers—or published output—having influence, it is the policy analytic capacity—or human capital—that has long term influence and resonance inside government, and increasingly international organizations.

Some think tanks attract more media than government attention. The capacity to gain funds from foundations, governments, and corporations to undertake their policy analysis is indirect recognition of the value of many institutes. Others value the pluralism of debate that think tanks can bring to liberal democracies, and this is one rationale behind the think tank capacity building initiatives of development agencies. In neopluralist thinking, independent think tanks are often portrayed as creating a more open, participatory and educated populace and represent a counter to the influence of powerful techno-bureaucratic, corporate, and media interests on the policy agenda. Moreover, a more informed, knowledge-based policy process—a role that think tank experts help fulfill—could enlighten decision making (Weiss 1990).

Early American studies of think tanks often adopted power approaches to the role of think tanks in decision making. Elite studies of institutes such as the Brookings Institution (Dye 1978) emphasized how think tanks are key components of the power elite where decision making is concentrated in the hands of a few groups and individuals. Similarly, some Marxists argued that establishment think tanks are consensus-building organizations developing and debating the ideology and long-range plans that convert problems of political economy into manageable objects of public policy. As the common economic interests and social cohesion among the power elite or ruling class is insufficient to produce consensus on policies, agreement on such matters requires "research, consultation and deliberation" to form a coherent sense of long-term class interests (Domhoff 1983, 82) and maintain hegemonic control (Desai 1994). However, these studies direct analysis toward well-known policy institutions with solid links to political parties or the corporate sector, neglecting the role of smaller, lesser-known institutes which thrive in much larger numbers than the elite think tanks.

In general, contemporary analysts are skeptical of think tanks exerting consistent direct impact on politics (see essays in Stone and Denham 2004). Instead, they develop wider and more nuanced understandings of think tank policy influence and social relevance in their roles as agenda-setters who create policy narratives that capture the political and public imagination. This ability to set the terms of debate, define problems and shape policy perception has been described elsewhere as "atmospheric" influence (James 2000, 163). Moreover, the fluctuating and changing influence of think tanks has much to do with the way in which think tanks interact over time in epistemic communities, advocacy coalitions, and discourse coalitions. The epistemic community concept (Haas 1992) focuses on the specific role of experts in the policy process and the heightened influence of consensual knowledge in conditions of policy uncertainty (Ullrich 2004). In this perspective, think tanks wield their expertise and analysis as objectified scientific input to policy. The advocacy coalition approach emphasizes an alternative view that analysis has a long-term enlightenment function in altering policy orthodoxies, and highlights the role of beliefs, values and ideas as a neglected dimension of policy making (Lucarelli and Radaelli 2004). By contrast, discourse approaches emphasize the role of language and political symbolism in the definition and perception of policy problem. It is a constructivist approach that emphasizes intersubjective knowledge—common understandings and shared identities—as the dynamic for change and in which think tanks are wordsmiths. In these perspectives, it is in the *longue duree* that think tank policy analysis and activity has achieved wider social relevance and shaping patterns of governance and moving paradigms.

REFERENCES

Abelson, Donald. (2002) *Do Think Tanks Matter?* Montreal, McGill-Queen's University Press.

Boucher, Stephen, et al, (2004) *Europe and its think tanks; a promise to be fulfilled. An analysis of think tanks specialised in European policy issues in the enlarged European Union*, Studies and Research No 35, October, Paris, Notre Europe.

Critchlow, D. T. (1985) *The Brookings Institution, 1916–52: Expertise and the Public Interest in A Democratic Society*, Dekalb, Northern Illinois Press.

Denham, Andrew & Garnett, Mark. (2004) "A Hollowed Out Tradition? British Think Tanks in the Twenty First Century," in Diane Stone and Andrew Denham (eds) *Think Tank Traditions: Policy Research and the Politics of Ideas*, Manchester, Manchester University Press.

Desai, Rhadika. (1994) "Second-hand Dealers in Ideas: Think Tanks and Thatcherite Hegemony," *New Left Review*, No. 203: 27–64

Domhoff, William. G. (1983) *Who Rules America Now? A View for the '80s*, New Jersey, Prentice Hall.

Dror, Yehezkel (1984) "Required Breakthroughs in Think Tanks," *Policy Sciences*, 16: 199–225

Dye, Thomas. R. (1978) "Oligarchic tendencies in national policy making: The role of private planning organisations," *Journal of Politics*, 40(May): 309–31.

Haas, Peter (ed.) (1992) "Knowledge, Power, and International Policy Coordination," *International Organization*, 46(1).

Heineman, Robert A. et al. (2003) *The World of the Policy Analyst*, Chatham House Publishers 2002.

James, Simon. (2000) "Influencing government policymaking" in Diane Stone (ed.) *Banking on Knowledge: The Genesis of the Global Development Network*, London, Routledge.

Johnson, Erik. (1997) "Improving Public Policy in the Middle East and North Africa: Institution Building for Think Tanks," Washington D.C.: Center for International Private Enterprise.

Krizsán, Andrea and Zentai, Violetta. (2004) "From Civil Society to Policy Research: The Soros Network and Roma Policy," in Diane Stone and Simon Maxwell (eds.) *Global Knowledge Networks and International Development: Bridges Across Boundaries*, London, Routledge.

Ladi, Stella. (2004) *Globalization, Policy Transfer and Think Tanks*, Cheltenham, Edward Elgar.

Lucarelli, Sonia and Radaelli, Claudio (2004) "Italy: Think Tanks and the Political System," in Diane Stone and Andrew Denham (eds.) *Think Tank Traditions: Policy Research and the Politics of Ideas*, Manchester, Manchester University Press.

McGann, J. & Weaver, K. eds. (2000) *Think Tanks and Civil Societies*. Transaction Press.

Miller, Christopher. and Struyk, Raymond. "Policy Research in Bosnia and Herzegovina: The role and Impact of Local Thinks," *Southeast European Politics,* 5(1): 45–59.

Minggiu-Pippidi, Alina. (2003) "Designing the new social contract: trends and threads in CEE public policy research," in United Nations Development Program (ed.) *Thinking the Unthinkable: From Thought to Policy. The Role of Think Tanks in Shaping Government Strategy: Experiences from Central and Eastern Europe*, Bratislava, UNDP Regional Bureau for Europe and the Commonwealth of Independent States.

Reinicke, Wolfgang and Deng, Francis. (2000) *Critical Choices: The United Nations, Networks and the Future of Global Governance*, Ottawa, International Development Research Centre.

Simon, Sheldon, (2001) "Evaluating Track II Approaches to Security Diplomacy in the Asia Pacific: The CSCAP Experience," *National Bureau for Asian Research Special Report*, September.

Smith, James (1991) *The Idea Brokers: Think Tanks and the Rise of the New Policy Elite*, New York, Free Press.

Stone, Diane (2003) "The 'Knowledge Bank' and the Global Development Network," *Global Governance*, 9: 43–61.

Stone, Diane and Denham, Andrew. Eds. (2004) *Think Tank Traditions*, Manchester, Manchester University Press.

Struyk, Raymond J. (2002) *Managing Think Tanks: Practical Guidance for Maturing Organizations*, Budapest, Local Government and Public Service Reform Initiative and Washington DC., the Urban Institute.

Ullrich, Heidi. (2004) "European Union think tanks: generating ideas, analysis and debate," in Diane Stone and Andrew Denham (eds.) *Think Tank Traditions: Policy Research and the Politics of Ideas*, Manchester, Manchester University Press.

UNDP (2003) *Thinking the Unthinkable: From Thought to Policy*, Bratislava, United Nations Development Program.

Weiss, Carol. (1992) *Organizations for Policy Analysis: Helping Government Think*, London, Sage.

Part IV

Policy Decision Making:
Rationality, Networks, and Learning

12 Rationality in Policy Decision Making

Clinton J. Andrews

Policy decisions should be rational but sometimes they are not. The same goes for policy advice, according to critics who use the word "rational" in particular ways. The task in this chapter is to build a concise yet nuanced account of rationality in policy decision making that counters shallower complaints while providing points of departure for deeper critical probing.

The chapter begins by discussing implied links between policy analysis and science. It then explores the substantive and procedural dimensions of policy decision making, and the distinct roles of analysts and decision makers. It reviews progress in developing tools for rational policy analysis, confronts the normative divide between adherents of theoretical and practical reason, shows how public participation can augment the rationality of public decisions, and closes by noting that the status of rationality in public decision making is insecure.

POLICY ANALYSIS AS SCIENCE

Historical perspectives on policy analysis highlight the great modern urge to bring science to bear on society's problems. This urge has deep roots in the writings of Plato, Bacon, Descartes, Bentham, and Marx, among others, who all advocate variants of a scientifically guided society (Lindblom 1990). Progressive-era think tanks, Great Society systems analysis, and Lasswellian policy analysis are only the most recent manifestations of this ancient impulse. Surely any "good" society will take advantage of new knowledge to promote progress.

If policy analysis has scientific aspirations, then the scientific enterprise itself warrants a closer look. Science has proven to be a wonderfully productive enterprise, generating useful knowledge faster and cheaper than any other social activity the world has ever known. Given adequate resources, the wheel of science spins happily along, cycling from induction to deduction, from gathering evidence, to detecting patterns in the evidence, to formulating conceptual explanations for those patterns, to testing these hypotheses against additional empirical evidence (Wallace 1971). Focused research communities form around particular phenomena and shared conceptual frameworks, thereby promoting rapid progress within narrow domains. Norms of ideal science include universalism (apply only impersonal, objective criteria, disregard the personal and social characteristics of the scientist), communality (freely share new knowledge), disinterestedness (avoid a personal stake in a specific research outcome), and organized skepticism (require empirical and logical evidence for claims) (Merton 1973). In these ways, the scientific enterprise rapidly produces, validates, and disseminates knowledge.

Yet science remains a social activity, as fraught with weaknesses as any other human enterprise. Scientists have suffered from enforced orthodoxies, nepotism and favoritism; and ideal norms have been corrupted so that some science appears biased, proprietary, self-interested, or credulous (Jasanoff 1990). Scientific facts and truths are in any case temporary and provisional, representing only the current consensus—sometimes very long-lived—within a community of researchers. Thus science has a communicative context, and scientific knowledge claims are contingent.

Science is an elite enterprise that systematically excludes or marginalizes incompetent practitioners. Scientific norms, practices of peer review, and credentialing institutions all work to filter out poorly trained and less talented researchers, although these arrangements can also encourage a stifling orthodoxy. Democracy, it is worth noting, also has elements of exclusivity—madmen, children, and noncitizens do not vote (Guston 1993). Yet it remains true that only a tiny segment of society produces, communicates, and advocates on behalf of the scientific knowledge used in public decision making. Its moral autonomy has "helped create science in an Old Testament style, that is, respect without comprehension" (Toumey 1996, 34).

There are other sources of relevant, elite-based knowledge. The legal expertise of attorneys, the moral authority of religious leaders, the sharp pencils of accountants, and the contributions of many types of professionals all might contribute to better public decision making.

Difficulties emerge when deciding whose knowledge counts the most. Citizens vary in their education, life experience, raw intelligence, and particular knowledge. It makes sense to delegate certain decisions to experts. We ask engineers to design our bridges, neurosurgeons to operate on our brains, and economists to set monetary policy. Yet sometimes the value of elite expertise is less clear. Thus toxicological knowledge may be no more relevant than local fishing lore when setting fish consumption advisories in polluted waters. Experts also have limited domains of expertise, so it is not clear whether a biologist or a priest has a stronger claim in helping politicians decide the ethics of embryonic stem cell research. Some scientific knowledge is uncertain or irrelevant, some relevant knowledge is local rather than general, and some decisions turn on values as much as on the facts.

SUBSTANTIVE AND PROCEDURAL DIMENSIONS

Simon (1976) offers one solution to the dilemma of whose knowledge counts by distinguishing between substantive and procedural rationality. He measures substantive rationality relative to optimal outcomes, and procedural rationality relative to optimal decision processes.

Scientifically produced knowledge contributes to substantive rationality. Such knowledge describes phenomena and explains causal factors. It provides the factual basis for better decisions. It satisfies scientific criteria of validity and reliability, and it justifies authoritative knowledge claims. Scientific knowledge is a key input that contributes to the "best" outcome.

Yet every decision also has a procedural component: Who makes the decision, and what are the prescribed steps in making the decision? Procedural rationality helps improve decisions by specifying their "who" and "how" aspects. Optimal processes are legitimate, reasoned, and transparent.

Simon's distinction between substantive and procedural rationality maps nicely onto a distinction made decades earlier by Weber (1922) regarding sources of legitimacy. Public decisions are legitimate if they are legal, authoritative, and appropriate for the context. There are two very different sources of legitimacy. First, there is the legitimacy of authority, based in status, as enjoyed by divine rulers, revered elders, and scientific experts. Second, there is the legitimacy of consent, based in civil society, and deriving from following constitutional rules and open, democratic procedures. These distinctions make intuitive sense, but they also raise a troubling question: Are these two sources of legitimacy complementary or does one displace the other? Symmetrically, does increased procedural rationality come at the expense of decreased substantive rationality?

Lindblom (1990) argues forcefully that substantive rationality should not be allowed to displace procedural rationality. Especially regarding social phenomena, he doubts that science ever rises above mere confirmation of common sense. He believes that social scientific expertise should not be privileged over lay judgment in public decision making, and he advocates a *self-guided* rather than a *scientifically guided* society. Science should play only a minor supporting role. Lindblom's argument draws strongly on his famous "muddling through" conception, which asserts that scientific planning frequently fails in decentralized capitalist democracies because power is shared and no one has full information (1959). His solution is to encourage incrementalism in policy-making, and continual, mutual adjustment among policy actors.

Critics of Lindblom assert that incrementalism is the rational procedure sometimes but not all of the time (Breheny and Hooper 1985; Smith and May 1980). There are decisions in which expert contributions to substantive rationality are essential, such as the bridge-building example mentioned earlier. There are also "big" decisions that cannot be easily or cheaply reversed or subdivided, such as damming a major river, starting a nuclear power plant, or going to war. In such cases, the goodness of decisions depends equally on their procedural and substantive elements. However, the critics face a daunting task in explaining which decisions should be incremental and which should not.

RATIONAL AND REASONABLE

There is a way to relieve some of the inconsistencies identified in the preceding paragraphs, by distinguishing between decision making and analysis. Decision making is the art of choosing reasonable decision rules, ones that are appropriate for each decision context. Reasonable decision rules are internally consistent and an outcome of moral argumentation, they are values-based. Analysis is the science of applying those decision rules rationally, according to appropriate standards. Rational analysis is logical, valid, reliable, and empirically tested, it is fact-based. Values and facts are distinct intellectual categories although they can be hard to distinguish from one another in practice.

"Irrational" decisions are often nothing more than the rational application of unreasonable decision rules. For example, given a "net social benefit" decision rule, it may seem quite rational to dam a major river like the Yangtze. If a "no losers" test had been applied instead, then the rational choice might be to leave the river alone. Rationality in policy decision making thus requires both reasonable decision rules and rational applications of those rules.

Often the jobs of analysis and decision making are separated because of the scale and complexity of modern society. This opens up the possibility that analysts will not check with decision makers to determine which decision rule is reasonable. Equally, decision makers may not bother to check with analysts regarding the rationality of the rule's particular application. Rationality in policy decision making thus depends crucially on effective communication between decision makers and analysts.

The troubling word "appropriate" appears twice in this section, raising difficult questions. How does a decision maker know that a decision rule is reasonable, that is, appropriate to its context? Also, how does an analyst know that the logical and empirical standards applied are rational, that is, appropriate to the decision rule and its context? The answer to both questions is that appropriateness is socially determined. Both decision makers and analysts thus must communicate with others—the population at large as well as a range of experts—to confirm that they have acted appropriately.

SINGLE AND MULTIPLE DECISION MAKERS

Some decisions *seem* private: you choose your breakfast items, your day's clothes, and whether to get out of bed in the morning. Yet even despots do not get to make truly independent decisions. If you know that others strongly influence your own choice of food, clothing, and schedule, you also suspect that even Adolf Hitler and Julius Caesar needed to consult with confidantes and mollify the masses. Almost all policy decisions are truly multi-party decisions. This implies, first, that there *must* be a procedural component to public decision making that specifies how the parties interact. Second, this multi-party context implies that communication among parties will strongly influence outcomes.

As the next section illustrates, a close look at the tools of rational policy analysis shows that some of the most widely used methods blithely assume a single omniscient decision maker. For example, a hypothetical social planner acts on behalf of the whole population when selecting socially optimal policies by means of benefit-cost analysis. The risk assessor likewise weighs expected aggregate social risks and benefits when selecting optimal regulations. Such tools simplify away the procedural and communicative challenges of public decision making. We need to move beyond them (Andrews 2002).

TOOLS OF RATIONAL POLICY ANALYSIS

The science of public decision making has in fact evolved rapidly over the past century. A quick tour spanning welfare maximization, public choice, multi-agent simulation, and decision support follows.

WELFARE MAXIMIZATION

Starting from a microeconomic notion of individual utility, rationally pursued, Bergson, later extended by Samuelson, developed an additive social welfare function, with optimal public policy being that which maximizes the aggregate utility across members of the population. This individualistic formulation contrasts with competing concepts such as Benthamite utility ("the greatest good for the greatest number").

Benefit-cost analysis is a widely used tool that attempts to guide policymakers to welfare-maximizing choices. At its heart is the Kaldor-Hicks decision criterion that directs the "social planner" to choose the alternative providing the greatest net social benefits. It depends on two very strong assumptions, first, that it is reasonable to add gains and losses across individuals when calculating the societal net benefit; and, second, that the things individuals gain or lose are easily substitutable so that the winners can, at least hypothetically, compensate the losers. Thus it offers substantive equivalence to the Pareto criterion that underlies the microeconomic conception of free markets, because both can yield efficient outcomes.

However, the Pareto criterion also has a procedural component that promotes fairness as well as efficiency: it requires unanimous and voluntary participation in transactions to ensure that decisions have no losers, only mutual gains. The Kaldor-Hicks criterion is more procedurally coercive, implying majority rule at best, and dictatorship by the social planner at worst. Yet, realistically, many things that civilizations need impose costs on a few in order to reap broad social benefits. Examples include public education, progressive income taxation, highways, power plants, sewage treatment plants, and jails.

Benefit-cost analysis thus has a place in the policy analysis toolkit. As a decision aid, it is teachable, replicable, quantitative, and offers progressive insights that help narrow choices. Done properly, it requires a comprehensive enumeration of costs and benefits—this is both a strength and a weakness, since comprehensiveness is technically impossible even if it is conceptually desirable. Practitioners have attempted to include an ever-broader range of tangible, intangible, and temporally distant costs and benefits.

Public Choice

The microeconomic approach has led to a variety of contributions under the rubric of public choice theory that show how individual interests influence both marketplace and public policy outcomes. Self-interested bureaucratic actors maximize their budgets (Niskanen 1971), and citizens form clubs to collectively provide some forms of public goods (Buchanan 1965), for example. The plausibility of social welfare functions has been challenged by Arrow (1951) on logical grounds, because under reasonable assumptions it is possible to show that any democratic aggregation process leads to inconsistent and unstable results.

Our collective decision-making mechanisms are deeply flawed, so that neither markets nor politics on their own serve us adequately. Markets are sometimes inequitable because they concentrate wealth while making one dollar equal one economic vote, and because future generations get no votes. Also, market imperfections abound, with monopoly power, public goods, externalities, and information problems being the most severe weaknesses. Government failures also abound. Bureaucratic self-interest can encourage agents within government to maximize their budgets or allow regulatory agencies to be captured. Also, as discussed earlier, democratic decision making according to "reasonable" criteria can become arbitrary and unstable (Arrow 1951). Given criteria of collective rationality, a Pareto (no losers) principle, independence of irrelevant alternatives, and non-dictatorship, Arrow presents an impossibility theorem for the existence of social welfare functions. He shows that pairwise voting such as is currently practiced in most elections leads to endless cycling, majority rule can select no winner non-arbitrarily, society's preferences do not exhibit collective rationality and do not aggregate individual preferences consistently, and that by not counting the intensity of preferences, voting will lead to inconsistent outcomes (Pearce 1986). Formal democratic decision-making mechanisms thus need to be supplemented sometimes.

One solution is to relax some of Arrow's reasonable criteria. By relaxing the Pareto postulate, we open up the solution domain to allow winners, losers, and compensation. By relaxing the independence postulate, we move from pairwise comparisons to multiple options. By relaxing the unlimited domain postulate (part of collective rationality), we allow efforts to foster unanimity prior to a vote. We maintain transitivity (the other part of collective rationality) and nondictatorship. Public participation is one way to relax Arrow's criteria while preserving elements of democracy, as will be discussed shortly.

There have been many important extensions to the microeconomic approach that have broadened its reach. Game theorists have usefully characterized responses to governmental interventions as mixed-motive (competitive-cooperative) negotiations (Axelrod 1984). Decision theorists have introduced concepts of risk preference and multi-criteria tradeoffs (Keeney and Raiffa 1976), thereby forcing into daylight the issues of risk and priority associated with policies. Psychologists have demonstrated that individuals rely on heuristics and suffer from systematic biases that are not reflected in standard utility functions (Tversky and Kahneman 1974), thereby weakening the policy optimality claims of microeconomic analysts, and highlighting the roles of communication and perception in public management. Most of these contributions have the effect of making the science more effective in describing, explaining, and prescribing changes in public decision making, in accord with an individualistic, utilitarian form of rationality.

Modern microeconomic theory now explicitly acknowledges both the independence and interdependence of decision makers. Theory now has much to say about the importance of rules and access to information, pinpointing conditions leading to stable, efficient, and (sometimes) equitable outcomes. Equally important, an emerging emphasis on collection of experimental evidence has made microeconomics a more realistic behavioral science.

Multi-Agent Simulation

Multi-agent simulation is a relatively new modeling approach that seeks to generalize from micro-economic game theory by incorporating more actors, imbuing them with more realistic cognitive limitations in the form of bounded rationality and imperfect knowledge, and investigating out-of-equilibrium conditions. Access to cheap computing power has allowed modelers to explore cases that used to be mathematically intractable, involving heterogeneous actors, evolutionary processes, and emergent structural relationships. In policy simulations, preferred governmental interventions sometimes diverge dramatically from those identified as optimal under neoclassical microeconomic assumptions.

The multi-agent approach has been useful in the innovation, anti-trust, environmental, and security policy domains, among others (Axelrod 1997; Barnett et al. 2000; Epstein and Axtell 1996; Gilbert and Troitzch 1999). One early application shows how a widespread individual preference for having as few as one-third of your neighbors share your own ethnicity will lead to highly segregated housing patterns, even in the absence of discriminatory real estate market actors and policies (Schelling 1978). Another application shows how modeling with adaptive agents can yield results that are at variance with those of neoclassical economics. In particular, in perfectly competitive markets, regulation is either distorting and inefficient or irrelevant. However, when agents—firms in this model—are heterogeneous, boundedly rational, and interact directly with one another out of equilibrium, regulations can be demonstrated to have positive welfare effects (Teitelbaum 1998).

Decision Support Systems

Another important innovation has been to reframe policy analysis as a decision support activity rather than a surrogate for actual decision making. The distinction is important. Traditional policy analysis accepts a request for a study from the decision makers, sets the scope of the research question, establishes key assumptions, carries out the analysis, and delivers policy recommendations back to the decision makers. Decision support systems instead reserve key decisions for decision makers, and plan for repeated interactions between analysts and decision makers. It is a humbler approach but its analytics are often more complex.

An example of a decision support system is a regional electric power planning tool used a few years ago in New England (Andrews 1992). Its purpose was to help break an impasse among utility companies, regulators, environmentalists, and other interested parties regarding public utility investment policy. Analysts built a complex scenario analysis tool for simulating the operation of the regional power system under various assumptions over a multi-decade time horizon, and then they convened a planning process that involved all of these parties. Iteratively, the analysts proposed the scope of analysis and the stakeholders approved it, the analysts offered assumptions for review and the stakeholders approved them, when stakeholders disagreed among themselves about certain assumptions the analysts ran their model both ways and reported back whether their answers diverged, the stakeholders suggested policy alternatives and the analysts evaluated their multi-attribute impacts, the stakeholders evaluated these simulated impacts and drew their own conclusions about which solution was optimal from their point of view, and out of this interaction emerged broad consensus on a new set of energy policies for the region. Decision support systems have found application in an increasing number of fields spanning urban planning, environmental policy, health policy, energy policy, international relations, and military policy, among others (Sauter 1997; Brail and Klosterman 2001).

Readers will detect that the key distinction between traditional policy analysis and decision support systems is that the latter have an explicit procedural component. Decision support analysts devote much effort to mapping the points in a decision process at which analysts might helpfully intervene. They then apply themselves to the design of potentially fruitful interactions at those few key points. They are shifting the practice of policy analysis away from a major focus on substantive rationality to giving equal consideration to procedural rationality.

In sum, the tools of rational policy analysis have evolved over a century toward a richer conception of rationality that acknowledges substantive and procedural dimensions, rational applications of reasonable decision rules, an expectation that interested parties hold diverse views, and more limited roles for experts. These tools must appropriately blend facts and values as they produce actionable policy advice.

PUBLIC PARTICIPATION

Public participation has several potential roles in policy decision making, and the reasons offered for encouraging it are diverse (Wengert 1976). One can pursue participation as policy, that is, with a normative perception that it is desirable in and of itself because, in the words of Susskind and Elliott (1983), it democratizes, decentralizes, deprofessionalizes, and demystifies public policy. One can pursue participation as a strategy, as a means for achieving other ends. Participation can operate as communication, leading to improved information flows that produce better decisions. Participation can serve as therapy, a way to coopt alienated groups into the mainstream. It can function as conflict resolution, so that participation may (or may not) lead to reduced tensions and stable outcomes in controversial decisions. More intuitively, the best way to find out what people want and value is to ask them (Feiveson et al. 1976).

There is a spectrum of participation mechanisms available (FEARO 1988):

- Public information (ads, newsletters, exhibits)
- Public information feedback (polls, focus groups, surveys)
- Consultation (hearings, workshops, panels, games)
- Extended involvement (advisory committees, charrettes, task forces)
- Joint planning (arbitration, conciliation, mediation, negotiation, partnership)
- Delegation (citizen control, home rule)

Choosing which mode of participation to solicit is important because each has distinctive strengths and weaknesses. Steps in choosing a mechanism typically include informal early consultation to identify major issues and actors, confirmation of an organizational mandate to proceed in an accountable and open fashion, identification of potentially interested participants including those who are unlikely to receive representation, analysis of the specific situation, setting objectives for the participation process, determining information exchange requirements, planning the length of the activity and the complexity of involvement, implementation, and evaluation of how it worked (FEARO, 1988).

Cultivating public participation as a conscious strategy or policy does not mean that it may not arise "naturally" in spontaneous occurrences. The existing pattern of public interaction sets the stage. Susskind and Elliott (1988) describe patterns of paternalism (elites govern, they inform the public of decisions), conflict (members of the public begin to distrust the elites, they second-guess decisions and demand participation), and coproduction (elites and members of the public share decision-making power and constructively resolve conflicts).

Like other collective decision-making mechanisms, public participation also has flaws. These include potential tyranny of the majority or minority, instability of decisions, poor information, apathy and stakeholder fatigue, adverse reactions to perfunctory involvement, and the nonrepresentativeness of participants in any small group process.

In evaluating the success of public participation processes, Webler and Renn (1995) argue that the key criteria are fairness and competence. A fair process gives all interested parties equal opportunities to participate in the discourse, make validity claims, challenge validity claims made by others, and determine when closure is reached. A competent process operates in direct tension with fairness, however, by setting minimal standards for cognitive and lingual competence, ensuring reliance on appropriate knowledge, using a consensually approved translation scheme, and relying on the most reliable methodological techniques available. In addition to balancing fairness and competence, traditional measures of effectiveness and value also figure into perceived success. Participation increases the rationality of public decision making to the extent that it overcomes the failings of markets and politics, as well as its own internal weaknesses.

THEORETICAL AND PRACTICAL REASON

Philosophers identify theoretical and practical reason as two distinct approaches to the facts-values dichotomy in public decision making. Theoretical reason is the rationality underlying pure science, and it helps us evaluate whether our theories have empirical validity. Practical reason is the rationality underlying decision making, and it helps us evaluate the normative validity of our actions. Marrying facts and values—analysis and decision making—requires integrating theoretical and practical reason.

Is such a marriage necessary or even desirable? Perhaps only one type of reason is enough. Theoretical reason, for example, is a consequentialist, outcome-oriented doctrine that prizes usefulness in linking facts and values. For its disciples, good science generates testable hypotheses and credible data that usefully advance knowledge, and good decision making leads to useful, utility-enhancing outcomes.

Practical reason, by contrast, is a deontological, obligation-oriented doctrine that prizes wide acceptance in linking facts and values. For its disciples, good science produces widely accepted knowledge, and good decision making is also widely accepted.

Unfortunately, neither theoretical nor practical reason offers truly universal lessons. Theoretical reason delivers only temporary truths because science is always contingent. Practical reason delivers only useful norms because experience is never adequate to support the formulation of absolute moral laws. Both doctrines offer plausible ways to integrate facts and values in decision making, as long as one is willing to accept an extremely limited, relative form of rationality.

INSTRUMENTAL, STRATEGIC, AND COMMUNICATIVE RATIONALITY

Jantsch (1975) points out that different contexts demand different rationalities. When the task is simply to rationalize the use of scarce resources in the absence of uncertainty or conflict, an *instrumental* response is appropriate. Instrumental rationality optimizes the allocation of resources according to an efficiency criterion. For example, a public works manager operates instrumentally to allocate a fixed budget among pipes, valves, filters, pumps, concrete, excavation equipment, and labor when designing a water supply system.

When the task is to rationalize a set of steering principles for managing uncertainty and complexity, a *strategic* response is appropriate. Strategic rationality optimizes strategies for responding to change induced at least partly by the actions of others, according to an effectiveness criterion. For example, a mayor operates strategically when deciding whether to build a water supply system ahead of or in response to demand, even as developers and prospective residents decide whether to build and buy new homes in her city.

When the task is to rationalize a set of collective preferences—norms—for managing conflict, then a *communicative* response is appropriate. Communicative rationality optimizes opportunities for achieving consensus, according to a criterion of ethical behavior. For example, the mayor may ask a municipal planning commission to develop, in consultation with stakeholders and the general public, a widely accepted land use plan that represents the community's vision of where and when future development will happen, including any required water supply system improvements.

A devotee of theoretical reason, say, a utilitarian, will respond instrumentally in a non-social context and strategically in a social, multi-party context. This person will test the validity of scientific facts by considering the empirical evidence. She will test the validity of decision-making values by confirming that her utility increases.

A devotee of practical reason, by contrast, will respond instrumentally in a non-social context but she will act communicatively in a social, multi-party context. She will test the validity of both facts and values with reference to the degree of consensus each enjoys.

So, in a non-social context, devotees of both theoretical and practical reason operate instrumentally. But in a social context—which is far more prevalent—there is divergence because a theoretical reasoner will operate strategically and a practical reasoner will operate communicatively (see Table 12.1). Thus, if the mayor is a theoretical reasoner, she will extend her town's water supply system strategically, seizing opportunities as they arise, without consultation, and maximizing her own expected benefits along the way. On the other hand, if she is a practical reasoner, the mayor will operate in a more deliberative manner, seeking broad input and acceptance of the water system's expansion plans and ensuring that neither she nor developers and residents are blind-sided by any aspect of the development process.

Such an argument overstates the differences, however, because there can be utilitarian reasons to operate communicatively. First, conflict can be a source of scarcity and uncertainty, giving communication both instrumental and strategic value. Second, the contingent and socially constructed nature of scientific knowledge implies communication challenges, and highlights the value of achieving consensus on "serviceable facts." Third, since every public decision has a procedural component, interested parties will have opportunities to reward conformance with widely shared norms of ethical behavior. Fourth, the contemporary common division of labor between analysts and decision makers can impose costly communicative distortions. Distortions also can appear as experts communicate across disciplinary boundaries, or with members of the lay public. Thus, communicative action offers utility for avoiding unintended misunderstandings and needless conflicts. All public decisions need to achieve at least a limited degree of communicative rationality, as every mayor knows.

TABLE 12.1
Rationality in Philosophical and Social Context

Social Context:	Single Party	Multi-Party
Philosophical Context:	**Decision Context**	**Decision Context**
Utilitarian Perspective (consequentialist, optimizing, theoretical reason)	Instrumental Rationality (rationalize use of scarce resources, valid facts are empirically tested, valid values increase utility)	Strategic Rationality (rationalize steering principles given uncertainty, valid facts are empirically tested, valid values increase expected utility)
Communicative Perspective (deontological, consensus-seeking, practical reason)	Instrumental Rationality (rationalize use of scarce resources, valid facts are empirically tested, valid values increase utility)	Communicative Rationality (rationalize norms for managing conflict, valid facts enjoy consensus, valid values enjoy consensus)

Norms of ideal communication include comprehensible, sincere, legitimate, and truthful speech (Forester 1980; Habermas 1979). A typology of communicative distortions distinguishes two dimensions: origins and intentions. Individual and unintentional distortions include poor writing or speaking capabilities, for example. Individual and intentional distortions include such acts as lying and deception. Systemic and unintentional distortions are due to such problems as miscommunication across disciplinary and organizational boundaries. Systemic and intentional distortions are particularly problematic, and examples include propaganda and misleading advertising. Reducing any of these distortions directly increases communicative rationality.

Conflicts nevertheless persist between devotees of theoretical and practical reason because the underlying moral values differ. For the same reasons that we see the tragedy of the commons play out in many policy domains, so we see that strategic action frequently displaces communicative action. Individuals often have too much to gain by strategic action not to pursue it, even if it damages the public good. Consensus has limited value in a world with great scope for independent action.

CONCLUSIONS

The desire to apply rationality to public decision making is a modern desire, bundled in with other tenets of modernity. These include a faith that humankind is making qualitative progress, that there is a definable "public good," that individual actions matter, and that human inventiveness will create more good things than bad things. These tenets are by no means universally accepted. Some see a grimmer world in which public decision making is purely a pluralistic game, a play of power, an unequal contest whose outcome is determined by social or economic structure, or a simple series of do-able deals. Others see a world in which values are the only essential element of decision making, and the factual element is secondary and perhaps even indeterminate. Rationality in public decision making will be of little interest to partisans and demagogues, and efforts to improve the scientific or procedural basis of public decisions are unlikely to win their support.

This chapter began by linking rationality in public decision making with science, with substance and logic. It then added a procedural dimension that greatly enriched our notion of rationality, by bringing in communicative and legitimacy concerns. It showed that popular tools of policy analysis such as benefit-cost studies are deficient when judged against this broader definition of rationality; hence, better tools are under development. Rationality may even be improved by resorting to procedural solutions such as public participation. Ultimately, rationality is a characteristic of public decision making that some people desire some of the time. It has no guaranteed seat at the table. Its very vulnerability should make us value it and pursue it all the more passionately.

REFERENCES

Andrews, C.J. (1992). Sorting out a consensus: Analysis in support of multi-party decisions. *Environment and Planning B: Planning and Design* 19(2): 189–204.
Andrews, C.J. (2002). *Humble Analysis*. Westport, CT: Praeger.
Arrow, K.J. (1951). *Social Choice and Individual Values*. New York: John Wiley and Sons.
Axelrod, R. (1984). *The Evolution of Cooperation*. New York: Basic Books.
Axelrod, R. (1997). *The complexity of cooperation: Agent-based models of competition and collaboration.* Princeton, NJ: Princeton University Press.
Barnett, W.A., Chiarella, C., Keen, S., Marks, R. and Schnabl, H., eds. (2000). *Commerce, Complexity, and Evolution: Topics In Economics, Finance, Marketing and Management*, Proceedings of the Twelfth International Symposium in Economic Theory and Econometrics, International Symposia in Economic Theory and Econometrics. Cambridge: Cambridge University Press.
Brail, R., and Klosterman, R., eds. (2001). *Planning Support Systems*. Redlands, CA: ESRI Press.

Breheny, M.J., and A.J. Hooper, eds. (1985). *Rationality in Planning*. London: Pion Limited.

Buchanan, J. (1965). An Economic Theory of Clubs. *Econometrica* 32: 1–14.

Epstein, J.M., and Axtell, R. (1996). *Growing artificial societies: Social science from the bottom up*. Cambridge, MA: MIT Press.

Federal Environmental Assessment Review Office (FEARO). (1988). *Public Involvement: Planning and Implementing Public Involvement Programs*. Prepared by Praxis, Inc. for FEARO, Hull, Quebec, Canada.

Feiveson, H.A., Sinden, F.W., and Socolow, R.H., eds. (1976). *Boundaries of Analysis: An Inquiry into the Tocks Island Dam Controversy*. Cambridge, MA: Ballinger.

Forester, J. (1980). Critical Theory and Planning Practice. *APA Journal* 46(3): 275–286.

Gilbert, N., and Troitzsch, K.G. (1999). *Simulation for the Social Scientist*. Milton Keynes: Open University Press.

Guston, D.H. (1993). The essential tension in science and democracy. *Social Epistemology* 7(1): 3–23.

Habermas, J. (1979). *Communication and the Evolution of Society*. Boston: Beacon Press.

Jantsch, E. (1975). *Design for Evolution*. New York: Braziller.

Jasanoff, S. (1990). *The Fifth Branch: Science Advisors as Policymakers*. Cambridge, MA: Harvard University Press.

Keeney, R., and Raiffa, H. (1976). *Decisions with Multiple Objectives: Preferences and Value Tradeoffs*. New York: John Wiley.

Lindblom, C.E. (1959). The science of 'muddling through.' *Public Administration Review* 19: 78–88.

Lindblom, C.E. (1990). *Inquiry and Change*. New Haven: Yale University Press.

Merton, R.K. (1973.) The Normative Structure of Science. Reprinted in Merton's *The Sociology of Science*. Chicago: University of Chicago Press.

Nash, J.F. (1950). Equilibrium points in N-Person Games. *Proceedings of NAS*.

Niskanen, W. (1971). *Bureaucracy and Representative Government*. Chicago: Aldine-Atherton.

Pearce, D. (1986). *The MIT Dictionary of Modern Economics*, entry on social welfare functions. Cambridge, MA: MIT Press.

Sauter, V.L. (1997). *Decision Support Systems*. Hoboken, NJ: John Wiley and Sons.

Schelling, T.C. (1978). *Micromotives and Macrobehavior*. New York: W. W. Norton.

Simon, H.A. (1976). *Administrative Behavior: A Study of Decision-making Processes in Administrative Organization*. New York: Harper & Rowe.

Smith, G., and May, D. (1980). The Artificial Debate Between Rationalist and Incrementalist Models of Decision-Making. *Policy and Politics* 8: 147–161.

Susskind, L., and Elliott, M. (1983). Paternalism, Conflict, and Coproduction. New York: Plenum Press.

Teitelbaum, D. (1998). *An Adaptive Agent Approach to Environmental Regulation*. Ph.D. disseratation, Pittsburgh, PA: Carnegie Mellon University.

Toumey, C.P. (1996) *Conjuring Science*. New Brunswick, NJ: Rutgers University Press.

Tversky, A., and Kahneman, D. (1974). Judgment under uncertainty: Heuristics and biases. *Science* 185:1124–1131.

von Neumann, J., and Morgenstern, O. (1944). *Theory of Games and Economic Behavior*. Princeton, NJ: Princeton University Press.

Wallace, W. (1971). *The Logic of Science in Sociology*. New York: Aldine deGruyter.

Weber, M. (1922, 1957.) *The Theory of Social and Economic Organization*. New York: Free Press.

Webler, T., and Renn, O. (1995). A brief primer on participation: philosophy and practice. In O. Renn, T. Webler and P. Wiedemann, eds. *Fairness and Competence in Citizen Participation*. Dordrecht: Kluwer Academic Publishers, pp. 17–33 (Ch. 2).

Wengert, N. (1976). Citizen Participation: Practice in Search of a Theory. In A. Utton, ed., *Natural Resources for a Democratic Society*. Boulder, CO: Westview Press, pp. 1–40.

13 Rational Choice in Public Policy: The Theory in Critical Perspective

Steven Griggs

Rational choice theory seeks to generate, from a set of parsimonious assumptions that privilege the instrumental actions of individual policy actors, a predictive and universal explanation of the policy process. This quest for predictive and universal explanation has challenged orthodox accounts across a range of different contexts, problematizing not least group mobilization and the vagaries of collective action (Olson 1962, 1982), coalition building (Riker 1962), the dynamics of bureaucracies (Downs 1967; Niskanen 1971; Dunleavy 1991) and political-business cycles (Nordhaus 1975; Alt and Chrystal 1983). Indeed, rational choice theory has itself become, if not quite the orthodox approach to policy analysis, at the very least the dominant yardstick against which to assess explanations of the policy process. However, this somewhat hegemonic advance of rational choice theory from its origins in party competition and voting behavior has not been without contestation (Lichbach 2003). In recent years, the limits of rational choice have come under increasing scrutiny. Notably, Green and Shapiro (1994) have alleged that rational choice is founded upon concededly unrealistic and inadequately tested assumptions. Others have derided its tendency simply to confirm trivial findings in complex mathematical models, condemning rational choice for simply restating the obvious (Johnson 1997). What generates such critiques, and indeed debate within rational choice theory itself, is not only differential conceptions of the complexity of the policy process that rational choice actually seeks to model (Hay 2004, 46), but also rival conceptions of epistemology and appropriate scientific inquiry often within rational choice theory itself (MacDonald 2003, 551).

This chapter examines the contribution of rational choice theory to our understanding of the policy process. It begins with an investigation of the common assumptions that underpin rationalist approaches before analyzing how rational choice has engaged in debates surrounding institutions and ideas in its quest to explain strategic equilibria in policy-making. In so doing, we seek to problematize the challenges to and limitations of rational choice theory. There are for example divisions within rational choice theory itself over the boundaries to rationality and definitions of self-interest *and* its applicability to all areas of social inquiry (MacDonald 2003, 551). Indeed, whilst some posit the restriction of rational choice to appropriate domains, others begin to loosen core assumptions or even downgrade rational choice to a partial explanation, to a useful heuristic device or set of tools to be deployed in conjunction with other approaches. The chapter thus concludes by questioning the limits of rational choice theory through bringing to the fore the constitutive logic of all policy theory (Howarth 2000, 130). It is against this background that we first turn to an examination of the building blocks of mainstream rational choice theory and the search for strategic equilibria before addressing the challenges and limits to rational choice theory.

THE BUILDING BLOCKS OF RATIONAL CHOICE THEORY

Rational choice theory is best characterized as a school or an approach to understanding the dy-namics of public policy; it is a "family of theories" rather than a single theory (Green and Shapiro 1994, 28). The likes of game theoretical accounts of strategic interactions (Axelrod 1984), social choice critiques of the impossibility of a democratic aggregation of interests (Arrow 1951), and public choice applications of economics to politics (Niskanen 1971; Olson 1982) all sit shoulder to shoulder under the auspices of rational choice. In this opening section, we identify a set of com-mon building blocks that arguably provide the foundations that hold such mainstream rationalist approaches together; foundations that have however been stretched or applied over time with varying levels of consistency as we shall discover below. Our first common building block is the assumption of rationality, which posits that individuals in the policy process are rational, and that the behavior of agents is best explained by imputing rationality on to them (Dowding and King 1995, 1). We then go on to examine further heroic qualities associated with individuals in the form of consistent and rank-ordered preferences before addressing the premises of methodological individualism and deductive reasoning.

THE ASSUMPTION OF RATIONALITY

Within rational choice accounts of public policy, individuals are characterized as instrumental actors, pursing courses of actions "not for their own sake, but only insofar as they secure desired, typically private ends" (Chong 1996, 39). In this instance, rationality is entwined with utility-maximization. Rational individuals are those individuals who, when faced with distinct courses of action or policy options, choose the feasible course of action, which is most likely to maximise their own utility. Rationality thus emerges from an actor's capacity to calculate and attach costs and benefits to avail-able policy options, and to select the course of action that best maximises her own utility (Dunleavy 1991, 3; Majone 1989, 13; Elster 1986, 4). Policy actors are constructed as egotistical, self-regarding instrumental actors, "choosing how to act on the basis of the consequences for their personal welfare (or that of their immediate family)" (Dunleavy 1991, 3). As such, mainstream rational choice lends itself towards explanations of policy outcomes grounded in the goal-oriented action of individuals (MacDonald 2003, 552) where the desires, beliefs, and preferences of individual actors are identified as the causes of their actions (Green and Shapiro, 1994: 20). Of course, such rational behavior by individuals will not necessarily produce positive collective outcomes. Rational utility-maximizing individuals will and do deliver collectively unintentional outcomes or socially irrational outcomes (Levi 1997, 20) as the "tragedy of the commons" demonstrates (Hardin 1969). Rational choice thus explains the irrational collective outcomes of the individual actions of rational actors.

RANK-ORDERED AND CONSISTENT PREFERENCES

As we suggested above, this assumption of rationality hinges upon a number of heroic qualities attached to individual actors, not least that rational actors possess, even when faced with complex situations, the capacity (in terms of information, time, and objectivity) to choose the optimum course of action open to them (Ward 2002, 68). Importantly, individual rational actors must, if the assump-tion of rationality is to hold, possess preferences or wants that are ranked-ordered, and consistent in that they are both transitive and stable over time. First, the rank-ordering of preferences asserts that individuals are able to establish a hierarchy of wants or preferences; preferences of course have to be comparable. Second, the condition of transitivity establishes a particular consistency of preferences in that if an individual prefers oranges (x) to pears (y) and pears (y) to apples (z), she will prefer oranges (x) to apples (z). Under such conditions, preferences are said to be transitive. Finally, an individual's preferences are taken to be both stable over time (at least in the short-term), and to be given. In terms of this latter condition, that which assumes the given-ness of preferences, mainstream rationalist accounts are simply saying that for the purposes of explanation, they are not overly concerned with the origins of individuals' preferences. For Shepsle and Bonchek, rational choice accounts "take people as we find them," less concerned with "why they want what they want" (1997, 17).

METHODOLOGICAL INDIVIDUALISM

Mainstream rational choice builds its explanations of policy outcomes on the actions of individuals, privileging the role of actors over and beyond that of social structures. Social structures are attributed no "independent status apart from the individuals who constitute them. Only actors choose, prefer, believe, learn and so on: society does not act independently of them" (Lichbach 2003, 32–33). This privileging of actors locates the explanation of macro-level phenomena at the micro-level of the individual, or at the aggregated behavior of individuals (Van Thiel 2004, 180). Social structures are thereby conceptualized through the intentional behavior of individuals, interpreted as the aggregate result of the calculations and utility-maximizing strategies of individual actors, such that institutions become "instrumental products used by individuals to maximise their respective utilities" (Blyth 2002, 19). As such, rational choice stresses the production of causal mechanisms, underplayed in structural and functionalist explanations (Chong 1996, 42–43). For, as Laver argues, "the primitive motivational assumptions" of rational choice "relate to the individual as a self-contained unit of analysis" (1997, 9).

DEDUCTIVE REASONING

In applying deductive reasoning, rational choice explanations of policy outcomes advance through first establishing sets of propositions and statements about real world phenomena and the rational behavior of individuals, and then testing these propositions through comparison with events and the actual behavior of actors (Laver 1997, 4). Indeed, Laver (1997) makes an emblematic defence of the value of what he calls the *a priori* approach of rational choice over and beyond predominant empirical approaches to policy analysis (for another defense see Ward 2002, 69–70). Such predominant empirical approaches, Laver argues, simply extrapolate generalized propositions about political behavior from "systematic observations of what real people actually do," which "in the last analysis more or less says that the world is as it is because that's how it is" (1997, 10). Drawing upon the work of Nozick and Rawls, Laver argues, however, that the very value of deductive reasoning in rational choice accounts lies in the fact that the explanation of political outcomes derives from motivational assumptions defined in another realm, that of the individual.

What these building blocks of mainstream rational choice theory offer is a "convenient short-cut which makes possible a naturalist science of the political such as is capable of generating through a process of deduction, testable and predictive hypotheses" (Hay 2004, 40). The complexity of both individual motivations and the decision-making process is thus necessarily mobilised out of rational choice accounts in the quest for universal and parsimonious explanation. Issues of interpersonal variation and personal identity are, for example, neatly sidestepped under the guise of rational instrumental utility-maximising individuals, with preferences given, stable over time, and common across individuals (see below). However, rather than acknowledging the contested nature of such oversimplifications, mainstream rational choice theorists laud such interchangeability, for it "constitutes a conscious effort to apply standards of scientific explanation in the social sciences" (Tsebelis 1990, 45).

THE SEARCH FOR EQUILIBRIUM SOLUTIONS

In discussing the building blocks of mainstream rational choice approaches, we have set our analysis within the conditions of parametric decision making. Under the conditions of parametric decision making, individuals calculate the costs and benefits of particular courses of action with no risk or uncertainty over either the outcomes of particular courses of action or over how the actions of others might impinge upon potential outcomes. Particular courses of action are known by individual actors to lead to specific outcomes, and the actions of other individuals are fixed in that they do not affect the relationships between the particular courses of action open to an individual and the outcomes associated with each of these particular courses of action (Ward 2002, 68). Here we now move on from the conditions of parametric decision making to examine the conditions of strategic decision making and the implications of such conditions for our understanding of the motivations of rational individuals in the policy process. Understanding the conditions of strategic decision making brings to the fore the search for strategic equilibria and questions earlier assumptions of methodological individualism. It leads us first to clarify the assumption of rationality, moving from the maximisation of utility to the maximisation of expected utility.

In fact, rather than the simplifying assumptions of parametric decision making, most policy making will take place under the conditions of strategic decision making. Strategic decision-making assumes that actors operate under conditions of interdependence where the actions of others will impinge upon the relationship between courses of action and potential outcomes; such that personal outcomes for individuals will depend upon the collective expectations and action of others. Individual actors are thus obliged to act strategically, to anticipate what from a range of policy options other actors will do and equally what these other actors believe she herself will do (Elster 1986, 7). Under such conditions, and given that rational actors cannot guarantee the outcomes of particular courses of action, or necessarily know the consequences of their actions, individuals will make calculations over the efficacy of particular policy instruments and the probability of particular instruments delivering potential outcomes. In other words, rational individuals will maximise the expected utility attached to policy instruments.

This recognition of strategic independence privileges the conceptualisation of the processes of decision-making as complex interactive games played out between individual policy actors whereby the coordination of the actions of individual actors is at a premium. In such complex interactive games, the primary analytical concern of rational choice theorists is the search for, or identification of, the necessary conditions for optimum strategic equilibrium solutions. Equilibrium solutions occur when individual actors involved "in a recurring course of action are considered as not having any incentives to deviate from this course" (Tsebelis 1990, 41). Equilibrium solutions are thus by definition self-reinforcing. However, there is no single equilibrium solution in any game being played out by rational actors (as the Folk Theorem demonstrates), bringing to the fore the question of why particular equilibrium solutions emerge over others and how stable interactions ensure between policy actors. Indeed, accounting for such patterns of stability challenges assumptions of unstable patterns of competition inherent within mainstream rational choice accounts of public policy.

This search for strategic equilibria is problematized by the logic of collective action, presented as the difficulties of overcoming strategic coordination in multiple actor games. Recurring games do offer actors the opportunity of trial-and-error learning (see evolutionary game theory). However, rational choice theory has tended to couch explanations of stability within the framework of institutions. Institutions, it is argued, place constraints upon actors, lessen information costs, and offer "nests" for focal points which when taken together facilitate coordination and cooperation between actors and explain the emergence of specific equilibrium solutions over others (North 1990, Goldstein and Keohane 1993). Indeed, Garrett and Weingast (1993, 173–207) demonstrate how the 1979 Cassis de Dijon ruling of the European Court of Justice established the principle of the mutual recognition of goods and services that facilitated moves toward the European single market through its capacity to operate as a focal point to overcome collective action and coordination difficulties between member states keen to guard their domestic interests and uncertain of the outcomes of any further moves towards economic competition. Ideas thus operate in this instance "*ex post* as auxiliary hypotheses designed to explain disconfirming outcomes" (Blyth 2002, 26).

This search to explain stability fuels questions over how far the assertion of methodological individualism best characterizes rational choice theory. Rational choice accounts of policy making specify prevailing institutional rules of the game such that, as Dowding and King (1995, 1) assert, rational choice theory explains how context informs the preferences of actors, offering explanations of political outcomes "where the reasons for individual action are specified, and the structural conditions under which those reasons of action have been modelled and explained." The behavior of individuals becomes an optimal response both to other actors and the dominant institutional rules and norms, such that "the prevailing institutions (the rules of the game) determine the behaviour of the actors, which in turn produces political or social outcomes" (Tsebelis 1990, 40); or, in other words, "preferences provide the motivation of individual action; institutions provide the context allowing causal explanation" (Dowding and King 1995, 1). This assertion does not necessarily contest the fundamental assumption of methodological individualism, which is that macro-social outcomes are the product of the micro-actions of individuals whose behaviour and identity are not determined by such structures. However, Ward argues that the existence of multiple equilibria requires actors to coordinate beliefs through common conjectures and that such patterns of beliefs are intersubjective, forming "a *system* that cannot be reduced to the beliefs of any one player considered as a 'social atom'" (Ward 2002, 71). Indeed, for Ward, rational choice models, "in ontological terms partly comprise taken-as-given socio-structural elements," informing us how decisions are taken within social structures (Ward, 2002, 71).

Overall, therefore, the conditions of strategic decision making pose a number of internal challenges to rational choice accounts of the policy process, not least the explanation of the emergence of particular stable patterns of policy making or strategic equilibrium solutions. The predominant response to such challenges has been the turn toward further incorporation into rational choice of the role of institutions and ideas. However, moves toward institutions and ideas strain assumptions of rationality and potentially hamper quests for universal explanation. Indeed, the very acceptance of multiple equilibria weakens the predictive power of rational choice. With these strains in mind, we now examine the challenges and limits to rational choice theory.

CHALLENGES TO RATIONAL CHOICE THEORY

The rationality assumption that we have addressed so far parsimonious and universal explanations founded upon the actions of rational utility-maximizing individuals. However, this very assumption of rationality is often challenged as the Achilles' heel of mainstream rational choice theory, labeled as being reductionist and falsely biased toward economistic arguments, as attributing overoptimistic heroic qualities to individuals, and as lacking empirical foundation (see, for example, the work of Green and Shapiro 1994). At their strongest, such challenges summarily dismiss short-term utility-maximization as historically and culturally specific to capitalist societies, with rational choice theory characterized as "more an ideological expression of the United States' interests in the post-Cold War period than an attempt at social science" (Johnson 1997, 171). Indeed, it is somewhat ironic for its detractors that such a culturally bound theory as rational choice is "sophomoric [...] when contending that [it] contains a unique capacity to transcend culture and reduce all human behaviour to a few individual motivational uniformities" (Johnson 1997, 1).

Typically, the alleged primacy of self-interest is said to fail to recognise the complex motivations of individuals in the policy process. As Udehn (1996) argues in an attack on the assumption of self-interest, policy actors are just as likely to be motivated by group interests or altruistic public concerns as their own narrow self-interest; and, as such, self-interest cannot be simply imputed on or read into every action of an individual throughout the process of decision-making. Exploring rationalist explanations of bureaucratic behavior, Udehn thus questions Niskanen's characterization of bureaucrats (1971) as self-interested budget-maximizers, eager to increase departmental budgets in order to provide themselves with opportunities to award themselves higher salaries, gain promotion, or enhance their own reputation. For Udehn there is "no necessary connection between budget-maximisation and self-interest [...] the way to make a career might be to reduce budgets or, at least, to save money" (1996, 75). Budget-maximisation might not necessarily be a case of self-interested behavior, but an example of the altruistic desire to serve the common good. In fact, the imposition of a utility function in rational choice accounts attributes similar motivations to individuals such that context comes to dominate in explanations over and beyond the agency of individual actors (as we have suggested above). As such, rational choice is charged with ignoring the origins of preferences and over-riding the past history and identity of policy actors, stripping individuals of differences that emerge from their individual personal identity or history; with no account of identity-formation, actors in the policy process become interchangeable (Tsebelis 1990, 43). Whilst prized by mainstream rational choice theorists as a short-cut to scientific explanation, this interchangeability is derided by detractors as a "homogeneity assumption" that "is justified on the grounds of theoretical parsimony" (Green and Shapiro 1994, 17). It elevates the policy context or institutional environment to the exclusion of individuals and choice, such that "it is surely tempting to ask: 'When is a choice not a choice?' Answer: 'When it is a rational choice.'" (Hay 2004, 53).

Such short cuts toward parsimonious and universal explanation are alleged ultimately to underplay the uncertainty and complexity of much of the decision-making process. Here, policy making is far removed from the strategic cost-benefit calculations of informed and instrumental individuals. Rather, it is characterized by the politics of ambiguity and uncertainty where the information available to policy-makers is inconclusive, where their capacity to process such information remains limited, and where consequently policy making becomes less about problem-resolution and more about persuasion, communication, advocacy, and the setting of norms (Majone 1989). Indeed, uncertainty, unlike complexity and risk, hampers the definition by individuals of both interests and distinct courses of action. It obliges actors to operate within policy frames that establish norms and codes for making sense of problems and guiding their behaviour through the policy process (Griggs and Howarth 2002). Under such conditions of ambiguity, individual policy actors are thus best conceived of as satisfiers rather than maximizers, operating under the conditions of bounded rationality (Simon 1957) or following institutional logics of appropriateness (March and Olsen 1989).

In fact, methodological pathologies and inadequate empirical testing are, in the work of Green and Shapiro (1994), said to fuel these untenable rationalist characterisations of the dynamics of policy-making. Labelling rational choice as method rather than problem-driven, Green and Shapiro do indeed argue that rational choice theory betrays a bias towards post hoc theory development (1994, 34–39), epitomized by the process of retroduction whereby rational choice theorists deliver post hoc explanations of known facts. Such post hoc theorizing undermines the empirical testing of rational choice inspired models, for as they argue:

> Data that inspire a theory cannot, however, properly be used to test it, particularly when many post hoc accounts furnish the same prediction. Unless a given retroductive account is used to generate hypotheses that survive when tested against other phenomena, little of empirical significance has been established. (Green and Shapiro 1994, 35–36)

Indeed, Green and Shapiro claim that this absence of empirical testing is amplified by the recourse to a comparatively large number of unobservable entities in rational choice explanations (1994, 39–41). Thus, they posit that when rational choice models confront unexpected outcomes or patterns of behavior, they are able to dismiss such outcomes as some unobservable thought process or "offsetting tendency or temporary aberration"; evidence for which it is difficult to establish empirically (1994, 40).

What holds such methodological and theoretical challenges together is the argument that rational choice fails to address the empirical, both in its methodological pathologies, which constrain its empirical testing, *and* in its parsimonious and universal assumptions over the motivations and roles of individuals, which fail to conceptualise the complexity of the decision-making process. Nowhere is this more clearly illustrated than in the debates surrounding the veracity of rational choice theories of collective action. Here Olson's problematization of collective action and the requirement to offset the tendency of rational actors to free-ride through the generation of selective pecuniary incentives are simply said to be refuted empirically by the range of established patterns of group mobilization and social movement protest and contestation across political systems (see, for example, the work of Jordan and Maloney 1997). Such forms of mobilization are not temporary aberrations, but point arguably to the limitations of instrumental accounts in modelling the complex motivations of individuals and the need for rational choice theory to address rival explanations of group identity and its expression if it is to understand the limits to its universalist aspirations. It is to the response of rational choice theorists to such challenges that we now turn.

MEETING THE CHALLENGES TO RATIONAL CHOICE

All research communities are composed of "pragmatists," "synthesizers," and "competitors" (Lichbach 2003, 4–7). Whilst "pragmatists" work solely within the confines of their chosen approach, "synthesizers" complement their chosen approach with the insights of rival theories in the desire to converge towards a unified centre, and "competitors" advance the engagement and evaluation of their chosen approach against other theories, stressing the incompatibility of fundamental competing assumptions between approaches. In this section, drawing on the work of Lichbach (2003), we present three stylized accounts of such potential responses to the challenges to rational choice theory. Protectionist pragmatists, the default position of much of rational choice theory, seek to ward off challenge and maintain the fundamental building blocks of rational choice intact. Expansionist synthesizers start from the assumption that rational choice should deliver an effective portrayal of the reality of decision making and thus seek to rearticulate the assumptions of rational choice theory to ward off claims of simplification and lack of complexity. Finally, confrontational competitors privilege the fundamental assumptions of rational choice, but call for further engagement of rational choice theory with its rival approaches based upon a dynamic testing of rival predictions; a process that has the potential to reach a substantive amelioration of rational choice theory. Let us begin our analysis by examining the responses of pragmatic protectionists.

PRAGMATIC PROTECTIONISTS

The standard defense of such pragmatic protectionists is to adopt what is termed the Friedman defence (Friedman 1953). Here advocates of rational choice acknowledge that the simplifying assumption of rationality in no way mirrors or represents the complexity of policy making. However, they argue that this is somewhat immaterial for the strength of any theory lies not in the accuracy of its basic assumptions, but rather in its predictive and explanatory power (Green and Shapiro 1994, 30–31; Hay 2004, 48). And against these evaluative criteria, rational choice has demonstrated its value, not least through the problematization of collective action. In addition, however, such pragmatic protectionist responses tend to draw upon the "covering law" defense. Here, rationalists deny the complexity of the policy process and argue in fact that the assumption of rationality does indeed represent the actual practice of decision-making (Green and Shapiro 1994, 30–31; Hay 2004, 48). Finally, a further pragmatic protectionist defence is to invoke the defence of domain restriction. Tsebelis typically argues that rationality is best defined as a "subset of human behaviour" (1990, 32). Thus rational choice cannot claim to explain all political phenomena. Rather, in a relaxation of its universal aspirations, rational choice should be confined to episodes where "the actors' identity and goals are established and the rules of interaction are precise and known to the interacting agents" (1990, 32).

Such responses tend to keep the fundamental assumption of rationality intact in that they either dismiss challenges as to the requirement of any theory of the policy process to portray the reality of decision making, deny the complexity of the decision-making process, or limit the applicability of rational choice to particular domains of decision-making. However, these pragmatic protectionist rebuttals are far from complementary and draw upon contradictory justifications (see below). More importantly, they all run the risk of ignoring disconfirming evidence, being biased in other words towards the privileging of evidence that simply reinforces the assumption of rationality (Green and Shapiro 1994, 42–43). Indeed, domain restriction abandons whole areas of the policy process to alternative explanations, which is not without implications for both the applicability and empirical testing of rational choice models: "If the appropriate domain within which a theory is to be tested is defined by reference to whether the theory works in that domain, testing becomes pointless" (Green and Shapiro 1994, 45).

Expansionist Synthesizers

Expansionist synthesizers, in what could be construed as a hegemonic move to expand the boundaries of rational choice (Lichbach 2003), rearticulate the fundamental assumptions of rationalist accounts in order to offer an effective portrayal of the reality of decision making. In so doing, they adopt to varying degrees the position of the expansionist synthesizer. Thus, on the one hand, Dunleavy (1991) enriches the work of Niskanen by refining the utility function of bureaucrats and the conditions associated with the following of budget-maximizing strategies by bureaucrats, arguing that budget-maximization will depend upon the position or rank of the bureaucrat within the bureau and the nature of the budget that is to be maximised. Where conditions are not opportune, senior bureaucrats will bureau-shape rather than budget-maximise. On the other hand, other rational choice models begin to re-articulate conceptions of self-interest further away from the pursuit of narrow pecuniary benefits in order to portray more effectively the reality of the motivations of individuals in the decision-making process. In the words of Ward, such accounts remove the straitjacket of rational choice and allow for the likes of bounded rationality, choice under uncertainty and nonegotistical and "moral motivations" (Ward 2002, 84). Typically, work on collective action has thus come to privilege the role of 'soft' selective incentives, such as expressive or social incentives that can only been gained from participation (see the work of Chong (1991) and Opp (1986) and Opp and Gern (1993)). Altruism thus becomes a dominant utility-function, although rational choice theorists have recognized its importance in the past (Ward 2002, 79).

Such moves toward identity-based interpretative explanations are firmly endorsed by the work of Ferejohn (1991). His starting point is to claim that both rational and interpretative accounts of public policy are incomplete, unable on their own to offer a full account of social action. Indeed, a complete account of social action, he argues, is only possible if we are to view rational and interpretative approaches as complementary (1991, 279). Rational choice is thus defined for Ferejohn as "an interpretive theory that constructs explanations by 'reconstructing' patterns of meanings and understandings (preferences and beliefs) in such a way that agents' actions can be seen as maximal, given their beliefs" (1991, 281). Indeed, the logics of rational choice and interpretative approaches are similar in that they are both intentional accounts that

> start with observed data (behaviour including documents and letters, practices and institutions) and reconstruct actors and their inner attributes (meanings, beliefs and values) in such a way that the data are as fully explained or accounted for as possible. (Ferejohn 1991, 281)

And, as for interpretative accounts, they require a form of rationality embedded in them (1991, 281). This expansionist account is thus that of a fully-fledged "synthesizer"

Underpinning such responses is the distinction between "thin" and "thick" accounts of rationality. Mainstream rational choice accounts of policy change "posit not only rationality, but some additional description of agent preferences and beliefs" (Ferejohn 1991, 282), imputing onto agents a dominant utility function so that for example all politicians across different contexts will seek to maximize votes whilst bureaucrats will seek to maximise budgets. However, "thin" accounts assume no more than instrumental accounts of rationality that agents "efficiently employ the means available to pursue their ends" and impute no dominant utility function onto individuals (Ferejohn 1991, 282). Indeed, as we said above, what these accounts are doing is not so much loosening the assumptions of rational choice, as questioning how far self-interest has to be defined in terms of narrow "selfish" or hard pecuniary benefits. They thus focus upon the re-articulation of self-interest as utility maximisation in order to problematize the rationalist conception of individuals as selfish individuals. The conception of self-interest comes to mean simply that individuals pursue preferences in pursuit of benefits that may or may not be "selfish" or material in nature. Indeed, utility replaces the notion of self-interest, such that "formally speaking, self-interest is not required for rational choice, utility maximisation can suffice" (Dowding and King 1995, 14). In short, what this means in practice is that utility is to be privileged over self-interest, but also that the very conception of utility itself is to be stretched. Such accounts run the risk of tautological explanation for there is no course of action that cannot be explained away as some form of utility-maximisation once rational choice accounts move away from the preoccupation with hard pecuniary benefits. Equally, claims to universalism and prediction are further weakened.

CONFRONTATIONAL COMPETITORS

Negating the potential hegemonic drives of expansionists, confrontational competitors call for the further engagement with, and testing of rational choice theory against, its rivals. Thus, Lichbach (2003, 209) asserts that the "success of rational choice depends on how it treats its foils." Rational choice theory should tackle concrete problems, establishing sets of competing predictions against which it can engage in "creative competitions" (2003, 209). This is not to negate the fundamental assumptions of rational choice, for as Lichbach suggests (2003, 62):

> Rational choice theorists should begin with thin theories (that assume pecuniary self-interest) as their baseline model, determine how much of the phenomena under question can be explained by such theories, and only then adopt thicker theories to account for phenomena that remain inexplicable. [...] But before they attempt to synthesize their major competitors, rational choice theorists should initially remain consistent with the core of rational choice theorizing.

Rather it is ultimately to call for a more "modest modelling tradition" of rationalist narratives: "the historical and comparative analysis of strategic decision-making'" (Lichbach 2003, 211).

In fact, through the construction of analytic narratives, Bates and colleagues (1998) bolster rational choice explanations of events and outcomes through drawing systematic explanations from "thick descriptive" case studies, which underline the importance of social context and history. In doing so, Bates and colleagues move toward a problem-driven approach that employs deductive reasoning and thin accounts of rationality, but retreats from the production of universal laws of human behaviour (Bates et al. 1998, 11). Such an approach offers a narrative approach that both examines "stories, accounts and context" *and* "extracts explicit and formal lines of reasoning, which facilitate both exposition and explanation" (Bates et al. 1998, 10). It establishes the origins of individual preferences and dominant rules and patterns of strategic interaction, building up from the contextual reconstruction of events as observed and interpreted by actors. As such, it combines inductive qualitative and descriptive methods to establish actors' preferences and perceptions with deductive methods to understand the behavior of actors within the game being analysed (Bates et al. 2000, 697). The pursuit of analytic narratives thereby addresses the tendency of mainstream rational choice to "take people as we find them" (see above), deploying narratives in the context of actor-centric extensive-form games.

The employment of analytic narratives responds directly to challenges over the tendency of rational choice accounts to impute beliefs and preferences onto actors in the policy process. Indeed, the recourse to "thick descriptive" case studies becomes a central step in rational explanation, for it produces in the words of Bates and his colleagues "such intimacy with detail" that "we argue, *must* inform the selection and specification of the model to be tested and *should* give us a good grasp of the intentions and beliefs of the actors" (Bates et al. 2000, 698). Like the approaches discussed above, however, the construction of analytic narratives is not without its criticisms. First, it leads to the questioning of the actual value that the assumption of rationality adds to explanations. Second, it is claimed that the approach is prone towards tautological explanations (Elster 2000). For as Bates and his colleagues argue, "Should we possess a valid representation of the story, then the equilibrium of the model should imply the outcome we describe—and seek to explain" (Bates et al. 1998, 12).

Overall, therefore, rational choice has tended to generate three types of responses to the challenges posed by alternative accounts or indeed generated by its own internal contradictions. Whilst default responses have sought to keep the assumption of rationality broadly intact, other responses have sought either to reinterpret the primary assumptions of rational choice to adopt a more synthetic approach that brings together rational and interpretative approaches. What these more expansionist accounts, as with confrontational accounts, deliver is the relaxation of the universalist and parsimonious aspirations of rational choice through the investigation of the origins of preferences and individuals' conceptions of utility. However, as we suggested above, we have to be wary of the potential to confuse the different epistemological positions of instrumental-empiricism and scientific-realism that underpin such accounts. Although often grouped together, the Freidman inspired "as if" defense builds upon instrumental-empiricism whilst domain restriction is based upon scientific-realism. These different epistemological positions in rational choice theory require clarification (MacDonald 2003).

Equally, we have to guard against the metaphorical reduction of rational choice theory to the status of a neutral or pliable toolkit within the armoury of policy analysts; albeit a more than useful tool in the armoury open to analysts. Indeed, in pursing the development of analytic narratives, Bates and his colleagues challenge Elster, one of their critics, to "offer us a better set of tools" (Bates et al. 2000, 702). This position is not without its detractors. Udehn argues that such a tactic of reducing rational choice to a heuristic device is undoubtedly limited "unless it is argued that the failures of a simplifying assumptions are as enlightening as its success" (1996, 93). However, rather than enter into further discussion of the validity of the assumption of rationality, we argue that the conception of rational choice as a heuristic device or a "set of tools" misunderstands the constitutive nature of policy theory. It is to this misunderstanding that we turn in our conclusion.

ASSESSING THE LIMITS OF RATIONAL CHOICE: IT IS WHAT IT IS, ISN'T IT?

Theories of the policy process constitute the social reality they seek to describe and to interpret, offering particular explanations of the research problems and data they themselves have constituted (Howarth 2000, 130). Policy theories do not exist outside of the data. This starting point places limitations on rational choice theory and its responses to its internal and external challenges. First, it questions the empiricist methodology of mainstream rational choice accounts and undermines its claims to predictive universal explanation. Second, it challenges specifically recent attempts to relegate rational choice to a toolkit or partial explanation to be deployed in conjunction with other approaches, for these accounts of the limits of rational choice are predicated upon the existence of empirical data that somehow exists as valid outside of theory and neglect how particular theories selectively determine the definition of what is data and indeed what are the relevant research questions to be explored. In fact, this flaw can arguably be associated with the arguments of Green and Shapiro in their seminal critique of rational choice theory. Green and Shapiro condemn rational choice because in rational choice accounts "evidence is projected from theory rather than gathered independently from it" (1994, 42). Thus, they themselves fail to acknowledge the constitutive logic of policy theory. There is not a set of empirical data that can be generated by neutral tools independent of theory and that can then be subjected to different theoretical approaches. To even approach explanation requires some initial or partial understanding (Howarth 2000, 131).

What does this mean for the limits of rational choice? In short, it offers an understanding of rational choice that is best summarized as "it is what it is." This is not to call for the absence of dialogue between different approaches to the explanation of policy outcomes. Neither is it to necessarily adopt the Freidman defense or that of the covering law or domain restriction. Rather, it is to argue that rational choice theory, like all policy theory, offers a particular explanation of research problems and data it itself has constructed. It cannot be reduced to a neutral toolkit or heuristic device or integrated into other approaches. Its limitations are thus to be judged through debate within the community of policy analysts through the likes of creative confrontations. After all, there is no neutral body of data that can be constructed through the use of impartial tools and against which we can test theories. Rational choice is what it is, isn't it?

REFERENCES

Alt, J.E., and Chrystal, K.A. (1983). *Political Economics*. Brighton: Wheatsheaf Books.

Arrow, K.J. (1951). *Social Choice and Individual Values*. New York: Wiley.

Axelrod, R. (1984). *The Evolution of Co-operation*. New York: Basic Books.

Bates, R.H., Greif, A., Levi, M., Rosenthal, J-L., and Weingast, B.R. (1998). *Analytic Narratives*. Princeton, NJ: Princeton University Press.

Bates, R.H., Greif, A., Levi, M., Rosenthal, J-L., and Weingast, B.R. (2000). The Analytic Narrative Project. *American Journal of Political Science, 94*, 696–702.

Blyth, M. (2002). *Great Transformations. Economic Ideas and Institutional Change in the Twentieth Century*. Cambridge: Cambridge University Press.

Chong, D. (1991). *Collective Action and the Civil Rights Movement*. Chicago: University of Chicago.

Chong, D. (1996). Rational choice theory's mysterious rivals. In J. Freidman (ed), *The Rational Choice Controversy*, pp. 37–57. New Haven: Yale University Press.

Dowding, K., and King, D. (1995). Introduction. In K. Dowding and D. King (eds), *Preferences, Institutions and Rational Choice*, pp. 1–19. Oxford: Clarendon Press.

Downs, A. (1957). *An Economic Theory of Democracy*. Harper and Row: New York.

Downs, A. (1967). *Inside Bureaucracy*. Boston: Little Brown.

Dunleavy, P. (1991). *Democracy, Bureaucracy and Public Choice. Economic Explanations in Political Science*. Hemel Hempstead: Harvester Wheatsheaf.

Elster, J. (1986). Introduction. In J. Elster (ed), *Rational Choice*, pp. 1–33. Oxford: Basil Blackwell.

Elster, J. (2000). Rational Choice History: A Case of Excessive Ambition. *American Political Science Review*, *94*, 685–695.

Ferejohn, J. (1991). Rationality and Interpretation: Parliamentary Elections in Early Stuart England. In K.R. Monroe (ed), *The Economic Approach to Politics. A Critical Reassessment of the Theory of Rational Action*, pp. 279–305. London: Harper Collins.

Friedman, J. (1996). (ed). *The Rational Choice Controversy. Economic Models of Politics Reconsidered*. New Haven: Yale University Press.

Friedman, M. (1953). The Methodology of Positive Economics. In M. Friedman (ed), *Essays in Positive Economics*, pp. 3–46. Chicago: University of Chicago Press.

Garrett, G., and Weingast, B.R. (1993). Ideas, Interests, and Institutions: Constructing the European Community's Internal Market. In J. Goldstein and R.O. Keohane (eds), *Ideas and Foreign Policy: Beliefs, Institutions and Political Change*, pp. 173–207. Ithaca: Cornell University Press.

Green, D.P., and Shapiro, I. (1994). *Pathologies of Rational Choice Theory. A Critique of Applications in Political Science*. New Haven: Yale University Press.

Griggs, S., and Howarth, D. (2002). The Work of Ideas and Interests in Public Policy. In A. Finlayson and J. Valentine (eds), *Politics and Post-Structuralism: An Introduction*, pp. 97–111. Edinburgh: Edinburgh University Press.

Goldstein, J., and Keohane, R.O. (eds) (1993). *Ideas and Foreign Policy: Beliefs, Institutions and Political Change*. Ithaca: Cornell University Press.

Hardin, G. (1969). The Tragedy of the Commons. *Science, 162*, 958–962.

Hay, C. (2004). Theory, Stylized Heuristic or Self-Fulfilling Prophecy? The Status of Rational Choice Theory in Public Administration. *Public Administration, 82*, 39–62.

Howarth, D. (2000). *Discourse*. Buckingham: Open University Press.

Johnson, C. (1997). Preconception vs. Observation, or the Contribution of Rational Choice Theory and Area Studies to Contemporary Political Science. *PS: Political Science & Politics, 30*, 170–174.

Jordan, G., and Maloney, W. (1997). *The Protest Business? Mobilizing Campaign Groups*. Manchester: Manchester University Press.

Laver, M. (1997). *Private Desires, Political Action. An Invitation to the Politics of Rational Choice*. Sage: London.

Levi, M. (1997). A Model, A Method, and a Map: Rational Choice in Comparative and Historical Analysis. In M.I. Lichbach and A.S. Zuckermann (eds), *Comparative Politics. Rationality, Culture and Structure*, pp. 19–41. Cambridge: Cambridge University Press.

Lichbach, M.I. (2003). *Is Rational Choice Theory All of Social Science?*, Ann Arbor: University of Michigan.

MacDonald, P.K. (2003). Useful Fiction or Miracle Maker: The Competing Epistemological Foundations of Rational Choice Theory. *American Journal of Political Science, 97*, 551–565.

Majone, G. (1989). *Evidence, Argument and Persuasion in the Policy Process*. New Haven: Yale University Press.

March, J., and Olsen, J. (1989). *Rediscovering Institutions*. New York: Free Press.

Mueller, D.C. (2003). *Public Choice III*. Cambridge: Cambridge University Press.

Niskanen, W. (1971). *Bureaucracy and Representative Government*. Aldine-Atherton: Chicago.

Nordhaus, W.D. (1975). The Political Business Cycle. *Review of Economic Studies, 42*, 169–190.

North, D.C. (1990). *Institutions, Institutional Change and Economic Performance*. Cambridge: Cambridge University Press.

Olson, M. (1965). *The Logic of Collective Action: Public Goods and the Theory of Groups*. Cambridge, MA: Havard University Press.

Olson, M. (1982). *The Rise and Decline of Nations: Economic Growth, Stagflation and Social Rigidities*. New Haven: Yale University Press.

Opp, K-D. (1986). Soft Incentives and Collective Action: Participation in the Anti-Nuclear Movement. *British Journal of Political Science*, *16*, 87–112.

Opp. K-D., and Gern, C. (1993). Dissident Groups, Personal Networks and Spontaneous Cooperation; The East German Revolution of 1989. *American Sociological Review*, *58*, 659–680.

Riker, W. (1962). *The Theory of Political Coalitions*. New Haven: Yale University Press.

Schweers Cook, K., and Levi, M. (1990). (eds). *The Limits of Rationality*. Chicago: University of Chicago Press.

Shepsle, K.A., and Bonchek, M.S. (1997). *Analyzing Politics. Rationality, Behavior and Institutions*. New York: W.W. Norton and Company.

Simon, H. (1957). *Administrative Behaviour*. New York: Free Press. 2nd edition.

Tsebelis, G. (1990). *Nested Games. Rational Choice in Comparative Politics*. Berkeley: California University Press.

Udehn, L. (1996). *The Limits of Public Choice*. London: Routledge.

Van Thiel, S. (2004). Trends in the Public Sector. Why Politicians Prefer Quasi-Autonomous Organizations. *Journal of Theoretical Politics*, *16*, 175–201.

Ward, H. (2002). Rational Choice Theory. In D. Marsh and G. Stoker (eds), *Theory and Methods in Political Science*, pp. 65–89. Basingstoke: Palgrave Macmillan, 2nd edition.

14 Taking Stock of Policy Networks: Do They Matter?

Jörg Raab and Patrick Kenis

INTRODUCTION

Almost two decades of research in public policy using the concept of policy network has resulted in considerable output.[1] A great number of articles on policy networks can be found in major journals in political science and public administration and even more chapters in edited volumes, special issues of journals (Marin and Mayntz 1991; König 1998) or more specialized policy journals. Therefore, the concept can be regarded as being one of the major analytical concepts in the field of public policy partly competing, partly complementing other major approaches like veto players/game theory (Tsebelis 1999), ideas (Weir 1992), or the advocacy coalition approach (Sabatier and Jenkins-Smith 1993). The concept has been used to analyze policy making and implementation at the local and regional (Melbek 1998; Schneider et al. 2003), the national (see, among others, Laumann and Knoke 1987; Rhodes 1991; Schneider and Werle 1991), the European (Bretherton and Sperling 1996; Héritier 1993; Nölke 2003), and the international level (Grundmann 1997; Reinicke 1998). Moreover, the concept has been applied in the analysis of policy making in many different industrial sectors such as nuclear energy (Zijlstra 1979), chemicals, and telecommunication (Schneider 1992), and policy fields such as environmental (Carpenter et al. 2003) or science policy (Grande and Peschke 1999).

If we look at the nationality of the authors, however, it seems that the concept has been used much more frequently by European than by North American, especially U.S., scholars. This can be largely attributed to different research traditions but also to different political cultures of European welfare states with coalition governments and a consensus oriented policy style which make the development of policy networks much more likely than in a political system that is characterized by majority voting rule, party competition, and a pluralistic interest intermediation system as in the United States (Peters 1998, 32). Moreover, as we will see below, the policy network concept followed and largely replaced the framework of corporatist interest intermediation (very popular in the 1970s and 1980s in Europe) as a more general analytical framework. The policy network concept has widely been used in the 1990s to analyze policy making within the European Union, which is now frequently characterized as a new system of governance based on negotiations between national governments, the European Commission, the European parliament, large companies and national or European associations (Börzel 1997).

Common to all studies in this area is a relational perspective, i.e., a focus on actors, their interests, and especially their relations as the key explanatory factors, whether they are conducted qualitatively or quantitatively, whether they use network as a mere metaphor or with a clear definition that is subsequently operationalized.

The role of networks in policy making became an important issue on the research agenda in the late 1980s. Policy researchers began to both theoretically and empirically focus on how networks

---

1. A search for the term "policy network(s)" on the ISI Web of Science covering ISI journal articles from 1988 to July 2006 resulted in 155 hits for titles only and 323 hits as a general topic.

between public, private and non-profit actors shape processes of policy making and governance. This increasing popularity can be attributed, first, to a transformation of political reality, second, to a subsequent transformation of the conceptual and theoretical framework in policy analysis, and, third, to the development of a methodological apparatus for structural analysis (Kenis and Schneider 1991, 33). As a consequence, scholars not only started to describe these more horizontal forms of governance that developed out of a changed distribution of power, but also tried to argue normatively why these forms of governance were the most effective and efficient for certain types of policy and organizational problems. The term "network" was claimed to becoming the new paradigm for the "architecture of complexity" (Simon quoted in Kenis and Schneider 1991, 26) or the major device to reintegrate differentiated systems of actors in modern societies (Mayntz 1993a). At the beginning of the 1990s, it was stated that policy network analysis was not just a "new fad," but was employed "due to the growing insight that public policies emerged from the interaction of public and private actors" (Windhoff-Héritier 1993, 143). It was further seen as a "promising instrument of political research" because different theoretical approaches could be combined and because it offered the possibility to go beyond the mere description of formal institutional structures and to investigate which actors dominate the political decision-making process in different policy fields (Windhoff-Héritier 1993, 143).

These were high hopes, but to what extent were they fulfilled? Using a network perspective, policy researchers have been able to describe the various formal and informal structures of policy making in different policy fields. In some but still rather rare instances, quantitative network analysis was used in order to gain a more detailed description and analysis. Describing these policy-making structures is no little achievement, since the description of the nature of the beast is a fundamental step for any further inquiry. But how much progress was there beyond the mere description? Have more insights been gained into how certain structural configurations influence policy processes and outputs, i.e., did scholars manage to go beyond network as a metaphor or an analytical tool? In short, do policy networks matter?

In answering this question, we will look at where and how the concept originated. Then we will discuss what progress has been made toward a network theory of policy and what further steps could be taken in order to further advance such a theory.

WHERE DOES THE POLICY NETWORK CONCEPT COME FROM?

Looking at the literature the term *policy network* is used with different meanings and analytically with different purposes. One can identify at least three dimensions of the concept: (1) network as an analytical framework and as an empirical tool, (2) network as social structure, and (3) network as a form of governance. Network theory is often talked about as a fourth dimension. However, there is still a lot of uncertainty as to what exactly a network theory is. At times, network is the object of the study (dependent variable) in network theories (comparable with organizations in organization theories). At other times, one can also find network as the independent variable, and policy out-comes, organization behavior, etc. are explained by its characteristics (Kenis and Knoke 2002). In this second form, however, one should not talk about network theories but about a network theory of policy or a network theory of organizations.

NETWORK AS AN ANALYTICAL FRAMEWORK AND AS AN EMPIRICAL TOOL

The network concept is often used merely metaphorically in policy analysis. However, even in those instances, the researcher takes a particular perspective, namely focusing the analysis on the actors, their interests but especially on the existing and non existing ties among each other. Therefore, the policy network approach takes a middle position between undersocialized approaches like rational choice or oversocialized approaches like Marxist approaches (Granovetter 1985).

Network analysis as an empirical tool has been one of the major innovations in the social sciences in the last 30 years and has recently been applied more and more in policy analysis. Three reasons have lead to the success of network analysis as a paradigm and an empirical tool. First, concepts were based on relations rather than attributes. By concentrating their attention on the ties between social entities, rather than on the qualities possessed by them, it forces social scientists to think in terms of constraints and options that are inherent in the way social relations are organized (van Poucke 1979, 181). Network analysis is therefore based on an "anticategorical imperative, which rejects all attempts to explain human behavior or social processes solely in terms of categorical attributes of actors, whether individual or collective" (Emirbayer and Goodwin 1994, 1414). At the center of analysis are not attributes such as age, gender, social status, political affiliation, religious beliefs, ethnicity, or psychological predisposition, but the relations between social entities as a means of explaining why people behave the way they do and why certain outcomes come about (Emirbayer and Goodwin 1994, 1414). The two basic components of all network analyses are a set of objects (called nodes, positions, or actors) and a set of relations among these objects (called edges, ties, or links) (Knoke 1990). Network analysis is not a neutral statistical method, nor is it a theory. It is an empirical tool to describe social structure on the basis of relations between social entities (Kenis and Schneider 1991). It is nonetheless analytically formal in that it mandates systematic and replicable routines, requires strict coding rules and has an internal logic or algorithm that produces descriptive or inferential results (Griffin and van der Linden 1998). The strength of the methodology is based first on well-developed data collection procedures. Second, standard methods are available for analyzing and measuring the structural properties of whole systems (centralization, hierarchization, density, etc.) as well as of the social positions of the single social entities within these systems (centrality, clique membership, prestige, structural equivalence, etc.). Third, the statistical procedures to calculate these measures are implemented in standard calculation and visualization software. Based on this "toolbox," the principal achievement of network analysis "has been to transform a merely metaphorical understanding of the embeddedness of actors in networks of social relationships into a more precise and usable tool for social analysis" (Emirbayer and Goodwin 1994, 1446). It is now possible to operationalize and measure the relational properties of social and political systems and the encompassing units by collecting data on virtually any social relation between the units of interest to the researcher.

Besides the formalized quantitative approach, a second more qualitative direction evolved in political science arising from the discussion on interest intermediation and corporatism (Schmitter and Lehmbruch 1979; Börzel 1998), the coordination of industrial sectors (Hollingsworth et al. 1994), as well as the discussion on political planning and implementation (Scharpf 1993; Mayntz,1996) all of which were later integrated in the general analytical approach of policy analysis. Here, "network" is applied as an analytical framework, which guides the empirical perceptions in research on policy making and directs the researchers' perception and attention towards the actors and their relations. Laumann and Knoke's study of the U.S. energy and health policy domains (1987) can serve as a classical example for the formalized approach on a large scale as well as Schneider and Werle's research in the German telecommunication domain (1991) on a smaller scale. In these studies, quantitative information is rigorously collected about the actors and their relations within a certain policy field. These data are then used to gain insight into the (power) structure of a policy field by using indices such as density, centrality or influence reputation or by analyzing the cliques (coalitions) that were formed in a policy process. The advances in computer hardware and software now make it possible to use quantitative data for elaborate visualizations of networks (Brandes et al. 1999). Examples for the qualitative branch of the policy network approach include case studies such as Toke and Marsh's study on genetically modified food (2003) in which they describe the network structure and how it changed over time and use these insights to explain how network were mutually affected by each other in this case.

NETWORK AS SOCIAL STRUCTURE

One of the fundamental assumptions in network analysis is the belief that structures have a certain stability, which leads to its rather static character. When applying the "network" notion in the analysis of economic, political, and social processes and outcomes, it is assumed that after some time actors have built more or less stable exchange relations, which are not changed fundamentally by "superficial" every day events (Windhoff-Héritier 1993, 144). In most cases, the nodes within a policy network represent corporative or collective political or administrative actors like ministries, government agencies, or societal actors like associations, unions, or even private actors like companies which occupy specific positions or roles. "Network" in this respect, is seen as a social structure with very specific features. In policy making it is regarded as an arrangement characterized by a predominance of informal communicative relations, a horizontal as opposed to a hierarchical pattern of relations and a decentralized pattern of actors' positions (Kenis and Schneider 1991, 32). The difference between the first and the second understanding of network is that in the first it is possible to conceptualize any social structure (even pure hierarchies) as a network and apply the analytical toolbox of network analysis, but that the second dimension reveals specific structural features.

NETWORK AS A FORM OF GOVERNANCE

Starting with Williamson's *Markets and Hierarchies* in 1975, in which he elaborated Coase's basic ideas about the determinants for the organization of economic activities, a rich body of literature has developed on different forms of governance over the last two decades (Williamson 1975). For some time, transaction costs as the major factor to explain special forms of social organization was applied only in economics. It was only some years ago that the discussion in economics, organization theory, and political science converged in a common literature. Central to this discussion were the questions about the factors leading to hierarchical, network, or market arrangements and about the conditions under which the different forms have comparative advantages (Hollingsworth et al. 1994). An important point in this discussion was the question whether networks are simply a combination of elements of market and hierarchy—and could therefore be placed on a continuum somewhere between market and hierarchy—or whether they are better understood as unique forms of governance in their own right (Powell 1990).

Parallel to the Anglo-Saxon discussion in economics, an independent discussion about networks and other governance forms started in Germany in political and administrative science. Since the beginning of the 1970s, a debate about steering (*Steuerung*) had been developing. Originally, scholars were interested in understanding and improving policy planning and implementation processes through the state. But the high hopes were profoundly disappointed. The state as the central actor lost more and more of its strong and independent position and had to face the claims of the ever stronger societal actors, which made it impossible to hierarchically implement policy decisions especially in complex policy fields. As a consequence, scholars not only started to describe these more horizontal forms of governance, which developed out of a changed distribution of power, but also tried to explain normatively why these forms of governance were the most effective and efficient for certain types of policy problems. Central to this discussion is the understanding of network as an emergent organizational entity, i.e., as a new form of social organization. Although network as a form of governance is characterized by a plurality of autonomous actors, as they are found within markets, and the capability to pursue collective goals through deliberately coordinated actions, which is one of the major elements of hierarchies (Mayntz 1993b), it is claimed that a new form of governance develops. This new form is more than the sum of the actors and their links and more than a combination of elements of hierarchy and markets (Mayntz 1993b). In this approach, "network" is conceived and interpreted as a discrete form of governance and together with market and hierarchy as an ideal type of coordination. The characteristics of this ideal type are not only seen in a specific structural feature of the system of production and exchange, but also for example in the mode of conflict resolution, the basis of legitimacy, the general (cognitive) orientation and incentives of the actors.

It is claimed by the proponents of this approach (Schneider and Kenis 1997) that it is not only possible to achieve more conceptual clarity but also to develop a refined analytical instrument with which actor coordination in concrete policy or economic systems can be modeled as a specific mixture of these ideal types (Schneider and Kenis 1997, 20).

The integration of the discussion in economics, organization theory, and political science has had two consequences. First, scholars now have a less normative and more flexible notion for the description of new arrangements in policy making. Second, the discussion on and comparison of markets, hierarchies, and networks, which was taken from economics, had a strong functionalist and economic touch (Perrow,1981). A major concern was effectiveness and efficiency and the classical questions of political science were more and more superseded. In empirical policy network studies one rarely reads about power and influence, legitimacy, interests, democracy, etc. This was substantively different in the early network studies such as the community power studies (Laumann and Pappi 1973). They focused explicitly on the analysis of political structures, especially on power structures. Therefore, it is necessary to separate the discussion on network as a governance form, network as a specific social structure, and network as an analytical tool in order to address questions of power, influence, and responsibility more accurately. With network as an analytical tool, influence and power can be operationalized in terms of centrality or prestige of actors. On the other hand, thinking in terms of governance and not only in terms of social structure opens up yet another perspective. Systems of governance made up of different organizations, whether their features come close to a network or rather represent a mixed type, can be seen as an organization of "higher order" (Teubner 1996) or "emergent" (Scharpf 1993) form of organization, which produce outcomes that cannot be attributed to any single organization alone. Moreover, the process and therefore the outcome cannot be completely controlled by any individual organization. The different views on networks, therefore, have great implications not only for the analysis of the structure and the processes but also for the evaluation of the outcome.

TOWARD A NETWORK THEORY OF POLICY?

Despite the frequent talk in the literature about network theory, we claim that the utilization of such a theory regarding policy making is a long way off. Strictly speaking, we should be able to demonstrate that a difference in structural network characteristics, i.e., the presence and absence of ties, has a significant impact on the policy output. Only in this instance could something be explained other theories are not able to and only then could one seriously talk about a *network* theory of policy (see Salancik 1995) with regard to a network theory of organization). Network analysis might be used as a descriptive tool to collect data but that does not automatically lead to a network theory if the data is used to develop or test other theories.

In the literature on policy networks, ample attention has been given to the conditions for the development of policy making. Some of the case studies mentioned before tried to explain why a specific policy network has developed. Others set out to explain why policy networks as a specific form of governance developed since the 1970s (e.g., Kenis and Schneider 1991; Mayntz 1993b). Here, policy network is seen as the dependent variable.

If we look at publications from the second half of the 1990s and in the last few years, we can observe that scholars try to bring together at least some of the different perspectives on governance (the German and American version), interorganizational networks, interest intermediation, and studies in political sociology sometimes using quantitative network analysis beginning with the community power studies in the 1970s (Dowding 1995; Klijn 1997; Raab 2002).

However, despite the achievements mentioned earlier, we feel that we are not really making enough progress in creating empirical generalizations especially when it comes to explaining policy outputs or outcomes with network characteristics. Using the framework of scientific inquiry proposed by Wallace (1969) as a heuristic tool it will therefore be evaluated what building blocks of a network theory of policy are already assembled and what is still missing. The model by Wallace distinguishes five components of scientific inquiry: theories, hypotheses, observations, empirical generalizations, and methods. The first four components form the major steps of the research cycle, while methods play a role in and connect all transitory steps between the components, from logical deduction through operationalization and measurement to logical induction. Scientific work is hereby conceptualized as a succession of manipulations of information each of which is controlled by a particular kind of method. Whereas methods are seen here as the principal controls over the way in which scientific inquiry is pursued, theories are the most important informational product of this pursuit. Wallace points out that individual observations contain only very small amounts of information about a given phenomena, and that empirical generalizations and hypotheses are limited to moderate amounts of information but that theories (insofar as each theory is synthesized from several different generalizations, and each empirical generalization is synthesized from several different observations) can contain the maximum amount of information (Wallace 1969, x).

In his perspective, theory is not just a storehouse of information, but theory itself actively performs two crucial roles in generating the information that is stored within it: first, it specifies the factors one should be able to measure before doing research, and, second, it serves as a common language into which the results may be translated for purposes of comparison and logical integration with results of other researchers after the research has been completed. In order to arrive at a network theory of policy making, a "theory storehouse" (Wallace) can therefore only be developed by recurrently going through the research cycle as described above.

Consequently, the policy network literature will in the following be assessed on the basis of what has already been assembled in each of the components "observation," "empirical generalizations," "theories," and "hypotheses." Before we can start however, we first have to identify that part of the policy network literature that falls within the definition of "network theory of policy making," since we are interested in the information in the literature on how and why networks influence the structure, process, and outcomes of policy making. Only the literature in which network is considered the *explanans* and policy is considered the *explanandum*, can logically contribute to the development of a network theory of policy making. As we will see, the so-called policy network literature is a miscellany of analytically quite different approaches. Consequently, the literature identified can, following the principal logic of the model presented, be assessed on how and whether information is produced which can be added to the "network theory of policy making"-storehouse. Such a contribution can be made, again according to the logic of the model, by any of the four "method"-steps presented: developing theory from empirical generalizations, developing empirical generalizations from observations, developing observations from hypotheses, or developing hypotheses from theory. If we look at the literature, the vast majority of contributions being published so far contain empirical observations. This is no surprise, because usually after a phenomenon is discovered the natural first step is to describe it as thoroughly as possible. We will therefore start with "observations."

Main Observations in the Literature on Policy Networks

Numerous quantitative and qualitative studies describing networks were published in the 1980s until the mid-1990s. Important publications in this regard were the *Organizational State* (1987) and subsequent work by Pappi, Knoke, and colleagues (Knoke et al. 1996) in which the importance of large formal organizations for policy making in modern industrialized countries was demonstrated and analyzed what kind of structures had developed in certain policy fields like energy, health, and labor.

Other empirical articles that were influenced by the "Organizational State" but came from a European tradition and were published in the edited volume *Policy Networks* by Marin and Mayntz (1991), i.e., Schneider and Werle (1991), Jansen (1991), and Kenis (1991). A somewhat different strand developed in the British context (Rhodes 1990; Rhodes and Marsh 1992).

Further empirical work was done among others by Bulkeley (2000) on the Australian climate change network, Daguerre (2000) on child care policy in England and France, Daugbjerg (1998) on nitrate policy making in Denmark and Sweden, Forrest (2000) on drought policy in post-apartheid Namibia, Nunan (1999) on the implementation of European Union environmental policy in Britain, Schneider (1992) on the chemicals control and telecommunication policy in Germany, and Sciarini (1996) on the Swiss agricultural policy and the GATT negotiations.

Further and more recent work encompasses studies on policy networks by Greer (2002) as well as Toke and Marsh (2003) in the English, Montpetit (2002) and Carpenter et al. (2003) in the North American, and Raab (2002) in the German context.

Studies that combine a policy network and a rational choice/game theoretic approach, i.e., that attempt the integration or reconciliation of structure and agency related approaches encompass among others König and Bräuninger's study on network formation in the German labor-policy domain (1998), Pappi and Henning's study on the organization of influence on the EC's common agricultural policy (1999), Stokman and Berveling's study on decision outcomes and network dynamics in Amsterdam (1998), and van Assen et al.'s (2003) study on decision making in the EU regarding support for fishery infrastructure.

Although or because we, meanwhile, have a myriad of empirical studies using network as a concept to describe structures in policy making, it is very hard to come up with some robust and consistent findings (see below) that go beyond some superficial descriptions. However, some notable patterns emerge.

First, in the roughly first two decades of research and discussion on policy networks it was demonstrated that policy making structures indeed existed in which corporate actors negotiated solutions for certain policy fields. The strong involvement of private and societal actors led to a wider perspective from a state centered to a more encompassing perspective of public policy making.

Second, despite the very different usages of the concept "network," almost all studies see organizations or parts of them as the main actors and conceptualize them as corporate actors and more technically as nodes in the network. Thus organizations are generally accepted as boundedly rational actors and are characterized by intentional actions that have a certain consistency and stability (Jansen 1997). They are seen as being able to control collectivized events (Coleman 1990) and to follow a long-term strategy (Jansen 1997).

Third, there are only few studies in which "network" is used as the independent variable, i.e., in which policy outputs or outcomes are explained with certain structural features of the policy making arrangement. Moreover, there are—in our view—hardly any studies in which the outputs or outcomes are evaluated in terms of effectiveness whatever the criteria might be. If we, therefore, have to answer the question "what do networks do?" we have to come to the conclusion that we know very little based on empirical research when it comes to their effectiveness. This might be due to the fact that one of the—sometimes implicit—assumptions by network scholars has been for a long time that policy networks produce better policies and are, consequently, a better form of policy making compared to more traditional forms. Accordingly, the quality of policy outputs or outcomes and especially the democratic quality of policies made in and through policy networks has rarely been questioned (for some exceptions see Schneider 1999 and Guéhenno 1994).

Fourth, most of the studies have a static character, i.e., the policy networks are seen as stable and the structural characteristics are described for a certain period or in a snapshot mode for multiple periods or points in time. This involves a methodological and a theoretical problem. In network analysis, it is generally assumed that these structures, i.e., the actors and their relations, should have a certain stability. However, it is common knowledge that social structures, including policy networks, are nothing else than repetitive patterns of social interactions (Giddens 1979) that are slightly changed every time they are repeated.

Besides the methodologies difficulties, there is also a theoretical problem. Because agency, structure, process, and outputs are so closely linked in reality the question arises whether the sequence of structural configurations makes a difference for an ongoing policy making process and the subsequent output. For example, does it make a difference if a policy network first develops a high internal density and a high internal legitimacy and then maximizes external ties and external legitimacy as has been suggested by Human and Provan (2000) for interorganizational networks?

Furthermore, there are hardly any studies that try to track policy networks for a longer time either retrospectively or through repeated measurements. This is partly due to the fact that the approach is relatively young, but, also partly, because data requirements are considerable, retrospective data collection is problematic, and repeated collection of network data is risky and very expensive.

EMPIRICAL GENERALIZATIONS IN THE LITERATURE ON POLICY NETWORKS

According to the model by Wallace presented above, it is possible to arrive at a general theory through logical induction by first making empirical generalizations over a multitude of observations. Unfortunately, to our knowledge, no encompassing meta-analysis has yet been conducted, that tries to come up with more general and more abstract categories and indicators for the dependent as well as independent variables, count the observations and make statements about the effects (consequences, outputs, outcomes, results), for example, in terms of the number and types of actors, the types of relationships, clique structure, density, centralization, etc.

In general, we have not gone beyond some very preliminary attempts to summarize some results by constructing descriptive categories (see, for example, van Waarden 1992) that have resonated in the field only to a limited extent.

What we would need, on the one hand, are studies in which the questions should be addressed how networks influence outputs/outcomes (performance) and how particular aspects of networks matter (assuming that the basic question—do networks matter?—has already been answered affirmatively). On the other hand, as it was stated before, the number of studies reporting specific effects of policy networks is rather limited so far. Therefore, at this time it is doubtful whether a comprehensive meta-analysis with a limited number of cases will already lead to meaningful results.

THEORETICAL BUILDING BLOCKS IN POLICY NETWORK RESEARCH

In our view, which seems to be the general opinion in the field (among others König,1998; Peters 1998, 26; Peterson 2003, 8), a consistent body of hypotheses does not exist that could be called a network theory. To be precise, since a theory is defined by its dependent variable it is likely, if there is progress in that direction at all, that different theories will be developed that might share some important traits but would be considerably different from each other. They could be called a network theory of policy, of effectiveness, of organizations, etc., depending upon what the main phenomenon-to-be-explained is.

The decisive question in this endeavor, however, is whether it is possible to come up with more general categories both for the dependent and independent variables compared to the ones constructed for the step "empirical generalizations." The question to be asked at this point would be "of what factors are the structural features of a network a special case?" and "of what categories are the different policies a special case?" (see Wallace 1969, ix). The three categories usually used to categorize policies, i.e., distributive, redistributive, and regulative, might be a good starting point in this respect). This should then allow us to formulate causal relationships of a more general kind between structural features of the policy making arrangements and policy outputs/outcomes.

Hypotheses in Policy Network Research

If we start with making empirical observations and through empirical generalizations manage to formulate a theory, the next step is to come up with hypotheses derived from the theory that can subsequently be tested by making empirical observations. Hypotheses in this respect are concise about what is expected to occur, not why it is expected to occur (Sutton and Staw 1995, 377).

Since there is no unified theoretical body, it is logical that we hardly find specific hypotheses making statements about what to expect in terms of policy outputs or outcomes given certain structural features of the network in the literature. There are, however, bits and pieces in the literature that formulate propositions based on a range of theories, using network as a dependent or an intervening variable.

A sober evaluation of the research and findings in terms of developing a network theory of policy so far reveals that the situation seems to be rather bleak. Despite the multitude of observations, we have not been able to really go beyond the merely metaphorical use of the network concept. From this perspective, the strategy to start at empirical observations and arrive at a theory through logical induction from empirical generalizations seems highly doubtful. Also, most of the studies reporting empirical observations do this without any hypothesis. Therefore, it is no surprise that the results seem to lack the necessary consistency in terms of time, institutional frame, number of actors, importance of the policy, and the like in order to come to empirical generalizations. Given the effort especially necessary in conducting comparative quantitative network studies, it does not seem very promising to engage in studies that simply add empirical observations without any hypotheses based on a network theory of policy. Therefore, we will evaluate in the next section, how such a theory could be developed as a starting point for further empirical research.

WHERE TO GO FROM HERE?

From the analysis above it can be concluded that the "network theory of policy-making" storehouse is rather empty. There seems to be hardly any knowledge on the effects of network attributes on the characteristics of policy making. In order to hold the claim that networks are relevant in policy making, one has to demonstrate that the presence and absence of relationships between actors in a policy-making setting makes a difference to the policy making (i.e., its structure, processes and outcomes). Only if we can demonstrate the types of effects of interactions or links between actors on policy making, can we create a genuine and exclusive basis for a network theoretical approach to policy making. Rather than claiming again and again that relations are important, one should arrive at theoretical propositions about whether interactions make a difference with respect to policy making, i.e., linking structural characteristics to outcomes. Studies in adjacent fields such as sociology, organization studies, or public management could hereby serve as guiding examples that look at the influence of network characteristics, for example, on innovation (Owen-Smith and Powell 2004) or on the quality of service delivery in health and human services (Provan and Milward 1995).

Instead of using the network terminology just as a tool, one should use it for understanding policy making per se. How do interactions support policy making? How does policy-making function in terms of interactions? How does adding or subtracting an interaction in a policy setting change the policy making? How should interactions be structured ideally to increase, for example, innovation in policy making. An information rich theoretical storehouse should be able to answer these types of questions.

But what happens in the absence of such a storehouse or better, how could the storehouse be filled? Here again, the classical model of Wallace might be useful. On the basis of this model, we can identify what has to be achieved in order to develop theory.

Since network theory building on policy making is in such a premature state, the most logical place to start at in the Wallace model is "observations." This might, at first glance, appear to contradict the earlier remark that claimed that we have an abundance of observations but a deficit of theories. The issue seems, however, that we need different types of observations. Since we are primarily interested in the effects of a specific independent variable (i.e., the absence and presence of relations) and not just in the dependent variable (i.e., traits of policy making), we cannot just start collecting information about policy-making cases, which vary on a specific trait. The reason being, that we are at this point not so much interested in explaining differences in certain traits of policy making (e.g., its degree of innovation) but are interested in the effect of a specific explanation (i.e., the absence and presence of relations).

Therefore, in order to develop a network theory of policy making we need to select observations in function of the operationalization of hypotheses. These hypotheses on their part should be logically deduced from some kind of theoretical statement, which proposes that the presence or absence of interactions between policy actors affect a specific characteristic of policy making. For example, a hypothesis could be: The higher the density within a policy field, the higher the chance that it produces an innovative outcome. This hypothesis does obviously not result from a strong or sophisticated network theory of policy making, but it is at least consistent with the general theoretical claim that networks play an important role in policy making. Moreover, such a hypothesis can be operationalized and thus guide our empirical observations.

On the basis of these observations, the hypothesis can be falsified or rejected and thus leads to an empirical generalization: policy fields with high density rates have higher innovation rates compared to policy fields with low density rates. In order to transform this type of information to the level of "theory," the "why" question must be answered. Why is it that the degree of density in a policy field increases its level of innovation? This question can be answered by first finding an answer to the question what other distinctive characteristics policy fields do have in common, because they either have a high or low level of density (which can explain differences in the level of innovation). Second, one needs to answer the question of what the degree of innovation is a special case of. In other words, in which way can the phenomenon-that-explains (i.e., the density of the policy field) and the phenomenon-to-be-explained (i.e., innovation in policy fields) be inductively generalized beyond its original formulation and thus increasing the scientific information.

CONCLUSION: ARE WE EXPECTING TOO MUCH?

The answer is yes and no. We are not expecting too much for at least two reasons. On the one hand, there is a constant and increasing stream of claims from the academic and practice literature that relations and networks are important in the functioning, process and outcome of policy making. As our review of the literature has demonstrated, however, the evidence for this claim is hardly present. On the other hand, network analysis has been providing more and more sophisticated and widely used methods for describing and analyzing relational structures (also in the field of policy making). But in order to be productive in understanding policy making, network analysts will also need to become more theoretical about the study of policy making. As convincingly argued by Salancik (1995), network analysts tend to use other theories (such as resource dependency theory or diffusion theory) to explain phenomena but often do not ask how their perspective addresses a theoretical problem. In line with Salancik, it seems that we are not expecting too much that if network analysis is used, its theoretical advantages should go beyond other well-developed theories. Consequently, in case networks are considered important in policy making and network analysis wants to be productive in describing policy making arrangements and in explaining policy outputs or outcomes, we do expect two things: first, the formulation of propositions about how adding or subtracting a particular interaction in a policy network will change the policy coordination among the actors; and second, the formulation of propositions on how a network structure enables or disenables the interactions between two parties in a policy setting (see e.g., Kenis and Knoke 2002).

But, at the same time, we could also say that, at least at this time, we are indeed expecting too much. The main reason being that developing a theory as a rich "information storehouse" in the sense of the Wallace model is an extremely complicated journey. It assumes that we study a substantive number of policy-making cases, agree on the most important independent variables, use comparable operationalizations and measurements, concentrate on comparable traits of policy making, develop causal reconstructions that will ultimately have to be based on a theory of action, etc.

We have to admit that this chapter has not contributed much to this journey, except, perhaps, by demonstrating how such a journey could look (and, as we all know, real journeys always look different than those in travel catalogs).

REFERENCES

Assen van, M., Stokman, F., and Oosten van, R. (2003). Conflict measures in cooperative exchange models of collective decision-making. *Rationality and Society*, 15, 85–112.

Börzel, T. A. (1997). What's So Special About Policy Networks? — An Exploration of the Concept and Its Usefulness in Studying European Governance. *European Integration online Papers (EIoP)*, 1, http://eiop.or.at/eiop/texte/1997-016a.htm.

Börzel, T. A. (1998). Organizing Babylon — On the Different Conceptions of Policy Networks. *Public Administration,* 76, 253–274.

Brandes, U., Kenis, P., Raab, J., Schneider, V. and Wagner, D. (1999). Explorations into the Visualization of Policy Networks." *Journal of Theoretical Politics,* 11, 75–106.

Bretherton, C., and Sperling, L. (1996). Women's Networks and the European Union: Towards an Inclusive Approach? *Journal of Common Market Studies,* 34, 487–508.

Bulkeley, H. (2000). Discourse coalitions and the Australian climate change policy network. *Environment and Planning C: Government and Policy,* 18, 727–748.

Carpenter, D., Esterling, K., and Lazer, D. (1998). Strength of Weak Ties in Lobbying Networks: Evidence from Health-Care Politics in the United States. *Journal of Theoretical Politics*, 10, 417–444.

Carpenter, D., Esterling, K., and Lazer, D. (2003). The Strength of Strong Ties: A Model of Contact-Making in Policy Networks with Evidence from U.S. Health Politics. *Rationality and Society*, 15, 411–440.

Coleman, J.S. (1990). *Foundations of Social Theory*. Cambridge, MA and London: Harvard University Press.

Daguerre, A. (2000). Policy networks in England and France: the case of child care policy 1980-1989. *Journal of European Public Policy*, 7, 244–60

Daugbjerg, C. (1998). Linking Policy Networks and Environmental Policies: Nitrate Policy Making in Denmark and Sweden 1970-1995. *Public Administration*, 76, 275–294.

Dowding, K. (1995). Model or Metaphor? A Critical Review of the Policy Network Approach. *Political Studies,* 43, 136–158.

Emirbayer, M. and J. Goodwin (1994). Network Analysis, Culture, and the Problem of Agency. *American Journal of Sociology,* 99, 1411–54.

Forrest, J.B. (2000). The Drought Policy: Bureaucracy, Decentralization, and Policy Networks in Post-Arparthaid Namibia. *American Review of Public Administration*, 30, 307–333.

Giddens, A. (1979). *Central Problems in Social Theory. Action, structure and contradiction in social analysis.* London: The Macmillan Press Ltd.

Grande, E., and Peschke, A. (1999). Transnational cooperation and policy networks in European science policy-making. *Research Policy,* 28, 43–61.

Granovetter, M. (1985). Economic Action and Social Structure: The Problem of Embeddedness. *American Journal of Sociology,* 91, 481–510.

Greer, A. (2002). Policy Networks and Policy Change in Organic Agriculture: a Comparative Analysis of the UK and Ireland. *Public Administration,* 80, 453–474.

Griffin, L.J., and van der Linden, M. (1998). Introduction. In L.J. Griffin and M. van der Linden (eds), *New Methods for Social History,* pp. 3–8. Cambridge: University of Cambridge Press.

Grundmann, R. (1998). Policy networks and global ecological problems: The case of the ozone layer. *Law and State,* 58, 7–35.

Guéhenno, J.-M. (1994). *Das Ende der Demokratie.* München: Artemis und Winkler.

Héritier, A. (1993). Policy Netzwerkanalyse als Untersuchungsinstrument im europäischen Kontext: Folgerungen aus einer empirischen Studie regulativer Politik. In A. Héritier (ed), *Policy-Analyse. Kritik und Neurorientierung (PVS Sonderheft),* pp. 432–447. Opladen: Westdeutscher Verlag.

Hollingsworth, J.R., Schmitter P.C., and Streek, W. (eds) (1994). *Governing Capitalist Economies: Performance and Control of Economic Sectors.* Oxford: Oxford University Press.

Human, S. E. and Provan, K. G. (2000). Legitimacy Building in the Evolution of Small Firm Multilateral Networks: A Comparative Study of Success and Demise. *Administrative Science Quarterly,* 45, 327–365.

Jansen, D. (1991). Policy Networks and Change: The Case of High-Tc Superconductors. In B. Marin, and R. Mayntz, (eds), *Policy Networks. Empirical Evidence and Theoretical Considerations,* pp. 132–159. Boulder/Colorado, Frankfurt: Campus Verlag/Westview Press.

Jansen, D. (1997). Das Problem der Akteurqualität korporativer Akteure. In A. Benz and W. Seibel (eds), *Theorieentwicklung in der Politikwissenschaft - eine Zwischenbilanz,* pp. 193–237. Baden-Baden: Nomos Verlagsgesellschaft.

Kenis, P. (1991). The Preconditions for Policy Networks: Some Findings from a Three-Country Study on Industrial Restructuring. In B. Marin, and R. Mayntz, (eds.). *Policy Networks. Empirical Evidence and Theoretical Considerations,* pp. 297–330. Boulder/Colorado, Frankfurt: Campus Verlag/Westview Press.

Kenis, P., and Schneider, V. (1991). Policy Networks and Policy Analysis: Scrutinizing a New Analytical Toolbox. In B. Marin and R. Mayntz (eds), *Policy Networks. Empirical Evidence and Theoretical Considerations,* pp. 25–62. Boulder/Colorado, Frankfurt: Campus Verlag/Westview Press.

Kenis, P., and Knoke, D. (2002). How Organizational Field Networks shape Interorganizational Tie-formation Rates. *Academy of Management Review,* 27, 275–293.

Klijn, E.-H. (1997). Policy Networks: An Overview. In W.J.M. Kickert, E.-H. Klijn, and J.F.M. Koppenjan (eds), *Managing Complex Networks. Strategies for the Public Sector,* pp. 14–34. London: Sage Publications.

Knoke, D. (1990). *Political Networks. The Structural Perspective.* Cambridge: Cambridge University Press.

Knoke, D., Pappi, F.U., Broadbent, J., and Tsujinaka, Y. (1996). *Comparing Policy Networks: Labor Politics in the U.S., Germany, and Japan.* New York: Cambridge University Press.

König, T. (ed) (1998). Modeling Policy Networks. *Journal of Theoretical Politics (special issue).* London: Sage Publications.

König, T., and Bräuninger, T. (1998). The formation of policy networks. Preferences, institutions and actors' choice of information and exchange relations. *Journal of Theoretical Politics,* 10, 445–471.

Laumann, E.O., and Pappi, F.U. (1973). New Directions in the Study of Community Elites. *American Sociological Review,* 38, 212–230.

Laumann, E. O., and Knoke, D. (1987). *The Organizational State. Social Choice in National Policy Domains.* Madison/Wisconsin: University of Wisconsin Press.

Marin, B., and Mayntz, R. (eds). (1991). *Policy Networks. Empirical Evidence and Theoretical Considerations.* Boulder/Colorado, Frankfurt: Campus Verlag/Westview Press.

Mayntz, R. (1993a). Modernization and the Logic of Interorganizational Networks. *Knowledge and Policy: The International Journal of Knowledge Transfer and Utilization,* 6, 3–16.

Mayntz, R. (1993b). Policy-Netzwerke und die Logik von Verhandlungssystemen. In A. Héritier, *Policy-Analyse. Kritik und Neurorientierung*, pp. 39–56. Opladen: Westdeutscher Verlag.

Mayntz, R. (1996). Politische Steuerung: Aufstieg, Niedergang und Transformation einer Theorie. In K. von Beyme and C. Offe (eds), *Politische Theorien in der Ära der Transformation*, pp. 148-169. Opladen: Westdeutscher Verlag.

Melbeck, C. (1998). Comparing local policy networks. *Journal of Theoretical Politics*, 10, 531–552.

Montpetit, É. (2002). Policy Networks, Federal Arrangements, and the Development of Environmental Regulations: A Comparison of the Canadian and American Agricultural Sectors. *Governance*, 15, 1–20.

Nölke, A. (2003). Multi-level Governance in the European Union: The Evolution of Transnational Policy Networks. In Boehnke, K. (ed), *Israel and Europe: A Complex Relationship*, pp. 137–154, Wiesbaden: Deutscher Universitätsverlag.

Nunan, F. (1999). Policy network transformation: the implementation of the EC Directive on packaging and packaging waste. *Public Administration,* 77, 621–638.

Owen-Smith, J., and Powell, W.W. (2004). Knowledge Networks as Channels and Conduits: The Effects of Spillovers in the Boston Biotechnology Community. *Organization Science* 15, 5–21.

Pappi, F. U., and Henning, C.H.C.A (1999). The organization of influence on the EC's common agricultural policy: A network approach. *European Journal of Political Research,* 36, 257–281.

Perrow, C. (1981). Markets, Hierarchies and Hegemony. In A.H. van de Veen (ed). *Perspectives on Organization Design and Behaviour,* pp. 371–386. New York: Wiley.

Peters, G. (1998). Policy networks: myth, metaphor and reality. In Marsh, D. (ed), *Comparing Policy Network,* pp. 21–32. Buckingham/Philadelphia, Open University Press.

Peterson, J. 2003. Policy Networks. *Reihe Politikwissenschaft des Instituts für Höhere Studien.* Wien. http://www.ihs.ac.at/publications/pol/pw_90.pdf.

Poucke, W. van (1979). Network Constraints on Social Action: Preliminaries for a Network Theory. *Social Networks*, 2, 181–190.

Powell, W.W. (1990). Neither Market Nor Hierarchy: Network Forms of Organization. *Research in Organizational Behavior,* 12, 295–336.

Provan, K. and Milward, H. B. (1995). A Preliminary Theory of Interorganizational Network Effectiveness: A Comparative Study of Four Community Mental Health Systems. *Administrative Science Quarterly*, 40, 1–33.

Raab, J. (2002). Where Do Policy Networks Come From? *Journal of Public Administration Research and Theory*, 12, 581–622.

Reinicke, W. H. (1998). *Global Public Policy. Governing without Government?* Washington D.C: Brooking Institution Press.

Rhodes, R.A.W. (1990). Policy Networks. A British Perspective. *Journal of Theoretical Politics*, 2, 293–317.

Rhodes, R. A.W. (1991). Policy networks and sub-central government. In G. Thompson (ed), *Markets, Hierarchies and Networks. The Coordination of Social Life*, pp. 203–214. London/Newbury Park, Calif.: Sage Publications.

Rhodes, R.A.W., and Marsh, D. (1992). Policy Networks in British Politics. In Rhodes, R.A.W., and Marsh, D. (eds), *Policy Networks in British Government*. Oxford: Clarendon Press.

Sabatier, P.A., and Jenkins-Smith, H.C. (1993). *Policy change and learning: an advocacy coalition approach*, Boulder, Colo.: Westview Press.

Salancik, G.R. (1995). Wanted: A Good Network Theory of Organization. *Administrative Science Quarterly,* 40, 345–349.

Scharpf, F. W. (ed) (1993). *Games in Hierarchies and Networks. Analytical and Empirical Approaches to the Study of Governance Institutions*. Frankfurt A.M., Boulder (Col.): Campus Verlag and Westview Press.

Schmitter, P.C., and Lehmbruch, G. (1979). *Trends Towards Corporatist Intermediation*. Beverly Hills, London: Sage Publications.

Schneider, V. (1992). The Structure of Policy Networks: A Comparison of the Chemicals Control and Telecommunications Policy Domains in Germany. *European Journal of Political Research*, 21, 109–129.

Schneider, V. (1999). Möglichkeiten und Grenzen der Demokratisierung von Netzwerken in der Politik. In J. Sydow and A. Windeler (eds), *Steuerung von Netzwerken: Konzepte und Praktiken*, pp. 327–346. Wiesbaden: Westdeutscher Verlag.

Schneider, V. , and Werle, R. (1991). Policy Networks in the German Telecommunications Domain. In B. Marin and R. Mayntz (eds), *Policy Networks. Empirical Evidence and Theoretical Considerations*, pp. 97–137. Boulder/Frankfurt: Westview Press/Campus Verlag.

Schneider, V. and Kenis, P. (1997). Verteilte Kontrolle: Institutionelle Steuerung in modernen Gesellschaften. In: P. Kenis and V. Schneider (eds), *Organisation und Netzwerk. Institutionelle Steuerung in Wirtschaft und Politik*, 9–44. Frankfurt/New York: Campus Verlag.

Schneider, M., Scholz J., Lubell, M. Mindruta, D., and Edwardsen, M. (2003). Building consensual institutions: Networks and the National Estuary Program, *American Journal of Political Science*, 47, 143–158.

Sciarini, P. (1996). Elaboration of the Swiss Agricultural Policy for the Gatt Negotiations: A Network Analysis. *Schweizer Zeitschrift für Soziologie*, 22, 85–115.

Sutton, R.I., and Staw, B.M. (1995). What theory is not. *Administrative Science Quarterly* 40, 371–384.

Teubner, G. (1996). Die vielköpfige Hydra: Netzwerke als kollektive Akteure höherer Ordnung, In P. Kenis, and V. Schneider (eds), *Organisation und Netzwerk. Institutionelle Steuerung in Wirtschaft und Politik*, pp. 535–562. Frankfurt, New York: Campus Verlag.

Stokman, F.N., Berveling, J. (1998). Dynamic modelling of policy networks in Amsterdam. *Journal of Theoretical Politics*, 10, 577–601.

Toke, D., and Marsh, D. (2003). Policy networks and the GM crops issue: Assessing the utility of a dialectical model of policy networks. *Public Administration*, 81, 229–251.

Tsebelis, G. (1999). Veto players and law production in parliamentary democracies: An empirical analysis. *American Political Science Review*, 93, 591–608.

Wallace, W. L. (ed) (1969). *Sociological Theory. An Introduction*. Chicago: Aldine Publishing Company.

Waarden, F. van (1992). Dimensions and types of policy networks. *European Journal of Political Research*, 21, 29–52.

Weir, M. (1992). Ideas and the politics of bounded innovation. In Steinmo, S.; Thelen, K. and F. Longstreth (eds), *Structuring politics. Historical institutionalism in comparative analysis*, pp. 188–216. Cambridge/New York: Cambridge University Press.

Williamson, O. (1975). *Markets and Hierarchies: Analysis and Antitrust Implications*. New York: Free Press.

Windhoff-Héritier, A. (1993). Policy Network Analysis. In H. Keman (ed), *Comparative Politics. New Directions in Theory and Method*, pp. 143–160. Amsterdam, University Press.

Zijlstra, G. J. (1979). Networks in Public Policy: Nuclear Energy in the Netherlands. *Social Network,* 1, 359–389.

15 Theories of Policy Learning: Agency, Structure, and Change

John Grin and Anne Loeber

1 INTRODUCTION

In the Big Quest for an appropriate model of the policy process that has been driving policy science since its inception, theories on learning form a recurrent theme. Learning as a concept showed up in the policy process debate in reaction to the primeval approach to understanding policy making, that is, to Easton's (1953, 1967) system theory. Basically, the system model portrays the policy process as a "conveyer belt" (Stone 1998, x). Pressures from society are turned into inputs (demands and supports) for the political system, within which politicians authoritatively order and translate the societal pressures and requests into problems to be processed by policy makers. It is the latter's task to thereupon transform them into policies that, after having been politically sanctioned, are to yield policy outputs that resolve the problems as experienced. Subsequently, governmental administrators implement these policies according to their best potential. In return, society may respond by a new round of demands being articulated and pressures building up.

This stagist depiction of the policy process over the past few decades has been the dominant interpretation in the otherwise widely diverging field of the policy sciences, aptly characterised by Edella Schlager as a landscape of "mountain islands of theoretical structure, intermingled with, and occasionally attached together by foothills of shared methods and concepts and empirical work, all of which is surrounded by oceans of descriptive work not attached to any mountain of theory" (1997, 14). The systems approach mountain riffs hold in common the rather strict analytic distinction between the realm of politics, located exclusively in the governmental institutions of the nation state, and society at large; as well as an emphasis on power and conflict in explaining policy change. Learning theories entered the scene when cognition and knowledge utilisation were taken into consideration to rival power as an explanatory factor of policy change. As Hugh Heclo (1974, 305) put it in what may justifiably be called the earliest seminal study on policy-oriented learning: "Tradition teaches that politics is about conflict and power. This is a blinkered view of politics.... Politics finds its sources not only in power but also in uncertainty ... Policy making is a form of collective puzzlement on society's behalf." By focusing attention to, and opening up the hitherto black box of "puzzling on what to do," learning theories have sought to address the complex relation between power and knowledge in the policy process and to consider changes in ideas as a central factor in understanding policy change.

Learning theories drew much attention between about 1980 and the late 1990s. In an often cited "midterm review" of learning theories, Bennett and Howlett (1992) showed that different approaches employ different conceptualisations of learning which cannot be easily reduced to one umbrella definition. They formulated three descriptive questions to usefully distinguish between the prevailing approaches: what are the subjects of learning in an approach, what are the objects of learning, and what is learning supposed to contribute to? Now that the attention cycle for policy-oriented learning seems over its top, we think it is time to go beyond identifying the varieties of approaches and clarifying the insights gained. In this chapter, we wish to identify the upshot of learning literature for the literature on governance, which seems to be the next major mountain isle in policy science's evolving landscape.

It is our contention that the governance perspective involves more than changes in the actual institutional design and organization of the governing process to which many authors limit their focus (e.g., Kickert et al. 1997; Rhodes 1997). Rather, a change can be observed in the dominant way in which the relation between state and society is conceived of and acted upon, which comes out in a change in institutions in the realm of the political *and* elsewhere in society (Hajer 2003; Grin 2006). To assess the merits of the learning approaches to conceptualizing governance as a process of transforming relations between government and society, we will go beyond, or, maybe better, behind, the questions singled out by Bennett and Howlett. We will take their first question (*who* learns?) beyond the straightforward question of who are included as learning actors, into an investigation of how these actors are situated in relation to each other and to social and political institutions. In discussing the final question (*learning to what effect?*), we will pay attention not only to the relation between learning and policy change, but, more specifically, to the relation between learning and the reproduction and transformation of institutions. Thus, in our discussions, we will give particular attention to the way in which the relation between agency and structure is depicted—an issue that any social science theory should address, but which is particularly important to theorizing "governance."

The learning theories discussed in this manner are organized into three broad categories. First, theories are discussed that focus on learning *from one domain to another*, that is, on the transfer of insight and information produced within some context to a policy area located elsewhere in space and/or time (section 2), and on theories that focus on the relation between learning and policy change *within* one particular domain (section 3). Strikingly, while both types of policy-oriented learning theories typically focus on governmental institutions as the locus of change resulting from learning processes, the *organizational* aspect of learning often remains implicit. Section 4 addresses approaches that deal with a core aspect of learning that the former two categories of theories leave largely undiscussed: what does it mean to consider (governmental) organizations as learning actors? In conclusion, we will draw inferences from the upshot of this variety of learning approaches in terms of their contribution to the evolving literature on governance.

2 LEARNING BETWEEN DOMAINS: LESSON DRAWING AND POLICY TRANSFER

One major branch of literature on learning concerns processes of lesson drawing between policy domains that are at some distance from each other in time and/or space. As we shall see, these approaches have gradually evolved from accounts with limited explanatory power (and ambition) to something close to a full-fledged theory of learning and policy change. We therefore wish to pay attention to them as approaches that may contribute to governance literature, much of which emphasizes the need to confront the fact that "the constraints of social time and geographical space no longer impose fixed barriers to many forms of social interaction" (Held and McGrew 2000, 3).

2.1 DIFFERENT APPROACHES

At the cradle of the literature on lesson drawing is the work of Richard Rose (1991, 1993, 2004), who in his theorising starts from the claim—which he considers self-evident (cf. Page 2000 for some critical remarks)—that policy makers in their work increasingly make use of insights gained elsewhere. Convinced that "problems that are unique (...) are abnormal," Rose holds that policy makers can draw lessons from the experiences of their counterparts in other cities, regional or national governments regarding comparable problems that will help hem deal better with their own issues (Rose 1991, 4). To Rose, the agents of learning are civil servants (and maybe their external advisers, but certainly not politicians). The author conceives of these agents not as political theorists but as social engineers seeking to apply knowledge instrumentally to improve the feasibility of policy programs (Rose 1993, 2004). They engage in lesson-drawing, when they experience a "gap between present aspirations and achievements" (1991, 11) or when there is "uncertainty in the minds of policymakers" (1991, 12).

In the attention paid to the motives of actors in the policy formation process to produce and apply practical knowledge lays the merit of Rose's work. By focusing on the ways in which policy makers draw lessons and improve their practices, Rose emphasises the unique status of practical considerations and experience in policymaking. This focus his work shares with that of Anne Schneider and Helen Ingram who, however, differ from Rose in taking a less technical stance on lesson drawing and pay more attention to explaining the ways in which experiences shape processes of policy formation. A more fundamental difference is their central concern with the biases introduced in policy designs.

Schneider and Ingram (1988) discuss the notion of "systematically pinching ideas" by exploring the rules of thumb employed by policy makers during policy design, that is, by studying what Simon (1945) called the decision heuristics. The authors argue that policy design is "less a matter of invention than of selection" (1988, 63). Biases in design result from the ways in which past experiences and experiences in other domains are called upon by policy makers through associative reasoning, the reconstruction of memories, and the anchoring of incremental reasoning in some particularly chosen starting point. Examples from very different contexts are supposed to help in deliberately mitigating the biases introduced by decision heuristics, thus promoting opportunities for nonincremental policy change. In later work, Schneider and Ingram (1990; cf. 1997) have proposed "learning tools" for that purpose.

The "sequential adoption of the same program by two ore more independent states," lies at the heart of Colin Bennett's work on policy transfer. Building on the conceptual notions and empirical findings of Rose, Bennett (1991) seeks to explain policy "import" on the basis of system-level socio-economic characteristics, existing interdependence between the two states involved, and transnational communication. In regard to the third factor, Bennett distinguishes five types of motives for utilizing evidence from other contexts, varying from mollifying political pressure by using foreign experiences to searching for the best policy to deal with a problem. On basis of a case study, Bennett claims that in most cases a mix of motives will be present, depending on the interests of the "importer." Other case studies (e.g., Tavits 2003) have provided further evidence for this finding.

Building on the work of Bennett and Rose, David Dolowitz and David Marsh (1996) have further explored the notion of policy transfer as "a process in which knowledge about policies, administrative arrangements, institutions etc. in one time and/or place is used in the development of policies, administrative arrangements and institutions in other time and/or place" (1996, 343). Knowledge transfer may concern policies, institutions, ideologies, or justifications, attitudes and ideas, and negative lessons (Dolowitz 1997). Treating it primarily as the dependent variable, they seek to understand knowledge transfer as the result of strategic decisions by actors inside and outside government. They pay specific attention to policy entrepreneurs and experts as well as to intergovernmental and international organizations, which may encourage exchanges of ideas. In a later article, they add think tanks, transnational corporations and nongovernmental institutions and consultants, arguing that the latter two are increasingly important because they "tend to offer advice based upon what they regard as 'best practice' elsewhere" (Dolowitz and Marsh 2000, 7).

According to Dolowitz and Marsh, there are three types of transfer. *Voluntary transfer* is driven by dissatisfaction with current policy, for instance because of policy failure or elections (cf. Rose's "lesson drawing" and Schneider and Ingram's "systematically pinching of ideas"; and also Cox's (1993) policy borrowing or Ikenberry's (1990) policy band-wagoning). *Direct coercive transfer* results less from learning than from obligations imposed by international or transnational treaties or entities (cf. Bennett's (1991) "penetration" notion, or Ikenberry's (1990) "external inducement"). *Indirect coercive transfer* is driven by externalities that result from interdependence, such as regional or global environmental problems or migration patterns, by global economic constraints, or by rivalry or emulation considerations. In their 2000 article, the authors note that the role of international corporate or NGO consultants blurs the distinction between voluntary and coercive transfer. Furthermore, they extend their analytical scope by considering policy transfer as a variable explaining policy failure or success. They mention three factors explaining policy failure: *uninformed transfer*, when sufficient information about the foreign policy's institutional context and its conditions for success is lacking; *incomplete transfer*, when policies are adopted without the crucial contextual and institutional conditions in place; and *inappropriate transfer*, when a policy is included in a wider program that is based on a very different set of values. This resonates with their earlier conclusion that—contrary to what Rose holds—more attention to institutional factors is needed, especially because policy transfer may simply reinforce existing power relations unless a less pluralist, state-centric stance is taken. Moreover, a less positivist conceptualisation is needed, to pay more attention to the role of judgement in the definition of problems and solutions (Dolowitz and Marsh 1996, 10–11).

These important conclusions on policy transfers/lesson-drawing approaches are pushed further, and put into a more fundamental light, by Diane Stone. Much of the earlier lesson-drawing literature, Stone argues, too easily assumes that policy transfer may lead to an increased rationality in policy making, ignoring the tendency that policy transfer will privilege lessons which are in line with the fundamental assumptions underlying current policies. Directly related is her claim that "lesson-drawing is not politically neutral" (Stone 1999, 52). While this claim is shared by Dolowitz and Marsh, Stone adds the corollary that "the value of lessons lies in their power to bias policy choice" (ibid.), suggesting (like Schneider and Ingram) a more critical stance on methodical-prescriptive aspects. In addition, she remarks that policy transfer literature has the potential to contribute not only to comparative public policy, but to "global policy studies" and public policy studies "attempts to directly address globalisation." Here, Dolowitz and Marsh's claim resonates that students of policy processes always need to consider policy transfer. Yet, Stone suggests a deeper understanding by observing that "the policy transfer concept problematises the division between the domestic and the international" (cf. Rose 2004, 9–101). Her discussion on how global phenomena impinge upon the nation state suggests a more fundamental interpretation on Dolowitz and Marsh's (2000) finding that voluntary and coercive transfer may be difficult to distinguish, and suggests that this should not be seen as an analytical problem, but rather as an analytical clue.

Stone argues that contextual and institutional factors deserve more attention than they now get in policy transfer literature, implying a need for a less ahistorical treatment of policy learning. She conceives of policy transfer as one type of policy change. Taking it as a consequence of policy learning (1999, 51; 2004, 548), she emphasizes that the transfer not only consists of policies per se, but also of "ideas, ideals, expertise, programmes and personnel" that may significantly influence "the development and implementation of public policy" (Stone 1999, 55). Regarding the agents of learning, she focuses on the "third sector": NGOs, foundations, pressure groups, thinks tanks, and so on. In later work, Stone has further elaborated what she calls the "privatisation of policy transfer," particularly focusing on think tanks (Stone 2000) and on global networks (Stone 2004), which are epistemic communities (Haas 1989; 1992) that can create and disseminate policy knowledge.

Another attempt at synthesizing earlier approaches to policy transfer and lesson-drawing has been made by Mark Evans and Jonathan Davies (1999). With Stone they share an understanding of policy transfer as one particular form of (or input in) policy change, and an interest in the interaction of structure and agency. An important addition is that they subsequently develop a framework for the latter, building on Wendt's (1987) elaboration of Giddens' (1984) structuration theory, which conceives of structure as both the medium of action and as its outcome. The framework also builds on literatures on globalization, internationalization, transnationalization, and policy transfer. It identifies how a variety of structural factors (economic, technological, ideological and institutional) may interact with each other and with "globalizing tendencies" in shaping policy transfer processes.

2.2 IN SUM

As approaches to theorizing the policy process and, especially, as contributions to the emerging governance literature, lesson drawing/policy transfer concepts seem to be coming of age lately. First, the role of non-governmental agents has become included and elaborated in especially the later approaches (Dolowitz and Marsh, Stone, Evans and Davies; but cf. Schneider and Ingram 1988). Second, an important advance has been the work by Stone who not only draws attention to agency and, more particularly, the role of different types of agents, but also to the need to overcome methodological nationalism. A third crucial development has been Stone's call for, and Evans and Davies' elaboration of, the interaction between structure and agency. Taken together, these elements offer a good basis for a full fledged theory of policy change through policy transfer *between* different domains—of obvious importance in a transnational world.

An emphasis on social construction, such as found in the work of Stone and Evans and Davies, will also help to meet criticism (e.g., James and Lodge 2003) that the focus on the relation between policy transfer and policy failure (in Dolowitz and Marsh 1996) neglects the connecting processes. These will codepend on the "theories-in-use" (Schön 1983; Argyris 1990, see below) of the actors involved as they deal with contextual and structural factors. Only an explanatory theory of this kind will provide a basis for the "prescriptions for practice" that Stone seeks, and to which Schneider and Ingram's (1997) notions of "systematically pinching ideas" and learning tools provide a contribution. Such a theory may contribute to an important issue in governance literature: the understanding of *institutional* change as both a condition for, and an outcome of, policy change.

3 LEARNING WITHIN DOMAINS: SOCIAL LEARNING AND THE ADVOCACY COALITION FRAMEWORK

While literature on policy learning *across* domains has gradually evolved into an increasingly comprehensive theory of the policy process, as the previous section shows, work on learning *within* a particular policy domain has been motivated from its onset by the intention to provide an integral theory of the policy process, taking into full consideration the role of ideas and arguments.

3.1 SOCIAL LEARNING

A major contribution to the field of policy learning within domains is the work on social learning by Peter Hall. His oeuvre grew out of an attempt to understand long-term policy change in British economic policy between the 1930s and the emergence of Thatcherite policies. His objective was to conceptualise policy making in a way that pays due attention to both societal developments and the active role of the state "apparatus" (1993, 275). Building on the work by Hugh Heclo, he outlined an image of learning with three central features. First, Hall argues, "one of the principal factors affecting policy at time-1 is policy at time-0" (1993, 277); second, the key agents who push forward the learning process are the experts within the state or those located at the "interface between the bureaucracy and the intellectual enclaves of society" (1993, 277) in a given policy domain; and, third, of key importance is the capacity of states to act autonomously from societal pressure. Hall defined social learning as "a deliberate attempt to adjust the goals or techniques of policy in response to past experience and new information," adding that "learning is indicated when policy changes as the result of such a process" (Hall 1993, 278).

Crucial in Hall's theory is the distinction between three forms of learning:

- First order learning, which leads to a change in the "levels (or settings) of the basic instruments of (...) policy, such as the minimum lending rate or fiscal stance";
- Second order learning, leading to a change in both policy instruments and their settings;
- Third order learning, leading to not only a change in policy instruments and their settings, but also to a change of the "policy paradigm," that is, the "framework of ideas and standards that specifies not only the goals of policy and the kind of instruments used to attain them, but also the very nature of the problems they are meant to be addressing" (1993, 279). The policy paradigm is conceived of as part of the context in which policymaking takes place.

Hall draws on the Kuhnian image of scientific development to hypothesise on the conditions for third order change. First, change depends on the arguments of competing factions, their positional advantages within a broader institutional framework, the ancillary resources they can command and exogenous factors affecting power relations. Second, Hall argues, "the movement from one paradigm to another is likely to be preceded by significant shifts in the locus of authority over policy" in the eyes of politicians. Third, "third order change is likely to involve the accumulation of anomalies, experimentation of new forms of policy and policy failures that precipitate a shift in the locus of authority over policy and initiate a wider contest (...) [which] will end only when the supporters of a new paradigm secure positions of authority (...) [and] institutionalise the new paradigm" (Hall 1993, 280–81).

Various authors have applied Hall's social learning approach and significantly added to it. Criticizing an article by Hall and Taylor (1996), Colin Hay and Daniel Wincott (1998) stress the need to pay better attention to the relation between structure and agency (a point largely accepted by Hall and Taylor 1998). Stressing the dialectic nature of the relation between structure and agency, Hay and Wincott (1998, 953) consider it quintessential to go beyond rational choice approaches into theorizing "institutional innovation, evolution and transformation capable of linking the subject in a creative relationship with an institutional environment." As a corollary, (policy) "[c]hange is seen as the consequence (...) of strategic action (...). Since individuals (and groups of individuals) are knowledgeable and reflexive, they routinely (...) monitor the consequences" (1998, 954) of, e.g., the developments in British economic policy (cf. Hay 2001).

This trail has been further followed by Hugh Pemberton, who proposes and explores further adaptations of Hall's model. Pemberton (2000) proposes a synthesis between Hall's social learning model and policy network approaches (e.g., Marsh and Rhodes 1992), making up for the network theory's alleged capability to explain change, and at the same time providing the structural dimension (based on network theory) that is inadequately represented in social learning theory. His model of the "policy making terrain" encompasses a range of possible policy actors linked to one or more networks (e.g., the cabinet ministers, industry networks, think tanks and issue networks). The policy terrain is embedded in a three-level environment: organizational culture, international context, and the broader historical-sociological-political context. Interestingly, the schematic representation includes a feedback loop, indicating how actors and networks in turn change the environment through policy output and implementation. Empirically, Pemberton (2000, 789) finds that "policy networks can change their configuration and that different networks are associated with different orders of policy making."

In a later article, Pemberton (2003) elaborates on Hall's (1993, 288) suggestion that it may be interesting to explore the link between networks and third order change. Reanalysing Hall's case, he finds that networks "were a particularly important *intermediate* variable in a recursive process. Policy change was brought about by learning in policy networks, but networks were also shaped by changes in the policy environment. Negative feedback from past policies brought the new 'growth' network into being." Furthermore, this new analysis confirms that "peripheral actors with little obvious power may exert great influence over policy through the medium of a policy network." Maybe most fundamental is the finding that third order learning may occur and lead to changes in the terms of the debate, but not necessarily to lasting policy changes. This may be explained by the fact that implementation may escape the changes in the world of policy making, and by the fragmentation of the polity.

Using the same case, Oliver and Pemberton (2004) show that "the paradigm change seems to be far more evolutionary than Hall's typology of change allows" (2004, 435). They suggest "punctuated equilibrium" as a more fitting metaphor than "revolution," and posit a more sophisticated understanding of "the mechanics of policy learning and policy change." Third order change occurred, they argue, through a "complex iteration" of first and second order changes over a decade, which, while involving an ideational battle in which outsiders played a key role, primarily took place within government." Full institutionalisation of a new paradigm required an "exogenous shock [namely a war announcing itself] capable of destroying confidence in the possibility of stabilizing the existing policy framework" (ibid.).

3.2 POLICY-ORIENTED LEARNING: THE ADVOCACY COALITION FRAMEWORK

Probably the most debated and employed approach to understanding policy-oriented learning has been the Advocacy Coalition Framework (ACF). Its primeval version grew from Paul Sabatier's (1986) attempt to synthesize "bottom-up" and "top-down" approaches in implementation studies. From the bottom-up approaches it first and foremost borrows its unit of analysis. Rather than on a policy program, the focus of an analysis should be on a policy *problem*, Sabatier argues, so that the unit of analysis should be the variety of policy makers (including e.g., opinion leaders), policy implementers and target groups involved in dealing with a particular problematic—the *policy subsystem*.

From top-down approaches, he maintains the attention devoted to the ways in which social, economic and other factors, events and processes, that are exogenous to the subsystem, affect the policy process. In addition, the ACF imports from top-down approaches the idea to account for "the attempts by various actors to manipulate (. . .) governmental programs in order to achieve their objectives over time, and actors' efforts to improve their understanding of (. . .) the problem (. . .) as they learn from experience." Obviously, "[a]ttention thus shifts from policy implementation to policy change over periods of 10–20 years."

To the first outline thus emerging the ambitions were added to "integrate the hitherto largely separate literatures on (1) knowledge utilization and (2) policy change" (Sabatier 1987, 650). This reflects Sabatier's (1978) recognition that technical information may have a significant influence on the policy process, through its role in advocacy, as well as through its enlightenment function. The ACF thus meets a major criticism against the stagist model, by fully appreciating the role of ideas and arguments in policy evolution (Sabatier 1993, 15).

The ACF conceives of the policy subsystem as comprising a wide range of actors, aggregated into *advocacy coalitions* (AC) that by definition share a *policy belief system* and "often act in concert" (Sabatier 1987, 652) or, in a more recent formulation, "engage in a non-trivial degree of coordinated activity over time" (Sabatier 1999, 120). Advocacy coalitions interact to produce policy programs. Their actions are mediated by so-called brokers, and influenced by the constraints and resources implied by their contexts. The composition of coalitions is assumed to be relatively stable over periods of a decade or so. A coalition's policy belief system comprises "deep-core beliefs" that include basic ontological and normative convictions considered relevant across virtually all policy domains; policy core beliefs which "represent a coalition's basic normative commitments and causal perceptions across an entire policy domain," and "secondary aspects" that is, a narrower set of beliefs that pertain to a particular policy problem and its context (Sabatier 1999, 121–22; see chapter 9, this volume).

The policy programs that evolve from the (inter)actions of various advocacy coalitions reflect the way in which these "seek to understand the world in order to further their policy objectives." This is called *policy oriented learning* which, following Heclo (1974, 304), is defined as "relatively enduring alterations of thought or behavioral intentions that result from experience (...) [and] involve (...) perceptions concerning external dynamics, and increased knowledge of the state of the problem parameters and the factors affecting them" (Sabatier, 1987, 654). Conceptually, learning is conceived of lasting changes in the policy belief systems. As a consequence, three types of learning are distinguished, pertaining, respectively, to changes in the various layers of policy belief systems.

Of the extensive debates triggered by the ACF, a crucial one concerns the heart of the framework: the definition of the policy subsystem. Sabatier (1993) considers it quintessential that, as the unit of analysis, it must be stable over the prolonged period (10–20 years) over which policy change is to be studied. Thomas (1996) has disputed this notion, arguing that literature shows an evolution of the concept from a mostly static interpretation based on the iron triangle metaphor, to a more dynamic interpretation that recognises the potential for significant changes in the order and organization of subsystems over time. Grin, Hoppe, and Van de Graaf (1997) pick up on this point, arguing on theoretical and empirical grounds (Loeber and Grin 1996 [2006]; Eberg 1997), that a policy subsystem can never be defined without some historical-institutional analysis. They point to examples (e.g., Hoppe and Peterse 1993; Hoppe et al. 1987) in which policy problematics arise in the interstitches between two or more established policy subsystems, which may *compete* over new policy problems, to conclude that policy subsystems are under continuous political (re)construction. The relations between policy subsystems, agency and policy change have more recently been developed further by Howlett and Ramesh (2002), who show that subsystems shape the policy process, *and* conversely, that policy learning and policy change may contribute to subsystem transformation.

In response, Sabatier and Jenkins-Smith (1999, 135–37) acknowledge the interaction between related subsystems along functional and territorial lines (cf. also Zafonte and Sabatier 1998), recognize the possibility of "nested" and of "overlapping" systems and introduce a welloperationalized distinction between a nascent subsystem and a mature one. They do, however, *not* wish to adopt the more fundamental claim that subsystems must be seen as continuously under construction. This stance is rooted in their critical-rationalist methodological position: as a unit of analysis, the subsytem is a *researcher's* construct that must be held stable over the period investigated. Denying the stability of a subsystem would undermine the possibility to define, and distinguish between, the three layers of relevant policy belief systems.

Not surprisingly, against this background, Sabatier and Jenkins-Smith are even less tempted to adopt Hajer's (1995, 68–72) fundamental contention that the idea of a policy belief system as the basis of action of advocacy coalitions reflects an individualist ontology. In Hajer's view, individuals are characterized by and through the practices they engage in. Action is not rooted in beliefs that are a priori given. Rather than holding stable values, Hajer (1995, 71) argues, people hold "vague, contradictory and unstable 'value positions'" that may be influenced by new discourses "for instance because [these create] new subject and structure positionings." Fischer (2003, 94–104) shares this position, and criticizes the ACF's emphasis on causal argumentation in "professional forums" that is informed by pre-given policy beliefs. Closely related, both authors criticize the ACF's presumption that policy core beliefs are resistant to change. Because of this erroneous view, Fischer argues, and because of its neglect of the role of strategic action, the ACF seems to explain policy stability better than policy change.

It is interesting to view this debate in the light of empirical work on long-term policy change, which combines a nonrationalist, interpretive, epistemological position with the assumption that action is being informed by policy beliefs. Eberg's (1997) comparative study of waste policy change empirically shows that core beliefs indeed are stable over a prolonged period and that learning regarding core beliefs is mainly induced by crises and surprises; but also that the likelihood of learning on core beliefs, and thus of radical policy change, codepends on (social and physical) structural elements, among which discursive elements such as images of nature. In a comparative study of the development of wind energy policy and practices, Van Est (1999) empirically finds coalitions that are based on shared core beliefs and, through their interaction, shape policy development. Interestingly, their interactions strongly depend on the learning alliances that these coalitions form, which reflect (and shape) dominant discourses.

3.3 IMPLEMENTATION AS LEARNING

John Grin and Henk Van de Graaf have extended the notion of policy learning to the realm of policy implementation. Their point of departure is that—ironically, in view of the ACF's roots—policy implementation processes are obscured in the framework. If, as implementation literature suggests, implementation may *transform* policy, it is important to understand how implementation may be conceived of as learning—and to use that insight to further elaborate Elmore's (1985) idea of policy design as a combination of "forward and backward mapping" (Grin and Van de Graaf, 1996a).

Central to Grin and Van de Graaf's (1996b) depiction is the idea that policy target populations do not necessarily share a *policy* belief system. They may be characterized by belief systems ("theories of action") which are rooted in the sort of practices they are professionally engaged in when contributing (or *not* contributing) to policy implementation: managing a firm, farming, developing technology, and so on (Grin and Van de Graaf, 1996a). The finding from implementation studies that policy implementation generally implies policy change (Majone and Wildavsky 1979), Grin and Van de Graaf can thus explain empirically, showing that implementing actors, from their own context and theories of action, are likely to attribute to policy objects and objectives a meaning that differs from that of policy makers.

In contrast to Sabatier, Grin and Van de Graaf assume a constructivist ontology and a hermeneutic epistemology. Consequently, even though they (1996a, b) too conceive of belief systems as structurally layered, they do not assume a hierarchical relation between the layers. Building on Fischer's (1980; 1995) idea of the four layers of evaluative discourse and Schön's (1983) empirical-phenomenological work on "reflection-in-action," they conceive of action as being guided by an actor's (four-layered) "theory of action," which comprises notions regarding the *evaluation of solutions* (empirical-analytical arguments), *problem definitions and the meaning of solutions* (phenomenological arguments), *empirical and normative background theories* (hermeneutic-interpretive arguments), and *normative-ontological preferences* (philosophical arguments).

The idea is that this structure applies to theories of action of policy makers, implementers, and target groups alike, yet that these actors' theories of action are *substantively* different. This has an important implication. Rather than shared meanings or value consensus, effective implementation of policy plans in line with policymakers' intentions merely requires a *congruency* of meaning regarding the main policy objects or artifacts. Actors attribute congruent meanings to an artifact "if they perceive the artifact's properties in such a way that the artifact has a sensible meaning to all of them. Congruency or incongruency of meaning is what determines the degree to which artifacts (…) impede or facilitate joint action" (Grin and Van de Graaf, 1996b, 304).

Learning during the "implementation game" (in a process of "communicative action") is supposed to contribute to achieving congruency. In analyzing the conditions for such learning, Grin and Van de Graaf, following Schön (1983) and Argyris et al. (1985), distinguish between first and second order learning and describe the conditions under which the latter, most fundamental type of learning is possible. Several of the hypotheses on these matters that the authors formulated have been tested in an empirical study on 66 cases of implementing environmental policy plans in the Netherlands

(Van de Graaf and Grin, 1999). This study yielded an understanding of the precise ways in which the proper use of policy instruments may induce learning that may help produce a congruency of meaning between policy makers, policy implementers, and target groups and thus contribute to the realization of policy goals.

3.4 IN SUM

The ACF deserves credit for being theoretically comprehensive, rigorous, and integrative. However, its contribution to understanding policy processes is essentially limited by its underlying positivist epistemology and methodology (cf. Fischer 2003, 100). Approaching its constitutive elements from a constructivist-hermeneutic view, the ACF is seen to synthesize various crucial insights in the relation between learning, action and structure. It holds that theories-in-use (policy beliefs) guide action, and posits that the relations between action, learning, structural context, and policy change must be understood from the broader perspective of the mutual shaping of structure and agency. When viewing the ACF in this light, it follows that (other than Hajer and Fischer seem to suggest) discourse analysis is not an alternative to the idea of learning by coalitions that share theories of action, but rather that discourses are *an element of* the structures that shape learning, and that learning is part of the processes through which discourses (like other structural elements) are being reproduced and transformed. Taking this perspective, the ACF is however exposed as undervaluing the role of strategic, reflexive action (which is both shaped by and a shaping structure) in these processes and thus in policy change. It is here that insights from (Hall's) social learning tradition—especially analyses from authors like Hay and Wincott and Pemberton, who give adequate attention to the relation between structure and agency, may essentially add to the ACF.

From the perspective set out in our introduction, the main pitfall of Peter Hall's social learning approach is that it adopts a rather classical picture of a polity, namely as separated from society at large. Society mainly enters the policy process through exerting pressure and through the contribution of experts and other elite players to policy making. While this point is partly repaired by the merger with network theory, a more comprehensive solution is provided by the ACF's more inclusive notion of a policy subsystem.

Still, both approaches have in common that they treat implementation as exogenous to the polity. This conceptual isolation of the implementation process, that learning theories share with many other theories of the policy process, not only describes but also shapes policy practice and thus may interfere with the relation between learning and policy change, as Pemberton's (2003) work shows. The main merit of Grin and Van de Graaf's work on implementation—understood as a dynamic process of mutually making sense of policy objects between policy makers, implementers and target groups—may well be that it remedies this lack of attention to the well-known fact that "implementation is the continuation of politics with different means" (Majone and Wildavsky 1979, 175). To fully comprehend implementation as an integral part of policy making, we must take into account the relations between learning, policy change, and organizational dynamics.

4 THEORIES ON ORGANIZATIONAL LEARNING IN A PUBLIC SETTING

The theories on learning discussed above typically focus on governments as the loci of change and presuppose the individual policy maker or policy analyst to be the learning subject. Remarkably, the *organizational* aspect of learning in these theories remains largely implicit. Since processes of policy-oriented learning generally imply a change in organizational action, this aspect arguably deserves due attention (Argyris and Schön 1978; Huber 1991; Busenberg 2001). The theories discussed are unclear about the implications that learning at the level of the individual may have for higher levels of aggregation in an organization. In addition, little attention is paid to the manner in which the context influences an individual's learning potential.

The need to focus on the dynamics in organizations is the more pressing when the original focus on governmental agency in the policy sciences is broadened to include "non-state" actors as well (as in e.g., Schneider and Ingram, Dolowitz and Marsh, Stone, Evans and Davies, Sabatier and Grin and Van de Graaf). As we have seen above, in these theories, there is a development toward understanding policy change as the resultant of learning processes among *and between* governmental and non-governmental actors, be they members of a policy target group (cf. Grin and Van de Graaf), a policy network (cf. Pemberton) or an advocacy coalition (Sabatier). Such inclusive approaches imply a need to take the institutional contexts of all learning subjects, state and non-state, into consideration.

4.1 The Learning Government

One of the first political scientists to address the phenomenon of the learning government as an organization is Lloyd Etheredge.[1] In his early work, Etheredge couples an ambition of developing a full-fletched theory of governmental learning to detailed empirical work on American domestic and foreign policy making (Etheredge 1981, 1985; Etheredge and Short 1983). What makes this work of particular interest to the study of policy change is that the author unravels the concept of the "learning government" into a kaleidoscope of theoretical and empirical building blocks which he then sets out to explore.

Etheredge distinguishes between five types of learning which each correspond to a different academic literature. Of these, the first ("scientific method learning") refers to the dominant interpretation of learning in cognitive developmental psychology as the effective mastering and processing of new and explicit knowledge. The other four types of learning involve an increase in the tacit knowledge and personal skills of an individual. By emphasising the noncognitive and nonexplicit elements in learning processes, Etheredge is ahead of his field. The importance of skills to implement intentions is underscored, for instance, some 15 years later by Scott (1998) who invokes the Greek notion of *mētis* to make this point. Likewise, a decade after Etheredge, the policy philosophers that gave a name to the argumentative turn in policy analysis (see Fischer and Forester 1993) rekindled the interest in the aspect of judgement and wisdom in government—with reference to the Aristotelian notion of *phronèsis* (Torgerson 1995; Flyvbjerg 2001; Loeber 2004)—in line with the pragmatist tradition of the 1920s and 30s (cf. Dewey 1991 [1927]; Merriam 1931). In the field of organizational learning, the distinction between codified and tacit knowledge (Polanyi 1967) was later elaborated by Lam (1998).

Another aspect of governmental learning that Etheredge sets out to unravel is the relation between the learning individual and the learning organization. Etheredge clearly posits the often assumed tenet that organizational learning may be defined "by analogy with individual learning" (Etheredge and Short 1983, 48). He proceeds to distinguish between three aggregation levels at which such learning may occur: the level of the individual decision maker, of a team, and of the collective. Characteristic of the latter type of learning in an organization is that it cannot be reduced to the accumulated learning of "any of its constituent parts" (1983, 49). With this three-tier conceptualization, Etheredge can be said to have outlined the contours of a comprehensive program on learning, which has yet to be implemented integrally. Separately, the identified levels correspond to a strand in organizational learning literature, which each has its counterparts in the literature on the public sector. Below, these are discussed in view of the policy-oriented learning theories described above.

---

1. A comparable yet not specifically government-focused attempt at providing a comprehensive overview of concepts of learning vis-à-vis organizations at the time was provided by Shrivastava 1983.

4.2 Learning Individually In and By "The Learning Organization"

Theories on learning at the level of the individual in an organization are of relevance to the theories discussed above, as many of these treat (policy) organizations as singular learning actors. Grin and Van de Graaf's invoking of the work of Donald Schön is a case in point. In the latter's work on learning, which in regard to organizations he elaborated with Chris Argyris (Argyris and Schön 1974, 1978, 1996; Argyris 1990, 1993, 1999), the "theories-in-use" that Grin and Van de Graaf refer to, form a central tenet. They are understood as a mental map of theoretical, normative, and empirical considerations that professionals bring to bear on their problem-solving activities. This map is what is being reviewed in the process of learning: when through observation and experience unexpected problems (surprises) are detected that indicate a misfit between the specificities of the problem situation and the theory-in-use, the latter is adjusted accordingly. Such adaptations Argyris and Schön refer to as "single loop learning," a type of learning that leaves intact the map's fundamental notions. Consequently, this type of learning generally results in incremental changes in an actor's problem-solving strategies. In the case of "double loop learning," the core elements themselves are the object of reflection, as a result of which major changes in an actor's strategic choices, objectives, and preferences may occur.

Insights into the conditions under which single or double loop learning may occur are relevant to policy-oriented learning theories. On the basis of such insights, governments can draw and implement inferences from policy and program evaluation. Under the straightforward title "Can governments learn?", Leeuw et al. (2000) bring together a large number of studies that relate policy evaluation to organizational learning, understood as a change in a governmental body's theory-in-use. Conceptualisations of organizational learning are linked to the knowledge utilization literature (e.g., Weiss 1977, 1980; Knott and Wildavsky 1980) and amount to a focus on the conditions and institutional arrangements under which learning in the public sector may be promoted (e.g., Rist 2000; Busenberg 2001).

Building on Agyris' and Schön's conceptualization of the relation between the learning individual and his or her organizational context, is a literature that addresses the organization itself as a learning entity. Of this body, notably the work of Peter Senge on the "learning organization" (1990) has fed into policy-oriented literature.[2]

The core theme in Senge's work is the exploration of the prerequisites required for organizations to successfully and effectively adapt to, and anticipate, a changing environment. In order to engage in the "adaptive learning" and "generative learning" required, Senge argues, an organization must master five basic competences ("disciplines") such as the ability to facilitate its employees to explicate their deeply held images and assumptions and to have employees develop a joint understanding of a desirable future. The possibility of successfully applying all of these disciplinary requirements crucially hinges on the organization's ability to master the "fifth discipline," the capacity to view and appreciate the organization as a whole rather than as an accumulation of its constituent parts.

It is notably for this latter focus on systems dynamics that Senge's work has found a receptive audience among policy scientists, policy makers, and representatives of the business sector who engage, separately and jointly, in experimenting with strategies to realize public policy ambitions by tapping into the dynamics of private organizations (e.g., Cramer and Loeber 2004). In search for a new role of the state vis-à-vis major environmental and societal problems in late-modernist network society, of recent, literature on learning and societal change speaks of a shift in the teleology

---

2. In particular, it has been invoked in approaches that can be roughly grouped together under the elastic heading of "New Public Management" that seek to parallel the management of organizations in the public sector to that in the corporate sphere (e.g., Reschenthaler and Thompson 1996).

of learning.[3] The initial focus in policy-oriented learning theories on the intelligence of government and, in the learning organization approaches, on the flexibility and adaptability of enterprises converge in a concern with improving the learning capabilities of society as such (see e.g., Loeber et al. forthcoming). The traditional focus on the learning individual-in-context hence shifts to addressing learning processes at the level of the collective.

4.3 Learning Collectively

When Etheredge addressed the issue of "systems intelligence"—an intelligence that cannot be reduced to a system's individual components or even to "any set of its members"—over two decades ago, he did so in then-prevailing terms. Criticizing governments' attempts at rational and synoptic planning, he praised the market system for its intelligent efficiency (e.g. in regard to the long-term allocation of resources). In the current discussions on systems innovation in the light of environmental and social goals (see e.g., Beck 1999; Grin 2006), it is precisely the "intelligence" of the market system of the past epoch that is called into question. The challenge now is to organize for a systems intelligence at the level of the collective that comprises both market and public sphere.

With this shift, also the basic premises of the dominant approaches to learning (the idea that an individual, rational actor is the locus of learning, and that organizations that operate as more or less coherent agents are equally capable of acting rationally) have become subject to critical reflection. Learning theorists in search for new ground have come to realize that "perhaps more than learning itself, it is our *conception* of learning that needs urgent attention" (Wenger 1998, 9; italics in the original).

Of recent, learning theories have been articulated that, for all their differences, share the view that the learning process is situated (and observable) *in social interaction*, and that it involves more than a mere change in cognition in the actors involved. Among the most radically innovative is Etienne Wenger's interpretation. Starting from the premise that human knowing is fundamentally a social act, Wenger (1998) perceives of learning as a process of transforming meanings and identities in what he dubs "communities of practice." Such a community is an identifiable group of people who interact regularly in regard to some shared concern or passion "for something they do," and who learn from their mutual engagement about how to improve their practice. In contrast to earlier interpretations of learning, in Wenger's depiction the dichotomy between individual learning and collective learning is non-existent, as is the distinction between tacit and explicit knowledge.

This line of reasoning links up with the discourse-analytical tradition in policy-focused literature that emphasizes the embedding of individually held beliefs and problem frames (theories-in-use) in their wider social context. Emphasized in particular are the linguistic systems (vocabularies, repertoires, narratives) through which an individual's perception of a concrete situation is understood to be given shape (e.g., Potter and Wetherell 1987; Radaelli 1999). The reciproque relationship between individuals' attempts at constructing meaning and reality, and the contextual dynamics that coshape their perceptions, is captured aptly in Wenger's notion of reification: "We

---

3. Senge's notions on the learning organization have strongly affected the coining of such concepts as "Sustainability Focused Organisational Learning" (Molnar and Mulvihill 2003), not in the least as Senge himself in later publications and through the establishment of the SoL Sustainability Consortium promotes the belief that "non-systemic ways of thinking and acting" are at the core of unsustainable practices, and that these can be tackled by "building [learning] enterprises that operate in greater harmony with larger social and ecological systems" (Senge 2000). Senge's work thus oddly connects cutting-the-red-tape approaches to public administration (cf. Aucoin 1996, Osborne and Gaebler 1992) which root predominantly in conservative political perspectives, to thoughts on a new 'governmentality' to use a Foucaultian phrase, notably to those with an ideological orientation toward the pursuit of a sustainable development.

project our meanings into the world and then we perceive them as existing in the world [in the form of abstractions, tools, symbols, stories, terms and concepts] as having a reality of their own" (1998, 58–59).

A comparable conceptualization of organizational learning is provided by S. D. Noam Cook. Cook (Cook and Yanow 1993; Cook and Brown 1999; Wagenaar and Cook 2003) links up the notion of learning to practice, that is, to doing and knowing in an organizational or group context. By approaching organizations as *a culture* in the anthropological sense of the word, the author argues, a researcher may conceptualize learning beyond the traditional reductionist focus on the changing actions and views of an organization's individual members. Rather, learning is to be understood in terms of continuity and discontinuity of practices over time (which may, for instance, involve learning *not* to change but to maintain one's identity in the face of new developments).

Such an interpretivist view, with emphasis on the social, interactive dimension of learning and its situated and collective nature, may provide useful insights in practices of, *and* possibilities for, governance. While underlining the limits to control (see Yanow 1996), it directs the attention to the potential of any actor irrespective of his or her affiliation with formal government, to operate as active creators of meaning, to take initiative and to engage in independent thought and action in regard to collective problems. It also implies a need to reconsider the stagist depiction of implementation which assumes a sharp distinction between policy makers and target groups, that is, between government and society.

5 CONCLUDING REMARKS

Learning theories in the policy sciences present a highly dynamic domain of thought. Several major changes can be observed since Bennet and Howlett's (1992) mid-term review of the field. First, the initial focus on governmental actors was broadened to include societal actors in the theories. Second, in more recent theory, learning has come to be looked at as a collective rather than an individual act. A third major development is the more adequate account given of the relation between agency, structure, learning, and societal change.

Underlying these changes, two paradigmatic shifts may be observed to take place. First, underlying the change in focus from the learning individual to the learning collective, and the growing attention for the relation between agency and structure, is a shift away from the individualist ontology implied in the focus on the intended meanings (as in the theories-in-use of a professional, or in the belief system of an advocacy coalition), to a relational understanding of interpreted meanings. Second, interdependently, a shift can be observed in the methodological orientation of research on learning. The original learning theories that took the stagist depiction of the policy process as a point of departure (e.g., Etheredge; Sabatier) adopted a neopositivist, hypothesis-testing approach to analyzing learning and policy change. With the recent changes toward a relational interpretation of the construction of knowledge and meaning, an interpretivist (phenomenological, constructivist) perspective on learning is winning ground (Grin and Van de Graaf; Wenger; Cook).

Given these changes and shifts, learning theories may arguably contribute largely to the development of a full-fletched theory on governance. At the heart of such a theory, then, would be an understanding of ideas and (espoused and tacit) knowledge, as well as the symbolic artefacts (language, acts, objects) in which these are embedded, that are no longer projected as a rival to power as an explanatory factor of (policy and societal) change, or as mere conveyors of power, but as an expression of power itself. Furthermore, because theories of learning in a policy context are inevitably linked up with an understanding of action, they may be crucial to understanding governance in present-day networked society. In the absence of clear-cut demand-and-control options of a central government, "constructive action that moves the community from a flawed present toward an improved future" (Jennings 1987, 129) may be perceived of as being planned, discussed, and implemented in (society-centered) practices that exist as situated expressions of the connection between agency and structure. Learning, then, may hold the key to enabling mutually shaped, collective change.

REFERENCES

Argyris, Ch. (1990). *Overcoming organizational defences — Facilitating organizational learning.* Needham Heights: Allyn and Bacon.

———— (1993). *Knowledge for Action. A Guide to Overcoming Barriers to Organizational Change.* San Francisco: Jossey-Bass.

———— (1999). *On Organizational Learning.* Oxford: Blackwell.

Argyris, Ch. and Donald A. Schön (1974). *Theory in Practice. Increasing professional effectiveness.* San Francisco: Jossey-Bass.

———— (1978). *Organisational Learning: A Theory of Action Perspective.* Reading, Mass.: Addison-Wesley Publishing.

———— (1996). *Organisational Learning II; Theory, Method, and Practice.* Reading, Mass,: Addison-Wesley Publishing.

Aucoin, P. (1996). "Operational Agencies: From Half-Hearted Efforts to Full-Fledged Government Reform." *Choices: Institute for Research on Public Policy* 2, no. 4.

Bennett, Colin J. (1991). "How States Utilize Foreign Evidence," *Journal of Public Policy* 11, no 1: 31–54.

Bennet, Colin J. and Michael Howlett (1992). "The Lessons of Learning: ReconcilingTheories of Policy Learning and policy change," *Policy Sciences* 25: 275–294.

Burstein, P. (1991). "Policy Domains: Organization, Culture, and Policy Outcomes," *Annul Review of Sociology* 17: 327–350.

Busenberg, George J. (2001). "Learning in Organizations and Public Policy." *Journal of Public Policy* 21, 2: 173–189.

Cook, Scott D.N. and Dvora Yanow (1993). "Cultural and Organizational Learning." *Journal of Management Inquiry* 2, no. 4: 373–390.

Cook, Scott D. N. and John Seely Brown (1999). Bridging Epistemologies: The Generative Dance between Organizational Knowledge and Organizational Knowing *Organization Science* 10, no. 4 (Jul.–Aug., 1999): 381–400.

Cox, Robert Henry (1999). "Creating Welfare States in Czechoslovakia and Hungary: Why Policy Makers borrow Ideas from the West," *Government and Policy* 11, no. 3: 349–364.

Cramer, J. and A. Loeber (2004). Governance Through Learning: Making Corporate Social Responsibility in Dutch Industry Effective From a Sustainable Development Perspective *Journal of Environmental Policy & Planning* 6, No. 3/4 (September/December 2004): 1–17.

Dahl, Robert A. (1956). *A Preface to Democratic Theory.* Chicago: University of Chigaco Press.

Davis, Charles and Sandy Davis (1988). "Analyzing Change in Public Lands Policymaking: From Subsystems to Advocacy Coalitions," *Policy Studies Journal* 17: 324.

Dewey, J. (1991 [1927]). *The Public and its problems.* Athens: Swallow Press.

Dolowitz, David (1997). "British employment policy in the 1980s: learning from the American Experience," *Governance* 10, no. 1: 23–42.

Dolowitz, David and David Marsh (1996). "Who learns what from whom: A review of the policy transfer literature," *Political Studies* 44, no. 2: 343–357.

———— (2000). "Learning from Abroad: The Role of Policy Transfer in Contemporary Policy Making," *Governance* 13, no. 1: 5–24.

Eberg, Jan (1997). *Waste policy and learning. Policy Dynamics of Waste Management and Waste Incineration in the Netherlands and Bavaria.* Delft: Eburon.

Elmore, Richard F. (1985). "Forward and backward mapping," in: K. Hanf and D. Toonen, eds., *Policy Implementation in Federal and Unitary Systems.* Dordrecht: Martinus Nijhoff, 33–70.

Etheredge, Lloyd S. (1981). Government learning: an overview. In S. Long (ed.) *Handbook of Political Behavior, Vol. 2,* New York: Plenum Press.

———— (1985). *Can Governments Learn? American Foreign Policy and Central American Revolutions*. New York: Pergamon Press.

Etheredge, Lloyd S. and James Short (1983). "Thinking about Government Learning," *Journal of Management Studies* 20, no. 1: 41–58.

Evans, Mark and Jonathan Davies (1999). "Understanding Policy Transfer: A Multi-level, Multi-disciplinary Perspective," *Public Administration* 77, 2: 361–385.

Evans, Mark and Jim Buller (Eds.) (2003). *Policy Transfer in Global Perspective*. Hants: Ashgate.

Flyvbjerg, B. (2001). *Making Social Science Matter. Why Social Inquiry Fails and How It Can Succeed Again*. Cambridge, Cambridge University Press.

Fischer, Frank (1980). *Politics, Values and Public Policy. The Problem of Methodology*. Boulder, Col.: Westview Press.

———— (1995). *Evaluating Public Policy*. Chicago: Nelson-Hall.

Fischer, F. and J. Forester (Eds.) (1993). *The Argumentative Turn in Policy Analysis and Planing*. Durham, N.C.: Duke University Press.

Forrester, J.W. (1968). *Principles of systems*. Cambridge, Mass.: Wright-Allen Press.

Giddens, Anthony (1984). *The Constitution of Society*. Cambridge: Polity Press.

Grin, John and Graaf, Henk Van de (1996a). "Technology Assessment as Learning," *Science, Technology and Human Values* 20, no. 1: 72–99.

Grin, John and Henk Van de Graaf (1996b). "Implementation as Communicative action. An Interpretive Understanding of Interactions between Policy Actors and Target Groups," *Policy Sciences* 29, no. 4: 291–319.

Grin, John, Rob Hoppe and Henk Van de Graaf (1997). "Towards a Theory of the Policy Process: Making the ACF More Ambitious, Encompassing *and* Simpler to Apply," Paper presented on a Workshop on Policy-Oriented Learning, organized by Polybios, Amsterdam, February 4, 1997.

Grin, John (2006). Reflexive Modernization as a Governance Issue — or: Designing and Shaping *Re*-structuration (49–71). In: Voß, Jan-Peter; Bauknecht, Dierk; Kemp, René (eds.), *Reflexive Governance for Sustainable Development*. Cheltenham: Edward Elgar.

Haas, Peter M. (1989). "Do Regimes Matter? Epistemic Communities and Mediterranean Pollution Control," *International Organization* 43: 377–403.

———— (1992). "Introduction: Epistemic Communities and International Policy Coordination," *International Organization* 46, No. 1: 1–35.

Hajer, M. A (2003). "Policy without Polity: Policy Analysis and the Institutional Void," *Policy Sciences* 36, no. 2: 175–195.

Hall, Peter A. (1993). "Policy Paradigms, Social Learning and the State. The Case of Economic Policymaking in Britain," *Comparative Politics* 25, no. 3: 275–296.

Hall, Peter A. and Rosemary C.R. Taylor (1996). "Political Science and the Three New Institutionalisms," *Political Studies* 46. no. 54: 936–957.

———— (1998). "The potential of historical institutionalism: A response to Hay and Wincott," *Political Studies* 46, no. 5: 958–962.

Hay, Colin (2001). "The 'crisis' of of Keynesianims and the Rise of Neo-Liberalism in Britain: An Ideational Institutionalist Approach," pp. 193–218 in: Campbell, J.L. and O.K. Pedersen (Eds.), *The Rise of Neo-Liberalism and Institutional Analysis*. Princeton, N.J.: Princeton University Press.

Hay, Colin and Daniel Wincott (1996). "Structure, Agency and Historical Institutionalism," *Political Studies* 46, no. 5: 951–957.

Heclo, Hugh (1974). *Social Policy in Britain and Sweden*. New Haven, CT: Yale University Press.

Held, David and Anthony McGrew (2000). "The Great Globalization Debate: an Intriduction," pp. 1–45 in *idem* (eds.) *The Global Transformations Reader. An Intriduction to the Globalization Debate*. Cambridge: Polity Press.

Hoppe, Robert (1993) Political Judgment and the Policy Cycle: The Case of Ethnicity Policy Arguments in the Netherlands. In: F. Fischer and J. Forester (eds.) *The Argumentative Turn in Policy Analysis and Planning*. Durham and London: Duke University Press.

Hoppe, Robert, Henk Van de Graaf, Asje van Dijk (1987). "Implementation research and policy design: problem tractability, policy theory, and feasibility testing," *International Review of Administrative Sciences* 53: 581–604.

Hoppe, Rob and Aat Peterse (1993). *Handling Frozen Fire. Political culture and risk management*. Boulder, CO: Westview Press.

Howlett, Michael and M. Ramesh (2002). "The Policy Effects of Internationalization: A Subsystem Adjsutment Analysis of Policy Change," *J. Comparative Policy Analysis: Research and Practice* 4: 3150.

Huber, G. (1991). "Organizational Learning: The Contributing Processes and the Literatures," *Organization Science* 2, no. 1: 88–115.

Ikenberry, G. John (1990). The International Spread of Privatization Policies: Inducements, Learning and "Policy Bandwagoning," pp. 88–110. In: Ezra Suleiman and John Waterbury (Eds.), *The Political Economy of Public Sector Reform and Privatization Policy*, Boulder, CO: Westview Press.

James, Oliver and Martin Lodge (2003). "The Limitations of 'Policy Transfer' and 'Lesson Drawing' for Public Policy Research," *Political Studies Review* 1: 179–193.

Jennings, B. (1987). Interpretation and the Practice of Policy Analysis. In: F. Fischer and J. Forester (Eds.) *Confronting values and policy analysis: The politics of criteria*. Newbury Park, CA: Sage.

Kickert, Walter J.M., Erik-Hans Klijn and Joop F.M. Koppenjan (Eds.) (1997). *Managing Complex networks. Strategies for the Public Sector.* London: Sage.

Knott, J.H. and A. Wildavsky (1980). If Dissemination Is the Solution, What Is the Problem? *Knowledge: Creation, Dissemination, Utilization*, 1, no. 4.

Lasswell, Herbert D. (1971). *A Pre-view of Policy Sciences*. New York: Elsevier.

Leeuw, Frans L, Ray C. Rist, Richard C. Sonnichsen (Eds.) *Can Governments Learn? Comparative Perpsectives on Evaluation & Organizational learning*. New Brunswick, N.J.: Transaction Publishers

Lindblom, Charles E. and Edward J. Woodhouse (1993 [1968]). *The Policy-Making Process*. Eaglewood Cliffs, N.J.: Prentice Hall.

Loeber, A. (2004). *Practical Wisdom in the Risk Society. Methods and Practice of Interpretive Analysis on Questions of Sustainable Development*. Thesis. University of Amsterdam.

Loeber, Anne and John Grin (1996 [2006]). "From Green Waters to 'Green' Detergents: Processes of Learning between Policy Actors and Target Groups in Eutrophication Policy in the Netherlands, 1979–1987." Paper delivered at the 1996 Annual Meeting of the Western Political Science Association, San Francisco, CA, March 1416.

Loeber, Anne, Barbara van Mierlo, John Grin, Cees Leeuwis (forthcoming). The Practical Value of Theory: Conceptualising Learning in the Pursuit of a Sustainable Development. In: Arjen E.J. Wals (Ed.) *Social Learning toward a more Sustainable World: Principles, Perspectives, and Praxis*. United Nations University Press.

Majone, Giandomenico (1991). "Cross-National Sources of Regulatory Policy Making in Europe and the United States," *Journal of Public Policy* 11, no. 1: 79–106.

Mars, D. and R.A.W. Rhodes (Eds.) (1992). *Policy Networks in British Government*. Oxford: Clarendon Press.

Mawhinney, Hanne B. (1993). "An Advocacy Coalition Approach to Change in Canadian Education," ch. 4 (pp. 59–82) in Sabatier and Jenkins-Smith (1993).

McCool, Daniel (1993). "Subgovernments as Determinants of Political Viability," *Political Science Quarterly* 105, no. 2: 269–293.

Merriam, Ch. E. (1931). *New Aspects of Politics* (3rd ed.). Chicago: University of Chicago Press.

Mintrom, Michael and Sandravergari (1996). "Advocacy Coalitions, Policy Entrepreneurs and Policy Change," *Policy Studies Journal* 24: 420–434.

Molnar, E. and P.R. Mulvihill (2003). Sustainability-focused Organizational Learning: Recent Experiences and New Challenges, *Journal of Environmental Planning and Management*, 46, no. 2: 167–176.

Newman, Janet (2001). *Modernising Governance. New Labour, Policy and Society.* London: Sage.

Oliver, Michael and Hugh Pemberton (2004). "Learning and Change in Twentieth-Century British Economic Policy," *Governance* 17, no. 3: 415–441.

Osborne, D. and T. Gaebler (1992). *Reinventing Government*. Reading, MA: Addison-Wesley.

Page, Edward C. (2000). *Future Governance and the Literature on Policy Transfer and Lesson Drawing*. Economic and Social Research Council, Future Governance paper no. 1.

Pemberton, Hugh (2000). "Policy Networks and Policy Learning: UK Economic Policy in the 1960s and 1970s," *Public Administration* 78, no. 4: 771–792.

——— (2003). "Learning, Governance and Economic Policy," *British Journal of Politics and International Relations* 5, no. 4: 500–524.

Polanyi, M. (1967). *The Tacit Dimension*. London: Routledge and Kegan Paul.

Polsby, Nelson W. (1984). *Political Innovation in America: The Politics of Policy Innovation*. New Haven, CT: Yale University Press.

Potter, J. and M. Wetherell (1987). *Discourse and Social Psychology. Beyond Attitudes and Behaviour*. London: Sage.

Radaelli, C. M. (1999). "Harmful Tax Competition in the EU: Policy Narratives and Advocacy Coalition," *Journal of common Market Studies* 37, no. 4: 661–682.

Rist, Ray C. (2000). The Preconditions for Learning: Lessons from the Public Sector. In: Leeuw, Frans L, ray C. Rist, Richard C. Sonnichsen (eds) *Can Governments Learn? Comparative Perpsectives on Evaluation & Organizational Learning*. New Brunswick: Transaction Publishers

Schön, D. A. and M. Rein (1994). *Frame Reflection. Toward the Resolution of Intractable Policy Controversies*. New York, Basic Books.

Reschenthaler, G.B. and F. Thompson (1996). The Learning Organization Framework and the New Public Management. Paper prepared for the conference on The New Public Management in International Perspective. St. Gallen (Sw) 11–13, July 1996.

Rhodes, R.A.W. (1997). *Understanding Governance. Policy Networks, Governance, Reflexivity and Accountability*. Buckingham and Philadelphia: Open University Press.

Robertson, David Brian (1991). "Political Conflict and Lesson-Drawing," *Journal of Public Policy* 1, no. 1: 55–87.

Rose, Richard (1991). "What Is Lesson-Drawing?," *Journal of Public Policy* 11, no. 1: 3–30.

——— (1993). *Lesson-Drawing in Public Policy. A Guide to Learning Across Time and Space*. Chatham, N.J.: Chatham House Publishers.

——— (2004). *Learning from Comparative Public Policy. A Practical Guide*. London and New York: Routledge.

Sabatier, Paul A. (1978). "The Acquisition and Utilization of Technical Information by Administrative Agencies," *Administrative Science Quarterly* 23: 286–411.

——— (1986). "Top-down and Bottom-up Approaches to Implementation Research: A Critical Analysis and Suggested Synthesis," *Journal of Public Policy* 6: 21–48.

——— (1987). "Knowledge, Policy-oriented Learning, and Policy Change. An Advocacy Coalition Framework," *Knowledge* 8: 649–692.

——— (1988). "An advocacy Coalition Framework of Policy Change and the Role of Policy-Oriented Learning Therein," *Policy Sciences* 21: 129–168.

Sabatier, Paul A. and Hank C. Jenkins-Smith (1993). *Policy Change and Learning. An Advocacy Coalition Approach*. Boulder, Col.: Westview Press.

Sabatier, Paul, Susan Hunter and Susan McLaughin (1987). "The Devil Shift: Perceptions and Misperceptions of Opponents," *Western Political Quarterly* 42: 229–261.

Sabatier, Paul and Anne Brasher (1993). "From Vague Consensus to Clearly Differentiated Coalitions: Environmental Policy at Lake Tahoe, 1964/1985," pp. 149–276 in Sabatier and Jenkins/Smith (1993).

Sabatier, Paul A. (1999). "The Advocacy Coalition Framework: An Assessment," pp. 117–166. In: Paul A. Sabatier (ed.), *Theories of the Policy Process*. Boulder, Col: Westview Press.

Schlager, Edella and William Blomquist (1996). "A Comparison of Three Emerging Theories of the Policy Process," *Political Research Quarterly* 49: 651–672.

Schlager, Edella (1997). "A Response to Kim Quaile Hill's *In search of Policy Theory*," *Policy Currents* 7: 14–15.

Schneider, Anne and Helen Ingram (1988). "Systematically Pinching Ideas: A Comparative Approach to Policy Design," *Journal of Public Policy* 8, no. 1: 61–80.

——— (1990). "Behavioral Assumptions of Policy Tools," *Journal of Politics* 52, no. 2: 510–529.

——— (1997). *Policy Design for Democracy*. Lawrence: The University of Kansas Press.

Schön, Donald A. (1983). *The reflective practitioner. How professionals think in action*. New York: Basic Books.

Scott, J.C. (1998). *Seeing Like a state: how certain schemes to improve the human condition have failed*. New Haven, CT: Yale University Press

Senge, Peter (1990). *The fifth discipline*. New York: Doubleday/Currency.

Simon, Herbert A. (1996). Bounded Rationality and Organizational Learning. In: M.D. Cohen and L.S. Sproull (Eds.), *Organizational Learning*. Thousand Oaks, CA: Sage Publications, 175–187.

Shrivastava, Paul (1983). "A Typology of Organizational Learning Systems," *Journal of Management Studies* 20 (10): 7–28.

Stone, Deborah (1997 [1988]). *Policy Paradox. The Art of Political Decision Making*. New York and London: W.W. Norton.

Stone, Diane (1999). "Learning Lessons and Transferring Policy across Time, Space and Disciplines," *Politics* 19, no. 1: 51–60.

Stone, Diane (2000). "Non-Governmental Policy Transfer: The Strategies of Independent Policy Instuitutes," *Governance* 13, no. 1: 45–70.

Stone, Diane (2004). "Transfer Agents and Global Networks in the 'Transnationalisation' of Policy," *Journal of European Public Policy*, 11(3) 2004: 545–566.

Sewell, Granville (1999). "Advocacy Coalition and the Implementation of the Framework Convention on Climate Change." To be published in Sabatier (2005).

Tavits, Margit (2003). "Policy Learning and Uncertainty: The Case of Pension Reform in Estonia and Latvia," *The Policy Studies Journal* 31, no. 4: 643–660.

Thomas, Gerald (1996). "Policy Subsystems, the Advocacy Coalition Framework and the US Civilian Land Remote Sensing (Landsat) Policy," paper delivered at the 1996 Annual Meeting of the Western Political Science Association, San Francisco, CA, March 1416.

Torgerson, D. (1995). Policy Analysis and Public Life: The Restoration of Phronesis? In: J. Farr, J.S. Dryzek, S.T. Leonard (Eds.), *Political science in history: Research programs and political traditions*. Cambridge: Cambridge University Press.

Van de Graaf, Henk and Rob Hoppe (1989 [1992]). *Beleid en politiek. Een inleiding tot de beleidswetenschap en de beleidskunde*. Bussum: Coutinho.

Van de Graaf, Henk and John Grin, "Towards a new conception of policy discourse", ….

Van de Graaf, Henk and John Grin (1999). "Policy Instruments, Pratiques Réfliches et Apprentisage. Implications pour la Gouvernabilité à Long Terme et la Démocratie," *Espaces et Sociétés* 97–98: 63–90. [English version available from the authors].

Van Est, R. (1999). *Winds of Change. A Comparative Study of the Politics of Wind Energy Innovation in California and Denmark*. Utrecht: International Books.

Wagenaar, Hendrik and S.D. Noam Cook (2003). Understanding Policy Practices: Action, Dialectic and Deliberation in Policy Analysis. In: M.A. Hajer and H. Wagenaar (eds.) *Deliberative Policy Analysis. Understanding Governance in the Network Society*. Cambridge.

Walker, Jack L. (1969), "The Diffusion of Innovations Among the American States," *American Political Science Review* 63: 880–899.

Walt, Gill Louisiana Lush and Jessica Ogden (2004). "International Organisations in Transfer of Infectious Diseases Policy: Iterative Loops of Adoption, Adaptation and Marketing," *Governance* 17, no. 2: 189–210

Weiss, C. (1977). *Using Social Research in Public Policy Making*. Lexington: D.C. Heath.

——— (1980). "Knowledge Creep and Decision Accretion," *Knowledge: Creation, Diffusion, Utilization* 1, no. 3.

Wendt, A. (1987). "The Agency-structure Problem in International Relations," *International Organization* 41: 335–370.

Wenger, E. (1998). *Communities of Practice. Learning, Meaning, and Identity*. Cambridge: Cambridge University Press.

Yanow, D. (1996). *How Does a Policy Mean? Interpreting Policy and Organizational Action*. Georgetown: Georgetown University Press.

Zafonte, Matthew and Paul Sabatier (1998). "Shared Beliefs and Imposed Interdependencies as Determinants of Ally Networks in Overlapping Subsystems," *Journal of Theoretical Politics* 10, no. 4: 473–505.

Part V

*Deliberative Policy Analysis:
Argumentation, Rhetoric, and
Narratives*

16 Deliberative Policy Analysis as Practical Reason: Integrating Empirical and Normative Arguments

Frank Fischer

During the past two decades a growing number of policy scholars have focused on the role of argumentation in policy analysis, giving rise to what has been described as the "argumentative turn" (Fischer and Forester 1993) and the practice of "deliberative policy analysis (Hajer and Wagenaar 2003). The argumentative turn in policy analysis emerged to deal with the epistemological limitations of "neopositivist" or empiricist policy analysis and the technocratic decision making practices to which it gave rise. After examining the limits of technocratic policy analysis, in particular its difficulties in supplying "usable knowledge" to policy decision makers, the essay takes up the argumentative turn and the processes of policy argumentation. It then offers a dialectical communications model of policy decision making and supplies it with an informal logic of practical reason, presented as an alternative to the formal logic of neopositivism. Practical reason, as an informal logic of evaluation, is delineated as four interrelated levels of policy discourse that systematically connect facts and values, empirical and normative inquiry in framework for policy deliberation. The ability of the methodological framework to organize policy discourse is briefly illustrated with a particular policy issue.

TECHNOCRATIC POLICY ANALYSIS: THE LIMIT OF NEOPOSITIVISM

The practice of policy analysis that emerged in the 1960s and 1970s was, in large part, technocratic in form. It was, as such, narrowly designed to serve managerial practices of public agencies. Toward this end, the field was mainly shaped by a methodological framework derived from the neopositivist/empiricist methods that dominated the social sciences of the day. The result was an emphasis on rigorous quantitative analysis, the objective separation of facts and values, and the search for generalizable findings whose validity would be independent of the particular social context from which they were drawn. Such a policy science, it was argued, would be able to develop generalizable knowledge and tested solutions applicable to a range of policy problems in different political contexts. In no small part, this was driven by the dominant influence of economics and its positivist scientific methodologies on the development of the field.

Policy analysis thus emerged to inform a "rational model" of decision making, or what Stone (1988) has called the "rationality project." In this model, rational decision makers are seen to follow steps that closely parallel the requirements of scientific research. Decision makers first empirically identify a problem, and then formulate the objectives and goals that would lead to an optimal solution. After determining the relevant probabilities and consequences associated with the alternative means to the solution, analysts assign numerical values to the various costs and benefits related to the predicted outcomes. Combining the information and evidence about probabilities, consequences, and costs and benefits, they select the most efficient, effective alternative.

Basic to the approach has been an effort to sidestep the partisan goal and value conflicts generally associated with policy issues (Amy 1987). Policy analysis, in this model, seeks to translate political and social issues into technically defined ends to be pursued through administrative ends. Difficult economic and social problems are treated as issues in need of improvement management and better program design; their solutions are to be found in better collection of data and the application of technical decision approaches. Much of policy analysis has thus been a matter of applying empirically-based technical methodologies, such as cost-benefit analysis and risk assessment to the technical aspects of all policy problems.

Despite the devotion of a large amount of time, money, and energy to this form of policy analysis, it has confronted considerable difficulty supplying policy decision makers with the kinds problem-oriented knowledge that was expected from policy analysis. Missing have been the often promised solutions to pressing economic and social problems. The field is seen to have generated far too little "usable knowledge" (Lindblom and Cohen 1979; Fischer 1995). This concern first emerged as a problem of "knowledge utilization," with new journals and discussions emerging to examine the gap between policy research and the needs of policy makers. Why did policy makers so often express frustration with both the forms and relevance of the finding offered by such policy analysis (Fischer 1995)? From other quarters it gave rise to the argumentative turn.

The "postpositivist" argumentative turn does not hold that policy science has had no impact on public issues. Rather, it recognizes that its role has been more to stimulate the political processes of policy deliberation than to provide answers or solutions to the public problem facing contemporary societies. Although deliberation is generally acknowledged to be important to effective policy development, the field's reliance on neopositivist, empirical approaches has done more to hinder than facilitate deliberative processes. In this view, it has impeded policy analysis's ability to more directly do what it can do well—improve the quality of policy argumentation in public deliberation. The argumentative turn is in significant part an effort to revive and strengthen this policy-analytic function by setting it out on its own epistemological footing. It has developed as an effort to both understand the nature of the problem and to find new and more relevant ways of dealing with policy analysis and advice giving. Anchored to an alternative epistemological orientation that understands knowledge to be the product of interaction—even conflict—among competing interpretations of a policy problem, it brings empirical and normative inquiry together in a deliberative framework. At the same time, it is seen to provide a better description of what real-world analysts and policy makers actually do when they examine a particular problem—namely bring together the relevant considerations and argumentative deliberations about both their relationships to one another and their resultant implications for action.

THE ARGUMENTATIVE TURN

The argumentative turn starts from a recognition that multiple perspectives are involved in the interpretation and understanding of social and political reality and the competing definitions of policy problems to which they give rise. Toward this end, an argumentatively-oriented deliberative policy analysis seeks to disarm epistemologically the one-dimensionality objectivity of conventional policy analysis, often advanced as *value-neutral* scientific policy analysis (Fischer 2003). As Hawkesworth (1988, 191) puts it, recognition of "the theoretically constituted and essentially contestable character of empirical claims requires policy analysis to understand its task in terms of identifying the diverse dimensions of debate pertinent to particular policy questions." From the argumentative perspective, moreover, the identification and clarification of contentious issues related to theoretical assumptions and empirical findings of policy inquiry also facilitates political choice and thus democratic decision making.

Beyond serving the needs of administrative policy makers, the deliberative practitioner seeks to represent a wider range of interests, arguments and discourses in the analytical process. This is done in part by emphasizing citizen participation, including the examination of the ways in which citizens' interests are discursively constructed, as well as how they come to hold specific interests. For the argumentative orientation, this means exercising much more political insight in the processes of policy definition and formation. By getting more deeply involved in the discursive and symbolic sides of politics, argue such theorists, policy analysts help decision makers and citizens develop alternatives that speak to their own needs and interests, rather than those defined and shaped for them by others.

Toward this end, such theorists and practitioners stress the need for participatory democracy and the development of techniques of participatory policy analysis, approaches that emphasize deliberative interaction between citizens, analysts, and decision makers (Fischer 2000; Hajer and Wagenaar 2003). In so far as the goal is to provide access and explanation of data to all parties, and to empower the public to understand analyses, it promotes democratic governance. By supplying citizens with the information citizens need about their circumstances to make intelligent choices about the actions they can take, deliberative policy analysts adopts a methodological stance designed to dispel the technocratic mystique of conventional policy analysis through greater citizen involvement. Argumentative analysis, as such, focuses on the crucial role of language, rhetorical argument, and stories in framing debate, as well as on structuring the deliberative context in which policy is made. It also brings in the local knowledge of citizens—both empirical and normative—relevant to the social context to which policy is applied.

POLICY AS ARGUMENT

This discussion elaborates a particular aspect of deliberative policy analysis—the need to integrate empirical and normative analysis and how that can be done.[1] From this perspective, it is the argument that constitutes the basic unit of real-world policy analysis. As Majone (1989, 7) has explained, most of the work of the policy analyst "in a system of government by discussion…has less to do with the formal techniques of problem-solving than with the process of argument." As he writes, "the job of the analyst consists in large part of producing evidence and arguments to be used in the course of public debate." In view of this discursive nature of policy analysis, policy itself is thus best understood as "crafted argument" (Stone 1988). In an attempt to improve policy arguments, writes Hawkesworth (1988, 191), the goal of policy analysis is to illuminate "the contentious dimensions of policy questions, to explain the intractability of policy debates, to identify the defects of supporting arguments, and to elucidate the political implications of contending prescriptions." Such a task involves both empirical and normative analysis.

The interest in argumentation in policy analysis draws from both theoretical and practical perspectives. On the one side, its diverse theoretical influences run through British ordinary-language analysis, the Frankfurt School of critical social theory, French poststructuralism, and a renewed appropriation of American pragmatism. On the other hand, it is based in practical terms on experiments on the part of policy analysts and planners, from stakeholder analysis and participatory research to citizen juries and consensus conferences. These rich sources have assisted "postempiricists" in recognizing how language and modes of representation both enable and constrain their work. They have come to appreciate how their practical rhetoric depicts and selects, describes and characterizes, includes and excludes. The discussion here is oriented around a particular line of development in the argumentative turn—a dialectical communications approach based on the informal or good-reasons logic of argumentation. The productive capacities of the approach is emphasized, in particular its ability to generate ways of thinking and seeing that open new possibilities for problem-solving and action.

Persuasion and justification play important roles in each stage of the policy process. Starting with the problem-setting stage of analysis, well before recommendations and alternatives can be delineated, the very determination of what "the problem" is depends on deeply rhetorical and interpretive practices. Even after acceptable alternatives have been selected and implemented, political justification has to receive continual attention. New arguments have to be constantly made to give "the different policy components the greatest possible internal coherence and the closet fit to an ever-changing environment" (Majone 1989, 31). Policy development is thus guided by a discursive process of developing and refining ideas.

Although these processes are not well understood, they are basic to the construction and reconstruction of policy problems. To better understand them, the argumentative policy analyst turns from the study of abstracted epistemological problems of analysis to the political and sociological significance of actual practices. Emphasizing the context-specific rhetorical character of analytical practices—the ways the symbolism of language matters, the ways audiences needs to be taken into account, how solutions depend on problem construction, and so forth—the argumentative approach recognizes that policy arguments are intimately involved with the exercise of power. Beyond an emphasis on efficiency and effectiveness, it calls attention to the inclusion of some concerns and the exclusion of others, the distribution of responsibility as well as causality, the assigning of praise and blame, and the use of particular political strategies of problem framing as opposed to others.

At times the discursive role is explicit. This is particularly the case when policy analysts are asked to assume the role of advocate. In the advocacy role, the analyst is generally asked by the client to go beyond the issues of efficiency and offer advice about what the objectives themselves should be. Given the uncertainty of many policy problems, often including the very definition of the problem, the job also involves, as Majone (1989, 35) puts it, not only finding "solutions within given constraints" but also taking the initiative and pushing "out the boundaries of the possible in public policy."

Given that policy problems can be represented in many languages, discourses, and frames, the connection between the language of the analyst's arguments and the language of the political setting is necessarily important. Moreover, the ways in which analysis has to be sensitive to the shifts in political power—from election to election, elite to elite, or coalition to coalition—are reflected not only in policy decisions but in the very language in which policy issues and choices are made available to the public. In so far as policy makers and affected publics alike can be stymied or mystified by technical languages of expertise, the argumentative approach is put forward to help refine both public understanding and ethical imagination.

Thanks to the careful inquiries of writers like Forester (1999) and Hoch (1994), such discursive practices are documented in the everyday work of policy analysts. By exploring policy argumentation in concrete institutional settings, this research calls attention to the kinds of organizational networking that analysts must do to forge working policy relationships. A narrow focus on technical evaluation of the content of the final document misses the kinds of work that precede and follow the presentation of outcomes and proposals—including the scanning of the political environment for support and opposition to potential recommendations, anticipating the counter-reactions that policy measures might provoke, as well as being alert to the subtle form of negotiation that transpires among agency staff interested in maintaining their own strategic work relationships. The argumentative approach, in this respect, counsels the analyst to move beyond the separation of the political and the rational. Working in complex organizations structured by political processes, policy analysts are—or have to become—political actors, whether or not they wish to. Confronting messy issues involving diverse populations with multiple and conflicting interests, they have to learn to balance the technical and the political components of the assignment.

And, not least important, the argumentative turn draws attention to the democratic potential of policy analysis. Policy arguments cannot be presumed to be optimally clear, cogent, true, and free from political and institutional biases. Democratic deliberation, to be sure, is always precarious and vulnerable. But through thoughtful, informed and passionate argumentative processes citizen can learn. Policy analysis, in this respect, can facilitate the process by promoting communicative competencies and social learning. To do this, though, it has to take into account the ways policy arguments can be skewed by inequalities of resources and entrenched relations of power.

ARGUMENTATIVE POLICY ANALYSIS: THE COMMUNICATIONS MODEL

Various efforts have been made to develop procedures for an argumentative policy analysis. An important case in point is the "communications" approach to policy analysis that began to evolve in the late 1970s and early 1980s. This orientation has turned the analytical problem on its head (Churchman 1971; Fischer 2003). Recognizing that the normative dimensions of policy questions cannot be dealt with through the empirical analysis—that is, by converting them into variables to be operationalized—these scholars have sought a viable alternative by reorienting the task to begin from the normative perspective and fit the empirical in. Indeed, as they demonstrate, this is how policy deliberation actually works. In politics, politicians and policy decision makers put forth proposals about what to do based on normative arguments. Empirical analysis comes into play but only when there are reasons to question or explore the factual aspects of the argument.

In this perspective, normative-based analysis can be facilitated by an organized dialogue among competing normative positions. Designed to identify and create potential areas of consensus, the approach emphasizes the interactive and productive role of communication in cognitive processes. Unlike the process of pure or abstract thinking, the power of critical judgment depends on potential agreement with other participants. In fact, such judgment anticipates such communication.

One influential approach to such a communications model has been to follow the example of law and legal argumentation. In such a scheme, policy analysts and decision makers each take on the assignment of preparing arguments for and against particular policy positions. As Rivlin (1973, 25) suggested, they would "state their side of the argument, leaving to the brief writers of the other side the job of picking apart the case that has been presented and detailing the counter evidence." Such policy argumentation begins with the recognition that the participants do not have solid answers to the questions under discussion, or even a solid method for getting the answers. With this understanding the policy analysts and decision makers attempt to work out a meaningful synthesis of perspectives. Churchman and his followers have suggested that the procedure follow the form of a debate. They maintain that the problem presented by the absence of appropriate evaluative criteria can be mitigated by designing rational procedures to govern a formal communicative exchange among the various points of view that bear on the decision-making process.

In such a policy debate, each party would confront the others with counterproposals based on varying perceptions of the facts. The participants would organize the established data and fit them into the world views that underline their own arguments. The criteria for accepting or rejecting a proposal would be the same grounds as those for accepting or rejecting a counterproposal and must be based on precisely the same data. Operating at the intersection where politics and science confront practice and ethics, both policy analysts and decision makers would explore and compare the underlying assumptions being employed.

This involves a different approach to empirical and normative inquiry. Where conventional social science attempts to build in qualitative data about norms and values to an empirical model through quantification, the communications model reverses the task by fitting the quantitative data into the normative world view. In this case, pragmatic validity is tested, criticized, and interpreted by qualitative arguments based on world views and their value orientations. The locus of the interpretive process shifts from the scientific community to the practical-world of the public realm. In the transition, the outcome of an evaluation is pursued by the giving of reasons and the assessment of practical arguments rather than scientific demonstration and verification. As in interpretive explanation generally, the valid interpretation is the one that survives the widest range of criticisms. In the proposed debate model, each party would cite not only causal relationships but also norms, values, and circumstances to justify a particular decision. As practical arguments, such interpretive evaluations connect policy options and situations by illuminating those aspects of the situations that supply relevant grounds for policy decisions.

In this scheme, the formalized debate itself is taken to be the most instructive part of the assessment process. The technique is designed to clarify the underlying norms and goals that give shape to competing world views, and enables the exercise of qualitative judgment in as unhampered a way as possible. The free exercise of normative judgment, released from the constraints of the formal policy model, increases the chances of developing a synthesis of normative perspectives that can provide an acceptable, legitimate basis for decisions and actions based on the strongest possible argument. Even if analysts cannot agree on the final assessment, a communicative approach supplies a procedure for probing the normative implications of recommendations and for indicating potentially consensual conclusions that offer productive ways to move forward. In the process, it also clarifies the basic points of dissensus that stand in the way of reaching agreement.

At minimum, then, the technique goes a considerable distance toward removing the ideological mask that often shrouds policy analysis. Such a communications approach, moreover, would not need to be limited to the interactions between organizational policy makers and policy analysts. Ideally, it could be extended to the full range of differing interests and political perspectives drawn from the larger policy environment (George 1972; Porter 1980). The communications approach is thus an important step toward the development of a methodology designed to facilitate complex dialectical explorations of facts and values throughout the policy-analytic process. As with any step forward, however, it only brings us to the next set of hurdles. The inevitable question that arises is this: if both decision makers and analysts are to employ the same criteria in their respective policy arguments, what are these criteria? Here the technique encounters the basic fact-value problem: are there criteria or grounds for mediating normative-based practical discourse? Practical debate brings the value dimensions of policy argumentation into sharper focus, but this is not to be confused with methodology per se. Given the long history of arguments about value judgments in philosophy and the social sciences, it is reasonable to assume that the methodological success of a communications model ultimately rests on the elaboration of rules that govern the exchange of normative arguments. Rational inquiry—whether scientific or normative—depends on the availability of rules and standards that can serve as grounds for valid judgment (i.e., operational rules permitting the formulation of more or less general propositions or conclusions that are not included in the data but legitimately deduced, inferred, or extracted from them). In a normative exchange, it is often easy to agree that one argument is more persuasive than another, but it is not always easy to say how that is known. Indeed, the absence of such normative judgments that has long contributed to the epistemological demise of normative theorizing in the contemporary social sciences.

ARGUMENTATION: THE SEARCH FOR RATIONAL PROCEDURES

Other writers have sought to deal with the problem or rational procedures by further extending the legal-oriented analogy of brief writing to include the concept of "rules of evidence." By examining the rules and procedures that govern legal arguments in the courtroom, the policy sciences might gain insight into rules of argumentation that can be adapted to the policy deliberation process. Such an approach would allow analysts to concede the limitations of empirical decision-making methods but, at the same time, salvage the contributions that they do offer. By combining empirical analysis, policy deliberation and the development of rules of evidence, policy scientists can, in this view, move the policy evaluation process toward a judicious mix of pragmatism and rigor.

Duncan MacRae, Jr., for instance, has emphasized the value of supplying policy analysis with a regulated discourse that commands the kind of rigor characteristic of legal argumentation. The advantage of regulated communication, in MacRae's (1971; 1976, 85) view, is that it stands "apart from the discourse of ordinary life in several attributes such as precise definitions, stress on written rather than oral communication, and limitation of meaning to what has been specified in advance." A statement or judgment in such a discourse can be given a precise definition and interpretation by a larger audience. For example, a legal essay written by trained lawyers directs the attention of similarly trained readers to statements and conclusions that can be systematically re-examined by shared rules and methods.

The concept of rules of evidence in law suggests the development of logical rules of evidence for policy argumentation (Majone 1989, 49). Both MacRae and Anderson have urged policy analysts to examine the possibility of borrowing and adapting the rules of normative analysis employed in political philosophy. As Anderson (1978, 22) states, policy analysts typically fail to appreciate that "their concern with cost-benefit analysis is only an episode in a long Western tradition of defining principles appropriate to judge the legitimacy and propriety of political activity." As a suggestive attempt to bridge this gap, MacRae (1976, 93) has introduced three logical tests basic to political philosophy: logical clarity, logical consistency, and generality.

More systematically, Dunn (1981) has presented a model for policy argumentation founded on Toulmin's "informal logic" of practical reason and argumentation. This scheme offers a more dynamic picture of policy argumentation that moves from empirical data to the conclusions via a normative warrant and its backing. Of special importance is the model's incorporation of rebuttal arguments and qualifications to the concluding claims or recommendations. Nonetheless, it fails to supply a sufficiently detailed delineation of the line of argument that supports the backing of the normative warrant. Without this line of argumentation, the scheme is unable to clarify the full integration of empirical and normative judgments. But this problem can be remedied, as we outlined below.

The critical question, then, is how to develop a practical framework that integrates both empirical and normative components of a policy argument. Although the basic task of epistemology and methodology in philosophy and the social sciences is to analyze and clarify the basic concepts and rules that govern the logic of the discourse in which humans do their thinking, the realm of normative discourse, as we have seen, is far less developed than the logic of empirical discourse. Theorists working in this tradition have been unable to offer sufficient precision about these rules to make them useful. The contribution of ordinary-language philosophers has been an important exception. Examining practical discussion in everyday life, they have shown the study of practical reason to offer a useful avenue of methodological exploration for policy evaluation (Fischer 1995). From this tradition we gain insight into two fundamental questions: what does it mean to evaluate something? And how can such evaluations be justified?

PRACTICAL REASON: THE LOGIC OF POLICY ARGUMENTS

The logic of practical reason pertains to the systematic study of the rational processes related to human reason about action. It deals with cases in which decisions have to be taken among various action alternatives. The concern is with the justification of real-world decisions, rather than with a formal system of logic applied to action. Practical reason, also called the "theory of argumentation," holds that a decision depends on the person making it, and that formal rules of decision-making cannot be abstracted from persons and their actions into formal systems of demonstration modeled on deductive logic, as attempted by the methodologies of positivist social science. Reasoning refers here to a method for convincing or dissuading adversaries, and for coming to an agreement with others about the legitimacy of a decision.

Practical reasoning operates between the logic of demonstration and theories of motivation and action. Not only does it include an empirical assessment of the situation, it also takes into consideration the actor's motives for an action. In practical reasoning, motives that have successfully undergone the test of argumentation can count as "good reasons." In contrast to positivist theories of behavior, which downplay or deny the importance of the reasons people give for their actions, practical reasoning takes seriously the arguments offered for a particular action. An argument as to whether position A or position B can be accepted and used as the basis for an action is judged on the merits of the evidence in the case, rather than as an acting out of the psychological or sociological forces that are behind the debate.

Pactical arguments are, in this regard, propositions that seek to establish if particular acts are good and should be performed. Practical reasoning takes into account, however, the conditions under which actors in real life accept these implied norms as meaningful and commit themselves to them personally. In seeking a decision on which action should be taken, a practical argument begins with the norms to which the participants in the controversy are committed and then seeks, by means of argument, to ground the decision on them. Practical reasoning thus requires normative commitments. Such norms are never universal or ever-lasting; all that is necessary in practical reasoning is that they be recognized by the audience—larger or smaller—to whom the discourse is addressed at the specific time of the argument. Practical reasoning, as such, takes place among individuals or groups in a social context and in historical time. In contrast to the timelessness that is fundamental to deductive reasoning, the notion of temporality is essential to practical reasoning.

Practical reason is thus basic to deciding among the interpretations of various subject matters and activities. This applies to both empirical and normative inquiry. As a social practice, empirical social science is itself related to the judicial-rhetorical mode of inquiry as much as or more than to formal demonstrative logic. Whereas a mathematical or logical proof is either true or false (and if it is true, purportedly accepted by those who understand it), practical arguments are only more or less convincing, more or less plausible to a particular audience. What is more, there is no unique way to construct a practical argument: data and evidence can be chosen in a wide variety of ways from the available information, and there are various methods of analysis and ways of ordering values.

Practical argumentation thus differs from formal demonstration in three important considerations. Whereas formal demonstration is possible only within a formalized system of axioms and rules of inference, practical argumentation begins from opinions, values, or contestable viewpoints rather than axioms. It employs logical inference but is not exhausted in deductive systems of formal statements. Second, a formal demonstration is designed to convince those who have the requisite technical knowledge, while informal argumentation always aims to elicit the adherence of the members of a particular audience to the claims presented for their consent. Third, practical argumentation does not strive to achieve purely intellectual agreement but rather to offer acceptable reasons for choices relevant to action (such as a disposition to act at a appropriate moment).

Writers such as Toulmin (1958) and Perelman (1984) point to legal reasoning as the exemplifying case of practical reasoning. An analysis of legal reasoning, they demonstrate, provides important insights into the process of practical reasoning. Judicial procedures and proceedings, including the arguments of counsel and the decisions of judges and legislative decisions regarding the formation of laws, represent forms of practical reasoning that help to clarify principles of argumentation. Drawing as well on traditional procedures of rhetoric, Perelman's offers his theory of argumentation as a "new rhetoric" that avoids the negative image long associated with rhetoric by supplying it with a more complete theory of practical reasoning.

Thanks to these scholars, the neglected study of rhetoric has more recently returned to the social sciences. After having long been denigrated as a negative concept referring to verbal manipulation, theorists such as McClosky (1985; 1994), and Nelson, Megill, and McCloskey (1987) have labored to restore rhetoric's traditional meaning and to employ it in fields such as economics and political science. In this regard, as Battistelli and Ricotta (2001, 7) put it, rhetoric is characterized by a form of argumentation and practical reason "that is not driven by apodictic syllogisms, but rather uses probable premises to develop relativized arguments, pragmatically oriented to obtain the consent of the receiver." Respecting the rules of conversation, issues of fact and value in this "new rhetoric" are judged in the broader light of historical context, affective influences, and motivational factors. Most important, it recognizes the partiality of the premises in practical argumentation and their dependency on situational circumstances.

POLICY ARGUMENTATION AS PRACTICAL REASON

One of the first policy theorists to call for such a reorientation is Majone. The structure of a policy argument, Majone (1989, 63) explains, is typically a complex mix of factual statements, interpretations, opinion, and evaluation. The argument supplies the links that connect the relevant data and information to the conclusions of an analysis. Majone's conceptualization of the features of a policy argument are an important contribution to the development of an argumentative policy analysis. But his efforts do not sufficiently account for or clarify the normative dimensions that intervene between findings and conclusions. From the preceding discussion, we can formulate the task as a matter of establishing interconnections among the empirical data, normative assumptions that structure our understandings of the social world, the interpretive judgments inherent in the data-collection process, the particular circumstances of a situational context (in which the findings are generated or the prescriptions applied), and the specific conclusions. The scientific acceptability of the conclusions depends on the full range of interconnections, not just the empirical findings. While neopositivists social scientists see their approach as more rigorous and therefore superior to less empirical, less deductive methods, this model of policy argumentation actually makes the task more demanding and complex (McClosky 1994; Fischer 1995a; 1990). Not only does it include the logic of empirical falsification, it encompasses the equally sophisticated normative questions within which it operates. The researcher still collects the relevant data, but now has to situate or include them in the interpretive framework that gives them meaning. No longer is it possible to contend that such normative inquiry can be ignored, as if it somehow relates to another set of concerns.

In *Evaluating Public Policy* (Fischer 1995b), I have outlined a multimethodological framework for integrating these empirical and normative components. The approach takes its initial insight from Toulmin's informal logic of argumentation. It begins by sketching out the logical connection between the empirical data collection process, the measurement of the data against a warrant, which leads to the statement of a concluding claim. But the defining feature of a postempiricist policy analysis is the elaboration of the normative line of argument involved in justifying the backing of the norm or standard employed as evaluative criterion. Toward this end, the framework provides a logic of four interrelated discourses that outlines the concerns of a postempiricist policy evaluation. Extending from concrete questions related to efficiency of a program up through its situational context and the societal system to the abstract normative questions concerning the impact of a policy on a particular way of life, the scheme demonstrates how empirical concerns can be brought to bear on the full range of normative questions. Facilitating a dialectical communication between the policy analyst and the participants relevant to a deliberation, the discourses organize and illuminate the discursive components of a complete policy argument.

As guidelines for deliberative inquiry, these four discourses are broken down into twelve more specific questions designed to probe policy arguments. The first two discursive phases of the logic of policy discourse, constituting the first-order level of evaluation, are technical verification and situational validation. First-order discourse focuses on the specific action setting of a policy initiative, probing both specific program outcomes and the situational (or circumstantial) context in which they occur. The second two discursive phases of the logic, or the level of second-order discourse, are societal vindication and ideological choice. Here argumentation shifts to the larger social system of which the action context is a part; it focuses on the instrumental impact of the policy goals on the societal system as a whole, and an evaluation of the normative principles and values underlying this societal order. Each of these discourses has specific requirements that must be addressed in rendering a complete justification of a practical judgment. For a reason to be considered a "good reason," it must satisfy all four discursive phases of this methodological probe.

The logic of policy argumentation thus works on two fundamental levels, one concretely concerned with a program, its participants, and the specific problem situation to which the program is applied, and the other concerned with the more abstract level of the societal system within which the programmatic action takes place. The evaluation of a policy argument, in this sense, must always look in two directions, one micro, the other macro. For instance, a policy to introduce a multicultural curriculum in a particular university should not only indicate specific course offerings, but also address the larger requirements of a pluralist society, such as the need for a set of common integrating values capable of holding the social system together.

It is important to emphasize that the logic of policy argumentation organizes four interrelated *discourses* rather than a single methodological calculus per se. The task is not to "plug in" answers to specific questions or to fulfill prespecified methodological requirements. It is to engage in an open and flexible examination of the kinds of concerns raised in the various discursive phases of the problem. In this respect, the questions do not constitute a complete set of rules or fixed requirements that must be dealt with in any formal way. Rather, they are designed to orient argumentation to a particular set of concerns. Within the discursive framework, deliberation may follow its own course in the pursuit of understanding and consensus. Policy argumentation, moreover, can commence at any one of the phases. Choosing the place to begin is determined by the practical aspects of the policy to be resolved.

Toward this end, the questions serve as guideposts for deliberative inquiry. The methodological orientations accompanying each of the discursive phases are tools that can support and assist the deliberative process, but need be brought into play only where deemed appropriate. It is, for instance, in no way mandatory to carry out a cost-benefit analysis in the verification of a program outcome. Cost-benefit analysis is understood to be a methodological technique that addresses empirical concerns of verification, but need be employed only when deemed suitable to the specific concerns to hand. There are, in this sense, no hard and fast rules that have to be followed. Rather, the goal is to initiate and pursue reasoned dialogue and consensus at each of the four discursive phases of deliberation. Short of consensus, the objective is clarification and mutual understanding among the parties engaged in deliberation.

TECHNICAL-ANALYTICAL DISCOURSE: PROGRAM VERIFICATION

In the policy sciences verification is the most familiar of the four discursive phases. In the logic of practical discourse it is addressed to the consideration of facts; in policy research it pertains to the basic technical-analytical or methodological questions that define empirical policy analysis. Concerned with the measurement of the efficiency of program outcomes, the methodologies typically employed to pursue questions of verification are the established tools of conventional policy analysis (Sylvia, Sylvia, and Gunn 1997). The basic questions of verification are:

- Does the program fulfill its stated objective(s)?
- Does the empirical analysis uncover secondary or unanticipated effects that offset the program objectives?

- Does the program fulfill the objectives more efficiently than alternative means available?

The task is to produce a quantitative assessment of the degree to which a program fulfils a particular objective (standard or rule) and a determination (in terms of a comparison of inputs and outputs) of how efficiently the objective is fulfilled (typically measured as a ratio of costs to benefits compared with other possible means.

CONTEXTUAL DISCOURSE: SITUATIONAL VALIDATION

From the empirical verification of program outcomes, first-order policy argumentation leads to questions of validation. Validation focuses on whether or not the particular program objectives are relevant to the situation: that is, in the language of informal logic, it takes up the question of situational relevance. Instead of measuring program objectives per se, validation examines the conceptualizations and assumptions underlying the problem situation that the program is designed to influence. Validation centers around the following questions:

- Is the program objective(s) relevant to the problem situation?
- Are there circumstances in the situation that require an exception to be made to the objectives?
- Are two or more criteria equally relevant to the problem situation?

Validation is an interpretive mode of reasoning that takes place within the frameworks of the normative belief systems brought to bear on the problem situation. It draws in particular on qualitative methods, such as those developed for interpretive sociological and anthropological research geared to the situation (Farr 1987).

SYSTEMS DISCOURSE: SOCIETAL VINDICATION

At this level, the logic of policy argumentation shifts from first-order to second-order discourse, that is, from the concrete situational context to the societal context as a whole. The task here is to show that a policy goal (from which the program objectives were drawn) addresses a valuable function for the existing societal arrangements. As such, it engages the issue of instrumental or contributive consequences in the informal logic of practical reason. Societal vindication is organized around the following questions:

- Does the policy goal have instrumental or contributive value for the society as a whole?
- Does the policy goal result in unanticipated problems with important societal consequences?
- Does a commitment to the policy goal lead to consequences (e.g., benefits and costs) that are judged to be equitably distributed?

Here evaluation might ask if a focus on particular programs designed to achieve particular objectives tends to facilitate a particular type of social order. Second-order vindication, as such, steps outside of the situational action context in which program criteria are applied and implemented in order to assess empirically the consequences of a policy goal in terms of the system as a whole. Coming to grips with unexpected consequences often involves testing the policy's underlying assumptions about a system's functions and values.

Ideological Discourse: Social Choice

The fourth discursive phase of the logic of policy deliberation turns to ideological and values questions. Here the informal logic criteria of consistency and transcendent values come into play. Social choice seeks to establish and examine the basis for making rationally informed choices about societal systems and their respective ways of life. Social choice raises the following types of questions:

- Do the fundamental ideals (or ideological principles) that organize the accepted social order provide a consistent basis for a legitimate resolution of conflicting judgments?
- If the social order is unable to resolve basic values conflicts, do other social orders equitably accommodate the relevant interests and needs that the conflicts reflect?
- Do normative reflection and empirical evidence support the justification and adoption of alternative principles and values?

Social choice involves the interpretive tasks of social and political criticism, especially as practiced in political theory and philosophy. Most fundamental are the concepts of a "rational way of life" and the "good society." Based on the identification and organization of a specific configuration of values—such as equality, freedom, or community—models of the good society serve as a foundation for the adoption of higher-level evaluative criteria. Although the task of such discourse is to tease out the value implications of policy arguments, it involves more than mere value clarification. It is also concerned with the ways in which ideological discourse structures and restructures the social order.

A critical judgment in the logic of policy argumentation is presented here as one that has been pursued progressively through the four phases of evaluation. The logic of an empirical assertion moves from the data to the conclusion, mediated by a warrant backed by normative and empirical assumptions. In normal discussion, these assumptions typically serve as part of the background consensus and are called into question only during disputes. The goal of a comprehensive-critical evaluation is to make explicit these assumptions through a progressive critique extending from societal validation to ideological choice (or from ideological choice to validation). As reflected through the logical link of an empirical assertion to the level of ideological choice, a full delineation of the logic of an evaluation discloses its meaning and implications for the pursuit of a particular conception of the ideal society.[2]

The starting point for an evaluation generally depends on the particular policy issue and the debates that it has generated. Typically, the contentious issue relates most specifically to one of the levels, potentially expanding to one or more of the others as an argument progresses. In highly contentious policy issues, however, there can be arguments emerging at all levels at the same time (Fischer 1995, 47–68).

The ability to logically analyze policies offers insights into the construction of acceptable alternative policies. After organizing a policy argument into its component parts, analysts can turn their attention to political consensus formation. The process involves an attempt to convert a static conception of a policy position into a dynamic argument with persuasive power. After identifying the potential areas of policy consensus and conflict, analysts can design an alternative policy proposal that addresses the key issues of conflict. The test of the alternative argument is how well it stands up to the criticisms and objections of the political audiences it has to persuade, the breadth of its appeal, the number of views it can synthesize, and so on. In many cases, this means the analyst has to attempt to dialectically move the proposal beyond a narrow defense of a particular argument in order to present a more comprehensive picture of the political situation. As a narrow argument can be defended only within a limited context of belief, the policy analyst must at times try to offer a new or reformulated view to replace or revise a belief system that impedes the construction of consensus.

The development of such policy proposals remains as much an art as a science. The process involves conjecture, analogy, and metaphor, and logical extrapolation from established causal relationships and facts. Unlike the scientist's analysis based on a closed, generalized model, the policy analyst's proposal is of necessity open and contextual. Where the former model follows the formal principles of inference, the latter is geared to the rules and procedures of informal logic.

CONCLUSION

This chapter has explored the "argumentative turn" in policy analysis. Policy analysis is understood here as "crafted argument." The task is to improve policy argumentation by illuminating contentious questions, identifying the strengths and limitations of supporting evidence, and elucidating the political implications of contending positions. In the process, the task is to increase communicative competencies, deliberative capacities, and social learning.

Drawing on a several related theoretical perspectives—in particular ordinary language philosophy and the informal logic of good reasons—the discussion presented a dialectical communications model of policy analysis that reverses the standard approach by fitting empirical findings into normative argumentation. Guided by the informal good-reasons logic of policy discourse, such policy analysis is organized around four interrelated discourses, taken here to be levels of argumentation. Extending from the concrete questions concerning programmatic efficiency up through the situational context of action and the societal system to the questions involving the relation of a policy to the good life, the levels constitute the discursive components of a comprehensive or complete policy judgment. Working across two fundamental levels of discourse, the four levels are as such concerned both with the level of the program (its participants and the specific problem situation to which the program is applied) and with the more abstract level of the societal order within which the programmatic action takes place. Each of the four discourses has specific empirical and normative requirements that must be addressed in making a complete justification of a policy argument For a reason to be considered a "good" one, the analyst much convince the discursive participants that it satisfy all four discursive phases of the methodological probe.

The approach is designed to help the analyst and other participants to better understand the structure of the policy argument—as a complex blend of factual statements, norms, interpretations, opinions, and evaluations—than does the empirical approach to policy analysis. At the same time, it also more closely links the analytical task to the ordinary-language policy argumentation of real-world politicians and policy makers. Indeed, the argument here is that the approach is a more accurate representation of how politicians, policy analysts, and citizens actually argue and deliberate about policy in the real world of politics. It offers, as such, an approach better suited to real world policy making than the conventional positivist model which emphasizes empirical analysis at the expense of normative investigation. By demonstrating how both the empirical and normative concerns that emerge in policy argumentation are interrelated, the model is offered as way forward in the search for a more socially relevant postpositive alternative.

NOTES

1. A longer version of this chapter appears in chapter 9 of *Reframing Public Policy: Deliberative Politics and Discursive Practices* by the author.
2. The basic types of empirical knowledge that can be brought to bear on normative judgments can all be located across the four levels of discourse: knowledge about the consequences that flow from alternative actions and knowledge about alternative means available (basic to technical verification); the particular facts of the situation and knowledge of the established norms that bear on the decision (situational

validation); the general causal conditions and laws relevant to the problem (systems vindication); and knowledge about values that bear on the decision and about the fundamental needs of humankind (ideological social choice).

REFERENCES

Anderson, C. W. (1978). "The Logic of Public Problems: Evaluation in Comparative Policy Research," in D. Ashford (ed.), *Comparing Public Policies: New Concepts and Methods*. Beverly Hills, CA: Sage.

Battistelli, F. and Ricotta, G. (2005). "The Rhetoric of Management Control in Italian Cities: Constructing New Meanings of Public Action." *Administration & Society*, 36: 661–687.

Churchman, C. W. (1971). *The Designing of Inquiring Systems*. New York: Basic Books.

Dunn, W. N. (1981). *Public Policy Analysis*. Englewood Cliffs, NJ: Prentice-Hall.

Farr, J. (1987). "Resituating Explanation," in T. Ball (ed.), *Idioms of Inquiry: Critique and Renewal in Political Science*. Albany, NY: SUNY Press.

Fischer. F. (1990). *Technocracy and the Politics of Expertise*. Newbury Park, CA: Sage.

——— (1995). *Evaluating Public Policy*. Belmont, CA: Wadsworth.

——— (2003) *Reframing Public Policy: Discursive Politics and Deliberative Practices*. Oxford: Oxford University Press.

Fischer, F. and J. Forester (1993) (eds), *The Argumentative Turn in Policy Analysis and Planning*. Durham, NC: Duke University Press.

Forester, J. (1999). *The Deliberative Practitioner: Encouraging Participatory Planning Processes*. Cambridge: Cambridge University Press.

George, A. (1972). "The Case of Multiple Advocacy in Making Foreign Policy." *American Political Science Review*, 66: 761–85.

Hajer, M. and Wagnaar, H. (2003). *Deliberative Policy Analysis*. Cambridge: Cambridge University Press.

Hawkesworth, M . E. (1988). *Theoretical Issues in Policy Analysis*. Albany: SUNY Press.

Hoch, C. (1994). *What Planners Do?* Chicago: APA Planners Press.

MacRae, D. Jr. (1971). "Scientific Communication, Ethical Argument and Public Policy." *American Political Science Review,* 65: 38–50.

——— (1976). *The Social Function of Social Science*. New Haven, CT: Yale University Press.

Majone, G. (1989). *Evidence, Argument, and Persuasion in the Policy Process*. New Haven: Yale University Press.

McCloskey, D. N. (1985). *The Rhetoric of Economics*. Madison: University of Wisconsin Press.

——— (1990). *If You're So Smart: The Narrative of Economic Expertise*. Chicago: University of Chicago Press.

——— (1994). *Knowledge and Persuasion in Economics*. Cambridge: Cambridge University Press.

Nelson, J. S., Megill, A., and McCloskey, D. N. (1987). *Rhetoric of the Human Sciences: Language and Argument in Scholarship and Public Affairs*. Madison: University of Wisconsin Press.

Perelman, C. (1984). "Rhetoric and Politics." *Philosophy and Rhetoric*, 17/3: 129–34.

Porter, R. B. (1980). *Presidential Decision Making*. Cambridge: Cambridge University Press.

Rivlin, A. (1973). "Forensic Social Science: Perspectives on Inequality." *Harvard Educational Review* (Reprint Series, No. 8). Cambridge, MA: Harvard University Press.

Stone, D. A. (1988). *Policy Paradox and Political Reason*. Glenview, IL: Scott, Foresman and Company.

17 Rhetoric in Policy Making: Between Logos, Ethos, and Pathos

Herbert Gottweis

INTRODUCTION[1]

How can we develop a better understanding of the public policy process, its actors, modes of decision making, outcomes and consequences? This question lies at the heart of contemporary public policy research. Different schools of thought in policy research give different answers to this question. Whereas neopositivist approaches embrace the rationality model of policy making and attempt to provide unequivocal, value-free answers to major questions, argumentative policy analysis rejects the focus of policy studies being the application of scientific techniques and rationality, instead moving language and the process of utilizing, mobilizing and weighing arguments and signs in the interpretation and praxis of policy making and analysis into its center.

But it is stunning to realize that neither "rationalistic" nor "post-rationalistic" approaches in policy studies have paid much attention to a number of phenomena that, no doubt, play crucial roles in many policy-making processes: phenomena such as trust, credibility, virtue, emotions, feelings, and passions (Putnam 1993). Many key policy decision processes seem to be neither the outcome of the application of scientific rationality nor the result of deliberation processes, but can only be explained by the appeal and impact of the personality of a key decision maker and his or her skills to persuade, the credibility of certain actors, or the anxieties or hopes that influence the dynamics of decision making. Some policy topics are endlessly negotiated with armies of stakeholders; other policies are simply imposed onto the citizenry without much discussion. Both types of policies (and many others) occur simultaneously in the same policy context, such as on the local level, in a particular country, or on the transnational/global level. Whereas certain policy-making processes, such as the reform of banking regulations, seem to be dominated by the exchange of rational argumentation and deductive reasoning, other policy-making processes, such as the introduction of a law dealing with aspects of global warming or legal measures dealing with abortion, are characterized by impassioned speech, expressions of anger or language ridden with anxiety. A style of arguing that would cause consternation in one policy milieu might be perfectly legitimate in another.

It is not far-fetched to assume that such differences in dealing with policy issues must significantly affect the dynamics, composition of actor networks and outcomes of policy processes. Although policy analysts surely are aware of the role of such factors in policy making, and history provides countless examples of the importance of passion and ethos in the political world, policy analysis has not yet found an adequate analytical language to deal with them. The growing irresolvable nature of many contemporary policy questions, the crisis of scientific rationality, the new

1. I am grateful to Anna Durnova for research assistance and Ursula Naue for comments.

politics of religion, and the rise of a new culture of uncertainty further emphasize the need to develop a policy analysis well suited for increasingly complex policy settings. In this chapter I will suggest that argumentative policy analysis and some traditions in the study of rhetoric provide important connecting points to extend our notion of argumentation and bring back passion and ethos to the study of policy making.

POLICY ARGUMENTATION, RATIONALITIES, AND COGNITIVISM

Conflicting views about the role and nature of rationality in policy making are at the root of different strategies of theorizing about the public policy process. "Rationalistic" models emphasize the importance of scientific, instrumental rationality in the study and solution of policy problems. However, one of the most important alternative directions in current, critical policy analysis in the last decade is argumentative policy analysis. The term *argumentative policy analysis* subsumes a group of different approaches toward policy analysis that share an emphasis on language as a key feature and thus as a necessary key component of policy analysis. Argumentative policy analysis links post-positivist epistemology with social theory and methodology and encompasses theoretical approaches such as discourse analysis, frame analysis and interpretative policy analysis. Although these different approaches are hardly synonymous, they nevertheless share the special attention they give to argumentation and language and the process of utilizing, mobilizing and weighing arguments and signs in the interpretation and praxis of policy making and analysis (Fischer 2003; Gottweis 2006).

Proponents of argumentative policy analysis do not believe that policy analysis can be a value-free, technical project, and argue that both policy making and policy analysis involve argumentation that needs to be at the center of policy. One of the key characteristics of argumentative policy analysis is its conceptualization of the role of policy analysis and of the policy analyst in the policy process. This viewpoint sweepingly rejects the idea of the "neutral" and "objective" policy analyst qua social technician and, rather, espouses the idea of the policy analyst as something like a lawyer (Majone 1989), an advocate, deeply engaged in the policy process itself. Although authors such as Majone and Stone (1988) have not gone further than rejecting the "objectivist" idea of the policy analysist, in the wake of Fischer and Forester's *Argumentative Turn* and Dryzek's *Discursive Democracy*, the notion of argumentative policy analysis as fostering and encouraging political participation and deliberation has become very influential. With the departure of the idea that the main task of the policy analyst is to identify solutions for objective problems, the image of the professional expert is reconstructed as one of the facilitators of public learning and political empowerment (Fischer 2003). Torgerson argues that "just as positivism underlies the dominant technical orientation in policy analysis, so the post-positivist orientation now points to a participatory project" (1986, 241). Forester, Healy, and Innes (1999; 1996; 2003) have advocated communicative policy analysis, the idea that the main task of the policy analyst is to facilitate process of deliberation and to help planners to critically reflect on their own discursive practices.

Underlying this "policy model" is an approach toward communication and argumentation strongly influenced by the late work of Jürgen Habermas. In his *Theory of Communicative Action* (1985, originally in German 1981), Habermas has developed the idea of "communicative rationality," which he defines as rational what is communicatively, intersubjectively justified or justifiable. Rationality comes into existence via intersubjectively grounded argumentation. This advocacy for a "communicative policy analysis" is elaborated in greatest detail in Dryzek's *Discursive Democracy*, which discusses Habermas's critique of instrumental rationality: the idea to devise, select, and effect good means to clarified ends; and the alternative model of a communicated rationality, oriented toward the coordination of interactions via communication (Dryzek 1990). This idea of policy analysis as a deliberative, participatory, communicative project can be followed from Torgesen, via

Dryzek, the "Argumentative Turn" and, most recently in *Deliberative Policy Analysis* by Hajer and Wagenaar (2003), who bluntly state that policy analysis *is* deliberative (21–23).

Through the Habermasian "Communicative Action" model, another important feature of argumentative policy analysis has been introduced in argumentative policy analysis: a certain tendency toward cognitivism. Discourse ethics in the Habermas tradition starts from the assumption that moral problems are capable of being solved in a rational and cognitive way. However, it needs to be questioned whether policy disputes are always solved or settled by appeal to reason. Although argumentative policy analysis clearly recognizes this phenomenon, much of the analysis in this tradition pays only scant attention to phenomena such as passion and emotions in policy making, probably because of an understanding of discourse and argumentation that reduces argumentation to the operation of logos rather than a tendency to integrate pathos and ethos into argumentation, to phenomena that have received much attention in the tradition of Greek rhetoric. In fact, there seems to be a propensity in argumentative policy analysis to confine reasoning to deliberative and judicial reasoning, as apart and separated from manipulative, negative rhetoric. Propaganda is clearly differentiated from "genuine argumentation," and, in this respect, argumentative policy analysis seems to be closer to the Platonic ideal for science as a search for truth than to the Aristotelian/ Sophistic tradition (Turnbull 2005). In its attempt to avoid what is seen as one of the main mistakes in neopositivist policy analysis, namely the confusion of reason with instrumental rationality, the communicative model suggests communicative rationality as the democratic version of bringing reason into the world. But the underlying construction of the policy process is guided by rationality assumptions, in particular, by the idea that the policy process needs to be structured in a way to allow for the operation of communicative rationality. This, however, constitutes a new form of constraint for the notion of reason—and narrows down the scope of application of this policy model.

BRINGING IN EMOTIONS AND ETHOS

It is probably not exaggerated to argue that major strands of reasoning in contemporary political science and political philosophy are obsessed with the idea to eliminate passion and anything remotely irrationally sounding in politics. There is a line in reasoning about politics from Plato to Kant and Hegel that emphasizes reason as the sound foundation of politics, versus uncontrolled, passionate behavior leading to disaster. Historically, the image of the wild and uncontrolled passions as a deep threat to humankind and civilization is deeply rooted in Western philosophy. For Plato, passion is the name of a problem for which reason is the answer (Meyer 1991, 38). Nagging philosophical suspicion concerning the dark powers of passion continue in the history of thought also in philosophers such as Kant or Hegel, for whom reason was the path to freedom and truth, and passion threatened the moral and society order (Meyer 1991; Svasek 2002, 13).

However, we might also interpret passion in a more benign fashion. And this conceptualization of passion has also important implications for opening up argumentative policy toward a new understanding of the policy process. For Aristotle, emotions were "all those feelings that so change men as to affect their judgement" (Aristotle 1991). No contradiction existed for him between reason and emotion. Aristotle construed thought and belief as the efficient cause of emotion and showed that emotional response is intelligent behavior open to reasoned persuasion. As W. W. Fortenbaugh puts it in his classic study on Aristotle and emotions: "When men are angered, they are not victims of some totally irrational force. Rather, they are responding in accordance with the thought of unjust result. Their belief may be erroneous and their anger unreasonable, but their behaviour is intelligent and cognitive in the sense that it is grounded upon a belief which may be criticised and even altered by argumentation" (1975, 17). Thus, it might be useful to return to a close reading of the Classical tradition of rhetoric in order to advance a more comprehensive model of argumentation.

Much later in Western philosophy, this tradition of reasoning was further developed by David Hume in his *Treatise on Human Nature* (1739). Hume famously argued that reason itself could not motivate us to act and, further, that it could not oppose the only true motive of the will, our desires, or what Hume calls the passions. No doubt, despite its negative image in the history of philosophy, emotions have figured largely as a topic of interest in a variety of scientific contexts, such as in psychiatry and psychology.

But much of the work on emotions in this direction has been characterized by an essentializing attitude toward emotions, as they are conceptualized as predictable outcomes of universal psychobiological processes or "things" the social systems must deal with (Abu-Lughod and Lutz 1990, 2–3). In contrast, emotions could also be conceptualized as a discursive practice. Emotions belong to the repertoire of rhetoric, and emotional display and the language of passion may very well coexist with argumentative and ethical discourse. This rhetorical position allows us to explore how speech and language provide the means by which emotions have their effects and therefore take on significance. Thus, this view emphasizes the interpretation of emotions as pragmatic acts and communicative performances, and thus as modes of argumentation. Emotions, then, should not be seen as "things" being carried by the vehicle of discourse and rhetoric, but as a form of rhetorical praxis that creates effects in the world (Abu-Lughod and Lutz 1990, 11–3; Lutz and White 1986).

Emotional discourse is always bound up with structures and hierarchies of power. It is part of complex scenographies (see below) in which argumentation takes place. Power relations determine what can or what cannot be said about self and emotion, and emotional discourse can establish, assert, or reinforce power or status differences (Abu-Lughod and Lutz 1990, 14). In a congressional debate about the pros and cons of human embryonic stem cell research, when a member of the U.S. Senate tells a moving story about his son who suffers from diabetes, when scientists invite wheelchair-bound Christopher Reeve to tell his story of despair and hope, or when pro-life advocates talk about baby farms producing organs, we see not only the classical instruments of rhetoric being used to move the passions of audiences, but also efforts to stabilize or destabilize existing structures and practices in research and medical practice. Policy analysis needs to pay attention to such aspects of political decision making. To some extent in subfields of political science, such as in public opinion or electoral research, doubts are few that emotions and persuasion matter in politics. However, as uncertainty become more pronounced in many policy fields, it might be useful to reconsider pathos and emotion not as a "force" in its own, as a "fact of political life," but as being intrinsically linked to the everyday practice of policy making, as a rhetorical device that takes considerable impact in many policy areas and is a key element of policy argumentation (Gottweis 2006).

RHETORIC AND ARGUMENTATION

Rhetoric is broadly acknowledged as an important feature of the political process. Often associated with the art of persuasion, rhetoric is typically defined as an integral moment of policy making, and the idea of rhetoric points to the necessity to convince, persuade, and communicate efficiently in the context of shaping and implementing public policies. A highly publicized national speech given by a country's president can set the agenda in a policy field, push decision making into a particular direction, or put pressure on policy makers of all parties. Although the power of rhetorical presentation in politics is hardly contested, at the same time, maybe simultaneously, the term *rhetoric* suffers under an image problem : while rhetoric is widely seen as closely linked with politics, it nevertheless often has a pejorative connotation, as describing intellectually vacuous or empty statements that mainly serve to manipulate, to cover up something or to distract from the real sequences of events. As I will argue, this rhetoric's image problem dates back to Plato, and it has played a major role in the relative negligence of rhetoric in policy research. It is time to restore the place of rhetorical analysis in policy studies in order to throw an analytical light on highly important aspects of the policy-making process. Rhetoric is genuinely linked to the idea of persuasion, but it also has a much neglected performative dimension: in the play of language not only signs are communicated.

One of the key texts in contemporary argumentative policy analysis, Giandomenico Majone's *Evidence, Argument and Persuasion in the Policy Process* (1989), explicitly defines the ancient tradition of rhetoric as the obvious and necessary point of departure for modern policy analysis. "The centuries-old tradition of humanistic disciplines, from history and literary criticism to moral philosophy and law, proves that argumentative skills can be taught and learned. Thus, if the crucial argumentative function of policy analysis is neglected in university departments and schools of public policy, this is due less to a lack of suitable models than to serious misconceptions about the role of reason in human affairs and about the nature of the 'scientific method'... when mathematicians acknowledge that mathematics is not the antithesis of rhetoric... it should not be left to policy analysts to fight the last battles of positivism" (xii). Majone then goes on to discuss in great detail the virtues of rhetoric for policy analysis, and the "argumentative character" of the policy process itself, which calls for systematic attention to the role and function of words in and the ways of "doing things with word" (7). "Its crucial argumentative aspect is what distinguishes policy analysis from the academic social sciences on the one hand , and from problem-solving methodologies such as operations research on the other" (7). In a similar way, James A. Throgmorton has pointed to the importance of rhetoric in planning and policy making (1991). However, both texts reduce the notion of rhetoric to the idea of persuasion via the argument itself, the process of demonstrating that something is the case or not, such as through induction and deduction. Aristotle has called this form of reasoning argumentation through logos. While emphasizing the fact that policy analysts themselves are part of a process of argumentation that ties observer close with the observed, both authors focus on rhetoric as constitutive of the meaning of policy and planning, without elaborating further on the analytical instruments of rhetoric. Thus, the notion of rhetoric remains closely tied to the idea of logos, the appeal to reason by means of words, deduction and induction, which, already in the classical tradition of Aristotle was seen as only one among other "rhetorical proofs."

Argumentation theory and rhetoric have a long history that dates back to pre-Aristotelian philosophy. It is always connected to considerations and reconsiderations of the notions of logic, communication and persuasion. Mobilizing, positioning, and transmitting arguments also requires appropriate socio-political conditions: argumentation is the antithesis to revelation; it is not about revealing a truth but attempts to convince (Breton and Gauthier, 2000, 3–5). The Sophists emphasized the importance of rhetoric in politics and the idea that facts are what we are persuaded of (Danzinger 1995). Plato accused the Sophists of only dealing with the appearances of truth, whereas philosophy's role was to deal with establishing the true and the good (Meyer 1994, 50–51). Every since, the discipline of rhetoric must live with its image problem of superficially dealing with surface phenomena and deceit, instead of serving the establishment of the good and the true.

Aristotle, by contrast, attempted to accord a positive place to rhetoric by positioning it as part of dialectic, along with poetics and the study of topics (Meyer 1994, 119–23). As Michel Meyer points out, rhetoric appears forcefully in times of crisis for the lack of directing principles in settling questions that are being submitted to controversial answers. In the absence of leading principles that could offer some definitive, unequivocal answers, problems are bound to be disputed and solved "equivocally." Just as the Peloponnesian Wars in ancient Greece led to a collapse of previous and well-established values and modes of thought and to the rise of rhetoric, the upheavals of our times have led to a new reconsideration of rhetoric, argumentation, persuasion, and its relationship to logic and communication (Meyer 1994, 36–37). Rhetoric is a discourse in which one can hold opposite judgments on the same question. What is problematic remains so through the displayed multiplicity of judgments (Meyer 1994, 52).

In contemporary times, the theory of argumentation and rhetoric were taken up and further developed by Stephen Toulmin (1958) and Chaim Perelman (Pereleman and Olbrechts-Tyteca 1958) in the late 1950s, and the work of both had a lasting influence in the field of political science. Closely related to the development of argumentation theory was the rise of hermeneutics, phenomenology, structuralism and post-structuralism not only in philosophy but also in the social sciences from the 1970s on. The ascent of argumentative policy analysis must be seen in this complex intellectual environment as a result of a political constellation of transformation and upheaval, when, during the 1980s, largely unanticipated by the international political science community, the Soviet Union broke down, the "end of history" was proclaimed, the European Union finally rose to the status of an international economic super power, and the traditional models of economic growth and the nature-society interaction came to be deeply questioned. The crisis of the major political metanarratives, powerfully analyzed by Francois Lyotard (1979), and the limits of growth and scientific progress seemed to call for new, more nuanced confrontations and understandings of the nature of policy making. Majone's *Evidence, Argument, and Persuasion in the Policy Process* (1989) contextualizes the need for argumentative policy analysis by reference to the "crisis of scientific expertise" in regulation policy, which was to became visible during the 1970s: "Increasingly, public debates about regulatory decisions, nuclear safety, technology assessment, and similar trans-scientific issues tend to resemble adversary proceedings in a court of law, but with an important difference—the lack of generally accepted rules of procedure" (4). This "crisis of scientific rationality," identified by Majone in the late 1980s, has hardly ceased to define everyday life of regulation and other fields of policy making.

BRINGING BACK RHETORIC

Classical rhetoric found its culmination in the work of Aristotle. "Let rhetoric be (defined as) an ability, in each (particular) case, to see the available means of persuasion," Aristotle suggested (1991, 36). He defined three kinds of proofs (*pisteis*) that are crucial in rhetoric: "Of the *pisteis* provided through speech there are three species: for some are in the character (ethos) of the speaker, and some in disposing the listener in some way [pathos, H.G.], and some in the argument [logos] itself, by showing or seeming to show something.... [There is persuasion] through character whenever the speech is spoken in such a way as to make the speaker worthy of credence.... [There is persuasion] through the hearers when they are led to feel emotion (pathos) by the speech.... Persuasion occurs through arguments (logoi) when we show the truth or the apparent truth from whatever is persuasive in each case" (37–39).

Thus, in the Aristotelian perspective, the term *ethos* designates a certain quality of a speaker, but does not refer to any internal attitude or a system of abstract values. Ethos is a procedural phenomenon that comes into existence in action; it is a discursive praxis that is based on exchange and interaction and depends on the perception of audiences. On the other side is pathos, which emphasizes the importance of feelings and passions in the mobilization of opinion. Pathos refers to the fact that the knowledge of other people's emotions is vital for politics. While logos convinces by itself, pathos and ethos are tied to specific circumstances and, above all, the persons implied in these situations.

Aristotle's rhetoric always had a prominent place in the history of occidental philosophy. In the twentieth century, the work of Stephen Toulmin (1958) and Chaim Perelman (1958) was key for reintroducing the notion of rhetoric into contemporary social and political theory. In the humanities and social sciences, based on the path-breaking studies of Perelman (1977), discourse theory has begun increasingly to focus on the study of rhetoric as an elaboration of the theory of language acts and of pragmatics (Maingueneau 2002).

While in the ancient tradition, the concept of rhetoric is mainly organized around oral speech; its consideration can also be seen as the acknowledgement of the complexity of discourse. If we apply rhetoric in the context of the study of policymaking, it is useful to reconceptualize the notion of argumentation. If we look at political discourse, we can understand a mode of argumentation in

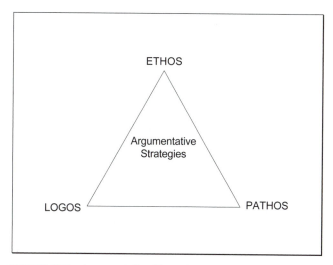

FIGURE 17.1   Argumentative Strategies

a policy context as being dominated by one of these three elements, logos, ethos, and pathos, that take on different weight in the argumentation (Adam 1999). As mentioned above, in the Aristotelian tradition logos instructs and applies reason, ethos refers to the "morality" of the speaker, and pathos has the function to move and refers to the passions. Any text or genre of discourse can be analyzed with respects to its dominant modes of argumentation and related, dominant constructions and presentations of individual and collective selves. Although a mode of argumentation dominated by logos is characterized by reasoning and the presentation of facts, evidence and empirical proofs, pathos operates with empathy, sympathy, sensibilities, while ethos functions with trust, respect authority, honesty, credibility and considerations of the desirable. Any communication or speech act combines elements of logos, pathos and ethos, though different weight might put by a speaker on these three elements of persuasion.

What the differentiation of logos, pathos, and ethos in argumentation brings into focus is a more differentiated conceptualization of the notion of persuasion in policy making than usually offered in argumentative policy analysis. While political argumentation always entails the notion of persuasion, rhetoric emphasizes that argumentation is not always or necessarily persuasion via logos, the words of the speech, such as the scientific exchange of information and knowledge, but can also use different channels of persuasion, such as pathos and ethos, which in this perspective become key factors to be considered in the policy-making process (Stone 1988, 304).

SITUATING RHETORICAL PRAXIS

If we follow this interpretation of argumentation and therefore identify rhetoric as a key element in policy making, we have identified an analytical problem or challenge in policy analysis rather than offered an analytical solution. We have identified the "what" of the problem, the necessity to "bring back in rhetoric into our consideration of argumentation," but not discussed the "how" of the solution of the problem, in which conceptual way this could be accomplished. While in the past policy and political science scholars have occasionally paid attention to the importance of rhetoric (Fontana, Nederman, and Remer 2004), very little work has been done to integrate this acknowledgment of rhetoric into the praxis of policy analysis. Thus, the next question important to address in the context of rhetoric in policy making is which analytical strategies should be applied to develop a more differentiated picture of the policy-making process.

The consideration of the interplay among logos, ethos, and pathos in policy making brings into focus the performative nature of the policy process. Aristotle's discussion of rhetoric must be located in a historical context in which the appearance of the public space is simultaneous with the emergence of theater and performance as a new dimension of public life. The flourishing of rhetoric as a form of public political activity was a complex phenomenon closely associated with developments such as the rise of the *stoa* as site of deliberation and as an oratorical setting during the fifth century in ancient Greek (Johnstone 1996, 102). Jeffrey C. Alexander has recently pointed to the fact that in earlier, more archaic forms of complex societies, such as the imperial orders of Egypt, social hierarchies simply could issue commands and were dominated by ritualized performances. In more loosely knit social organizations, such as in ancient Greece, authority became more open to challenge. Social spaces opened up for negotiation, and social processes became more subject to conflict and argumentation. This rise of the public sphere (Habermas 1987) or public stage opened up a public forum in which actors increasingly enjoyed the freedom to enact and project performances of their imagination tailored to various audiences (Alexander 2004, 544–45). Thus, the rise of rhetoric in ancient Greece is to some extent also related to a process of deep social, cultural and political transformation in which rhetoric expresses the increasingly performative, nonritualistic, staged nature of the political process. It therefore is not far-fetched to argue that bringing back in rhetoric into the study of policy making not only requires attention to phenomena such as pathos and ethos but also to the performative and open nature of policy making in contemporary political settings.

Policy making always has a strong performative dimension and thus is a way of doing things with words. J. L. Austin in his performative speech act theory, most famously developed in his *How to Do Things with Words* (1962), interprets sentences as forms of actions. Performative utterance does not refer to an extra-linguistic reality but enacts or produces what it refers to. We can therefore speak of argumentative performativity as a crucial element in policy making. During a discussion on unemployment policy measures, a politician of one party might suggest the image that many unemployed simply lack the will to find a job; thus, regulations to obtain unemployment benefits should become more restrictive. This argumentation is not only an interpretation of the nature of unemployment, it also, at least to some extent, redefines the unemployed as poorly motivated, lazy individuals who should try harder to change their situation. Hence, this argumentation "makes up" a particular group of individuals and potentially exposes them to specific, new, tougher policy measures. We might say that this argumentation not only describes but produces what it refers to.

While this reading of the power of discourse is relatively undisputed within the tradition of argumentative policy analysis, the wider implications of performative argumentation have received relatively little attention. Following Goffman's ethnomethodological approach, Hajer (2005) has recently begun to study the performative dimensions of deliberative settings in policy making and pointed to the importance of the dramaturgy of policy settings. Goffman's dramaturgical approach is partially based on insights from the study of theater that emphasize the importance of dramaturgy for linking the written word with its "translation" into the acting of a theater play (Goffman 1969; 1974). Nevertheless, Goffman's work has a strong sociological orientation and is less interested in the language-analytical aspects of social performativity. This is precisely where rhetoric comes in with its specific interest in how "things are done with words." Apparently, any policy-making process is determined by the way it is located or "produced" in time, in space, and in its social make-up. In this process of *mise-en-scène*, important differences of the policy-making process are shaped, such as the difference between a policy-making process that operates top–down via a quick, undisputable decision of policy makers, or a policy process that is characterized by lengthy deliberations in a deliberative setting.

Policy making never takes place in any kind of economic, political, social, cultural, or semantic vacuum. It is always a contextualized and situated process. At the same time, policy making is about the definition of policy settings, policy actors, policy institutions and policy dynamics.

Any unemployment policy in a given country will very much depend on existing and established patterns of policy making and networks, institutions, resources, and economic circumstances. But a newly elected government might want to change or revamp many of these pre-established structures, redefine the nature and causalities of unemployment, and choose a new strategy to fight unemployment. Such a situation calls for the crafting of a new scenography (Maingueneau 2002), the creation of a setting, the identification of a group of key actors and the development of a temporal structure for the policy setting. A new unemployment policy might come about by bringing together the various interest groups at a table to negotiate the future policy or by quickly passing a law that introduces the new measures to fight unemployment. It is in such moments that words not only matter because they signify but also because they perform, shape, create, and transform policy-making dynamics.

RHETORIC IN ACTION

Policy making thus must be seen as a multifaceted process that involves as much argumentation as a process of shaping and creating a dynamic, a rationality, a logic of reasoning, a basis for decision making. We can differentiate between different models of argumentative performativity, or models of argumentative orientation (Caron 1983, 140) depending on their emphasis on pathos, ethos, or logos in argumentation.

The way a certain policy problem is depicted and defined gives rise to particular scenarios of interaction and involvement, describes involved actors, a particular timing and the location for a policy development to take place. In turn, such a scenography explains and justifies why it is precisely that chosen scenography which is needed for a policy-making process to take place, to take form and to solve a problem.

A government might, for example, decide that a particular desirable solution for a policy problem is best attained if it capitalizes from trust in certain of its key policy makers; conversely, it might want to keep issues of trust and emotions on the backburner and create a mainly rational decision-making process around an issue. It might be also an issue of bringing in or leaving out particular actors in a policy setting. In issues of reproductive medicine, emotive language, and appeal to religious feelings will mobilize Christian groups that otherwise do not necessarily get involved in this issue. An emphasis on a "rational solution" or the refusal to engage in religious argumentation might favor a more expert-dominated model of problem solving. An anti-abortion grassroots groups might decide to try to define the policy dynamic of stem cell research support by linking the research with the question of abortion and a language of "defending life." Clearly, policy making is always a highly constrained process, but policy actors do have a choice in determining settings, and often a fierce struggle to determine a particular "solution model" is part of the actual policy-making process. Thus policy making is hardly only about argumentation, the creation of exchange of arguments, but also a performative process in which the boundaries of argumentation are defined. Finally, the selection of a particular policy model (see below) is always temporary and subject to modification. It might very well be the case that the used policy model changes during the process of policy making.

For the purpose of demonstrating the usefulness of the proposed analytical framework, I will discuss six configurations of a policy scenography: the *etho-centric*, *logo-centric,* and *patho-centric* as the basic models of a policy scenography, and the *logo-pathetic,* the *etho-pathetic,* and the *etho-logical* models as subforms of the basic models. They are conceived as models of argumentative orientation (Caron 1983, 140) to show the hegemony and structure of the three rhetoric elements: logos, ethos, and pathos. These models result from concepts such as enounced, enunciation, and scenography, mentioned before, and they reflect the dramaturgical character of this performance.

Ethnocentric policy performances tend to occur, for example, at the occasion of a presidential

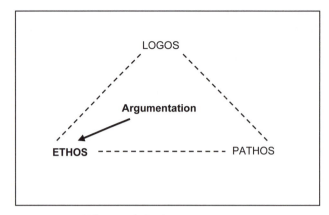

FIGURE 17.2   Etho-centric Performance

speech, when the audience expects the moment of acknowledgement of a particular policy view. This means that the speaking subject will adopt the *role of authority* and will often perform this role connected to his position or function in the institutional hierarchy of the state. When President Bush gives a speech about what needs to be done to fight an environmental disaster, he will not negotiate or discuss his policies but, very much based on the powers of his office, state what will happen in the near future. He also "can do this" because he is the president of the United States, and he can be assured that most of his fellow citizens will acknowledge his "aura," dignity, and right to take action. At a different occasion, President Bush might also decide to present his new educational policy "as president " (i.e., based on the aura of his office). In that case there is no time pressure to act quickly, but he might decide to use his status and weight as a policy maker simply to avoid lengthy and broad discussion.

The difference between the etho-centric model and the logo-centric model is the mode of presenting arguments. In the logo-centric model the speaking subject has an ideal space and time to show the arguments, to *discuss* them, to problematize the topic of the policy (Turnbull 2003). The stage and discussion is very favorable to this kind of argumentation, an argumentation that does not necessarily need to end and has a univocal meaning. Nevertheless, the speaking subject should, more than in any other model, emphasize the central arguments, their weight from the factual point of view and not from a personal one. Generally, we observe this type of the performance in a

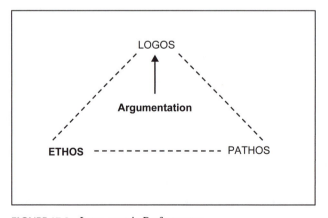

FIGURE 17.3   Logo-centric Performance

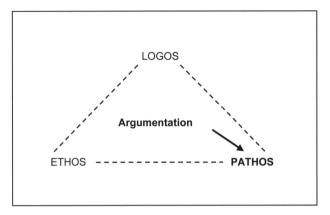

FIGURE 17.4   Patho-centric Performance

parliamentary plenum or subcommittee discussion, or in a working-group discussion. A delibera-tive policy context might also be characterized by the dominance of a logo-centric scenography, in which highly elaborated rules of discourse structure exchange with a strongly cognitive tendency that rules out displays of emotion.

The patho-centric performance is based on a focus on emotions that are implemented in the discourse. These emotions are vehicles of the argumentation of the speaking subject, who this time has a central role. The strategy of the speaking subjects emphasize the emotions of the audience in order to respond to them not in the terms of bringing in a new constructed proposition but in the terms of mobilization of this audience *against* an elite. Patient groups might mobilize the complex iconography of their health condition and suffering as an argument for more liberal regulations in stem cell research or for more financial resources for medical research. Public hearings with "sufferers," with patients visibly handicapped by a particular disease or who are disabled, like wheel-chair-bound Christopher Reeve, create stages where patho-centric argumentation gains a performative space.

Typically, policy scenographies neither follow one of the ideal types outlined above, but involve a particular combination of those central elements of persuasion. We might think of a *etho-pathetic* constellation with the combined dominance of two basic categories of persuasion: the ethnocentric and the patho-centric argumentation. Generally, the emotions that mobilize the audience are not only related to the issue at stake but are also connected with the person who mobilizes. The speak-ing subject mobilizes passions, but at the same time uses his ethos, for example, to speak to the nation as a president. This kind of performance tends to occur in uncertain moments, even in the chaotic ones, when the individual looks for a fulcrum that can change his situation, get it better. The environmental disaster is discussed in all its horror and impact, but, at the same time, the person, the president who speaks, gives hold and confidence not because he necessarily has a solution in hands, but because he can be trusted, relied on.

Furthermore, we can identify a *logo-pathetic* constellation, in which the treatment of a particular topic combines and focuses a consideration of emotions with nuanced rational discussion of the pros and cons of a particular mode of action. Political decision making about euthanasia might involve a subtle consideration of the many aspects of the topic that have to do with feelings and emotions and, at the same time, consider in a logical-deductive manner the weight of the various arguments speaking for and against euthanasia.

Finally, an *etho-logical* constellation of policy making refers to a policy scenography in which a logos-dominated argumentation is closely connected with the ethos of a speaker. A politi-cian whose many decades in politics have given him an authoritative voice in the political process and government might present a complicated argument in favor of better measures against global warming and speak as an experienced, seasoned member of the parliament.

This list of different applications of rhetoric in policy making is neither exhaustive nor will any of the described constellations define a policy setting indefinitely. But, over time, a particular process of policy making will be characterized by a particular style of reasoning, a particular distribution of roles, and a location for the policy-making process to take place. The different models describe scenarios for policy making that are contested, change over time, but nevertheless constitute a key explanation for the course of policy-making processes in different policy fields.

CONCLUSIONS

In this chapter I tried to sketch an analytical strategy that gives rhetoric an appropriate place in argumentative policy analysis. Argumentative policy analysis rejects the idea of the "neutral," "objective" policy analyst qua social technician and instead espouses the idea of the policy analyst as something like a lawyer (Majone), an advocate, deeply engaged in the policy process itself. From this perspective, it is not far to the reconstruction of the position of the policy analyst as called upon to foster and encourage political participation and deliberation. If "truth" escapes the grip of the rationalistic/positivistic policy analyst but becomes a project of communication, the study of the construction, dissemination, exchange, and impact of argumentation *qua logos* becomes the obvious agenda of policy analysis. The rejection of the neopositivist identification of reason as an expression of instrumental rationality leads in deliberative/participatory policy analysis to a predominant interest in the study of the conditions for communicative rationality to materialize in policy making.

While this approach is well suited to the study of particular policy settings and constellations, I have argued that a number of other policy constellations seem to call for a different theoretical orientation and approach. The tradition of rhetoric in history and in political science provides excellent connecting points for such a reorientation. From this perspective, a reflexive or deliberative staging of a policy-making process seems to be only one among many other, different models. The effort to solve an intractable policy conflict, such as euthanasia, through deliberative techniques—"reframing" (Schön and Rein, 1994)—might be a pretty hopeless project. During the negotiation of particular regulatory polices, such as those dealing with issues of life and death, the transparency of regulatory institutions could be as important as creating the institutional possibility for emotional display, the articulation of hopes and anxieties. Public participation and involvement might often simply not be what the different stakeholders in a conflict constellation are seeking. The growth industry of staging consensus conferences and citizen mediations might well work in certain fields of policy making but fail miserably in others. I have argued for a better consideration of the performative dimension of policy making that can take on a variety of different expressions.

By bringing back the tradition of rhetoric to policy analysis, I have tried to widen the focus of policy analysis toward a consideration of undisputed features of many policy-making processes, in particular the importance of ethos, virtue, trust, feelings, and emotions. I suggested to conceptualize these elements in policy making not as expressions of irrationality but as inseparable from the operation of reason. Just as politicians might use emotional language in a very calculative manner, citizens might decide in a very reasonable manner that they refuse to consider a particular matter, for example, the question of euthanasia in severely disabled newborns, only from the perspective of utilitarian philosophy. The attempt to shape and define policy constellation through rhetoric is not a privilege of policy elites but constitutes everyday life practice of the many policy actors dispersed in contemporary multilayer governance networks.

The implications of this perspective for argumentative policy analysis are considerable. I have tried to discuss how the staging of policy making has an impact on a number of different models of policy making that impact style, composition, content, and implementation. These are always contested and object to change, but, at some point in a policy-making process, they will be determinants in a particular course of action.

On the normative side, the idea of the different rhetorical strategies for poliy making can become a tool to create scenarios for policy solutions based on an assessment of a particular constellation in a policy field. A regulatory policy-making process dealing with emission standards in the car industry that has a high likelihood to involve a well-established and experienced group of policy makers will invite a logo-centric staging of a policy-making process with a focus on deliberating and negotiating scientific data and evidence. At the same time, the preparation of a law regulating human cloning that most likely will involve highly emotionally charged discussions and attract a broad scope of actors and interests will lend itself more toward policy forms that allow more expressive forms of articulation or seek early the parliamentary forum for dealing with the issue. Such options for policy making are open for the different policy actors in contemporary networks of governance, ranging from citizen groups that attempt to create a policy agenda to governments that want to pass a law in a particular policy field.

The rapid pace of scientific-technological development from genetic engineering to nanotechnology, major challenges related to socio-economic development, such as the problem of global warming and breakthroughs in modern medicine, seem to radically question existing notions of humanity, progress and the future of humankind. Today, political controversies about technology and science and other social key questions such as the environment and unemployment seem to emphasize uncertainty more than ever. For policy analysis, this new constellation of uncertainty, the old and new ambivalences of our time, have significant implications. This situation points to the need that policy analysis brings argumentation in all its complexities, including rhetoric, into the center of its analytical and epistemological project.

REFERENCES

Abu-Lughod, Lily and Lutz A. Catherine (1990). Introduction: Emotion, Discourse, and the Politics of Everyday Life, in Abu-Lughod/Lutz (eds.). *Language and the Politics of Emotion* (Cambridge: Cambridge Unversity Press 1990), 1–23.

Adam, J-M (1999): *Linguistique Textuelle et Analyse des Pratiques Discursives*, Paris. Nathan.

Alexander, J. C. (2004). Cultural Pragmatices: Social Performance between Ritual and Strategy. *Sociological Theory, 22:* 527–573.

Aristotle (1991). *On Rhetoric*. A Theory of Civic Discourse: Newly Translated with Introduction, Notes, and Appendixes by George A. Kennedy. Oxford: Oxford University Press.

Austin, J. L. (1962). *How to Do Things with Words*. Cambridge, MA: Harvard University Press.

Benveniste, E. (1966). *Problèmes de Linguistique générale*, Paris: éd. Gallimard.

Benveniste, E. (1972). *Problèmes de Linguistique Générale*, Vol. 2. Paris: éd. Gallimard.

Breton, P. and G. Gauthier (2000). *Histoire des Théories de l'Argumentation*. Paris: La Decouverte.

Caron, J. (1983). *Les Régulations du Discours: Psycholinuistique et Pragmatique du Langage*. Paris : Presses Universitaires de France.

Danzinger, M. (1995). Policy Analysis Postmodernized: Some Political and Pedagogical Ramifications. *Policy Studies Journal,* 23(3): 435–450.

Dryzek, J. S. (1990). *Discursive Democrary: Politics, Policy, and Political Science*. Cambridge: Cambridge University Press.

Fischer, F. (2003*). Reframing Public Policy: Discursive Politics and Deliberative Practices*. Oxford: Oxford University Press.

Fontana, B., Nederman, C.J., and Remer, G. (eds.) (2004). *Talking Democracy. Historical Perspectives on Rhetoric and Democracy.* University Part, Pennsylvania: The Pennsylvania University Press.

Forester, J. (1999). *The Deliberative Practioner. Encouraging Participatory Planning Processes*. Cambridge: Cambridge University Press.

Fortenbaugh, W. W. (1975). *Aristotle on Emotion*. London: Duckworth.

Goffman, E. (1969). *The Presentation of Self in Everyday Life.* London: Penguin Books. Original work published 1959.

Goffman, E. (1974). *Frame Analysis.* Cambridge, MA: Harvard University Press.

Gottweis, H. (2006). Argumentative Policy Analysis. In B. Guy Peters & Jon Pierre (ed.) *Public Policy Handbook.* London: Sage.

Habermas, J. (1985). *The Theory of Communicative Action.* Vol.1, 2. Cambridge, MA: Polity.

Healy, P. (1997). *Collaborative Planning.* London: Macmillan.

Hajer, M. (2005). Setting the Stage: A Dramaturgy of Policy Deliberation. *Administration & Society*, 36, 624–647.

Hajer, M. and H. Wagenaar. Introduction. In Hajer, M. & Waagenaar H. (eds.) *Deliberative Policy Analysis: Understanding Governance in Network Society.* Cambridge: Cambridge University Press, 2003.

Hume, D. (1986). *A Treatise on Human Nature.* Ernst C. Mossner (ed.). Viking Press. (Originally published 1739)

Innes, J. J. (2003). Collaborative Policy Making: Governance through Dialogue. In M. Hajer and H. Wagenaar (ed.), *Deliberative Policy Analysis: Understanding Governance in the Network Society.* Cambridge: Cambridge University Press.

Johnstone, C. L. (1996). *Greek Oratorical Settings and the Problem of the Pnyx: Rethinking the Athenian Political Process*, 97–127.

Lutz, C., and G. M. White (1986). The Anthropology of Emotions. *Annual Review of Anthropology, 15:* 405–435.

Lyotard, J-F (1979). *The Post-Modern Condition.* Manchester: Manchester University Press 1984. Maingueneau, D. (2002) *Analyser Les Textes de Communication.* Paris: Nathan.

Majone, G. (1989). *Evidence, Argument and Persuasion in the Policy Process.* New Haven, Conn: Yale University Press.

Meyer, M. (1986). *De la Problématologie. Philosophie, Science et Langage* Bruxelles: Pierre Mardaga. Meyer, M. (1991). *Le Philosophe et les Passions: Esquisse d'une histoire de la nature humanine. Paris:* Le Livre de Poche.

Meyer, M. (1994). *Rhetoric, Language, and Reason.* University Park: Pennsylvania State University Press.

Nussbaum, M. C. (2001*). Upheavals of Thought: The Intelligence of Emotions.* Cambridge: Cambridge University Press.

Perelman, C., and L. Olbrechts-Tyteca. (1958). *Traité de l'Argumentation, la Nouvelle Rhétorique.* Paris: Presse Universitaire de France.

Perelman, C. (1977). *L'Empire Rhétorique.* Vrin: Paris.

Patillon, M. (1990). *Éléments de Rhétorique Classique.* Paris: Nathan.

Putnam, R. (1993). *Making Democracy Work: Civic Traditions in Modern Italy.* Princeton, N.J.: Princeton University Press.

Schön, D. A. and M. Rein (1994). *Frame Reflection: Towards the Resolution of Intractable Policy Controversies.* New York: Basic Books.

Searle, J. (1969). *Speech Acts: An Essay in the Philosophy of Language.* Cambridge: Cambridge University Press.

Stone, D. (1988). *Policy Paradox: The Art of Political Decision Making.* New York: W. W. Norton.

Svasek, M. (2002). The Politics of Emotions. Emotional Discourse and Displays in Post-Cold War Contexts., *Focaal–European Journal of Anthropology, 39:* 9–27.

Throgmorton, J. A. (1991). The Rhetorics of Policy Analysis. *Policy Sciences, 24,* 153–179.

Torgersen, D. (1986). Between Knowledge and Politics: The Three Faces of Policy Analysis. *Policy Sciences, 19,* 33–59.

Toulmin, S. (1958). *The Uses of Argument.* Cambridge: Cambridge University Press.

Turnbull, N. (2003). The Implications of the Division of Logic and Argumentation for Policy Theory. Paper given at the 2nd ECPR Conference, Marburg, 18–21 September 2003.

Turnbull, N. (2005). *Policy in Question: From Problem Solving to Problematology.* Ph.D. Thesis, School of Social Science and Policy, University of New South Wales. Syndey.

White, H. (1981). The Value of Narrativity in the Representation of Reality. In W.J.T. Mitchell (ed.), *On Narrative.* Chicago: University of Chicago Press.

White, H. (1987). *The Content of the Form: Narrative Discourse and Historical Representation.* Baltimore: Johns Hopkins University Press

18 Narrative Policy Analysis

Michel J. G. van Eeten

Given the ubiquitous presence of stories in every aspect of policy, it seemed inevitable that sooner or later, stories would become a central object of study within policy analysis. As it turns out, it was later rather than sooner. For a long time, the field of policy analysis treated stories as inferior forms of information and reasoning, to be passed over in favor rigorous scientific methods and objective data.

It took until the late 1980s before a policy analyst—ironically, one with a background in statistics—demonstrated that good policy analysis revolves around crafting an argument, rather than applying logic and science (Majone 1989). This insight was part of a wider development which has received many labels, but which many have come to know as the "argumentative turn" in policy analysis (Fischer and Forester 1993). According to Fischer (2003), this development has resulted in a set of new approaches that present a "postempiricist" alternative to the dominant technocratic and empiricist models in policy analysis.

Among these new approaches is narrative policy analysis—even if the leading book on narrative policy analysis (Roe 1994) does not subscribe to all elements of the postempiricist agenda. According to Roe (1994, 2), the key practical insight of narrative policy analysis is this: "Stories commonly used in describing and analyzing policy issues are a force in themselves, and must be considered explicitly in assessing policy options." Rather than stories per se, Roe (1994, p. 3) focuses on policy narratives, which he defines as: "those stories—scenarios and arguments—that are taken by one or more parties in the controversy as underwriting and stabilizing the assumptions for policymaking in the face of the issue's uncertainty, complexity or polarization."

This chapter first asks what it means to explicitly consider narratives in policy analysis. It then discusses the variety of answers that researchers have given to that question. Next, we turn to the use of narrative policy analysis as a methodological approach procedure to deal with controversial policy issues marked by conflicting policy narratives. An important concept in this procedure is the notion of the metanarrative, which we explore in some detail. The last part of the chapter presents two brief case studies of actual applications of narrative policy analysis, focusing on the last step: identifying a metanarrative.

NARRATIVE COMMA POLICY COMMA ANALYSIS

What does it mean to explicitly consider narratives in policy analysis? While Roe connects narrative policy analysis with a very specific approach, it is not the only way to take stories into account. Other authors have developed different approaches which could be shared under the same label. What they demonstrate is how the label can be read to imply different methods, units of analysis, and research goals. These approaches configure the terms in the label in different ways. For example:

- the *narrative analysis of policy*, where the methods of narrative analysis are applied to the world of policy, often showing the narrative and symbolic structures that operate in policy processes (e.g., Stone 1997);

- the *analysis of policy narratives*, where different methods—often from the social sciences—are used to reconstruct the stories that actors tell about a policy issues, often showing how the same policy terms or measures are given meaning in different and conflicting ways (e.g., Bedsworth 2004);
- the *policy analysis of narratives*, where different methods—both from literary theory and social science—are used to analyze the relations among conflicting policy narratives in order to develop policy advice on how to proceed, e.g., how to recast the policy issue (e.g., Roe 1994);
- the *narrative of policy analysis*, where narrative analysis is used to excavate the narrative foundations of policy analysis itself, often showing hidden ideological assumptions and power structures and calling for more professional reflexivity and pluralism (e.g., Fischer and Forester 1993).

This is by no means an exhaustive set of configurations, but it does make us sensitive to the diversity of approaches that could lay claim to the label narrative policy analysis. In the literature, we see different choices—or rather, trade-offs—being made with regard to the methods, unit of analysis, and research objective.

As far as methods are concerned, the term *narrative analysis,* strictly speaking, refers to the branch of literary theory knows as narratology.[1] Narratology has developed concepts and methods with the specific aim to study the characteristics of narratives—or more precise—to study texts, broadly defined, in as far as they are narratives. Of course, there is much more going on in any specific text than narrative only, but narratology focuses primarily on the latter. Narrative is, generally speaking, defined as the narration of a sequence of events, where an event is defined as the transition from one state to another (e.g., Bal 1998).

The field has developed concepts to study three key aspects of any narrative: story, text, and narration (Rimmon-Kenan 1983, 3). Story refers to the set of events that are being narrated, abstracted from their specific representation in the text. Here, narrative analysis focuses on events, characters and plot. Text refers to the telling of the story in spoken or written discourse, although narrative analysis has been extended to also study narratives in other media than text. When studying text, narrative analysis tries to make sense of how the story is told, e.g., timing (the narration may not follow the chronology of the story) and so-called "focalization." Focalization is the perspective or prism through which the narrative content is being represented. The third aspect, narration, concerns the act of producing the narrative. The analysis of narration focuses on the narrator(s) and narratees that may be explicitly present in the text, even as characters, or may be implied by it. Of the three aspects, only the actual text is immediately available to the analyst as a unit of analysis. Story and narration can only be studied through the text.

In narrative policy analysis, the term *narrative analysis* sometimes refers to the abovementioned set of concepts and methods from literary theory. An example is the use of Propp's folktale framework to analyze policy narratives around a flooding disaster (Van Eeten 1999b) or development projects (Roe 1989). In addition, the term is used as a loose label to cover a much broader set of methods—basically any method that focuses on language may be used. For Roe, for example, narrative policy analysis is not limited to narrative analysis per se, but employs a variety of methods and concepts from the much wider field of contemporary literary theory (1994, 2).

The term *narrative analysis* may also refer to a related field in the social sciences—a study of how narratives function in the interactions among individuals. Often, these studies employ an ethnographic set of methods. Wagenaar (1995), for example, has made detailed studies of the stories that public servants tell to make sense of the situation in which they or their organizations find themselves. The focus is on what the story tells us about policy practice, more than on the story itself. The stories contain metaphors, distinctions, and other sense-making elements that help the analyst to connect the language of actors to their actions. These types of narrative analysis are quite similar to approaches like frame analysis (Schön and Rein 1994), analysis of belief systems

(Sabatier and Jenkins-Smith 1993), and discourse analysis (Hajer 1995). In terms of methods, this research may apply methods from narratology, but more often the term *narrative analysis* indicates primarily that narratives are taken as the starting point, as the unit of analysis, rather than indicating the use of specific methods.

With regard to the unit of analysis, we also see interesting differences in the literature—and these are related to the tradeoffs regarding methods. Given the origins of narrative analysis, the most straight-forward unit of analysis is an "existing text" of a specific author—e.g., policy papers, news reports, bureaucratic forms, speeches or the oral histories offered by respondents. Like their counterparts in literary theory, some analysts have extended these existing texts to also include other nonverbal artifacts from the world of policy and politics, such as buildings, television images, photographs, and paintings (e.g., Yanow 1995a; Edelman 1995).

While specific, individual texts are a natural unit of analysis, they do pose limitations regarding the kind of generalizations and conclusions the analyst can reason toward. Policy analysis is typically interested in studying processes of collective decision making. Individual texts can be used for this task, insofar as they can be shown to be representative of a certain position or phenomenon at the collective level. Usually, however, this is difficult. One official's speech or oral history is likely to be slightly—or not so slightly—different from that of another official, even if they belong to the same administration. One policy paper is unlikely to reflect perfectly the range of official policy statements made on a specific issue.

Therefore, the analyst often needs a more aggregate unit of analysis than individual texts. For this reason, when analysts write about policy narratives, they often are talking not about a specific text, but about a constructed narrative that is attributed to an actor in a policy issue—in other words, the position of a group, an organization, or even a coalition of organizations. Yanow (1995b, 113) calls this a "constructed text" as opposed to an "authored text," which is the same as the abovementioned existing text. Bridgman and Barry (2002), for example, reconstructed two key policy narratives from a set of unstructured interviews with key stakeholders. On the issue of number portability in the New Zealand telecommunication sector, they aggregated all accounts into two narratives: the dominant telecom's story and the story of its competitors. Others (e.g., Bedsworth et al. 2004; Roe 1994; Van Eeten 1999a) have followed a similar approach.

One step further brings us to even more aggregate units of analysis. Dicke (2001, 10), following Czarniawska (1997), speaks of "societal narratives," which she defines as a "similar lines of reasoning" that is shared by many "little stories"—the latter are what we have called specific existing texts or authored texts. Edelman (1977, 1988) has written extensively about stories and symbolism in the wider political discourse, only loosely connecting his analysis to specific texts.

How these "aggregated" policy narratives are constructed is to be decided by the analyst. Narrative policy analysis does not prescribe any method for this part of the research. The literature shows a variety of methods, including, but not limited to, content analysis (Linder 1995), actor or stakeholder analysis (Bridgman and Barry, 2002), network analysis (Hukkinen et al. 1990), semiotics (Van Eeten and Roe, 2000), and Q-methodology (Van Eeten 2001). In many cases, an explicit method may even be absent and the researcher relies on the plausibility and reconcilability of the positions (e.g., Bedsworth et al. 2004). Typically, this means that the constructed narratives are built on a (presumably) shared idea of what the relevant perspectives on the issue are—often following straight-forward distinctions among actors, along the lines of, say, industry, government, and environmental groups.

Whatever method is followed, the narrative analysis itself starts only *after* the narratives have been (re)constructed—or, in the case of authored texts—identified. How the policy narratives are reconstructed does have consequences for the methods one can apply to them. Many of the methods of narratology rely heavily on "close readings" (i.e., on the specifics of the texts being analyzed). The same could be said of the methods used in the ethnographic approach to narrative analysis. If the text is a highly aggregate construction, then it typically offers less meaningful specifics, providing a less fruitful ground for these methods. The tradeoff is, of course, that the constructed, less specific narrative, allows for a wider generalizability of the conclusions coming out of the analysis. For many policy analysts operating in processes of collective decision making, that generalizability is a prerequisite for their work. So they adopt methods for their narrative analysis that can work with aggregated narratives. Roe's use of the semiotic square to compare and contrast policy narratives is an example of such a method (Roe 1994).

This brings us to the third set of tradeoffs: the research objective. Many of the tradeoffs regarding methods and units of analysis can be understood best by looking at the kind of conclusions the analyst is interested in. The type of conclusion that is preferred also guides what methods and units of analysis are suitable.

Much of the earlier work on narrative and symbolism in policy language set out to unveil and critique hidden ideological and power structures. Murray Edelman (1971, 1977, 1988) has published famous research in this direction. One of his book titles indicates his objective fairly clearly: *Political Language: Words That Succeed and Policies That Fail* (Edelman 1977). Typically, he shows how political and professional elites use language to reinforce the existing power structure and facilitate the quiescent acceptance of chronic poverty and large inequalities. Edelman explicitly admits not subjecting the critics of the current "regimes" to the same analysis, because he is interested in the regimes themselves precisely because of their power. "The whole point," Edelman (1977, 14) writes, "...is to examine the evocation of alternative cognitions." Often, these alternatives are overlooked or actively resisted by the powers that be, he argues.

In certain policy areas, Edelman's goal may have become reality, to some extent. Here, researches are confronted with multiple and conflicting perspectives on the same policy issue—often even on the same evidence (e.g., Throgmorton 1993). Many have turned to language in an attempt to explain how these very different perspectives are possible and what their implications are. Narrative has provided a natural way with which to describe and make sense of these perspectives. For many researchers, the main objective is to demonstrate not only to explain the dynamics of the policy process by demonstrating the presence of multiple and conflicting policy narratives, but also that each of these narratives is valid on its own terms and should be taken into account in the policymaking process. In the words of Bedsworth and colleagues (2004, 406): "These...policy narratives demonstrate how policy actors differ in their drivers for action, bases for trusting claims, and response to uncertainty."

Using narrative to explain action makes clear why most of these researchers do not adhere to a strict definition of narrative, but also incorporate argumentative forms of language. They are interested in what drives the action of actors, how they make the "normative leap" from "is" to "ought" (Schön and Rein 1994). Actors use both narrative and argumentation for this goal—where narratives in a strict sense are stories about a sequence of events with beginning, middle, and ends, as in scenarios, and where arguments are built from premises to conclusions. This is why researchers like Roe and others incorporate both forms in their definition of policy narrative—even if others have argued that arguments and narratives present two different modes of knowing and thinking (Bruner 1986).

Within this strand of literature, researchers explicitly reject judging the different narratives in terms of truth value or establishing the primacy of one narrative over another—though some do try to explain empirically why a specific narrative has become dominant (e.g., Bridgman and Barry 2002). Implicitly or explicitly, this research often critiques the dominant narrative, given the presence of equally valid alternatives often voiced by less powerful stakeholders. This point is equally important at different stages in the policy process—from competing problem definitions to competing evaluations of policies (Abma 1999). Along the same lines, this research critiques technocratic approaches in these cases, since issues can no longer be decided by appealing to "objective facts."

The end point of this strand of literature—demonstrating the presence of conflicting, but equally valid policy narratives with opposing implications for action—is the starting point for other researchers: Given that the presence of these narratives often makes issues intractable, how can we recast the issue? Their research objective is to come up with policy advice that helps actors to move out of the existing impasse. Here, the challenge is to deal with the fact that in these cases is no way to arbitrate between the competing narratives, either on scientific or on other grounds. Several researchers have concluded that in those cases, actors and analysts would do best to develop a new narrative that takes into account the existing narratives, but at the same time is more amenable to deliberation or policy making. This is what Roe (1994) has called identifying a metanarrative. Others have called it recasting or reframing (Rein and Schön 1993). Schön and Rein (1994) describe reframing as an attempt to shift the paradigm of a problem. The approach is an open, deliberative process grounded in argument, evidence, and policy debate where participants can critically reflect and reappraise their initial framing of the issue. Roe's breakthrough insight was to understand how narrative analysis could be used to support this difficult process. We will return to this insight shortly.

As stated earlier, the choice for a research objective influences the choice of methods and unit of analysis. This is not a mechanical or deterministic relationship, but we can indicate certain patterns here. In principle, the research objectives outlined above do not preclude each other. One could make a critical analysis of the hidden power structures of a policy narrative, do the same for the competing narratives, explain how they guide the actions of actors in different directions and try to come up with policy advice on how to proceed, given these conflicting narratives.

In practice, however, narrative policy analysis tends to reflect constraints on time and resources and focus on one of the objectives. Analyzing and critiquing a specific dominant narrative is quite amenable to close readings and the methods of narratology, because one has time to get into the specifics of that narrative—perhaps looking at a set of relevant texts in detail. Similarly, an ethnographic narrative analysis of, say, social service employees' stories about their clients, can devote attention to the oral accounts and specific phrasings of individual respondents. This is different for analysts who are interested in (constructed) narratives that capture the positions of stakeholders in a decision making process. Here, we see more effort going into identifying, constructing and elaborating these narratives, and less to detailed analysis of actual existing texts. We see a similar shift when the objective is to recast a policy issue that is intractable because of conflicting policy narratives. This objective draws resources and attention away from reconstructing the narratives—though that obviously has to be done here too, as the first step—and toward analyzing the relations between those narratives. We can now also see why Roe (1994) employs the semiotic square as a method: it allows him to analyze the relations between the different narratives, which hopefully points to a possible metanarrative. He spends less time applying methods of narrative analysis to the narratives themselves and even less time on methods to identify and reconstruct the individual narratives. Most of his cases simply present the policy narratives as if they are already given and can readily be divided in stories and non-stories. This has given rise to some confusion with researchers trying to adopt his approach. For this reason, we'll slightly revise his approach to make it more transparent and replicable. First, however, we turn to his notion of the metanarrative.

FINDING THE METANARRATIVE

The concept of the metanarrative has drawn considerable attention and, at the same time, generated considerable confusion. The confusion seems to relate to two issues: How is the metanarrative identified and what is its status?

Roe's approach follows four steps (1994, 3–4): First, the analyst identifies the conventional narratives that dominate the issue. Second, he or she identifies the narratives that do not conform to the conventional definition, i.e., "non-stories," such as a circular argument or those that run counter to the dominant narratives. Third, the analyst compares and contrasts the two sets of narratives—stories on the one hand and the non-stories or counter stories on the other—in order to generate a metanarrative "told" by the comparison. Fourth, and last, the analyst determines if or how the metanarrative recasts the issue in such a way as to make it more amenable to deliberation, analysis, and policy making.

Quite literally, the metanarrative is a narrative about other narratives. For Roe, it is a story that can account how the conflicting policy narratives on a certain issue can all be the case at the same time. Furthermore, the analyst—or policy maker or stakeholder—is not looking for just any metanarrative, but for a metanarrative that enables the parties involved to recast the issue to make it more amenable to deliberation, analysis, and policy making. In that sense, the metanarrative is a proposal for a new policy agenda (Van Eeten 1999a). As with all policy advice, it depends on the actors if and how a metanarrative is adopted and indeed successful in recasting the issue.

The metanarrative is not a compromise or common ground. To use a simple illustration: if one narrative says the issue is "black ' and the other says it is "white," then the metanarrative is not "grey" but a term that is both "black" and "white" at the same time (i.e., "coloredness")—or neither "black" nor "white" ("colorlessness"). This is the logic of the semiotic square (Schleifer 1987). The two latter terms can be understood as metaterms which comment on the possibility of the first black-white opposition. Figure 18.1 presents a more interesting illustration of the semiotic square.

By comparing and contrasting the policy narratives on an issue, the relations among them become visible, which may point to a metanarrative. In that sense, Roe (1994, 4) describes the metanarrative as the story that is being "told" by the comparison. Needless to say, the comparison may point to different metanarratives or even to none at all. Furthermore, the comparison may be executed in different ways, leading also to different possible outcomes. This need not be problematic. In fact, more options are welcome. The search is not for the one "correct" metanarrative, but for *a* metanarrative that seems most promising in recasting the issue.

Roe's procedure is unclear in several important respects. First, how is the analyst to identify the stories and the non-stories. Most of his case studies simply present the narratives, as if it is self-evident which narratives are out there, as well as what their structures are—that is, whether they are stories or non-stories. Given the lack of methodological guidance on how the narratives are reconstructed, the first two steps become problematic.[2] If the analyst loosely reconstructs these policy narratives, then especially qualifying a narrative as a non-story runs the risk of being little more than an artifact of the analysis. For this reason, the analyst needs to incorporate more methodological support for the first two steps in his or her research design. The case studies presented in the next sections of this chapter show one way of doing this: by applying Q-methodology, a very appropriate and effective companion to narrative policy analysis.

The second problem with the procedure is that it is unclear why the metanarrative can only be generated by contrasting the stories with the non-stories. To be sure, this is an interesting and promising comparison. To understand the structural differences among the two sets is likely to tell the analyst something about the characteristics of the policy discourse. But the procedure need not be restricted to that comparison only. As we will see in the case studies, different comparisons can

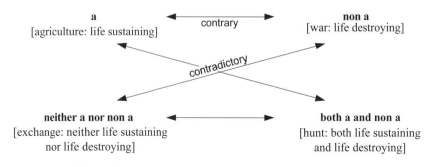

FIGURE 18.1   The semiotic square.

also generate a metanarrative. The semiotic square can help to unravel meaningful relations among the narratives in different ways.

Fischer (2003, 174–75) has lodged three further criticisms to Roe's approach. First, he states that Roe relies on the stories offered by the immediate participants to the story. This is problematic, according to Fischer, because "often the real problem to be dealt with in a public controversy is created by considerations outside the scope of everyday arguments." While Fischer raises a legitimate concern that there may be important perspectives outside the arguments currently present in the debate, his use of the term *the real problem* is awkward and does not seem to fit very well with the postempiricist approach. It is unclear how any consideration could lay claim to describing the "real" problem. While some may consider, say, a Gramscian critique of hegemonic social structures to be helpful and informative, stakeholders trying to influence policy making may find it more helpful to understand the different policy narratives and the relations among them. In short, Fischer's criticism should serve as a warning on the limitations of the method, but it does not seem to invalidate Roe's approach.

Fischer's second criticism is that Roe has failed to incorporate the participation of actors in his approach. While it is true that participation is remarkably absent as a theme in Roe's book, the approach itself seems to have no problem with it. All steps of the procedure could be done in a participatory way. Having the stakeholders actively contrasting different (sets of) narratives may indeed generate interesting results, as well as provide checks on the analytic process. Should a metanarrative come out of this process, chances are it will have more support that a metanarrative that is the product of a lone analyst. That said, the crucial contribution of Roe is that now the analyst at least has some methodological support to facilitate the process of recasting and finding metanarratives—in other words, the analyst can add value to the process.

The third and final criticism that Fischer brings forth, states that Roe should have applied narrative analysis to policy analysis itself. He also takes issue with what he sees as the technocratic orientation of Roe's approach. Roe explicitly acknowledges that a critique of the technocratic foundations of conventional policy analysis can and should be done. It is, however, not the objective of his book. There is already a rich literature that has argued "the argumentative turn" of policy analysis. Roe chooses a more instrumental orientation, aiming to contribute a new methodology to the field of policy analysis. Whatever one may think of these choices, they are not inherent to the approach itself, but rather reflect the agenda under which it is employed. Narrative policy analysis can be employed by different actors—not just analysts—and is quite compatible with different agendas, be they empiricist, postempiricist or otherwise.

This discussion brings us to the last part of this chapter: an application of the approach in two case studies. Given the constraints of the chapter, we briefly go through the steps to illustrate how the approach can be implemented in practice, with the abovementioned considerations in mind.

TWO APPLICATIONS OF NARRATIVE POLICY ANALYSIS

The first case study deals with the conflicting stakeholder views during the formation of the most recent Dutch National Transportation Plan. The second case concerns the controversial expansion of the Amsterdam Schiphol Airport. In both cases the first two steps of the narrative policy analysis were performed using Q-methodology—for more details on the case studies, see Van Eeten (2001; 2003).

How can stakeholders' arguments be identified without forcing a specific problem definition upon them? Q-methodology is especially suited to the task of uncovering positions really held by participants in a debate rather than accepting the predefined categories of decision makers, analysts, or participants. In recent years, Q-methodology has received increasing attention in the policy analysis community, particularly regarding its performance in supporting public involvement initiatives and uncovering and representing stakeholder positions and their interrelations (Dryzek and Berejikian 1993; Durning 1993, 1999; Gargan and Brown, 1993; Maxwell and Brown, 2000; Pelletier et al, 1999; Steelman and Maguire, 1999; Weimer 1999). The method has proven to be fruitful in capturing rich understandings of stakeholder views and positions, thereby making the method an important tool for deliberative democracy, as recognized by Dryzek (1990) over a decade ago.

Q-methodology condenses the variation of views, opinions, and ideas into a set of underlying problem definitions. In a nutshell, the procedure is this: respondents sort a set of statements on the problem. Using factor analysis, the method then identifies factors, which are clusters of statements that are correlated in the sorts of some respondents. These clusters can be interpreted as policy narratives. The elegance of this method is that it is not sensitive to the narratives that the analyst a priori expects to be there—unlike open qualitative interview techniques that often end up reproducing a priori categories such as the different stakeholder groups. This makes the procedure more robust and reliable for the first two steps of narrative policy analysis. Q-methodology also manages to avoid some important drawbacks of surveys, as explained by Dryzek (1990).

Q-methodology was applied in both case studies through a number of steps introduced briefly here.[3] First, in an attempt to reflect the range of opinion, some 200 statements were collected from media archives, advocacy papers, stakeholder meetings, interviews, and policy reports. Especially useful were verbatim reports from several stakeholder meetings, because of the range of arguments and positions expressed in them.

From this collection, a sample of statements was selected to be used in subsequent interviews with stakeholders (75 statements for the case on the Transportation Plan; 80 for the case on airport expansion). To check the representativeness of the sample, a control question was added to the interview protocol: Subjects were asked if they missed any aspect of the issue they believed was relevant to their position. Answers given during the interviews raised no questions as to the sample's validity.

Next, representatives were selected from the stakeholders—24 for the case on Transportation Plan; 38 for the case on airport expansion. For the latter the sample of respondents included representatives of airline corporations, airport management, different levels and sectors of government, national environmental organizations, local citizens, and environmental interest groups, and commercial or regional economic interest groups.

Each representative was asked to perform a Q-sort, in which the respondent models her or his point of view by rank-ordering the statements from the sample along a continuum. The extremes of the distribution were coded "most agree" and "most disagree," with 0 indicating indifference. In standard Q-sort fashion, the respondents were also asked to place the statements in a quasi-normal distribution (Figure 18.2). This encourages the respondents to think about the relationships among the statements more systematically, as well as prioritize the statements in relation to each other. During and after the sorting process, respondents were interviewed to ascertain the reasoning behind their specific ordering.

Last, the Q-sorts were factor-analyzed to identify patterns and commonalities among individuals.[4] In the case study on the Transportation Plan, this led to four significant factors. The case study on airport expansion identified five factors. The policy narratives represented by the factors were

Number of Statements

3	8	16	26	16	8	3
–3	–2	–1	0	+1	+2	+3
most			statement			most
disagree			scores			agree

FIGURE 18.2   The opinion continuum for the Q-sort in the case of airport expansion.

identified by calculating the statements' scores, that is, the weighted average of the scores given to each statement by the Q sorts associated with the factor.

For each case, starting with the case on the Transportation Plan, we briefly summarize the policy narratives that were found and compare and contrast these narratives, in search of a metanarrative that allows us to recast the issue.

CASE STUDY: DUTCH NATIONAL TRANSPORTATION PLAN

Dutch transportation policy had been controversial for years, with stakeholder chastising the last plan for its ineffectiveness with regard to reducing environmental problems, massive congestion, underperforming public transportation, and fragmented administrative relations, among other issues. The last plan, officially presented by government in 1990, had very ambitious objectives on these issues. It fell short on virtually all of its ambitions.

In the spring of 1998, the Ministry of Transportation, Public Works and Water Management initiated a deliberative process to inform the development of the new National Transportation Plan. After several brainstorm sessions with potential participants, the ministry identified eight recurrent themes in the discussion it saw as important for writing the new plan.[5]

Around these themes, eight deliberative platforms were organized with around ten participants each and chaired by the participants themselves. The invitation to participate was sent out widely, though for the most part to people who, in one way or the other, had a professional involvement in transportation. The result was a mix of representatives from different sectors of local, regional, provincial and national government, academics and consultants, and stakeholder representatives from environmental organizations, the transportation sector, labor unions, and industry. In total, over a hundred persons participated in the deliberative process. Funds were allocated to each platform so they could be fairly self-organizing.

Over the course of the summer, the process peaked in intensity. In just a few months, the eight platforms produced over 65 documents adding up to several inches of fact finding reports, opinions, problem descriptions, discussions, vision statements, recommendations, feedback from outsiders, and observations on the process itself. Although officially authored by each platform as a whole, the documents were actually multi-authored and multi-varied statements and recommendations on transportation issues.

The task to capture the outcomes of the platform deliberations quickly proved much more difficult than anticipated. There was a plethora of positions, recommendations and, more tangible, documents. The connections among the themes seemed elusive and the topic of much debate within the project. Beforehand, the project team expected that the stakeholders would form coalitions around different sets of policy measures, which could then be identified as alternatives to developed and prepared for decision-making in the plan. Things turned out differently. Many policy measures had support from a wide range of actors, but for different reasons.

In support of its task, the project team then commissioned a policy analysis using Q-methodology to distill the main perspectives underlying—or, if you will, overarching—the many views on the eight themes of the platforms. This way, it hoped to get a better sense of what the different directions were for transportation policy, as well as identifying the agenda for subsequent deliberations. Following are the main policy narratives that were identified by the Q study.

A. Scarcity Narrative

Starting from a market approach to transportation, the narrative takes note of all manner of "scarcities" in the transport systems (as reflected in, e.g., traffic congestion and externalities associated with car pollution), whose costs need to be better allocated, i.e., the economic distribution of costs and benefits associated with these scarcities is asymmetrical. More rational allocation of transportation infrastructure and services is inhibited by the fact that the prices governing the transportation system rarely reflect the true costs and benefits of transport. The use of infrastructure, for example, is "free" after paying what is basically an entrance fee in the form of road tax. Moreover, the cost is fixed, no matter how much of the infrastructural capacity one uses or how much capacity is available. The demand for transport mobility is therefore not matched optimally to the supply of infrastructure for that mobility. Similarly, the externalities of transport, such as environmental damage and the use of natural resources, are not reflected in the price.

From this narrative, the policy answer is to implement measures that price transportation toward "telling the truth," i.e., reflecting the real costs. For example, government should stop treating road infrastructure as a collective good to be financed through public investments, and instead deal with it as a private good whose price structure more rationally matches individual willingness and ability to pay.

B. Logistics Narrative

Here the overriding concern is to optimize the logistical performance of the transportation system as a network. According to the narrative, the system generates all manner of socio-economic benefits, not the least of which is the crucial part the network plays in a Dutch economy heavily reliant on transportation and the efficient distribution of goods and services. "The Netherlands, Gateway to Europe," was the shorthand phrase for this narrative. The main problem is that there are logistical bottlenecks which cause inefficiencies and harm the environment. Transport arteries are clogged and economic centers become increasingly difficult to reach. In this view, the growing demand for transportation mobility is not intrinsically problematic. Quite the contrary, the real problems—the bottlenecks—accordingly require better governmental management and interventions.

Policy answers to reduce or otherwise alleviate bottlenecks include building new infrastructure and measures aimed at more efficient use of the existing network infrastructure. These latter incorporate proposals aimed at enhancing traffic flows as well as ensuring the economically most beneficial road uses, such as cargo transport, get priority over uses deemed less important, such as commuter traffic. The instruments used depend on the specific bottleneck and may include regulation, pricing, and changes in road design, among others.

C. Pragmatic Narrative

In contrast to other narratives, the dominant storyline here is not about the state of transportation, but about the lessons from past policies. Past experience has taught officials that transportation problems are complex, manifold and cannot be understood from a single, coherent perspective. In this estimation, our understanding is permanently incomplete, best reflected in the fact that the track record of the answers proposed by the other narratives has been very mixed. Anyway, what works has proven to be highly context-dependent. The officials and stakeholders advocating this narrative are weary of any "new" transportation policy or framework and instead argue that what is needed are not "new" answers (assuming they are even possible), but more intelligent and flexible uses of what is already known pragmatically.

In principle, the policy answers to problems in the transportation system include the whole repertoire of known measures. The real challenge is customize case- and region-specific, tailor-made policy packages for the panoply of transportation issues. One instrument, like prices, may work for one problem and region, but you need different sets of instruments for other problems and regions.

D. TECHNOLOGICAL NARRATIVE

The transportation system faces serious problems, including congestion and environmental harm. The system, however, is a highly valued public service, and what is needed to address its problems are major technological innovation and experimentation. The large-scale adoption of new technologies will result in a high quality transport system that is, moreover, sustainable and accessible to all social groups, the two core values in this narrative. One example is to transform public transport systems into "individualized collective transport systems," i.e., electric cars for the city combined with parking lots and connections to other transport modes at the periphery. Many technologies, in the view of this narrative's advocates, are already available but remain unused because of a variety of institutional and economic barriers. The task of government is to eliminate these barriers.

Here the policy answers are a variety of measures to bring about technological innovation. Such measures may include governmental investments in the technologies as well as other policy instruments such as pricing and regulation.

Each of the narratives has very different policy implications, even when they appear to ask for the same measures. Take the issue of ameliorating congestion by reducing the number of cars on the road—a major objective of the previous plan which it had spectacularly failed to achieve. From the scarcity narrative, reduction in car numbers would never be a goal in and of itself, but rather would only be a byproduct of full-cost pricing. From the logistic narrative, it already is current Dutch policy to reduce the number of cars on the road, but only at certain times and places. Cars are a problem in so far as they are linked to certain logistical bottlenecks. From the pragmatic narrative, reduction in car numbers is always a live policy option, but its relevance would have to be judged on a case-by-case basis and would certainly never be a system-wide goal or priority. From the technological narrative, reducing the number of cars on the roads means a technologically different kind of car or a solution which may not even be car-based. The real goal is not to get fewer cars on the road but to develop technology to get the right cars on the road.

What can narrative analysis tell us about the relations among these narratives? Here, the semiotic square appears to be helpful. A first starting point is the opposition between the logistics narrative and the scarcity narrative. These two captured the main division in the public debate at that time.

The logistics narrative had been the main rationale behind the existing policy and had driven implementation programs for years. The scarcity narrative, on the other hand, was the new contender which had rapidly gained support. Its emphasis on pricing and markets was more and more underwritten by different governmental agencies as the future direction for transportation policy. Actual attempts to implement it, however, faced fierce resistance and failed almost without exception. It took about ten years for government to develop and agree upon an initiative for electronic road pricing around the three largest Dutch cities, only to see its political support crumble as soon as the system moved toward implementation. So far, the scarcity narrative is by and large policy and very little implementation. The overall result has a completely inert transportation policy, notwithstanding the broadly-felt need for change in light of the current problems.

Taking the scarcity-logistics opposition as the starting point, we can see how the complex terms that rises out of opposition (both policy and implementation, neither policy nor implementation) denote the two remaining narratives. In an important sense, both are alternatives arising from the opposition between logistics and scarcity. Together, the four narratives form a semiotic square about interventions, i.e., the way they relate to the day-to-day implementation of policy (Figure 18.3).

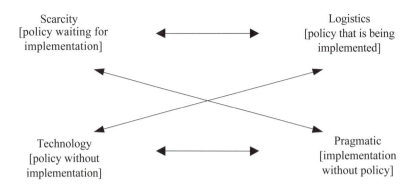

FIGURE 18.3 Semiotic square on future transportation policy.

If we read the first opposition to be about policy that is being implemented or not being implemented, then pragmatic argument clearly signifies the position that is both implemented and not implemented. Here, it is all implementation without policy. Or rather, whatever happens in implementation *is* policy. Some of its proponents even expressed hostility regarding what they felt was an overkill of "new" policy that never made it to implementation. In fact, many respondents indicated they saw the national transportation policy as a major obstacle, not a source of support, to getting effective and innovative regional initiatives off the ground. The reason that it does not propose a transportation policy in the way the others do, also explains why this narrative has a marginal presence, if any, in most formal documents—indeed, why it is hardly recognized as a policy narrative at all.

In sharp contrast to this stands the technological narrative that neither is accepted as policy, nor guides implementation. Narrative D has an aura of science fiction around, ironically by being too specific. That is, there are futuristic videos and computer presentations of major technological innovations that, according to this narrative, need to be adopted by government. The imagery is almost too operational, while for many the systems portrayed seem far removed from current transportation policy and practice. As a result, the option seems all the more unbelievable. In fact, proponents of D have tried to come up with proposals that connect with existing government programs, in order to get out of the sci-fi realm, but many people think the government will never get there. It's simply too far fetched. But if far-fetched is measured by government adoption, then the real issue is how unbelievable it would be as a government policy.

As a whole, the semiotic square raises another opposition: between policy narratives that tightly couple policy to implementation (A, B) and those that decouple them (C, D). Narrative C argues that innovation—defined as the implementation of change—is only possible if the constraints of policy on operations are lifted, while D argues that real innovation has to be freed from the constraints of here-and-now feasibility and implementation in a fragmented policy sector. This could be cast as a new semiotic square (Figure 18.4).

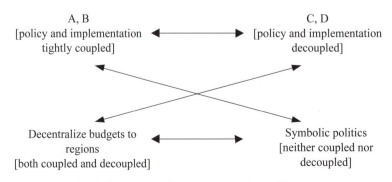

FIGURE 18.4 Semiotic square on future transportation policy.

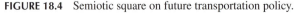

The metanarrative this may point to is to massively decentralize the transportation budgets. Such a move would by and large decouple between national policy and regional implementation, but at the same time it would couple regional policy—which is now the policy that matters in terms of funding—to regional implementation. This puts in a different light the failure of the road pricing initiative around the three biggest cities taken under the scarcity narrative. If the congestion of these cities is indeed as problematic as many argue, why did these cities themselves not initiate a road pricing scheme, irrespective of the national support for such a measure?

The neither/nor term points to an alternative that could never explicitly become official policy, but is nevertheless a real live option: national transportation policy becomes a game of symbolic politics. The transportation ministry sees its policies as a symbolic means to influence regional activities. Whatever implementation efforts may occur in practice, when needed, the ministry would try to appropriate them as belonging to the policy.

CASE STUDY: THE CONTROVERSIAL EXPANSION OF AMSTERDAM AIRPORT

Since the mid 1980s, the Dutch government has struggled with the trade-off between the economic importance of Schiphol and the environmental impact of the increasing air traffic. It took some ten years to forge the difficult political compromise the cabinet eventually agreed upon. The plan set out a twofold objective: expand Schiphol Airport with a fifth runway, and reduce the airport's environmental impact. New and more stringent standards were established for noise pollution. One intent of expansion was to reduce the number of people experiencing aircraft noise as a severe nuisance by spreading aircraft movements over a larger area. Besides reducing noise pollution, the plan adopted a standstill policy for safety, local air pollution, and odor nuisance (meaning their levels may not increase beyond 1990 levels).

Parliament reluctantly accepted the plan in 1995, but not before significantly amending it. Members of parliament were afraid that if the rate of growth exceeded predictions, the Civil Aviation Authority might grant the airport too much leeway regarding the noise standards. Therefore, they added an amendment limiting Schiphol's growth not to exceed a maximum volume of 44 million passengers and 3.3 million tons of cargo per year. Unfortunately, in the very year the plan was published, 1995, the actual passenger and cargo volumes equaled those the model predicted for 2004. Equally unfortunate, economic growth had actually been lower than the model assumed. The limit on Schiphol's growth was rapidly coming closer.

So once again, government faced an expansion decision for the airport. In 1996, at parliament's request, the central government set up an interagency project called Future Dutch Aviation Infrastructure (TNLI). TNLI was to address the issue through extensive deliberation with stakeholders, answering the core question (TNLI 1997, iii): "Do we want to accommodate further growth of civil aviation in the Netherlands? The central question is whether further growth is beneficial and necessary. What are the advantages and disadvantages, the costs and benefits, the challenges and risks?"

This framing of the problem mirrored the debate's polarized agenda. Stakeholders clustered around the positions for or against further growth, along well-established lines. The positions marked the ends of a continuum of available alternatives, placing more moderate policy arguments, such as "selective growth" and "mitigate negative effects," somewhere toward the middle.

Stakeholder deliberations were already underway, when the TNLI-project commissioned a policy analysis using Q-methodology in order to map the stakeholder positions and find leads on how to proceed with the controversial expansion decision. The analysis identified five policy narratives.

A. Societal Integration Of A Growing Airport

This narrative argues that the societal benefits of the airport are highly valued. On the other hand, the problem of noise pollution is of utmost importance. In no other policy narrative are costs and benefits articulated so clearly alongside one another. Balancing the two is at the core of the narrative. Furthermore, the costs and benefits are conceptualized mainly from a regional, spatial perspective, that is, in terms of their effects on the region surrounding the airport. Respondents consider noise pollution a much more important costs of the growing airport than, say, carbon dioxide (CO_2) emissions. The benefits are also recognized to have this regional spatial ambit—society must provide space for civil aviation because it greatly contributes to the region's international business climate.

In sum, this policy narrative insists that in the region a positive balance must be struck between these costs and benefits, if integration of the airport into the wider society is to succeed.

B1 Expansion of Aviation Infrastructure as a Necessity In the Face of International Economic Competition

B1 is the narrative driving the original Schiphol Airport expansion proposal and its continuing support. Like policy narrative A, this one values highly the economic benefits of civil aviation, albeit the focus is now international rather than regional. B1 emphasizes the international context of civil aviation and the need to invest in the sector to retain the socioeconomic benefits.

If the Netherlands does not invest in expansion, it will lose its strong position in this sector, so this narrative claims, because other countries do invest and with substantial effect. Since transport and infrastructure are considered to be the backbone of the Dutch economy, the international position of the national economy as a whole will suffer accordingly. This will lead to a variety of negative consequences, most notably, loss of jobs and its multiplier effect.

All in all, this narrative calls for investment in expansion while there are still opportunities to do so. Respondents recognize the environmental problems of expansion, but in this narrative the environmental problems do not affect the perceived necessity for growth. Expansion can occur within noise and safety standards because airport growth can be accommodated at a new location where the effects on the human population are considerably lower, e.g., on a artificial island off the coast. As far as the global environmental effects of aviation are concerned, it agrees with the preceding policy position: No expansion in the Netherlands will lead to a displacement of pollution elsewhere or even an increase in pollution overall. In other words, whatever happens, the effects of further growth are unavoidable.

B2 Expansion of Civil Aviation Infrastructure as an Unjustified Use of Public Funds

Since the current controversy is polarized, interviewers would expect to find a passionate narrative against airport expansion, and, indeed, the Q analysis strongly confirms this. Policy narrative B2 is B1's opposite. The same cluster of statements from the Q-sort articulates both narratives. As would be expected in polarization, they treat the same aspects as central, but their assessment of these statements is diametrically opposed. Where B1 claims that infrastructural expansion is a necessity from the perspective of international economic survival, B2 casts serious doubt on the importance of the civil aviation sector for the Dutch economy.

Investing in the expansion of aviation infrastructure is not only unnecessary, it is an unjustified use of scarce public resources. The policy of "The Netherlands, Gateway to Europe" entails costs that are too high in terms of infrastructure and environmental damage, while its socioeconomic benefits, if real, are fairly low. The capacity problem for Schiphol Airport is not considered real, but rather a self-inflicted difficulty. It is therefore nonsensical, according to this policy narrative, to claim that the current growth of civil aviation somehow forces the Netherlands to expand. Because the benefits of and necessity for expansion are absent, it is much better to refrain from, if not actively resist, accommodating further growth. Much better opportunities for investment are available, such as information and communication technology. These show more economic promise while entailing fewer disadvantages.

C. Ecological Modernization of the Civil Aviation Sector

The narrative advanced by position C, as in B2, is critical of civil aviation in the Netherlands. But unlike B2, the critical stance does not stem from an assessment of the disadvantages of further growth. Growth or no growth is a secondary issue here. Instead the narrative focuses on the conditions under which civil aviation as a sector and its key industries operate.

Civil aviation is controversial in this narrative because the conditions are absent that would ensure that the sector functions in a sustainable way. A central point in the line of narrative is that the sector has not internalized the real costs of aviation, particularly environmental externalities. This is partly because government treats the sector differently from other branches of industry. Standards for noise pollution and acceptable risks are less stringent than for other industries and there is no levy on kerosene or value-added tax on tickets and related services. There are also hidden subsidies.

The sector needs to take the real costs of its operations into account. When done, this will more or less automatically lead to a sustainable mode of operating. In this way, civil aviation will become more like other sectors, such as the chemical industry, in undergoing what has been called ecological modernization (Hajer 1995). The price structures of air traffic should start to reflect the true costs of aviation. Implementation of a levy on aviation fuel and a value-added tax on tickets is a good starting point, as are upgrading noise and safety standards. According to this policy narrative, what hampers ecological modernization, and what needs critical evaluation, is government's multiple roles in the civil aviation sector.

D. Sustainable Solutions To a Growing Demand for Mobility

Narrative D approaches the issue mainly as a problem of the growing demand for mobility; that is, people want to travel more, whatever the means of transportation (land, air, or otherwise). On the one hand, the regional and global environmental problems of civil aviation are deemed severe. On the other, the growing mobility—of which increased air traffic is an important part—is a largely independent development that has proceeded irrespective of government policy to intervene.

Accommodating further growth of mobility, and the demand for it, is less an option than a necessity according to this narrative. Mobility will increase one way or another. At the same time, the narrative underscores the severity of the environmental problems associated with mobility growth. Combining these two elements, leads this narrative to emphasize the search for sustainable solutions to the growing demand for mobility. No other narrative pays so much attention to the need to substitute air traffic with other forms of transportation that have fewer environmental consequences. Also, the narrative calls for "greening" the design and management of the aviation infrastructure needed to accommodate growth.

We are now in a position to determine whether and how these narratives recast the issue. Arguments B1 and B2 reflect the prevailing polarization for or against further growth and infrastructure expansion. Arguments A, C, and D, however, define related but different problems and call for different measures. The analysis indicates that these narratives are relatively independent.[6]

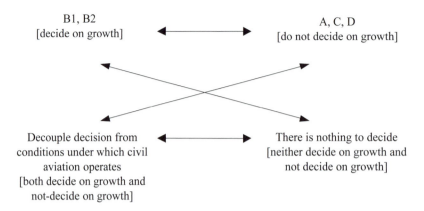

FIGURE 18.5   Semiotic square on airport expansion.

However, A, C, and D are habitually collapsed into and treated as part and parcel of the positions for or against growth. In that sense, we can qualify them as non-stories. Instead of conflating the non-stories into B1 or B2, the data insist that they can be more sensibly viewed as relatively independent from (indeed orthogonal to) the continuum of for-or-against further growth. For example, three respondents subscribe to both narrative C and B1, while five others subscribe to C and B1's opposite, B2.

When we contrast B1 and B2—the dominant narratives—with A, C, and D—the non-stories—we get a semiotic square that points to a metanarrative (Figure 18.5).

In opposition to the dominant narratives, it is clear that non-stories do not see the decision on growth as the key issue for policy. To illustrate: Evaluating the costs and benefits of further growth is a non-issue in the ecological modernization argument (C). The argument is chiefly concerned with the conditions under which the civil aviation sector operates and the conditions needed to bring about sustainable development. Whether further growth will occur under these conditions is another question—one that does not need answering—according to this policy argument, since the market will answer it after the fact. Similarly, A and D do not see the decision on the expansion itself as the core issue.

This opposition points to a metanarrative: decouple the expansion decision from the issues articulated by A, C, and D. Give the latter narratives their own policy agendas. This way, whatever the outcome of the expansion decision, the government can still make important advances with regard to A, C, and D. It could, for example, begin to put into place "normal" operating conditions for the civil aviation sector: fuel taxes, enforceable noise standards that actually offer legal protection to citizen, and the dismantling of hidden subsidies. This would cut across the polarized stakeholder positions marked by B1/B2, given that in both camps there is support for A, C and D. And at least as important: Of 38 stakeholder representatives, 13 had stronger affinity with the arguments A, C, or D and the proposals these represent, than with arguments B1 or B2. This means that for them it is more important that action is taken on these issues, than that the expansion decision goes one way or the other.

The neither/nor term of the semiotic square is also a kind of metanarrative, albeit one that is not very amenable to further deliberation and analysis: it argues that there is really nothing to decide. This is the cynical view that some stakeholders ended up with after the arduous deliberative process. They saw the whole ordeal as a ritual. In reality, no political authority would ever stop airport expansion.

IN CONCLUSION

The emergence of narrative policy analysis has been a remarkable innovation within policy analysis. True enough, the identification of metanarratives have not put an end to controversy and polarization in the policy world. It seems unlikely that any product of policy analysis and advice could meet such a test. That said, the method has been able to generate surprising insights and valuable advice, if the recipients of the studies I was involved in are any measure. These insights and advice did not make their work much easier, but it did help them to identify areas where some progress was possible. Marginal progress, some would say. But as policy veterans Neustadt and May (1986, xvii) have said, "Marginal improvement is worth seeking. Indeed, we doubt that there is any other kind."

In this sense, narrative policy analysis has taken up Majone's advice on how to "improve the quality of public deliberation" for complex policy problems. "Good policy analysis," he argues, "[. . .] provides an intellectual structure for public discourse." This structuring is especially important "when factual or value premises are moot, when there are no generally accepted criteria of rightness, [because then] the procedure of decision making acquires special significance and cannot be treated as purely instrumental." The structure needs to "facilitate a wide-ranging dialogue" among the advocates of different views (Majone, 1989, 7, 17, 183).

Narrative policy analysis has not generated a sweeping professional movement, by any stretch of the imagination. However, it did manage to find appeal both within the postempiricist movement, as well as within mainstream policy analysis. Roe's work has been widely reviewed and cited. On a more personal note, my case study on the expansion of Amsterdam Schiphol Airport managed to receive the Vernon Prize of 2001 for best paper in the *Journal of Policy Analysis and Management*. Other authors using some form of narrative analysis have managed to get published in the major journals. All this is good news.

The attention given to narrative policy analysis from mainstream—"technocratic," if you will—policy analysis has raised some eyebrows and attracted suspicion in the postempiricist community. While some may frown on instrumentalism per se—a somewhat paradoxical view for a field that was founded to be exactly that: instrumental to decision making—one can also see this as a crosswalk to get across some of the important messages of the postempiricist agenda.

NOTES

1. For a brief overview of narratology, see: http://www.press.jhu.edu/books/hopkins_guide_to_literary_theory/narratology.html.
2. In the appendix to *Narrative Policy Analysis*, Roe does offer a methodological elaboration on how "ideally" his approach should be implemented. While he presents an interesting and valid methodological approach that is more specific about the first two steps of the analysis, it does not address our concerns. First of all, the proposed "ideal" method seems unnecessarily restrictive. It is really just one way, and a rather unusual one at that, to operationalize the first two steps. Second, Roe himself applied this ideal procedure in only one of his case studies. Apparently the other were possible without it. This also points to the fact that there are other ways to achieve the same goal.
3. For an excellent general discussion of Q-methodology, see Brown (1980).
4. After calculating the correlations, a centroid factor analysis was performed, which was then rotated according to the varimax principle. The number of extracted factors was limited to four because additional factors did not contribute more than a handful of percentage points to the total explained variance and had negligible statistical significance.
5. The eight themes were: (1) the tension between individual needs and collective interests; (2) accessibility: destinations and connections; (3) using infrastructure: doing more with the same; (4) the environment as a crucial aspect of developing and implementing policy; (5) technology: mobility without drawbacks;

(6) the state and the market; (7) administrative relations: decentralization where possible, centralization where needed; (8) the international dimension of transportation policy.

6. For a full explanation of why these narratives are relatively independent, see Van Eeten (2001, p. 404).

REFERENCES

Abma, T. (1999), *Telling Tales: On Evaluation and Narrative. Advances in Program Evaluation*, Vol. 6, JAI Press, 1999.

Bal, M. (1998), *Narratology: Introduction to the Theory of Narrative*, University of Toronto Press.

Bedsworth, L.W., M.D. Lowenthal, W.E. Kastenberg (2004), Uncertainty and Regulation: The Rhetoric of Risk in the California Low-Level Radioactive Waste Debate. *Science, Technology & Human Values*, 29 (3): 406–427.

Bridgman, T. and D. Barry (2002), Regulation is evil: An application of narrative policy analysis to regulatory debate in New Zealand. *Policy Sciences*, 35: 141–161.

Bruner, J. (1986), *Actual Minds, Possible Worlds*, Cambridge, MA: Harvard University Press.

Czarniawska, B. (1997), *Narrating the Organization: Dramas of Institutional Identity*, Chicago: Chicago University Press.

Dicke, W.M. (2001), *Bridges and Watersheds: A Narrative Analysis of Water Management in the Netherlands, England and Wales*, Amsterdam: Aksant.

Dryzek, J.S. (1990), *Discursive Democracy: Politics, Policy, and Political Science*, Cambridge: Cambridge University Press.

Dryzek, J.S. and J. Berejikian (1993), Reconstructive democratic theory. *American Political Science Review*, 87: 48–60.

Durning, D. (1993), Participatory policy analysis in a social-service agency: A case-study,. *Journal of Policy Analysis and Management*, 12 (2): 297–322.

Durning, D. (1999), The transition from traditional to postpositivist policy analysis: A role for Q-methodology. *Journal of Policy Analysis and Management*, 18 (3): 389–410.

Edelman, M. (1971), *Politics as Symbolic Action: Mass Arousal and Quiescence*, New York: Academic Press.

Edelman, M. (1977), *Political Language: Words that Succeed and Policies that Fail*, New York: Academic Press.

Edelman, M. (1988), *Constructing the Political Spectacle*, Chicago: University of Chicago Press.

Edelman, M. (1995), *From Art to Politics: How Artistic Creations Shape Political Conceptions*, Chicago: University of Chicago Press.

Fischer, F. (2003), *Reframing Public Policy: Discursive Politics and Deliberative Practices*, New York: Oxford University Press.

Fischer, F. and J. Forester (eds.) (1993), *The Argumentative Turn in Policy Analysis and Planning*, Durham/ London: Duke University Press.

Gargan, J.J. and S.R. Brown (1993). What is to be done? Anticipating the future and mobilizing prudence. *Policy Sciences*, 26: 347–359.

Hajer, M.A. (1995), *The Politics of Environmental Discourse: Ecological Modernization and the Policy Process*, Oxford: Clarendon.

Hukkinen, J., Rochlin, G.I. and Roe, E.M. (1990). A Salt on the Land: A Narrative Analysis of the Controversy over Irrigation-Related Salinity and Toxicity in California's San Joaquin Valley. *Policy Sciences*, 23 (4): 307–329.

Linder, S.H. (1995), Contending Discourses in the Electric and Magnetic Fields Controversy: The Social Construction of EMF Risk as a Public Problem. *Policy Sciences*, 28: 209–230.

Majone, G. (1989), *Evidence, Argument, and Persuasion in the Policy Process*. New Haven: Yale University Press.

Maxwell, J and S.R. Brown (2000). Identifying problems and generating solutions under conditions of conflict. *Operant Subjectivity*, 23 (1): 31–51.

Pelletier, D., Kraak, V., McCullum, C., Uusitalo, U., Rich, R. (1999). The shaping of collective values through deliberative democracy: An empirical study from New York's North Country, *Policy Sciences*, 32 (2): 103–131.

Rein, M. and D. Schön (1993), Reframing Policy Discourse, in: Fischer, F. and J. Forester (eds.) (1993), *The Argumentative Turn in Policy Analysis and Planning*, Durham/London: Duke University Press, 145–166.

Rimmon-Kenan, S. (1983), *Narrative Fiction: Contemporary Poetics*, London: Methuen.

Roe, E.M. (1989), Folktale Development. *The American Journal of Semiotics*, vol. 6 (2/3): 277–289.

Roe, E.M. (1994), *Narrative Policy Analysis: Theory and Practice*, Durham/London: Duke University Press.

Hukkinen, J., G.I. Rochlin, E.M. Roe (1990), A Salt on the Land: A Narrative Analysis of the Controversy over Irrigation-Related Salinity and Toxicity in California's San Joaquin Valley. *Policy Sciences*, 23 (4): 307–329.

Sabatier, P.A. and H.C. Jenkins-Smith (eds.) (1993), *Policy Change and Learning: An Advocacy Coalition Approach*, Boulder, CO: Westview Press.

Schleifer, R. (1987), *A.J. Greimas and the Nature of Meaning: Linguistics, Semiotics, and Discourse Theory,* London/Sydney: Croom/Helm.

Schön, D.A. and M. Rein (1994), *Frame Reflection: Toward the Resolution of Intractable Policy Controversies*, New York: Basic Books.

Steelman, T.A. and L.A. Maguire (1999), Understanding participant perspectives: Q-methodology in national forest management. *Journal of Policy Analysis and Management* 18 (3): 361–388.

Stone, D.A. (1997), *Policy Paradox and Political Reason*, Boston: Harper Collins.

The Rhetoric of Risk in the California Low-Level Radioactive Waste Debate. *Science, Technology & Human Values*, Vol. 29 No. 3: 406–427.

Throgmorton, J. (1993), Survey Research as Rhetorical Trope: Electric Power Planning Arguments in Chicago, in: Fischer, F. and J. Forester (eds.) (1993), *The Argumentative Turn in Policy Analysis and Planning*, Durham/London: Duke University Press, 117–144.

TNLI (Project of Ministry of Transport, Public Works, and Water Management, Ministry of Housing, Spatial Planning, and the Environment, and Ministry of Economic Affairs) (1997). Hoeveel ruimte geeft Nederland aan luchtvaart? Perspectievennota. The Hague: SDU.

Van Eeten, M.J.G. (1999a), *Dialogues of the Deaf: Defining New Agendas for Environmental Deadlocks*, Delft: Eburon.

Van Eeten, M.J.G. (1999b), Morality, Uncertainty, and Controversy: A Metanarrative about Flooding and Dike Improvement, in: Abma, T. (1999), *Telling Tales: On Evaluation and Narrative. Advances in Program Evaluation*, Volume 6, JAI Press, 1999, 53–78.

Van Eeten, M.J.G. (2001), Recasting Intractable Policy Issues: The Wider Implications of the Netherlands Civil Aviation Controversy. *Journal of Policy Analysis and Management*, vol. 20 (3): 391–414.

Van Eeten, M.J.G. (2003), *Taking the Public Seriously: Linking Deliberative Democracy and Collective Decisionmaking*. Manuscript under review.

Van Eeten, M.J.G. and E.M. Roe, (2000), When Fiction Conveys Truth and Authority: The Netherlands Green Heart Planning Controversy. *Journal of the American Planning Association*, vol. 66 (1): 58–76.

Wagenaar, H. (1995), Urgent Stories: Morality and Narrative in Public Administration. *Administrative Theory and Praxis*, 17 (1): 92–104.

Weimer, W.L. (1999). Comment: Q-method and the isms. *Journal of Policy Analysis and Mangement*, 18 (3): 426–429.

Yanow, D. (1995a), Built Space as Story: The Policy Stories that Buildings Tell. *Policy Studies Journal*, 23: 407–422.

Yanow, D. (1995b), Practices of Policy Interpretation: Editors Introductory Essay to the Special Issue "Policy Interpretation." *Policy Sciences*, 28: 111–126.

Part VI

Comparative, Cultural, and Ethical Perspectives

19 Comparative Public Policy

Martin Lodge

INTRODUCTION

Why do some states adopt seemingly coercive measures to achieve particular policy goals while others rely on voluntary compliance? How significant is a particular regional policy initiative? Do parties in government matter in terms of policy outputs and outcomes? These are the type of questions that are at the heart of comparative public policy research. Comparison, arguably the oldest social science activity in the world, has allowed for the generation of many accounts seeking to explain particular policy developments. Generalizations from comparatively informed research has established the following particular conventional wisdoms:

- The past two decades have been decades of neoliberalism, with the United Kingdom (UK) at the forefront. The widespread adoption of economic and social policy reforms is said to have led to a "regulatory state" (Majone 1997; Moran 2003). One example that is said to be representative of this period of sustained policy change in Britain has been the regulatory reform of the British railways.
- The UK has the "fastest law of the West" (Dunleavy 1995, 60). Largely manufactured by the plurality electoral system, single-party governments can usually rely on stable majorities in parliament and, given the absence of any other powerful and potentially countervailing political institutions, the majority party in the House of Commons is able to form an "elective dictatorship." Two decades of bureaucratic slimming down and de-hierarchisation have caused the UK to be seen as *the* political system that is most likely to produce policy failures, if not fiascos (see Dunleavy 1995). One widely used example of such policy pattern has been the 1991 Dangerous Dogs Act, which, for a time, held the dubious title ("awarded" by the UK government's Better Regulation Task Force) of being a prime example of the knee jerk response type of policy making (see Hood, Baldwin, and Rothstein 2000). Although the 1991 Act received initial cross-party and media support, it was consequently seen as a disproportionate and ill-considered government response to a public outcry after the killing in public of innocent and vulnerable people by dogs deemed particularly aggressive.
- To achieve desired outputs, credible commitment of the regulatory framework is necessary. In situations where private investors cannot be sure of the motivations of the government, and therefore fear expropriation, governments need to develop devices to signal credible commitment in order to attract investment. For Levy and Spiller (1994), the story of designing credible regulatory mechanisms lies at the heart of the success story of Jamaican telecommunications over the past decade or so. According to their account, without a system that minimized the discretion of national administrative and political actors via a licensing regime, investment by the incumbent, Cable & Wireless, in the expansion of the telecommunications network would not have been achieved.

So far, so normal. All three stories seem to perform to type, in terms of following the usual interests of public policy analysis in explaining policy developments and in terms of concerns such as "party matters" or "institutions matter." Similar accounts could have been developed for other

273

countries, for example the *Rechtsstaat* and gridlock nature that is said to dominate policy making in Germany or the supposedly statist instincts that allegedly characterise policy making in France. Is, therefore, the confirmation of stereotypes all that comparative public policy can contribute to our understanding of public policy? Let us consider three qualifications to the above stories:

- If vertical separation is regarded as the indicator of neoliberalism that was present in the British administration when the British Railways Act 1993 was adopted and which led to the adoption of a vertical separation between infrastructure and operational services as well as to large-scale organizational privatization and fragmentation (and a public subsidy regime relying on franchising), then it should not be expected that other countries would follow a similar path at the same time. However, Sweden had already separated its infrastructure and services in the late 1980s and Germany, at the same time as the UK, also separated infrastructure from its railway operational services—although both Sweden and Germany opted for different ownership and wider structural solutions as well as different pricing regimes. These similarities could also not be blamed on EU-related processes ("Europeanisation"), as the relevant Directive (91/440) only required a separation in accounting terms and was applicable to cross-border services (which was irrelevant for Britain as it did not have a trans-jurisdictional railway line in the early 1990s) (Lodge 2002; 2003).
- The UK was far from being the only country to respond to dog-related fatal incidents with a breed-based policy approach that assumed particular types and breeds of dogs to be specifically and inherently aggressive. The breed-based approach that usually placed particular restrictions on American pit bulls and American Staffordshire Terriers flourished in the early and late 1990s, as well as in the first decade of the twenty-first century across (Western) Europe and other countries (including Trinidad, various counties in the United States, and a number of provinces in Canada, with some variations across states and subnational states). The UK was part of a first wave of countries (including Scandinavian countries, Ireland, and the Netherlands) to adopt breed-based dangerous dog legislation. Some Länder in Germany also sought to adopt breed-based provisions in the early 1990s, but failed because of challenges in the administrative courts. But it was not only the content of the legislation that was similar across states. In terms of response time, the UK was far from being the frontrunner in the race for the fastest law of the West. In 2000, when a dog incident in Hamburg involving the killing of a young boy caused German Länder to respond with legislative or regulatory measures, their reaction time was faster than the UK in the 1991 episode and their responses were far from coordinated (as one would have expected from that country's implicit policy norm to aspire toward legal harmonization) (see Lodge and Hood 2002; Hood and Lodge 2005; Hood, Rothstein, and Baldwin 2001).
- If credible commitment in terms of a nondiscretionary licensing regime was so important for the development of Jamaican telecommunications from the late 1980s, then why did the Jamaican government during the 1990s manage to challenge the initial licensing regime by facilitating rival operators (such as Voice over Internet), committing itself to liberalization and competition in international forums (i.e., the WTO) and by establishing, in a consensual agreement with the incumbent, a far more discretionary regime in 2000. More significantly, Jamaica did not appear to pay a penalty in terms of lower investment and thus decelerating network expansion. Such a claim is inherently difficult to make given the absence of counterfactuals, however, network expansion did not decrease, but increased continuously. In fact, compared to other English-speaking Caribbean island states, the Jamaican performance looks even more impressive—especially as Barbados and Trinidad and Tobago are usually thought of as having more credible political institutions than Jamaica (admittedly, Barbados and Trinidad and Tobago started from more advanced positions in terms of network expansion) (Lodge and Stirton 2005, 176; 2002). Why, despite doing everything that went *against* the prescriptions of Levy and

Spiller (and the World Bank) did Jamaica achieve such an extent of network expansion that outperformed both Barbados and Trinidad (see Stirton and Lodge 2003)?

These cases are hardly representative of the enormous field of studies that could be defined as falling under the comparative public policy label (instead, they are unrepresentative not only because they (1) are largely biographical and (2) originate in only one subdomain of comparative public policy, regulation). However, they seek to be representative of two central objectives of comparative public policy: comparative public policy is inherently about seeking to establish what accounts for the observed patterns in public policy. In addition, as illustrated by the three episodes briefly illustrated above, comparative public policy is also about questioning stereotypes by exploring somewhat paradoxical or counterintuitive developments (see also Castles 1989).

Although these two purposes of comparative public policy research may appear largely uncontroversial, how different literatures have sought to go about such endeavours has led to considerable diversity, in terms of research methodology, questions explored and policy domains investigated. In many ways, therefore, trying to identify the core of comparative public policy somewhat resembles the quest for a mystical essence. As with any religious and quasi-religious entity, searches for divinities encourage the emergence of diverse social movements that advocate particular roads to salvation. The search for the essence of comparative public policy is further complicated by many studies not accepting the comparative public policy label. Therefore, any search for the essence of comparative public policy as a practice rather than as a common label needs to move across different academic disciplines and departments, ranging from social policy (and education), political science, sociology, and law to economics. Given the extent of studies that could be broadly defined as comparative public policy, this chapter seeks to narrow the search for the essence of comparative public policy in three stages. First, this chapter takes a broad view as to what roughly constitutes comparative public policy. Second, it turns to the standard approaches in the study of comparative public policy and then considers diverse fields in which comparative public policy has developed. The conclusion considers whether there is more to comparative public policy than a broad label. Given the width and breadth of the literature, this chapter can only attempt to survey some trends, without any claim toward covering the literature in any comprehensive manner.

WHAT IS COMPARATIVE PUBLIC POLICY?

In order to begin the quest for the discovery of an essence of comparative public policy, this section considers issues of the logic and methods of comparative public policy research before considering whether there are any natural limits as to what comparative public policy constitutes. It is argued that comparison is largely driven by a joint logic, but not necessarily a common method, while the subject of public policy is arguably a matter of definitional boundary-drawing as to what constitutes a state activity.

As already noted, the logic of comparative public policy is driven by the search for determinants of public policy. Increasing the number of observations provides inbuilt control against assuming particular patterns. It hardly needs stating that comparison is at the heart of any endeavour that makes this discipline a social science: in the light of the inability to conduct real experiments, comparing across time, states or sectors offers one way to explore and evaluate patterns of state intervention in order to identify and isolate variables. In short, we compare to draw inferences. The logic of comparison allows the analysis, as Francis Castles notes (1989, 4), to move beyond the overparticularistic (in the form of a single event history) and the overgeneralized (in the sense of grand narratives). In addition, there is hardly disagreement that without a shared commitment toward appropriate research design issues (see, for example, Keman 1999), comparison is meaningless, in terms of cumulating knowledge for academic knowledge and of providing policy makers with potential lessons about policy experiences elsewhere. Thus, questions of, for example, choosing cases, observations (and number of observations), and domains (what we compare) are central to any endeavour that seeks to fall under the comparative public policy label.

However, what the appropriate tools of the comparative method represent is controversial. Without seeking to develop an argument about comparative research methodology (see Geddes 2003; Rueschemeyer 2003; Munck 2004; McKeown 2004; also Whitehead 2002, chapter 8; for a critical approach, see Fischer 2003), among the methods for conducting comparative public policy, large-n type studies, for example, comparing different "family of nations" (Castles 1998) have been particularly prominent. They have offered approximations of different national welfare state developments, pointed to interesting paradoxes and put many myths to rest (such as those of "convergence" and "races to the bottom," see Castles 2004). Studies that utilize cross-national aggregate data across a larger number of countries, have been crucial in terms of establishing insights as to what factors (or variables) are associated with commonalities and differences across states, domains and time periods. Regardless of the attraction of statistical methods in establishing some form of robust insight that moves beyond that of anecdote, the insights produced by these methods should nevertheless be regarded with considerable caution, given the (mostly inevitable) reliance on officially produced data. In many ways, students of comparative public policy have been studying what states, international organizations or non-governmental organizations, such as Transparency International, allow (or want) them to study (by producing particular data sets) in ways determined by research methodologies that fulfil particular understandings of appropriate (statistical) methods (see also Castles 1989, 5).

Relying on broad indicators statistical association comes, of course, at the price of detailed understanding of why particular choices were taken at specific times (for example, those studies interested in the various stages of the policy cycle, see chapter 4 in this volume). Thus, different methods of comparison have dominated the study of different definitions of policy, such as whether policy is defined as an output, outcome, content, or style. Even if similarities can be established at more than just the superficial level, these similarities may hide substantial variation in motives: history is littered with examples of similar policy options being adopted for opposite reasons. What may appear at one level as similar patterns may reveal itself as immensely distinct at another level.

Thus, talking about comparative public policy should be seen as a commitment to a particular logic of doing research, namely a commitment to the systematic investigation across states, domains and time, not a particular method in terms of research strategies and instruments. As a consequence, small-n, qualitative studies have a role to play in advancing our understanding of public policy, and this also includes appropriately framed single-n studies (see Gering 2004). Considerable efforts have been made to generate substantial insights from small-n studies, by trying to increase the number of observations. One example of such a strategy has been the explicit use of cross-country and cross-sectoral approaches and careful case selection (see Levi-Faur 2004, building on Vogel 1996).

Despite a largely common interest in the comparative logic, there are also questions as to what the public policies are that comparative public policy is interested in; for example, studies of dangerous dogs regulation may not necessarily be regarded by some as being of equal standing when compared to the study of welfare state expenditures. The study of public policies is, however, the study of state intervention in social life, or, put differently, the study of the interaction between the state and its subjects, whether it relates to welfare state expenditure, utility regulation, or policies regarding dogs.

In addition, the past two decades have witnessed two particularly prominent trends that challenge the centrality of the state in the study of public policy; first, the study of interaction effects between international and supranational regimes, in particular the European Union and its member states, and second, a greater sensitivity toward the fact that many public policies are executed at the wider societal level leading to a greater interest in the interorganizational relationships within the economy. While some countries have traditionally relied on third-sector welfare provision, developments such as privatisation as well as a greater interest in relationships within the economy have led to an increase in the societal localities of public policies. If, therefore, public policy has traditionally been interested in the diverse ways in which the state did things, labels such as *political economy* point to a more extensive understanding of what public policy is about—namely about how economic activity is shaped by relations among societal actors themselves; an extension to public policy that could be regarded as pointing to the continuous and indirect attempts at expanding the tactics of government into further domains of social life.

The notion of *Staatsaufgabe* (as utilized by Grimm, 1996) points to these changing trends in the delivery and organization of particular public policies. *Staatsaufgabe* translates badly into English as it defines both activity as well as obligation. If we consider the study of comparative public policy in the sense of state activities, there may some grounds to suggest that the field should be focused on those areas where the state (however defined and operationalized) does things to its subjects (in the coercive or liberating sense). However, if we take the wider definition in terms of state obligations, comparative public policy can be understood in terms of the beyond the state areas as well, namely all those domains where the state' is somehow expected to bear responsibility for outputs and outcomes. In an age where distinctions between private and public are in any case difficult to draw (and have encouraged the inflationary use of the word *governance*), where there is at least a greater prominence of private actors taking on regulatory functions (such as credit card companies in Internet gambling) and where national autonomy is said to be severely constrained by international commitments or dynamics, it makes sense to follow the second definition rather than the first—with implications on the choice of policy domain and type of research methodology.

Thus, comparative public policy is united in its search for explanations of observed patterns of state activities, using, most prominently, cross-national, but also cross-time, and cross-sectoral analysis. It is this logic of comparing that allows us to speak of comparative public policy—exploring puzzles enhances our understanding of the persuasiveness of explanations that may be widely held, but may rely on less solid foundations. In all other respects, a definition of comparative public policy is necessarily marred by controversy in terms of methodological issues as well as diversity in terms of domains investigated.

WHAT ARE THE QUESTIONS OF COMPARATIVE PUBLIC POLICY?

Traditionally, comparative public policy accounts have drawn on a number of core questions and literatures. These core questions relate to an interest into the degree and nature of political units' responsiveness to external challenges. For convenience, these can be separated into three distinct analytical approaches, with further subdivisions in each approach respectively (without claiming to establish a mutually exclusive or fully exhaustive list). These three broad approaches toward accounting for public policy trends in comparative perspective are labeled here *habitat, responsive government,* and *institutions.*[1] The first two point to external sources shaping government policies, whereas the latter highlights the importance of internal factors. The rest of this section considers each of these three broad approaches in turn.

Habitat-based accounts stress the importance of socio-economic factors in shaping public policies, whether in terms of economic structure or in terms of exposure to particular industrial production method. Thus, policy developments are said to be particularly evident at certain levels of economic development (however measured), leading to convergence. Among the key claims of the literature stressing socio-economic determinants has been the shift in the developed world toward post-Fordism. In the light of increasing individualization of modes of production and life-styles, welfare states as well as other form of collective policy provision are said to be facing particular problems: the individualization of social experiences makes universal welfare coverage, as well as

1. The notion *habitat* is taken from Hood (1994).

easy tax collection, problematic. In addition, given the coverage of the basic societal needs, they encourage the growth of an anti-tax electoral constituency that opposes (collectivist) redistribution.

The degree of openness of national economies is often seen as crucial for explaining policy patterns, in particular in terms of available rents for politically motivated redistribution to constituencies. In other words, the more open the economy (or a particular economic sector), the more difficult it is for states to engage in corruption or other forms of predatory behavior, given likely penalties for such behavior on international markets (assuming, of course, the portability of the factors of production). Finally, the internationalization of the economy is said to expose national states to similar challenges which are, however, met by different degrees of distress and opportunity structures for incurring policy change, given institutional differences (see Scharpf 2000). These challenges of internationalization are particularly stark in areas where national states have lost their national economic border control—for example, in the European Union, the mutual recognition principle places the European Court of Justice as final arbiter as to what constitutes legitimate trade barriers (as defined in treaties). At the same time, it should be recognized that the contemporary interest in internationalization is merely a continuation in the interest in the viability of particular policy approaches given changing environmental conditions (in the case of taxation, see Hood 1994, 116–22).

Accounts that broadly fall under the responsive government label point to the different ways in which governments respond to external pressure for change. Governments take some form of opinion as a "thermostat" (see Wlezien 1995; Taylor-Gooby 1985) and respond by seeking to establish congruence between public demands and policy outputs. Although it is a basic premise of liberal democracy that governments should be responsive to the wider electorate, different sources of such responsiveness can be distinguished. First, in the pure form of responsive government, policies are seen as emerging as a response to public salience. Thus, a majority anti-tax coalition in the wider electorate is said to encourage long-term shifts toward a different policy-mix on inflation and acceptable unemployment levels. Elsewhere, public opinion responsive government is regarded as outright bad, for example in the area of risk regulation where criticism focuses on political knee jerk responses to short-lived moral panics following high visibility incidents (see Breyer 1992; Sunstein 2003).

Second, and arguably representing the most well-established research tradition in comparative public policy, is the "do parties matter" question. Research in this tradition traditionally focuses on macro-economic policy trends under left- and right-of center parties (Hibbs 1977; Castles 1982; Blais et al. 1996; Berry and Lowry 1987) or on whether party manifestos have an impact on eventual government policy (Laver et al. 2003). With regard to the former, there has been only limited evidence, for example, Richard Rose over two decades ago stressed that inheritance outweighed any form of marginal change parties in government could make (Rose 1990). Others point to changes at the margins that provide clear evidence of partisan preferences (e.g., in taxation, see Steinmo 1993, 145–54). With regard to research on the impact of party manifestos, there has been considerable evidence that points to an association between manifesto commitments and subsequent government policies (Laver et al. 2003; Budge et al. 1987; Laver and Budge 1992).

Third, according to the seminal work by George Stigler regulation is "as a rule […] acquired by the industry and is designed and operated primarily for its benefit" (Stigler 1971, 3). Although this universal law-like statement has been modified over time (by friends and foes of this so-called economic theory of regulation, see Wilson 1980; Peltzman 1976 and 1989; Keeler 1989), it nevertheless points to the well-established tradition in political science that stresses to the importance of special interests in the development of public policies, across sectors and states. Similar interest, although based on a very different research approach, is related to the literature in policy networks and its claims about the importance of the features of the policy network (such as the distinction between issue networks and policy communities). Other types of special interests are "advocacy coalitions" (Sabatier 1988) and other forms of coalitions of various organizations and individuals united by common policy belief systems (such as epistemic communities)—these accounts to some extent also relate to literatures that attach causality to ideas themselves.

Turning finally to institutions, it has become a platitude over the past two decades to declare that "institutions matter" and that policies are "path dependent" (see Pierson 2000a). Such an interest in the institutions was partly a result of the absence of similar responses by different political systems to similar external inputs or shocks. Thus, comparative public policy accounts have explored why certain developed states survived the years of economic stagflation in the 1970s in better shape than others (see Scharpf 1991). Similarly, as the three examples at the outset of this chapter noted, political institutions came to be associated with different degrees of responsiveness in terms of policy bandwagons (such as privatization of publicly owned utility companies). And as already noted above, internationalization and universal budgetary constraints caused different degrees of adaptation pressure on national systems—partly challenging those recipes of success of the 1970s.

Whatever stripe of institutionalism one chooses to be associated with, three distinct institutional impacts are particularly noteworthy when it comes to comparative public policy. The first is that "nations matter"—in the sense that there are particular "national styles" (emerging from an interaction between informal norms and formal institutions, Richardson et al. 1982) or that broad formal policy system factors impact on how systems respond to various policy challenges—either at the level of macro-institutional political system features, such as rules concerning electoral systems or federalism, or at more meso-level institutional mechanisms, such as the so-called politico-institutional nexus, interaction patterns between state and societal groups (see Hall 1986) or the rules and loci of decision making (Steinmo 1993). In contrast, others stress the importance of "sectors" or policy domains—pointing to distinct sectoral characteristics that pose distinct challenges to policy makers. Following this dichotomy, comparative research has increasingly utilized these two approaches for their investigation (e.g., using two policy domains in two states to explore which "logic," the national or the sectoral, seems to dominate).

In contrast, less attention in comparative public policy research has been paid to the idea that "policies are their own cause" and that they "self-destruct" (see Hood 1994, 13–17). According to this argument, any intervention triggers responses that provoke further self-stimulating responses (Wildavsky 1980, 62–85), while environmental reactions and wider changes reduce the effectiveness (or even reverse) of the chosen policy instruments (e.g., free meals for school children instituted during times of malnutrition being carried forward in times of widespread obesity). In addition, such issues also point to different accounts regarding sources of policy change (see below). In contrast to the approaches explored earlier, this idea about how institutions matter has been far less widely explored, especially in comparative perspective.

The above section is by no means comprehensive, and, in many cases, the different approaches overlap and are used in a complementary fashion. Nevertheless, they highlight a relatively concentred interest in broadly similar questions. In this sense of certain questions dominating academic attention, something called "comparative public policy" seems to exist.

DOMAINS OF COMPARATIVE PUBLIC POLICY

If public policy is about what states do (directly and indirectly) to us, its subjects, then we are confronted by a large number of different types of state intervention and tools—from before the cradle to beyond the grave. Among the many ways to classify comparative public policy literatures, the following categorizes these literatures according to their dominant policy instrument, or tool. An adaptation of Christopher Hood's typology of Nodality, Authority, Treasure and Organisation (or NATO; see Hood 1983, chapter 1) allows for one particular way of classifying different lines of enquiry that are associated with comparative public policy while also moving beyond a mere

TABLE 19.1

Treasure	Nodality
Interest in how governments raise and spend money *Literatures*: Taxation and Welfare State spending, total public expenditure	Interest in how governments acquire knowledge or use information to affect behavior *Literatures*: Policy transfer & learning; government information
Organization	**Authority**
Interest in how governments directly organize their own architecture or directly provide services *Literatures*: public management policy change, privatization	Interest in how governments use authority *Literatures*: Regulation of societal actors

listing of literatures in terms of subject or chronological ordering. Nevertheless, this choice of breath comes at the expense of depth and comprehensiveness. Table 19.1 provides an overview of the ways in which different comparative public policy literatures can be organized according to the NATO scheme (organized in Table 19.1 according to the degree of direct resource depleteability on the horizontal dimension (nodality and authority scoring low) and the degree of constraint on the "target" on the vertical dimension (with the use of treasure and nodality being generally more discretionary than the application of organization or authority; Hood 1983, 145). The rest of this section surveys these different literatures. While clearly not being able to do justice to the breadth and depth of these literatures, this highly selective survey points to some recurring themes across these different literatures which relate to common questions, as noted above.

Nodality focuses on the way in which governments "traffic in information" (Hood 1983, 4). Governments require the provision of information for the development of policy responses and they are engaged in the dissemination of information (occupying, for example, large shares of national advertisement markets). Such activities range from at-large and bespoke forms of propaganda encouraging regime or party-in-government support to particular health advice (smoking kills), food health warnings or education (national curricula for schools). At the information receiving end, governments have traditionally taken great care in receiving reports, taking notice and registering individuals and activities. Arguably, the rise of an "audit society" (Power 1997) points to an extension of tactics of government in order to both extend its knowledge about certain activities and influence ever more activities—with all their intended and, arguably, more significantly (in their extent and their potential impact on social systems), unintended consequences. While not necessarily taking up the implications of the "audit society" thesis, the interest in new modes of governance, such as benchmarking and target setting has been of considerable degree of attention in a diversity of literatures (e.g., on the EU's open method of co-ordination or the growth of certification schemes instead of regulation for the classification of goods).

Related, there has been a recent resurgence in interest in how governments learn and how policies get transferred from one place to another (Rose 1993, 2004; Dolowitz and Marsh 1996, 2004; James and Lodge 2003). These accounts, seeking to explore lesson-drawing and policy transfer connect to a wider and well-established literature that has explored the transfer of institutions to post-colonial and developing countries (Jacoby 2000, chapter 1). While these earlier studies (linked to some extent to the ambitions of the comparative public administration movement of the immediate post-Second World War period) linked the learning about and transferring of public policies to stages in economic development, later studies have highlighted the importance of partisan preferences for selective learning as well as institutional processes, for example, ranging from explanations why particular policy templates are regarded as more appropriate than others (Lodge 2003), claims regarding the "fungibility" of particular policies due to their institutional complexity or close fit with a specific environment (Rose 1993) to arguments pointing to the inevitability of encouraging 'irritant' rather than straightforward accept/reject responses as may be assumed when using the term *policy transplants* (Teubner 1998).

Authority is defined as the use of legal or official power to "determine" (Hood 1983, 5), in the "allowing" and "forbidding" sense. Regulation combines interests of numerous social science disciplines, ranging from economics, political science, socio-legal studies and sociology to "black letter" law (i.e., generally known principles of law thought to be free of doubt or contention). And in many ways, the study of regulation has explored questions that characterise the study of public policy (such as noted above), for examples, questions concerning commonalities and differences in regulatory objectives as well as their change, the comparison of institutional architectures (especially the supposed growth of quasi-independent regulatory agencies in Europe and elsewhere) or the comparative study of enforcement practices, especially with regard to environmental regulation (Vogel 1988).

While very much encouraged by the rise of the regulatory state (Majone 1997), studies of authority go back in time, even outside the United States where, arguably, a regulatory state has been part of the institutional furniture since at least the beginning of the twentieth century (Skowronek 1992). For example, the evolution of regulation in nineteenth-century Britain (in particular relating to railways) generated a literature on "the growth of the state" (see MacDonagh 1958; Parris 1960). Turning to the studies interested in comparative regulatory change in the past two or three decades, there has been some attempt at explicit comparative work, usually relying on either cross-national and historical analysis of a single domain (Thatcher 1999; Lodge 2002) or cross-domain analysis in a single country (see Hood et al. 2001). Some studies have moved toward an explicit "across-country, across-domain" approach (see Vogel 1996; Levi-Faur 2004; Lodge and Stirton 2005). In addition, while for some the emergence of regulatory institutions is a phenomena best studied as part of an international diffusion process (at a large-n level: Levi-Faur 2003), more limited comparative analysis also points to increasing similarities across countries, even though they may have arrived at these similar points via diverse routes. If countries with very different political and economic institutions are diagnosed to arrive at similar points in terms of institutional arrangements, such as in telecommunications (Thatcher 2004) or dangerous dogs regulation (see Hood and Lodge 2005), then institutions therefore, at least to some extent, don't seem to matter. However, taking a more fine-grained institutional analysis points to ongoing significant differences in regulatory approaches and institutions that reflect particular constellations at particular conjunctures as well as more long-standing assumptions and norms (Döhler 2002).

As already noted, in other areas of studies regarding authority (or regulation) there has been substantial interest in different ways of enforcement—see for example Vogel's seminal study regarding enforcement in environmental regulation that pointed to the importance of national legal traditions (Vogel 1986). At the same time, regulation is hardly the only way in which states utilize authority. One key area of, arguably, growing interest has been immigration and states' attempts at classifying immigrant populations (see King 1999, 97–134; Joppke 1999)

Treasure is defined here as the receipt and the expenditure of monetary resources. In many ways, the accounting for different expenditure patterns as part of welfare state programs—in combination with differences in organization of the welfare state—have been at the forefront of the comparative public policy literature, highlighting the existence of different types of welfare state families, as well as the well-established "do parties matter" accounts that stress the importance of public expenditures for attempts at securing re-election.

Taxation has been one of the key areas of contemporary public policy, whether in terms of the impact of partisan governments (Steinmo 1993, 2003; Rose and Karran 1987), the strategic incentives of rulers (see Levi 1988), the interaction between state and domestic elites (Lieberman 2003), or the differential impact of international competition on domestic tax rates (Ganghof 2000; Kemmerling 2005; Kato 2003). Similarly, there have been attempts to establish families of tax states (relying on different degrees of direct and indirect taxation, see Peters 1991). Arguably, a habitat of emerging technologies that allow for relatively costless monitoring of monetary exchange as well as growing voter resistance to direct (or, in other words, visible forms of) taxation, has encouraged a move toward indirect taxation, such as taxes on consumption. At the same time, certain types of tax are likely to be related to different types of technologies. For example, the difficulty of controlling Internet gambling has led to credit card companies acting as gatekeepers to control such activities.

Similar to the questions to what extent states are able to tax (or, rather, what sorts of activities it is able to tax), considerable (and, in comparison to tax, considerably more) attention has been paid to the question whether states can still spend in times of perceived fiscal constraint, due to government debt, international commitments, such as the budgetary and fiscal rules shaping the European single currency, or pressures on social budgets (especially pensions), due to changing demographics. The literature has therefore partly moved beyond questions as to whether there is a universal "race to the bottom" (answer: no) or whether "parties matter" (it depends, see Garrett 1998; Iversen 1999) to the study of institutional factors in shaping the ways in which governments seek to retrench in the light of their institutional commitments and path dependencies (Pierson 2000b; Hopkin and Blyth 2004), seeking to explore why members of similar welfare state families respond in different ways (Bechberger 2005). In many ways, the interest in the "treasure" activities of national states has been at the heart of the comparative public policy literature, partly because of the existence of hard data that suited statistical treatment, partly because of the extension of the welfare state in the post-Second World War. It allowed for many crucial debates in comparative public policy, such as debates whether and why governments grow or whether political business cycles exist (Alesina, Roubini, and Cohen 1997). Given budgetary constraints and long-term demographic changes, the study of "treasure," especially of the effecting type (i.e., expenditure), remains one core activity of those studies that fall under the comparative public policy label.

Organization is defined by the possession of capacity to mobilize people or rely on buildings, land or equipment directly without reliance on negotiations with third parties (see Hood 1983, 6). The study of direct action in comparative perspective has widely taken place within a single country, but much less in cross-national context Nevertheless, if one accepts that administrative reform policies can be regarded as public policies that the state does to itself and, more importantly, therefore affects its subjects, then the boom industry in cross-national accounts of administrative change (often labeled "public management") in the past two decades can be counted as a central part of contemporary comparative public policy studies. For example, Michael Barzelay employs the notion of public management policy change in order to apply a Kingdon-type approach (with some added ingredients) toward comparative case study research (see Barzelay 2001, 2003; Kingdon 1995). In contrast, Christopher Pollitt and Gert Bouckaert offer a more historical institutionalist narrative of comparative administrative reform (Pollitt and Bouckaert 2004).

Comparison is very much at the heart of studies of the changes in the organization of the state itself in that authors identify different degrees (of comprehensiveness) of change and seek to explore different reform trajectories. Outright comparison has proven more difficult, partly given difficulties in measuring the extent of administrative reform even at the broadest level, given the need to take different institutional starting positions into account as well as different cultures. Nevertheless, broad comparison across countries throws up central puzzles, both at the level of medium-sized samples and small-n comparisons. For example, claims that extensive administrative reform policies seem to have been an "English-speaking disease" in that countries such as New Zealand, Australia, and the United Kingdom (although to a lesser extent in its Northern Irish part) were far ahead in terms of extent and speed of administrative reform over the course of the past two decades face problems given the extensive reforms that took place in Sweden at the same time and the absence of any major administrative reform beyond the level of announcements in the United States. Similarly, issues such as party in government or economic well-being seem not to be associated with the extent of administrative reform. With diagnosed policy developments not fitting the standard public policy accounts, comparing organizations at the level of administrative reform has maintained an inherently institutionalist flavor in the sense of describing national and subnational changes—even when trying to force a common narrative onto different case studies that highlight the role of particular policy entrepreneurs, issue framing, and other mechanisms (see Barzelay 2003 and further contributions in that special issue of *International Public Management Journal*). Administrative reform seems largely a matter of motive and opportunity for political and administrative actors set within particular institutional constellations.

While comparison of administrative reform "at large" (in the sense of broad administrative reform movements) has largely remained at the level of stressing the institutional distinctiveness of national experiences, the analysis of more specific issues in administrative policy challenges stereotypes regarding 'path dependency' of particular countries or policy domains. For example, the UK and Germany (at the federal level) are often regarded as being on opposite ends of the spectrum when it comes to the extent and speed of the introduction of managerial reforms into government processes. However, when focusing on the issue of competency, Germany seemed to be thinking of competency in the 1980s (but then forgetting about it in the wake of unification until the late 1990s), whereas the UK senior civil service only discovered competency in the early 1990s (see Hood and Lodge 2004).

Related, the past two decades have witnessed the shift in many developed and developing countries from the direct public service provision by the state to the delivery of these services through (often regulated) private providers. One particular prominent area has been the literature on the privatization of state-owned enterprises, in particular in the area of utilities, such as telecommunications. Such changes in organization are notable, if alone for the fact that Max Weber defined the railways and the telegraph as defining features of the occidental state over a century ago.

The above classification and overview of the literature is hardly exhaustive and is likely to generate substantial criticism for its incompleteness. This section's main purpose was to highlight the key domains in which comparative public policy literatures have evolved. Regardless of the differentiation in terms of activities, there is a distinct commitment toward raising similar questions, suggesting that there remains something at the heart of comparative public policy that makes it identifiable, namely the type of questions it asks. Certain literatures do not easily fit into any of the four categories—and in many cases, even the above-mentioned literatures often stretch across different areas. For example, the study of regulation often involves the study of organization (such as regulatory institutions and questions of ownership). More generally, key areas in the comparative public policy literature stretch across numerous, if not all, four types of activities. For example, "varieties of capitalism" accounts (see Hall and Soskice 2001) cut across a number of different types of activities and policy instruments, ranging from cross-national expenditure patterns, the organization of particular forms of relationships (in the economy) to the impact of legal instruments on the wider system of law. The "varieties of capitalism" literature also highlights the importance for the analysis to move beyond the state into the institutions that govern the relationships within the market.

Classifying writings on comparative public policy according to NATO points to the difficulty of assessing any claims concerning big government. The usual measures of big government—expenditures—have hardly witnessed a universal cut despite the contemporary emphasis on containment. However, how to measure the size of government activity becomes even more difficult when trying to assess the combined effect of other types of policy instruments, such as those of information or authority. For example, one of the attractions of using regulation is the shift of compliance costs to (largely) private parties, whereas a simple reliance on rule-making is relatively costless (apart from the production costs of writing the rule).

Finally, taking a NATO perspective allows the analysis to move toward an assessment whether there have been some larger trends in the evolution of state activities. Indeed, as Hood (1983, 154–63) noted over two decades ago, we may be witnessing a return to an age that is less characterized by checkbook government than by regulatory government that largely relies on authority.

In contrast, some may point to the growth of media-management within central government as one indicator of government via information (in fact, some argue that certification schemes rather than a reliance on regulation point to a move away from authority to nodality). However, just as there are potential difficulties in putting the ruler over the size of the regulatory state in terms of extent of rules and their cost (and benefits), any attempt at trying to "metrify" government by information is also limited, especially in comparative perspective, for example because of differences in political-media relations.

CONCLUSION

At the outset, it was noted that comparative public policy appeared in many different guises. The purpose of this chapter was to discover whether there was anything that unified studies that (explicitly or implicitly) carried the comparative public policy label. One key risk of the ever-differentiating analysis of public policies, across existing disciplines and newly forming fields, is that unifying themes are lost in the variety of different languages that emerge with each academic subfield. Similarly, the risk is the different subfields have differentiated to such an extent that they no longer communicate to each other even if they ask similar questions and share research interests.

This chapter has sought to identify an essence in comparative public policy in three respects. It has been argued that there are certain elements that unite comparative public policy, namely a shared commitment toward the logic of comparison and a broad interest in asking related questions. At the heart of the academic study of comparative public policy in all its fields and methods is the interest in exploring the determinants for state action—and such exploration requires a willingness to move beyond description to explore puzzles and challenge received wisdom, as the three brief examples noted at the outset.

In terms of active engagement with the world of practicing public policy, comparative public policy plays a distinctive role. In a world, where Herbert Simon's complaint regarding the prominence of "proverbs in administration" (1946) still holds true, the role of comparative public policy is to inform and challenge national developments and arguments. While appropriate comparison is likely to add information to the policy-making process and allows for a critical estimation as to the extent and nature of contemporary policy developments, contemporary comparative public policy analysis should nevertheless seek to avoid falling into the "what works" trap. Drawing lessons for application, especially in partisan contexts where short-term interests dominate, is most likely to lead to unintended and unforeseen irritation effects. Instead, comparative public policy is most likely to contribute to the intelligence of decision making by critically assessing any proclamation of national innovation in public policy and by pointing to and exploring comparative experiences that move beyond the casual anecdote. Comparative public policy, therefore, is hardly the divinity that through its questions and empirical investigations is going to lead to the nirvana of well-functioning state interventions (potentially it is more likely to represent the role of the chorus in ancient Greek tragedies), but its essence is that of critical and continuous questioning, not more, but, more importantly, not less.

ACKNOWLEDGMENTS

I am deeply indebted to Jan Meyer-Sahling, Nick Sitter, Lindsay Stirton, and Kai Wegrich for extremely perceptive comments on various drafts of this chapter.

BIBLIOGRAPHY

Alesina, A., Roubini, N., and Cohen, G.D. (1997). *Political Cycles and the Macroeconomy*. Cambridge, MA: MIT Press.

Barzelay, M. (2003). Introduction: The Process Dynamics of Public Management Policymaking. *International Public Management Journal* 6(3), 251–281.

Barzelay, M. (2001). *The New Public Management*. University of California Press.

Baumol, W.J. (1967). The macroeconomics of unbalanced growth. *American Economic Review* 57, 415–26.

Bechberger, E. (2005). Regaining Control over the Social Budget: Welfare Reforms in Corporatist-Continental Europe. Paper presented at Political Studies Association annual conference, Leeds 5-8 April 2005.

Berry, W.D. and Lowry, D. (1987). Explaining the size of the public sector. *Journal of Politics* 49, 401–40.

Blais A., Blake, D., and Dion, S. (1996). Do Parties Make a Difference: A Reappraisal. *American Journal of Political Science* 40, 514–520.

Breyer, S. (1992). *Breaking the Vicious Cycle*. Cambridge/MA: Harvard University Press.

Budge, I., Robertson, D. and Hearl, D. (1987/eds.). *Ideology, Strategy and Party Change*. Cambridge, Cambridge University Press.

Castles, F.G. (2004). *The Future of the Welfare State: Crisis Myths and Crisis Realities*. Oxford: Oxford University Press.

Castles, F.G. (1998). *Comparative Public Policy*. Cheltenham: Edward Elgar.

Castles, F.G. (1989). Introduction: Puzzles of Political Economy. In F.G. Castles (ed.), *The Comparative History of Public Policy*, 1–15. Cambridge: Polity Press.

Castles, F.G. (1982/eds.). *The Impact of Parties*. Beverly Hills, CA: Sage.

Castles, F.G., and McKinlay, R.D. (1979). Does Politics Matter? An Analysis of the Public Welfare Commitment in Advanced Democratic States. *European Journal of Political Research* 7, 169–186.

Döhler, M. (2002). Institutional Choice and Bureaucratic Autonomy. *West European Politics* 25(1), 101–124.

Dolowitz, D. and March, D. (2000). Learning from Abroad: The Role of Policy Transfer in Contemporary Policy-Making. *Governance* 13(1), 5–24.

Dolowitz, D. and March, D. (1996). Who learns what from whom: A review of the policy transfer literature. *Political Studies* 44, 343–357.

Dunleavy, P. (1995). Policy Disasters: Explaining the UK's record. *Public Policy & Administration* 10(2), 52–70.

Esping-Andersen, G. (1990). *The Three Worlds of Welfare Capitalism*. Cambridge: Polity Press.

Fischer, F. (2003). *Reframing Public Policy*. Oxford: Oxford University Press.

Ganghoff, S. (2000). Adjusting national tax policy to economic internationalization. In F.W. Scharpf and V. Schmidt (eds.) *Welfare and Work in the Open Economy* (vol. 2), 597–645. Oxford: Oxford University Press.

Garrett, G. (1998). *Partisan Politics in the Global Economy*. Cambridge: Cambridge University Press.

Geddes, B. (2003). *Paradigms and Sand Castles: Theory Building and Research Design in Comparative Politics*. Ann Arbor: University of Michigan Press.

Gerring, J. (2004). What is a case study and what is it good for? *American Political Science Review* 98(2), 341–354.

Grimm, D. (1996/ed.). *Staatsaufgaben*. Frankfurt/M: Suhrkamp.

Hall, P.A. (1986). *Governing the Economy*. Cambridge: Polity.

Hall, P.A. and Soskice, D. (2001). Introduction to Varieties of Capitalism. In P.A. Hall and D. Soskice (eds.). *Varieties of Capitalism*, 1–68. Oxford: Oxford University Press.

Hibbs, D.A. (1977). Political parties and macroeconomic policy. *American Political Science Review* 71, 1467–1487.

Hood, C. (1994). *Explaining Economic Policy Reversals*. Buckingham: Open University Press.

Hood, C. (1986). *Tools of Government*. Basingstoke: Macmillan.

Hood, C. and Lodge, M. (2005). Pavlovian innovation, pet solutions and economising on rationality? Politicians and dangerous dogs. In J. Black, M. Lodge and M. Thatcher (eds.) *Regulatory Innovation: A comparative analysis*. Cheltenham: Edward Elgar.

Hood, C., Baldwin, R. and Rothstein, H. (2000). Assessing the Dangerous Dogs Act: When Does a Regulatory Law Fail? *Public Law* (Summer), 282–305.

Hood, C., Rothstein, H., and Baldwin R. (2001). *The Government of Risk*. Oxford: Oxford University Press.

Hopkin, J. and Blyth, M. (2004). How many varieties of capitalism? Structural reform and Inequality in Western Europe. Paper presented at American Political Science Association annual conference, 1-5 September 2004.

Imbeau, L.M., Pétry F. and Lamari, M. (2000). Party Ideology and Government Policies: A Meta-Analysis. *European Journal of Political Research* 40, 1–29.

Iversen, T. (1999). *Contested Economic Institutions*. Cambridge: Cambridge University Press.

Jacoby, W. (2000). *Imitation and Politics*. Ithaca: Cornell University Press.

James, O. and Lodge, M. (2003). The Limitations of 'Policy Transfer' and 'Lesson Drawing' for Public Policy Research. *Political Studies Review* 1(2), 179–193.

Joppke, C. (1999). *Immigration and the Nation–State*. Oxford: Oxford University Press.

Kato, J. (2003). *Regressive Taxation and the Welfare State: path dependence and policy diffusion*. Cambridge: Cambridge University Press.

Keeler, T. (1989). Theories of Regulation and the Deregulation Movement. *Public Choice* 44(1), 103–45.

Kemmerling, A. (2005). Tax mixes, welfare states and employment: tracking diverging vulnerabilities. *Journal of European Public Policy* 12(1), 1–22.

King, D. (1999). *In the Name of Liberalism*. Oxford: Oxford University Press.

Kingdon, F.W. (1995). *Agendas, Alternatives, and Public Policies* (2nd ed.). New York: Harper Collins.

Laver, M., Benoit, K., and Garry, J. (2003). Extracting Policy Positions from Political Texts Using Words As Data. *American Political Science Review* 97(2), 311–31.

Laver, M. and Budge, I. (1992/eds.). *Party Policy and Government Coalitions*. London: Macmillan.

Levi, M. (1988). *Of Rule and Revenue*. Berkeley: University of California Press.

Levi-Faur, D. (2004). Comparative Research Designs in the Study of Regulation: How to increase the number of cases without compromising the strength of case-oriented research. In J. Jacint and D. Levi-Faur (eds.), *The Politics of Regulation: Institutions and Regulatory Reforms for the Age of Governance*, 177–199. Cheltenham: Edward Elgar.

Levi-Faur, D. (2003). The Politics of Liberalization: Privatization and regulation-for-competition in Europe's and Latin America's Telecoms and Electricity industries. *European Journal of Political Research* 42(5), 705–774.

Levy, B and Spiller, P (1994). The Institutional Foundations of Regulatory Commitment: A Comparative Analysis of Telecommunications Regulation. *Journal of Law, Economics and Organisation* 10, 201–246.

Lieberman, E.S. (2003). *Race and Regionalism in the Politics of Taxation in Brazil and South Africa*. New York: Cambridge University Press.

Lodge, M. (2003). Explaining Institutional Choice and Policy Transfer: The Case of British and German Railway Reform. *Governance* 16(2), 159–178.

Lodge, M. (2002). *On different tracks: designing railway regulation in Britain and Germany*. Westport: Praeger.

Lodge, M. and Hood, C. (2002). Pavlovian Policy Responses to Media Feeding Frenzies? Dangerous Dogs Regulation in Comparative Perspective. *Journal of Contingencies and Crisis Management* 10(1), 1–13.

Lodge, M. and Stirton, L. (2005). Well Connected? Building Capacity for Pro-Competitive Telecommunications Regulation in Three Caribbean States. In G. Harrison (ed.), *Global Encounters: International Political Economy, Development and Globalization*, 171–194. Basingstoke: Palgrave.

Lodge, M. and Stirton, L. (2003). Rethinking Institutional Endowment in Jamaica: Misguided Theory, Prophecy of Doom or Explanation for Regulatory Change? Paper presented to CARR/CRC/ABS workshop, University of Manchester, 26–27 June 2003.

Lodge, M. and Stirton, L. (2002). Regulatory Reform in small developing states: Globalisation, regulatory autonomy and Jamaican telecommunications. *New Political Economy* 7(3), 415–33.

MacDonagh, O. (1958). The Nineteenth-Century Revolution in Government: A Reappraisal. *The Historical Journal* 1(1), 252–67.

Majone, G. (1997). From the Positive to the Regulatory State. *Journal of Public Policy* 17(2), 139–167.

McKeown, T.J. (2004). Case Studies and the Limits of the Quantitative Worldview. In H.E. Brady and D. Collier (eds.). *Rethinking Social Inquiry: Diverse Tools, Shared Standards*, 139–167. Lanham, MD: Rowman & Littlefield.

Moran, M. (2003). *The British Regulatory State*. Oxford: Oxford University Press.

Munck, G. (2004) Tools for Qualitative Research. In H.E. Brady and D. Collier (eds.) *Rethinking Social Inquiry: Diverse Tools, Shared Standards*, 105–121. Lanham, MD: Rowman & Littlefield.

Keman, H. (1999). The Comparative Method and Political Science. In P. Pennings, H. Keman and J. Kleinnijenhuis (eds.), *Doing Research in Political Science*. London: Sage.

Parris, H. (1960). The Nineteenth-Century Revolution in Government: A Reappraisal Reappraised. *The Historical Journal* 3(1), 17–37.

Peltzman, S. (1976). Towards a More General Theory of Regulation. *Journal of Law and Economics* 19(3), 211–40.

Peltzman, S. (1989). The Economic Theory of Regulation after a Decade of Deregulation. Brookings Papers on Economic Activity (Microeconomics), 1–44.

Peters, B.G. (1991). *The Politics of Taxation*. Oxford: Blackwell.

Pierson, P. (2000a). Increasing Returns, Path Dependency, and the Study of Politics. *American Political Science Review* 94, 251–267.

Pierson, P. (2000b/ed.). *New Politics of the Welfare State*. Oxford: Oxford University Press.

Pollitt, C. and Bouckaert, G. (2004). *Public Management Reform*. Oxford: Oxford University Press.

Power, M. (1997). *The Audit Society*. Oxford: Oxford University Press.

Richardson, J. (1982/ed.). *Policy Styles in Western Europe*. London: Allen & Unwin.

Rose, R. (2004). *Learning from Comparative Public Policy*. London: Routledge.

Rose, R. (1993). *Lesson-drawing in Public Policy*. NJ: Chatham House.

Rose, R. (1990). Inheritance before choice in public policy. *Journal of Theoretical Politics* 2(3), 263–91.

Rose, R. (1988). *Understanding Big Government*. London: Sage.

Rose, R. and Karran, T. (1987). *Taxation by Political Inertia*. London: Allen & Unwin.

Rueschemeyer, D. (2003). Can one or a few cases yield theoretical gains. In J. Mahoney and D. Rueschemeyer (eds.), *Comparative Historical Analysis in the Social Sciences*, 305–336. Cambridge, Cambridge University Press.

Sabatier, P.A. (1988). Advocacy Coalition Framework of Policy Change and the Role of Policy Learning. *Policy Sciences* 21, 128–168.

Scharpf, F.W. (2000). Economic Changes , Vulnerabilities, and Institutional Capabilities. In F.W. Scharpf and V. Schmidt (eds.), *Welfare and work in the open economy* (vol. 1), 21–124, Oxford: Oxford University Press.

Scharpf. F.W. (1991). *Crisis and Choice in European Social Democracy*. Ithaca: Cornell University Press.

Simon, H. (1946). Proverbs of Administration. *Public Administration Review* 6, 53–67.

Skowronek, S. (1977). *Building a New American State.* New York: Cambridge University Press.

Steinmo, S. (2003). Bucking the trend? The welfare state and the global economy: the Swedish case up close. *New Political Economy* 8(1), 31–48.

Steinmo, S. (1993). *Taxation and democracy*. New Haven: Yale University Press.

Stigler, G. (1971). The Theory of Economic Regulation. *Bell Journal of Economics and Management Science* 2(1), 3–21.

Sunstein, C. (2003). *Risk and Reason*. Cambridge: Cambridge University Press.

Taylor-Gooby, P. (1985). *Public Opinion, Ideology and the State of Welfare*. London: Routledge.

Taylor-Gooby, P. (2001). Sustaining state welfare in hard times. *Journal of European Social Policy* 11(2), 133–148.

Teubner, G. (1998). Legal Irritants: Good Faith in British Law or how unifying law ends up in new divergences. *Modern Law Review* 61(1), 11–32

Thatcher, M. (2004). Winners and Losers in Europeanisation; Reforming the National Regulation of Telecommunications. *West European Politics* 27(2), 284–309.

Thatcher, M. (1999). *The Politics of Telecommunications*. Oxford: Oxford University Press.

Vogel, D. (1986). *National Styles of Regulation: environmental policy in Great Britain and the United States*. Ithaca, NY: Cornell University Press.

Vogel, S. (1996). *Freer Markets, more rules: regulatory reform in advanced industrial countries*. Ithaca, NY: Cornell University Press.

Wagner, A. (1887). *Finanzwissenschaft, parts 1 and 2*. Leipzig: CF Winter.

Wildavsky, A. (1980). *The Art and Craft of Policy Analysis*. London: Macmillan.

Wilson, J.Q. (1980). The Politics of Regulation. In J.Q. Wilson (ed.), *The Politics of Regulation*.

Wlezien, C. (1995). The Public as Thermostat: Dynamics of Preferences for Spending. *American Journal of Political Science* 39, 981–1000.

20 Applied Cultural Theory: Tool for Policy Analysis

Robert Hoppe

1 INTRODUCTION: CULTURE MATTERS IN PUBLIC POLICY

More than ever before, in our late or postmodern condition of civil societies and polities, governance implies the active creation of shared, or, at least, congruent political and policy frameworks. For policy analysis this means that culture matters. The challenge is to intelligently and creatively cope with pluralism and diversity. One important way of doing this is develop a kind of policy analysis that pays attention to cultural differences more than current practice, which frequently violates even existing precepts to take culture into account. This is by no means easy, for it takes some counter-intuitive assumptions to see that the proposal makes sense. After all, from a cultural perspective, public policy making appears to invent and impose a unitary, supposedly consensual governance culture on the many different cultures "out there" in society (Van Gunsteren 2002). Yet, taking cultural difference seriously and making it an ally instead of an enemy is the only sensible response for a policy analysis profession in tune with its times. The thesis of this chapter is that we need grid-group cultural theory to do a better policy analytic job. Group-grid cultural theory speeds up and facilitates acting on precepts already in the toolkit of analysts; and it suggests a couple of new ones. In a sentence, applied cultural theory offers the policy analyst an approach to his job, responsive to the needs of modern governance systems.

Given this justification for the need of a culturalist approach, the central question of this chapter is, What, if any, is the contribution of group-grid cultural theory for the analysis of public policy? In section 2, I will first provide a very concise overview of cultural theory, limited to what is minimally necessary for understanding the possibilities for application in policy analysis.[1] Next, in section 3, I show how group-grid cultural theory can be used as a tool to enrich policy analysis as conventionally understood. It is demonstrated (in section 3.1.) how group-grid cultural theory is used in the analysis of basic value orientations and institutional implications of policy discourses and elite policy belief systems; (in section 3.2.) how it may be used in spotting overlooked options and constructing productive hybrid policy alternatives in policy brokerage and policy design; and (in section 3.3.) how it helps in predicting side effects and intelligent policy learning. Yet, its most important contribution (demonstrated in section 3.4.) is in facilitating frame reflection in problem structuring. More particularly, paraphrasing one of Wildavsky's aphorisms, an inch of group-grid cultural theory gives scholars and practitioners miles of frame-reflective policy analysis.

2 WHAT IS GROUP-GRID CULTURAL THEORY?

Within a culturalist approach, one may distinguish between the attitudinal and the inclusive approach. The attitudinal approaches, like the civic culture (e.g., in Almond and Verba 1963) and (post)materialist culture traditions in political science (Inglehart and Baker 2000), use a restrictive definition of culture as mental products of individuals, i.e., meanings, values, norms, and symbols. In research, culture is operationalized as the aggregate of individual attitudes; where individuals are seen as single units of analysis, free from social contexts. In policy analysis, this social-psychological theorizing leads to the assumption of congruence or harmony between policy and political culture; where differences in culture have to be bridged by an "imposed," unifying governance culture. The inclusive approach defines culture more comprehensively. First, in social-constructivist fashion culture is seen as ways of world making, or ways of creating conceptual order and intelligibility through labels, categories, and other principles of vision and division (Bourdieu). Second, culture is studied as part and parcel of a way of life; individuals are seen in the context of prior social solidarities and institutions. In research and policy analysis the inclusive approach leads to "an institutional theory of multiple equilibria, in which different cultural contexts have opposing effects upon the thought and action of the individual" (Grendstad and Selle 1999, 46).

Within the inclusive approach, there is a further split between the romantic vision of culture, and modernist ones, like in Marxist and technological thinking (Van Gunsteren 2002). In the former version, the study of culture is a life-long undertaking; only "going native" provides the feel for detail and fine-grained distinction necessary fur truly grasping the essence of another (sub)culture; and the set of cultures is infinite in complexity and variety. In policy analysis, this would lead to advocacy for one particular culture, or becoming a specialist, like country specialists in the analysis of international politics. In Marxist and modern technological visions, culture is a dependent variable of underlying economic and technological realities. For policy analysis, quick analysis and practical understanding of culture is possible, but at the cost of seeing it as false consciousness in need of a reality correction. Group-grid cultural theory avoids both extremes. Being familiar with its four ideal-typical cultures speeds up analysis and orientation because it is a continuous warning sign against assuming universal culture or applying just one particular cultural lens to analyze a policy problem; and the social-constructivism underlying cultural theory will prevent one from falling in the trap of reducing culture to false consciousness.

Cultural theory originates from Mary Douglas' effort to remedy the failure of anthropologists to systematically compare cultures (Douglas 1978). Subsequently, Douglas herself developed the theory (esp. Douglas, 1987), but it was also quickly put to use in understanding policy debates on environmental problems and risks (e.g., Douglas and Wildavky 1982). In the 1980s and 1990s, the cultural theory bandwagon was joined by authors from many different social science disciplines, like Michael Thompson, Steve Rayner, Chris Lockhart, Richard Ellis, and Christopher Hood. In 1990, Thompson, Ellis, and Wildavsky produced what still stands as the most comprehensive statement and justification of cultural theory between the covers of one book (Thompson, Ellis, and Wildavsky 1990). In this way, cultural theory came to political science. Thompson, Grendstad. and Selle 1999) and policy analysis. Yet, it remains puzzling that Mary Douglas, as founding mother, and especially Aaron Wildavsky, as intellectual founder of Berkeley's school of public policy analysis and later lead user and advocate of group-grid cultural theory in political science (Wildavsky 1987), did so little in formally (as opposed to "inspirationally") linking cultural theory and policy analysis (but see Geva-May 1997, xiii; Swedlow 2002).

Cultural theorists claim that the social world ticks the way it does due to selective affinity and mutual dependency between social relations, cultural biases, and behavioral strategies. Therefore, group-grid cultural theory belongs in the inclusive camp. The group and grid dimensions of human transaction are constructed as the ultimate causal drivers in ordering social relations. These give rise to cultural biases as justifications for particular social orders. As justifications and sets of available orientations to action, the cultural biases influence behavior by making it patterned. The properties of social relations in group-grid cultural theory are about relational patterns, or stable types of transactions between people. The theory distinguishes between internal structures called "grid" and external structures called "group" Grid refers to the types of rules that relate one person to others on an ego-centered basis. Grid is low when there are few binding rules, and when people negotiate rules among themselves. Therefore, if grid is low, you have symmetrical transactions. Grid is high when rules are numerous and complex, and when they are imposed without people having much of a say in accepting or rejecting them. Therefore, if grid is high, you get asymmetrical transactions. Group refers to the experience of belonging to a bounded social unit. High group means people identify strongly with those they see as "members." Thus, if group is high, you get restricted transactions. Low group means people don't care for membership but for people who are intrinsically interesting for some reason or other. If group is low, you get less exclusive, unrestricted transactions.

Combining the group and grid dimensions gives you a social map with four types of relationships (see Figure 20.1). Two of them, markets or networks and hierarchy, are well known and thoroughly analyzed in previous social science literature (e.g., Lindblom 1977; Williamson 1975). But if the known types of social relationships are classified by two discriminators, a full typology should pay attention to the other two possibilities: clans or enclaves, and systems of isolation or zero-networks.

Corresponding to these four types of social relationships, so grid-group cultural theory's fundamental claim, are cultural biases. They refer to sets of shared values and beliefs (Thompson et al.,1990, 1), or stable orientations to action (Eckstein 1988, 790) or dispositions/habitus (Bourdieu 1998, 6). They are thought of as judgments of value which function as justifications of specific organizational structures. It is supposed that each develops its own typical set of beliefs, a cognitive and moral bias that contributes to reflexivity in the social organization (Douglas, gridgroup.listserv, March 10, 1998). In the language of complexity theory, the cultural biases function as stable attractors in socio-cultural landscapes. Group-grid cultural theory posits four viable or long-term sustainable cultural biases, called active or competitive individualism (Thompson et al. 1990, 34–35),

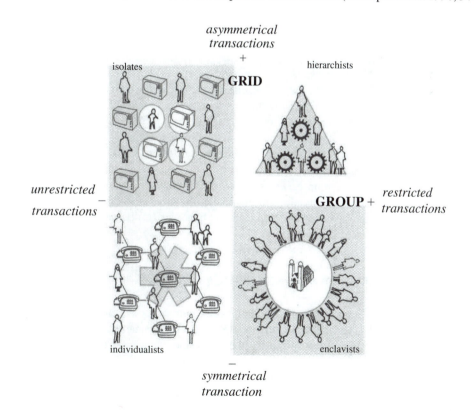

FIGURE 20.1 Cultural Theory's Grid/Group Typology. Source: Thompson, 1996; symbols taken from front page of Schmutzer, 1994.

pattern-maintaining or conservative hierarchy (Douglas and Wildavsky 1983, 90–92), egalitarian sects or dissident enclaves (Douglas 1986, 38–40; Sivan 1995, 16–18), and backwater isolates or fatalists (Schmutzer 1994; Douglas, 1996, 183–87). Michael Thompson claims the existence of a fifth cultural bias—indifference to and active avoidance of the group and grid dimensions of life results in hermit-like autonomy.

The orientations or dispositions underlying cultural biases guide judgment and action in many ways. Cultural theorists have inquired into the interpretive and more practical correspondences between the cultural biases and strategies in many social fields (Mamadouh 1999, for an overview). Perhaps the theory's most important claim here is its rigorous demonstration of the poverty of (individualist) *homo economicus* as dominant model for individual behavior, and thus the existence of "missing persons" in much of contemporary social science (Thompson et al. 1990, 40–47; Douglas and Ney 1998).

To some, the group/grid scheme is basically a descriptive taxonomy or typology. If looked at as a construction of ideal types, to which reality does not correspond in a one-to-one way, cultural theory as group/grid analysis offers considerable conceptual resources for comparative research and theory development. Real life phenomena can be analyzed as dyadic or triadic hybrids (Hood 1998); hybridization can take different time paths and have different critical junctures; and, therefore, some such hybrids may show more stability through time than others. Other theories conceptualize social change as faster or slower movement from one to another pole on a one-dimensional scale (modernism- postmodernism, materialism-postmaterialism). Group-grid analysis obliges you to perform the more demanding task to trace (simultaneous) changes between the four quadrants of its two-dimensional socio-cultural space (Thompson et al. 1990, 75ff).

One more element deserves brief elucidation, i.e., group-grid cultural theory's explanation of social change. Culturalist approaches generally have often been rejected as too static, better geared to explaining social stability than transformation. Social stability is unlikely as group-grid cultural theory views the mutual engagement of the four cultures/solidarities as continuous social and political struggle. Mary Douglas (1996, 43) stresses the institution-based (Douglas 1986) and constitution-making nature of human choice: "In the social sciences a choice is treated as ... arising out of the needs inside the individual psyche ... (In t)he theory of culture a choice is an act of allegiance and a protest against the undesired model of society. ... each type of culture is by its nature hostile to the other three cultures. ... (A) all four coexist in a state of mutual antagonism in any society at all times." The continuous struggles for cultural hegemony in different social fields imply agonistic interactions between people. Therefore, the theory hardly predicts the social harmony characteristic for theories of social stability. Group-grid cultural theory's model of social change as political and social struggle for cultural hegemony and learning makes the theory eminently suitable as a theoretical building block for a theory of long term policy dynamics (cf. Sabatier and Jenkins-Smith 1993; Baumgartner and Jones 1994; Eberg 1997).

3 CULTURAL THEORY AS A TOOL IN POLICY ANALYSIS

In this section I will show how group-grid cultural theory contributes to policy analysis as conventionally understood. I will argue that although existing policy analysis methods admonish analysts to map cultural context, they leave analysts mostly in the dark about how to go about it. All these tools lean on group-grid cultural theory's vision of the four cultures. Familiarity with this view speeds up a policy analyst's tasks considerably. From this perspective, although the ideas are not entirely new, applied group-grid cultural theory contributes substantially to the policy analytic toolkit (also Swedlow 2002). More particularly I will argue four points:

- cultural theory helps policy analysts in quick scans of basic value orientations and institutional as well as instrumental implications inherent in different strands of policy discourse and in elite policy belief systems (section 3.1);
- cultural theory allows policy analysts to quickly spot overlooked options and create culturally hybrid, but productive policy alternatives in policy brokerage and policy design tasks (section 3.2);
- cultural theory systematically helps policy analysts predict a policy's side effects and design policy-oriented learning processes (section 3.3);
- and last but not least, deriving from the prior points, cultural theory is an excellent heuristic in problem-structuring and frame-reflective policy analysis (section 3.4).

In illustrating these four points, I will draw on examples from many different policy problems and domains. Compared to using one or two running examples, I have thereby sacrificed background and depth of understanding to the (for my purposes in this chapter) more important goal of demonstrating the surprising versatility and flexibility of cultural theory in policy analytic applications. However, those interested in the former may consult the referenced works.

3.1 ANALYSIS OF BASIC VALUES AND INSTITUTIONAL IMPLICATIONS IN POLICY DISCOURSE AND POLICY BELIEF SYSTEMS

A first application of group-grid cultural theory is to perform a discourse analysis and map the belief systems (Sabatier and Jenkins-Smith 1993) or policy frames (Schön and Rein 1994) of protagonists and antagonists in a policy issue. In Sabatier's layered depiction, deep core beliefs involve fundamental normative and ontological beliefs that apply to all policy domains without exception. Grid-group cultural theory's four core-value systems—conservative hierarchy, active and competitive individualism, egalitarian enclavism, and fatalist isolates—can be used as an analyst's compass in finding his bearings in the ideals espoused in policy frames and belief systems. Table 20.1 is an illustration of a cultural typology of transport and mobility policy discourses developed by Robert Hoppe and John Grin (2000) in comparative research about technology assessments on transport and mobility issues. To develop the cultural theory-compass into a typology of discourses that also covers lower-order belief layers like policy core beliefs (fundamental problem definitions, positions, and strategies) and instrumental secondary beliefs (preferred policy instruments and information), considerable substantive familiarity and interactional expertise (Collins and Evans 2002) with the particulars of discourses in a particular policy domain is necessary. In this case, core values, policy cores, and secondary aspects had to be based upon intensive interpretive analyses of the discourse of spatial planning (Hoppe 1992) and car mobility policies in Britain, the Netherlands, and Germany (Hendriks 1999).

The typology was subsequently used to discover and unearth the cultural biases of members in policy issue networks through careful interpretation of document and interview data. The result is a detailed map of cultural biases prevalent in the policy discourses in a particular domain. Table 20.2 gives the results of the comparative study performed on the basis of the cultural typology for the transport and mobility domain (Hoppe and Grin, 2000). The final step, of course, is interpreting and explaining the distributive pattern found. In this particular case, the frequency of hierarchical policy frames is the most striking feature. This was explained by the position of parliamentarian TA institutes as knowledge producers and advisors to national parliaments. Only policy options plausibly available to national parliaments and national governments are taken into account. Being comprehensive and balanced, with a niche for every aspect, is the political strength of the hierarchist

TABLE 20.1
A Cultural Typology of Transport Policy Belief Systems

Policy core values	Hirarchist/Etatiste	Individualist/Market	Egalitarian/Public
Spatial organization of society	Stable, predictable part-whole pattern; preference for vertical relationships; preference for larger scale	Location/distance in horizontal space geared to efficient task performance; indifference to scale	Equally strong = equal size = rather small; preference for smaller scale
Mobility	Orderly and controlled mobility	Self-determination, individual mobility, accessibility	Equal access by all — residents, pedestrians, cyclists, motorists, public transport users — to a livable, sustainable public space
Dominant problem definition	*Chaos or stagnation*; too little inefficiently used capacity; how to keep transport "stream" in the "bed" of existing transport infrastructure; *supply problem* (unless demand stretches technical possibilities)	*Shortage of space*, passable roads, useful transport information; loss of valuable time and opportunities; *supply problem* (demand is always a given)	*Excessive demand for (car) mobility*; oversized infrastructure; erosion of public space; deterioration of environment and residential areas; *demand problem* (too much supply, anyway)
Preferred policy instruments	Regulation > market	Market > regulation	Inner conviction > regulation > market
External costs	Public acceptance of external transport costs; if unavoidable, private imposition of external transport costs	Disregard: if unavoidable, private acceptance of, or compensation for external transport costs	Public prevention, or (as second-best alternative) private imposition of external transport costs
Supply-oriented	Production of adequate supply, according to expert views	Increase supply of all possible transport modes, preferably through public funding	Resist all possible supply inceases
Demad-oriented	External, administrative demand regulation through (physical, technological, legal) prohibitions, mandates	Pay for supply shortages through marke regulation, i.e., individually focused pricing systems	Manage demand down-ward through education/persuasion (preferably) or (if need be) through administrative or market demand regulation
Favorite technology	Love of high-tech, large-scale transport technologies, technical fix	Love of cars, foremost; technical fixes	Love of low-tech, small-scale transport technologies; resist technical fixes

Reprinted by permission from *Parliaments and Technology: The Development of Technolgy Assessment in Europe* edited by Norman J. Vig and Herbert Paschen, the State University of New York Press. ©2000 State University of New York. All Rights Reserved.

position. This also explains why in lower-order layers of the policy belief system individualist and egalitarian elements do occur (Hoppe and Grin 2000, 312).

Of course, this research procedure may be formalized and quantified. In her study of so-called NIMBY (Not-In-My-Backyard)-type resistance to local waste facility siting decisions in the Netherlands, Van Baren (2001) used Q-methodology (Brown 1980; Durning 1999) to measure which policy frames could be assigned to different policy actors. They were asked to evaluate several statements on waste policy, physical planning and the attributes of decision-making processes in this domain in general, especially about their duration and tendency for deadlocks. For this purpose a set of statements was formulated on the basis of a factorial design reflecting the fundamental variance found in group-grid cultural theory. After performing hierarchical cluster analysis and (inverted) factor analysis on the data set of the evaluation of all statements by key actors, she identified three policy belief systems. Table 20.3 summarizes her findings.

TABLE 20.2
Cultural Biases in the Contents of TA Studies

PBS Element/ TA Study	Policy core: Spatial Organization	Policy core: Mobility	Problem definition	Policy instruments: External costs	Policy instruments: Supply oriented	Policy instruments: Demand oriented	Favorite technology
POST							
p&q	n.a.	H	H				
c&r			H	H		E	H, E
TN							
p&q*		H	H, E	H, E		H, I, E	
c&r	H, E	H, E	H, E	H, E	H, E,	H, I, E	H, E
RI							
p&q	n.a.	H	H, E	H			
c&r				H	H	E	
OPECST							
p&q	H, I	H, I	H (I)		H, I	I	H
c&r	H, I	H, I	H (I)		H, I	I	H
STOA							
p&q	E	H	H, E	I	H, I (E)	H (E)	H, I, E
c&r				I	H, I	H, I	H, E

Legend: The acronyms on the left vertical axis stand for parliamentarian Technology Assessment institutes in several countries involved in the study; p&q stands for problem definitions and questions asked; c&r for conclusions and recommendations. H, I, and E stand for the three active cultural biases.
*Considered here are TN's social problem definition in the broad sense (from which ecotaxation is a derivative), and topics identified for the consensus conference.
Reprinted by permission from *Parliaments and Technology: The Development of Technolgy Assessment in Europe* edited by Norman J. Vig and Herbert Paschen, the State University of New York Press. ©2000 State University of New York. All Rights Reserved

Datasets and analyses like the ones mentioned in this section provide the policy analyst with what Wildavsky called the first step in culturally sensitive policy analysis: the drawing of a sort of cultural baseline, or the (historically dynamic) description of the relative strength of the cultural biases in traceable sources of policy actors' statements and beliefs. Of course, such readily traceable sources should sometimes be complemented and verified by studies of more invisible sources of power and influence. Studies of the second and third faces of power may correct findings as the ones presented above.

3.2 FINDING OVERLOOKED OPTIONS AND CONSTRUCTING PRODUCTIVE CULTURALLY HYBRD POLICY ALTERNATIVES IN POLICY BROKERAGE AND DESIGN

The claim here is that group-grid cultural theory offers a parsimonious, yet sufficiently variegated system for up-close monitoring of movements in the belief systems and discursive practices of the myriad of policy actors populating the policy subsystems. Group-grid cultural theory's constrained relativism gives you four cultural-institutional focal points or "attractors." For the analysis of sub-politics in policy issue networks the ascertaining of the relative strength of the four cultural biases obviously, as proposed by Swedlow (2002), gives you more and better information about people's belief systems than rounding up the usual suspects of left versus right, or materialism versus post-materialism. Cultural theory constructs a society's political discursive space: how many plausible stories there are to tell, which actors are likely to tell which story, and which audiences are likely to find which story more credible (Ney and Thompson 1999, 215). This discursive space consists

TABLE 20.3
Policy Belief Systems (PBS)

	PBS 1	**PBS 2**	**PBS 3**
	"More waste capacity? Yes, on condition that careful through decisive decisions are made."	"More waste capacity is necessary! Government intervention is needed."	"More waste capacity? No, only in consultation with actors involved."
Style of thinking and acting	• Moderately egalitarian and individualistic	• Hierarchical and moderately individualistic	• Strongly egalitarian
Waste policy	• Waste prevention • Method of waste treatment	• Realizing sufficient waste facility capacity	• Impact of waste facility on environment
Physical planning	• Careful, but decisive	• Speeding up decision-making process is necessary	• Carefulness instead of speed

Source: Van Baren 2001, 267.

of the three meta-narratives of the active biases, i.e., hierarchy, individualism, and enclavism; and a suppressed, at least underarticulated, isolationist bias (Hoppe and Peterse 1993, 36–38). Every policy debate is about the argumentative and rhetorical "grip" these four metanarratives can exert on each other's manifest and latent adherents. They constrain and enable the types of political rhetoric that can be legitimately and successfully used by politicians and policy actors.

In analyzing the dynamics of her cases of local waste facility siting, Van Baren (2001, 202–10, 267–68) observed a pattern that could be exploited more generally by policy analysts applying group-grid cultural theory to their jobs. In cases where the hierarchist policy belief system was the dominant one, its adherents attempted to fix, and put closure on, the agenda of the entire decision making process. They actively worked to exclude or marginalize policy actors that held other policy frames; and thus prevented them from putting their issues on the agenda. Due to their frustration, these other actors initiated antagonistic, but non-dominant advocacy coalitions that could be linked to the strongly egalitarian third policy belief system. Not surprisingly, it is this kind of belief system that is dubbed NIMBY by their hierarchic opponents. In the resulting deadlock, policy talk and negotiations could only be resumed after brokers occurred on the scene. In cases in which planned capacity was eventually realized, such brokers had policy beliefs linked to the first, moderately egalitarian and individualist belief system. Obviously, this policy frame could function as a discursive bridge to get negotiations between advocates of hierarchist and egalitarian frames going again. Where no such brokers were found, deadlocks continued and planned capacity was not realized.

The generalizable lesson of Van Baren's comparative case studies is that by zooming in on the four ways of life and their (likely) hybrids, you have a heuristic for systematically construct-ing compromises, zones of productive engagement and possible convergence, and triangulating for culturally robust solution directions at relevant system levels (Schwarz and Thompson 1990; Roe 1998). Peterse and Hoppe (1998, 252–53), looking for cultural hybrids in their analysis of the controversy over Schiphol Airport's night flight regime, observed the absence of an enclavist-indi-vidualist alternative. From an individualist point of view, one would desire clear regulations and a transparent allocation of decision-making competences over public and private organizations. An individualist would insist on the flexibility of such arrangements, which can be guaranteed by rene-gotiating them on regular time intervals. From an egalitarian point of view, one would not object in principle, provided the decision making process would be institutionally designed so as to express public accountability and civic responsiveness. Based on this diagnosis of the state of public debate, they identified two groups potentially interested in pursuing such a policy alternative; entrepreneurs interested in sustainable air transport and their ecology-friendly potential clients.

Thus, it is useful and legitimate for a policy analyst to assess the accessibility for and loudness of voices of the four different cultural biases in a particular policy arena. In these kinds of "democracy audits" (Thompson 2002) or "plurality testing" (Peterse and Hoppe 1998, 246ff), the analyst sets out to demonstrate certain prejudices and imbalances between the four cultural biases; some of which may have to do with normal politics, but others may result from in-built institutional practices that need redressing. For example, Hendriks (1999) found that the differences in car mobility policies in Munich and Birmingham were, to a considerable extent, due to institutional differences between the local political and administrative infrastructures of both cities. Such institutions influence the penetration of the cultural biases in the policy process: their relative influence or force, and their inclusion or exclusion from a given policy arena. This, in turn, influences the mutual interaction between the biases, in terms of policy change, policy-oriented learning, and coalition strategies. Hoppe and Peterse (1993) have shown how to conduct such plurality tests in the example of debates on LPG-related external risks and Schiphol Airport's night flight regime (Peterse and Hoppe, 1998). Subsequently, they engaged in meta-policy design by suggesting ideas for adding temporary informal policy forums to the normal institutional arrangements in the government/business interface to hold risk-imposing firms publicly accountable for the risky externalities of their so-called private business strategies. Similarly, we engaged in some institutional redesign to build more civic responsiveness into large airport management. Thompson (2002) has applied similar methods to assess the democratic quality of development aid projects. The general idea is that zones of productive engagement or compromise are easier detected when all biases, but in the right proportions, have access to a particular policy domain. Apart from observing whether all the cultural policy frames are present in the debate and are taken seriously, the analyst should take care to assess the strength in numbers of the voices of isolationism/fatalism and autonomy that are usually absent in public debate. Too large quantities of these are supposed to undermine democracy and the quality of public debate. Similarly, an analyst should check if in policy domains or political regimes *in toto* the number of apparently uncontested issues is conspicuously large for a considerable time (Thompson 2002).

3.3 USING CULTURAL THEORY IN ANTICIPATING SIDE EFFECTS AND LEARNING

Group-grid cultural theory gives you a more developed heuristic for anticipating normally overlooked, undesirable side effects of program implementation. Even though many frame reflective analysts engage in backward mapping (Elmore 1985) of relevant policy frames held by implementing agencies and target groups, and in reconstructions of the belief systems of policy stakeholders, the major tacit assumption of policymakers still is that dismantling bureaucracy miraculously transforms bureaucrats and their citizen-clients alike in entrepreneurial individualists (Hood 1998; Hoppe et al. 2004). Smit and Van Gunsteren (1997), on the basis of cultural theory dynamics, predicted that Schiphol Airport management's stubborn monocultural, top-down imposed, and standardized implementation of noise-abating programs for nearby housing would lead to more and more egalitarian protest, individualist-induced law suits, and fatalist withdrawal. They recommended experiments in negotiating the meaning and policy implications of noise-abatement with bottom-up, responsive and flexible compensatory programs. Similarly, Van Gunsteren (2002) has criticized Dutch policy initiatives for toll roads and road pricing as means to tackle traffic jams. Policymakers mistakenly construct drivers as individualist choosers. But this overlooks that having chosen a job, a house, and a car, there is not much space left for choice. Given these choices, car drivers become fatalists that resign to chronic traffic jams, and make the best of it by transforming the interiors of their cars in comfortable individual spaces. Treating car drivers as individualist choosers will bring a government only loss of votes and confidence.

Jensen (1999) has criticized Danish legislators for designing regulation for social housing that imposes on tenants an "unworkable (enclavist) monoculture": "Though just one of the trio of possible destinations—egalitarianism—is the explicit goal of the reforms, these reforms actually operate in a way that ensures that most tenants end up at one or other of the other two destinations, either exiting into privately owned housing or sinking into fatalism" (Jensen 1999, 184). In her view, local-based intercultural institutional designs are to be preferred over nation-wide, uniform legislative reform. Of course, this would imply that hierarchist interpretations of consistency and absolutely equal treatment in legal science and the practice of law would have to give way to thinking among legislators, judges and lawyers in terms of more custom-made, individualist and egalitarian responsive law. As a final example of cultural theory's possibilities in anticipating undesirable side effects, I mention Van Asselt and Rotmans' (1996) method for systematic group support scenario writing in global climate change policymaking. Based on cultural theory's typology of surprises through mismatches (dystopias) between politically dominant (individualistic, say) constructions of how the world "out there" appears to work, and how it actually works (egalitarian, say), both quantitative models and qualitative scenarios can be systematically varied so as to tease out various undesirable and desirable future trajectories. These methods may play an important role in identifying "safe landing" scenarios in the way states and industries deal with this global problem.

Normal or conventional policy analysis uses methods of forward mapping from the ideals and ethical universals of politicians and policy analysts. In doing so, unwittingly, one optimistic assumption about goal-conform behavior is put on top of the next. Small wonder such an accumulation of optimism usually results in positive conclusions about a policy's feasibility and effectiveness. It is hard to break such habits of thinking in linear causality, simple systems and cybernetics, and goals-means relations, given the rationalist teleology prevalent in many policy analytic heuristics and methods. Not to mention that a policy's potentially undermining or negative side effects are not getting serious attention for reasons of political opportunism. One of the advantages of cultural theory is that its roots in institutionalism (Douglas, 1986) and complexity science (Thompson 1996) remind the policy analyst that next to rational teleology there are other teleologies to consider (Stacey 2001). The four ways of life or solidarities each have their own ways of unfolding over time (formative teleology), but may shift from one form to the next due to changes in context (transformative teleology). One of cultural theory's gifts to policy analysis therefore is the inclusion of the full range of teleologies involved in policy analysis and design.

3.4 Cultural Theory as Frame-Reflective Policy Analysis in Problem Structuring

The special problem of defining the nature of the problem has been recognized in policy analysis a long time ago quite independent from group-grid cultural theory. Following Dunn (2004) and many others, problem framing and structuring are the heart of good policy analysis. There exist several methods and techniques for problem framing and structuring. How can group-grid cultural theory help a policy analyst do a quicker, better, more systematic job here? Group-grid cultural theory's contribution in this field is that it teaches analysts which problem definition strategies to expect. It also gives them clues about which types will confront each other in policy arenas. This is potentially usable knowledge for teaching and practicing frame-reflective analysis (based on Hoppe 2002).

3.4.1 What Is a "Problem"?

Standard definitions speak of an unacceptable gap between normative ideals or aspiration levels and present and future conditions. Problems become public or policy problems if governments are supposed to deal with them. It follows that a "problem" is an analytical compound of three elements straddling the fact-value distinction: an ethical standard; a situation (present or future); and the construction of the connection between standard and situation as a gap which should not exist. Policy makers can agree or disagree on any of these elements. Concerning standards, one may distinguish between those with much and little consent. Regarding the situation (and its future development), there are those with highly certain and highly uncertain knowledge. About the relationship between standard and situation, people may disagree about the political sense to construct it as an intolerable gap in need of mending; or about the extent to which this is a government's responsibility. To simplify, I use only two dimensions—degree of certainty about knowledge, and degree of consent on relevant standards—to distinguish four types of problems (Hoppe 1989, based on Douglas and Wildavsky 1983; also Thompson and Tuden 1959).

Structured problems are characterized by high degrees of certain knowledge and consent. Road maintenance, or (as in The Netherlands) the application of rules for the allocation of social housing facilities, are some obvious examples. Dealing with such problems belongs to daily administrative routine. Moderately structured problems come in two distinct forms. In one variation, (moderately structured problems/ends) consent on relevant standards is high, i.e., relevant values and appropriate ends are not contested. But policy makers cannot agree on the effectiveness and efficiency of means to be used and (financial) resources and risks to be allocated. Many traffic safety problems belong here. Even though everybody sincerely supports the goals, neither experimental research, nor pilot projects, nor negotiations can usher in a definitive solution. The other variation (moderately structured problems/means) features substantial agreement on certain knowledge, but sometime intense disagreements about values at stake and ends to be pursued. Examples here are abortion, euthanasia, or voting rights for foreigners. We can easily do all of these things, but disagreement on the ethical desirability or acceptability of the values and goals continues and, sometimes, intensifies.

Finally, there are those problems where both the knowledge base and ethical support remain hotly contested. The most urgent and virulent political problems, unfortunately, frequently belong to this type. Such problems remain ill-defined, "wicked," "messy," or "ill-structured," or unstructured, a term I prefer. Technical methods for problem solving are inadequate; there is uncertainty as to which disciplines, specializations, experts, and skills to mobilize; conflicts over values abound, and many people get intensely involved, with strong but divisive opinions. Car mobility problems frequently belong to this type of unstructured problems. Fighting traffic jams is a permanent battlefield of value conflicts. Road pricing mechanisms increase costs versus equal access to car mobility, also for lower income groups; or the need for cheap road transport facilities as a basis for regional or national economic competition versus the accompanying rise in transport volume, which may clog major transport arteries. The knowledge base for choosing among policy instruments is weakly developed. There remains high uncertainty about the effectiveness of policy measures, due to inseparable interaction effects in field experiments, the long maturation time for effects to become visible and measurable, and confounding influences from other policy domains and international developments.

What value can be gained from bringing cultural theory to bear on this well-known problem typology? Could we say anything about how policy makers or analysts belonging to one of the four ways of life would cope with different problem types? Can we predict the primary orientation of an adherent of a particular solidarity to frame a problematic situation as a particular type of problem? I will proceed by presenting the starkest contrasts first. I start with the hierarchist policy maker or analyst who is an expert in framing and then solving structured problems. Then, I will contrast him[2] with the frequently overlooked one, the isolate policy maker or analyst who sees unstructured problems everywhere, and identifies solving them with personal and organizational survival. Finally, I will come to enclavists who see value conflicts as the root cause of every problem and their overcoming as precondition to any solution; and individualist types, who want to move away from problems, if only a few inches.

3.4.2 Hierarchists: "Structure It!"

Policy makers and analysts working in *complex bureaucracies* are exposed to strong hierarchical social relationships and interaction patterns. These organizational structures express a cultural bias or disposition to world making characterized as paradigm protection (Thompson and Wildavsky 1986, 280–81) or belief in *strong theories or methods*—certified by science, or more traditionally, founded in religion. Although these two are often believed to be mutually exclusive, in a modern handbook on socio-cybernetic policy analysis (Rastogi 1992, 12), we find them both, side by side.[3] Rastogi professes that any effort at problem solving begins with an ordered knowledge base, generated by a scientific methodology and an interdisciplinary theoretical language fit for complexity (Rastogi 1992, 12). Turning to the topic of long-term, lasting solutions, Rastogi (1992, 16) opines that the root causes of social problems are "the abnormal or disturbed emotions/motives of the social actors participating or involved in the problem situations." To "nullify" these, we need a belief system of religious, or religiously inspired, "super-rational values." Given these world-making orientations, the hierarchist's *rationality is functional and analytic*. It is functional, in the sense of starting from a supposedly agreed objective, as a function of which the most effective and efficient means is worked out. It is analytic, in the sense that problem solving is considered an intellectual effort, best left to experts. In his *Administrative Behavior,* Simon (1947) has shown how this type of rationality, exactly because it does not deny, but actively uses the inevitable boundaries on our intellectual capacity as a building block in organizational design, can be systematically applied to create complex bureaucratic structures in which everyone expertly solves his partial problem within the decision premises of the organization's leadership. The whole idea presupposes that problems come neatly packaged; and if they don't, they can be made to come that way. "Structure it!" is the hierarchist's primary orientation to the definition of problems.

3.4.3 Isolates: "Surviving without Resistance"

Isolates experience themselves as outcasts, subjected to a fate determined by dark forces or far-away ruling circles. "God is high, and the King is far" is a good expression of the isolates' state of mind. We may think of the isolate as belonging to the contemporary underclass, those who, at the margins of modern society, live a life of exclusion. It is a way of life not seen and heard in policy-making circles. This is why in many policy studies applying cultural theory only the three "active" voices—hierarchy, enclavism, individualism—are heard, and the "passive" isolate is absent. Isolates perceive the institutional settings in which they find themselves in one of two different ways. It is inherent in their world-making disposition to see the world as a *lottery*, and risk absorption as the only way of coping with this "fact of life" (Thompson and Wildavsky 1986, 280). Transferred to social, organizational, and political relations, their life worlds are constructed as *unstable casinos.* If they believe the unstable casino is ruled by mere randomness, they may define the institutional environment as *anarchy.* Alternatively he could define the institutional situation as a *barracks*, if he believes the unstable casino is actually run by an all-powerful but unpredictable human despot or tyrant. The "rationality" of the isolate and fatalist is a gaming or gambling one. According to Dror (1986, 168–69), under conditions of adversity, policymakers resort to "fuzzy gambling." In its extreme, fatalist form, any decision making is senseless. Surprise dominates life, better intelligence cannot improve ignorance, having goals and values is a luxury, and decisions make no sense because experience and past performance have lost their anchoring functions in a highly volatile environment. In an effort to make the best of it, fatalist policymakers or analysts could gamble to maximize their chances for maximum gain, or a maxmax strategy; or, alternatively, try the policy principle of minmin-avoidance, i.e., choose a strategy which prevents the worst outcome, or at least minimizes the damage (Dror 1986, 10). The isolate, fatalistically inclined or more optimistic, will be predisposed to define any problem as unstructured. Believing that the world is a lottery and the social world an unstable casino, he will be extremely reluctant to impose any definitive framing on a problematic situation. "Survival" and "resilience" are the isolate's watchwords (Schwarz and Thompson 1990; Hood 1998), and they proscribe him to have any fixed ideas, let alone theories and methods, about the nature of the problem and how to solve it. Instead, he must be totally flexible, keep options open in order to be maximally resourceful and alert at every opportunity to escape fate and grab the lucky number.

3.4.4 Enclavists: "It's Not Fair!"

When one prefers a way of life permitting only relations with like-minded people and as little interference as possible from outsiders, one joins a clan, club, or commune. In group-grid cultural theory such people are called enclavists. They choose to inhabit an enclave encircled by a 'hostile' world. The world-making disposition of enclaves is best described as enlarged groupthink (Janis 1982). The enclavist way of life institutionalizes itself by systematically instilling the groupthink cultural bias in most of its adherents. Guarding the group boundaries by picturing the outside world as evil and mean is the principal way of keeping a society of enclavists together. This is exactly what the enlarged groupthink symptoms achieve. If they fail, expulsion, always disgraceful and sometimes violent, is the enclavist's means of last resort. The world-making disposition of enlarged groupthink is imbued with a communicative form of value rationality. It is communicative, because verbal means of persuasion, from public debate to speeches to propaganda campaigns, are the only allowed means of creating consent among equals. It is value rational, in the sense of normative standards and goal-finding being the major issue of problem-solving efforts, because the mix of inside moralism and outside criticism makes enclavists never miss an opportunity to point out the value conflicts between "us" and "them." The major route to a solution is that "they" give up their "wrong" values and change their ways accordingly. Enclavists proselytize, and outsiders should convert to the enclavist's values and life style. This assumption of ubiquitous value conflicts leads enclavist policymakers and analysts to structure problems as moderately structured/means. The valu- ative problem dimension is stressed. This does not mean that enclavist policy makers and analysts scrupulously survey all relevant values. Opposing "our" values to "theirs"—frequently attributed on the basis of stereotypes—is sufficient. The same logic breeds close monitoring of differences between groups in society; particularly differences in treatment by government. Thus, frequently, the value conflict is shaped as an issue of distributive justice, equality, or (broadly understood) fairness.[4] The fairness problem frame spills over into a problem of trust in the sphere of interaction and institutions.

3.4.5 Individualists: "Let's Make Things Better!"[5]

In the low group/low grid cell, we find the individualist way of life. In terms of interaction patterns, adherents prefer freely chosen exchange relations to other people. Except in the institutional domains of markets, they find and (re)create them in social networks. In networks, individuals "socialize" with partners, which results in a flurry of networking activity, with persons continuously moving in and out and between networks as they see fit. In networking, they live out their world-making disposition of seizing opportunities for individual benefit. The individualist type of rationality is functional and strategic. It is functional, in the sense that he searches for usable knowledge, i.e., data and informa- tion which help him maximize his utility, or at least "satisfice" at the self-selected aspiration levels (Simon 1947). It is strategic, in the sense that individualists are adept in getting usable knowledge by exploiting their personal networks. It is about "shifting the really vital discussions away from the formalized information-handling system and on to the informal old boy net. We characterize this strategy as individualist manipulative" (Thompson and Wildavsky, 1986, 280–81). The individualist's basic orientation to problems and problem solving is: "Let's make things better; let's get usable knowledge." What is a policy problem, so that it may be properly defined for an individualist policy maker or analyst? Essentially, "problems" are opportunities for improvement.[6] Defining a problem is framing it as a choice between two or more alternative means to seize that opportunity (Dery 1984, 27). Individualists don't care much for explicit value search and goal formulation. Always taking present conditions as evaluative baseline, individualists limit their preferences to comparisons of incremental change (Braybrooke and Lindblom 1963, 85). This largely implicit, meliorative way of treating values and goals fits the individualist networking style of political interactions hand-in-glove. Being casual about political ideology and explicit policy values allows individualist policy makers to identify shared interests, concerns and threats easily—even with potential opponents (cf. Sabatier and Jenkins-Smith 1993, 223–25). Likewise, preference aggregation among many individualist policy makers comes about as an epiphenomenon of the ongoing partisan mutual adjustment in policy networks (Braybrooke and Lindblom 1963, 15; Lindblom,1965). On the cognitive side of problems, the individualist policy makers' and analysts' instrumental outlook logically values know-how over know-that. They need usable knowledge (Lindblom and Cohen 1979), irrespective of its source. Sometimes the source is scientific or professional inquiry. But they rely as much or more on common sense and practical knowledge. Here again, their interaction style helps them mobilize the usable knowledge or "intelligence of democracy" (Lindblom 1965) implicitly stored in their networks. It follows that the individualist policymaker clearly prefers defining a problem as moderately structured/ends.

3.4.6 A Typology of Cultures of Problems

Figure 20.2 summarizes the results achieved by bringing cultural theory to bear on one particular problem definition. It shows that there is a straightforward match between the four cultures and policy problem types. Each way of life corresponds to one primary problem-framing strategy.

Thus, group-grid cultural theory's most important contribution is in the crucial, but very difficult task of problem structuring. Elsewhere I have argued why deliberate cognitive *problem structuring* by analysts and *reasoned problem choice* by democratically accountable politicians is indispensable in avoiding policy controversies and breaking deadlocks (Hisschemöller and Hoppe 1996; reprinted in Hisschemöller et al. 2001). It involves the confrontation, evaluation, and integration of as much contradictory information as possible. Apart from many social and political conditions, problem structuring requires forensic policy analysts endowed with skills of problem reframing or "the capacity to keep alive, in the midst of action, a multiplicity of views of the situation" (Schön 1983, 281). The forensic policy analyst considers it his task to use the differences between problem frames to forge an innovative policy design from a combination of plausible and robust arguments (frame-reflective analysis), or to test and bolster some frames (frame-critical analysis). Knowledge about different types of problem frames, and different repertoires of problem definition strategies, is a basic element in building a best practice or craft of doing forensic analysis (Anderson 1987; Jennings 1987). Precisely at this point cultural theory offers a valuable contribution. Thompson et al. (1990) have defended the thesis that at the intersection of grid and group on the socio-cultural map sits a fifth ideal-type—the "hermit"—named for this type's self-conscious withdrawal from commitment to and involvement in the other four ways of life. Schmutzer (1994) stresses another aspect of aloofness from the four ways of life, i.e., free access and movement between them. He therefore interprets the fifth ideal-type as a *Hermes*, the fast running messenger and clever translator, the god of commerce and traffic of the Greeks. Policy analysis needs Hermes-like problem structuring to become an accepted and feasible, teachable tool of the trade.

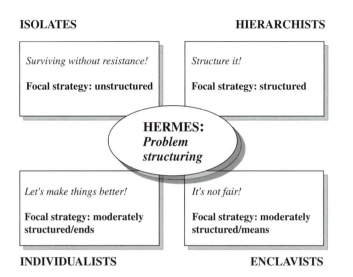

ISOLATES

Surviving without resistance!

Focal strategy: unstructured

HIERARCHISTS

Structure it!

Focal strategy: structured

HERMES:
Problem structuring

Let's make things better!

Focal strategy: moderately structured/ends

It's not fair!

Focal strategy: moderately structured/means

INDIVIDUALISTS

ENCLAVISTS

FIGURE 20.2 Cultural Bias and Problem Definition. Source: Hoppe 2002, 320 (reprinted from *Journal of Comprative Policy Analysis: Research and Practice*).

Group-grid cultural theory gives the policy analyst a conceptual basis and clues for more productive problem structuring. Consider the way Mamadouh (2002) decides to reframe the entire issue of dealing with multilingualism in the European Union (EU). At present the EU has 11 official and working languages; after expansion of its membership this number will even go up. Although dissatisfied about the practical problems and costs of institutional multilingualism and the factual linguistic homogenization through informal use of English, politicians avoid the issue; obviously there is no compromise between preserving national linguistic identities and improving EU communication. Academics and professionals—mostly language teachers—frame the problem as how many and which language(s) are going to survive? Which language(s) should dominate curriculums? Rational choice theory, reflecting the individualist culture, predicts that English will be the new *lingua franca*; it supposedly contributes most to your within-Europe communication potential. From a cultural theory perspective, Mamadouh argues, the professional and rational choice ways of framing the problem are one sided. She shows that the four cultural logics all have their own, sometimes contextually influenced, preferred repertoires for dealing with the plurality of languages as a barrier to social interactions: "...the pertinent question is not so much 'how many languages' or 'which language(s)?', but 'how is the mediation between speakers of different languages organized?'" (Mamadouh 2002, 341). In this perspective, the present situation can be analyzed as not so irrational, and many more strategies by stakeholders and policymakers alike appear likely and defensible. Thereby, cultural theory contributes to opening up the solution space for the problem of multilingualism.

4 APPLIED CULTURAL THEORY FACILITATES FRAME-REFLECTIVE ANALYSIS

In this chapter I have highlighted four contributions of cultural theory to policy analysis. Of course, this is not to say that applying cultural theory to questions of policy is easy and unproblematic. More particularly, some problems with the theory's structure and validation itself (Mamadouh,1999) spill over into its application to policy analysis. An important issue is level of analysis. It is not always easy to carefully specify whether one's analysis applies to policy preferences (bias), institutional ensembles (policy making relations), or policy behavior (implementation strategies, say). The theory itself is about coherent configurations of these three levels of analysis, but inconsistent combinations do occur in policy practice, and they should not be overlooked. Another level of analysis problem is the relationship between individuals, groups and larger human ensembles. Some consider it an advantage that the theory applies to all levels. Indeed, from a political and policy perspective it is familiar to distinguish egalitarian "wings" in political parties or government departments that, overall, are hierarchic or individualist. But this also leads to problems of interpreting an individual's position or behavior as carrier of cultural bias. Are individual policy actors coherent in the sense of consistent over time as carriers of one specific bias/relation/behavior set? Or are they sequential, in the sense of supporting one set but being open or vulnerable to other ones? Or are they even synthetic, in the sense of supporting different sets at different times for different audiences? (Olli 1999) Are only policy and political elites coherent; and the masses sequential or synthetic? Or does the plurality of present day political systems force leading politicians to be synthetic too? If the latter would be true, cultural theory interpretation runs headway into the problem of stolen rhetoric and stolen strategy in politics, i.e. using one type of policy discourse to achieve one's true goals in another, more true discourse. Especially in multiparty systems with compromise governments this would be a serious problem for applying cultural theory to policy analysis (Stenvoll 2002). A problem compounded by the fact that cultural theory itself predicts adherents of different bias/relations/behavior sets to have inherently different preferences for political and policy analysis at different levels of analysis and scale. Another problem to do with the level of analysis issue is that it is very difficult to use ordinary survey or poll data to infer cultural baselines. Although especially Norwegian political scientists Grendstad and Selle have developed this art to some extent (Grendstad and Selle 1997; Grenstad 1999; Grendstad and Selle 2000; Grendstad 2003), more qualitative and interpretive approaches to establishing the relative strength and weakness of cultural bias on higher-than-the-individual level look more convincing. In spite of many applications to many different policy fields, it remains the task of the individual policy analyst to devise a culturalist compass by himself for his own policy field. At best, the methodological guidelines given in section 3.1 provide him with some suggestions of how to proceed.

This brief list of problems serves to warn the reader that using applied cultural theory as a tool in policy analysis is not without its problems; and certainly does not absolve the analyst from proceeding cautiously and prudently. Nevertheless, as shown mainly by Christopher Hood (1998), being alert to cultural hybrids and different levels of analysis should steer the analyst clear of circular arguments and invalid conclusions. But in summary of all of the above, it bears repeating and stressing that cultural theory, if used with discretion and good judgment, contributes a fast-working and systematic heuristic for doing frame-reflective and frame-critical policy analysis. This mode of doing policy analysis fits the new pluralism hand in glove. It focuses on the cultural-institutional origins of people's preferences and multiple and pluriform frames of thinking and acting—the stuff of frame reflective analysis. But what stops the forensic analyst from becoming overwhelmed? Which people and which frames to include in her analysis? What is the meaning of a robust policy alternative if an analyst has no clue about the substantive and participatory closure of an issue? How does she distinguish between a merely accidental, local consensus and the political acceptability of policy proposals for nation-wide, perhaps transnational audiences? How does a forensic, frame reflective analyst not become a contemporary Sophist? This is where cultural theory's constrained relativism contributes most to good policy analysis. Without cultural theory, forensic analysis is easily overwhelmed by variety and complexity; it would fail to see the cultural wood for the symbolic trees, become a prey of cultural, interpretive and rhetorical stamp collection (Hood 1998), and postmodern epistemological and moral relativism. One remedy for the new pluralism would be to retrain policy analysts as applied political philosophers, as recommended by Hodgkinson (1983) and the policy philosophers (see Bobrow and Dryzek 1987). But a more efficient way of achieving the same is to use group-grid cultural theory as a simple but effective tool for frame reflective, argumentative policy analysis. If modern democracy and citizenship are indeed about the constructive organization of dealing with otherness and plurality (Van Gunsteren, 1998), policy analysis needs group-grid cultural theory to do a better job. This is because, to paraphrase Wildavsky, an inch of group-grid cultural theory gives an analyst miles of frame reflective analysis.

NOTES

1. See Thompson et al., 1990 for the best full exposition of the theory; for a more complete introduction and overview, see Mamadouh, 1999.
2. Needless to say that in this article he/him everywhere can also be read as she/her.
3. Of course, Rastogi is eccentric, but honest, in founding his normative position on religion. Policy analysts usually take either a cognitivist or a non-cognitivist meta-ethical stance. Cognitivism in policy analysis is frequently identified with Brecht's Scientific Value Relativism (or Alternativism). Scientists cannot scientifically determine whether or not something is valuable; but 'given' an ultimate value, they can use their scientific methods to clarify the implications and consequences of adhering to this 'given' value. Most policy analysts, e.g. cost-benefit analysts and pragmatic incrementalists, adhere to some form of emotive non-cognitivism, i.e. they deny ethical statements any cognitive status beyond emotional expressions of ephemeral and temporary preferences. The only thing scientists may do is observe people's preferences as manifested in their behavior, and adopt these 'observed' preferences as normative lodestars. Paradoxically, these more frequent meta-ethical positions, in practice, amount to the same hierarchical bias as Rastogi's in favor of experts who claim the right to force-feed their 'scientific' interpretations and 'empirical' indicators for values to politicians, policymaking officials, and citizens (Van de Graaf and Hoppe, 1989: 141–157; Fischer, 1990).
4. So strong is this tendency that in many versions of cultural theory enclavists are called 'egalitarians'.
5. Any similarity with an advertisement slogan of a multi-national company is wholly intentional.
6. The Pareto optimum in cost benefit analysis – choose the alternative(s) which make at least one person better off, and nobody else worse off—is the algorithmic form of the individualist position.

REFERENCES

Almond, G.A. and Verba, S. (1963). *The civic culture. Political attitudes and democracy in five nations*, Newbury Park, CA/London: Sage.

Anderson, Ch. W. (1987). Political philosophy, practical reason, and policy analysis. In F. Fischer and J. Forester (eds) *Confronting values in policy analysis. The politics of criteria*, 22–44. Newbury Park, CA: Sage.

Baumgartner, F.R. and Jones, B.D. (1993). *Agendas and instability in American politics*. Chicago and London: Chicago University Press.

Bobrow, D.B. and Dryzek, J.S. (1987) *Policy analysis by design*. Pittsburgh, PA: University of Pittsburgh Press.

Bourdieu, P. (1998). *Practical reason: on the theory of action*. Cambridge: Polity Press.

Braybrooke, D. and Lindblom, Ch.E. (1963) *A strategy of decision. Policy evaluation as a social process.* New York: Free Press.

Brown, S.R. (1980). *Political subjectivity: applications of Q-methodology in political science*. New Haven, CT: Yale University Press.

Collins, H.M. and Evans, R (2002). The third wave of science studies: studies of expertise and experience, *Social Studies of Science* 32, 2, 235–296.

Dery, D. (1984). *Problem definition in policy analysis*. Lawrence, KS: University Press of Kansas.

Douglas, M. (1978). *Cultural bias*. Occasional paper, Royal Anthropological Institute, 35.

Douglas, M. (1986). *How institutions think*. Syracuse, NY: Syracuse University Press.

Douglas, M. (1996). *Thought styles: Critical essays on good taste*. London: Sage.

Douglas, M. and Ney, S. (1998). *Missing persons: A critique of personhood in the social sciences*. Berkeley: University of Califormia Press.

Douglas, M. and Wildavsky, A. (1982). *Risk and culture*. Berkeley, CA: University of California Press.

Dror, Y. (1986). *Policymaking under adversity*. New Brunswick, NJ: Transaction Publishers.

Dunn, W.N. (2004). *Public policy analysis. Anintroduction* (3rd ed.). Upper Saddle River, NJ: Pearson Prentice Hall.

Durning, D. (1994). The transition from traditional to postpositivist policy analysis: a role for Q-methodology, *Journal of Policy Analysis and Management* 18, 3, 389–410.

Eberg, J. (1997). *Waste policy and learning. Policy dynamics of waste management and waste incineration in the Netherlands and Bavaria*. Delft: Eburon.

Eckstein, H. (1988). A culturalis theory of change, *American Political Science Review* 82, 3, 789–804.

Elmore, R.F. (1985). Forward and backward mapping: reversible logic in the analysis of public policy. In K. Hanf and T. Toonen (eds) *Policy implementation in federal and unitary systems*, 33–50. Dordrecht: Kluwer.

Fischer, F. (1990). *Technocracy and the politics of expertise*. Newbury Park, CA: Sage.

Geva-May, I. (2002). Cultural theory: The neglected variable in the craft of policy analyis. *Journal of Comparative Policy Analysis: Research and Practice* 4, 243–266.

Grendstad, G. (1999). A political cultural map of Europe. A survey aproach. In *GeoJournal* 47, 463–475.

Grendstad, G. (2003). Grid-group theory and political orientations: Effects of cultural biases in Norway in the 1990s. *Scandinavian Political Studies* 23, 3, 217–241.

Grendstad, G. and Selle, P. (1997). Cultural theory, postmaterialism and environmental attitudes. In R. Ellis and M. Thompson (eds.), *Culture matters. Essays in honor of Aaron Wildavsky*, 151–168. Boulder, CO: Westview Press.

Grendstad, G. and Selle, P. (1999). The formation and transformation of preferences. Cultural theory and postmeterialism compared. In M. Thompson, G. Grendstad and P. Selle (eds.), *Cultural Theory as Political Science*, 43–58.

Hajer, M. (2000). *Politiek als vormgeving*. Vossiuspers: Amsterdam.

Hendriks, F. (1999) *Public policy and political institutions: The role of culture in traffic policy*. Aldershot: Edward Elgar.

Hisschemöller, M. and Hoppe, R. (1996). Coping with intractable controversies. The case for problem structuring in policy design and analysis, *Knowledge and policy: the International Journal of Knowledge Utilization and Transfer* 8, 4, 40–60.

Hisschemöller, M., Hoppe, R., Dunn, W.N., and Ravetz, J.R. (2001). *Knowledge, power, and participation in environmental policy analysis. Policy studies review annual, 12*. New Brunswick, NJ: Transaction Publishers.

Hodgkinson, Chr. (1983). *The philosophy of leadership*. Oxford: Basil Blackwell.

Hood, Chr. (1998). *The art of the state*. Oxford: Clarendon Press.

Hoppe, R. (1989). *Het beleidsprobleem geproblematiseerd: Over beleid ontwerpen en probleemvorming*. Muiderberg: Coutinho.

Hoppe, R. (1992). Enkele opmerkingen over de bestuursgeografische bijdrage aan een constructivistisch-critische bestuurskunde. In H. van den Brink (ed.), *Bestuur en Territoir. Opstellen aangeboden aan drs. A. Bours*, 69–81. Amsterdam: Het Sprinhuis.

Hoppe, R. (2002). Cultures of policy problems. *Journal of Comparative Policy Analysis: Research and Practice* 4, 305–326.

Hoppe, R and. Grin, J. (2000). Traffic problems go through the technology assessment machine: a culturalist comparison. In N. Vig and H. Paschen (eds), *Parliaments and technology. The development of technology assessment in Europe*, 273–324. Albany: State University of New York Press.

Hoppe, R. and Peterse, A. (1993). *Handling frozen fire. Political culture and risk management*. Boulder: Westview Press.

Hoppe, R., Jeliazkova, M.I., Grin, J. and Van de Graaf, H. (2004). *Beleidsnota's die (door)werken*. Bussum: Coutinho.

Inglehart R., and Baker, W.E. (2000). Modernization, cultural change and the persistence of traditional values, *American Sociological Review* 65, 19–51.

Janis, I.L. (1982). *Groupthink. Psychological studies of policy decisions and fiascoes* (2nd ed.). Boston: Houghton Mifflin Comp.

Jennings, B. (1987) Interpretation and the practice of policy analysis. In F. Fischer and J. Forester (eds) *Confronting values in policy analysis. The politics of criteria*, 128–152.

Jensen, L. (1999). Images of democracy in Danish housing. In M. Thompson et al (eds) *Cultural Theory as Political Science*, 173–185.

Lindblom, Ch.E. (1965) *The intelligence of democracy*. New York: Free Press.

Lindblom, Ch.E. (1977). *Politics and markets. The world's political-economic systems*. New York: Basic Books.

Lindblom, Ch. E. and Cohen, D. (1979). *Usable knowledge*. New Haven: Yale University Press.

Mamadouh, V. (1999). Grid-group cultural theory, *GeoJournal* 46, 3, 395–500.

Mamadouh, V. (2002). Dealing with multilingualism in the European Union: Cultural theory rationalities and language policies. *Journal of Comparative Policy Analysis: Research and Practice* 4, 327–346.

Olli, E. (1999). Rejection of cultural biases and effects on party preference. In M. Thompson, G. Grendstad, and P. Selle (eds.) *Cultural Theory as Political Science*, 59–74.

Peterse, A. and Hoppe, R. (1998). Argumentatieve beleidsanalyse toegepast op het debat over Schiphols vluchtregime tussen 06.00 en 07.00 uur. In R. Hoppe and A. Peterse (eds.) *Bouwstenen voor Argumentatieve Beleidsanalyse*, 221–261.

Rastogi, P.N. (1992). *Policy analysis and problem solving for social systems. Toward understanding, monitoring and managing complex real world problems*. New Delhi: Sage.

Roe, E. (1998). *Taking complexity seriously: Policy analysis, triangulation, and sustainable development*. Boston/Dordrecht: Kluwer.

Sabatier, P. and Jenkins-Smith, H. (eds) (1993). *Policy change and learning: an advocacy coalition approach*. Boulder: Westview Press.

Schmutzer, M.E. (1994). *Ingenium und individuum. Eine sozialwissenschaftliche theorie von wissenschaft und technik*. Wien und New York: Springer Verlag.

Schön, D.A. (1983). *The reflective practitioner. How professionals think in action*. New York: Basic Books.

Schön, D.A. and Rein, M. (1994). *Frame reflection: Toward the resolution of intractable policy controversies*. New York: Basic Books.

Schwarz, M. and Thompson, M. (1990). *Divided we stand: Redefining politics, technology, and social choice*. New York: Harvester Wheatsheaf.

Simon, H.A. (1947). *Administrative behavior*. New York: Wiley.

Sivan, E. (1995). The enclave culture. In M.M. Marty (ed) *Fundamentalism comprehended*. Chicago: Chicago University Press.

Stacey, R.D. (2001). *Complex responsive processes in organizations. Learning and knowledge creation*. London and New York: Routledge.

Stenvoll, D. (2002). Norwegian politics of abortion: Perspectives, arguments and values. *Journal of Comparative Policy Analysis* 4, 287–304.

Swedlow, B. (2002). Toward cultural analysis in policy analysis: Picking up where Aaaron Wildavky left off. *Journal of Comparative Policy Analysis: Research and Practice* 4, 267–286.

Thompson, J.D. and Tuden, A. (1959). Strategies, structures and processes of organizational decisions. In J.D. Thompson et al (eds) *Comparative Studies in Administration*. Pittsburgh, PA: Pittsburgh University Press.

Thompson, M. (1996). *Inherent relationality. An anti-dualist approch to institutions*. Bergen: LOS Report 9608.

Thompson, M., Ellis, R. and Wildavsky, A (1990). *Cultural theory*. Boulder, CO: Westview Press.

Thompson, M. and Wildavsky, A. (1986). A cultural theory of information bias in organizations, *Journal of Management Studies* 23, 3, 273–286.

Thompson, M., Grendstad, G. and Selle, P. (eds.) (1999). *Cultural theory as political science*. London and New York: Routledge.

Thompson, M. (2002). Don't let it put you off from dinner: First steps towards ethical policies shaped by cultural considerations. *Journal of Comparative Policy Analysis* 4, 347–363.

Van Asselt, and M. Rotmans,J. (1996). Uncertainty in perspective. *Global Environmental Change* 6, 2, 121–157.

Van Baren, N. (2001). *Planhiërarchische oplossing: een bron voor maatschappelijk verzet*. PhD dissertation, University of Amsterdam, Amsterdam.

Van de Graaf, H. and Hoppe, R. (1989). *Beleid en politiek*. Muiderberg: Coutinho.

Van Gunsteren, H.R. (1998). *A theory of citizenship. Organizing plurality in contemporary democracies*. Boulder: Westview Press.

Van Gunsteren, H. (2002) Regimes as cultures (unpublished paper).

Van Gunsteren, H. and Smit, P. (1997). Cultuur en constitutievorming rond Schiphol. *Beleid en Maatschappij* 2, 62–73.

Wildavsky, A. (1987). Choosing preferences by constructing institutions: A cultural theory of preference formation. *American Political Science Review* 81, 1, 3–21.

Williamson, O.E. (1985). *The economic institutions of capitalism*. New York: Free Press.

21 Ethical Issues and Public Policy

Eileen Sullivan and Mary Segers

INTRODUCTION

Public policies distribute resources and values, shaping social and political life in the process. Elected and appointed public officials inevitably make normative decisions; in the classic words of David Easton, "Politics is the authoritative allocation of values." The candidate for office who is sure his victory depends on a deal with a corrupt local leader, the analyst evaluating a program who feels pressure to overemphasize benefits or underemphasize costs, the public health administrator developing a state-wide program to distribute organ transplants, the administrator of a public university contemplating an affirmative action plan, and the deputy who sees his superiors violating the law all face important ethical choices.

Because politics inevitably requires such choices, political science and public policy programs generally include at least one course on ethics and politics. These courses are not easy to teach because they have to impart some knowledge of moral and political philosophy, an ability to recognize ethical issues in specific political situations, and an understanding of the ways ethical theories can be applied both to clarify those situations and to provide criteria for satisfactory resolutions.

As professors teaching ethics and politics for many years, we have developed a course that challenges our students to realize the complexity of the ethical decision-making they will confront in their professional lives. The course draws upon writings in political theory as well as contemporary cases of ethical dilemmas in policy and public administration. We approach this material from the perspective of the public official. We select case studies that show the types of ethical conflict that arise for people in government positions, including elected and appointed officials, those responsible to take action, and those who conduct research or provide policy or legal advice. The cases illustrate how officials define ethical situations, how they think through their options, how and why they reach a particular decision and, where possible, how they reflected on those decisions afterward.

The cases often involve officials at relatively high levels of government dealing with unusually important cases involving war and peace, equality and discrimination, abortion and stem cell research. Our task is to make clear the ways in which the official thinking and our analysis of that thinking can be applied to people at all levels of government dealing with cases of all degrees of importance.

In this chapter, we describe how we teach this course in ethics, politics, and public policy. We begin with a brief definition of ethics and discuss prevailing theories of ethical decision making—consequentialist approaches, deontological or Kantian theories, and the contemporary renaissance of virtue ethics. We illustrate how public officials have used these ethical approaches in an actual decision-making process. We then consider what is distinctive about politics, why the complexities of public life make it different from private life, and what implications this has for applying ethics to politics. We include the cases of two public officials who at a time of crisis behaved ethically and effectively. The most distinctive aspect of politics is the fact that public officials often have to decide whether to use morally dubious means like violence, lying, and deception to promote the interests of those they represent. We discuss briefly some of the literature on "dirty hands" in politics and include a final case study on the use of violent means in warfare. We conclude with some suggestions about how to approach ethical decision making in public service—through a mix of appreciation of consequences, fidelity to duty, and respect for oneself and one's organization as moral agents.

ETHICS AND ETHICAL PERSPECTIVES

Ethics deals with values, with good and bad, with right and wrong. The fundamental questions raised by Socrates and Plato in ancient Greece are central to the study of ethics: How should one live? What is the good life? What makes an action the right, rather than the wrong, thing to do? What should our goals be? As Peter Singer notes, "We cannot avoid involvement in ethics, for what we do—and what we don't do—is always a possible subject of ethical evaluation. Anyone who thinks about what he or she ought to do is, consciously or subconsciously, involved in ethics" (Singer 1991, v). As applied to politics, the central ethical questions are what ends or goals should government serve? And what processes or means should government use to achieve those ends?

From the standpoint of philosophy, ethical theory or normative ethics is concerned with developing and justifying the standards or norms that should guide action. Applied ethics is concerned with the ways those norms or standards can be applied to actual situations, to clarify the ethical issues involved and to suggest standards and modes of reasoning that might be appropriate to resolving them. The study of ethics and politics is an example of applied ethics.

Three approaches currently dominate the landscape of normative ethics: consequentialism, deontological ethics, and virtue ethics. *Consequentialism* emphasizes good results as the basis for evaluating human actions. The core idea of consequentialism is that what makes an action or a policy right is that it brings about better consequences than any of its alternatives. Consequentialist theories offer various definitions of the best outcome, including the greatest possible increase of pleasure over pain of classic utilitarianism, and the greatest possible satisfaction of preferences of welfare economics (Pettit 1997). Theories of the common good, rooted in the writings of Plato, Aristotle, and Cicero, can also be examples of consequentialist approaches. They urge us to view ourselves as members of the same community who share mutual goals, and

> focus on ensuring that the social policies, social systems, institutions, and environments on which we depend are beneficial to all. Examples of goods common to all include affordable health care, effective public safety, peace among nations, a just legal system, and an unpolluted environment. (Velasquez et al., 2002, 2)

Consequentialism is the ethical approach taken by most public officials. The public health administrator who spends a state's limited resources on primary health care that will serve many rather than on expensive organ transplants that will serve few, the research analyst who conducts a cost benefit analysis of a proposed program, and the university that adopts an affirmative action program to promote diversity all are taking this approach.

Despite the popularity and currency of consequentialism, however, critics are quick to point out its deficiencies. They argue, first, that this approach countenances sacrificing the interests of a few for the sake of the many, treating some as the means to the ends of others. The public health official preferring to devote resources to primary care sacrifices the interest of those in need of transplants, and the affirmative action program that seeks diversity for the university and the country may sacrifice the interests of some white male applicants.

Critics of consequentialism also point out that we cannot foresee or estimate all the possible or even probable consequences of a particular action or policy. In 1920, who would have imagined that Ford Motor Company Model T cars would result, generations later, in gridlock and air pollution? This "problem of unintended consequences" is exacerbated by our inevitable bias as actors. Our situations and our interests will affect our conception of consequences and the importance or weight we assign to them. The candidate considering whether to lie is likely to consider his victory as essential to the common good; he is also likely to see only the short-term consequences of the lie and not the long-term effect on public trust and respect for authority.

A third criticism concerns the calculation of consequences itself. Whose interests should be taken into account? How should costs and benefits be weighed or measured? Should intensity of preference be measured? For example, should a U. S. president considering armed intervention to prevent massacres in Darfur consider only the consequences for U.S. troops and resources or should he also include the lives in Darfur? And should he weigh those lives equally? How should a state governor weigh the very intense preference of a small minority for organ transplants against the preference of a large majority for primary care?

Deontological ethics starts from the premise that there are moral obligations or duties we ought to fulfill apart from consideration of consequences. In this sense the right takes priority over the good, or the end of action. Deontological ethics is rooted in the moral philosophy of Immanuel Kant. The basic moral duty is to treat people as ends rather than as means to purposes outside of themselves (Baron 1997). One example of deontological theory that influences contemporary discussions of ethics and politics is based on the premise that our roles in society give specific content to our moral obligations or duties. The early twentieth-century British idealist F. H. Bradley in his essay "My Station and Its Duties" developed the argument that our moral duties are determined by our social station or role and the responsibilities that come with it (Bradley 1876). As parents, daughters, neighbors, and members of professions—doctors, lawyers, analysts, administrators, elected officials—we have jobs to do and a moral obligation to do them well. The research or budget analyst facing pressure to underestimate costs for a favored program who asks what is the role of an analyst and what are the obligations that flow from it illustrates this approach to ethics.

Another example of deontological ethics, derived most recently from the moral philosophy of John Rawls, focuses on the duty to treat people as ends and on the premise that they are so treated when they are able to consent to the actions that affect them.

> What makes human beings different from mere things is that people have dignity based on their ability to choose freely what they will do with their lives, and they have a fundamental moral right to have these choices respected. People are not objects to be manipulated; it is a violation of human dignity to use people in ways they do not freely choose. (Velasquez et al., 2002, 1)

The right action in this view is what free, equal, and rational persons, including those affected by the action, would be able to consent to. Some versions of human rights theories are also examples of a deontological approach to ethics, that is, respecting rights is a mark of respecting people as ends with life goals and plans to achieve them.

The candidate considering whether to lie who asks if other people, including the victims of the lie, would consent to lying in this situation takes this deontological approach to ethics. So does the governor who, before deciding on the allocation of resources between transplants and primary care, asks if there is a policy that all parties could consent to after debate and deliberation.

Virtue ethics is the third major approach to ethics. Proponents view moral questions from the standpoint of the moral agents and focus on the sources of morality in their inner life and character (Slote 1997, 177). They maintain that "Perhaps 'What ought I to do?' is the wrong question. We might ask instead: 'What kind of person should I be?'" (Pence 1991, 249). Derived from Aristotle, virtue ethics assumes that there are certain ideals toward which we should strive because they provide for the full development of our humanity. These ideals are discovered through thoughtful reflection on what kind of people we have the potential to become. Honesty, courage, compassion, generosity, fidelity, integrity, fairness, and prudence are all examples of virtues that we can emulate and seek to cultivate. The assumption is that a person who has developed virtues will be naturally disposed to act in ways consistent with them.

The orientation of who am I and who should I be also has a social dimension. Moral agents also ask who are "we" and who should "we" be. For example, during the debate on the North American Free Trade Agreement, Vice President Albert Gore and House Minority Leader George Mitchell defended the agreement on grounds that rejecting it would mean America had adopted a cringing, fearful, and despairing attitude to the world and to its own future (Slote 1997).

Public officials, in deciding on actions in specific situations, make use of these ethical approaches, even if they do not usually articulate their thinking in precisely these terms. The decision of the Clinton administration not to intervene to stop the genocide in Rwanda in 1994 is a good illustration of how officials at various levels of the hierarchy actually thought through their choices and how they reflected on those choices in subsequent years.

RWANDA: CASE STUDY OF ETHICAL APPROACHES

Rwanda raised profound ethical issues: it was the worst instance of genocide since the Nazi killings of the Jews during World War II. Over the space of about three months from April through June 1994, nearly one million Tutsis in Rwanda were murdered by their Hutu neighbors. Rwanda had endured a civil war between the Hutu-dominated government and a Tutsi rebel force for years, but, in the spring of 1994, a cease fire was in place, monitored by a UN peacekeeping force. The genocide—the targeted killings of Tutsis—effectively ended the cease fire. Within one day, ten Belgian troops in the peacekeeping force were murdered by Hutu militias. In the United States, the Clinton administration immediately ordered the evacuation of all Americans including the embassy staff. The United States also strongly supported a UN Security Council decision to reduce the peacekeeping operation to a skeleton force. When the UN Secretariat proposed a replacement peacekeeping operation, the United States successfully opposed it as vague and unrealistic. Efforts by some within the Clinton administration to advance intermediate measures, such as U.S. logistical or financial support for an African peacekeeping force or action to jam the hate-filled Hutu radio stations, were opposed and stalled within the bureaucracy. The killings ended only when the Tutsi rebel force seized control of the Rwanda government.

At the time, U.S. officials at the highest levels based their decision on a calculation of consequences for U.S. national interests. They concluded that Rwanda was not a strategic interest and accordingly they could not justify the costs of intervention in terms of troops or resources by any benefit to the nation. Moreover, they thought that a UN-led intervention with or without U.S. forces was not likely to succeed and would provoke a public failure for the administration, the United States, and the United Nations like the one that had ended the peacekeeping operation in Somalia the previous year. As they saw it, the costs were clear, including the cost of failure, and the benefits highly uncertain. These considerations greatly outweighed the costs of the deaths in Rwanda. Once this overall decision was taken, the highest level officials turned to other pressing issues and left it to deputies and assistants to consider any intermediate actions (Carlsson et al., 1999, 1; Ferroggiaro 2004; Powers 2001, 2003).

The decision-making process illustrates some of the challenges of a consequentialist approach when officials are involved in many issues and have limited time to decide. In particular, it shows that the end or good sought is not always easy to define and also that the past experience and interests of the officials themselves—the moral agents—influences their definition of the end, and their analysis of alternatives.

The definition of national interest is not always obvious. Donald Steinberg was senior director for African Affairs at the National Security Council. He remembers "struggling without success to convince people that Rwanda's genocide actually did threaten our national security...Now we understand that our lives here in America can be touched in the most immediate ways imaginable" by events in other countries but this was not the "prevailing reasoning" at the time (Steinberg 2004, 16–17). Anthony Lake was National Security Advisor to President Clinton. In an interview after he left office, he acknowledged that he did not, at the time, give much consideration to the idea that when states collapse they can become breeding grounds for terrorism, which certainly affects our interests (Lake 2003, 11).

The U.S. officials, without much deliberation either inside the government or with the public, reached their decision not to intervene very quickly. Lake and Madeline Albright, who was U.S. ambassador to the UN, agreed that officials at the highest policy making level gave serious consideration only to the alternative of drawing down the U.N. presence. Other options were "not even vaguely in the cards at the time," said Albright (Albright 2004, 5). Lake recalls that at his level "the issue" of U.S. intervention or assistance to a UN intervention "just never arose . . . it was almost literally inconceivable" (Lake 2003, 2). And Lake acknowledges that he and others knew that "hell was breaking loose in Rwanda" (Lake 2003, 5).

The challenge of consequentialism here was not in identifying all the alternatives but in being willing to analyze them. Because of their past experience and current fears, officials preferred a quick selection of one alternative because they gave weight to the costs for the agent—the United States—and not to the costs for the Rwandans—the others.

Michael Barnett was a political-military officer at the U.S. Mission to the UN in New York on a Council on Foreign Relations Fellowship at the time of the Rwanda crisis. In writings since he left that position, he has sought to explain the tendency of officials like himself to give all the weight in their calculations to the interests of their organizations, to assign those interests moral value, and to be indifferent to people and events outside the organizations (Barnett 1997).

Barnett quickly adopted the prevailing view that the United States should not risk failure by intervening or supporting intervention. He identified with the interests of the U.S. Mission, the State Department, and the U.S. government. The identification developed over time as he worked long hours with his colleagues, and acquired status and influence within the organization. He was seen as the "expert" although he had been working on Rwanda for only four months and had no prior knowledge of the country. His expertise came from his official position: his contacts, attendance at meetings, and knowledge of official papers and correspondence.

What is most interesting about Barnett's reflections is that preserving the organizations' interest also seemed the moral or the right thing to do. He did not see himself as preferring the interests of the United States and the United Nations to the moral good; he saw saving the United States and the United Nations from another failure as the moral alternative compared to saving lives in Rwanda. Albright also reflects this orientation when she recalls, "I was trying very hard to make sure that we could continue to support peacekeeping operations," so that not risking failure now would preserve the United Nations and the United States support for future conflicts (Albright 2004, 5).

Barnett's point is not that preserving the United States and the United Nations from another failure was an immoral alternative; his point is that, given the exigencies of life in bureaucracies, organizational interests will come to seem as moral interests and persons outside the organization will not receive much consideration in the calculations of consequences. Barnett thinks this tendency could be counterbalanced if officials had more knowledge of, and contact with, the people who will be affected by their decisions. But what also can counterbalance this tendency, in the opinion of other officials involved in the Rwanda decision, is for officials to maintain a sense of duty or commitment to basic moral principle, not to replace the calculation of consequences, but to inform it.

The officials, who in retrospect regret some aspects of their behavior at the time of the crisis, often seem uncomfortable speaking in moral terms, preferring to speak of a "human" rather than an ethical or moral orientation. Lake, for instance, is reluctant to speak of "moral obligation . . . because that's presumptuous." But he says that government officials are "human beings" and not just "interest calculating machines" (Lake 2003, 11). Prudence Bushnell was deputy assistant secretary of state for African Affairs and chair of the interagency task force that tried unsuccessfully to gain approval for intermediate actions in Rwanda. She voices a similar idea in retrospect, suggesting a duty or obligation independent of consequences that we have as human beings.

> And for all of the reasons that make sense for rational policy analysis, we did nothing, and, in terms of our hard core national interest, it didn't matter…In many respects they were right. So we got out of it without having to use a great deal of resources. Certainly nobody was killed; no American was killed…and we did the right thing by the taxpayer…But did we do the right thing as human beings? (Bushnell 2003, 23–24)

These officials, like Barnett, are not suggesting that decisions should be made without reference to consequences for the nation's interest, but they are suggesting that the costs of deaths in Rwanda should have factored more in their thinking and behavior. And they should have factored more because the officials had a basic moral duty to prevent deaths if they could. Lake argues that as officials and even as citizens we tend to think of national interest in an abstract way that blinds us to the reality of the lives that are affected. Hundreds of thousands of deaths are an important reality too, he says, and should be taken into account. As human beings, given "the fact of so many deaths," he and others at his level should at least have exerted a greater degree of leadership and demanded a more rigorous analysis of all the alternatives.

Lake also says that he and others should have assigned more weight to the deaths in Rwanda in calculating the costs of the various alternatives. He asks us to compare two countries and to suppose that the United States has more of a national interest in the first—"lets say it's 10 times as big"—but in the first 15,000 to 20,000 people are at risk of death compared to two million deaths in the second. "So even if the national interest gets more weight than the humanitarian obligation, when you look at the scope of each we ought to be paying a lot more attention to" the second country than we do (Lake 2003, 11).

Lake is offering an approach to thinking about humanitarian intervention that is suggestive even if it cannot be done in this numerical way. But the variables are his: how great is the evil to be stopped, how much even indirect national interest do we have in stopping it, how onerous is the cost, and how likely is the chance of success? And interestingly what would have made this more rigorous calculation of consequences more likely in the case of Rwanda was if officials had clung to a fundamental moral commitment to prevent suffering that preceded and informed their calculations.

Even in the case of Rwanda, where a policy consensus developed very quickly, there were some within the Clinton administration who urged a different course, if not direct U.S. intervention, at least U.S. support for interventions by others or for intermediate range options. These voices tended to be lower in the hierarchy and responsible for Africa desks either at the National Security Council (NSC) or the State Department, suggesting that the abstract thinking Lake referred to or the indifference Barnett highlighted is less likely among those who have some knowledge and contact with the people affected. None of these officials resigned, or leaked, or protested publicly. None really considered those actions at the time. In retrospect they ask if there were other things they could have done to alter the administration's decision making, giving us some ideas about the types of actions available to those whose policy preferences are overruled.

Steinberg says, "sometimes you make your case" and the decision goes against you. "Then you have to decide personally if this is so important to you that you are going to resign or ask to be transferred, or if you are going to continue to give your views and lose out occasionally" (Steinberg 2004, 9–10). Prudence Bushnell, however, wishes in retrospect that she had done more; that bureaucrats like her should be more prepared to take risks within the hierarchy when their principles are being "walked upon." It never occurred to her to call Lake or the secretary of state, for instance; it was just not something a person at her level did (Bushnell 2003, 22). Even Albright recalls that people in Washington would have thought her "crazy" if she seriously proposed another alternative but nevertheless she wishes now that she had done more to fight for a large humanitarian intervention. "It would never have happened. But I would have felt better about my own role in this," she said (Albright 2004, 5–6).

The lessons that officials derived from their participation in the decision about Rwanda are relevant to officials at many levels dealing with many types of issues. The researcher evaluating a program of his organization will feel the same sense of identification as Barnett and the same temptation to evaluate the program positively not only for the usual self-interested motives but also because preserving the reputation of the organization seems like a moral interest. Saving an organization—a child welfare agency or a church—from a public scandal may seem like a moral good, even at the risk of some children some of the time.

THE POLITICAL ENVIRONMENT

As the case of Rwanda illustrates, applying ethics to political decision making is not easy. Politics is a distinctive realm, different from private life. It deals with the life of the community and transcends the private lives of individuals with their circles of particular friends and relatives. It involves government and governors protecting the life of the community and the liberty of citizens, or promoting a fair and just society. Politicians and policy makers act for others but also serve themselves, they rule over others and can coerce people, and their decisions have broad, cumulative effects on present and future citizens.

Political life is different from private life in several crucial respects. Public officials act on behalf of others and their acts have consequences for others as well as themselves. A private individual may decide to risk his own life and fortune to do the right thing but if a politician does the same, she is harming not just her own interests but the community she has pledged to serve. A U.S. president who committed troops to Rwanda would be risking not his own life but the lives of those troops. And if the United States and the United Nations failed in an intervention, it might well have consequences for their ability to intervene in future crises. It is because public officials are responsible for the interests of others that consequentialist approaches to ethics are appropriately so pervasive in the literature of political science and public policy.

Because they represent others, public officials may face a moral conflict between their personal beliefs and the beliefs of their constituents. Former New York Governor Mario Cuomo faced such conflicts in deliberating about the death penalty and abortion and wrote eloquently about how to resolve such conflicts (Cuomo 1984). Former Democratic presidential candidate John Kerry faced similar conflicts in the 2004 presidential campaign when he was taken to task by a handful of Catholic bishops who threatened to deny him sacramental communion because of his position on abortion (Segers 2005).

Decision making in public life will usually involve a conflict among values, or choices among goods, and not just between goods and evils. For officials debating Rwanda, preserving the United States and the United Nations from a potential failure was a good to be sought but so was saving lives in Rwanda. Similarly, officials responsible for rebuilding ground zero in New York City have to reconcile or choose among the moral claims of the families who want a fitting memorial, local businessmen who want a vibrant economic space, local residents who want a living community, and a city that needs a tax base to fund services and programs of all types.

Politics is also different in ways that concern the very essence of moral agency and responsibility. Dennis Thompson speaks of "the problem of many hands" in political life. "Because many different officials contribute in many different ways to decisions and policies of government, it is difficult even in principle to identify who is morally responsible for political outcomes" (Thompson 1987, 40). This makes it difficult not only for citizens to hold officials accountable, but also for officials themselves to decide on their own moral responsibility. Those reflecting on their decisions in Rwanda, for instance, certainly take some responsibility, but they also make it clear not only that the primary culprits are those who led and did the killings but also that responsibility for standing by is widely shared—by the U.S. government in general, other member states of the UN, the international community, the Western world, and the world.

The fact that politics is a distinct realm and private morals cannot be applied so readily does not mean that ethics has no place but it "does require us to take into account the special characteristics of politics as we frame our moral judgments" (Gutmann and Thompson 2006, xi). The German sociologist, Max Weber regarded an absolutist ethic of ultimate ends that insisted on morally correct means regardless of the circumstances and consequences as utterly inappropriate and dangerous in politics. For Weber, adopting this stance, "Let justice be done though the world may perish," showed a vain preference for personal moral purity at the cost of everyone and everything else. Weber offered instead an ethic of responsibility, which focused on the politician's commitment to a cause or end, her dispassionate and selfless assessment of the means necessary to achieve it, and her acceptance of responsibility for the consequences. But even Weber saw a final limit to this consequentialist approach, calling on an ultimate sense of duty beyond consequences. At some point, the public official has to draw a line and say with Martin Luther "Here I stand" regardless of consequences because "I can do no other." (Weber 1918, 127). In Weber's terms the moral failure of officials in Rwanda was certainly not their determination to consider U.S. national interests in the short- and long-term, nor their fear of provoking another failure for the United States or the United Nations. The failure, as Lake acknowledged, was in not taking serious responsibility for the consequences that would follow from their decision and, in that light, making sure to rigorously evaluate all of the options available to them.

BEHAVING MORALLY AND EFFECTIVELY

While it is all too easy to find instances of moral failure in public life, it is important to also highlight instances in which officials at all levels behaved ethically and effectively, and to understand the variables that made this possible. Gerald Pomper, in his recent contribution to the ethics and politics literature, *Ordinary Heroes and American Democracy,* analyzes the institutional and individual sources of such ethical behavior.

Two of the ordinary heroes Pomper identifies are Representative Peter Rodino, who oversaw impeachment proceedings against President Richard Nixon, and Dr. Frances Kelsey, who prevented the deadly drug thalidomide from being commercially marketed in the United States. These officials adopted multiple ethical approaches to guide them. They certainly were aware of the consequences of their decisions but it was a conception of duty derived from their professions and institutional positions that directed them to the course of action that would produce the best outcome. They also had some qualities of character—some moral virtues—that made it possible for them to fulfill those duties.

Congressman Peter Rodino was not a "great man" either before or after the Nixon Watergate investigation; he was an ordinary congressman, not well known to the public. Yet at a decisive moment, he met the challenge posed by the Watergate burglary in 1972 and the subsequent cover-up by the Nixon White House, a crisis that dominated the federal government's work for two years, from 1972 to 1974 (Pomper 2004, 31).

In chairing the hearings of the House Judiciary Committee that voted to impeach President Nixon, Rodino was certainly aware that his actions would have momentous consequences for the country in the short and long run. "People thought we would impeach Richard Nixon. That was the furthest thing from my mind. I was hopeful, I was prayerful that we wouldn't, that what we would find out was exculpatory" (Bernstein 2005, C-11). Rodino was also aware that the consequences that would follow from the impeachment process were just as important as those that would follow from the actual decision. If a sizeable section of the people regarded the process as unfair, they would lose confidence not only in the decision but also in the institutions that brought it about. In his statement to the House, Rodino said, "Let us now proceed with such care and decency and thoroughness and honor that the vast majority of the American people and their children after them will say: 'That was the right course. There was no other way'" (Rodino, 1974). Rodino took his own responsibility for the consequences of his actions seriously. "To impeach a President is an awesome responsibility. Indeed after we voted to impeach Nixon, I...called my wife and, when she answered, broke down and cried" (Rodino 1999, A-19; Pomper 2004, 49).

To perceive the process as fair, Rodino concluded, the public would have to see it as nonpartisan, would have to conclude that members voted their best judgment of the facts regardless of party. Having been a congressman for more than twenty years, Rodino knew that partisanship could never be eliminated entirely but he believed it could and must be minimized.

To attain this goal, Rodino fulfilled his duties as they were defined by the norms of the Congress and the role of committee chair. For the committee investigation, Rodino worked diligently to prepare a thoroughly researched handbook on the arcane subject of impeachment. He instructed the committee staff to prepare a report for the members that analyzed facts and outlined arguments on both sides of the question but took no position and made no recommendation. As special counsel for the investigation he hired John Doar, a Republican. He insisted on secrecy in the Judiciary Committee deliberations so that his committee would not be split prematurely on party lines. He used his powers as chair to prohibit the staff and the counsel from making public statements and to ensure that Republican members had as much chance to speak and pose questions as the Democrats. He also used his powers to reject any arbitrary time deadlines so that committee staff could assemble the evidence and the members could deliberate about it (Pomper 2004, 45–48). Rodino was effective as well as dutiful; in the end, a majority of the Republican members of the committee joined the Democrats in voting for three articles of impeachment.

During the process, Rodino also gave evidence of moral virtues, not all moral virtues to be sure and certainly not sainthood or the heroism of myths and legends. We do not know many aspects of Rodino's moral character, including his behavior as a husband, son, father, or neighbor. We do not even know how he behaved as a congressman or a politician in other circumstances. But he was courageous and patient in his determination in this case. He refused to be rushed by House leaders such as Speaker Tip O'Neill.

> I told O'Neill in no uncertain words that I was going to do it my way. I don't mind being called cautious, because I believe that when one is responsible for making decisions that are going to affect the future of the country, one doesn't treat those issues by making snap judgments. Maybe we ought to have a little more of that. (Pomper 2004, 46)

He also was modest and did not grab the limelight. He avoided public statements and allowed others—especially the Republicans—ample space and credit.

A second example of an "ordinary hero of American democracy" is Frances Kelsey, a staff scientist with the Food and Drug Administration (FDA), who in 1962 prevented the introduction of the drug thalidomide into the United States. Sold abroad as a mild sedative, this drug was widely used to treat nausea in pregnant women. It was subsequently discovered that, if taken during early pregnancy, thalidomide caused serious harm to fetuses—major defects such as being born without arms and legs. By doing her job as a bureaucrat with the FDA, Kelsey prevented similar damage from occurring to thousands of children born in the United States (Pomper 2004, 134).

Highly educated, with both a doctorate and a medical degree, Kelsey came to the FDA in 1960 after ten years of medical research experience that included reviewing drug studies submitted for publication. This proved to be valuable preparation for her work as a bureaucrat at the FDA since it taught her to emphasize the ordinary canons of scientific investigation and to approach drug studies with a certain amount of judicious skepticism.

As an FDA staff investigator, Kelsey's job was to ensure that drug companies' applications for approval of new drugs demonstrated that the drug met certain safety standards. The application for thalidomide was Kelsey's first assignment at the FDA. As she later said, my superiors "thought it would be an easy one to start on. As it turned out, it wasn't all that easy" (Burkholz 1997, 2). Kelsey approached the application as a cautious bureaucrat. She found the drug company's application sloppy—"It was so superficial and anecdotal." She was troubled by the lack of evidence, poor record-keeping, incomplete test results (Pomper 2004, 143).

At first Kelsey stalled for time to give herself and her staff the opportunity to rigorously examine the application material and other relevant literature. Then she began to worry about possible connections between thalidomide and peripheral neuritis, based on a research note in a British scientific journal that she read. She felt the drug manufacturer bore the burden of proof that the drug was safe and repeatedly declared the application incomplete, asking for more data. Over time, she also began to wonder about long-term effects of thalidomide on fetuses. The manufacturer complained about Kelsey's foot-dragging to her superiors, and ultimately visited the head of the FDA to pressure him to overrule Kelsey on the application. As Kelsey reported, "They telephoned my superiors and they came to see them too... Most of the things they called me you wouldn't print" (Mulliken 1962, 28; Pomper 2004, 144).

Ultimately, Kelsey wanted the drug application to be withdrawn, based on the reports from Europe of deformed neonates being born to German and British women who had taken the drug. Eventually, the German government forced the German manufacturer to withdraw the drug from the market. In March, 1962, the American manufacturer withdrew its FDA application. Kelsey had prevented an American catastrophe.

The consequences of Kelsey's decisions were a matter of life and death and she was certainly aware of that. But like Rodino she was able to rely on the norms of her profession and institutional role to determine the best alternative course of action. Kelsey did her job as a scientist; she used professional judgment and followed the norms of data collection, analysis, and presentation of evidence. And she also did her job as a professional bureaucrat; she insisted on adhering precisely to bureaucratic routines and to the impersonal procedures of the FDA in handling drug applications. In this way she avoided arbitrary decision making and showed neither favoritism nor prejudice to the applicant. As Pomper notes, "Kelsey and her colleagues displayed the virtues of bureaucrats. They showed how bureaucracy can enhance life, quite literally, and extend individual freedom" (Pomper 2004, 157). Kelsey also displayed some aspects of a virtuous character that she brought to the FDA job. For more than a year, she was courageous enough to stand her ground against the drug manufacturer.

Once Kelsey's work became known, Congress debated and strengthened drug enforcement policy, requiring manufacturers to submit additional data on the safety and effectiveness of new drugs before they could be marketed in the United States. Kelsey's example indicates, then, that conforming to the norms of institutions and professions in a democracy can also be a way of highlighting areas where those norms need to be improved.

THE PROBLEM OF DIRTY HANDS

Of all the reasons why the political environment differs from private life, the most crucial is the fact that public officials often face the choice of using what are regarded as evil means for the sake of the people and communities they represent. The political environment is different because what is regarded as virtue in private life will often harm a community. The political world is "largely impersonal and intractable... populated by powerful people and formidable institutions that are hostile to the purposes of public-spirited officials" (Gutmann and Thompson 2006, xi).

A classic statement of this position is Machiavelli's *The Prince*. For rulers, Machiavelli states, vices such as miserliness or parsimony with the people's money are preferable to virtues of generosity or liberality. Whereas promise-keeping is important in private life, in public life political leaders should be prepared to violate treaties and alliances when circumstances change and it is no longer in the public interest to keep them. Deceit may at times be prudent, but a politician must conceal the fact that he is being deceitful. Also rulers must be prepared to use cruelty in order to better maintain order in society (Machiavelli 1995, chs.16–19).

Max Weber's ethic of responsibility that we referred to earlier is another approach to the problem of dirty hands or evil means in politics. An ethic of responsibility would allow public officials to justify means like violence, deception, manipulation, and lying in pursuit of their ends, but it also allows us to morally evaluate them in terms of the ends they seek and the dispassionate, selfless way they assess the means actually necessary to achieve them. And, of course, Weber also left open the possibility that a responsible public official would draw a line he would not cross for any end.

In a famous 1973 essay, Michael Walzer reflects further on this problem of dirty hands in politics. He suggests that the dilemma is a central feature of political life, that the need to use morally dubious means in pursuit of good ends arises not merely as an occasional crisis in the career of this or that unlucky politician but systematically and frequently. Walzer thinks this explains the convention that politicians are typically thought to be morally corrupt. He agrees with Weber that consequentialism is the appropriate ethical orientation for a public official charged with the care of a community. But he pays more explicit attention than Weber to an official's sense of moral duty and moral character independent of consequences. "A particular act of government may be exactly the right thing to do in utilitarian terms and yet leave the man who does it guilty of a moral wrong" (Walzer 1973, 161).

The politician's recognition of the moral wrong reflects three things: his character, our judgment of him, and the status of morality itself. For Walzer, the moral politician should be conscious that he has "done something wrong even if what [was]...done was also the best thing to do on the whole in the circumstances." The politician's consciousness of wrong should also influence our judgment of him. Walzer uses the example of a reform politician who must make a deal with a corrupt ward boss in order to win election. "Because he has moral scruples about this, we know him to be a good man. We want him to make the deal, precisely because he has scruples about it. We know he is doing right when he makes the deal because he knows he is doing wrong" (Walzer 1973, 166). For the status of morality itself, Walzer argues that even as we judge an action as right from a consequentialist perspective, we should at the same time acknowledge that the means are wrong, moral standards of right and wrong still stand; they have been overridden in this case but have not "been set aside, canceled, or annulled" (Walzer 1973, 171). Because the moral standards have not been annulled, they continue to function as requirements for public officials and as bases for our evaluation of them.

CASE STUDY OF DIRTY HANDS: THE USE OF TORTURE IN WARTIME

The problem of dirty hands in politics is most clearly illustrated by decisions to use violence in war. Political theorists since St. Augustine have developed a concept of a just war, articulating the ends for which wars may justly be fought and the means that may be employed in the pursuit of victory. The most basic ethical principle governing the means of warfare is that noncombatants are to be protected unless the violence to them is an unavoidable necessity in the pursuit of military targets. Noncombatants include, most obviously, civilian populations but also those enemy forces who have been taken prisoner (Walzer 1977). In recent years, the Bush administration and the American people have confronted this issue in dealing with captives taken in the wars in Afghanistan and Iraq.

After the attack on the World Trade Center in September 2001, the administration declared a "war on terror" and subsequently commenced actual warfare in Afghanistan. Administration officials then had to decide how the United States would treat captured members of al Qaeda, the terrorist organization, and the Taliban, the Afghan forces. The officials justified their positions primarily in legal and in what they called "policy" terms. They usually did not justify them with explicit ethical arguments but their policy positions reflect their views on the relationship between ethics and politics, specifically whether there are moral limits to the means that can be used to promote a nation's interests.

The legal questions concerned both international and domestic law. The international law was the Geneva Conventions, an international treaty that is considered the basic law of war. Among other things, the Conventions regulate the treatment of different types of captives, soldiers and civilians for instance. The requirements vary but basically the Conventions state that all captives must be treated humanely, and they prohibit physical and mental torture as well as cruel, humiliating and degrading treatment.

The Bush Administration concluded that the United States was not obliged to follow the Geneva Conventions in the conflict with Afghanistan. In a February 2002 confidential memorandum with the subject line: "Humane Treatment of al Qaeda and Taliban Detainees," the president wrote that the captives were not covered by the Conventions (Bush 2002, 2). Al Qaeda was not a state and so could not be a party to a treaty and the Taliban were "unlawful combatants." Essentially the president declared that the detainees had no rights in international law—they were not legally entitled to humane treatment.

Nevertheless, the president wrote, given "our values as a nation" the United States would, as a matter of policy, treat detainees humanely. The U.S. Armed Forces, in particular, would act in accordance with the principles of Geneva "to the extent appropriate and consistent with military necessity" (Bush 2002, 2). The president did not mention the CIA, although it was responsible for many of the interrogations in Afghanistan and in Guantanamo Bay Cuba (GTMO), where captives were taken for longer term detention.

In referring to our values as a nation, the president makes use of a form of virtue ethics, saying that we are the kind of nation that behaves humanely, but he does not say we do so independent of consequences. Rather, we behave humanely when it is appropriate and consistent with military necessity, terms that the president failed to define. The basic stance of the memorandum then is Machiavellian; the nation is at war and its leaders must be able to choose the means necessary to protect it.

The president's decision reflected the legal interpretation of the Geneva Conventions articulated by the Department of Justice Office of Legal Counsel (OLC) particularly by then Deputy Assistant Attorney General John Yoo. It also reflected the briefing memos prepared by the White House Counsel Alberto Gonzales.

Gonzales maintained that the Geneva Conventions requirements were not in the national interest because they would not protect the country from attacks. The war on terror was a new type of war requiring a "new paradigm" that "renders obsolete Geneva's strict limitations on questioning of enemy prisoners." To wage the new type of war, the United States needed "flexibility" in conducting interrogations in order to obtain information about the enemy's capacities and plans. Moreover, Gonzales wrote, declaring that the Conventions did not apply reduced the threat that interrogators or their superiors would be prosecuted as war criminals if future special counsels decided to pursue "unwarranted charges" on the basis of such hard to interpret terms as "inhuman treatment" (Gonzales 2002, 2).

Unlike the decision on Rwanda, there was disagreement within the administration on the applicability of the Geneva Conventions. The main objections came from the State Department's Adviser William H. Taft IV and then from Secretary of State Colin Powell. Like the president and Gonzales, they argued in consequentialist terms, but they emphasized different consequences for U.S. national interests. They reflected the State Department's responsibility for maintaining U.S.

relationships with other countries and illustrate again the way our situations affect our conception of consequences.

Taft and Powell disagreed with the OLC legal analysis and said that acting on it would undermine the country's credibility and moral authority (Taft 2002a, 1; Powell 2002, 3). They did not say exactly that bypassing the law was immoral or unethical; rather it would hurt the country's reputation for moral conduct, and that would have costs. A presidential decision that Geneva did not apply, Powell wrote, "will reverse over a century of U.S. policy and practice" (Powell 2002, 2). In addition, bypassing international law would undermine the U.S. ability to secure the cooperation of other nations, raise issues about our relationships with other questionable governing regimes, and lower the bar for other countries' treatment of captured U.S. forces. Taft and Powell also rejected the idea that following Geneva would impose costs on U.S. security, arguing that the Conventions provided a sufficiently robust framework for interrogations.

Having concluded that the United States was not bound by international law, administration officials turned to the U.S. laws that governed the interrogations, especially the Federal Anti-Torture Statute of 1996. The anti torture law prohibits U.S. nationals from committing torture outside the United States under penalties that include lengthy imprisonment and death. The statute defines torture as "an act ... specifically intended to inflict severe physical or mental pain or suffering ... upon another person within his custody or physical control." In late spring 2002, the administration received requests to clarify requirements under the statute from the CIA.

Again, the legal position was articulated by John Yoo at OLC in a memorandum to Gonzales over the signature of Jay S. Bybee, then assistant attorney general and now a federal judge on the 9th circuit. Yoo interpreted the statute very narrowly, leaving wide discretion to policy makers to decide on the appropriate methods of interrogation. He interpreted specific intent to mean that the person must "expressly intend" or have the "express purpose" or the "precise objective" to inflict the severe pain (OLC 2002, 3, 4). And "severe" pain or torture is not the "mere infliction of pain and suffering;" even "cruel, inhuman or degrading treatment" may not meet the criterion of severe (OLC 2002, 13, 1). Torture inflicts pain that is difficult to endure, that is "equivalent in intensity to the pain accompanying serious physical injury, such as organ failure, impairment of bodily function or even death" (OLC 2002, 1). Mental pain or suffering is torture only if it results in significant psychological harm lasting for months or even years. In interviews and articles after he had left office, Yoo said that reduced sleep, stress positions, isolation from other prisoners, and solitary confinement were not torture in the U.S. definition of the term. "The purpose of these techniques is not to inflict pain or harm, but simply to disorient," he wrote (Yoo 2005a, 3; 2005b, 15).

Yoo's memo also outlined legal defenses that would be available to an official who was charged with torture, even under the restricted definition. First, the president has "complete discretion" in wartime to manage a military campaign, including detaining and interrogating the enemy (OLC 2002, 33). Thus, a government defendant could claim that if his actions were properly authorized he was fulfilling the executive branch authority to protect the federal government and the nation from attack (OLC 2002, 45).

Second, Yoo argued that government interrogators and their superiors charged with torture could justify or defend their actions on the overlapping grounds of necessity and self defense. Torture or other violation of the "literal language of the criminal law" might be justified if it were necessary to prevent even greater harm to the nation. If a detainee *might* possess information that could enable the United States to prevent attacks, torture might be justified since "clearly any harm that might occur during an interrogation would pale to insignificance compared to the harm avoided by preventing such an attack" (OLC 2002, 40, 41).

The argument that Yoo sets forth could constitute the frame for a moral justification of torture or lesser forms of coercive interrogation: the person adopting the admittedly evil means has reasonably certain knowledge that the one to be tortured has relevant information, that great harm in the form of an attack is very likely to occur, that the information will be necessary to prevent the attack, and that there are no alternative ways to obtain the information in time to prevent it. This justification would be some form of the "ticking time bomb" scenario. But the crucial parts of this argument are: What does it mean to be reasonably certain that a detainee has, and will give, useful information or that an attack is imminent or very likely to occur? In suggesting that torture is a defensive response to a potential attack that can be used when the opportunity is available and that since September 11, 2001 the president can authorize torture or an act of torture in the general name of national security, Yoo says in effect that under the law U.S. interrogators could torture any captives they thought had useful information about al Qaeda. This is a Machiavellian position.

Although they defined the law to allow them maximum flexibility, the Bush administration had not developed a policy on the exact interrogation techniques that would be permitted. They developed these policies over time in an ad hoc way, first for GTMO and then for other theaters. Secretary of Defense Rumsfeld did not make a final decision for GTMO until fifteen months after detainees first arrived there. During that time he approved one set of techniques, including many that he acknowledged were seen as violations of Geneva, then rescinded the approval and established an intradepartmental working group to advise him, and then finally approved a set of methods which included a smaller number of those regarded as violations.

Over the course of the decision, debate and conflict about the methods to be approved took place first at GTMO and then in the working group at the Department of Defense. The opposition to the use of aggressive methods in both places came from attorneys from the Judge Advocate General Corps (JAG). Lt. Col. Thomas Berg was one of the JAG attorneys at GTMO. He had "irreconcilable differences" and "hostile" conflicts with the military intelligence people and with their JAG attorney, whom he "despised" (Berg 2005, 9, 12). He cited the example of Red Cross visits. According to Geneva and the Army's Field Manual (FM), which is seen to be in accord with it, the Red Cross should be able to register captives as soon as they arrive at a facility but when the "intel" people had high value prisoners "they would want to prevent the Red Cross from knowing about them for a while" (Berg 2005, 10).

On his side of the conflict, Berg said he was determined to apply the Geneva Conventions and the FM. He traces his determination to three main factors. First was his sense of professional duties as a lawyer, and as a JAG lawyer in particular, to enforce the law. The job of the JAG lawyer is to tell the military commanders "No you can't do that," said Berg, "by doctrine, we are the conscience of the command" (Berg 2005, 6). Second, Berg relied on his own individual conception of moral duty. "I thought there was a right and wrong principle involved and I wanted to be on the right side" (Berg 2005, 12). Third and, it seems, least important in his considerations, he did not think coercive tactics produced real benefits. These sorts of tactics, he said, "will make them [detainees] even less willing ... to give anything up. And we degrade ourselves in the process" (Berg 2005, 16). Berg was willing to endure conflict and the anger of the intel commander as the price of his position, but he acknowledges that he had some advantages as a reservist who could go back to a "pretty good civilian job, so I didn't view it as my career being at stake" (Berg 2005, 12).

Within the working group in Washington, opposition to more aggressive techniques also came from JAG officers from the four armed services, who were members. They objected to the OLC legal analysis and to the recommendations for what they called extreme or aggressive methods, that "on their face" violated or "may appear to violate" military law, army doctrine, domestic criminal law, and the Geneva Conventions. Major General Thomas Romig of the Army said the legal analysis would generate international criticism "that the U.S. is a law unto itself" (Romig 2003, S8794).

The JAG officers' arguments focused on consequences, namely the costs of authorizing such techniques, and they pointed to a broad range of costs. Some concerned the self-interests of the military interrogators and their superiors. Using the proposed methods placed them at risk of criminal prosecutions in the United States and abroad. Major General Jack Rives of the Air Force said,

Although a wide range of defenses...theoretically apply, it is impossible to be certain that any defense will be successful at trial; our domestic courts may well disagree with DoJ/OLC's interpretation of the law. Further, while the current administration is not likely to pursue prosecution, it is impossible to predict how future administrations will view the use of such techniques. (Rives 2003b, S8796)

The JAG officers also saw costs to the interests of the U.S. military overall, fearing that the proposed methods lowered the bar for treatment of U.S. POWs in this and future conflicts. Brigadier General Kevin Sandkuhler of the Marines wrote, "OLC does not represent the services; thus, understandably, concern for servicemembers is not reflected in their opinion" (Sandkuhler 2003, S8794).

More broadly the JAG officers feared for the military's sense of itself, for who and what they were as an organization. They asked the question posed by virtue ethics: who are we and who will we become? The officers answered that the proposed methods did not conform to the military's sense of itself. General Rives:

The use of the more extreme interrogation techniques simply is not how the U.S. armed forces have operated in recent history. We have taken the legal and moral "high road" in the conduct of our military operations regardless of how others may operate. Our forces are trained in this legal and moral mindset from the day they enter active duty. (Rives 2003b, S8796)

The officers feared that the proposed methods, in undermining military culture, would also undermine discipline and, in that sense, the moral character of individual servicemembers. General Rives was concerned that giving official approval and legal sanction to interrogation techniques that the military had regarded as unlawful "may create uncertainty among interrogators regarding the appropriate limits of interrogations." The idea that the detainees were unlawful belligerents not entitled to protections of Geneva was "a legal distinction that may be lost on the members of the armed forces" (Rives 2003a, S8795).

Rear Admiral Michael Lohr of the Navy said, "I recommend we consider asking decision makers directly is this the 'right thing' for U.S. military personnel." He also said the proposed methods were not consistent with the American people's conception of moral duty or sense of itself as a people.

More broadly, while we may have found a unique situation in GTMO where protections of the Geneva Conventions, U.S. statutes, and even the Constitution do not apply, will the American people find we have missed the forest for the trees by condoning practices that, while technically legal, are inconsistent with our most fundamental values?" (Lohr 2003a, S8795)

In this way the JAG officers informed their consequentialist thinking with considerations derived from other ethical approaches: a basic conception of moral obligation, duty to professional norms, and concern for the moral character of organizations and individuals. Their arguments can be seen as another version of Lake's suggestion that our moral commitments or duties as individuals, organizations, and communities should affect our calculation of consequences. Our commitments tell us what to include among the consequences. For Lake, his moral values should have influenced him to give more weight to the large number of deaths in Rwanda. For the JAG attorneys, effects on the military's sense of itself and the country's sense of itself should be included among the costs and benefits of policies on interrogations.

To summarize, despite opposition from the State Department, the Bush administration justified exemption from international law and a very narrow interpretation of U.S law on Machiavellian grounds: the end justifies the means; the nation is at war and its leaders must be able to choose the means necessary to protect it. Given the threat of deadly attacks by terrorist groups such as al-Qaeda, the use of torture to extract information from detainees may be justified since any harm that might occur during an interrogation would be relatively mild compared to the harm avoided by preventing such an attack.

The strongest opposition to the administration's policy came from JAG attorneys who were concerned about U.S. national interests, the self-interests of service members, and also about the moral duties and character of the military as individuals and as an organization. In these terms, they found that the disadvantages of using torture outweighed the advantages.

CONCLUSIONS

In this chapter, we have analyzed case studies in ethics and politics to illustrate how public officials make normative decisions on important policy issues. We have discussed prevailing ethical theories and pointed out how officials have used these ethical approaches in actual decision making. Our goal has been to clarify the ways in which public officials' thinking and our analysis of that thinking can be applied fruitfully to people at all levels of government dealing with many different types of cases. We now summarize what we have learned.

First, it is clear that ethical decision making in public life is highly complex. There are multiple factors and interests to consider and many centers of allegiance making claims on public officials—ranging from fidelity to duty, to law, to professional norms, to conscience, to constituents, to the public interest, and to the interests of humanity. Officials have to be sensitive to nuance and to shades of gray, and they must be willing to balance costs and benefits, and to seek compromise where appropriate.

Second, in the cases we have discussed, public officials usually adopt a consequentialist mode of analysis. This is not surprising since they represent or act for others, and their actions directly affect the lives of ordinary citizens. However, our analysis of the cases suggests that elements of deontological ethics and virtue theory often become part of the officials' consequentialist reasoning, and make up for some of the deficiencies of that approach in complex situations where decisions have to be made quickly on the basis of limited information. The elements of other ethical approaches also help the officials compensate for the tendency, highlighted by Barnett, to equate the immediate interests of their organizations with the moral good. The different ethical approaches may be incompatible in their first principles but the cases suggest that they all can be useful in guiding officials making actual decisions

For Peter Rodino, Frances Kelsey, and Thomas Berg the norms of their professions and of their positions in the bureaucracy helped them determine the course of action that would yield the best consequences. They did not have to analyze alternatives or weigh costs and benefits to figure out where the public interest lay. In other cases, the alternative ethical approaches did not so directly lead to a decision but gave the officials, or could have given them, a richer conception of the effects of proposed actions. Anthony Lake suggested that his own values or principles or conception of moral duties should have influenced him to give more weight to the scope of the killing in Rwanda. The JAG lawyers worried that harsh interrogation techniques would undermine the military's conception of itself as a moral agent, which would have consequences for self-respect and discipline.

Third, qualities of individual moral character played an important role in some of the cases we examined. Peter Rodino and Frances Kelsey had in common personal virtues of modesty, persistence, and courage. They shunned the spotlight, and took risks that probably few others would accept—ridicule in Rodino's case, and her job in Kelsey's. Although Pomper explains their success by emphasizing their conformity to institutional norms and roles, it seems clear that individual moral character also helped them to be effective under pressure and in times of crisis (Pomper 2004, 244).

Fourth, context matters in ethics, and contextual factors matter here with respect to ethical decision making. For the public officials mentioned in this chapter, background experience, the responsibilities of a position, and the bureaucratic level of that position in an executive hierarchy influenced ethical priorities. Secretary of State Colin Powell's background as a general and former head of the Joint Chiefs of Staff made him especially sensitive to the fact that not following the Geneva Conventions would lower the bar for other countries' treatment of captured U.S. soldiers. In addition, his position as secretary of state undoubtedly led him to emphasize the consequences of U.S. renunciation of Geneva standards for our relations with other nations. Frances Kelsey's experience as a scientific investigator and medical practitioner sensitized her to the need for pharmaceutical companies to demonstrate drug safety and to the public health consequences of their failure to do so. In several cases, an official's position in the bureaucracy influenced the conception of consequences. Donald Steinberg, Prudence Bushnell, and other mid-level officials in the NSC and the State Department, who were closer to the Africa desks than Anthony Lake or Madeline Albright, emphasized the negative consequences of a do-nothing policy for the people of Rwanda as well as for U.S. national security. On the issue of torture, it was JAG attorneys rather than White House Counsel and Department of Justice lawyers who were cognizant of the impact of torture upon U. S. servicemen and women. This suggests that the lower one is in the bureaucratic hierarchy and the more contact one has with the ordinary people affected by policy decisions, the less likely one is to engage in the kind of abstract thinking that Lake saw as typical of top decision-makers. In other words, our situations affect our conceptions of consequences and our framing of ethically justifiable public policies.

Finally, deontological ethics could play a more prominent role in ethical decision making than it currently does. Consequentialism is said to be appropriate because politicians represent others, act for others, and their actions impact directly upon the lives of others. However, another way that politicians could represent us would be to consult us directly and elicit our consent through public discussion and debate. On this view, the basis of morality is what various parties can rationally and freely agree to. This is the rationale underlying deliberative democracy (Fishkin 2003). Such a deontological ethics focuses on the duty to treat people as ends in themselves rather than as means to the ends of others. And people are treated as ends when they are able to consent to the actions, policies, or institutions that affect them.

In terms of the cases discussed in this chapter, perhaps Rodino's chairing of the House Judiciary Committee hearings comes closest to responding to public debate about the Watergate scandal. On issues of Rwanda and torture during wartime, the public was not consulted at all. Ironically, later revelations of torture at prisons such as Abu Ghraib provoked a fierce public debate about whether such policies should be carried out in the name of the American people. Proponents of deontological ethics might ask why such a debate could not have happened much earlier, when the administration was considering the relevance of the Geneva Conventions to the war on terror in 2002. From this perspective, the task of public officials facing difficult ethical decisions would be to ask what the people affected by the decision would consent to and, when possible, to implement procedures to solicit the views of those people.

REFERENCES

Albright, Madeleine (2004). Interview, Frontline: Ghosts of Rwanda. Public Broadcasting Company, pp. 1–11. http://www.pbs.org/wgbh/pages/frontline/shows/ghosts/interviews/albright.html.

Barnett, Michael N. (1997). The UN Security Council, Indifference, and Genocide in Rwanda. *Cultural Anthropology*, 4(4); 551–578

Barnett, Michael (2002). *Eyewitness to a genocide: The United Nations and Rwanda.* Ithaca, NY and London: Cornell University Press.

Baron, Marcia W. (1997). Kantian Ethics. In *Three Methods of Ethics*, edited by Marcia Baron, Philip Pettit, and Michael Slote, pp. 3–91. Malden, MA: Blackwell Publishers.

Berg, Thomas (2005). Interview, Frontline: The Torture Question. Public Broadcasting Company, pp. 1–18. http://www.pbs.org/wgbh/pages/frontline/torture/interviews/berg.html.

Bernstein, Adam. Rep. Peter Rodino 95; Presided over Nixon impeachment hearings. *The Washington Post*, May 8, 2005, C-11.

Bradley, Francis Herbert (1876). My station and its duties. In *Ethical Studies*. New York: Oxford University Press, Second Edition, 1988.

Burkholz, Herbert (1997). Giving Thalidomide a second chance. *FDA Consumer Magazine,* pp. 1–4. http://www.fda.gov/fdac/features/1997/697_thal.html.

Bush, George (2002). Memorandum: Humane treatment of al Qaeda and Taliban detainees, pp. 1–2. http://www.gwu.edu/~nsarchiv/NSAEBB/NSAEBB127/02.02.07.pdf.

Bushnell, Prudence (2003). Interview, Frontline: Ghosts of Rwanda. Public Broadcasting Company, pp. 1–25. http://www.pbs.org/wgbh/pages/frontline/shows/ghosts/interviews/bushnell.html.

Carlsson, Ingvar, Sung-Joo, Han, and Kupolati, M. (1999). *Report of the Independent Inquiry into United Nations Actions During the 1994 Rwanda Genocide.* New York: United Nations.

Cuomo, Mario (1984). Religious belief and public morality: A Catholic governor's perspective. In *A Wall of Separation? Debating the Public Role of Religion,* edited by Mary C. Segers and Ted G. Jelen, pp. 144–159. Lanham, MD: Rowman and Littlefield.

Ferroggiaro, William, ed. (2001). The U.S. and the genocide in Rwanda 1994: Evidence of inaction. *The National Security Archive*, Electronic Briefing Book, pp.1–10. Government documents cited in this paper were obtained by the National Security Archive under the Freedom of Information Act.

Ferroggiaro, William (2004). The U.S. and the genocide in Rwanda 1994: Information, intelligence and the U.S. response. *The National Security Archive*, Electronic Briefing Book.

Fishkin, James S. and Laslett, Peter, eds. (2003) *Debating Deliberative Democracy*. Malden MA: Blackwell Publishers.

Gonzales, Alberto R. (2002). Memorandum for the president: Decision re application of the Geneva Convention on prisoners of war to the conflict with Al Qaeda and the Taliban, pp. 1–4. http://www.gwu.edu/~nsarchiv/NSAEBB/NSAEBB127/02.01.25.pdf.

Gutmann, Amy and Dennis Thompson (2006). *Ethics & Politics: Cases & Comments* (4th ed.). Belmont, CA: Thomson Wadsworth.

Lake, Anthony (2003). Interview, Frontline: Ghosts of Rwanda. Public Broadcasting Company, pp. 1–12. http://www.pbs.org/wgbh/pages/frontline/shows/ghosts/interviews/lake.html.

Lohr, Rear Admiral Michael F. (2003a). Memorandum: Working group recommendations relating to interrogation of detainees. *Congressional Record: July 25, 2005*, S8795, pp. 17–18. http://www.fas.org/irp/congress/2005_cr/s072505.html.

Lohr, Rear Admiral Michael F. (2003b). Memorandum for the Air Force general counsel: Comments on the March 6 2003 detainee interrogation working group report. *Congressional Record: July 25, 2005*, S8795-S8796, pp. 18–20. http://www.fas.org/irp/congress/2005_cr/s072505.html.

Machiavelli, Niccolo (1994). The discourses. In *Machiavelli: Selected Political Writings*, edited by David Wooton, pp. 81–217. Indianapolis, IN: Hackett Publishing.

Machiavelli, Niccolo (1995). *The Prince.* Edited and translated by David Wootton. Indianapolis, IN: Hackett Publishing.

Mulliken, J. (1962). A woman doctor who would not be hurried. *Life Magazine 53*, 28–29.

OLC, Office of Legal Counsel, U.S. Department of Justice (2002). Memorandum for Alberto R. Gonzales counsel to the president re: Standards of conduct for interrogation under 18 U.S.C. Sections 2340-2340A, pp. 1–46. http://www.gwu.edu/~nsarchiv/NSAEBB/NSAEBB127/02.08.01.pdf.

Pence, Greg (1991). Virtue theory. In *A Companion to Ethics*, edited by Peter Singer, pp. 249–258. Cambridge, MA: Blackwell Reference.

Pettit, Philip (1997). The consequentialist perspective. In *Three Methods of Ethics*, edited by Marcia Baron, Philip Pettit, and Michael Slote, pp. 92–174. Malden, MA: Blackwell Publishers,

Pomper, Gerald M. (2004). *Ordinary Heroes and American Democracy.* New Haven: Yale University Press.

Powell, Colin L. Secretary of State (2002). Memorandum to counsel to the president: Draft decision memorandum for the president on the applicability of the Geneva Convention to the conflict in Afghanistan, pp. 1–5. http://www.gwu.edu/~nsarchiv/NSAEBB/NSAEBB127/02.01.26.pdf.

Power, Samantha (2001). Bystanders to genocide: Why the United States let the Rwandan tragedy happen. *The Atlantic Monthly, 288*(2), 84–106.

Power, Samantha (2003). *A Problem from Hell: America and the Age of Genocide.* New York: Harper Collins Publishers.

Rawls, John (1996). *Political liberalism.* New York: Columbia University Press.

Rives, Major General Jack L. (2003a). Memorandum For SAF/GC: Comments on draft report and recommendations of the working group to assess the legal, policy and operational issues relating to interrogation of detainees held by the U.S. armed forces in the war on terrorism. *Congressional Record: July 25, 2005,* S8794-S8795, pp. 15–17. http://www.fas.org/irp/congress/2005_cr/s072505.html.

Rives, Major General Jack L. (2003b). Memorandum: Final report and recommendations of the working group to assess the legal, policy and operational issues relating to interrogation of detainees held by the U.S. armed aorces in the war on terrorism. *Congressional Record: July 25, 2005,* S8796, pp. 20–22. http://www.fas.org/irp/congress/2005_cr/s072505.html.

Rodino, Peter W. (1974). As quoted in *Congressional Record,* July 19, 2005, pp. S8484,

Rodino, Peter W. (1999). The vote that changed America. *New York Times,* July 27, 1999, pp. A-19.

Romig, Major General Thomas J. (2003). Memorandum for general counsel of the department of the Air Force: Draft report and recommendations of the working group to access [sp] the legal, policy and operational issues related to interrogation of detainees held by the U.S. Armed Forces in the war on terrorism. *Congressional Record: July 25, 2005,* S8794, pp. 14–15. http://www.fas.org/irp/congress/2005_cr/s072505.html.

Sandkuhler, Brigadier General Kevin M.(2003). Memorandum for general counsel of the Air Force: Working group recommendations on detainee interrogations. *Congressional Record: July 25, 2005,* S8794, pp. 12–13. http://www.fas.org/irp/congress/2005_cr/s072505.html.

Segers, Mary (2005). Catholicism and democracy: Bishops, politicians, and voters in the 2004 presidential campaign." Unpublished Paper. Proceedings of the American Political Science Association, September 2005, Washington, D.C.

Singer, Peter, ed. (1991). *A Companion to Ethics.* Cambridge, MA: Blackwell Reference.

Slote, Michael (1997). Virtue Ethics. In *Three Methods of Ethics,* edited by Marcia Baron, Philip Pettit, and Michael Slote, pp. 175–239. Malden, MA: Blackwell Publishers.

Steinberg, Donald K. (2004). Conflict, gender, and human rights: Lessons learned from the field. Joan B. Kroc Distinguished Lecture Series, Institute for Peace and Justice, University of San Diego, pp. 1–28.

Taft, William H. IV (2002a). Memorandum to John C. Yoo: Your draft memorandum of January 9, pp. 1–40. http://www.cartoonbank.com/newyorker/slideshows/01TaftMemo.pdf.

Taft, William H. IV (2002b). Memorandum to counsel to the president Alberto Gonzales: Comments on your paper on the Geneva Convention, pp. 1–5. http://www.gwu.edu/~NSarchiv/NSAEBB/NSAEBB127/02.02.02.pdf.

Thompson, Dennis F. (1987). *Political Ethics and Public Office.* Cambridge, MA: Harvard University Press.

Velasquez, Manuel, Thomas Shanks, Claire Andre, and Michael Meyer (2002). *Thinking Ethically: A Framework for Moral Decision-making.* Markkula Center for Applied Ethics, Santa Clara University, pp. 1–3. http://www.scu.edu/Ethics.

Walzer, Michael (1973). Political action: The problem of dirty hands. *Philosophy and Public Affairs* 1 (Winter 1973): 160–180.

Walzer, Michael (1977). *Just and Unjust Wars: A Moral Aargument with Historical Illustrations.* New York: Basic Books.

Weber, Max (1918). Politics as a vocation. In *From Max Weber: Essays in sociology,* edited by H. H. Gerth and C. Wright Mills, pp. 77–128. New York: Oxford University Press, 1958.

Yoo, John (2005a). Commentary: Behind the 'torture memos.' *UC Berkeley News.* January 4, 2005, pp. 1–4. http://www.berkeley.edu/news/media/releases/2005/01/05_johnyoo.shtml.

Yoo, John. (2005b). Interview, Frontline: The torture question. Public Broadcasting Company, pp. 1–24. http://www.pbs.org/wgbh/pages/frontline/torture/interviews/yoo.html.

22 Public Policy and Democratic Citizenship: What Kinds of Citizenship Does Policy Promote?

Anne Larason Schneider and Helen Ingram

INTRODUCTION

> Citizenship (n). The state of being vested with the rights, privileges, and duties of a citizen. The character of an individual viewed as a member of society; the behavior of citizens in terms of the duties, obligations, and functions of a citizen. (*Random House Dictionary of the English Language*, 1988).

Public policy in the United States and most other Western democracies always has been used to promote one or another vision of democratic citizenship and nationhood. When citizenship is conceived broadly to encompass the rights and opportunities people should be able to expect from the governance of their society as well as their obligations, then almost every public policy impinges on citizenship in ways either large or small, positive or negative. Citizenship, however, is not just about rights and opportunities, but also about identity and whether ones identity is fully embraced by the society. Public policy teaches powerful lessons about rights, opportunities, and identity—but it carries different messages for different people, and produces more than one kind of citizen. Policy analysts and political leaders are acutely aware that policy may encourage or thwart participation, increase knowledge or obfuscate citizen learning, include or marginalize different groups, and advantage some at the expense of others. There is nothing neutral about the relationship between public policy and democratic citizenship.

This chapter begins by examining the concept of citizenship in its many diverse and partially conflicting meanings as explored by academic theorists, public intellectuals, and civic educators. We then turn to the types of citizenship that policy produces and to the concerns raised by policy analysts and others.

DEMOCRATIC CITIZENSHIP: IDEALS AND CONCERNS

Democratic citizenship refers to the characteristics and actions that people should exhibit in a democracy if they are to be considered worthy and deserving of the privileges and rights of the society. Because democracies are self-governing entities, their citizens are expected to support the values and engage in the behavior needed to sustain a democratic way of life. Democratic citizenship also refers to the ways the society and its public policies should treat people—namely, that all are created equal and entitled to equal rights, to equal opportunity, and to equal inclusion in membership of the nation. Democratic citizenship, then, is a socially constructed concept grounded in the moral values and legal framework of the society. The construction of citizenship has evolved over time, but beyond the basic notion that citizens have rights and are expected to support democratic ideals, there is not all that much agreement on specifics. As the discussion that follows illustrates, academic literature has drawn some fairly distinct differences between philosophies of citizenship. Contemporary left and right ideologies echo some of these distinctions even though the broader public discourse and those engaged in civic education, tend to embrace a blend of theories and a series of personal characteristics that are not reflected much in the academic treatments.

In the scholarly literature on democratic citizenship a number of issues have emerged, including: (1) whether the primary obligation of citizens as they participate in politics is the rational pursuit of self-interest or whether they should support that which is in the public interest; (2) whether democracy requires that citizens be active in holding government accountable or whether passivity and disinterest actually are necessary for democratic governance; (3) whether citizenship is mainly concerned with political participation, especially voting, or also with civic engagement and voluntary activities; (4) whether the emphasis should be on rights and opportunities as opposed to obligations or duties; (5) whether rights should be confined to the so-called "negative" rights of limiting government interference with liberty or expanded to include the social rights insuring everyone the basic necessities of life; (6) whether there should be a national homogeneous culture defined mainly by the traditional values (white, European, Christian, male leadership, and female domesticity) or whether being "truly American" (or "truly Canadian" or "truly French") embraces a wide range of values drawn from diverse race, ethnic, nationality, religious, and gender identities; and (7) whether voters need to be "competent" and where the competency line should be drawn. The different emphases sometimes are grouped roughly into three categories, although there are numerous distinctions within each one: liberal/pluralist, civic republican/communitarian (including deliberative, participatory, and discursive versions), and nativist perspectives (e.g., see Almond and Verba, 1963; Conover, et al. 1991; Mansbridge 1990; DeLuca 1995; Boyte 2003; Verba et al. 1995; Bellah et al. 1985; Dryzek 1996; deLeon 1997; Ingram and Smith 1993; Landy 1993; Nie et al. 1996; Putnam,2000; Shklar 1991; Skocpol 1999; Smith 1986; Etzioni 2004).

One of the long-standing tensions between the liberal and civic republican models of citizenship is in the emphasis placed on pursuit of self-interest through politics and pursuit of a collective interest or common good. The traditional liberal perspective contends that good citizens should pursue their own interests in the political market place just as they are expected to do in the economic system. Beginning at least with Schumpeter's work in 1935, the idea of balancing self- and public interest that had been common since the initial formulation of the republic was replaced with the contention that there is no common good or public interest (Mansbridge 1990; Lowi 1979; Schumpeter 1987) . Instead, the pluralist idea of democracy was articulated in which citizens and public officials both are expected to pursue self-interest. The dynamic interplay of these would, on the one hand, hold elected officials accountable, and on the other hand, produce a temporary balance among the competing interests that is the closest possible to the interests of both sides (Downs 1957).

The traditional liberal view of a limited role for citizens was supported by many of the early studies of voting behavior, which claimed that the classical theory of democracy was inconsistent with the actual functioning of U.S. democracy (Berelson et al. 1954). The authors first posited a "classic" version of citizenship (which some theorists such as Patemen, 1970, say actually never existed), that viewed citizens as active, informed, and rational individuals. They were not only able to connect their self-interests with the positions of candidates and political parties, but were expected to vote accordingly. They also were expected to have a coherent set of beliefs corresponding to general ideas of either liberal or conservative political ideologies. Finding these characteristics lacking, the authors posited that "lack of interest by some people is not without its benefits (Berelson et al. 1954, 314).

Theories of participatory and discursive democracy (Landy 1993; Barber 1984) contend that, through discourse and communication, citizens are able to identify what is in the best interests of the collectivity, and also will be willing to pursue it (Fischer 2003). Liberalism, in the view of the communitarians and participatory democrats, has envisioned only a "thin" version of citizenship, rather than one featuring an active, engaged populace that creates and belongs to a community, bringing meaning and inclusion into people's lives. Communitarians such as Etzioni (2004) and those stressing the importance of social capital, such as Putnam (2000), conceptualize citizenship as including community-oriented voluntary activities, which co-produce (along with local government) many of the services needed by the least advantaged people in the community. Citizens are not simply subjects who should obey the laws, be loyal to the nation and support the leadership, but are active, competent, and contrarian people, willing to criticize leaders and policies.

Liberal and communitarian visions of citizenship also differ on the role of rights, with some of the latter contending that rights claims have crowded out the discussion of issues needed for people to come to a genuine deliberative understanding of the collective good (Landy 1993). Some accuse communitarians of being too orientated toward the public good and the duties of citizenship, without an adequate understanding that citizenship must have a balance between duties and rights and a balance between self-interest and the public interest.

National identity has always been an issue in the United States and is especially salient at this time in the creation of a united Europe from among the very strong national identities of the traditional countries. "Nativism" is posited by some scholars as a third version of citizenship, (Smith 1986), and one that sees a common cultural identity and common values as central to citizenship (Abizasdeh 2002). Nativists see national identity threatened by new immigrants and other social changes reflected in multi-culturalism and the decline in the "Christian way of life."

These conceptions, although at times "cruelly narrow-minded" (Smith 1986, 2) reflect a love of community and a desire for inclusion in a community of like-minded people with whom one shares a common social and cultural identity—a place where a person "like me" can truly belong.

The "moral values" movement that emerged during and after the 2004 presidential election reflects the deep-seated beliefs of some Americans that religious values as defined mainly by Christian traditions are synonymous with American values. This movement focuses on anti-abortion, anti-gay rights such as marriage or civil unions, restoring prayer in schools, permitting the Ten Commandments to be shown in public spaces, and a preference for candidates who converse with God as part of their deliberations about public issues. These types of principles may well reflect the re-emergence of nativism in that they represent a preference for homogeneous belief systems grounded in religion that are not subject to debate or discourse, except for arguments over "correct" interpretation of the will of God.

Within the broad recognition that beliefs in democratic principles include beliefs in individual rights, there is a long-standing disagreement between those who advocate mainly the rights to be free from an overreaching government, the so-called "negative" rights that prohibit government from interfering in free speech, assembly, religious observation; and those who include "social" rights to the basic necessities of life including food, shelter, and safety (Marshall 1964). The liberal tradition in America leans toward the former (although there certainly is some support for social rights); whereas the British and European tradition typically includes embraces a much more expansive welfare state (Conover 1990). This type of disagreement about the proper reach of public policy extends into the contemporary liberal–conservative debates over whether the national government in the United States should be a pro-active force for social and economic justice, or whether the welfare state should be sharply limited and the province of local government and civic organizations.

The competence of voters is an issue with a long tradition in the United States, and one that has two distinct facets. The first is the re-emergence over questions of restrictions on the right to vote that still exist for many of those who are mentally ill, who have had felony convictions, who are disenfranchised because of strict residency requirements (Shriner 2005; McDonald 2004), or who are sixteen to eighteen years old. The second issue of competence involves the role of experts and whether the rapid advances in science and technology, along with the increased complexity of policy making, means that policy making should be largely left to expertise in the bureaucracy with citizens and elected officials both having a much reduced role.

These philosophical debates have generated considerable research on how well citizens are able to perform the responsibilities of citizenship, but only a surprisingly small amount of research on what citizens, themselves, believe citizenship is all about. Two studies, however, stand out. The first was conducted by Dryzek who concluded that there are four discourses of democracy (1996) among U.S. citizens. *Contented republican* refers to those who are trusting of government, believe in an active and informed citizenry, and believe that discussion can bring about an "identity between what is good for me and what is good for society" (Dryzek 1996, 133). *Deferential conservatism* reflects the notion that politics is only for the elites and people simply do not know enough or care enough to be involved. Government should be very limited, but left to experts to govern, as they are best equipped to look after the national interest. *Disaffected populism* also reflects beliefs that power is in the hands of conservatives and business elites, but differs in that populists believe elites will govern in their own interest, not in the national interest. People need to mobilize and take back power. Ordinary people, not elites, can be trusted. *Private liberalism* refers to ideas that government has too large a role in society and in life, but active citizenship is not desirable, either. The private realm of work and family are more important and one needs to rely on family, friends, and the market rather than government. Conover's comparative study of U.S. and British citizens found that the U.S. citizens focused far more on civil rights, such as free speech, whereas the British focused more on social rights (Conover et al. 1991). Although there were other differences, there also was considerable overlap in ideas across these two nations, and the authors concluded that the meaning of citizenship is more complex and ambiguous than found in the philosophical debates.

WHAT KIND OF CITIZENSHIP DOES POLICY PRODUCE?

Policy impacts citizen attitudes and behaviors through explicit "citizenship education" initiatives, but primarily through the messages, models, and actual allocation of values for the society. In this section, we begin with the vision of citizenship found in specific citizenship education initiatives in the United States, Britain, and the European Union; we then turn to policy across a number of different substantive fields and illustrate how differences in policy design produce different kinds of citizenship.

CITIZEN EDUCATION INITIATIVES

What is most noticeable about the citizenship initiatives in Western democracies, is that they do not reflect any one of the philosophical constructions of citizenship "types" but rather reflect ideas from all of the philosophical perspectives. Our review of the recent initiatives in the United States indicates broad agreement that citizenship requires knowledge of democratic institutions and principles, skills for influencing politics and policy, and dispositions that reflect beliefs in democracy.[1] The more specific ideas about citizenship lean more toward an active and engaged citizen especially at the local level than toward a passive subject, more toward civic volunteer activities than toward political action other than voting, (Boyte 2003); more toward civil rights than toward social rights; more toward limited and decentralized government than activist government; and toward a set of exemplary personal characteristics that are generally individualistic, passive, and not overtly political in nature. For example, the Indiana General Assembly in 1995 listed thirteen character traits to be taught as part of their state-wide mandated public instruction on "good citizenship." These included: (1) being honest and truthful, (2) respecting authority, (3) respecting the property of others, (4) always doing one's personal best, (5) not stealing, (6) possessing the skills necessary to live peaceable in society and not resorting to violence to settle disputes, (7) taking personal responsibility for obligations to family and community, (8) taking personal responsibility for earning a livelihood, (9) treating others the way one would want to be treated, (10) respecting the national flag, the Constitution of the United States, and the Constitution of the State of Indiana, (11) respecting one's parents and home, (12) respecting one's self, and (13) respecting the rights of others to have their own views and religious beliefs. (IC 20-10.1-4-4.5).

Much greater emphasis on the idea of public responsibility, however, is found in a popular guide for teaching citizenship to K-5 students in the United States (Six Pillars of Character 2004). This guide refers to two educational goals: "that good citizens do their part to make their community a good place to live," and "that they have the power to make a positive difference in the world" (Six Pillars of Character 2004). The six principles are: (1) do your share to make your school, your community, and the world a better place; (2) take responsibility for what goes on around you; (3) participate in community service; (4) help take care of the environment; (5) be a good neighbor; (6) treat other people with respect and dignity; and (7) follow the rules of your family, your school, and your society.

The National Civic Education Association has developed a comprehensive curricular model for K-12 years that emphasizes the rights, participatory responsibilities, political institutions, and dispositions—including tolerance and respect for others—that are needed to sustain democracy. The focus in these standards is more on the questions and topics to be considered, however, than it is on providing an agreed-upon framework that could be embraced by contemporary left and right ideologies in the United States. Interestingly, the details of this framework are buried deep in the implement chain—undoubtedly as a way of avoiding the seriously divisive arguments that emerge whenever left, right, and religious right ideologues engage one another on the issue of the appropriate moral values of citizenship.

Britain initiated a major citizenship education project in the late 1990s with the general goals of teaching social and moral responsibility, community involvement and political literacy (Lockyer et al. 2003; Crick 2003). The revival of interest in citizenship in Britain emerged at least partly from "the excesses of possessive individualism" during the Thatcher years, the low levels of voting participation especially among youth, and the immigration into England of many people from different cultural backgrounds (Lockyer et al. 2003). The goal of the report is to "create a new model of active citizen, fitted for participatory democracy, rather than to reproduce a minimally engaged law-abiding subject." (Lockyer 2003, 3).

Striking a very similar cord, the Council of Europe's project, Education for Democratic Citizenship" emerged out of concerns about low levels of participation, the "rise of intolerance, xenophobia, and racism throughout Europe," and alienation of youth (Education for Democratic Citizenship 2003, 2). The report noted multiple themes and general principles for each: (1) from a *political* perspective, to enhance participation; (2) in terms of *cohesion*, to respond to the "fragmentation of increasingly individualist, pluralist, and complex societies;" (3) in terms of *dignity, respect, identity*, control over choices and quality of life; (4) in *cultural* terms, "the point is to create conditions for complete individual fulfillment and participation of everyone in creating a democratic culture;" (5) in terms of *rights*, "democratic citizenship is supposed to provide everyone with information about one's rights;" (6) in terms of *responsibilities*, "democratic citizenship corresponds on the one hand, to a spirit of solidarity and a sense of the inherent limits of individual rights in order to respect others and contribute to the common good and, on the other hand, the possibility of being independent and assuming that independence." (All quotes are from Education for Democratic Citizenship, 2.)

The visions found in the Council of Europe and the British projects embrace an expansive view of citizenship in political, social, economic, and cultural terms. Citizenship, in this vision, is about the quality of ones life as an individual, as a member of the society, and as a participant in insuring the quality of life of others. These visions posit a national identity based not on a homogenous culture or on a set of guaranteed freedoms, but on a sense of place and culture that embraces diversity.[2]

HOW PLURALISM PROMOTES POSITIVE CITIZENSHIP

The significant point about pluralist democracy, when it works as envisioned rather than in one or another of its perverted forms, is that it can produce policy that provides the opportunities, resources, positive identities, and incentives for a vibrant citizenship.

Examples of the positive effects of pluralist democracy are not difficult to find. The progression of suffrage laws from highly restrictive ones that permitted only white, male, property owners to vote to the much more expansive system that now includes almost all citizens eighteen and older is a good example of the direct effects of public policy on citizen opportunities to be involved in politics. Over time, as the issues shifted from the right to vote, to actually having the resources, incentives, and removal of local barriers, new policies were adopted including the Civil Rights Act of 1964, the Voting Rights Act of 1964, the Twenty-fourth and Twenty-sixth Amendments, the 1993 National Voter Registration Act (the "motor voter act"), and the Help America Vote Act of 2002.

Equal treatment under the law is a guaranteed right in the Constitution, but a host of policies have been adopted to insure and extend these rights of nondiscrimination and fair treatment to all aspects of ones life, not just to voting or political participation. The Civil Rights Act of 1964, for example, prohibits discrimination on the basis of race, color, sex, religion, or national origin by employers, labor unions, hotels, restaurants, theaters, gas stations, and all other public accommodations involved in interstate commerce. Workplace discrimination also was attacked through the 1967 Age Discrimination Act and the 1990 Americans with Disabilities Act.

Many initiatives exist to promote the health and safety of the people, including the clean air and water act—which also promote a new level of respect for the integrity of the planet—policies to ensure safety of the food supply, provide health care access for older Americans and for the poor, creation of a massive health research program under the National Institute of Health and the Centers for Disease Control to reduce the incidence of disease. Regulatory policies have been adopted to insure a right to a reasonable level of safety in the workplace, such as the creation of the Occupational Safety and Health Act of 1970.

Although the United States has never acknowledged that people have the types of "social rights" that British and European citizenship embrace, dozens of policies exist to either provide social welfare for those who cannot provide for themselves, or to provide the means and opportunities for self-sufficiency. Education policy has always been the most central means to insure equal opportunity for economic success in the United States. Free public education remains open to all children in the United States (including those of noncitizens) regardless of test scores or grades. As the nation developed, the Morrill Act created a system of higher education that would be available at very low cost to all people—not just to the elite and wealthy families of the East Coast. Education provides the resources, knowledge, and "standing" that enables people from all walks of life, race, nationality, and income to participate on a relatively equal basis (Nie et al. 1996). The 1935 Social Security Act and other New Deal programs of the 1930s and 1940s established a federal role in providing social safety nets, and even though these programs did not guarantee a "right" to the basic necessities of life, their intent was to insure a livable income for all people.

The Great Society programs of the 1960s were prompted by the growing recognition that the federal government was distrusted and was unable to take effective action to reduce poverty, solve the problems of racism, or inequality in society, and that the energy going into the massive demonstrations taking place on behalf of civil rights movement, women's movement, and the anti-war movement could be directed toward positive change at the grassroots level. A very different policy design was used in these programs—one in which the federal government set broad policy goals, allocated resources, but permitted wide discretion at the local level on the means to achieve those goals. Among the most prominent examples of this type of loosely coupled policy was the 1964 Economic Opportunity Act (EOA) which created the community action programs and the well-known provision that they be administered with "maximum feasible participation" of the residents of the areas and members of the groups served (Public Law 88-452, sec 202(a)(3))..

A very large number of other policies could be cited here that strengthen one or another aspect of citizenship or shape citizen beliefs and values in certain directions. Policy restrictions on immigration common during the first two centuries privileged white northern Europeans, signifying a form of nativism about who the most appropriate citizens are; whereas changes to a more race/nationality neutral immigration policy purportedly signals support for traditional American ideals of equality (Sniderman et al. 2004). Policy support of scientific and technological research signals the centrality of scientific ways of thinking and the superior value of technological progress as compared to other notions of progress, such as progress in human capacity for empathy or progress in indigenous beliefs in the sanctity of the planet and its resources. Policy protection of the environment, on the other hand, signals the importance of citizen commitment to environmentalism and restricts certain kinds of economic development, even as policy exploitation of natural resources signals the centrality of economic progress that depends on energy. Many public policies reflect complex and sometimes conflicting ideas of the appropriate beliefs and actions of the "good citizen," but this simply means that policy tends to represent the multiplicity of values in an open society. Provision of safety from crime, terrorists, and other threats strengthens national identity and shows that government cares about people's quality of life, even as other acts—such as the Patriot Act—undermine traditional notions of privacy and protection of civil rights. Policy to reduce hunger, provide better housing, improve nutrition, and develop effective drug therapies for disease all contribute to the way that citizens ought to be treated by their society.

Pluralist democracy has produced policy that, in turn, forges a particular pattern of citizenship. But there are a host of concerns about the state of citizenship in the United States.

CONCERNS ABOUT POLITICAL INFLUENCE OF INTEREST GROUPS AND WEALTH

Many academics and public intellectuals have voiced concerns about the influence that special interests and wealth have in policy making. There are, of course, policy regulations regarding interest groups and the use of wealth in politics, but the number of interest groups grows steadily, wealth continues to be used in numerous ways both obvious and hidden. The demands on government for constant improvement in the quality of life and the need to compete with other nations for economic, cultural, and military superiority are so extensive that government grows until citizens cannot relate to it, enormous budget deficits are created, and government is no longer capable of solving problems or serving the national interest (Lowi 1979; Greider 1992; Dionne 1991; Rauch 1994).

Lowi (1979) was one of the first scholars to posit that the problems with pluralism are not a "natural" byproduct of constitutional arrangements, but actually are created by the form that public policy has taken in the United States. Lowi was especially critical of the fact that most policies (excluding some forms of regulatory policy) are characterized by a particular kind of policy design in which statutes are vague, lack transparency, delegate most authority to agencies or local governments, and grant lower-level implementing agencies wide discretion in meeting the needs and demands of the various interest groups. Neither the statute nor the implementation specifications contains clear standards or rules of law. The result is "interest group liberalism," which undermines government, Lowi says, because it precludes planning (relying on bargaining instead); undermines public morality and citizenship in that the self-seeking interests of organized groups dominate the policy process; is unable to pursue justice because justice is not at the bargaining table and is not even considered, and teaches wrong lessons about citizenship and democracy. Lowi's solution focused on "juridical" democracy where statutes contain clear, specific rules of law that enables citizens to know exactly what is being done, to whom, why, and with what resources. This type of statute provides a clear point of contention for those who oppose it, which leads (if needed) to positive policy change.

Although many contemporary commentators are concerned about the influence of interest groups, and many of them believe in an activist government, their prescriptions tend to take on a different angle than Lowi, and prescribe greater citizen participation and activity (Greider 1992); greater responsibility from the media to unveil special interests and false arguments (Fallows 1997); greater exercise of integrity by elected officials (Rausch 1994); and the reinvention of government and devolution of government to lower levels and nonprofits led by Vice President Al Gore in the mid-1990s.

Concerns about "Big Government" and "Moral Lessons": The Conservative Critique

Many conservative observers of American government also are concerned about interest group influence, but they have quite a different set of prescriptions grounded mainly in strategies to reduce the role of public policy in society, leaving far more to philanthropists, civic volunteers, non profits, faith-based organizations, and private enterprise. The conservative critique has found a comfortable intellectual setting in public choice or rational choice theories of public policy. Public choice theory assumes a certain type of "natural" human behavior: the self-interested, utility-maximizing individual. Since this is the way people "naturally" behave, the theory contends, then social and political institutions have to be designed to accommodate such behavior. The problem, however, is that public choice theorists have deduced that if people pursue self-interests through politics, then public policy inevitably grows to cover more and more aspects of life and results in inefficient policies that do not solve problems and waste resources. Thus, the classical public choice theory contends that as much as possible should be left to markets, rather than government. The vision of citizenship here is very limited: citizens are "naturally" self-interested and unable to conceptualize or pursue a common interest.

The conservative critique extends beyond concern about big government to the moral lessons taught by a society that provides "too much" for its citizens. Also drawing from public choice theory, conservative views of citizenship focus on a particular form of individual secular morality: citizens should be self-sufficient, able to provide for themselves and their families, and disciplined enough to insure that they take advantage of the educational and other opportunities that are offered by the state. The debate about "privatized" security accounts within the Social Security system is a prime example of how the conservative and contemporary liberal perspectives of citizenship differ. The conservative agenda emphasizes a citizenship of individual self-reliance in which each provides for his/her own retirement; whereas liberals view security beyond the working years as a collective problem in which the society as a whole should share responsibility for insuring the quality of life for the elderly. The moral lesson of privatized social security is one of the self-reliant citizen; the moral lesson of collective social security is one of community care and compassion for those beyond the working years.

Other conservative commentators, such as Lawrence Mead (1987) and Charles Murray (1994), argue that all aspects of the welfare state create dependency and fail to teach good citizenship lessons. For example, the Welfare Reform Act of 1996 ends the entitlement that children previously had of a life with a family of at least one parent who had sufficient income to provide for housing, food, and other necessities, and replaces it with a time-limited entitlement of five years over the lifetime of the adult guardian. The act is intended to teach young women not to have more children than they can support, to not have children out of wedlock, and to take advantage of educational opportunities before they have children because education. The act teaches that parents must work and do not have the privilege of staying at home with their children even when the children are very young.

A New Nativism? The Religious Right's Critique

A host of other policies and policy proposals over the past few years also are intended to re-introduce through public policy notions of morality grounded in Christian belief systems. The support of marriage act (that would ban same-sex marriage or civil unions) is an example. So is the policy insuring that faith-based institutions are eligible as service-delivery systems for federal grants; efforts at the local, state, and national levels to permit school-sponsored prayer, display of Christian symbols such as the Ten Commandment, proposals to overturn the *Roe v. Wade* grant of a woman's right to the control of her own body during the first trimester of pregnancy; proposals to limit the teaching of evolution in school or to add various forms of "intelligent design" as a theory of human origin. These policies are intended mainly to regulate individual behavior and to teach different beliefs so that policy will reflect the moral teachings of fundamentalist Christians. The "good citizen" in this view, is one who exemplifies religious values—mainly fundamentalist Christian values. The vision here is of a society where all citizens are part of a common community because they share the same basic religious ideas.

The religious critique of contemporary public policy is quite different from the conservative one, in that it does not advocate the same type of "hands off" restraint of politics nor aversion to the use of federal power. The religious critique is directed at the secular culture of pluralist democracy and at the multicultural, multiracial heterogeneity of the culture. To the religious right, there is a "right way" to be an American, and public policy should teach this through its directives, symbols, and messages.

Concerns about Citizens and Experts

Many policy arenas have become exceptionally complex due to the scientific and technical advances of the twentieth and twenty-first centuries, the global economy, and the new forms of war that terrorism has advanced. From a policy science point of view, sophisticated analysis is needed to determine the facts, to provide the best estimates of benefits and costs, the best estimates of risk or probabilities, and to combine the facts into a scientific version of the problem to be solved and to design solutions (Quade 1991). From a policy science perspective, policy designs should not be determined through bargaining as interest groups have conflicts of interest and ordinary citizens simply do not know enough about science or technology or the law to be helpful in policy design. Taken to its logical extreme, public officials should only set broad national goals and leave the details to experts in the agencies, guided by scientific findings and professional management strategies (Kennan 1995). The role of citizen is limited to reacting when policy goes seriously wrong, and even then, it is up to the scientists, managers, and legal experts to design effective solutions. Citizen life would be largely divorced from complex policy issues and can focus on things such as civic engagement, participating in broad-gauged agenda setting activities, helping insure integrity in elected government leaders, and providing support for the advancement of science and technology.

Others see a variety of potential negative impacts on citizenship when policy arenas become dominated by the language and knowledge systems of science or highly professionalized experts (Stone 1997; Fischer and Forrester 1993; Guston 2004; Sarewitz 1997; deLeon 1997; Ingram and Schneider 2005). The issues come to be constructed in scientific terms and choices are defined by technically oriented or scientifically oriented decision making models. The use of quantitative decision making or other forms of "clinical reason" often disempowers citizens, substitutes scientific knowledge for ordinary knowledge, and in other ways precludes citizen understanding and input. From these perspectives, scientific knowledge and expertise do not necessarily produce the best public policy, as policy has to serve numerous roles in society, of which one is problem solving, but others include justice, support of democratic processes, and the exercise of citizenship itself. Engagement in policy making and collective problem solving should be part of the meaningfulness in people's lives—not just a technocratic exercise.

Recognizing the increased alienation from politics of many citizens in the United States, either because of the power of interest groups or the science/professionalism of policy arenas, a number of policy scholars have proposed discursive and participatory policy designs that are intended to increase the capacity of ordinary citizens to participate in policy development and implementation (Fischer 2003; Hajer and Wagenaar 2003; Feldman and Khademian 2002). Instrumental rationality, upon which policy science solutions depend, Dryzek argues, simply does not work to produce solutions in highly complex policy situations characterized by multiple values, multiple ways of framing the problem, multiple possible causal agents, multiple possible solutions,and high degrees of uncertainty regarding the means/ends connections. There simply is no single right or best or "most scientific" answer in highly complex situations and discourse among interested parties is the better way to arrive at a collective "best answer." Communication among the diverse perspectives can be expected to lead to better understanding of interests and to solutions—even if only partial ones—that reflect the collective good. A similar conclusion has been reached from the extensive research program of Elinor Ostrom (1990) who, although working out of a public choice paradigm rather than the critical theory paradigm, has found in studies of common pool resources that communication among participants often permits them to come together—sometimes with and sometimes without external government intervention—and design policy strategies that come close to an optimal solution.

Discursive and participatory models of many different kinds are being used in complex and scientific policy arenas (Hajer and Wagenaar 2003; Feldman and Khadmanian 2004). Policy analysts have devised a number of techniques to bring the citizen back in, including focus groups, citizen juries, community advisory boards, consensus conferences, adaptive management, inclusive management, and participatory integrated assessment. Even though there are problems with these, and outcome evaluations are not usually conducted, participants and observers tend to make the argument that the groups often devise innovative policy designs that experts, alone, would not have developed (Innes and Booher 2003; Healey et al. 2003). Deliberative policy arenas constitute a dramatic change in the role of citizens compared with pluralist democracy. When deliberative policy making works, it brings together the citizenship of political participation with that of civic engagement by providing institutional arenas where citizenship can flourish. It creates inclusion and belonging; it brings new meaning into people's lives.

Concerns about Equality: Policy Design and Inequality in Citizenship

One of the most persistent findings from empirical studies of citizen participation in politics and civic engagement in the United States is not only that the levels are low, in comparison with other developed democracies, but that the levels are very uneven across a range of demographic characteristics including income, education, age, gender, and race (Nie et al. 1996). The issue here is not which of these is most important, but rather why it is that persons who are the least advantaged also have the lowest participation levels. Some attribute this to the welfare state itself—that the comfortableness of welfare guarantees whether through direct welfare, minimum wage, unemployment insurance, social security, homeless shelters and the like, creates dependency that undermines active, full participation in the polity (Mead 1997). Others attribute it to the contentment of the lower class—that even the least well off people in the United States believe that policy is treating them fairly and therefore they see no need to participate because they are basically contented. Others believe that persons with lower levels of income and education simply do not have the resources (time, money, expertise, skill) to participate at the same level as others. Critical theorists attribute the discrepancy in participation to the manipulation by the state and specific ways that institutions of participation systematically discourage or prohibit participation, such as the felony exclusion, difficulties in registration, harassment and fear-inducing messages to potential voters, and to the purposeful complexities of voting procedures (Piven and Cloward 1988; McDonald 2004; Hacker et al. 2004).

Those working from the perspective of policy design and interpretive frameworks have begun to advance theories of policy feedback that explain how public policy plays a significant role in unequal participation both through direct effects (such as the rules of participation or allocation of resources) and indirect or interpretive effects that shape citizen orientations to the state (Schneider and Ingram 1993, 1997, 2005; Ingram and Schneider 1993, 2005; Mettler 2002; Soss, 1999; Hacker et al. 2004; Sidney 2003).

Schneider and Ingram's theory of policy design and citizenship proposes that some (not all) policy-making systems become "degenerative," such that issues are not considered on their own merits in terms of problem solving or improving the quality of life for the populace, but instead are manipulated for strategic gain through the manipulation of images. Policy making in these contexts relies on divisive social constructions of social groups for legitimation. The social construction of target populations refers to the image, characteristics, and values that tend to be associated with the group. Social constructions can take on many forms, and sometimes are so hegemonic that they seem absolutely natural and appropriate, and at other times are heavily contested. The constructions of target populations range from very positive, such as "deserving" or "entitled" to very negative, such as "greedy" or "violent."

Policy designs, Schneider and Ingram argue, depend on two aspects of target populations: their traditional political power resources (such as interest groups, wealth, voting patterns) and on their social constructions. By combining these dimensions, Schneider and Ingram propose four types of target populations: *advantaged, contenders, dependents, and deviants. Advantaged* groups have high levels of political power resources and also carry a strongly positive social construction. *Contenders* are powerful but are negatively constructed; *dependents* are socially constructed as "good" people, although weak or even helpless and they lack political power resources; *deviants* lack political power and are very negatively constructed. Policy directed toward each of these groups will tend to take on distinctive and different characteristics. Design elements, they contend, are interpreted by target populations in ways that influence their orientation toward government and their patterns of political participation. For example, policy designs for advantaged populations tend to focus on distributing benefits through capacity building programs with rules that are inclusive and expansive. Because there is so much political capital to be gained by providing benefits (subsidies, positive regulations) to advantaged groups, this domain will become oversubscribed, with far more public resources and favorable regulations than are actually warranted. Rationales for policies directed to advantaged groups emphasize that these policies are necessary for the national interests (such as economic competitiveness) and are an efficient way to achieve common societal goals. When burdens are being delivered to advantaged groups—such as taxes or undesired regulations—design elements tend to focus on self-regulation and learning at first; positive inducements, standards, or schemes where the target group can avoid the regulation or can buy its way out. Rationales associated with delivering burdens to advantaged populations explain that the group is sacrificing for the good of the country or that the burden really is in their own interests in the long run.

In contrast, policy design elements for delivering benefits to dependents tend to be means-tested with exclusionary rules, strict eligibility requirements, and punishment for noncompliance with the rules. Rationales tend to be in terms of justice, equal opportunity, need, or fairness rather than contributions to the national interest. For deviants, most of the policy consists of burdens or costs, especially discipline or punishment, delivered with strict rules and legitimated through the notion that the groups deserve to be punished for their violations of the law and that the public needs to be protected from them. Contenders are a difficult group as they have significant political power but are negatively constructed as "greedy" or "dangerous." Policy designs whose primary impact is on contenders tend to take on several other characteristics, including a high level of deception that makes it difficult for a lay person to know exactly what the policy will actually do. These policies may appear to regulate and discipline the target population, but in fact, offer numerous opportunities for the target group to thwart policy intent during implementation. Policy designs in this sector tend toward public tokens of discipline or regulation but with significant loopholes during the implementation that enable the target populations to escape most of the regulatory environment.

Secrecy and deception come to characterize much of policy designs, as policy makers shape their rationales to fit the social constructions they believe will generate the most political capital from the broad public, but contain actual policy design elements that will generate political capital from the powerful. These dynamics extend not just to specific policy designs, but to the design of the entire public policy agenda, as the issues that are taken up by political decision makers tend to be those that will confer benefits to the advantaged, punishment to the deviants, rhetorical policy without resources to the dependents, and token regulations to curb the dangerousness or greediness of powerful but negatively constructed groups.

Policy designs send very different messages to target populations that are interpreted by citizens and, in turn, impact their political participation and their orientation toward government. For example, Schneider and Ingram (1993, 2005) posit that advantaged populations will come to believe that their problems actually are national concerns that should be dealt with by government in its role of protecting the public interest, but that the problems of others are mainly special interests. Their orientations toward government tend to be disdainful (government is not very efficient, for example, and attempts to solve problems that should be left to the private sector), but they support limited government and tend to believe that the "rules of the game" are open, fair, and winnable. High levels of traditional political participation are expected from advantaged populations (voting, contacting, interest group activity, campaign contributions) and low levels of other types such as social movements, demonstrations, or violence.

Dependents, on the other hand, are expected to learn that they truly are helpless and needy; that their problems are more the responsibility of the private sector, philanthropy or faith-based organizations. They tend to have a disinterested and passive orientation toward government and may even come to believe that their own interests are not as important as the interests of other groups. They see the "political game" as hierarchical and elitist. Very low participation patterns of all types are expected. However, positive policy directed at dependents may in some cases be justified more on the basis of merit or deservedness than of helpless need; or policy entrepreneurs may mobilize dependents, reframe the issues, so that they obtain a more positive construction. These dynamics may, over time, create social movements or new interest groups that protect the advantages they have gained and protect their image as deserving of what they are receiving. Deviants come to understand that they have been labeled as bad and dangerous people; that their problems are their own fault and that government agents will treat them with disrespect or even hate. Orientations toward government are expected to be distrustful, alienated, and angry. They are expected to see the "rules of the game" as the abuse of power by privileged people. Traditional forms of participation are expected to be largely ignored in favor of the occasional social movement, demonstration, strike, or violence

Jensen's study (2005) of the pensions awarded to veterans of the Revolutionary War illustrate how policy created the group, constructed rationales of deservingness, provided resources and benefits, and over time produced the powerful veterans interest group that exists today. Suzanne Mettler's (2002) study of the effects of the G. I. Bill on the political participation and civic engagement of World War II Veterans illustrates how a beneficial policy, its rationales, and delivery mechanisms combined to produce significant higher levels of political participation for those who participated in it than for those who did not. Her project then turns to explaining the relationship—how and why is it that a generous social program such as the G. I. Bill had such effects on citizenship practices? Drawing on ideas from policy design and policy feedback, she notes that the G. I. Bill's educational benefits were generous; were not means-tested; were easy to access; did not label the recipient as a welfare case but treated the person with dignity since all veterans were on an equal basis rather than some being stigmatized as less advantaged. Using both qualitative and quantitative methodologies, she found support for the idea that these policy design elements of the G. I. Bill had positive effect on citizenship, especially for persons who had come from low and moderate income backgrounds.

The evolution of the policies enacted by the Social Security Act of 1935 illustrate that it is not simply the provision of a benefit that makes a difference in citizenship practices, but the rationales, rules, tools, and the implementation structure through which the recipient has a direct experience with government operatives. The target populations of the social security section of the act cut across racial, ethnic, social class, and economic lines and, most importantly, did not require means testing. All eligible persons had to pay into the fund if they were ever to be recipients. The policy was justified on the ground that it actually was just an insurance plan: people pay into it, and later after reaching the eligibility age, they receive funds from it. All who pay are entitled to receive. The Social Security Act did not cover everyone, however. It was originally intended for citizens in the industrial cities and excluded self-employed farmers, most agricultural workers, and domestic workers. However, those omitted were soon brought into it through amendments in 1950 that expanded coverage to all three of these groups who were expected to bring enormous new resources into the fund, which was quite strapped to meet the payouts that were being made. One of the rationales used in expanding the policy was that this was a better type of welfare system than simply providing a handout to the poor, as the policy required that people had to pay if they were to participate.

The long-term effects of the Social Security program are well known. Among them, this policy created, defined, and constructed as worthy citizens the elderly population and dramatically increased the political participation level of this group until today the American Association of Retired Persons (AARP) is one of the largest and most powerful interest groups in the United States. The statute also had some other interesting effects (Campbell 2002) in that among those who are recipients of social security, those with higher income levels are not the most active participants. In fact, Campbell (2002) has shown that social security recipients with lower incomes actually participate at a higher level than those with higher incomes—completely reversing the usual positive correlation between income and participation. Campbell attributes this compensatory effect to the fact that lower income social security recipients are more dependent on social security than others.

The 1935 act also created the Aid to Dependent Children (ADC) program, whose initial target group consisted mainly of white widowed mothers who could not provide for their children. This act presumed that mothers should be at home with their children, rather than working. The demographic composition was overwhelmingly white (about 86%) and most (85%) of the recipients were children whose fathers had died (Berkowitz 1991). The ADC program was means tested from the outset. Women had to prove that they were poor and unable to care for their children. By 1962, however, only 7 percent of the ADC caseload involved children whose fathers had died. By the time of the 1996 welfare reform that basically eliminated this entitlement, minority recipients were not only disproportionately represented but by most accounts actually outnumbered whites (Schram 2005). The recipients had become increasingly negatively constructed as welfare "queens," or as people who cheated the system.

In commenting on the welfare reform of 1996, The Personal Responsibility and Work Reconciliation Act of 1996 (Public Law 104-193), and the Temporary Assistance to Needy Families (TANF) Soss noted that "Over the past two decades, the question of how to cultivate 'good citizenship' has come to play a remarkable role in American welfare politics" (Soss 2005, 293). A new paternalism underlies this welfare reform whose purpose is to impose moral teaching and personal discipline to (mainly) mothers of minor children. Mead (1997) argues that paternalistic welfare programs are necessary because of the irresponsibility and lack of self-restraint among the poor.

Soss compares the citizenship practices of recipients of AFDC and Social Security Disability Insurance (SSDI), and finds marked distinctions that almost certainly have been produced by the rhetoric, rules, and the personal experiences recipients have had in obtaining the benefit to which they, presumably, are entitled. The SSDI program is designed so that recipients, although they have to meet strict requirements to document their disability, have a detached relationship with government that is the same, regardless of income level. They apply through a toll-free phone and can send supporting documents through the mail. If they are denied benefits, they can appeal to a superior in the office. Even though the requirements are strict, Soss's interviews indicate that SSDI recipients feel they are treated with respect (Soss 2005, 2 99). Similar types of comments were made by the G. I.'s included in Mettler's analysis of the G.I. Bill—efficient administration of the program that treated the recipients in a respectful manner. AFDC applicants, in contrast, had to appear in person at a local office that had made no provision for the children who usually accompany the parent. Applicants have to prove that they are poor, unable to care for their children, and are not cheating "the system" in some way (Soss, 2005:300).

AFDC clients come to understand that disagreeing with the case worker is generally futile. There are significant barriers to social mobilization—including the fact that AFDC clients (in contrast with SSDI) tend to believe that others in the group, in fact, exhibit the negative constructions attributed to the group as a whole but that they, personally, are different. They adopt mainly passive and subject orientations toward government and are far less likely than SSDI clients to believe that their individual actions would make any difference or that government listens to people like them (Soss 2005, 313). SSDI recipients, on the other hand, participate in politics and hold political beliefs that are generally indistinguishable from the general population.

CONCLUSION

It is often supposed that constitutions, guided by traditional political philosophies such as liberalism or civic republicanism, determine citizenship and that public policies, which operate on a much narrower plane and deal with power and values, and have little to do with the form citizenship takes in a nation. The perspective in this chapter is that citizenship and democracy are contested concepts, with meanings that are constantly under contention and constantly evolving. Public policy both explicitly and implicitly affects those meanings as well as the material conditions that enable or thwart the practice of citizenship.

We have set out some broad perspectives about citizenship. Citizenship encompasses the quality of life that a society is expected to provide to its people, and there are numerous examples of how public policy is related to the quality of life. There are also disagreements about the level that should be provided by government and whether the inequality in the quality of life is tolerable. Citizenship encompasses the quality of engagement and participatory arenas that are available to the people; and public policy makes these arenas available or controls the access and ease of access to them. Citizenship involves the rights and privileges that people have. Public policy defines and secures rights and privileges, or fails to do so, or does for some but not others. Citizenship involves the qualities of mind and behavior that citizens are expected to have, but again there are disagreements over what "morality" means in the context of citizen beliefs, and whether policy should teach and support secular morality or religious morality; whether it should emphasize the self-interested, self-sufficient individualism or the empathic, community-oriented citizenship. There are disagreements over whether political participation is at an appropriate level or whether inequalities in participation are a matter of concern. There are concerns about the competence of citizens to engage in policy deliberations in a meaningful way; there are concerns that interest groups and experts are crowding out the ability of ordinary citizens to participate.

Citizenship is about identity and about whether one's identity is embraced fully by the community and the nation. Public policy helps shape identity and, in ways both instrumental and symbolic, influences whether people belong to the society and are "full-fledged" members of a community or not. We have shown that public policy sends different kinds of messages, provides for (or permits) different levels of quality of life, different access, and different identities to different social groups. Public policy produces the equality that exists in citizenship, but it also produces (or permits) an unequal citizenship in the United States. This chapter has demonstrated that the types of citizens in a society depend largely on the cumulative public policy choices that are made.

NOTES

1. In the United States, major initiatives have been undertaken by several national foundations, including a cosponsored annual Congressional Conference on Civic Education, first held in 2003, and the first annual National Conference on Citizenship held in December, 2004. Generally, these initiatives all indicate that democratic values should be taught in the schools through civic education, but there is no broadly-agreed-upon statement of "ideal citizenship."

2. This brings up the issue of whether there are any common international themes on the meaning of democracy or citizenship. In 1999, the International Association for the Evaluation of Educational Achievement launched its first international assessment of citizenship knowledge and engagement at age fourteen (Torney-Purta et al. 2001). Eventually including twenty-eight countries, they contend that there is a core agreement about a very few fundamental democratic principles and processes, including core beliefs in competitive political parties, political rights (such as voting and standing for election), free elections, free speech, limits on the influence of the wealthy, limits on political influence over the courts, obligations to obey the law, and obligations to vote in elections.

REFERENCES

Abizasdeh, Arah. (2002). Does liberal democracy presuppose a cultural nation? Four arguments. *American Political Science Review* 96(3, September): 495–509.

Almond, Gabriel and Sidney Verba (Eds.). (1989). *The civic culture revisited*. Newbury Park, CA: Sage.

Barber, Benjamin. (1984). *Strong democracy: Participatory politics for a new age*. Berkeley: Univeristy of California Press.

Bellah, Robert Neelly, Richardd Madsen, William M. Sullivan, Ann Swidler, and Steven M. Tipton. (1985). *Habits of the heart: Individualism and commitment in American life*. Berkeley: Univeristy of California Press.

Berelson, Bernard, Paul Lazarsfeld, and William McPhee. (1954). *Voting. A study of opinion formation in a presidential campaign*. Chicago: University of Chicago Press.

Berkowitz, Edward D. (1991). *America's welfare state from Roosevelt to Reagan*. Baltimore: Johns Hopkins University Press.

Boyte, Harry C. (2003). A different kind of politics: John Dewey and the meaning of citizenship in the 21st century. *The Good Society* 12: 1–15.

Broder, David S. (2000). *Democracy derailed: Initiative campaigns and the power of money*. New York: Harcourt, Inc.

Campbell, Andrea Louise. (2002). Self-Interest, social security, and the distinctive participation patterns of senior citizens. *American Political Science Review* 96(3, September): 565–574.

Conover, Pamela Johnston, Ivor M. Crewe, and Donald D. Searing. (1991). The nature of citizenship in the United States and Great Britain: Empirical comments on theoretical themes. *Journal of Politics* 53 (3, August): 800–832.

Crick, Bernard. (2003). The English citizenship order 1999: Context, content and presuppositions. In Lockyer, et al. *Education for democratic citizenship.*

Dewey, John. (1996). *Democracy and Education.* Free Press. New York.

deLeon, Peter. (1997). *Democracy and the policy sciences.* Albany: SUNY Press.

DeLuca, Tom. (1995). *The two faces of apathy.* Philadelphia: Temple University Press.

Dionne, E. J. (1991). *Why Americans hate politics.* New York: Simon and Schuster.

Downs, Anthony. (1957). *An economic theory of democracy.* New York: Harper and Row.

Dryzek, John S. (1996). Political inclusion and the dyamics of democratization. *American Political Science Review* 90:475–87.

Education for Democratic Citizenship. (2004). http://www.coe.int/T/e/Cultural_Co-operation/education/E.D.C. Council of Europe.

Etzioni, Amitai. (2004). *The common good.* Cambridge: Malden Press.

Fallows, James. (1997). *Breaking the news: How the media undermine American democracy.* New York: Random House.

Feldman, Martha S., and Anne M. Khademian. (2002). To manage is to govern. *Public Administration Review* 62 (5, September/October): 529–541.

Fischer, Frank. 2003. *Reframing public policy: Discursive politics and deliberative practices.* New York: Oxford University Press.

Greider, William. 1992. *Who will tell the people? The betrayal of American democracy.* NY: Simon and Schuster.

Guston, David. (2004). Forget politicizing science. Let's democratize science! Issues in Science and Technology, Fall, 2004. http://www.issues.org/21.1/21.1preview.html.

Hacker, Jacob, Suzanne Mettler, Dianne Pinderhughes, and Theda Skocpol. (2004). Inequality and Public Policy. Task Force on Equality and American Democracy. American Political Science Association.

Hajer, Maarten, and Hendrik Wagenaar. (Eds.). (2003). *Deliberative policy analysis: Understanding governance in the network society.* Cambridge, UK: Cambridge University Press.

Healey, Patsy, Claudio de Magalhaes, Ali Madanipour, and John Pendlebury. (2003). Place, identity and local politics: analyzing initiatives in deliberative governance. In *Deliberative policy analysis: Understanding governance in the network society*, edited by Maarten Hajer and Hendrik Wagenaar. Cambridge, UK: Cambridge University Press.

Henry, William A. (1994). *In defense of elitism.* New York: Doubleday.

Hetherington, Marc J. (2004). *Why trust matters: Declining political trust and the demise of American liberalism.* Princeton, NJ: Princeton University Press.

Huntington, Samuel. (2004). *Who are we?* New York: Simon and Schuster.

Ingram, Helen, and Steven R. Smith. (1993). *Public policy for democracy.* Washington, D.C. Brookings Institute Press.

Ingram, Helen, and Anne Schneider. The social construction of public policy. In *Deserving and entitled: Social construction and public policy*, edited by Anne L. Schneider and Helen Ingram, pp. 1–34. Stoneybrook: State University of New York, 2005,.

Innes, Judith, and David E. Booher (2003). Collaborative policymaking: governance through dialogue. In *Deliberative policy analysis: Understanding governance in the network society,* edited by Maarten Hajer and Hendrik Wagenaar. Cambridge, UK: Cambridge University Press

Jensen, Laura S. (2005). Constructing and entitling America's original veterans. In *Deserving and entitled: Social construction and public policy*, edited by Anne L. Schneider and Helen Ingram, pp. 35–62. Stoneybrook: State University of New York, 2005.

Landy, Marc K., and Martin A. Levin. 1995. *The new politics of public policy.* Baltimore: Johns Hopkins University Press.

Landy, Marc. 1993. Public policy and citizenship. In *Public policy for democracy*, edited Helen Ingram and Steven Rathgeb Smith. Washington, D.C.: The Brookings Institution. Reprinted by US Information Agency. New Delhi, India, 1996.

Lockyer, Andrew, Bernard Crick, and John Annette (2003). *Education for democratic citizenship* (Ed). Burlington, VT: Ashgate Press. (Lockyer.... Introduction and Review. Pp. 1–14).

Lowi, Theodore. (1979). *The end of liberalism.* New York: Norton.

Mansbridge, Jane. (Ed.) (1990). *Beyond self interest.* Chicago: University of Chicago Press.

Marshall, Thomas H. (1964). *Citizenship and social development.* Garden City, NY: Doubleday.

McDonald, Michael P. (2004). United States Elections Project. http://elections.gmu.edu/Voter_Turnout_2004. htm (accessed Nov. 23, 2004).

Mead, Lawrence.(Ed.) (1997). *The new paternalism: Supervisory approaches to poverty.* Washington, D.C.: Brookings Institution Press.

Mettler, Suzanne, and Joe Soss. (2004). The consequences of public policy for democratic citizenship: Bridging policy studies and sass politics. *Perspectives on Politics* 2 (1, March): 55–73.

Mettler, Suzanne (2002). Bringing the state back in to civic engagement: Policy feedback effects of the G. I. Bill for World War II veterans. *American Political Science Review.* 96(2): 351–365.

Monroe, Kristen, James Hanking, and Renee Bukovchik Van Vechten. (2000). The psychological foundations of identity politics. *Annual Review of Politics* 3:419–447.

Murray, Charles A. (1984). *Losing ground: American social policy, 1950–1980.* New York: Basic Books.

National Civic Education Association. (2004). Standards. http://www.civiced.org/stds.html (accessed February, 2005).

Nie, Norman H., Jane Junn, and Kenneth Stehlik-Barry. (1996). *Education and democratic citizenship in America.* Chicago: University of Chicago Press.

Ostrom, Elinor. (1990). *Governing the commons: The evolution of institutions for collective action.* New York: Cambridge University Press.

Pierson, Paul. (1996). The new politics of the welfare state. *World Politics* 48(2): 143–179.

Piven, Frances Fox, and Richard A. Cloward. (1988). *Why Americans don't vote.* New York: Pantheon Books.

Putnam, Robert D. (2000). *Bowling alone: The collapse and revival of American community.* New York: Simon and Schuster.

Quade, E. S. (1991). *Analysis for public decisions.* New York: Elsivier Science.

Rauch, Jonathan. (1994). *Demosclerosis: The silent killer of American government.* New York: Random House.

Sarewitz, Daniel. (1997). *Frontiers of illusion: Science, technology and the politics of progress.* Temple University Press.

Schneider, Anne L., and Helen Ingram. (1993). Social construction of target populations. *American Political Science Review* June.

Schneider, Anne Larason, and Helen Ingram. 1997. *Policy design for democracy.* University of Kansas Press.

Schneider, Anne L., and Helen Ingram. (Eds.) (2005). *Deserving and entitled: Social construction and public policy.* Stoneybrook: State University of New York.

Schram, Sanford. (2005). Putting a black face on welfare: The good and the bad. In *Deserving and entitled: Social construction and public policy*, edited by Anne L. Schneider and Helen Ingram, pp. 261–290. Stoneybrook: State University of New York.

Schumpeter, Joseph A. (1987). *Capitalism, socialism and democracy.* London: Unwin Paperbacks.

Shklar, Judith N. (1991). *American citizenship: The quest for inclusion.* Cambridge: Harvard University Press.

Sidney, Mara S. (2003). *Unfair housing: How national policy shapes community action.* Lawrence: University Press of Kansas.

Skocpol, Theda, and Morris R. Fiorina. (Eds.). (1999). *Civic engagement in American democracy.* Washington, D.C., New York: Brookings Institution Press and Russell Sage Foundation.

Skocpol, Theda. (2003). *Diminished democracy: From membership to management in American civic life.* Norman: University of Oklahoma Press.

Smith, Rogers M. (1986). The meaning of American citizenship. *News for Teachers of Political Science* (Spring), http://www.apsanet.org/CENnet/thisconstitution/smith.cfm (accessed February, 2005).

Smith, Steven Rathgeb, and Helen Ingram. Forthcoming. "Implications of Choice of Policy Tools for Democracy, Civic Capital and Citizenship" in *The Tools of Government. A Public Management Handbook for the Era of Third-party Government*, Lester Salomon, ed. Oxford University Press, New York.

Sniderman, Paul, M., Louk Hagendoorn, and Markus Prior. (2004). Predisposing factors and situational triggers: Exclusionary reactions to immigrant minorities. *American Political Science Review* 98(1, February): 35–49.

Soss, Joe. (1999).Lessons of welfare: Policy design, political learning, and political sction. *American Political Science Review* 93(2, June): 291–328.

Soss, Joe. (2005). Making clients and citizens: Welfare policy as a source of status, belief, and action. In *Deserving and entitled: Social construction and public policy* , edited by Anne L. Schneider and Helen Ingram. Stoneybrook: State University of New York.

Stockman, David A. (1986). *The triumph of politics.* New York: Harper and Row.

Stone, Deborah. (1997). *Policy paradox: The art of political decision making.* New York: W. W. Norton.

The Six Pillars of Character (2004). Teaching guide: Citizenship for grades K-5. http://www.goodcharacter. com/pp/citizenship.html (accessed February, 2005).

Torney-Purta, Judith, Rainer Lehmann, Hans Oswald, and Wolfram Schulz (2001). Citizenship and education in twenty-eight countries: Civic knowledge and engagement at age fourteen. International Association for the Evaluation of Educational Achievement (IEA) The Civic Education Study. Amsterdam, The Netherlands. http://www.canberra.edu.au/civics/projects/iea_summary.html.

Uggen, Christoher, and Jeff Manza. (2002). Democratic contraction? The political consequences of felon disenfranchisement in the United States. *American Sociological Review* 67(6):777–803.

Verba, Sidney, Kay Lehman Schlozman, and Henry E. Brady. (1995). *Voice and equality: Civic voluntarism in American politics.* Cambridge, MA: Harvard University Press.

Part VII

Quantitatively Oriented Policy Methods

23 Quantitative Methods for Policy Analysis

Kaifeng Yang

INTRODUCTION

Policy analysis involves using quantitative and/or qualitative techniques to define a policy problem, demonstrate its impacts, and present potential solutions. It often requires sophisticated methods to assess how identified policy problems are impacted by numerous variables, including both policy interventions and contextual factors. Quantitative methods help demonstrate whether a relationship exists between policy designs and policy outcomes, test whether the relationship can be generalized to similar settings, evaluate magnitudes of the effects of policies on social, economic, and political factors, and find better policy alternatives. The use of such methods is part of the scientific expertise with which policy analysts claim their relevance. Techniques such as modeling, quantification of inputs and outputs, descriptive statistics, statistical inference, operations research, cost-benefit analysis, and risk-benefit analysis are frequently used in policy studies.

This chapter discusses the use of quantitative methods in policy analysis. It aims to provide a general understanding of the use of quantitative methods in policy analysis, using examples from the policy analysis literature and linking quantitative methods with the development of policy analysis as a profession and an applied discipline. The chapter has two major sections. The first section briefly reviews the emergence and evolution of quantitative methods in policy analysis, discussing their origin, change, use, and education. The second section introduces some quantitative methods that are widely used in policy analysis.

Due to page limits, this chapter does not cover such basic topics as sampling, level of measurement, reliability, validity, and hypothesis testing, nor does it go into the details of the statistical procedures. Interested readers may find the details in many research methods textbooks. This chapter does not address several important quantitative analysis methods either, such as cost-benefit analysis, survey research, evaluation research, Q methodology, and environment impact assessment, since they are dealt with in other chapters of this handbook. For the same reason, the debate between positivist and post-positivist perspectives is not elaborated here.

HISTORY OF QUANTITATIVE METHODS IN POLICY ANALYSIS

The need for quantitative policy analysis reflects elected officials' desire to design better policies, understand how policies have performed, and assess what impacts policies have made. The use of quantitative methods in policy analysis has its intellectual roots in Harold Lasswell (1951, 1970, 1971), who envisions an overarching policy science discipline based on social science knowledge and methods to analyze policy choices and decision making for the democratization of the society. Policy science, as a multimethod, multidisciplinary, and problem-oriented filed, is concerned with mapping the policy process, policy alternatives, and policy outcomes. Like other social science disciplines, it has to use analytic methods to model policy dynamics and solve policy problems.

Quantitative Analysis as Policy Analysis: 1950s–1960s

Quantitative methods have long been used in public decision making. The New York Bureau of Municipal Research in the 1910s started to use social science methods to systematically study urban problems. In 1922, the Bureau of Agricultural Economics was created within the U.S. Department of Agriculture to examine the relationships between agriculture and the economy and to develop better economic policies. However, more sophisticated use of quantitative methods did not emerge until World War II. The Office of Scientific Research and Development was established in 1941 to coordinate scientific activities during War World II. The Employment Act of 1946 created the Council of Economic Advisors, the first step as Congress formally acknowledged that the executive branch should utilize expert knowledge.

Regarding quantitative methods being used, World War II was a watershed that stimulated new analytic techniques such as systems analysis and operations research. Social scientists began to play more important roles in government decision making by adopting positivism and normative economic reasoning. The economic models dominated the field. For example, scientists and engineers in Great Britain created operations research in World War II in order to help effectively allocate and mange military resources. The technique became widely used in the United States in the early 1950s. It has also been called as management science, systems engineering, and cost-effectiveness analysis. The Rand Corporation, founded in 1948 to do policy analysis work for the government especially the Department of Defense, finally developed the technique into systems analysis, a tool used in the military throughout the 1950s. It was quite successful in solving simple and some complex problems such as inventory management, production scheduling, equipment reliability assessment, and investment risk minimization (Brewer and deLeon 1983).

The 1960s became a "Golden Age" for systems analysis and policy analysis. During this time, policy analysis was essentially quantitative analysis and the research emphasis was on methodology rather than on subject matter. Policy analysis expertise or specializations were in the quantitative methods and techniques, not in their application in specific policy areas. As Radin (2000) observed, professional papers and conferences in the 1960s primarily addressed quantitative analytic procedures such as linear programming, Markov analysis, dynamic programming, game theory, stochastic modeling, Bayesian analysis, quasi-linearization, invariant embedding, and general systems theory. One reason for the quantitative orientation was that most policy analysts during this time were experts in economics. Radin (2000) observed that most of the policy analysts of the time, who were trained as economists or operations researchers, had Ph.D.'s in those areas. Most policy analysis positions were on economic analysis. For example, the Bureau of Agricultural Economics was the center for economic policy research. The Council of Economic Advisers was another prominent policy analysis organ. During this time, policy analysis was influenced by the methodology development of other disciplines, such as the positivism in social science generally, econometrics in economics, and the behavioral revolution in political science.

The domination of quantitative methods in policy analysis during this period was also apparent in the practice. To a large extent, the use of Planning, Programming, and Budgeting Systems (PPBS) is characteristic of policy analysis at this stage. Actively promoted by President John Kennedy's Secretary of Defense, Robert McNamara, PPBS had antecedents in the work of the Rand Corporation. McNamara invited Charles Hitch from Rand to establish a Systems Analysis Unit with responsibility for the PPBS process linking planning with budgeting. The research unit also introduced some other quantitative methods to the federal government such as cost-benefit analysis, operations and systems research, and linear programming. President Johnson, in 1965, required all federal agencies to prepare planning documents and issue-analysis papers to back up their recommendations to the Bureau of Budget. PPBS consisted of three main types of reports: (1) program memoranda, comparing the cost and effectiveness of major alternative programs and describing the agency's strategy; (2) special analytic studies on current and long-term issues; (3) program and financial plans, summarizing agency outputs, costs, and financing needs over a five-year period. In 1965, the Bureau of the Budget issued a directive to all federal departments and agencies, requiring them to establish central analytic offices that would apply PPBS. In 1969, the National Environmental Policy Act mandated impact analysis in environment policy making.

From the very beginning, statistics has been a curricular requirement. Policy analysis program was thought to help students establish a sense of critical awareness for the general utility of quantitative information (Leinhardt 1981). The early policy literature introduced systems analysis and operations research methods, especially as applied in the defense area (Hitch 1965; Quade 1966; Quade and Boucher 1968). Contents such as how to apply operational research methods, welfare economics, and cost-benefit analysis were common topics in popular textbooks on policy methods during the time.

In public affairs or policy programs, which were first established in the late 1960s, economics was the primary theory, coupled with a number of quantitative techniques. For example, at the University of Minnesota's School of Public Affairs, economics was the core of the required curriculum. Its policy analysis core sequence includes cost effectiveness analysis and PPBS. It also had a quantitative methods sequence teaching the logic of inference and regression analysis (Brandl 1976). In 1968, the University of Michigan reorganized its Institute of Public Administration into the Institute of Public Policy Studies. The program had eight core courses for first year students. Among them, four courses are analytical tools such as statistics, micro and macro economics, cost benefit analysis, and systems analysis. Other course included two in organizational theory and two in political theory and institutions. The purpose was to help students combine latest tools of problem solving and quantitative analysis with a subtle understanding of the social, political, and economic contexts (Walker 1976).

USE OF QUANTITATIVE POLICY ANALYSIS METHODS: 1970s–1980s

The use of quantitative techniques such as PPBS had its critics since its emergence. Wildavsky (1969) called for rescuing policy analysis from PPBS, arguing that preconditions for successful PPBS implementation usually do not exist in government. In fact, three years after President Johnson's announcement of a government-wide PPB system, President Nixon issued a memorandum abolishing it. By the 1970s, many limitations of the positivist approach have been acknowledged. In general, those quantitative techniques failed to effectively deal with many complex social problems because those problems cannot be represented with a rational scientific model and do not have a single unitary goal. Operations research places a heavy burden on mathematicians and quantitative analysts to come up with mathematical representation, while overlooking qualitative and soft data, concepts, and methods (Brewer and deLeon 1983). Systems analysis, heavily relying on economics and objective measurements and proxies, does not work well when a full range of human values, interests, and perspectives are considered. Other tools such as flow charts and decision trees were found helpful when there were agreed-upon goals and values. But in reality, policies tend to have multiple and conflicting goals.

Nevertheless, in the 1970s and 1980s, quantitative methods stemming from the systems analysis framework were still widely used and economic models remained dominant although other techniques were also drawn from positivist social sciences. Radin (2000) concluded that "despite the differentiation in practice, the economists' framework, drawn from the market model, continued to dominate" (p. 113). The cost-benefit analysis was extensively used to quantify costs and benefits of policy solutions and thus identify the solution providing the greatest net benefit. For example, the California Legislative Analyst's Office conducted cost-benefit studies for all legislation before the legislature during the 1970s and 1980s. Cost-benefit analysis was required in the federal government in the 1970s and 1980s for all proposed regulations to be issued by agencies, although the benefits of health, education, and welfare programs are diverse and often intangible. The Executive Order 12291 signed by President Reagan, required detailed cost-benefit analyses for all new federal regulations to assure that federal regulatory agencies thoroughly study the impact of proposed regulations on all concerned parties before promulgation. The order specifies that administrative decisions shall be based on adequate information concerning the need for and consequences of proposed government action, and regulatory objectives shall be chosen to maximize the net benefits to society.

The development of quantitative methods in policy analysis was affected by several historical social events. For example, the Energy Crisis impelled academia to set up energy supply and demand models based on mathematics. The War on Poverty generated a series of new social welfare programs that produced great opportunities for policy analysis. As a result, professional journals and research institutes in public policy were created in a large amount. Significant resources were available for evaluation studies sponsored by the federal government. In the 1950s and 1960s, policy analysis was primarily prospective in that it attempted to assess policy alternatives before a program was actually established. Retrospective policy analysis, which evaluates the impact of an established program, was used in the 1960s but did not become a common practice until the 1970s. At the same time, program failures of some Great Society initiatives prompted policy analysts to address the implementation issues during the policy design stage (Nakamura and Smallwood 1980). Analysis on implementation and program impact entailed the use of more sophisticated methods in order to include more contextual variables. While the measurement of efficiency and filed study were emphasized in the 1960s, experimental studies became important in the 1970s, when social experiments such as Negative Income Tax and Head Start programs were widespread (Daniels and Wirth 1983).

In general, during the two decades, analytic capacity was significantly enhanced due to greater demands for policy analysis, stronger computing capabilities, and advances in economic modeling such as micro-analytic simulation models. However, although policy analysis became more sophisticated, its limits were also exposed (May 1998). The debates between qualitative and quantitative methods, positivist and post-positivist approaches also took momentum. Quantitative techniques were no longer the sole set of skills for policy analysts, and many people realized that political skills were as important as technical skills (i.e., Meltsner 1976).

With support from private foundations, in the late 1970s, public policy graduate programs were set up at Harvard, the University of California at Berkeley, Carnegie-Mellon, the Rand Graduate Institute, the University of Michigan, the University of Pennsylvania, the University of Minnesota, and the University of Texas at Austin. At the University of Michigan, the policy program introduced several new courses on advanced analytical techniques such as modeling and forecasting, policy evaluation, and operations research with emphasis on statistical decision theory. A math refresher course was added to prepare students for advanced statistics (Walker 1976). The National Association of Schools of Public Affairs and Administration established policy analysis as one of five fundamental subject areas. Wildavsky (1976) described the principles for graduate education of public policy based on Berkeley's experiences in the 1970s. He emphasized the importance of multiple analytic perspectives and techniques, arguing that no single set of operations can be taught as the essence of analysis. He viewed analysis as a traveling skill of creatively applying analytic tools to solve various policy problems in a short time period.

Engelbert (1977) reviewed the experiences of policy graduate programs in the early and middle 1970s and pointed out that there was a core subject matter built around: (1) quantitative methodology including mathematical programming and modeling and descriptive and inferential statistics; (2) the political and institutional environment of policy formulation and implementation; (3) economic theory and analysis with emphasis on public-private sector relationships in the allocation of resources; (4) behavioral and nonbehavioral decision making and implementation strategies and processes; and (5) program management, control, and evaluation. There was a heavy reliance upon quantitative tools of evaluation: "Not only is training in quantitative methodology emphasized in course subject matter . . . but students are expected to demonstrate some proficiency in the application of quantitative techniques to problem-solving exercises" (Engelbert 1977, 231). Intensive instruction was given to techniques such as operations research, model building, cost-benefit analysis, and linear programming.

DEMOCRATIZATION FOR POLICY ANALYSIS: 1990s~

In the 1990s, quantitative analysis became far more common and informed, largely because statistical software, such as SPSS, SAS, and STATA, facilitated the use of quantitative methods to deal with complex models and huge datasets. Those statistical packages can calculate numerous statistics and allow their user to manipulate the dataset and transform the variables. Today, policy analysis bears the imprint of the positivist heritage, which is evident in the curricula of policy schools requiring various statistics as core courses. The power of the heritage is also seen in the journals such as *Journal of Policy Analysis and Management (JPAM)*, *Policy Studies Review (PSR)*, *Review of Policy Research (RPR)*, among others. These journals are filled with policy studies using various statistical analyses of particular policies. It is also evident in the annual conferences sponsored by the Association of Public Policy and Management, which, in recent years, have been dominated by papers that employ positivist economic and other research models (Durning 1999).

Meanwhile, there have been methods wars between quantitative and qualitative research; between internal and external validity; and between experimental and statistical control (Brewer 1983; Krane 2001). The quantitative versus qualitative debate reflects the larger battle between "positivists" and "post-positivists." Since the 1980s, the rational positivist approach to policy analysis has been criticized on many grounds. The basis of quantitative methodologies is empirical falsification through objective hypothesis testing of rigorously formulated models. The fundamental positivist principle in policy analysis is to separate facts and values, by which normative issues are translated into technical considerations. In pursuit of replicable relationships, positivists emphasize empirical research designs, causal modeling, scientific sampling, and quantification of outcomes. However, when studying social phenomenon, we can not isolate ourselves from the objects of the research, nor can we separate facts from values.

In the methodology curriculum, positivism equips the students with empirical research designs and statistical methods. Many writers criticize that students trained in this tradition often have little training in understanding the normative and interpretive foundations of the tools they have learned, as well as the social settings to which these techniques are to be applied (Fischer 1998). Therefore, post-positivism has been proposed as an alternative, which is treated as a marriage of scientific knowledge with interpretive and philosophical knowledge about norms and values. In terms of epistemology, post-positivism incorporates deliberative theories and democratic participation.

The tension between positivism and post-positivism has not faded away. On the one hand, one can justifiably argue that positivism is feeble in the face of intractable or wicked problems (Fischer 1995). On the other hand, it is not clear whether post-positivism can specify a common goal of its own and offer their own set of solutions, especially in the operational aspects of policy research (deLeon 1998). Nevertheless, since the 1990s, more efforts have been made to democratize the policy analysis design and process. Participatory design, stakeholder involvement, citizens' input, qualitative methods, and mixed methodology, among others, have contributed to an area with a multidisciplinary theoretical and methodological base (Krane 2001).

Currently, positivism still constitutes the discipline's intellectual infrastructure and is supported by the training, practice, and specialization of the academicians who teach policy analysis methods (Durning 1999). Morçöl (2001) finds that there is considerable support for positivism among policy professionals, especially among practitioners and professionals with educational background in economics, mathematics, and science. Policy analysis skills in the 1990s include: case study methods, cost-benefit analysis, ethical analysis, evaluation, futures analysis, historical analysis, implementation analysis, interviewing, legal analysis, microeconomics, negotiation and mediation, operations research, organizational analysis, political feasibility analysis, public speaking, small-group facilitation, specific program knowledge, statistics, survey research methods, and systems analysis (Radin 2000).

Vijverberg (1997) recommends that a quantitative methods curriculum should include: (1) Course 1: introduction to probability theory, hypothesis testing, statistical distributions, difference of means test, ANOVA, and rank tests; (2) Course 2: research design and survey methods; (3) Course 3: introduction to regression analysis; (4) Course 4: continuation of regression analysis including maximum likelihood estimation, logit/probit, tobit, simultaneous equations, factor analysis, and LISREL models; (5) Course 5: advanced topics in research methods, including Box-Jenkins (ARIMA), unit roots and cointgration, the introduction to nonparametric statistics, and sample selectivity models. In addition, the economic analysis and operational research traditionally are essential to quantitative policy analysis, so we add them as another category of courses. It can be described as advanced topics in economic analysis and operational research, which includes macroeconomics, microeconomics, cost-benefit analysis, econometrics, operations research, and applied economics.

Take the Master of Public Policy program in the Harris School of Public Policy, University of Chicago as an example, students must finish required and elective courses including Mathematical Preliminaries, Statistical Methods for Policy Research I, Survey Research Methodology, Survey Questionnaire Design, Statistical Methods for Policy Research II, Applied Regression Analysis and some economic analysis courses. Students use computer programs to apply these techniques to real situations (e.g., the effect of sales taxes, labor market discrimination, and redistributive programs). It is also apparent from the curricula and syllabi that economic analysis dominates the teaching for policy analysis.

QUANTITATIVE STATISTICAL METHODS

Statistics is the theory and procedure of analyzing quantitative data obtained from samples of observations in order to study and compare sources of variances of phenomena, to help make decisions to accept or reject hypothesized relationships. Descriptive statistics enable policy analysts to summarize data effectively and meaningfully. Inferential statistics is the use of quantitative techniques to generalize from a sample to a population. In order to choose the right technique policy analysts have to consider the research purpose, the sample size, the distribution of the data, the number of dependent and independent variables, and the type of measurement scale employed by the variables. One can refer to other statistical books for detailed information (i.e., Hair et al. 1998).

UNIVARIATE AND BIVARIATE ANALYSIS

Univaraite or descriptive statistics summarize a body of raw data so that the data can be more easily understood. Before descriptive statistics are calculated, policy analysts sometimes use graphs and tables to map the data and have a general sense of the data. For example, frequency polygon displays the trend, Ogive (cumulative frequency polygon) shows percentage of cases following below or above a standard, and both of them can be used to compare different samples. Histograms and bar charts help demonstrate differences among subgroups. Percentages can be calculated to show the proportions, such as the percentage of welfare receipts who are satisfied with the service. Those proportions are sometimes difficult to interpret—as too high or too low, for example—if policy analysts are not familiar with the context. A 5 percent dissatisfaction rate can be interpreted either as an alarming sign or as prove of quality.

Measures of central tendency indicate the typical value of the data. The mean is the arithmetic average and affected by extreme values. Thus it is not useful for a skewed distribution such as income. The median is the middle observation in a rank-ordered dataset and is insensitive to the observations' values but sensitive to sample size. The mode is the most frequent value, insensitive to the values and sample size. Researchers should find out whether the appearance of two or more modes is due to the mixing-together of different subgroups (e.g., weights of third graders and their parents) in one dataset. The relative value of the mean, median and mode inform policy analysts the shape of the distribution. The choice of an appropriate measure depends on not only the distribution, but also the level of measurement and the analysts' purpose. Also important are measures of dispersion, which sometimes indicate reliability, consistency, and safety. For example, decision makers may be interested in which police department has shorter average emergency response time, but they should also be interested in how consistent those departments are. Analysts should use several descriptive statistics to summarize different aspects of their data to produce a clearer picture. The standard deviation is the most commonly used measure, although it is not useful for a skewed distribution. Another measure, the Inter-quartile range (the distance between the upper and lower quartiles), is hard to calculate mathematically but useful for a skewed distribution.

Bivariate analysis tests whether and how one variable is statistically related with another variable. It helps demonstrate the existence, statistical significance, the direction, and the strength of the relationship. The procedure depends on the level of measurement of the independent and dependent variables. When the independent and dependent variables are categorical (nominal or ordinal), contingency table analysis (cross-tabulation) is generally used. When the independent variable is categorical and the dependent variable is interval or ratio, the difference of means test (t test) or analysis of variance (ANOVA) is preferred. When both variables are interval or ratio, correlation or regression is conducted.

In contingency table analysis, analysts first separate the observations into groups based on their values for the independent variable, then calculate percentages within the independent categories, and finally compare the percentages across one of the dependent categories. The percentage difference tells analysts whether the independent variable makes a difference (Meier and Brudney 2002). The chi-square (χ^2) test is then used to assess the statistical significance of the relationship—whether we can reject the null hypothesis that assumes no relationship between two variables in the population based on our sample observations. Chi-square test indicates the probability that the results can be generalized to the population. However, chi-square is not a measure of substantive importance or strength because chi-square result is affected by the sample size: if the sample size N is large (say, greater than 1, 500), χ^2 will usually be large even if the association is weak. The importance or the strength of the relationship is better measured, especially when dealing with large samples, by a measure of association that ranges from +1.0 (prefect positive relationship) and –1.0 (perfect negative relationship). When both variables are ordinal, the most frequently used measures of association are Kendall's tau-b (for square tables), Kendall's tau-c (for non-square tables), Somer's d, and Goodman and Kruskal's gamma. In general, the tau measures are used more commonly then the Somer's d measures. Many analysts often use both gamma and either tau-b or tau-c. When one or both of the variables are nominal, Goodman and Kruskal's lambda should be used.

The difference of means test and the analysis of variance have similar logic. Analysts first divide observations into categories based on the values of the independent variable. A relationship exists if the values of the dependent variable are quite different across groups and have smaller within-group variance than before (Johnson and Reynolds 2005). To determine the statistical significance, the difference of means test uses t test and compares the result with the appropriate criterion (large t values lead to rejection of the null hypothesis). The analysis of variance uses F statistic to measure the statistical significance. F is the ratio of between-group mean square to within-group mean square. The F ratio is compared with an F-ratio table to decide whether to reject the null hypothesis.

Linear regression, or ordinary least squares regression, is to find the best line function to describe a relationship that can minimize the squared errors. Its general form is $Y = a + bX + e$, in which a is the intercept, b is the slope, and e is the error term. The formula for b, the regression coefficient, is

$$\frac{\Sigma(X_i - \bar{X})\,(Y_i - \bar{Y})}{\Sigma\,(x_i - \bar{x})^2}.$$

The coefficient shows how much the estimated average Y value will change if X is changed one unit. The goodness of fit may be measured by the standard error of the estimate, which indicates the amount of error that one makes when predicting a Y value for an X value. Another common goodness of fit measure is the coefficient of determination (r^2) ranging from zero (lack of fit at all) to one (perfect fit). The coefficient of determination is the ratio of the explained variation to the total variation in Y, or the ratio of the reduction of the error by using the regression line to the total error by guessing the mean.

ANALYSIS OF VARIANCE (ANOVA)

ANOVA is a dependence technique that explains the variation of a metric dependent variable based on a set of nonmetric (categorical) independent variables. Its general form is:

$$\underset{\text{(metric)}}{Y_1} = \underset{\text{(nonmetric)}}{X_1 + X_2 + X_3 + \ldots + X_n}$$

ANOVA helps determine whether samples from two or more groups come from populations with equal means. It is a primary tool for analyzing experimental data. ANOVA examines within-groups variances (MS_W) and between-groups variances (MS_B). The ratio of MS_B to MS_W, which is the F statistic, measures how much variance is attributed to the different treatments versus the random sampling error. Large values of the F statistic lead to rejection of the null hypothesis assuming no treatment effects. Consider a study on job training and job placement. Policy analysts want to compare the effect of two programs, School Training and On-the-Job Training (OJT), on job placement in terms of salary. Participants are randomly assigned to one of the two programs. ANOVA is used to test the difference between the two groups. The independent variable here is the type of job training programs and the dependent variable is participants' monthly earnings. ANOVA is widely used in policy studies. For example, Wells, Layne, and Allen (1991) used ANOVA to assess whether learning styles differed for supervisory, middle, upper middle, upper, and executive managers in the Georgia Department of Corrections.

To use ANOVA, the data has to satisfy the assumptions of linearity, normality (the dependent variable is normally distributed), and equal variance (variances are equal for all treatment groups). However, F tests in ANOVA are robust regarding these assumptions except in extreme cases. The equal variance assumption is often ignored if the number of cases in each group is similar. Analysts are encouraged to examine the data first to assess the presence of nonlinear relationships and outliers.

MULTIPLE REGRESSION ANALYSIS

Multiple regression analysis examines the relationship between a single metric dependent (criterion) variable and a set of metric independent (predictor) variables. Its general form is:

$$\underset{\text{(metric)}}{Y} = \alpha + \underset{\text{(metric)}}{\beta_1 X_1 + \beta_2 X_2 + \beta_3 X_3 + \ldots + \beta_n X_n} + \varepsilon$$

α is a regression constant, representing the value of Y when all the independent variables have values of zero. β is a regression coefficient indicating the relationship between X and Y controlled for all other independent variables. ε is an error term that incorporates the cumulative effect on Y of factors not included in the model. Regression may be used to calculate the predicted value of Y for any given value of X. And the residuals or distances between the predicted and observed values of Y lead to a measure (R^2) of how well the equation fit the data.

Regression analysis is the most widely used and versatile dependence technique in policy analysis for the purpose of prediction or explanation. For example, regression analysis is the foundation for forecasting models that predict national economy or other performance based on certain inputs. It is used to examine how decisions are made and how attitudes are formed. It is also used to identify quality determinants of policy implementation and program design. Hunter (2001) used multiple regression to explain the difference of states' economic growth by lobbying efforts in selected categories and a sample of demand-side economic policies, controlling for net business growth, expenditure, and republican control of the government and legislature. The economic growth was measured by the change of a state's per capita gross state product (GSP) between 1986 and 1991. The regression results suggest that two categories of lobbying efforts explain more of the variance in GSP than the demand-side policies and the other variables. With multiple regression, the author was able to show that the control variables contributed to 9 percent of the variation in changes in GSP while the dependent variables contributed to an additional 34 percent variation.

A very important but often ignored step is to assess whether the model satisfies the assumptions of regression analysis, such as existence, linearity, homoscedasticity (equal residual variances), independence of the residuals, and normality. The principal diagnostic method is to examine the residual—the difference between the actual dependent variable value and its predicted value—though partial regression plots and statistical tests (i.e., the Kolmogorov-Smirnov test and the Shapiro-Wilks test for normality; the Durbin-Watson test for independence). In graphical analysis, a triangle-shaped or a diamond-shaped pattern indicates the presence of heteroscedasticity, which can also be assessed with the Levene test in SPSS. Also important is to avoid multicollinearity, which can substantively affect explanation and estimation of the regression coefficients and their significance tests. Analysts can use correlation matrix for the independent variables to observe whether high correlations are present (.90 and above). More common measures are the tolerance value and the variance inflation factor (VIF, rule-of-thumb cutting value at 10.0), which measures the degree to which each independent variable is explained by the other independent variables. Analysts may use some remedial strategies to solve the above problems, and data transformation (i.e., from Y to log Y or Y^2) is one of the options. In the final steps, analysts also need to identify outliers and determine whether they should be excluded from the analysis. Common indicators for this purpose are the leverage h and the Cook's distance, which measures the extent to which the regression coefficients change when the particular observation is deleted.

TIME SERIES ANALYSIS

Time series analysis identifies the pattern of change across time in order to explain the phenomenon and to predict the future based on historical and existing patterns. It enables policy analysts to examine a variable, such as unemployment rate and economic growth, over equally spaced intervals of time such as month and year. Its general form is

$$X_t = a_1 X_{t-1} + a_2 X_{t-2} + \ldots + a_n X_{t-n}$$

Time series analysis is important to policy analysis since policy change is a crucial question and time series analysis permits data-based forecasting. Many policy studies are cross-sectional, and the results may be strengthened by replicating the study in different times. In addition, time-series analysis can address questions of causation that would be impossible to tackle with cross-sectional analysis, given that the temporal sequencing of changes can be established with a time-series. For example, to answer the question whether the incidence of crimes in a region changed following the establishment of a new crime-fighting program, interrupted time-series experiment is an appropriate strategy. To predict the pattern over time based on Gallup polls of presidential popularity, time-series regression is an appropriate strategy.

In general, time series analysis can serve three purposes: analyses of trends and forecasting; causal analyses; and program and policy analyses (Burbridge 1999). Especially, interrupted time-series is useful because the introduction of a program or policy will produce a break in the time-series trend for certain variables affected by the program or policy. Analysts need to have enough pre-program data to establish a pre-program trend, to know the exact time of the introduction of the program and reasonable assumption about how long it will take for the program to affect the long term trend (Burbridge 1999).

There are six basic steps in a time series analysis. First, plot the data. Second, examine the plot and determine if any short-term fluctuations exist. Third, if the data show a cyclical trend, determine the length of the short-term trend and filter the trend. Fourth, determine whether a relationship exists. Fifth, use linear regression to estimate the relationship between time and the variable being analyzed. Sixth, make a forecast by using the regression equation (Meier and Brudney 2002).

For example, in a research on policy design, bureaucratic incentives, and policy enforcement, Keiser and Meier (1996) hypothesized that local-level implementation environment and resources committed to implementation affect the actual enforcement levels. Using pooled time series data of federal laws on child support enforcement from 1983 to 1991, they were able to confirm the hypotheses. Albritton (1979) measured impacts of the Title XX amendments to the Social Security Act with an interrupted time-series analysis. The Auto-Regressive Integrated Moving Averages (ARIMA) model was adopted and the results showed that the policy innovation led to dramatic, nonincremental changes. Morgan and Pelissero (1980) used an interrupted time-series quasi-experiment to test the hypothesis that reformed cities tax and spend less than unreformed cities. Eleven cities, with a population of 25,000 and above, which reformed their political structure between 1948 and 1973, were compared with eleven matched cities that did not reform. The results showed that government structure did not affect cities' fiscal behavior.

Event History Analysis (EHA)

Event history analysis is used to explain why certain units of analysis (individuals, organizations, or states, etc.) are more likely to experience the event(s) of interest than others. It is a specialized subfield of time series analysis that analyzes rare events (time series in which most data are non-events). The data in EHA measures the number, timing, and sequence of changes in a variable of interest. EHA can be a form of panel study in which the periods of observation are not arbitrarily spaced but instead measurement is taken at each stage of a sequence of events. The dependent variable is qualitative and taking values between zero and one, but the independent variables can take any real numbers.

The key concepts of EHA include a risk set (a set of unit of analysis that have yet to experience a particular event), a survivor function (the decline in the size of risk over time), and the hazard rate (the rate at which particular events occurring at a particular time). EHA assumes that it is possible to predict the dependent variable (e.g., marriage, employment changes, higher education, and death) within certain time frames. The rationale stems from the life table analysis used by demographers to calculate survival and mortality rates in a given population over time. For example, if x number of the population is alive at time t, it is possible to predict the survival rate of that population at time t + 1. The hazard rate in EHA is the other side of the survival rate and refers to the probability of a dependent variable occurring to an individual within a specified time frame, given that individual is at risk (Cohen, Manion, and Morrison 2000). The problem is solved by taking a logit transformation of the dependent variable and then estimating with maximum likelihood techniques (Allison 1984).

EHA began to be used in social sciences in the 1970s. It was prominent in the field of international relations, where it was used to analyze time series of international conflict and diplomatic events. Policy analysts applied EHA in other areas later on. Plotnick (1983) used EHA to study the entry to and exit from the Aid to Families with Dependent Children (AFDC) program. The estimates were applied to projected changes in lengths of time spent on and off AFDC and in AFDC caseloads due to changes in the dependent variables. The results demonstrated that age and wage have significant, negative effects on the rate of entering AFDC, and significant, positive effects on the exit rate.

Berry and Berry (1990), examining state lottery adoptions, used EHA to explain how states' internal characteristics (political and economic) and regional diffusion influenced the probability that the state adopted a lottery. An EHA model was developed as:

$$ADOPT_{i,t} = \Phi \left(\begin{array}{c} b_1 FISCAL_{i,t-1} + b_2 PARTY_{i,t} + b_3 ELECT1_{i,t} + b_4 ELECT2_{i,t} + b_5 INCOME_{i,t-1} \\ + b_6 RELIGION_{i,t-1} + b_7 NEIGHBORS_{i,t} \end{array} \right)$$

$ADOPT_{i,t}$	=	the probability that state i will adopt a lottery in year t
$FISCAL_{i,t-1}$	=	the fiscal health of a state's government in the previous year
$PARTY_{i,t}$	=	the degree to which a political party controls the government
$ELECT1_{i,t}$	=	dummy, 1 for the year of gubernatorial election
$ELECT2_{i,t}$	=	dummy, 1 for neither the year of an election nor the year after
$INCOME_{i,t-1}$	=	personal income
$RELIGION_{i,t-1}$	=	the proportion population adhering to fundamentalism religion
$NEIGHBORS_{i,t}$	=	the number of previously adopting neighboring states

The results showed that previous adoption by neighboring states and declining fiscal health affect the probability of adopting the lottery. The authors noted that lottery adoption was most likely to occur in the years immediately following the election. In addition, states with lower per capita income and states with higher percentage of religious fundamentalists were least likely to adopt lotteries. With EHA, Berry and Berry (1990) concluded that regional diffusion and internal determinants were valid explanations of state lottery adoption. They proposed that EHA should be used in other subfields of political science because it takes advantage of both temporal and cross-sectional variation in political behavior, and it remains valid for rarely occurred events such as wars and switching political party identification. Box-Steffensmeier and Jones (1997) illustrated EHA methods with three issues: overt military interventions, challenger deterrence, and congressional career paths. They called for greater use of EHA models as well.

FACTOR ANALYSIS

Factor analysis is an interdependence technique in which all variables are simultaneously considered and factors are created to explain the variable set. Factor analysis has three basic purposes: to identify factor structure underlying the variables, to achieve data reduction, and to test the relationships among variables. Factor analysis is based on the fundamental assumption that some underlying factors, which are smaller in number than the number of observed variables, are responsible for the covariation among observed variables. The emphasis on an underlying factor structure reflects a belief that there are real qualities in the world, such as trust, motivation and satisfaction, which are not directly measurable but can be revealed through the covariation of related variables. Its general form is:

$$X_1 = b_1(F_1) + b_2(F_2) + \ldots + b_n(F_n) + d_1(U_1)$$

where

X_1	=	the subject's score on observed variable 1
b_n	=	the weight for underlying common factor n, as used in determining the subject's score on X_1
F_n	=	the subject's score on underlying factor n
d_1	=	the regression weight for the unique factor associated with X_1
U_1	=	the unique factor associated with X_1

Factor analysis has two types: exploratory and confirmatory. Confirmatory factor analysis is used with path analysis for structural equation modeling. For exploratory factor analysis, if cases are being grouped then it becomes Q method or cluster analysis; if variables are being grouped then it is the R-type factor analysis. Factor analysis differs from the principal components analysis in that the components of principal component analysis account for total variance in the data while the factors of factor analysis account for common variance in the dataset. Factor analysis assumes that the observed variables are linear combinations of the underlying factors. In contrast, principal component analysis assumes that components are linear combinations of observed variables. Therefore, factor analysis can be used to identify the number and nature of the factors that are responsible for covariation in the dataset, but principal component analysis cannot. Nevertheless, many writers do not make the distinction especially when the purpose is to reduce items or variables.

For example, Winter and May (2001) measured Danish farmers' social motivation to comply with regulations with six survey items about farmers' perceptions of the enforcement style of municipal inspectors. They then used the principal component analysis, treated as factor analysis, and identified two underlying dimensions of enforcement style: formalism and coercion. Warner and Hebdon (2001) studied factors affecting local governments' restructuring choices among privatization and its alternatives. In addition to fiscal stress and control variables such as per capita income, municipal type, size of government and tenure of office, the authors developed fourteen items to measure economic and political conditions of the local governments. They conducted principal components analysis and reduced the fourteen items to three distinct components: information and service quality; efficiency; and unionization and political factors. In Table 23.1, the first seven items have factor loadings higher than 0.5 on Information and Service Quality, with lower loadings for the other two components. Therefore, the seven items can be used together in the future analysis. The eighth item, local employment impact, has similar loading on the first component (0.476) and the third (0.452). Therefore, this item should have been deleted from future analysis.

PATH ANALYSIS

Path analysis is used to test the indirect and casual relationships among the variables specified in the model. Policy analysts first draw a path diagram based on a theory or a set of hypotheses, then estimate path coefficients using regression techniques, and finally determine indirect effects (Nachmias and Nachmias 1996). It is very useful when dealing with mediating effects, where an independent variable had an impact on an intervening variable which, in turn, had an impact on a dependent variable. Path analysis assumes perfect reliability of the instruments used to operationalize variables. Therefore, all variables in the path model are considered to be observed, not latent or underlying factors. When it is used mathematically with confirmatory factor analysis (CFA), it becomes structural equation modeling (SEM) and can deal with latent variables. SEM allows

TABLE 23.1
Principal Components Analysis Results from Warner and Hebdon (2001)

	Information & Service Quality	Efficiency	Union
Information (1)	0.792	0.17	0.038
Legal	0.643	−0.048	0.407
Community Values (2)	0.614	0.2	0.27
Monitoring (3)	0.613	0.189	0.301
Service Quality (4)	0.604	0.481	−0.003
Leadership	0.563	0.434	−0.009
Experience	0.529	0.125	0.132
Local Employment Impact	0.476	0.196	0.452
Economic Efficiency	0.147	0.832	0.092
Budgetary Impact	0.07	0.793	0.339
Management	0.321	0.693	0.112
Labor	0.457	0.471	0.419
Union	0.076	0.075	0.799
Political (5)	0.216	0.243	0.573

Note: N = 201; Based on a 1997 survey on New York State towns and counties.

assessment of the reliabilities of the latent variables, more precise estimation of the indirect effects of the exogenous variables, and multiple dependent variables.

Path analysis is used to both simplify and depict complex theoretical relationships. LISREL (Linear Structural Relations) has been the popular program since 1981, and statistical packages such as SAS and Stata can conduct the analysis as well. Ellickson (1992) used path analysis to explain the impact of personal, environmental, and institutional factors on legislative success with data drawn from the 1987–88 Missouri House of Representatives. The results showed that institutional variables, seniority and political party, have the strongest impact. The path analysis was able to show that formal office is an intervening variable between legislative success and other independent variables such as age, urbanism, seniority, and political party.

Cohen and Vigoda (1998) used path analysis to compare two different models explaining the relationship between citizenship behavior and work outcomes. Figure 23.1, the direct model, has no mediating variables. The results show that political participation, community involvement, and general altruism have statistically significant direct impact on perceived performance, while disillusionment with government has significant direct impact on turnover intentions. Figure 23.2, the indirect model, has four independent variables (political participation, community involvement, general altruism, and disillusionment with government), one mediating variable (participation in decision making), and two dependent variables (turnover intentions and perceived performance). Among the independent variables, only community involvement has a statistically significant path to participation in decision making. In comparison, model fit indices suggested that the direct model is better than the indirect model.

GAME THEORY

Game theory is a mathematical approach to individual decision making that employs games as paradigms of rational decision-maker interactions. A game is any interaction between agents that is governed by a set of rules specifying the possible moves for each participant and a set of outcomes for each possible combination of moves. A game of "pure strategy" consists of the following inter-related components: The *players*, who may be people or organizations, choose from a list of *options*

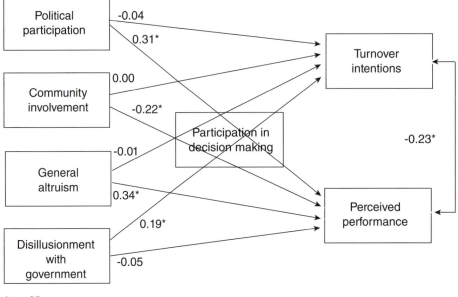

FIGURE 23.1   An Indirect Path Model from Cohen and Vigoda (1998).

or *strategies* available to them. At each stage of the play, the players choose their course of *action* from a set of possible decisions, which are not usually the same for each player. The actions lead to *outcomes* or *consequences*. It assumes the players have fixed *preferences* for the outcomes: they like some outcomes more than others. After the decisions have been made, each player receives a certain *payoff* measured in a common unit for all players (Morrow 1994).

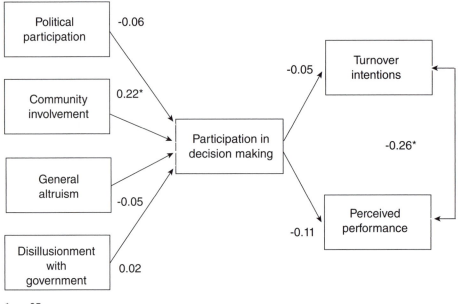

FIGURE 23.2   A Direct Path Model from Cohen and Vigoda (1998).

The assumptions of game theory are: (1) individual action is instrumentally rational, (2) common knowledge of rationality held by all the players, (3) the players will draw the same inferences on how a game is to be played, (4) players know the rules of the game and their motive is independent of the rules, (5) fixed preferences, (6) transitivity (if A>B and B>C then A>C) (Heap and Varoufakis 2004; Gates and Humes 2000). Apparently, those assumptions are simplistic and subject to criticisms. For example, individual identities and preferences may not be pre-fixed; rather, they are socially embedded and constituted. They are often generated during the specific social interactions.

In a policy situation, we may encounter different occurring events that result from decisions made by others. When actors seek to maximize their own interests but their actions affect one another, a game condition involving both conflict and cooperation exists. Game theoretic models help actors make decisions when confronted with competing policy alternatives or decision consequences. Both politics and games involve the moves and interactions of players attempting to maximize their interests; the selection of strategies with specific consequences; and, at times, coalition formation (Kelly 2003).

There are several game forms. The simplest one is the two-person, zero-sum game in which two players are involved and one player's gains are the other player's losses, and vice versa. Consider the Prisoner's Dilemma, one of the classic games, as an example. The two players are partners in a crime who have been captured by the police. Each suspect is placed in a separate cell and offered the opportunity to confess. Each prisoner has two choices: strategy A (confess) or strategy B (do not confess). The payoff for a prisoner in any particular round depends on both prisoners' choices in that round. As shown in the tradeoff table (Table 23.2), there are four possible scenarios: (1) both choose to confess (strategy A), and each of them earns the same payoff of 3; (2) both choose not to confess (strategy B), and each of them has the same payoff of 2; (3) Prisoner 1 chooses to confess (strategy A) while Prisoner 2 chooses not to (strategy B). As a result, Prisoner 1 earns a payoff of 5 while Prisoner 2 earns a payoff of 1; (4) Prisoner 1 chooses not to confess (strategy B) while Prisoner 2 chooses to confess. As a result, Prisoner 1 earns a payoff of 1 while Prisoner 2 earns a payoff of 5.

The Prisoner's Dilemma relates to the issue of trust, the free rider problem, public goods, negotiation, regulation, corruption, and conflict resolution. Axelrod (1984) demonstrated that *Tit-for-Tat,* a program starting with a co-operative move and then following whatever the opponent did on the previous move, is the best strategy in repeated Prisoner's Dilemma games. It indicates that although cooperation is not a Nash equilibrium in the one-shot game, it is in indefinitely repeated games. Both Axelrod's analysis (1984) and Smith's (1982) analysis have led to many other applications in the filed of political science (see Axelrod and Dion 1988). Game theory has been used in political science since the 1950s, especially in areas such as voting, group preference, coalition formation, bargaining, diplomacy, and negotiation (Shubik 1982). After Harsanyi (1967) introduced the concept of incomplete information to game theory in the late 1960s, incomplete information models have been applied to voting, political activism, bureaucratic control, crisis bargaining, arms control agreements, and alliance formation (Gates and Humes 2000).

TABLE 23.2
The Prisoner's Dilemma

		Prisoner 1	
		Strategy A	**Strategy B**
	Strategy A	(3,3)	(1,5)
Prisoner 2			
	Strategy B	(5,1)	(2,2)

SIMULATION

Simulation is a quantitative procedure by which analysts build mathematical models of policy process that are difficult to solve analytically and then run the models on a series of organized trial-and-error experiments in order to simulate the behavior of the system over time. It helps analysts understand the system by simulating it in the environment and determining the likely course of events and conditional changes in public policy. It helps answer questions such as: "What would happen to our local economic development policies if the inflation rate is 4 percent instead of 3 percent in the coming year?" Or, "How would this growth management strategy influence the traffic of this county in twenty years?" Simulation sometimes is the only method available if the actual environment or system is difficult to observe or model, or if the model is too complicated to be solved analytically. In some other times, it is infeasible (i.e., too expensive or disruptive) to actually operate and observe a system. For example, if analysts are comparing two ways of providing benefits to veterans, operating two different systems may cause great confusion and legal problems.

A good simulation should satisfy the following conditions: (1) Calibrated. Accurate data are included in the construction of the simulation, and the values for the parameters match empirical observation as closely as possible; (2) Checked. The functioning of the model is comparable to the actual functioning of the real world; (3) Flexible. The model is flexible enough to answer a variety of questions (Kane 1999). The general steps are: (1) define the system one intends to simulate, (2) formulate the model one intends to use, (3) identify and collect data necessary to test the model, (4) test the model and compare its behavior with the actual environment, (5) run the simulation, (6) analyze the results and revise the solution if desired, (7) rerun the simulation to test the new solution, (8) validate the simulation (Levin et al. 1989).

Despite the criticism that it lacks mathematical elegance and precision, simulation is one of the most widely used operations research techniques. In the 1960s, it was used in international relations and urban affair issues such as municipal budgeting, election, and political recruitment (see Coplin 1968). Its use has grown considerably with the development of mathematical modeling and informational technology. It is especially useful in answering "what if..." questions (Zagonel et al. 2004). At the University of Rhode Island, the Department of Environmental and Natural Resource Economics created a Policy Simulation Laboratory (SimLab) to apply interactive tools based on modern computer technologies to help understand the consequences of policy actions. For example, the town council in one of the Group Decision Rooms of SimLab might design a plan for managing growth in the town. Computer systems then simulate the environment and predict the economic and social consequences of the plan. Geographic Information Systems are used to present the consequences for the town with electronic maps.

Simulation is used in a variety of policy settings such as the construction of electoral districts (Gelman and King 1994), the making of foreign policy (Taber 1992), the effects of emission controls on the earth's climate (Bankes and Lempert 1996), social security reform (Weller 2000), and alternate approaches to health insurance expansion (Remler, Zivin, and Glied 2004). Tengs et al. (2004) created a Tobacco Policy Model to examine the potential consequences of mandating tobacco companies to improve the safety of cigarettes. Through simulation of the U.S. population over a fifty-year time span, the results show that even if the safety mandate makes smoking more attractive and increases tobacco use, it is still possible to obtain a net gain in population health. Robins, Michalopoulos, and Pan (2001) used a simulation model to examine whether welfare recipients would work full-time if offered an earnings supplement conditioned on full-time employment. The simulation model extended a traditional microeconomic model of the income or leisure choice to include the choice to receive welfare, assuming that welfare recipients' decisions about employment and welfare were based on the intention to maximize their economic well-being. Outcomes were simulated with three different financial incentives: AFDC (pre-TANF environment), TANF (currently used in the sample states as required by the Temporary Aid to Needy Families Act), and SSP (Self-Sufficiency Project).

The results suggested that the earning supplement would increase full-time employment while the TANF incentives would encourage primarily part-time employment.

CONCLUSION

Quantitative methods help assess the relative and joint effects of a variety of independent variables on some dependent variables. They inform citizens and clients about policy choices with numbers, graphs, and tested relationships. They enable citizens and clients to see the benefit and risks of policy alternatives with mathematical eyes. Development of more sophisticated quantitative techniques is a crucial task for many current policy analysts (Wagle 2000). As policy problems become more complex, environments become more turbulent, and time and budgets become more constrained, policy analysts must be able to choose the most appropriate (valid, reasonable, and realistic) strategy and implement the study in a short period of time.

REFERENCES

Albritton, R. B. (1979). Measuring public policy: Impacts of the supplemental security income program. *American Journal of Political Science*, *23*(3), 559–578.

Allison, P. D. (1984). *Event history analysis*. Newbury Park: Sage.

Axelrod, R. (1984). *The evolution of cooperation*. New York: Basic Books.

Axelrod, R., and Dion, D. (1988). The further evolution of cooperation. *Science 242*. 1385–1390.

Bankes, S., and Lempert, R. J. (1996). Adaptive strategies for abating climate change. In Fogel, L. J., Angeline, P. J., & Back, T. (eds.), *Proceedings of the fifth annual conference on evolutionary programming*, pp. 17–25. Cambridge, MA: MIT Press.

Berry, F. S., and Berry, W. D. (1990). State lottery adoptions as policy innovations: An event history analysis. *American Political Science Review*, *84*(2), 395–415.

Box-Steffensmeier, J. M., and Jones, B. S. (1997). Time is of the essence: Event history models in political science. *American Journal of Political Science*, *41*(4), 1414–1461.

Brandl, J. E. (1976). Public service education in the 1970s. *Urban Analysis*, *3*, 105–114.

Brewer, G. D., and deLeon, P. (1983). *The foundations of policy analysis*. Homewood, IL: The Dorsey Press.

Brewer, M. B. (1983). Evaluation: Past and present. In E. L. Struening and M. B. Brewer (eds.), *Handbook of evaluation research*, Beverly Hills, CA: Sage.

Burbridge, L. (1999). Cross-sectional, longitudinal, and time-series data: Uses and limitations. In G. J. Miller and M. L. Whicker (eds.), *Handbook of research methods in public administration*, pp. 283–300. New York: Marcel Dekker.

Cohen, A., and Vigoda, E. (1998). An empirical assessment of the relationship between general citizenship and work outcomes. *Public Administration Quarterly*, *21*(4), 401–431.

Cohen, L., Manion, L., and Morrison, K. (2000). *Research methods in education*, 5th ed., New York: Routledge.

Coplin, W. D. (1968). *Simulation in the study of politics*. Chicago: Markham Publishing.

Daniels, M. S., and Wirth, C. J. (1983). Paradigms of evaluation research: The development of an important policy-making component. *American Review of Public Administration*, *17(1)*, 33–45.

deLeon, P. (1998). Introduction: The evidentiary base for policy analysis: Empiricist versus postpositivist positions. *Policy Studies Journal*, 26(1), 109–113.

Durning, D. (1999).The transition from traditional to postpositivist policy analysis: A role for Q-methodology. *Journal of Policy Analysis and Management*, 18(3), 389–410.

Ellickson, M. C. (1992). Pathways to legislative success: A path analytic study of the Missouri house of representatives. *Legislative Studies Quarterly*, 17(2), 285–302.

Engelbert, E. A. (1977). University education of public policy analysis. *Public Administration Review*, 37(3), 228–236.

Fischer, F. (1995). *Evaluating public policy*. Chicago: Nelson-Hall.

Fischer, F. (1998). Beyond empiricism: Policy inquiry in postpositivist perspective. *Policy Studies Journal*, 26(1), 129–146.

Gates, S., and Humes, B. D. (2000). *Games, information, and politics*. Ann Arbor: The University of Michigan Press.

Gelman, A., and King, G. (1994). Enhancing democracy through legislative redistricting. *American Political Science Review*, 88(3), 541–559.

Gottman, J. M. (1988). *Time-series analysis*. New York: Cambridge University Press.

Hair, J. F., Tatham, R. L., Anderson, R.E., and Black, W. (1998). *Multivariate data analysis* (5th ed.). Upper Saddle River, NJ: Prentice Hall.

Harsanyi, J. (1967). Games of incomplete information played by Bayesian players. *Management Science*, 14, 159–182, 320–334, 486–502.

Heap, S. P. H., and Varoufakis, Y. (2004). *Game theory*. New York: Routledge.

Hitch, C. J. (1965). *Decision-making for defense*. Berkeley, CA: University of California Press.

Hunter, K. G.. (2001). An analysis of the effect of lobbying efforts and demand-side economic development policies on state economic health. *Public Administration Quarterly*, 25(1), 49–78.

Johnson, J. B., and Reynolds, H. T. (2005). *Political Science Research Methods* (5th ed.). Washington, D.C.: CQ Press.

Kane, D. (1999). Computer simulation. In G. J. Miller and M. L. Whicker (eds.), *Handbook of research methods in public administration*, pp. 511–533. New York: Marcel Dekker.

Keiser, L. R., and Meier, K. J. (1996). Policy design, bureaucratic incentives, and public management: The case of child support enforcement. *Journal of Public Administration Research and Theory*, 6(3), 337–364.

Kelly, M. A. (2003). Game theory. In J. Rabin (ed.), *Encyclopedia of public administration and public policy*, pp. 533–536. New York: Marcel Dekker.

Krane, D. (2001). Disorderly progress on the frontiers of policy evaluation. *International Journal of Public Administration*, 24(1), 95–123.

Lasswell, H. D. (1951). The policy orientation. In D. Lerner and H. D. Lasswell (eds.), *The policy sciences*, pp. 3–15. Stanford: Stanford University Press.

Lasswell, H. D. (1970). The emerging conception of the policy sciences. *Policy Sciences*, 1, 3–14.

Lasswell, H. D. (1971). *A pre-view of policy sciences*. New York: Elsevier.

Leinhardt, S. (1981). Data analysis and statistics education in public policy programs. In J. P. Crecine (ed.), *Research in public policy analysis and management*, pp. 53–61. Greenwich, CT: JAI Press.

Levin, R. I., Rubin, D. S., Stinson, J. P., and Gardner, E. S. (1989). *Quantitative approaches to management*. New York: McGraw-Hill.

May, P. J. (1998). Policy analysis: Past, present, and future. *International Journal of Public Administration*, 21(6-8), 1089–1114.

Meier, K. J., and Brudney, J.L. (2002). *Applied statistics for public administration* (5th ed.). Belmont, CA: Wadsworth.

Meltsner, A. J. (1976). *Policy analysis in the bureaucracy*. Berkeley: University of California Press.

Morçöl, G. (2001). Positivist beliefs among policy professionals: An empirical investigation. *Policy Sciences*, 34, 381–401.

Morgan, D. R., and Pelissero, J. P. (1980). Urban policy: Does political structure matter? *American Political Science Review*, 74(4), 999–1006.

Morrow, J. D. (1994). *Game theory for political scientists*. Princeton, NJ: Princeton University Press.

Nachmias, C. F., and Nachmias, D. (1996). *Research Methods in the Social Sciences* (5th ed.). New York: St. Martin's Press.

Nakamura, R. T., and Smallwood, F. (1980). *The politics of policy omplementation*. New York: St. Martin's Press.

Quade, E. S. (Ed.). (1966). *Analysis for military decisions*. Chicago: Rand McNally.

Quade, E. S., and Boucher, W. I. (Eds.). (1968). *Systems analysis and policy planning: Applications for defense*. New York: American Elsevier.

Plotnick, R. (1983). Turnover in the AFDC population: An event history analysis. *The Journal of Human Resources*, 18(1), 65–81.

Radin, Beryl A. (2000). *Beyond Machiavelli: Policy analysis comes of age*. Washington DC: Georgetown University Press.

Remler, D. K., Zivin, J. G., and Glied, S. A. (2004). Modeling health insurance expansions: Effects of alternate approaches. *Journal of Policy Analysis and Management*, 23(2), 291–313.

Robins, P. K., Michalopoulos, C., and Pan, E. (2001). Financial incentives and welfare reform in the United States. *Journal of Policy Analysis and Management*, 20(1), 129–150.

Shubik, M. (1982). *Game theory in the social sciences*. Cambridge: The MIT Press.

Smith, M. (1982). *Evolution and the theory of games*. Cambridge: Cambridge University Press.

Taber, C. S. (1992). POLI: An expert system model of U.S. foreign policy belief systems. *American Political Science Review*, 86(4), 888–904.

Tens, T., Ahmad, S., Moore, R., and Gage, E. (2004). Federal policy mandating safer cigarettes: A hypothetical simulation of the anticipated population health gains or losses. *Journal of Policy Analysis and Management*, 23(4), 857–872.

Vijverberg, W. P. (1997). The quantitative methods component in social sciences curricula in view of journal content. *Journal of Policy Analysis and Management*. 16(4), 621–629.

Wagle, U. (2000). The policy science of democracy: The issues of methodology and citizen participation. *Policy Sciences, 33*, 207–223.

Walker, J. L. (1976). The curriculum in public policy studies at the University of Michigan. *Urban Analysis, 3*, 89–103.

Warner, M. and Hebdon, R. (2001). Local government restructuring: Privatization and its alternatives. *Journal of Policy Analysis and Management*, 20(2), 315–336.

Weller, C. E. (2000). Risky business? Evaluating market risk of equity investment proposals to reform social security. *Journal of Policy Analysis and Management*, 19(2), 263–273.

Wells, J. B., Layne, B. H., and Allen, D. (1991). Management development training and learning styles. *Public Productivity & Management Review*, 14(4), 415–428.

Wildavsky, A. B. (1969). Rescuing policy analysis from PPBS. *Public Administration Review*, 29, 189–202.

Wildavsky, A. B. (1976). Principles for a graduate school of public policy. *Journal of Urban Analysis, 4*, 3–28.

Winter, S. C., and May, P. J. (2001). Motivation for compliance with environmental regulations. *Journal of Policy Analysis and Management*, 20(4), 675–698.

Zagonel, A. A., Rohrbaugh, J., Richardson, G. P., and Anderson, D. F. (2004). Using simulation models to address "what if" questions about welfare reform. *Journal of Policy Analysis and Management*, 23(4), 890–901.

24 The Use (and Misuse) of Surveys in Policy Analysis

Jerry Mitchell

Once upon a time in the distant past, Neanderthals were undoubtedly crouched in a cave somewhere in present day Europe wondering if they should relocate because of a shrinking bear population. If the Neanderthal's Leviathan was inclined toward a social contract way of thinking, the early humans might have been polled about their support and opposition to the move elsewhere. The results could have been used as a rationale for the risk-filled decision to budge or stay put. The reason for the eventual extinction of the Neanderthals was possibly because the populace perceived the correct policy direction, but the sovereign misinterpreted the data.

There is certainly no speculation involved in knowing that people have been formally and informally polled about different courses of action in many venues and for all sorts of reasons throughout human history. Pontius Pilate decided to put Jesus to death after taking an unsystematic survey of the local populace, President Bill Clinton decided to fib about his affair with Monica Lewinsky after his pollster told him the public would strongly disapprove of such a dalliance, and the Hungarian Parliament decided to withdraw its troops from Iraq after a poll showed 55 percent of the public favored the pull out.

It could very well be human nature for leaders and followers to question one another about what they believe or what they should do. Perhaps there is an evolutionary pressure for people to ask each other how well they have adapted or fail to adapt to environmental circumstances. After all, the pervasive propensity to gossip is nothing more than a small scale, unscientific survey that describes what other people have said and done. At the institutional level, yesterday's royal privy council and today's corporate advisory board are kindred mechanisms for eliciting opinions about particular actions. Voting is really nothing more than a state-sponsored, self-selected survey that provides a legal mandate for office holding and making laws. The fact is that people are polled about their preferences before they go to the polls and then polled again after they have been to the polls to explain why they marked their ballots one way or another.

The fascination with surveys has reached epidemic proportions. Practically every nation on the globe conducts a poll before and after the election of their leaders. In the months leading up to the 2004 U.S. presidential election, voter surveys were undertaken on a daily, if not hourly, basis by news organizations, advocacy groups, and political parties. Although politicians decry surveys and contend they are not beholden to polls, it was easy to witness the impact of surveys in the 2004 election because the two presidential candidates campaigned almost exclusively in states where surveys showed a neck and neck race. In the eccentric winner take all system of the American electoral college, there was no sense in running commercials or making personal appearances in a state where one candidate had a dominant lead according to survey research.

But it is not only in political campaigns where survey research has become popular. Viewer surveys establish which television shows survive and thrive every season, which celebrities are liked and disliked, and which commercials succeed and fail. It is a rare consumer product that has not been subjected to a marketing survey at one time or another. Customer opinion polls affect where products are placed on store shelves and the form of advertising that appears in store windows. In fact, the University of Michigan's survey of consumer sentiment has become a leading indicator of the health of the U.S. economy. Even the determination of what is good and bad to eat is based to some degree on the longitudinal responses to questionnaires about the eating habits of some specially selected population. The extraordinary deference to surveys and the ease of their administration has led them to become a part of every school of thought, so that it is commonplace to find survey results reported in the professional journals of anthropology, psychology, sociology, education, political science, and public administration.

The use of survey research is also a part of policy analysis. Surveys are conducted to identify public needs, to discover support and opposition to policies, and to evaluate satisfaction and dissatisfaction with programs. Surveys may be employed by policy makers as the foundation for making decisions about whether to create new policies or terminate old ones, to gain a better understanding of issues, and to advocate for changing policies, programs, and services. Surveys can be applied to every stage of the policy process: to identify problems, consider the worth of solutions, determine legislative support for laws, appraise implementation difficulties, and measure outcomes. Surveys are relevant to many policy areas: the environment, social welfare, economic development, education, healthcare, civil rights, criminal justice, and foreign affairs (Christenson and Taylor 1983; Glaser and Bardo 1994; Swindell and Kelly 2000; Thompson 1997). To influence public policy, surveys are conducted by every sector—public, private, and nonprofit—from the San Francisco Zoo to the *Chicago Tribune* to the New York City Council. They can be used at every level of government: federal, state, and local. Whenever and wherever surveys are conducted, there is money to be made in putting them together and analyzing the results. In 2001, George W. Bush's administration spent nearly one million dollars alone on operations to gauge the public's reaction to alternative Social Security proposals and energy policies (Green 2002).

It does not take much noticing to notice that surveys are important part of the policy process, but surprisingly policy analysis textbooks all too often leave survey methods out of the analyst's methodological toolbox. For example, in the 499 pages of the 4th edition of David L. Weimer's and Aidan R. Vining's *Policy Analysis: Concepts and Practices* (2005) there is a mere page and half discussion of interviews, not even the inclusion of the word survey or poll in the index. Who knows the reason for this neglect, but it is surely no time to be a Neanderthal when comes to understanding how to study policies that affect the lives of countless people. The purpose of this chapter, therefore, is to examine the use of surveys in policy analysis. The first part identifies the elements of survey research, the second part provides examples of how surveys address various policy questions, and the last part examines problems with the survey research enterprise.

THE ELEMENTS OF SURVEY RESEARCH

There are four things to consider when undertaking a survey: (1) selecting the best type of survey to use, (2) developing good questions, (3) determining who should be surveyed, and (4) analyzing the results.

TYPE OF SURVEYS

There are three types of surveys: telephone, in-person, and self-administered. Telephone surveys are the easiest to conduct because all that is required is a phone, phone numbers, and a caller (although large-scale telephone surveys do necessitate elaborate systems, such as telephone assisted computers and a large, well-trained staff). Interviewing people by telephone is by far the most common way of polling large numbers of people—the nation, a state, or a large metropolitan area. Telephone surveys are advantageous because of their immediacy, standardized format, and potential for inter-viewers to explain questions to the respondents. However, it is impossible to reach people without telephones (the homeless, hospital patients, prisoners, etc.) and it often difficult to contact certain populations (judges, doctors, elected officials, etc.) with gatekeepers (i.e., secretary, assistant, etc.). Yet another problem is getting responses from people who employ their answering machines and caller Id systems as screening devices. Pollsters are also legally prohibited from using automated dialing equipment to call wireless numbers.

In-person surveys involve face-to-face contact between interviewers and respondents. This may involve a formatted questionnaire with a set number of responses that come one right after another or it can be unstructured with the questions evolving like a conversation between two friends. In-person surveys are not appropriate for large populations, but they are very useful when wanting to contact a select group of people in a natural setting—on the streets, in a mall, or inside a waiting room. A major advantage is to permit interviewers to explain questions to the respondents. To be done well, trained interviewers are critical because voice inflections, body language, and other physical cues can shape responses. In-person interviews are expensive and time consuming.

Self-administered surveys are distributed to respondents for completion. Surveys can be dis-tributed in four ways: (1) sent through the mail and returned in the mail, (2) sent through e-mail or posted on a Web site and return via e-mail or by entering information on a Web site, (3) left at particular sites (on a table or counter) and either returned by mail or to the site (drop box, etc.), and (4) passed out to people as they enter or leave buildings, streets, rooms, or other venues. The advantages of self-administered surveys include anonymity for the respondents, the ability to ask sensitive questions, the potential for gaining access to difficult-to-reach populations, and the absence of interviewer bias. On the negative side, it is a difficult to obtain responses—questionnaires can be easily tossed in the trash, email can be deleted, and surveys left lying around may not be picked up. It is critical to make sure that one person does not complete more than one survey, otherwise the sample is biased. Asking good questions is extremely important because the interpretation of questions is left to the respondents.

QUESTIONNAIRES

Surveys are all about questions. The conundrum is that questionnaire construction is more of an art than a science. There is no exact prescription for how any question should be asked in sur-veys, although there are books that provide some guidelines for asking questions, such as Peter M. Nardi's *Doing Survey Research* (2003) and Don Dillman's *Mail and Internet Surveys: The Tailored Design Method* (2000). Sometimes questions from previous surveys are repeated, but in most instances questions are crafted ad hoc from one survey to the next. Two general kinds of questions can be posed: (1) close-ended questions that provide a set of response categories for the respondents to complete, and (2) open-ended questions that allow respondents to write in their responses.

Survey questions operationalize variables. An independent variable is one that explains a be-havior, attitude, or need. For example, partisan affiliation may be used as an independent variable to explain support or opposition to some policy. A dependent variable is what is being explained or accounted for. Some typical dependent variables include policy satisfaction, the use of services, and the support of public programs.

Both independent and dependent variables have different values or properties with them. For instance, age can take different values for different people or for the same person at different times. Similarly, country of origin is a variable because a person's country can be assigned a value. There are two traits of variables that should always be achieved. Each variable should be exhaustive, it should include all possible answerable responses. For instance, if the variable is "religion" and the only options are "Protestant," "Jewish," and "Muslim," there are quite a few religions that haven't been included. The list does not exhaust all possibilities. Since it is not possible to list all possibilities with some variables, it typical to explicitly list the most common properties and then use a general category like "Other" to account for all remaining ones. In addition to being exhaustive, the properties of a variable should be mutually exclusive, no respondent should be able to have two attributes simultaneously. While this might seem obvious, it is often rather tricky in practice. For instance, it would be inappropriate to represent the variable "employment status" with the two properties "employed" and "unemployed." The problem is these attributes are not necessarily mutually exclusive—a person who is looking for a second job while employed would be able to check both attributes. The solution may to have another category "employed but looking for a job" or to have the respondent check all that apply.

Survey questions can be nominal, ordinal, or interval level measures. A nominal level measure is one that contains distant categories without any ordering. For example, if a survey asked if a person owed or rented their home. An ordinal measure is one that has a set of ordered categories. Age could be measured by a series of ordered ranges, such as from eighteen to thirty, thirty-one to forty, and so on. An interval level measure is one where every value is its own category. An example is asking an open-ended question that requires the respondent to write in the number of years they have been employed. Each response would be its own value. The level of measurement of the questions is important because it determine the kind of statistical analysis that can be performed.

There are many additional items to consider when constructing a survey instrument (Miller and Miller-Kobayahsi 2000). Respondent must be told how to answer questions and there should be a statement about whether the survey is confidential or not. Most surveys start off with questions that are relatively easy to answer, followed by more difficult questions. Demographic questions (income, age, residence, etc.) are usually posed at the end of a survey. Typically, survey researchers want to obtain an intensity of feeling in their questions, so that they would not ask if someone were satisfied or dissatisfied, but rather they would inquire whether an individual was very satisfied, somewhat satisfied, somewhat dissatisfied, or very dissatisfied. Questions should not be biased or leading. They should be easy for the respondents to understand, which requires the analyst to carefully to match questions to the units of analysis. This is one reason that surveys should be pilot tested before they are actually administered.

RESPONDENTS

There are two approaches to deciding who to survey: (1) the entire population of interest, or (2) a sample of the population. When there is a small population, everyone is usually surveyed. For instance, if one were surveying twenty-five juvenile offenders about their opinions of an alternative-to-incarnation boot camp they had just completed, then all twenty-five participants would be surveyed. There would be no need to sample them. When there is a larger population involved, then it is worthwhile to engage in sampling, that is, to draw a subset of the population. There are two types of samples: probability and non-probability.

A probability sample is one in which names are drawn from a population whose size and characteristics (such as gender, age, residence, etc.) are known. In other words, there is means to know statistically whether the sample is representative of the population. In a probability sample, it is possible to calculate a sampling error—the difference between the sample statistics and the true parameters of the population. Sampling error is a function of the number of respondents—the larger the number of people from whom data are collected, the smaller the sampling error (and, of course, the higher the cost of the survey). A survey of one thousand respondents would have a sampling error of ± 3.1 percent, while in one with two hundred respondents the sampling error would be ±6.9 percent. Random assignment is the most common form of probability sampling, which involves giving every subject in a population the exact same chance of being selected. Another type of probability sample is a systematic sample, which involves selecting names or items from a population list at set intervals (e.g., every tenth person).

A non-probability sample is one where names are selected from a population whose size and characteristics are unknown. For example, if the Chicago Transit Authority wanted to survey its riders it would know there is a population of riders, but it would not have a master list from which to draw names. In non-probability sampling the effort is to estimate whether the sample is representative of a population that is known to exist, but whose exact parameters are unknown. To construct a representative distribution of respondents, there may be a purposive effort to obtain responses according to particular categories, such as gender, ethnicity, or occupation.

Whether it is a probability or non-probability sample, a survey researcher endeavors to have a large enough sample size to approximate the population, to have a response rate above 50 percent, and to make sure that all of the questions in the survey instrument are answered. The quality of a sample is dependent on the sample and how it will be used. If a state were considering the value of creating a new enterprise zone program and wanted to know how well it has worked in other places, it might be good enough to have a sample of the experiences of nearby states in using enterprise zones. Someone from a think tank examining the perceptions of enterprise zones in the nation would probably want a sample of American states from every region of the country.

Data Analysis

Surveys yield numbers. The irony is that subjective questions produce objective statistics. Every question in a survey is a univariate analysis that may be presented, depending on the format of the question, as a frequency distribution or measure of central tendency. Bivariate statistics depict the relationship between two questions. Multivariate statistics are about the relationship among two or more questions, which often involves the use of regression analysis. In other words, a survey assessing support for school vouchers could indicate how many of the respondents supported or opposed vouchers (a univariate analysis). It could also show whether Republicans or Democrats were more or less likely to support school vouchers (a bivariate analysis). And it could point out whether support or opposition to vouchers was affect by one variable more than others, such as partisan affiliation, gender, residence, or income (a multivariate analysis).

There are many techniques for determining the accuracy of survey results, which can be calculated using a statistical software package. For example, the Chi Square statistic measures the significance of bivariate relationships between nominal level variables while correlation coefficients measure the strength of the relationship among multiple interval level variables. Another statistic is Pearson's r, which is a measure of the strength of association between two interval level variables. The type of statistic used to assess the value of relationships is dependent on how questions are measured, the sample size, and the audience for the analysis. Complicated statistical discussions may be more appropriate for scholarly readers than for policy makers or the public.

Survey data can be presented in a narrative or in graphs and tables. If tables are used, it is important that enough information is presented for easy interpretation, but not so much information that comprehension becomes difficult. Tables should have a descriptive title, all variables and their corresponding categories should be clearly labeled, the independent variables should be listed in a column and the dependent variable should be listed along the row, statistical measures should be listed at the bottom of the table, and the number of cases used in the analysis should be indicated. After a conclusion or recommendation section, it is common for a policy report to contain an appendix which includes the survey instrument with the responses to each question.

THE USE OF SURVEYS

There are several ways surveys are used to examine public policies. Three uses are illustrative: (1) assessing the need for policies, (2) understanding the support and opposition to solutions, and (3) evaluating the responsiveness of policies to individuals and groups.

NEED ASSESSMENT

Policy analysts commonly assess the need for policies among various segments of the public. How are policy makers supposed to know that policies should be adopted if they don't know what is needed? Although need is a somewhat ambiguous concept that can vary from one person or group to another, a straightforward way to understand need is to ask people what they need, letting them self-define the concept. Once the level of need has been assessed for a particular population, then a more intelligent discussion of program planning can be instigated. Ideally, policy makers and policy advocates seek to develop a service or intervention to the help the population achieve or approach a satisfactory state (Posavac and Carey 2003).

   An example of a need assessment is a survey conducted by the New York City Department of Small Business Service to determine the need for a business improvement district (BID) in a local neighborhood. A BID is a professionally-managed enterprise whose purpose is to improve a locale using funds from mandatory special taxes or fees paid by property and/or business owners in a legally designated area. The issue is whether or not a BID is needed. To determine need, a survey is distributed to all of the businesses and property owners asking them to indicate whether they agree or disagree about several neighborhood conditions, such as dirty streets, pick pocketing, deteriorated facades, and retail vacancies. When the surveys results show overwhelming agreement on the severity of the problems in an area, the city council has more of a reason to approve the establishment of a BID. In fact, nearly all of the New York City's forty-seven BIDs have been established after surveys found businesses believed they were needed.

OPINION POLLING

It is common to assess the level of support and opposition to alternative solutions in the policy process. Anyone and everyone can be involved in the assessment of solutions, including elected officials, public administrators, policy advocates, and journalists. Studies are done all the time to discover opinions about limiting abortion, privatizing Social Security, installing charter schools, or constructing mass transportation systems. In effect, surveys become a kind of plebiscite on the worth of policy options. If most people support some alternative, then that gives it credence, no matter whether it will or will not be effective. Conversely, if there is general opposition to an alternative, then that make may make an alternative less worthwhile, even though it might have a great chance of succeeding.

   There is no more important example of how surveys are used to measure the support and opposition to public policy than in the decision of cities to build sports stadiums. Every city where new baseball, football, basketball, or multipurpose stadiums have been considered, there have been polls undertaken to diagnose the views of city residents and elected officials. These surveys are conducting by citizen groups opposed to publicly financed stadiums, business groups in support, and local media interesting in a more balanced assessment. Generally, positive survey results can give a stadium proposal the aura of respectability and negative results can make it extremely difficult to go forward. In 2001, a proposal to construct a publicly financed stadium in Minneapolis-St. Paul was seriously affected by a public opinion survey conducted by the *St. Paul Pioneer Press*. In a front page story, the paper reported that public financing for sports facilities was an unattractive proposition among residents in the Twin Cities. Based on a telephone survey of 406 residents, 62 percent of likely voters polled in St. Paul and 71 percent of those queried in Minneapolis opposed any significant public financing for a new ballpark for the Twins. Subsequent to the survey, the stadium proposal was rejected by the city council. Although the survey was not the only reason for its demise, it was certainly a major factor

IMPACT ASSESSMENT

Surveys are also conducted to assess policy outcomes. People may be surveyed about whether they are aware of a public advertisement, if they have every used a revamped service, or if they are satisfied or dissatisfied with a new or ongoing program. The premise is that the capacity of a political system to respond to the preferences of its citizens is central to democratic theory and practice. From a democratic perspective, it may not really matter if a policy is effective or efficient, but instead the issue is whether or not it satisfies some segment of the public according to the results of a survey.

The evaluation of the Drug Abuse Resistance Education (D.A.R.E) program is a good example of how surveys trump other methodologies in the assessment of impact. The D.A.R.E. program involves specially trained, uniformed police officers giving lessons to elementary school students (typically, eight to twelve year olds) on how to resist drugs. By employing law enforcement officers to teach the curriculum, D.A.R.E. brings the firsthand accounts of the officers' experiences from the street to the classroom. The lessons provide factual information about drugs, with an emphasis on gateway drugs (marijuana, alcohol, and tobacco), and teach refusal skills through role-playing and other techniques. When it comes to evaluation of D.A.R.E, cost-benefit studies have consistently found it to be inefficient, and quasiexperimental designs have concluded it is not that effective in preventing young people from using drugs (Lynman et al. 1999). Nonetheless, the program survives in school districts because surveys consistently find parents, teachers, administrators, and students are satisfied with its performance. For example, a 1995 survey of 1,800 parents, teachers, and D.A.R.E. graduates in Illinois found the program was valuable and worth maintaining. Over 92 percent rated it "very good" or "good." This impact assessment is reported on the D.A.R.E Web site (2004), which, when combined with other similar surveys, is a rationale for the program's continuing presence in public schools.

THE MISUSE OF SURVEYS

The fact that surveys are used all the time does not mean they are perfect. Surveys have three problems: (1) surveys are frequently completed that are methodologically flawed, (2) surveys are regularly conducted that are politically biased, and (3) surveys are used inappropriately as a substitute for other forms of democratic engagement.

SURVEY FLAWS

It is not easy to create the perfect survey, perhaps it is impossible. It is all together too easy to find surveys with unrepresentative samples comprised of a small number of people who choose to participate, abysmally low response rates, highly ambiguous questions, ill-defined words in the questionnaire, responses to complex subjects limited to yes and no answers, and statistics that provide percentages, but not the actual number of people who responded to the questions. The fact is that anyone can conduct a survey, without any expertise whatsoever, and there is no survey police to hall bad researchers away. The penalty for poor research is to critique the analysis, which happens only occasionally, or to ignore the results, which happens all the time.

An example of a poorly constructed survey is a needs assessment conducted by the Los Angles Downtown Women's Action Coalition in 2001, the purpose of which was to understand the problems confronting homeless women on Skid Row. One question asked, "Overall, how would you rate the treatment you received from the staff of the various missions, shelters, and social services agencies of the Skid Row area?" The response categories were: (1) very good, (2) good, (3) average, (4) poor, (5) very poor, and (6) no opinion. The problem with the question is that it is actually three questions: one about missions, another about shelters, and third about social service agencies. The question also does not define what is meant by staff and it assumes the respondents are in agreement on where Skid Row is located. In addition, the response categories are indistinctive; is it really possible to distinguish between very good and good, or very poor and poor? The survey sample was 399, but no effort was made to show whether it was representative of the population of homeless women. The survey was completed on only one day in the summer, so it is impossible to know if there are were any seasonal variations in the opinions of the women. Simply put, the survey had many methodological flaws, although that did not stop the Coalition from publicizing the results and citing them in policy-making forums. Perhaps the methodology was not that important because the results confirmed the Coalition's advocacy work on behalf of homeless women in Los Angles.

Survey Bias

Surveys can be methodologically sound, yet biased. A tendency in policy analysis is for surveys to be created for no other reason than to rationalize, advocate, and attack public policies. In other words, surveys in policy analysis are often more political instruments than scientific endeavors. Does anyone really believe that someone with a conservative ideology would ever produce a survey that shows parents are not satisfied with school voucher programs? Has the American Association of Retired Persons (AARP) once presented statistics showing a general opposition for seniors to buy cheap drugs in Canada? Would the Sierra Club really undertake a survey to prove that most people do not believe sprawl is a major problem? It is obvious why President George W. Bush in 2004 cited a survey that showed 70 percent of Iraqis supported his policies and equally obvious why he rejected a survey that found 70 percent of Europeans were opposed to his policies.

The space between objectivity and subjectivity is ephemeral. For example, the New Haven, Connecticut Town Green District conducted a survey in 1999 with 900 surveys mailed or hand delivered to property owners and businesses, resulting in 131 responses for a response rate of 15 percent, which the district proudly noted in a newsletter was a 173 percent increase in responses over the previous year's survey. To the question—"Are you generally pleased with the impact that the Town Green has had on downtown?"—71.8 percent said "yes" and 6.9 percent said "no." To the question, "Do you see/feel a positive change downtown since the creation of the district in January 1997?"—70.2 percent said "yes" and 7.6 percent said "no." It stretches common sense to think the Town Green District would have ever conducted a survey that found over 70 percent in the no category for either of these questions. It seems apparent that this survey was more about advocacy than an empirical description of public opinion.

Undemocratic Surveys

A final issue in survey research is the presumption that the best measure of any public policy is to have a set of responses to survey questions. In effect, responding to surveys has become a substitute for other forms of forms of democratic engagement—attending public hearings, writing letters to public officials, and voting in elections. A survey is one of a few ways that citizens can express their views about alternative garbage disposals methods in a locality or a proposal in a state to reduce a budget deficit by issuing bonds and reducing services. The assumption is that surveys are a corrective to the influence of rich elites and professional interest groups in the policy process. Other than voting, surveys are one of the few opportunities for the disadvantaged and people with busy lives to analyze and shape public policy. There is even a sense that the act of being interviewed might reduce a citizen's feeling of alienation from politics and government (Benson 1981; Web and Hatry 1973).

One problem with the use of surveys to reflect democracy is the low cost and benefits to those being interviewed (Berinsky 2004). Respondents do not contact pollsters, but instead pollsters and their political sponsors assume the costs of participation by contacting people and mobilizing them into a limited form of political action. But this only half of the equation, answering polls is also a low-benefit activity. Respondents are no better off at the beginning of an interview than at the end. In effect, to use surveys in the policy process is to rely on the lowest common denominator of democratic participation.

Another problem is that not all respondents react the same to questionnaires. Consequently, surveys tend to reinforce social inequality. Few surveys are multilingual and most require the respondents to be familiar with processing bureaucratic information. All kinds of people are excluding from survey research, such as children, people in institutions (prisons, hospitals, etc.), and individuals who for one reason or another lack the time or interest to answer survey questions. When it comes to telephone interviews, households without phone service are excluded, thereby devaluing the opinions of those with lower incomes, less stable jobs, and fewer group and community attachments (O'Sullivan, Rassal, and Bermer 2004). It is doubtful that a telephone survey on housing policy would be meaningful if it excluded those without telephones.

Polls tend to include mostly people who like putting forth their opinions about issues. There is an argument that understanding the public interest should be more than counting the opinions of individuals who enjoy giving their views on everything and anything. In fact, one of the ideas of representative democracy is that elected officials and public administrators have a responsibility to understand the silent majority. The intent of surveys is surely not to force people to have opinions. There are many policy issues when people do not have enough information to make an informed assessment. Most Americans have heard of the No Child Left Behind Act, for instance, but nearly seven in ten say they don't know enough to form an opinion about the educational initiative of the federal government.

A final problem is that surveys tend to boil complicated issues down to the level of platitudes, catch phrases, and easy to answer questions. Is it really good for democracy to think about public policy in the most simple of terms? Simplistic surveys may do nothing more than produce a convoluted mishmash of ideas and opinions that don't indicate anything other than most people are confused. Consider, for example, a *Harris Poll* conducted online in 2002 among a nationwide sample of 2,118 adults. The data was weighted to be representative of all U.S. adults. The poll found:

- Almost everyone, 93 percent of all adults, support "the United States continuing to fight...the war on terrorism in order to kill or capture those who planned or supported the attacks...on September 11th."
- When it comes to U.S. support for other countries fighting against their terrorists, the public is much more equivocal. Modest majorities favor U.S. support for Israel (63%) and Britain in Northern Ireland (56%). The public is almost equally divided as to whether the U.S. government should support the Indian government, the Russian government or the Spanish government against those attacking them in Kashmir, Chechnya and the Basque region. And most people oppose U.S. support for the Chinese government in Tibet (68%) or for "undemocratic, totalitarian or military dictatorships" (64%).

- A 58 percent majority of all adults believes that "the use of bombs and guns against...governments that do not give their people the right to decide their own future by free democratic elections" can be justified.
- A 57 percent majority of the public says they "think of people fighting to overthrow dictatorial, military or undemocratic governments" as freedom fighters, and only 11 percent think of them as terrorists.
- When the government is bad enough, almost everyone thinks that the use of bombs and guns against the government is justified. When told of the attempt by German officers to bomb and kill Hitler during World War II, fully 89 percent of adults say that "it is morally justified to kill people if you have no other way to fight against a really bad government or leader."

The conclusion of this poll is that the public is confused about what is and is not terrorism. It is unclear how this information helps policy makers or, for that matter, how it helped the people who responded. Terrorism is a complicated subject that requires thinking about many events in human history, weighing the advantages and disadvantages of various forms of participation in different contexts, and understanding a wide range of human behaviors. It is difficult to comprehend how simplifying reality through a series of questions that yield conflicting results will ever contribute to the improvement of public policy, one of the obvious goals of policy analysis.

CONCLUSION

The fact that there are problems with the use of surveys does not mean they should be removed from the policy process. What is needed is more careful consideration of how they are used and a better sense of the ways they can be misused. Simply put, knowledge is key to the key to good utilization. In this regard, educators must spend more effort to examine surveys in policy analysis textbooks and in college classrooms. Academics should be especially cognizant of how they report survey results in professional journals because they are implicitly setting standards for how to judge the worth of surveys conducted in the world of politics and administration. When presenting the findings of survey research, it is incumbent on everyone to be thorough in the description of their methodology. Thoroughness may go along way to eliminating mistakes, exposing bias, and indicating how the results should be used. A survey report that details how questions were asked, notes all aspects of the sampling procedure, and explains the statistics analysis will be much more likely to be utilized and understood. And when the elements of survey research are followed closely and the problems with survey research are avoided, the use of surveys in policy analysis will be less Neanderthal and more likely to lead to good public policy.

REFERENCES

Benson, Paul R. (1981). Political Alienation and Public Satisfaction With Police Services. *Pacific Sociological Review* 24(1): 45–64.
Berinsky, Adam J. (2004). *Silent Voices: Public Opinion and Political Participation*. Princeton, NJ: Princeton University Press.
Christenson, James A., and Gregory S. Taylor. (1983). The Socially Constructed And Situational Context For Assessment of Public Services. *Social Science Quarterly* 64(2): 264–274.
Dillman, Don. (2000). *Mail and Internet Surveys: The Tailored Design Method*. New York: Wiley.
Downtown Women's Action Coalition. (2001). *Downtown Women's Needs Assessment: Findings and Recommendations*.
Glaser, Mark A., and John W. Bardo. (1994). A Five Stage Approach For Improved Use of Citizen Surveys in Public Investment Decisions. *State and Local Government Review* 26(3): 161–172.

Green, Josuha. (2002). The Other War Room: President Bush Doesn't Believe in Polling—Just Ask his Pollsters. *The Washington Monthly*, (April).

Harris Poll. (2004). http://www.harrrispoll.com.

Kelly, Janet, and David Swindell. (2002). A Multiple-Indicator Approach To Municipal Service Evaluation: Correlating Performance Measurement and Citizen Satisfaction Across Jurisdictions. *Public Administration Review* 62(5): 610–621.

Lynam, Donald R., Richard Milich, Rick Zimmerman, Scott P. Novak, T. K. Logan, Catherine Martin, Carl Leukefeld, and Richard Clayton. (1999). Project DARE: No Effects at 10-Year Follow-Up. *Journal of Consulting and Clinical Psychology* 67, No. 4 (August): 590–593.

Miller, Thomas L., and Michelle A. Miller-Kobayahsi. (2000). *Citizen Surveys: How To Do Them, How To Use Them, What They Mea*n. Washington, DC: International City Management Association.

Nardi, Peter M. (2003). *Doing Survey Research: A Guide to Quantitative Methods*. New York: Longman.

O'Sullivan, Elizabethann, Gary R. Rassal, and Maureen Berner. (2004). *Research Methods for Public Administrators*. New York: Longman.

Posavac, Emil J., and Raymond G. Carey. (2003). *Program Evaluation: Methods and Cases*. Upper Saddle River, NJ: Prentice Hall.

Project D.A.R.E. (2004). http://www.dare.com.

St. Paul Pioneer Press. (2001). Little Support for Public Financing for Twins' Stadium, (November 1), Internet edition.

Swindell, David, and Janet Kelly. (2000). Linking Citizen Satisfaction Data to Performance Measures. *Public Performance & Management Review* 24(1): 30–52.

Thompson, Lyke. (1997). Citizen Attitudes about Service Delivery Modes. *Journal of Urban Affairs* 19(3): 291–302.

Weimer, David L. Weimer, and Aidan R. Vining. (2005). *Policy Analysis: Concepts and Practices.* New York: Prentice Hall.

Webb, Kenneth, and Harry P. Hatry, H. (1973). *Obtaining Citizen Feedbac*k. Washington, DC: The Urban Institute Press.

25 Social Experiments and Public Policy

Caroline Danielson

INTRODUCTION

Social experiments randomly assign people (or sometimes sets of people, i.e., neighborhoods or communities) either to a group that is subject to one or more policy "treatments" or to one that continues to be subject to the prevailing policy norm ("controls"). For example, a social experiment might test the efficacy of a welfare-to-work program by randomly assigning welfare applicants to the new program (perhaps an intensive, coached job search combined with the provision of services like transportation assistance and subsidized child care) and to the old standard, which leaves the initiative to find a job nearly completely up to the welfare recipient.[1]

It is standard for those who conduct experiments to make the claim that theirs is the only methodology that can with certainty isolate the impact of the program under evaluation. Social experiments alone can assure that "any differences that emerge over time in employment, earnings, or other relevant outcomes can reliably be attributed to the program" (Berlin 2002, 3). Yet this is not simply a claim that circulates in the research community. Social experiments also hold the respect of those crafting social policy (Baum 1991; Greenberg, Linksz, and Mandell 2003; Greenberg, Mandell, and Onstott 2000; Haskins 1991). Social experiments generate this respect because they appear to offer a readily-accessible, incontrovertible answer to the most pressing question in evaluation research: does X program cause Y outcome?[2]

In this chapter, I examine the key factors that make social experiments attractive to both researchers and policy makers. These features of social experiments seem worth exploring because there appears to be a consensus among researchers and policy makers that experiments constitute a gold standard in policy evaluation. To the extent that this consensus exists, it removes one obstacle to the application of social science research to policy making. Social experimentation promises to be a rigorous, straightforward arbiter among political choices—a method well-suited to the division of labor that leaves the choice of ends to policy makers and the evaluation of means to technical experts.

Such a consensus clearly does not imply that only evidence from social experiments will be used in the policy process, or even that any research at all will guide policy making. The literature describing the actual use of research in policy making is also extensive. Greenberg, Linksz, and Mandell (2003) explore the influence of social experiments in the welfare policy arena on state policy makers, and Weaver (1999) examines the role of policy research in the debates on "ending

---

1. I use examples from the arena of welfare policy to illustrate principles and pitfalls of social experiments; however, social experiments are also used in other social policy arenas, including crime, education, and health. For a list of major social experiments conducted in the United States, see Greenberg and Shroder (2004).

2. I focus on tests of the efficacy of a program, although experimental data can be turned to other purposes—for instance, computing cost-benefit calculations.

welfare as we know it" that occurred in the 1990s. Aaron and Todd (1979) reports on the influence of earlier social experiments on policy. For examples of other research examining more generally the use of social science research in policymaking (see Danziger 2001; Haveman 1976; Hird 2005; Jones 1976; Lindblom and Cohen 1979; Rich 2001; Shulock 1999; Stone 1997; Szanton, 1981). Obviously, legislators can choose whether to request, or to use, social scientific research to evaluate policy proposals although their choices are constrained by the prevailing norms regarding the applicability of research to policy development and evaluation. This chapter will examine key aspects of the prevailing norms regarding social experiments.

A number of important aspects of social experiments have been discussed extensively elsewhere: technical issues (e.g., selective attrition, determining the effect of the treatment), the definition of treatments (are only certain types of policies tested? are programs tested in an intensive enough way?), and the practicalities of running experiments (obtaining the committed participation of agencies that implement policies, adequately getting the message across). Recent discussions include Gennetian et al. (2002), Grogger and Karoly (2005), Haveman (1987), Heckman in Manski and Garfinkel (1992), Lalonde (1995), and Orr (1999).

I focus here on unpacking two accepted aspects of experiments that make them attractive to policy makers: their ability to isolate causes and their methodological transparency. Experiments offer these virtues, but not in an unqualified way: they are not a complete recipe for policy evaluation. I also take up ethical questions that social experiments pose. I argue that the absence of a real debate over ethics is more evidence that social experiments are an established methodology from the point of view of both researchers and policy makers. My argument is in line with other discussions of the ways in which methodology can take precedence over substantive debates about the ends that democratic societies seek to achieve and the permissible means that they can use to achieve them (Fischer 1990; Fischer 2003; Stone 1993).

After sketching the history of social experiments in the next section and summarizing essentials of conducting experiments in the third, I take up the primary intellectual attraction of experiments in the fourth—their ability to isolate the program from other events that shape subjects' outcomes—and in the fifth I discuss a central political attraction of experiments—what I call their transparency. In the sixth section I review standard ethical justifications of social experimentation.

EVOLUTION OF SOCIAL EXPERIMENTATION

Greenberg, Linksz, and Mandell (2003) review the history of social experiments and *The Digest of Social Experiments* describes all social experiments conducted to-date in the United States (Greenberg and Shroder 2004). When large-scale social experiments were first proposed in the 1960s, they were a departure from the normal practice of policy research. Evidence of this is that organizational capacity had to be built to handle the new demand: the Manpower Demonstration Research Corporation (now simply MDRC) a non-profit, non-partisan research organization, with seed funding from the Ford Foundation, was purpose-built in the early 1970s to conduct the National Supported Work Demonstration (Gueron 2000; Manski and Garfinkel 1992).[3] A handful of other organizations also retooled to undertake experiments (e.g., Mathematica Policy Research, Abt Associates, Rand, organized research units at a few large universities). The scale and scope of cooperation between civilian agencies and researchers was also unprecedented.

Haveman (1987) notes that poverty research, and the organizations capable of training researchers and carrying out the research, were fundamentally shaped by the War on Poverty, which provided the funding and the federal agency loci to stimulate policy research in this field. The *Digest*

---

3. The Ford Foundation also funded the development of several public policy schools (Haveman 1987), presumably to develop capacity to conduct rigorous, policy-relevant research.

of Social Experiments reveals that the majority of social experiments have been conducted with poor populations as subjects in program areas that include health, employment, and education and training (see Greenberg and Shroder 2004).

The first social experiment, the New Jersey Negative Income Tax Experiment (NIT), was conducted by Mathematica under contract from the University of Wisconsin's Institute for Research on Poverty. This experiment had several treatment groups, each of which was subject to a different combination of a minimum guaranteed income and a tax rate on income earned above the guarantee. The core aim was to test whether adults would reduce their hours of work if they knew they were guaranteed a minimum income. According to an observer, it was not obvious that experimentally altering individual's incomes was ethical. Conducting the New Jersey NIT was justified on the grounds that there was no other way to obtain answers to the question of individuals' responses to a guaranteed income (Haveman 1987).

It is important to realize that experiments were first intended to be used in conjunction with simulation to provide a way of projecting the impact of a broad range of policies. According to Haveman (1987), writing after the first wave of social experimentation in the 1970s had ended, a goal of all of these experiments was to estimate structural parameters like the behavioral response (expressed, for instance, in hours of work) to manipulations of income by tax policy. That is, so long as the assumption could be maintained that individuals' behavior in response to incentives like additional income was constant across time and place and varied smoothly, an experiment that assigned groups to several gradations of tax policy treatments could be used to estimate the impact of a whole range of tax policies on hours of work.

According to economist James Heckman, however, as the NIT experiment in particular progressed, its aims grew more constrained: it came to be to compute the mean impacts of the program (Heckman in Manski and Garfinkel 1992). Instead of one or several experiments providing the raw material that would enable researchers to simulate behavioral responses to a range of hypothetical policies, an experiment would supply simply the difference in outcomes between the treatment and the control group for the policy or policies under study. This type of experiment gets called a "black-box" experiment because researchers make no strong claims about the underlying causes of the outcomes; their focus is on reporting the results of a particular policy treatment.

The scaling back of researchers' ambitions had partly to do with technical difficulties in collecting data adequate to the task of simulating responses to a range of hypothetical policies. The results of the NIT, in particular, were not as clean as expected. Apparently the implied responses to different tax policies the researchers computed relied on self-reported, and therefore incomplete, income data as well as on the experimental data, and the computations did not produce a smooth pattern of responses. But dropping this more theory-laden approach to experiments perhaps also betrays the insight that a more easily-communicated approach is more compelling to policy makers. Black-box experiments report the outcome, attribute it to the treatment, and stop there.

The goal in conducting social experiments has decidedly shifted to estimating mean impacts of the treatment (Greenberg, Linksz, and Mandell 2003). It is this way of setting up social experiments that has won the approbation of policy makers and that backs confident statements that organizations like MDRC make about the methodological rigor of experimental evaluations. As the then president of MDRC has stated, "With random assignment, you can know something with much greater certainty and, as a result, can more confidently separate fact from advocacy" (Gueron 2000, 1).

The sense that black-box experiments are the gold standard of evaluation research had developed by the late 1980s. According to those pivotal in developing the legislative language for the 1988 overhaul of the Aid to Families with Dependent Children (AFDC) program, Family Support Act (FSA), experimental evidence from a number of welfare-to-work projects that MDRC was conducting played a decisive role (Baum 1991; Haskins 1991). This was the case for a number of reasons (fortuitous timing, MDRC's ability to both disseminate results widely and in a timely fashion and to maintain a non-partisan stance), but included the absence of debate among researchers about the outcomes and the concomitant respect that the methodology commanded. The FSA included provision for the evaluation of its effects using randomized experiments.

A few years later, a little-used provision of Title IV-A, Section 413 of the Social Security Act stating that federal requirements for AFDC could be waived by the Secretary of the US Department of Health and Human Services was exploited to allow states broadly to experiment with their AFDC programs in the early- and mid-1990s. Section 413 states that "The Secretary may assist States in developing, and shall evaluate, innovative approaches for reducing welfare dependency and increasing the well-being of minor children living at home". It continues, "In performing the[se] evaluation[s]…, the Secretary shall, to the maximum extent feasible, use random assignment as an evaluation methodology" (42 U.S.C. 613).

While obtaining approval for waivers to existing AFDC program regulations apparently became quite straightforward by the mid-1990s—the Clinton administration did not want to be perceived as obstructing states' reform efforts—the Administration for Children and Families did typically require states to perform randomized experimental evaluations of their programs, a requirement that produced a wealth of data that would not otherwise exist. Forty-three states obtained waivers between January 1993 and August 1996, although not every state actually implemented its waiver program (Boehnen and Corbett 1996; Gordon, Jacobson, and Fraker 1996). With this impetus, a large number of social experiments was initiated in the 1990s.[4] One might say, then, that the early- and mid-1990s marked a high point in policy evaluation because of the widespread use of experimental methodology.

Although the pace of experimentation has since slowed in the welfare policy arena, commentators continue to call for experimental evaluations of policy proposals newly on the national agenda. For example, a policy brief published by the Brookings Institution endorses experimental evaluations of government programs to encourage marriage as a means of defusing controversy over their appropriateness—if programs that encourage couples to marry raise marriage rates, then, presumably, concerns about intervening in individuals' private lives will diminish (Haskins and Offner 2003). At the same time, the case for experimental evaluation of policy proposals is building in other policy arenas. As evidenced by the language of the 2002 No Child Left Behind act policy makers are now advocating evaluations of policy proposals the field of education using experimental methodology (Glenn 2004; Mosteller and Boruch 2002).

NUTS AND BOLTS OF EXPERIMENTS

To conduct an experiment, researchers randomly assign some members of a target group to the program under study and some to the current program. The impact of the treatment is measured as the mean difference between the treatment and control groups on relevant measures (e.g., income, educational achievement, mental health). That is, how much more (or less) income did the treatment group earn at the end of the study period than the control group did? Or, how much higher (or lower) did the treatment group score on a standardized test administered to both groups?

Internal validity is the core methodological strength of experiments. Assigning members of a target group at random to treatment and control comparison groups ensures that they are statistically equivalent on both measured and unmeasured characteristics. Since adjustments can be made for differences on measured characteristics, the problem that other research methods face is their inability to methodologically rule out systematic differences between nonexperimental comparison

---

4. The evaluated programs include the Minnesota Family Investment Program (MFIP), Florida's Family Investment Program (FIP), Vermont's Welfare Restructuring Project (WRP), Arizona's EMPOWER program, Connecticut's Jobs First program, Iowa's Family Investment Program (FIP), and the Indiana Manpower Placement and Comprehensive Training Program (IMPACT).

groups on *unmeasured* characteristics.[5] Experiments make it possible to confidently assert that there are no differences (statistically speaking) between experimental comparison groups on unmeasured characteristics. Any differences between groups measured subsequently can therefore be confidently attributed to the treatment, within the bounds of certainty provided by statistics.

To insure the internal validity of experiments, researchers must successfully randomize participants between the test and the standard programs. This involves developing a protocol for initial randomization that is straightforward and not susceptible to manipulation by those implementing the protocol. It further involves ensuring that members of the control group do not cross over and obtain the program reserved for the treatment group. It also requires that members of the treatment group realized that they were subject to different program rules than the control group. For more extensive treatments of the practicalities of conducting experiments, see Boruch (1997), Hausman and Wise (1985), and Orr (1999).

It is important to be clear about what the outcomes that can be measured experimentally are. The experimental outcomes that can be measured depend on the point at which randomization occurred. For example, if some welfare recipients are assigned to have a limit on the number of months they are eligible to receive cash assistance and some are not, then the experimental outcomes that can be measured are in relationship to *exposure* to a time limit. For example, did those who were subject to a time limit find a job sooner than those who were not? Or, did they use fewer months of welfare over a particular period of time? The effect of the time limit on the income and well-being of those who reach it in the experimental group is not an experimental outcome, since the two groups were not randomly assigned to *reach* the time limit. It is possible to compare subgroups defined by initial characteristics of the treatment and control groups because the groups are (stastistically) identical on those measures. For example, it would be possible to compare the differences between long-term welfare recipients assigned to the groups subject and not subject to the time limit.

A related point is that experimental outcomes are measured as differences between those assigned to the program and those not assigned to it. The effect of the new program is often not identical to the impact measured by the experiment because not everyone gets the program. For example, some of those assigned to a treatment group that is eligible for a range of job search services will not avail themselves of any of the services, or of only some of them.[6] Finally, the impact of the program either on participants or on those randomized to be eligible for the program is not the identical to the impact on the population if the new program were to become policy because experiments typically do not randomly assign entire target populations to treatment and control groups. The first crucial point here is that a new program may very well change the applicant pool. For example, in the presence of time limits, some of those who would earlier immediately have applied for cash assistance when they experienced a job loss might hold out for a few months, realizing that they now only have a limited number of months of eligibility for cash aid.[7] The second is that if a new program is widely implemented, it may change the broader environment in which it operates (so-called "macro" effects) in ways that a small pilot program that is experimentally tested would not. For example, a job search program, if implemented for all welfare recipients, may alter the labor market for low-income workers, thus altering the effectiveness of the job search program.

---

5. Researchers using nonexperimental methods can argue that, for theoretical or practical reasons, it is unlikely that the comparison groups in question differ on unmeasured characteristics.

6. Random assignment experiments, under certain assumptions, have a built-in instrumental variables estimator that can be used to estimate the average effect of the treatment on the treated (Angrist et al., 1996; Gennetian et al., 2002).

7. While it would be possible to randomly assign a sample of the entire target population to treatment and control groups, it would be more expensive (and in many cases prohibitively so) because a large enough sample would have to be randomized in order to detect the effect of the treatment. The size of this sample would depend on the expected rate of application to the program among members of the target population.

CONCEPTION OF CAUSALITY

Here is a stripped-down version of the core question to which policy makers seek an answer when they commission a policy evaluation: If we implement X program, will Y outcome result (or, in the case of a program already implemented: Did X program produce Y outcome that we envisioned)? Policy evaluation is fundamentally a testing of means. Simplifying the real complexities of the process of policy making, one can say that policy makers seek to achieve an end. The ideal evaluation of a policy would answer the question, does one particular means as compared to another advance us toward that end?

Here is the question that social experiments address: On average, there was (or was not) a statistically significant difference (at conventional levels) between the outcomes of treatment group T and control group C on measure M (of outcome Y) in an experiment in which X program was tested. For example, if policy makers want to know whether a welfare-to-work program that emphasizes quick immersion into a process of searching for a job (X) improves child well-being (Y), researchers would design an experiment that randomly assigned some (T) to participate in a sequence of job search activities and others not (C). Child well-being (Y) might be measured, among other things, by surveying parents about problem behaviors their children might be exhibiting (M).

Is the question that policy makers implicitly pose identical to the question that researchers address? The central difference between the two questions posed above is generalizability. It seems clear from the way that the first query above is framed that policy makers are interested in a general result, or something resembling law-like behavior. If program X is funded, then Y outcome will always (or usually) obtain. But experiments tell us nothing directly about law-like behavior. Their methodological soundness comes exactly from their internal validity. That is, experiments are a powerful means of attributing the impact of the intervention, and not other factors, to the outcomes observed by researchers. Experiments accomplish this by posing a counterfactual: what would have happened had the program *not* existed? Thus researchers use experiments to identify causes using the evidence from unique occurrences, rather than that obtained from observing regularities or from logical deduction.[8]

Given policy makers' interest in the more general question, the natural inclination is to generalize. Thus a natural slippage occurs: researchers and policy makers treat the experiment as predictive of outcomes in other times and places that are "similar enough." But what counts as similar enough? What would the outlines of an argument that generalized from one particular experiment look like? There are two key elements: (1) identify the most important behavioral mechanisms that produced the result, and (2) identify key features of situations that make them enough like the experimental situation so that individuals placed in those like situations will interact with the context in the same manner that the experimental subjects did.

Because experiments take a black-box approach, they do not address the behavioral responses that the program may have induced (although researchers can and do use other methodologies to understand such mechanisms). And unlike researchers conducting laboratory experiments, those carrying out social experiments do not control the context in which the treatment and control group programs unfold. In this sense, they cannot rigorously specify the context. There is at least one strong reason to believe that experimental situations are exceptional: those who are "treated" are not blind to their situation, and those who administer the treatment often know the circumstances of the experiment—this is a crucial difference between double-blind medical trials where both treatment and control groups are treated and neither researcher nor subject knows who received the treatment and social experiments.

Those interpreting experimental impacts must make additional inferences in order to generalize beyond the particular instance, and they must do so on grounds other than the soundness of the

---

8. Max Weber (1949) developed this conception of causality.

internal validity of the experiment.[9] The causal question to which policy makers seek an answer thus differs crucially from the question that researchers answer by conducting a social experiment.

METHODOLOGICAL TRANSPARENCY

Perhaps experiments must be interpreted with caution because they do not unpack causal mechanisms and because conclusions drawn from them do not extend in a straightforward fashion to programs put in place in other contexts. But as freestanding exercises, experiments have the virtue of employing a methodology that is more readily grasped than other evaluation methodologies. In addition, experiments are attractive because they promise to sidestep the debates of "dueling witch doctors" that heighten the politicization of policy debates: when technical experts disagree, it undermines the credibility of the policy proposal (Baum 1991).

The promise that social experiments make of a more immediate, incontrovertible truth than other research methodologies offer appears to rest on two factors. First, grasping the essentials of social experiments seems to require no arcane technical training inaccessible to policy makers and their advisors. Second, and relatedly, the outcomes of experiments are not murky: experiments reliably allow observers to sharply distinguish between programs that worked and those that had no effect on outcomes of interest.

One might complain that a key test of a social scientific methodology in the policy arena should not be its (apparent) lack of technical complexity, but this complaint would be misplaced. Garfinkel, Manski, and Michalopoulos claim that social experiments receive funding preference over basic research in the social sciences because policy makers are unable to interpret the disputes that social scientists enter into over the results of quasi-experimental research (in Manski and Garfinkel 1992). But when, for example, engineers and biologists are hired by policy makers, they produce proof of the viability (or lack thereof) of their efforts: an unmanned air vehicle that can track a highway, a fly-sized drone that collects photographic evidence. Social scientists in general face precisely the problem that they cannot produce tangible proof that social programs are working without simultaneously justifying and explaining the methodology by which they arrived at their conclusions. That is, a welfare-to-work program must be shown to be effective; it is not evident from simple observation whether the program increased subjects' hours of work or not.

There is, in fact, a large literature on subtle technicalities of experimentation. These subtleties range from the step of the program at which randomization occurs (experimental differences must be measured in relationship to this step) to the difference between intention to treat and the effect of the treatment to macro effects that experiments do not fully capture like information diffusion, norm formation and altered market equilibria.[10] These subtleties typically receive only scant attention when researchers communicate their results to policy makers (see, for example, Hamilton et al. 2001, ES-9; Beecroft et al. 2003, ii).

It is worth noting in this context that the experimental evaluations of welfare-to-work programs, among them those that so impressed the framers of the FSA in the late 1980s, have now been subject to several reanalyses that raise questions about the internal validity of the findings (Hotz, Imbens, and Klerman 2001; Walker et al. 2003). That is to say, there is debate among researchers about the outcomes of the very experiments that had such an influence on the formulation of the work-first approach in state reforms and eventually on the shape of the Temporary Assistance for Needy Families (TANF) program that replaced Aid to Families with Dependent Children (AFDC) in 1996. As is probably often the case, this scholarly debate took longer to mature than did the policy debate.

---

9. Other sorts of evaluation methodologies also pose problems for generalization. Manski (1995) addresses this issue in a broader sense.

10. For examples of these discussions, see Manski and Garfinkel 1992. See Haveman (1987) for a discussion of problems that the first set of social experiments shared.

In fact, it is plausible that the aims of social experiments and the manner in which their results are reported is heavily influenced by the desire to communicate in a transparent way. As I described in section two, economists' original aim for experimentation was to recover structural behavioral parameters that could be used to simulate the impact of arbitrary policies. But this more ambitious aim was quickly dropped, possibly partly because it was not compelling to policy makers.

Further, it might seem puzzling that experiments are typically agnostic about the outcome. Even if theory or intuition predicts that welfare recipients who receive job search assistance should find employment at a higher rate than those who do not, researchers perform a two-tailed hypothesis test (i.e., that the alternative hypothesis is the difference of means is equal to zero, not the difference of means is greater than zero).[11] This unwillingness to begin from theory is perhaps more evidence that experiments are meant to be transparent, or assumption-free. Alternatively, it is possibly evidence that researchers seek to be as conservative as possible.

Thus it might be fair to say that the way social experiments have been carried out has been influenced by policy makers' need for simplicity and clarity. But it would be misleading to state that experiments are simply methodologically transparent.

ETHICAL JUSTIFICATIONS

As I noted in the second section, conducting the first NIT experiment was acceptable because it was seen as a last resort: those who proposed it and those who supported its implementation could envision no other way of testing individuals' responses to a guaranteed minimum income. Social experiments must no longer meet this severe standard. They are now presumed to be appropriate: randomized trials are ethical except in special circumstances. For an example of the standard defense, see the statement by the then-president of MDRC (Gueron 2000): In short, resources can generally be presumed to limited, and as long as more people are potentially eligible for the program than can actually be served, random assignment is a fair way of allocating scarce resources. More fundamentally, random assignment is a means of determining whether programs benefit target populations or not. Both individual and social ends can be better achieved if only successful programs are pursued with government dollars.

Although it is apparent that not every situation of policy interest is susceptible to experimentation for ethical reasons, versions of random assignment seem to be. For example, it is not possible to imagine assigning children to parents, or education to children, even though it is vitally important to know how much difference family background, and how much education, makes to children's achievement. But it is possible to contemplate assigning parents to programs that increase their likelihood of developing positive relationships with one another and their children (Haskins and Offner 2003; Dion et al. 2003). While proposed programs are not identical to "assigning children to parents," the shaping of choices that these programs, if successful, would have in effect imply that some children will have relationships with parents that they would not otherwise have had.

It appears that they are presumed to be ethical because of aspects of the methodology employed. Researchers point out if resources are limited so that only a subset of applicants can be accommodated in the program, then random assignment—the core distinctiveness of social experiments—is a fair way of distributing the opportunity to participate, and is more fair than the most likely other means of allocating it (e.g., first come, first served). This argument can be challenged. Researchers must ensure that the treatment and control groups are large enough to produce reliable estimates of the impact of the program. Depending on the size of the program being evaluated, they may warn sponsors that evaluation sites will need to ramp up recruitment efforts in order to enroll enough subjects to randomize (see, e.g., Dion et al. 2003). In such situations, everyone who sought the service or program being evaluated could be accommodated, and it is the experiment that produces

---

11. There are also standard phrases to repeat here—Type I error, Type II error, replication—I will just note them here in passing. They also bear on the reliability of the distinction made in crucial ways.

the need to deny some access.

In cases where programs are mandatory for all applicants, or are open to all who request it, random assignment can be thought of as a fair way of assigning recipients to programs of unknown efficacy. That is, if it is unknown whether the old or the new program produces better outcomes, a social experiment can determine whether the new program should continue. Once the experiment has run its course, the knowledge that it produces will benefit all future applicants. Note that if experiments are the gold standard, then it is tautologically true that the program's effects are not known—at least not with any credibility—in the absence of one or several social experiments conducted to establish the efficacy of the program.[12]

It is also the case that, in the United States, the provision of social supports are typically not seen as rights and poor people are not taken to be a group that requires special protections. Just as the government can grant or withhold tax relief at will, denying an individual access to a program to which she does not have a strong claim, even if comparable others do have access to the program, poses a weak ethical dilemma. This ethical dilemma is further weakened by an individualist ethic. Social experiments do not deny individuals access to services that they might desire because those in the control group can often, through their own initiative, acquire the education or job search assistance that the experimental program provides to some.

In these ways it has become easy to justify random experiments as an evaluation tool for any program that Congress or a state legislature might decide to authorize. Randomization to be eligible for (temporary) income supplements, to have time-limited welfare benefits, and to receive job search assistance have all recently passed muster. So while on the ground there are apparently ethical qualms about assigning participants to treatment and control groups that are serious enough to cause agencies to refuse to participate in experiments—see , for example, Gueron (2000)—the research community's justifications for experimentation makes clear that researchers see no serious ethical barriers to randomization in a broad range of instances. To an extent, social experiments are even treated as establishing a baseline for the ethical evolution of social policy: random assignment is a fair means of allocating scarce resources and experiments can tell us which programs help, and which harm, target populations.

There is a related question that is a natural follow-on for those who promote social policy evaluation via experimentation: Why does a society aim to understand the effects of programs on outcomes? A straightforward answer is that its members seek to improve the lot of disadvantaged groups. Since social programs can appear promising without in fact producing intended effects, evaluating their effects again makes sense, and social experiments are the most reliable means of evaluating their effects.[13]

In this sense, the ethical question has been turned on its head: Is it ethical to assign (or even invite) individuals to participate in programs *without* knowing whether the treatment has the intended effect? After all, social choices are about achieving ends. While they may limit permissible means, programs like TANF are primarily aimed at achieving certain outcomes (broadly speaking, ameliorating the lot of children in poor families). Social experiments are a means of achieving social ends by helping to determine which programs further social goals Without delving into mechanisms for social choice and their justifications, it appears to be at least possible to assert that research methodologies that seek to isolate the impact of programs on participants advance social choice-making by advancing the achievement of social ends like that of improving the well-being

---

12. Because of the large number of factors outside of the control of those orchestrating the experiment, it is probably quite difficult to replicate a social experiment. All the same, the argument in favor of replication does not lose its punch: as is the case with all research that relies on statistics, experimental impacts are subject to random error. Then the questions becomes: at what point do researchers decide that they know whether the program works or not, and thus whether this ethical justification for randomization still holds?

13. See O'Connor (2001) for the claim that poverty research focuses narrowly on individual circumstances and behaviors instead of on the social and economic opportunities that these individuals face.

of low-income children.[14] Social experiments achieve particularly high marks in this regard because it is accepted that they are methodologically rigorous.

The ethical questions posed by experimentation are no longer ones that set up serious obstacles to the implementation of experiments because the technical merit of experimentation is unquestioned. A number of researchers have explored different aspects of the push toward neutral, efficient decision-making in the policy arena, often noting a link to anti-democratic practices (Fischer 1990; Fischer 2003; Stone 1993). Fischer (1990) argues that the objective of technocrats is to remove as many decisions from the political arena as possible, shifting them into the arena of administration. In the case of social experiments, it appears that placing faith in their methodological virtues has allowed policy makers to largely finesse ethical questions.

CONCLUSIONS

To recap, social experiments appear to offer three core strengths: fairness, simplicity, and rigor. Random assignment offers a fair way (perhaps the most fair way) of allocating scarce resources, no special training is required to grasp the essentials of the method, and experiments reliably isolate "the program" from other factors influencing subjects' outcomes thus informing policy makers how to further social ends. Experiments do possess these virtues, but they do not possess them in an unqualified way. I have argued that, in fact, the conclusions that can be drawn from social experiments, like other evaluation methodologies, rest on crucial assumptions, and they have important limitations. The manner in which social experimentation has evolved in the United States has reduced the apparent complexities of evaluating social policies, but it has not actually erased them. Policy makers would do well to keep these complexities and limitations in view, even as they point to the strengths of experimentation. Finally, the fact that experiments are methodologically attractive should not be a reason to sideline ethical questions.

REFERENCES

Aaron, Henry J., and John Todd. 1979. "The Use of Income Maintenance Experiment Findings in Public Policy, 1977–78." *Industrial Relations Research Association Proceedings, 1979.* Madison, WI: IRRA.

Angrist, Joshua D., Guido W. Imbens, and Donald B. Rubin. 1996. "Identification of Causal Effects Using Instrumental Variables." *Journal of the American Statistical Association* 91(434, June): 444–455.

Baum, Erica. 1991. "When the Witch Doctors Agree: The Family Support Act and Social Science Research." *Journal of Policy Analysis and Management* 10(Fall): 603–615.

Beecroft, Erik, Wang Lee, and David Long. 2003. *The Indiana Welfare Reform Evaluation: Five-Year Impacts, Implementation, Costs and Benefits.* Cambridge, MA: Abt Associates, September.

Berlin, Gordon L. 2002. "Encouraging Work, Reducing Poverty: The Impact of Work Incentive Programs." New York: Manpower Demonstration Research Corporation, March.

Boehnen, Elisabeth, and Corbett, Thomas. 1996. "Welfare Waivers: Some Salient Trends." *Focus* 18(1): 34–41.

Boruch, Robert F. 1997. *Randomized Experiments for Planning and Evaluation: A Practical Guide.* Thousand Oaks, CA: Sage.

Brady, Henry E., Nancy Nicosia, and Eva Y. Seto. 2002. "Establishing Causality in Welfare Research: Theory Application. Unpublished Manuscript.

Burtless, Gary. 1995. "The Case for Randomized Field Trials in Economic and Policy Research. *The Journal of Economic Perspectives* 9(2, Spring): 63–84.

Danziger, Sheldon. 2001. "Welfare Reform from Nixon to Clinton: What Role for Social Science?" In *Social*

---

14. For a critical review of some issues in social choice literature, see Sen 1982.

Science and Policy-Making: The Search for Relevance in the Twentieth Century. D. L. Featherman and M. A. Vinoviskis, eds. Ann Arbor: University of Michigan Press, 137–164.

Dion, M. Robin, Barbara Devaney, Sheena McConnell, Melissa Ford, Heather Hill, and Pamela Winston. 2003. "Helping Unwed Parents Build Strong and Health Marriages: A Conceptual Framework for Interventions. Final Report submitted to the Administration for Children and Families, US DHHS, January.

Fischer, Frank. 1990. *Technocracy and the Politics of Expertise*. Newbury Park, CA: Sage.

Fischer, Frank. 2003. *Reframing Public Policy: Discursive Politics and Deliberative Practices*. Oxford: Oxford University Press.

Gennetian, Lisa A., Johannes M. Bos, and Pamela A. Morris. 2002. "Using Instrumental Variables Analysis to Learn More from Social Policy Experiments." MDRC Working Papers on Research Methodology. New York: Manpower Demonstration Research Corporation, October.

Glenn, David. 2004. "No Classroom Left Unstudied." *Chronicle of Higher Education* 50(38): A12.

Gordon, Anne, Jonathan Jacobson, and Thomas Fraker. 1996. "Approaches to Evaluating Welfare Reform: Lessons from Five State Demonstrations." Cambridge, MA: Mathematica Policy Research, October.

Greenberg, David and Mark Shroder. 2004. *The Digest of Social Experiments* (3rd ed.). Washington, D.C.: Urban Institute Press.

Greenberg, David, Donna Linksz, and Marvin Mandell. 2003. *Social Experimentation and Public Policymaking*. Washington, D.C.: The Urban Institute Press.

Greenberg, David, Marvin Mandell, and Matthew Onstott. 2000. "The Dissemination and Utilization of Welfare-to-Work Experiments in State Policymaking." *Journal of Policy Analysis and Management*. 19(3): 367–382.

Grogger, Jeffrey and Lynn A. Karoly. 2005. *Welfare Reform: Effects of a Decade of Change*. Cambridge, MA: Harvard University Press.

Gueron, Judith M. 2000. "The Politics of Random Assignment: Implementing Studies and Impacting Policy. New York: Manpower Demonstration Research Corporation.

Gueron, Judith M. 2003. Fostering Research Excellence and Impacting Policy and Practice: The Welfare Reform Story. *Journal of Policy Analysis and Management* 22(2, Winter): 163–174.

Gueron, Judith M. "Learning About Welfare Reform: Lessons from State-Based Evaluations." *New Directions for Evaluation* 76 (Winter 1997):79–94.

Hamilton, Gayle, Stephen Freedman, Lisa Gennetian, Charles Michalopoulos, Johanna Walter, Diana Adams-Ciardullo, and Anna Gassman-Pines. 2001. "National Evaluation of Welfare-to-Work Strategies: How Effective Are Different Welfare-to-Work Approaches? Five-Year Adult and Child Impacts for Eleven Programs." New York: MDRC, December.

Haskins, Ron, and Paul Offner. 2003. "Achieving Compromise on Welfare Reform Reauthorization." Policy Brief: Welfare Reform and Beyond #25. Washington, D.C.: The Brookings Institution, May.

Haskins, Ron. 1991. "Congress Writes a Law: Research and Welfare Reform." *Journal of Policy Analysis and Management* 10(4, Fall): 616–32.

Hausman, Jerry, and David Wise, eds. 1985. *Social Experimentation*. Chicago: University of Chicago Press for National Bureau of Economic Research.

Haveman, Robert H. 1987. *Poverty Policy and Poverty Research: The Great Society and the Social Sciences*. Madison, WI: University of Wisconsin Press.

Haveman, Robert. 1976. "Policy Analysis and the Congress: An Economist's View." *Policy Analysis* 2: 235–250.

Heckman, James J. and Jeffrey A. Smith. 1995. "Assessing the Case for Social Experiments." *The Journal of Economic Perspectives* 9(2, Spring): 85–110.

Hird, John A. 2005. "Policy Analysis for What? The Effectiveness of Nonpartisan Policy Research Organizations." *Policy Studies Journal* 33(1, February): 83–105.

Hotz, V. Joseph, Guido Imbens, and Jacob Alex Klerman. 2000. "The Long-Term Gains from GAIN: A Re-Analysis of the Impacts of the California GAIN Program." National Bureau of Economic Research Working Paper w8007, November.

Jones, Charles O. 1976. "Why Congress Can't Do Policy Analysis (Or Words to that Effect)." *Policy Analysis* 2(2): 251–264.

Lalonde, Robert J. 1995. "Promise of Public Sector Training Programs." *The Journal of Economic Perspec-

tives 9(2, Spring): 149–168.

Lindblom, Charles E., and David K. Cohen. 1979. *Usable Knowledge: Social Science and Social Problem Solving*. New Haven, CT: Yale University Press.

Manski, Charles F. 1995. *Identification Problems in the Social Sciences*. Cambridge, MA: Harvard University Press.

Manski, Charles F., and Irwin Garfinkel. 1992. *Evaluating Welfare and Training Programs*. Cambridge, MA: Harvard University Press.

Mosteller, Frederick, and Robert Boruch. 2002. *Evidence Matters: Randomized Trials in Education Research*. Washington, D.C.: Brookings Institution Press.

O'Connor, Alice. 2001. *Poverty Knowledge: Social Science, Social Policy, and the Poor in Twentieth-Century U.S. History*. Princeton, NJ: Princeton University Press.

Orr, Larry L. 1999. *Social Experiments: Evaluating Public Programs with Experimental Methods*. Thousand Oaks, CA: Sage.

Rich, Andrew. 2001. "The Politics of Expertise in Congress and the News Media." *Social Science Quarterly* 82(3): 583–601.

Sen, Amartya. 1982. *Choice, Welfare and Measurement*. Oxford: Basil Blackwell.

Shulock, Nancy. 1999. "The Paradox of Policy Analysis: If It Is Not Used, Why do We Produce So Much of It?" *Journal of Policy Analysis and Management* 18(2): 226–244.

Stone, Deborah A. 1993. "Clinical Authority in the Construction of Citizenship" In *Public Policy for Democracy*. Ingram, Helen and Steven Rathgeb Smith, eds. Washington, D.C.: The Brookings Institution, 45–67.

Stone, Deborah. 1997. *Policy Paradox: The Art of Political Decision Making*. New York: Norton.

Szanton, Peter. 1981. *Not Well Advised*. New York: Russell Sage Foundation.

Walker, Robert, David Greenberg, Karl Ashworth, and Andreas Cebulla. 2003. " Successful Welfare-to-Work Programs: Were Riverside and Portland Really that Good?" *Focus*. 22(3): 11–18.

Weaver, R. Kent. 1999. "The Role of Policy Research in Welfare Debates, 1993-1996." Unpublished Manuscript.

Weber, Max. 1949. *The Methodology of the Social Sciences*. Translated and edited by Edward A. Shils and Henry A. Finch. New York: The Free Press.

26 Policy Evaluation and Evaluation Research

Hellmut Wollmann

DEFINITIONS, CONCEPTS, AND TYPES OF EVALUATION

Evaluation in the field of public policy may be defined, in very general terms, as an analytical tool and procedure meant to do two things. First, evaluation research, as an analytical tool, involves investigating a policy program to obtain all information pertinent to the assessment of its performance, both process and result; second, evaluation as a phase of the policy cycle more generally refers to the reporting of such information back to the policy-making process (see Wollmann 2003b, 4).

Yet, a bewildering array of concepts and terms has made its appearance in this field, especially given the recent "third wave" development of new vocabulary (such as management audit, policy audit, and performance monitoring). In light of a definition that focuses on the function of evaluation and, thus, looks beneath the surface of varied terminology, it becomes apparent that the different terms "cover more or less the same grounds" (Bemelmans-Videc 2002, 94). Thus, analytical procedures, which have come to be called "performance audit" would be included in our definition, except, however, "financial audit," which checks the compliance of public spending with budgetary provisions and would not be counted as evaluation (see Sandahl 1992, 115).

TYPES OF EVALUATION: FUNCTIONS AND TIMING

In terms of the different temporal and functional linkages with the "policy cycle," often the following distinctions are made (see Wollmann 2003b).

Ex-ante evaluation, preceding decision making, is meant to (hypothetically) anticipate and pre-assess the effects and consequences of planned or defined policies and actions in order to "feed" the information into the upcoming or ongoing decision-making process. If undertaken on alternative courses of policies and actions, ex-ante evaluation is an instrument of making the choice between alternative policy options (ideally) analytically more transparent, more foreseeable, and politically more debatable. It includes *implementation pre-assessment* is meant to analytically anticipate the course of policy implementation in focusing on its process, as well as *environmental impact assessment,* designed for anticipating or predicting the consequences which envisaged policies and measure may have on the environment.

Ongoing evaluation has the task of identifying the (interim) effects and results of policy programs and measures while, in the policy cycle, the implementation and realization thereof is still under way. The essential function of "ongoing" evaluation is to feed relevant information back into the implementation process at a point and stage when pertinent information can be used in order to adjust, correct or redirect the implementation process or even underlying key policy decisions. In a nearly synonymous usage, some speak of *accompanying evaluation* running parallel to the policy implementation process. Within "ongoing" or "accompanying" evaluation one can discern

between a primarily "analytical" modality that remains "detached" and "distanced" from the implementation process in order to ascertain objectivity. Further, the term interventionist accompanying
evaluation has been applied when, besides the analytical mandate, the evaluators are also expected,
if not obliged to actively intervene in the implementation process in order to rectify shortcomings
and flaws in the implementation process jeopardising the attainment of the pre-set policy goals. In
such an "interventionist" orientation "accompanying" evaluation would approximate the concept
of *action research.*

Finally, monitoring can be seen as an (ongoing) evaluative procedure which aims at (de-
scriptively) identifying and, with the help of appropriate, if possible operationalized, indicators,
at "measuring" the effects of ongoing activities. In the most recent upsurge of "performance indicators" (PIs) in the concepts of New Public Management, indicator-based monitoring has gained
great importance.

Ex-post evaluation constitutes the classical variant of evaluation to assess the goal attainment
and effects of policies and measures, once they have been completely As such, summative (Scriven
1972) has been directed at policy *programs* (as a policy action form combining policy goals and
financial, organisational as well as personnel resources), typical of early reform policies in the
United States, but also in European countries, ex-post policy evaluation has often been identified
with *program evaluation* (see Rist 1990). Characteristically, policy (or program) evaluation has
been given primarily two tasks.

First, it was meant to produce an assessment about the degree to which the intended policy
goals have achieved ("goal attainment"). The *conceptual problems* following from this task revolve
around the conceptualising the appropriate, if possible measurable, indicators in order to make such
assessments of goal attainment. But, besides identifying the "intended" consequences, the assessment
of the effects of policies and programs came to pertain also to the non-intended consequences.

Second, the evaluation of policies and programs was also expected and mandated to answer the
(causal) question as to whether the observed effects and changes have be really (causally) related to
the policy or program in question. From this the *methodological* issue of applying the methodological tools and skills (possibly and hopefully) capable of solving the "causal puzzle."

Meta-evaluation is meant to analyse an already completed (primary) evaluation using a kind
of secondary analysis. Two variants may be discerned. First, the meta-evaluation may review the
already completed piece of (primary) evaluation as to whether it is up to methodological criteria and
standards. One might speak of methodology-reviewing meta-evaluation. Second, the meta-evaluation
may have to accumulate the substantive findings of the already completed (primary) evaluation and
synthesise the results. This might be called a "synthesising" meta-evaluation.

While (rigorous) evaluation aims at giving a comprehensive picture of what has happened in
the policy field and project under scrutiny, encompassing successful as well as unsuccessful courses
of events, the best practice approach tends to pick up and tell success stories of reform policies
and projects, with the analytical intention of identifying the factors that explain the success, and
with the applied (learning and pedagogic) purpose to foster lesson drawing from such experience
in the intranational as well as in the inter- and transnational contexts. On the one hand, such good
practice stories are fraught with the (conceptual and methodological) threat of ecological fallacy,
that is, of a rash and misleading translation and transfer of (seemingly positive) strategies from
one locality and one country to another. On the other hand, if done in a way which carefully heeds
the specific contextuality and conditionality of such good practice examples, analysing, telling and
diffusing such cases can provide a useful fast track to evaluative knowledge and intra-national as
well as trans-national learning

Vis-à-vis these manifold conceptual and methodological hurdles full-fledged evaluation of
public-sector reforms is bound to face a type of quasi-evaluation has been proposed (see Thoenig
2003) that would be less fraught with conceptual and methodological predicaments than a full-fledged

evaluation and more disposed toward focusing on, and restricting itself to, the information- and data-gathering and descriptive functions of evaluation rather than an explanatory one. A major asset may be a conceptually and methodologically pared-down variant of quasi-evaluation that may be conducive to more trustful communication between the policy maker and the evaluator that will promote a gradual learning process that fosters an information culture (Thoenig 2003).

Finally, an evaluability assessment can be undertaken. This happens before an evaluation, be it of the ex-post, but also of the ex-ante and ongoing type. It is used to find out in advance which approach and variant of evaluation should be turned to on the basis of the criteria of technical feasibility, economic viability, and of practical merits.

"Classical" evaluation is, first of all, directed at (ex-post) assessing the attainment or nonattainment of the policy and program goals or at (ex-ante) estimating the attainability of goals. It deals essentially with the *effectiveness* of policies and measures the amount of resources employed (or invested) in order to reach that goal. This is in contrast to a cost-benefit-analysis which compares the outcomes to the resources devoted to achieve them. Emphasizing efficiency cost-benefit analysis may thus also have an ex-post orientation.

TYPES OF EVALUATION: INTERNAL AND EXTERNAL

For one, evaluation may be conducted as an internal evaluation. Such evaluation is carried out in-house by the operating agency itself. In this case, it takes place as self-evaluation. In fact, one might argue that informal and unsystematic modes of self-evaluation have been practiced ever since (in the Weberian) bureaucracy model) hierarchical oversight has taken place based on forms of regular internal reporting. But evaluation research involves more formal approaches. Evaluation research has become a key component of various theories of public administration. In recent years, New Public Management has emphasized the concept of monitoring and controlling based on evaluation performance indicators. Such indicators play, for example, a pivotal role in operating systems of comprehensive internal cost-achievement accounting (see Wollmann 2003b).

External evaluation, by contrast, is initiated or funded by outside sources (contracted out by an agency or actor outside of the operating administrative unit). Such an external locus of the evaluation function may be put in place by institutions and actors that, outside and beyond administration, may have a political or structural interest employing evaluation as a means to oversee the implementation of policies by administration. Parliaments have shown to be the natural candidates for initiating and carrying out the evaluation of policies and programs inaugurated by them. In a similar vein, courts of audits have come to use evaluation as an additional analytical avenue for shedding light on the effectiveness and efficiency of administrative operations.

But also other actors within the core of government, such as the Prime Minister's Office or the Finance Ministry, may turn to evaluation as an instrument to oversee the operations of sectoral ministries and agencies. Finally, mention should be made of ad hoc bodies and commissions (i.e., enquiry commissions) mandated to scrutinize complex issues and policy fields. Such commissions may employ evaluation as an important fact-finding tool before recommending policy implementation by government and ministries.

The more complex the policies and programs under consideration are, and the more demanding the conceptual and methodological problems of carrying out such evaluations become, the less the institutions, initiating and conducting the evaluation, are capable to carry out such conceptually and methodologically complicated and sophisticated analyses themselves. In view of such complexities, evaluation research is ideally based on the application of social science methodology and expertise. Thus, in lack of adequately trained personnel and of time the political, administrative and the other institutions often turn to outside (social science) research institutes and research enterprises in commissioning them to carry out the evaluation work on a contractual basis (see Wollmann 2002). In fact, the development of evaluation, since the mid- 1960s, has been accompanied by the (at times rampant) expansion of a "contractual money market" which, fed by the resources of ministries, parliament, ad hoc commissions, etc., has turned evaluation research virtually into a "new industry of considerable proportion" (Freeman and Solomon 1981, 13), revolving around contractual research" and has deeply remolded the traditional research landscape in a momentous shift from "academic to entrepreneurial" research (see Freeman and Solomon 1981, 16), a topic to which we return.

THE THREE WAVES OF EVALUATION

Three phases can be distinguished in the development of evaluation over the past forty years: the first wave of evaluation was during the 1960s and 1970s, the second wave began in the mid-1970s, and a third wave set in since the 1990s.

During the 1960s and 1970s, the advent of the advanced welfare state was accompanied by the concept of enhancing the ability of the state to provide proactive policy making through the modernization of its political and administrative structures in the pursuit of which the institution-alization and employment of planning, information, and evaluation capacities were as seen as instrumental. The concept of a "policy cycle" revolved, as already mentioned, around the triad of policy formation, implementation, and termination, whereby evaluation was deemed crucial as a "cybernetic" loop in gathering and feeding back policy-relevant information The underlying scientific logic (Wittrock, Wagner, and Wollmann 1991, 615) and vision of a science-driven policy model was epitomized by Donald Campbell's famous call for an *experimenting society* ("reforms as experiments," Campbell 1969) .

In the United States, the rise of evaluation came with the inauguration of federal social action programs such as the War on Poverty in the mid-1960s under President Johnson with evaluation almost routinely mandated by the pertinent reform legislation, turning policy and program evaluation virtually into a growth industry. Large-scale social experimentation with accompanying major evaluation followed suit.[1] In Europe, Sweden, Germany, and the United Kingdom became the frontrunners of this "first wave" of evaluation (see Levine 1981; Wagner, and Wollmann 1986; Derlien 1990); in Germany social experimentation (experimentelle Politik) was undertaken on a scale unparalleled outside the United States (see Wagner, and Wollmann 1991, 74).

Reflecting the reformist consensus, which was widely shared at the time by reformist political and administrative actors as well as by the social scientists, involved through hitherto largely unknown forms of contractual research and policy consultancy, the evaluation projects norma-tively agreed with and supported the reformist policies under scrutiny and were, hence, meant to improve policy results and to maximize output effectiveness. (Wittrock, Wagner, and Wollmann 1991, 52).

The heyday of the interventionist welfare state policies proved to be short-lived, when, following the first oil price rise of 1973, the world economy slid into a deepening recession and the national budgets ran into a worsening financial squeeze that brought most of the cost-intensive reform poli-cies to a grinding halt. This lead to the "second wave." As policy making came to be dictated by the calls for budgetary retrenchment and cost-saving, the mandate of policy evaluation got accordingly redefined with the aim to reducing the costs of policies and programs, if not to phase them out (see Wagner, and Wollmann 1986; Derlien, 1990). In this second wave of evaluation focusing on the cost-efficiency of policies and programs, evaluation saw a significant expansion in other countries, for instance, in the Netherlands (see Leeuw 2004, 60).

The "third wave of evaluation" operates under the influence of sundry currents. For one, the concepts and imperatives of New Public Management (see Pollitt and Bouckaert 2003, 2004) have come to dominate the international modernization discourse and, in one or the other variant, the public sector reform in many countries (see Wollmann 2003c) with "internal evaluation" (through the build-up and employment of indicator-based controlling and cost-achievement-accounting, etc.) forming an integral part of the "public management package" (see Furubo and Sandahl 2002, pp. 19 ff.) and giving new momentum to evaluative procedures (see Wollmann 2003b.). Moreover, in a number of policy fields, evaluation has gained salience in laying bare the existing policy shortcomings and in identifying the potential for reforms and improvements. The great attention (and excitement) raised recently by the European-wide "PISA" study, a major international evaluation exercise on the national educational systems, has highlighted and, no doubt, propelled the role and potential of evaluation as an instrument of policy making. Third, mention should be made that, within the European Union, evaluation has been given a major push when the European Commission decided to have the huge spending of the European Structural Fund systematically evaluated (see Leeuw 2004, 69 ff.). As the EU's structural funds are now being evaluated within their five-year program cycle in an almost text book-like fashion (with an evaluation cycle running from ex-ante through ex-post evaluation), the evaluation of EU policies and programs has significantly influenced and pushed ahead the development of evaluation at large. In some countries, for instance Italy (see Stame 2002; Lippi 2003), the mandate to evaluate EU programs was, as it were, the cradle of the country's evaluation research, which had hardly existed before.

In an international comparative perspective at the beginning of the new millennium, policy evaluation has been introduced and installed in many countries as a widely accepted and employed instrument of gaining (and of "feeding back") policy-relevant information. This has been impressively analysed and documented in a recent study[2] based on reports from twenty-two countries and on a sophisticated set of criteria (see Furubo et al., 2002, with the synthesising piece by Furubo, and Sandahl 2002). While the United States still holds the lead in the "evaluation culture" (Rist, and Pakiolas 2002, 230 ff.), the upper six ranks among European countries are taken by Sweden, the Netherlands, the United Kingdom, Germany, Denmark, and Finland (see Furubo, and Sandahl 2002; Leeuw 2004, 63).

METHODOLOGICAL ISSUES OF EVALUATION

Evaluation research is faced with two main conceptual and methodological tasks: (1) to conceptualize the observable real world changes in terms of intended (or non-intended) consequences that policy evaluation is meant to identify and to assess (as, methodologically speaking, "dependent variables"); and (2) to find out whether and how the observed changes are causally linked to the policy and measure under consideration (as "independent" variable).

In coping with these key questions, evaluation research is seen to be an integral part of social science research at large; it includes, as such, most of social science's conceptual and methodological issues and controversies. In fact, it seems that the methodological debates that have occurred in the social science community at large (for instance in the strife between the "quantitative" and the "qualitative" schools of thought) have been one of the most pronounced (and at times fiercest) struggles in the evaluation research community.

Two phases can be discerned in this controversy. The first, dating from the 1960s to the early 1980s, has been characterized by the dominance of the neopositivist-nomological science model (with an ensuing preponderance of the quantitative and quasi-experimental methods). The second and more recent period has resulted from advances in the constructivist, interpretive approach (with a corresponding preference for qualitative heuristic methods).

Accordingly, from the neopositivist perspective, evaluation has been characterized by two premises. The first is the assumption that in order to validly assess whether and to what degree the policy goals (as intended consequences) have been attained by observable real world changes, it is necessary to identify in advance what the political intentions and goals of the program are. In this view, the intention of the "one" relevant institution or actor stands in the fore.

Second, in order to identify causal relations between the observed changes and the policy/program under consideration, valid statements could be gained only through the positivist application of quantitative, (quasi-) experimental research designs (Campbell, and Stanley 1963). Yet, notwithstanding the long dominance of this research paradigm, the problem of translating these premises into evaluation practice were obvious to many observers. For example, in identifying the relevant objectives serious issues arise (see Wollmann 2003b, 6): (1) goals and objectives that serve as a measuring rod are hard to identify, as they often come as "bundles"—goals are hard to translate into operationalizable and measurable indicators; (2) good empirical data to fill in the indicators are hard to get, and the more meaningful an indicator is, the more difficult it is to obtain viable data; (3) the more remote (and, often, the more relevant) the goal dimension is, the harder it becomes to operationalize and to empirically substantiate it; (4) side effects and unintended consequences are hard to trace.

Moreover, methodologically robust research designs (quasi-experimental, controlled, time-series, etc.) are often not applicable, at least not in a methodologically satisfying manner (Weiss and Rein 1970) Here one needs to observe the *ceteris paribus* conditions (on which the application of quasi-experimental design hinges) are difficult, if not impossible, to establish. While the application of quantitative methods is premised on the methodological requirement "many cases (large N), few variables," in the real world research situation often the constellation is the opposite: "few cases (small N), many (possibly influencing) variables." These problems tend to rule out the employment of quantitative methods and, instead, proceeding qualitatively. And finally, the application of time series methods (before/after design) has often narrow limits, as the "before" data are often not available nor procurable.

In the second phase, the long dominant research paradigm has come under criticism on two interrelated scores. For one, the standard assumption that evaluation should seek its frame of reference first of all in the policy intention of the relevant political institution(s) or actor(s) has been shaken—if not shattered—by the advances of the *constructivist-interpretive* school of thought (Mertens 2004, 42 ff.). It advocates questioning on epistemological grounds the possibility of validly ascertaining "one" relevant intention or goal and call instead for identifying a plurality of (often) perspectives, interests, and values. For instance, Stufflebeam (1983) has been influential in advancing a concept of evaluation called the "CIPP model," in which C = context, I = input, P = process, P = product. Among the four components, the "context" element (focusing on questions like: What are the program's goals? Do they reflect the needs of the participants?) is meant to direct evaluator's attention, from the outset, to the needs (and interests) of the participants of the program under consideration (and its underlying normative implications). This general line of argument has been expressed in different formulations, such as "responsive," "participatory," or "stakeholder" evaluation. Methodologically the constructivist debate has gone hand-in-hand with (re-)gaining ground for qualitative-hermeneutic methods in evaluation (Mertens 2004, 47). Guba and Lincoln (1989) have labeled this development "fourth generation evaluation."

While the battle lines between the camps of thought were fairly sharply drawn some twenty years ago, they have since softened up. On the one hand, the epistemological, conceptual and methodological insights generated in the constructivist debate are accepted and taken seriously, the mandate in evaluation to come as close as possible to "objective" still remains a major objective. The concept of a "realistic evaluation" as formulated by Pawson and Tilley (1997) lends itself to serve that purpose. Furthermore, it is widely agreed that there is no "king's road" in the methodological design of evaluation research; instead, one should acknowledge a pluralism of methods. The selection and combination of the specific set and mix of methods depends on the evaluative question to be answered, as well as the time frame and financial and personnel resources available.

EVALUATION RESEARCH: BETWEEN BASIC, APPLIED, AND CONTRACTUAL RESEARCH

The emergence and expansion of evaluation research since the mid-1960s has had a significant impact on the social science research landscape and community. Originally the social science research arena was dominated by *academic* (basic) research primarily located at the universities and funded by independent agencies. Even when it took an *applied policy* orientation, social science research remained essentially committed to the academic/basic formula. By contrast, evaluation research, insofar as it is undertaken as "contractual research," commissioned and financed by a political or administrative institution, involves a shift from "academic to entrepreneurial settings" (Freeman and Solomon 1981).

Academic social science research, typically university-based, has been premised on four imperatives. The first has been a commitment to seeking the truth as the pivotal aim and criteria of scientific research. The second relates to intra-scientific autonomy in the selection of the subject matter and the methods of its research. The third has been independent funding, be it from university sources or through peer review-based funding by research foundations such as the National Science Foundation. The final component has been the testing of the quality of the research findings to an open scientific debate and peer review.

While applied social science still holds on to the independence and autonomy of social science research, *contractual research,* which now constitutes a main vehicle of evaluation research, hinges on a quite different formula. It is characterized by a commissioner/producer or consumer/contractor principle: "the consumer says what he wants, the contractor does it (if he can), and the consumer pays" (to quote Lord Rothschild's dictum, see Wittrock, Wagner, and Wollmann 1991, 47). Hence, the "request for proposal" (RFP) through which the commissioning agency addresses the would-be contractors (in public bidding, selective bidding, or directly), generally defines and specifies the questions to be answered and the time frame made available. In the project proposal the would-be contractor explains his research plan within the parameters set by the customer and makes his financial offer which is usually calculated on a personnel costs plus overhead formula.

Thus, when commissioned and funded by government, evaluation research confronts three crucial challenges related to the subject-matter, the leading questions, and the methods of its research. In contract research, unlike traditional evaluation research, these considerations are set by the agency commissioning the evaluation. Also, by providing the funding, the agency also jeopardises the autonomy of the researchers ("who pays the piper, calls the tune"). And finally, the findings of commissioned research are often held in secret, or at least are not published, thus bypassing an open public and peer debate. So, contractual research is exposed and may be vulnerable to an *epistemic drift* and to a colonization process in which the evaluators may adopt the "perspective and conceptual framework" of the political and administrative institutions and actors they are commissioned to evaluate (Elzinga 1983, 89).

In the face of the challenges to the intellectual integrity and honesty of contractual research, initiatives have taken by professional evaluators to formulate standards that could guide them in their contractual work, in particular in their negotiations with their "clients" (Rossi, Freeman, and Lipsey 1999, 425 ff.). Reference can be made here, for example, to *Guiding principles of Evaluation,* adopted in 1995 by the *American Evaluation Association* in 1995. Among its five principles the maxims of integrity and honesty of research are writ large (Rossi, Freeman, and Lipsey 1999, 427 ff.; and Mertens 2004, 50 ff.).

Professionalization

In the meantime, evaluation has, in many countries, become an activity and occupation of a self-standing group and community of specialized researchers and analysts whose increasing professionalization is seen in the formation of professional associations, the appearance of professional publications, and in the arrival of evaluation as a subject matter in university and vocational training.

As to the foundation of professional associations, a leading and exemplary role was assumed by the American Evaluation Society (AES), formed in 1986 through the merger of two smaller evaluation associations, Evaluation Network and the Evaluation Research Society. As of 2003, AES had more than three thousand members (Mertens 2004, 50). An important product was the formulation of the aforementioned professional code of ethics laid down in the "Guiding Principles for Evaluators" adopted by the AES in 1995. In Europe, the European Evaluation Society was founded in 1987 and the establishment of national evaluation societies followed suit, with the UK Evaluation Society being the first[3] (see Leeuw 2004, 64 f.). In the meantime, most of them have also elaborated and adopted professional codes of ethics which expresses the intention and resolve to consolidate and ensure evaluation as a new occupation and profession.

Another important indicator of the professional institutionalization of the evaluation is the extent to which evaluation has become the topic of a mushrooming publication market. This, not least, includes the publication of professional journals, often in close relation to the respective national association. Thus, the American Evaluation Association has two publications: The *American Journal of Evaluation* and the *New Directions for Evaluation* monograph series (Mertens 2004, 52). In Europe, the journal *Evaluation* is published in association with the European Evaluation Society. Furthermore, a number of national evaluation journals (in the respective national languages) have been started in several European countries. All of these serve as useful sources of information on the topic of evaluation research.

NOTES

1. For example, see the "New Jersey Negative Income Tax experiment," which involved $8 million for research spending (Rossi and Lyall 1978).
2. For earlier useful overviews, see Levine et al. 1981; Levine 1981; Wagner and Wollmann 1986: Rist 1990; Derlien 1990; Mayne et al.. 1992.
3. European Evaluation Society, http://www.europeanevaluation.org. Associazione Italiana de Valuatazione, http:// www.valutazione.it. Deutsche Gesellschaft für Evaluation, http://www.degeval.de. Finnish Evaluation Societ, e-mail: petri.virtanen@vm.vn.fi. Schweizerische Evaluationsgesellschaft, http://www.seval.ch. Société Française de l'Evaluation, http://www.sfe.asso.fr. Société Wallonne de l'Evaluation et de la rospective, http://www.prospeval.org.UK Evaluation Society, http://www.evaluation.org.uk

REFERENCES

Campbell, Donald T. (1969). "Reforms as Experiments." *American Psychologist*, pp. 409 ff.

Campbell, Donald T., and Stanley, Y. (1963). *Experimental and Quasi-Experimental Evaluations in Social Research.* Chicago: Rand McNally.

Bemelmans-Videc, M. L. (2002). Evaluation in The Netherlands 1990–2000.Consolidation and Expansion. In Jan-Eric Furubo, Ray C. Rist, and Rolf Sandahl (eds.), *International Atlas of Evaluation.* London: Transaction, pp. 115–128.

Derlien, Hans-Ulrich (1990). Genesis and Structure of Evaluation Efforts in Comparative Perspective. In Ray C. Rist (ed.), *Program Evaluation and the Management of Government.* London: Transaction, pp. 147–177.

Freeman, Howard, and Solomon, Marian A. (1981). The Next Decade of Evaluation Research. In, Robert A. Levine, , Marian A. Solomon, Gerd-Michael Hellstern and H. Wollmann. (eds.), *Evaluation Research and Practive. Comparative and InternationalPperspectives.* Beverly Hills: Sage, pp. 12–26.

Furubo, J., Rist, R. C., and Sandahl, Rolf (eds.) (2002). *International Atlas of Evaluation*. London: Transaction.

Furubo, J., and R. Sandahl (2002). A Diffusion-Perspective on Global Developments in Evaluation. In Jan-Eric Furubo, Ray C. Rist, and Rolf Sandahl (eds.), *International Atlas of Evaluation*. London: Transaction, pp. 1–26.

Elzinga, Aant. (1985). Research Bureaucracy and the Drift of Epistemic Criteria. In Björnand Wittrock, and Aant Elzinga (eds.), *The University Research System*. Stockholm: Almqvist and Wiksell, pp. 191–220.

Guba, Y., and Lincoln E. (1989). *Fourth Generation Evaluation*. London: Sage.

Lasswell, H. D. (1951). The Policy Orientation. In Daniel Lerner and Harold D. Lasswell, (eds.), *The Policy Sciences*. Palo Alta, CA: Stanford University Press, pp. 3–15

Leeuw, F. L. (2004). Evaluation in Europe. In R. Stockmann (ed.), *Evaluationsforschung* (2nd. ed.). Opladen: Leske + Budrich, pp. 61–83.

Levine, Robert A., Solomon, M. A., Hellstern, G., and Wollmann, Hellmut (eds.) (1981). *Evaluation Research and Practice. Comparative and International Perspectives*. Beverly Hills: Sage.

Levine, Robert A. (1981).. Program Evaluation and Policy Analysis in Western Nations: An Overview. In, Robert A. Levine, Marian A. Solomon, , Gerd-Michael Hellstern and H. Wollmann. (eds.), *Evaluation Research and Practive. Comparative and International Perspectives*, Beverly Hills: Sage, pp. 12–27.

Lippi, Andreas. (2003). As a voluntary choice or as a legal obligation? Assessing New Public Management policy in Italy. In Hellmut Wollmann (ed.), *Evaluation in Public-Sector Reform*. Cheltenham, UK: Edward Elgar, pp. 140–169

Mayne, J. L., Bemelmans-Videc, M. L., Hudson, J., and Conner, R. (eds.) (1992). *Advancing Public Policy Evaluation*. Amsterdam: North-Holland

Mertens, Donna M. (2004). Institutionalising Evaluation in the United States of America. In Reinhard Stockmann (ed.), *Evaluationsforschung* (2nd. ed.). Opladen: Leske + Budrich, pp. 45–60

Pawson, Ray, Tilley, Nick. (1997). *Realistic Evaluation*. London: Sage.

Pollitt, Christopher. (1995). "Justification by Works or by Faith? Evaluating the New Public Management," *Evaluation*, 1(2, October), 133–154.

Pollitt, Christopher/ Bouckaert, Geert (2003). Evaluating Public Management Reforms. An International Perspective. In Hellmut Wollmann (ed.), *Evaluation in Public-Sector Reform*. Cheltenham, UK: Edward Elgar, pp. 12–35.

Pollitt, Christopher, and Bouckaert, Geert. (2004). *Public Management Reform* (2nd ed.). Oxford: Oxford University Press.

Rossi, Peter H., Freeman, Howard E., and Lipsey, Mark W. (1999). *Evaluation. A Systematic Approach* (6th ed.). Thousand Oaks, CA: Sage.

Rist, Ray (ed.) (1990). *Program Evaluation and the Management of Government*. London: Transaction.

Rist, Ray, and Paliokas, Kathleen. (2002). The Rise and Fall (and Rise Again?) pf tje Evaluation Function in the US Government. In Jan-Eric Furubo, Ray C. Rist, and Rolf Sandahl (eds.), *International Atlas of Evaluation*. London: Transaction, pp. 225–245.

Sandahl, Rolf. (2002). Evaluation at the Swedish National Audit Bureau. In J. L. Mayne, M. L. Bemelmans-Videc, J. Hudson, and R. Conner. (eds.), *Advancing Public Policy Evaluation*. Amsterdam: North-Holland, pp. 115–121.

Scriven, Michael. (1972). The Methodology of Evaluaiton. In Carol H. Weiss (ed.), *Evaluating Action Programs*. Boston, pp. 123 ff.

Stufflebeam, D. L. (1983). The CIPP Model for Program Evaluation. In G. F. Madaus, M. Scriven, and D. L. Stufflebeam (eds.), *Evaluation Models*. Boston: Kluwer-Nijhoff, pp. 117–142.

Stame, Nicoletta. (2003). Evaluation in Italy. An inverted Sequence from Performange managent toprogram Evaluaton? In Jan-Eric Furubo, Ray C. Rist, and Rolf Sandahl (eds.), *International Atlas of Evaluation*. London: Transaction, pp. 273–290.

Thoenig, Jean-Claude. (2003). Learning from Evaluation Practice: The Case of Public-Sector Reform. In Hellmut Wollmann (ed.), *Evaluation in Public-Sector Reform*. Cheltenham, UK: Edward Elgar, pp. 209–230.

Vedung, Evert (1997). *Public Policy and Program Evaluation*. New Brunwick: Transaction.

Wagner, Peter, and Wollmann, Hellmut. (1986). "Fluctuations in the Development of Evaluation Research: Do Regime Shifts Matter?" *International Social Science Journal*, 108, 205–218.

Wagner, Peter, and Wollmann, Hellmut. (1991). "Beyond Serving State and Bureaucracy: Problem-oriented Social Science in (West) Germany." *Knowledge and Policy* 4 (12), pp. 46–88.

Weiss, R. S, and Rein, Martin. (1970). "The Evaluation of broad-aim programs. Experimental Design, its difficulties and an alternative." *Administrative Science Quarterly,* pp. 97 ff.

Wittrock, Björn, Wagner, Peter, and Wollmann, Hellmut (1991). Social science and the modern state. In Peter Wagner, C. Weiss, C. Hirschon, Björn Wittrock, and Hellmut Wollmann (eds.), *Social Sciences and Modern State.* Cambridge: Cambridge University Press, pp. 28–85.

Wollmann, Hellmut. (2002). Contractual Research and Policy Knowledge. In *International Encyclopedia of Social and Behavioral Sciences* (vol. 5), pp. 11574– 11578.

Wollmann, Hellmut. (ed.) (2003a). *Evaluation in Public-Sector Reform*, Cheltenham, UK: Edward Elgar.

Wollmann, Hellmut. (2003b). Evaluation in Public-Sector Reform. Towards a "third wave" of evaluation. In Hellmut Wollmann, *Evaluation in Public-Sector Reform*. Cheltenham, UK: Edward Elgar, pp. 1–11.

Wollmann, Hellmut. (2003c)., Evaluation in Public-Sector Reform. Trends, Potentials and Limits in International Perspective. In Hellmut Wollmann (ed.), *Evaluation in Public-Sector Reform*. Cheltenham, UK: Edward Elgar, pp. 231–258.

Wollmann, Hellmut. (2005). Applied Social Science : Development, State of the Art, Consequences. In UNESCO (ed.), *History of Humanity* (vol. VII). New York: Routledge (forthcoming), chapter 21.

Part VIII

*Qualitative Policy Analysis:
Interpretation, Meaning, and Content*

27 Qualitative-Interpretive Methods in Policy Research

Dvora Yanow

The use of qualitative methods in policy research is not new. Academic scholars and policy analysts have for some years been venturing out into the "field" as ethnographers or participant-observers to study first-hand the experiences of legislators, implementors, agency clients, community members, and other policy-relevant stakeholders. Others have based qualitative studies on in-depth interviews with various policy actors; and still other studies draw on legislative, agency, and other documents.

What is new, however, in methodological circles is a greater attention to making the steps of such analyses more transparent. On the one hand, this makes it easier for students and others to learn how such studies are carried out. At the same time, such transparency enables critics and skeptics of the scientific standing of such research to see that they are not impressionistic, that they have regularized procedures, and that they can yield trustworthy analyses, although these procedures and standards may be—indeed, are—different from those used in other forms of research. Part of this transparency involves making clear that qualitative methods have a longstanding history of philosophical exploration and argumentation that supports their procedures and evidentiary claims at a conceptual level. It has become increasingly important to be explicit about what these philosophical groundings are, and so this chapter includes a brief summary of several of the central presuppositions and their ideational sources. Another part of this transparency involves attending quite carefully to the language used in talking about methodological concerns and methods procedures. This has led to a shift in many circles from talking about "qualitative" methods to a discourse of "interpretive" methods. This shift has taken place because of the so-called "interpretive turn" in the social sciences quite broadly (see, e.g., Rabinow and Sullivan 1979, 1985), but also because of the greater awareness of the philosophical presuppositions undergirding *all* research methods and an increased desire to ground methods discussions in their attendant methodologies.

The approach I sketch out here rests, then, on "taking language seriously" (to draw on Jay White's article and book titles; White 1992, 1999) and also on the very philosophical presuppositions that undergird these methods and methodologies. I begin with an explanation and defense of the interpretive turn, not only in conceptual terms but in methodological ones as well, as a more fitting name for this form of research. As this rests on philosophical argumentation, in the second section I summarize some of the main points from interpretive philosophies that inform interpretive methods. These suggest some of the central characteristics and themes of interpretive methods, including some of the central issues raised today in methodological discussions. Entire chapters and volumes have been written about these several interpretive methods. Here, I will sketch out the entailments of interpretive methods for accessing or generating data. The chapter concludes with very brief notes on some of the interpretive methods used in analyzing such data in the context of policy research. There are many more than I have space for here, and the reader is encouraged to use the references to pursue these.

WHAT'S IN A NAME? INTERPRETIVE METHODS

Researchers in many fields who use those methods traditionally called "qualitative"—field research methods such as participant-observation and analytic methods such as frame analysis or ethno-methodology—are increasingly using a different umbrella term to refer to them: "interpretive." The reasons are both historical and contemporary, having to do with the origins of the term qualitative and current issues in the philosophy of science, including social science.

The language of qualitative methods came into being to distinguish field research methods, such as those developed prominently in Chicago School sociology and anthropology from the 1930s to 1960s, from the survey research design and statistical methods being developed at the same time, notably at Columbia University and later at the University of Michigan's Institute for Social Research. As the latter were designated "quantitative" methods, the former must, by the logic of language and category construction, be "qualitative." Qualitative research, then, was that research that drew on one or more of three methods for gathering, accessing or generating data: observing, with whatever degree of participating; interviewing in a conversational mode; and the close reading of topic-relevant documents.[1]

One difficulty with the qualitative-quantitative nomenclature is that the category structure sets up an opposition that does not hold. "Qualitative" researchers count things (although what they do with numbers, how they treat them analytically, is characteristically quite different from the ways that quantitative researchers treat them; see, e.g., Gusfield 1976, 1981); "quantitative" researchers interpret their data. And so the distinction is both erroneous and misleading.

Two other differences further complicate the two-part category structure. First, its focus on numeracy diverts attention from underlying ontological and epistemological differences that are far more significant. Different methods presume different "reality statuses" for the topic of research. A simplistic example would be that tables, chairs, and other office furniture, which one can physically touch, have a different ontological standing than, say, the organization whose offices they furnish—something that might matter, for instance, in analyses from different perspectives of space planning for that organization (which, as a concept, denotes more than its material reality). Different reality statuses in turn presume different ways of knowing and different rules of evidence (that supports the "truth claims" of the analysis) or criteria for assessing its trustworthiness. An analysis of the allocation of office space and furnishings to members at various levels of the organization requires a different kind of "know-ability" than an assessment of the meanings of those allocations to those members and their interpretations of the differences. The qualitative-quantitative terminology has become a shorthand proxy for referring to philosophical differences between methods informed by interpretive philosophies and those informed by logical positivism and its emendations. This masking, through the qual/quant language of the category structure, of ontological and epistemological presuppositions undergirding methodological debates and methods procedures exacerbates the lack of attention to philosophical presuppositions common in the way methods courses are typically taught—that is, as a set of tools divorced from any underlying assumptions.[2]

Second, under pressure to meet the evaluative standards of quantitative methods—the validity and reliability criteria that are grounded in the presuppositions of logical positivism—some qualitative researchers are increasingly doing work designed to resemble more closely the characteristics

1. Examples of such qualitative studies include many that focused on bureaucracies, such as Blau 1953, Gouldner 1954; Kaufman 1960, Selznick 1949, or on workers and work practices, such as Becker et al. 1961; Dalton 1959.
2. Note that "pre"suppositions are not prior in time but in logic. Most researchers do not first decide what their ideas about reality and knowledge are. It is far more common to simply begin with a research puzzle and proceed to a research design. What is "prior" precedes in the sense of logic: research designs presume certain ideas about or attitudes toward ontological status and epistemological possibilities. These are embedded in research methods.

of large "n" research and to conform more to the research processes associated with quantitative methods. "Qualitative" research looks less and less like the traditional field research methods associated with that term. Such efforts include, for example, the adoption of computer programs (such as NU'DIST or Atlas-Ti) to "process" words and phrases from interview and field notes or focus groups, as well as highly structured interviews, Q-sort and other techniques, rather than the ethnographic, participant-observer, ethnomethodological, semiotic, narrative, and other approaches that are the hallmarks of qualitative methods.[3] The social sciences, including policy studies, are increasingly characterized by a tripartite methods categorization: quantitative, qualitative-positivist, and qualitative-interpretive. The distinction is made clearer when one considers the presuppositional grounding that informs the methods used in this latter category.

INTERPRETIVE METHODOLOGICAL PRESUPPOSITIONS

The Continental philosophies of phenomenology, hermeneutics, and critical theory developed in Europe during the first half of the twentieth century engaged some of the same questions that nineteenth- and early twentieth-century positivist philosophies did: what is the character of human social reality, as compared with the ontological status of the physical or natural world? And, in light of that reality status, how can aspects of the human social world be known in a "scientific" fashion—again, as compared with the ability to know something, with any degree of certainty, about the physical or natural world? Early nineteenth-century positivist philosophers advanced the argument that the social world should be know-able in the same way that planetary motion and physical mass, for example, could be known: through systematic application of human reason, restricted by the later logical positivist philosophers to sense-based observation alone. Such study should yield principles or "laws" of human behavior that were not only discoverable, but universal. Observation from a vantage point external to the subject of study—an Archimedean point or "God's-eye view" (see, e.g., Harding 1988)—was not only desirable; it was deemed possible.[4]

From the perspective of the interpretive philosophers, however—those Continental philosophers and their American counterparts in symbolic interactionism, pragmatism, and the later ethnomethodology—the human social world is different in significant ways from the world of nature and physical objects and forces. One difference is the centrality of meaning-making to human life. A second is that that meaning-making of lived experience—the interpretive processes through which one generates meaning and is able to understand another's meaning—is highly context-specific. From this perspective, the researcher cannot stand outside the subject of study: more than just the five senses is involved in interpreting people's acts, the language they employ, and the objects they create and use; objectivity is not possible—from this perspective, general laws look more like a "view from nowhere" (Nagel 1986; see also Haraway 1988, Harding 1993), as situational sense-making draws on prior knowledge and builds on intersubjective understanding.

Interpretive researchers, then, do not feel the need to transform words into numbers for analysis. This is the most immediately visible characteristic of interpretive methods: they are word-based, from data "collection" instruments to data analysis tools to research report formats and contents. Interpretive researchers stick close to the character of the data they are encountering: as policy-relevant actors deliberate through words, whether written or oral (or, for that matter, nonverbal), researchers use those words as their data in seeing meanings and sources of meanings. When those actors use numbers, as in counting the numbers of drivers arrested for driving drunk (Gusfield 1981), researchers read those numbers as sources of meaning (for instance, to explore category-construction). This

3. For further discussion of these points and for illustrations of these and other interpretive methods beyond what is discussed in this chapter, see, e.g., Prasad 2005 and Yanow and Schwartz-Shea 2006.
4. This has come to be one understanding of "objectivity." For a critique of that understanding, see, e.g., Bernstein 1983, Hawkesworth 2006, Yanow 2006a.

makes interpretive methods particularly suitable for argumentative, deliberative, and other such approaches to policy research (e.g., Fischer and Forester 1993, Hajer and Wagenaar 2003).

Because they are ontologically constructivist (rather than realist) and epistemologically interpretivist (rather than objectivist), interpretive researchers are attuned to the ways in which their own presence might, in many ways, potentially affect what they are learning in their research. Unlike survey researchers, however, who exert efforts in questionnaire design and administration to minimize these so-called "interviewer effects," interpretive researchers increasingly deny the possibility that interviewers or participants or, in fact, readers can be nonimpacting in this way. Instead—and here is a second hallmark of interpretive research—interpretive methodologists call for heightened degrees of reflexivity on the part of the researcher: explicit attention to the ways in which family background, personality, education, training, and other experience might well shape who and what the researcher is able to access, as well as the ways in which he makes sense of the generated data. This is the enactment of the phenomenological argument that selves are shaped by prior experiences, which in turn shape perception and understanding. It is an argument that has also been advanced in feminist theories and race-ethnic studies concerning "standpoint" perspectives (see Hartsock 1987). Contemporary research reports are increasingly expected to include reflexive accounts of these "standpoints" and their role in shaping interpretations.

A related implication of taking a context-specific view "from somewhere" that denies the possibility of "discovering" generalizable, universal laws in policy research is the potential for multiplicity of meaning, depending on context and phenomenological experience. A hermeneutic argument, this goes beyond the interpretation of biblical texts—its historical antecedent—to the interpretation of other sorts of texts (e.g., policy documents) and other sorts of physical artifacts (e.g., agency buildings), as well as to human acts (e.g., legislating or implementing)—what Taylor (1971) called "text analogues" (see also Ricoeur 1971), to which we might also add nonverbal behaviors. It posits a representational—a symbolic—relationship between human artifactual creations and the values, beliefs, and sentiments that comprise their underlying meanings. Central to this position is an appreciation for the ambiguities that may, and often do, especially in policy arenas, arise from multiple interpretations of the same artifacts—especially as the reasons for such interpretational differences are rarely made explicit in everyday policy discourse. This is, or can be, the researcher's task.[5]

For this reason, among others, interpretive researchers insist on grounding analytic inferences in the clear and detailed enumeration of acts, of interview language, and of objects necessary for supporting inferences. Such grounding is one of the ways in which interpretive researchers argue for the evidentiary bases for their truth claims. It is why narrative reports often read like novels—a third hallmark: without such detailed grounding, reports could read like imaginative flights of fancy. This is also why interpretive research data often cannot be condensed in tables, leading to reports that are typically longer than those based on quantitative data that can be summarily presented in such a fashion. (This acceptance of the social realities of multiple meanings is also the reason that interpretive policy analysts include the study of underlying values in their research, negating the

---

5. I develop the argument about symbolic relationships further in Yanow (2000, ch. 1). I disagree with those who claim that a hermeneutic approach requires, per se, a realist approach to texts and text analogues, a point discussed in Hendriks (2005b: 25). For those of us who follow a "reader-response" approach to textual meaning, meaning does not necessarily reside in the text itself, nor does it reside necessarily in the author's intended meaning—analogous in the policy world to legislators' intent. A phenomenological hermeneutics—the point I have sought to articulate in my work—sees meaning also in readers' responses to texts, and it can be seen as well as emerging out of an interaction among these three (text, author, reader; see, e.g., Iser 1989). This position is well suited for the analysis of policies because of its appreciation for the ambiguities of lived experience and its interpretation.

fact-value dichotomy that has held sway in some other areas of policy analysis.[6])

These characteristics—word-based methods and writing, researcher reflexivity, and the exploration of multiple meanings and their ambiguities, especially in policy contexts in which contention over the policy issue under study is common—are three of the central hallmarks of interpretive research, informed by a constructivist ontology, an interpretivist epistemology, and other attendant philosophical presuppositions. These presuppositions are enacted in methods of generating and analyzing data.

METHODS OF GENERATING DATA

Terminology comes into play again in talking about what in methods texts has customarily been termed "collecting" or "gathering" data. This language suggests that the data are just lying around waiting to be found and assembled and brought back for analysis, much like a botanist might collect or gather specimens to mount in the lab. Indeed, even the words "datum/data" in their literal meanings denote things that are given, underscoring the positivist notion that the researcher can stand outside the research setting and its details and discover (or uncover) their characteristics objectively.

From an interpretive perspective, by contrast, the evidentiary material that the researcher analyzes is constructed by participants in the event or setting being studied. To the extent that the researcher herself is seen as a participant, one might even speak of the co-construction or co-generation of evidence. This language draws on the social constructionist argument that is central to phenomenology (see, e.g., Schütz 1962; Berger and Luckmann 1966). Methods of generating data are threefold: observing, interviewing, reading. Interpretive research typically draws on one or more of these three.

1. OBSERVING

Observing, with whatever degree of participation in the setting, acts, and events being observed, is the heart of participant-observer and ethnographic research. These methods entail more than just a set of tools; they rest on what might be called, in both cases, an "ethnographic sensibility" (Pader 2006). This means an intention to understand acts and actors as much as possible from within their own frame of reference, their own sense-making of the situation. In ways similar to those articulated by Erving Goffman (1959) concerning symbolic interactionism and Harold Garfinkel (1977) concerning ethnomethodology, the researcher seeks to understand the everyday, common sense, largely unarticulated, yet tacitly known "rules" that members of the situation have mastered and which enable them to navigate the interactions and settings that comprise their daily lives.

In the context of housing policy, for example, and specifically of occupancy rates, Ellen Pader's experience as a guest in the home of a Mexican family opened her eyes to the fact that the lived experience of "crowding"—the number of bodies occupying a given square footage of domestic space—is not universal. Yet United States housing policy sets occupancy rates that disallow the person:space ratios common in other parts of the world, even when immigrants to the United States from those places would themselves be more comfortable at the higher ratios familiar from their countries of origin. Enforcement of lower ratios mandated by law can, in her view, be discriminatory. It was her first-hand observation of different ways of constructing space and its meanings that led her to her analyses of these policies (see, e.g, Pader 1994, 1998, 2002, 2006).

---

6. For a critique of the fact-value dichotomy, see Rein (1976). For a critique of other ways of treating that dichotomy, see Hawkesworth (1988).

Herbert Gans (1976) makes the important point that participant-observation can entail varying degrees of participation. Ranging these along a continuum, we have at one end what most would probably consider the typical participant-observer role: much like Pader participating in the Mexican household, sleeping in the same bed with the daughters, the researcher assumes a situation-specific role and acts out of the requirements of that role. One might take on the role, for instance, of community organizer or agency department head (Yanow 1996) to study policy implementation at the local level. Gans notes, however, that it is also possible to be a participant-observer in the explicit or public role of researcher, rather than in an "insider" role. Here, the emphasis is more on "observer" than on "participant," although the researcher is present on site, accompanying policy-relevant actors as they attend to daily tasks and so on, according to the needs of the study. When called upon to act, the researcher does so in keeping with her research role, rather than her member role. Ingersoll and Adams' (1992) study of the Washington State Ferry system is an example of extended observation where the researchers mingled their observational roles as researchers with participation as system riders. Lin's (2000) comparative analysis of state prisons and criminal justice policy is another example of a study that drew on on-site observation, in which she was clearly in a researcher's role rather than that of either guard or prisoner.

All along this continuum, the researcher is ever-mindful of his researcher role, even in a situational role, as Gans stresses, even when constrained from acting as a researcher by the demands of his member role. This casts the researcher in an "undercover" role, which raises the classic questions of ethical research practice connected to disguised identity (that is, is it ethical for the researcher to disguise the fact that she is conducting research?). Different researchers take different positions on this question.[7]

2. INTERVIEWING

Interpretive interviewing bears a family resemblance to common conversation, although the interviewer typically takes a more active role in directing the trajectory of the conversation than, say, a friend or family member might. As with participant-observation or ethnographic research, the interpretive interviewer is interested in understanding how those he is talking to make sense of their lived experiences. This enacts a phenomenological position. Unlike the survey researcher, whose training stipulates that she not depart from the text of the written questions—neither in tone of voice nor delivery nor in wording or question order—the interpretive researcher typically seeks to draw the speaker out, much as one would a conversational partner, in order to gain further understanding of the terms being used or the perspective being articulated. Frederic Schaffer's "ordinary language interviewing" (2006) is an example. He sought to understand how those he spoke with in Senegal made sense of the concept of "democracy" (Schaffer 1998): was it, in their eyes and in their experiences, the same thing that Americans call democracy, or did it have a particular, local coloration? He shapes his follow-up questions to respond to what he has just been told or, at times, to clarify a point made earlier in the conversation (see Schaffer 2006).

Policy-related research often draws on interviews, especially of legislators or agency executives. Yet interviewing need not be restricted to "elites" (see, e.g., Soss 2006, Walsh 2004). From an interpretive research perspective, especially one informed by critical theory, non-elite actors are also seen as playing a role in shaping policies, especially in rejecting top-down acts such as in policy implementation; and the researcher would want to understand their perspectives as well. Jeanette Hoffman (1995), for instance, found that technology policy was determined not only by

---

7. In institution-based research in the United States where the investigator is required to comply with institutional review boards' (IRB) interpretations of protection of human subjects regulations, this question might also arise in the context of whether lack of such disclosure might potentialy harm research "subjects." There are many more questions about ethical practices and about IRB procedures than I can address in this chapter. See, e.g., Katz (2004).

policy-makers, but also in a complex interaction that included members of technology firms and university researchers.

Interviewing can be the sole source of data for an interpretive study. It can also be the "talk" part of a participant-observer or ethnographic study. However, if the researcher observes, say, office activities before, during, and after conducting interviews, that would not commonly be considered generating ethnographic observational data. The latter requires more systematicity to provide trustworthy evidence: "being there" through prolonged observation over time and space, in various circumstances (e.g., times of day, days of the week, time of year, level or part of the organization), depending on how these bear on the research question.

3. READING DOCUMENTS

The third source of interpretive data is documents of various kinds, depending on the research topic. These can be legislative records, bills and their marked-up drafts, notes on meetings, personal diaries, daily calendars, agency memos, annual reports, correspondence, and so on. For historical data, the researcher might also read back issues of newspapers; depending on the research question, editorial columns might constitute data alongside reportage. Rather than reading these as event evidence, they might be read for a sense of the times—of how people responded at that time to particular events or ideas. The focus is on meaning-making. One is, in a way, interrogating the written record when one was not or could not be present oneself. Phyllis Chock's (1995) study of Congressional "talk" during debates on immigration policy is an example of such usage of legislative records. By examining the written record of spoken language, she was able to analyze the ways in which legislators' and expert witnesses' embedded ideas about immigrants reflected and shaped immigration reform and policy contentions.

Document reading can also be part of an observational study or an interview-based project. Documents can provide background information prior to designing the research project, for example, or prior to conducting interviews. They may corroborate observational and interview data—or they may refute them, in which case the researcher is "armed" with evidence that can be used to clarify or, perhaps, to challenge what he is being told, a role that observational data may also play.

METHODS OF ANALYZING DATA

Once one has data in hand, so to speak, how might one analyze them interpretively? Analysis and data generation are not so clearly separable—analysis begins, in fact, with the very design of the research project, and fieldwork, deskwork, and textwork (the "writing up") are intertwined; but in a short chapter, it is easier to treat them as if they were temporally distinct.

There is a vast array of interpretive methods of analysis, among them action research (or participatory action research), case study analysis (either single or explicitly comparative), category analysis, content analysis (word-based, not incidence rate counts), conversational analysis, discourse analysis, dramaturgical analysis, ethnomethodology, frame (-reflective) analysis, genealogy, grounded theory, life histories, metaphor analysis, myth analysis, narrative analysis (of various sorts), poststructural analysis, science studies, semiotics, space analysis, story-telling analysis, and value-critical analysis. Some of these have been drawn on in policy research more than others, perhaps for reasons of familiarity rather than anything else (although one might argue that the subjects of policy studies are marked by a degree of contention that lends themselves to some methods, such as frame or value-critical analysis, more than others). Here, I will touch on a few of these as exemplars.

1. Frame or Value-Critical Aanalysis

Interviewing, sometimes together with observing (e.g., meetings, public hearings) and document analysis, lends itself to frame analysis or value-critical analysis (see, e.g., Linder 1995; Schmidt 2000, 2006; Schon and Rein 1994; Swaffield 1998; see also Luker 1984). Here, the researcher identifies two or more interpretive communities (also called communities of meaning, communities of practice, speech or discourse communities, etc.) and the language each uses to "frame" the policy issue, typically in conflicting ways. Analysis consists of identifying the values underlying the respective frames. Undertaken in an action research mode, this analysis might also suggest interventions to enable each interpretive community to understand why the other reasons in the way that it does and possibly to broker a mediated resolution to the conflict. Graham Allison's (1971) multiple-lens study of the Cuban missile crisis was an earlier version of this kind of research. It is an approach that has been taken up in organizational studies at a theoretical level (see, e.g., Morgan 1986 or Bolman and Deal 1991). I have extended the interventionist implications of this approach also to implementation analysis (Yanow 1987).

2. Story-Telling Analysis

Drawing on an interesting combination of interviewing with directed diary writing, Steven Maynard-Moody and Michael Musheno (2003) and their colleagues have developed a method of accessing stories told by front-line workers concerning their actions in implementing public policies. Michael Lipsky's (1980), Jeffrey Prottas' (1979), and Richard Weatherly's (1979) first-generation studies of workers at the front lines themselves rested on intimate familiarity with what teachers, social workers, police officers, and others actually do in the field—how they interact with clients, students, and so on—generated through some combination of observing people in action and talking with workers and others.

3. Narrative Analysis

Other researchers see narrative analysis as distinct from story analysis. Carolyn Hendriks (2005a), for example, treats narratives as the overall development of a line of argument, rather than as stories in the way used by Maynard-Moody and Musheno—narratives with plot lines that have beginnings, middles, and ends. Emery Roe's (1993) theory of narrative policy analysis draws on a stream of literary theory that uses "counter-narratives" as ways of making the line of argument clearer, through juxtaposing the narrative argument with a contrasting hypothetical. Tineke Abma (1999) has treated narrative analysis in a number of ways in the context of program evaluations. What all of these have in common is a focus on the importance of attending to policy-relevant actors' language in discerning the character of disputes and the potentials for interpretation.

4. Dramaturgical Analysis

Maarten Hajer (2005) draws on the approach developed by the literary theorist Kenneth Burke for analyzing dramas. His analytic pentad situates dramatic action in the context of its setting, looking also at the actors in question, their acts, and their agency and purpose (Burke 1945). This provides a systematic framework for the analysis of policy "acts," which Hajer has extended most recently to the analysis of events surrounding the murder of the Dutch public figure Theo van Gogh. Burke's theory also suggests a systematic approach to the analysis of policy and organizational settings and their spatial meanings (Yanow 2000, 2006b).

5. CATEGORY ANALYSIS

One of the analytic steps that characterizes the work of interpretive researchers is the impulse to, in the words of some, "destabilize" received or commonplace meanings. Others talk about this using the language of "deconstruction": accepted policy meanings are deconstructed in the sense that the typically unspoken, commonsense assumptions built in to them are named and subjected to inquiry. One of the most common sets of assumptions are those embedded in policy issue categories, such as classifications of welfare recipients or prisoners, or of school children and their learning levels. Analyzing the language and structure of these categories along with practices of category-making is another area of interpretive method. As creating categories for administrative purposes through policy-making is a common state activity, category analysis is especially useful in policy research. I have developed one approach to category analysis and used it in the context of race-ethnic policy and administrative practices, such as those used in hospitals, census-taking, and employment (Yanow 2003).

There are many more forms of interpretive (qualitative) approaches to policy research than there is space to discuss here. The references point to some of these, as well as to primary and secondary sources for their theoretical and philosophical background. Additional forms will continue to be developed as more and more policy researchers discover the utility of analyses grounded in the actual lived experiences of policy-relevant actors and in the meanings they make of the policies that engage and affect their lives.

REFERENCES

Abma, Tineke, ed. 1999. *Telling Tales: On Narrative and Evaluation.* Advances in Program Evaluation, v. 6. Stamford, CT: JAI Press.

Allison, Graham. 1971. *Essence of Decision.* Boston: Little, Brown.

Becker, Howard S., Geer, Blanche, Hughes, Everett C., and Strauss, Anselm L. 1961. *Boys in White.* Chicago: University of Chicago Press.

Berger, Peter L. and Luckmann, Thomas. 1966. *The Social Construction of Reality.* New York: Anchor Books.

Bernstein, Richard J. 1983. *Beyond Objectivism and Relativism.* Philadelphia: University of Pennsylvania Press.

Blau, Peter. 1963 [1953]. *The Dynamics of Bureaucracy.* Chicago: University of Chicago Press.

Bolman, Lee G. and Deal, Terrence E. 1991. *Reframing Organizations.* San Francisco: Jossey-Bass.

Burke, Kenneth. 1945. *A Grammar of Motives.* New York: Prentice Hall.

Chock, Phyllis Pease. 1995. "Ambiguity in Policy Discourse: Congressional Talk About Immigration." *Policy Sciences* 28: 165–84.

Dalton, Melville. 1959. *Men Who Manage.* New York: Wiley.

Fischer, Frank and Forester, John, eds. 1993. *The Argumentative Turn in Policy Analysis and Planning.* Durham, NC: Duke University Press.

Gans, Herbert. 1976. "Personal Journal: B. On the Methods Used in This Study." In *The Research Experience,* ed. M. Patricia Golden, 49–59. Itasca, IL: F.E. Peacock.

Garfinkel, Harold. 1977. "What is Ethnomethodology?" In *Understanding and Social Inquiry,* ed. Fred R. Dallmayr and Thomas A. McCarthy, 240–61. Notre Dame, IN: University of Notre Dame Press.

Goffman, Erving. 1959. *The Presentation of Self in Everyday Life.* New York: Doubleday.

Gouldner, Alvin Ward. 1954. *Patterns of Industrial Bureaucracy.* Glencoe, IL: Free Press.

Gusfield, Joseph R. 1976. "The Literary Rhetoric of Science." *American Sociological Review* 41: 16–34.

Gusfield, Joseph R. 1981. *The Culture of Public Problems: Drinking-driving and the Symbolic Order.* Chicago: University of Chicago Press.

Hajer, Maarten. 2005. "Setting the Stage: A Dramaturgy of Policy Deliberation." *Administration and Society* 36: 624–647.

Hajer, Maarten A. and Wagenaar, Hendrik, eds. 2003. *Deliberative Policy Analysis.* NY: Cambridge University Press.

Haraway, Donna. 1988. "Situated Knowledges: The Science Question in Feminism and the Privilege of the Partial Perspective." *Feminist Studies* 14: 575–99.

Harding, Sandra. 1993. "Rethinking Standpoint Epistemology: What is 'Strong Objectivity'?" In *Feminist Epistemologies*, ed. Linda Alcoff and Elizabeth Potter, 49–82. New York: Routledge.

Hartsock, Nancy C. M. 1987. "The Feminist Standpoint." In *Feminism & Methodology*, ed. Sandra Harding, 157–80. Bloomington: Indiana University Press.

Hawkesworth, M. E. 1988. *Theoretical Issues in Policy Analysis.* Albany, NY: SUNY Press.

Hawkesworth, Mary. 2006. *Feminist Inquiry: From Political Conviction to Methodological Innovation.* New Brunswick, NJ: Rutgers University Press.

Hendriks, Carolyn M. 2005a. "Participatory Storylines and Their Influence on Deliberative Forums." *Policy Sciences* 38: 1–20.

Hendriks, Carolyn M. 2005b. "Stories from Policy Praxis: The Case of Deliberative Governance." Presented at the European Consortium for Political Research Conference, Budapest (September).

Hofmann, Jeanette. 1995. "Implicit Theories in Policy Discourse: An Inquiry into the Interpretations of Reality in German Technology Policy." *Policy Sciences* 28: 127–48.

Ingersoll, Virginia Hill and Adams, Guy. 1992. *The Tacit Organization.* Greenwich, CT: JAI Press.

Iser, Wolfgang. 1989. *Prospecting: From Reader Response To Literary Anthropology.* Baltimore: Johns Hopkins University Press.

Katz, Jack. 2004. "Subterranean Fieldworkers' Blues: Scratching Toward a Common Law of Social Research Ethics." Presented to the Center for the Study of Law and Society, Boalt Hall School of Law, University of California, Berkeley (February 17).

Kaufman, Roger. 1960. *The Forest Ranger.* Baltimore, MD: Published for Resources for the Future by Johns Hopkins Press.

Lin, Ann Chih. 2000. *Reform in the Making.* Princeton, NJ: Princeton University Press.

Linder, Steven. 1995. "Contending Discourses in the Electric and Magnetic Fields Controversy." *Policy Sciences* 28: 209–30.

Lipsky, Michael. 1980. *Street-Level Bureaucracy.* New York: Russell Sage Foundation.

Luker, Kristin. 1984. *Abortion and the Politics of Motherhood.* Berkeley: University of California Press.

Maynard-Moody, Steven and Musheno, Michael. 2003. *Cops, Teachers, Counselors: Stories from the Front Lines of Public Service.* Ann Arbor, MI: University of Michigan Press.

Maynard-Moody, Steven and Musheno, Michael. 2006. "Stories for Research." In *Interpretation and Method: Empirical Research Methods and the Interpretive Turn*, ed. Dvora Yanow and Peregrine Schwartz-Shea, ch. 18. Armonk, NY: M.E. Sharpe.

Morgan, Gareth. 1986. *Images of Organization.* Beverly Hills, CA: Sage Publications.

Nagel, Thomas. 1986. *The View from Nowhere.* New York: Oxford University Press.

Pader, Ellen J. 1994. "Spatial Relations and Housing Policy: Regulations that Discriminate Against Mexican-Origin Households." *Journal of Planning Education and Research* 13: 119–35.

Pader, Ellen-J. 1998. "Housing Occupancy Codes." In *The Encyclopedia of Housing*, ed. Willem van Vliet, 288–90. Thousand Oaks, CA: Sage.

Pader, Ellen J. 2002. "Housing Occupancy Standards: Inscribing Ethnicity and Family Relations on the Land." *Journal of Architecture and Planning Research* 19: 300–18.

Pader, Ellen. 2006. "Seeing with an Ethnographic Sensibility: Explorations Beneath the Surface of Public Policies." In *Interpretation and Method: Empirical Research Methods and the Interpretive Turn*, ed. Dvora Yanow and Peregrine Schwartz-Shea, ch. 8. Armonk, NY: M.E. Sharpe.

Prasad, Pushkala. 2005. *Crafting Qualitative Research: Working in the Postpositivist Traditions.* Armonk, NY: M.E. Sharpe.

Prottas, Jeffrey Manditch. 1979. *People Processing: The Street-Level Bureaucrat in Public Service Bureaucracies.* Lexington, MA: Lexington Books.

Rabinow, Paul and Sullivan, William M., eds. 1979. *Interpretive Social Science.* Berkeley: University of California Press.

Rabinow, Paul and Sullivan, William M., eds. 1985. *Interpretive Social Science*, 2nd ed. Berkeley: University of California Press.

Rein, Martin. 1976. *Social Science and Public Policy.* New York: Penguin Books.

Ricoeur, Paul. 1971. "The Model of the Text." *Social Research* 38: 529–62.

Roe, Emery. 1994. *Narrative Policy Analysis: Theory and Practice.* Durham, NC: Duke University Press.

Schaffer, Frederic Charles. 1998. *Democracy in Translation: Understanding Politics in an Unfamiliar Culture.* Ithaca, NY: Cornell University Press.

Schaffer, Frederic Charles. 2006. "Ordinary Language Interviewing." In *Interpretation and Method: Empirical Research Methods and the Interpretive Turn*, ed. Dvora Yanow and Peregrine Schwartz-Shea, ch. 7. Armonk, NY: M.E. Sharpe.

Schmidt, Ronald, Sr. 2000. *Language Policy and Identity Politics in the United States.* Philadelphia, PA: Temple University Press.

Schmidt, Ronald, Sr. 2006. "Value-Critical Policy Analysis: The Case of Language Policy in the United States." In *Interpretation and Method: Empirical Research Methods and the Interpretive Turn*, ed. Dvora Yanow and Peregrine Schwartz-Shea, ch. 17. Armonk, NY: M.E. Sharpe.

Schon, Donald A. and Rein, Martin. 1994. *Frame Reflection: Toward the Resolution of Intractable Policy Controversies.* New York: Basic Books.

Schütz, Alfred. 1962. "On Multiple Realities." *Collected Papers,* ed. Maurice Natanson, 3 vols., 207–59. The Hague: Martinus Nijhoff.

Selznick, Philip. 1949. *TVA and the Grass Roots: A Study in the Sociology of Formal Organization.* Berkeley: University of California Press.

Soss, Joe. 2006. "Talking Our Way to Meaningful Explanations: A Practice-Centered View of Interviewing for Interpretive Research." In *Interpretation and Method: Empirical Research Methods and the Interpretive Turn*, ed. Dvora Yanow and Peregrine Schwartz-Shea, ch. 6. Armonk, NY: M.E. Sharpe.

Swaffield, Simon. 1998. "Contextual Meanings in Policy Discourse: A Case Study of Language Use Concerning Resource Policy in the New Zealand High Country." *Policy Sciences* 31: 199–224.

Taylor, Charles. 1971. "Interpretation and the Sciences of Man." *Review of Metaphysics* 25: 3–51.

Walsh, Katherine Cramer. 2004. *Talking About Politics: Informal Groups and Social Identity in American Life.* Chicago: University of Chicago Press.

Weatherley, Richard A. 1979. *Reforming Special Education: Policy Implementation from State Level to Street Level.* Cambridge, MA: MIT Press.

White, Jay D. 1992. "Taking Language Seriously: Toward a Narrative Theory of Knowledge for Administrative Research." *American Review of Public Administration* 22: 75–88.

White, Jay D. 1999. *Taking Language Seriously: The Narrative Foundations of Public Administration Research.* Washington, DC: Georgetown University Press.

Yanow, Dvora. 1987. "Toward a Policy Culture Approach to Implementation Analysis." *Policy Studies Review* 7, 103–115.

Yanow, Dvora. 1996. *How Does a Policy Mean? Interpreting Policy and Organizational Actions.* Washington, DC: Georgetown University Press.

Yanow, Dvora. 2000. *Conducting Interpretive Policy Analysis.* Newbury Park, CA: Sage.

Yanow, Dvora. 2003. *Constructing American "Race" and "Ethnicity": Category-making in Public Policy and Administration.* Armonk, NY: M.E. Sharpe.

Yanow, Dvora. 2006a. "Neither Rigorous Nor Objective? Interrogating Criteria for Knowledge Claims in Interpretive Science." In *Interpretation and Method: Empirical Research Methods and the Interpretive Turn*, ed. Dvora Yanow and Peregrine Schwartz-Shea, ch. 4. Armonk, NY: M.E. Sharpe.

Yanow, Dvora. 2006b. "How Built Spaces Mean: A Semiotics of Space" In *Interpretation and Method: Empirical Research Methods and the Interpretive Turn*, ed. Dvora Yanow and Peregrine Schwartz-Shea, ch. 20. Armonk, NY: M E Sharpe.

Yanow, Dvora and Schwartz-Shea, Peregrine. 2006. *Interpretation and Method: Empirical Research Methods and the Interpretive Turn.* Armonk, NY: M E Sharpe.

28 Qualitative Research and Public Policy

Alan R. Sadovnik

Over the past two decades, the use of qualitative research in the social sciences has increased significantly (Riehl 2001). Although quantitative methodologies remain the dominant paradigm in policy research and recent federal policy initiatives privileging experimental designs and randomized field trials as the gold standard for evaluation research have bolstered its position, qualitative methods remain an important tool for policy researchers (Maxwell 2004; Chatterji 2005). The purpose of this chapter is to discuss the evolution of qualitative research, its strengths and weaknesses, how it differs from quantitative research, and its important contributions to public policy research, especially in educational research. Based upon this discussion, I will argue that qualitative research should be part of any mixed-method approach to policy research.

WHAT IS QUALITATIVE RESEARCH?

Qualitative research involves research that uses observational, communicative, and documentary methods in natural settings (Riehl 2001, 116) in an effort to understand the social world. According to Denzin and Lincoln, it is

> multi-method in focus, involving an interpretive, naturalistic approach to its subject matter. This means that qualitative researchers study things in their natural settings, attempting to make sense of, or interpret, phenomena in terms of the meanings people bring to them. Qualitative research involves the studied use and collection of a variety of empirical methods—case study, personal experience, introspective, life story, interview, observational, historical, interactional, and visual texts—that describe routine and problematic moments in individuals' lives. (1994, 2)

Some qualitative researchers have remained squarely in the scientific tradition of post-positivism: insisting on objectivity, rigorous research design, and examining causality (Maxwell 2004). Others are more rooted within interpretive traditions, including symbolic interactionism, ethnomethodology, hermeneutics, postmodernism, feminism, critical theory, and cultural studies (Riehl 2001, 116) and in varying degrees reject post-positivist notions of scientific rigor.

HISTORY OF QUALITATIVE RESEARCH

Logical positivism has been the foundation for social science methods since the nineteenth century. From Comte's introduction of a positive science of society, later to be termed positivism, to Durkheim's codification of positivist empiricism in his classic *The Rules of Sociological Method*, quantitative methods dominated social science, especially in the United States (Denzin and Lincoln

1994, 1–17). However, there has been a rich, concurrent qualitative tradition, beginning with cultural anthropology and institutionalized in sociology by the Chicago School in the 1920s–1940s (Vidich and Lyman 1994, 23–59).

The Chicago School sociologists, such as Robert Park, Ernest W. Burgess, W.I. Thomas and Louis Wirth produced a series of ethnographic studies on Chicago neighborhoods that was part of the larger project of producing an ecological theory of urban life. These sociologists moved away from the "missionary" perspective of earlier sociologists such as Albion Small and early cultural anthropologists seeking to bring a Christian attitude to the study of "primitive" cultures. The Chicago School made ethnographic studies an important feature of American sociology (Vidich and Lyman 1994, 32–35).

Working within this tradition, William Foote Whyte's *Street Corner Society* (1943, 1955, 1981) about Italian Americans living in the North End of Boston introduced participant observation as an important part of ethnography. Whyte lived in the neighborhood, interacted daily with his "Cornerville" boys and became a subject of his own study. Like his mentors in Chicago's Sociology Department, Whyte's work was "initially motivated by a sense of moral responsibility to up-lift the slum-dwelling masses," but became the model for future ethnographic research in which the researcher became part of the group he was studying. Such immersion required ethnographers to move back and forth between their roles as "objective" observers and their roles as "subjective" participants (Vidich and Lyman 1994, 34).

Some Chicago School researchers, like Park, worked from an assimilationist model, with their works exploring how to assimilate new immigrants into the urban Protestant middle class culture. Others like Hollingshead (1949/1961) celebrated nineteenth-century small town values and relied on Durkheim's distinction between mechanical and organic societies and Tonnie's distinction between *gemeinschaft* and *gesellschaft*. Neither model, however, could account for the racism within American society and the opposition to the assimilation of African Americans into mainstream culture. Another Chicago trained sociologist, African-American E. Franklin Frazier produced a series of works (1937a, 1937b, 1957) that "stands apart, not only because it points to the exclusion of blacks from the American ideal of brotherhood and the then-emerging civic otherhood, but also because its research orientation drew on the life histories of his subjects and his own experience (Vidich and Lyman 1994, 34).

From World War II to the present, American sociology moved away from the assimilationist model to a more pluralist one, with ethnographies rejecting a linear pattern of the integration of immigrants and African Americans into white, middle-class culture. Recent works such as Portes and Rumbaut's *Legacies: The Story of the Immigrant Second Generation* (2001) provides much more nuanced ethnographic accounts of the tensions between assimilation and separation and introduces the term "segmented assimilation" to reject a linear model of cultural integration. What *Legacies* has in common with earlier ethnographic accounts is its rich descriptions of immigrant life and an understanding of the subjective perspectives of individuals and groups, the hallmark of qualitative research.

From the early twentieth century, qualitative research has been influenced by interpretive and phenomenological paradigms in the social sciences (Giddens 1975). From the symbolic interactionism of G.H. Mead and Herbert Blumer with its emphasis on the social construction of reality, to the sociological analysis of everyday life by Erving Goffman (1961a, 1961b, 1963a, 1963b, 1967) and ethnomethodologist Harold Garfinkel (1967), qualitative researchers sought to uncover the contextual use of symbols, such as language and dress and the problematic nature of meanings (Collins 1975; Sadovnik 1994). These micro-sociologies of everyday discourse and interactions laid bare the ways in which social actors constructed meaning in the context of social interactions and how everyday life is often confused, problematic and uncertain. When combined with more macro-structural approaches, these sociologies of everyday life became powerful analyses of social order and change (Collins 1975, 2005).

From the 1980s to the present, qualitative research has been heavily influenced by postmodernism. Postmodernism developed out of a profound dissatisfaction with the modernist project of enlightenment and reason. Beginning with the poststructural writings of Jacques Derrida (1973, 1981, 1982) and Jean Baudrillard (1981, 1984), social theorists, particularly in France, questioned the appropriateness of modernist categories for understanding what they saw as a postmodern world, a world that transcended the economic and social relations of the industrial world that modernist thought had sought to understand. In particular, the work of Jean Francois Lyotard (1982, 1984) rejected the Marxist perspective and the Enlightenment and modernist assumptions underlying Marxist theory and sought to create a different theory for the late twentieth century.

There is a vast body of literature on the definition of postmodernist theory (Aronowitz and Giroux 1991; Giroux 1991; Harvey 1989; Jameson 1982, 1992; Jencks 1987; Lyotard 1984), as well as a growing body of literature on postmodern approaches to education (Aronowitz and Giroux 1991; Cherryholmes 1988; Doll 1989; Ellsworth 1989; Giroux 1988, 1991; Lather 1989; McLaren 1986, 1991; McLaren and Hammer 1989; Wexler 1987).

It is important to begin by defining modernist social theory. In both sociology and philosophy, modernist theory traces its intellectual heritage to the Enlightenment. From the classical sociological theory of Marx (1971), Marx and Engels (1947), Weber (1978), and Durkheim (1938/1977, 1947), to the pragmatist philosophy of Dewey (1916, 1927/1984), and to the social theory of Jürgen Habermas (1979, 1981, 1982, 1983, 1987), what is usually referred to as modernist theories had a number of things in common. First, they believed in progress through science and technology, even if they were skeptical of positivist social science. Second, they emphasized the Enlightenment belief in reason. And third, they stressed Enlightenment principles such as equality, liberty, and justice.

Postmodernist thought consists of many interrelated themes. First, postmodernism insists on what Lyotard (1984) has labeled the rejection of all metanarratives. By this, Lyotard meant that modernist preoccupation with grand, total, or all-encompassing explanations of the world need to be replaced by localized and particular theories. Second, postmodernism stresses the necessary connection between theory and practice as a corrective to the separation of them in much modernist thought. Third, postmodernism stresses the democratic response to authoritarianism and totalitarianism. In particular, Stanley Aronowitz and Henry Giroux (1991), Giroux (1991), and Peter McLaren and R. Hammer (1989) call for a democratic, emancipatory, and antitotalitarian theory and practice, with schools seen as sites for democratic transformation. Fourth, postmodernism sees modernist thought as Eurocentric and patriarchal. Giroux (1991), Patricia Lather (1991), Elizabeth Ellsworth (1989), and others provide an important critique of the racism and sexism in some modernist writings and of the failure of modernism to address the interests of women and people of color. Fifth, postmodernist theorists believe that all social and political discourses are related to structures of power and domination. Sixth, postmodernism stresses what N. Burbules and S. Rice (1991) term "dialogue across differences." Recognizing the particular and local nature of knowledge, postmodern theorists call for the attempt to work through differences rather than to see them as hopelessly irreconcilable. Thus, postmodern theories of education call for teachers and students to explore the differences between what may seem like inherently contradictory positions in an effort to achieve understanding, respect, and change.

In qualitative research the works of Norman Denzin and Yvonne Lincoln (1994, 2000, 2005) have influenced what has been termed the postmodern turn. Rejecting the modernist approaches of earlier qualitative researchers such as Howard Becker, whose *Boys in White* (Becker 1961/1976), applied rigorous scientific methods of quantitative research to qualitative analysis, postmodernists rejected the principles of logical positivism and crossed theoretical and methodological boundaries. These researchers produced small case studies, celebrated stories and narratives, and questioned the possibility of objectivity. These researchers often blurred the lines between social science and literature, with traditional methodological concerns with objectivity, sample size, and reliability and validity rejected as Eurocentric and oppressive (Kincheloe and Steinberg 1998; Lather 1989,

1991). Sadovnik (1995) provides a critique of postmodern research in education, arguing that they often lack empirical evidence to support their claims. Nonetheless, in the last decade they have increasingly become an important school of qualitative research.

Insufficient empirical evidence is certainly a problem for policy research, where policy makers rely on sound empirical findings to influence policy. Despite the problems with much postmodern research, there remains a significant body of qualitative research that is methodologically sound and is important for policy research. Riehl (2001, 117) argues that there have been numerous important qualitative studies in the sociology of education that have influenced policy in a number of areas, including studies of inequality and the differential effects of schooling on student achievement, schooling and socialization, schools as social organizations, and policy issues in education.

THE NATURE OF QUALITATIVE RESEARCH

Qualitative research is based on what sociologists term social constructionism and interpretivism. Unlike quantitative research, which is usually deductive (theory testing), qualitative research is usually inductive (theory construction). Social scientists do not simply discover or find knowledge; they are not detached from the world they are researching. Rather, they actively construct knowledge by inventing tools and instruments to collect and produce data. These tools and instruments are constantly renewed and revised. Social scientists formulate concepts to make interpretations of the data. The language coined to interpret data is distinguished from everyday talk, but also enters everyday talk. As concepts enter everyday talk they shape everyday practices and activities. There are a number of different forms of constructionism:

- Weak Constructionism: "Scientific knowledge is in part the product of processes of social negotiation without claiming that such knowledge is *only* a matter of social negotiation." This position avoids the relativist view that any interpretation is as good as another (Schwandt 2000, 199).
- Strong Constructionism: "Radical social constructionists ... argue that knowledge is the product of social processes and that all statements of the true, the rational, and the good are the products of various particular communities of interpreters and thus to be regarded with suspicion" (ibid., 199).

Interpretivism views human action as inherently meaningful and therefore qualitative researchers interpret the subjective meaning of action (grasping the actor's beliefs, desires, etc.) from an objective manner. Within this context, understanding is an intellectual process whereby the researcher (the inquirer as subject) gains knowledge about an object (the meaning of human action). Researchers refer to the hermeneutic circle of understanding which is "object oriented": it directs the researcher to the texts, institutions, practices or norms of life that are the object of inquiry. No reference is made to the researcher (Schwandt 2000).

A more radical branch of interpretivism is derived from philosophical hermeneutics, which is radical departure from other interpretivist methods. This perspective challenges the Cartesian binary or dichotomy between the inquirer (subject) and the object of inquiry (research object) and argues that:

- research knowledge cannot simply reproduce the meanings or understandings of the empirical world without taking into account the researchers' biases;
- understanding is something that is *produced* in the dialogue of research;

- a naive realism or objectivism is opposed with respect to meaning and endorses the position that there is never a finally correct interpretation;
- meaning is negotiated. (Schwandt 2000, as cited in Singh 2005)

Based upon the view that reality is socially constructed and negotiated, qualitative researchers attempt to uncover this situated, contextual, and changing nature of reality. In order to do this, qualitative researchers use a variety of methodological approaches and sampling techniques.

ETHNOGRAPHY

Ethnography refers to an in-depth study of a group of people or individuals in their or his context. It is both descriptive and interpretive, providing an insider view of the subjects. This includes what is called an emic view, the view of the insiders of themselves, and an etic view, the view of the outsiders of the culture. The ethnographic method includes the following:

- Selection of the group/site
- Gaining entrance
- Identification of area of interest
- Immersion in the context
- Gaining informants
- Data gathering (observations, interviews, artifacts)
- Data analysis and theory development—intermittent with collection—"thick description"
- Avoidance of theoretical preconceptions. (Singh 2005)

ACTION RESEARCH

This type of qualitative method is aimed at improving a certain practice, organizational context or a way of life. Action research is characterized by the following:

- It understands practice as a social phenomenon;
- It involves the people within the practice in the research process—it is participatory;
- It involves people working collaboratively with each other and with people from the outside;
- It is critical—asks why, why not, whose voice is being heard, and whose interests are being served;
- Aims at empowering people inside the practice. (Singh 2005)

Researchers who want to directly influence the practice within organizations most often use action research. For example, educational researchers often conduct action research with teachers and principals in schools in order to discover what works and what does not work and to collaboratively implement organizational change. From a positivist standpoint, such a priori political goals violate the objective norms of science and make the researcher part of the processes under investigation. Action researchers reject this stance of objectivity and argue that the purpose of research is to help improve the organizations under investigation. Although action research has become an important tool for policy research, it remains controversial.

CASE STUDY

A case study is a holistic, in-depth investigation that uses multiple sources of data that can be either quantitative or qualitative. There are three types of case studies: *Exploratory*, *Explanatory*, and *Descriptive*. The researcher selects cases for either intrinsic or instrumental reasons; it can be different from ethnography because it does not necessarily aim to see the emic view and different from action research because it does not necessarily aim to change a practice or involve the people from the inside (Singh 2005).

GROUNDED RESEARCH

Based on the grounded theory of Strauss and Glaser (1967) and Strauss and Corbin (1990), the general goal of grounded theory research is to construct theories in order to understand phenomena. Its main contribution is in generating theory from data in a systematic way—theory grounded in the data. Using the process of analytic induction, grounded theory research examines cases in detail and continues to build theory from the bottom up—based on observations of particular data. In the process of examining these cases over time, the researcher continually refines and develops new theories to explain the observed phenomena.

These types of qualitative approaches involve a number of different methods, some or all of which can be used in a given study. These include interviews, focus group interviews, observation (participant and non-participant), archival and content analysis.

Interviews may be conducted face-to-face, by e-mail, or telephone and may be informal, semi-structured, or formal, structured interviews. They are sometimes audiotaped and then carefully transcribed. These transcripts can be analyzed using a number of different qualitative software packages, which organize the data according to a number of themes.

A selected group of individuals may be interviewed on a common topic; the group dynamics provide valuable information. These focus groups are often organized around a topic, scenario, or dilemma. Although focus groups can provide the interviewer with important insights, they can also be manipulated by the presence of a strong personality in the group. Skilled focus group interviewers have to manage the group dynamics carefully.

Observation may be participant observation or non-participant observation. In participant observation, the researcher becomes a part of the context he/she is studying. For example, in *Street Corner Society*, William Foote Whyte lived in the North End of Boston and became a member of the group he was studying. In *Home Advantage*, Annette Lareau served as a teaching assistant in the schools she was studying. The purpose of such immersion is to allow the researcher to become part of the culture and to understand the subjective perception of members. The danger is that participant observers can lose their objectivity or begin to see the world as members rather than researchers.

Non-participant observation involves observing individuals or groups from the outside, often without any direct interaction. The work of Erving Goffman (1971) is the best example of such an approach. Goffman observed people in their natural settings, including theaters, cafeterias, train stations, public restrooms and built a dramaturgical theory of human interaction. This approach saw social actors as in a continual state of performance and interpretation. Adler and Adler (1994) note that the major problem with this form of research concerns its validity, as without interacting with people, the researcher is always interpreting their behavior from his perspective, without benefit of learning the subjective perspective of the individuals involved.

Qualitative researchers sometimes study situations and organizations of which they are a part. This type of research, observer as participant is a potentially fruitful but difficult form of qualitative research. Sadovnik (1994) and Semel (1994) provide accounts of the difficulties of conducting research in schools in which they were teaching and of the need to bracket out their insider perspective as a member of the group from their outside perspective as researcher.

One of the most controversial issues in observational research is the question of consent. Although IRB (Institutional Review Board) regulations require that researchers inform their subjects that they will be studying them, some researchers argue that deception may be necessary to uncover the workings of some organizations. Journalists, for example, sometime pose as members without consent in order to do an expose. For example, Emily Sachar taught as a New York City public school teacher for a year and then wrote a series of articles in *Newsday*, later published as *Shut Up and Let the Lady Teach* (1991). The principal, teachers, and students in the school did not know she was a journalist until the series was published. Punch (1994) argues that although deception is generally a violation of social science research codes, there may be times when the public good outweighs this restriction, so long as the ethical dictum, "do no harm" is followed.

CRITERIA FOR EVALUATING QUALITATIVE RESEARCH DESIGNS

Qualitative policy research must be conducted in a systematic manner if policy makers are going to take its recommendations seriously. Therefore, we must be able to evaluate the research designs of qualitative studies. The criteria for such evaluation include:

- Identification of comments about participant/site selection-sampling procedures, ethical clearance procedures, design of data collection protocols, and data analysis instruments;
- Rationale for sampling procedures—choice of sites, participants, and size of cohort;
- Deployment of different data collection instruments—interviews, observation, documents, and audio/video recordings;
- Systematic procedure for recording data—protocols, and transcription conventions;
- Systematic procedure for analyzing data;
- Reliability of sample size: Although qualitative research does not require the type of reliability and generalizabilty of quantitative research, the question of sample size remains an important one. Whether educational policy makers can or should make policy based on one classroom or school is an important question. The evaluation of sample size usually revolves around whether or not the case or cases can be seen in some way as representative of a larger population of which it or they are a part. (Creswell 2005, in cited in Singh, 2005)

STRENGTHS AND WEAKNESSES OF QUALITATIVE RESEARCH

Johnson and Onwuegbuzie (2004, 20) provide a useful discussion of the strengths and weaknesses of qualitative research:

Strengths

- The data are based on the participants' own categories of meaning.
- It is useful for studying a limited number of cases in depth.
- It is useful for describing complex phenomena.
- Provides individual case information.
- Can conduct cross-case comparisons and analysis.
- Provides understanding and description of people's personal experiences of phenomena (i.e., the "emic" or insider's viewpoint).

- Can describe, in rich detail, phenomena as they are situated and embedded in local contexts.
- The researcher identifies contextual and setting factors as they relate to the phenomenon of interest.
- The researcher can study dynamic processes (i.e., documenting sequential patterns and change).
- The researcher can use the primarily qualitative method of "grounded theory" to generate inductively a tentative but explanatory theory about a phenomenon.
- Can determine how participants interpret "constructs" (e.g., self-esteem, IQ).
- Data are usually collected in naturalistic settings in qualitative research.
- Qualitative approaches are responsive to local situations, conditions, and stakeholders' needs.
- Qualitative researchers are responsive to changes that occur during the conduct of a study (especially during extended fieldwork) and may shift the focus of their studies as a result.
- Qualitative data in the words and categories of participants lend themselves to exploring how and why phenomena occur.
- One can use an important case to demonstrate vividly a phenomenon to the readers of a report.
- Determine *idiographic* causation (i.e., determination of causes of a particular event).

Weaknesses

- Knowledge produced may not generalize to other people or other settings (i.e., findings may be unique to the relatively few people included in the research study).
- It is difficult to make quantitative predictions.
- It is more difficult to test hypotheses and theories.
- It may have lower credibility with some administrators and commissioners of programs.
- It generally takes more time to collect the data when compared to quantitative research.
- Data analysis is often time consuming.
- The results are more easily influenced by the researcher's personal biases and idiosyncrasies.

Based upon these strengths and weaknesses, it is clear that qualitative research should be an important part of public policy research. Riehl (2004) argues that qualitative research in the sociology of education has made valuable contributions to our understanding of educational problems and has offered policy makers useful data for school improvement. In an age where educational research is dominated by the Institute of Education Sciences at the U.S. Department of Education labeling experimental research design and randomized field trials modeled after the pharmaceutical and medical research communities as the "gold standard" for evaluating what works and recommending policy and programmatic interventions, it is imperative that qualitative research is recognized as an important tool for policy makers. Whether studies are totally qualitative or part of a mixed-method approach that uses both quantitative and qualitative methods, qualitative research provides important data for public policy. Chatterji (2005) argues convincingly that a mixed-method approach rich in qualitative methods must be part of extended-term mixed-method (ETMM) evaluation designs to ensure researchers provide policy makers with the best evidence of what works in education. This is certainly true in other areas such as public administration, health care, transportation, criminal justice, and other public policy realms.

A number of examples of how qualitative research informs public policy are in order. Annette Lareau's *Home Advantage* (1989) and *Unequal Childhood: Class, Race and Family Life* (2004) provide in-depth ethnographic accounts of the relationship between family and schools. These books provide policy makers with an understanding of how families and schools can work together to improve student achievement. Pierrette Hondagneu-Sotelo's *Domestica* provides a qualitative investigation of the world on Latina immigrant domestic workers in Los Angeles and offers important findings to improve the working and living conditions of immigrants. Lois Weis's *Class Reunion* examines how a group of working class adults in a northeastern de-industrialized city have adapted to the new service economy. A follow-up to her *Working Class without Work* (1990), Weis re-interviewed the graduates of the high school she studied in 1985. Using what she terms qualitative longitudinality (2005), Weis provides two ethnographic snapshots of the same individuals over two decades and how they responded to changing economic and social conditions. Weis's work provides important data for policy makers concerned with improving the lives of workers in a rapidly changing global economy. Roger Sanjek, *The Future of Us All* is a detailed qualitative ethnography of the Elmhurst-Corona section of Queens in New York City. Based on fifteen years of ethnographic research, Sanjek chronicles how the new waves of immigrant groups turned the area into one of the most racially and ethnically diverse neighborhoods in the United States. Through an analysis of how these immigrant groups interacted with neighbors who had been their longer and with the New York City political and economic elites, Sanjek provides valuable data for urban planners and policy makers. These are just a few of the important qualitative studies that have made significant contributions to public policy debates. They are all methodologically rigorous, scrupulously researched, and illustrate the importance of qualitative research for public policy research.

REFERENCES

Adler, P. A., and Adler, P. (1994). Observational Techniques. In N. K. Denzin & Y. S. Lincoln (Eds.), *Handbook of qualitative research* (pp. 377–392). London: Sage.

Aronowitz, S., and Giroux, H. (1991). *Postmodern education: Politics, culture and social criticism*. Minneapolis: University of Minnesota Press.

Baudrillard, J. (1981). *For a critique of the political economy of the sign* (Charles Leaven, Trans.). St. Louis: Tellos Press.

Baudrillard, J. (1984). The precession of simulacra. In B. Wallis, (Ed.), *Art after modernism: Rethinking representation* (pp. 213–281). Boston: David Godine.

Becker, H. (1961/1976). *Boys in white*. Somerset, NJ: Transaction Books. (Originally published in 1961)

Burbules, N., and Rice, S. (1991). Dialogue across differences: Continuing the conversation. *Harvard Educational Review*, 61(4), 393–416.

Burbules, N., and Rice, S. (1992). Can we be heard? A reply to Leach. *Harvard Educational Review,* 62(2), 264–271.

Chatterji, M. (2005). Evidence on "What Works": An argument for extended-term mixed-method (ETMM) evaluation designs. *Educational Researcher*, 34(5):14–24

Cherryholmes, C. (1988). *Power and criticism: Poststructural investigations in education*. New York: Teachers College Press.

Collins, R. (1975). *Conflict sociology*. New York: Academic Press.

Creswell, J. W. (2005). *Educational research, planning, conducting, and evaluating quantitative and qualitative research* (2nd edition). Upper Saddle River, NJ: Pearson Education

Denzin, N. K., and Lincoln, Y.S. (Eds.) (1994). *Handbook of qualitative research*. Thousand Oaks, CA: Sage.

Denzin, N. K., and Lincoln, Y.S. (Eds.) (2000). *Handbook of qualitative research* (2nd ed.). Thousand Oaks, CA: Sage.

Denzin, N. K., and Lincoln, Y.S. (Eds.) (2005). *Handbook of qualitative research* (3rd ed.). Thousand Oaks, CA: Sage.

Derrida, J. (1973). Speech and phenomenon. Evanston, IL: Northwestern University Press.

Derrida, J. (1981). *Positions*. Chicago: University of Chicago Press.

Derrida, J. (1982). *Of grammatology*. Baltimore: Johns Hopkins University Press.

Dewey, J. (1916). *Democracy and education*. New York: Free Press.

Dewey, J. (1984). The public and its problems. In John Dewey: *The later works*, Vol. 2: 1925–1927. Carbondale & Edwardsville, IL: Southern Illinois University Press. (Original work published 1927)

Durkheim, E. (1947). *The division of labor in society*. Glencoe, IL: Free Press. (Original work published 1893)

Durkheim, E. (1952). *The rules of sociological method*. London: Routledge & Kegan Paul.

Durkheim, E. (1977). The evolution of educational thought (P. Collins, Trans.). London: Routledge (Kegan Paul. (Original published in 1938)

Ellsworth, E. (1989). Why doesn't this feel empowering? Working through the repressive myths of critical pedagogy. *Harvard Educational Review*, 59(3), 297–324.

Frazier, E. F. (1937a). The impact of urban civilization on Negro family life. *American Sociological Review*, 2: 609–618.

Frazier, E. F. (1937b). Negro Harlem: An ecological study. *American Journal of Sociology*, 43: 72–88.

Frazier, E. F. (1957). *Black bourgeoisie: The rise of a new middle class in the United States*. Glencoe, IL: The Free Press.

Giddens, A. (1975). *The new rules of sociological method*. London: Cambridge University Press.

Giroux, H. (1981). *Ideology, culture and the process of schooling*. Philadelphia: Temple University Press.

Giroux, H. (1983). *Theory and resistance in education*. South Hadley, MA: Bergin & Garvey.

Giroux, H. (1988). *Teachers as intellectuals*. South Hadley, MA: Bergin & Garvey.

Giroux, H. (1991). *Postmodernism, feminism, and cultural politics: Redrawing educational boundaries*. Albany, NY: SUNY Press.

Goffman, E. (1959). *The presentation of self in everyday life*. Garden City, NY: Doubleday.

Goffman, E. (1961a). *Asylums*. Garden City, NY: Doubleday.

Goffman, E. (1961b). *Encounters*. Indianapolis, IN: Bobbs-Merrill.

Goffman, E. (1963a). *Stigma*. Englewood Cliffs, NJ: Prentice-Hall.

Goffman, E. (1963b). *Behavior in public places*. Garden City, NY: Doubleday.

Goffman, E. (1967). *Interaction ritual*. Garden City, NY: Doubleday.

Habermas, J. (1979). *Communication and the evolution of society*. Boston: Beacon Press.

Habermas, J. (1981). Modernity versus postmodernity. *New German Critique*, 8(1), 3–18.

Habermas, J. (1982). The entwinement of myth and enlightenment. *New German Critique*, 9(3), 13–30.

Habermas, J. (1983). Modernity: An incomplete project. In H. Foster (Ed.), *The anti-aesthetic: Essays on postmodern culture* (pp. 3–16). Seattle, WA: Bay Press.

Habermas, J. (1987). *The philosophical discourse of modernity* (F. Lawrence, Trans.). Cambridge, MA: MIT Press.

Harvey, D. (1989). *The condition of postmodernity: An inquiry into the origins of cultural change*. Cambridge, MA: Basil Blackwell.

Hemmings, A. (2006). Great ethical divides: Bridging the gap between institutional review boards and researcher. *Educational Researcher*, 35(4), 12–17.

Hondagneu-Sotelo, P. (2004) *Domestica*. Berkeley: University of California Press.

Jameson, F. (1982). Postmodernism and consumer society. In H. Foster (Ed.), *The antiaesthetic: Essays on postmodern culture* (pp. 11–125). Seattle: Bay Press.

Jencks, C. (1987). *What is post-modernism?* New York: St. Martin's.

Johnson, R. and Onwuegbuzie, A. (2004). Mixed methods: a research paradigm whose time has come. *Educational Researcher*, 33(7):14–26.

Kincheloe, J. L., and Steinberg, S. R. (Eds.). (1998). *Unauthorized methods: Strategies for critical teaching*. New York: Routledge.

Lareau, A. (1989). *Home advantage*. New York: Routledge.

Lareau, A. (2004). *Unequal childhood: Class, race and family life*. Berkeley: University of California Press.

Lather, P. (1989). Critical theory, curriculum transformation, and feminist mainstreaming. *Journal of Education*, 1966 (March), 49–62.

Lather, P. (1989). Postmodernism and the politics of enlightenment. Educational Foundations, 3 (3), 8–9.

Lather, P. (1991). *Getting smart: Feminist research and pedagogy with/in the postmodern*. New York: Routledge.

Lyotard, J. F. (1984). *The postmodern condition* (G. Bennington & B. Massumi, Trans.). Minneapolis: University of Minnesota Press.

Maxwell, J. Causal explanation, qualitative research and scientific inquiry in education. *Educational Researcher*, 33(2): 3–11.

Marx, K. (1971). *The poverty of philosophy*. New York: International Publishers.

Marx, K., and Engles, F. (1947). *The German ideology*. New York: International Publishers. (Original work published 1846)

McLaren, P. (1991). Schooling and the postmodern body: Critical pedagogy and the politics of enfleshment, In H. Giroux, *Postmodernism, feminism, and cultural politics: Redrawing educational boundaries* (pp., 144–173). Albany, NY: SUNY Press.

McLaren, P., and Hammer, R. (1989). Critical pedagogy and the postmodern challenge: Toward a critical postmodernist pedagogy of liberation. *Educational Foundations*, 3(3), 29–62.

Portes, A., and Rumbaut, R. (2001). *Legacies: The story of the immigrant second generation.*

Punch, M. (1994). Politics and ethics in qualitative research. In N.K. Denzin & Y.S. Lincoln (Eds.), *Handbook of qualitative research* (pp. 83–97). Thousand Oaks, CA: Sage.

Riehl, C. (2001). Bridging to the future: The contributions of qualitative research to the sociology of education. *Sociology of Education*, 74 (Extra Issue): 115–134.

Sacher, E. (1991). *Shut up and let the lady teach*. New York: Poseidon Press.

Sadovnik, A. R. (1994). *Excellence and equity in higher education*. New York: Peter Lang.

Sadovnik, A. R. (1995). Postmodernism and the sociology of education: Closing the rift among scholarship, research, and practice. In George Noblit & William Pink (Eds.), *Continuity and contradiction: The futures of the sociology of education*. Cresskill, NJ: Hampton Press.

Sanjek, R. (2000), *The future of us all*. Ithaca, NY: Cornell University Press.

Schwandt, T. A. (2000). Three Epistemological Stances for Qualitative Inquiry: Interpretivism, Hermeneutics and Social Constructionism. In N. K. Denzin & Y. S. Lincoln (Eds.), *Handbook of qualitative research* (pp. 189–213). Thousand Oaks, CA: Sage.

Semel, S. F. (1994a). Writing School History as a Former Participant: Problems in Writing the History of an Elite School. In G. Walford (ed.) *Researching the powerful in education* (pp. 204–220), University College London Press.

Singh, P. (2005). Data collection in qualitative research. Brisbane, Queensland, Australia: Queensland University of Technology, CD ROM of course EDN611, possession of author; also at http://olt.qut.edu.au/edu/EDN611/sec/index.cfm?

Strauss, A. and Glaser, B.G. (1967) *Discovery of grounded theory: Strategies for qualitative research.* Somerset, NJ: Aldine Transaction.

Vidich, A. J. and Lyman, S. M. (1994). Qualitative Methods: Their History in Sociology and Anthropology. In N. K. Denzin & Y. S. Lincoln (Eds.), *Handbook of Qualitative Research* (pp. 23–59). London: Sage.

Weber, M. (1978). *Economy and society* (Vols. 1 & 2). (G. Roth & C. Wittich, Eds.) Berkeley: University of California Press.

Wexler, P. (1987). *Social analysis: After the new sociology*. London: Routledge & Kegan Paul.

Whyte, W. F. (1981). *Street corner society: The social structure of an Italian slum* (3rd ed.). Chicago: University of Chicago Press. (Original work published 1943)

Weis, L. (2004). *Class Reunion*. New York: Routledge.

29 Interpretation and Intention in Policy Analysis

Hendrik Wagenaar

1 INTERPRETATION IN POLICY ANALYSIS: CAUSAL VERSUS INTENTIONAL EXPLANATION

The interpretative approach to policy analysis is not one singular method, but rather a family of approaches. Different approaches to interpretive theory have varying takes on the object of interpretation (intentions, reasons, traditions, stories, discourses, systems of signs), follow different methods, and operate on different philosophical preconceptions, but their shared assumption is that policy formation and implementation, or broader, the activities and interactions of government agencies, public officials and their publics in civil society, cannot be properly understood unless we grasp their relevant meanings (Bevir and Rhodes 2003). For example, as Yanow puts it in characterizing interpretive policy analysis: "An interpretive approach to policy analysis (...) is one that focuses on the meanings of policy, on the values, feelings, or beliefs they express, and on the processes by which those meanings are communicated to and 'read' by various audiences." (Yanow 2000) This is the standard definition of interpretive policy analysis, and obviously it makes sense as it couples a particular mode of inquiry and explanation to a particular image of the social-political world. That world, which is both the object and context of policy analysis, is characterized by "values, feelings and beliefs" (Weiss and Rein 1970) and the way these are expressed and communicated among various groups. It is also—something that is undercharacterized in Yanow's definition—about acting in a world of uncertainty that originates in complexity (Bohman 1996; Dryzek 1990), irrepressible ambiguity and contingency (Schwandt 1997), and the inevitable conflict and incompatibility that spring forth from pluralistic practices and institutional positions (Kekes 1993; Wagenaar 2002).

To understand such a world, explanations in terms of causal connections between an entity *x* and an entity *y* don't make much sense. For example, to say that, when one declines to vote for candidate A because one disagrees with his position on abortion, that his or her nonvoting behavior is "caused" by a position on abortion would be seriously misleading. After all, despite his or her stand on abortion, one could still have decided to vote for him because one believes he is a better leader in times of crisis, or because he is the lesser of two evils, or because one feels affinity with his personality, or because one has always been voting Republican/Democrat and to do otherwise now just doesn't feel right, or because one's father-in-law votes for him, and so forth. Not only does the terminology of causation suggest an airtight level of determination that simply isn't warranted in the world of human action, but more importantly, it is beside the point. The very concepts that figure in the explanation—voting, position, abortion, strong leader—are not mere behaviors but *action* concepts, that is activities that are defined and constituted by an intrinsic *intention* (Fay 1975; Taylor 1977). Differently put, we, as voters and citizens of Western liberal states, grasp these concepts, and the associated behaviors, in terms of what they *mean* to us.

Meanings are not causally connected, but intentionally. An action is explained intentionally when we are able to specify the future state of affairs that required the specific action. (Elster 1983; von Wright 1971).[1] The difference with causal explanation is in the different *explananda*. An example suggested by von Wright will make this clear. When an experimental psychologist stimulates the cortex of a monkey to elicit certain movements of the monkey's left arm, the language of intentions plays no role in the explanatory scheme. We could perhaps be tempted to say that the electrical stimulation made the monkey wave his hand, but that would be irrelevant to the causal explanation of the arm movement as an effect of the stimulation. By saying that the electrical current to the cortex, triggered certain neurological activities in certain nerve strata, which in turn made the muscles of the left arm contract so that the monkey lifted his arm, is to exhaustively explain the monkey's arm movement. To add that the stimulation of the cortex made the monkey wave at us would be to ascribe something to the monkey that greatly and unwarrantedly, transcends the explanatory scheme. What is explained is how parts of the monkeys body move under the causal influence of electrical stimulation of the cortex.

Now consider the following situation. At the time of this writing, a small controversy erupted in the Dutch media over a Moroccan Imam who, upon being presented to the Minister of Immigration in a meeting—who, a fact that is essential to this small drama, is a woman—refused to shake hands with her. The scene, including the minister's defiant reaction, was broadcast on television, and instantly a wave of indignation at the Imam's rude behavior engulfed the media. Now, to explain the Imam's behavior in causal terms would be wholly incommensurate to the situation at hand. In fact, in the days following the incident, various actors in the media, including the Imam himself, stepped in to explain the refusal to shake hands. The Imam referred to the words of the Prophet that prohibit men and women from shaking hands because of the close association of touching and sexual intercourse. The refusal to shake hands was, in fact, meant as a sign of respect to the female minister. Other Muslims, however, saw this as a particularly strict interpretation of the Koran that was inappropriate for Muslims in a modern, urban society. Others thought the minister's behavior rude and lacking in respect and pointed out that in many religious communities relations between men and women are strictly regulated. Among orthodox Jews, for example, men and women are also not allowed to shake hands.

To summarize the situation around the Minister and the Imam, the *explanandum* in this case, is not a particular muscular movement, but an *action*, a particular behavior that is constituted by an intention. Or, as von Wright puts it, an *inner* aspect that is behind the action, and the results that the action is supposed to bring about or the *outer* aspect of the action (von Wright 1971, 86). In human affairs the inner and the outer aspect of action always go together, for most of the time we act because we intend to bring about some result. In fact, by taking the intention (not to violate the commands of the Koran) out of the explanatory scheme of the Imam refusing to shake hands with the minister, we wouldn't be able to make sense of the situation. The physical movements alone are not even a necessary condition of the action "avoid shaking hands," because there are other ways of doing that like walking out of the room, turning one's back, or ignoring the minister altogether. In this particular case, intentions literally *constitute* the situation, from the expectation of shaking hands in situations like this to refusing to acknowledge the minister's extended hand. The whole storm erupted because a social code exists that defines extending and accepting (or refusing) hands as the patterned activity we recognize as greeting (Geertz 1973).

2 HOW NOT TO THINK ABOUT INTENTION

This is what we mean when we speak of actions having *meaning*. This is also the bare-bone formulation of how we explain meaningful action; how we acquire valid knowledge of it, through intentional explanation. But having said this, it leaves many questions open, some of which will be discussed in this section. First, the immediate conclusion after stating the necessity of intention in understanding human situations is that to be appropriate to their subject, the social sciences require a different kind of inquiry than the natural sciences, namely interpretive inquiry. In general terms this seems to be the proper conclusion, but in the actual practice of doing interpretive inquiry, there are so many complexities and confusions that this becomes an almost meaningless, and in some cases even misleading, statement. But let's first state the case of an interpretive approach to the social sciences, and for the purpose of this chapter, policy sciences.

The central fact that necessitates interpretive explanation in the social sciences is that the unit of analysis, the "brute" data of the social and policy sciences, are not hardwired into social reality, but require interpretation to make them "visible" at all. Terms such as "voting," "marrying," or "negotiating" can only be inferred from the physical movements that carry them by assuming a particular purpose or intention that makes this particular movement or verbal utterance a recognizable case of marrying or negotiating. In the social sciences observation requires interpretation.

Some analysts infer from this that interpretive inquiry is, by inference, a subjective enterprise. There are two reasons why the evocation of the term subjective without any further qualification is misleading. First, the acceptability of interpretive statements is as constrained by the empirical world as is the acceptability of causal statements (Thomas 1979), but, it should be added, constrained in a different way. Second, the term "subjective" suggests that interpretation is something that takes place within the mind, or is about objects that can only be grasped by mental processes. Both objections to the term "subjective" hang together.

Let's clarify the misunderstandings about the alleged subjective character of the word "intention" by looking at an example. What does it mean when in a police report, it is stated: "The suspect was arrested because he intended to rape the victim." This statement does certainly not refer to some mental state that preceded the act of rape, that is only accessible by the person himself and that only he can avow or deny. Intention has "no experiential essence," as Jeffrey Coulter puts it. The word "intend" in the above phrase does not denote some subjective state of the suspect's mind that can only be reflected upon by the subject himself, or inferred, through empathic identification of an observer with a subject. The seemingly mentalistic word "intend" here refers as much to an observable action as the seemingly objective word "rape" later in the sentence. As Coulter states:

> To learn the expression "I intend" is not to learn, miraculously, to assign a label to some introspected experience—for how could one be trained to make the correct identification of his introspected percept?—but consists, rather in learning how to perform what Austin termed a "commisive."[2] To declare one's [or disavow, as in this example—HW] intention is to perform a specific sort of illocutionary act, which, like all such acts, require appropriate "felicity" conditions. Thus there is a clear and crucial connection between particular sorts of intentions and particular sorts of circumstances.... Thus: A description of an intention is a description of an action (an envisaged action), not of an experience. Avowals and ascriptions of intentions, then, are organized by, and gain their intelligibility from, not some mental divinations but from the particulars of public states of affairs. (Coulter 1979)

This whole process of grasping intentions takes place in, what one could call, a semiotic public space; or, more precisely, is made possible at all by being suspended in this shared linguistic realm. If a detective weighs the evidence that will or will not lead to the conclusion that the suspect had the intention to rape the victim, this whole process hinges on the public availability, and the possibility for public inspection of, such categories as "victim," "rape," and "consent." All actors in this drama—victim, suspect, detective, and later, district attorney, lawyer, judge—are bound by these pre-given cultural categories, and are unable to overstep the boundaries of these concepts-in-use (to use a famous phrase by Donald Schön) on peril of being misunderstood in the best case and ostracized in the worst. A different way to put this is that "data," judgments and conclusions (and the warrants for the conclusions), in this social event are all situated. They make sense only within a particular context. The rape claim is predicated on a complex set of (mostly tacit) background knowledge about value systems surrounding gender, about the relation between men and women, about the set of conventions that guide the initiation of sexual contact, and so forth. Data, conclusions, as well as the grounds for those conclusions are constituted by the shared expectations, beliefs, values, routines, and practices of the members of a culture; "constitutive" indicating that the shared background knowledge "creates the very possibility of certain activities," and, I would add, certain categories (Searle 1995, see also Fay 1975, 76; Taylor 1977). This is the meaning of those oft-used words "public" and "transparent" here. Terms such as "rape," "sexual," "intending," (or "voting," "promising," "shaking hands") are publicly available for everyone to see. They are transparent in that:

> The public criteria for . . . "intending" are circumstantially bound and not restricted to some codified set of associated behaviors or experiences, as if these could be listed as a fixed set of "conditions"; members of a culture must exercise situated judgments, must analyze contexts for what could account as criteria for proper ascription or for the ratification of an avowal in those specific cases. (Coulter 1979, 44)

One way to try to end these convolutions about subjective and objective meaning is to follow Geertz and simply say that the whole dichotomy is misconceived. If we insert "meaning" where he uses "culture," we would conclude then that meaning "though ideational, (...) does not exist in someone's head, though unphysical, (...) is not an occult entity" (1973, 10). Geertz is perfectly right here, of course. It doesn't make sense to try to locate meaning, ontologically, in the mind or in some reified cultural or institutional pattern. Actions are meaningful in that they signify something, and the question is then: What does this particular action (a disavowal of rape; the refusal to shake hands) signify? Something larger then than the particularity of that singular action is being said, and this expressive force hinges on these actions being embedded in something larger in the first place, something that exists before, and independently of, the individual acting. But that something is not some reified "deep structure" or some axiomatic set of rules, but more a shared set of understandings that are linguistically inscribed in the world, and that are invoked, and, in an ongoing dialectical movement sustained, whenever we "read" the symbolic meaning of a particular behavior. So perhaps this is the place to insert what is perhaps Geertz's most often quoted statement on culture, the analysis of meaning, and the continuity between observation and explanation in interpretive analysis: "Hopping back and forth between the whole conceived through the parts that actualize it and the parts conceived through the whole that motivates them, we seek to turn them, by a sort of intellectual perpetual motion, into explications of one another" (1983, 69).

Finally, this digression on the meaning of meaning in interpretive analysis can be concluded with a more practical hands-on statement of methodological import. The dual nature of meaning implies that, whatever our research interest—for example, the intentions of mental patients navigating the revamped social service landscape of a large American city in the 1980s (Lewis et al. 1991; Wagenaar 1987), or the emergence of the school as we know it from the vagaries of institution building in the Prussian state (Hunter 1996), or the evaluation of a particular educational reform (Dunne 1993)—our work begins with the careful and precise registering of the concrete behaviors of concrete actors. Now, these behaviors can have many different guises and many different substrates. They can be statements in interviews, observed activities, written statements in documents, both formal (reports, laws, position papers) and informal (letters, diaries). They can take the form of stories that people tell to explain their actions in particular circumstances. They can be our renderings (in research notes) of what we believe we have observed. They can be descriptions (part descriptive, part interpretive) of artifacts such as buildings, cartoons, or office spaces, or of performances or rituals. Or they can be a carefully put together reconstruction of some developmental trajectory. But what ties all these different forms of registering behaviors together is that we regard them as the expressions of, the carriers of, social meaning. Behaviors are a window upon meaning; and, safe for the a priori imposition of theoretical schemes upon the research material (a practice that Glaser and Strauss call, "pseudo-verification"), there exists no shortcut to the extrapolation of meaning from concrete, microscopic behavior. As Geertz puts it, "Behaviors must be attended to, and with some exactness, because it is through the flow of behavior—or more precisely social action—that cultural forms find articulation" (2003, 17). The interpretive analyst acts on the assumption that the general is folded into the particular. The analogy is with chromosomes here. As chromosomes carry the full complexity of particular life form in their genetic code, so the cultural life form in all its meaningful complexity is carried within the minutiae of observed behavior.

3 VARIETIES OF INTERPRETATION IN POLICY ANALYSIS

Although the various approaches to interpretation all focus on the meanings that shape actions, they differ in important ways in how they understand and explain meaning, how they view the position of the subject in analysis, in their philosophical assumptions, and in how they articulate the role of the policy analyst. This sections describes and gives examples of two well-known approaches to interpretation in policy analysis. In the course of doing this, the discussion will also explore some further complications with interpretive analysis. I will discuss respectively Dvora Yanow´s hermeneutical approach to interpretive analysis, and Mark Bevir and Rod Rhodes' interpretivist third way between hermeneutics and poststructuralism. This doesn't exhaust the family of interpretive approaches. It is often overlooked, for example, that qualitative research is, in method, analytical thrust, and explanatory logic, an interpretive approach. Some of the best known examples (Estroff 1981; Liebow 1967; Wiseman 1979) succeed in imaginatively reconstructing the experiential world of the subjects of study. In strictly numerical terms, qualitative research is the method of choice for most policy researchers (at least in Europe). Narrative analysis, discourse analysis (including poststructuralist analysis), the analysis of social practices, and deliberative policy analysis are also significant, vibrant ways of engaging in interpretive policy analysis that have resulted in important work. These are discussed in other sections of the book.

3.1 Dvora Yanow: How Does A Policy Mean?

It is probably not an overstatement to claim that Dvora Yanow´s *How Does A Policy Mean?* (Yanow 1996) was one of the books that put the interpretive approach on the agenda in post-empiricist policy analysis. For many people, her approach to interpretation has become synonymous with interpretive policy analysis proper. The book's argument is cleverly organized around a puzzle: according to any instrumental criterion, such as efficacy or efficiency in reaching the policy's goal, the Israeli policy of creating community centers in new settlements in the 1970s was deemed a failure. Nevertheless, the policy remained well-funded for a period of over twenty years, and drew continuing support from a range of political actors in Israel. How could this be? Yanow's answer to this seeming anomaly is that in the context of Israeli society and Israeli politics, the policy had a particular *meaning* for key audiences. Yanow urges the policy analyst to become sensitive to the expressive, symbolic aspect of policy. Not as an add-on to the "real"—read instrumental, material, power-related—aspects of policy making, but as an intrinsic aspect of each and every act of policy making. These meanings reside in all aspects of a policy; not just the legislative texts that state the policy's intent, but also in the actions of key groups to implement the policy and in the artifacts, such as agency buildings, their furnishings, and, one could add these days, their Web sites (Yanow 1996).

In a small and useful successor to the first book, Yanow explains how to conduct interpretive policy analysis. Conceptually, interpretive policy analysis, according to her, consists of the following elements: (1) identify the artifacts (language, objects, acts) that are the carriers of meaning; (2)

identify the interpretive communities, relevant to a policy, that are the perceivers of this meaning; (3) identify the discourses through which these meanings are communicated; (4) identify any point of conflict that suggests that different groups attach divergent meanings to some aspect of a policy (Yanow 2000).

The French philosopher Paul Ricoeur has famously claimed that social behavior can be seen as a text. Yanow uses this metaphor to further clarify her position in conducting interpretive policy analysis. Public policies, both in their formulation and their enactment, should be seen as texts that are "read" by various stakeholder groups and, of course, by the analyst. Apart from a limited metaphorical value, it is not always completely clear what the added value of the text metaphor is in Yanow's approach. (And in one, important way, it introduces a questionable element of meaning realism in the analysis. I will return to this later.) Yanow's methodological approach, in its careful reconstruction of the perspective of the groups that are involved and the wider context from which the policy derives its meaning, is in fact quite close to the steps in traditional qualitative analysis. For example, in one key step in her approach to interpretive policy analysis, "identifying interpretive communities," Yanow suggests to the reader that relevant information may be found in written sources (newspapers, magazines, agency newsletters, annual reports, government documents, etc.), oral sources (interviews with key actors), observation (of actions, interactions, and the material context in which these actors move about), and participation. In accessing these sources and gathering research materials, the analyst is urged to begin the process of analysis, for: "The interpretive policy analyst needs to build a context in which to access local knowledge. Knowing what specific object or piece of language has significance comes from situational familiarity—understanding what is important to stakeholders, to policy-relevant publics" (2000, 38). The actual process of analysis entails two steps: "(1) a daily sense making, out of which (2) puzzles emerge (events or acts or interactions that contradict what the analyst expected, or which he cannot make sense of, given what he knows at that moment, or which contradict one another)" (ibid.). In short, these are the very same data sources and analytical steps that make up any good qualitative study. Finally, in addition to identifying interpretive communities and how they understand a particular policy, Yanow suggests some interesting other foci of analysis that open up windows on public policy. These are the analysis of metaphors, of policy categories (the contradictions and ambiguities that reveal the hidden assumptions behind the way a particular policy carves up the world), the analysis of policy artifacts (particularly buildings), policy programs (by which Yanow, going by her text, seems to mean policy instruments), and of policy rituals.

Yanow's version of interpretive policy analysis, as expounded in her two books and various articles, pairs clarity of exposition to practicality in its presentation of how to go about doing it. Yet it also suffers from two problems: (1) a tendency to reify meaning, and a concomitant instrumental notion of the stance of the interpretive analyst' and (2) the absence of conflict and power in her analytic scheme.

Yanow's version of interpretive policy analysis suffers from what is sometimes called "meaning realism." Meaning realism is the view that "meanings are fixed entities that can be discovered and that exist independent of the interpreter" (Schwandt 2000). Meaning realism is a feature of those versions of hermeneutic analysis that aim at exegesis, the elucidation of the meaning of texts. The method of exegesis revolves around two related premises: (1) the interpreter and the object of interpretation are distinct, and (2) the first is not involved with the latter. The second premise must be taken in an epistemological way. The analyst is not necessarily emotionally uninvolved, but he is, or more precisely, he must always remain external to and unaffected by the act of interpretation (Schwandt 2000). To get the interpretive analysis started, the analyst not only has to project an a priori, and in practice more or less distinct and monolithic, "meaning" in the world, the exact nature of which is to be discerned by the analyst, but simultaneously, the analyst has to place himself outside the process of meaning-making (despite protestations that the analyst is part of the world that he analyzes) to function as an Archimedean point. The analyst gains knowledge about an object (the meaning of human action), and the (implicit) implication is that there is one right meaning to be discovered out there. Meaning is objectified

It is at this point in particular that Yanow's text-analogy is significant. She introduces the claim that policies can be seen as texts not to elucidate a decentered, relational system of meaning-formation (such as is common in poststructuralist and deliberative approaches to interpretation. See the respective chapters in this book.), but to set out her exegetic approach to interpretation. The meaning of the policy as a "text analogue" is then "read" by the various constituencies *and* the analyst. In fact, it is the task of the analyst to "clarify" meanings, while remaining aloof from the interactions between actors by which meaning is established (Yanow 2000, 17–18). This puts Yanow squarely in the hermeneutical-essentialist tradition of finding the true meaning of texts, as some relation of correspondence between some fixed meaning "out there" and its representation by the analyst. Differently put, her aim is not to explore the internal relations (consonances and differences) between the elements of her policy system, and so to infer meaning, more or less a la Geertz, but to read the meaning that is somehow residing in the policy (Yanow 2000, 19). And although Yanow's "reading" is methodologically sophisticated, this doesn't detract from the point that meaning is pulled from the slice of social reality as a rabbit out of a hat. To quote Schwandt once again: "Thus, in interpretive traditions, the interpreter objectifies (i.e., stands over and against) that which is to be interpreted. And, in that sense, the interpreter remains unaffected by and external to the interpretive process" (2000, 195). This is a problem that affects most hermeneuticaly oriented approaches to interpretive policy analysis.

Second, and related to the preceding point, in Yanow's version of interpretive analysis there is little room for ambiguity, indeterminacy, power, and conflict. In general, for policy analysis to be appropriate to its intended use, it must be consonant with its political setting. This is not a "secondary consideration," as Dryzek rightly points out, for policy analysis differs from pure social science in that it is intended to be used in practical political settings. Thus, "social science may fail as policy analysis as it fails to address its political setting" (Dryzek 1982, 310). And as countless analysts have pointed out, that setting is characterized by interaction, power play, structural inequality, deep complexity, indeterminacy, dispersed decision making, lack of trust among actors, value pluralism, and a fundamental orientation to practice (Bohman 1996; Dryzek 1982, 1990; Forester 1999; Hajer and Wagenaar 2003b; Stone 1997; Wagenaar and Cook 2003). Very little of this resonates in Yanow's version of interpretive analysis. At best, she is willing to "map" the various meanings that populate the particular policy landscape that is the object of analysis. For a more direct rendering of the typical characteristics of the setting of policy analysis, we need to turn to such approaches as frame analysis, poststructuralism, and deliberative policy analysis.

3.2 MARK BEVIR AND ROD RHODES: INTERPRETING BRITISH GOVERNANCE

Bevir and Rhodes' approach to interpretive political analysis distinguishes itself from Yanow's approach in that it attempts to supply to interpretation a deeper philosophical context. Toward this end, it centers on three concepts: *tradition, dilemma,* and *decenteredness.* In their main text *Interpreting British Governance* (Bevir and Rhodes 2003), the authors argue the case for interpretation in political science by stating two key assumptions: (1) people act on their beliefs and preferences, and (2) we cannot infer people's beliefs from objective facts about them (such as income level) or general assumptions (such as the rationality of human actors) (2003, 19). Taken together these two premises lead to the conclusion that we cannot get around interpretation in political science. Bevir and Rhodes' version of interpretive analysis is sophisticated in that it shows awareness of the strengths and weaknesses of a large chunk of the family of interpretive approaches. In fact, it explicitly announces itself as providing a "third way" between hermeneutics and poststructuralism that, although indebted to both traditions, attempts to avoid some of the problems that the authors ascribe to both of them.[3] In particular, Bevir and Rhodes are sympathetic to the decentered approach of poststructuralists such as Foucault, who see meaning as emerging from an almost randomly thrown together assemblage of practices, beliefs, and meanings that make the very existence of certain social categories possible. To understand a social object or a particular behavior is to interpret it in the wider discourse that makes that object of behavior possible (2003, 23). On the other hand, they reject the poststructuralists´ hostility toward the role of human agency in social affairs, which makes these approaches "come dangerously close to denying any scope to the subject and reason" (2003, 43). Hermeneutic interpretivism departs from an epistemologically dubious subjectivity and essentialism (the all-knowledgeable, autonomous subjects who "think and act according solely to their own reasons and commands" (2003, 32), so that this approach can "come dangerously close to embodying an analysis of the subject as autonomous and an analysis of reason as pure and universal" (ibid.).

Bevir and Rhodes introduce the concept of "tradition" to balance agency and determinism in understanding intention and meaning in the world of politics. As they state:

> (A) rejection of autonomy need not entail a rejection of agency. To deny that subjects can escape from all social influences is not to deny that they can act creatively for reasons that make sense to them. On the contrary, we must allow for agency if only because we cannot separate and distinguish beliefs and actions by reference to their social context alone. Different people adopt different beliefs and perform different actions against the background of the same social structure. Thus, there must be a space on social contexts where individual subjects decide what beliefs to hold and what actions to perform for their own reasons. . .This view of agency suggests that we see social context not as episteme, languages or discourses, but as traditions. The concepts of episteme, language and discourse typically invoke social structures that fix individual acts and exist independently of them. In contrast the notion of tradition implies that the relevant social context is one in which subjects are born, which then acts as the background to their beliefs and actions without fixing them. Traditions allow for the possibility of subjects adapting, developing and even rejecting much of their heritage. (2003, 32)

Bevir and Rhodes take pains not to reify tradition. Traditions are not immovable superstructures with an inexorable inner logic that determine people's beliefs and actions. Traditions are not cultural prisons. Rather, traditions are an "initial influence" on people that "colors their later actions." Whenever the situation calls for it, people may feel the need to alter traditions. Traditions are "contingent products of the way in which people develop specific beliefs, preferences and actions" (2003, 34). Traditions emerge from "local reasoning" and "micro-practices" (2003, 35). It is here that that Bevir and Rhodes stake out the middle position between hermeneutics and poststructuralism. On the one hand: "We have to redefine tradition in a nonessentialist, decentered manner to aid any lingering sense of objective reason." On the other hand: "While a rejection of the autonomous subject prevents a belief in a neutral or universal reason, the fact of agency enables us to accept local reasoning in a way that Foucault often seems reluctant to do" (2003, 35).

How do traditions change? They change because actors struggle with dilemmas. Sticking to their nonessentialist program, the authors emphasize that dilemmas are not hardwired into reality. Dilemmas may arise from people's experiences, but this need not be the case. "Dilemmas can arise from both theoretical and moral reflection and from experiences of worldly pressures" (2003, 36). The point is that traditions and dilemmas are both defined in a *decentered* way. Traditions, dilemmas, and local practices are mutually constitutive: "Because people confront these dilemmas in diverse traditions, there arises a political contest over what constitutes the nature of the failings and what should be done about them" (2003, 64). Bevir and Rhodes' version of interpretivism thus hinges on a decentered approach to the study of political phenomena. Basic categories such as policy institutions, problems, programs, networks, or governance, are not pre-given, but should be explained as the contingent products of actors' ongoing actions, struggles, and negotiations. They summarize their decentered version of interpretivism by commenting on the concept of policy networks: "We build change into the heart of our account of networks by exploring how individual actors respond to dilemmas to reinterpret and reconstruct practices and the traditions they embody" (2003, 71). Methodologically, Bevir and Rhodes propagate the microsociological approach that Geertz argued for. Decentered studies of political phenomena require that we "build a multifaceted picture of how the several actors understand and construct" the phenomenon. We should not expect to find one overarching truth, but rather, as Yanow also noted, a fundamentally pluralistic world; a world made up of "narratives about how (. . .) people understand what they are doing in networks, where these understandings usually both overlap and conflict with one another" (2003, 66).

In its nonfoundational understanding of meaning, and in its emphasis on the micro-analysis of the beliefs and actions of all actors who are involved with a particular policy sector, this approach attempts to steer free from the meaning realism of more exegetically minded forms of hermeneutic analysis. And with its singular focus on actors' struggles with and over policy dilemmas and un-intended consequences, it is consonant with the complex, contested world of public policy. Yet, it suffers from the problem that it is not always clear what the epistemic status of traditions is. On the one hand, traditions are observer-independent entities, or phenomena, out there in the world that form the object of study. ("Traditions are contingent products of the ways in which people develop specific beliefs, preferences and actions" (Bevir and Rhodes 2003, 34)). On the other, they are described as analytical categories that serve as an explanatory tool that is specifically tailored to the goals of the analyst. ("Political scientists construct traditions in ways appropriate to explaining the particular sets of beliefs and actions in which they are interested" (2003, 33)). In their examples, the authors vacillate between both. Their analysis of Thatcherism, for example, is mostly a categorization of the different understandings of the academic literature on the Thatcher reforms organized according to the four well-known, but preconceived political traditions in Britain (liberal, Tory, Whig, and social-ist). The four "narratives" are not based on any empirical inquiry into the way the Thatcher reforms were experienced by local administrators, professionals at public service agencies, or residents in public housing projects. Their analysis of the reforms by New Labor, however, trace the tortuous emergence of joined-up government as the result of labor officials struggling with a series of political dilemmas, policy problems, and the unintended consequences of Thatcherite reforms.

4 CONCLUDING REMARKS: POLICY INTERPRETATION, GOVERNANCE, AND DEMOCRACY

To what extent has interpretive policy analysis succeeded in becoming a viable alternative to insti-tutionalized empiricist policy analysis? The answer must be guarded and qualified. As a theoretical endeavor, as manifested by the number and sophistication of the articles, books, and conferences that are devoted to one or another form of interpretive policy analysis, it is by now a blossoming branch of the academic discipline of policy studies. Most scholars working in this tradition no lon-ger have much trouble in getting their work published, even in the mainstream policy and public administration journals. Certain books, such as Fischer and Forester's *The Argumentative Turn in Policy Analysis and Planning* (1993), or Deborah Stone's *Policy Paradox* (1997), have found their way into undergraduate policy curricula. And both the American Political Science Association and its European counterpart, the European Consortium of Political Research regularly devote space in their conferences to interpretive approaches to the policy sciences.

In the professional field the picture is less clear. If we restrict the interpretive approach to qualitative research, then the interpretive turn is resounding success, certainly in Europe. Much applied policy research is qualitative, generally following the format of a short case study, followed by some conclusions and recommendations. However, it must be feared that a lot of this work is what Glaser and Strauss despairingly call "opportunistic," with "tacked-on conclusions" (and ditto recommendations, one should add), and with little guarantee of the quality of the interviewing and data-analysis. Solid studies that, for example, shed light on the implementation of a policy initiative by inquiring into interpretive communities and the language and artifacts of a policy program (Yanow 2000), or that map stubborn policy controversies (Rein 1983) are much harder to find within government agencies and for-profit think tanks. In this sense, it must be feared that the lack of relevance that has been ascribed to empiricist policy analysis (Fischer 2003; Rein 1976) has not been alleviated by a shift to quick-and-dirty qualitative research. In practical professional terms, in these instances the interpretive turn amounts to not much more than "interpretation-lite."

Yet, this is not all that there is to it. Interpretive policy analysis, rooted in a different understanding of what amounts to valid and justified knowledge of the social world, has always held out a different conception of democracy; a different understanding of the role of experts and citizens in the organization of democratic policy making. Interpretive social science, with its focus of making the meaning of actions transparent—both one's own and those of others—is seen to increase the possibility of increased communication between different groups in society (Fay 1975, 80; Geertz 1973, 24). With hindsight, this promise of enlightenment and the subsequent increase of communication in a pluralistic society was overly optimistic. In a complex, conflicting world with deep, structural inequalities of power and access to essential resources, there is little chance that constructive communication spontaneously increases when competing groups are informed about the meaning that a particular government action has for different groups (Bohman 1996). For that to happen, more conditions have to be fulfilled, and it is precisely along these lines that interpretive approaches have made their greatest inroads in the last two decades.

Looking back, what has become clear is that policy analysis has not changed policy making, but instead that changes in policy making have created the possibilities, and in many cases the *necessity*, for allowing interpretive inquiry into policy analysis. Spurred by the emergence of what has become known as the network society, policy is increasingly made in complex, more or less autonomous networks of governmental and societal actors, often blurring the boundaries between the traditional levels of government (Pierre 2000; Rhodes 1996). Participants in these networks, realizing their mutual dependency in getting things done, have to find ways to collaborate—even in the face of conflicting interests and values. In addition, due to the technical and social complexity of various policy fields, government actors increasingly run into the limits of hierarchical-instrumental policy styles (Hajer and Wagenaar 2003a). The usual strategies to deal with policy complexity—such as disaggregating a complex problem in its constituent parts to solve the problem piecemeal, step by step, or to design a systems model of the problem—are extensions of instrumental rationality. In actual practice they fall short of solving the problem because they are unable to capture the dynamic interaction between the parts that is the hallmark of complexity (Urry 2003). For this reason Dryzek suggests that only nonreductionist strategies, in particular the collaboration of a wide range of participants in a communicatively rational way, will be able to deal with policy complexity (Dryzek 1990).

In many advanced liberal democracies, this situation has led to efforts to involve those affected by policy initiatives in governing through interactive policy making or coproduction. Although initially these experiments in governance were often dominated by administrators, and amounted to little more than elaborate consultation models, increasingly nongovernment actors are given genuine decision power, leading to collaborative policy making (Innes and Booher 2003), empowered participatory governance (Fung and Wright 2003), and deliberative planning (Forester 1999; Healy 1997) In this changing and fragmented policy landscape where policy is often made outside official hierarchical channels, and with actors who were, until recently, removed from any decision-making power, the consonance between an interpretive epistemology, communicative rationality, and a participative, deliberative mode of democracy, has the chance to achieve greater institutional expression. In this way, policy analysis seems to return to Lasswell's ideal of a policy science of democracy. In the "contextual orientation" that is the heart of Lasswell's vision, policy analysis was always to include the knowledge and judgments of citizens in the solution of collective problems. Articulating and grasping meaning is a central part of this endeavor, because meaning making, as Hajer and Wagenaar conclude (Hajer and Wagenaar 2003a), although ambiguous and open-ended, is remarkably well adapted to the inconsistencies and contradictions that are characteristic of the pluralistic, complex, and indeterminate everyday policy world; where rationality is no longer seen as the efficient achievement of predetermined goals, but rather as the difficult task of trying to imagine the other's perspective through a process of open, reciprocal, and respectful communication.

NOTES

1. In the philosophy of science literature a distinction is often made between "explanation" and "understanding." The term "explanation" is used for causal explanation in the natural sciences, and "understanding" for a different kind of explanation in the humanities or "Geistewissenschaften." The difference is sometimes said to reside in the fact that understanding has a certain psychological ring to it. Methodologically, this implies that understanding requires empathy, or the "re-creation in the mind of the scholar of the mental atmosphere, the thoughts and feelings and motivations, of the objects of his study" (von Wright 1971, 6). Hermeneutic philosophy, the branch of philosophy that takes the interpretation of the meaning of language as its entrance into grasping the world of human affairs, also rests on the same distinction between (causal) explanation and (interpretive) understanding. However, it considers the latter not as a psychological but as a language-oriented, semantic category. The empathic and the language-based version of understanding have in common that they see it as a distinct, *sui generis*, form of obtaining knowledge about the world that derives its special character from the nature of its object, namely human action. In this chapter I tend to steer clear from the debates and controversies that surround the alleged distinction between explanation and understanding. Instead I use the word "explanation" to refer both to causal and intentional explanation (Elster 1983; von Wright, 1971).
2. "The whole point of a commissive is to commit the speaker to a certain course of action. Examples are: promise, covenant, contract, undertake, bind myself, give my word, am determined to, intend, declare my intention, mean to....(etc.)" (J. L. Austin, in Coulter, 1979, 163).
3. Poststructuralism in policy analysis encompasses a variety of approaches such as narrative analysis, Foucauldian genealogical analysis, governmentality, and discourse analysis, with different methodological emphases and varying substantive interest. They have in common that they consider meaning not as residing in the external world (in which meanings could be "read" by an observer, and in which language would be an expression of this external meaning), but as immanent to language systems. Meaning is in the *relation* between elements. (Howarth,2000) Where poststructuralism differs from structuralism is that it situates the interplay of symbols in a wider context of language and action that informs the meanings thus derived. The assumption is that semantic meaning—and in its wake, institutional and personal identity—derives from the interplay of the elements of the symbolic system in relation to the wider world—itself a structure of symbols. Differently put, poststructural approaches share the insight that language is *constitutive* of social reality.

REFERENCES

Bevir, M., & Rhodes, R. A. W. (2003). *Interpreting British Governance*. London: Routledge.

Bohman, J. (1996). *Public Deliberation. Pluralism, Complexity, and Democracy*. Cambridge, MA: The MIT Press.

Coulter, J. (1979). Transparancy of Mind: the Availability of Subjective Phenomena. In J. Coulter (Ed.), *The Social Construction of Mind. Studies in Ethnomethodology and Linguistic Philosophy*. Totowa, NJ: Rowman and Littlefield.

Dryzek, J. S. (1982). Policy Analysis as a Hermeneutic Activity. *Policy Sciences, 14*, 309–329.

Dryzek, J. S. (1990). *Discursive Democracy. Politics, Policy, and Political Science*. Cambridge: Cambridge University Press.

Dunne, J. (1993). *Back to the Rough Ground: 'Phronesis" and 'Techne' in Modern Philosophy and in Aristotle*. Notre Dame, IN: University of Notre Dame Press.

Elster, J. (1983). *Explaining Technical Change*. Cambridge: Cambridge University Press.

Estroff, S. E. (1981). *Making It Crazy. An Ethnography of Psychiatric Clients in an American Community*. Berkeley: University of California Press.

Fay, B. (1975). *Social Theory and Political Practice*. London: George Allen & Unwin.

Fischer, F. (2003). Beyond Empiricism: Policy Analysis as Deliberative Practice. In M. Hajer & H. Wagenaar (Eds.), *Deliberative Policy Analysis. Understanding Governance in the Network Society* (pp. 209–227). Cambridge: Cambridge University Press.

Forester, J. (1999). *The Deliberative Practitioner. Encouraging Participatory Planning Processes*. Cambridge, Massachusetts: The MIT Press.

Fung, A., & Wright, E. O. (Eds.). (2003). *Deepening Democracy. Institutional Innovations in Empowered Particpatory Governance*. London: Verso.

Geertz, C. (1973). Thick Description: Toward an Interpretive Theory of Culture. In C. Geertz (Ed.), *The Interpretation of Cultures* (pp. 3–32). New York: Basic Books.

Hajer, M., & Wagenaar, H. (2003a). Introduction. In M. Hajer & H. Wagenaar (Eds.), *Deliberative Policy Analysis. Understanding Governance in the Network Society* (pp. 1–33). Cambridge: Cambridge University Press.

Hajer, M., & Wagenaar, H. (Eds.). (2003b). *Deliberative Policy Analysis. Understanding Governance in the Network Society*. Cambridge: Cambridge University Press.

Healy, P. (1997). *Collaborative Planning: Shaping Places in Fragmented Societies*. London: Macmillan.

Howarth, D. (2000). *Discourse*. Buckingham: Open University Press.

Hunter, I. (1996). Assembling the School. In A. Barry & T. Osborne & N. Rose (Eds.), *Foucault and Political Reason. Liberalism, Neo-liberalism and Traditionalities of Government* (pp. 143–167). London: UCL Press.

Innes, J. E., & Booher, D. E. (2003). Collaborative Policymaking: Governance through Dialogue. In M. Hajer & H. Wagenaar (Eds.), *Deliberative Policy Analysis: Understanding Governance in the network Society*. Cambridge: Cambridge University Press.

Kekes, J. (1993). *The Morality of Pluralism*. Princeton, NJ: Princeton University Press.

Lewis, D., Riger, S., Rosenberg, H., Wagenaar, H., Lurigio, A. J., & Reed, S. (1991). *Worlds of the Mentally Ill. How Deinstitutionalization Works in the City*. Carbondale, IL: Southern Illinois University Press.

Liebow, E. (1967). *Tally's Corner. A Study of Negro Streetcorner Men*. Boston, MA: Little, Brown and Company.

Pierre, J. (Ed.). (2000). *Debating Governance: Authority, Steering, and Democracy*. Oxford: Oxford University Press.

Rein, M. (1976). *Social Science and Public Policy*. Harmondsworth: Penguin Books.

Rein, M. (1983). Value-Critical Policy Analysis. In D. Callahan & B. Jennings (Eds.), *Ethics, the Social Sciences, and Policy Analysis*. New York: Plenum Press.

Rhodes, R. A. W. (1996). The New Governance: Governing without Government. *Political Studies, 44*, 652–667.

Schwandt, T. A. (1997). Evaluation as Practical Hermeneutics. *Evaluation, 3*(1), 69–83.

Schwandt, T. A. (2000). Three Epistemological Stances for Qualitative Inquiry. Interpretivism, Hermeneutics, and Social Constructivism. In N. K. Denzin & Y. S. Lincoln (Eds.), *Handbook of Qualitative Research* (2nd ed., pp. 189–215). Thousand Oaks, CA: Sage.

Searle, J. R. (1995). *The Construction of Social Reality*. New York: The Free Press.

Stone, D. (1997). *Policy Paradox. The Art of Political Decision Making*. New York: W.W. Norton.

Taylor, C. (1977). Interpretation and the Sciences of Man. In F. R. Dallmayr & T. A. McCarthy (Eds.), *Understanding and Social Inquiry*. Notre Dame, IN: University of Notre Dame Press.

Thomas, D. (1979). *Naturalism and Social Science. A Post-Empiricist Philosophy of Social Science*. Cambridge: Cambridge University Press.

Urry, J. (2003). *Global Complexity*. Cambridge: Polity.

von Wright, G. H. (1971). *Explanation and Understanding*. Ithaca, NY: Cornell University Press.

Wagenaar, H. (1987). *Virtual Institutions: Community Relations and Hospital Recidivism in the Life of the Mental Patient.* Unpublished doctoral thesis, Massachusetts Institute of Technology, Cambridge, MA.

Wagenaar, H. (2002). Value Pluralism in Public Administration: Two Perspectives on Administrative Morality. In J. S. Jun (Ed.), *Rethinking Administrative Theory. The Challenge of the New Century* (pp. 105–130). Westport, CT: Praeger.

Wagenaar, H., & Cook, S. D. N. (2003). Understanding Policy Practices: Action, Dialectic and Deliberation in Policy Analysis. In M. Hajer & H. Wagenaar (Eds.), *Deliberative Policy Analysis: understanding governance in the network society.* Cambridge: Cambridge University Press.

Weiss, R. S., & Rein, M. (1970). The Evaluation of Broad-Aim Programs: Experimental Design, Its Difficulties, and an Alternative. *Administrative Science Quarterly* (March), 97–109.

Wiseman, J. P. (1979). *Stations of the Lost. The Treatment of Skid Row Alcoholics.* Chicago: The University of Chicago Press.

Yanow, D. (1996). *How Does a Policy mean? Interpreting Policy and Organizational Action.* Washington D.C.: Georgetown University Press.

Yanow, D. (2000). *Conducting Interpretive Policy Analysis* (Vol. 47). Thousand Oaks, CA: Sage.

30 Context-Sensitive Policy Methods

Susan E. Clarke

I. WHY CONTEXT-SENSITIVE POLICY METHODS?

Talking about "context-sensitive policy methods" seems an awkward and unnecessarily cumbersome way to characterize policy research. Why not just refer to qualitative methods or even post-positive orientations to distinguish contextual policy approaches from conventional policy analysis strategies? Context-sensitive policy methods share some, but not all, of the assumptions of qualitative and post-positive approaches. Most importantly, context-sensitive methods highlight policy research tools and analytic strategies that allow more systematic and rigorous research in situations where variations in context and setting are important aspects of data observations. Where data is not obvious or not easily available, both data collection tools and analysis procedures must be sensitive to the contextual specificity of the information and measurements in play.

Policy researchers often—but not always—deal with policy problems where variations in context and setting are important elements to be retained in data collection and analysis. More conventional variable-wise strategies often divorce the observations from their context in order to meet assumptions of independence for testing purposes. As a result the meaning of the observation also disappears. Contextual approaches redress this through use of analytic tools and strategies that do not rely on these conventional assumptions. Context is a critical explanatory element, not a residual category in context-sensitive research (Maxwell 2004). This chapter makes the case for context-sensitive policy research methods, describes some tools that support this approach, and identifies some of the issues raised by context-sensitive policy research.

A. CONFRONTING DUALISMS

Weimer (1999) characterizes the stance of many policy researchers in saying that, as a policy analyst, he is willing to "embrace any method that can potentially help me give better advice." The argument here is that contextually-sensitive methods—whether they be quantitative or qualitative—are likely to generate better advice because their findings and inferences are interpretable—that is, can be plausibly defended (Collier, Brady, and Seawright 2004, 238). In addition, they are accessible and knowable to policy makers and citizens because the case-oriented tools retain the contextual features that give the observation meaning and emphasize the processes that connect events and factors to outcomes. Methods sensitive to context, therefore, contribute to valid inferences as well as increase the potential impact of policy research on policymaking.

To move toward context-sensitive policy research, rejecting, or at least sidestepping, the dualism of quantitative and qualitative methods is an important first step. Although the rhetoric in some disciplines and many departments continues to reify this purported research divide, only the most primitive form of empiricism or positivism continues to assume such stark differences (see Brower et al. 2000; Miles and Huberman 1994). The most influential book on social science research in the last few decades, King, Keohane, and Verba's *Designing Social Inquiry* (1994) explicitly rejects this dualism. Brady and Collier's (2004) path-breaking *Rethinking Social Inquiry* now pushes this debate further by claiming these methods share a similar epistemological foundation, share similar inferential challenges stemming from their reliance on observational data, but employ diverse tools in their analyses and approach these challenges in different ways (Brady, Collier, and Seawright 2004, 11). Their call for developing shared standards for social science research underscores the need to more systematically document both the diverse tools and often implicit standards used in different research traditions.

1. The Quantitative Methods Template

This dualism is grounded in the distinctive attributes associated with these research approaches. Briefly, using quantitative methods allows the researcher to make inferences and possibly predictions about the generalizability of their findings to a larger population. To do so requires a probability sampling strategy that will allow such generalizations and a large enough number of cases to permit statistical analyses with a narrow margin of error. Researchers often approach their experimental or correlational projects armed with research designs testing theories and hypotheses generated by other scholars; both the cases and the populations are given (Ragin 2004). These assumptions and procedures encourage the researcher to choose falsifiable research questions, to rely on precise quantitative measures (especially interval or ratio-level measures), to test alternative hypotheses with statistical tools, to seek outcomes or dependent variables with sufficient variation across cases, to focus on the discrete variables "explaining" the greatest amount of variation in the dependent variable, and to set aside outliers that don't fit the most parsimonious explanations (see Ragin 2004; Maxwell 2004). Causation is inferred through correlations of variations in independent and dependent variables rather than through direct observation. Most researchers using these methods see their findings as amenable to replication by other researchers and as contributions to testing and building a larger body of theory.

2. The Qualitative Methods Template

Qualitative research is, unfortunately, often defined in terms of the absence of these features of quantitative research. As an inductive research strategy, qualitative research does not necessarily rely on hypotheses and theory. An emphasis on "thick analysis" is one of the most distinctive features of qualitative research.[1] This entails direct observation to gain detailed knowledge about a case in order to understand the meaning of the behaviors observed to the actors involved. Trying to understand "how" things happen, what the "facts" mean is a key goal and such understandings can only be developed through observing particular settings. As a result, researchers focus on a small number of cases that are theoretically or substantively important; these cases may indeed change in the process of research (Ragin 2004). Large N studies are not feasible since detailed knowledge of each case is less possible and less important in such approaches.

Making causal inferences is not necessarily the goal of all qualitative researchers. Indeed testing theory and linking findings to broader theories often appears sacrificed to the "unique" character of the particular case (Blee 2004). To some extent, qualitative researchers seem to be collecting and analyzing data simultaneously, rather than the more sequenced procedures of more quantitative research. Sampling is seemingly erratic and unstructured and theory-testing is not always a high priority. The focus often is on the processes linking events (Maxwell 2004); this emphasis on process and causal mechanisms constitutes a distinctive approach to explanation and causality (Maxwell 2004).

In order to build theory, qualitative researchers find it essential to remain open to all the possible factors that might be important in the research setting rather than an a priori list of factors to investigate. These attributes are especially likely to characterize more ethnographic approaches which emphasize the importance of "letting the data speak for themselves" rather than constraining it with preconceived frameworks and categories (see Bayard de Volo and Schatz 2004). Overall, as Bashi (2004) points out, qualitative researchers put a premium on the virtue of avoiding "control" of all the factors that quantitative researchers see as important—the subjects, the research protocols, the relationship of the researcher and the respondent, and the context itself. They emphasize that the researcher is constructing knowledge or data, not relying on some package of assembled data. The fluidity and unstructured nature of these processes make qualitative research methods appear "nearly antithetical to the scientific method influenced by a longstanding positivist tradition" (Bashi, V. 2004; see also, Flick 2002).

B. WHICH TEMPLATE BEST GUIDES RESEARCH?

NSF's recent workshop on qualitative methods characterized many of the "best practices" for qualitative research as systematic and rigorous approaches that can document the reliability and validity of their findings (NSF 2004; Blee 2004). They also emphasized the importance of using research questions rather than descriptive goals to frame the research as well as designing a sampling and analytic framework allowing exploring alternative explanations, even if these change during the course of research (Blee 2004). Validity issues, often the bane of qualitative research, should be continuously assessed. Nevertheless, the major assets of qualitative research—the emergence of nonparsimonious explanations and stories, the contextual focus, the information of respondent's perceptions, the long-term engagement of the researcher—are to be highlighted (Bless 2004, 56).

To many, the NSF report sounded like a set of mixed messages. Neither data nor methods are inherently quantitative or qualitative. Social science research overwhelming draws on observational data—data that is amenable to analysis through any number of techniques, often both quantitatively or qualitatively. This is especially so for documents, interviews, and text—there is nothing about this "data" that is obviously quantitative or qualitative. Even naturalistic observations can be coded and analyzed with quantitative methods although the researcher may well complain that doing so robs the "data" of the meanings so laboriously collected. Similarly, characterizing some analysis strategies as more obviously qualitative or quantitative is open to challenge. Positivism does not encompass only quantitative research (Weimer 1999). And as Lin (1998) points out, there are many different approaches under the umbrella of "qualitative methods." In addition to the more interpretivist views noted above, qualitative researchers also engage in tracking processes that appear to lead consistently to one set of outcomes rather than another, in determining which characteristics are—and are not—typically associated with certain policy problems, and in mapping patterns across settings and actors (see NSF 2004).

These are different modes of inquiry although perhaps more similar than some adherents are willing to admit (Brady and Collier 2004). The more effective research approach is likely to draw on the strengths of both traditions in a multi-method strategy rather than "improving" qualitative research with a template derived from a narrow quantitative approach. More specifically, policy researchers are better served by developing and documenting the diverse array of tools that meet their needs rather than feeling pushed into either the quantitative or qualitative camp. The question then is what is it about policy analysis that makes neither qualitative nor quantitative methods the obvious research template?

C. Does Policy Research Require a Distinctive Context-Sensitive Template?

Most policy researchers are problem-oriented rather than concerned with theory development. Theory development is not an irrelevant concern but often a secondary one. Unless the analyst is concerned with evaluating the impact of a program (see Geva-May and Pal 1999), the focus tends to be on a set of problems in distinctive settings. This usually engenders a smaller number of cases to study since the researcher is looking at the whole case rather than extracting variables from each for analysis. Falsification is not a relevant criterion for designing the research question; rather, the research question is about the problem itself. Some qualitative researchers would reject the notion that reliability and validity are the appropriate primary criteria for evaluating qualitative research. Policy researchers rarely can afford that stance, however, although many would agree that these criteria need to be adapted for qualitative or contextual research (Weitzman 2004, 1999). Parsimony is less important than gaining a full and accurate understanding of the trends and conditions contributing to the problem and understanding the likely impacts of alternative solutions. Policy researchers are less likely to see data in terms of theory testing or building but they are also not likely to "let the data speak for themselves" either. Finally, one of the most important departures from conventional analyses is the need in context-sensitive research to abandon the assumption that variables or factors operate—and thus can be analyzed—independently of each other. Instead, policy researchers are acutely aware of the interdependence and complexity of the problems they are involved in.[2]

Context-sensitive policy researchers are more likely to be interested in understanding causal mechanisms than in searching for causal relationships (Lin 1998). Yet this is not to argue that causal explanations are not possible in more qualitative and contextual research: Miles and Huberman (1984) argue that field research is better than quantitative methods in developing understandings of what they call "local causality"—the causal mechanisms—while Maxwell (2004) details a number of process-oriented approaches that can rule out alternative explanations in developing a causal argument.

An interest in context in itself does not necessarily distinguish quantitative and qualitative approaches. Some researchers might argue that context is an interaction term and can be incorporated in more conventional regression analyses. As Collier, Seawright, and Brady (NSF) note, such practices have become increasingly common in regression analyses: they cite Franzese's study (2003, 21) reporting that between 1996 and 2001, interaction terms have been used in 25 percent of the quantitative articles in major political science journals." Although this may well encourage further multi-method analyses, interaction terms are not appropriate surrogates for the contextual effects important to policy researchers. They tell little about the processes that contribute to the problems and potential solutions of interest to policy analysts.

To meet the problem-oriented needs of policy researcher, to allow for interdependent configurations and processes, to truly understand contextual effects, it is necessary to work with tools that do not separate the observation and the context. This generally requires case-wise rather than variable-wise analysis. This also affects both how the researcher collects and analyzes the data. In a word, it requires a research template featuring context-sensitive tools.

II. CONTEXT-SENSITIVE TOOLS FOR CONSTRUCTING AND COLLECTING DATA

While policy researchers can identify a number of factors that distinguish their methodological needs from those of more conventional qualitative and quantitative researchers, one of the most important issues is their very direct involvement in the data collection and analysis process. Although it is disingenuous to assume that problem selection, data collection, and data analysis in more conventional approaches is not vulnerable to researcher bias, it is nevertheless important to recognize that the close engagement of policy researchers with respondents makes the issue more visible. This also makes the need for reflectivity especially significant. This is standard practice in most policy analysis protocols; it is emphasized particularly in Lasswell's policy sciences approach where researchers devote significant resources to locating their own values and perspectives relative to the problem being analyzed.

In its recent report, NSF (2004) recommends that any researchers working with qualitative methods assess the "possible impact of the researcher's presence and biography" at every step of the research process. While there is no reason not to extend this admonition to all researchers (witness the unquestioned decades of NSF-sponsored research on gender-less political behavior), the potential for bias is seen as especially acute when researchers are present during the data collection process.

A. CONSTRUCTING AND COLLECTING POLICY-RELEVANT DATA

But most policy researchers have little recourse to constructing their own data. To the extent they are problem-oriented, they generally are dealing with a specific problem in a particular setting. With luck, there will be data available on the trends and conditions contributing to the problem but it is up to the researcher to gain a better understanding of the problem from the perspective of those involved with it and affected by it. Collecting and constructing data about these perceptions and contextual factors is the task.

In contrast to more qualitative research, policy researchers are more likely to begin with a relatively "structured data collection plan." That is, as the researcher becomes oriented to the problem, some types of data collection become obvious and can be planned in advance. Other data, admittedly, may be identified during the research process but this is a strength of contextual research, not a flaw in research design. Few policy researchers face such questions as "what are my cases" or "what are their relevant features" as may be the case in qualitative research (NSF 2004). Most begin with an analytic framework that helps them select the cases and identify the factors to take into consideration in their research. These frameworks are relatively straightforward and convergent; the most distinctive is the policy science's emphasis on problem orientation, decision processes, and mapping. All these frameworks emphasize a series of categories and features to take into account, not to impose a priori constraints on the researcher but to overcome the bounded rationality limiting every researcher.

B. Q-METHODOLOGY

Given the task of understanding perceptions about policy problems and the context in which these occur, it is not surprising to rely on interview methods. There is a long and honorable tradition in the social sciences of gaining observational data through interviewing those directly involved in the situation being researched (see Leech 2002; also, Beamer 2002; Lieberman 2004; Maestas 2003; Morgan 1996; Murphy 1980; Sturges and Hanrahan 2004; Stroh 2000; Roulston et al. 2003). This is also the point at which researchers are most vulnerable to charges of bias. To overcome some of these concerns, alternative interview techniques allow the interviewer to collect information without imposing her values and biases on the process. Indeed, it is possible to argue these strategies are less vulnerable to researcher bias than the categories and closed-ended options imposed on respondents in survey research.

One of the more innovative interview strategies involves Q-methodology, a tool in use for over 50 years in business and management, psychological, and planning research but less well known to policy researchers. Its advocates see it as an empirical tool for charting subjective perceptions, preferences and values. The objective is not to create causal arguments based on individual actions and choices but to work with a "subject-centered" perspective. Indeed, it was referred to as the foundation for "a science of subjectivity" by its founder (Stephenson 1953) because it relies on the self-reference of the respondent and depicts the world as experienced from their point of view.[3] The assumption is that these internal frames of reference have a structure and form that can be made manifest and comparable by using the same formal interview instrument across respondents (Brown 1980). Q-methodology allows each respondent—rather than the researcher—to model their own views about an issue in terms of their intensity. At the end of each interview, the researcher has the respondent's unique schematic configuration of ideas, beliefs, and opinions that can then be compared with the similarly unique configurations of other respondents to identify areas of agreement, overlap, and potential conflict.

1. Doing Q

While the core activity is an interview with those seen as holding a representative range of views and understandings of a problem (usually 25–30), the interview tool is distinctive. In becoming oriented to the problem and the different values and interests potentially in conflict, the researcher constructs a matrix or factorial design of the dimensions most important to explore with the participants. This matrix often is based on a theoretical or analytical framework and is specific to the problem being analyzed. One axis usually includes dimensions of the problem under study while the other axis of the matrix often includes the policy attributes considered especially salient for this issue. This could include, for example, the different aspects of problem orientation—the goals, the varying views on the trends and conditions contributing to the problem, possible alternative solutions, and projections of future conditions.

Here is where Q-methodology diverges from traditional interviewing (see Brown 1980; Durning 1999). Rather than asking the respondent their views on each of these dimensions, the researcher devises statements for each cell by drawing on newspaper accounts, reports, expert interviews, and other sources of information. In each cell, the researcher puts two to three items that reflect the intersect forming that cell, e.g., policy goals about growth. These include positively as well as negatively constructed statements; developing unambiguous statements is as important in Q research as in survey research. This is not a standard "sample" of statements but one that is broadly representative of the discourse on the topic being analyzed. This usually means around 40–60 statements distributed across the cells. After pre-testing the statements, the researcher randomly numbers each statement and puts each statement on a 3×5 card—this deck of cards constitutes the Q sort.

In meeting with each of the purposively selected participants, the researcher sets out a strip of paper with 0 in the middle and a continuum of ± on each end up to +5 and –5. These represent the extent to which the participant agrees or disagrees with each statement. The respondent is asked to rank the statements relative to each other by arraying the cards across the continuum, putting those she is uncertain of on the 0 position but encouraged to distribute the others in a normal distribution. This allows the respondent to model their own point of view by sorting and "bundling" their values, beliefs, and ideas in ways that reflect both the direction and the intensity of their overall belief structure. At the end of the session, the researcher records the distribution of statements in each cell. Both cases and items can be analyzed; for policy purposes, cluster analysis is often the most useful analytic tool because it retains the case while mapping belief structures systematically and reliably across cases in terms of those who sorted their statements in similar or dissimilar ways. Essentially, people are correlated across a sample of statements (Durning 1999).

What are the advantages of this seemingly odd procedure? The primary advantage is that this method takes the self-referential perspective of the respondent seriously (Durning 1999). This is especially important in exploring values, preferences and other views not easily articulated or anticipated (Durning and Osuna 1994; Steelman and Maguire 1999). These bundles of statements often reveal unexpected juxtapositions of interests and values, in many cases indicating common ground in a policy conflict where none was anticipated. Clarke and Moss (1990), for example, found that housing needs provided common ground among environmentalists, social service providers, and developers in Boulder, Colorado. In addition, Q is often appealing and engaging to participants, especially those elites fatigued by conventional interview tools and too likely to give canned responses to easily anticipated questions. The potential reduction of interviewer bias also is often cited as an advantage of using Q over other techniques. The interviewer is present but more distant from the interview "process" than in phone or mail surveys or other conventional interview settings; thus the pressure to give the socially desired response is lessened.

For the researcher, the matrix provides the researcher with a direction for initial analysis by illustrating the areas and dimensions with greatest convergence, divergence, intensity, and so on. Thus Q method does not remove bias but certainly limits it (Robbins and Krueger 2000). To Durning (1999, 403), it holds the promise of "subtly subverting the premises of positivist policy analysis" by providing "procedures for the empirical study of human subjectivity." Q also contributes to discursive democracy, according to Dryzck (1990; see also Steelman and Maguire, 1999), by acknowledging the analyst and the respondents as active participants in the research process.

Being a nonrandom sample, it is not possible to make inferences about the findings or to generalize beyond the relatively small number of cases. But the goal is often to understand viewpoints within a particular group, such as agency officials or citizens involved in disputes (e.g., Steelman and Maguire 1999). Q provides contextually-sensitive quantitative data in settings where usually only qualitative data exists (Brown 1980), and is amenable to replication (see Durning 1999). In doing so, it can give the policy researcher an invaluable means of understanding complex views on complex problems, insights that are often "unavailable through other methods" (Durning 1999).

B. Rapid Ethnographic Assessment Procedure (REAP)

Using a Rapid Ethnographic Assessment Procedure (REAP) is another data collection technique helpful in context-sensitive policy research, particularly when time and money are limited. REAP is a tool brought to more developed societies from policy research on public health (Rapid Assessment Procedures), poverty (Participatory Wealth Ranking), and agricultural issues (Rapid Rural Appraisal) in less developed areas. In the United States this tool is increasingly used for societal impact assessments, community needs assessments, and cultural resource management issues (Low et al. 2005). Less structured than Q method, REAP relies on triangulation and iteration to strengthen the validity and reliability of the findings. As Low and her colleagues point out (2005, 664), "the semi-structured interview, expert interview, and the community focus group, are the characteristic elements of a triangulated methodology." Participants are not chosen through formal sampling techniques so the generalizability is low but the accuracy in characterizing situations, attitudes, and values is high. Less than 100 interviews are often sufficient, given the time frame involved. With an often multidisciplinary team rather than an individual researcher in the field, different data collection elements can unfold simultaneously with frequent and intense interaction among team members. Similar to more qualitative approaches, as the new data comes in and the findings are reevaluated, it is possible that new research questions emerge in the process of the research project. Given the rapid pace—often a four month or less time frame—of the data collection and the multiple researchers, construct validity can also be an issue. Low et al suggest that triangulation and the multidisciplinary nature of the research teams can correct these problems and mitigate concerns with internal validity.

REAP data is analyzed by collaborative exchanges on themes emerging from the multiple data collection projects. These themes are used to develop more detailed coding schema for the transcribed field notes and interview materials. While these are amenable to more quantitative analyses, the priority is on retaining the contextual detail in each case.

C. Introducing Intensive and Contextual Dimensions to Survey Research

Satterfield (2004) argues that the intensive and contextual aspects of qualitative research methods can be incorporated into telephone survey research by using CADI (Computer Aided Design Instrument) systems. These systems allow a programmed sequence of questions to be created in which the queries, contingent on each respondent's previous response, resemble a conversation rather than the flat responses generated by conventional surveys. Such "pathway surveys" (Satterfield and Gregory 1998; Gregory et al. 1997) map participant perceptions of complex policy decisions as well as their accounts of how they move from their goals and values to actual decision choices. As Satterfield points out, these "linked question sets" can be used to trace the reasoning processes that lead participants down one decision pathway and not another. The survey design incorporates the major pathways and opinion streams identified in pre-survey interviews. Although many potential decision pathways can be incorporated in the survey instrument, most responses tend to cluster around a few key pathways (Satterfield and Gregory 1998). Advocates see pathway studies as taking standard survey methods to a more subtle and nuanced level; from a contextual perspective, they support mapping participants' subjective perceptions, perspectives, and values about complex issues and allow the researcher to identify whether these responses are conditional on other factors.

D. Emerging Data Collection Technologies

Technological advances clearly are changing the data collection landscape. As noted above, CADI systems are transforming survey research in ways that incorporate contextual sensitivities of qualitative methods. PDAs and other hand held devices now allow the researcher to record and transmit interview data, whatever the interview process, in a matter of minutes. The agreement between data collected with paper forms and data collected with handheld computers was greater than 95 percent in a recent study (Fletcher et al. 2003; see also, Ice 2004.). EthnoNotes, an Internet-based field note management tool, facilitates the writing, sharing, and analyzing of field notes in collaborative and multisite research projects (Lieber et al. 2003). It also supports indexing and coding of text and integration with quantitative materials. These improvements in the speed, efficiency, and sensitivity of data entry and collection are especially important when analysis overlaps data collection in the field as is often the case in policy research

III. ALTERNATIVE ANALYSIS STRATEGIES IN CONTEXT-SENSITIVE POLICY RESEARCH

It is becoming increasingly common to characterize methodological approaches as emphasizing variable-wise or case-wise analysis (Ragin 1987; Brunner 1996). The former is associated with conventional quantitative analyses in which an observation is converted into a series of discrete variables that are comparable across observations; the relationships between variables can be compared while "holding constant" the effects of other discrete variables. To achieve this, the meaning of each variable is determined prior to the observation—e.g., educational achievement is presented as cumulative years in formal schooling—and is presumed to be invariant across observations. By divorcing the meaning from the context of the observation—it is not important whether a respondent sees her educational achievement in different terms—the researcher gains enormous analytical leverage by comparing patterns across cases.

But case-wise analysis retains the case as a whole, without divvying it up into variables determined on an a priori basis. Separating variables out on the basis of prior assumptions and categories introduces researcher bias and results not only in distorted interpretations of the research findings but in missed opportunities to uncover the patterns that give meaning to the data. The case-wise rationale is that the context for each observation is essential to understanding the meaning of the information gathered. Rather than discrete variables, the important factors in each case are assumed to be interactive and multi-collinear, with distinctive process configurations within each case. Accordingly, Collier, Brady, and Seawright (2004, 252) characterize this as causal process observations rather than the variable-wise data set observations. Case-wise analysis demands complex analytic strategies, given the uncategorized (and often unstructured) data (Becker 2004) and the interest in preserving the contextual features.

A. DISCOURSE, NARRATIVES, AND ARGUMENTATION

Analysis of discourse, narrative and argumentation is a bridge between more traditional qualitative methods and contextual policy research methods. Narratives are important elements in both approaches. Satterfield (2004, 117) describes narratives as "both the storied talk that characterizes conversation, musings, and social discourse in everyday life as well as more formal definitions pointing to the attributes of this form including plot, narration, the imagistic and affective valence of a narrative vignette, and so on." Ethnographic research puts a premium on such materials; researchers often use participant observation and other ethnographic tools to collect individual narratives in relatively unstructured fashion.

1. Narrative and Argumentation in Policy Research

Narratives and argumentation figure prominently in policy concepts such as discourse coalitions (Hajer 1993), causal stories (Stone, D. 1989), frames (Morth 2000; Pal 1995; Wanta 1993; Hershey 1994) and other approaches featuring problem definition processes (Rochefort and Cobb 1994; Rydin, 1998; Pollock et al. 1994; Sharp 1994;). These approaches share a perspective emphasizing the multiple ways in which people come to understand an event or phenomenon. The emphasis can be interpretivist—assuming multiple realities, uncovering the meanings different situations or ideas have for people in everyday life, and asking how they explain what they do and believe (Lin 1998; Yanow, 2000; Gamson, 1992). It can also be more directly constructivist—the processes by which people construct meanings and rationales for their acts (Ingram and Schneider 1994). Narratives do not merely illuminate an issue but represent blueprints for understanding how issues are identified, who is assigned blame or responsibility for problems, how groups are mobilized around some policy solutions and not others, and other processes.[4]

Narratives also serve to connect events and processes in a specific context (Maxwell 2004). Tracing processes through narratives or stories about sequences of events is an important dimension of using narratives as evidence (Abbott 1992; Stryker 1996; Buthe 2002; Franzosi 1998). These "connecting strategies" are essential to understanding causal processes although they are also subject to the criticism that they tend "to underspecify causality" and "often miss the distinction between chronology and causality" (Maxwell 2004, 256).

2. Discourse Analysis Using Computer-Aided Tools

Discourse analysis is one of the more loosely applied terms in the humanities and social sciences. While there is general agreement that language and rhetoric are important subjects of analysis in themselves—since they are used to shape and frame policy issues—there are few standards guiding such analyses and directing the researcher in how to analyze discourse in order to understand policy problems (deLeon 1998). For example, content analysis is often mistaken for discourse analysis (see Herrera and Braumoeller 2004). While its emphasis on the frequency of certain phrases and terms can be important, content analysis in itself is often less relevant to problem-oriented research. The relevance or salience of the frequency distribution is not always obvious unless there is an analytical framework available for interpreting these trends. Brunner (1987), for example, traces the symbolic dissociation in the meaning of the term "Watergate" from reference to the actual burglary at the Watergate residential complex during the Nixon administration to its subsequent use to refer to numerous instances of lack of trust in government. Few exercises in content analysis meet this analytic standard, however.

Discourse analysis examines the structure and the content of different "strings" of reasoning or beliefs expressed by a range of respondents or in documentary materials. The links between these strings and different actors as well as the ways in which these strings can shape problem definitions and privilege some solutions and exclude others are amenable to analysis, using software developed for this purpose. Basically, these software tools allow the researcher to find, display, and analyze "patterns of co-occurrences of codes, text strings and case-variables" in consistent and reliable ways (Weitzman 2004). Or in Lewis' (2004, 439) more instrumental terms, the researcher can use these programs to "associate codes or labels with chunks of text, sounds, pictures, or video; to search these codes for patterns; and to construct classifications of codes" that are amenable testing.

One of the earliest programs developed for discourse analysis was the unfortunately named NUD*IST software for Non-Numerical Unstructured Data with Indexing Searching and Theorizing (Richards and Richards 1995). NUD*IST evolved over time to allow the researcher to code text of any sort, to develop categorizations based on the data, to sort and analyze patterns in the data, and to perform various statistical tests ranging from crosstabs to measures determining whether the patterns appearing to emerge from the data were "statistically significant." Sidney (2002), for example, analyzed the different problem definitions used by Latinos, African Americans, Asians, and Anglos to describe "the problem with schools" in their cities. Her discourse analysis, using NUD*IST, indicates that these varying problem definitions across racial and ethnic boundaries hinder coalitional strategies for those interested in reforming urban public schools. Similarly, Clarke (1999) compared abortion narratives over time in Denver by using NUD*IST to analyze newspaper accounts of abortion conflicts. Over time both pro-choice and anti-abortion advocates shifted their frames away from their original value-driven perspectives; an alternative narrative emphasizing public order emerged as city officials become concerned about the city's image in the face of these conflicts.

Computer-aided analysis is particularly important for discourse analysis and other text analysis tasks. This use of computers for analysis of qualitative research marks a number of distinctive approaches that promise more rigorous and consistent contextual analyses (see discussion of software tools in Weitzman and Miles 1995; Weitzman 1999, 2000). These promises of greater rigor and reliability place contextual research on discourse closer to conventional quantitative research and beyond ethnographic research. They also promise greater ability to integrate qualitative and quantitative data. Critics argue, of course, that the meaning of the text can be lost in the coding and categorization. Collier, Brady, and Seawright (2004, 266) disparage this as the "trend toward technification" as an end it itself, displacing simpler and more sensitive tools. But the more recent versions of NUD*IST, its successor NVivo, and Atlas.ti provide for categorization based on patterns of relationships in the text. Although these computer-aided tools increase the speed and consistency of discourse analysis, there is little evaluation to date of the effects of the software on the outcomes

(Weitzman, 2004). And most software is limited to analysis of text although analysis of media such as audio and video is now possible with some programs, e.g. Atlas.ti 5.0, NVivo 2.0, HyperResearch, interClipper, C-I-SAID, and Transana (see Weitzman 2004; Lewis 2004).

B. QCA AND FUZZY SET APPROACHES

Case studies are a mainstay of policy research but also remain significant methods in political science, sociology, and public administration (see Bennett et al. 2003; Brower et al. 2000; also, see Yin 1994; "Symposium" 2000). Within-case analyses of a single case are valued in many fields as well, with a rich intellectual tradition supporting their contributions to theory development as well as their relevance in policy research. But since multiple sites or analyses over time provide opportunities for comparison and stronger arguments about causal processes, many researchers are interested in contextually-sensitive comparisons of larger numbers of cases. One of the most significant breakthroughs for social science researchers and policy researchers is Ragin's adoption of Boolean algebra for Qualitative Comparative Analysis (QCA) of multiple case studies. QCA allows the researcher to work with relatively large numbers of cases using Bayesian inference to evaluate necessary and sufficient causes of outcomes.

QCA highlights the different assumptions about causality characterizing contextual policy research methods. As Ragin (2004) points out, conventional positivist research tests the independent effects of competing explanations of the outcome but more qualitative research sees causation in terms of a combination of causes. Indeed different combinations or configurations of characteristics may produce the same outcome through distinctive causal paths. This potential for "multiple, conjunctural causes" is especially relevant to policy research.

The Bayesian logic in Ragin's QCA yields "truth tables" to sort out these causal paths, sorting out the different combinations of dichotomous factors in each case associated with the presence and absence of the outcome being studied. The researcher identifies the dichotomous factors to be included in the tables—generally informed by some theoretical or analytical framework—and also determines whether they were present or absent in each case being compared (Amenta and Poulson 1994; Wichkam-Crowley 1991). This makes the analysis vulnerable to claims of researcher bias since any shift in coding from the dichotomous characteristics can alter the findings substantially.

In his fuzzy set approach, Ragin introduces continuous variables and a software program that makes QCA an efficient and rigorous means of testing hypotheses about the necessary and sufficient conditions associated with the outcomes. Mahoney (2004) points out that fs/QCA allows researchers to: (1) analyze probabilistic patterns of necessary or sufficient causation, (2) explore how different combinations of variables are each jointly sufficient for an outcome, and (3) assess the statistical significance and statistical relevance of necessary and sufficient causes. Kilburn (2004) uses QCA to identify the necessary and sufficient conditions for different regime types in 14 U.S. cities. His analysis considers market conditions (a city's fiscal resource base and mobility of local capital) and democratic conditions (local civic participation and ward-style representation) but he finds that neither is necessary or sufficient for supporting the emergence of a more progressive, as opposed to a developmental or caretaker, regime. Instead, three interactions between the components of market and democratic conditions explain the presence of progressive regimes.

C. CLUSTER ANALYSIS

Cluster analysis is appropriate when the researcher is interested in determining how cases are similar and different in the absence of a priori categorization or classification. The assumption is that each case is unique but that they can be classified based on their similarity to other cases; this is a common classificatory device we all do in everyday life. Available as part of SPSS (Statistical Package for the Social Sciences) and STATA, cluster analysis is a variant of factor analysis in which the cases (rather than the variables) are systematically and sequentially paired in terms of the means of each attribute.

Any type of data is amenable to cluster analysis; it is an innovative way to integrate quantitative and qualitative data in case-wise analysis. Cluster analysis is useful for exploratory research rather than causal predictions;[5] by retaining the case and systematically comparing to other cases, it is especially useful for context-sensitive policy research.

Although the researcher can specify a certain number of clusters to get a quick sense of the data, the most effective strategy is to decide on cluster methods and distance measures and run the cluster procedure to view the emerging clusters. Using a variety of algorithms, the cluster procedure will pair up cases until it is clear that the coefficients of any additional cases are different enough from the established cluster to indicate a new cluster is called for. That cutoff point is subjective; it can be determined visually or preset. A dendogram displays the formation of clusters or groupings by plotting each step of agglomeration in terms of the coefficients of the cluster and the potential new case.[6] Tables present the means of each variable in the cluster and report the F statistic and F significance values to determine how "loose" or "tight" the clusters are as well as how different each cluster is from the others. These allow the researcher to characterize the clusters by looking at the mean values for the attributes defining the cluster; it is also possible to identify the demographic features associated with each cluster if the data involves human subjects.

The now familiar labels of "soccer moms" and "NASCAR dads" were derived from cluster analysis—rather than variable-wise analysis—of polling results. This highlights one of the main virtues of cluster analysis: it offers a systematic, rigorous, valid means of presenting data in a narrative or story format intuitively understandable by policy makers and citizens. By focusing on the interaction of different features within a case, cluster analysis also illustrates the importance of variations within categories as well as across grouping. Indeed, it often illustrates unexpected interactions among conventional factors. In Staeheli and Clarke's (2004) analysis of the differential effects of work and household responsibilities on political participation, it became clear that the generational differences among Latinos were equally or more important than the differences between Latinos and Anglos. Needless to say, assuming that ethnic differences are the critical factor prior to the analysis would obscure such findings. Brunner (1986) used cluster analysis to demonstrate the multiple meanings of poverty and the importance of understanding which type of poverty is being targeted by policy interventions. This demonstrates the utility of cluster analysis for needs assessments and other diagnostic tasks, especially with underserved populations with complex, distinctive needs.

As an inductive research tool, cluster analysis is open to criticism that the classifications—the clusters—are too fluid and too vulnerable to changes depending on the items being considered. On the other hand, the claim that it is an improvement over a priori categorization must be tempered with the recognition that the researcher is still selecting data, cutoff points, and making a number of other subjective choices. If the researcher is clear on the advantages as well as limitations of cluster analysis, it is a powerful and versatile tool for context-sensitive policy research.

V. ISSUES RAISED BY CONTEXT-SENSITIVE RESEARCH METHODS

The NSF workshop recommendations for more qualitative researchers are deceptively simple. The researcher should provide an account of how the conclusions were reached, why the reader should believe the claims and how one might go about trying to produce a similar account. Most researchers would agree with the importance of transparency and the need to provide evidence for the claims made.[7] Making evidence-based claims based on contextually-sensitive research, however, is a more challenging issue. Some of the most thought-provoking issues raised in context-sensitive research center on these issues of transparency and systemization and sources of leverage for causal inference.

A. Transparency and Systemization

Throughout the research process, contextual policy methods provide a means for conducting consistent, systematic, and rigorous data collection and analysis when important data is not readily available. As noted above, there are many challenges to this approach, from both qualitative and quantitative researchers. Nowhere are these challenges greater, however, than in the writing up of contextual policy research and the responsibility for providing evidence for the claims and conclusions drawn from the research.

One of the most important ways to strengthen reporting of contextual policy research materials is also the simplest—documenting the research question, the methods used and why, the time frame, the number of cases or respondents, how they were selected, the assumptions being made about causality and evaluative criteria, and other nuts and bolts features of doing good research. This material can be woven into the text or included in an appendix (see Huff 1999). The failure to include such detail weakens the persuasiveness of whatever findings are presented and raises unnecessary doubts about the reliability of the results.

At this point there are few explicit guidelines for carrying out context-sensitive policy research. Although there is some dispute over the need for "rules for a more systematic use of qualitative evidence" (Tarrow 2004, 179; Collier, Brady, and Seawright 2004), steps can be taken to move toward a more coherent, systematized body of context-sensitive policy research methods. Clarifying some of the epistemological common ground shared by quantitative and qualitative methods would encourage more integrative strategies as would better training in contextual research methods (see Bennett et al. 2003; also CQRM 2003). In addition to setting out some of the available methods for contextual policy research, it is useful to consider how we might think about the "best practices" for collecting and analyzing context-sensitive materials (see e.g. Brower et al. 2000).

B. Sources of Leverage for Making Evidence-Based Claims

Since the contextual policy researcher lacks the tropes or accepted language of reliability and validity available to the quantitative researcher—particularly measures of "significance"—making claims based on the findings is contested terrain (Kritzer 1996; see also, Brady and Collier 2004; Brower et al. 2000). Few policy researchers are willing to settle for "illuminating" rather than "convincing" findings (NSF 2004). But the nature of the problem-oriented enterprise and the unique data collection and analysis demands of contextual policy research exacerbate the difficulties of supporting the validity and plausibility of the research findings.

Yet this is a critical task facing policy researchers, whether using quantitative or contextual approaches; more qualitative researchers, however, seem more vulnerable to validity claims. Weitzman (2004) recollects Miles and Huberman's (1994, 247) warning: "Qualitative analyses can be evocative, illuminating, masterful, and wrong. The story, well told as it is, does not fit the data. Reasonable colleagues double-checking the case come up with quite different findings. The interpretations of case informants do not match those of the researchers."

The standards of evidence for qualitative data remain contested and unstandardized, with little agreement on what constitutes "proof" or "plausibility" (NSF 2004). Both qualitative and quantitative researchers are concerned with causal inference. Some techniques, such as Ragin's fuzzy set approach, provide for testing hypotheses in the same manner as more traditional quantitative methods. But most contextual policy research will rely on a broader set of strategies to address the issue of causal inference and causal validity in contextual research. Contextual researchers are more likely to see causality in process terms or as a series of necessary and sufficient conditions than the positivist notion inferring causality from the statistical association between discrete factors. Contextual researchers often direct their attention to the processes appearing to link cause and effect —"process analysis" (Brady and Collier 2004) in order to infer causality.

A brief inventory of strategies to increase the leverage of contextual research findings would highlight Miles and Huberman's (1994) extensive list of innovative logical exercises that allow the researcher to eliminate alternative explanations and support the conclusions presented.[8] Maxwell (2004) also takes on this challenge, sketching a set of strategies for assessing causal claims such as searching for discrepant or disconfirming evidence, triangulation of different sources of information, different investigators, or different methods of data collection (Weitzman 2004; Creswell 1994), feedback on interpretations from participants themselves. Munck (2004) systematically tracks qualitative tools relevant for each step of the research process and able to shore up context-sensitive evidence. Tarrow (2004, 175) reviews tools capable of bridging the quantitative –qualitative divide, emphasizing process tracing, a focus on tipping points, framing qualitative research within quantitative profiles, triangulation, and sequencing qualitative and quantitative studies.

Brady and Collier (2004) also emphasize the strong leverage to be gained by employing both thick analysis and statistical tests—"nested analysis" featuring the strength of each approach.[9] The large N analysis sets out the patterns among the variables while case studies, if carefully selected, can provide some understanding of the processes underlying these patterns. There are many grounds for case selection but multimethod strategies beginning with the aggregate analysis offer several prospects: using outliers to select cases, using cluster groupings to identify prototypical cases, and other means of selecting cases to clarify processes that distinguish among outcomes (Collier and Mahoney 1996; Collier, Mahoney, and Seawright 2004; Geddes 1990). In contrast, some scholars may start with case studies in order to identify the critical factors for an aggregate level analysis.

Despite the obvious advantages of research using both quantitative and qualitative techniques, multi-method strategies are often sequential rather than truly integrative and iterative. To some extent, this occurs from thinking of methods in a dualistic manner—seeing qualitative methods as only suited to certain types of information and considering quantitative methods as able to provide better measures of other features (e.g., NSF 2004). Truly integrative strategies are rare but involve iterative methods rather than placing quantitative and qualitative research side by side in a project. As Tarrow (2004) and others note, bridging strategies recognize the distinctive research traditions shaping both qualitative and quantitative research but find intermediate means to link these specializations.

VI. CONCLUSION

Good research depends on matching the research question with the appropriate research methods—for policy researchers that often means contextually sensitive research methods. As the previous sections sketch out, there are several contextually sensitive techniques that policy researchers can add to their kit of analytic tools. The premium is on methods that attempt to balance rigor and flexibility; policy researchers, particularly those working outside academe, continually face challenges to the validity and reliability of their work. Context-sensitive tools allow them to make persuasive and accessible arguments and provide evidence to back their claims. They also encourage engagement with a broader public and thus contribute to democratic discourse (Fisher 1993; Geva-May and Pal 1999; Drycek 1990).

NOTES

1. Clifford Gertz's characterization of "thick description" is the most familiar phrase (Geertz 1973). Brady, Seawright, and Collier refer more generally to "thick analysis" (2004).
2. As I often say in my seminars, "the world is multi-collinear—get over it."
3. The term "Q" derives from the contrast with the "objectivist" assumptions of "R" methodology, with data collected through surveys, etc. for correlational analyses in which measurement is independent of the individual's self-reference and it is assumed the answers have the same meaning and intensity for all respondents (see Brown, 1980).
4. For these more structured purposes, policy researchers often turn to more systematic data collection processes such as interview protocols or REAP (above; see Low 2005) and often rely on more structured text analysis procedures.
5. But see Schrodt and Gerner (2000) for an example of developing early warning indicators using cluster analysis.
6. Clustergrams (Schonlau, 2002) can be used to demonstrate how cluster members are assigned to different clusters for nonhierarchical clustering in addition to the dendograms used to illustrate hierarchical clustering processes. It is also possible to graphically represent the structure of cluster linkages with cluster maps (Austrian, 2000).
7. The importance of doing so can not be overstated, although Brower et al. (2000, 376) note the "paradox of transparency and fallibility" in qualitative research—the more transparent the qualitative researcher, the more vulnerable she is to alternative interpretations of the findings.
8. Weitzman reminds us that Miles and Huberman's list (1994) includes: Checking for representativeness, checking for researcher effects, triangulation across sources and methods; checking the meaning of outliers; looking for negative evidence; making if-then tests; ruling out spurious relations; replicating a finding; checking out rival explanations; and getting feedback from informants. They also offer a wide variety of methods for building matrices and other kinds of displays that can assist the analyst in seeing larger patterns, both within and between cases, and performing the kinds of checks referred to above consistently and on broad scales.
9. Brady and Collier adapted this term from Coppedge's (2001) "nested induction" and from Lieberman's "nested analysis" (2003).

BIBLIOGRAPHY

Abbott, Andrew. 1992. "From Causes to Events." *Sociological Methods & Research* 20: 428–455.

Amenta, E. and J.D. Poulsen. 1994. "Where to Begin–A survey of 5 approaches to selecting independent variables for QCA." *Sociological Methods and Research* 23: 22–53.

Austrian, Ziona. 2000. "Cluster Case Studies: The Marriage of Quantitative and Qualitative Information for Action." *Economic Development Quarterly* 14: 97–110.

Bashi, Vilna., 2004. "Improving Qualitative Research Proposal Evaluation," Report on NSF Workshop on Scientific Foundations of Qualitative Research, 39–43.

Bayard de Volo, Lorraine and Ed Schatz. 2004. "From the Inside Out: Ethnographic Methods in Political Research." *PS* 37: 267–71.

Beamer, Glenn. 2002. "Elite Interviews and State Politics Research." *State Politics and Policy Quarterly* 2: 86–96.

Becker, 2004. "The Problems of Analysis." *Report on NSF Workshop on Scientific Foundations of Qualitative Research*, 45–47. http://www.nsf.gov/pubs/2004/nsf04219/nsf04219–6.pdf

Bennett, Andrew, Aharon Barth, and Kenneth R. Rutherford. 2003. "Do We Preach What We Practice? A Survey of Methods in Political Science Journals and Curricula." *PS: Political Sciences & Politics.*

Blee, 2004. NSF Workshop on Scientific Foundations of Qualitative Research.

Brady, Henry E. and David Collier, eds. 2004. *Rethinking Social Inquiry: Diverse Tools, Shared Standards.* Boulder, CO and Berkeley, CA: Roman & Littlefield and Berkeley Public Policy Press.

Brady, Henry E., David Collier, and Jason Seawright. 2004. "Refocusing the Discussion of Methodology." In

Brady, Henry E. and David Collier, eds. *Rethinking Social Inquiry: Diverse Tools, Shared Standards.* Boulder, CO and Berkeley, CA: Roman & Littlefield and Berkeley Public Policy Press. Pp. 3–20.

Brower, Ralph S., Mitchel Y. Abolafia, and Jered B. Carr. 2000. "On Improving Qualitative Methods in Public Administration Research." *Administration & Society* 32:363–397.

Brown, Steven R. 1980. *Political Subjectivity: Applications of Q-methodology in political science.* New Haven CT: Yale University Press.

Brunner, R.D. 1986. "Case-wise Policy Analysis: Redefining Poverty." *Policy Sciences* 19:201–223.

Brunner, Ronald. D. 1987. "Key Political Symbols: the Dissociation Process." *Policy Sciences* 20: 53–76.

Buthe, Tim. 2002. "Taking Temporality Seriously: Modeling History and the Use of Narrative as Evidence." *American Political Science Review* 96: 481–493.

Clarke, Susan. 1999. "Ideas, Interests, and Institutions: Abortion Politics in Denver." In *Culture Wars and Local Politics.* Edited by Elaine Sharp, Lawrence: University Press of Kansas.

Clarke, Susan E. and Anne K. Moss. 1990. "Economic Growth, Environmental Quality, and Social Services: Mapping the Potential for Local Positive-Sum Strategies." *Journal of Urban Affairs* 12: 17–34 (Winter).

Collier, David and James Mahoney. 1996. "Insights and Pitfalls: Selection Bias in Qualitative Research." *World Politics* 49: 56–92.

Collier, David, Henry Brady, and Jason Seawright. 2004. "Sources of Leverage in Causal Inference: Toward an Alternative View of Methodology." In Brady, Henry E. and David Collier, eds. 2004. *Rethinking Social Inquiry: Diverse Tools, Shared Standards.* Boulder, CO and Berkeley, CA: Roman & Littlefield and Berkeley Public Policy Press, 229–266.

Collier, David, James Mahoney, and Jason Seawright. 2004. "Claiming Too Much: Warnings about Selection Bias." In Brady, Henry E. and David Collier, eds. 2004. *Rethinking Social Inquiry: Diverse Tools, Shared Standards.* Boulder, CO and Berkeley, CA: Roman & Littlefield and Berkeley Public Policy Press, 85–102.

Collier, David, Jason Seawright, and Henry E. Brady. 2004. "Qualitative v. Quantitative: What Might this Distinction Mean?" *Report on NSF Workshop on Scientific Foundations of Qualitative Research,* 71–76. http://www.nsf.gov/pubs/2004/nsf04219/nsf04219–6.pdf

Coppedge, Michael. 2005. "Explaining Democratic Deterioration in Venezuela through Nested Inference," in Frances Hogapian and Scott Mainwaring, eds., *The Third Wave of Democratization in Latin America.* Cambridge: Cambridge University Press, 389–316.

CQRM. 2003. "Teaching Qualitative Methods Courses." http://www.asu.edu/clas/polisci/cqrm/Qualitative MethodsAPSA.html.

Creswell, J.W. (1994). *Research design: Qualitative and quantitative approaches.* Thousand Oaks, CA: Sage

deLeon, Peter. 1998. "Models of Policy Discourse: Insights versus prediction." *Policy Studies Journal* 26: 147–161.

Dion, Douglas. 1998. "Evidence and Inference in the Comparative Case Study." *Comparative Politics* 30: 127–146.

Durning, Dan. 1999. "The Transition from Traditional to Postpositivist Policy Analysis: A Role for Q-Methodology." *Journal of Policy Analysis and Management* 18: 389–410.

Durning, Dan and Will Osuna. 1994. "Policy Analysts' Roles and Value Orientations: An Empirical Investigation Using Q Methodology." *Journal of Policy Analysis and Management* 13: 629–657.

Dryzck, John. 1990. *Discursive Democracy.* Cambridge MA: Cambridge University Press.

Fletcher, Linda A., Darin J. Erickson, Traci L. Toomey, and Alexander C. Wagenaar. 2003. "Handheld Computers: A Feasible Alternative to Paper Forms for Field Data Collection." *Evaluation Review* 27:

Fischer, Frank. 1993. "Citizen Participation and the Democratization of Policy Expertise." *Policy Sciences* 26: 165–187.

Flick, Uwe. 2002. "Qualitative Research: State of the Art." *Social Science Information*: 4: 5–24.

Franzese, R. J. 2003. "Quantitative Empirical Methods and Contest Conditionality." *CP*: Newsletter of the Comparative Politics Organizaed Section of the American Political Science Association, 20–24.

Franzosi, Roberto. 1998. "Narrative as Data: Linguistic and Statistical Tools for the Qualitative Study of Historical Events." *International Review of Social History* 43:81–104.

Gamson, William. 1992. *Talking Politics.* Cambridge: Cambridge University Press.

Geddes, Barbara. 1990. "How the Cases You Choose Affect the Answers You Get: Selection Bias in Comparative Politics," *Political Analysis* 2: 131–150.

Geertz, Clifford. 1973. "Thick Description: Toward an Interpretive Theory of Culture." In Clifford Geertz, *The Interpretation of Cultures*. New York: Basic Books, 3–32.

George, Alexander L., and Andrew Bennett. 2005. *Case Studies and Theory Development*. Cambridge, MA: MIT.

Geva-May, Iris and Leslie A. Pal. 1999. "Good Fences Make Good Neighbors: Policy Evaluation and Policy Analysis—Exploring the Differences." *Evaluation* 5: 259–277.

Gregory, R., Flinn, J., Johnson, S., Satterfield, T., Slovic, P., and Wagner, R. 1997. "Decision Pathway Surveys: A Tool for Resource Managers." *Land Economics* 72: 240–254.

Hajer, Maarten A. 1993. "Discourse Coalitions and the Institutionalization of Practice: The Case of Acid Rain in Great Britain." In Fischer and Forester (eds.) *The Argumentative Turn in Policy Analysis and Planning*. Durham, NC: Duke University Press, pp. 43–71.

Herrera, Yoshiko M. and Bear F. Braumoeller. 2004. "Symposium: Discourse and Content Analysis." *Qualitative Methods*. Newsletter of the American Political Science Association Organized Section on Qualitative Methods. Vol. 2, #1: Spring.

Hershey, Marjorie R. 1994. "The Meaning of a Mandate: Interpretations of "Mandate" in 1984 Presidential Election Coverage." *Polity* 27: 225–254.

Huff. A. S. 1999. *Writing for Scholarly Publication*. Sage.

Ice, Gillian H. 2004. "Technological Advances in Observational Data Collection: The Advantages and Limitations of Computer-Assisted Data Collection." *Field Methods* 16: 352–375.

Kilburn, H. Whitt. 2004. "Explaining U.S. Urban Regimes: A Qualitative Comparative Analysis," *Urban Affairs Review* 39: 663–651.

King, G., R. Keohane, and S. Verba. 1994. *Designing Social Inquiry*. Princeton, NJ: Princeton University Press.

King, G., R. Keohane, and S. Verba. 1995. "The Importance of Research Design in Political Science." *APSR* 89: 475–481.

Kritzer, Herbert M. 1996. "The Data Puzzle: The Nature of Interpretation in Quantitative Research." *AJPS* 40: 1–32.

Leech, Beth L. et al. 2002. "Symposium: Interview Methods in Political Science." *PS* XXXV: 663–688.

Lewis, R. Barry. 2004. "NVivo 2.0 and ATLAS.ti 5.0: A Comparative Review of Two Popular Qualitative Data-Analysis Programs." *Field Methods* 16: 439–469.

Lieber, Eli, Thomas S. Weisner, and Matthew Presley. 2003. "EthnoNotes: An Internet-based Field Note Management Tool." *Field Methods* 15: 405–425.

Lieberman, Evan S. "Symposium: Field Research." *Qualitative Methods*. Newsletter of the American Political Science Association Organized Section on Qualitative Methods. Vol. 2, #1 (Spring).

Lin, A.C. 1998. "Bridging positivist and interpretivist approaches to qualitative methods.(The Evidentiary Basis of Policy Analysis: Empiricist vs. Postpositivist Positions)." *Policy Studies Journal* (March 22): 162–180.

Low, Setha, Dana H.Taplin, and Mike Lamb. 2005. "Battery Park City: An Ethnographic Field Study of the Community Impact of 9/11." *Urban Affairs Review* 40: 655–682.

Maestas, Cherie, et al. 2003. "The State of Surveying State Legislators: Dilemmas and Suggestions." *State Politics and Policy Quarterly* 3 (Spring): 90–108.

Mahoney, James. 2004. "The Distinctive Contributions of Qualitative Data Analysis." *Report on NSF Workshop on Scientific Foundations of Qualitative Research*, 95–799. http://www.nsf.gov/pubs/2004/nsf04219/nsf04219–6.pdf

Maxwell, Joseph A. 2004. "Using Qualitative Methods for Causal Explanation." *Field Methods* 16: 243–264.

Miles, Matthew B. and A.M. Huberman. 1994. *Qualitative Data Analysis*. Sage.

Morgan, David L. 1996. "Focus Groups." *Annual Review of Sociology* Vol. 22: 129–152

Morth, U. 2000. "Competing Frames in the European Commission: The case of the defence industry and equipment issue." *Journal of European Public Policy* 7: 173–189.

Munck, G. 2004. "Tools for Qualitative Research." In Brady, Henry E. and David Collier, eds. 2004. *Rethinking Social Inquiry: Diverse Tools, Shared Standards*. Boulder, CO and Berkeley, CA: Roman & Littlefield and Berkeley Public Policy Press, 102–121.

Murphy, Jerome. 1980. *Getting the Facts: A Fieldwork Guide for Evaluators & Policy Analysts*. Santa Monical, CA: Goodyear.

NSF. 2004. *Workshop on Scientific Foundations of Qualitative Research*. Washington DC: NSF.

Pal, L.A. 1995. "Competing Paradigms in Policy Discourse: The Case of International Human Rights," *Policy Sciences* 28: 185–207.

QCA. http://www.u.arizona.edu/~cragin/QCA.htm

Ragin, C. 1995. "Using Qualitative Comparative Analysis to Study Configurations." In U. Kelle, *Computer-aided Qualitative Data Analysis*. Newbury Park, CA: Sage. Pp. 177–189.

Ragin, Charles C. 1987. *The Comparative Method: Moving Beyond Qualitative and Quantitative Strategies*. Berkeley: University of California Press.

Ragin, Charles C. 2000. *Fuzzy-Set Social Science*. Chicago: University of Chicago Press.

Ragin, Charles. 2004. "Turning the Tables: How Case-Oriented Research Challenges Variable-Oriented Research." In Henry E. Brady, and David Collier, eds. *Rethinking Social Inquiry: Diverse Tools, Shared Standards*. Boulder, CO and Berkeley, CA: Roman & Littlefield and Berkeley Public Policy Press, 123–138.

Ragin, Charles C. 2004. "Combining Qualitative and Quantitative Research." *Report on NSF Workshop on Scientific Foundations of Qualitative Research*, 109–115. http://www.nsf.gov/pubs/2004/nsf04219/nsf04219–6.pdf

Richards, T. and L. Richards. 1995. "Using Hierarchical Categories in Qualitative Data Analysis." In U. Kelle, *Computer-aided Qualitative Data Analysis*. Newbury Park, CA: Sage, 80–95.

Robbins, Paul and Rob Krueger. 2000. "Beyond Bias? The Promise and Limits of Q Method in Human Geography." *The Professional Geographer* 52: 636–648.

Rochefort, David and Roger Cobb. 1994. *The Politics of Problem Definition*. Lawrence: University Press of Kansas.

Roulston, Kathryn, Kathleen deMarrais, and Jaime B. Lewis. 2003. "Learning to Interview in the Social Sciences." *Qualitative Inquiry:* 643–668.

Rydin, Y. 1998. "Managing Urban Air Quality: Language and rational choice in metropolitan governance." *Environment and Planning A* 30: 1429–1443.

Satterfield, Theresa (Terre). 2004. "A Few Thoughts on Combining Qualitative and Quantitative Methods." *Report on NSF Workshop on Scientific Foundations of Qualitative Research*, 117–119. http://www.nsf.gov/pubs/2004/nsf04219/nsf04219–6.pdf

Satterfield, T. and Gregory, R 1998. "Reconciling Environmental Values and Pragmatic Choices." *Society and Natural Resources* 11, no. 7: 629–647.

Schneider, Anne L. and Helen Ingram. 1994. "Social Constructions and Target Populations: Implications for Politics and Policy." *American Political Science Review* 87: 334–47.

Schonlau, Matthias. 2002. "The clustergram: A graph for visualizing hierarchical and nonhierarchical cluster analyses." *The Stata Journal* 2: 391–402.

Schrodt, P.A. and D. J. Gerner. 2000. "Using Cluster Analysis to Derive Early Warning Indicators for Political Change in the Middle East, 1979–1996." *American Political Science Review* 94: 803–818.

Sharp, Elaine. 1994. "Paradoxes of National Anti-drug Policymaking." In Rochefort, D. and Roger W. Cobb (Eds.), *The Politics of Problem Definition*. Lawrence: University Press of Kansas, 98–116.

Sidney, Mara. 2002. "The Role of Ideas in Education Politics: Using Discourse Analysis to Understand Barriers to Reform in Multiethnic Cities." *Urban Affairs Review* 38: 253–279.

Small n Web site: http://www.smalln.spr.ucl.ac.be.

Staeheli, Lynn A. and Clarke, Susan E. 2004. "The New Politics of Work and Time." *Urban Geography* 24:103–126.

Stark, Andrew. 2002. "Why Political Scientists aren't Public Intellectuals" *PS* September. http://www.apsanet.org/PS/sept02/stark.cfm.

Steelman, Toddi A. and Lynn A. Maguire. 1999. "Understanding Participant Perspectives: Q-Methodology in National Forest Management." *Journal of Policy Analysis and Management* 18: 361–388.

Stephenson, W. 1953. *The Study of Behavior: Q-technique and its methodology*. Chicago: University of Chicago Press.

Stone, Deborah. 1989. "Causal Stories and Formation of Policy Agendas." *Polical Science Quarterly* 104: 281–300.

Stroh, Matt. 2000. "Qualitative Interviewing." In *Research Training for Social Scientists*, Dawn Burton, ed. Thousand Oaks, CA: Sage, 196–217.

Stryker, Robin. 1996. "Beyond History Versus Theory: Strategic Narrative and Sociological Explanation." *Sociological Methods & Research* 24: 304–352.

Sturges, Judith E. and Kathleen J. Hanrahan. 2004. "Comparing Telephone and Face-to-Face Qualitative Interviewing: A Research Note." *Qualitative Research* 4: 107–118.

"Symposium: The Case of Case Study Research." 2000. Comparative and Historical Sociology Newsletter Advanced Industrial Democracies, 1974–1980." http://www.sla.purdue/academic/soc/comphist/chs-00Fall1.html.

Tarrow, Sidney. 2004. "Bridging the Quantitative-Qualitative Divide." In Brady, Henry E. and David Collier, eds. 2004. *Rethinking Social Inquiry: Diverse Tools, Shared Standards.* Boulder, CO and Berkeley, CA: Roman & Littlefield and Berkeley Public Policy Press, 171–179.

Thomas, D., C. McCoy, and A. McBride. 1993. "Deconstructing the Political Spectacle: Sex, race, and subjectivity in public response to the Clarence Thomas/Anita Hill "sexual harassment" hearings." *American Journal of Political Science* 37: 699–720.

Wanta, W. and Y.W. Hu. 1993. "The Agenda-setting Effects of International News Coverage: An Examination of Differing News Frames*." International Journal of Public Opinion Reseach* 5: 250–264.

Weimer, David L. 1999. "Comment: Q-Method and the Isms." *Journal of Policy Analysis and Management* 18: 426–429.

Wichkam-Crowley, Timothy P. 1991. "A Qualitative Comparative Approach to Latin American Revolutions." *International Journal of Comparative Sociology* 32: 82–109.

Weitzman, E. A. 1999. Analyzing qualitative data with computer software. *Health Services Research* 34 (5), 1241–1263.

Weitzman, E. A. 2000. Software and qualitative research. In N. Denzin & Y. Lincoln (Eds.) *Handbook of qualitative research*, 2nd ed. Thousand Oaks, CA: Sage, 803–820.

Weitzman, E. A. 2004. "Advancing the Scientific Basis of Qualitative Research." *Report on NSF Workshop on Scientific Foundations of Qualitative Research*, 145–148. http://www.nsf.gov/pubs/2004/nsf04219/nsf04219–6.pdf

Weitzman, E. A. & Miles, M. B. 1995. *Computer programs for qualitative data analysis: A software sourcebook.* Thousand Oaks, CA: Sage.

Yanow, Dvora. 2000. *Conducting Interpretive Policy Analysis.* Sage University Papers Series on Qualitative Research Methods, Vol. 47. Thousand Oaks, CA: Sage.

Yanow, Dvora. 2003. *Constructing 'Race' and 'Ethnicity' in America: Category-Making in Public Policy and Administration.* Armonk, NY: M. E. Sharpe.

Yin, Robert K. 1994. *Case Study Research: Design and Method.* Thousand Oaks, CA: Sage, 99–146.

Part IX

Policy Decisions Techniques

31 Cost-Benefit Analysis

Gerald J. Miller and Donijo Robbins

1.1 INTRODUCTION

The cost-benefit analyst's pursuit of evidence to support the one most efficient allocation of economic resources deserves critical analysis. The analyst who uses the cost-benefit approach, we argue, recommends action based on analysis following vaguely defined methods. No matter how vague, these methods derive from a distinct belief about social relations and define a good citizen.

Policy analysts seek intuitive, popular appeal for their work when debate widens to include many frames of reference. A single frame of reference limits participation in determining the value of action for the common good, wide participation being the equivalent to a free market in good analyses. This chapter has two goals: to describe and then to examine critically cost-benefit analysis (CBA) as a single frame of reference for policy analysis.

Policy analysis, in the comparing the costs, benefits, risks, and timing of government action—policy consequences—can inform decisions. The decisions may also cause or realize (spawn) a less desirable distribution of costs and benefits among individuals. Despite its straightforward, intuitive nature, cost-benefit analysis rests on difficult choices about what are costs and what are benefits. Little agreement exists about how to calculate the impact of risk and timing on costs and benefits.

The cost-benefit idea represents a tradeoff between efficiency and equality in social and economic affairs. Equity guides policies and programs that give to each according to his needs from each according to her abilities whereas efficiency advises that public projects should result in at least one person being better off and no one worse off. Controlling what analytical methods to employ in making allocation choices has great allure and controversy.

1.2 WHAT COST-BENEFIT ANALYSIS IS AND IS NOT

Cost-benefit analysis refers to the collection and organization of data relevant to a government leader's decision to intervene when markets fail, through public projects, programs, or regulatory regimes (Krutilla 1961, 226; Musgrave 1969). Cost-benefit analysis is a form of evaluation research concerning: either continuing or discontinuing a program, program strategy, a technique, or an improvement, or allocating resources among competing programs (GAO 1991; Poister 1978, 8; Weiss 1972, 16–17).

Evaluation criteria vary. They include effectiveness of a program's performance in light of specified objectives, efficiency in maximizing value or minimizing cost through technological, economic, or productivity analysis, adequacy of the program in the degree to which the program eliminates a problem, appropriateness or worth of the program objectives, and program responsiveness to the needs and desires of its users and clients. Moreover, evaluation research may take place in the research and development or even planning stage of a program, any time during the program's operation as a formative evaluation, or as a full scale evaluation in response to a sunset provision in the law creating the program, a summative evaluation (Rossi and Wright 1984; Rossi and Williams 1972; Poister 1978; Scriven 1972; Suchman 1967).

The net benefit criterion steers government decision makers in pursuing government action. Graham (1981) has defined net-benefit as a norm signaling appropriate government intervention because intervention's benefits outweigh its costs. Analysts use the criterion after they discount benefits and costs with a figure called the social discount rate (Baumol 1970; Tullock 1964; Marglin 1963; Pigou 1932). Analysts also account for the sensitivity of their discounted costs and benefits to risk, uncertainty, and price level inflation (Arrow and Lind 1970; Hirschleifer 1958; Hirschleifer and Shapiro 1970).

Cost-benefit analysis differs from two other well-known policy analysis tools, cost-effectiveness analysis and risk analysis. Cost-effectiveness analysis collects and arranges data to facilitate a comparison of the costs of achieving a desired public program objective required by various alternative treatments, interventions, programs or policy designs. The criterion for judging the best alternative is either least cost for a given level of effectiveness or greatest effectiveness for a given level of spending. For example, within a health ministry, having a given amount budgeted to spend from the treasury or finding alternatives with the same cost, the analysts would evaluate alternative public health programs in terms of mortality, morbidity, or quality of life. The analyst would recommend the alternative optimizing the combination or perhaps any single effectiveness measure (mortality, morbidity, or quality of life). In other decisions, the analyst might compare two or more ways of getting the same results and recommend the cheapest.

Cost-effectiveness has a more specific use than cost-benefit analysis. For example, cost- effectiveness analysis addresses the goals of a ministry rather than the general welfare of the population served. While government program effectiveness and general welfare improvement may appear to be distinctions without a difference, the administrative idea of effectiveness may limit the use of effectiveness analysis far more than the socially desirable and intuitively appealing concept of net-benefit. However, an analyst may have great difficulty finding the amount of actual benefit that may result from a program even if costs are known. Missing data make cost-effectiveness analysis the analytical technique of choice.

Cost-benefit also differs with risk analysis or risk-benefit analysis. In the latter, risk becomes a primary factor in the analysis rather than a secondary one in cost-benefit analysis. If we define risk as the probability of an event multiplied by the event's severity, the risk estimate takes the place cost holds in analysis. The benefit calculation rests on an estimate of society's willingness to pay to reduce a risk or to forego a benefit (Wilson and Crouch 2001, 137). The discounting and sensitivity analysis are similar in both techniques. The major difference between a cost-to-benefit and a risk-to-benefit comparison lies in the perception of risk (Miller 2005, 486-487; Tversky and Kahneman 1981; 1974; Douglas and Wildavsky 1982).

The question of whose estimates should prevail captures much of the legitimacy question affecting analyst use of cost-effectiveness, risk-benefit, and cost-benefit analysis.

1.3 ROOTS OF COST-BENEFIT ANALYSIS

Cost-benefit analysis developed in practice and application first, then theory followed much later. Persky (2001) credits French engineers, especially Jules Dupuit, with the pioneering use of cost-benefit analysis. Dupuit (in translation; 1952) uses Jean-Baptiste Say (1826) as a vehicle for development and analysis of public works decisions in which one could find the "power or capacity of an article to satisfy our wants or gratify our desires" (p. 87). Utility to Dupuit and Say was "the difference between the sacrifice the purchaser [taxpayer] would be willing to make in order to get [the project] and the purchase price [tax] he has to pay in exchange" (p. 90). Later, Dupuit defines utility as the power to satisfy or gratify arising from the expenditure of public funds on a project. The power resides in the project's effects—cost savings, inventive new uses for the public project, and competition with cost reduction in competing forms of goods the public project supported.

Dupuit illustrates with a canal. A town, he explains (1952, 91–96), may use 10,000 tons of stone each year, perhaps delivered by path and ox cart, for house construction and repair. A canal built to carry the stone reduces the cost of stone production by 25 percent. Moreover, the canal, if longer than the present ox cart path, opens up new quarries to extraction, increasing competition and the variety of stone, and thereby reducing costs of production even more. The greater variety of stone and stone's lower cost may lead to other uses—more durable housing, tile instead of thatch roofs, paved streets, and more durable drainage canals opening more land for cultivation or some other net positive use. The public expenditure has reduced production costs and has satisfied wants and gratified desires. Did anyone, if asked, agree to pay the canal construction tax with full knowledge of the canal's consequences? Perhaps not. Did the canal benefits outweigh the costs? According to Dupuit, they did.

Watkins (2005) and Porter (1995) credit French engineers with transmission of analysis abroad, especially to the United States through their close relationship with officers in the U.S. Army. The French helped found the U.S. Corps of Engineers during the American Revolution as well as the U.S. Military Academy's engineering school, the sole engineering school in the country until the establishment of one at Rensselaer Polytechnic Institute in 1824.

Thus, modern uses of cost-benefit analysis in the United States came with the U.S. Army Corps of Engineers. As the Corps rose as a major force in public works, the U.S. Congress mandated, within its Rivers and Harbors Appropriations Act of 1902, that engineer analysts

> shall have in view the amount and character of commerce existing or [a reasonable prospect of what will exist] which will be benefited by the improvement, and the relation of the ultimate cost of such work, both as to cost of construction and maintenance, to the public commercial interests involved, and the public necessity for the work and propriety of its construction, continuance, or maintenance at the expense of the United States (U.S. Congress 1902, 372).

Although general, the 1902 Act outlined a Dupuit-style cost-benefit analysis.

Standardization of analytical terms and concepts, as well as federal responsibility for flood control when analysis justified it, arrived with the Flood Control Act of 1936. The Act allowed government improvement or participation in the improvement of benefits "to whomsoever they may accrue" when those benefits exceed estimated costs "and if the lives and social security of people are otherwise adversely affected" (U.S. Congress 1936, 1570). No theory and no generally accepted definition of costs and benefits existed. In fact, Key (1940, 1137) could still ask, "On what basis shall it be decided to allocate x dollars to activity A instead of activity B?" His answer: "impressionistic judgment." He argued that few cost standards exist leaving analysts to rely on judgment and administrative surveys.

Nevertheless, cost-benefit analysis advocates were everywhere. Pearce (1998) describes the increasing acceptance of the analytical approach to include a federal interagency committee on analysis in 1946, a Bureau of the Budget Circular in 1952 formalizing concepts and providing guidance, and major academic economists' justification for the technique in 1958 (Eckstein, 1958; Krutilla and Eckstein 1958; McKean 1958). Moreover, President Lyndon Johnson added cost-benefit analysis as a tool within the Planning, Programming Budgeting System (PPBS) to advance his Great Society in 1965. To Johnson cost-benefit analysis was a modern-day management tool. From that point on, all presidents have called for some form of economic analysis. For example, Presidents Reagan and Clinton issued executive orders (12291 in 1981 and 12866 in 1993, respectively) requiring federal agencies to prepare cost-benefit analyses for all major federal regulations (Hahn and Dudley, 2004). These RIAs (Regulatory Impact Analysis under Reagan and Regulatory Impact Assessment under Clinton) "require agencies to consider all significant costs and benefits" even unquantifiable ones, as well as alternatives (Hahn and Dudley 2004, 5).

1.4 PROVISION THEORY

Jules Dupuit's ideas have found a place in public finance and government's provision of public services. Generally, the problem is to decide how much and what type of goods to provide when rationing by the market is not feasible or desirable or both. Public policy makers need some mechanism for deciding these questions, and luckily, they have not just one but four mechanisms: basic economic feasibility, Pareto optimality, the Kaldor criterion, and democratic voting.

1.4.1 ECONOMIC FEASIBILITY

Economic feasibility or economic efficiency exists when the benefits from a public program exceed the costs of that program. Consider the following two programs, each costing society $10,000 but yielding different benefits. The first program, program A (see Table 31.1), is not economically feasible; benefits are less than costs. Program B (see Table 31.2) is economically feasible because benefits to society as a whole, the summation of all individual benefits, exceed societal costs. Policy makers, if only using this method, would choose program B. In the end, however, program B does not meet productivity standards; that is, economic efficiency and equity may not be realized because one person is made worse off in the end.

1.4.2 PARETO CRITERION

Named after the nineteenth-century economist, the Pareto criterion guides selection of a policy. The criterion formalizes the definition of economic efficiency by favoring those projects or policies in which at least one person is better off and no person is worse off as a result. The Pareto criterion goes one step further than economic feasibility to allow for more equity.

Consider program B where efficiency is achieved but equity is lacking. Using the Pareto criterion, although the majority of individuals are made better off, there is one person, C, whose position

TABLE 31.1
Program A

Individual	Benefits ($)	Costs ($)	Surplus (Loss) ($)
A	3,000	2,000	1,000
B	2,500	2,000	500
C	500	2,000	(1,500)
D	500	2,000	(1,500)
E	2,000	2,000	0
Total	8,500	10,000	(1,500)

TABLE 31.2
Program B

Individual	Benefits ($)	Costs ($)	Surplus (Loss) ($)
A	3,000	2,000	1,000
B	3,500	2,000	1,500
C	1,000	2,000	(1,000)
D	3,000	2,000	1,000
E	2,500	2,000	500
Total	13,000	10,000	3,000

TABLE 31.3
Program C

Individual	Benefits ($)	Costs ($)	Surplus (Loss) ($)
A	3,000	2,000	1,000
B	3,500	2,000	1,500
C	2,000	2,000	0
D	3,000	2,000	1,000
E	2,500	2,000	500
Total	14,000	10,000	4,000

is made worse; the individual costs are more than the individual benefits. Under this criterion, then, policy makers would not fund program B.

Program C (see Table 31.3), on the other hand, deserves funding because it is both economically feasible and achieves Pareto optimality; at least one person, here A, B, D, and E, is made better off without making anyone worse off.

1.4.3 KALDOR CRITERION

Another method of dealing with general welfare of the population, the Kaldor criterion, is slightly less demanding. This method begs the question: Should we or should we not accept a policy if those in the community benefiting from the policy compensate those who lose by the policy, especially if the winners or beneficiaries still have some gain left over?

Consider this example. If the strict private goods only requirement were not relaxed (libertarianism), we would never get such goods as pristine ocean beaches. One finds it extremely difficult to slice up pieces of the ocean in order to allocate maintenance responsibilities to protect the beach. Moreover, nature's ways in forcing erosion and beach sand movement would make such coercion folly. Will one person maintain the beaches? Not by the table of benefits, especially when those benefits are held down by the inability to divide the resource or exclude others from its use.

But should the beaches be sustained? If costs equal the expense of maintaining the beaches and benefits equal the sum of everyone's perception of betterment, if economic feasibility occurs, then common sense would tell us yes. For example, the $10,000 program, program C, provides greater benefits to some than to others. The gains range from $500 for E to $1,500 for B.

We might say that the $10,000 version of beach cleanup is less equitable than it is efficient. Defining performance as a balance between equity and efficiency, analysts want to find the program that would achieve both. The Kaldor criterion suggests a way to find that program.

Recall the Kaldor criterion provides for winners compensating losers in a given situation. Without assuming any losers, however, we can still create a Kaldor-like result, as Table 31.4 illustrates.

TABLE 31.4
Program C

Individual	Benefits ($)	Costs ($)	Surplus ($)
A	3,000	2,999	1
B	3,500	3,500	0
C	2,000	2,000	0
D	3,000	3,000	0
E	2,500	2,500	0
Total	14,000	13,999	1

To ensure that the winners bear their fair share of the costs and still reap some gain, the maximum project would have to be $13,999. We can compute this amount by distributing the costs in the same way as the original surpluses so that one person gains $1 of surplus, whereas all others have benefits that equal their costs.

The dispersion of benefits and costs underlies the progressive tax structure and distribution of income programs that have guided the construction and maintenance of the U.S. version of the welfare state. More to the point of this chapter, however, the Kaldor criterion underlies cost-benefit analysis. The Kaldor criterion argues that as long as the benefits exceed the costs of a project, the project should go forward.

1.4.4 VOTING

The problem with mathematical approaches to determine public program funding is the quantification of benefits, especially those that are intangible and immeasurable. In countries where the values of individualism and decentralized decision making reign, we assume that each person can judge a policy alone. The sum of those judgments becomes the public welfare. Referenda voting can establish the public welfare.

But what vote should be required: Unanimity? Three-fourths? Two-thirds? Fifty percent plus one? Plurality? The answer lies in the analysis of voting by legislative bodies. Following Buchanan and Tullock (1962), the analysis reduces to the interaction of two variables. The first variable is the loss of value that occurs by not including every individual's vote, every individual's calculation of benefit from a given project. The second is the cost of the effort to ascertain each individual's preferences.

Voting analysis demands that we know individuals' preferences toward a project. Obviously, 100 percent voting participation resulting in a consensus decision on the project would guide decision makers in making a valid decision. The first variable in voting analysis, therefore, is the probability of violating the Pareto criterion as we depart from unanimous consent. Such a problem occurs in sampling as well as in choosing majority rule over consensus.

Finding an appropriate system of voting involves trading off the cost of exclusion against the cost of the election, a calculation easier than it looks. We seldom have a single issue where an individual has two choices and perfect information about them both. Rather, we have a continuous stream of issues about which individuals have varying levels of intensity of preferences.

Such arrays of preferences yield themselves to vote trading—logrolling—as well as coalition building. In cases where we have public provision of private goods, we have the conditions for bargaining: costly participation, isolated issue salience, and unclear estimates of who benefits through policies and by how much. These conditions create one of two things: overspending (Buchanan and Tullock 1962) and underspending (Downs 1960).

1.5 COST-BENEFIT ANALYSIS

The four mechanisms discussed above are the underlying theory of provision and allocation that guides cost-benefit analysis. With a cost-benefit analysis, at least one project needs to be studied—a microanalysis approach. In this case, the concept is straightforward: determine benefits and costs; then find the ratio of dollar-quantified benefits, at their current value, to dollar-quantified costs, at their current value (B/C). If that ratio is greater than one, the analysis suggests, because benefits are greater than costs, that the project should be considered for inclusion in the government's budget. At the macro level, however, the analysis is more complex. Analysts have to ask, what is happening in the aggregate if we do or do not provide this project. For example, if we build a canal, we have to determine the opportunity cost to society—the cost of giving up something else like a new bridge, a new sewer system, or higher taxes (and, consequently, lower private consumption) to pay for the project.

The technical concept includes two major ideas influencing the analysis. First is the notion of measuring benefits and costs. This involves estimating, forecasting, and costing them, all difficult to do in the public goods sector. The second idea is measuring benefits and costs at their current value. Current value requires the knowledge of social preferences about the time value of money—discount—and the impacts of inflation. That these are contested concepts understates the vagueness, the amount of deference given the analyst—the controversy—surrounding them.

1.5.1 UNCERTAINTY AND THE MEASUREMENT OF BENEFITS AND COSTS

Measuring benefits and costs involves careful consideration. An analyst must consider both the obvious and not so obvious consequences of a project, forecasting changes that will occur and affect these consequences over time, and costing the consequences properly, in both accounting and economic terms. Here, we describe the hazards of estimating, forecasting, and costing.

The first element of measurement is estimation. Estimation deals with the type of cost or benefit to be counted and includes benefits and costs that are real or pecuniary types, tangible or intangible, as well as direct or indirect. First, real benefits and costs are those that have an absolute consequence for society as a whole. That is, on balance the benefit or cost to society was not one in which the cost to one group of individuals was offset by the benefit to another group of individuals. The benefit or cost was not merely redistributed—as a pecuniary benefit or cost would describe—but an absolute change in the wellbeing of society as a whole.

Second, estimates of tangible and intangible benefits and costs describe the difference between those that can be priced, or about which members of society can agree relatively easily on price, and those they cannot. A tangible cost and benefit to many is a project such as a dam, with its measurable construction costs and irrigation, flood control, and recreation benefits. An intangible cost might be the value of endangered species that are destroyed as a result of the dam's displacement and destruction of the species' habitat by the construction of the dam.

The last type of benefit and cost that an analyst must confront in estimating the numbers that feed the cost-benefit analysis is the direct-indirect contrast. Direct costs are those immediately apparent from the project. The dam example, both tangible costs and tangible benefits, illustrates this idea. The indirect or secondary costs from the dam's construction might include such things as poorer or better drainage of streams and marshes that fed the undammed stream; greater air and noise pollution as a result of recreational equipment used on reservoirs created by the dam; and even climate changes that result from large bodies of water replacing water flows.

In each case, the analysis would not be complete without considering the pecuniary, intangible, and indirect benefits and costs of a project. Most analyses suggest this to be difficult and controversial.

The second element of measurement is forecasting. The policy problems and consequences of forecasting are often not based on political differences. Rather, they are based on quantitative and qualitative methods using unknown data about the future. Cost-benefit analysts cannot predict the future any better than any other analyst, and, instead, must monitor various data sets. Judgments must be made about what to consider important enough to follow closely, what is novel, and what is a trend. For example, forecasters use time-series information on inflation, interest rates, revenue, expenditures, surpluses, and debt to help guide the cost-benefit process. Thus, forecasting has a great interpretive potential. Likewise a forecase can influence the course of events. If one's view is substantially influential, the guidance this forecast provides can influence the expectations of others (Pierce 1971, 41). As Klay (1985) has pointed out, what one wants to see can happen; views do become self-fulfilling prophecies. Thus, forecasting is often a judgmental process, one especially influenced by forecasters' social construction of reality, a process now acknowledged, used, and called dynamic forecasting or dynamic scoring (Mankiw and Weinzierl 2004; Auerbach 1996).

Finally, cost-benefit analysts must cope with the assignment of some quantitative value to the stream of benefits and costs. Assignment has special difficulty in the public goods sector, since markets have not "priced" these goods, owing to market failures in either rivalry or divisibility. Specific costing problems that bedevil analysts are estimating shadow prices, final prices, opportunity costs, transfers, and inflation.

First, the cost of a project or the benefit of it may often be estimated by analogy, i.e., shadow prices. Some equivalent market may exist for a project, somewhere; that equivalent is employed as the basis for costing out the elements of the project for analysis. The problems associated with finding such a shadow price, or of using the most nearly correct one, still create problems. Would a roller coaster ticket price shadow a subway fare?

Second, the lack of a shadow price leads to additional problems. That is, most public goods tend to be oriented toward outcomes rather than mere outputs. Therefore determining final prices becomes a difficult task. Outcomes are extremely hard to envision much less estimate in dollar-denominated consequences. For example, street sweeping and cleaning are often touted as popular programs, even though they have no meaningful outputs (pounds of garbage collected, raves from residents) but they have definite outcomes. "Clean streets" has a meaning all its own and is an end in itself. Such an end-in-itself is hard to measure for cost-benefit analysis especially when the outcome may not have roots in sensible, consequential, and measureable outputs.

Next, a project without a shadow price always carries an opportunity cost that might be measurable and meaningful for analysis. The opportunity cost of any project is the benefit and cost of another project foregone to proceed with the present one. The true worth of any project, therefore, is the cost (and benefit) of the most obvious substitute. Clean streets may carry the cost of an opportunity foregone, such as a rat amelioration program. The illustration also suggests the problem of lack of adequate quantifiability in opportunities foregone, the biggest problem in calculating costs.

Fourth, a transfer of payment from one individual to another should not be included in the calculation of benefits and costs. Transfers are not included because "there are no economic gains from a pure *transfer payment* because the benefits to those who receive such a transfer are matched by the costs borne by those who pay for it" (U.S. Office of Management and Budget 1992, 5).

Finally, inflation has an impact on the future values of benefits and costs. The U.S. Office of Management and Budget suggests that "analysts should avoid having to make an assumption about the general rate of inflation whenever possible" (U.S. Office of Management and Budget 1992, 7). But if a rate is necessary, they recommend that "the rate of increase in the Gross Domestic Product deflator from the Administration's economic assumptions for the period of the analysis."

1.5.2 Valuation Over Time and by Different Selection Criteria

The method of selection of projects through cost-benefit (CB) analysis comes from the concept of investment. The investment theory utilizes policy or project comparisons between a stream of benefits and a stream of costs measured at their current value—discounting future values into today's values. Generally, these comparisons are made on the basis of one or the other of two calculations, net present value (NPV) or internal rate of return (IRR).

The NPV measures future streams of benefits and costs by "netting" or subtracting current value costs from current value benefits (benefits minus costs). A variation of this measure is the more popularly known ratio of current value benefits over current costs—cost-benefit ratio (B/C). The criterion for selection in the former is a positive number greater than unity (1).

A second method of selecting a project involves determining the project's internal rate of return (IRR). This calculation suggests projects with current value benefits exceeding their current value costs by a given rate, or percentage, are better than those that do not.

The difference between NPV and IRR is that the NPU discriminates in favor of larger numbers. That is, IRR corrects for extremely large differences in scope among projects. IRR is more appropriately applied at the macrolevel where projects compete against other projects than at the microlevel where a project's benefits compete against its costs.

Nevertheless, the B/C ratio calculation depends on establishing of current value benefits and costs. Current value benefits and costs are also known as discounted elements. Analysts use different discount rates and time frames for comparison purposes.

Discounting is based on a preference for the time value of money. For example, if given the choice between $100 now and $100 a year from now, most people would prefer to have the $100 now. If forced to wait, people would want the year-from-now choice to be equal in value to the $100 received today. The amount that would make the $100 a year from now equivalent in value to the $100 received today is a person's, or a society's, willingness to wait to receive some benefit. The benefit and its magnitude influence a person in a societies a time value of money. Under some circumstances, some would prefer more money than others. To illustrate: The delay in getting the $100, such as when parents lend money to a college student daughter or son to buy an automobile in return for the promise to repay it, the parents might want compensation for the delay. What would the value and time preference be? Would the value and time preference be the same when the student wanted to buy a house or summer on the beach in Xanadu?

1.5.3 An Example

For cost-benefit analysis we begin with future values over multiple years but must convert these future values (FV) into present values (PV) so we can compare all costs and all benefit. For example, $100 two years from now has a different present value than $100 three years from now. To find the present value, the future value is discounted based on the interest or discount rate (i) and the timeframe (t). Mathematically, the present value formula is presented as follows: $PV = FV [1/(1+i)^t]$. The portion of the equation in brackets is called the discount factor. Assuming a 7 percent discount rate, the present value of $100 two years from now is $87.34. The present value of $100 three years from now is $81.63. The longer the period of time before a future value appears, the smaller the present value. The same is true with different discount rates. The larger the discount rate, the smaller the present values over time.

This logic applies to cost-benefit projects. The B/C ratio is calculated by adding up the discounted benefits and dividing by the total value of all discounted costs. Consider the simplistic Programs D and E presented in Table 31.5. Each project has a stream of benefits and a stream of costs; all are future values. Each value must be discounted for its respective time period assuming the same discount rate for all time periods. Using a 7 percent discount rate, the discount factor is determined for each year. The discount factor for each year is then multiplied by the respective future value of each benefit and cost. For example, for program D the present value of $300,000 three years from now is $244,889. Next discounted benefits are added, yielding a present value total of $1,248,984, and divided by the total discounted costs of $1,621,096. The B/C ratio is 0.77. This ratio is less than unity suggesting costs are greater than benefits. For Program E, the B/C ratio is 1.01; indicating benefits are greater than costs.

By adding discount rate sensitivity to these two programs, different B/C ratios are calculated. For example, Table 31.6 presents the same process but with a 6 percent discount rate. Both B/C ratios are larger than with a 7 percent discount rate. Why? Because in both programs the benefits are much larger than costs, making the magnitude of change (in dollar value) greater. That is, the dollar value of 5 percent of $100 is less than 5 percent of $1000.

Using the 7 percent discount rate as our comparison (Table 31.5), increasing the rate 1 percent to 8 percent decreases the B/C ratio for both Programs (see Table 31.7). In fact, Program E where

TABLE 31.5
Cost-benefit Analysis for Two Programs Using Seven Percent Discount Rate

Program D at 7 percent

Year	Benefits ($)	Costs ($)	Discount Rate (7%)	Discounted Benefits ($)	Discounted Costs ($)
1	0	1,000,000	0.9346	0	934,579
2	0	500,000	0.8734	0	436,719
3	300,000	60,000	0.8163	244,889	48,978
4	300,000	60,000	0.7629	228,869	45,774
5	300,000	60,000	0.7130	213,896	42,779
6	300,000	60,000	0.6663	199,903	39,981
7	300,000	60,000	0.6227	186,825	37,365
8	300,000	60,000	0.5820	174,603	34,921
			TOTAL =	1,248,984	1,621,096
			B/C =	**0.77**	

Program E at 7 percent

Year	Benefits ($)	Costs ($)	Discount Rate (7%)	Discounted Benefits ($)	Discounted Costs ($)
1	0	1,500,000	0.9346	0	1,401,869
2	50,000	900,000	0.8734	43,672	786,095
3	600,000	80,000	0.8163	489,779	65,304
4	600,000	80,000	0.7629	457,737	61,032
5	600,000	80,000	0.7130	427,792	57,039
6	600,000	80,000	0.6663	399,805	53,307
7	600,000	80,000	0.6227	373,650	49,820
8	600,000	80,000	0.5820	349,205	46,561
			TOTAL =	2,541,640	2,521,026
			B/C =	**1.01**	

TABLE 31.6
Cost-benefit Analysis for Two Programs Using Six Percent Discount Rate

Program D at 6 percent

Year	Benefits ($)	Costs ($)	Discount Rate (6%)	Discounted Benefits ($)	Discounted Costs ($)
1	0	1,000,000	0.9434	0	943,396
2	0	500,000	0.8900	0	444,998
3	300,000	60,000	0.8396	251,886	50,377
4	300,000	60,000	0.7921	237,628	47,526
5	300,000	60,000	0.7473	224,177	44,835
6	300,000	60,000	0.7050	211,488	42,298
7	300,000	60,000	0.6651	199,517	39,903
8	300,000	60,000	0.6274	188,224	37,645
			TOTAL =	1,312,920	1,650,979
			B/C =	**0.77**	

Program E at 6 percent

Year	Benefits ($)	Costs ($)	Discount Rate (6%)	Discounted Benefits ($)	Discounted Costs ($)
1	0	1,500,000	0.9434	0	1,415,094
2	50,000	900,000	0.8900	44,500	800,997
3	600,000	80,000	0.8396	503,772	67,170
4	600,000	80,000	0.7921	475,256	63,367
5	600,000	80,000	0.7473	448,355	59,781
6	600,000	80,000	0.7050	422,976	56,397
7	600,000	80,000	0.6651	399,034	53,205
8	600,000	80,000	0.6274	376,447	50,193
			TOTAL =	2,670,341	2,566,203
			B/C =	**1.04**	

TABLE 31.7
Cost-benefit Analysis for Two Programs Using Eight Percent Discount Rate

Program D at 8 percent

Year	Benefits ($)	Costs ($)	Discount Rate (8%)	Discounted Benefits ($)	Discounted Costs ($)
1	0	1,000,000	0.9259	0	925,926
2	0	500,000	0.8573	0	428,669
3	300,000	60,000	0.7938	238,150	47,630
4	300,000	60,000	0.7350	220,509	44,102
5	300,000	60,000	0.6806	204,175	40,835
6	300,000	60,000	0.6302	189,051	37,810
7	300,000	60,000	0.5835	175,047	35,009
8	300,000	60,000	0.5403	162,081	32,416
			TOTAL =	1,189,012	1,592,398
			B/C =	**0.75**	

Program E at 8 percent

Year	Benefits ($)	Costs ($)	Discount Rate (8%)	Discounted Benefits ($)	Discounted Costs ($)
1	0	1,500,000	0.9259	0	1,388,889
2	50,000	900,000	0.8573	42,867	771,605
3	600,000	80,000	0.7938	476,299	63,507
4	600,000	80,000	0.7350	441,018	58,802
5	600,000	80,000	0.6806	408,350	54,447
6	600,000	80,000	0.6302	378,102	50,414
7	600,000	80,000	0.5835	350,094	46,679
8	600,000	80,000	0.5403	324,161	43,222
			TOTAL =	2,420,891	2,477,564
			B/C =	**0.98**	

---

benefits exceeded costs at a 7 percent discount rate now has a B/C ratio less than one; costs are larger than benefits.

The application of the time value of money preference to policy analysis grows more difficult because of our inability to estimate and forecast accurately. Theorists offer different views on technology but argue differences most often on political rather than technical grounds. Tullock (1964) argues that low discount rates justify too many public projects, redistributing income from present to future generations. Baumol (1968, 800) argues that a Tullock redistribution tends to "take from the poor to give to the rich." Baumol would let the future take care of itself but avoid taking tax money from obviously high-yielding projects to spend on obviously low-yielding projects. Baumol calls for one exceptional use of tax money at the expense of high-yielding private projects, a category of public goods he calls "irreversibilities" (p. 800). He suggests, "If we poison our soil so that never again will it be the same, if we destroy the Grand Canyon and turn it into a hydroelectric plant, we give up assets which like Goldsmith's bold peasantry, '... their country's pride, when once destroyed can never be supplied.' All the wealth and resources of future generations will not suffice to restore them" (p. 800). In a more practical sense, Dunn (2004) points out that high discount rates result in a minimal role for government action and a maximal one for the private sector with lower discount rates reversing the roles. Without a complex analysis of monetary policy, Dunn suggests the government-borrowing rate as appropriate, given the fact that taxpayers who are also willing bond buyers express their preferences by stepping up and buying the government's bonds. As such the U.S. OMB (1992) continues to suggest using a 7 percent discount rate along with sensitivity and scenario analysis—changing the discount rate and time frames when conducting a cost-benefit analysis. As the detailed scenarios show above, the slightest change in the interest rate could significantly change the conclusion of a decision maker.

1.6 POLICY ANALYSIS AND COST-BENEFIT ANALYSIS

Where is cost-benefit analysis's place in policy analysis? It depends on whom you ask. Amartya Sen maintains it is a daydream; Henry Richardson declares it stupid. Yet cost-benefit analysis was a modern-day marvel to President Johnson (Wolfson 2001). In the end, cost-benefit analysis can serve as a management tool, where applicable, to help guide, the decision-making process because not all cost-benefit analyses are useful or even conducted properly. For example, Hahn and Dudley (2004, 11) evaluated cost-benefit analyses (RIAs) from the Reagan, Bush, and Clinton Administrations. They found the overall quality of the RIAs to be low. Costs and benefits often went unreported. Where they were reported, they were not analyzed together. Seventy-one percent of the RIAs did not report net benefit information. In addition, where data were available and quantified, cost-benefit comparisons were not present.

One difficult and controversial approach to estimation comes from "structured conversations" about hypothetical choices. The choices involve individual preferences for the hypothetical existence and value of projects and courses of action (Larson 1992). Measuring benefits contingently requires an analyst to ask individuals to "vote" a willingness to pay for or accept compensation for the loss of a project, program, or policy despite no direct, active consumption of the fruits of the policy change. Voting—responding to survey research questions—allows the members of the group to estimate an option value or "an amount someone is willing to pay to keep available the option for future consumption of the good" or the amount "one might be willing to pay . . . to preserve a wilderness that one anticipates possibly visiting some time in the future" (Weimer 2005, 74–75). The willingness to accept compensation—what the respondent would be willing to give up—may involve higher pollution levels, greater use of a park or beach, greater police efforts to constrain movement, or releasing drug offenders serving a mandated prison sentence (Kahneman and Knetch 1992, 69; Brown 2004).

Milgrom (1993, 417–422) critiques the theory of contingent valuation on the basis of its violation of the utilitarian philosophy from which cost-benefit analysis developed. He argues that existence value in any standard economic approach must be pecuniary value to the individuals, a value realized only through their "own personal economic motives" (p. 431). He calls the contingent valuation supporters optimistic. They believe that all factors that shape individual perceptions of the world may yield estimates of value. They also believe that individual perceptions alone can drive valuations. Valuations, in fact, may lead to unacceptable conclusions, perhaps that "the secret [or natural] destruction of a [wilderness] does no damage . . . the real damage is wrought by the journalist who first publicizes the destruction" (p. 419). He calls for cost-benefit analysis to use only the most complete and undistorted information about what individuals prefer expressed in economic terms—what they would actually pay or accept—if given the opportunity in a market and only what people can think of paying or accepting in strict economic terms.

Feelings, knowledge, and values are some of the noneconomic factors that sway responses to surveys valuing existence of some economic resource. Whether individuals feel that policy should dictate preservation of a wilderness, whether a person knows the extent of the risk the wilderness faces, and whether someone can value the wilderness if never seen, directly used, or thought about in economic terms are not likely candidates for strict measurement of economic preferences, Milgrom says. Instead, wilderness will exist because there is some other reason, one that cannot be traded off against economic values; environmental preservation is a deep-seated concern, possibly even a belief held by individuals on which public policy develops.

Altruism also violates the principles of cost-benefit analysis. A survey asking the value of the continued existence of a wilderness may elicit a response based on the moral satisfaction of increasing the supply of public goods, with the respondent thinking that more public goods will make everyone better off. Does the altruism actually make everyone better off economically? Milgrom asks (p. 419–420). No, he says, altruism is not consistent with the idea that each person is independent of every other and that personal value "is treated as a purely personal matter that is related to the personal benefits each individual receives from the project" (p. 420). Altruism leads to double-counting of the individual valuator's benefits.

Valuing the distribution of benefits also runs afoul of strict economic analysis through the measurement and comparison of costs and benefits. For example, individual survey respondents may report that preserving jobs is worth the cost of opposing free trade, that "it is more efficient to protect the habitat of spotted owls [than] the jobs of Oregonian lumberjacks" (p. 421). Some individuals, he says, would report being willing to pay to enforce "racially or ethnically homogeneous neighborhoods" (p. 421). He asks whether any policy analysts facing such problems use contingent valuation.

Valuing outcomes presents unique problems. Valuing an outcome can attribute cause and status to those who are responsible for the change in existence, nature or people. Cause and status definitions of the situation can have unwarranted consequences in surveys. Willingness to pay (WTP) or accept (WTA) in a national park fire situation illustrates the process. Asked in a survey, an individual might answer in one way to the WTP or WTA in firefighting for those events caused by lightning and in another way to those events caused by careless campers and in still another way, fires set by foresters to reduce undergrowth and prevent future wildfires. Milgrom argues that the survey respondent must be consistent irrespective of the method the policy used to mitigate the public problem. He also states the obvious in that cost-benefit analysis should not cope with individual valuations made without adequate information.

Valuing from rights and obligations confuses the cost-benefit analysis as well. The environmental debate and the debates about almost all policy issues have elements of rights extensions and exclusions—perhaps a right an animal has to be kept free from harm in laboratory experiments or the rights of animals not to be used for food, clothing, or shelter. The debates also have elements involving obligations, especially ecosystem preservation, for its own sake or for future generations or for the preservation of animals and plant species. A right is a right, irrespective of economic value, Milgrom states. An obligation is a feeling a respondent has, one often affected by the feeling about those to whom the person might owe the obligation. For example, an obligation to preserve the rainforest in Brazil may fall on respondents' obligations owed scale according to a feeling about Brazilians.

Political leaders willing to read into cost-benefit analysis any of these concepts go beyond the theory of cost-benefit analysis and, some say, misuse the analysis or use an invalid one. These leaders simply read into the substance and process of median voter models—majority rule—the utilitarian model of moral philosophy. The good citizen is one who accepts the benevolence of political leaders as well as the leaders' choice of the moments to bestow their recognition of feelings, knowledge, altruism, equity, responsibility, rights, and obligations.

1.7 ECONOMIC REASONING IN GOVERNMENT FINANCIAL MANAGEMENT RATHER THAN POLICY ANALYSIS

We now place cost-benefit analysis within the even larger body of literature characterizing economic reasoning in government. This review forms a critique and supports the literature of the previous section, and suggests the larger sources and consequences of the cost-benefit analysis approach for choice.

Economic decision making tends to be deductive. Because of that, economics has an elegant and mathematics-based precision in detailing "proof." Economics also provides a sense of practical worldliness. Having based microeconomics, or the theory of the firm, on the idea that firm owners maximized, economic theory asserts something called optimal, public decisions.

The fundamental principle of economic reasoning applied to the public sector states that "bureaucratic officials, like all other agents in society, are motivated by their own self interests at least part of the time" (Downs 1957, 2). That is, political actors seek advantage for both themselves and their constituents and tend to maximize gain and minimize loss. Both bureaucratic and political actors reach their targets through a maze of rules, communication and coordination rules for bureaucratic officials and voting rules for political actors. The world within which behavior bends around rules is an unpredictable one. The actors, therefore, constantly calculate what is literally a risk-return relationship, given their original preferences for different kinds of advantages.

The CBA approach has its limits in government decision-making. That is, CBA is often used to justify *ex post facto* a position already taken; the most significant factor in CBA is often its sponsor, as was President Lyndon Johnson in the Great Society and the institution of PPBS. Cost-benefit analysis tends to neglect the distributional consequences of a choice. The method, logically and systematically, undervalues projects that even the distribution of wealth and overvalues projects that exacerbate economic inequality. In the Kaldor terminology, cost-benefit analysis would recommend a course of action that could potentially allow the winners to compensate the losers so that no one is worse off, but the method does not guarantee that the winners *will* compensate the losers.

Over and above the operational problems with CBA, and by extension economic reasoning in government, there are intangibles of fundamental importance that CBA cannot conceive. For example, a moral significance in the duties and rights of individuals to each other and of government to all individuals is not comprehended in the measurement of consequences alone. With cost-benefit analysis, certain rights such as due process of the law or broad public participation and discourse, cannot be conceived simply because they are processes valued for themselves rather than outcomes.

Cost-benefit analysis has been blamed for damaging the political system. Some argue that politics is superior to analysis because of the wider scope of ideas and concepts the people practicing politics can fathom. Others argue that analysis enfranchises unelected policy analysts and disenfranchises those who do not understand, do not believe, or cannot use analysis to make their arguments to government. Such a situation creates a loss of confidence in government institutions, at the very least, and, more fundamentally, subverts democratic government.

To return to CBA's basis in economics, others argue that the basis insofar as it describes or prescribes government action has flaws. That is, CBA assumes that there can be no market failure. There are always opportunity costs and shadow prices with which public sector goods and services can be valued. Research on markets suggests that markets are not perfectly competitive, that the lack of competition leads inevitably to failure, and that public goods are produced to remedy that failure. Without a way to value public goods and services, therefore, cost-benefit analysis fails to inform the decision-making process.

Another economic idea—that any alternative must be judged in terms of other alternatives—lends support to analysis. These proponents of CBA argue that there is no alternative to CBA, none as explicit or systematic. In fact, CBA analysts' formalized, explicit nature allows the public to hold its public officials accountable to a larger extent than under normal politics and management. Systematic analysis is less likely to overlook an important fact or consideration which when placed in an adversarial process such as politics, may lead to the determination of the public interest far sooner than mere impressionistic surmise.

However, opponents of cost-benefit analysis argue about what it systematically reveals. They say that it reveals only values related to conserving resources to the exclusion of all others; the overriding value, in fact, is economic efficiency rather than others that are possible: those associated with justice, domestic tranquility, the general welfare, and the blessings of liberty. As Dryzek (1993, 222) points out, "[A]ll that matters is how much of the target value [efficiency] is achieved." Moreover, cost-benefit analysis never questions the existing resource constraints, a matter that is questioned in political debate.

The controversy over the use, misuse, or lack of use of analysis often pits those who believe in government against those who see the market as the predominantly positive force in society. Typically, what CBA overlooks is what most pro-government action proponents find government most useful in providing—equity—and to an even larger extent broad participation in self-government. Pro-market proponents argue that government intervenes for spurious reasons and, in doing so, creates more problems than it solves, certainly leading to less rather than more economic efficiency.

1.8 CONCLUSION

This chapter described and examined cost-benefit analysis. Cost-benefit analysis has had a brief and controversial history. Policy analysts, decision makers, and politicians alike find themselves arguing over its purpose, theory, and application. Understandably, differences arise where costs and benefits are difficult, and sometimes impossible to measure. Used correctly, however, cost-benefit analysis can lend itself to the decision-making process not as the deciding factor but as a technique to identify economically efficient policies, one of many quantitative and qualitative factors in political decision making.

REFERENCES

Arrow, K.J. and Lind, R.C., Uncertainty and the evaluation of public investment decisions, *American Economic Review*, 60, 364, 1970.

Auerbach, A.J., Dynamic revenue estimation, *J. Economic Perspectives*, 10, 141, 1996.

Baumol, W.J., On the social rate of discount, *American Economic Review*, 58, 788, 1968.

Baumol, W.J., On the discount rate for public projects, in *Public Expenditures and Policy Analysis*, Haveman, R.H. and J. Margolis, J. Eds., Markham, Chicago, 1970, 273–290.

Brown, D.K., Cost-benefit analysis in criminal law, *California Law Review*, 92, 325, 2004.

Buchanan, J.M. and Tullock, G., *The Calculus of Consent*, University of Michigan Press, Ann Arbor, 1962.

Douglas, M. and Wildavsky, A., *Risk and Culture*, University of California Press, Berkeley, 1982.

Downs, A., *An Economic Theory of Democracy*, Harper & Row, New York, 1957.

Downs, A., Why the government budget is too small in a democracy, *World Politics*, 12, 541, 1960.

Dryzek, J.S., Policy analysis and planning: From science to argument, in *The argumentative turn in policy analysis and planning*, Fischer, F. and Forester, J., Eds., Duke University Press, Durham, 1993, 214–232.

Dunn, W. N., *Public Policy Analysis*, Prentice-Hall, Alpine, 2004.

Dupuit, J. (1844). De la mesure de l'utilite des travaus publics, Annales des Ponts et Chaussees, 2d series, 8. Cited in Dupuit (1952).

Dupuit, J. (1952). On the measurement of utility of public works, trans. R.H. Barback, in *International Economic Papers*, Peacock, A.T., Lutz, F.A., Turvey, R, and Henderson, E., eds., MacMillan, New York, 1952, 84–110.

Eckstein, O., *Water resource development: The economics of project evaluation*, Harvard University Press, Cambridge, 1958.

GAO (General Accountancy Office), *Designing evaluations*, PEMD-10.1.4, GAO, Washington, 1991. http://www.gao.gov/policy/10_1_4.pdf. Accessed January 18, 2005.

Graham, D.A., Cost-benefit analysis under uncertainty, *American Economic Review*, 71, 715, 1981.

Hahn, R.W. and Dudley, P., How well does the government do cost-benefit analysis? Working Paper 04-01, AEI-Brookings Joint Center for Regulatory Studies, 2004.

Hirschleifer, J., On the theory of optimal investment decision, *J. Political Economy*, 66, 329, 1958.

Hirschleifer, J. and Shapiro D.L., (1970). The treatment of risk and uncertainty, in *Public Expenditures and Policy Analysis*, Haveman, R.H. and Margolis, J., Eds., Markham, Chicago,1970, 291–313.

Kahneman, D. and Knetch, J.L., Valuing public goods: The purchase of moral satisfaction, *J. Environmental Economics and Management*, 22, 57, 1992.

Key, V.O., The lack of a budgetary theory, *American Political Science Review*, 34, 1137, 1940.

Klay, W.E., The organizational dimension of budgetary forecasting: Suggestions from revenue forecasting in the states, *International J. Public Administration, 7*, 241, 1985.

Krutilla, J.V., Welfare aspects of benefit-cost analysis, *J. Political Economy*, 69, 226, 1961.

Krutilla, J.V. and Eckstein, O., *Multipurpose River Development*, Johns Hopkins Press, Baltimore, 1958.

Larson, D.M., On measuring existence value, *Land Economics* 69, 116, 1992.

Mankiw, N.G. and Weinzierl, M., Dynamic scoring, NBER Working Paper 11000. 2004. http://www.nber.org/papers/w11000. Accessed December 2004.

Marglin, S.A., The social rate of discount and the optimal rate of investment. *Quarterly J. Economics*, 77, 95, 1963.

McKean, R., *Efficiency in government through systems analysis*, Wiley, New York, 1958.

Milgrom, P., Is sympathy an economic value? Philosophy, economics and the contingent valuation method, in *Contingent valuation*, Hausman, J.A., Ed., North-Holland, New York, 1993, 417–435.

Miller, G.J., Government fiscal policy impacts, in *Handbook of Public Sector Economics* Robbins, D., Ed., CRC Press, New York, 425–521.

Musgrave, R.A., Cost–benefit analysis and the theory of public finance, *J. Economic Literature*, 7, 797, 1969.

Pearce, D., Cost-benefit analysis and environmental policy, *Oxford Review of Economic Policy* 14, 84, 1998.

Persky, J., Retrospectives: Cost-benefit analysis and the classical creed, *J. Economic Perspectives* 15, 199, 2001.

Pierce, L.D., *The Politics of Fiscal Policy Formation*, Goodyear, Pacific Palisades, 1971.

Pigou, A.C., *The Economics of Welfare*, MacMillan, London, 1932.

Poister, T.H., *Public Program Analysis*, University Park Press, Baltimore, 1978.

Porter, T.M., *Trust in Numbers*, Princeton University Press, Princeton, NJ, 1995.

Rossi, P.H. and Wright, J.D., Evaluation research: An assessment, *Annual Review of Sociology*, 10, 331, 1984.

Rossi, P. H. and Williams, W., *Evaluating Social Programs*, Seminar Press, New York, 1972.

Say, J.B, Traite *d'Economie Politique (A Treatise on Political Economy)*, Lippincott, Grambo & Co. Philadelphia, 1826. Trans. C. R. Prinsep. Ed. Clement C. Biddle. Library of Economics and Liberty, 1855. Accessed July 2005 http://www.econlib.org/library/Say/sayT0.html.

Scriven, M., The methodology of evaluation, in *Evaluating Action Programs*, Weiss,C.H., Ed., Allyn & Bacon, Boston, 1972, 123–136.

Suchman, E.A., *Evaluative Research*, Russell Sage Foundation, New York, 1967.

Tullock, G., The social rate of discount and the optimal rate of investment, *Quarterly J. Economics*, 78, 331, 1964.

Tversky, A. and Kahneman, D., Judgment under uncertainty: Heuristics and biases. *Science*, 185, 1124, 1974.

Tversky, A. and Kahneman, D., The framing of decisions and the psychology of choice, *Science*, 211, 453, 1981.

United States Congress, An act making appropriations for the construction, repair, and preservation of certain public works on rivers and harbors, and for other purposes, Public Law 57-154, Statutes at Large, 1, 1902.

United States Congress, Authorizing the construction of certain public works on rivers and harbors for flood control, and other purposes, Public Law 74-738, Statutes at Large, 32, 1936.

United States Office of Management and Budget, Memorandum for heads of executive departments and establishments, Circular No. A-94 Revised, Washington, 1992. http://www.whitehouse.gov/omb/circulars/a094/a094.html. Accessed March 7, 2005.

Watkins, T. (2005). Introduction to cost-benefit analysis. http://www2.sjsu.edu/faculty/Watkins/cba.htm. Accessed March 7, 2005,

Weimer, D.L., The potential of contingent valuation for public administration practice and research, *International J. Public Administration*, 28, 73, 2005.

Weiss, C.H., *Evaluation Research*, Prentice-Hall Englewood Cliffs, 1972.

Wilson, R. and Crouch, E.A.C., *Risk Benefit Analysis*, 2nd ed., Harvard University Press, Cambridge, 2001.

Wolfson, A., The costs and benefits of cost-benefit analysis, *Public Interest*, Fall, 93, 2001.

32 Environmental Impact Assessment: Between Bureaucratic Process and Social Learning

Yaakov Garb, Miriam Manon, and Deike Peters

INTRODUCTION

Environmental Impact Assessment (EIA) is a relatively new tool for decision making involving a standardized set of procedures designed to evaluate the prospective impacts a planned measure will have on the natural environment, and by extension, on human health. An EIA does not, however, relieve public policy and lawmakers from the duty of (pre-)determining at which point prospective impacts should be deemed too great to justify a particular project. EIA processes are typically located at the center of the most contentious public policy decisions, involving difficult trade offs between nature, society and economy. For example, do the projected time savings from a new highway justify routing it through a nature preserve where it will disrupt the habitat of several rare and endangered species? What are the cumulative traffic and pertaining pollution impacts from a new shopping mall, and do the people in the immediate vicinity have to tolerate these negative effects for the economic benefit of the city as a whole? What kind of preventive measures are needed before the new airport runway becomes acceptable to the surrounding neighborhoods? The results of EIAs are often challenged in court and, even if this is not the case, EIAs still often provide starting points rather than final answers or solutions to contentious public policy debates.

ORIGINS OF EIA

Environmental impact assessment came into being as a formally required, legislatively mandated, decision-making tool on January 1, 1970 in the United States with the inception of the National Environmental Protection Act (NEPA). This was a groundbreaking and revolutionary moment in the legislative history of the environmental movement that can be felt today around the world and at all levels of the development process.

The roots of EIA, and impact assessment in general, however, can be traced back far earlier in the history of development decision making. There is nothing new about the idea of incorporating information gathering into planning and design, and we can find examples of the use of analytical tools to make predictions as far back as the sixteen century. In 1546 the Royal Commission of England issued a report investigating the impacts of iron mills and furnaces in Southern England that incorporated many elements of a modern EIA (Barrow 1997; Shrimpton 2000). In the 1930s, the Design and Industry Association in the UK issued Cautionary Guides that set guidelines for good and bad environmental practices in urban design in an attempt to influence the direction of planning and decision making at that time and to incorporate greater environmental sensitivity (Caldwell 1988). Before NEPA, however, all attempts to measure impacts and make predictions were done at the discretion of the individual developer or government agency, with no established procedures or regulatory oversight. These tended to involve the public in only a limited way, if at all, and many development projects escaped any assessment process. Thus, apart from these ad hoc precursors to formal evaluation processes, the dominant approach to development decisions prior to NEPA incorporated only two major considerations, financial viability and technical feasibility (Barrow 1997).

The rapid development of the twentieth century brought with it a rise in public concern about the impacts on the environment and human health. On a legislative level, this brought many new laws governing human health, consumer protection, and workplace safety. However these early measures still failed to make any systematic connection between the impacts of development and the quality of the natural environment (Caldwell 1988). It was not until the growth of the environmental movement in the 1960s, and the high profile controversies over the use of pesticides and other chemicals, that there was sufficient pressure for the government to take action regarding the environment. There were other factors, too, that helped to lay the groundwork for the eventual passage of NEPA. The information revolution that began in the 1950s, developments in assessment techniques and planning theory, and a growing desire to integrate science and other technical and analytical tools into the decision-making process, all contributed to the birth of NEPA, and with it the modern EIA (Bailey 1997; Shrimpton 2000).

On January 1, 1970, President Nixon signed NEPA into law, making EIA a statutory requirement with set guidelines and broad objectives. This bold action opened a new chapter in the history of public policy and decision making, for the first time requiring a systematic approach to assessing and predicting impacts and presenting the results. The main objective of NEPA's drafters was to reform both the decision-making process and the dominant development and design priorities in a way that would be enforceable and subject to external review (Caldwell 1988).

To achieve this goal, they laid out the general framework for the EIA process. Section 102(2)(c) of NEPA lists three requirements: First, the assessment of all environmental impacts of the proposed action, including the residual effects that could not be mitigated, and of alternatives to the proposed action; second, a statement of the relationship between short-term economic gains and the long-term advantages of maintaining a productive ecosystem; and third, a statement of any irreversible environmental or social consequences should the proposed action be implemented (O'Riordan and Sewell 1981). Importantly, NEPA is a procedural legislation, mandating a set of actions to be followed, as opposed to specifying environmental outcome (Cashmore 2004).

It is important to note that NEPA itself establishes a broad definition of the word *environment*, one that includes the social as well as the biophysical components, although this has not always been the case in the application of NEPA, particularly in its earlier days. In addition, NEPA specifically mandates the disclosure of information to the public and to other relevant government agencies, by requiring the preparation and release of the Environmental Impact Statement (EIS). With its bold goals and sparse details, NEPA's drafters left much room for interpretation, thus beginning what has now been more than 30 years of discussion, debate, and legal battle over just how the EIA process should look and what it is meant to accomplish. This debate has grown to include people and governments around the globe, and participants from nearly every disciplinary background, including planners, scientists, economists, political theorists, and of course, developers, environmentalists, and the general public: a veritable EIA industry.

STEP-BY-STEP: THE EIA PROCESS

Despite the wide variety in EIA legislation and practices around the world, the basic structure of the EIA process is more or less the same. The EIA occurs through six major stages: screening, scoping,

---

TABLE 32.1
The Basic EIA Process

1. Screening of project proposal
2. Scoping:
   a. Definition of key issues
   b. Establishment of parameters of study
   c. Collection of base-line data
3. Impact Assessment (EIS)
   a. Identification and prediction of impacts
   b. Evaluation of impact significance
   c. Recommendation of mitigation and management strategies
   d. Release of final EIS
4. Review of EIS—decision is made
5. Implementation—development begins
6. Monitoring and Auditing

---

impact assessment, review, implementation, and monitoring/auditing (see Table 32.1). The initial screening process determines whether or not a project requires an EIA. The goal of this phase is to assure that unnecessary assessments are not carried out, while developments requiring assessment are not missed. The criteria for which development projects are subject to EIA laws varies greatly across national lines; some countries have no specific regulations regarding the screening process at all or adopt very weak criteria whereas in others, like the United States and Canada, the screening process is quite rigorous and well defined (Barrow 1997).

Once a project is determined to be subject to EIA procedures, it undergoes a scoping process to set its parameters and identify the key issues. Scoping presents a chance early in the assessment process to focus the study and establish its key goals and the level of detail, geographic boundaries, and temporal scale that will be considered. At this stage, relevant baseline data is collected and a team is gathered to conduct the assessment. Scoping can resemble a brainstorming session of experts and others associated with the proposal (Barrow 1997). Additionally, scoping presents a good opportunity to integrate the public into the EIA process. Local residents, in particular, may be the most aware of the particularities of the local area and can help EIA practitioners in identifying potential impacts that might otherwise go unnoticed or arise as points of conflict further down the road.

Following these initial stages, the formal impact assessment is carried out and the Environmental Impact Statement (EIS) is prepared. The goals of this stage are to identify, measure, and evaluate all the potential impacts and to suggest mitigation or avoidance measures. There is a wide range of technical and analytical tools available for impact assessment; the data collected should be both qualitative and quantitative and should, ideally, incorporate impacts on both the bio-physical environment as well as the cultural and socio-economic sphere. Assessment methods can range from simple to highly complex and include check lists, matrices, GIS mapping, and mathematical modeling. Traditional cost-benefit analysis and other related evaluative techniques may also be incorporated in the EIS in order to determine the significance of the impacts predicted. It is critical that alternatives to the development proposal, including no development, be considered at this time and that assessment take place for each scenario. After the completion of the assessment and evaluation process, recommendations should be made for how to proceed and how to minimize or mitigate the negative effects that will result, either through modification of the original design or through subsequent management. These recommendations should be included in the EIS document in addition to a list of impacts that are unavoidable or cannot be mitigated. There is a wide range in presentation of the final EIS in terms of both length and style of the document produced. Some EIS total thousands of pages and are laden with technical detail, whereas others present only a cursory overview of the situation. A good EIS must be both understandable and thorough, a challenge given the scale of the assessment task.

Once completed EIS is made public and reviewed and a decision is made on whether to allow a project to go through as proposed, rejecting it altogether, or allowing it with stipulations. The review process differs in different legislative contexts and may be done by a panel that includes members of the public, by a group of government officials, or by the judiciary (Barrow 1997).

The final stages of the EIA process, auditing and monitoring, take place largely after the project is completed but are nonetheless crucial in assuring the integrity of the process. The post-assessment audit seeks to answer the question of how closely the predicted impacts resemble those that actually occurred. In addition, auditors may review the effectiveness of the recommended mitigation and management strategies. Auditors should evaluate the EIA process, its thoroughness and cost-effectiveness, and the accuracy of its results. Monitoring differs from auditing in that it is an ongoing process that focuses on collecting technical data on the impacts of development and can occur throughout the process, before and after project completion. Monitoring feeds into both the assessment and auditing process. Post-development, monitoring is important in order to assess compliance with EIA recommendations and to assure that the EIA process produces results on the ground and not simply a good EIS document. Unfortunately, many countries, particularly in the developing world, lack the resources, technical abilities, or political will to implement good monitoring and auditing procedures.

Outlined below is the basic structure of the EIA process. It is important to note that this process does not occur in a linear fashion as it might appear, but rather is a cascading and at times cyclical process in which various stages may be occurring simultaneously with results feeding both subsequent and previous stages. Furthermore, the EIA process does not occur in a vacuum but is embedded within a much larger context that includes planning priorities, development needs, scientific research, and political frameworks, to name just a few. Obviously, these and other factors influence the EIA process at every stage and allow for considerable play and variation along the way, as will be discussed in greater detail in subsequent sections.

LIFE AFTER NEPA: ADAPTATION AND SPREAD OF EIA LEGISLATION

The 35 years since the conception of the modern EIA has been marked by a rapid spread of EIA legislation to over 100 countries around the world (Glasson et al. 2005) . This often follows a cycle in which some EIAs are conducted through donor or company requirements even in the absence of EIA requirements in the country, then a surge of EIAs when national regulations come into force, followed by a period of EIA maturity, in which the requirements are fine-tuned (Glasson 2005, pp. 293–4). With that spread has come an ever-growing volume of both critique and refinement of the EIA process. Within the United States, the passage of NEPA on the federal level was followed by similar actions by many individual states, such as California's 1970 Environmental Quality Act and Vermont's Act 250, for example. By 1991 there were 16 state-level bills that either added requirements to the national ones or replaced national procedures altogether. Collectively, these bills are known as "little NEPA's" and tend to be more demanding than the federal laws. On both a state and federal level, refinement of EIA requirements evolved out of a great deal of litigation following the passage of NEPA. NEPA's drafters chose to use relatively vague language, allowing the courts to hammer out the details of the EIA procedure (O'Riordan and Sewell 1981). For better or for worse, it is clear that litigation remains a central focus of the U.S. model of EIA. The emphasis on litigation is something that many other countries have tried to avoid in their adaptation of EIA legislation and it is the source of much criticism of the U.S. model (Caldwell 1988; Bailey 1997). Others point to the positive role of the courts in clarifying procedures and encouraging the growth and evolution of EIA within the United States (O'Riordan and Sewell 1981).

On an international level, countries such as France, Canada, Australia, and Thailand followed the lead of the United States and adopted their own EIA legislation as early as the 1970s. By 1985 there were already signs that EIA was becoming an international norm, at least in the developed world; in that year, the European Community passed a directive requiring EIA procedures in all member states.[1] EIA again gained prominence on the world stage at the 1992 Earth Summit in Rio de Janeiro when the UN passed Agenda 21 encouraging all countries to "integrate environment into decision-making" and requiring EIA procedures as part of the Convention on Bio-Diversity (CBD). Since then quite a few international agreements have included EIA requirements, and many international aid agencies, like the UN and the World Bank, require that recipients complete an EIA for any development project that receives funding. These measures have expanded the reach of EIA beyond just the developed world, and today EIA legislation can be found in more than 100 countries across almost every continent.

That said, it is important to note that there is much variety in both EIA legislation and its effectiveness. Laws and procedures are adapted by each country to fit within its own decision-making framework. Some nations have followed the U.S. model and created their own EIA legislation whereas others, like Sweden, Denmark, and the UK have chosen to integrate EIA into existing planning procedures without new legislation (Barrow 1997). On a procedural level, differences arise from the unique challenges that are present in certain settings, such as in the developing nations. And even within a Western European countries, there are differences, for example in the volume performed (20 EIAs are done a year in Austria, versus 7,000 in France), in the degree of public participation, and in which projects require an EIA (Glasson 2005, p. 296). These differences make it impossible to imagine a one-size-fits-all EIA process or to generalize about the success of EIA globally without acknowledging the variety of legislative contexts and EIA experiences.

One of the most obvious examples of cross-national variation in EIA legislation is the extent to which EIA is used to integrate the public into the decision-making process. In much of the developed world, EIA legislation includes public participation or disclosure as one of its stated goals, however the interpretation of this concept varies greatly. In the United States, EIA procedures have evolved to incorporate and require more and more participation over the years as a result of several court decisions. Allowing public lawsuits that challenge EIA findings is one way that people in the United States can engage with the EIA process that is not permitted in other contexts. There are also attempts to integrate the public earlier in the process before a decision is made, in the scoping and assessment phases. Outside of the United States, New Zealand is known for having some of the highest levels of public participation at all stages, both before and after a decision is made, and including project design (Barrow 1997). In Europe, on the other hand, even the most recent amendments to the EIA Directive require only the disclosure of information to the public, not the active engagement that is present in the other contexts (Hartley and Wood 2005). The lowest levels of public participation can be found in the developing world, where there tends to be little political will to include the public; this, together with low levels of education and limited experience of the public in the political arena tends to lead to top-down EIA procedures that pay little attention to the opinions of the local residents (Petts 1999). Yet in almost all contexts, the EIA does provide an entry point through which pressure groups (which are often linked to activist counterparts globally) can access information about and challenge disturbing projects.

Some theorists see direct links between the openness of a country's political system and the extent to which adopting EIA procedures has led beyond the procedural level to substantive policy review. Some of the key political factors include the level of government accountability, the openness of the democratic process, the influence of interest groups, and the procedures for settling disputes. In contexts where the political climate is such that people have access to information, a means of engaging the decision-making process, and the ability to challenge results,

---

1. Directive on the assessment of the effects of certain public and private projects on the environment (85/337/ EEC).

the influence of EIA seems to be much greater than in countries where people do not (O'Riordan and Sewell 1981).

EIA IN PRACTICE: PROCEDURAL CHALLENGES AND CRITIQUES

The political contexts and legislative requirements are only part of what assures the effectiveness of the EIA process. It is also important to look at the procedural level in terms of how requirements are actually carried out. Public participation is a recurring area in which the complications of putting EIA goals into practice are evident. There is a wide range of procedural norms even within a given legislative context relating to how, when, and to what extent public participation is sought. At the lowest level is the simple provision of information to the public, through leaflets, newspapers, and other one-way forms of communication. Accessibility of information is critical; one of the most common procedural critiques levied against EIA is that the documents produced are often highly technical and lengthy, and thus don't really accomplish the goal of informing the general public. Creating a document that is at once thorough and accessible is a central challenge for EIA practitioners both in terms of relations with the public and usefulness for decision-makers, themselves not technical experts (Alton 2003).

Providing information is only a small part of meeting the goal of public participation, however; participation implies a two-way process that goes beyond the disclosure of information. The collection of feedback from the public, through surveys or interviews, is one common method. Though a good first step, this, too, falls short of true participation, as the power is still entirely in the hands of the experts to collate and present this feedback and to integrate into the EIS produced (Petts 1999). Public meetings can sometimes be a more meaningful way of incorporating participation that can lead to greater accountability of decision makers and developers. These, however, can become quite contentious and can be dominated by NIMBY and LULU concerns.[2] Public participation needn't imply opposition, however. It can also be a constructive process that will improve a project's design and the ultimate decision and lead to better relations in the future. In some cases, the local residents may have more knowledge of the local area than outside experts and can provide valuable assistance to developers. For this reason, timing is crucial; for participation to be effective it must be done when done early, so that concerns can be adequately addressed and input integrated before entrenching antagonism (Kwiatkowski 2003).

Establishing a community advisory group, or a body of key stakeholders that represent the greater public, is another way to integrate participation at a very high level by inviting the public to play an active role in shaping the outcome of a development decision. This approach acknowledges that the public is not just to be placated, but may genuinely have something to contribute to the assessment and design process. This representative approach, too, has its limitations, as it relies heavily on a select group of individuals to speak for the entire public and therefore does not result in a truly open process or the education of the general population (Petts 1999). The complications of meaningfully integrating the public and providing them with accessible information illustrate some of the procedural challenges that are imbedded throughout the EIA process and the wide range of procedural norms that exist. Overall, there has been growing attention to the need for meaningful integration of local stakeholders, largely as a result of outside pressure from NGO's and community

---

2. The abbreviations stand for "Not In My Back Yard" and "Locally Unwanted Land Uses." Note that, as Fischer (2000, 125) has pointed out, "Basically, NIMBY reflects a public attitude that seems to be almost self-contradictory: namely. That people feel it is desirable to site a particular type of facility somewhere as long as it is not where *they* live." Typical NIMBY and LULU projects are landfills, hazardous waste facilities, power plants, prisons, homeless shelters, or drug clinics.

activists (Shrimpton 2000; Petts 1999). Many countries that previously had little or no provisions for public disclosure are adopting disclosure practices and there is growing pressure to make EIA documents accessible to a wider audience rather than just technical experts.

The timing in which impact assessment takes place is another procedural variable that is often the focus of critique. For an EIA to have meaning, to be able to influence the outcome of development, it must take place early on, where options are still open and alternatives truly exist. Too often, EIA is done only after a great deal of project planning has taken place and is used only as a tool to justify and give legitimacy to a predetermined decision or design plan (Alshuwaikhat 2005). There can still be some value in a retrospective EIA, as it can provide valuable information on mitigation options and on-going management, but it falls short of the goal of EIA to be a proactive tool that institutionalizes foresight (Bailey 1997).

The link between EIA and on-going project management, or how the EIA is used after the point of decision making, is another important challenge receiving increasing notice. Critics have argued that though EIA documents may contain a wealth of data and information, they are too often ignored or even discarded as soon as a decision is made and a project moves forward and that the entire process has been too focused on producing the EIS (Robinson 1992). One of the goals of the EIA has always been to provide information and recommendations to improve the development project throughout its life cycle. Unfortunately, procedures are not always in place to translate that goal into a reality and the value of EIA as a management tool can often go untapped. But there has been a shift in EIA away from narrowly focusing on the accuracy of predictions toward linking EIA recommendations with project management (Morrison-Saunders 2005). In some cases, EIS documents may even contain legally binding prescriptions for on-going management and impact mitigation or a special management document may be required (Bailey 1997).

With all of its imperfections, there is little question that EIA has firmly established itself as the dominant means for incorporating environmental considerations into development decision making. At the same time, the EIA process remains in a constant state of evolution and flux, as it has since its inception, driven by an ever-growing body of experience and critique. In the years since NEPA, there has been much progress in both recognizing and addressing the procedural and technical challenges of EIA practice. The following list of "best practices" summarizes some of the key characteristics identified as necessary to assure EIA effectiveness.

EIA "BEST PRACTICES"

(adapted from Barrow 1997)

- *Timing*: assessment should be initiated early in process, before major project/policy decisions are made and alternatives are ruled out.
- *Assessment techniques*: systematic and interdisciplinary analysis should be performed using a variety of assessment techniques and incorporating biophysical, social, cultural, and economic impacts as well as indirect and cumulative impacts.
- *Independence*: objective review of results should occur to ensure scientific integrity.
- *Public disclosure*: EIA results should be published before decision is made in a way that is accessible and widely available for review.
- *Public participation*: participation should take place at various stages and suggestions incorporated into project design and decision making .
- *Follow-up*: EIA results should be integrated into on-going management and compliance monitored.

BEYOND PROJECT-LEVEL EIA:
THE RISE OF STRATEGIC ENVIRONMENTAL ASSESSMENT

At the same time that these improvements to the EIA process are taking place, there are others who hold that such refinements are not enough and that more sweeping changes are needed in order to meet the goal of sustainable development. This level of critique does not look at the EIA process in isolation, but focuses, rather, on the interfaces between the EIA process and the surrounding development context, thus adopting a more radical, bigger-picture view of the changes that are needed in order to move forward. These critics play an integral part in promoting the continued evolution of EIA, particularly the most cutting edge developments that we see today.

Perhaps the best example of such a critique, and the progress it has spurred, can be seen in the development of the Strategic Environmental Assessment (SEA), a relatively new tool for impact assessment that is gaining ground around the world. This tool came out of the critique that the project-based characteristic of EIA makes it, on its own, intrinsically antithetical to the promotion of sustainable development. The goal of EIA is to institutionalize damage prevention and to further an anticipatory, proactive approach to dealing with the environment, and yet the very nature of EIA makes it, in one sense, reactive in that it can only be done once a project is already proposed (Alshuwaikhat 2005).

SEA addresses this by establishing a process similar to EIA that can be carried out at the policy, planning or program level. In other words, SEA mandates that before a development policy, whether national or international, is passed, its impacts should be assessed and evaluated just as we do for individual projects. Sustainability goals, then, would "trickle down" from the highest levels of decision making to the project level based on the results of the assessment and decisions that followed (Alshuwaikhat 2005). This helps assure that the full range of development options are truly considered instead of waiting until many are ruled out to begin the assessment process. In addition to being more anticipatory and broadening the scope of EIA, SEA also provides a way of capturing cumulative and indirect impacts that can go unnoticed as a result of the narrow focus of project-level EIA. It is important to note that though SEA emerged out of the recognition of the short-falls of EIA, it is not meant as a substitute or replacement, but rather acts in conjunction with current EIA procedures.

In the past ten years, there has been growing recognition internationally about the important role that SEA can play in promoting sustainable development and the limitation of the project-based EIA. Significant challenges still exist, however, in terms of the implementation of SEA procedures. Current policy and planning procedures lack triggers to set the SEA process in action, and once initiated there is insufficient guidance on how SEA should be carried out. Advocates of SEA point out that this should not be surprising given the relatively short life of SEA development, and that the current challenges facing SEA resembles those faced with EIA in the 1970s (Shrimpton 2000).

SEA may have the most important role to play in the developing world, where the development challenges are the greatest and there are the most significant barriers to adopting good EIA practices. Currently, developing countries around the world have established various forms of EIA legislation and yet these are often ineffective in promoting ecologically sound development. Focusing on using impact assessment tools to make big-picture plans and decisions might be more effective in this context than the project-based EIA. Experience with the implementation of SEA in the developing world remains limited, however there are some promising examples. In Asia, for example, SEA has been used to develop Nepal's forest management plan and Pakistan's water program, and a few developing countries around the world have adopted legislation mandating some form of SEA, including Brazil, South Africa and China (Alshuwaikhat 2005).[3]

---

3. For an extensive, up-to-date review of SEA approaches in international financial and development organizations as well as SEA implementation in twelve different countries, see Chaker et al. (2006).

EIA AS PUBLIC POLICY: NOT "HARD SCIENCE," BUT A MEANINGFUL TOOL FOR DELIBERATIVE DECISION MAKING

The above sections have already indicated that EIA can hardly be regarded as "hard" or "exact" science. With all the procedural and technical challenges, scientists themselves are in fact some of the harshest critics of the EIA process. For one, the "scientific" goals of EIAs have largely proven impossible to attain: natural ecosystems and human populations are simply too complex to make accurate, "objective" predictions about the precise environmental and health impacts of any given project. Scientists critical of EIA often focus on the lack of a peer review-process and question the independence of the consultants hired by developers to complete the EIA (Robinson 2001; Treweek 1996). Assuring the legitimacy of EIA findings is one of the critical roles that the courts and the public can play, and this is why it is essential that there be a process to challenge findings. Measuring and predicting impacts is not simple, even with the highest level of independence. Furthermore, there is often a lack of good base-line data that can be used as a basis for making predictions, and certain impacts, particularly indirect and cumulative impacts, are often ignored because they are difficult and costly to quantify, despite the fact that they may be quite significant (Parr 1999).

In the end, the process of scientific inference is always laden with interpretative elements. However, if properly acknowledged, the value-ladenness of EIA does not necessarily discredit it as a tool for decision making. Quite the contrary, it can also be seen as an opportunity. Yet to date, few EIA experts are willing to radically rethink the core nature of EIA as a soft tool that "is political to its roots" (Richardson 2005, 350). The role of interpretation and valuation in EIA remains a contested issue—one that is, in fact, very much linked to larger debates in public policy and planning about the nature of decision making. More specifically, the so-called communicative, or argumentative turn in policy analysis and planning (see e.g., Fischer and Forester (1993), Dryzek (1993) or Healey (1993)) has also begun to affect some people's thinking about EIA. Bringing some of the insights from planning theoretical debates related to the communicative turn to bear on this issue, Richardson (2005, 341) argues that environmental assessment "needs to engage with competing multiple rationalities, and the inescapable presence of value conflicts." The question of values has indeed become a very difficult issue within EIA, as the line between facts and opinions can easily become quite blurred. The fact that the assessing experts typically carry out their work in the midst of various power struggles and processes of political maneuvering and a look into the daily practice of environmental assessment quickly confirms that EIAs or SEAs are highly politicized sites of struggle. Thus, a simplistic, technocratic interpretation of EIA (and SEA) is clearly falling short of its reality in practice, and it may be more appropriate to instead measure the usefulness of the EIA process by its ability to increase the overall sustainability of the decision-making process. In this context, Wilkins (2003, 404), calls for an even greater subjectivity in EIA, arguing that

> subjectivity [is] ... one of the positive attributes of the process that should be encouraged in order to promote sustainability and to inspire confidence in EIA. A satisfactory decision at the end of a specific EIA is not the only goal of the process. As a forum in which the public, proponents and regulators deliberate on the design and implementation of development plans, the creation of discourse around the pertinent issues at stake is also an important result. EIA promotes the development of values that foster greater social responsibility and has the capacity to increase the importance of long-term environmental considerations in decision-making.

Here, EIA is seen less as a tool for environmental decision making than for social learning (also see Wandesforde-Smith and Kerbavaz 1988, 161–163). Clearly, promoters of this view are typically more interested in the EIA process than in its results. But one does not have to go this far to acknowledge the fact that subjective value assessments and power struggles are inescapable in the practice of EIA.

CONCLUSION

In the late 1970s, sustainable development became an increasingly important public policy goal. In this context, EIA entered the stage as a new, now indispensable, decision-making tool. Far from being a foolproof scientific exercise, EIA remains a relatively malleable evaluation device that is always dependent on judgment calls and value assessments from experts. Also, as practical experience has shown, EIAs are not free from political and other influences. Even the most professional and independently prepared EISs are useless unless the results are taken seriously in the subsequent decision-making context. Regardless of this persistent element of subjectivity, however, the overall usefulness of the tool remains unquestioned. Today, most countries require EIAs for a host of large-scale projects, from transport infrastructures to housing estates and commercial or industrial developments. Assessment techniques have also been expanded to more specifically include health or social aspects (HIAs, SIAs) or to be applied at the level of plans and programs (SEA). EIAs are particularly contentious in the case of very high-profile, large-scale mega projects. Even short of rejecting a mega-project outright, an EIA might call for such extensive mitigation measures so as to render the entire project economically unviable, which is especially problematic in cases where politicians and public decision makers have tied their political futures to the construction of a particular project. In the end, any EIA process is only as good as the public policy environment it is embedded in.

REFERENCES

Alshuwaikhat, Habib M. 2005. Strategic Environmental Assessment Can Help Solve Environmental Impact Assessment Failures in Developing Countries *Environmental Impact Assessment Review* 25: 307–317.

Alton, Charles. 2003. Let Us Make Impact Assessment More Accessible. *Environmental Impact Assessment Review* 23: 141–153.

Bailey, John. 1997. Environmental Impact Assessment and Management: An Underexplored Relationship. *Environmental Management* 21, no. 3: 317–327.

Barrow, C. J. 1997. *Environmental and Social Impact Assessment: An Introduction.* London: Arnold Publishing.

Caldwell, Lynton. 1988. Environmental Impact Assessment: Origins, Evolution, and Future Directions. *Policy Studies Review* 8: 1, 75–83.

Cashmore, Matthew. 2004. The Role of Science in Environmental Impact Assessment: Process and Procedure Versus Purpose in the Development of Theory. *Environmental Impact Assessment Review* 24: 403–426.

Chaker, A., El-Fadl, K., Chamas, L., and B. Hatjian (2006) A review of strategic environmental assessment in 12 selected countries. *Environmental Impacts Assessment Review*, 26: 15–56.

Dryzek, John. 1993. Policy Analysis and Planning: From Science to Argument. In: Fischer, Frank and Forster, John, *The Argumentative Turn in Policy Analysis and Planning.* Durham and London: Duke University Press.

Fischer, Frank. 2000. *Citizens, Experts, and the Environment: The Politics of Local Knowledge.* Durham and London: Duke University Press.

Fischer, Frank, and Forster, John (Eds). 1993. *The Argumentative Turn in Policy Analysis and Planning.* Durham and London: Duke University Press.

Frank, David J., Hironaka, Ann, and Evan Schofer. 2000. The Nation-State and the Natural Environment over the Twentieth Century. *American Sociological Review* 65, 1: 96–116.

Glasson, John, Therivel, Rikki, and Andrew Chadwick. 2005. *Introduction to Environmental Impact Assessment*, 3rd ed. New York: Routledge.

Hartley, Nicolas, and Christopher Wood. 2005. Public Participation in Environmental Impact Assessment—Implementing the Aarhus Convention *Environmental Impact Assessment Review* 25: 319–341.

Healey, Patsy (1993) Planning Through Debate: The Communicative Turn in Planning Theory. In: Frank Fischer and John Forster, eds., *The Argumentative Turn in Policy Analysis and Planning.* Durham and London: Duke University Press, 234–257.

Kwiatkowski, Roy E., and Maria Ooi. 2003. Integrated Environmental Impact Assessment: A Canadian Example. *Bulletin of the World Health Organization* 81, no. 6: 434–438.

Morrison-Saunders, Angus, and Bailey, John. 2000. Exploring the EIA/Environmental Management Relationship: Follow-up for Performance Evaluation. Paper presented at IAIA '00 Back to the Future conference (EIA Follow-up Stream). Hong Kong Convention and Exhibition Centre, 19–23 June 2000, Hong Kong.

O'Riordan, Timothy, and Sewell, W. R. D., eds. 1981. *Project Appraisal and Policy Review.* Chichester: John Wiley and Sons.

Parr, S. 1999. *Study on the Assessment of Indirect and Cumulative Impacts, as well as Impact Interactions.* Volume 1: Background to the Study.

Petts, Judith. (ed.) 1999. *Handbook of Environmental Impact Assessment,* vol. 1. Oxford: Blackwell Publishers.

Richardson, Tim. 2005. Enviornmental Assessment and Planning Theory: Four Short Stories about Power, Multiple Rationality, and Ethics. *Environmental Impact Assessment Review* 25, 341–365.

Robinson, Nicholas A. 1992. International Trends in Environmental Impact Assessment. *Boston College Environmental Affairs Law Review* 19, no. 3: 591–621.

Robinson, Nicholas A. 2001. Legal Systems, Decision Making and the Science of Earth's Systems: Procedural Missing Links . *Ecology Law Quarterly* 27, no. 4: 1077–1161.

Shrimpton, Mark, and Storey, Keith. 2000. *Assessing and Managing Socio-Economic Effects: Improving the Process of Environmental Impact Assessment.* Paper presented at the European Centre for Occupational Health, Safety and the Environment (ECOHSE) Symposium, 4–7 Oct 2000, Kaunus, Lithuania (available online at http://www.gla.ac.uk/ecohse/2000papers/shrimpton-storey.pdf, 1-31-2006).

Treweek, J. 1996. Ecology and Environmental Impact Assessment. *The Journal of Applied Ecology* 33, no. 2: 191–199.

Vries, Michiel S. de. 1999. *Calculated Choices in Policy-Making: Theory and Practice of Impact Assessment.* New York: St. Martin's Press.

Wandesforde-Smith, Geoffrey, and Kerbavaz, Joanne 1988. The co-evolution of politics and policy: elections, entrepreneurship and EIA in the United States. In: Wathern P. (ed.) *Environmental impact assessment: theory and practice.* London: Allen and Unwin, 161–91.

Wilkins, Hugh. 2003. The need for subjectivity in EIA: discourse as a tool for sustainable development. *Environmental Impact Assessment Review* 23: 401–414.

33 Technology Assessment as Policy Analysis: From Expert Advice to Participatory Approaches

Bernard Reber

Technological innovations are key issues in politics and economics. They also legitimize—if it's new, it's good. Today, political discourses on employment increasingly concern innovation capacities in a competitive international race. Thus technological choices are strategic. If the private sector and the market play an important role in this, the political dimension is also vital, from educational options to choices between different fiscal incentives. The political decision makers need expert advice—decision makers who are not able to understand and anticipate all aspects of many complex questions—this is the genesis of Technological Assessment (TA). But every technology, like the two-faced Janus, has two sides. Innovations carry with them risks as well as advantages. In the extreme, "meliorism" is in competition with responsibility: to put it in terms of the opposition between Ernst Bloch (1959) and Hans Jonas (1979), doing "better" technologically may also incur grave costs and "rampant apocalypticism." In this case, risk policy must be some part of innovation policy. Sometimes innovations are unwelcome and a source of controversy in the wider population, and even among scientists. In certain cases, like genetically modified (GM) foods or brain sciences, the scientists are not in a position to produce robust evidence and to declare a given innovation innocuous, contrary to the hopes of politicians or other stakeholders. Are politicians then condemned to take strong decisions on the basis of weak certainties, given that they are accountable for public welfare and must safeguard the common good?

TA research—principally in the United States and in Europe has for 30 years tried to make these choices less arbitrary, better informed, and more clearly justified. The need for advice is driven not only by the so-called pure technological questions (existing largely in the realm of fiction), but most often by socio-technological aspects of innovations. The interrelationships between science, technology and society are becoming more and more complex and difficult to predict—and yet the TA guiding policy responses has arguably not kept pace with these developments. As we will see, TA can be many different things, from scientific advice to Participatory Technological Assessment (PTA), matching "facts" and "values" in contexts of uncertainty. These sociopolitical innovations—implemented in the complexity of European technologies and societies—constitute rare occasions to confront directly philosophical questions like the interrelations of fact and value, issues of pluralism in both political and moral philosophy, as well as questions concerning the proper role of the precautionary principle (PP) in risk analysis.

In this chapter we will first present TA as scientific advice, as was embodied in the U.S. Office of Technology Assessment (OTA) before it was terminated by Congress and then in some counterpart institutions and innovations—Participatory Technological Assessment (PTA)—in Europe. Second, we will describe briefly some procedures and criteria for evaluating PTA thus conceived. Third, we'll discuss roles and impacts of TA. In conclusion, we will consider anew two further questions: the relationship of facts and values in TA (or PTA) procedures, and the articulation between ethics and TA (or PTA) and the precautionary principle in risk assessment.

I. DILEMMAS OF EXPERTISE BETWEEN SCIENCES AND POLITICS: SHORT-TERM AND LONG-TERM ASSESSMENT

After a long debate, the United States Congress created the OTA in 1972 (Bimber 1996; Herdman and Jensen 1997; Kunkle 1995). This office was to provide "early indications of the probable beneficial and adverse impacts of the applications of technology and to develop other coordinate information which may assist the Congress" (OTA, 1995). On the political side, OTA was governed by the Technology Assessment Board (TAB), consisting of six representatives and six senators, evenly divided between the two parties, and chaired in a rotating term by one of its own. On the expert side, OTA was advised by the Technology Assessment Advisory Council (TAAC), consisting of ten expert members of the public, appointed by the TAB, the comptroller general, who heads the General Accounting Office, and the director of the Congressional Research Service. TAB had formal control over OTA's analytical agenda and remained engaged over OTA's history. TAAC had no formal operational authority and was, perhaps in consequence, less active and engaged (Herdman and Jensen 1997).[1] OTA could generally not conduct an assessment without a specific remit from Congress to do so. Assessments were often stimulated by discussions among congressional members. Before work began, the TAB had to approve each proposal for an assessment, preventing the agenda from being high jacked by individual committee aims or politically-driven partisan interests. To help frame and determine the scope of the assessment, a staff of two to six analysts would then organize an advisory panel of stakeholders and (typically) nongovernmental experts. Staff would pursue the assessment through a variety of methods, circulating preliminary drafts to the members of the advisory panel and, often, to additional outside readers. The final draft was then subject to further formal external and internal review before being submitted to the director and the TAB for approval and release. The TAB exercised high standards vis-à-vis its procedures and the objectivity of its reports. Congressional testimony and discussion with Administration officials, stakeholders, public groups and press, often followed the issuing of reports.

The OTA slowly grew in status and recognition. By 1980, its budget (about 22 million dollars (Bimber 1996)), reached the plateau at which it would stay till its demise, the year of its closure[2] in 1995.[2] The number of its staff hovered around 200, but the specific number of full-time OTA employees was often difficult to determine because many of them were contractors only for a limited duration. Most employees were analysts with advanced degrees, working in a relatively flat organizational structure.

The OTA is often mentioned as pioneer of TA. Curiously, however, relatively little attention was paid to it at the outset (Coates 1999), despite a burgeoning literature on the philosophy and methods of technology assessment during its formative years. Only toward the end of the term of its first director, did the OTA make an effort to consolidate knowledge about methods of technology assessment in the private sector and in government. A review, culminating in a report based on hearings before the TAB (OTA 1977), concluded that technology assessment was an increasingly useful tool for medium and long-term management in both sectors.[3] It could provide early warning of unanticipated consequences as well as analysis of options and alternatives. It should be "tailor-made to fit the resources, timing, and needs of the decision makers." Under its second director (1977–1979), the OTA engaged in a priority-setting enterprise that solicited input from more than 5,000 members of the public (OTA 1979). Analyst Bruce Bimber (1996) writes critically that the "exercise was a classic policy analyst's attempt at determining national priorities through technical non-political means. It outraged many legislators who recognized it as a rejection of Congress's own agenda-setting processes." Nevertheless, the senior staff members who participated in the process devised criteria for determining whether OTA might fruitfully conduct an assessment on any given topic. The critical questions were:

- Can OTA do the assessment?
- Does the assessment involve the impact of technology?
- Is there congressional interest?
- Does the technology impact significantly on the quality of life and human needs?
- Would the assessment provide foresight? (OTA 1979)

The OTA began a self-review process in September 1992 to scrutinize its aims and operations. That marked a break from the past, identifying the OTA's work as a specific form of policy analysis, although the printed report begged the question of what policy analysis is by defining it as the activity of policy analysts (OTA 1993). The study identified two standard aspects of OTA's policy analysis: (1) the description of the context of a policy problem and the presentation of the relevant information that might require congressional attention, and (2) the discussion of potential solutions or options that Congress might choose to adopt. It was not clear, however, what was the appropriate balance of attention to context and options. This work identified three primary criteria of good policy analyses: objectivity, reader-friendliness, and timeliness. Congressional staff acknowledged the OTA's reputation for objectivity as one of its "chief assets" (OTA 1993). However, there was no consensus among the staff about what it meant to be "objective" and the term was variably used to signal a range of different virtues, from the absence of issue-related bias to evidence of scientifically based literature and data.

Reforms, some hastily planned, were in the works in the summer of 1995, when Congress eliminated the OTA by refusing to appropriate funds for it. In retrospect, the motivations behind this action can be traced in part to the OTA's own self-review: the criticisms articulated in that report—and particularly the recognition by the OTA staff—that they were "expected to do more better, faster—without compromising the integrity of the assessment process" (OTA, 1993) were prescient, foreshadowing the congressional hostility that spelled its demise. But perhaps more importantly, it got caught in a struggle between the Clinton administration and a new conservative Congress dominated by Newt Gingrich. The conservatives had promised to eliminate federal agencies, and OTA was the easy one, as an agency that prided itself on nonpartisanship had not natural constituency to lobby for its survival.

Even this brief history of the OTA reveals an organization poised on the awkward boundary between politics and science, charged to provide technically oriented, unbiased foresight to a traditionally short-sighted, partisan, and politically-motivated legislative body. As such, the OTA's trajectory illustrates the essential question concerning strong bipartisan support for using forms of peer review in regulatory science, in congressional, federal regulatory agencies, courtrooms (Berger 2000; Breyer 2000), and states (CGS 1999).[4]

II. FROM EXPERTISE ADVICE TO PARTICIPATORY TECHNOLOGICAL ASSESSMENT (PTA)

The example of the OTA inspired ideas in other countries, particularly in Europe, where new developments arose within a diversity of regulatory institutions. These institutions basically followed the OTA model. And, as we will see, the same conflicts and questions emerged concerning the roles, the methods and the impact of TA. Although the OTA made extensive use of stakeholders as members of panels and reviewers of drafts, it made little effort to include lay-citizens in its assessment (Bereano 1997). But somewhat later, the concept of TA began to evolve in new direction, including greater lay participation. First, the addressees of TA studies were not always legislators but increasingly also the bureaucracy and other levels of government. Moreover, while the United States approach to assessment was based on technological expertise, it later began to involve stakeholders and a wider public in the processes. European TA, in contrast, struggled from the outset with the challenge to integrate interests and values of all parties throughout the assessment. TA practitioners have subsequently adopted more participatory methods (Dürrenberger, Kastenholz, and Behringer 1999; Van Eijndhoven 1997), such as focus groups, citizens' panels (Joss and Durant 1995; Brown 2006; Guston 1999; Hörning 1999), and scenario workshops (Andersen and Jaeger, 1999; Sclove 1999). Devices of this kind provoke some key political questions concerning the form of participation and different implicit social ontologies (Kahane 2002).

After the European BSE (mad-cow) crises, consumers became more recalcitrant about issues such as GM food. Important normative notions (such as the precautionary principle) now[5] set an important moral and juridical meta-standard, serving to frame certain political decisions concerning scientific and technological choices.[5] In February 1992, the Maastricht Treaty had introduce the PP as one of the foundational principles for a European policy on the environment, and the Resolution of the European Council at Nice[6] explored PP in greater detail in more than 20 articles.[6] The need for a stronger, more pluralist participation in the assessment process has become a high priority (Fischer 1999; Reber 2005b). The politicization of TA activities by integrating participatory elements has its origins in the recognition that the state is accountable to often conflicting demands: new developments in science and technology put public authorities under pressure as they are faced with *uncertainty* about the consequences of these developments and with a plurality of values and interests about them. In this sense, the development of PTA arrangements is a kind of partial response to the wider problem of the legitimacy and scope of state authority.

We have to recognize that these questions are not easy ones. Who is qualified to speak to them and decide? How is it possible to map the values concerned (Fischer and Forester 1987; Hill 1992)? The profound impact on everyday life and the political system bring to varying degrees of uncertainty with them: cognitive (what are they really?), normative (linked with a plurality of values, compatibility with ethical standards or notions) and pragmatic (what should we do given the situation?) (Hennen 1999).

With a wide diversity of approaches, PTA has opened up spaces in which different agents exchange views, deploy diverse modes of communication such as narration, interpretation, argumentation, and reconstruction, to mention only a few.[7] The recent methodological wealth in this can be illustrated by a simple enumeration of the types of procedures now in play: citizen juries, consensus conferences, deliberative conferences, *Delphi* and *Charette* methods, expert panels, focus groups, planning teams, scenarios workshops, perspective workshops, consumer workshops focused on "visions of the future," global cafés, direct initiatives and referendums, public surveys, public auditions, opinion polls (with or without deliberation), multiple choice questionnaires, discussion and negotiation between interest groups, citizens' councils and committees, voting conferences, interactive technological evaluation (TE), constructivist TE of consumers, interdisciplinary working groups and political role-playing.[8]

These experiments can take place in a synchronous or asynchronous manner, with the real presence of participants or by means of information and communication technology (ICT). They vary according to the motivations driving them (e.g., focus on counseling or decisions), their aims (e.g., cartography of the diversity of positions, consensus building or deliberative disagreement), their themes (e.g., public or little-known, complex and controversial), the social and institutional context, the moment of their realization, the human and financial means which they have, and lastly, their modes of "arrangement"—from the definition of the objectives, recruitment, and equity in the implementation of the procedures, to carrying out the decisions and perhaps involving political figures in the procedures) (Reber 2005a).

It is clear that TA exploits many methods. It is impossible to describe each of them in detail here. Nevertheless, some methods constitute the core of the TA "method toolbox," while new methods are continually being introduced. In fact, the TA method toolbox expands with time and with new institutions joining the TA community.[9] We can trace back the TA historical trajectory to the first expansion of the toolbox in the TA history the first expand of the method toolbox when classical or scientific expertise (expertise in the "hard" sciences) was supplemented with *participatory* or interactive methods. These two types of methods are now considered as current TA practice.

We will now show how some of these methods of PTA reflect explicit choices, which privilege and take charge of certain phases of public evaluation.

A. SUBMITTING AN ISSUE TO DISCUSSION: CITIZEN JURIES

As its name indicates, this was originally a type of legal deliberation, specifically, in jury procedures and Assize Courts (Stewart, Kendall, and Coote 1994). A group of 12 to 24 people, selected at random, is invited for a period of three days to a week to give its opinion, by vote or in an agreement, on a given issue (Veasey 2002). Jurors are selected according to their degree of closeness to the issue, as well as certain socio-demographic categories (age, profession, gender, place of residence, cultural identity). A significant amount of work, over four to five months, is done by an advisory committee, a working group and two moderators. These three groups are responsible for laying out the "mandate" or "charge" (*chef d'accusation*), in keeping with the trial metaphor. This distinctive methodological stage is elaborated with great care. (For instance, the "charge" can end up being divided.) Persons selected in phone interviews are asked to offer judgments, and to base these on what they hear from witnesses and experts, presented either alone or in panels. The issue is explained to the jurors by these experts, but other, more "neutral" individuals are also available to assist the jurors, either at the beginning of the auditions, or as long as they last. At least half of the time allotted to this phase is devoted to answering the questions of the jurors. The deliberation which follows can take up to a day, in order to arrive at a consensus, if possible. This deliberation either focuses on a single question or, when appropriate, on work done in subgroups on a number of themes. All information derived from the arguments presented and the votes cast is surveyed in the final report, which then becomes a key source for the individuals initiating the procedure. It follows that the moderators must have a great deal of skill, since they must not only chair the discussions, but facilitate deliberation and synthesis, while ensuring that answers remain on track in terms of the question posed.

B. LARGE-SCALE PARTICIPATION: ÉTATS GÉNÉRAUX

Many PTA-type processes have been criticized for being too inward-looking and fostering a *Loft Story*[10] environment which fails to engage an adequate number and diversity of participants. In response to this criticism (and to revive the old French tradition of General Assemblies or *États Généraux*), questions addressing food and health in particular have been more widely debated. I will examine one example of this alternative assessment procedure: the *Etats généraux de l'alimentation. Que voulons-nous manger?* (General assemblies on food issues entitled "What do we want to eat?"), (Joly and Marris 2002; Whiteside 2003). This assessment separated into two phases, a preparatory stage and an institutional stage.

The preparatory stage involved three modes of consultation:

1. An opinion poll, both qualitative and consultative, was conducted by the IPSOS agency, so as to identify the expectations, inquiries, contradictions, and overall perception of the

information pertaining to food. The results were made public in five regional forums, which were held for ten days in Lille, Lyon, Nantes, Marseille, and Toulouse.

2. Five "pre-forums" brought together approximately 100 people (eight tables of twelve people each), citizens, consumers, and professionals from the food industry. These discussion groups were filmed and took place in the presence of sociologists who also were in charge of evaluating the entire process. Each forum was organized in the same five cities. The discussions were meant to reach consensus but also to identify contradictory consumer expectations. They were completed by public debates organized throughout France by three consumer groups, on the specific theme of genetically modified organisms.

3. During the entire process of the *États Généraux*, a Web site was provided both inform the public and to receive questions.

The institutional stage fell into two parts:

1. Regional forums with 500 people were established in order to allow for an interactive discussion between local figures in the food sector, grass-roots organizations, elected officials, and health and education professionals. The themes that were discussed stemmed from opinion polls but also from pre-forums. The setting resembled a TV set, with a seven-person table for the experts, an eight-person podium for "members of civil society," and a third space for the journalist, accompanied by a philosopher or sociologist in charge of synthesizing or reinitiating the discussion.

2. The National Conference of the *États Généraux*, held on December 13, 2000 at the *Grande Arche de la Défence*, brought together more than 700 people, some of whom participated in the regional forums. Also present were figures from the agricultural and food industries, health professionals, consumer associations, representatives of local government, public health officials, members of the press, scientific experts, and three ministers. The speeches alternated between institutional discourse, excerpts from the "pre-forums" and the regional forums (including filmed excerpts), statements regarding four possible scenarios for the future, and debates with the audience. The prime minister pronounced the concluding remarks.

C. Group Inquiries: Consensus Conferences, Citizen Conferences or Publiforums

Consensus-oriented conferences (Andersen and Jaeger 1999; Joss and Durant 1995; Gossement 2003) citizen assemblies or publiforums comprise the emblematic apparatus of what has been called (somewhat facilely) "technical democracy" (Callon, Lascoumes, Barthe 2001; Sclove 1995; Kleinman 2000). A group of ten to thirty people is brought together for a total of seven days during three weekends. Their goal is prepare a conference at which experts will be heard, regarding questions stemming from a public scientific controversy. These citizens can be chosen by a polling organization, in a lengthy process designed to select "the most neutral individuals" or "the most naïve (*candide*)"[11] ones; they can also be selected through newspaper advertisements.[11] The first two weekends focus on acquiring knowledge about the premises and consequences of the chosen theme, collectively laying out the topics and questions for the roundtables, and choosing the experts. After the latter have been auditioned, the citizens put together a final report, which is released to the press. A scientific steering committee advises the institution in charge of the conference, and a moderator is always present to assist participants in the discussions.

Significant variations exist in the implementation of these procedures, which initially were carried out in Denmark. We will point out two major modifications with two examples of such experiments.

The first was akin to the format of consensus-oriented conferences and extended its perimeter to Europe: the "European Citizen's Deliberation Initiative. The Present and the Future of Brain Science"[12] (nine different countries; 2005–2006).[12] This project is the successor to several unsuccessful attempts, pan-European or trans-European, such as the "Euro-Forums on Human Genetics" (2001–2002), organized within the framework of the European Council.

The second was the *Debate on GMOs and Crop Experimentation*, organized by the Conseil Économique et Social[13] (Reber 2006). This assembly was comprised of three types of participants: (1) "citizens," represented by high school students, unemployed people, and young academic; (2) "experts," and (3) "sages"[14] who were in charge of writing up the final report, several weeks later. To be sure, this experiment is to be distinguished from a citizens' conference by the short time that was allotted for its preparation and organization.[15] The organizers themselves hoped in vain for a true citizens' conference on the subject, which would have taken place at the end of 2002.

D. Reflexive Evaluation: Inventory, Control, and Participative Evaluation (ICPE)

In the event of a crisis or as an intermediate stage in the development of a project, this methodology focuses on the act of evaluation proper. It asks the participants to share control and responsibility for evaluation with respect to questions such as: Assessment according to which methods? Involving whom? Using what data? Aiming at what type of restitution (Booth et al. 2001)? The duration of the process varies according to the theme and the number of people invited to participate. During the first meeting, which is open and informal, the participants discuss what they want to learn, the goals of the evaluation and the activities that are to be evaluated. Participants can suggest questions to be prioritized by the evaluation procedures and choose the type of indicators (direct or indirect) to best serve this end. Ideally, the indicators are well-chosen in relation to the participants' goals, and the overall quality, pertinence and availability of information. In this case, the entire process is simplified with respect to the quantity and scope of data collection. If appropriate, the evaluation group can choose to accumulate additional information, within the initially set deadline. At the end of this process, discussion centers on how to best analyze, synthesize, and present the data, based on the specific audience, the type of results that are expected, the decisions they might entail, and the available time and resources. This can be a moment for re-evaluating the questions posed at the outset. The presentation makes it easier to inquire into which conclusions should be drawn, what can be learned from the results, which new questions might have emerged, and what options there are for responding to existing problems, or problems emerging in the course of the survey. A plan of action is then drawn up and included in a report reviewing the entire process, focusing on what has been learned and identifying different available courses of action.

E. Secondary Evaluations

The extension of methods, from classical TA to PTA has broadened the kind of quality criteria a TA project should meet. Besides scientific quality criteria assessing the TA output, quality criteria for the TA process itself have been developed. The first comparative European evaluations of these practices were recently published, including "Methods of participation in evaluation and decision-making on technological matters" (EUROPTA) (Joss and Belluci 2003), "Technology Assessment in Europe; between Method and Impact" (TAMI) (Decker and Ladikas 2004), and the study entitled "Governance of the European Research Area: the role of civil society."[16] Other publications have contributed to this evaluation of PTA as well (Rowe and Frewer 2000; Fiorino 1990; Renn, Webler, and Kastenholz 1996; Callon, Lascoumes, and Barthe 2001; Joss 1999a: Klüver 2003). Having screened and evaluated technologies according to different methods, the organizers and researchers proceed in these latter publications to comparatively evaluate the process and the methodologies they used. Notwithstanding the reservations noted above, these meta-evaluations are principally concerned with the degree of public participation. Some studies speak of "participative democracy," importing a concept born in quite another context. Some authors who classify diverse PTA experiments, often suggest new standards in such diverse arenas as theories of democracy (borrowed from authors like Barber, Beck, Giddens, Habermas, and Luhmann in theories of participative, deliberative, and dialogic democracy), procedural justice, communication theories, and even views on modernity. Among the criteria these authors propose are: representativeness, independence, openness, quality of arguments, early commitment, influence, transparency, accessibility of the information, relevance, definition of the tasks, structuralization of the decision, equal power to every participant, loyalty in interpersonal relations, flexibility allowing participants to make their own agenda and the cost-efficiency balance of the operation.[17]

These interesting lists could be expanded. Such criteria, however, have evident weakness. They arguably place a disproportionate weight on participation over technological and evaluative (especially moral) aims. This is a point to which I shall return in my conclusion. We will see before how TA, mainly in its participative form, combines sciences, technologies and policy.

III. GOALS AND IMPACTS OF TA

TA is a generic term for nonuniform (Joss and Belluci 2003) and even partly contradictory approaches and activities. Therefore definitional problems have arisen (Grunwald 2002). Some TA definitions are based on its goals and functions of it: focusing on the contribution of TA to the social problem solving; certain special aims, like early warning against technically induced risks or the aims of innovation funding. Other definitions attend to methods used and the main categories TA uses regarding participation. Still others focus on the subject matter of the TA process—its concrete targets of investigation and which aspects of technology it concerns. Finally, the TAMI project, involving both researchers and practitioners, put forward a common definition that also reflects the "addresses" of the TA process: "Technology assessment is a scientific, interactive and communicative process which aims to contribute to the formation of public and political opinion on societal aspects of science and technology."

Thus defined, what are the possible roles (Bütschi and Nentwich 2002), goals, and impacts of TA?

A. Scientific Assessment on Consequences and Options

Two classic roles of TA are related to its function of making scientific knowledge available for decision makers as comprehensive as possible: (1) comprehensive overview of consequences, and (2) technical options assessed and reconstructed. The first role provides a presentation of the possible[18] consequences connected with a specific technology. Growing demands to apply scientific methods to anticipate long-term effects are increasing awareness of the ways in which techno-scientific progress almost always incurs unintended consequences for society, economy, and the environment. To this end TA draws on a range of scientific procedures such as risk assessment or economic modeling.[19]

The second role tries to objectivize technical options and to assess the viability of different technological paths by means of foresight studies or scenario writing, to facilitate rational decision making in innovation policies. The added value of TA lies in a comprehensive overview of possible effects (including but not restricted to economic cost-benefit calculations) as a fundamental prerequisite for policy making (OECD, 1983; Paschen and Petermann 1991). It is true that research and development policy making has to deal with high degrees of uncertainties with regard to future outcomes in contexts in which stakes are often high and decisions are urgent (Funtowicz and Ravetz 1992). New technologies or research areas are often promoted by powerful techno-scientific communities that might overestimate chances and underestimate risks. TA can help to broaden the analysis, including views of other expert communities (inter- and intradisciplinary pluralism) (Reber,2005b), and give a more complete and comprehensive view on possible effects of implementation of a technological innovation.

B. Extending the Scope and Efficacy of Research and Development Policy

If an identified problem requires additional research, a TA project might update the research agenda. The assessment of various research options may in turn lead to recommendations for a re-orientation of research policy. Research and development policy may be interpreted in part as a response to "market failure": it can steer technological developments according to societal needs—needs to which the market might be indifferent. In this way it stands to influence the social shape of upcoming new technologies (creating supply-push driven needs) as well as triggering the development of new, socially useful technologies (responding to demand-pull driven needs). Thus knowledge of the spectrum of possible technological solutions available to meet social requirements is strategic. This dimension of TA had its genesis in the Dutch concept of "Constructive TA" (CTA) (Rip, Misa, and Schot 1995; INRA 2003). It promotes the technology that is sensitive to social objectives such as environmental protection (e.g., reducing the consumption of natural resources as well as the environmental waste and pollution). It also increases the interaction between assessment and analysis on the one hand, and the design of new technologies on the other and tries to serve a constructive role in technological and societal choice, maximizing the benefits and minimizing the problems that may be associated with knowledge-based innovation. It conceives of technological products as flexible entities, co-produced by the social contexts of their invention and use rather than as black boxes to which society must adapt. Thus, the tenets of CTA include: (1)early and controlled experimentation to identify and possibly ameliorate unanticipated consequences, (2) interaction between innovators and the public, (3) socio-technical mapping, (4) and combination of traditional stakeholder analysis with the plotting of technical activities.

C. Evaluating the Consequences of Policies and Laws

Within the preparation phase of a political or legislative decisions (and following its implementation), it is essential to explore that decision's objectives in light of its foreseeable consequences, including its scientific and social effects. Some critics of the precautionary principle (Sunstein 2005a, 2005b) precisely target the consequences of new laws. Over the past few decades, there has been growing debate about the role of the public in determining policy regarding issues of science and technology, and evolving it in policy decision making when feasible (e.g., Rosener 1978; Renn 1992; Bradbury 1994; Klauenberg and Vermulen 1994).

D. Agenda-setting

Raising awareness of the consequences of new technologies in controversial cases might be an important goal for TA, particularly if these are not already included in the political or public agendas. TA institutes working on behalf of parliaments can collaborate with the agenda-setting processes in different ways. Sometimes TA agents are charged to solicit comments on governmental policy papers, or the TA institute is asked to give advice or to provide additional researches on a specific issue during congressional hearings. These interventions need not result in political decisions, but they certainly serve to increase political awareness.

E. SOCIAL MAPPING IN CONTROVERSIAL ENVIRONMENTS

Technological controversies often highlight the fact that different actors, social groups, epistemic communities, and at times,researchers, arrive at different assessments depending on their interests, preferences, values (Kuhn 1977), epistemic, and moral evaluations (Reber 2005b). The analysis of these competing elements—and of the conflicting expectations to which they give rise—may enhance awareness of the social context of policy making and may provide opportunities for conflict resolution in novel ways (Bellamy and Schönlau 2004; Sunstein 1996; Reber 2006a). "It can also be seen as an integral part of the assessment of risks and benefits since such assessment depends on values held by the assessor. Discourse analysis used to clarifying the interconnectedness of scientific arguments and expert judgments in debates revolving around ethical beliefs and world views, may separate facts from values and establish awareness of the fundamentally political character of technology debates which on the surface might appear as debates on scientific facts" (TAMI Report 2004, 63).

F. THE ROLE OF MEDIATION

A TA project might aim at overcoming "blockade" situations by stimulating self-reflection on the part of the actors or by developing bridge-building alternatives (INES 2004).[20] Here PTA procedures provide different types of "communication spaces," which, in turn, permit actors the opportunity to confront conflicting aims and interests with a minimum of normative constraints (e.g., constraints dictating minimal civility) (Chambat Fourniau 2001; Pharo 1991, 2004). They can also promote different forms of agreement and ways of achieving a convergence of views: compromise (Pennock and Chapman 1979), *modus vivendi*, deliberative disagreements (Rescher 1993), consensus (Habermas 1992), or compensation for violated interests. In cases of very new technologies with uncertain consequences and significant ethical implications, TA practitioners can take into account the need for parties to be heard equally, while restricting the modus of communication to relevant arguments (Klüver 2003; Habermas 1991;[21] von Prittwitz 1996). In this way participants can be gently compelled to stick to certain standards of civility and other minimal procedural rules in their discourse.[22] This process can promote the values of openness and fairness (Joss S. and Browlea 1999) among the representative actors, and hence TA can contribute to meta-level policy debates on the "political culture." Ideally, the decision-making process would approximate to the rules of democratic deliberation.[23] The task is both ambitious and tricky, however any commitment to a formal process of discourse can (from a stakeholders' perspective) be perceived as dangerous, either because its outcomes are unpredictable (van den Daele 1995) or because it may promise to promote an unwanted asymmetry (Stengers 1997).[24]

G. REFRAMING THE POLICY DEBATE

With the growing importance of technologies for societal development, the issue of trust (Durant 1999) in experts is moving to the center of the technology debate (Giddens 1991). TA projects stand to increase the comprehensiveness of the debate. New ways must be found for science and society to negotiate uncertainties (Nowotny, Scott, and Gibbons 2001). TA know-how can contribute to this aim, particularly through participatory procedures based on special cooperative arrangements between scientists and nonscientists. This collaboration can mitigate differences in problem definition, interpretations, and evaluations of data and knowledge, and do so in a manner more responsive to wider social perceptions and interests. Comprehensiveness might be increased by taking into consideration the viewpoints of more actors, their different perspectives, and rationales (technical, ethical, social, economical, environmental). It may yield a clearer evaluation of the conflicting policy options and participants' (relevant actors) reasons for consent and dissent, giving way to more finely tuned policies. In these ways TA holds the promise of reframing discussions on policy options, including policy goals and means of political intervention.

H. New Forms of Governance and Decision-Making Processes

TA can contribute to the decision-making process by assessing how existing policies tally with salient assumptions and preferences. It may explore alternative policy options, probable effects, and the efficacy of different instruments such as financial measures (environmental tax, voluntary agreements) or legal regulations. With regard to technologies (often subject to international standards), TA needs more frequently to benchmark policies and deliver information on options for an internationally sound system of regulation. It might even be a goal for TA to recommend alternative forms of governance, both responsive and accountable to informed public debate (Callon, Lascoumes, and Barthe 2001).

I. New Policies

A TA-project might recommend concrete policy activities, if a new technology signals the need for an extension or modification of existing laws, as in the case of legislation concerning bioethics and informatics. Another possible goal is the assessment of different technology policy alternatives.

Of course, a TA project might address several objectives at once and aim both at improving knowledge of a new emerging technology and informing the public about it. Goals must be flexibly and realistically defined in accordance with the particular situation within which the TA institution operates. Perhaps the demise of the OTA was in part because of its failure to acknowledge in this way how its specific circumstances determined the aims it could reasonably achieve.

CONCLUDING PERSPECTIVES

Knowledge, as Albaek (1995) has put it, including scientifically-produced knowledge, "flows into the decision making process through obscure channels from many different sources, and this results in a more general awareness of the way the world appears and is structured."

Scientific advice (and TA in particular) often increases the complexity of decision making since it provides a largely unbiased and pluralist picture of the problem (including areas of uncertainty). Science does not make the decision-making process a straightforward one. It does not, however, diminish the degree of a problem's complexity and uncertainty (Banse, Hronszky, and Nelson 2005). Rather, it increases that complexity and makes the uncertainties more vivid, leaving politicians with the task of making decisions within a context of scientific controversy (von Schomberg 1992; Reber 2006c). Thus, TA cannot easily be exploited to promote the agendas of particular agents; it seldom yields the direct solutions so often sought by policy makers.

New data, more sophisticated interpretations, and informed arguments should not be regarded as "magic bullets" that can directly target legislation, fiscal policies, or the design of political programs.

That has been made clear in studies on the uses of TA. Those studies also show that while policy makers can reasonably expect TA to provide "conceptual clarifications" (Caplan 1979) of scientific knowledge, TA results rarely deliver a "guideline" for political action. "Conceptual clarification" typically confers three benefits: (1) an increased awareness of the complex interconnection of the target problems with different fields of policy making, (2) a better awareness of previously unforeseen effects, and (3) changes in the policy makers view on priorities for political action.

The constraints on the use of TA in policy making are manifold (Paschen and Petermann 1991), owing to the resources needed to facilitate interaction between TA researchers and policy makers, as well as time restriction on the collection, consolidation, and dissemination of results. We have to recognize too that the scientific staff of a TA organization often lacks experience of policy culture, despite the fact that some lead double career paths and are trained both in the hard sciences and in policy making. Scientific analysis and political action are based on different "logics" and procedures that are quite simply worlds apart. Scientific knowledge is likely to be strategically used (or ignored) opportunistically in the negotiation of different policy-making interests. The relations between science, technology, and politics are also subject to different modes of articulation (Shapin and Schaffer 1985; Latour 1999). In addition to the necessity for technocratic and institutional legitimacy, the demand for justification arose (Habermas 1968), explicit or implicit, especially in a media world, insisting on reasons after or before political actions. TA, and particular PTA, have the comparative advantage: they demand deeper justifications for political policies and create a structure within which normative and scientific issues are granted a clearer voice.

In practice, democratic politics in today's complex societies are subject to numerous rules and constraints. In practice, democratic procedures tend too often to be rather perfunctory and replace the richness of deliberation with referenda (not direct) or elections by acclamation. The linguistic/rhetorical potential of the citizen in a contemporary democracy is arguably reduced to his capacity to declare, "I choose this candidate" or "I agree with/reject this position on this issue," or even "I abstain and shall go fishing.[25] Curiously enough, the possibility of more innovative discursive rules, enabling a greater degree of "publicity" (the Kantian *Öffentlichkeit*) and opportunity for participation, emerges at a locus of particularly great complexity—at the interface between the sciences and society, in the area of participative technological assessment. To be sure, there is nothing new about taking account of the impact of technological innovations on society.[26] Neither is it new to voice concern for the democratic response to this impact (i.e., to the consequences of such innovations on the society) on the affected people and on the political process. In John Dewey's pragmatism, for instance, one finds these issues considered within an overall program for the human and social sciences (Dewey 1927). It was precisely in order to bring to light and evaluate these consequences that Dewey developed an entire (and voluminous) theory of inquiry (Dewey 1938). Increased participation on the part of the public, as called for in PTA, is not unique to this arena.[27] TA's main innovations (aside from the currency it has conferred on principles such as the participation of the public and the principle of precaution)[28] have to do with rethinking our procedural and methodological commitments and our opportunities to make different socio-ontological choices with respect to our ultimate goals. Beyond these policy considerations, I wish to mention two topics that merit further attention.

Too few philosophers are willing to confront the empirical and moral implications of PTA. Perhaps, like Jean-Pierre Dupuy,[29] we find the point of view of Sirius less demanding and prefer to inhabit the subsidiary regions of bioethics or environmental ethics, avoiding the thorny problem of how to mediate social and political interests.

From this point of view, Armin Grunwald's work (1999) and studies like that of the INES project ("Institutionalisation of Ethics in Science Policy: Practices and Impacts")[30] seem to me more fruitful, for they, at least, attempt to identify objectives for research in ethics and PTA. But still the question remains difficult, because of the distance between two asymmetric normative traditions—the ethics of technology and TA—each of which is based on fundamentally different assumptions and epistemic standpoints concerning technology policy. The first emphasizes the normative implications of decisions on technology and the importance of moral or ethical conflicts (Grunwald 1996), while the second relies mainly on descriptive sociological research (Petermann 1991).[31] But prominent sociological descriptions (like other kinds of sociological constructivism) have had "precious little to say about science and technology policy" (Giere 1993). Radder (1996) recognized that they often tap into normative issues in the course of their empirical studies but accuses them of failing to develop systematic responses to the inevitable normative dimensions. Some authors invite sociologists to practice "naturalistic epistemology," "to extrapolate from *is* to *ought*" (Fuller 1988), but the matter is not so simple between sociology (Pharo 2004) and philosophy. Many philosophers, after all, recognize the distinction of facts and values without insisting on a strict dichotomy between them (Putnam 2002; Lee 1985). Surely research methods in the sciences and policy making could be followed (as in Fischer 2003)[32] that permit an interpretative bridge between the empirical and normative dimensions of a given issue.

Perhaps a more stable approach is on offer from contemporary philosophy (Kagan 1998; Rachels 1998). A research program integrating discourse analysis and moral philosophy, I believe, would be both ground-breaking and fruitful. One way to pursue this would be to investigate the implicit moral theories of different actors in a policy scenario. Philosophical ethics need not be purely normative nor in line with the Habermasian approach to the justification and management of political procedures. Styles of argumentation taken from moral philosophy and used for purposes of justification merit our attention in this context (Reber 2006b). The evaluation of PTA devices from the interface of moral philosophy and the descriptive sciences could provide insight into the relations between ordinary speech, normative democracy and moral theories. Current scientific controversies targeting the precautionary principle cry out for attention of this kind.

Comparing U.S. and European studies and policies on risk, we find a powerful difference based on the putative distinction the "precaution principle" vs. "science-based regulations" in cost-benefit analysis (CBA) (Burgess 2004; Sunstein 2005).[33] However, this suggests a false and misleading dichotomy (Stirling 1999; Zaccaï and Missa 2000; Gossement 2003). A more accurate distinction might be made between "narrow" bases for regulation provided by the formal concept of risk and the broad framework associated with "precaution" where the latter includes an acknowledgement of the multidimensional scope of risk, the incommensurability of different classes and aspects of risk, and the formal conditions of strict uncertainty and ignorance (Godard 1997). If scientific practice itself is more often guided by such considerations, then the precautionary approach may be, in fact, the more "scientific" one (Stirling 1999). It emerges that more systematic attention needs to be paid to the formulation of the exogenous and intrinsically subjective "framing assumptions" and to their validity in the context of the values and priorities co-existing in a pluralistic society. An essential complement to science lies in the development of procedures such as PTA, providing vital contextual information on values and priorities, with which to frame scientific practice and to foster social appreciation of the different dimensions of risk. It is clear that there exists a positive role for dissent as well as for the recognition of consensus: PTA holds out the promise of a better understanding of the different aspects of technological risks, and of more effective regulatory instruments[34] manifesting the very "precautions" today's democracies so urgently need.[35]

NOTES

1. They describe a change over time in the TAB from a kind of joint committee to a Board of directors, and in TAAC from active managers to a visiting committee.
2. This work is archived in OTA (1995) and at Web sites maintained at the National Academy of Sciences and at Princeton University. http://www.wws.princeton.edu/ota/
3. The hearing highlighted research managers from industry who praised technology assessment as a

managerial tool, in part, perhaps, to defuse some criticism and fears from industry that OTA was created to be a regulatory body. See "The Debate over Assessing Technology," *Business Week* (April 8,
1972).

4. See also Chubin and Hackett (1990), Jasanoff (1990), Smith (1992).
5. Certainly, this principle enjoys recognition at the international level with the Declaration of Rio on the
    environment and sustainable development, adopted on June 10, 1992, or the agreement on the access to
    information, the participation of the public in decision making and the access to justice on the environ-
    ment, of June 25, 1998, called the Agreement of Aarhus.
6. Held December 7–20, 2000.
7. To use the categories proposed by Ferry J-M, 1991. Research in this area pays more attention to the
    manner in which data bases are constituted by analyzing the computer technologies and communication
    techniques made use of in these procedures, whether through imagery projected on the screen, cyber
    cards or sophisticated software for simulation purposes. See for example, Latour 2005.
8. For more detailed, but not (exhaustive) presentations, see Slocum (2003), for France, see *Le catalogue
    des instruments*, published for the National Commission on Public Debate, 2004.
9. See European Parliamentary Assessment Web site: http://www.eptanetwork.org/EPTA/
10. The term refers to a French reality TV show, *Loft Story*, which filmed a group of about ten people shar-
    ing an apartment in the course of about 24 hours.
11. "Naïve" (*candide*) is the astonishing term used by the organizers of the French Conference on GMOs
    in Food and Agriculture (Conférence française sur les OGM dans l'alimentation et dans l'agriculture)
    held in 1998.
12. See http://www.meetingmindseurope.org.
13. "Débat sur les OGM et les essais au champ," held in Paris February 4th, 2002. See the Web site: http://
    www.conseil-economique-et-social.fr/ces_dat2/plan.htm.
14. Four different public personalities responsible for their institutions and who were asked to organize
    this conference: Jean-Yves Le Déaut, President of the *Office Parlementaire d'Evaluation des Choix
    Scientifiques et Technologiques* (OPECST), (French *Parliamentary Office of Scientific and Technologi-
    cal Assessment* (POSTA)), Jacques Testart, President of the *Commission Française du Développement
    Durable*, (French *Commission for Sustainable Development*), Didier Sicard, President of the *Comité
    Consultatif National d'Ethique pour les sciences de la vie et de la santé* (CCNE), (*National Advisory
    Committee on Ethics*) and Christian Babusiaux, President of the *Conseil National de l'Alimentation*,
    (National Council for Food Consumption).
15. To such an extent that some people described it as a "parody of a citizens' conference."
16. See http://europa.eu.int/comm/research/science-society/documents_en.html.
17. For a presentation of these stimulating essays and a critic see (Reber 2005b).
18. That should be done with all the modal nuances like plausibility, possibility, probability (different sorts)
    and necessity. We have to recognize that it's rarely the case.
19. As we will see with the precautionary principle and risk assessment.
20. It could be a role for TA practitioners and sometimes for ethicists.
21. With all the empirical limits of this theoretical and reconstructed approach, with is much more concerned
    with social theories than socio-linguistics analyses.
22. Which are sometimes far to be respected if researchers try to empirically check if they are always
    respected or not (Reber 2003).
23. See "Legitimisation by process" (Luhmann 1992) or (Gutman and Thompson 1996; Leydet 2002; Cohen
    1989).
24. For a critic of the strong and original position of this philosopher of sciences regarding the questions
    of tolerance, impartiality and attachment, see (Reber 2006b).
25. To be sure, results of elections or referendums can be interpreted as one likes, *ad libitum*; moreover,
    one can also distinguish between electoral democracies and democracies of expression, implication and
    intervention (Rosanvallon 2004).
26. They already were a particular concern of the philosopher Hans Jonas, as early as 1959.
27. For instance, Robert A. Dahl (1998), but also the experiments in local democracy that have become
    increasingly frequent in the last ten years (i.e., the possibility of voting on a small participative budget,
    as in the Parisian suburb of Saint-Denis).
28. See, e.g., the French law on local democracy (*démocratie de proximité*) that redefined the statutes of the

National Commission on Public Debate (law 2002-276 of February 27, 2002), or, further, law 95-101 of February 2, 1995, known as the "loi Barnier" that reinforces the protection of the environment.

29. In Dupuy (2002). As a "rationalist extremist" the urgency is for him "conceptual before being moral or political." "Before imagining political and technical procedures which would allow a technical and scientific democracy to envisage what it wishes to accomplish (...) we need to define the nature of the evil we are faced with." As a skeptic with regard to collective rationality, particularly as regards its procedural and deliberative aspect, he caustically took a swipe at the French Prime Minister's Report on the precautionary principle under the direction of Kourilsky P. and Viney G. (1999), whom he styles "post-modernists" still resigned to using collective procedures. He is not more kindly inclined toward sociologists of the "hard" sociology of history of sciences. See pp. 24, 13, 21–23.

30. The Institutionalisation of Ethics in Science Policy: Practices and Impacts. See http://www.cesagen.lancs.ac.uk/research/related/ines.htm.

31. Ethics is not the only normative field. Law, economy, and part of political sciences are normative too.

32. Four interrelated discourses that outline the concern of postempiricist policy evaluation, or in a minimal moral methodology like in (Kaiser and Forsberg, 2000; Mepham, 2000).

33. Very often these studies depart widely from the minimal legal conceptions of risk such as those enshrined in the European Communication, the Nice Resolution, the Barnier law 1995, and the Environmental Chart of the French Constitution (2004).

34. Incremental regulatory instruments embodying varied degrees of "precaution," including a wide range of permutations on the relatively prominent themes of consultation, freedom of information, planning research, monitoring, corporate responsibility, compensation, tax incentives, insurance, liability, criteria of best practice, minimum standards, phase-outs, and the burden of proof.

35. Thanks to Prof. Alison Deham, Fellow and Tutor in Philosophy at St Anne's College, Oxford University, for helping with the translation of this chapter.

BIBLIOGRAPHY

Albaek, E. (1995). Between Knowledge and Power. Utilisation of Social Science in Public Policy Making. *Policy Sciences, 28*, 79–100.

Andersen, I. E., and Jaeger, B. (1999). Scenario Workshops and Consensus Conferences: Towards More Democratic Decision-Making. *Science and Public Policy, 26*(5), 331–340.

Banse, G., Hronszky, I., and Nelson, G. (eds.), (2005). *Rationality in an Uncertain World.* Berlin: Sigma.

Bellamy, R., and Schönlau, J. (2004). The Normality of Constitutional Politics: An Analysis of the Drafting of the EU Charter of Fundamental Rights. *Constellations, 11*(3), 412–433.

Benjamin, M. (1990). *Splitting the Difference. Compromise and Integrity in Ethics and Politics.* Lawrence: Kansas University Press.

Bereano, P. L. (1997). Reflections of a Participant-Observer: The Technocratic/Democratic Contradiction in the Practice of Technology Assessment. *Technological Forecasting & Social Change, 54*(2&3), 163–176.

Berg, M. R., Michael, D. N., and Brudney, J. L. (1978), *Factors Affecting Utilisation of Technology Assessment in Policy Making.* Centre for Research on Utilisation of Scientific Knowledge. University of Michigan.

Berger, M. A. (2000). Expert Testimony: The Supreme Court's Rules. *Issues in Science and Technology, 16*(4), 57–63.

Bimber, B., (1996). *The Politics of Expertise in Congress: The Rise and Fall of the Office of Technology Assessment.* Albany: State University of New York Press.

Bloch, E. (1959). *Das Prinzip Hoffnung.* Frankurt-a-Mainz: Suhrkamp.

Booth, W., Ebrahim, R., and Morin, R. (2001). *Participatory Monitoring, Evaluation and Reporting: An Organisational Development Perspective for South African NGOs,* Braamfontein: Pact/South Africa.

Bradbury, J. A., (1994). Risk Communication in Environmental Restoration Programs. *Risk Analysis, 14*(3), 357–363.

Breyer, S. G. (2000). Science in the Courtroom. *Issues in Science and Technology, 16*(4), 52–56.

Brown, M. (2006). Citizen Panels and the Concept of Representation. *The Journal of Political Philosophy* 13(2), 203–225.

Burgess, A. (2004). *Cellular Phones. Public Fears, and Culture of Precaution.* Cambridge: Cambridge University Press.

Bütschi, D., and Nentwich M. (2002). The Role of Participatory Technology Assessment in the Policy-making Process, in S. Joss, and S. Bellucci (eds.), *Participatory Technology Assessment—European Perspectives,* pp. 253–256, London: Westminster University Press.

Callon M., Lascoumes P., and Barthe Y., (2001). *Agir dans un monde incertain. Essai sur la démocratie technique.* Paris: Seuil.

Caplan, N. (1979). The two Communities Theory and Knowledge Utilisation. *American Behavioral Sciences,* 459–470.

Chambat, P.. and Fourniau, J.-M. (2001) Débat public et participation démocratique. In Vallemont S. (ed.), *Le débat public: une réforme dans l'État. LGDJ,* 9–37.

Chubin, D., and Hackett, Ed. (1990). *Peerless Science: Peer Review and US Science Policy.* Albany: SUNY Press.

Coates, V. (1999). Technology Forecasting and Assessment in the United States: Statistics and Prospects. *Futures Research Quarterly, 15*(3), 5–25.

Cohen, J. (1989). Deliberation and Democratic Legitimacy, in Hamlin A. and Pettit, P. (eds.), *The Good Polity. Normative Analysis of the State,* pp. 17–34. Oxford: Basil Blackwell.

Coote, A., Kendall, E., and Stewart, J. (1994). *Citizens' Juries.* London: Institute for Public Policy Research.

Council of State Governments (CSG). (1999). *A State Official's Guide to Sound Science.* Lexington, KY.

Dahl, R. A., (1998). *On Democracy.* New Haven, CT: Yale University Press.

Decker, M., and Ladikas, M. (eds.). 2004. *Bridges between Science, Society and Policy; Technology Assessment—Methods and Impacts.* Berlin: Springer.

Dewey, J. (1927), 1946. *The Public and its Problems,* Chicago: Gateway Books, Chicago.

———. (1938). *Logic: The Theory of Inquiry,* New York: Henry Holt.

Dupuy, J-P. (2002). *Pour un catastrophisme éclairé. Quand l'impossible est certain.* Paris: Seuil.

Durant, J. (1999). Participatory technology assessment and the democratic model of the public understanding of science, *Science and Public Policy, 26*(5), 313–319.

Dürrenberger, G., Kastenholz, H., and Behringer, J. (1999). Integrated Assessment Focus Groups: Bridging the Gap Between Science and Policy. *Science and Public Policy, 26*(5), 341–349.

Fiorino, D. J. (1990). Citizen Participation and Environmental Risk: A Survey of Institutionnal Mechanism. *Science,Technology & Human Values, 15*(2), 226–243.

Fischer F. (2000). *Citizens, Experts and the Environment: The Politics of Local Knowledge.* Durham, NC: Duke University Press.

———. (2003) *Reframing Public Policy. Discursive Politics and Deliberative Practices.* Oxford: Oxford University Press.

———. (1999). Technological Deliberation in a Democratic Society: The Case for Participatory Inquiry. *Science and Public Policy, 26*(5), 294–302.

Fischer F. and Forester J. (eds.) (1987). *Confronting Values in Policy Analysis. The politics of Criteria.* London: Sage.

Fuller, S. (1988). *Social Epistemology.* Bloomington, IN: University Press.

Funtowicz, S. O., and Ravetz, J .R. (1992), Three Types of Risk Assessment and the Emergence of Post Normal Science, in Krimsky, S. and D. Golding, *Social Theories of Risk,* pp. 252–274. Westport, CT: Praeger.

Giddens, A. (1991). *The Consequences of Modernity.* Cambridge: Polity Press.

Giere, R. N. (1993). Science and Technology Studies: Prospects for Enlightened Postmodern Synthesis. *Science, Technology, & Human Values, 18*(1), 102–112.

Godard, O. (1997). *Le principe de précaution dans la conduite des affaires humaines.* Paris, Ed. de la Maison des Sciences de l'Homme and INRA-Editions.

Gossement A., *Le principe de précaution. Essai sur l'incidence de l'incertitude scientifique sur la décision et la responsabilité publique.* Paris: L'Harmattan, 2003.

Grunwald, A. (2002). Technikfolgenabschätzung – Eine Einführung. Berlin: Sigma.

———. (1999). Technology Assessment or Ethics of Technology? Reflections on Technology Development between Social Sciences and Philosophy. Ethical Perspectives. *Journal of European Ethics Network, 6*(2), 170–182.

Guston, D. H. (1999). Evaluating the First US Consensus Conference: The Impact of the Citizens' Panel on Telecommunications and the Future of Democracy. *Science, Technology, & Human Values, 24*(4), 451–482.

Gutmann, A., and Thompson, D. (1996). *Democracy and Disagreement.* Boston: Harvard University Press.

Habermas, J. (1992). *Faktizität und Geltung. Beiträge sur Diskurstheorie des Rechts und des demokratischen Rechtsstaats.* Frankfurt-a-Mainz, 1992.

———. (1968). *Technik und Wissenschaft als "Ideologie."* Frankfurt-a-Mainz: Suhrkamp.

Hennen, L. (1999). Participatory Technology Assessment: A Response to Technical Modernity? *Science and Public Policy, 26*(5), 303–312.

Herdman, R. C., and Jensen, J. E. (1997). The OTA Story: The Agency Perspective. *Technological Forecasting & Social Change*, 54 (2&3), 131–144.

Hill, C. (1997). The Congressional Office of Technology Assessment: A Retrospective and Prospects for the Post-OTA World. *Technological Forecasting & Social Change*, 54(2&3), 191–198.

Hill S. (1992). *Democratic Values and Technological Choices.* Stanford, CA: Stanford University Press.

Hörning, G. (1999). Citizens' Panels as a Form of Deliberative Technology Assessment. *Science and Public Policy, 26(5),* 351–359.

INES Project. (2004–2006), *The Institutionalisation of Ethics in Science Policy. Practices and Impacts.*

INRA. (2003). *Co-construction d'un programme de recherche: une expérience pilote sur les vignes transgéniques.* Paris, INRA.

Jasanoff, S. (1990). *The Fifth Branch: Science Advisers as Policymakers.* Cambridge: Harvard University Press.

Joly P-B., and Marris C. (2002). "Que voulons-nous manger?," *Les Etats généraux de l'alimentation: enseignement d'une expérience de mise en débat public des politiques alimentaires,* Rapport Direction Générale de l'Alimentation, Paris. Available online at http://www.agriculture.gouv.fr/ega/presentation.

Jonas, H. (1979). *Das Prinzip Verantwortung.* Frankfurt-a-Mainz, Insel Verlag.

Joss, S. (ed.). (1999a). *Special Issue on Public Participation in Science and Technology. Science and Public Policy, 26*(5), 290–373.

Joss S., and Belluci, S. (eds.). (2003). Participatory Technological Assessment. European Perspectives. London: Westminster University Press.

Joss, S., and, Browlea, A. (1999b). Considering the concept of procedural justice for public policy and decision-making in science and technology , *Science and Public Policy, 2*(5), 321–330.

Joss, S., and Durant, John. (1995). *Public Participation in Science: The Role of Consensus Conferences in Europe.* London: Science Museum.

Kagan, S. (1998). *Normative Ethics.* Oxford: Westview Press.

Kahane, D. (2002). Délibération démocratique et ontologie sociale. *Philosophiques, 29,* 251–286.

Kaiser, M., and Forsberg, E. M. (2000) Assessing Fisheries—Using an Ethical Matrix in a Participatory Process. *Journal of Agricultural and Environmental Ethics, 14,* 91–200.

Klauenber, B. J., and Vermulen E. K. (1994). Role for Risk Communication in Closing Military Waste Sites. *Risk Analysis, 14*(3), 351–356.

Kleinman, K. L. (ed.). (2000). *Science, Technology & Democracy.* Albany: State University Press of New York.

Klüver, L. (2003). Project Management. A Matter of Ethics and robust Decision, in Joss S. and Bellucci S. (eds.), *Participatory Technology Assessment. European Perspectives.* London, Westminster University Press. From the Report: See http://www.tekno.dk/subpage.php3? article=345&language=uk&category=11&toppic=kategori11

Kourilsky, P., and Viney, G. (1999). *Le principe de précaution. Rapport au Premier ministre,* Paris: Odile Jacob and La Documentation française.

Kuhn, T. S. (1977). *The Essential Tension. Selected Studies in Scientific Tradition and Change.* Chicago:, University of Chicago Press.

Kunkle, Gregory C. (1995). New Challenge or the Past Revisited? The Office of Technology Assessment in Historical Context. *Technology in Society, 17*(2), 175–196.

Latour B., (1999). *Politiques de la Nature.* Paris: la Découverte.

Lee, K. (1985). *A New Basis for Moral Philosophy.* London: Routledge & Kegan.

Leydet, D. (ed.) (2002). *La démocratie délibérative. Philosophiques, 29*(2), 175–370.

Luhmann, N. (1992). *Beobachtungen der Moderne*. Opladen: Westdeutscher Verlag.

Mepham, T. B. (2000) A framework for the ethical analysis of novel foods: the ethical matrix. *Journal of Agricultural and Environmental Ethics, 12*, 165–176.

(French) National Commission on Public Debate. (2004). *Le catalogue des instruments*, Paris.

Nowotny, H., Scott, P., and Gibbons, M. (2001), *Rethinking Science — Knowledge and the Public in an Age of Uncertainty*. Cambridge: Polity Press.

OECD, (1983). *Assessing the Impacts of Technology on Society*. Paris: OECD.

Office of Technology Assessment (OTA). (1995). *OTA Legacy*. http://www.wws.princeton.edu/ota/

———. (1993). *Policy Analysis at OTA: A Staff Assessment*.

———. (1979). *OTA Priorities*. http://www.wws.princeton.edu/ota/

———. (1977). *Technology Assessment in Business and Government: Summary and Analysis*. http://www.wws.princeton.edu/ota/

Paschen, H., and Petermann, T. (1991), Technikfolgen-Abschätzung. Ein strategisches Rahmenkonzept für die Analyse und Bewertung von Techniken, in T. Petermann (ed.), *Technikfolgenabschätzung als Politikberatung*, pp. 19–42. Frankfurt: Campus.

Pennock, J. R., and Chapman, J. R. (1979) *Compromise in Ethics Law and Politics, Nomos XXI*. New York: New York University Press.

Pharo, P. (2004). *Morale et sociologie. Le sens et les valeurs entre nature et culture*. Paris: Gallimard.

———. (1991). *Politique et savoir-vivre. Enquête sur les fondements du lien civil*. Paris: L'Harmattan.

Putnam, H. (2002). *The Collapse of the Fact/Value Dichotomy, and Other Essays*. Cambridge: Harvard University Press.

Rachels, J. (ed.). (1998). *Ethical Theory*. Oxford: Oxford University Press.

Radder, H. (1996). *In and about the World: Philosophical Studies of Science and Technology*. Albany: State University of New York Press.

Reber, B. (2006a). Pluralisme moral: les valeurs, les croyances et les théories morales. *Archives de philosophie du droit, 48,* (forthcoming)

———. (2006b). Théories morales et *Cosmopolitiques*. L'épreuve de l'évaluation technologique participative. J. Lolive and O. Soubeyran (eds.), *Émergence des Cosmopolitiques et refondation de la pensée aménagiste*, Paris: Centre Culturel International de Cerisy-la-Salle, *La Découverte*, (forthcoming).

———. (2006c). Les controverses scientifiques. Paris, *Encyclopaedia Universalis, La Science au présent* 156–159.

———. (2005a). Public Evaluation and new Rules for 'Human Park', in B. Latour and P. Weibel, *Making Things Public. Atmospheres of Democracy*, pp. 314–119. Cambridge: MIT Press.

———. (2005b). Technologies et débat démocratique en Europe. *Revue Française de Science Politique, 55*, 811–833.

———. (2004). Ethique et évaluation technologique participative, in B. Castagna, S. Gallais, P. Ricaud, and J-P Roy (eds.), *La situation délibérative dans le débat public*, pp. 387–405 Tours: Presses Universitaires François Rabelais, vol. 2.

———. (2003). Les controverses scientifiques publiques au secours de la démocratie, *Cosmopolitiques, Cahiers théoriques pour l'écologie politique, 3*, 93–107.

Renn, O. (1992). Risk Communication: Towards a Rational Discourse with the Public. *Journal of Hazardous Materials, 29, 3*, 465–519.

Renn, O., Webler T., and Kastenholz, H. (1996). Procedural and substantive fairness in landfill sitting: a Swiss case study, *Risk: Health, Safety and Environment*, 145–168.

Rescher, N. (1993). *Pluralism. Against the Demand for Consensus*. Oxford: Oxford University Press.

Rip, A., Misa, Th. J., and Schot, J. (eds.). (1995). *Managing Technology in Society — The Approach of Constructive Technology Assessment*, London: Pinter.

Rosanvallon, P. (2004). Le mythe du citoyen passif, *Le Monde*, June 20–21, 1, 14.

Rosener, J. B. (1978). Citizen Participation: Can We Measure Its Effectiveness? *Public Administration Review*, *38(5)*, 457–463.

Rowe, G., and Frewer J. L. (2000). Public Participation Methods: A Framework for Evaluation. *Science, Technology and Human Values, 25*(1), 3–29.

———. (2004). Evaluating Public Participation Exercises: A Research Agenda *Science, Technology & Human Values, 29*(4), 512–557.

Sclove, R. (1999). The Democratic Politics of Technology: The Missing Half. The Loka Institute. Available online at http://www.loka.org/idt/intro.htm.

———. (1995). *Democracy and Technologies.* New York: Guilford Press.

Shapin, S., and, Schaffer, S. (1985). *Leviathan and the Air-Pump.* Princeton, NJ: Princeton University Press.

Slocum, N. (2003). *Participatory Methods Toolkit. A Practitioner's Manual.* Bruges: United Nations University.

Smith, B. L. (1992). *The Advisers: Scientists in the Policy Process.* Washington, DC: The Brookings Institution Press.

Stengers, I. (1997). *Cosmopolitiques,* tome 7: *Pour en finir avec la tolérance,* Paris: La Découverte-Les Empêcheurs de penser en rond.

Stewart, J., Kendall, E., and Coote, A. (1994) *Citizens' Juries.* London: IPPR.

Stirling, A. (1999). *Precautionary and Science-Based Approaches to Risk Assessment and Environnental Appraisal.* Sevilla: Institute for Prospective Technology Studies.

Sunstein, C. R. (2005a). *The Laws of Fear: Beyond the Precautionary Principle.* Cambridge University Press.

———. (2005b). Environmental Protection and Cost-Benefit Analysis. *Ethics, 115*(2), 351–385.

———. (1996). Incompletely Theorized Agreements, *Legal Reasoning and Political Conflict,* New York, Oxford: Oxford University Press, 35–61.

Van Den Daele, W. (1995). Technology Assessment as a Political Experiment, in von Schomberg, R. (ed), *Contested Technology,* pp. 63–90. Tilburg: International Centre for Human and Public Affaires.

Van Eijndhoven, J. C. (1997). Technology Assessment: Product or Process? *Technological Forecasting and Social change, 54,* 269–286.

Von Prittwitz, V. (ed.). (1996). *Verhandeln und Argumentieren.* Opladen: Leske und Budrich.

Von Schomberg, R. (ed.). (1992). *Science, Politics and Morality. Scientific Uncertainty and Decision Making.* Dordrecht: Kluwer Academic Publisher.

Veasey, K. (2002). *Citizen Jury Handbook,* Minneapolis, MN: Jefferson Center.

Whiteside, K. H. (2003). French Regulatory Republicanism and the Risks of Genetically Modified Crops. *French Politic, 1,* 153–174.

Zaccaï, E., and Missa, J-N. (2000). *Le Principe de précaution. Significations et conséquences.* Bruxelles: Ed. de l'Université de Bruxelles.

34 Public Policy Mediation: From Argument to Collaboration

David Laws and John Forester

In this chapter we explore the resonance between the work of policy analysis and the work of public policy mediation. Mediators' practice turns out not only to be a form of policy analysis but to have implications for advancing the broader practice of policy analysts as well. We examine public policy mediation as a form of practice that has developed in the United States over the past twenty years—a practice that "deform[s], constrain[s]...and enable[s]" policy-making in ways that can be practically instructive for all those interested in "exploring the communicative dimensions of collective debating and deciding on matters of collective concern," including, of course, debates about the substantive content of policy issues.[1]

Mediation responds in a practical and institutional way to the plural perspectives in contemporary policy analysis that challenge efforts to root choices in a single privileged viewpoint or a monopoly upon systematized reason. So our exploration of mediation takes on theoretical as well as practical significance. Assessing public policy mediation can also give us insight into what it means to "engender a practice" of deliberation as a response to a policy problem. Many features that shape contemporary policy analysis—from the reworking of policy's institutional base to the need to negotiate knowledge *in situ*, to demands to enhance democratic legitimacy directly in policy arrangements—all imply efforts best understood in this way, as constituents of deliberative practice (Laws and Hajer 2006).[2]

Such reflection on mediated negotiation practice can help us better understand the problems and tensions that have triggered recent interest in deliberative forms of policy assessment. Understanding policy analysis as it integrates features of mediation practice can help us to highlight institutional and deliberative opportunities that narrower epistemological notions of methods of inquiry neglect, distract us from, and undermine. Such institutional and performative features of mediators' work are just those that the turn to deliberative policy analysis has emphasized: the carefully selective framing of interests and concerns, the networks of actors that develop around policy problems, and the potential for practical deliberation on questions that draw together facts and values in the face of uncertainty (Hajer and Wagenaar, 2003; Forester).

Normatively, our account highlights failures of conventional forms of policy analysis that may leave the players in many policy settings with the equivalent of poorly negotiated policy outcomes, as well as without the benefits of the processual and substantive learning that mediated negotiations can enable. In short, if we can easily become more stupid (or strategically misinformed) when we're kept apart, acting unilaterally and poorly able to listen—either because of our defensiveness,

---

1. Gomart and Hajer 2002, p. 10.
2. Chambers (1996) in an effort to work out the practical implications of communicative ethics, notes that "[I]mplementing practical discourse, then, is not so much a question of setting up a constitutionally empowered 'body' of some sort as it is of *engendering a practice*." (171–172, emphasis added)

513

cynicism, arrogance, or overconfidence—policy analysis and planning can learn practically and productively from settings in which parties meet each other in ways that enable them to learn interactively, craft new options and, in the process, transform or rebuild their relationships. In improving policy analysis in these ways, we might further develop democratic policy-making practice and the possible meanings of democratic politics as well.

By "mediation" we refer to a form of practice that brings together diverse stakeholder representatives to listen to one another's concerns, to learn about environmental contingencies, and to negotiate consensus agreements on courses of action that they can then implement (Susskind et al. 1999). Students and practitioners of mediation share a set of terms that they actively contest—including, for example, "consensus," "stakeholder," and "neutrality"—in a continuing conversation about the commitments that define the practice. Because internal reflection on these issues is well developed, the debates in the mediation field resonate well with basic concerns of policy-makers in this period of institutional fragmentation and shifting bases of political legitimacy. We focus on a form of mediation practice called "mediated consensus building" that seeks to inform the development and implementation of public policy.[3] In consensus building processes a "mediator" engages, supports, and shapes the participation of diverse individuals who represent stakeholders. In what follows, we describe mediation with special attention to practicing mediators' points of view as they move through and develop a process that proceeds in a series of stages, from conflict assessment, through convening or constituting a deliberative process, to fact-finding and learning, to negotiating agreements that commits them to future action.

WHAT DO MEDIATORS DO?

In this section we provide a sense of what mediators do when they become involved in policy-making, echoing the model that mediators most often use to describe their practice.[4] This account elaborates mediation as a sequence of stages, each with a distinct character and focus, stages that anticipate and build on one another and are linked by the efforts of the mediator. Success in mediation typically means navigating the stages in this sequence and the transitions between them.[5] These stages pose distinct challenges and demands; each one requires that mediators bring competency to complex and contested policy controversies.

We focus here on four steps in this sequence of stages that animates public policy mediation. The first is the effort to assess the conflict or controversy to determine whether a fuller mediated conversation among interdependent stakeholders offers any promise for successfully negotiating an agreement on the policy issues at stake. The second is the convening of a diffuse assembly of representative actors as a group that will construct a sense of its own identity and its own ability to act. Third comes the parties' efforts to learn, to deal with disputed facts. We close by looking at the effort to negotiate practical solutions in light of strong differences of opinion and interest. Together, these moments illuminate a kind of pragmatic public deliberation whose theoretical and practical significance political scientists and analysts have recently discussed quite widely (Bohman and Rehg 1997; Dryzek 1987, 2000; Fischer 2000). All along the way we hope to address contemporary policy analytic themes like learning and reframing, at a performative as well as at a substantive level.

---

3. See Susskind, McKearnan, and Thomas-Larmer (1999) for a comprehensive view of the core commitments in public policy mediation.
4. The Consensus Building Institute describes the major phases of consensus building as: "Convene; Clarify Responsibilities; Deliberate; Decide; Implement Agreement." http://www.cbuilding.org/research/Cards/CB_ESSENSTEPS.pdf.
5. Mediators are also careful to note that success can involve parties reaching the agreement that it does not make sense to continue or to move on to the next stage.

ASSESSMENT

Public policy mediation usually starts with a request for help. Historically these appeals have been occasioned by controversies—for example, about the need to build something or prevent something from being built, about the need to make a rule, or about the allocation of risks or resources. Disputes over building affordable housing, siting waste treatment plants and halfway houses, creating standards for the cleanup of contaminated sites, the allocation of federal housing funds, or the federal regulation of crane safety operation are just a few of the situations in which public action has been contested and in which the public officials responsible have turned to mediation to find an alternative to traditional forms of policy development and implementation.

A mediator's first response—upon receiving any invitation to intervene—would be to undertake a "conflict assessment." Assessment is the institutional device that "enables the [mediator]—and thereby the convenor—to identify the relevant stakeholders, map their substantive interests, and begin to scope areas of agreement and disagreement among them" (Susskind and Thomas-Larmer 1999, 104). The formal focus of such a conflict or convening assessment is to determine whether it makes sense to take the next step and organize a formal meeting of stakeholder representatives given their diverse perspectives and goals and varying degrees of trust, and, if so, to suggest a design and preliminary agenda.[6] The mediator develops the assessment by interviewing the "stakeholders."[7] The mediator draws on the authority of the sponsoring agency to initiate these contacts and provide a context for discussion, but acts at arms length and by her own standards.

For the mediator, assessment provides a kind of "intake" mechanism that roots the intervention in direct interaction with everyone "[w]ho is involved and affected by the issues, ... [w]ho will need to implement any agreement that is reached ... [and] [w]ho could potentially block implementation of an agreement" (Carlson 1999, 179) This foundation of direct engagement expresses a practical sense of the demands of action and mediators' sense of the sources and importance of their legitimacy. Mediators, of course, are neither judges nor arbitrators. They seek to enable stakeholders to learn together, to assess and invent options creatively, and to negotiate mutually beneficial agreements upon action or policy.

> The legitimacy of consensus building processes, which are often used as adjuncts to more traditional democratic forums, depends on whether they are viewed by stakeholders and the public at large as representative of all interests and points of view. A bedrock principle of consensus-based processes, therefore, is that everyone with a stake in the decision should be represented at the table. This principle helps to ensure that any consensus agreement reached will be seen as legitimate by all relevant parties and have broad support when implemented. (Carlson 1999, 185)

The interview process by which mediators initially engage stakeholders is already a step in the process. The interview setting creates a sphere of intimacy in which the mediator tries "to get to know each stakeholder individually." At the same time mediators test the practicality of moving forward by educating "the stakeholders about what it takes to bring a consensus process to a successful conclusion." (Susskind et al. 1999, 104)

Finally, the interview process is a relational transaction in which stakeholders "assess the assessor" and gauge whether that person is likely to be impartial and effective as a mediator" (ibid). As mediator Susan Podziba (1998) put it:

---

6. Mediation originates in settings where advocates who press contending views reach impasse and request help in seeing if they can move forward. This anchors mediation in the need to act and in the disruption of action by anger, confusion, and disagreement over what is to be done. This anchors mediation in the particulars of problems, of time and place, and of the experience and aspirations of people affected by the action.

7. The term "stakeholder" provides legitimacy to parties' involvement and guides analysts' mapping of the issue networks (Heclo 1978) that exist around the problem.

When the process team began its work in Chelsea, its members were clearly 'outsiders' and, therefore, suspect. In seeking entry into the community, the mediator met with community leaders, the people others sought out for needed information. In meeting with these individuals, the mediator learned about the city, but perhaps more importantly, she let them know who she was. She answered questions about her work and family because she understood that the information shared with these leaders would be spread throughout the city. Thus, the interviews were a mechanism for informing the community about the 'outsiders' and they provided an opportunity for trusted people to obtain, and then share, real information with peers. (23)

In her account of working successfully to build consensus on a new city charter in Chelsea, Massachusetts, Podziba provides a sense of the scale and focus of the assessment process and the relationship between the substantive and relational facets of careful assessment practice:

The Chelsea Process commenced with approximately 40 interviews with community leaders—formal leaders and informal opinion makers. Interviewees ranged from sitting aldermen to heads of community organizations to the city Santa Claus. The interviews had multiple goals. First and foremost was to learn of the perceived causes of Chelsea's problem, why the city was put into receivership, the elements needed for its new government, and what would be required for the new government to last over time ...

In addition to gathering information about the city, the interviews allowed leaders of the community to be personally apprised of the process, and initiated the creation of relationships between the mediator and the community. The interviews served as an opportunity to let people know the mediator and her assumptions regarding her role in the process. (9)

Thus the assessment phase roots the prospective mediation process in the history and particulars of the conflict as expressed in the diverse narratives of the groups and individuals affected by the decision and whose commitment is needed to act. It combines analysis of these views and begins to build relationships between the mediator and the stakeholders.[8] The effort to assess and initially catalogue interests is balanced by the consistent appreciation by the mediator that she is engaging a story that is still unfolding—and that her ability to shape this unfolding story hinges on enabling these interviewees (and later participants) to depart from their publicly proclaimed scripts and refine their stories, their objectives, fuller interests, possible actions, new suggestions or demands, and so on.

Conflict assessment, like subsequent stages of mediation, is organized to help the interviewees retain the ability to surprise the assessors and participate as authors of the process and outcome. Mediators work to explain "why the assessment is being done, who is sponsoring it, and why it is important for all stakeholders' views to be heard" (Susskind et al. 1999, 110). Assessing the contested issues and relationship at hand, mediators pursue their analysis through "open-ended questions" that "allow interviewees to share their perception of reality...without the imposition of an alien framework of analysis" (Moore in Susskind et al. 1999, 112) .

The tension between these facets spills over to the output of the assessment process, a report that summarizes the views of stakeholders and recommends whether or not to continue, and (in the case of a positive recommendation) presents a design for how to bring stakeholders together.[9] This document is shared with all the stakeholders and is supposed to "provide...the parties with an impartial map of the underlying conflicts that will need to be addressed" (Susskind et al. 1999, 104).

---

8. Susskind et al. 1999, 116–117 cf. Susskind and Cruikshank 1987, 86. Forester, 2006a.
9. Readers can review examples at http://www.podziba.com or http://www.cbuilding.org.

A positive convening assessment will also engage stakeholders by rendering the perspective they have described accurately and, at the same time, framing the variety of perspectives in relationship to the problem and to one another.

> Seeing their own interest described in print often helps each party feel heard and understood. Reading about other parties' interests provides everyone with an accurate portrait of opposing views and the prospects for agreement. (Susskind et al. 1999, 104)

Thus the conflict assessment phase of the convening process—and this is characteristic of mediation more generally—combines information gathering and relationship building in the context of the specific case-defined logic.

CONVENING STAKEHOLDERS

Conflict assessment concludes with a decision by the sponsoring public agency to move ahead or not to start at all.[10] A decision to go ahead then means bringing together a group of stakeholders who may never have met, or have only met across a barricade, to discuss face-to-face the very issues over which they are in conflict. The focus of the convening process is to constitute these diverse individuals as a group with a sense of its identity and its role in the policy process: a group convened now less to debate issues than to negotiate agreements upon action or policy.

To get a feel for the distinctive way in which this transition occurs in mediation, we turn to a transcript of an actual convening meeting. The sponsoring agency is the Maine Low-Level Radioactive Waste Authority (the Authority). The stakeholders are a diverse group that includes representatives of state agencies, advocacy organizations, and general interest organizations (e.g., hospitals and the teachers' union). They have come together at the sponsoring Authority's invitation to discuss convening a citizens' advisory group (CAG) to advise the Authority on how to best fulfill Maine's responsibilities for managing low-level radioactive waste as set by federal law.

Discussing the decision to move ahead involved reviewing commitments on all sides. The convening authority must consider whether it is willing to support the process and it must specify how it will act on the outcome if consensus is reached. The members must consider their obligations to each other and to the convening authority. Will they commit to procedural responsibilities,[11] agree to uphold principles of participation, and "[i]f the process generates a consensus . . . to support and advocate for the agreement within their own organization and stakeholder groups as well as with the public" and, if they do form agreements, to honor them by agreeing to "refrain from commenting negatively on the agreement?" (Susskind et al. 1999, 126) The mediators clarify their role and their managerial responsibilities, both by describing it and, as we will show, more convincingly, by starting to act on it. Convening is the time at which these commitments are first made explicit and explored directly through interaction. It often provides participants with their first experience of working together under a consensus decision rule.[12]

---

10. Conditions for the latter might include the refusal of a key stakeholder to participate.
11. "Member and alternates agree to 1. Attend all of the regularly scheduled meetings. 2. Arrive at each meeting full prepared to discuss the issues on the agenda . . . 3. Present their own views and the views of the members of their constituencies and be willing to engage in respectful, constructive dialogue with other members of the group. 4. Strive through the process to bridge gaps in understanding, to seek creative resolution of differences, and to commit to the goal of achieving consensus." (Susskind et al. 1999, 125)
12. "Consensus means that there is no dissent by any member. There will be no formal votes taken during deliberations. No one member can be outvoted. Members should not block or withhold consensus unless they have serious reservation with the approach or solution selected by the rest of the group, they should make every effort to offer an alternative satisfactory to all stakeholders." (Susskind et al. 1999, 125)

We focus here on the accounts the sponsoring Authority and the mediator provided, the way these procedural commitments are reflected within them, and the efforts of the stakeholders to respond by reframing their roles and the agenda and, in the process, testing, specifying, and securing further those procedural commitments that animated their practical agreement to deliberate and negotiate. In becoming authors of the agenda, the stakeholders clarify their roles by taking ownership of their process and beginning to function as a group (public).

The sponsoring Authority's account of its role and the role of the CAG was articulated in a letter sent to stakeholders inviting them to attend the first meeting. This letter described the Authority's eagerness "to create a Citizen's Advisory Group to advise it on key decisions that will need to be made in the siting process" for a low level radioactive waste disposal facility. The letter went on to frame "the first task of the group": "to assist the Authority in developing environmental and other technical criteria by which portions of the state will be excluded from consideration as possible sites of a low-level radioactive waste disposal facility." The letter concluded by underscoring how "crucial" it was "that all groups with a stake in this decision participate in each and every step of the siting process."[13]

This invitation already began to parse the role of the Authority—asking questions—and the role of the citizens, expressing preferences and offering advice on these questions. The comments by a member of the sponsoring Authority that opened the first meeting of the Citizens' Advisory Committee re-expressed this interpretation as the context for the meeting:

> The Authority's job, as given to us by the Maine legislature, is to plan, design, and operate if needed, a low-level radioactive waste facility in Maine within the framework of Maine laws and federal law and regulations.

This institutional context, expressed in legal mandates and responsibilities, framed the Authority's role and, reflected through this, its sense of roles for its consultants and the citizens it had invited to consult. Objecting to this framing would mean taking on the history and framework of rules and responsibilities that the Authority embodied, as mandated by the state legislature, in the context of the meeting. This context tied the desire "to attain the widest possible consultation in order to assure that any Maine facility that is developed takes into account the wisest possible technical information and the widest interests of the people of Maine" to expectations that the "work of the Citizens Action Group" will uphold this framework by "proceeding at a reasonable pace so that everyone can ask questions and learn what they need to learn to offer well informed and wise advice."

The mediator's opening statement restated these expectations and their implications for the group whose members were eyeing each other for the first time around the table:

> The goal I think, from the Authority's standpoint is to get the best possible advice they can get on a series of questions that they *have to answer* if a facility is going to be sited. We will obviously be operating within the framework of federal and state law . . . I hope people around this table—and others we may want to add—will make the best effort to give the best advice we can to the Authority in making the decisions it is obliged by law to make.

The mediator then went on to describe his role and, in the process, to set up a contrasting set of expectations that focused on giving fair value to the rights and standing of the stakeholders within the process:

---

13. Letter from the Maine Radioactive Waste Authority, May 8, 1989. All quotes from the Citizen's Advisory Committee are from Laws 1989.

My job is to serve as facilitator—or you might say, referee—perhaps for today's and we hope a series of subsequent conversations…My task is not just to convince myself I'm neutral, but to convince all of you throughout the conversations that *I'm working to ensure that everybody's voice is heard and that collectively the voices on this advisory group communicate a set of concerns to the Authority in as clear and compelling a fashion as possible.*

Framing his task in terms of ensuring that the advisory group had a voice, tying his legitimacy to his ongoing ability to convince the group of his "neutrality,"[14] and thereby deputizing them as agents of the process, led to an account of the CAG that broadened its role beyond giving the Authority advice on specific questions. The mediator began by describing the Authority's desire to stand convention on its head and "engage the entire community in what the appropriate criteria are for choosing a site [and] choosing a technology."

He then extended this account in two ways. First, in substantive terms, he framed a broader role of stakeholders as authors who "invent policy suggestions," rather than "merely respond to decisions." Second, by asking for their consent, the mediator framed the group as the final arbitrator of questions about the legitimacy of the process:

I think that this process that we're about to enter into with your concurrence, if that is to be, is one in which we will be inventing policy suggestions, not merely responding to decisions made by the Authority.

The latter commitment was deepened in subsequent comments by the mediator, comments that gave the citizens the responsibility for monitoring the process, control over its future, and suggested norms for evaluating the process as a conversation:

I'm not, however, in the public relations business, not in business—like some—of getting hired on to suppress conflict, not in the business of steering this group toward any one outcome. The moment any of you feels that we're in some way biased in how we're behaving, please tell us, give us a chance to try to make a correction, and if we can't correct it then we will bow out. Our job is for you to perceive us as neutral and we're willing to be held accountable on that score.

If you ever have concern about how the discussion is going, please interrupt the discussion and raise the point about the process. If you feel someone else or you are not being recognized, interrupt. We do not operate by Robert's Rules of Order. *We seek to talk to each other in the way that you would normally carry on a dialogue.* The only concern is the logistics, not the formalities.

These two accounts of the role of the CAG contrast sharply. In the Authority's account, the CAG is an auxiliary body, defined by the Authority's responsibilities and drawing its legitimacy from the Authority's institutional status. The mediator's account raised the possibility of a broader role, defined by the CAG, and rooted in a legitimacy that is generated directly by the representative character of the group and the self-given character of the agenda and rules. The dramatic tension between these accounts was raised, and resolved, in an interaction that started with a presentation by one of the Authority's consultants.

The consultant was, by most accounts of consulting in such circumstances, acting in good faith. He entered the process with a monologue that shifted the focus of the conversation, got down

---

14. Neutrality is a problematic phrase that is the subject of much disagreement. It is probably best thought of as a term of art that describes a nonpartisan attitude and actions.

to work, and begin to talk about substance, implicitly moving on from the review of these institutional conventions:

> What I'm here to do today is to talk about low-level radioactive waste. What is it? Why are we here?

This defined part of his role, which worked to help each CAG member "put everything in context...[by] trying to show you relatively, "Is this bad? Is this high? Is this low? Where does this stand in the norm of the type of radiation we get?" He would also help the CAG "[g]et into some of the engineering disposal technologies that are either in existence today or are being planned to be used by other states, compacts, or counties." This shifted the focus even further to the technical features of options like "shallow land burial...[that] relies solely on the geology and hydrology of the site to contain the movement of radionucleides."

To the stakeholder sitting at that table, this self-evident transition to substantive concerns also interpreted and presumed the role of the CAG as listening, trying to understand, asking questions, and commenting on the difficult choices that the Authority faced.[15] The substantive orientation began to insulate the reflection on roles and on the ground rules for interaction that was opened by the tension raised in the mediator's comments. This tension was deepened as the consultant described the process that he took the Authority to be in the midst of:

> We developed the BEP (Board of Environmental Protection) rule last year. The methodology development—the exercise we're going through right now—is underway in the '89–early 1990 timeframe, followed by site selection leading into a detailed characterization. I say characterization—as we identify sites we will have to go in and do exhaustive geotechnical hydrological, and environmental studies of those sites, which will then require NRC licensing in this particular case. We're looking optimistically at a construction completion in either late 1995 or early 1996, if all the approvals can be maintained. Any glitch in any of those approvals will obviously have a potential major effect on the overall schedule.

By participating in this conversation, the citizens around the table are now assenting to an entire process that has the self-evident character of an institutional backdrop that sets the stage. The agenda and sequence are set, they can be taken for granted, and with them the topics of the conversation and roles within the conversation. The focus is technical issues about siting. The schedule is tight and any effort to question the process could disrupt the ability of the Authority and the State of Maine to meet their mandated responsibilities and put it at risk at in the national policy process.[16]

Some CAG members accepted the role that had been offered by responding with factual question like, "How much waste will go into the facility?" and, "Should we discuss radioactivity in terms of curies or rems?" Others chipped away at the conventions, asking questions like, "Do these facilities require permanent staffing?" or, "Is there any technology today that will isolate nuclear

---

15. By focusing on geology and technology the consultant invites stakeholders to take up his implicit interpretation of the proper role of the committee, thereby rendering less visible and problematic the nontechnical role of the committee. See Austin (1962, 117) on understanding this process as a sequence of illocutionary acts.

16. Rendering this as a recitation of facts also set truth or accuracy as the basis for discussion. And there was not much to dispute. The Authority *had* developed the BEP and *was* in the process of methodology development that *would* lead to site characterization. The presumption that these prior activities legitimately mandated the current process—that might have been controversial — was insulated from just the kind of scrutiny the facilitator had invited.

waste for thousands and thousands of years?"—questions that called for limited reflection but did not challenge the role framing that was being taken up in the meeting.

This went on until the representative of the Friends of Maine Woods entered the discussion:

> On that particular point...I would argue at great length. The type of containment we've seen here *is entirely irrelevant*. Murphy's Law is going to work on every one of them and I think you've admitted that...you don't know how long it's going to take to watch these: a thousand years or a hundred and ten. I certainly would dispute your saying that it is very clear they will have something to do with the nature of the site that might be selected. *I think they have no bearing at all.*

The incompleteness of this statement is contextually eloquent. Its force cannot be explained in its content and this disjuncture inserted the thin end of a wedge between the perspectives of the citizen participants and those of the Authority and its consultants, reopening the possibility for reflection. The critique is hardly explicit and could easily be dismissed as unintelligible or out of order. It opened an interaction with the mediator in which his earlier commitments, and his invitation to "interrupt the discussion" "[i]f you ever have concern about how the discussion is going," were invoked and were now re-expressed performatively: the mediator's "call me on it" had been called indeed. The mediator's response treats the comment as reasonable and understandable, despite its surface inarticulateness:

> What would in your mind have the most bearing on the selection of sites?

This helps the citizen make his critique more explicit:

> I think you have not demonstrated—and we're a long way from being convinced—that there is safe way to dispose of this. You're asking us today to make assumptions.

The mediator's response moves reflexively from questions about available technologies and levels of exposure to the very assumptions and categories on which the whole conversation was being pursued:

> Let me come back to that. I'm glad you raised it. The Authority has to operate as if there might be a need to site a facility, because the state law and the federal law require them to do so.

This opened the possibility, immediately embraced by the participants, that the CAG might operate on a different basis. As citizens, the stakeholders might try to be independent, even skeptical, in order to keep questions regarding the safety and the operation of a facility open to scrutiny.

> Then the state law and the federal law had better convince us that they are safe.

The mediator further developed the reflexive opening by reframing this comment into a question that the CAG members could try to answer as a group. He continued,

> The question, I think, for the group is, 'Can you operate in the light of the Authority's request to seek advice on siting criteria, while holding your view that it would be preferable not to have a facility or a need for a facility at all?

Once this question was posed explicitly, the basis for critique and the disagreement about the proper way to frame the process become more explicit. A CAG member articulated the disagreement in terms of preserving the right to say, "No":

> I think we're saying [that] "None of the above" might be our choice. And also you reassured me, when you first spoke, that we may say "exclude," and you didn't say "only one area." We might say, "Exclude the State of Maine."

Another citizen in the group turned this critique into an opportunity for the CAG members to reflect in positive terms on what goals they would choose for themselves as a group, given the opportunity. His proposal tied the notion of a self-generated goal to the common good and suggested a direct and deliberative expression of democracy.

> On your last question, I'm not yet certain I can participate in the siting evaluation of preference criteria or any of that, but I do think it may be an appropriate time when we come back to try to decide for ourselves just exactly what the goal of this citizens' body is.
>   I have a proposal for a goal for this body. If you would like to think about it and discuss it, my proposal would be that the goal of this body is to make recommendations to the Authority which will result in the safest possible management of radioactive waste in the State of Maine. That would be my recommendation. That means that other decisions of risk, of technology, all will fall out at a later time after we have been able to obtain the information we need to make those kinds of decisions.

The speaker ties the goal to the participants' common status as citizens of the State of Maine. This question opened further reflection on the "logic of appropriateness" (March and Olsen) that mediated the relationship between CAG's goals, its institutional status, and the behavioral implications of both. The sponsoring Authority members present found the new proposal relatively easy to accept because they could differentiate between their responsibilities and the role that citizens might choose to play. A representative from a state agency had a more difficult time with the new goal. He was concerned that it would require him to participate in discussion that would raise tensions with professional responsibilities that implied limits on what he could say or do. This give and take eventually circled around to the speaker who had originally proposed that the CAG reflect on its goals:

> The goal is the safest possible management of nuclear waste in the State of Maine. I don't know that, I'm certainly not convinced that an in-state facility is the safest possible management of the low-level radioactive waste in the state. I'm not convinced that the continued operation of Maine Yankee is the safest possible management. I don't know yet that a compact is the safest possible management of the waste we have in this state. I think that remains to be seen. But I think that the goal of doing the best we can with that waste is what we should be shooting for.

This statement provided the kernel around which the question about goals was eventually resolved by interaction among the members of the CAG. The outcome reflected these concerns and proposals. The goal was amended to address the perceived need for a "debate of ideas": "To understand and share information about this issue with interested groups of citizens in order to help the Authority reach the wisest and fairest decision." The phrase "for the people of the State of Maine" was added. Another amendment addressed the tie to the Authority's obligations and responsibilities: "To assist the authority in evaluating potential specific sites in more detail using these [siting] criteria and in assessing possible incentive and compensation packages."

Citizenship defined the basis for participation and for reflecting on what kinds of questions and behavior were appropriate, along with setting behavioral expectations for a process that the participants would stand behind as legitimate and valid. This initial round of "constitutional" process constituting deliberation more or less concluded with a comment by a citizen member who differentiated the role of citizens from the responsibilities of the Authority. He underscored the dual responsibilities that had been used to define the office of citizen: First, he noted the "strong tie" standard of the common good that others had articulated— to address the safest management of the radioactive waste in Maine for the people of the State of Maine. Second, to fulfill their deliberative obligations, he argued that participants also needed to cultivate and respect each other's independence of thought:

> While I can sympathize with the uneasiness and need of the Authority to try to get some sense of what to do—that's why they're asking us for our ideas and recommendations—when you ask somebody for advice, you want to know for sure that you're getting the straight story—whether it's what you want to hear or whether it's not what you want to hear. The reason I'm uncomfortable in specifically addressing disposal site criteria—exclusion criteria, preference criteria, all that stuff—is because it's exactly what they want to hear.
>
> I think that this body ought to keep itself aloof enough, independent enough, and become educated enough, that it can tell the Authority what the Authority may not want to hear, if we deem it in the best interest of the safety of the people of the state. If that means ignoring the federally mandated time limits, so be it. That's not what the Authority wants to hear because they're mandated to work under those state and federal time frames and constraints. But I think we should be free to say, "That's full of beans and you ought to do something about it.
>
> I think that's our role. I think we're supposed to reflect the public, not to be subsidiary staff to the Authority. That's how I sense the role that you want to pick—as subsidiary staff—in order, in other words, when it comes around to fish and wildlife you can say, 'Well these lakes are not good. This pond doesn't have any trout any more, so it probably is a better site for a facility. That's what staff do. That's not what a *citizens'* advisory group ought to do.

This summary rooted the legitimacy of the process in interaction of citizens who are free to state their minds in the context of a collective effort to come to agreement. If this conflicts with rules and mandates—so be it. Through this effort to reflect on and articulate the goals and ground rules that would bind them, the CAG convened itself as a public in relation to the Low-Level Radioactive Waste Authority. This process drew on the procedural commitments articulated by the mediator, and it was given fair value in part by his interventions in the development of the conversation. This interplay that drew on and created a directly democratic quality of self-generated terms of interaction distinguished the convening phase and opened the possibility of the continuous questioning of all parties interests and possible options that adept mediators sustain throughout duration of consensus-building processes.

DELIBERATION: LEARNING VIA FACT-FINDING AND DEALING WITH INTERDEPENDENCE

The next phase of mediation is broadly characterized by its deliberative character. This relates to questions of knowledge and the potential of mediation to draw on the domain specific knowledge of participants as well as to manage the "contradictory certainties" (Swartz and Thompson 1990) that characterize many policy controversies. Mediators, we shall see, focus attention on action that frames questions in terms of how to act, in terms of "what can we do?" rather than upon whose argument is more right or more true.

Here, in processes of mediated negotiations, we see a surprising shift of attention from that typical of policy debates. Indeed, while policy debates are adversarial encounters, in which arguments are used strategically, whether face-to-face or waged through the media of think tanks, funded research, advocacy science, and the newspapers, mediated negotiations displace the argument-focused work of debate and substitute instead an action-oriented negotiation that calls selectively upon knowledge generation via joint fact finding rather than adversary science to support its claims.

Here the cultivated judgment of mediators can help inform and broaden the policy analysis that sharply demarcates knowledge from action. Mediators know that all parties to a dispute come with their justifications and reasons and so shift the focus from reconciling beliefs to creating new bases for action. Mediators know that many public policy disputes resist resolution through identifying the definitive facts or getting them in order. Each side typically has its own definitive facts, its own experts, its own advocacy organizations. As a result, mediators know that working in such contexts cannot be reduced to moderating debate or arbitrating truth. Mediating negotiations calls forth practical efforts that reach beyond what "moderators" do and suggest new roles from which policy analysts can learn (Forester 2006b).

We consider briefly two strategies used by mediators. Both have direct implications for policy analytic practice. The first concerns joint fact finding, the second concerns a studied movement past gullibility that attempts to assess parties' interests in ways that will not be held hostage to the gamesmanship and creation of mutual ignorance by deliberate misrepresentation that leads to stalemate or suboptimal public outcomes.

LEARNING AND JOINT FACT-FINDING

Canadian mediator Bill Diepeveen recounts a case involving city neighborhood representatives, the city planning department, and a local hospital whose nuclear magnetic resonance imaging machine seemed threatened by the nearby placement of a new light rail line (Forester 2005a). The hospitals wanted the light rail buried in tunnels underground. The city argued that the underground placement of the line would be prohibitively expensive. We quote Diepeveen at some length so that we can then draw lessons about issues of adversary science, fact-finding, and the risks of nonmediated, nondeliberative policy analysis. This case, he tells us, offered lessons "related to the 'my expert versus your expert' routine," surely an abiding problem of policy analysis. As we will see, Diepeveen's and other mediators' work on fact-finding offers lessons for policy analysts too.[17] He tells us:

> We were debating one issue: The impact of the light rail transit on the nuclear magnetic resonance imaging (MRI) machines that are in the hospitals—because the trains, which are powered by electricity supplied by overhead lines, go by and create a magnetic field which interferes with the operation of the MRI ...

---

17. Diepeveen's and related mediators' accounts are part of an on-going research project by Forester to assess oral history based "practice stories" of mediators' work. These accounts represent not full histories of cases but rather revealing representations of mediators' own framing of their practice. These frames give us not last words but first words, albeit from the trenches of engaged practice, to explore as they characterize and pose institutional and micro-political aspects of mediated negotiations and public deliberations, as assessed, for example in J. Forester, *The Deliberative Practitioner*, MIT Press. 1999. All quotes from Diepeveen come from Forester 2005a.

We had a big debate about that. The institutions were saying that the train needed to go underground because the concrete tunnel and the steel rebar in the tunnel will dissipate the magnetic fields.

The City's saying, "Absolutely not—it's too expensive to put this thing underground. We've got to keep it above-ground."

So for me, this learning experience was about, "Well, how do you deal with these conflicting opinions?" We weren't getting anywhere in the argument, and each group had their own expertise to support their positions."

So far, of course, Diepeveen has found himself in the traditional policy analytic role. The hospitals and health care interests press for one alternative and bring experts and analyses and the facts to bear; the city representatives make a contrary argument, not taking on the scientific analysis of the hospitals immediately, but bringing yet other considerations of cost and viability to bear. Diepeveen wondered, as policy analysts must often wonder in the face of incommensurable arguments, how are we to settle such debate?

Diepeveen continued:

As a group, they had to realize firstly that they were stuck and secondly that as long as they remained fixed on those positions, they weren't going to get anywhere. Now one of the things we had talked about at the beginning was that when the negotiating group members took the agreement back to their various organizations for ratification, they would be able to do so in the full confidence that the information on which the agreement was based was sound and defensible. That meant that they wouldn't have to go away and say, "We agreed to this because so and so in the negotiating group said it would work."

What this situation did was force us to answer the question, "Well, let's see if we can get some information jointly—let's get something we can all agree on."

Notice here that the mediator and negotiators and stakeholder representatives anticipated and prepared themselves to deal with questions based fully on suspicion and prior distrust of the other parties. No party would be asked to sign on to an agreement or to believe an option to be viable simply because someone in the negotiating group, one of the other parties, said it should be so. Here we see realpolitik drive procedure and caution and foster the capacity for all parties to build confidence. The entire mediation process had been founded on the expectation that blind trust would be required of no one. The initially adversarial, quasi-deliberative conversation built in the expectation, the assurance, that stakeholders would somehow gain confidence together in pursuing the soundness of crucial underlying information. But what did this mean practically? Diepeveen continues to explain:

So we sat down as a group and said, "What's the question?" We jointly defined the question clearly and got agreement on it.

Then we asked, "Well, what are the skills that are needed in order to actually answer the question? What kind of skills does a person need?" After we reached an agreement on that, then we said, "Ok, who's out there?"

Here the deliberative conversation moves from debate to negotiation, from questions of "What do we know?" to questions of "What can we do?" Debate, of course, remains important: the stakeholders are deeply divided in their beliefs about the threats to the MRI equipment and the effectiveness of feasible options. But they are beginning to see that they are divided not only on questions of what's true and right, but on questions of what they might do, including, crucially, how they can learn together. Here, the mediator becomes pivotal, not so much by moderating debate—assuring fairness and turn-taking and various rules of procedure—as by posing questions for joint action that explore and specify the theme of "What can we now do?" (Forester 2006b). Diepeveen helped the stakeholders define what they needed to know and where they would turn to find someone with the background to answer the technical and economic questions they had. So far, we have all "information," but the mediator here, unlike a moderator of debate, has been preparing the way for joint action:

> And we did a request for proposals and ended up agreeing on a European consulting firm...All of the information was sent to them, and it was information that the committee had agreed that they would need.
>
> So, in fact, what happened was that this consultant became a servant of the negotiating team, the entire negotiating team. It wasn't your person, it wasn't my person: it was *our* person. That was really important because it gave people the comfort they needed in order to take the agreement back to their constituents with confidence.

At this point, as Diepeveen makes clear, negotiation had displaced debate, and everyone had learned in the process. The implications for policy analytic work could hardly be more striking. An argumentative process of adversarial science has been transformed into a political deliberation among deeply suspicious and skeptical parties who have moved from the warfare of "my expert against your expert" to facilitated negotiation in which their commitment to quality of information was intact, but the rules (and behavior) of procedure had been radically transformed. We wish to note particularly the mediator's enabling this move by contentious, distrusting parties to joint fact-finding (choosing appropriate expertise together and learning jointly from a jointly legitimated source) and to open alternatives to argument as their sole mode of conversation.

Policy analysts, we suspect, may also often be similarly caught: these stakeholders have experts who claim "A" and those stakeholders have experts who claim "B" (and so on). The analysts themselves have little option but—if they are not simply to limit themselves to the claims of "A" and "B"—to try to find yet other sources of expertise "C" to help them to assess the questions at hand, including of course the views "A" and "B" of the other experts. But a mediator works with the parties so that they choose and thereby legitimate the experts and sources that ground their beliefs about contested questions. The policy analyst without the benefit of a mediated deliberation, in contrast, may only choose (and hardly legitimate) yet another source of (nevertheless perhaps suspect) expertise.

Diepeveen's account helps us understand what's at stake in this move from debate to another model of policy inquiry:

> The consultant then came back with a recommendation that said, "In this particular case, above ground or below ground, it's still going to impact the MRIs. You're going to have to protect the MRIs...
>
> As a result they ended up talking about putting one-foot thick lead walls all around these machines. But because it was independent, the city people could go back to their political bosses and say, with confidence, "This is what we have to do."
>
> The health care and academic reps could go back to their Boards of Governors and say, "You know, yes, we thought that [going] underground would solve the problem, but technical expertise says that it's not going to make a difference [to put it underground]." This group in particular was very concerned about the issue because while the initial concern had been about the impact on the MRIs, there was also an issue of aesthetics, their desire to keep the power lines and tracks and train underground.

The mediated deliberation, Diepeveen suggests, makes joint action possible because it provides confidence by upholding independence in the context of a shared sense of "This is what we have to do." He summarizes:

> We started out with my expert vs. your expert. What turned the corner was a realization by the parties that that wasn't going to get them anywhere. They realized that they could talk until they were blue in the face, and the other wasn't going to convince them. So now it was a matter of saying, "Guys, how are we going to get around this?" What do you need in order to get around this? '
>
> They all said, "Sound technical information that's independent." As a [community] guy I'm not making my decision because you, the health care reps, say it's a good deal, or because you say it's not going to have an impact. And the health care reps aren't going to make their decisions because the City rep says it's not going to make an impact. We're going to make a decision based on sound technical expertise that's coming from the outside, that is defensible, that's independent from someone who's not working for you, not working for me.

Diepeveen's story of what he'd learned in this joint fact finding process can teach us about more than the shift from adversarial debate to legitimate action. What distinguishes his practice from the work of a "moderator of debate" is a practical sense of how to continue to open possibility in a policy controversy that otherwise conveys the feeling of going nowhere, of stakeholders stuck in perpetual rhetorical warfare, launching broadsides for their positions, against one another, with little mutual recognition accomplished and less agreement upon joint action.

MEDIATING NEGOTIATIONS: DEALING PRACTICALLY WITH INTERDEPENDENCE

We turn now to the part of mediated negotiations that might be most visible to outsiders—the negotiation itself—even if it builds directly upon and depends wholly for its success upon the prior work of conflict assessment, convening, and mutual learning or fact-finding as we have discussed them so far. We turn once more to Diepeveen's account now to pose a puzzle that we will then try to solve with our account of negotiation. The puzzle emerged in Diepeveen's work to mediate inter-municipal disputes in Canada. He tells us:

> We had one situation where I was meeting with a municipality, and the Reeve (their chief elected officer) and his chief administrative officer both said, "You know what, you might have 100% success rate now, but you won't by the time this one ends. Because this one isn't gonna go. There's no way there's gonna be an agreement, there's too much bad blood between the two municipalities."
>
> It was an annexation dispute, a small annexation. It was really not a big chunk of land—it might have only been an acre or two. It was quite small, but what made it look so impossible were the negative relations between the two municipalities—the total lack of trust.

So Diepeveen sets the stage: conflict between politically established entities, "total lack of trust," predictions from elected leaders and administrative staff as well that face-to-face discussions will be pointless, will only fail. Diepeveen as mediator has been given the good counsel of years of experience and political judgment: "There's no way there's gonna be an agreement."

The puzzle is set by Diepeveen's account of what happened in this "impossible" case:

> They ended up getting an agreement—but the fascinating thing is that I have heard from
> both these two guys, who now have said to us, "You know what? The fact that we got this
> deal, that was nice. But the thing that has been beneficial to us is the fact that we have
> now established a working relationship that has gone far beyond this little land issue to
> a whole bunch of other things."[18]
>
> He said, "That's been the amazing thing for me: the transformation that has come
> about—as a result of what was a small annexation—has translated into a lot more coop-
> eration in a whole bunch of other areas."

We get our first glimpse into what might explain the shift in the administrators' comments to
Diepeveen regarding their interdependence and connectedness. He continued:

> You see these municipalities have shared boundaries for years—there are long standing
> relationships. The parties aren't going away. So whatever the specific issue happens to
> be, it's always in the shadow of those relationships. The relationship building is critical.
> It really is.

The tie between substantive terms ("the specific issue") and relationships that Diepeveen highlights is described in more detail by Kelman (1996) in the interplay among three "central implications for what happens—or ought to happen—in the negotiating process" when it is understood as
interactive problem solving (99). To approach a problem through negotiation means,

> treat[ing]…the conflict or disagreement between the parties at the table as a problem that
> they have in common…The problem the two parties share is that each side's pursuit of
> its own interests…undermines or threatens the interests, values, and needs of the other.
> As a result, each party is stymied in the pursuit of its interests. (Kelman, 1996, 100)

Negotiation involves moving from these conditions for stalemate (as predicted by the local
experts in Diepeveen's case) by first,

> acknowledging that there is a shared problem, calling for a joint effort to identify ways in
> which both parties can pursue their interests and satisfy their needs without undermining
> or threatening each other. (ibid)

The stakeholders in Diepeveen's story eventually came to recognize, deeply and directly, just
this interdependence—that the problem was a shared problem in the relationship between them, and
that recognition opened the door to more productive negotiations. As one captured it vividly:

> One administrator…all of a sudden said to me, "Until I realized that I could divorce my
> wife easier than I could divorce my municipal neighbor, things weren't going that well.
> But when I realized that I had to have an ongoing relationship, all of a sudden the incen-
> tive to negotiate with the other side was there."

We take this comment to reveal more about the depth of the speaker's perception of his interdependence with his municipal neighbor than it reveals about his feelings for his wife. Such rec-

---

18. Other mediators describe such discovery of broader relationships. See H. Bellman in Harrington (1996 p.
    132—133)

ognition of interdependence sets the stage for efforts to solve the problem, the second of Kelman's three "central implications" of treating negotiation as interactive problem solving. Once parties recognize their interdependence, integrative solutions help them to prove to themselves and each other that pursuing their own interests need not "undermine or threaten the interests, values, and needs of the other" (100).

Mediation practice in this final stage is directed at helping the parties to fashion these integrative solutions that respond to deep and persistent perceptions of interdependence by fashioning policy proposals that take account of the needs and interests of both parties and thereby "move from a mutually destructive to a cooperative, mutually enhancing relationship" (Kelman 101). This process usually starts with getting parties to "push behind [their] incompatible position[s] to identify the needs that underlie their position. Focusing on underlying needs—just like focusing on underlying interests rather than opposed positions—enables the parties to search for solutions that are unlikely to emerge from positional bargaining" (Kelman 1996, 111; Fisher et al. 1981).

The comments of Lawrence Susskind, an experienced public policy mediator, suggest how mediators can make the prospect of integrative, "mutual gains" outcomes practically accessible to stakeholders.

> I am modeling the process that I'm hoping they're going to use in dealing with each other. I'm taking this person's side when he says "No" and I'm saying, "You're saying, 'No' to him. I can see why you're saying, 'No,' but what else could he have said that would have satisfied you?" I'm getting him into the mode of making proposals in response to things that he doesn't like rather than negative statements, and the participants see that that's the way to deal with other they disagree with in this kind of process....
>
> At some point I see the light bulb go on. They next time something comes up that this person doesn't like, he or she says, "I don't like that as much as this and this. Could you live with that?" and the person looks over and smiles at me. You can just see it; it is a very obvious event. They get it, and it's very intriguing. (Susskind in Kolb 1994, 342–343)

In such work with the stakeholders we get to the "essence of the process" which works by,

> acknowledging the other's needs as well as your own, and making proposals that respond to both. Arguing that you don't like what the others want, and you want something else instead (which is the old model of bargaining), doesn't produce agreement. Remember, we're trying to get an agreement. We're not done until we get an agreement." (Susskind in Kolb 1994, 343)

When the parties "get" this insight at a practical level,

> [t]hey stop saying, 'That's crazy! We're not going to that. I'm opposed to that.' They realize that the way to get what they want is to offer the others something that, in fact, responds to their needs but also responds to the speaker's own needs... (Susskind in Kolb 1994, 342)

For the stakeholders to work together in this way, the negotiation process has to be "a joint effort, in which the parties work together to generate ideas for a solution that meets both of their needs." The "hallmark" of such negotiation—such social and political interaction—is "that each participant tries to enter into the other's perspective and take the other's role, thus gaining an understanding of the other's concerns, expectations, and intentions" (Kelman 1996, 101). This can generate the understanding needed to engage in the kind of reasoning Susskind describes above and opens the way for parties to influence one another, not by entrenching their commitments to their positions and demands, but by enabling them to be "responsive to each other's needs" (Kelman 1996, 101).

These three steps—acknowledging interdependence with the recognition that the problem is a shared one in the relationship among the parties, trying to solve the problem by generating integrative solutions that respond to the needs and interests of all parties, and drawing on an understanding of each sides' "concerns, expectations, and intentions"—open the way for negotiations in which solving the problem inherently means changing the relationship between the parties. This is just what Diepeveen's municipal administrators were reporting above.[19]

The mediator's ability to sustain a hard-nosed and realistic sense of political possibility—in the face of well-entrenched nay-saying—represents, in a moment in practice, a deep challenge of democratic politics and policy analysis, a challenge of what Hannah Arendt called "natality," bringing new relationships into the world. In mediation, parties' perceptions of interdependence complement their hard-edged concerns with self-interest so typical of distributive politics. Mediation works because of—not in spite of—the tension that exists between "creating and claiming value" and between the distributive and relational elements of negotiation.[20]

The implication here is practical and institutional. Because the tie between interest and interdependence often offers more possibilities than initially meet the eye, mediators (and potentially policy analysts) can often uncover possibilities where stalemate seemed inevitable. Because processes like public hearings and adversarial science can harden positions by promoting exaggeration and corrupting "the facts" (as opposed to promoting mutual learning and joint inquiry), mediators know how to design and manage institutional alternatives that do not hold stakeholders hostage to defensiveness, fear, and mutual manipulation of information, but at the same time do not require them to give up their concern for their own needs and interests.

Notice that we see no talk here of compromise, giving in, betraying principle, no talk even of splitting differences. We see instead that the institutional process changed the nature of the discussions. Diepeveen implies not only that the agendas of deliberation were broadened from a narrower single issue problem-solving discussion, but that the interests of both parties, in his case one more urban and one more rural municipality, were considered by the convened representatives as equally legitimate, deserving of attention and respect.

So mediators not only may teach policy analysts about the dangers of narrow agendas set by powerful parties or the dangers of taking too narrow a problem-solving orientation, but the mediators are actually conducting policy focused deliberations themselves. These deliberations have been both participatory and practical and outcome oriented—so that Diepeveen's stakeholders quoted above spoke of these sessions as "amazing," noting a "transformation that...has translated into a lot more cooperation in...other areas."

Diepeveen extended his account to institutional analysis, comparing these mediated processes to the scope and character of the conventional institutional mechanism available to resolve such disputes:

> What was happening was something that wouldn't happen in front of a tribunal. The administrative tribunal looks at a proposal on the table, and everyone focuses on that. You're always attacking that annexation or that land use. It's an argument: you are trying to convince the board of the merit of your case and to destroy the case of the other.
>
> But what happened here was that, when the mediators came in and reframed the situation, it became a situation of, "Ok, so what's important to both sides here?"
>
> The rurals could tell their story, and all of a sudden there was—if I can use the term

---

19. Starting with the "problem" in negotiations parties are led to their "relationship." Starting with their "relationship," they are led to their "problem." Once parties perceive a problem as shared, and thereby in their relationship, solving that problem invariably involves changing that relationship.

20. Mnookin, Peppet, and Tulumello (2000) Lax and Sebenius (1987)

loosely—an "obligation" on the part of the urbans to respond to that, and to say, "In order for us to resolve this, you have concerns too, and we're going to have to address them."

So that was a real transformation point, and I think that that, in itself, has been one of the real selling points of the whole mediation process—that it has legitimized both sides of the debate, both sides of the "argument."

So Diepeveen helps us see how the institutional process of mediation itself shapes the process of policy analysis. In mediated negotiations, parties move from debate, from pro and con argument, to collaboration, a joint effort to generate proposals for action that respond to the question, "What's important to both sides here?" This process does not come at the expense of debate and argument, but it extends the process of inquiry to the creation of a self-generated process of mutual recognition, even a legitimation of the stakeholders' agreements upon action now that "both sides" may feel "legitimized," respected, taken seriously.

Policy analysts can learn from mediators how to better to assess stakeholders' interests—especially those interests so far unarticulated and hardly made public. Policy analysts can learn from mediators to focus not only on stakeholders' passionately defended positions but also, more crucially, on the conditions of interdependence and on-going relationships between the parties. Policy analysts can learn from mediators that even in the face of well-established claims that there's "no way" a dispute can resolved, facilitated deliberative processes can generate surprising transformations of policy options as stakeholders glimpse new possibilities of relationships, new possibilities of recognizing and addressing issues heretofore ignored.

CONCLUSIONS

In the sections above we have tried to convey the grain and texture of mediation practice as well as its outlines and formal organization. This move into the details of institutional, and even micro-political, interaction matters because it is precisely at this level that public policy mediators build the relational ties, secure the commitments of stakeholders, develop shared perspectives on contentious issues, and design the policy options that make mediation a revealing practice from a policy perspective. We have tried to show here how these designs in action can open up new policy possibilities in situations that otherwise seem to promise only stalemate or escalating conflict.

Mediators' actions in these moments are practical, political moves. They have the immediate, tacit quality of the intuitive responses of experienced athletes who can anticipate the movement of a ball in play and a defender in a sequence of action likely to unfold, as David Halberstam has put it, "at the speed of thought" (Bourdieu 1977). Mediators' moves function at the margin of possibility to chip away at pre-established positions and to encourage subtle reframings of perspectives and claims that can, at any moment in the evolution of a policy discussion, open onto broader and deeper transformations of possibilities of action. A significant part of the effectiveness of mediation practice involves this persistent attention to actions that test and enact newly negotiated relationships, float new proposals, and try out emergent insights about policy options and implementation.

We have also tried to show that this procedural sophistication is not simply deal making in another form. The key feature of mediation practice is the way mediators' "designs in action" align with broader features of policy development and implementation. For example, the interactions between a mediator and stakeholders that take place in a conflict assessment constitute an applied form of network analysis that responds to the dynamic character of the institutional spaces in which contemporary public policy is made.[21] Unlike analysts relying on stable bureaucratic processes of policy-making, mediators map networks *in situ* and in relation to the policy controversies that frame

21. See Hajer and Wagenaar, 2003; Kickert, Klijn, and Koppenjan, 1997; Sabel, Fung, and Karkkainen, 2000.

both the interactions in a network at a given point in time and the stakes different actors have in the problem. This applied network strategy ties historical relationships to substantive interests and draws on the interdependence embodied in shared problems to open new possibilities for development. Mediators develop the potential that inheres in fluid institutional relationships by convening representative policy actors as stakeholders, creating a shared, public account of the issues, and framing initial questions about relationships, vulnerabilities and relevant facts in ways that make the exploration of interdependence practically accessible.

As de facto policy analysis, mediation strategies then help these practical stakeholders to integrate their self-interest in problems at hand with a recognition of their interdependence. In so doing, mediators enable parties to frame collective action problems together, as an interdependent group of negotiators, so that they can act on the problems that they could not deal with separately.[22] Mediators engage stakeholders in the assessment phase to recognize subsidiary as well as primary interests, differing priorities, opportunities to trade across differences, and areas of shared uncertainty and needs to learn. Then, as we showed, stakeholders can begin to confront and refine the expectations they have of one another, to rework agendas and barely explored relationships, and to begin to probe freshly imagined and negotiated possibilities together. As our example illustrated, a key feature is that mediators convene practical discussions in ways that uphold stakeholders' independence and capacities for critical reflection even as they ask the parties to respond to their perceptions of interdependence by generating practical policy proposals and options. In these ways mediators create the possibility of transforming a loosely connected network of actors with an unclear institutional pedigree into a group—a practical public even—that generates the conditions for its legitimacy directly via its representative character and its accountability to stakeholder constituencies.

Here the mediators are not working as substantive policy experts giving opinions or predictions about desirable policy outcomes, but they are creating the conditions and processes that enable the convened stakeholders to work together to take advantage of the best available information and expertise, to assess one another's interests and priorities, to learn about pressing uncertainties and vulnerabilities, and then to invent options that address their real, separate and shared, interests. In these ways, mediators turn reflection on the conditions of stakeholders' interdependence and vulnerability into designs for cooperative inquiry and invention that can be enacted in conversation to enable stakeholders to negotiate relationships that both satisfy their self-interests and respond to the broader democratic significance of the issues at hand.

But mediators' work of conflict assessment and convening stakeholders opens, more than exhausts, the effort to plumb the possibilities of interdependence. Joint fact-finding reframes disputes and debates about who is right into questions about how to act and learn together in light of disagreements and in the face of persistent uncertainties. Reframing variations on the theme, "How can I convince you that you're wrong?" into versions of "What do we do about our disagreement?" opens new ways forward. As in the assessment and convening stages, mediators helping parties to confront, but not dissolve, differences in perspectives, interests, and priorities adds to the experience and growing confidence that makes it a bit easier and more plausible that, having negotiated cooperative ways of addressing their differences once, the group can do it again.

The turn to a kind of joint problem solving in negotiation makes this process even more practical and specific, without devolving into simple deal making. As we showed, this move to negotiation heightens perceptions of interdependence, underscoring the need for mutual recognition, reciprocity and cooperation across differences. The fashioning of agreements gains in momentum when stakeholders acknowledge that to get what they want separately they have to design terms that meet the interests of others as well.

---

22. Charles Sabel describes this as the "pragmatic trick" of framing "a collective action problem such that a collective actor emerges that has a natural interest in solving it" (1994).

Lawrence Susskind describes how this modulation of difference and understanding occurs through the stakeholders' emerging sense of facts, interests, and possibilities:

"People start this process with needs, desires, want, concerns, ideology, uncertainty, and interests—all of them. And I expect people to change—to alter their sense of what they would or wouldn't like to have happen by listening to what other people say...Learning and inventing goes on, reconsideration goes on, and argument matters. People discover something about their own interests along the way...People are not just collection of preset interests; they also have all kinds of tacit wants and needs that come into play." (Susskind in Kolb 1994, 348)

So stakeholders' practical contemplation of their interdependence in negotiation forces acceptance of the possibility that "their views of themselves, of the work, and the interests arising from both—their identities, in short—will be changed unexpectedly by [their] explorations." (Sabel, 1994 pp. 247-248.)[23] Negotiated agreement on policy designs or plans for implementation then occasion shifting boundaries between the self, the other, and the common in the face of innovative policy designs—and so, too, new associative ties that constitute an element of democratic renewal.[24] Here again we see the resonance in which particular moments in mediation practice, moments of dawning and transformative recognition of new relationships of self and other—newly appreciated interdependence and newly engaged cooperative inquiry and design as a result—become focal points in processes of political and institutional development that can produce new policy measures and extend to renew the available forms of democratic practice.

BIBLIOGRAPHY

Austin, John. 1962. *How To Do Things With Words*. Cambridge, MA: Harvard University Press.

Bohman, J. and W. Rehg, Eds. 1997. *Deliberative Democracy*. Cambridge, MA: MIT Press.

Bourdieu, P. 1977. *Outline of a Theory of Practice*. Cambridge

Carlson, Chris. 1999. "Convening," in L. Susskind, S. McKearnan, and J. Thomas Larmer, Eds. *The Consensus Building Handbook*. Thousand Oaks, CA: Sage.

Chambers, Simone. 1996. *Reasonable Democracy*. Ithaca, NY Cornell University Press.

Cohen, J. and J. Rogers, Eds. 1995. *Associations and Democracy*. London: Verso.

Cohen, J. and C. Sabel. 1997. "Directly-Deliberative Polyarchy." *European Law Journal*, 3(4):313–340.

Dryzek, J. S. 1987. "Discursive Designs: Critical Theory and Political Institutions." *American Journal of Political Science,* 31: 656–679.

———..2000. *Deliberative Democracy and Beyond*. Oxford: Oxford University Press.

Fischer, Frank. 2000. *Citizens, Experts, and the Environment: The Politics of Local Knowledge*. Durham, NC: Duke University Press.

Forester, J. 1999. *The Deliberative Practitioner*. Cambridge, MA: MIT Press.

———. 2005a. "From Environmental to Urban to Inter-Municipal Disputes: A Profile of Bill Diepeveen's Mediation Practice." Cornell University Department of City and Regional Planning. May.

———. 2005b. "If Parties Often Misrepresent Their Interests, How Can We Evaluate Negotiated Policy Agreements?" in John Scholz and Bruce Stiftel, Eds. *Adaptive Governance and Florida's Water Conflicts*, Washington, D.C.: Resources for the Future.

---

23. These modulations are of a family with what a moment that is referred to in the institutional and public lawyering literature of pragmatism as bootstrapping. See Simon, 2003 p. 56ff.

24. The potential of policy processes to develop associative environments features prominently in theories of institutional and legal pragmatism. See Sabel (1992, 1993, 1994, 1995), Fung and Wright (2001, 2003), and Cohen and Sabel (1997). Cohen and Rogers (1995) develop this insight explicitly in terms of a theory of associative democracy.

———. 2006a. "Rationality and Surprise: The Drama of Mediation in Rebuilding Civil Society," in Penny Gurstein and Nora Angeles, Eds. *Engaging Civil Societies in Democratic Planning and Governance*. U. Toronto Press.

———. 2006b. "Making Participation Work When Interests Conflict: From Fostering Dialogue and Moderating Debate To Mediating Disputes." *Journal of the American Planning Association* (Fall), 73: 4.

Fung, Archon. 2001. "Accountable Autonomy: Toward Empowered Deliberation in Chicago Schools and Policing." Politics and Society 29.

Fung, Archon and E. O. Wright. 2001. "Deepening Democracy: Innovations in Empowered Participatory Governance." *Politics and Society* 29(1): 5–41.

———. 2003. *"Deepening Democracy: Institutional Innovations" in Empowered Participatory Governance*. London: Verso.

Gomart, Emilie and Maarten Hajer. 2002. "Is That Politics? For an Inquiry into Forms in Contemporary Politics," in Joerges, B., Nowotny, H. (Eds), *Looking Back Ahead: The 2002 Yearbook of the Sociology of the Sciences*, Kluwer Publishers, Dordrecht.

Hajer, Maarten and Hendrik Wagenarr, Eds. 2003. *Deliberative Policy Analysis*. Cambridge: Cambridge University Press.

Heclo, H. 1978. "Issue networks and the executive establishment" in A. Kind, Ed. *The New American Political System* (87–124). Washington D.C.: American Enterprise Institute for Public Policy Research..

Kelman, H.C. 1996. "Negotiation as Interactive Problem Solving." *International Negotiation* 1:9987–124123.

Kickert, Walter J. M., Erik-Hans Klijn, and Joop F.M. Koopenjan. 1997. *Managing Complex Networks. Strategies for the Public Sector*. London, Sage.

Kolb, Deborah. 1994. *When Talk Works*. San Francisco: Jossey Bass.

Laws, David. 1989. Transcripts of the Citizen's Advisory Committee to the Maine Low Level Radioactive Work Authority, June 8–22. Transcribed by and on file with D. Laws.

Laws, David and Maarten Hajer. 2006. "Policy in Practice," in Michael Moran, Robert Goodin, and Martin Rein, Eds. *The Oxford Handbook of Public Policy*. New York: Oxford University Press.

Lax, D. A. and J. K. Sebenius. 1987. *The Manager as Negotiator*. New York: The Free Press.

Mnookin, R. H., S. R. Peppet, and A.S. Tulumello. 2000. *Beyond Winning: Negotiating to Create Value in Deals and Disputes*. Cambridge, MA: Belknap Press.

Podziba, Susan. 1998. "Social Capital Formation, Public Building and Public Mediation: The Chelsea Charter Consensus Process." Dayton, OH: Kettering Foundation Press.

Sabel, Charles. 1992. "Studied trust: Building new forms of co-operation in a volatile economy," in F. Pyke and W. Singenberger, Eds. *Industrial Districts and Local Regeneration* (215–250). Geneva: Institute for Labour Studies..

———. 1993. Constitutional Orderings in Historical Context. *Games in Hierarchies and Networks*. F. W. Scharf. Boulder, CO: Westview, 65–123.

———. 1994. "Learning by Monitoring: The Institutions of Economic Development," in N.J. Smelser and R. Swedberg, Eds., *The Handbook of Economic Sociology* (137–165). Princeton: Princeton University Press..

———. 1995. "On the New Pragmatism of Firms and Public Institutions," Paper presented to the conference on Liberal Institutions, Economic Constitutional Rights, and the Role of Organizations, European University Institute, Florence, December 15–16.

Sabel, Charles, Archon Fung, and Bradley Karkkanien. 2000. *Beyond Backyard Environmentalism*. Boston: Beacon Press.

Schwarz, Michael and M. Thompson. 1990. *Divided We Stand: Redefining Politics, Technology and Social Choice*. London: Harvester Wheatsheaf.

Simon, William H. 2003. "Solving Problems v. Claiming Rights: The Pragmatist Challenge to Legal Liberalism" Columbia Law School, Pub. Law Research Paper No. 03-58. Available on online at http://ssrn.com/abstract=459325.

Susskind, Lawrence and Jennifer Thomas-Larmer. 1999. "Conducting a Conflict Assessment," in L. Susskind, S. McKearnan, and J. Thomas Larmer, Eds. *The Consensus Building Handbook*. Sage.

Part X

Country Perspectives

35 Policy Analysis in Britain

Wayne Parsons

INTRODUCTION

The development of public policy and policy analysis as distinct fields of academic research and practice in government emerges in Britain in the 1970s. This chapter examines the growth of a "policy orientation" in Britain since this period and reviews how this has been manifested in academia, think tanks, and government. However, although the policy orientation has been a relatively recent development in Britain, it is important to place the emergence of policy studies (as knowledge of the policy process) and policy analysis (as knowledge in and for the policy process) in a broader historical and intellectual context.

British politics from the early nineteenth century onwards was greatly influenced by political economy. Classical political economists, such and Adam Smith, David Ricardo, Thomas Malthus, Jeremy Bentham, and J. S Mill, and others were very much public intellectuals. They theorized not only in order to both understand and explain the wealth of nations, but also to shape the policies of their day. An *analytical* approach to public problems has therefore been a defining characteristic of British politics and government for some time. This analytical approach also extended into other areas of public life and opinion. The development of a financial press that discussed and propagated economic theories was an important aspect of the formation of political opinion in the nineteenth and twentieth centuries. The *Economist*, for example, was founded to campaign for free-trade, and journalists (most notably Walter Bagehot) took a leading role in disseminating economic theories. Indeed, this role of journalism in framing economic opinion was also to be a characteristic of the British financial press in the twentieth century (Parsons, 1989). The triumph of *laissez-faire* political economy from the 1840s onwards meant that so many (noneconomic) issues of public policy were, for the most part, framed by the ideas of the political economists. As Keynes argued, Ricardo "conquered" England as completely as the Holy Inquisition had conquered Spain (Keynes, 1936, 32).

It is necessary, therefore, to understand how political or policy debates in Britain have, since the nineteenth century, taken place within the context of a widely accepted *economic* paradigm. In this sense, British policy making was analytical a long time before the emergence of policy analysis—*qua* a rational mode of political argument. Philanthropic social reformers in the nineteenth century may also be read (along with the political economists) as contributing to an analytical mode of policy making. Here we may refer to three exemplars of this approach: Florence Nightingale, Charles Booth, and the Rowntrees. Florence Nightingale (1820–1910) is most famous for her role in the history of nursing profession, but she is rather less well known for her part in promoting the use of statistics in analyzing problems and devising solutions. During the Crimean War she had developed her abilities in the collation and analysis of statistical data and showed how this data could be used to improve medical care. Afterwards, she was to apply her methods more broadly and showed how (objective) statistical analysis and graphical presentation could be a powerful instrument for policy making (Stinnett, 1990). Another contributor to the development of a more analytical approach to social problems was Charles Booth (1840–1916) whose survey into life and labor in London between 1886 and 1903 was aimed at molding public opinion and policy. His mapping of wealth and poverty in London served both to influence policy, and to shape the development of urban sociological analysis (Booth, 2005). His methods greatly impressed Jane Addams

(1860–1935) and led to a similar study of Chicago (published as the Hull-House papers in 1895). Addams's work, of course, contributed much to the founding of the Chicago school of (applied) sociology. The Chicago school, in turn, was to prove highly influential in the development of the policy orientation in the applied social sciences in Britain as in the United States. Booth also inspired the efforts of father and son (chocolate) philanthropists Joseph and Benjamin Seebohm Rowntree (1834–1925 and 1871–1954 respectively) in their attempts to *understand* and measure poverty and its causes *and thereby* help to ameliorate it. They were both strong supporters of the Liberal Party and were active in promoting policies to improve welfare provision. One of the lasting memorials to their efforts was the creation of the *Joseph Rowntree Foundation* and *Charitable Trust* which have remained active in policy research to the present day (Rowntree 2005) . This commitment to an analytical or empirical approach to problems and policy was also a feature of the development of socialist politics in Britain in the late nineteenth and early twentieth centuries. Amongst one of the lasting achievements of this period was the creation of perhaps one of the first "think tanks," the *Fabian Society* in 1884. Founded by some of the leading intellectuals of the day, including George Bernard Shaw, H. G. Wells, and Sydney and Beatrice Webb, the society believed in promoting gradual and pragmatic change through rational argument and discussion of public problems. Later, this commitment to promoting change through rational argument and inquiry prompted the Webbs to lead the campaign to establish the London School of Economics (LSE) in 1893. The society was to have a major influence on shaping the policies of the Labour Party—an influence that has continued in the present century (Fabian, 2005).

ECONOMICS AND PUBLIC POLICY

British public policy has been framed by economics more than by any other of the social or policy sciences. For a long period of time the dominance of *laissez-faire* political economy meant that other policies were constructed in the context of the doctrine that the state should have a minimal involvement in solving problems which could best be addressed by the working out of market forces. However, by the early twentieth century this paradigm was being challenged by liberals and Fabian socialists (amongst others) who argued that the state also had a role in making Britain a fairer society: liberty had a positive and negative dimension. The "new liberalism" associated with L. T. Hobhouse (Professor of Sociology at the LSE) and Liberal politicians Asquith and Lloyd George, argued that the state should have responsibilities in respect of social and welfare policies. In the twentieth century J. M. Keynes (1884–1946) was, like the classical political economists, driven by the desire to both explain economic conditions and relationships and change policy, and in so doing laid the foundation for an era of economic policy associated with his name. In the period between the two great wars, Keynes successfully undermined the dominance of the so-called Treasury ortho-doxy in both academic and journalistic publications. This campaign against *laissez-faire* economic policy culminated with the publication of the *General Theory of Employment Interest and Money* in 1936. During World War II, Keynesian economists came to prominence in policy making and in due course Keynesian economics became the ruling orthodoxy in British economic policy—until the late 1970s. One of the consequences of the "Keynesian revolution" in British government was that it paved the way for a growth in the numbers and influence of economists in British economic policy making. And, as in the days of *laissez faire*, it could be said that the new Keynesian policy framework, constituted the dominant paradigm within which other policy problems were considered in the decades following World War II. British policy making process thus gave economists a pre-eminent position in shaping core policies. For his critics, Keynes's economics provided the impetus for a highly technocratic approach to economic management which served to legitimate the claims that policymaking was in the "public interest," when in reality politicians and bureaucrats were far more self-serving than Keynes believed (Parsons, 2003).

However, if the Keynesian revolution in government ensured the primacy of economics and economists in the policy-making process in terms of national economic policy, it is important to note that in many other policy domains, another, less noticeable economic revolution also took place in the decades following World War II. This other revolution had been launched by a Cambridge economist who was somewhat overshadowed by Keynes—A. C. Pigou (1877–1959). Although Keynesian economics defined the framework within which macro economic policy was formulated, *policy analysis* as a tool-box of rational analytical techniques for decision making has its roots in Pigou. Policy analysis in Britain (as elsewhere) has been dominated by the use of rational techniques. These include cost-utility techniques, social and environmental impact assessments, evaluation research, forecasting/futures research, and the use of social and performance indicators. These techniques owe much to the development of welfare economics from the work of Pigou. His book *The Economics of Welfare* (1920), initiated a line of theory and empirical research which paved the way for the introduction of rational analysis in the 1960 and 1970s. Pigou's economics, when mixed with Pareto's theory and refined by Kaldor and Hicks (together known as the new welfare economics), gave rise to a powerful and elegant theoretical framework for thinking about public policy issues and provided a methodology for determining the use of taxes and subsidies as a way of distributing and balancing public and private welfare. It thus served as a basis for thinking about policy issues which involved questions of how the pie could be divided up, and how political conflicts over the public versus private interest could be (apparently objectively) resolved. Much attention has been given to the "Keynesian Revolution" in British government but perhaps more attention should be given to appreciating the extent to which the welfare economics that developed out of Pigou's work came to frame so many aspects of British public policy. Positivistic policy analysis, with its belief in measuring costs and benefits has its roots deep in the soil of welfare economics. Related to the growth of policy analysis from welfare economics was another product of the 1940s—systems thinking. Operational research (OR)—or operations research as it became known outside Britain—was devised by military planners during World War II. This, in due course, evolved into systems analysis, which complemented the development of other techniques derived from welfare economics. Systems thinking was to permeate both the development of rational policy analytical methods, but also to constitute a dominant discourse within the study of policy making as a systems process. This meant that OR and systems analysis complemented the influence of the Eastonian "black box" approach to policy making in the British political system.

THINK TANKS

Policy analysis in the UK as an activity in government may be said to begin with the Conservative government of Edward Heath in the 1970s. The Conservatives introduced a variety of techniques into the policy making process such as PPBS and Programme[.] Analysis and Review (PAR); both enjoyed a short life span. However, a more long-lived innovation was the establishment of the Central Policy Review Staff (CPRS) (Blackstone and Plowden, 1988). Although Britain had—since the Fabian society—a history of (what we *now* call) think tanks, it was only with the establishment of the CPRS that the term really entered into common usage in British politics and political science. Indeed, for many years, the CPRS was simply known as *the* think tank. The CPRS was an important attempt to create a unit at the heart of government with a remit to the think strategically, across departmental boundaries and drawing on a broad range of expertise from the civil service and "outsiders." It survived under successive Prime Ministers Wilson, Callaghan, and Thatcher, but was eventually abolished by the latter in 1983. The CPRS was replaced with a policy unit at number 10 under Derek Rayner, head of Marks and Spencer. The remit of the unit was far narrower than that of the CPRS: in turn this led to the creation of an efficiency unit in the Cabinet Office. This marked a change in emphasis away from trying to make government "smarter" and more strategic, towards the effort to make government more efficient, economical, and effective—in business terms. The idea of a CPRS was, in due course, to be revived in Blair's first administration. But, in general terms British central government proved to be indifferent, if not hostile, to analytical or strategic approaches to policy making aimed at breaking down the longstanding "policy silos" in Whitehall.

The growth of think tanks *outside* government has been a major feature of the policy orientation in British politics. It was during the inter-war period that a number of major policy institutions were established. Amongst the most important was the *Royal Institute for International Affairs* founded in 1920—although since 2004 it has re-branded itself as Chatham House. It was conceived in the aftermath of World War I as an Anglo-American institute of foreign affairs to "study international problems with a view to preventing future wars." However, the Institute was subsequently established independently in 1920. (Its American sister organization was later set up in New York as the Council on Foreign Relations) The Chatham House states that it is:

> an independent research institute, think tank and membership organization for individuals, corporations, governments and NGOs, and is precluded by its Charter from expressing any institutional view or policy on any aspect of international affairs. It does not receive any statutory government funding and is not a government organization, although some government departments are corporate members of Chatham House and, like many other organizations, sometimes fund specific projects at the Institute.

The institution has long served as a place where insiders and outsiders can exchange ideas. To facilitate this exchange the "Chatham House Rule" was devised (originally in 1927 and subsequently refined). The rule states that when a meeting, or part thereof, is held under the Chatham house rule, participants are free to use the information received, but neither the identity nor the affiliation of the speaker(s), nor that of any other participant, may be revealed. The rule has been used world-wide as a convention to facilitate frank and open exchange of opinions and information. Another think tank set up in the inter-war period was the *Policy Studies Institute* (PSI) which was original established as *Political and Economic Planning* (PEP) in 1931. PEP was in its heyday in the 1930s highly influential; not least in its promotion of the concept of a National Health Service. Later in the 1960s its work on racial discrimination played an important role in the race relations policy. PEP subsequently became PSI (1978) and in 1998 became a wholly owned subsidiary of the University of Westminster.

An important figure associated with the early says of PEP was Michael (later Lord) Young (1915–2002), a leading policy/social entrepreneur of his and subsequent generations. Young was (it is not an exaggeration to say) a *one man* think tank whose career is almost a potted history of British politics and society (Briggs, 2001). From PEP he went to head the Labour Party's research department and was responsible for writing Labour's manifesto for the 1945 general election—a document that pretty much defined the post-war policy consensus for decades afterwards. He set up the *Institute for Community Studies* (ISC) in 1953 the Consumers Association; *Social Sciences Research Council; Economic and Social Science Research Council* in 1956, and was the first chairman of the Social Science Research Council (later the Economic and Social Science Research Council (ESRC)). He also thought up the idea of the Open University. As an academic he was responsible, with Peter Wilmott and Peter Townsend, for some of the defining work in British sociology which addressed major policy areas such as urban development, education and poverty. He was passionately committed to research and problem solving. Young was responsible for literally dozens of organizations that helped to shape public policy in his long lifetime. In the last few years of his life he set up the *School for Social Entrepreneurs* (1998). Following his death the *Young Foundation* was established (by the merger of the ISC and another of his creations, the *Mutual Aid Centre*) to take his work and ideas forward.

Another important independent think tank set up of the period between the two world wars established in 1938 and still in business is the *National Institute for Economic and Social Research* (NIESR).

> The Institute's objective is to promote, through quantitative research, a deeper understanding of the interaction of economic and social forces that affect people's lives so that they may be improved. The Institute is independent of all party political interests. It receives no core funding from government and is not affiliated with any single university, although the staff regularly undertakes projects in collaboration with leading academic institutions.

However, although the inter-war period was to witness the establishment of early examples of independent think tanks, a notable aspect of the story of think tanks in Britain is the lack of a British Brookings, which had been set up around the same time as the RIIA. This meant that Britain has really lacked a well-funded, large independent organization on the Brookings model. Life in think tank jungle in Britain has consequently evolved without the emergence of a big (Brookings type) well-resourced, authoritative, and independent policy beast. The result is that the think tank community is mostly populated by small, financially less robust creatures seeking to influence policy and opinion. Hence, the most significant aspect of the expansion of think tanks in the post-war period (and especially since the 1970s) has been the rise and rise of the more ideologically and/or more niche focused organizations. Perhaps the most important of these is the *Institute of Economic Affairs* (IEA), established in 1955 to promote free-market economics and counteract the influence of Keynesian economics in government and academia (Cockett, 1994). The IEA proved highly effective in putting forward marked-based alternatives in public policy. With the emergence of the "new right" in the 1970s and 1980s there was a veritable explosion of conservative/free market think tanks. In 1974 Margaret Thatcher and Sir Keith Joseph established the *Centre for Policy Studies,* which was very influential in shaping the policy agenda of the Conservative Party in government under Margaret Thatcher. Many others followed—most notably the Adam Smith Institute (ASI). Founded in 1977, ASI (modestly) describes itself as "Britain's leading innovator of free-market economic and social policies... [which] has played a key role in developing practical initiatives to inject choice and competition into public services, extend personal freedom, reduce taxes, prune back regulation, and cut government waste" (Adam Smith Institute, 2005).

In the battle of ideas that took place in the 1970s and 1980s, it was unquestionably organizations such as the ASI that outnumbered and out-gunned advocates of more left of center policy ideas. However, in the 1990s the balance of influence was redressed somewhat with the establishment of a variety of think tanks aiming to combat the dominant position of "new right" policy "wonks" and "wonkettes" (as they were increasingly being termed in Britain and the United States) in shaping the policy agenda . These new wave of think tanks included the *Institute of Public Policy Research* (IPPR) and *Demos*. IPPR was founded as an independent think tank in 1988, in the aftermath of Labour's election defeat in 1987. The first chair was Tessa Blackstone, who had been a member of the defunct CPRS. It describes itself as the:

> UK's leading progressive think tank. Through our well-researched and clearly argued policy analysis, reports and publications, our strong networks in government, academia and the corporate and voluntary sectors and our high media profile, we play a vital role in maintaining the momentum of progressive thought... Since its inception, IPPR has built up a well-deserved reputation for generating new and imaginative ideas. Our aim is to continue to be a force for change by delivering far-reaching and realistic policy solutions that we hope will produce a fairer, more inclusive and more environmentally sustainable world. (IPPR, 2005)

The institute has been close to Labour: one of its directors (Patricia Hewitt) became a member of Blair's cabinet, and another (Mathew Taylor) was a former assistant general secretary of the Labour Party. It had an important role in shaping "New" Labour policies in opposition, and subsequently in government. Another director, Nick Pearce, was also special adviser to David Blunkett in the Home Office and the Department of Education and Employment.

Demos was established in 1993 by the former editor of *Marxism Today*, Martin Jacques. It describes itself as concerned with "building an everyday democracy."

> We believe everyone should be able to make personal choices in their daily lives that contribute to the common good. Our aim is to put this democratic idea into practice by working with organizations in ways that make them more effective and legitimate. (Demos 2005)

Its first director, Geoff Mulgan, had close ties to New Labour and later became director of the *Performance and Innovation Unit* (see below) in Blair's first administration. Amongst the first big ideas was its championing of the "communitarianism" associated with Amitai Etzioni. Mulgan's successor, Tom Bentley (1999–) had (like Pearce) previously been a special adviser to David Blunkett as Secretary of State for Education and Employment. Other think tanks followed in the 1990s and in 1996, the *New Local Government Foundation* was created to promote a more local/decentralized approach to policy. In 1998 another "left," or Labour orientated, think tank (*Catalyst*) was set up to apply labour values to the policy issues of the day. In 1999 the *New Politics Network* was established following the winding up of the "Democratic Left"—the remnants of the British Communist Party. This phase of growth in left(ish) think tanks was followed by the continued expansion of policy organizations covering most positions on the ideological spectrum and representing areas of national policy and international issues and relations. The role of think tanks and and wonks for hire in British politics and policy making is also diverse. But they are all in the same business—making friends and influencing people. Inevitably, not all think tanks are equal in influence: some are more equal than others. In the 1980s the Thatcher governments were, for example, close to the IEA and ASI; whereas the Blair governments tended to import people and ideas from IPPR and *Demos*. However, it is noticeable that with the (managerialist/market) consensus which has dominated British politics in the late 1990s and early 2000s, think-tanks are adapting so as to appeal across the political or partisan spectrum. This also enables them to draw on a wider range of potential individuals and organizations (and corporations) to fund their activities. A case in point is the ASI, which was close to the new right in the 1980s, but was subsequently very successful in attracting business from the New Labour government. Indeed, the Blair government proved to be one of its biggest clients. *Demos*, perhaps one of the most successful British think-tanks attracts funding from a very wide range of partners from the public and voluntary sectors, as well the corporate sector, including IBM, Shell, British Gas, Nat West Group, Northern Foods, Orange, Tesco, and Unilever. It is also, for an organization so close to Labour, not above giving the Conservative party advice on how to win elections (Boys Smith, 2005). If think tanks like *Demos* are to continue to be successful (in getting money and influencing policy debate) then this kind of post-ideological/post-partisan re-configuration will become increasingly the norm.

THE DEVELOPMENT OF A POLICY ORIENTATION IN ACADEMIA

The Keynesian era was also to be associated with the rise of the welfare state and it was in the field of *social administration* that some of the defining influences on the emerging policy approach were to occur. Policy studies as it was to develop in Britain from the 1960s grew more out of the study of social administration than economics. Policy analysis, on the other hand, as we noted above, was to develop from *welfare economics*. We can trace the beginnings of policy focus in social administration back to the contribution of a number of scholars in this field who were based at the London School of Economics. One of the defining contributors to social administration was R. M. Titmuss (1939–1973). As professor of social administration at the school (1950–1973), Titmuss had a major role in both shaping the field, and made important contributions to thinking about welfare policies in his books and articles. Another professor of social administration who had an impact on both academic research and policy was Brian Abel-Smith (1926–1996), who also served as an advisor in two Labour governments. Social administration of the kind advanced by Titmuss and Abel Smith was to be an important aspect of the development of the policy approach as it was to emerge in Britain in the 1960s and 1970s. However, in the 1970s social administration was being refashioned into social policy. Alcock argues that this shift towards an emphasis [on] policy marked the desire by many in the field to "move beyond the narrow confines of Fabian welfare statism" (Alcock, 2003, 7). This culminated in a decision (in 1987) of the *Social Administration Association* to change its name to the *Social Policy Association*. The old name was thought (by the majority at least) to be too closely associated with the existing welfare state: "whereas social policy encompassed also a more general concern with the analysis of the political and ideological bases of welfare provision" (Alcock 2003, 7). A number of volumes published during this period, when the shift from Fabianism to greater theoretical pluralism and from administration to policy occurred, illustrate this. Michael Hill 's *The Sociology of Public Administration* (1972) and *Understanding Social Policy* (1980), and Hall, Land, Parker, and Webb's *Change, Choice and Conflict in Social Policy* (1975) made important contribution to the development of a more specific policy focus. But perhaps the most important text to emerge from social policy in the early 1980s was Ham and Hill's, *The Policy Process in the Modern Capitalist State* (1984). Ham and Hill developed their approach while teaching a master's course at the *School of Advanced Urban Studies* (SAUS) at Bristol University from 1979. Chris Ham, a political scientist, was an expert on health policy, and Michael Hill, a professor of social policy, combined their interests to write a book aimed at students following courses in a variety of disciplines and policy areas including social administration, sociology, political science, policy, and organizational studies. This instantly became one of the standard texts for students of policy analysis and public policy in many disciplines. SAUS—later (in 1995) renamed the *School of Public Policy* at Bristol University—was one of the hot spots in the development of public policy in Britain in the 1970s and 1980s. Other notable hotspots included the *Centre for the Study of Public Policy* (founded in 1976) at the University of Strathcylde and the *Institute of Local Government* (INLOGOV) (founded in 1966) at the University of Birmingham.

The British policy approach also developed out of teaching and research in the field of public administration. A number of volumes may be referenced as marking a shift towards a more discernable focus on policy process and policy analysis. The first is Sir Geoffrey Vickers' (1894–1982) *The Art of Judgement: A Study of Policymaking,* published in 1965. This did much to shape the policy approach as it developed in the 1970s. If there was one book that facilitated the shift from thinking in terms of *administration* to *policy making* it was this book. *The Art of Judgement*—together with his subsequent publications—drew on Vickers' extensive practical administrative and managerial experience as well as his expertise in systems theory to illustrate how thinking in terms of policy making advanced our understanding of public administration . Peter Self (1920–1999) was amongst the first to explore the implications of techniques such as Cost-Benefit Analysis and PPBS. *Econocrats and the Policy Process: The Politics and Philosophy of Cost-Benefit Analysis,* published in 1975, was one of the defining statements on the impact of policy analysis in the British policy making process. CBA, he famously noted, was little more than "nonsense on stilts." Self was to be a lifelong critic of the way in which economics had come to dominate policy making.

Welfare economics (along with OR) had, as Self argued, considerable influence in the development of physical planning in post-war Britain. The development of planning in British universities in the post-war era was also a source of an emergent policy approach. British planning theory and practice was informed by the notion of improving the rationality of decision making, and also by the idea of thinking in terms of systems (Allmendinger, 2002). This gave rise to the belief that planning towns and regions could be understood as a means by which planners could, through better—more rational and systematic—analysis anticipate, manage, and control change in a holistic way rather than leave it to the vagaries of the market. This meant that planning depended on acquiring data and building models so as to assess the likely impacts—costs and benefits—of changes. Planning methodologies thus sought to combine the insights of systems thinking with the rationale of welfare economics. It was a paradigm which was, for the most part, dominated by engineers and architects. Together, rational systems approaches constituted the dominant paradigm of planning in Britain until the emergence of so-called neo-liberal approaches in the 1980s. An important response to the theoretical and practical policy issues raised by both rational-analytical methods of planning and "new right planning" was the emergence of approaches to planning influenced by "communicative" modes of rationality. In this model, planning ceases to be process dominated by claims to rational-analytical knowledge and instead is open to becoming a communicative and collaborative enterprise. The leading exponent of the view that planning processes should be redesigned so as to realize the potential of communicative rationality has been Patsy Healey, whose work has contributed to the development of an argumentative turn in policy analysis and planning (Healey, 1993).

Amongst the earliest publications in the field of political science that contributed to this move towards a distinctive policy was by an American (who became a long-term resident of the UK), Richard Rose. Rose was the founder director of the *Centre for the Study of Public Policy* at Strathclyde University. His edited book *Policy-Making in Britain* (1969) was for many students (including the present author) the first introduction to a *policy* perspective on British politics at a time when teaching (and research) was dominated by a highly institutional focus. Even so, a few years later (in 1975), Rose could note that there was still little use of the term "policy studies," even though British academics had long been concerned with "policy" and "problems" (Rose, 1975, 58). Rose and his colleagues at Strathcylde were to do much to promote the growth of public policy in Britain. The growth of a policy approach in British political science may be seen in several books that were the outcome of both teaching and research programs in the 1970s. Amongst the earliest of these was W. I. (Bill) Jenkins's *Policy Analysis: A Political and Organizational Perspective.* (1978). This was amongst the first books by a British academic that sought to cater for a market for policy analysis which had (in his words) "taken off" in the 1970s. Jenkins had been involved in developing (with several colleagues) one of the earliest courses on public policy in Britain at the University of Loughborough in 1970–1971. The book covered both theoretical aspects of the field and reflected on the implications of rational techniques being imported in government—PPBS and PAR. Above all, the book took an interdisciplinary approach and showed how the study of policy and the teaching of policy studies had to utilize a variety of disciplines and approaches. One swallow does not make a summer, and it took a few more years before policy analysis became a more distinctive field. As Rudolf Klein (1980) noted in a review of Aaron Wildavsky's *The Art and Craft of Policy Analysis,* the policy approach still had to overcome a fair amount of doubt, indifference, and hostility. Academics and practitioners, he argued could claim to be involved in analyzing problems and devising solutions—but why call it policy analysis or describe themselves as "policy analysts"? Hence, he argued, academic interest was low, and the take up by the government and civil service was poor. But, perhaps the situation was not so grim. The academic interest in policy continued to grow, even if the take up by central government of policy analysis was less marked. In a few years, a number of publications blossomed—signs that British academics were increasingly finding public policy an attractive framework for research and teaching. The publication in 1980 of Michael Carley's *Rational Techniques in Policy Analysis* was also a sign of the fact that, by the early 1980s, there was a growing interest in policy analysis amongst policy researchers and civil servants. This volume provided a comprehensive guide to the dominant techniques being employed by analysts working in government think tanks, NGOs, and international organizations. The book was funded by the PSI and the SSRC.

In 1984 Brian Hogwood and Lewis Gunn published their *Policy Analysis for the Real World*. This differed from Jenkins's and Ham and Hill's books in that it was a "how to do" policy analysis textbook. That is, it aimed to introduce students and practitioners to the techniques of analysis that could then be plugged into other material and experience. This volume also emerged from teaching for a course on Policy Analysis, at Strathclyde University, funded by the Nuffield Foundation. Brian Hogwood had earlier published a book on *Policy Dynamics* with B. Guy Peters (1983), and his co-author Lewis Gunn was, at the time, director of the Public Management Unit—also at Strathclyde University. In addition, by the 1980s a range of texts were published examining the British policy-making process as a distinct way of understanding British politics and government and included: Richardson and Jordon (1979), Burch and Wood (1983), Jordan and Richardson (1987). Such texts drew both on the standard (mainly American) theoretical literature and the growing literature in articles and books dealing with specific *areas* of British public policy. During the 1980s and 1990s, therefore, there was steady growth in policy studies in British universities, both in term of undergraduate and postgraduate courses and doctoral research. As an indicator of this expansion, a number of texts were published to cater to this growing market. Michael Hill published a valuable reader, The *Policy Process* (1993), which in due course was followed by *The Policy Process in the Modern State* (1997); the present author's volume, *Public Policy* (1995); and Peter John's *Analysing Public Policy* (1998) were all adopted as texts for courses in public policy in the UK and elsewhere. Therefore, it is possible to say that policy studies in Britain as a distinct academic activity had, by the 1990s, apparently, finally taken off.

A key factor underpinning this shift towards a focus on policy was the growth of managerialism in central and local government. In central government this took the form of experimenting with strategic planning techniques and the CPRS. But perhaps the more significant development was in the spread of corporate management and planning techniques in local government and in urban/land use and regional planning. The policy approach as it evolved in the 1970s became closely associated with "planning" and the redesign of local government on corporate lines. Effectively, corporate planning was what passed policy analysis. The "rational model" was adopted less as an analytical device than as a prescriptive model of what the planning process/cycle ought to look like. Journals such as *Policy and Politics*, *Local Government Studies*, *Public Administration*, and *Town Planning Review* published numerous articles in the period that reflect the managerialist turn in British policy analysis. A volume published by the *Institute of Local Government Studies*, entitled *Approaches in Public Policy* (Leach and Stewart 1982) well illustrates the extent to which corporate management and planning discourse—and the wisdom/sophistry of management consultants (Skelcher 1982, 36)—came to dominate "policy approaches" in policy making in British local government. However, by the time the INLOGOV volume was published, other changes were on the way, driven by the Thatcher government. Britain's first women Prime Minister had no great love for local government—not least because it was a source of opposition to her reforms—and the result was that in the 1980s local government in Britain was fast replaced by local administration of central government policies. The Thatcher/Major governments aimed to get local government to become more business like, and in which case, it would not be planners who would rationally decide but citizens as *consumers*. This meant that whereas previous decades had been about *smarter* government (more rational policy making and planning), the Thatcher era introduced more emphasis on *smaller* government (more market rationality and less planning). Nonetheless, the managerialist context has remained an important aspect of the development of a policy orientation in British government. This was to be evident in with the election Blair's "New" Labour party in 1997.

OLD POLICY ANALYSIS AND NEW LABOUR

A new chapter in the story of social science and British government opened with David Blunkett's speech to the Economic and Social Research Council (ESRC) in February 2000: *Influence or Irrelevance: Can Social Science Improve Government?* In his speech Blunkett called for a new relationship between social science and government that would bring to an end the "irrelevance" of social science to the policy-making process. This new relationship would be for social scientists to "tell [the government] what works and why and what types of policy initiatives are likely to be most effective" (Blunkett, 2000). He argued that:

> We're not interested in worthless correlations based on small samples from which it is impossible to draw generalisable conclusions. We welcome studies which combine large scale, quantitative information on effect sizes which allow us to generalise, with in-depth case studies which provide insights into how processes work. (Blunkett, 2000)

After years of "irrelevance" and "worthless correlations" the government was giving the social sciences and opportunity to become relevant to policy making. The government wanted to know what caused problems and what solutions worked best. As part of the drive towards evidence-based policy the ESRC, in 1999, funded the *UK Centre for Evidence Based Policy and Practice* with the aim of bringing "social science research much nearer to the decision making process." In 2000 an *Evidence Network* was created to develop the capacity for EBP in the UK forming a hub in a number of nodal points for various research organizations involved in evidence-based policy. There was a precedent for this in the previous government's support for the development of evidence-based medicine in the National Health Service Research and Development Programme that led to the creation of the UK Cochrane Centre in 1992. Evidence-based policy was to be a core aspect of the government's modernization agenda for government.

New Labour under Blair was a party that adopted a "third way" in thinking about public policy. It was an approach that was far less ideologically driven than previous Labour governments: this meant that policy had to be framed less by the ideas of the past, than by what works. In practice this involved a reform of government so as to modernize the way in which policy was made. If what counted was what works, then policy making had to be predicated on finding out what works (Davies, 2000). A number of policy documents set out a commitment to modernizing and professionalizing the policy process. In 1998 a *Performance and Innovation Unit* (PIU) was created as a result of a review of effectiveness in government by the Cabinet Secretary, Sir Richard Wilson. PIU signaled the return to the kind of CPRS model abandoned by Thatcher in 1983. Drawing on the experience of the CPRS and that of similar strategic units in other countries, the PIU aim was to "improve the capacity pf Government to address strategic, crossing-cutting issues and promote innovation in the development of policy and in the delivery of the Government's objectives." This involved developing projects involving long-term thinking, using teams of civil servants and non-civil servants, which had a strong bias towards analysis and "analytically-driven solution." Later, the government published a statement of its approach to policy making in the *Modernizing Government* White Paper of 1999 (Cabinet Office, 1999a). The White Paper argued that policy making would aim to be "forward looking in developing policies to deliver outcomes that matter, not simply reacting to short-term pressures" (Cabinet Office, 1999a, 1.23).

> Policy making is the process by which governments translate their political vision into programs and actions to deliver "outcomes," desired changes in the real world. Many of the other issues considered in this White Paper cannot be seen in isolation from the policy-making process. Government cannot succeed in delivering the outcomes people

want if the policies and programs they are implementing are flawed or inadequate. (Cabinet Office 1999a, 2.1)

Subsequently, the white paper was followed by perhaps the most wide-ranging review of the role of policy analysis in British government to date. This took the form of a report by a Cabinet Office team, *Professional Policy Making for the 21st Century* (Cabinet Office, 1999b).

The professional model (see Figure 35.1) is significant in the history of British policy making in that it marks the latest reincarnation or mutation of "planning" into the language of "strategic policy making." The model characterizes professional policy making as driven by evidence and framed with the long-term in mind to secure policy that delivers. In this respect, it is a classic strategic planning type model. The more contemporary addition is the emphasis in the model for the need for *stakeholder* analysis and management. But, apart from this addition, it is the "rational model" of policy making as developed in the corporate planning/management approaches of the 1970s. The report on professional policy making was followed up by a survey (*Better Policy Making*) on how actual policy accords with the (above) model. As with the original report, *Better Policy Making*, whatever its strengths and weaknesses, does constitute one of the "most comprehensive surveys that have ever been undertaken" (Cabinet Office, 2001, 16) into the policy-making processes of British government. For this much alone it is of considerable value. In addition to *Better Policy Making,* the National Audit Office published a report on *Modern Policy making: Ensuring Policies Deliver Value for Money* (NAO, 2001) to coincide with the PSD's report. The PIU contributed to the discussion on policy making with a paper on the theme of *Better Policy Delivery and Design* (PIU, 2001). In 2001, the PIU was joined by a Prime Minister's *Forward Strategy Unit* (FSU) that used a similar approach to the PIU, but also made use of outside advisers.

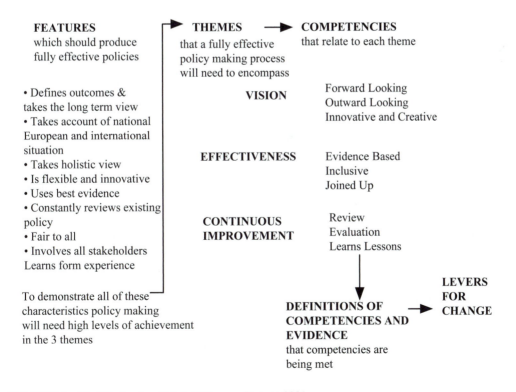

FIGURE 35.1   The "Professional Model." Source: Parsons 2001.

The PIU was in the forefront of seeking to promote a more "joined-up" and "wired-up" policy process that was more driven by evidence and policy analysis. The unit was, above all, an instrument of strategic policy making and much of its work was directed to developing a strategic capacity within government. As an acknowledgement of this, in 2002 a new unit (the Prime Minister's Strategy Unit (PMSU)) was created and combined with the PIU and the FSU. The Strategy Unit "provides the Prime Minister with in-depth strategy advice and policy analysis on his priority issues." It states that its main aims are: carrying out strategy reviews and providing policy advice in accordance with those policy priorities; supporting government departments in developing effective strategies and policies—including helping them to build their strategic capability; and conducting occasional strategic audits; and to identify and disseminate thinking on emerging issues and challenges for the UK government.

At the time of writing, the work of the PMSU represents the cutting edge of policy analysis in the British policy-making process. The work of the unit is grounded in an evidence-based approach. This means that it is involved in analyzing "statistical trends, causal relationships, [and] evidence of what works." It is also concerned to promote "analyzing major policy issues and designing strategic solutions" across government departments. A look at the *Strategy Survival Guide* (PMSU, 2004) provides an insight into the analytical approach which is at the core of the unit's mission. The guide provides tools for building skills in analytical capacity. These include: structured thinking, appraising options, building an evidence base, and managing stakeholders and communications. Apart from stakeholder analysis, what is most notable about the analytical tools is how they rely on the kind of methodologies one finds in textbooks on rational policy analysis, such as in Michael Carley book (1980), and in American texts in the 1960s combined with the standard techniques of strategic management developed twenty or thirty years ago. The guide recommends systems thinking, SWOT and Pestle analysis, brainstorming, and techniques to map brainstorming outcomes. Appraising options involves: cost-benefit/effectiveness analysis and multi-criteria analysis. Building an evidence base involves skills in data handling and use of surveys and focus groups; use of modeling and market/organizational analysis. Something new, compared to the policy analysis of the past, is the emphasis on policy transfer, but the skills in looking forward are well established techniques: futures and forecasting and counter-factual analysis (plus the more recent technique of scenario planning). An additional toolbox is available for the would-be futurist, particularly the techniques developed by the consultancy, *Synectics (inc),* who trade on being "pioneers in innovation" and helping organizations to promote "strategic renewal"; greater creativity, and to "develop, qualify and execute executive breakthrough solutions." It is perhaps, the relationship between corporate strategic management and the reliance generally on management consultants and modernized/professionalized policy making that is the most notable and defining feature of the development of policy analysis in the Blair government (see Craig, 2006). This is confirmed by the fact that Blair appointed David Bennett, a former McKinsey executive, to head the Downing Street policy unit. The *Times* reported that the Blair government has spent a record amount on hiring management consultants—over one billion pounds in 2004 alone (Baldwin and Ashworth, 2005). Significantly, when the government needed some strategic thinking on the thorny issue of pensions, it was not an internal policy unit, or outside think-tank they asked for advice, but (Lord) Adair Turner—yet another McKinsey alumnus (Pensions Commission, 2005). While the emphasis on evidence- based policy and what works has stressed the need to define a new relationship between policy relevant research by academics and policy users in government, the most important aspect of the development of policy analysis in the Blair government has been the way in which is has stressed the relationship between policy making and corporate strategic management techniques. As Richard Reeves notes:

> If politics has indeed become as essentially technocratic exercise, bright management consultants make good partners. Unhindered by history and free of political philosophy, they are interested only in finding the right technical solution to any given problem...If

"what counts is what works," McKinsey is more help than Marx. If a Mckinseyite thinks Tawney is a bird, who cares? (Reeves, 2005)

In practice, the approach to policy analysis developed in the Blair governments has been a fusion of well-established positivistic techniques of policy analysis and the equally well-worn tools of strategic management. Another indicator of the commitment to a highly positivistic conception of policy analysis came with the establishment of a master's course at London University's *Institute of Education* in Policy Analysis and Evaluation (in 2005) in collaboration with the Cabinet Office's Government Social Research Unit. This initiative was part of the civil service's Professional Skills for Government program. The course was designed "to provide students with an understanding of the major quantitative research skills relevant to designing, analysing and evaluating government policy." Teaching modules include: Sampling Data and Data Collection, Experimental and Quasi-Experimental Design, Longitudinal Research and Analysis, Statistical Analysis, Economic and Econometric Analysis, and Qualitative Research and Analysis.

POLICY ANALYSIS AND MANGERIALIZATION

Keynes once noted that it is ideas that (ultimately) shape policy for good or ill: but not immediately. It takes time for an idea to get into practice. The ideas that inform policy, he argued, are invariably past their use by the time they actually get applied: "the ideas which civil servants and politicians and even agitators apply to current events are not likely to be the newest" (Keynes, 1936, 384). In the case of policy analysis in British government, Keynes's point is entirely appropriate. The model of "better," "professional," "modernized" policy making in Tony Blair's government has proved to be a case of déjà vu all over again. Apart from the inclusion of more recent techniques (such as stakeholder/risk analysis and scenario planning) Labour's approach to policy analysis was remarkable only for the degree of its continuity with the past, rather than anything especially "new." The toolboxes of the policy professionals, as developed by the PIU and the PMSU, are packed full of the same tools as those that were around when the Beatles were "top of the pops" on the British charts. At that time, there was little take up in British government. In central government there was a brief and unconvincing attempt to develop a strategic think-tank and to adopt some the PPBS approaches that had came out of the Pentagon. The story was rather different in local government, where rational techniques and corporate planning did make inroads into practice. However, as far as central government is concerned the position of policy analysis has to be related to the wider picture. In the 1970s under Heath and later Callaghan, the old policy framework that had dominated British politics since the 1940s—the Keynesian/Welfare state model—was simply no longer viable. Making government smarter was not enough in an age of stagflation. When the counter-revolution did strike back against the old consensus, it was to come out of the world of think-tanks inspired by Hayek and the free market. However, although the Thatcher governments were to decentralize through markets, they also ensured that what was left of the public sector would come under ever tighter central monitoring, regulation and control. This trade-off as between economic decentralization and political centralization was, for the most part, accepted by New Labour. Indeed, if anything New Labour, with its faith in driving improvements through targets and performance indicators, was to prove even more centralist in its approach to public policy (Travers, 2005).

What was "new" about the Blair government's approach to modernizing policy making from the efforts of the past was that the analytical (strategic) mode of policy making championed by the PIU and the PMSU was teamed with the drive to ensure that policy was "delivered." In other words, the professional model may be described less an exercise in rational policy *analysis*, than a form of policy *management*. Policy analysis became essentially a method of both finding out "what works," and "what makes policy happen." That is, evidence-based policy is fundamentally to do with ensuring policy delivery. Indeed, on this point it is interesting to note that the *National School for Government* (set up in 2005) has a program for civil servants on *precisely* that—policy management (National School for Government, 2005). This includes courses on: developing deliverable policy, economics for policy making, evaluation of programs and policies for practitioners, introduction to evidence-based policy making, making policy that happens, the policy environment, and risk analysis in the policy area.

Whereas in the 1970s and 1980s the real policy action was in the think tanks, the current managerialist consensus in British politics means that ideological conflict, or the "battle of ideas" is, if not over, then on hold. Think tanks thrived when the battle was at its height, and have inevitably become less influential in a world in which the policy agenda is essentially managerialist and characterized by a lack of fundamental ideological disagreement between the main parties. Even so, the number of think tanks and "policy wonks" continues to proliferate and carve out niches in the (crowded) market of ideas. And, given their dependence on corporate sponsors, and in order to position themselves in a highly competitive market, think tanks have become increasingly "trapped by their paymasters into a bland managerialism, and thus become depoliticised" (Blackhurst, 2005).

At the beginning of this chapter we argued that economics has had a dominant role in shaping both policy analysis (as the application of rational techniques to policy problems) and in framing the British policy agenda. However, it is also the case that the development of policy analysis has also taken place within a highly managerialistic approach to public policy. To coin a phrase closely associated with Blair's favorite firm of management consultants (aka: the Firm, the Brotherhood, the Jesuits of Capitalism), McKinsey, "everything can be measured and what gets measured can be managed." This is to say that policy making has been conducted less as problem "solving" (by rational analysis) than by problem "management" by numbers. This began with the attempt to import forms of strategic management into government (PPBS) in the early 1970s, continued with the drive towards efficiency, effectiveness, and economy in the Thatcher governments, and the shift towards so-called 'new public management' in the 1980s and 1990s. This emphasis on better policy making and "delivery" through better *management* was deepened and extended under the Blair governments. In power (New) Labour pushed forward with reforms designed to improve policy "delivery" by the use of performance-based management techniques reliant on targets and performance indicators, but in addition, a few years into the first term, the government also sought to "modernize" the management of the policy *process* itself. And, central to this ambition was, of course, the *management of knowledge* within a *strategic* process. Evidence-based policy is quintessentially a mode of policy making in which knowledge is itself an object of deliberate strategic planning and management. In which case, "better policy making" is a function of better knowledge management. The driving force behind policy analysis, therefore, has been the desire to improve the management of the corporate headquarters of "Brit Corp," whose primary purpose is to ensure that their portfolio of Business(like) operations "deliver" policy by hitting their specified and measurable targets.

In many ways, the development of policy analysis in the Blair governments is indicative less of change than continuity. In practice, from the 1970s policy analysis emerged out of a desire to make government more corporate and strategic. This was not an immediate success. However, with the transformation of the role of the state in the Thatcher period, the path was cleared for a more comprehensive restructuring of government on corporate lines. The modernization of policy making in strategic terms has been an integral part of this wider process of redesigning government.

BIBLIOGRAPHY

Adam Smith Institute. (2005). http://www.adamsmith.org.
Alcock, P. (2003). "The Subject of Social Policy" in P. Alcock, A. Erskine, and M. May (eds.) *The Student's Companion to Social Policy*, Blackwell, Oxford.

Allmedinger, P. (2002) *Planning Theory*. Palgrave: London.

Baldwin, T. and J. Ashworth. (2005). "No 10 risks row to hire new policy boss from the 'Jesuits of Capitalism." *Times*, June 11.

Blackhurst, R. (2005). "The sad decline of the policy wonks." *New Statesman*, January 31.

Blackstone, T. and W. Plowden. (1988). *Inside the Think Tank: Advising the Cabinet, 1971–1983*. London: Heineman.

Blunkett, D. (2000). *Influence or Irrelevance: can Social Science Improve Government?* Swindon: ESRC, and Department for Education and Employment, February.

Booth, C. (2005). The Booth archive at the London School of Economics: http://booth.lse.ac.uk/

Boys Smith, N. (2005). *True Blue: How Fair Conservatives Can win the Next Election*. London: Demos.

Briggs, A. (2001). *Michael Young: Social Entrepreneur*. London: Palgrave.

Burch, M. and B. Wood. (1983). *Public Policy in Britain*. Oxford: Martin Robertson.

Cabinet Office. (1999a). *Modernising Government* (Cmnd 4310). London: The Cabinet Office.

Cabinet Office. (1999b). *Professional Policymaking for the 21st Century*, London: The Cabinet Office.

Cabinet Office. (2001). *Better Policy-Making*. London: Centre for Management and Policy Studies.

Carley, F. (1980). *Rational Techniques in Policy Analysis*. London: Policy Studies Institute/Heinemann.

Cockett, R. (1994). *Thinking the Unthinkable: Think Tanks and the Economic Counter-Revolution*, 1931–1983. London: Harper Collins, London.

Craig, D. (2006). *Plundering the Public Sector*. London: Constable.

Davies, H. T. O, S. M. Nutley, and P. C.Smith. (2000). *What Works: Evidence-Based Policy and Practice in Public Services*. Bristol: The Policy Press.

Demos. (2005). http://www.demos.co.uk.

Fabian. (2005). http://www.fabian-society.org.uk.

Hall, P., H. Land, R. Parker, and A. Webb. (1975). *Change, Choice and Conflict in Social Policy*. London: Heinemann.

Ham, C. and M. J. Hill. (1984). *The Policy Process in the Modern Capitalist State*. London: Harvester Wheatsheaf.

Hill, M. J. (1972). *The Sociology of Public Administration*. Heinemann: London.

Hill, M. J. (1980). *Understanding Social Policy*. Oxford: Martin Robertson.

Hill, M. J. (Ed.) (1993). *The Policy Process*. London: Prentice Hall.

Healey, P (1993). "Planning Through Debate: The Communicative turn in Policy Analysis," in F. Fischer and J. Forrester (eds.), *The Argumentative Turn in Policy Analysis and Planning*. London: UCL Press, 233–253.

Hogwood, B.W. and B.G. Peters. (1983). *Policy Dynamics*. Brighton: Wheatsheaf.

Hogwood, B.W. and L. Gunn. (1984). *Policy Analysis for the Real World*. Oxford: Oxford Univeristy Press.

IPPR. (2005). http://www.ippr.org.uk.

Jenkins, W.I. (1978). *Policy Analysis: A Political and Organizational Perspective*. Oxford: Martin Robertson.

Jordon, A.G. and J. J. Richardson. (1987). *British Politics and the Policy Process*. London: Unwin Hyman.

Keynes, J.M. (1936). *The General Theory of Employment Interest and Money*, Published in the *Collected Writings of John Maynard Keynes*, as Volume VII. Macmillan/Cambridge University Press 1973.

Klein, R (1980). "Creating Problems" (Book Review). *New Society*, 53:141.

Leach, S. and J. Stewart. (Eds). (1982). *Approaches in Public Policy*. London: Allen and Unwin.

National Audit Office. (2001). *Modern Policy-Making: Ensuring Policies Deliver Value for Money, Report by the Comptroller and Auditor General, HC 289 Session 2001–2002: November 2001*. London: National Audit Office.

National School for Government. (2005). http://www.nationalschool.gov.uk.

Parsons, W. (1983). "'Keynes and the Politics of Ideas.", *History of Political Thought*, 4(2): 367–92.

Parsons, W. (1995). *Public Policy* Cheltenham: Edward Elgar.

Parsons, W. (2003). "Politics and Markets: Keynes and his Critics" in T. Ball and R. Bellamy (eds.), *The Cambridge History of Twentieth Century Political Though*. Cambridge: Cambridge University Press.

Pensions Commission. (2005). *A New Pension Settlement for the Twenty-First Century: The Second Report of the Pensions Commission*. London: The Stationary Office, 45–69.

Performance and Innovation Unit. (2001). *Better Policy Delivery and Design: A Discussion Paper*. London: PIU.

Pigou, A. C. (1920). *The Economics of Welfare*. London: Macmillan.

PMSU. (2004). *Strategy Survival Guide*. London: Strategy Unit.

Reeves, R. (2005). "Politics—Richard Reeves tells the time unaided." *The New Statesman*, June 20.

Richardson, J. J. and A. G. Jordon. (1979). *Governing under Pressure: The Policy Process in a Post-Parliamentary Democracy*. Oxford: Martin Robertson.

Rose, R. (ed). (1969). *Policy-Making in Britain*. London: Macmillan.

Rose, R. (1975). "Comparative Public Policy," in S. S. Nagel (ed.), *Policy Studies in America and Elsewhere*, Lexington Books, Mass.

Rowntree, Joseph and Benjamin Seebohm (2005). http://www.jrf.org.uk.; http://www.jrct.org.uk.

Self, P. (1985). *Econocrats and the Policy Process: The Politics and Philosophy of Cost-Benefit Analysis*. London: Macmillan.

Skelcher, C. (1982). "Corporate Planning in Local Government" in Leach and Stewart (eds.), *Approaches in Public Policy*. London: Allen and Unwin, 36–51.

Stinnett, S. (1990). "Women in Statistics: Sesquicentennial Activities," *The American Statistician*, May, 44(2), 74–80.

Synectics. (2005). http://www.synecticsworld.com.

Travers, T. (2001). "Local Government," in A. Seldon (ed.), *The Blair Effect: The Blair Government, 1997–2001*. London: Little Brown, 117–137.

Vickers, G. (1965). *The Art of Judgment*. London: Chapman Hall.

36 The Evolution of Policy Analysis in the Netherlands

Igor Mayer

No nation is even remotely in the same league as the United States in terms of the supply of skilled policy analysts and large, highly qualified policy analysis and research organizations that have unbelievable capacity to manipulate and distribute an amount of information and interpretation not dreamed of at the start of federal policy analysis, when calculators, not computers were found on the desks of individual analysts. (Williams 1999, 158)

Indeed, in Europe, policy analysis methodology has not yet succeeded in finding its way, de facto, into policymaking processes. (. . .) This situation does not mean that policy analysis is not undertaken in Europe; rather, for most European policy analysts, knowledge and professional skills are unarticulated, tacit level of experience. (Geva-May 2002, 251)

INTRODUCTION

Does policy analysis exist outside the United States, or are the arts and crafts of policy analysis across the Atlantic a weakened and disoriented branch of *the real thing,* as the citations above seem to suggest? If policy analysis exists outside the United States—and from our point of interest in the Netherlands in particular—did it come about through a mere transplantation of theories, institutions, and methods originally developed in the United States; or has policy analysis outside the United States an autonomous value, contribution, and evolution? The different contributions and evolutions of policy analysis for instance appear in the various and changing connotations of the word "policy analysis" in national languages. In the Netherlands, for instance, the notion *beleidsanalyse*—the literal translation of policy analysis—is an ambiguous and somewhat problematic concept. It was first introduced in the early 1970s as a deliberate and programmatic effort to rationalize public policy making in all public policy domains. During the early 1980s, the notion attracted a rather negative connotation, due to the failure of a governmental program by that name, the so-called committee for the development of policy analysis (COBA; *de Commissie voor de Ontwikkeling van BeleidsAnalyse*). Many now prefer to use equivalents such as applied policy research or research based advice instead. But as I shall demonstrate in this paper, the notion *beleidsanalyse* is making a remarkable comeback since the turn of the century while it is being used for financial and performance accountability in the public sector. Thus, starting from the observation that different countries show different connotations and evolutions of policy analysis, I will analyze in this paper the evolution of policy analysis in the Netherlands on the basis of the following questions: What are the main characteristics (features) of policy analysis in the Netherlands? What changes, if any, have occurred in policy analysis in the Netherlands since the Second World War and what triggered these changes?

A study attempting to analyze or interpret the evolution of policy analysis in the Netherlands, unavoidably touches upon the question how and what to compare over time? This could be, how policy analysis evolved in the Netherlands as compared to other countries such as the United States (cf. Bemelmans-Videc 1994); or, how policy analysis evolved in different agencies or in different policy subsystems within the Netherlands (cf. Mayer et al. 2002; Hoppe and Halffman 2004). In recent years, many studies have focused on policy analysis as an important factor for policy change (Hall 1993; for an overview see Kleistra and Mayer 2001) and policy oriented learning (Sabatier 1998; Bennett and Howlett 1992; Howlett and Rames, 1998). As has been argued convincingly in historic accounts of the evolution of policy analysis in the United States, the arts and crafts of the discipline seem to be subjected to various "carriers" and "barriers" on the demand and supply side of policy analysis (DeLeon 1988; William, 1999; House and Shul, 1991; Radin 1997, 2000; Lynn 1999). Few studies however have specifically focused on developments in policy analysis, in particular outside the United States, and the contributing factors (with notable exceptions in Howlett and Linquist 2004; Scott 2002; Mayer et al. 2002). The chapters on country perspectives in this book therefore make an important contribution to the field.

It may very well be that the claim of U.S. dominance in policy analysis as illustrated in the citations above, originates from the fact that in other countries, different styles of policy analysis are prevalent but that these styles are not readily acknowledged as (part of mainstream) policy analysis (Mayer et al. 2004). Other styles that are not very well established within the United States, such as interactive or participatory styles, may be more developed in other countries such as Denmark or the Netherlands (Mayer 1997; Fischer 2000). It may be necessary to widen the view of policy analysis styles and allow them to be considered worthy of the discipline. Otherwise we run the risk of falling into a tautological trap: (proper) policy analysis does not exist outside the United States because everything that is done outside the United States is not (proper) policy analysis. In my view, a comparative study on the evolution of policy analysis in one (or more) countries should focus on determining the changes in:

1. The underlying *beliefs,* e.g., the values, worldviews, and quality criteria that define what is and is not good or proper policy analysis, incl. the *roles* that policy analysis and analysts actually play in the policymaking process.
2. The preferred *methods* or *methodological approaches* of policy analysis.
3. The *institutions* and *institutionalizations* of policy analysis, e.g., the number of organizations, the characteristics of the policy analysis market, the rules and regulations that guide the relations with clients.

Changes in policy analysis over a period of decades, or differences among nations or agencies can be described in terms of these aforementioned aspects (Radin 2000; Howlett and Linquist 2004). But that leaves unexplained what triggers or prevents such changes in policy analysis? It seems unlikely that differences (in evolution of policy analysis) between systems (e.g., countries) or subsystems (e.g., policy domains or belief systems) can be explained by cultural or political factors alone—or other factors should then explain the cultural differences and cultural changes. The development of water management in the Netherlands for instance is first (and maybe foremost) the result of geographical conditions and significant events such as floods and droughts that have occurred since the early middle ages until today. Like changes in policy, changes in policy analysis are the result of a variety of factors: some are external to the system such as events; some are contextual such as cultural or political trends that are part of society at large; some are institutional such as changes in legislation or a swing from state to market; and finally there are factors that result from learning processes, e.g., a growing awareness of the problems incongruencies and incompatibilities of existing policy (analytic) practices. In my view, changes in policy analysis could therefore be explained by looking at:

4. External influences (e.g., certain physical or international events and incidents that create or stimulate a demand for particular type or styles of policy analytic studies.

5. Changes in the national political or cultural climate (e.g., a swing from consensus to polarization, or from public to market orientation that influences the demand for particular type or styles of policy analytic studies).

In the remaining part of this chapter, I will give a condensed and straightforward analysis of the evolution of policy analysis in the Netherlands focusing on what changes occurred in policy analysis (aspects 1–3 above) and what contributed or caused to these changes (aspects 4–5 above). Table 36.1 (see page 566) provides a summary of this analysis. Based upon my analysis, I will distinguish the following periods in the evolution of policy analysis in the Netherlands:

1. Policy analysis *avant la lettre* (1945–1971)
2. The introduction of policy analysis "American style" (1971–1982)
3. The expansion and diversification of policy analysis (1982–1992)
4. The interactive years of policy analysis (1992 onwards)
5. The managerial approach to policy analysis (1999 onwards)

POLICY ANALYSIS AVANT LA LETTRE (1945–1971)

TECHNOCRACY AND CORPORATISM

As with most countries in Europe, the Second World War left the Netherlands in a deplorable economic and social condition with much of the infrastructure, industry, and housing destroyed. The national reconstruction process of course was enhanced by the US-donated Marshall aid. With the economic crisis of the 1930s fresh in mind the *Central Planning Bureau* (CPB) was founded in 1945 and formally established in 1947. Its first objective was to support the reconstruction process with economic analysis. Under the supervision (from 1945–1955) of the famous Dutch economist and later Noble price winner, Jan Tinbergen (1903–1994), the CPB provided *policy analysis* from an economic perspective (Dror 1968; Vught 1995; Hoppe and Halffman 2004). In fact, whereas the literal English translation of its Dutch name is The Central Planning Agency, its formal English name is the Netherlands Bureau for Economic Policy Analysis. For reasons of scope, I am unable to go into much detail here about the evolution of the CPB since 1945, but nowadays the CPB has become one of the world's leading institutes in economic modeling (econometrics) to be used for policy support (CPB 2005). At home, it has managed to gain an almost inviolable position within the governmental budgetary and policy-making process. Cabinet and opposition plans and proposals, but also investment proposals tendering for governmental subsidy, election programs and coalition agreements are unavoidably evaluated *ex ante* for their economic effects in CPB economic models. From time to time, the CPB's influential but also monopolist position—and for some, the lack of transparency of their models—is under attack. So far, the stronghold has not been demolished (Hoppe and Halffman 2004). Furthermore, CPB's economists have proved to be influential political advisors, before or behind the political screen, and one former director of the CPB has been minister of finance in three recent coalition cabinets.

During the early reconstruction period after the Second World War, another influential governmental advisory body was founded. The *Social Economic Council* (SER), established in 1950, provided a platform where members representing employers, members representing unions, and independent, or "Crown" representatives appointed by the government could meet, discuss social economic issues, and give advice (SER 2005). The significance and influence of the SER for government policy has gone up and down over time (SER 2005). During the early reconstruction years, corporatism flourished and the SER became rather influential. During a notorious period of polarization in the seventies, the SER proved largely paralyzed by the rising conflicts between the social partners. And during the heyday of the so-called consensualist *polder model,* the Cabinet's obligation to ask the Council's advice on all significant social and economic policy intentions was reversed in law.

Looking back at the early decades after the war, the CPB and SER are two interesting exponents of different styles and contexts of policy analysis in the Netherlands—although at first, *avant la lettre.* The CPB was and still is one of the best examples of a highly institutionalized, methodologically skilled, and rationalist style of policy analysis. It was already recognized by Dror (1968) as a unique institution difficult to find a peer elsewhere in the world. CPB's views on policy analysis, their preferred methods, and roles, root firmly in rationalism and economic modeling. Some would describe the worldview of the CPB as *Decisionist*—aiming for a segregation of applied science (the facts) and politics (the values). For many, CPB is even *Technocratic or Econocratic*—in many ways closed and opaque to outsiders but with a marked influence on political decision making. The SER on the other hand, reflects a second important tradition of policy analysis in Dutch society—by corporatism and similar forms of elite consultation. In other words, the Netherlands show a strong and pervasive tendency for elites of economic, political, and societal institutions to settle conflicts and disagreements among themselves in sometimes lengthy consultation processes, often behind closed doors.

The period of post war economic and infrastructural reconstruction coincided with a catastrophic flooding of the South Western Delta area in 1953, caused by a storm tide. Two thousand people died during these floods and the economic damage was enormous. The conceivable reaction was that this may never happen again. The *Delta committee,* established soon after the event, published its important *Delta Plan* in 1960. It comprised a large set of engineering works to raise protection from the sea. The work of the Delta committee followed by the Delta law and execution of the Delta works greatly stimulated the demand for policy relevant knowledge and analysis in the field of water management. Policy analysis *avant la lettre* in water management, consisted of engineering studies to support dike-reinforcement and the closing off of estuaries, augmented with economic (cost benefit) analyses. A great body of policy relevant knowledge had been developed in water boards (established in the 12th century), government directorates such as *Rijkswaterstaat* (RWS, established In the late 18th century), and the engineering societies and firms (RWS 2005). The tools and methods of knowledge for policy making were principally derived from the engineering and economic sciences.

THE INTRODUCTION OF POLICY ANALYSIS "AMERICAN STYLE" (1971–1982)

CONTINUED INSTITUTIONALIZATION OF SCIENCE-BASED ADVICE

During the late 1960s and 1970s, the welfare state in the Netherlands expanded significantly. But the political and societal context gradually changed from political and societal consensus to political polarization (see for details Kickert and van Vugh, 1995; Kicker, 1999). Lijphart's famous *rules of pacification* were definitely buried in the "fighting coalition" cabinet (1973–1977) led by the social-democratic leader Joop den Uyl (Lijphart 1968, 1969; Daalder, 1974).

In the realm of planning and policy analysis, the CPB strengthened and expanded its position in policy formulation, and, in addition, new planning agencies and many policy advisory committees were also established (Doorn and van Vught 1978; Vught 1995). During the 1970s, "makability" became a political buzz word for social-democrats. The notion was generally based upon ideas of social engineering and comprehensive planning of society. "Makability" and a number of external events triggered a strong demand for forecasting and future studies. In 1973, the Netherlands were subjected to an oil boycott by OPEC, and, as a consequence, the Netherlands' long-term energy policy was put high on the political agenda. During this time, the CPB as well as industrial organizations and (ad hoc) governmental committees developed a number of early energy scenarios that were used for policy making but also gave rise to increasing controversies because of their suspected imbalance (Dammers 2000). It marked the beginning of a period of social controversy on (nuclear) energy that lasted for a decade or more. Furthermore, the Club of Rome's report "Limits to Growth" published in 1972, had significant impact in the Netherlands (Meadows et al. 1972). Many academics and policy analysts started familiarizing themselves and using the underlying method of *system dynamics* initially developed by Forrester (1971) and used by Donella and Dennis Meadows et al. (1972) for their report to the Club of Rome. "Makability" also contributed to the founding of more science-based planning agencies (and neo-corporatist advisory bodies) from the late to the mid 1970s. Some examples of RPD include: the spatial planning department (established 1968, now RPB-Netherlands Institute for Spatial Research), the SCP-Social and Cultural Planning Agency (established 1973), and most of all the Scientific Council for Public Policy (WRR) (cf Vught 1995; RPB 2005; SCP 2005; WRR 2005).

The Scientific Council for Public Policy, *Wetenschappelijke Raad voor het Regeringsbeleid* was founded, first on a preliminary basis in 1972, and later established formally in 1976. Between 1968 and 1973, two influential advisory committees had diagnosed an increasing complexity in society, lack of a comprehensive view on future developments in society and (too) many inconsistencies in policy making (Polak 1978; Staal and Vught 1987, 1988). More consistency in policy making, and better policy coordination was deemed necessary. The WRR would therefore advice government on long-term developments in society, identify potential bottlenecks, and offer policy alternatives to remedy these bottlenecks. It would develop a long-term framework for prioritizing different policy issues and support the development of coherent policies and advise about the improvement of long-term research. The council and the affiliated researchers first took upon them a major effort to develop a comprehensive, scientific and seemingly objective forecasting study. Such a naïve and all-encompassing notion of future research in a polarized political and societal climate soon led to failure and disappointment. The report finally published in 1977, had a horizon of 30 years and looked at all sectors of Dutch society (Kickert and van Vught 1995; Polak 1978). The ambitions needed to be lowered and the methodological approach redirected (Staal and van Vught 1987, 1988). The future studies of the WRR became more specific, policy oriented, and more responsive to differing political and societal values. Over the years and by learning from mistakes and failures, the WRR has indeed succeeded to become an important scientific advisory council for Dutch government and along with institutions such as the CPB, has contributed significantly in the field of future studies and publications on foresight in policy making up to this date (WRR 2005).

COBA AND THE BIRTH OF BELEIDSANALYSE

While government increased its planning scope, financial budgets expanded and political controversies increased, coherent and consistent policy formulation became more and more difficult (Boorsma et al. 1999). With one eye on other countries, policy makers were looking for programs and techniques to rationalize policy formulation. Inspiration was found in the Planning, Programming Budgeting System (PPBS) in the United States, which, at the time, was already strongly criticized (cf. Radin 2000). In 1971 a study group with representatives from CPB, other planning agencies, and a broad representation of senior civil servants presented their findings about the use of *beleidsanalyse* (policy analysis) and cost benefit analysis (CBA) in the Netherlands. A special committee was soon formed for the preparation, enhancement, and support of policy analysis in all government departments in the Netherlands—the infamous committee for the development of policy analysis COBA. An independent office was established within the Ministry of Finance. Two methodologies for policy analysis were selected, worked out and subsequently introduced as forming the heart of a policy analysis *Dutch style* (Boorsma et al. 1999). Furthermore, a training program about policy analysis was set up for public servants on both lower and senior levels (Hellendoorn 1985). In addition, special working groups where established for instance to conduct a cost-benefit analysis of the national airport. Progress and results of projects and studies were published in the journal *Beleidsanalyse*, established by COBA in 1972. The journal managed to outlive the COBA for a little less than two decades, until it was finally abolished in 2000. At the end of the 1970s, the work of the COBA was evaluated and a special conference was held in 1980 about its future. The evaluation merely confirmed that the results of COBA where ambiguous to say the least—but many had already concluded that it had proved a downright failure (Scholten 1980).

In retrospect, the COBA made some important methodological contributions for instance in furthering the techniques on Cost Benefit Analysis and the technique of Objectives Analysis (COBA 1976; COBA 1975). But these methods had been far from successful in their implementation. Much has been written in the Dutch literature about why the COBA experiments failed (and as we shall see later, some of the lessons now seem forgotten). In sum, the failure of the COBA was due to a combination of many factors—a rigid and bureaucratic implementation of objective analysis techniques but mainly a neglect of the multi-actor, interpretative and political dimensions of policy formulation (Scholten 1980). In fact, in many cases it proved virtually impossible and very time consuming to formulate and split up the main and lower level objectives of all government policies and make them consistent. And in many cases, the public servants involved could not see the return on the effort or more importantly their intuition led them to believe it was even politically unwise (Wilmer 1980; Scholten 1980). In the end, COBA was abolished in 1982. But even after COBA, many of the ideas, experiences, and tools of *beleidsanalyse* subsisted within a unit of the ministry of Finance. Government policies and budgets in the Netherlands at the time were reconsidered (i.e.,cut down) and policy analysis increasingly became a financial-economic policy instrument dominated by the ministry of Finance to support that (Boorsma et al. 1999).

As said, COBA had been more successful and influential in its general methodological contributions than in its original goals of making government policy more rational and consistent. In retrospect, the COBA greatly improved and diffused important policy analytic techniques such as Cost-Benefit Analysis. Today, Societal Cost Benefit Analysis (*Maatschappelijke Kosten baten Analyse*) plays an important financial and political role in governmental decision-making in particular in decisions about infrastructure planning such as high speed railways (de Jong and Geerlings 2002). Even more important, the technique of departmental goal analysis (*departementale doelstellingen analyse* (DDA) strongly interacted with an emerging policy sciences in the Netherlands (Hoogerwerf 1996; Kickert 2004). Generations of students as well as junior and senior public officials where educated in techniques for mapping existing and new policies into hierarchies—called trees– of objectives and were taught how to formulate policies with that (cf. Hoogerwerf 1972; Kuypers 1980; Hellendoorn 1985).

RAND AND THE DELTA CONTROVERSY

In the 1960s and early 1970s, most of the Delta works, initiated after the 1953 flood, were constructed according to plan. In the early seventies, most water works were completed except for the biggest and most ambitious challenge of the Delta plan: the closing of the Eastern Scheldt Estuary, in the south west of the Netherlands. Triggered by environmental concerns, i.e., the conservation of the tidal and salt-water ecology, and economic interests, largely fishery, the societal and political opposition against the closure of the Eastern Scheldt had risen significantly. The matter led to fierce political and societal debate and caused a deadlock situation which almost led to the fall of the then coalition cabinet. Two opposing views existed: (1) the closing of the estuary as proposed in the

Delta plan, and; (2) keeping open the estuary but enforcing the dikes along the estuary, as proposed by environmental pressure groups. A government committee was installed to break the stalemate. The committee found an alternative that could reconcile the values of safety, ecology and fishery and could therefore be acceptable to all parties. The innovative solution was to build a storm surge barrier, a dam that could be closed under severe weather conditions but would otherwise remain open to allow the free flow of seawater in and out of the estuary. On behalf of the Dutch Ministry of Public Works and Water management, the American Rand Corporation carried out its famous Polano-study to support the subsequent decision-making (Goeller et al. 1977). By and large, the Polano-study was an impact assessment of the three alternatives to flood protection: the original closure plan, the plan to raise the dikes around the estuary and the storm surge barrier. The results of the analysis conducted by the Rand-analysts were presented in colorful scorecards providing decision-makers with a comprehensive overview of possible options and their impacts. Government and parliament opted for the storm surge barrier. Because of its innovative approach, its high status and its great impact, the Polano-study and the Rand style of policy analysis of the time gained a high profile in Dutch water management and other areas. The storm surge barrier resolved most of the conflicts between values of safety, economy, and ecology, but the technological challenge and the financial costs would soon prove to be staggering.

The containment of floods is not the only challenge in the Netherlands. Periods of extreme drought can also cause serious problems and damage to the economy. In the summer of 1976, the Netherlands faced one of the most serious droughts of the 20th century. In response, the PAWN-study, an acronym for Policy Analysis of Water management in the Netherlands, was commissioned. The PAWN-study was a major research project carried out between1977–1980 and involved the Ministry of Public Works and Water management, the Rand Corporation, and an independent technological research institute from the Netherlands, Delft Hydraulics (Goeller 1983). The study included a thorough and comprehensive *systems analysis* of the Dutch national and regional water systems and its use[r]s. Various computer models, still main frame at the time, simulated the dynamics of water management. The outcomes of the PAWN-study were used to draft the second policy document on water management issued in 1984. This was also the year that the PAWN-study was awarded the Management Science Achievements Award by the Institute of Management Sciences, USA. In the wake of the PAWN-study, many courses and seminars were organized about systems analysis in order to disseminate the knowledge and methodology to regional water management authorities. A number of institutions developed as think tanks and system analysts in the field of water management.

RATIONALIZATION IN A TIME OF RISING CONTROVERSIES

In retrospect, the introduction of "American style" policy analysis took place in a time of strong polarization in Dutch society and politics. Policy makers and policy advisors had become more aware of the (political) complexity of policy problems. Whereas the rationalization of policy formulation by COBA was generally considered a failure, the more politically sensitive approaches by the Rand Corporation managed to contribute to solving a controversy on the Eastern Scheldt barrier. The main difference lies in the fact that the COBA attempted to rationalize or even neutralize politics, whereas the Rand-study rationalized decision-making with reconnaissance of the political multi actor context. For COBA, *beleidsanalyse* was a craft and with the support of experts, civil servants were educated in how to use the models and tools for policy formulation. The Polano-study conducted by the outside policy analysts from Rand, not only supported a decision-making process but also legitimized a historic compromise in the Netherlands. It further introduced to policy makers a new way of thinking: in terms of alternative solutions that can have different impacts on multiple criteria. Through the Polano-study, policy makers in the Netherlands got better acquainted with policy analysis American Style, but it was the PAWN-study issued after the 1976 period of drought, that really institutionalized the policy analysis/systems analysis approach in the field of water management and other policy areas.

EXPANSION AND DIVERSIFICATION OF POLICY ANALYSIS (1982–1992)

THE MARKET OF POLICY RESEARCH AND ADVICE

By the end of the 1970s and during most of the 1980s, the Netherlands faced severe and structural problems, in terms of public deficits, unemployment, housing shortage etc. Public expenditures among others for academic research and higher education were cut back in "efficiency operations." "Limits to governance" replaced "makability of society." Various coalition cabinets at the time also had their hands full with managing a number of political and societal controversies—in particular on nuclear energy and the possible installment of U.S. cruise missiles in the Netherlands. Both issues led to considerable societal unrest, strongly divided the population, and induced some memorable demonstrations of mass protest in the early 1980s.

In this social and political climate, public criticism on the role of science and technology—a trend set in much earlier—culminated. Alternative. nonpositivist paradigms in the social sciences prospered. The policy sciences increasingly broke away from the mother disciplines such as economics, political science, law and sociology etc. During the 1980s, semi-independent departments of public administration were constituted in about 10 out of 13 universities (Kickert 2004). Together they attracted hundreds of young students each year. They were taught by a new generation of public administration professors that criticized the rationalist paradigms and techniques of the policy sciences and policy analysis as put forward by, among others, Kuypers (1980) and Hoogerwerf, who had previously been their mentors. Their own competitive paradigms focused on multi actor settings, policy networks, and largely accepted and accommodated to, political rationality, multiple interpretations, and ambiguity in the policy process (Snellen 1984; Ringeling 1985; Bruijn and ten Heuvelhof 1991; Godfroij 1995, Kickert and Vught 1995).

In the mean time, the aforementioned planning agencies and advisory councils, CPB, WRR, SCP and others such as the RIVM-Research on Man and Environment and CBS-Central Bureau for Statistics prospered. They continued to play their technocratic and decisionist roles in the policy process, mainly as data suppliers and providers of policy relevant research and advice. Many governmental advisory committees, where societal groups were represented, professionalized. The notion *Beleidsanalyse* however merely slumbered within the beleidsanalyse unit, later to be the policy evaluation and instrumentation unit of the ministry of Finance. Beleidsanalyse was mostly associated with the journal by that name. Much emphasis at the time was put on policy evaluation research, such as in Environmental Impact Assessments (Milieu Effect Rapportages, MER) and Cost Benefit Analysis. Still, some new and interesting developments in the field of policy analysis started to take off: (1) an emerging market of policy research and advice, and (2) the emerging of new interactive and participative methods for policy analysis.

During 1980s, market parties started to become active in the field of policy research. The aforementioned success of Rand and the Polano and Pawn studies may have contributed to this. One of the earliest players Research voor Beleid (*Research for Policy*) was established in 1980, and numerous companies have followed since then (VBO 2005). Over the years, the Netherlands have developed a very high density of private companies/foundations that operate in the market of policy research and advice. Some are off springs of university faculties who, in the late 1970s, early 1980s and under financial and political pressures, started to enter the emerging market of applied social scientific research. Many professors and university staff members have since become affiliated with one or more policy research or public consultancy companies. In addition, specialized research organizations such as the Netherlands Institute for Spatial Research, Ruimtelijk Plan Bureau (RPB), and the Netherlands Organization for Applied Scientific Research (TNO), that used to be government directorates or publicly funded institutions, have gradually been privatized (RPB 2005; TNO 2005). Although are still very much dependent on government contracts, for a decade or more they have had to operate in a free and competitive market. Government cut backs in the 1980s and 1990s merely contributed to the growth of the market of policy research and advice. There have been cases where civil servants—in a so-called revolving door effect—exited the public service, only to re-enter as external researchers or consultants, at higher costs (Groen Links 2001; Etty 2000). Half-hearted attempts with little effect were made in 1997/1998 to reduce the costs for external consultants. At the time of writing, no reliable indications exist about how much the public sector actually spends on external policy research and advice but all indications are that it is substantial.

THE RISE OF PARTICIPATIVE METHODS

By the 1980s the aforementioned societal conflict about (nuclear) energy had risen to such a high level that the idea was put forward to hold a broad societal debate, een *Brede Maatschappelijke Discussie* (BMD), on the issue (Dammers 2000). From 1982 until the publication of the final report in 1984, this broad societal debate on energy took place in a rather polarized climate of mistrust and skepticism. As Dammers (2000) has shown, many organizations—CPB, independent research organizations, advocacy organizations, and ministries—fought each other over the future energy scenarios to be used for the societal debate. Subsequently, thousands of participants from all sorts of vociferous organizations joined the hearings, only to give a cacophony of voices. In 1984 the BMD committee finally advised to maintain the two already existing nuclear power stations in the Netherlands, but *not* to build any more (Dammers 2000). In 1985 the government made it public that it planned to build at least two more nuclear power stations—an ambition never realized partly due to the Chernobyl accident in 1986. For many years, the negative experience of the BMD, its process and its effect, damaged the very idea that public participation and debates could be used to develop better policies or give advice. Better and more controllable participative methods were needed as well as a better understanding on how they should be used in a political process.

However, as far as innovations and developments in policy analytic methods are concerned, the more familiar and traditional techniques of policy analysis were gradually adapted to a new sense of political rationality. Interesting mixtures of new and old policy analysis methodologies were tried out—the main concern was to make policy analysis more interactive and participative. Classical methods, such as the Delphi, System Dynamics, Impact Analysis, Computer Modeling and Scenarios were combined with stakeholder/expert workshops and Gaming to give a more or less coherent methodology of participative policy analysis (Geurts and Vennix 1989; Vennix, 1990). Not only would interactive policy analytic techniques overcome some of the utilization barriers for policy analysis, but the participative methods also accommodated better to multiple stakeholder perspectives and complex, messy policy problems.

THE INTERACTIVE YEARS OF POLICY ANALYSIS (1992 ONWARDS)

POLICY ANALYSIS IN A POLDER MODEL

The early 1990s mark the beginning of a full decade of steady and prosperous economic growth, but foremost it was an era of societal consensus and constructive dialogue among stakeholders. In 1994, the growing political consensus between former opponents culminated in the first—*purple cabinet*— a coalition between the larger social democratic (PvdA) and conservative (VVD) parties and a smaller liberal party (D'66) leaving the Christen Democratic Party (CDA) in the opposition for the first time since 1918. The formalized consensus between employers and employees on social issues—*Polder Model*—became an example for other policy domains where differences of opinions or potential conflicts of interest could be solved in a constructivist/consensualist fashion. Even environmentalists and industrialists engaged in constructive dialogues in the *Green Polder Model*. At the same time, a latent but growing democratic crisis was felt, at the local level at first. But just after the turn of the millennium, the crisis became manifest at the national level through the rise of a radical popular movement and by the political assassination of its leader by a radical environmentalist in May 2002.

For the policy sciences in the Netherlands, it implied that the earlier largely descriptive multi-actor perspectives on policy making evolved into more *prescriptive* theories of policy making from which practical guidelines and methodologies for interactive policy making were derived (Kickert et al. 1997; Edelenbos 1999; Bruijn et al. 2002, Koppenjan and Klijn 2004; Mayer et al. 2005). The theories and guidelines were put forward under headings such as interactive and participative policy making, open planning, co-production, and, somewhat later, process management and process design (Bruijn and Porter 2004; Mayer et al.,2005). Interactive policy making was defined as "the early involvement of individual citizens and organized stakeholders in public policy-making in order to explore policy problems and develop solutions in an open and fair process of debate that has influence on political decision-making" (cf. Edelenbos 2000, 39; Mayer et al. 2005). Although the precise approach taken varies from project to project, interactive policy development normally involved inviting representatives of all interested parties and groups at an early stage to provide considered input to the process of developing policy. In liaison, stakeholders, policy makers and, where appropriate, external consultants identify problems and present solutions. The process is often supervised by independent process managers, who utilize working methods and group techniques designed to promote creativity, openness and result-oriented working among the participants (Edelenbos 1999; Bruijn et al. 2002). Since the beginning of 1990s, numerous experiments—large and small—in interactive policy development have taken place in the Netherlands. Better-known examples include the *Infralab* approach used by the Department of public works, and the "testing grounds" projects run by the Dutch Centre for Political Participation (IPP) in various municipalities around the Netherlands (Mayer et al. 2005). Also at the national level, governments and other organizations such as the Dutch Technology Assessment Organization, the Rathenau institute, started to actively explore, develop and use innovative methods and techniques for participatory analysis, such as through consensus conferences on topics such as genetic screening and cloning (Mayer 1997). Manuals, handbook, and guides were written in order to diffuse experiences, approaches and tools from one field or government body to another (Grin et al. 1997; Most et al. 1998). Major interactive and participative projects flanked decision making on large infrastructure projects such as the future of Dutch National Airport or the construction of the Second Harbor Area in the port of Rotterdam. In some cases, narrative and argumentative approaches to policy analysis supplemented such interactive projects (Eeten 1999, 2001; Hoppe and Peterse 1998).

While interactive, participative, and, to a much lesser degree, argumentative approaches were in fashion, the earlier styles of policy analysis subsisted. The traditionalist planning agencies, of course, had their own methodological and organizational evolution and sometimes merely incorporated new interactive methods, such as stakeholder workshops, into their toolbox. Due to the growing concern about for instance (long-term) environmental issues, well-established research and advisory institutes such as the RIVM (environment and health), the Central Bureau for Statistics and the aforementioned SCP and CPB evolved but also adapted their policy analytic methodologies. In 1992 for instance, the methodologically conservative CPB, published two distinguished and influential qualitative scenario studies—one about the world's economy, *Scanning the Future*—and the other about the Dutch economy, *Nederland in Drievoud* (the Netherlands in Threefold) (CPB 1992a, 1992b). The scenario studies were subsequently used for many foresight studies and stakeholder workshops by other organizations both in and outside government.

THE MANAGERIAL APPROACH TO POLICY ANALYSIS (1998 ONWARDS)

Beleidsanalyse All Over Again?

During most of 1990s, the interactive and participatory styles of policy analysis definitely had the "wind beneath their wings," but the older rationalist and client-oriented styles subsisted (e.g., in the ministry of Finance, the aforementioned planning agencies such as the CPB and the policy evaluation approaches of the Netherlands Court of Audit). At the close of the 1990s, the interactive and participatory styles were not without criticism (Mayer et al. 2005). The participatory and interactive processes were seen to run void, losing substance, expert knowledge, and good solutions along the way. Furthermore, decision-making tended to become viscous. In other words, policy makers increasingly felt the need for more rational policy analytic techniques such as societal cost-benefit analyses and other forms of *ex ante* evaluations (de Jong and Geerlings 2003). Decision-making on infrastructure projects in the Netherlands therefore was not only supported with participatory methods, but also with sophisticated cost benefits analyses, which from 2000 became mandatory as Studies into the Economic Effects of Infrastructures, *Onderzoek Economische Effecten Infrastructuur* or *OEEI*, conducted by CPB (De Jong and Geerlings 2003; Hoppe and Halffman 2004).

Another important but rather complicated process contributes to a remarkable return of the rationalist style of policy analysis as witnessed in the COBA experiments. During the mid-1980s government started to experiment with semi-autonomous agencies—*agentschappen*—and during the 1990s many such agencies were established (Kickert 1999). At the same time, an accruals-based system of financing was introduced that relied on the idea that the agencies delivered measurable products or services and that they therefore could and should be financed and held accountable on the basis of performances, i.e., outputs and outcomes (Knaap et al. 1997; Knaap and Oosterom 1999). Within no time, performance thinking spread throughout government not only in product and service oriented agencies but also in policy departments and state-institutions, such as courts (Berkhout and Sanders 1999). The new managerial paradigm in the public sector contributed to the implementation of a new system for the yearly parliamentary budgeting and accounting process. The new system was first introduced in 1999 in the policy document *From Policy Budgets to Policy Accountability* (VBTB) (Ministerie van Financien,1999; ARK 2004; Boorsma et al. 1999; Berkhout and Sanders 1999). The framework was overall supported and enhanced by parliament on the assumption that clarity and readability of budget reports would improve and that the accountability *ex post* would be enhanced (Berkhout and Sanders 1999). In short, VBTB requires ministries to state not just monetary amounts and objects of expenditures in their budgets, but also their policy objectives, how they intend to achieve them and the estimated costs. Most important, and much like the COBA ambitions, the VBTB framework induced a rigid way of thinking about formulating hierarchies of objectives. But it takes this thinking even a step further by demanding that the objectives are explicitly related to effects on society or the organization of government. In an English summary of the recent VBTB evaluation conducted in 2004, the Netherlands Court of Audit for instance, states:

> Firstly, VBTB requires that a policy's general objectives mention an effect on society or the organization of government. Compliance with this requirement was not adequate in the budgets for 2003. Secondly, the intended effects of general and operational objectives must be expressed in terms of concrete effect indicators with target values. This requirement

was likewise not met sufficiently in the budgets for 2003. (...) Top priority should be given to the development of effects and performance indicators with target values and the explanation of expenditure using performance data (ARK 2004).

Not surprisingly, some of the experiences in the bureaucracy with the VBTB framework are remarkably similar to that of COBA—the impossibility to make a wide range of political objectives, often based upon differing values and compromises, logically consistent, to split them up into a coherent set of lower level goals, indicate the proper instruments and means and measure the achievements and performances of them, preferably in a quantitative manner both *ex ante* and *ex post* (Boorsma et al. 1999; Ministerie van Financien 2002). Policy evaluation studies became even more formalized and rigid when the Dutch government adopted a Regulation on Performance Information and Evaluation Research, *Regeling Prestatiegegevens en Evaluatieonderzoek Rijksoverheid* (RPE) in 2001 (Ministerie van Financien 2001). This regulation among others specified that (with exceptions) all government policies are to be evaluated at least every five years. Possible sources of input for performance evaluations are the Central Bureau for Statistics, the Netherlands Court of Audit, and internal policy evaluation studies.

As illustrated above, the Court of Audit has recently urged to put more effort into a rigid system of performance evaluations but has also recommended explicitly to use *beleidsanalyse* (policy analysis) more frequently and systematically in order to make policy more effective (ARK 2004, 41). By doing that, the Court seems to disregard the evolution of concepts, theories and methods in the discipline of policy analysis. But more importantly, the Court's understanding and descriptions of what *beleidsanalyse* is are vague and often contradictory. Much like with COBA, this contemporary Dutch way of policy analysis is an attempt to rationalize government by turning *beleidsanalyse* into an instrument to gain financial-economic control in and over the policy process. Nevertheless, the Court is an influential institution in the Netherlands and we will therefore have to see how and to what extent its recommendations will influence the further evolution of policy analysis in the Netherlands.

More Trends

We see a number of trends in policy analysis in the Netherlands. First, the focus of attention of policy analysis now lies on understanding and managing the institutional and stakeholder context rather than an analysis of the policy substance. In practice, this implies that stakeholder, network, and resource analyses are conducted, that possible strategic behaviors are explored, that meta decision-making procedures and arrangements are designed with insights and techniques of process management (Bruijn et al. 2002; Koppenjan and Klijn 2004; de Bruijn and Porter 2004). Policy analysts and their clients have come to realize that they operate in a multi stakeholder context and have learned to use their political skills to mediate between different interests and core values. More attention is given to aspects such as the deliberate interweaving of substantive (policy) analysis and process management, e.g., by thinking in terms of strategic games and working towards negotiated knowledge (Riet 2003; Koppenjan and Klijn 2004).

We further see a continued process of institutionalization, professionalization (or bureaucratization), and commercialization not only at the supply side of policy analysis but also at the demand side. The number of government advisory committees has been reduced from several hundreds to a few dozens. But ad hoc policy research and advice has become a big market and market parties act accordingly. Whereas respective institutes in the field of water management for instance, used to be closely tied to government authorities and were publicly funded, they now have to acquire commissions in competition with other institutes. Another trend in the public sector is the long-term programming of the needs and questions for applied policy research and advice. But we have also noticed that clients subsequently, tend to split up their comprehensive needs for research and advice into (too?) many small projects leading to many coordination problems between the consultancy and research institutes involved. Furthermore, policy makers increasingly act as clients and have learned to manage their policy analysts, researchers, and consultants professionally. Public bodies rightfully demand value for money but increasingly expect products and services on demand. Within many government bureaucracies, special units have emerged that have a full time job going over the judicial, financial, and project details of (potential) contracts for applied policy research and advice. This frequently leads to communication problems and frustrations among the policy analysts and clients involved. In 2002 for instance, the Parliamentary Research and Verification Office was established. Its task is to validate "scientific" reports and support parliament in tendering external contracts that support parliamentary investigations. Managerial control over policy analysis does not only take place at the organizational level—through tendering and contract conditions—but also at the level of the project itself through review committees, regular meetings of steering committees, co-determination by the client of the problem formulation, the research questions, and the methods (and sometimes results), editing and negotiating draft reports, and so forth.

CONCLUSION

In this chapter, the story of the evolution of policy analysis in the Netherlands has been interpreted. Table 36.1 above gives a short overview of the story, highlighting the main changes and what contributed to these changes. I am aware that more historic, analytic, and theoretical questions can be raised and that more detailed answers are needed. Delineations and limitations in the story had to be made, many details had to be left out. Nevertheless, the story allows us to draw a number of tentative conclusions.

First and foremost, we can conclude that there exists a well-established tradition of policy analysis in the Netherlands. It can hardly be characterized as an "unarticulated, tacit level of experience" (cf Geva-May, 2002). But policy analysis in Netherlands frequently occurs under different names. It is a multi-faceted phenomenon that has mostly been institutionalized in public advisory committees, planning agencies, policy research and consultancy companies, think tanks, universities, and the like. Second, and in comparisons to the United States, policy analysis in the Netherlands is perhaps not very well incorporated *inside* bureaucracy. But when and where it is, *Beleidsanalyse* is strongly associated with rationalization of policy formulation and financial control over means and performances—the remnants of COBA. Inside bureaucracy it is strongly influenced by the values and techniques of the Ministry of Finance and institutions such as the CPB, and since about the late 1990s this style of policy analysis might be making a remarkable comeback.

Third, the policy analysis tradition in the Netherlands was influenced by a transplantation of methods and policy analysis styles from the United States with significant contributions by the Rand Corporation in the Polano and Pawn studies for water management. But the story also indicates that relatively autonomous learning processes occurred and that the Netherlands were able to make some contributions to the field, in particular regarding interactive and participatory methods.

Fourth, evolution of policy analysis does not mean that older policy analysis styles are replaced by new ones, rather values, roles, and methods are supplemented and sometimes come together to produce innovation. There are heydays of policy analysis styles—certain periods when distinct values, roles, and methods are in fashion and widely used or propagated. These often diffuse from one subsystem to other subsystems or even countries. Styles of policy analysis continue to sub-

TABLE 36.1
The Evolution of Policy Analysis in the Netherlands

	External events with impact on PA	Political and cultural climate	PA paradigm (beliefs, roles)	PA methods	PA institutionalization
Avant la lettre (1945–1971)	Post war reconstruction. In 1953 —a catastrophic flooding in SW Delta marks beginning of the Delta Works and creates a high demand for 'PA-like' studies in the water sector.	A period of national consensus and post war (economic and infrastructural) reconstruction.	PA = mainly technocratic, econocratic and decisionist. PA is an important but implicit and unquestioned foundation for political decision-making.	PA methods are derived from the economic, engineering and legal sciences.	Rise and/or rapid growth of the large public planning agencies, CPB, CBS, RIVM. Important role of engineering firms and institutions s.a Waterboards.
American style (1971 – 1982)	'Energy' and natural resources are high on the political agenda. In 1973, the Opec Oil boycott and occurs and the report to the Club of Rome appears. In water management, there are periods of extreme draught.	A period that starts with increasing polarization the end of 'pacification' in Dutch politics. There is a dominant belief in the 'makability' or social engineering of society.	PA should rationalize policy making and make it more consistent and comprehensive. PA is a skill and appropriate techniques can be developed and taught to public servants.	New PA methods are forecasting and future studies (e.g. in WRR studies), and the CBA and Objective analysis (in COBA). In water management the Rand-Polano studies (using MCA) and Pawn studies (systems analysis) are a great success and an example to other policy domains.	Continued growth of (new) planning agencies (WRR); Government sets up the ambitious but infamous COBA program (1973–1981) with many working groups. PA inside bureaucracy!
Expansion and diversification (1982- 1992)	Chernobyl impacts government decisions on nuclear energy. Societal and political controversies on cruise missiles and nuclear energy culminate.	This period is marked by limits to governance, governmental cut backs and an increasing market orientation (also in universities).	Public policy making is political and multi actor. PA should mainly analyze and support the political context and process. After the failure of COBA, the notion 'beleidsanalyse' becomes discredited.	The 'large societal debate on energy' fails— participatory methods are discredited. Continuation and refinement of earlier PA-methods, like cba,	Strong growth of the (commercial) market of applied policy research and advice. Some are 'off springs' from universities. Remnants of COBA slumber within the ministry
The interactive years (1992–)	Steady prosperous economic growth.	The polder model represents a new period of societal and political consensus. Policy making = constructive dialogues among stakeholders.	PA should aid and support constructive and interactive policy making processes among stakeholders and with citizens.	Much attention for the development and application of interactive, participatory methods at the local, regional and national level in many policy domains.	Continuation of above. Traditional PA organizations, s.a. CPB and engineering firms, open up their toolbox for part. methods. Many new and small PA firms emerge on the market. Public policy makers increasingly rely on outside expertise and advice.
The managerial approach (1998–)	Rise of new popular movement and political assassination mark end of consensual politics.	Public management paradigm puts emphasis on accountability, performance and output measurement etc.	In addition to the above…PA serves the interest of accountability and performance based evaluation.	In addition to the above… Performance measurement and evaluation methods, impact assessments, ex ante evaluations, (societal) cba.	In addition to the above…Policy analysis again is embedded in the public sector. Ministry of finance and Court of Audit play key role. Evaluation units are set up within the bureaucracy.

sist. They are very likely to continue incremental evolution within certain agencies and can make remarkable returns. The rise and fall of COBA in the 1970s and the rise of the VBTB in the late 1990s nicely illustrate that dynamic.

ACKNOWLEDGMENTS

I am indebted to many people I have worked with in previous studies that have been used for this paper. My student research assistant, Jan Kwakkel, has done a great job finding useful information sources and writing an excellent paper on policy analysis. Yvonne Kleistra, a senior evaluator from the policy and operations evaluation department in the Netherlands' ministry of Foreign Affairs, has made invaluable contributions to my insights on policy analysis in the VBTB era.

REFERENCES

ARK. Netherlands Court of Audit (2004). Working towards VBTB compliant budgets: Progress in 2002–2003. Available at http://www.rekenkamer.nl (accessed March 10, 2005).

ARK. Netherlands Court of Audit (2005a). Available at http://www.rekenkamer.nl/ (accessed March 10, 2005).

ARK. Netherlands Court of Audit (2005b). Evaluatie VBTB. Den Haag: SDU. (TK 29949-1).

Bemelmans-Videc, M.L. (1994). De beleidsevaluatie bij centrale overheden: Ontwikkelingen in Europa, de Verenigde Staten en Canada. *Beleidswetenschap, 4,* 327–348.

Bennett, C.J., and Howlett, M. (1992). The lessons of learning: Reconciling theories on policy learning and policy change. *Policy Sciences, 25,* 275–294.

Berkhout, A., and Sanders, M. (1999). VBTB, begroten en verantwoorden met resultaat: Interviews met be-trokkenen, *Beleidsanalyse,* 1–2.

Boorsma, P., Meassen, F., and Schild, J. (1999). Van beleidsbegroting tot beleidsverantwoording in relatie tot beleidsanalyse en prestatiebegroting: Een historische vergelijking vanuit een beleidsanalytisch perspectief. *Beleidsanalyse, 1–2.*

Bruijn, H. de and Porter, A. (2004). The education of a technology, policy analyst – to process management. *Technology Analysis & Strategic Management, 16*(2), 261–274.

Bruijn, J. de, and Heuvelhof, E. ten (1991). *Sturingsinstrumenten voor de overheid. Over complexe netwerken en tweede generatie sturingsinstrumenten.* Leiden: Stenfert Kroese.

Bruijn, J. de, Heuvelhof, E. ten, and In 't Veld, R. (2002). *Process Management. Why project management fails in complex decision making processes.* Dordrecht: Kluwer.

CBS. Statistics Netherlands (2005). Available at http://www.cbs.nl/en/ (accessedMarch 10, 2005).

COBA. (1975). Kosten-baten-analyse 2, tweede deelrapport van de werkgroep 'Normen en maatstaven voor kosten-baten-analyse.' vergezeld van een beleidsnota van de COBA. *Beleidsanalyse, 4,* 9–67.

COBA. (1976). Handleiding voor de departementale doelstellingenanalyse. *Beleidsanalyse, 2,* 2–37.

CPB.- Netherlands Bureau for Economic Policy Analysis (1992a). *Nederland in Drievoud. Een scenariostudie van de Nederlandse economie 1990–2015.* Den Haag: SDU.

CPB. Netherlands Bureau for Economic Policy Analysis (1992b). *Scanning the future. A long term scenario study of the world economy 1990–2015.* Den Haag: SDU.

CPB. Netherlands Bureau for Economic Policy Analysis (2005). Available at http://www.cpb.nl/eng/ (accessed March 10, 2005.

Daalder, H. (1974). *Politisering en lijdelijkheid in de Nederlandse politiek.* Assen: Van Gorcum & Comp.

Dammers, E. (2000). *Leren van de toekomst. Over de rol van scenario's bij strategische beleidsvorming.* Delft: Eburon.

DeLeon, P. (1988). *Advice and consent; the development of the policy sciences.* New York: Russell Sage Foundation.

Doorn, J. van, and Vught, F. van (1978). *Planning. Methoden en technieken voor Beleidsondersteuning.* Assen: Van Gorcum & Comp.

Dror, Y. (1968). Public policy making reexamined (5th ed. 2003). Chicago: Chandler Publishing.

Edelenbos, J. (1999). Design and management of participatory public policy making, *Public Management Review, 1, 4,* 569–578.

Eeten, M. van, (1999). *Dialogues of the deaf: defining new agendas for environmental deadlocks.* Delft: Eburon.

Eeten, M. van. (2001). Recasting intractable policy issues: The wider implications of the Netherlands civil aviation controversy. *Journal of Policy Analysis and Management, 20*(3), 391–414.

Etty, W. (2000). Huurlingen. Externe adviseurs en hun invloed. *Binnenlands bestuur 21,* 27–31.

Fischer, F. (2000). *Citizens, experts and the environment. The politics of local knowledge.* Durham, NC: Duke University Press.

Forester, J. (1971). *World dynamics.* Cambridge, MA: Wright-Allen.

Geurts, J., and Vennix, J. (1989). *Verkenningen in beleidsanalyse: Theorie en praktijk van modelbouw en simulatie.* Zeist: Kerckebosch.

Geva-May, I. (2002). Cultural theory: the neglected variable in the craft of policy analysis. *Journal of Comparative Policy Analysis, 4,* 243–265.

Godfroij, A. (1995). Public policy networks: Aanalysis and management. Kickert, W. and Vught, F. van (eds.) *Public policy and administration sciences in the Netherlands.* Harvester Wheatsheaf: Prentice Hall.

Goeller, B. F. et al. (1977). *Protecting an estuary from floods—a policy analysis of the Oosterschelde. Vol. 1.* Summary report. Santa Monica, CA: Rand Corporation.

Goeller, B. F. et al. (1983). *Policy analysis of water management for the Netherlands. Vol. 1.* Summary report. Santa Monica, CA: Rand Corporation.

Grin, J., Graaf, H. van de, and Hoppe, R. (1997). *Interactieve technology assessment. Een eerste gids voor wie het wagen wil.* Den Haag: Rathenau Instituut.

GroenLinks (2001). *De staatsgreep van de zesde macht.* Utrecht: Wetenschappelijk Bureau Groen Links. Available at http://managementconsult.profpages.nl/man_bib/rap/groenlinks01.html (accessed March 12, 2005).

Hall, P. (1993). Policy paradigms, social learning and the state. *Comparative Politics, 25*(3), 275–296.

Hellendoorn, J. (1985). Tien jaar opleidingen beleidsanalyse. *Beleidsanalyse, 3,* 5–8.

Hoogerwerf, A. (1996). Veranderingen in het beleid en in de beleidswetenschap, *Beleidswetenschap,* 403–415.

Hoogerwerf, A. (ed.) (1972). Beleid belicht. Sociaal wetenschappelijke beleidsanalyse, Alphen aan de Rijn.

Hoppe, R. (2003). Werken op de grens tussen wetenschap en politiek: naar een typologie van grensarrangementen. *Beleidswetenschap, 2,* 144–145.

Hoppe, R., and Halffman, W. (2004). Wetenschappelijke beleidsadvisering in Nederland trends en ontwikkelingen. *Beleidswetenschap, 1,* 31–61.

Hoppe, R., and Peterse, A. (eds.) (1998). *Bouwstenen voor argumentatieve beleidsanalyse.* Den Haag: Elsevier.

House, P.W., and Shull R.D. (1991). *The practice of policy analysis; forty years of art and technology.* Washington: Compass.

Howlett, M., and E. Lindquist, (2004). Policy Analysis and Governance: analytical and policy styles in Canada. *Journal of Comparative Policy Analysis, 6*(3) 225–249.

Howlett, M., and Ramesh M. (1998). Policy subsystem configurations and policy change: Operationalizing the postpositivist analysis of the politics of the policy process. *Policy Studies Journal, 26*(3), 466–481.

Jong, M. de, and Geerlings, H. (2003). De opmerkelijke terugkeer van de kosten-baten analyse in het centrum van de bestuurspraktijk. *Beleid en Maatschappij, 30*(3), 166–178.

Kickert, W. (1999). Expansion and diversification of public administration in the postwar welfare state: the case of the Netherlands. In Kickert, W. and Stillman, R. (eds.) *The modern state and its study. New administrative sciences in a changing Europe and United States.* Cheltenham, UK: Edward Elgar, pp: 159–178.

Kickert, W. (2004). Wetenschappelijke oogst van de bestuurskunde. *Bestuurskunde 13*(1), 14–24.

Kickert, W., and Vught, F. van (eds.) (1995). *Public policy and administration sciences in the Netherlands.* Harvester Wheatsheaf: Prentice Hall.

Kickert, W., Klijn, E.H., and Koppenjan, J. (eds.) (1997). *Managing complex networks, strategies for the public sector.* London: Sage.

Kleistra, Y., and Mayer, I. (2001). Stability and Flux in Foreign Affairs: Modeling Policy and Organizational Change. *Cooperation and Conflict, 36*(4), 381–414.

Knaap, P. van der, and Oosterom, R. (1999). Zicht op resultaat? *Openbare uitgaven, 1*, 31–39.

Knaap, P. van der., Kraak, A., and Mulder, A. (1997). Aansturen op resultaat. *Openbare Uitgaven, 4*, 184–193.

Koppenjan, J., and Klijn, E.H. (2004). *Managing uncertainties in networks.* London: Routledge.

Kuypers, G. (1980). *Beginselen van beleidsontwikkeling*, deel A en B. Muiderberg: Countinho.

Lijphart, A. (1968). *The politics of accommodation: pluralism and democracy in the Netherlands.* Berkeley: University of California Press,

Lijphart, A. (1996). Consociational democracy. *World Politics 21* (2), 207–225.

Lynn, L.E. (1999). A place at the table: policy analysis, its postpositive critics, and the future of practice. *Journal of Policy Analysis and Management,* 411–424.

Mayer, I. (1997). *Debating Technologies: a methodological contribution to the design and evaluation of participatory policy analysis.* Tilburg: Tilburg University Press.

Mayer, I., Bots P., and Daalen, E. van (2004). Perspectives on policy analysis: a framework for understanding and design. *Journal of Technology, Policy and Management, 4*(2), 169–191.

Mayer, I., Edelenbos, J., and Monnikhof, R. (2005). Interactive policy development: undermining or sustaining democracy. *Public Administration, 83*(1), 179–199.

Meadows, D.H., Meadows, D.L., and Randers, J. (1972). *The limits to growth: a report for the Club of Rome's project on the predicament of mankind.* New York: New American Library.

Ministerie van Financiën (2001). *Regeling prestatiegegevens en evaluatieonderzoek rijksoverheid.* Den Haag: Ministerie van Financiën.

Ministerie van Financiën (2002). *VBTB, van beleidsbegroting tot beleidsverantwoording.* Den Haag: Ministerie van Financiën. [brochure]

Most, H. van der, Bots, P., and Koppenjan, J. (1998). *Informatief interacteren door interactief informeren.* Delft: RWS-RIZA, Aquest report.

Polak, J.M., (1978). De Wetenschappelijke Raad voor het Regeringsbeleid, *Beleid en Maatschappij, 5,* 140–142.

Pulles, J.W. (1985). *Beleidsanalyse voor de waterhuishouding in Nederland (PAWN).* 's-Gravenhage Rijkswaterstaat.

Radin, B.A. (1997). Presidential address: the evolution of the policy analysis field: from conversation to conversations. *Journal of Policy Analysis and Management,* 204–218.

Radin, B.A., (2000). *Beyond Machiavelli: Policy analysis comes of age.* Washington D. C.: Georgetown University Press.

Riet, O. van de (2003). *Policy analysis in multi actor policy settings.* Delft: Eburon (dissertation.)

Ringeling, A. B. (1985). Beleidstheorieën en theorieën over beleid, *Beleid en Maatschappij, 11,* 275–284.

RPB. Netherlands Institute for Spatial Research (2005). Available at http://www.ruimtelijkplanbureau.nl/en-gb/ (accessed on March 10, 2005).

RWS. Rijkswaterstaat (2005). Available at http://www.rijkswaterstaat.nl/ (accessed on March 10, 2005).

Sabatier, P.A. (1998). The advocacy coalition framework: revisions and relevance for Europe. *Journal of European Public Policy, 5*(1), 98–130.

Scholten, G.H., (1980). Beleid versus analyse: enkele kanttekeningen bij theorie en praktijk. *Beleidsanalyse, 3,* 5–9.

Scott, C, (2002). Policy analysis and policy styles in New Zealand: central agencies. Paper presented at the 24th conference of APPAM, November 2002, Dallas Texas.

SCP. Social and Cultural Planning Bureau of the Netherlands (2005). Available at http://www.scp.nl/english/index.shtml (accessed March 10, 2005).

SER. The Social and economic council of the Netherlands (2005). Available at http://www.ser.nl (accessed March 10, 2005).

Shulock, N. (1999). The paradox of policy analysis: if it is not used, why do we produce so much of it? *Journal of Policy Analysis and Management,* 226–244.

Snellen, I. Th. (1984). Beleidsontwerpen tussen bureaucratisch ambacht en politiek bedrijf, *Bestuurswetenschappen, 6,* 355–371.

Staal, P.M. van der, and Vught F.A van. (1987). Vijftien jaar toekomstonderzoek door de WRR: de uitgestelde methodologische reflectie deel 1. *Beleidsanalyse, 4,* 16–25.

Staal, P.M. van der, and Vught F.A. van (1988). Vijftien jaar toekomstonderzoek door de WRR: de uitgestelde methodologische reflectie deel 2. *Beleidsanalyse, 1,* 5–17.

TNO. Netherlands Institute for Applied Research (2005). Available at http://www.tno.nl (Accessed March 10, 2005).

VBO (2005). Vereniging voor Beleidsonderzoek. Available at http://www.beleidsonderzoek.nl (Accessed March 10, 2005).

Vennix, J.A.M. (1990). *Mental models and computer models, design and evaluation of a computer-based learning environment for policy-making.* Disertation, Universtity of Nijmegen.

Vught, F. van (1995). *National planning: The Dutch experience.* In: Kickert, W. and Vught, F. van (eds.) Public policy and administration sciences in the Netherlands. Harvester Wheatsheaf: Prentice Hall, 105–124.

Williams, W. (1999). Policy information and democratic governance: federal social policy analysis, 1965–1997. *Journal of Comparative Policy Analysis, 1,* 145–162.

Wilmer, C. J. (1980). Evaluatie van de departementale doelstellingenanalyses. *Beleidsanalyse, 1,* 22–24.

WRR. Scientific council for government policy (2005). Available at http://www.wrr.nl (accessed March 10, 2005).

37 Policy Analysis and Evaluation in Sweden: Discovering the Limits of the Rationalistic Paradigm

Jan-Eric Furubo

This chapter focuses on a country—and a political culture—which for a number of years had the largest public sector of all the OECD countries in terms of tax share, that is to say that a very large proportion of the country's total consumption is determined through political decisions.

This is a reflection of a political culture distinguished by a belief in the ability of government to deal with the problems confronting society. At the same time this political culture could be described in terms of its belief in the ability of scientific methods to answer questions related to how you could solve societal problems through governmental intervention.

It is therefore not a surprise that an elaborate system of evaluation and other forms of analysis developed in this society. Already seventy years ago discussions were taking place in governmental commissions about the role of counterfactual developments in measuring the effects of public intervention.

This chapter will give a more detailed picture of the actual character of this political culture with its belief in governmental intervention and scientific methods. It will also describe the actual system of policy analysis and evaluation in Sweden.

However, many of the factors that shaped this political and administrative culture have changed, so some of the assumptions underlying this culture can be questioned. And, at the same time, the long history of the experience of evaluations and other form of analysis leads to new questions. In its simplest form: Do we really manage society better in a system with numerous evaluations and studies about different interventions?

THE IMPACT OF SELF-PERCEPTIONS

Let us start with two central notions, or self-perceptions, that have underpinned the Swedish political and administrative culture. Aware that we are facing the risk of being too rhapsodic we will give an outline of these perceptions.

A self-perception of harmony and consensus is part of the political and administrative culture.

It is easy to describe Sweden in terms of harmony and stability. To start with one observation, Sweden has enjoyed one of the longest periods of unbroken peace in modern European history: the country has not been involved in military conflict since 1814. Sweden takes unfeigned pride in the fact that despite an earlier history of military adventures they were able during the latter period to resolve disputes over the country's geographical boundaries (1905 and 1917–21) by peaceful means.[1] Sweden also regarded herself as a homogeneous country in which such topics as religion, language, and ethnic identity which gave rise to tensions in many other countries were more or less absent.

Class conflict in Sweden has traditionally been regarded as an issue to be resolved within the framework of a common value system—a national consensus of interests. On the whole, the growth of the Swedish labour movement was a peaceful process distinguished by a spirit of conciliation and virtual absence of open conflict.

A summary account of this kind inevitably conjures up an idyllic picture of nearly utopian harmony. Indeed, the borderline between fact and fiction is not always immediately obvious. Defining its precise position is not, however, the important concern here. Rather, the point to be made in this connection is that the majority of Swedish *élites* would have readily endorsed some such account of conditions in Sweden during the period leading up to the 1980s, a fact which cannot have failed to exercise an influence on prevailing attitudes.

It was taken for granted in Sweden that conflicts should be resolved by negotiation, compromise, pragmatic solutions and regard for the facts of the case. And given that we more often than not agreed upon the fundamental goals it was more a question of the best way to reach the goals than the goals themselves.

… and a belief in the state and science

Hand in hand with this self-perception was the notion that the state, generally speaking, could solve the problems society was facing. The Danish political scientist Peter Dahler-Larsen has described this, with reference to Tocqueville's account of his visit to America in 1830–2, as a fundamental difference between the United States and Europe. The idea, says Dahler-Larsen "that a membership of the so-called 'permanent association' of society is mandatory; and the expectation that the state has a natural role to play in the regulation of public life within that association seems to be still with us today in Europe" (Peter Dahler-Larsen 2004).

A more elaborate discussion of this is beyond the scope of this chapter—and also the competence of its author. However, this historic line of explanation, which Peter Dahler-Larsen adheres to, implies an important difference between the United States and Europe. The creation of the United States can be regarded as a liberation *from* the state, a point of view which still has a bearing on how the state is regarded. This has to be compared with the situation in Europe in which the state has many times been trusted to be *an instrument* in the liberation from poverty and social injustice.

This discussion bears a resemblance to Wildavsky's observation about the welfare systems in Scandinavia, Austria and the Netherlands: "We may suspect a basic consensus, among both governing elites and the mass public, on the relation between state and society embodied in state guarantees of a wide variety of social services." In America, Wildavsky observes, state activity is "less widely accepted" (Wildavsky 1986, 368). Furthermore Jan Erik Lane notes that "The Nordic countries and Austria go together not only on trade union density and the acceptance of the legitimacy of corporatism, or the influence of hierarchically structured interest groups upon policy-making and policy implementation. They have in common also a party system where there is a large and often dominating social democratic party, often participating in governmental coalitions" (Lane 2000, 46).

So the belief in the state's ability to solve fundamental social problems is very deep-rooted. However, it can be said that these traditions gave rise in Sweden to an even stronger belief in the state than among her neighbors, at least if we use the actual size of the public sector as a measure of this belief.

This combination of a strong belief in the state's ability to solve societal problems and the self-perception of the political culture as a consensus culture in which the discussion was more oriented to discussion of means than the fundamental goals, was a breeding ground for the concept of the importance of empirical knowledge and research in the shaping of public sector decisions on different levels.

The term "social engineering" is also associated with the Nordic states and especially Sweden, where it is also used as an expression in the national discussion. In the concept of social engineering lies the notion that the best means should be selected to achieve a given goal. The selection became a science-infused process in which it was important to use knowledge and research.

The distinguished Norwegian historian Francis Sejersted characterizes both Norway and Sweden, but especially the latter, as nations with a belief in Science. This was furthermore a very salient feature of the Social Democratic Party in Sweden in its "hegemonic phase." There existed a belief that it was possible to create the good society with the help of science. Sejersted demonstrates also that individual scientists could heavily influence attitudes and discussions within the Social Democratic party (Sejersted 2005).

This approach and belief in the possibilities of science to shed light on social courses of events and thus provide a type of operating instruction, similar to those provided by IKEA, for building society and constructing interventions, did not only characterize what, in a somewhat limited sense of the term, can be regarded as the political sphere. It was supported to a considerable degree by the atmosphere that existed among intellectuals and researchers. Many of them believed in the possibilities of intervening in social courses of events with the support of empirical studies and social theories. It is possible that Swedish academic circles, in the first part of the last century, had a deeper interest and greater faith in the capacity to assess the effects of and preconditions for state interventions, than in corresponding circles in other countries.

The Swedish social context should then have strengthened what a leading European Evaluation expert Evert Vedung describes as the foremost component element in the rationalistic gigatrend, namely the disenchantment of the world—*Entzauberung der Welt*—that Weber speaks of (Vedung 2004, 14).

A DOMESTIC TRADITION

But besides this ideological fundament we can also find an important salient feature of the Swedish political system in the existence of channels between the political system and different research communities. We are to some extent talking about informal contacts between researchers and leading political groups, but there also existed formal structures and channels.

An important such channel was the Swedish system with appointed ad hoc policy commissions. Researchers were often used for studies of the effects of earlier interventions. There also existed an awareness of what we may call the fundamental problems of evaluation long before evaluations began to be referred to as such in Sweden, as is shown by the following quotation from an official commission in 1934 concerning the possibility of seeing the effects of certain measures of financial regulation. The author, later a Nobel Prize laureate, declares that an inquiry of this kind into the effects of regulation "must relate to the difference between the economic events which should be triggered by the employment of a different regulation. This other regulation (the norm of comparison) must therefore also be specified. In any other sense than as a difference between two sets of events initiated by alternative measures of financial regulation, all talk of effects will be devoid of definite content" (Myrdal 1934, 8).

These kinds of commissions played a great part in preparing the ground for many decisions, even in the first half of the last century. It has also been argued though that it celebrated its greatest triumphs in the sixties and seventies.

However, what is important in this context is that one important feature of the commissions system in Sweden was the importance attached to the collection of various kinds of factual material. In this way the commission system may also be regarded as a major channel for introducing knowledge of the current state of research in various fields of activity into the political decision-making process. In about one fourth of the commissions at least one academically trained specialist was involved during the period 1955–89 (Johansson 1992, 65).

Within the system of public official inquiries in Sweden, we find in numerous research reports and statements of expert opinion examples of what have more recently been designated as evaluations, even when we go back to the 1950s and the 1960s, or indeed even earlier. They are often to be found under such headings as "previous experience" or "the current situation" (Furubo 1994, 49).

The picture we have given of the commission system supports the contention that this system permitted Sweden to introduce the ex post assessment of effects early on and in a comprehensive manner.

AN AMERICAN IMPORT

Up to this point in time, the Swedish story has more unique features than it will have in the years to follow and can also been said to have followed another path than its Scandinavian neigbors. The *mixture* of factors we have described—attitudes towards the state, degree of consensus, the belief in rationalism and science and institutional prerequisites—created a sort of very early evaluative tradition, ad hoc oriented but still systematic, planned and based on scientific methods.

This very long domestic tradition met, half a century ago, a stream of intellectual commodities, mainly from the United States. The content of this import can be at least partly encircled with words like budget system, program budgeting, performance measurement, monitoring, evaluation, and so forth. It meant, among other things, that examinations and adjustments of governmental interventions should be part of the steering-system as such when it comes to these interventions. The pioneer-field was here the school-reforms in Sweden during the 1960s. After the introduction of the nine-year comprehensive school system in 1962, the Swedish Board of Education was given the responsibility of continuously monitoring and evaluating the system, the intention being that evaluations would provide the factual ground for successive revisions of the school system's general curricula (Franke-Wikberg and Lundgren 1980, 17). In the 1960s evaluation began to be viewed as an activity which should provide decision makers with briefing material for reassessments planned in advance.

But the school system was not the only sector where it was intended to bring evaluation activities into the decision-making process in a more continuous fashion. As early as the 1960s, many discussions were being conducted in this way and a more general grasp of the evaluative questions was maturing concerning the effects of various instruments of social and consumer policy, Thus, an interest in questions of evaluation was developing in several different policy areas. This led later to the creation of research bodies in a number of sectors, such as for example construction, crime prevention, and energy with evaluation as one of their principal tasks. Parallel to ideas of evaluation gaining a foothold within several specific policy areas a more general grasp of the evaluative questions was maturing.

And in the 1960s this interest in evaluation, even if the Swedish word for evaluation, *utvärdering,* wasn't invented at that time, is also linked to the budget-process through program budgeting.

It can therefore be said that the Swedish response to this American import was very quick. And one important reason for that was most probably that this import fitted so well into the ideological atmosphere which dominated Sweden.[2] Another reason, which, of course, in a way is interrelated with the first, is that Sweden in the 1960s and 1970s was very much influenced by American theories in fields like social science and public management.

The Introduction of the International Atlas of Evaluation points out that one possible explanatory factor for the diffusion of evaluative praxis to different countries can be the scope and patterns of each country's contacts with the American system, from academia to public administration. It is obvious that some countries were, during the 1960s and 1970s, more influenced by American theories in the social sciences and public management than others. This is, perhaps, related to language, general cultural factors, and to the linkages of American universities and knowledge systems to those in other countries (Furubo & Sandahl 2002a, 14).

The Swedish example illustrates this. Before the Second World War, the German language was the first foreign language in Swedish schools. After the War, the German language and the English language changed positions as the first foreign language at all levels in the educational system. This made it possible to reorient the academic system. At the end of the 1960s, the majority of all university social science textbooks even at basic levels were of American origin.

The leading Swedish sociologist for several decades, Torgny Segerstedt, made the following comment: "during the 1950s and 1960s, most younger Swedish sociologists spent a term—often a year—at some American University" (Blanck 1992, 92). He drew the conclusion that the significance of American scholarship in sociology and in the social sciences in general for developments in Sweden had been of "enormous importance." In the field of public management, a study showing the origin of the books in libraries and on bookstore sales lists gives further evidence of a very strong American influence (Blanck 1992, 92).

So, to conclude this discussion about the meeting between a rather unique domestic tradition and an import from the United States, it can be said that at the same time as the earlier tradition made it possible for Sweden to respond very quickly to the evaluative discourse in the United States, it also led to the consequence that Sweden from the 1970s adopted a more general international discussion about evaluation. Sweden was probably to some extent unique for a few decades but became like other European countries after the 1970s with respect to evaluation.

TODAY: AN ELABORATE EVALUATIVE STRUCTURE

Today we find an elaborate evaluative structure of evaluation commissioners, doers, and users. Basically this evaluative structure is, with few exceptions, directed by the government—it is part of the executive branch. However, the evaluative information, which is produced, is supposed to be used in two different settings. The first is within the government itself when the government controls and directs the agencies. The second is in the communication between government and parliament. One of the tasks of the government is to inform Parliament about the results of different activities financed by the tax-payers. And the information the government receives has therefore to some extent also to be channeled to Parliament. In the discussion transparency is also mentioned as a crucial argument when the importance of the government's information is discussed.

Ad Hoc Commissions

We described earlier how, traditionally, ad hoc commissions have played a great part in preparing the ground for many decisions. They still do, but it has been a topic in the discussion whether the role of the commissions, at least relatively speaking, has been diminished.

The commissions have been important for providing briefing and (evaluative) background materials both with respect to fundamental policy decisions and in connection with the day-to-day fine calibration of the arsenal of means available in various spheres of activity.

If we consider developments over a comparatively long period of time, we may ascertain that practically every policy issue of any significance at the national level has been addressed in a commission. The matters investigated might concern such things as the creation of a new agency, how to reorganize an existing agency or the preparation of a new act, a housing policy or a new pension system, and so forth. Commissions often include representatives of political parties and stakeholders such as trade unions, the employers' associations, organizations for students, teachers, consumers, environmental interests, and so on. This means that a number of different interested parties are briefed in relation to the same factual material and are able to influence the question of what factual material is to be considered relevant in assessing the matter at issue.

Another feature of the commission system in Sweden, as we have pointed out earlier, is the importance attached to the collection of various kinds of factual material and the involvement of researchers and specialists in different policy fields.

The commission system is still responsible for providing significant information input to politicians and other decision makers. An examination of the commissions that presented results in 1990 indicates that most of the 100 or so reports published in that year contain various kinds of ex post material answering questions such as "what developments have taken place in this sphere?", "how have the factors which central government has been trying to influence developed in reality?", "how have central government efforts been progressing in this sphere?", "how much have these efforts cost?", and such. In a number of reports, however, the question is also put as to whether the developments observed in fact depended on central government measures or if they would have occurred irrespective of them (Furubo and Sandahl 2002b, 117).

However, it must be added that even if the commission system still plays an important role studies indicate that its has lost relative weight in relation to other producers of policy analysis and evaluation during the last decades.

Sectorial Agencies[3]

Certain individual agencies have also been allotted a role as central evaluation bodies. In these cases, therefore, it is a question of agencies which have the task of examining developments in a certain area of society in general terms and not just in relation to their own activities. It may be stated that the task of evaluation in these cases is a special one lying outside the range of the other activities pursued by the agency.

We have pointed out the role education as a pioneer field had and the role allotted to the National Board of Schools. Another important area was, already in the 1970s, energy. It was an area where many programs were launched and in which evaluation activities took place over a long period of time. This was partly due to the huge investments made in the area in the search for alternative sources of energy and partly due to the existence of specific programs or projects, which in many cases were well-suited to evaluation. Between 1973 and 1993, some 200 different evaluations were carried out, either by the sectorial agency itself or by researchers from universities or other research bodies on the initiative of, or funded by, the sectorial agency (Vedung 1993).

Another area in which evaluation activities have been extensive is foreign aid. In an article whose purpose was to investigate the quality of evaluations in the aid field a choice of 277 evaluations produced over a period of 20 years was noted (Forss and Carlsson 1997). These examples show how extensive evaluation activities can be, at least within certain sectorial fields.

Research Bodies

An interest in evaluation issues developed in several different policy areas, as part of what we may call an intrasectoral development process. This led to the creation of research bodies in a number of sectors, such as construction, crime prevention, energy and regional policy with evaluation as one of their principal tasks. Evaluation activities also take place at the various research councils, where from time to time experts from other countries are invited in to assess various projects. If one reads the instructions for these research councils, we can see that many councils have the responsibility of conducting evaluations, even though the task is usually wider than pure evaluation, involving for instance following the developments in an area and providing the government with material that may be useful in its decision making. The National Council for Crime Prevention illustrates this. The council's assignment is to encourage crime prevention measures through evaluation, research, development and information activities within the field of criminal policy. The council is also responsible for official Swedish legal statistics. The council is a centre for information on crime, supplying information to the government, to Parliament and to other agencies within the legal system.

The assignment of another research body, the Office of Labour Market Policy Evaluation, is to promote, support and carry out research on the effects of labour market policies and study the functioning of the labor market (Furubo and Sandahl 2002b, 119).

EVALUATION AS A TASK FOR ALL AGENCIES

Even though some agencies have a special assignment to cover a sectorial field—what we have above referred to as sectorial agencies—all agencies have a responsibility to report back about the results of their own activities. One process in which information about results has long been demanded from agencies, in formal terms at least, is the budgetary process. The budgetary process usually refers to the regular official process by which agencies make their annual request to the government for new allocations for their activities, followed by the discussions subsequently ensuing within the government and Parliament. Traditionally and in practice, however, these discussions have usually been more concerned with the financial framework for the activities than with the activities themselves. Monitoring and evaluation were therefore introduced to help move the centre of gravity from input-control to output-control.

The first attempt, already mentioned above, to improve the budget process in Sweden came as in many other countries with the Program Budgeting trials at the end of the 1960s. These were not a success. Many factors contributed to the relatively poor results shown by the Program Budget Trials. Some of these failings were at ministerial level. The agencies received no support from the ministries, and politicians saw few advantages in the system, apart from some improvements in accounting and reporting. Other goals got in the way. More importantly, however, the requirements the agencies were expected to satisfy were far too general, lacking specific application to the capacities or the various kinds of activities pursued by the particular agencies concerned. Thus the initiative specified neither a particular client nor a focus (Sandahl 1993, 144).

However, changing economic circumstances in the mid-1980s led to different perspectives, which influenced the evolution of a new budgetary process. An important part of this revised budget process involved the replacement of the customary annual budget request by a variety of budget documents (Sandahl 1993). One of these was an extended (in-depth) budget request aimed to force the agencies to have more long-term perspectives and also to analyze the results attained in the immediately preceding years.

The following ten years or so can be described as an ongoing reform process with respect to the budget-system. Nowadays the emphasis is on the annual report. The annual report contains of course partly purely economic information However, the annual reports primarily contain information about what has actually been produced, that is output, and what this output has cost, and do not normally constitute outcome oriented evaluations. Many agencies, however, are often given special assignments by the Government to evaluate certain matters and to report back the results in their annual report.

The Ordinance for the Annual Report of government agencies states the following: "The agency shall report and comment on the results of its operations in accordance with the objectives and the demands for information stated by the Government in the annual directives or in any other decision. In cases where the Government has decided not to specify what information the agency should report back to the Government, the agency shall report and comment on changes in output with respect to volume, costs and quality." (ESV 2003, 8).

The more recent debate about the interplay between the agencies and the ministries has a certain resemblance to the debate which followed the efforts to introduce Program Budgeting. There is still a discussion about the lack of information at the same time as one often hears complaints from the agencies that the information they produce are not used within government or Parliament.

THE AUDIT OFFICE—PART OF THE LEGISLATIVE BRANCH

The present National Audit Office in Sweden was only established in July 2003 as an audit institution under Parliament. However, it has had two predecessors both of which attached great importance to performance audit (Lindström 2005). Sweden introduced performance audit as a distinct category of audit work in the 1960s. Pollit and colleagues' comparative study of Supreme Audit Institutions demonstrates that the Swedish Audit Office has the longest history of conducting Performance Audit (Pollitt et al. 1999).

The early introduction of performance audit in the 1960s can be explained on several levels and partly by the more general factors we have earlier tried to encompass. Sweden attempted to introduce program budgeting in the late 1960s and performance audit can be regarded as an important part of this rationalistic concept. Program budgeting fitted into the political and administrative culture in Sweden, with a belief in social engineering and a belief in the possibilities of evaluating and studying the effects of different governmental interventions and fine tuning the different instruments used in a certain policy. In all of this performance audit could play an important role.

There is an ongoing discussion how you can regard audit in relation to evaluation. It can be said that the fundamental rationale is different. However, and from a more practical point of view, it is an empirical fact that performance auditors do the same things as many evaluators do. If program evaluation, for example, is defined as a comprehensive and systematic ex post analysis of the implementation or effects of a given set of measures, a good many audit reports could be appropriately classified under the heading of program evaluation.

It is therefore natural to place the performance audit in an overview of the evaluative structure.

THE VALUE OF EVALUATIVE INFORMATION

In all discussions about evaluation, it can be said that a sort of common denominator is that evaluation will bring improvement, evaluation will make a difference in one way or another.

So, has evaluation made a difference for Sweden? Do we actually handle the stream of different topics in public life better than we should have done in a counterfactual world without evaluation?

Why is this discussion so important? Evaluation is today an extremely elastic term. It is used in different contexts, with different methods, different resources and with different ideas of how it can be utilized. So, we have to be very humble about what evaluation can be. However, it must be something that unifies in order to make it meaningful to have a common label. And that unifying point, the common denominator, is the notion that evaluations may contribute to improvement. This is a notion that things are done differently as a consequence of evaluation. It leads to other decisions and other practices, regardless of whether we are speaking about Parliament, a teacher in the classroom, or an individual consumer.

Evaluation can thus be said to have another raison d'être than other forms of knowledge production. With the aid of evaluation we can increase our knowledge about what causes different developments in society, but this is not the basic motive for evaluation, the explanation is a means to achieve improvement. Through evaluation we can exercise control but, in this context, control is a means of achieving the improvement of a certain activity or a certain program. Evaluation is derived from the conception that knowledge and understanding lead to improvement. The knowledge we acquire is assumed to have the effect that we do things differently and more wisely than we otherwise would have done.

And, at some point, after decades of evaluating, we must consider whether evaluation lives up to its aims and promises. Are things better through all this evaluation one can ask, with the same naivety that evaluators ask practitioners in other fields.

But when we discuss these questions we soon find that we cannot do it on a general level. The political and administrative systems on the national level produce many different forms of decisions, and we can guess that the discussion of our questions is not quite the same when it comes to a decision about a fundamental change in policy or a minor fine-tuning maneuver.

So, even if we are aware that all categorizations of decisions are relative and unstable, let us discuss the effects of evaluations in relation to a scale at which you, at one end-point, have more fundamental policy decisions on a rather *aggregated policy level*, decisions that can question the very *existence* of a governmental policy, its basic *goals* and its principal *means*. At the opposite end of the scale, we will find what we without further discussion may regard as pure and simple technique, e.g., operative decisions which are part of the ongoing implementation of an intervention or a program.

Between these points we can find a lot of other types of decisions, which perhaps can be labeled as a sort of policy maintenance. These decisions are related to more disaggregated goals and the use of instruments on a lower level in the end-means hierarchy.

When we empirically try to observe use, non-use and perhaps the misuse of evaluations in relation to this scale we often meet different players involved in the decision-making process depending upon where, on this scale, the decisions can be placed. In a country like Sweden it can even be said, at least on a text-book level, that the division between the ministerial structure and the different agencies, numbering about 300, reflects these categorisations. Somewhere, a borderline has been drawn between policy-making and implementation. On one side of the borderline we have what is regarded as implementation—the task of the agencies and on the other side is what is regarded as policy or policy making.

The earlier structure for the production of evaluative information reflects also, more or less on purpose, the different kinds of decisions. Internal evaluations are to some extent the task of all agencies. They have to report back on an ongoing basis about their activities, and it creates a stream of evaluative information. It is reasonable to assume that this stream of evaluative information is most relevant in more operative decisions. It also seems reasonable to assume that evaluation of and character produced by research institutions, governmental commissions and so on can be of use in what we have called policy maintenance and more fundamental policy decisions.[4]

Studies about how different forms of how evaluative information have actually influenced decisions or praxis, if the information has led to learning, improvements and changes are rare, in Sweden as in other countries.

There are only a few studies that try to estimate the use of evaluations in different kinds of decisions. So, to a great extent, what can actually be said in this field has a hypothetical character.[5]

However, the existing studies show that evaluations appear to be used by decision makers at operational levels for fine-tuning and implementation. It is evaluative information oriented towards output and performance.

If we move to the other extreme on our scale, the picture is entirely different. It is only in very exceptional cases that we can possibly find examples in which evaluations have been of importance for more significant changes in policies. This is said by the political system itself. A report from the Ministry of Finance (Ministry of Finance 2002) states that reassessments are made on an ad hoc basis, as a result of certain events or unsatisfactory states of affairs, and thus not as a consequence of evaluations indicating the need of reassessments. The same conclusion can be drawn from studies of policy developments in different social fields. Extremely rarely, if at all, are references made to evaluations as a motive for reassessments of the very existence of a policy/program or changes in the fundamental focus or its central means.

Some people may feel that this picture is disheartening. The question that stands out is, of course, how credible is this picture? Are there factors that make this difference between different decisions reasonable? Is it reasonable to believe that evaluations are of *no or little* importance for fundamental, significant decisions at the same time as they seem to play an important role where the detailed construction of a policy and its implementation are concerned? Yes, there are a number of explanations that make this plausible. I will, in this context, point out four explanations.

VALUE-BASED REASSESSMENTS

The first explanation is that the very nature of some decisions makes the evaluative information highly irrelevant.

A policy or intervention can be discussed and questioned both from a value perspective, and for more instrumental reasons. The value component can be expected to be more salient when we move towards the fundamental reassessments at the end-point in our scale, and the role of empirical information increases when we move in the other direction.

It is easy to point out that the existence or basic orientation of a program can sometimes be regarded purely as a question of values. We can, on one level, imagine that all politicians agree about the actual situation in some area, e.g., the standard of housing, the social distribution of education and so on. However, there can be quite different opinions about how a given situation should be judged. Some politicians may regard the situation as unsatisfactory, justifying political intervention. Other politicians may regard the same situation as quite satisfactory.

Even in those cases in which all politicians agree that a given situation is unsatisfactory, there can still be divergent opinions concerning whether or not it is a political issue at all, i.e., if the situation justifies political intervention.

And a politician arguing against an existing governmental intervention from such a value perspective has little use of evaluative-based information. If the evaluations show that the existing program has been successful, and perhaps indicate that some changes could make it even more successful, it is still irrelevant information for the politicians who are against the intervention as such. And the same can be said if the evaluations show the opposite; the intervention was a failure and that you perhaps need quite different instruments to make the intervention successful.[6] Even this information doesn't motivate a re-examination of the politicians own position regarding the intervention. However, in this case the politician is probably grateful for the information—it shows that his political adversaries were wrong even from their own value-premises.

In these situations, information from evaluations lacks relevance for future decision making, the political position towards the intervention or program is based on values about what is good and bad, better and worse and about the role of government. Your position does not depend on information concerning whether a *certain intervention* was a suitable means of reaching a certain goal or solving a certain problem in society or not.

But a very brief moment of reflection will probably also lead us to the conclusion that decisions concerning the basic orientation of policies are value-based to a much higher extent than decisions on lower policy levels. In other words, the relative weight of values and empirical information is quite different in more fundamental policy decisions compared with more technical and instrumental decisions concerning the more detailed construction of a given policy or its implementation.

THE CHARACTER OF THE EVALUATIONS

One second explanation concerns the actual character of the evaluations produced in Sweden and probably in many other countries. Most of the studies labeled evaluations in Sweden do not provide information at the fundamental goals-oriented level. Just to give one example: governmental agencies, governmental commissions and different research institutions in Sweden have produced literally hundreds of evaluations about the use of information as a policy instrument in areas such as energy consumption, health, and so on. These evaluations provide information about the dissemination of the information, how efficient different channels are compared with each other, the changes in knowledge and attitudes in different target groups that can be attributed to the information, and so on. In other words, the evaluations provide a lot of knowledge about the implementation of, in this case, a certain policy instrument. However, they do not provide answers to questions concerning in which situations information is a suitable policy instrument in relation to other policy instruments, in which situations information should be used instead of other policy instruments and in which situations information could lead to effects the opposite of what was intended.

There is even a tendency to produce fewer evaluations that deal with the basic assumptions about how a certain intervention can influence different causal relationships and the circumstances for governmental interventions. There has been a tendency over the past ten years or so to produce evaluations in a much shorter time and to provide more "easily captured" information.[7] More and more of the evaluations are oriented toward implementation, output and performance and are part of the system of agency reporting to the government. The information in the evaluations therefore is more relevant in decisions that are part of what I have called the maintenance of policies or operative decisions.

This explanation is empirical in character. It says that we, to some extent, produce the "wrong" evaluations if the intention is for them to be used in policy reassessments, and that we to some extent produce the "right" evaluations if the intention is that they be used in more operative decisions.

UNRELIABLE INFORMATION

We have discussed how the role of empirical information varies depending on where we are in our scale, and it is also obvious that the decision maker needs different forms of evaluative information depending on what kind of decisions we are talking about. When we want to know how we can improve the technical construction of a given policy instrument we need a certain type of information but when we are discussing whether or not it is a good idea to use this policy instrument at all, we need of course a quite different type of information. It is obvious that these different forms of information have many different characteristics. The first type of information is often of a character which makes it suitable for an ongoing production of information often based on routines and systems, which perhaps is not the case when we talk about the latter type of information.

It is also relevant to make a distinction between how exact and reliable different evaluative statements are. This is illustrated in the graph in Figure 37.1. On the Y-axis we can imagine, nearest the origin of coordinates, a limited measure, e.g., an information brochure on influencing a household's use of energy. A little further up we find the "package of information efforts" required to have an effect on energy consumption, and still higher up the total measures needed to influence energy use in society. On the X-axis we can imagine some kind of chain of effects where, in the example given, we see the reception of the information nearest the zero, and farthest to the right the influence on the environment, and the national economy that reduced energy consumption would have.

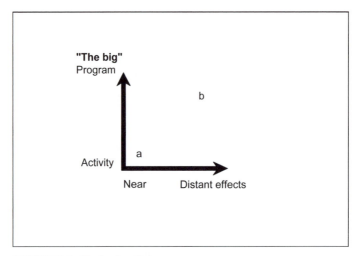

FIGURE 37.1 Evaluative Statements.

It is easily seen that we are talking about completely different kinds of information in "a" and "b" and without crossing over the line to a discussion about theories of knowledge we—and certainly the decision makers—can expect information in "a" to be very exact and, at the same time, reliable. Evaluative statements on the effects of complex interventions in still more complex social processes and courses of events are of a quite different nature. An evaluation that draws conclusions about the extent to which a reform of the school system, aiming to influence equality between men and women, has actually changed vocational choice, relationships in the home, and so forth, can hardly do so particularly well, and in any case not with a high degree of reliability. The nearer to "b," the more improbable it is that different evaluations will come to the same conclusions.

The problem is, of course, that the "b"—information is more relevant than the "a"—information, when it comes to decisions about the basic orientation of a policy. It is therefore difficult to imagine that this kind of often uncertain evaluative information should be transferred in a more immediate way to the political decision-making system. The lack of use in relation to fundamental policy reassessments can, therefore, seem very rational from the politicians' point of view in relation to handling the evaluative information, uncertain and inexact as it is. But on the other hand, we can also expect that the decision makers make more use of the evaluative information in relation to the maintenance of policies and operative decisions. The information they need in these processes is more of the "a" character and, hence, also more reliable. The difference when it comes to the use of evaluative information in different kinds of decision-making processes seems therefore reasonable even from this perspective.

EVALUATOR/DECISION MAKER RELATIONSHIP

In the discussion on evaluations and their use, we must address the relationship between evaluation and decision makers. Even if the discussion has long passed the point where it was a case of an immediate response by decision makers to a specific evaluation, there is still a notion that what the discussion is all about is evaluations and evaluation processes through which information is to be transferred to decision makers. Even if the interaction is complex, it is nonetheless the interaction between evaluators and decision makers. And the systems that have been built up within the framework of various control techniques, program budgeting, new public management, performance management, and the like, have also had this as their point of departure. They are systems which have also had the aim that decision makers, with the aid of evaluations, should be given fuel and data for fundamental reassessments of undertakings and activities.

However, if it was shown to be the case that this picture is not correct—that the program theory of evaluation can be questioned—this concept of a type of bilateral relationship between evaluation and decision-making can be criticized. In other discussions on policy changes it is emphasized that the trigger of the determination to make powerful changes is that something dramatic has happened, that we are in an extreme situation, that there is a feeling of crisis, which makes the search for other action alternatives necessary when it is felt that it is not possible to use the old methods.

If this picture is more true than the picture that emphasizes a type of regular rationality, where new knowledge of what we are doing leads to questioning and reorientation, this leads, of course, to the question of how the search for knowledge should proceed in this type of situation—in which new windows are opened and new alternative actions are sought. We can ask ourselves if it is credible that the decision-making system in a situation of this type asks the question of which evaluations have been made? Is it not more credible that the decision maker instead turns to those who are assumed to know, who are assumed to have knowledge of relevant theories and current empirical information, which is also, of course, based on evaluations? In other words, it is a case of knowledge structures that can, so to speak, receive and also absorb the often limited evaluations that are made of programs and interventions and relate them to more general knowledge.

We can imagine that evaluations make deposits into types of metaphorical knowledge banks that correspond to these knowledge structures. These are possibly the foremost users of certain types of evaluations. Evaluation has an important role in submitting contributions to knowledge structures of this type. The degree to which these knowledge structures are well defined varies from field to field. In some cases they are fairly self-evident, in other cases not. In the study of the stabilization policy (Jonung 1999), it is shown that in this case decision makers were easily able to distinguish the knowledge structures, professions, and disciplines in question.

Instead of discussing utility, use and a relationship problem between evaluations and decision-makers, it is rather a question of introducing the idea of intermediate structures that are possibly those that the decision makers communicate with more directly.

CONCLUSION OR THE PROMISE OF EVALUATION

We have described how different forms of systematic analysis—ex post and ex ante—have been adopted as a way to enhance rational decisions about governmental intervention in Swedish society. We have described how a country with a strong belief in state and science has built an elaborate structure for evaluation and how this structure feeds political and administrative decision making with a stream of information about different governmental activities. However, this chapter has also aimed to show that we today have to raise evaluative questions about evaluation itself.

Evaluation has promised a lot. One promise has been that we through evaluation can make better decisions, both regarding the practical implementation of policies and about the policies themselves. Therefore evaluation with all its subcategories has become an important tool in different governmental systems, reaching from cities to structures like the European Community. And organizations like OECD and the World Bank have become a sort of entrepreneurs for evaluation and the marriage between evaluation and different budget and management techniques.

Evaluation today represents a lot of intellectual resources and a lot of money. The time has certainly come to ask questions about the value of evaluation. To what extent can evaluation be said to have fulfilled its promises?[8]

This chapter has not given the answer to this question. However, we have pointed out some experiences and some factors that make it reasonable to question the more enthusiastic belief in evaluation.

The dissemination of evaluation praxis through budget and planning systems has been grounded in the implicit idea that political decision-making is very much the same as administrative decision making. Evaluation has very much been regarded as a *Mädchen für alles*, for all forms of decisions assuming that decision makers start to question earlier decision because they are questioned by evaluations. This can perhaps be true for some forms of decision making but it is probably not true that those on the political level start to question a fundamental policy—its goals and its principal tools—because even a few evaluations point out different problems in a policy, e.g., the lack of goal fulfillment and questions about the underlying rationale for the policy.

But evaluation has also given promises about what information it can deliver. Perhaps we have learned to regard statements about the effects of complex interventions in complex social processes, with more skepticism than when evaluation was in its pioneer phase.

A more critical discussion about evaluation leads also to questions about the relation between evaluation and other forms of knowledge production. We can ask to what extent evaluation is communicating with the knowledge frontiers in different disciplines more related to the substantial questions in different policy fields.

So, evaluation today has reached a degree of maturity and has since long passed (and this is certainly the case in Sweden) the optimistic phase when everything was possible. Today we have to adopt an evaluative attitude towards evaluation and ask questions about limitations in the role evaluation can play in different decisions and the limitations in the information that can actually be delivered by evaluation and its role in relation to disciplines and other forms of knowledge production.

NOTES

1. The union with Norway was dissolved in 1905. During 1917–21, there was considerable tension , which involved several states, regarding the position of Åland (an island or more precisely an island group in the Baltic Sea). A referendum took place among the population of Åland. The result of this was that an overwhelming majority of the population stated that they wanted to become a part of the Swedish state. However, the League of Nations finally settled for a solution which meant that Åland became part of the Finnish state, under special conditions. The tension was in periods so great that strong pressure groups both on Åland and in Sweden, even within government, discussed a Swedish military intervention to defend the interests of the population of the islands.
2. So, it can be noted that the reasons for the "import" of evaluation to Sweden do not necessarily have to be the same as the ones which contributed to the development of evaluation in the United States.
3. Swedish ministries are small and employ not more than a couple of hundred people each. Implementation is a task falling to the various agencies. There is several hundred agencies and their size varies considerably from a handful employees to several thousands. The agencies can be regarded as rather independent in their day-to-day work.
4. In this context the terms evaluation and evaluative information are used with great openness. However, even with such elasticity I do not include all kinds of descriptive information. We can assume that some notion of reality lies behind every policy or every governmental program. The foundation of an intervention is the perception that you need to do something, in other words that you are facing a problem or, perhaps, will be facing a problem in the future. The purpose of an intervention is to reduce the magnitude of this problem or to avoid it. And an important kind of information therefore relates to the fulfilment of political goals. Securing such information is not always a simple task. But basically our national statistics, as in many other countries, can tell us to what extent the "big goals" have been fulfilled. So a stream of such descriptive information is produced (Sjöström 2002).

    But when I discuss evaluations that can be used in the reassessments of policies, I am oriented toward the idea that evaluations will give us some information about how a certain action, on a micro or macro level, can be judged; to what extent the action has caused a certain development and how can this be explained?

    This perspective lies very near the definition by Evert Vedung (1997, 3). "Evaluation = df. careful retrospective assessment of the merit, worth, and value of administration, output, and outcome of government interventions, which is intended to play a role in future, practical action situations."

5. As is pointed out, there are few studies on the use of evaluations. In a presentation in OECD in February 2003, I tried to put together those that exist. The presentation was later published in the OECD Journal on Budgeting (Furubo 2003).

6. A similar situation is when it is agreed that something is a problem, and also that this problem is something which the government has to deal with, but some politicians do not think that they can afford it given other needs. You can, of course, say, "Yes, this is a very unsatisfactory situation and in my opinion this is something which should be resolved by governmental intervention, but we cannot afford it in the light of other needs." And the conclusion may be that a governmental program is abolished or a decision is made not to start a new program on grounds which at least limit the relevance of information in evaluations.

7. Indications of this are discussed in Furubo and Sandahl, 2002b (page 126). It is further indicated in reports from the National Financial Management Authority and also in the discussion about the system with Governmental Commissions (ESO 1998).

8. It has to be said that this is not in any way a new question. Mark S. Thompson wrote over 30 years ago "More than a decade has passed since structured analysis was introduced on a large scale in government. Throughout the world… systematic routines of analysis have been adopted in hopes that irrational social decision making would be reduced . . .The time has come to appraise as objectively as we can the net effects of these governmental changes (Thompson 1975, 1).

REFERENCES

Blanck, D. 1992. "The impact of the American Academy in Sweden" in R. Lundén and E. Åsard (eds.) *Networks of Americanization. Aspects of the American Influence in Sweden,* 80–93. Stockholm: Almqvist & Wiksell.

Dahler-Larsen, Peter *Is There a European Dimension in Evaluation?* Paper presented at Round Table discussion. The European Evaluation Societys 6th conference, Berlin, October 1, 2004.

ESO (expertgruppen för studier i offentlig ekonomi, the expert group on Public Finance) 1998. *Kommittéerna och bofinken. Kan en kommitté se ut hur som helst?* DS 1998:57

ESV (Ekonomistyrningsvereket, the Swedish National Financial Management Authority), 2003. *Performance Management in Swedish central government.* ESV 2003:22.

Finansdepartementet (Ministry of Finance) 2002. *Regeringskansliets kontroll och styrning av statlig verksamhet.*

Forss, Kim and Carlsson, Jerker. 1997. "The Quest for Quality — or Can Evaluation Findings be Trusted?" in *Evaluation* 5, no 4, 4811. 501. Sage Publications.

Franke-Wikberg, Sigbrit and Lundgren, Ulf P. 1980. *Att värdera utbildning.* Stockholm: Wahlström & Widstrand.

Furubo, Jan-Eric. 1994. "Learning from Evaluations: The Swedish Experience," in F. Leeuw, R. Rist, and R. Sonnichsen (eds.), *Can Governments Learn? Comparative Perspectives on Evaluation & Organizational Learning.* New Brunswick, NJ: Transaction Publishers.

Furubo, Jan-Eric and Sandahl, Rolf. 2002a. "Introduction — A Diffusion Perspective on Global Developments in Evaluation" in J. E. Furubo, R. Rist, and R. Sandahl (eds.), *International Atlas of Evaluation.* New Brunswick, NJ: Transaction Publishers.

Furubo, Jan-Eric and Sandahl, Rolf. 2002b. "Coordinated Pluralism — The Swedish Case," in J. E. Furubo, R. Rist, and R. Sandahl (eds.), *International Atlas of Evaluation.* New Brunswick, NJ: Transaction Publishers.

Furubo, Jan-Eric 2003. "The Role of Evaluations in Political and Administrative Learning and the Role of Learning in Evalaution Praxis" in *OECD Journal on Budgeting* 3, no.3, 67–85.

Johansson, Jan. 1992. *Det statliga Kommittéväsendet — Kunskap, Kontroll, Konsensus* (English summary). Edsbruk, Sweden: Akademitryck AB.

Jonung, Lars. *Med backspegeln som kompass — om stabiliseringspolitik som läroprocess,* Published by ESO (expertgruppen för studie i offentlig ekonomi, The expertgroup for Public Finance). DS 1999:9.

Lane, Jan-Erik. 1990. *New Public Management.* London: Routledge

Lindström, Eva. 2005. "A Swedish Challenge — a brand new SAI in an old Audit Culture" in *Public Audit in Europe – Achievments and Outlook. Selection of articles prepared by Supreme Audit Institutions of European States.* Moscow: Eurosai, 314–323.

Myrdal, Gunnar. 1934. "Finanspolitikens ekonomiska verkningar," AOU 1943:1

Pollitt, Chrstopher, Wavier Girre, Jeremy Lonsdale, Robert Mul, Hilka Summa, and Marit Waerness. 1999. *Performance Audit and Public Management in Five Countries.* Oxford: University Press.

Sandahl, Rolf. 1993. "Connected or Separated? Budgeting, Auditng and Evaluation in Sweden" in A. Gray, B. Jenkins, and B. Segsworth (eds.). *Budgeting, Auditing & Evaluation — Functions & integration in Seven Governments.* New Brunswick, NJ: Transaction Publishers.

Sejersted, Francis. 2005. *Socialdemokratins tidsålder, Sverige och Norge under 1900-talet.* Bokförlaget Nya Doxa: Nora

Sjöström, Olle. 2002. *Svensk statistikhistoria.* Södertälje: Gidlunds förlag

Thompson, Mark S. 1975. *Evaluation for decision in social programmes.* Wetmead, Farnborough, Hants: Saxon House.

Vedung, Evert. 1993. *Utvärderingar av Svensk energipolitik.* Närings- och teknikutvecklingsverket. R 1993:34

Vedung, E. 1997. *Public Policy and Program Evaluation.* New Brunswick, NJ: Transaction Publishers.

Vedung, Evert. 2004. *Utvärderingsböljans former och drivkrafter.* Stakes, FinSoc Working Papers 1/2004. Helsinki.

Wildavsky, Aaron (1986). *Budgeting: A comparative theory of budgetary process.* Second, revised edition. New Brunswick, NJ: Transaction Publishers.

38 The Policy Turn in German Political Science

Thomas Saretzki

INTRODUCTION

Policy analysis was not invented in Germany. Rather, both the term and the first concepts of policy analysis were imported from the United States. Such a conceptual transfer across the Atlantic is nothing new or unusual for political science in Germany. Even the whole discipline of political science had been (re-)established in Germany after the Second World War with the help of the American administration (Bleek 2001, 265–307). Policy analysis had precursors in the German academic tradition, the so-called Polizeywissenschaft (Maier 1966). Yet this tradition was rediscovered—one could even say: reinvented—by the discipline as a whole only after policy analysis became important in the United States (Beyme 1985; Bleek 2001, 72–76; Hartwich 2004). The turn towards policy was a challenge to academic political science on both sides of the Atlantic.

One thing worth noting in comparative perspective is the fact that the transfer of policy analysis to Germany happened with a certain time lag. In North America "the policy turn had, by the mid-1970s, developed to a point where both proponents and critics saw policy as central to the discipline, leading it into an interdisciplinary domain, even eclipsing its distinctly political perspective" (Torgerson 1995, 229). All of the points Douglas Torgerson described as central to the debate of the "policy turn" in political science in North America also played a significant role in Germany. But it took almost ten years until that stage of perception and critical discussion of the "policy turn" could be observed in Germany in the middle of the 1980s. "Policy studies" had already been mentioned in German introductory political science textbooks at the end the 1960s. But at that time they were portrayed as a research enterprise that took place in the United States (not in Germany)—and were sometimes seen by students as "the" characteristic American contribution to political science (Prätorius 2004, 75–76). To be sure, the transfer did not leave the transfered simply as it had been on the other side of the Atlantic. Rather, the reception and interpretation of policy analysis in Germany was influenced by the theoretical traditions developed in German political science. And the application of its concepts and methods were adapted and modified to fit with the specific problems of policymaking in the political system of the Federal Republic of Germany.

The interest in the Anglo-Saxon discussion on policy analysis brought a new word to German political science: policy. As in French, the German language does not possess a "term for policy that is distinct from that for politics" (Heidenheimer 1986, 3). In German, the word "Politik" signifies policy as well as politics. It is not possible, for instance, to shortly denote processes nicely described in English as the "politics of (environmental) policy." In order to be able to make such distinctions between different dimensions of the political, German political scientists did not work on their own language, but imported the English terms. In the years following the debate the policy turn, the differentiation of the German word "Politik" into the English triad policy, politics, and polity became a standard part of all textbook introductions to political science in Germany. Connected with this new awareness of the German language and its limits, the policy turn was also interpreted as a (re-)discovery of the content or material dimension of the political related to societal problems and political problem solving. Which societal problems are thematized and debated in the political realm, what political decisions are made and implemented to solve these problems? In that sense, i.e., as an orientation towards problems and problem solving strategies, the turn to policy clearly brought a differentiation to the terminology of German political science that is here to stay. Although as basic as such categorical differentiations of the subject of a discipline are, this terminological clarification is but one outcome of the debate on the policy turn in German political science—and clearly not the first nor the most important outcome the proponents of the policy turn were thinking of in the first place.

This chapter describes the development of policy analysis in Germany with a focus on its relation to political science. It starts with a look at the origin of policy analysis in Germany and its close connection with the program of domestic reforms pursued by a newly elected reform government of social democrats and liberals in 1969. While these discourse coalitions between political reformers and policy analysts soon faced some disillusionment on their way to change policies and policymaking in the 1970s, the growing importance and impact of the policy orientation led to a critical discussion of the policy turn in German political science in the middle of the 1980s. The chapter goes on to discuss the following questions: what do we know about the role of policy research for political science from empirical surveys? What infrastructure do we find in the field in terms of organisational foothold in the political science associations, journals publishing results of policy studies and institutional capacities in research and teaching? What points of reference matter when policy analysts relate their studies to political science? Are there specific German approaches to policy analysis? And finally: Can we identify clear future trends in policymaking and policy analysis in Germany?

POLICY ANALYSIS AND POLITICAL REFORM

The transfer of policy analysis from the United States to Germany in the late 1960s and early 1970s was not primarily driven by the cognitive value of its concepts and methods or by other internal scientific factors. Rather, the transfer corresponded with a growing demand for policy oriented expertise, especially from government and administration. While there were already some tendencies of involving more scientific expertise during the years of the "grand coalition" between christian democrats and social democrats (1966–1969), the real expansion of demand for policy oriented scientific knowledge could be observed after the coalition of social democrats and liberals came to power and formed the federal government in 1969. This so called "social-liberal coalition" started not only with a far-reaching program of "domestic reforms." It also began its term with very ambitious attempts to modernize the existing governmental and administrative structures and procedures and build up new informational, organizational and planning capacities for the kind of active policymaking (*aktive Politik*) deemed necessary to develop and realize its program of domestic reforms. It probably was primarily at this stage when "the concepts and tools of policy science and policy analysis (particularly of the PPBS sort) that German practitioners and researchers became acquainted with in the United States, had a conspicuous influence on concept formation in West Germany" (Wollmann 1984, 30).

To meet its demand for policy expertise, the social-liberal coalition expanded its offers for policy oriented contract research, created new advisory boards and established a number of major "reform commissions." A first group of commissions focussed on the modernization of government and administration, like the Projektgruppe Regierungs- und Verwaltungsreform (Project Group on the Reform of Government and Administration), which already began its work in 1968 under the grand coalition (Mayntz and Scharpf 1973), and the Studienkommission für die Reform des öffentlichen Dienstrechts (Commission on Civil Service Reform). A second group of commissions focusing more on developments in society was established somewhat later. The most comprehensive of these commissions was the Kommission für wirtschaftlichen und sozialen Wandel (Commission on Economic and Social Change), which published more than 150 reports on various societal trends in the middle of the 1970s (Wollmann 1984, 42–43).

In reviews of the policy turn written in the mid-1980s, the development of policy analysis in Germany was often characterized in the form of a three stage model build around the three key words: (traditional) consulting, reform, disillusionment (Sturm 1986, 231–232). By and large, this three stage model reflected the experience of those social scientists who were actively involved in consulting activities, reform commissions or contract research for government agencies. In the first two phases, these scholars had formed discourse coalitions with politicians and bureaucrats supporting the program of domestic reforms that the social-liberal coalition tried to bring about (Wagner 1990). Even before these reforms came to a halt as the economic conditions worsened and the resistance of powerful interest groups grew in the mid-1970s, the scholars engaged in reform of government and administration were confronted with various restrictions that hindered the attempts to establish methods and procedures of policy analysis in the federal bureaucracy. When returning to academia, most of these scientists started to work on the disillusioning experiences with the politics of policy reform in a specific way. Rather than trying to optimize rational planning processes they concentrated on problems of implementation and evaluation in the first place. So in Germany, implementation and evaluation were the first foci when policy analysis became part of "normal" scientific research at universities and research institutions (Wollmann 1984, 30). And after the disillusionment phase the critique of unreflected planning optimism became a recurring theme in the emerging policy research community.

POLICY ANALYSIS AND POLITICAL SCIENCE

In the beginning of the 1980s, the growing importance of contract research and consulting activities in the field of policy studies was generally perceived and discussed in the social sciences. Calls for a policy turn met with considerable scepticism and critique in German political science. In 1984, the policy turn and its implications for political science were discussed at a symposium on policy research in the Federal Republic of Germany, in which many leading political scientists took part (Hartwich 1985). This discussion about the relation of political science to policy research finally led to a debate about the self understanding of the discipline as a whole. In 1986 the first—and to date last—volume on the "state of the discipline" in German political science was published (Beyme 1986). In retrospect, the discussion on the role of policy research appears to be the last general debate on the collective self understanding of political science in Germany for almost 20 years. Only recently, some claim that now the time has come to start a new debate of this kind as the university reforms and the coming retirement of the third generation of political scientists pose serious challenges to the discipline (Greven 2004, 145–146).

There were several reasons for the controversies and ambivalent feelings of many German political scientists about the policy turn. First of all, there was the historical legacy. After the Second World War, political science was established as an academic discipline as part of the re-education campaign and with the support of the American administration. The basic political task for the country as a whole was to make sure that the Germans would again become part of the civilized world and build democratic institutions. For political science as an academic discipline the task was to help in this process of democratization and to make sense of the recent historic experience: Why did the first democratic state in German history, the Weimar Republic, fail? Why did the Nazis come to power? How did the NS dictatorship work? And how could the second German republic develop and sustain a democratic polity that would guarantee freedom and make sure that the Germans would live in peace with their neighbours? During the cold war, concepts of totalitarianism gained currency and provided a theoretical framework directed against fascist and sowjet forms of dictatorship.

Against this setting, i.e., the Nazi regime of the immediate past and the communist regime just across the border in the other part of Germany, the discipline developed a self-understanding of political science as a "science of order" with a strong emphasis on the normative foundations of political institutions. Since the order would have to be a democratic one, political science was seen as a "science of democracy."

In the 1960s the newly established democratic order seemed to have gained some stability in West Germany. Thus in political science, the emphasis on normative foundations of institutions was no longer strong. The focus was shifting "from polity to politics." At least this was the formula in the somewhat stylized short histories of the discipline presented later in the debates about the policy turn (Jürgens and Naschold 1983, 114–117). In the 1960s the younger generation of political scientists was much more interested in actual conflicts and crises within Western democracies. Moreover, as a consequence of university reforms and student protests, political science developed not only a new focus on politics as a subject of study, but turned into an openly politicized science itself.[1] Although the association managed to deal with these controversies without breaking apart in the 1970s, political scientists began to feel that they had an image problem that could have serious repercussions on the discipline as a whole.

While the open political controversies in the discipline diminished in intensity in the second half of the 1970s, the question remained whether it had anything useful to offer for society and political decision makers. A conference with the general topic political science and political praxis held in Bonn in autumn 1977 was intended to start a new dialogue with political and administrative practitioners in the capital of the West German Federal Republic, but failed to gain much attention from politicians and bureaucrats (Bermbach 2003, 32–33). At the end of the 1970s, political science had a problem of being accepted as an academic discipline producing socially relevant and useful knowledge both in the halls of power and in the public. Moreover, the usefulness of political science as a subject for graduate and postgraduate study was called into question. A large proportion of students graduating in political science lost their traditional perspectives on the labor market. Most of the professorships for political science had been established in the early 1970s as the demand for teachers in primary and secondary schools was increasing rapidly. In the second half of the 1970s these employment possibilities were drastically reduced as most of the available positions were filled and political education lost as a relevant political and scientific concern. Students interested in political science had to look for other career paths and job opportunities and hence for other qualifications than before.

In this situation, a turn towards policy looked like it had something to offer for political science (and its future graduates). A policy-oriented political science should and would be "practically relevant" (i.e., useful for policy makers and society). It would be "scientifically sound" (i.e., based on the latest—preferably quantitative—scientific methods). Moreover, a policy science orientation would lead political scientists into problem-oriented interdisciplinary cooperation. Thus, it would help in the process of "professionalizing" the discipline and its graduates that seemed to be necessary from this perspective. What looked promising for the advocates of a turn towards policy, was perceived as a critical threat to the discipline by their opponents. A turn towards policy, so the critics claimed, could and probably would have desintegrating effects on the discipline as a whole. Policy analysts could become specialists in their specific policy fields and engage more and more in problem-oriented interdisciplinary cooperation. But this would imply a turn away from basic questions of political order and from traditional core fields of political science which are constitutive

---

1. This process of politicization finally became obvious for anybody inside and outside the discipline at a meeting of the German political science association in Hamburg in 1973, when younger political scientists called for a joint resolution on the military coup against president Allende in Chile. After the meeting, political science was portrayed by the press primarily as a discipline caught in ideological struggles between neo-Marxists and conservatives (Bermbach 2003, 29–30).

for the discipline as such. Thus, a policy turn would undermine and finally threaten the unity and identity of the discipline. Policy analysis, as represented by the mainstream in the United States, implied a functional and technical understanding of policy making that came close to a conceptually induced depolitization on the level of the processes to be analyzed. What appeared to be a more scientific political science, so the critics claimed, turned out to be scientism, reducing the distinctive political qualities of the phenomena political science has to deal with. Furthermore, a policy science orientation with its emphasis on relevance and usefulness could threaten the integrity of the discipline. In order to be useful for decision makers, a closer cooperation with policy makers and other interest groups in the policy making process was necessary—and this could undermine the independence and professional competence of political scientists and finally lead to a politicization of the discipline.

All of these issues were more or less openly debated at the symposium on policy research in the Federal Republic of Germany organized by the chairman of the Deutsche Vereinigung für Politische Wissenschaft (DVPW) (German Political Science Association) (Hartwich 1985). Although sometimes ironically portrayed as a conflict of policy enthusiasts versus old institutionalists (representing grandpa's political science), the various aspects and implications of a turn towards policy were not only discussed in the form of a confrontational exchange between two camps where one camp was in favor of enhancing professionalization, relevance, and usefulness of political science via policy studies whereas the other wanted to safeguard the traditional core and identity of the discipline. There were advocates arguing in favor of policy analysis or a policy-oriented public administration. On the other side, representatives of the older generation articulated their criticism and scepticism about a policy turn in political science. But most discussants in the debate argued for some kind of complementarity or even integration, e.g., by trying to bring institutionalism to policy analysis.

POLICY RESEARCH IN POLITICAL SCIENCE

The debate on the role of policy research in relation to the core questions of political science was also informed by the first survey among political scientists on the state of the discipline conducted in 1984. The results of the survey were presented in the form of a report to the symposium (Böhret 1985). Critical collective scientific self reflection was supplemented by empirical self monitoring. The survey focused specifically on the relation of traditional or conventional "core areas" of the discipline and new fields, especially policy studies. Its findings were suited to take some of the hot air out of the discussion. A loss of interest in conventional "core areas" or a general trend towards policy studies could not be identified. Yet the percentage of political scientists engaged in policy studies apparently was about to increase (Böhret 1985, 240–241, 270–275). All in all, the report concluded with respect to the debates on the policy turn, "no drastic changes" could be established (Böhret 1985, 282, my translation).

A second survey on changes in theoretical orientation and thematic research interests of political scientists conducted two years later revealed that interest in policy analysis and public administration had already been growing during the 1970s and early 1980s (Honolka 1986, 53). While the 1970s and early 1980s are sometimes perceived as the boom years of policy analysis, this upward trend apparently came to a hold in the 1990s in Germany. In the third survey on political science in Germany, conducted in 1996/97, Hans-Dieter Klingemann and Jürgen Falter distinguished seven fields of research in political science. In their classification, policy research was put together with administrative science in a single category called "policy research and administrative science." About one third of the interviewees said that they would currently work in this field (Klingemann and Falter 1998, 311). Yet only one fifth declared that they regard this particular work as their personally most important field of research (Klingemann and Falter 1998, 313).

Did the debate about the policy turn have an impact on the structure of political science departments at German universities or on the denomination of professorships in political science? Some statistical information about the relevance and weight of policy studies can be obtained from a recent empirical study on political science as an academic discipline in Germany (Arendes 2005). Among other interesting historiographic information about the discipline it provides some data on the development of subdisciplines over time. As far as the debates that motivated the first survey on political science by Böhret (1985) are concerned, this study confirms the findings of the preceding surveys: the policy turn that caused so much debate in the discipline in the middle of the 1980s did not change the structure of political science in terms of its established subdisciplines. Most professorships are still assigned to the classical four subdisciplines of political science. The number of tenured political science professors dedicated primarily to policy fields and policy implementation has been increasing slowly but steadily both in absolute numbers and in percentage from 1.2 percent (N = 1) in 1969 to 6.2 percent (N = 22) in 1999 (Arendes 2005, 134). To be sure, these numbers are still rather small in comparison to the established four subdisciplines of political science. Yet in 1999, "policy fields and policy implementation" shares the sixth place on the list of „directions of specialization in political science" with the field of "political sociology" according to this assignment (Arendes 2005, 134).

POLICY STUDIES AND THE GERMAN POLITICAL SCIENCE ASSOCIATION

While the American Political Science Association established a public policy section in 1983 "as part of the vertical integration of the discipline" (Nelson 1996, 556), there is still no equivalent in its German counterpart. Some advocates of the policy turn in political science had called for such a section (e.g., Wollmann 1985, 77). Yet there is still no "Politikfeldanalyse" section integrating those who work on public policies in the DVPW. Consequently, there is no institutionalized forum in the discipline to work on a common understanding of the theoretical, methodological and practical issues involved in doing policy research.

JOURNALS

As in the United States (Nelson 1996, 557), there is no general German journal for political scientists specializing in public policy. Driven by newly invented evaluation schemes for German scientists that value publications in international peer reviewed journals much higher than publications in German, political scientists in general have increasingly strong incentives to publish in English. Some have been successful to get their manuscripts accepted by general policy journals (e.g., *Policy Sciences*). As in the United States (Nelson 1996, 557), the major German political science journals occasionally publish policy articles. This is the case in the leading journal, *Politische Vierteljahresschrift* (*PVS*) or in other general political science journals (*Leviathan, Zeitschrift für Politik, Zeitschrift für Politikwissenschaft*).

In some policy fields, a number of multidisciplinary journals on policy issues exist in Germany. These multidisciplinary policy-oriented journals provide opportunities for political scientists to publish. Some of them include a certain number of scientific disciplines. The *Zeitschrift für Umweltpolitik und Umweltrecht* (journal for environmental policy and environmental law) includes contributions on environmental problems from economics, law, and political science. Others include and address not only various disciplines, but reflective practitioners as well (e.g., *Zeitschrift für Sozialreform* (journal for social reform) in the field of social policy).

CAPACITIES IN RESEARCH AND TEACHING

The Wissenschaftszentrum Berlin für Sozialforschung (WZB) (Social Science Research Center Berlin) is the largest research institute, outside of those in universities, in Germany in the field of social research with a staff of about 150. Founded in 1969 by a group of MPs from the German Federal Parliament (Bundestag) from different parties, its primary political mission was to strengthen the ties of West Berlin with the Federal Republic of Germany by demonstrating that West Germany was still willing and able to establish new institutions in West Berlin in spite of protests from the East German government and the Soviet Union (Jahn 1994). The science center was planned to include several research institutes. The first research institute the founders wanted to realize was an International Institute of Management and Administration (Jahn 1994, 14). In the beginning of the 1970s, the establishment of a social science research institute, founded largely in secret as a private organization by a small number of politicians, but soon to get public funding from the Federal Ministry of Education and Science (Jahn 1994, 15), was not appreciated by the established scientific institutions. Rather, the establishment of the science center met with intensive criticism from universities in Berlin and outright protest from students opposing what they perceived as "new mandarins" of a commercialized "university incorporated" (Hirsch and Leibfried 1973).

In the 1970s and 1980s, the science center was primarily perceived as a research institute producing scientific studies and advice relevant for political reforms of the government formed by social democrats and liberals (Bleek 2001, 397–398). After the conservative-liberal coalition of Chancellor Kohl came to power in the beginning of the 1980s, the science center did not change to become a think tank of the new conservative-liberal government. Rather, after long negotiations, it experienced a shift from a problem- and policy-oriented focus towards questions more relevant in the context of basic research in the social sciences. In the press, this shift was reported as a change "from policy and politics to basics" (Altenmüller 1994, 23, my translation). In spite of this general trend, the science center still does a lot of research on public policy. Yet the focus shifted and some policy fields no longer appear in the current structure of research units. The science center still does research on economic and labor policy and public health, but reduced its emphasis on technology policy and stopped focusing on environmental policy.

The second research institute in the field of social research relevant for policy studies in Germany is the Max Planck Institute for the Study of Societies (MPIfG). Founded in 1985 in Cologne under the co-directorate of Renate Mayntz and Fritz W. Scharpf, the Max Planck Institute soon became very influential in policy research in Germany. Both directors had been former members of the famous project group on the reform of government and administration mentioned above (Mayntz and Scharpf 1973), Scharpf had also been the former director of the International Institute of Management and Administration at the Science Center in Berlin from 1973 to 1984. Although considerably smaller in size than the science center in Berlin (with a staff of about 40), the Max Planck Institute gained remarkable conceptual influence by developing a common analytical approach which was then applied in many policy studies in various policy fields (see below). This approach was later called the actor-centered institutionalism (Mayntz and Scharpf 1995; Scharpf 1997). When Wolfgang Streeck became director in 1995, the focus on political economy was strengthened and the approach of studies at the Max Planck Institute started to open up to include other forms of institutionalist theories such as historical institutionalism (Streeck and Thelen 2005).

Highlighting the WZB and the MPIfG does not mean that there are no other disciplinary or interdisciplinary research institutes outside the university system producing scientific knowledge and expertise relevant for specific policy fields. The Stiftung Wissenschaft und Politik (Foundation for Science and Politics), for example, provides advice to the German government in foreign policy (for think tanks in Germany see Thunert 2003). Yet the WZB and MPIfG are the biggest and most important social science research institutes still related to basic research in the social sciences. Within the German university system, some centers for policy studies run by or at least related to political science departments have gained reputation at the national and the international level. A case in point is the Zentrum für Sozialpolitik (Center for Social Policy) at the University of Bremen where Claus Offe and Manfred G. Schmidt worked for some years, or the Forschungsstelle Umweltpolitik (Environmental Policy Research Centre) at the Free University of Berlin directed by Martin Jänicke.

As far as capacities for teaching and studying are concerned, German universities are currently experiencing fundamental structural changes. During the last decades, one would not find a program of study with a degree in public policy at a German university. Students could enroll at universities to study political science or social science and then specialize in policy studies. But they would earn their degree in political science or sociology. With the forced introduction of bachelor and masters degrees in the course of the so called Bologna Process, which is supposed to create equivalent university degrees all over Europe, a lot of planning activities for specialized future courses of study are currently going on in the political science departments in German universities. Some of these activities may lead to bachelor or master degrees specializing in public policy.[2]

POLICY STUDIES AND POLITICAL SCIENCE: POINTS OF REFERENCE

In the debate on the role of policy research and its relation to the core questions of political science, the legacy, identity, and future direction of the discipline in Germany was an underlying theme. The debate partly showed signs of a generational conflict. To many representatives of the younger generation, the policy turn often appeared simply as a necessary and promising step towards more relevance and professionalization of political science. Some of the older generation kept on asking, what policy studies have to offer for answering the core questions of the discipline. Since that debate, the relation of policy analysis and political science is a recurring theme for German political scientists interested in analyzing policies and policy fields.

Yet in the normal proceedings of the following years, the fundamental differences concerning the identity and future direction of political science lost in importance. On the one hand, traditional political scientists realized that they had to pay tribute to the growing political importance of societal problems and the problem-solving capacity of political actors and institutions. Therefore, political scientists had to include the policy dimension in their concepts of the political much stronger than they did before. On the other hand, analysts adopting a policy perspective did so with implicit or explicit reference to more comprehensive concepts of the policy process and the political system in which societal problems were defined as political, policies for solving these problems were for-

---

2. In terms of public administration, earlier attempts to introduce new interdisciplinary courses of study beyond the traditional disciplines of law, political science, or sociology were more successful. The University of Konstanz—founded as a reform university in the 1960s—soon started an interdisciplinary program of study in public administration in 1968. This course of study offering a diploma in administrative science was probably the most successful program of this sort including undergraduate and graduate education in Germany (Timmermann 1982) up to now. Yet it remained the only program in administrative science at university level in German higher education for a number of years. In the 1990s, a similar course of study in public administration was introduced at the University of Potsdam. Situated near Berlin in the former GDR, this university had to look for new ways to compete with the programs offered at the old universities in the capital. At the postgraduate level, the Hochschule für Verwaltungswissenschaften (School for Administrative Science) in Speyer had teaching capacities for additional training offered primarily to graduates of law schools interested in careers in German civil service (König 1982). These capacities included elements of policy analysis (Wollmann 1984, 37). As the survey from 1996/97 showed, Konstanz and Speyer profited from the reputation of their teaching and training capacities in public administration (Klingemann and Falter 1998, 323–325).

mulated and implemented and policy outcomes were evaluated. And in doing their studies, some of them became aware of this reference, especially when they were confronted with the failure of their policy proposals or the critique of other scientists. Thus, the task was to reconsider the role of factors that are perceived as political on the generation of problems and the feasibility and acceptance of problem solving strategies. Forced to (re-)conceptualize the interplay of policies and features of political systems and processes, they often started to look at classical political science again. Such references to core concepts of political science could serve two functions: First, they could help overcome fragmentation and overspecialization in problem-oriented interdisciplinary policy research. Second, they could help to be accepted as a "true" political scientist working on problems related to the core questions of the discipline.

There are three prominent concepts that were implicitly or explicitly used in Germany when the question of relating policy analysis to political science arose: (1) the concepts of the state, (2) governing, and (3) steering. These concepts served as a kind of reference point for most policy studies to date. Recently, a fourth, currently popular, yet still ambiguous concept gained prominence in policy studies in Germany: the concept of governance. Finally, one can ask whether the concept of democracy played any role in the debate on the relation of political science and policy analysis.

The first concept that served as such a reference point for political scientists interested in policy studies is an old one—the concept of the *state*. To be sure, German history and the history of social science in Germany can generally be characterized as state-centered (Wagner 1990). Still, integrating or relating policy analysis to the concept of the state was not that self- evident for German political science after the Second World War. The tradition of political thought known as *Staatslehre* includes lawyers and social scientists emphazising the role of the state. The German term *Lehre* refers not only to a theory in the sense of empirical and analytical philosophy of science, but is strongly associated with the notion of a normative concept of what a good state essentially is and how it should function properly. In spite of the scepticism and critique of this tradition (Jann 1989, 40–45), however, there were some attempts to reinvent a concept of *Staatslehre* or to revitalize the old idea of integrative state sciences (*Staatswissenschaften*) in the 1980s (Hesse 1987).

The second concept or, rather concepts, that political scientists interested in policy analysis referred to are *Regierungslehre* and *Regieren* (government and *governing*). These are the concepts most members of the first generation of political scientists in Germany brought with them or adopted from the Anglo-saxon tradition after the Second World War. For the founding fathers of German political science, Staatslehre, was too static, too ahistorical, and too burdened with undemocratic traditions to serve as a concept for a science of democracy (Jann 1989, 46). Yet the version of "government" that came to dominate German political science textbooks until the 1970s focussed on political institutions and did not pay enough attention to the policy dimension. Thus, to work out a contemporary concept of governing was the task another group of political scientists set out for themselves. In this context, Hans-Hermann Hartwich and a number of younger collaborators tried to outline a concept of governing that goes beyond the institutional dimension and includes the policy dimension but does not fall back into the myths of the old *Staatslehre* (von Bandemer and Wewer 1989; Hartwich and Wewer 1990–1993).

Steering is the third category often referred to in policy studies in Germany. Originally introduced in the context of systems-theoretic frameworks, the notion of political steering played a significant role in the debate on planning and reform of public administration in the 1970s (Mayntz and Scharpf 1973). After the autopoietic turn of systems theory in Germany introduced by Niklas Luhmann (1984), the idea of steering a differentiated modern society, especially by a political system supposed to represent the top or center of society, was fundamentally called into question. This critique induced some conceptual clarifications on the part of those who frequently used the concept before (Mayntz 1987; Lange/Braun 2000). After Luhmann's (1989) debate with Fritz Scharpf (1989) at the opening session of the scientific conference of the DVPW in 1988, the possibility and limits, as well as the desirability, of political steering became a recurring theme in political science publications in general and in policy studies in particular (Mayntz 1995).[3]

In the last few years, there is a fourth concept coming to the fore and it is not clear yet whether and how it will replace or supplement other concepts that served as points of reference in policy studies. While some celebrate *governance* as a new concept open for interdisciplinary research on different forms of regulation, others think that it is just another buzz word that may well be forgotten again in a couple of years as it is still too ambiguous and not specific enough to successfully guide and structure empirical policy studies. Like the term "policy," the word "governance" has not yet been translated into German. The notion of "governance" was soon picked up in policy research to grasp and signify new forms of coordination and regulation beyond or in the shadow of the state (Benz 2004). Most prominent to date is still the idea of global governance as discussed in the context of international relations (Behrens 2005).

For a science originally introduced in Germany as a science of democracy, it is no wonder that the question arises whether there was or is a fifth concept that played a role as a point of reference in the debates on policy analysis. Yet in these debates, most political scientists referred to the concept of *democracy* primarily as a source of normative reflection, critique and reorientation, not as a point of reference that could serve as a basis for constructing an analytical and evaluative framework for policy studies. Moreover, the concept was mainly used as an adjective qualifying the other concepts as more or less democratic or even dichotomizing them on a single scale in two polar types that were either democratic or undemocratic. So, the notion of a democratic state was contrasted with a non-democratic, authoritarian or even totalitarian state, forms of governing or steering or types of governance could be more or less democratic. What got lost in this one-dimensional way of referring to the concept of democracy is the fact that there are indeed different models of democracy in the debate. One can distinguish between liberal, communitarian, republican, deliberative, or other models of democracy that are referred to not only in public controversies on policies or policymaking, but also in political scientists' debates on how a proper policy analysis of these controversial policies should be conceptualized and conducted in a democracy (Saretzki 1998, 301–317).

POLICY STUDIES: APPROACHES

In the first three decades since its transfer from North America, no specific German approach to policy analysis has been developed. While many observers noticed the absence of a specifically national approach to policy analysis in Germany, this was not considered to be a serious drawback. What appeared as a deficit of policy analysis criticized by proponents and sceptics alike was the lack of theory. On the first scientific conference of the DVPW officially devoted to policy studies which took place in West-Berlin in October 1982, the rapporteur of the working group on policy fields came to the conclusion that no common questions or problems, no common concepts, no hypothesis-generating typologies of policies or even approaches for generalizing theories showed up in the proceedings (Scharpf 1983, 504). Although there is still no generally accepted theory in the

---

3. Some political scientists tried to specify the meaning of the concept they suggested as frame of reference and clarify the difference between their concept and others. However, for another group of political scientists of the third generation, especially those engaged in comparative public policy research, these conceptual distinctions between state, governing and steering are irrelevant or do not make sense at all. Manfred G. Schmidt, the most important representative of the comparative approach to policy studies in Germany (see below), explicitly declared that he considers the terms "Staatstätigkeit," "Regierungspolitik," or "staatliche Steuerung" as synonyms (Schmidt 1988, 28). Conceptually differentiated or not, the three categories of state, governing, and steering served at least implicitly as points of reference in most policy studies done by political scientists. From the perspective of political science, concepts of new public management became relevant more as a subject of study than as a theoretical point of reference for policy studies.

field and even the theoretical points of reference differ in policy studies in Germany (see above), the landscape of approaches today is not as unstructured as it appeared in the beginning of the 1980s. Within the German discussion of policy analysis, two approaches appear as dominant or at least image forming in the sense that they are mostly referred to as mainstream when the question arises what policy analysis is. One indicator for their relative dominance in the German debate is the last available reputation analysis (Klingemann and Falter 1998, 326–336).

The first approach to be mentioned in this respect is the so-called *actor-centered institutionalism* developed by Renate Mayntz and Fritz Scharpf as an analytical framework for empirical policy studies at the Max-Planck-Institute for the Study of Societies (Mayntz and Scharpf 1995; Scharpf 1997). This approach "proceeds from the assumption that social phenomena are to be explained as the outcome of interactions among intentional actors— individual, collective, or corporate, that is—but that these interactions are structured, and the outcomes are shaped, by the characteristics of the institutional settings within which they occur." For the basic focus of their approach "on actors interacting within institutions" the authors "do not claim originality" (Scharpf 1997, 1)—and hence their approach is neither intended nor perceived to be in any way specifically German. Using some of the labels in the international debate, their approach can be classified as some version of new or rational choice institutionalism. While both authors agree on the importance of institutions (and hence can be called institutionalists), they differ somewhat on the conceptualization of the actors and their interaction. Scharpf (1997, 10–12) makes a clear distinction between problem-oriented and interaction-oriented policy research. Focusing on the latter, he finds game-theoretic modelling very fruitful—much more fruitful than Mayntz. To be sure, the "actor-centered institutionalism" is not a theory of the policy process or policy outcome, but an analytical framework or a heuristic device for empirical policy research (Mayntz and Scharpf 1995, 39). Yet as such it is open enough to provide an approach that has been picked up and tailored to explanatory tasks in many policy case studies carried out at the Max-Planck-Institute and elsewhere at German universities and research institutes.

The second approach that German political scientists will think of when it comes to policy studies cannot in any way be called typically German either—except for the name that its representatives have given it. The approach often called "*vergleichende Staatstätigkeitsforschung*" (Schmidt 1988) in Germany is basically what Anglo-Saxon political scientists call "comparative public policy" or "comparative policy analysis." The most prominent and most influential representative of this approach in Germany is Manfred G. Schmidt who also wrote some of the most frequently used German introductory essays into policy analysis (Schmidt 1997) and comparative policy research (Schmidt 2003). The comparative approach represented by Schmidt and others aims much more at empirical theory testing than at systematic theory building. Policy studies following this approach are mostly international in orientation, trying to include a large number of OECD countries where reliable empirical data is available. These studies are focusing on policy output or policy performance as the dependent variable to be explained. In his recent comparative study, Schmidt (2001, 23) argued for a combination of different "theory families" in order to precisely describe and explain welfare policies.

Apart from these two dominant or at least most prominent approaches, many other approaches are applied in policy studies in Germany with a focus on various aspects and actors, phases, or factors of policies the researchers are interested in. It is probably fair to say that almost all theoretical approaches presented in this volume have been discussed in Germany (and many have actually been applied in empirical policy studies).

What holds true for the mainstream, can also be said of its critics: a dominant orientation to the discussion going on in the English-speaking world—even the post-positive perspectives have been imported from the United States. In the last state-of-the-art volume on policy analysis with the subtitle "critique and new orientation," the editor Adrienne Héritier (1993) invited two prominent American authors to bring in new methodological perspectives and procedures for a participatory policy analysis (Fischer 1993; deLeon 1993). Within German political science, post-positivism is not a clearly identifiable approach or a clearly identified minority camp opposed to some kind of mainstream. Rather, the landscape of approaches and networks among policy researchers is very differentiated and has many overlaps with approaches that can be described as mainstream policy analysis.

When the debate on the new or rather rediscovered role of "ideational factors in policymaking" (Majone 1996, 611) reached German political science in the 1990s, a growing number of younger social scientists got interested in analyzing this dimension of the policy process. Their discussions were concerned with the conceptual and methodological questions related to the analysis of ideas, interpretations, discourses, metaphors, arguments, knowledge and cognitions, and their role in the policy process. In these debates it soon became clear that political scientists interested in these questions referred to a wide variety of different approaches to the analysis of this dimension ranging from some cognitively enriched version of rational choice theory to interpretive, discursive and poststructural frameworks with no common post-positivist vision emerging (Maier et al. 2003). In the debate on "ideational factors in policymaking," references to authors from other countries again play a dominant role in Germany. Concerning contributions by German political scientists, Frank Nullmeier's approach towards a "political science of knowledge" (Wissenspolitologie) is probably the concept quoted most often in the German discussion. Nullmeier suggested to start from a "rhetorical-dialectical" model of action and to analyse the role of knowledge in policymaking in analogy to economic models of markets introducing concepts like "knowledge markets" and "knowledge competition" (Nullmeier 1993; Nullmeier/Rüb 1993).

RECENT TRENDS

What are the future directions for policymaking and policy analysis in Germany? Upon first sight, many observers identify some general trends in policy making and implementation and in the way policy processes are conceptualized in political science in Germany. At a second look, however, there are also some countertrends that can be detected, albeit these countertrends are not simply a turning back. Hence, they pose some interesting puzzles or, at least, contradictory developments calling for further analysis and clarification in policy studies and political science in the future.

The first trend often proclaimed in the literature can be characterized as *decentering* of the classical model of the state as a unitary, hierarchical, centralized actor. What we are witnessing, many observers claim, is a trend *from the unitary state as central actor in policymaking and implementation to multi-actor spaces* where many public, private and civil actors are involved and no central agent or clearly identifiable hierarchy exists. Yet this is not the whole story. On the other hand, many policy processes in Germany can only be explained by referring to some sort of hierarchy in and between various state agencies, implying that these multi-actor spaces are not as decentered and symmetrically structured as it seems. Moreover, looking inside the many state agencies involved in policymaking and implementation, one can observe not only the re-emergence, but even the strengthening of hierarchy and centralization as a consequence of administrative reforms guided by output-oriented concepts of new public management.

The second trend proclaimed in many debates refers not to the model of the state as a central unitary actor, but to the interaction of state and government on the one hand and society on the other. Sometimes characterized as a socializing of the state, this change is often described as a shift *from the state and government to the market and civil society*. Yet, in spite of this image of growing societal self regulation by market or solidarity, a lot of policy processes in Germany have persuasively been analyzed as neocorporatist negotiations in the "shadow of the state" pointing to the limited capacity of societal self regulation in many policy fields. Moreover, procedures for alternative dispute resolution originally conceived of as a new form of participatory governance from below or at least as a societal alternative to conventional governmental forms of problem solving and conflict resolution have been transformed into new modes of governing complex and contested issues by established party governments.

A third trend is often characterized as a denationalizing of policy making implying a shift *from the national to the European or international level*. Proponents of this view point to the many transfers of political competence and power to the European Union or international regimes and institutions. Yet, as some policy studies on governance in multi-level systems have recently shown, europeanization and internationalization are not one way streets. The nation states and national political actors and institutions are not simply withering away or loosing power altogether. Some national political actors and institutions are also strengthened in this process, e.g., national governments can gain power in the EU (vis-à-vis their national parliaments or parties). Moreover, there are direct countertendencies that point to sometimes irritating forms of renationalization of certain policy issues and to a weakening of European institutions and international regimes.

A fourth trend reflects a shifting analytical focus concerning the main determinants of policy, i.e., a shift *from interests and institutions to ideas*. Yet some of the studies that tried to analyze more closely where these politically successful ideas came from were confronted not only with new ideas and learning mechanisms, but also with old questions of interests and power. Thus, at least implicitly, there are frameworks evolving in policy studies that try to reflect some kind of interaction between ideas, interests, and institutions. However, within these complex frameworks that account for ideas, interests, and institutions without neglecting one or the other, it is still an open question how the three interact in different contexts and policy fields.

A fifth trend reflects the relation of theory and practice in policy analysis. This trend can be characterized as a trend *from policy analysis to policy advice (and back)*. Just like in the boom years of policy analysis in Germany under the first social-liberal reform government at the end of the 1960s and 1970s, when the social democrats came to power a second time and formed the red-green government in 1998, the impression was widespread that now "the advisers are coming" again (Saretzki et al. 1999) and policy making would again be influenced by policy experts rather than by (conservative) party politicians or interest groups as in the Kohl era. Yet, the specific way in which Chancellor Gerhard Schröder made strategic use of policy expertise to circumvent his own party and parliamentary faction or even the whole parliament by establishing various new expert commissions led to various criticisms of this new mode of governing and the role of policy experts in the "Berliner Räterepublik" (Berlin Republic of Councils) (Heinze 2002). In the public this new relevance and utilization of expertise provoked critical debates about the role of policy experts in a parliamentary democracy. In the scientific community, it induced discussion and critical self-reflection on the impact that this specific kind of utilization and public involvement of scientific experts has on science and the scientific basis of policy analysis itself (Saretzki 2003).

OUTLOOK: ANOTHER POLICY TURN?

After the controversies on the policy turn in political science that took place in Germany in the mid-1980s, policy analysis was slowly accepted in the discipline. Policy studies were not only seen as a necessary and legitimate supplement to the traditional core questions of political science, but the policy perspective was slowly incorporated and became an integrated part of almost all subdisciplines in political science. Since the 1990s, political scientists interested in policy studies had their place firmly in the framework of the discipline. Seen from the perspective of political science, policy analysis led to a differentiation of the discipline by integrating one of the three basic dimensions of the political (policy, politics, and polity) more explicitly in its research and teaching.

This position of policy studies as a more or less integrated part of a differentiated discipline political science may change in the future as a consequence of reforms of universities and research institutions currently planned or under way in Germany. These reforms will change the institutional basis of political science as an academic discipline. Only a small number of new bachelor and master courses of study which are replacing the old diploma in Germany will lead to degrees in political science. Pushed to be more relevant and useful, most plans for new programs of study aim at practically oriented interdisciplinary courses of study (often including some sort of policy analysis).

Hence, on the one hand, many observers expect a trend towards disciplinary de-differentiation in German universities. This trend, some historians of political science claim when looking in the future, can have far reaching effects especially on the size of the political science professoriate. As many representatives of the third generation of political scientists in academia will retire in the next couple of years, their positions are unlikely to be filled by younger people representing the disciplinary core of political science because the number of classical disciplinary courses of study is drastically shrinking (Arendes and Buchstein 2004).

On the other hand, the dissolution of disciplinary programs at universities may not hit policy analysis as hard as it hits the other subfields of political science focusing on the classical core questions of the discipline. Some of these new bachelor and master programs deliberately choose public policy as their subject of study. Even the return of the old concept of Staatswissenschaften (state sciences) can be observed as label for new programs of study in German universities (including law, economics, political and administrative science, and other disciplines). In the context of the debate on the policy turn, this concept had mainly been interpreted as a precursor of policy analysis in Germany, representing an undifferentiated course of study for civil servants in the nineteenth century (Bleek 2004). Thus, in the next couple of years these developments taking place in the context of university reform may induce another sort of policy turn and lead to a new round in the debate on the relation of policy analysis and political science in Germany.

REFERENCES

Altenmüller, G.H. (1994). Einrichtung für Unkonventionelles. Ein Journalist sieht das WZB. Wissenschaftszentrum Berlin für Sozialforschung (ed.), *25 Jahre WZB — Art und Ort der Forschung*, pp. 23–58. Berlin.

Arendes, C. (2005). *Politikwissenschaft in Deutschland. Standorte, Studiengänge und Professorenschaft 1949–1999*. Wiesbaden: VS Verlag für Sozialwissenschaften.

Arendes, C., and Buchstein, H. (2004). Die Zukunft der Politikwissenschaft an Deutschlands Universitäten. *Politikwissenschaft, 130,* 136–150.

Bandemer, S. von, and Wewer, G. (eds.) 1989. *Regierungssystem und Regierungslehre. Fragestellungen, Analysekonzepte und Forschungsstand eines Kernbereiches der Politikwissenschaft*. Opladen: Leske und Budrich.

Behrens, M. (ed.) (2005). *Globalisierung als politische Herausforderung. Global Governance zwischen Utopie und Realität*. Wiesbaden: VS Verlag für Sozialwissenschaften.

Benz, A. (ed.) (2004). *Governance - Regieren in komplexen Regelsystemen. Eine Einführung*. Wiesbaden: VS Verlag für Sozialwissenschaften.

Bermbach, U. (2003). Die siebziger Jahre. In: J.W. Falter and F. Wurm (eds.), *Politikwissenschaft in der Bundesrepublik Deutschland. 50 Jahre DVPW*, pp. 29–34. Wiesbaden: Westdeutscher Verlag.

Beyme, K. von (1985). Policy Analysis und traditionelle Politikwissenschaft. In H.-H. Hartwich (ed.), *Policy-Forschung in der Bundesrepublik Deutschland. Ihr Selbstverständnis und ihr Verhältnis zu den Grundfragen der Politikwissenschaft*, pp. 7–29. Opladen: Westdeutscher Verlag.

Bleek, W. (2001). *Geschichte der Politikwissenschaft in Deutschland*. München: Beck.

Bleek, W. (2004). Deutsche Staatswissenschaften im 19. Jahrhundert – Disziplinäre Ausdifferenzierung und Spiegelung moderner Staatlichkeit. In E. Holtmann (ed.), *Staatsentwicklung und Policyforschung. Politikwissenschaftliche Analysen der Staatstätigkeit*, pp. 41–67. Wiesbaden: VS Verlag für Sozialwissenschaften.

Böhret, C. (1985). Zum Stand und zur Orientierung der Politikwissenschaft in der Bundesrepublik Deutschland. Ein Bericht für das 1. Wissenschaftliche Symposium der Deutschen Vereinigung für Politische Wissenschaft (November 1984) in Hannover. In H.-H. Hartwich (ed.), *Policy-Forschung in der Bundesrepublik*

Deutschland. Ihr Selbstverständnis und ihr Verhältnis zu den Grundfragen der Politikwissenschaft, pp. 216–330. Opladen: Westdeutscher Verlag.

deLeon, P. (1993). Demokratie und Policy-Analyse: Ziele und Arbeitsweise. In A. Héritier (ed.), *Policy-Analyse. Kritik und Neuorientierung,* pp. 471–485. Opladen: Westdeutscher Verlag.

Fischer, F. (1993). Bürger, Experten und Politik nach dem "Nimby"-Prinzip: ein Plädoyer für die partizipatorische Policy-Analyse. In A. Héritier (ed), *Policy-Analyse. Kritik und Neuorientierung,* pp. 451–470. Opladen: Westdeutscher Verlag.

Greven, M.T. (2004). Zur Situation der Politikwissenschaft in Deutschland - gegen einseitigen Alarmismus und für eine komplexere Selbstverständigungsdebatte der Disziplin, *Politikwissenschaft, 131,* 141–158.

Hartwich, H.-H. (2004). Die Staats- und Kameralwissenschaften als theoretische und empirische, immer aber nützliche Disziplinen gesellschaflicher Formierung im 17. und 18. Jahrhundert. In E. Holtmann (ed.), *Staatsentwicklung und Policyforschung. Politikwissenschaftliche Analysen der Staatstätigkeit,* pp. 21–35. Wiesbaden: VS Verlag für Sozialwissenschaften.

Hartwich, H.-H., and Wewer, G. (eds.) 1990–1993. *Regieren in der Bundesrepublik,* 5 Vols., Opladen: Leske und Budrich.

Heidenheimer, A.J. (1986). Politics, Policy and Policey as Concepts in English and Continental Languages: An Attempt to Explain Divergences. *Review of Politics, 48,* 3–30.

Heinze, R. G. (2002). *Die Berliner Räterepublik. Viel Rat - wenig Tat?.* Wiesbaden: Westdeutscher Verlag.

Héritier, A. (ed.) (1993). *Policy-Analyse. Kritik und Neuorientierung.* Opladen: Westdeutscher Verlag.

Hesse, J.J. (1987). Aufgaben einer Staatslehre heute. In *Jahrbuch zur Staats- und Verwaltungswissenschaft,* 1, pp. 55–87.

Hirsch, J., and Leibfried, S. (1973). *Materialien zur Wissenschafts- und Bildungspolitik.* Frankfurt am Main: Suhrkamp.

Honolka, H. (1986). Reputation, Desintegration, theoretische Umorientierungen. Zu einigen empirisch vernachlässigten Aspekten der Politikwissenschaft in der Bundesrepublik Deutschland. In K. von Beyme (ed.), *Politikwissenschaft in der Bundesrepublik Deutschland. Entwicklungsprobleme einer Disziplin.* pp. 41–61, Opladen: Westdeutscher Verlag.

Jahn, G. (1994). Es ging um Berlin. Rückblick auf die Entstehung des WZB. In Wissenschaftszentrum Berlin für Sozialforschung (ed.), *25 Jahre WZB - Art und Ort der Forschung,* pp. 11–22. Berlin.

Jann, W. (1989). Staatslehre - Regierungslehre – Verwaltungslehre. In S. von Bandemer and G. Wewer (eds), *Regierungssystem und Regierungslehre. Fragestellungen, Analysekonzepte und Forschungsstand eines Kernbereiches der Politikwissenschaft,* pp. 33–56. Opladen: Leske und Budrich.

Jürgens, U., and Naschold, F. (1983). Thesen und Materialien zur Arbeitspolitik. In H.-H. Hartwich (ed.), *Gesellschaftliche Probleme als Anstoß und Folge von Politik,* pp. 113–138. Opladen: Westdeutscher Verlag.

Klingemann, H.-D., and Falter, J.W. (1998). Die deutsche Politikwissenschaft im Urteil der Fachvertreter. Erste Ergebnisse einer Umfrage von 1996/7. In M.T. Greven (ed.), *Demokratie - eine Kultur des Westens?,* pp. 305–341. Opladen: Leske + Budrich.

König, K. (1982). Verwaltungswissenschaftliches Aufbaustudium: Speyer. In J.J. Hesse (ed.), *Politikwissenschaft und Verwaltungswissenschaft,* pp. 480–494. Opladen: Westdeutscher Verlag.

Lange, S., and Braun, D. (2000). *Politische Steuerung zwischen System und Akteur. Eine Einführung.* Opladen: Leske und Budrich.

Luhmann, N. (1984). *Soziale Systeme. Grundriß einer allgemeinen Theorie.* Frankfurt am Main: Suhrkamp.

Luhmann, N. (1989). Politische Steuerung: Ein Diskussionsbeitrag. *Politische Vierteljahresschrift,* 30, 4–9.

Maier, H. (1966). *Die ältere deutsche Staats- und Verwaltungslehre (Polizeiwissenschaft). Ein Beitrag zur Geschichte der politischen Wissenschaft in Deutschland,* Neuwied: Luchterhand.

Maier, M.L., Nullmeier, F., Pritzlaff, T., and Wiesner, A. (eds.) (2003). *Politik als Lernprozess? Wissenszentrierte Ansätze der Politikanalyse.* Opladen: Leske und Budrich.

Majone, G. (1996). Public Policy and Administration: Ideas, Interests and Institutions. In R.E. Goodin and H.-D. Klingemann (eds.), *New Handbook of Political Science,* pp. 610–627. Oxford: Oxford University Press.

Mayntz, R. (1987). Politische Steuerung und gesellschaftliche Steuerungsprobleme. Anmerkungen zu einem theoretischen Paradigma. In *Jahrbuch zur Staats- und Verwaltungswissenschaft,* 1, pp. 89–110.

Mayntz, R. (1995). Politische Steuerung: Aufstieg, Niedergang und Transformation einer Theorie. In K. von Beyme and C. Offe (eds.), *Politische Theorien in der Ära der Transformation,* pp. 148–168. Opladen: Westdeutscher Verlag.

Mayntz, R., and Scharpf, F.W. (1995). Der Ansatz des akteurzentrierten Institutionalismus. In R. Mayntz and F.W. Scharpf (eds.), *Gesellschaftliche Selbstregulierung und politische Steuerung,* pp. 39–72. Frankfurt am Main/New York: Campus.

Mayntz, R., and Scharpf, F.W. (eds.) (1973). *Planungsorganisation. Die Diskussion um die Reform von Regierung und Verwaltung.* München: Piper.

Nelson, B.J. (1996). Public Policy and Administration: An Overview. In R.E. Goodin and H.-D. Klingemann (eds.), *New Handbook of Political Science,* pp. 551–592. Oxford: Oxford University Press.

Nullmeier, F. (1993). Wissen und Policy-Forschung. Wissenspolitologie und rhetorisch-dialektisches Handlungsmodell. In A. Héritier (ed.), *Policy-Analyse. Kritik und Neubeginn,* Opladen: Westdeutscher Verlag, 175–196.

Nullmeier, F., and Rüb, F.W. (1993). *Die Transformation der Sozialpolitik. Vom Sozialstaat zum Sicherungsstaat.* Frankfurt am Main/New York: Campus.

Prätorius, R. (2004). US-amerikanische Prägungen der Policy-Forschung. In E. Holtmann (ed), *Staatsentwicklung und Policyforschung. Politikwissenschaftliche Analysen der Staatstätigkeit,* pp. 75–86. Wiesbaden: VS Verlag für Sozialwissenschaften.

Saretzki, T. (1998). Post-positivistische Policy-Analyse und deliberative Demokratie. In M.T. Greven, H. Münkler, and R. Schmalz-Bruns (eds.), *Bürgersinn und Kritik,* pp. 297–321. Baden-Baden: Nomos.

Saretzki, T. (2003). Aufklärung, Beteiligung und Kritik: Die „argumentative Wende" in der Policy-Analyse. In K. Schubert and N.C. Bandelow (eds.), *Lehrbuch der Politikfeldanalyse,* pp. 391–417. München/ Wien: Oldenbourg.

Saretzki, T., Rohde, M., and Leif, T. (1999). Ratlose Politiker, hilflose Berater? Zum Stand der Politikberatung in Deutschland. *Forschungsjournal Neue Soziale Bewegungen, 12,* 2–7.

Scharpf, F.W. (1983). Bericht aus der Arbeitsgruppe A: Politikfelder. In H.-H. Hartwich (ed.), *Gesellschaftliche Probleme als Anstoß und Folge von Politik,* pp. 504–509. Opladen: Westdeutscher Verlag.

Scharpf, F.W. (1989). Politische Steuerung und politische Institutionen, *Politische Vierteljahresschrift, 30,* 10–21.

Scharpf, F.W. (1997). *Games Real Actors Play. Actor-Centered Institutionalism in Policy Research.* Boulder, CO: Westview Press.

Schmidt, M.G. (1988). Einführung. In M.G. Schmidt (ed.), *Staatstätigkeit. International und historisch vergleichende Perspektiven,* pp. 1–35. Opladen: Westdeutscher Verlag.

Schmidt, M.G. (1997). Policy-Analyse. In A. Mohr (ed.), *Grundzüge der Politikwissenschaft,* Second Edition, pp. 567–604. München/Wien: Oldenbourg.

Schmidt, M.G. (2001). Einleitung. In M.G. Schmidt (ed.), *Wohlfahrtsstaatliche Politik. Institutionen, politischer Prozess und Leistungsprofil,* pp. 7–29. Opladen: Leske und Budrich.

Schmidt, M.G. (2003). Vergleichende Policy-Forschung. In D. Berg-Schlosser and F. Müller-Rommel (eds.), *Vergleichende Politikwissenschaft.* Fourth Edition, pp. 261–276. Opladen: Leske und Budrich.

Streeck, W. and Thelen, K. (eds.) (2005). *Beyond Continuity. Institutional Change in Advanced Political Economies.* Oxford: Oxford University Press.

Sturm, R. (1986). Policy-Forschung. In K. von Beyme (ed.), *Politikwissenschaft in der Bundesrepublik Deutschland. Entwicklungsprobleme einer Disziplin,* pp. 231–249. Opladen: Westdeutscher Verlag.

Thunert, M. (2003). Think Tanks in Deutschland — Berater der Politik?. *Aus Politik und Zeitgeschichte, B 51/2003,* 30–38.

Timmermann, M. (1982). Der eigenständige Studiengang: Das Konstanzer Verwaltungsstudium. In J.J. Hesse (ed.), *Politikwissenschaft und Verwaltungswissenschaft,* pp. 465–479. Opladen: Westdeutscher Verlag.

Torgerson, D. (1995). Policy Analysis and Public Life: The Restoration of Phronesis? In J. Farr, J.S. Dryzek, and S.T. Leonard (eds.), *Political Science in History. Research Programs and Political Traditions,* pp. 225–252. Cambridge: Cambridge University Press.

Wagner, P. (1990). *Sozialwissenschaften und Staat. Frankreich, Italien, Deutschland 1870–1980.* Frankfurt am Main/New York: Campus.

Wollmann, H. (1984). Policy Analysis: Some Observations on the West German Scene. *Policy Sciences, 17,* 27–47.

Wollmann, H. (1985). Policy-Forschung - ein "Kernbereich" der Politikwissenschaft. Was denn sonst? In H.-H. Hartwich (ed.), *Policy-Forschung in der Bundesrepublik Deutschland. Ihr Selbstverständnis und ihr Verhältnis zu den Grundfragen der Politikwissenschaft,* pp. 69–80. Opladen: Westdeutscher Verlag.

39 Policy Analysis in India: Research Bases and Discursive Practices

Navdeep Mathur and Kuldeep Mathur

INTRODUCTION

This chapter examines the patterns in policy analysis and its research bases in India. Due to India's post-colonial developing country orientation, policymaking and policy research have been framed through the terms of "development" and "planning." As a consequence, the conversation about policy research and analysis is inevitably about development policy as applied to various sectors such as poverty, industrialization, education, and employment, seen through an economistic framework. Moreover, Soviet-style central planning was the only broad methodological strategy that was considered to move India along that path of economic development. In this chapter, we identify the dominant paradigm of policy analysis (economic planning) and show how it evolved from factors rooted in the specific context of India's political development. More specifically, we discuss how the hegemony of economics as a discipline was central to the framing of political issues and consequent establishment of a particular pattern of policy analysis. We find that, while a well developed field of policy analysis has yet to be clearly identified, public administration as a subject of study and an applied field has received most attention in India. Currently, there is a strong trend in the growth of the activity of documentation of the institutional bases of policy analysis and research capacity, however a reflection on tools and methodologies of analyses has yet to emerge as an important theme in mainstream academia. We argue that the field of policy analysis, as it evolved in India, has developed in the interaction space between the state and the sphere of civil society organizations rooted in a participatory politics, and show how policy debates and research broke the economistic mould to take on a life of their own.

In order to provide an account of the dominant form of policy analysis in India, we direct attention towards the relationship between the political order and the practice of policy analysis (Fischer 1993, 21), where the initially dominant developmental paradigm termed "the Nehruvian Consensus"[1] created and maintained reliance upon economic-expert institutions as the primary tools of developmental policy research (Mathur 2001). From the 1950s onwards, this paradigmatic political program, framed through a technical rationality of economic development, was supported by a mainly generalist bureaucracy, whose key role was to manage the implementation of development policy in India. More recently, the growth of independent research institutions that variously play roles of advocacy and political campaigners has created a process of redefining of public problems. In terms of policy analysis, greater attention is paid to policy impacts at the level of target populations, and problems are increasingly reframed through a diversity of lenses, especially accounting for the protest movements against inappropriate or inadequate state action. As a challenge, social

---

1. Named after India's first Prime Minister, Jawahar Lal Nehru, who took the lead in articulating the strategy of India's Developmental framework.

analyses and methodologies began to poke holes in the rigid economistic system. Governmental institutions, experts and technocrats, in this current context, have been far from successful in settling such debates, faced with alternative experts and alternative sources of evidence that bring the hard experience of policy-community interaction to the table. The space for debate about alternatives has expanded and a new generation of policy professionals, both within and outside the bounds of state institutions has helped facilitate deliberation on issues that were previously in the domain of state control. Now, technocratic claims from the establishment elites are tested through alternative empirical evidence that incorporates the lived experience and counter-factual claims of those aca-demic-experts turned activists representing disadvantaged communities.[2] Environmental struggles have particularly highlighted governmental policy failures, and brought up critical perspectives on community-based governance and the need for expert institutions to pay attention to local knowl-edge (Guha 1989; Baviskar 1995; Dreze et al. 1997; Nanda 1999). The move from "Government to Governance" (Pierre 2000) rather than the consequence of the "hollowing out of the state" appears in India as a political struggle to redefine the nature of Indian democracy, from an elite one to a more participatory polity. These set of factors, in our assessment have contributed to the nascent emergence of policy analysis as a more diverse field in its own right, weakening the hegemony of economism to some extent.

POLICY ANALYSIS: FROM ECONOMIC PLANNING TO IMPLEMENTATION FAILURE

Policy analysis has not been a mainstream Indian research or academic tradition. The major policy goals emerged through a consensus between the Indian political leadership, industrial elite and the civil service intellectuals[3] that comprised the first democratic regime in India (from 1950 onwards). Apart from a basic democratic imperative, the overthrow of colonial rule was framed as a response to the growing impoverization of the vast mass of India's population. As a consequence, those major policy goals were framed as how can India achieve the standards of development, and as a corollary the quality of life that exists in Western developed nations in a shorter span of time. At a micro-level this translated into questions about how to end widespread hunger and illiteracy that were seen as the main obstacles on the path to Western developmental standards and for India's population to become productive in a modern sense. Within government therefore, policymaking was chiefly conceptualized as, and began with the acceptance of centralized economic planning as the overarching strategy of social and economic development. The Planning Commission was established as a core policy institution that would manage sectoral coordination of different plan-ning themes for achievement of socio-economic goals set by the political leadership. Planning was synonymous with policy making, and the value consensus over goals was not up for discussion. Goals were treated as fixed with only a process to technically design plans for their achievement. Such designing was based on theoretical exercises conducted by technical policy experts within the Planning Commission. In addition, the prime subactivity in policy analysis besides economet-ric modeling was the intense search and collation of more quantitative data, mainly as an effort to make models reflect reality more closely. Toward this end, the later establishment of public research institutes by the Planning Commission—often in conjunction with foreign funds such as from the United Nations, Ford Foundation, or USAID (United States Agency for International Develop-

2. Such as Dr. Medha Patkar in the Narmada Dam controversy.
3. This consensus or convergence between these groups is illustrated by the overlaps and dialogue between the Congress Party that led the national movement for independence, the Bombay industrialists and influential writings from well known civil service intellectuals.

ment) was geared towards developing external capacity and outsourcing the collection, collation, and supply of data.

Overtime, the base of expertise expanded to include national and internationally recognized economists. During the preparation of the Second (1956–61) and Third Five Year Plans (1961–66), the Planning Commission became an experimental school for those policy oriented economists who contested and debated models of social and economic development for developing countries. Economists from both the Western Bloc (such as J. K. Galbraith from Harvard University, Jan Tinbergen from The Netherlands) as well as the Eastern Bloc (Oskar Lange from Hungary) came to India and were part of this expert community that deliberated the models that should be followed in India to achieve its development objectives. However, the first three Five Year Plans were not able to achieve their expected targets. The rate of economic growth was lower than anticipated in the Plan while population growth was much higher resulting in an acute food crisis. The production and release of the Fourth Five Year Plan was postponed in order to buy time to correct the perceived weaknesses of earlier planning models and micro-level strategic interventions. Postponement of the introduction of the Fourth Five Year Plan in 1966 marked the end of a 15-year period of dominance of the technocratic policy analysis paradigm for policy analysis and research in India. The Planning Commission lost its hegemonic position of policy research and decision making, and policy decisions shifted to political and civil service leadership in the executive departments of Government of India. This shift, therefore, implied some loss of credibility of the Planning Commission's expertise and discussions about planning and policy became more open to the public, particularly once government ministers began to initiate discussions about specific policies. Ministers and other legislators further brought policy issues into public focus by raising discussions in parliament, an institution that provided relatively higher public access and transparency. The era of insulation of policy analysis from politics had come to an end. Planning related crises continued to worsen and public assessments helped policy analysis become more and more democratic over time, and this became apparent in varying forms in public debate as well as outputs from research institutions.

In the period from the late 1960s onwards, failure of plan objectives was blamed on poor implementation and projected in the public sphere as a crisis of implementation. Yet, there was no critical reflection of the econometric modeling or formulation methodologies of the Plans themselves. As a direct consequence, plan failures did not entail a critical thinking about policy analysis, rather the focus turned towards reform of administrative structures and process and ended up as an issue about the administration of plan objectives. For example, one of the major moves was to invite public administration experts from the United States and the United Kingdom to advise on the improvement and reform of administrative structures and process, the idea being that Western bureaucracies' attributes of efficiency and effectiveness need to be employed in the Indian situation to achieve success in plan implementation.

This closed policy analysis paradigm, as we have outlined above, had consequences for the development of policy research institutions as well as the development of the discipline and practice of public administration. Early policy research institutes were established to supply data, (because the failure of policy/plans was framed as lack of adequate or accurate data interlinked with, and also a consequence of poor implementation). Departments of public administration also were established in a large number of universities, independent institutes, towards the development of more professionalized practice. As a consequence, attention shifted to public administration and not towards policy analysis. Given that the policy process was understood as consisting of two successive stages—formulation then implementation, the key problems were framed as gaps in implementation, lack of coordination, and poorly developed roles of policy making and implementation professionals. Studies conducted in these public administration departments concerned relationships between bureaucrats and politicians, local administrators and politicians, which mainly demonstrated divergences in policy outlooks of these pairings. Following these studies, decision-making units and processes within ministries and departments were established to standardize and simplify rules and administrative processes of decision-making behavior and conduct. There was a strong influence of Zero-Base Budgeting (ZBB) and Performance-Based Budgeting (PPBM) from the United States. The entry-point for this influence came from the Ford Foundation and USAID, with both playing a major role in providing technical expertise and funds for adaptation of Indian institutions and bureaucratic processes.[4] The thrust of the U.S. influence was shaped by the recommendations of Paul Appleby of the Maxwell School at Syracuse University who had been invited by the Government of India in 1953 to study Indian administration and make suggestions of reform. His suggestions emanated from his belief that administration that served imperial rulers could not fulfill the aspirations of an independent India. The idea that there was a dichotomy between bureaucratic dispositions and development needs was widely accepted and the whole enterprise of implementation reform began to take shape under the American experience and influence. Professionalization of the administrative system through improved technical processes of decision making and imbibing a professional outlook among the administrators became the dominant themes of reform. Considerable American scholarly writing during this period emphasized these themes (see e.g., Braibanti and Spengler, 1963; Taylor et al. 1966). Most of the American scholars and consultants stressed the need to convert to a more flexible, freewheeling, administrative system where a clear responsibility of tasks is laid down. Indian public administration scholars began to move away from the legal framework of administering rules and regulations to behavioral orientations of commitment, dedication, and discretion. Led by the Indian Institute of Public Administration (IIPA), the graduate study of public administration in universities began to stress the role of individual behavior in attaining development goals and the relationships that bureaucrats forged with politicians.

There were only small voices of dissent against the dominance of the implementation failure framework. These came from within the field of economics too, mainly from B. R. Shenoy, the first major critic of the approach to planning and policymaking, who argued in favor of a more open economy and much less government control. Rather than argue for alternative methods of policy analysis and planning, Shenoy's critique was substantive and he appeared to be committed to laissez faire methods in so doctrinaire a manner that no one outside business circles took much notice of his criticisms (Hanson 1966, 128). He was among those economists who challenged the core strategy of investment in heavy (mother) industries that produced machinery to carry forward the process of industrialization and industrial production. The process of transfer of agricultural labour to the industrial sector to reduce rural unemployment and poverty and increase savings for investment by postponing consumption was seen as skewed in their view. Essentially, the argument of these economists was that centralized planning would stultify India's economic development rather than stimulate it, while accepting that economic growth has been achieved in some countries by this strategy. These economists argued that the implicit economic and political cost of this growth was disproportionately high in comparison with any long term benefits. However, these writings failed to provide clear alternatives for India and consequently did not engender widespread debates to seriously challenge India's dominant development paradigm.

To summarize, policy analysis emerged from the technical imperative of designing Five Year Plans and was supported by overseas economic development experts. Lacking a historical indigenous tradition and a failure to look at the enterprise of policy analysis in favor of implementation (a consequence of the classical economics tradition), the dominant paradigm in Indian policy analysis remained a technocratic and economics-led field of research and practice. This emphasis in government led to the establishment and further development of public administration, influenced primarily by trends in the United States. In turn, this influence was reflected in the focus of the curricula of university departments and institutes, to the neglect of policy analysis as an independent field of

---

4. The Ford Foundation alone spent $360,400 in grants to institutions and $76,000 in providing consultants and specialists to improve public administration in India during 1951-62 (Braibanti 1966:148).

study. Due to the multi-disciplinary character of the development of social science research in the 1970s and beyond and the participatory imperatives in the policy sphere, policy analysis began to emerge as a critique of the dominant paradigm. We illustrate these developments below by examining the trends in social research and the policy studies that were produced.

SOCIAL RESEARCH AND POLICY STUDIES

Apart from economics and history, other social science disciplines were slow to develop as major fields of study. Until the 1970s, political science was in infancy, and had focused its attention on legal and constitutional structures/institutions of government since colonial times. Sociology was oriented to and carried out by Western sociologists and was limited to describing and interpreting the "Indian social group, structure and interaction" to a primarily Western audience, and there was little direct analysis of public policy from sociological perspectives. The debate among Western analysts was concerned with the problem of "tribes" or traditional societies within developing countries—whether they would benefit from being incorporated in the mainstream of modernization or left untouched to pursue their own cultural norms (Guha 1999).

Empirical political science emerged from a focus on the impact of social groups on electoral behavior. Developed mainly as psephology, questions were restricted to electoral behavior, social basis of elections, participation of socially deprived groups.[5] It then turned its attention to implementation studies. With the acceptance of core planning objectives and goals, political science went on to do research about the implementation of *panchayati raj* (local self-governance at the village level). It neither attempted to theorize the appropriateness of decentralization in the face of diverse sets of local contexts nor sought to examine unintended consequences of *panchayati raj* institutions such as fragmentation of decision making and accountability. Political scientists rarely questioned the underlying norms of policy or planning objectives, rather analysis placed importance on their performance with respect to the procedural aspects of establishment and operation of *panchayats*.

Economics was the most well-established discipline in the Indian universities. Research institutes were also staffed by economists. Hence policy debates were chiefly initiated and conducted by economists, and therefore they were able to set the terms of the debate restricting it to this field. As economic planning was accepted as the dominant paradigm, voices of dissent were either suppressed or ignored, but dissent also came from economists. For example, the classical economist, A. D. Shroff established the Forum of Free Enterprise that attempted to offer free-market alternatives to centralized planning. The Forum was unable to make much impact given the dominant paradigm, yet it floated a political party based on the free enterprise philosophy and offered candidates for election in 1961.

Institutionally, universities had traditionally been organized as faculty of arts (that included political science, history, sociology, and mostly English-language literature) and technical faculties of medicine, engineering and pure sciences. There were changes in the 1970s with Jawaharlal Nehru University, New Delhi adopting a more multi-disciplinary mode of study in organizing its departments. Currently, policy analysis has been adopted as a full fledged topic of study at the university's Centre for the Study of Law and Governance. Many other institutions have followed this course.

More recently, policy studies in India have gained considerable ground. These have mainly drawn upon theoretical approaches developed in the West.[6] Here we briefly examine some exemplars for illustration and their theoretical approach to policy analysis in India. Broadly, recent mainstream

---

5. Kothari (1970) was an early book that employed structural-functional approach to study Indian politics and was published in the series edited by Gabriel Almond.

6. While this section is illustrative and summative rather than comprehensive and substantive, our selection of the literature is representative of wide-ranging policy analysis scholarship.

policy literature has drawn upon cost-benefit evaluation studies, neo-institutionalism (March and Olsen 1989), neo-Marxist analysis, and a mix of pluralist approaches. Through a program evaluation approach, evaluation studies of various policies and programs have been carried out that sought to identify factors responsible for policy failures and to suggest changes in program management and design to succeed in future iterations. Embedded within the centrally-planned developmental framework, problems of implementation took precedence in these studies under the guiding assumption that policies failed and/or could not achieve their objectives because of inadequacies in bureaucracy and administration related to values of efficiency and effectiveness.[7] There was an uncritical acceptance of the legitimacy of the goals of the policy, and sources of failure were seen to be located in the bureaucratic/managerial process rather than in program design and formulation of objectives. Little attention was paid to the appropriateness of particular policy goals or the means for their achievement.

The situation changed in the late 1960s when the country was confronted with a food crisis, industrial stagnation, a resource crunch and suspension of the central plan. Policies began to be assessed in relation to plan models, cross-sectoral relationships and the global economic context. While evaluation studies primarily focused on the efficiency and effectiveness dimensions of the bureaucratic structures and process, they failed to even explore the assumptions implicit in the officially stated policy goals and strategies. While this orientation was useful in collecting and collating basic data, the methodology failed to provide a conceptual framework for seeking policy alternatives. Consequently, economic evaluation studies began to take on a normative assessment element as well, where questions of appropriateness became more salient.[8] It was acknowledged that efficiency criteria may only promote particular types of programs or policies, and preclude others. The focus began to shift from narrow managerial bureaucratic considerations to challenging the very goals that a policy was seen to promote.

As a result, the theoretical focus shifted from state institutions per se to societal institutions that provide the arena for political contestation between groups. Derived from pluralist democratic theory (Dahl 1961), the assumption was made that the public interest is best served by a public policy that emerges from such competitions (Krueger 1974). Policy scholarship more recently began exploring the reasons and the context of the introduction of economic reforms. Scholars and practitioners from various academic persuasions joined in this exploration. Jenkins (1999) utilized an institutionalist approach to interpret the political mechanisms that facilitated reform processes in India. Through a discussion of incentives, institutional frameworks and skills, he highlighted the interaction between elite groups to explain the policy shifts that are labeled as "liberalization." Other influential studies have used a mix of pluralist-institutional approaches to model individual and group behavior through institutional incentives to achieve beneficial outcomes (Kohli 1989; Varshney 1999).

Neo-Marxist analysis has also grappled with this major recent move for economic reform posing the question of "why Indian capital, which was obviously a beneficiary of the protection offered under the earlier regime of intervention went along with and in fact celebrated *liberalization* of the

---

7. The literature concerning implementation is very large but the arguments cited in the reports of the Administrative Reforms Commission (1969) set up by the Government of India summarize the reasons of failures of achieving plan goals and targets.

8. The evaluations of the Integrated Rural Development Programme (IRDP) at the end of the Sixth Plan (1976-81) are an illustration of how the focus on the efficiency/effectiveness dimension circumscribed the discussion on finding ways to improve the implementation of a given policy and marked a departure from the kind of studies that were being conducted. It is only when the issue of appropriateness was raised-would you have a society of wage earners or entrepreneurs? — those policy alternatives came into sharper focus (Rath 1985, Dantwala 1985).

9. "It is plausible to argue, but difficult to prove, that any other government in office in mid-1991 would have done roughly the same in terms of fire fighting and crisis management simply because there was little choice" (Bhaduri and Nayyar, 1996:49).

kind introduced in 1980s and 1990s" (Ghosh and Chandrashekhar 2002). Their analysis identifies macro-level social and economic factors as explanatory variables to suggest that class linkages forged between domestic capital, international financial capital and the Indian middle class contributed to such a reform process. Other scholars suggest that such economic reforms were a normal/fire-fighting response to the economic crisis that the country faced in 1991 and was an instrument of crisis management by the government, given a neo-liberal international framework.[9]

Elements of March and Olsen's (1989) neo-institutional analysis are salient in Varshney's (1995) analysis of the design of India's "new" agricultural policy (1966–68). Using a neo-institutionalist view of institutions as a complex of routines, norms, rules, and understandings, he identified institutional incentives in the three ministries of Agriculture, Planning, and Finance that were directly involved in formulating agricultural policy. Such incentives are mediated through logic of appropriateness and logic of consequentiality of the political context within which institutional actors operate. Varshney points out that institutional actors involved in micro-process of production sought growth through increasing production, while at the same time making a political case for raising prices as well as subsidies. However, actors in the food department, concerned with feeding people, would make a case for lowering prices, acting on a different set of incentives. In his analysis, The Planning Commission was driven by dual and competing incentives, attempting to balance on the one hand raising agricultural production and on the other resisting raising food prices and subsidies. The Finance Ministry actors controlled spending and displayed resistance to subsidies and price rises to prevent imbalances in their budget. Varshney shows how the logic of consequentiality shaped individuals' roles within institutional parameters, and sketched out the state-institutional space for struggle over policy outcomes by political leaders and bureaucrats who held distinct visions of the agrarian economy.

Mathur and Bjorkman (1994) utilized an institutionalist perspective to explore the role of key individuals by focusing on cabinet ministers and civil servants in policy making. Their analysis identifies determinants such as actors' situational-institutional framework, nature of career and recruitment, and characteristics of professional experience that mediate the contribution of India's elite decision makers to policy making. Highlighting the predominance of political over administrative inputs into the policy process, their research suggests that the dominant image of rational decision-making articulated through the values of efficiency and technical optimality is undermined by a more dynamic interaction of values and beliefs of key actors and the framework of institutional constraints they impose on policy issues.

In a critical analysis of state action, Mathur and Jayal (1997) examined the policy process regarding drought in India. By examining the assumptions on which drought policy is formulated, they show how the powerful definition of "drought as crisis" led to the dominance of solutions that covered a short-time horizon, leading to the institution of measures to alleviate the immediate hardship of affected people. Blaming drought on unpredictable vagaries of nature, erratic monsoon, and, in some instances, on "the changing mood of the gods," this dominant view of drought then precluded the formulation of a long-term strategy that would include the provision of better infrastructural farming facilities in drought prone areas. Due to the assumptions of the causes of drought, long-term concerns simply did not enter the definition of the crisis. Thus policy contributed to exacerbating social consequences of drought even as political mileage is derived from drought management. Government performance evaluations were conducted at a technical level only accounting for responses to immediate needs, which, unsurprisingly, produced positive evaluations. An example of discursive policy analysis, this study identifies the frames through which the drought as crises discourse is formulated upon which, in turn, solutions are constructed. In addition to showing the substantive weakness of government response, their analysis carries a critique of the narrow technical focus of evaluations which are embedded within the dominant empiricist epistemological position. They suggest that the failure to consider policy alternatives is a direct consequence of the dominance of the crisis discourse and the consequent inability of other discourses (where radically different strategies emerge from alternative problem definitions) to arise and enter the deliberative space.

The field of environmental policy has attracted a rich contribution through a critical-analysis approach. Scholarship has examined the appropriateness of environmental policy and compared its social and cultural consequences with economic benefits. There have been a series of struggles and conflicts for water and forest rights which have raised issues regarding community rights in forests, rehabilitation, and displacement through large projects and the utility of large dams. Guha's (1973) study was among the early studies that played a crucial role in opening up the debate on environmental issues. In studying the Chipko (Tree-Hugging/Conservation) movement in North Indian Himalayan region of Garhwal, Guha highlighted the concerns and response of the local community to their loss of livelihood and control of local forest resources, in a context of commercial, state-sanctioned deforestation. Guha's analysis portrayed this movement as a challenge to India's national forest policy, and influenced both future public debate and policy reflection. A more recent issue, and a highly controversial and contested one is the case of the construction of the Sardar Sarovar dam on the Narmada River. It evoked sharp reactions from both its critics and supporters and led to a large number of research studies. With government oriented and international economists justifying construction of another big dam on technical and engineering attributes and its contribution to an abstract ideal of universal social progress, this technocratic growth narrative was challenged on grounded factors that drew attention to the displacement of inhabitants and the loss of their livelihoods based around the affected river systems. Not only has the popular struggle against the construction of the Narmada Dam attracted global attention, it has engendered policy argumentation that encompasses enormous amounts of technical concerns as well as challenges the basic meanings of development (D'Souza 2002; Dreze et al. 1997; Baviskar 1995). The movement against the dam project appeals to a participatory ideal of democracy where people not only have a right to information and be consulted about development plans likely to affect their lives, but where people have a right to play a role in the design and outcomes of such plans. As a consequence, the movement articulates a set of cultural rights to a way of life and the associated material rights to natural resources, in and by which they have lived (Jayal, 1999, 254).[10] Other studies in the postmodern tradition are too numerous to list here but have contributed immensely in opening the doors to a more grounded social science outlook and enriched policy research while facing tremendous resistance from the mainstream. However, this change in policy analysis has occurred simultaneously and partly due to the growth of a participatory politics in India, spearheaded through non-governmental organizations (NGOs), as we illustrate in the next section.

NGOS AND THE DEMOCRATIZATION OF POLICY ANALYSIS

In the past 15 years, India has undergone a process of market oriented economic reforms that have gone hand-in-hand with a "modernization program for government. Governmental reform, though slow, has helped expand the democratic space for dominant social and political values to be contested. For example, greater decentralization and capacity building in village councils (*panchayats*) were brought about through constitutional amendment, and have consequently provided a wider space for the expression of frustration and anger with the failure of state policies and action (Roy et al. 2001). The state's overall response to such demands of "deeper democracy" from civil society has been variable, ranging between greater cooperation and dialogue in some instances and ignoring them in others. And representing civil society in this democratic expansion and transformed relationship with the state have been NGOs, the civil sphere institutions of policy research and advice. Build-

---

10. As pointed out there is a large amount of literature that has responded to the issues raised by the construction of the Sardar Sarovar project. For a source of this literature see Jayal, 1999 and Baviskar 1995.

ing on a more general call for reform from the grassroots upwards, NGOs are becoming catalytic agents in facilitating a movement for deeper democracy in India. Several directories provide lists of NGOs that straddle the functions of research, advocacy, mobilization, and empowerment through campaigns and education (Shah, 1991). Estimates indicate that tens of thousands of NGOs operate in the sector broadly labeled "development" and receive US$9–10 billion from international sources and Rupees1,500 million (US$35 million) from domestic sources.

NGOs operate at several levels, ranging from service provision at the local level working to offset the impact of the failure of state provision to alternative program formulation to organizing protests. In time they have grown to coproduce and codeliver government services and facilitated communities to organize themselves to procure services or access entitlements. At the delivery level, their impact is limited to the demands of their target population, and statutory constraints. However, their micro-level experience and practice influences wider patterns of debate about policymaking and delivery. NGOs have attempted to apply their success models to other situations and other areas in the country. As alternative democratic mechanisms that consider development as a bottom-up approach, NGOs have argued for a nation-wide transformation in the developmental planning process in order to expand positive outcomes for a greater number of people at the local level.

NGOs attempt to directly shape public policy through advocacy rather than the above-described approach of replication of best-practice models. NGOs may enter policy advocacy directly by organizing campaigns and protest themselves or joining policy networks or issue-based coalitions.[11] In the context of poverty, participation, democratization, and equity concerns, Indian NGOs have engaged in organized advocacy in fields as diverse as informal, unorganized sector and child labor; affirmative action and protection for the disabled; a wide range of women's issues; environment, forests, and related issues such as displacement and rehabilitation; health; judicial reform; participatory management and governance; consumer rights; appropriate technology; shelter and other issues affecting the urban poor; and issues relating to their own working space (Khan 1997,13). The advocacy role of NGOs and their role in popular mobilization has contributed to successful policy changes such as the adoption of a joint forest management model (Joshi 1999; SPWD 1993), as well as enabling improvement in top-down policy changes such as the mandated representation of women in local government institutions (Vyasulu and Vyasulu 2000; Jha 2004).

In the space between service delivery and direct advocacy for policy change, NGOs have developed alliances with other non-state entities to further an alternative and participatory discourse of development. In concrete terms, NGOs have developed relationships with research institutions that tended towards a more progressive policy outlook. In turn, these institutes have played a key role as nodal institutions in the formation of policy networks and coalitions. For example, take the case of the alternative draft of national rehabilitation policy that was spear-headed by the head of the Indian Social Institute (Fernandes 1995). Using this institutionalized research base, a process of information sharing and deliberation among nation-wide NGOs was facilitated. This network of actors comprising NGOs—activists—researchers through extensive deliberations produced not only a set of abstract principles to underpin rehabilitation policy for internal displaced persons or

11. In a volume sponsored by Society of Participatory Research of Asia (PRIA), Khan (1997, op.cit) has provided several case studies of how grass root NGOs have pursued their advocacy activity. Of the five cases documented, the campaign for a comprehensive law for construction labour had a national perspective. Others were concerned with changes at the state or local level.
12. The Director of CWDS in her introduction to the Centre's Annual Report emphasizes that the CWDS 'is committed to creating integral links between women's studies and the women's movement and has continued to blend research, action and advocacy in its work while confronting the process of marginalisation of women.' and goes on to add that 'it does not view a positive value-based social intervention as being detrimental to social science research' (CWDS Annual Report, 1996-97:1).

refugees, but also concrete alternative policy objectives and strategies to achieve them. In another example, an independent statutory commission and research institute facilitated the formation of networks in the area of the rights of women. The National Commission of Women and Centre for Women's Development Studies (CWDS) has supported NGOs as umbrella organizations providing a research base and forum for influencing public policy going beyond their remit of "pure academic research" to an advocacy role.[12]

In the past few years, the support given by research institutes and NGOs that function as umbrella organizations to activists groups including other NGOs has enlarged the scope of public debate in searching for policy alternatives. However, government in its own right has been only half receptive to this alternative source of policy research and action. A case in point is the report of an Independent Commission on Health submitted by the Voluntary Health Association of India (VHAI) to the central government. Formulated through participatory research and deliberative processes organized by several NGOs, it contained more than 350 recommendations in pursuit of an overhauled national health policy. To say the least, the government response was not encouraging. In a letter to the VHAI, the Joint Secretary of Health in the Ministry of Health and Family Welfare referred to the tremendous effort that the government was already making by initiating new programs and then went on to defend government policy. The letter sought to absolve the government of its failures by suggesting that "a responsive and a conscious user will be able to revitalize the sector and make it more accountable than structural changes might be able to achieve" (Government of India 1999, 3).

However, the government has been more responsive in other instances. A demand by a network of women's groups for a more gender-just budget in 2005 was met with a surprisingly constructive response. The joint Action Group for Women, a forum of 50-odd NGOs working on gender issues had written to the finance minister pointing out the inherent failures in the bureaucratic approach and the need for greater participation of organized women groups in formulating the national budget (*Times of India* 2005, 8). The finance minister responded by making relevant budget performance data reports from 18 ministries and departments available to this network as a first step towards a gender-just budgeting process. Further alternative policy movements have used budget-setting as a key focus for transformation. The relevance of budget analysis lies in the fact that it has provided civil society with a tool through which it can effectively bring the perspectives and the concerns of the poor and marginalized into the process of policy formulation. More importantly, through budget analysis civil society organizations have successfully demonstrated the importance of strategic engagement with the state for promoting a people-centric discourse (Aiyar and Behar 2005).

NGOs have also developed an independent character to mobilize challenges to the dominance of governmental policy prescriptions envisioning an alternative kind of democratic order in India. For instance, a peoples' grassroots organization in the western state of Rajasthan, known as Mazdoor Kisan Shakti Sangathan (or Laborers & Farmers Solidarity Association), has led a struggle to fight corruption and demand government accountability, genuine decentralization and build real participatory democracy. This struggle has snowballed into a country-wide movement which led to the passage of a Right to Information statute (Roy et al. 2001).

The evolution of NGOs thus reflects a multi-layered transformation not only in filling gaps of state failure but articulating and acting through an alternative democratic discourse and providing alternative policy analyses. While early policy research institutes primarily acted as sources of data for fitting into government policy and subsequent institutes only partly succeeded in becoming more independent, influential and inter-disciplinary, NGO-type policy institutions marked a wholesale shift in the means of policy research, analysis and contestation. The cross-fertilization of ideas and strategies between NGOs and research institutes has developed into a vibrant dynamic of providing a clear set of alternative policy goals and action strategies in pursuit of an alternative democratic order. In some instances, governmental organizations have also been influenced to adapt and change through their interaction with NGOs. However, statutory constraints and often narrow targets imply limitations on the scope of NGOs to have a major impact on the new technocratic developmental discourse. Yet the success of their micro-models and widely credited expansion of democratic spaces do imply a constructive role in altering the terms of developmental politics. In this vein NGOs as reflexive organizations are engaged in developing strategic alliances to have a wider impact in the contested domain of public policy (Fernandes 1995, 291).

CONCLUSION

The field of policy research in India has received attention from different scholarly persuasions and institutions. While, initially, policy research was state-sponsored and had a narrow economic orientation, the successive waves of research institutions helped move towards a more interdisciplinary enterprise. The alternative development discourse broadly engendered by NGO-type policy research institutions moved policy research from an interdisciplinary focus towards the very reconceptualization of the meaning of democracy. The dominant mainstream in India is still an economics-technology discourse but has much more intellectual and practical expertise to contend with. Concurrently, policy studies scholarship has also moved on from a predominantly program evaluation orientation to the utilization of a variety of other approaches including neo-Marxist approaches where emphasis is placed on the nature of the (bourgeois) state and the outcomes of class struggles in society to explain emerging policies. Predominantly positivist in orientation, the pluralist approaches account for policy outcomes in terms of contextual incentives, informal and formal rules, and individual and group level bargaining and rational action. In an assessment of the literature, we find that institutionalized policy analysis still maintains a substantially rationalist character, and is less engaged with making a practical contribution to the emerging discourse of a participatory democracy. Expertise and knowledge is defined through the dominant frames of information technology and global management, and sanctioned by state institutions as well as research disciplines. At the same time, NGO activity in a dynamic interaction with state and non-state institutions have been the sources for alternative policy research and alternative sources of expertise. It is to this transformative space that policy research should (and has begun to) pay greater theoretical attention, going beyond the limitations of the traditional policy research orientations towards a postpositive approach.

Our account of the changes in the field of policy analysis in India draws upon the postpositivist critique of the dominant empiricist orientation of policy analysis and converges with its analysis of trends in the West. The postpositive perspective in policy studies seeks to provide an improved reflection of the world of practice as far as policy process is concerned. Instead of attempting to insulate decision making from everyday politics, it attempts to show that policy problems are defined in a subjective fashion and are dependent on the values and beliefs of the actors involved (Fischer 2003). Policy changes can then be as due to dynamics of complex relationships between societal actors that produce new constellations of social forces. Thus policy making can be recognized as a dynamic process occurring in a network society rather than one within hierarchies (Hajer and Wagenaar 2003). Emergence of the concept of governance brings into focus a new range of multi-level relationships among various governmental institutions, civil society organizations and international organizations. Policy analysis would then move away from the pretense of objective and value-neutral policy analysis assumed in the scientific approach (Fischer 2003, 15) and would open the door to a participatory democracy where citizens can take part in meaningful debates and contest policy issues that deeply affect them. The movement we have identified in this chapter in the Indian policy-making approach is of this order. As a normative project, the participatory imperatives seek to inform the kind of democracy that *should* evolve in India, rather than seeking to make corrections in programs alone. Moving beyond identifying incremental solutions to merely augment the skills of the politician and bureaucrat, this research orientation seeks to empower citizens to participate in decision making and to engage in a transformative democratic policy analysis.

REFERENCES

Aiyar, Y., and Behar, A. (2005). Budget Work in India: Civil Society Experiments in Democratic Engagement. *Economic and Political Weekly XL, 2,* 108–112.

Baviskar A. (1995). *In the Belly of the River: Tribal Conflicts over Development in the Tribal Areas.* New Delhi: Oxford University Press.

Braibanti, R. (1966). Transnational Inducement of Administrative Reform: A Survey of Scope and Critique of Issues. In J. D. Montgomery and W. J. Siffin. (eds.), *Approaches to Development: Politics, Administration and Change.* New York: McGraw Hill.

Braibanti, R. J., and Spengler, J. J. (eds.), (1963). *Administration and Economic Development in India.* Durham, NC: Duke University Press.

Center for Women's Development Studies (CWDS). (1997). Annual Report CWDS (1996–1997), New Delhi.

D'Souza, D. (2002). *The Narmada Dammed: An Inquiry into the Politics of Development.* New Delhi: Penguin Books.

Dahl, R. (1961). *Who Governs?* New Haven, CT: Yale University Press.

Dantwala, M.. (1985). Garibi Hatao (Eliminate Poverty) Strategy Options. Economic and Political Weekly, *XX, 11,* 475–476.

Dreze, J., Samson, M., and Singh, S. (eds.), (1997). *The Dam and the Nation: Displacement and Resettlement in the Narmada Valley.* New Delhi: Oxford University Press.

Fernandes W. (1995). An Activist Process around the Draft National Rehabilitation Policy. *Social Action, 45, July-Sept.,* 277–298.

Fischer, F. (2003). *Reframing Public Policy: Discursive Politics and Deliberative Practices.* Oxford: Oxford University Press.

Fischer, F. (1993). Policy Discourse and the Politics of Washington Think Tanks. In F. Fischer and J. Forrester (eds.), *The Argumentative Turn in Policy Analysis and Planning.* Durham and London: Duke University Press, 21–24.

Ghosh, J., and Chandrashekhar C.,P. (2002). The Political Economy of the Indian Reform Process. Paper presented at Seminar on The Politics of Economic Reform in India, Centre for Economic and Social Studies, Hyderabad, India.

Government of India. (1999). Letter to VHAI. January 8.

Guha, R. (1989). *Unquiet Woods: Ecological Change and Protest in the Himalaya.* New Delhi: Oxford University Press.

Guha, R. (1999). *Savaging The Civilized: Verrier Elwin, His Tribals and India.* New Delhi: Oxford University Press.

Hajer M. A., and Wagenaar, H. (eds.) (2003). *Deliberative Policy Analysis Understanding Governance in the Network Society* Cambridge: Cambridge University Press.

Hanson, A. H. (1966). *The Process of Planning: A Study of India's Five Year Plans 1950–6.* Oxford: Oxford University Press.

Jayal, N. G. (1997) Consolidating Democracy: Governance and Civil Society in India. Centre for Political Studies, Jawaharlal Nehru University, New Delhi (mimeograph).

Jayal, N. G. (1999) *Democracy and the State Welfare, Secularism and Development in Contemporary India.* New Delhi: Oxford University Press.

Jenkins, R. (1999). *Democratic Politics and Economic Reform in India.* New Delhi: Cambridge University Press.

Jha, A. K. (ed.). (2004). *Women in Panchayati Raj Institutions.* New Delhi, Anmol Publications.

Joshi, A. (1999). Progressive bureaucracy: An oxymoron? The case of Joint Forest Management in India. Paper 24a. Overseas Development Institute, London: Rural Development Forestry Network.

Khan, A. M. (1997). *Shaping Policy: Do NGOs Matter? Lessons from India.* New Delhi: Society for Participatory Research in Asia.

Kohli, A. (1989). Politics of Economic Liberalization in India. *World Development, 17, 3,* 305–328.

Kothari, R. (1970). *Politics in India.* Boston: Little and Brown.

Krueger, A. O. (1974). The Political Economy of the Rent-Seeking Society. *American Economic Review* 64, 3: 291–303.

March, J. G., and Olsen, J. P. (1989) *Rediscovering Institutions: The Organizational Basis of Politics.* New York: The Free Press.

Mathur, K. (2001). Governance and Alternative Sources of Policy Advice: The Case of India. In K. Weaver and P.B. Stares (eds.), *Guidance for Governance. Comparing Alternative Sources of Public Advice*, pp. 207–230. Tokyo and Washington, D.C.: Japan Centre for International Exchange and Brookings Institute.

Mathur, K., and Jayal, N. G. (1992). *Drought Policy and Politics: The Need for a Long Term Perspective.* New Delhi: Sage Publications.

Mathur, K., and Bjorkman, J.W. (1994). *Top Policy Makers in India Cabinet Ministers and Civil Service Advisors.* Delhi: Concept Publishers.

Nanda, N. (1999). *Forests for Whom? Destruction & Restoration in the U.P. Himalayas.* New Delhi: Har-Anand Publications.

Pierre, J. (ed.). (2000). *Debating Governance: Authority, Steering, and Democracy.* Oxford: Oxford University Press.

Rath, N. (1985). Garib Hatao (Eliminate Poverty): Can IRDP do it? *Economic and Political Weekly, 20, 6,* 238–246.

Roy, A., Dey, N., and Singh, S. (2001). Demanding Accountability. *Seminar,* 500, 2.

SPWD (Society for Promotion of Wastelands Development). (1993). Joint Forest Management: Regulations Update. New Delhi: SPWD.

Shah, G. (1991). *Non-Governmental Organizations in India.* Centre for Social Studies Surat/Centre for Asian Studies Amsterdam (mimeograph).

Taylor, C. C., Ensminger, D., Johnson, H.W.U., and Joyce, J. (1966). *India's Roots of Democracy: A Sociological Analysis of Rural India's Experience in Planned Development Since Independence.* Bombay: Orient Longmans.

Times of India. (1999). Letter to VHAI. January 18.

Varshney, A. (1995). *Democracy Development and the Countryside Urban Rural struggles in India.* Cambridge: Cambridge University Press.

Varshney, A. (1999). Mass politics or Elite Politics: India's Economic Reforms in Comparative Perspective. In J. D. Sachs, A. Varshney and N. Bajpai (eds.), *India in the Era of Economic Reforms,* pp. 222–260. New Delhi: Oxford University Press.

Vyasalu, P., and Vyasalu, V. (2000). Women in the Panchayati Raj: Grassroots Democracy in India. Proceedings of *Women's Political Participation and Good Governance: 21st Century Challenges*, pp. 41–48. New Delhi: UNDP.

40 Korean Policy Analysis: From Economic Efficiency to Public Participation

Changhwan Mo

INTRODUCTION

The Chosun dynasty in the Korean peninsula from 1392 to 1910 was a society governed by the philosophy of Confucianism. Policy making during this period was made by kings and elites who were called *seonbi*. The ideal *seonbi* were leaders who possessed high moral character, extensive knowledge of philosophy, poetry, manners, and history. But there was nothing like a formal discipline that dealt with politics or policy during the Chosun dynasty. The main guidance for statesmen was historical knowledge, stories that provided policy makers with some lessons relevant to the time. This remained the case until recent times when policy analysis as an academic field was introduced in Korea, largely taking its lead from American social science. This chapter examines the history of Korean policy analysis from 1960s to the present in order to understand its evolution and development.

One way to look at the evolution of policy analysis is by examining the nature and content of the articles published in the field. Toward this end, various Korean scholars (Kwon 1996; Hong and Kim 2001; Hur 1996; Kim 1992; Mok and Park 2002; Lee and Jung 1996; Song 1992) have reviewed the policy articles that had been published in major Korean journals. Kwon (1996) analyzed previous policy studies in *Korean Public Administration Review* (*KPAR*) from 1967 to 1995. According to him, 67 percent of those policy articles in *KPAR* applied a descriptive approach and 33 percent of them had a quantitative orientation. Following Kwon, Hong and Kim (2001) analyzed 77 articles that addressed policy issues in *KPAR* from 1996 to 2001. According to them, while 23 percent were descriptive in nature, the other 77 percent involved explanatory studies that investigated the correlation between social and political factors. Of the 70 percent, qualitative studies constituted 40 percent with quantitative studies constituting the rest.

Kim (1992) analyzed 210 policy articles in both *KPAR* and the *Korean Review of Political Science* (*KRPS*) from 1967 to 1992. He discovered that most of the articles addressed efficiency by applying a quantitative method and the scholars who adopted a quantitative method generally chose to study subjects that fitted that method. While Korean scholars, according to Kim, concentrated on specific subjects such as finance and welfare, they avoided more difficult subjects that could not be easily quantified, as well as those that took long-term perspectives. Seventeen percent of the articles from 1967 to 1976 were quantitative. They had increased to 38 percent from 1977 to 1987 and increased again to 58 percent from 1988 to 1991. Most of those quantitative studies focused on economic efficiency. According to Kim, out of 84 quantitative studies that addressed policy issues, 64 articles were based on economic efficiency, while 20 of them addressed policies from the perspective of social equality or political democracy. This trend reflected an attempt to separate values and facts in policy analysis.

Mok and Park (2002) analyzed all articles in the *Korean Policy Studies Review* (*KPSR*) from 1992 to 2001. They found that about 40 percent of articles applied a qualitative method and the rest of them, employed a quantitative method. According to Lee and Jung (1996), about 70 percent (106 out of 161 articles) of previous studies on policy decision making suggested alternatives after an analysis of specific policy issues such as social welfare and environment.

During the past decades, several U.S. scholars (Fischer 1993, 1995; deLeon 1997) have argued for the inclusion of normative values and the practical utility of including more participatory forms of policy analysis. Such participatory research incorporates the opinions of ordinary citizens into policy making, while experts act as a facilitator to help them to decide by themselves through a deliberative process.[1] This participatory paradigm has had increased influence in the field of policy analysis in Korea. Previous studies in Korea did not analyze the development of Korean policy analysis from a perspective of a participatory approach; this chapter includes an examination of the development in the latter part of the discussion.

REVIEW OF KOREAN POLICY ANALYSIS: BASIC BACKGROUND

In more than two thousand years of history, Korea had several kingdoms on the peninsula, all of which introduced policy measures to improve economic and social welfare of the citizenry. But there was no formal academic study of the effects of these policies; that only began in the 1960s as was the case elsewhere. "Public policy analysis" is taken here to refer an academic field that addresses policy issues in the public sector, while the term "policy sciences" refers to a field of study that addresses policy issues in both public and private sectors.

In the early 1960s, Korea was one of the poorest countries in the world and heavily dependent upon on aid from other countries. In 1961, a military coup took over the government and an Economic Planning Board was created as the most powerful planning and administration agency in Korea. The military government announced a five-year plan of economic development, as it put a priority on economic development. The model put into place pursued rapid economic growth. The economic plan was implemented twice in the 1960s, and the Korean government mainly utilized economists to address policy making.

The military regime took a top-down approach to policy making in an effort to overcome social and political opposition. The policy-making process was mainly dominated by military leaders and elites who supported the regime. The authoritarian regime resolved policy conflicts through an emphasis on control and order, with most policy studies during the period emphasizing state guided economic development and efficiency. In this political context, policy analysis was thus largely used as a tool to rationalize the power of the regime. Some of policy scholars, it is important to note, supported the military dictators with analytic techniques that helped them stay in power. Under the control of these political arrangements, citizens had no chance to participate in public policy making and implementation.

During this period, however, Korea did move from a country with a per capita income of less than $100 per year in 1961 to more than $15,000 in 2005. In the process, the government has engaged in planning the economy in ways that would control for market failures and promote export industries basic for economic growth. These economic policy measures, moreover, worked to draw attention to policy-making processes more generally.

Korean scholars who had interest in decision making and planning with respect to economic development also started to show interest in policy analysis more generally. Korean universities started to include policy analysis within their curricula in the middle of 1960s. A graduate program of public administration in a public university offered a course of policy formation in the spring of 1968. At this time, other graduate schools also began to change their curricula so that they could provide students with development theories and policy courses. Before then, the curriculum focused narrowly on public administration. The graduate school provided core courses, such as policy decision making and the content of policy analysis for students. Policy focus was beginning to broaden.

According to Hur (1996), policy analysis was taught under course titles such as "planning" or "decision-making" in the 1960s and 1970s. It was not taught as "policy analysis" per se until the 1980s. Most courses in policy analysis were offered in the departments of public administration rather than that political science. Most of the policy studies were carried out by scholars in public administration departments. As a result, it has become a tradition of Korean academic society that policy analysis is considered as a kind of sub field of public administration.

1970s: Importing Policy Analysis

The military regime of Park Jung Hee changed the Constitution in 1972 to solidify his political reign. Called *Yushin*, the regime initiated radical reforms based on practices of Japanese government in the late nineteenth century. Under the military dictatorship, any form of citizen participation in public policy making was strictly ruled out. The government took a harsh attitude toward citizen participation as it could lead to demands for democracy. This political situation led policy scholars to narrowly focus on the "value-neutral techniques" of policy analysis such as operations research (OR) and statistical methods rather than on democratic values and citizen participation in policy making. In the 1970s, there were no studies that addressed the participation of citizens and interest groups in the process of policy decision making (Lee and Jung 1996).

During this period, the government implemented an unequal development strategy and highly emphasized planning. According to Song (1992, 66), the unequal growth strategy of the Korean government increased social anomalies that made Korean scholars take interest in policy analysis as a new way to solve them. Those scholars who had an interest in planning and decision making started to study policy decision making. More importantly, young scholars who studied in the United States introduced theories of policy analysis, and a policy analysis textbook was published for the first time in Korea (Roh 1976). But, according to Song (1992), most of the policy studies in 1970s sought to supply the military regime with professional knowledge. They provided rationalizing tools for the military regime, serving to implement the repressive policies pursued by President Park.

Given the authoritarian nature of the Park Jung Hee's regime, the central government was largely a unitary actor in the policy-making process, maintaining strict control over budgetary allocations and personnel appointments. During the course of the decade, however, the regime became to regularly confront a civil society demanding democratization. University students, opposing political parties, and labor unions protested against the government. In face of rising social and political opposition, Park resorted to extraordinary measures to tighten his grip over the control of the country by establishing a new Constitution that allowed him to remain president until he passed away. As Chung (1990, 42) pointed out, "The Yushin regime was extremely authoritarian, eradicating any democratic channels in state-society relations and concentrating enormous power in the President and the executive."

The government had oppressed the protesting voices of citizens who were adversely affected by a particular public policy, often employing harsh coercive measures. In short, the military regime emphasized economic growth over democratic values and human rights.

It also should be emphasized that in the 1970s the Korean government established several government-funded institutes. These institutes provided the government with professional knowledge so that it could improve its policy decision making and implementation capabilities. Think-tank organizations, such as the Korea Development Institute and the Korea Industry Institute, belonged to the central government and, accordingly, they had to follow the government's policy directions.

Due to the influence of U.S. Army bases in Korea, with close relationships to the Korean army, the ministry of defense attempted to apply Planning-Programming-Budgeting Systems techniques

(PPBS) and Operations Research methods to public policy making during this period. Experts in policy analysis were significantly lacking, although the government was in need of many experts in the fields such as policy evaluation, PERT/CPM, system analysis, PPBS, and performance budgeting.

POLICY ANALYSIS IN THE 1980S

At the beginning of the 1980s the government was still occupied with economic growth, despite the public's increasing demands for more democratic governance. More and more, government-funded institutes supplied policy makers with the knowledge obtained from policy studies. Although researchers in those government-funded institutes addressed a range of public policies, they were mostly economists whose priority was on efficiency.

In 1987, the military rule finally came to an end, and the long-oppressed demands of the citizenry for more open government were answered by the victory of democracy movements. Most importantly, civic society took up the challenge of political democracy and many civic groups were formed in the 1980s. Since the inequalities of the development policy of the previous government had produced numerous social problems in the late of 1980s, Korean policy analysts had an opportunity to be taken in new directions, with Korean scholars expanding their perspectives beyond economic development to include various social issues.

In the1980s, new textbooks of policy analysis with titles such as *Introduction of Policy Sciences*, *Policy Evaluation*, and *Policy Analysis*, were published. In large part, they presented American policy concepts and practice. In 1981, graduate schools established new courses in policy analysis methods, policy implementation, policy development, and policy management. The curriculum change in the graduate programs for policy analysis widely impacted other programs in public administration. Also in the 1980s, a few studies emerged that addressed the participation of interest groups such as labor unions and coalition of farmers (Lee and Jung 1996).

President Roh Tae Woo took power in 1987. Since he was elected after the uprising of citizens in June 1987, he had to accept new democratic approaches in policy making and public administration. However, as he came from the military and was considered as a successor of the former military dictator, Chun Doo Hwan, his approach to citizen involvement in government left many unsatisfied. Although Korea became a democratic society after almost 30 years of dictatorships, the government still maintained elements of an authoritarian political culture..

NEW METHODS AND PRACTICES IN THE 1990S

An important step in the formal advance of policy analysis was the establishment of the Korean Association for Policy Studies and the Korean Association for Policy Analysis & Evaluation in 1992. In the early 1990s, thanks in significant part to these new associations, Korean policy analysis could now find its identity independently of both the academic fields of public administration and political science. At the same time, citizens and students stopped challenging the legitimacy of government since the country possessed a relatively democratic political system under the guidance of an elected president. But, as an extension of democratic politics, civic groups and labor unions began to struggle against government policies related to issues such as environment, trade and labor practices. This provided a favorable environment for policy scholars who wished to study a diverse array of policy issues in the Korean society.

The new democratic government required, of course, a different approach to resolving policy conflicts. Although the Korean government was looking for a peaceful way to resolve such conflicts, it was unsuccessful. One example was the difficulty that the government encountered in siting and constructing a nuclear waste facility in face of strong protests from citizens. If a military regime had still controlled the country, it would not have allowed citizens to launch such protests against government. The new government had to permit such demonstrations and found it difficult to make such decisions. Due to these protests, Korean scholars of policy analysis began to pay increasing attention to policy conflict and the democratic process of policy making (Roh 1996).

Then, in 1997, Korea experienced an economic crisis. The Korean economic and social systems collapsed, creating problems that had been unforeseen. No one had been able to forecast or prevent the collapse of the financial system. Due to the crisis, citizens became more and more aware of the importance of their involvement in policy making in the public sector. Several studies addressed the participation of interest groups such as labor unions and corporations in the process of policy making, but there were no empirical studies that addressed the participation of ordinary citizens in policy decision making (Lee and Jung 1996). Although there were a few studies of the participation of civic groups in the process of policy decision making, there was no research published in the *KPSR* during the 1990s that addressed public participation in public policy making .

At this time quantitative studies, as already noted, were dominant in the major journals of policy analysis in Korea, while qualitative studies that addressed social values were undervalued in Korean policy analysis. Policy analysts had not yet paid enough attention to the unique context of Korean policy making, focusing instead on the advanced techniques of statistical methods and operation research. Moreover, Korean scholars did not devote attention to philosophy and ethics with respect to public policy.

In the 1990s, the mass media and the Internet increasingly became import factors for Korean civil society. Since then ordinary citizens have freely used these media to express their voices against government policies. The policy analysis community, as a result, increasingly began to consider participatory approaches to solve the conflicts between citizens and government. Several scholars in the social sciences who had studied in Germany introduced the works of Habermas emphasizing participation and deliberation in public policy making. As the new century began, several articles argued for the rediscovery of "policy sciences of democracy" and emphasized the importance of participatory policy analysis.[2] For example, Moon (2003) and Kim (2003) wrote articles about the discursive theory of Habermas and the normative justification of public policy. In addition, Lee (2001) and Mo (2003) denied the dichotomy between facts and values and argued for a multi-dimensional framework of policy analysis. In 2000, several articles (Kim, D. H. 2004; Kim, G. 2004) published in the *KPSR* addressed issues of NIMBY (Not-in-My-Backyard) and citizen protests in policy implementation.

In recent years, Korea has been increasingly experiencing serious policy conflicts that the Prime Minister's Office has sought to deal with through a bill proposed in 2005 in which participatory approaches such as consensus conference, deliberative polling, scenario workshops, and citizen juries are made mandatory for so-called "wicked policy conflicts."[3] The goals of the bill are to contribute to social unity by resolving conflicts on the basis of participation and deliberation and to establish a framework of consensus through communication, compromise, the recovery of trust between public organizations and citizens, and the improvement of the capabilities of public organizations with respect to mitigation of conflicts by stipulating procedures designed to help prevent or solve them. The bill mandates a public organization to adopt a participatory approach in taking measures to manage or resolve conflicts. Given that the existing citizen participation methods such as public hearings and legislative hearings do not solve most serious conflicts that have been increasing in Korea, the bill offers a system that requires citizens to be partners in policy decision making. It requires government to fully consider participatory processes by utilizing decision-making methods in which citizens, interesting parties, and experts are all involved. As such, the bill is expected to improve both the efficiency of the policy implementation process and the democratic character of policy decision making by providing for deliberation among citizens and interesting parties. In addition to the mandatory requirement of participatory approaches, the bill proposes to establish conflict mediation methods, to establish conflict management committees, and create a conflict resolution support center.

PARTICIPATORY APPROACHES: PRACTICAL EXPERIENCES

These participatory approaches are reflected in a number of policy issues. As Korea established a democratic political system, President Kim Dae Jung, elected in 1997, stressed his intention to create a participatory democracy in which all people take part in policy decision making. Similarly, President Roh Moo Hyun, elected in 2003, called his administration "The Government of Participation," and declared that he intended to promote a genuine democracy with the people. He argued that a genuine democracy is possible only when the citizens voluntarily participate in the government rather than being mobilized for it. In so far as authoritarian governments had dominated the citizenry with the help of privileged elite groups, participatory government was intended to change the political culture and give citizens new experiences that would encourage their active involvement in the affairs of government.

Particularly important in this regard have been a number of serious policy conflicts, especially those related to environmental issues. One of those conflicts involved a dam on the Hantan River. This case is of special significance in the Korean policy community, as the central government has attempted to make it an exemplary model for resolving a conflict in a peaceful, democratic way. It was, as such, designed to serve as a model for how to deal with other policy conflicts in Korea. The Hantan River dam conflict was explicitly chosen in 2003 by the Presidential Commission on Sustainable Development (PCSD) as a model project to show that a participatory approach can work to resolve policy conflicts. The demonstration, however, largely failed. The government's approach was unable to resolve the conflict between government and residents who were adversely affected by the construction of a dam in the Hantan River.

The building of the Sapae Tunnel has attempted to employed deliberative opinion polling method, which allows a significant number of citizens to participate in resolving a conflict. It is the first attempt in Korea that has employed a deliberative polling approach to deal with a policy problem. Whereas the Hantan dam case allowed only a few representatives of those opposed to the dam to participate in the process of conflict resolution with the help of experts, the Sapae case permitted many more. But it too failed as Buddist monks successfully opposed it. Although the Korean government was again looking for a peaceful way to resolve them, it remained unsuccessful.

In 2003, the government attempted to designate a dump site on Wido Island in Puan County, North Cheonlla province. It designated the island as a nuclear depository site, but it dropped the designation due to fierce oppositions from residents and civic groups. The Puan residents and activists for environment protection staged violent demonstrations for several months in 2003, demanding that the bid initiated by the county mayor be scrapped. After the government failed in designating a site for the construction of nuclear waste dumps, it proposed a solution to solve the problem by a popular vote. It first accepted voluntary applications from local governments willing to allow the construction of the nuclear dump facility to house low- and intermediate-level radioactive wastes with the assistance of public subsidies. Four local governments applied as candidates for the project: Kyongju, Kunsan, Yongduck, and Pohang. Among them, the Kyongju-city's bid to accommodate it was overwhelmingly approved by residents (Kim 2005). As an initiative to raise public understanding on the safety of nuclear waste dump site, four regional governments embarked on extensive public relations campaigns. Before the voting, residents had a wide opportunity to access all information with respect to any issues related to the dump site. The government emphasized that the location of the site would be decided after there had been sufficient development of a social consensus among local residents.

The Kyongju-city residents approved the construction of the dump site by nearly 90 percent (Kim 2005). The city was automatically designated as the dump site in October 2005. The Ministry of Commerce, Industry and Energy (MOCIE) had pledged that it would select the final bidder based on the voting results. In addition to geological conditions, the rate of citizens' approval demonstrated by voting became the government's most important selection criterion.

For their willingness to accept the waste site, the Kyongju residents will receive major economic benefits. The government promised a financial support package of $300 million for regional development, in addition to an estimated $5–$10 million per year (depending on the amount of nuclear waste deposited at the site). Furthermore, the central government would relocate the headquarters of the Korea Hydro & Nuclear Power from Seoul to the area of the dump site. As South Korea is the world's sixth-largest nuclear power producing country, operating 19 nuclear reactors, these measures helped to deal with the rather disparate need to find a permanent solution for nuclear wastes. The fact that the conflict was resolved through political and deliberative processes, accompanied by economic compensation, rather than through rational decision making formally understood, illustrates the importance of the new interest in these approaches for the Korean policy process.

CONCLUSION

In the 1960s and 1970s, as we saw, policy analysis did not flourish under the authoritarian regimes that controlled Korea. To the degree that it developed, it was focused with economic development and economic efficiency. It is argued that some of policy scholars did work for the authoritarian regime, seeking to rationalize its policies. But it was not until the 1980s that Korean policy scholars were able to expand their research to include various issues related to the negative consequences of the authoritarian governments, such as poverty, education, environment, welfare, and labor issues. In the 1990s, Korean scholars also expanded their interest to citizen participation. As the Korea government increasingly democratized the political system, introducing various participatory practices, policy analysts also began to show interest in participatory policy analysis. Several studies have subsequently examined the feasibility of participatory approaches for resolving policy conflicts, especially as they have emerged in the policy-making process.

Many scholars, however, have noted the reliance of Korean policy researchers on foreign literatures, particularly the literatures of the United States and Western Europe. They argue that Korean policy analysis now needs to pay more attention to their own political context. Pointing out that most studies on policy decision making in Korea have applied policy theories borrowed from other political cultures and experiences to explain Korean cases, Lee and Jung (1996) criticized Korean policy scholars for not having created Korea-based policy theories that speak to the country's own culture, practices, and interests. The Korean policy analysis community, they argue, has not yet reached a state in which it can develop its own policy theories and analytic methods that are more appropriate for Korean politics and policy issues. This would appear to be the next important step in the development of the field.

NOTES

1. deLeon (1997, 111) pointed out that "fundamentally, the ideal behind [Participatory Policy Analysis] is that more-generalized and less-vested panels composed of citizens at large are empowered to participate in deliberations over public policy issues over an extended period of time (say, a year). A participatory policy analysis requires policy analysts to select Rose's 'ordinary citizens,' randomly chosen from a broadly defined pool of affected citizens (possibly formulated to take sociocultural variables into accout) so as to avoid the stigma of being 'captured' by established interests and stakeholders, to engage in a participatory a participatory analytic exercise."
2. The Prime Minister's Office of Government Policy Coordination has sent the proposed bill to Congress for legislation after several public hearings in May 2005.

REFERENCES

Chung, J. Y. (1990). South Korea strategies for dynamic transformation: 1961–88. In Lim, Gill-Chin, and Lee, Gi-Beom (eds.), *Dynamic Transformation: Korea, NICs and Beyond*, Seoul, Korea: Consortium on Development Studies, 37–51.

deLeon, P. (1997). *Democracy and the Policy Sciences*. Albany, NY: State University of New York Press.

Fischer, F. (1992). Restructuring policy analysis: A postpositivist perspective. *Policy Sciences* 25, 333–339.

Fischer, F. (1995). *Evaluating Public Policy*. Belmont, CA: Wadsworth.

Hong, S., and Kim, J. (2001). Research of policy science: Past, present, and future. A paper presented at a Conference of Korean Public Administration for 21st Century and Vision of Korean Association for Public Administration. Seoul: Korean Association for Public Administration.

Hur, M. H. (1996). Prospect and review of Korean policy sciences. A paper presented at 1996 Korea Association for Political Sciences. Seoul: Korea Association for Political Science.

Kim, D. H. (2004). A comparative study on the aspects of conflict in sitting policy for NIMBY and PIMFY public facilities: Cases of sitting Buk-gu crematorium and Ulsan station for Kyungbu Express Train. *Korean Policy Studies Review* 13, 157–188.

Kim, G. (2004). A case study on citizens' resistance on policy implementation. *Korean Policy Studies Review* 13, 159–184.

Kim, I. (1992). Scope and methods in policy studies: Works in KPAR and KPSR. *Korean Public Administration Review* 26, 1049–1068.

Kim, S. (2003). On concept of Habermas' discurs. Korean Policy Studies Review 12, 1–31.

Kim, Y. (2005). Kyongju to host nuclear dumpsite. *The Korean Times*, November 3, 1.

Kwon, K. D. (1996). An empirical analysis of trends in Korean public research: Focusing on the articles published in the Korean Public Administration Review (1967–1995). *Korean Public Administration Review* 30, 439–453.

Lee, H. (2001). Applying multidimensional theory into dichotomies of policy analysis: process and policy fact and values. *Korean Policy Studies Review* 10, 41–62.

Lee, S., and Jung, J. (1996). Analysis of the trends of empirical studies on policy decision making in Korea. *Korean Public Administration Review*, 30, 65–79.

Mo, C. (2003). An application of a multi-dimensional policy evaluation methodology on rail privatization: A case analysis of U.K. rail privatization. *Korean Policy Studies Review* 12, 249–272.

Mok, J. and Park, S. (2002). Ten years' history of Korean policy studies review. *Korean Policy Studies Review* 11, 319–332.

Moon, T. H. (2003). Discourse theory and the justification of public policy. *Korean Political Studies Review* 12, 125–144.

Roh, H. J. (1996). The development and characteristics of Korean public policy studies. *Public Administration Treatise* 31, 1–31.

Song, H. J. (1992). An analysis of the characteristics and contends of policy studies in the Korean policy analysis. *Korean Review of Policy Studies*, 1, 63–84.

Index